ENCYCLOPEDIA OF EDUCATION

SECOND EDITION

EDITORIAL BOARD

ENCYCLOPEDIA OF EDUCATION

SECOND EDITION

James W. Guthrie, Editor in Chief

VOLUME

8

Appendixes and Index

MACMILLAN
REFERENCE
USA™

THOMSON
GALE™

New York • Detroit • San Diego • San Francisco • Cleveland • New Haven, Conn. • Waterville, Maine • London • Munich

THOMSON

GALE

Encyclopedia of Education, Second Edition

James W. Guthrie, Editor in Chief

For more information, contact
Macmillan Reference USA
300 Park Avenue South, 9th Floor
New York, NY 10010
Or you can visit our Internet site at
http://www.gale.com

LIBRARY OF CONGRESS CATALOGING-IN-PUBLICATION DATA

Encyclopedia of education / edited by James W. Guthrie.—2nd ed.
p. cm.
Includes bibliographical references and index.
ISBN 0-02-865594-X (hardcover : set : alk. paper)
1. Education—Encyclopedias. I. Guthrie, James W.
LB15 .E47 2003
370'.3—dc21 2002008205

ISBNs
Volume 1: 0-02-865595-8
Volume 2: 0-02-865596-6
Volume 3: 0-02-865597-4
Volume 4: 0-02-865598-2
Volume 5: 0-02-865599-0
Volume 6: 0-02-865600-8
Volume 7: 0-02-865601-6
Volume 8: 0-02-865602-4

Printed in the United States of America
10 9 8 7 6 5 4 3 2 1

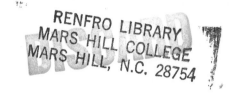

APPENDIX CONTENTS

APPENDIX I: Assessment and Achievement Tests **2751**

APPENDIX II: State-by-State Directory of Departments of Education **2759**

APPENDIX III: Court Cases, Legislation, and International Agreements **2763**

APPENDIX IV: Internet Resources **3189**

APPENDIX V: Bibliography **3193**

APPENDIX VI: Outline of Contents **3197**

APPENDIX I

ASSESSMENT AND ACHIEVEMENT TESTS

This list of commonly administered standardized assessments was compiled from information furnished by ERIC/AE Test Locator. The Test Locator is a joint project of the Educational Resources Information Center Clearinghouse on Assessment and Evaluation, the Library and Reference Services Division of the Educational Testing Service, the Buros Institute of Mental Measurements at the University of Nebraska in Lincoln, the Region III Comprehensive Center at George Washington University, and Pro-Ed test publishers. Information regarding tests not listed here may be obtained by using the Test Locator, located at <http://ericae.net/testcol.htm>. Additional information regarding the tests that follow is available through the testing services listed.

A

ABLE *see* Adult Basic Learning Examination, 2nd edition

ACT Assessment (ACT)
This multiple-choice test assesses high school students' general educational development and their ability to complete college-level work. Skill areas covered include English, mathematics, reading, and science reasoning. Grade 11 and above.

American College Testing, Inc.
P.O. Box 1008
Iowa City, IA 52243-1008
Phone: 319-337-1000
<www.act.org>

Adult Basic Learning Examination, 2nd edition (ABLE)
This multiple-choice exam measures adult achievement in these basic learning skills: reading comprehension, spelling, arithmetic computation, and problem solving. Age 17 and older.

Harcourt Brace Educational Measurement
19500 Bulverde Road
San Antonio, TX 78259
Phone: 800-211-8378
<www.harcourt.com/about/harcourt_educational_measurement.html>

AP Examination: Advanced Placement Program (AP)
This College Board-sponsored program gives high school students the opportunity to take college-level courses and exams in a variety of subjects while earning credit or advanced placement, or both, for college. Grades 11–12.

The College Board/Educational Testing Service
45 Columbus Avenue
New York, NY 10023-6992
Phone: 212-713-8000
<www.collegeboard.com>

Armed Services Vocational Aptitude Battery (ASVAB)
There are two audiences for this battery. First, it is the entrance exam for service in the U.S. Armed Forces. Second, this battery of multiple-choice tests is administered by guidance counselors to high school students as a diagnostic tool in order to determine possible civilian occupations and for career planning. The occupational composites are: mechanical and crafts, business and clerical, health, social and technology, and electronics and electrical. Grade 10 and above.

Testing Directorate Headquarters
Military Enlistment Processing Command
Attn: MERCT
Fort Sheridan, IL 60037
Phone: 800-USA-ARMY
<www.goarmy.com/util/asvab.htm>

ASSET
This multiple-choice exam assesses writing, reading, numerical, and advanced mathematical skills for course placement. Age 18 and above.

American College Testing, Inc.
P.O. Box 1008
Iowa City, IA 52243-1008
Phone: 319-337-1000
<www.act.org>

ASVAB *see* Armed Services Vocational Aptitude Battery

B

Ball Aptitude Battery (BAB)
This multiple-choice series of exams measures aptitudes for career exploration and self-knowledge. Subjects include: clerical, word association, writing speed, "ideaphoria," associative memory, inductive reasoning, auditory memory, spatial visualization, and vocabulary. Grades 8–12 and above.

Ball Foundation
800 Roosevelt Road, E-200
Glen Ellyn, IL 60137-5866
Phone: 800-469-8378
<www.ballfoundation.org>

Basic Achievement Skills Individual Screener (BASIS)
This test measures achievement in reading, mathematics, and spelling, and it assesses individual students' strengths and weaknesses with both norm-referenced and criterion-referenced information. Grade 1 and above.
Harcourt Brace Educational Measurement
19500 Bulverde Road
San Antonio, TX 78259
Phone: 800-211-8378
<www.hemweb.com>

Basic Inventory of Natural Language (BINL)
This oral exam measures language proficiency. It is used in bilingual language development, and speech and language remediation programs. Ages 4–adult.
CHECpoint Systems, Inc.
1520 North Waterman Avenue
San Bernardino, CA 92404-5111
Phone: 800-975-3250
Fax: 800-433-9330

BASIS *see* Basic Achievement Skills Individual Screener

Battelle Developmental Inventory (BDI)
This exam evaluates development in children by screening and diagnosing developmental strengths and weaknesses. Birth–age 8.
Riverside Publishing Company
425 Spring Lake Drive
Itasca, IL 60143-2079
Phone: 800-323-9540
<www.riverpub.com>

BINL *see* Basic Inventory of Natural Language

Brigance Diagnostic Comprehensive Inventory of Basic Skills (CIBS)
This assessment measures basic academic skills. Grades pre-K–9.
Curriculum Associates, Inc.
153 Rangeway Road
North Billerica, MA 01862
Phone: 800-225-0248
Fax: 800-366-1158
<www.curriculumassociates.com>

Brigance Diagnostic Inventory of Basic Skills
This assessment measures strengths and weaknesses in 14 major skill areas, provides system for performance record, and determines level of achievement. Grades K–6.
Curriculum Associates, Inc.
153 Rangeway Road
North Billerica, MA 01862
Phone: 800-225-0248
Fax: 800-366-1158
<www.curriculumassociates.com>

C

California Achievement Test (CAT/5)
This test assesses academic achievement in language arts and mathematics. Grades K–12.
CTB/McGraw-Hill
20 Ryan Ranch Road
Monterey, CA 93940
Phone: 800-538-9547
Fax: 800-282-0266
<www.ctb.com>

California Diagnostic Test (CDMT/CDRT)
This test assesses basic reading and mathematical skills. Grades 1–12.
CTB/McGraw-Hill
20 Ryan Ranch Road
Monterey, CA 93940
Phone: 800-538-9547
Fax: 800-282-0266
<www.ctb.com>

Career Programs Assessment (CPAt)
This multiple-choice exam is used for course placement to assess basic language, reading, and numeric skills. Age 18 and above.
American College Testing, Inc.
P.O. Box 1008
Iowa City, IA 52243-1008
Phone: 319-337-1000
<www.act.org>

CAT/5 *see* California Achievement Test

C-BASE *see* College Basic Academic Skills Examination

CDMT/CDRT *see* California Diagnostic Test

CIBS *see* Brigance Diagnostic Comprehensive Inventory of Basic Skills

CLEP *see* College-Level Examination Program

Cognitive Abilities Test Form 5 (CogAT)
This exam assesses students' abilities in reasoning and problem solving through use of verbal, quantitative, and spatial symbols. Grades K–12.
Riverside Publishing Company
425 Spring Lake Drive
Itasca, IL 60143-2079
Phone: 800-323-9540
<www.riverpub.com>

College BASE
This test consists of multiple-choice and essay components, which measure proficiency in English, mathematics, science, and social studies, as well as cross-disciplinary skills. College level.
Riverside Publishing Company
425 Spring Lake Drive
Itasca, IL 60143-2079
Phone: 800-323-9540
<www.riverpub.com>

College Basic Academic Skills Examination (C-BASE)
This multiple-choice and essay exam assesses knowledge of basic academic skills. Adults, college level.
College BASE Coordinator
Assessment Resource Center
University of Missouri–Columbia
2800 Maguire Boulevard
Columbia, Missouri 65201
Phone: 800-366-8232
Fax: 573-882-8937
<http://arc.missouri.edu/collegebase>

College-Level Examination Program (CLEP)
CLEP measures college-level achievement in 34 different subject areas, and students may earn up to two years of college credit. Grade 10 and above.
Educational Testing Service (ETS)
664 Rosedale Road
Princeton, NJ 08541
Phone: 609-921-9000 or 800-257-9558
Fax: 609-734-5410
<www.ets.org>

COMP Objective Test
This multiple-choice test assesses general education skills: communicating, solving problems, clarifying values, using the arts, using science, and functioning in social situations. Age 17 and above.
American College Testing, Inc.
P.O. Box 1008
Iowa City, IA 52243-1008
Phone: 319-337-1000
<www.act.org>

Comprehensive Testing Program (CTP III)
This test measures verbal and mathematical skills. Use of test is

restricted to Educational Records Bureau (ERB) members. Grades 1–12.

Educational Records Bureau
Educational Testing Service (ETS)
664 Rosedale Road
Princeton, NJ 08541
Phone: 609-921-9000 or 212-672-9809
Fax: 609-734-5410
<www.ets.org>

Comprehensive Test of Basic Skills, 4th edition (CTBS-4)
This multiple-choice test assesses basic skills in reading, language, mathematics, science, and social studies. Grades K–12.

CTB/McGraw-Hill
20 Ryan Ranch Road
Monterey, CA 93940
Phone: 800-538-9547
Fax: 800-282-0266
<www.ctb.com>

Cooperative Admissions Exam (COOP-Catholic HS entrance exam)
This Catholic high school entrance exam assesses language arts skills, such as reading comprehension, sequences, analogies, memory, verbal reasoning, language expression, as well as mathematical skills. It is used in the Archdiocese of New York, Archdiocese of Newark, Archdiocese of New Jersey, Diocese of Brooklyn, and Diocese of Rockland County. Grade 8. Materials available through school.

CPAt *see* Career Programs Assessment

CTB5-5 *see* TerraNova

CTBS-4 *see* Comprehensive Test of Basic Skills, 4th edition

CTP III *see* Comprehensive Testing Program

D

Differential Aptitude Test, 5th edition (DAT)
This is a multiple-choice exam that assesses aptitude and interest. It is used for educational and vocational guidance. Grades 8–12.

Harcourt Brace Educational Measurement
19500 Bulverde Road
San Antonio, TX 78259
Phone: 800-211-8378
<www.harcourt.com>

G

GIFFI *see* Group Inventory for Finding Interests

GIFT *see* Group Inventory for Finding Creative Talent

Graduate Management Admission Test (GMAT)
The Graduate Management Admission Council's exam is used by many graduate schools of business and management as a criterion in considering applications for admission. College level.

Graduate Management Admission Council
Educational Testing Service (ETS)
664 Rosedale Road
Princeton, NJ 08541
Phone: 609-921-9000
Fax: 609-734-5410
<www.ets.org>

Graduate Record Examinations (GRE)
The Graduate Record Examinations Board Program provides tests, publications, and services that assist graduate schools and departments in graduate admissions activities, guidance and placement, program evaluation, and selection of fellowship recipients. The GRE Program's tests include the General Test, which measures developed verbal, quantitative, and analytical abilities; the Subject Tests, which measure achievement in 8 different fields of study; and the Writing Assessment, which measures proficiency in critical reasoning and analytical writing. College level.

Educational Testing Service (ETS)
664 Rosedale Road
Princeton, NJ 08541
Phone: 609-921-9000
Fax: 609-734-5410
<www.ets.org>

Group Inventory for Finding Creative Talent (GIFT)
This assessment is used to screen elementary school students for programs for the creatively gifted. Available on three levels: Grades K–2, 3–4, 5–6.

Sylvia Rimm, Ph.D.
Educational Assessment Service, Inc.
W6050 Apple Road
Watertown, WI 53098
Phone: 800-795-7466
Fax: 920-261-6622
<www.sylviarimm.com>

Group Inventory for Finding Interests (GIFFI)
This assessment is used to identify students at middle and high school levels with attitudes and values associated with creativity. Available on two levels: Grades 6–9, 9–12.

Sylvia Rimm, Ph.D.
Educational Assessment Service, Inc.
W6050 Apple Road
Watertown, WI 53098
Phone: 800-795-7466
Fax: 920-261-6622
<www.sylviarimm.com>

H

HSPT *see* STS High School Placement Test

I

IEA *see* International Association for the Evaluation of Educational Achievement

Independent School Entrance Exam (ISEE) (middle and upper)
This test is a standardized admissions exam used by schools that are members of the Educational Record Bureau consortium (ERB). The ISEE is used to facilitate student placement in course levels and for identifying areas where the student may need reinforcement. Grades 6–12.

Educational Records Bureau
Educational Testing Service (ETS)
664 Rosedale Road
Princeton, NJ 08541
Phone: 609-921-9000
Fax: 609-734-5410
<www.ets.org>

International Association for the Evaluation of Educational Achievement (IEA)
This independent, international cooperative of national research institutions and governmental research agencies conducts large-scale comparative studies of educational achievement, with the aim of gaining a more in-depth understanding of the effects of policies and practices within and across systems of education. IEA studies are an important data source for those working to enhance students' learning at the international, national, and local levels. By reporting on a wide range of topics and subject matters, the

studies contribute to a deep understanding of educational processes within individual countries, and across a broad international context. IEA's most widely administered tests include: Trends in Mathematics and Science Studies (TIMSS), the Third International Mathematics and Science Study Repeat (TIMSS-R), and the Progress in International Reading Literacy Studies (PIRLS). Grades 4 and 8.

IEA–USA
International Study Center
Boston College
Manresa House
140 Commonwealth Avenue
Chestnut Hill, MA
Phone: 617-552-1600
Fax: 617-552-1203

IEA–Headquarters
Herengracht 487
1017 BT Amsterdam
The Netherlands
<www.iea.nl>

Iowa Tests for Educational Development (ITED) Form K & L or Form M
These exams assess the development of basic academic skills and identify students' strengths and weaknesses while also evaluating the effectiveness of instructional programs. Grades K–9.

Riverside Publishing Company
425 Spring Lake Drive
Itasca, IL 60143-2079
Phone: 800-323-9540
<www.riverpub.com>

ISEE *see* Independent School Entrance Exam

K

K-ABC *see* Kaufman Assessment Battery for Children

Kaufman Adolescent and Adult Intelligence Test (KAIT)
This exam is a comprehensive measure of general intelligence. Ages 11–85.

American Guidance Service
4201 Woodland Road
Circle Pines, MN 55014-1796
Phone: 800-328-2560
Fax: 800-471-8457
<www.agsnet.com>

Kaufman Assessment Battery for Children (K-ABC)
This exam measures individual cognitive assessment. Ages 2 years, 6 months–12 years, 5 months.

American Guidance Service
4201 Woodland Road
Circle Pines, MN 55014-1796
Phone: 800-328-2560
Fax: 800-471-8457
<www.agsnet.com>

Kaufman Brief Intelligence Test (K-BIT)
This test is used to obtain an estimate of intelligence. It is also used to assess giftedness, to reassess individuals, or as routine intake for patients, prisoners, or recruits. Ages 4–90.

American Guidance Service
4201 Woodland Road
Circle Pines, MN 55014-1796
Phone: 800-328-2560
Fax: 800-471-8457
<www.agsnet.com>

L

Law School Admission Test (LSAT)
This half-day, multiple-choice test measures acquired reading and verbal reasoning skills that law schools use as one of several factors in assessing applicants. The LSAT is required for admission to the 198 law schools that are members of the Law School Admission Council (LSAC). College level.

Law School Admission Council
661 Penn Street
Newtown, PA 18940
Phone: 215-968-1001
Fax: 215-968-1119
<www.lsac.org>

M

MAT *see* Miller Analogies Test

MCAT *see* Medical College Admission Test

Medical College Admission Test (MCAT)
This standardized, multiple-choice exam assesses problem solving, critical thinking, and writing skills in addition to knowledge of science concepts and principles prerequisite to the study of medicine. Subject areas include: verbal reasoning, physical sciences, and biological sciences. A writing sample is also part of the exam. Medical college admission committees consider MCAT scores as part of their admission decision process, and almost all U.S. medical schools require applicants to submit MCAT scores with applications. College level.

MCAT Program Office
P.O. Box 4056
Iowa City, IA 52243
Phone: 319-337-1357
<www.aamc.org>

Metropolitan Achievement Test (Metropolitan8)
This broad-ranging test measures foundation skills and critical-thinking processes and strategies. The test format is designed so that all students can easily focus on what's being asked in each question and so that they can navigate easily through the test. Grades K–12.

Harcourt Brace Educational Measurement
19500 Bulverde Road
San Antonio, TX 78259
Phone: 800-211-8378
<www.hemweb.com/trophy/achvtest/mat8.htm>

Middle Grades Assessment (MGA)
This test is composed of a student survey, a transcript study, and achievement tests in mathematics, science, and reading. A detailed school-level report presents the results of the students who have taken the assessment. Grade 8.

Educational Testing Service (ETS)
664 Rosedale Road
Princeton, NJ 08541
Phone: 609-921-9000 or 609-734-1987
Fax: 609-734-5410
<www.ets.org>

Miller Analogies Test (MAT)
This is a high-level mental ability test requiring participants to solve 100 multiple-choice, partial word analogies. Adults.

The Psychological Corporation
19500 Bulverde Road
San Antonio, TX 78259
Phone: 800-622-3231
<www.tpcweb.com>

N

National Assessment of Educational Progress (NAEP)
Also know as "The Nation's Report Card," this national assessment tests knowledge of reading, writing, mathematics, science, U.S. history, civics, geography, and fine arts. Scores are not reported to individual schools; rather, results are for populations of students and subgroups of those populations. Also, they are based on a sampling of students, not the entire group tested. There is a state-level NAEP that is administered as well. Grades 4, 8, and 12.
Office of Educational Research and Improvement
U.S. Department of Education
1990 K Street NW
Washington, DC 20006
Phone: 202-502-7300
<www.nces.ed.gov/nationsreportcard>

New York City Specialized Science High Schools Admission Test (SSHSAT)
This exam is used for admission to Stuyvesant High School, Bronx High School of Science, and Brooklyn Technical High School. It assesses verbal skills and mathematical problem solving. Grades 8–9.
New York City Board of Education
Division of Assessment and Accountability
110 Livingston Street
Brooklyn, NY 11201
Phone: 718-935-3767
Fax: 718-935-5268
<www.nycenet.edu/daa>

O

Otis-Lennon School Ability Test (OLSAT)
This multiple-choice test assesses general mental ability and scholastic aptitude. Measures verbal comprehension, verbal reasoning, pictorial reasoning, figural reasoning, and quantitative reasoning. There are seven different grade levels. Grade K–12.
Harcourt Brace Educational Measurement
19500 Bulverde Road
San Antonio, TX 78259
Phone: 800-211-8378
<www.hemweb.com/trophy/achvtest/mat8.htm>

P

PIRLS *see* International Association for the Evaluation of Educational Achievement

PISA *see* Program for International Student Assessment

PLAN
This precursor to the ACT helps 10th grade students prepare for the ACT, while measuring their academic development. Also, it focuses attention on both career preparation and improving academic achievement in high school. Grade 10.
American College Testing, Inc.
P.O. Box 1008
Iowa City, IA 52243-1008
Phone: 319-337-1000
<www.act.org>

Preliminary SAT/National Merit Scholarship Qualifying Test (PSAT/NMSQT)
This precursor to the SAT helps students prepare and practice for the SAT I: Reasoning Test and the SAT II: Writing Test. It is also the qualifying test for the scholarship competitions conducted by the National Merit Scholarship Corporation. Grade 10.
The College Board/Educational Testing Service
45 Columbus Avenue
New York, NY 10023-6992
Phone: 212-713-8000
<www.collegeboard.com>

Primary Test of Cognitive Skills (PTCS)
This test serves as a predictor of future academic achievement when given in conjunction with an achievement test. Skills assessed include verbal, nonverbal, memory, and spatial reasoning. This test can be used to identify giftedness, learning disabilities, or developmental delays. Grades K–1.
CTB/McGraw-Hill
20 Ryan Ranch Road
Monterey, CA 93940
Phone: 800-538-9547
Fax: 800-282-0266
<www.ctb.com>

Program for International Student Assessment (PISA)
This three-yearly survey coordinated by the Organisation for Economic Co-Operation and Development (OECD) assesses how well students nearing the end of compulsory education are able to apply the knowledge and skills developed at school, to perform tasks that they will need in their future lives, to function in society, and to continue learning. PISA is a collaborative effort among the governments of 28 OECD and 4 nonmember countries, and its assessment of reading literacy, mathematical literacy, and scientific literacy help educators measure students' ability in the area of life skills. Age 15.
Organisation for Economic Co-Operation and Development
DEELSA Statistics and Indicators Division
2 rue André-Pascal
75775 Paris Cedex 16
France
Phone: (33-1) 4524 9366
<www.pisa.oecd.org>

Progress in International Reading Literacy Studies (PIRLS) *see* International Association for the Evaluation of Educational Achievement (IEA)

PSAT/NMSQT *see* Preliminary SAT/National Merit Scholarship Qualifying Test

PTCS *see* Primary Test of Cognitive Skills

R

Riverside Performance Assessment Series (R-PAS)
This test assesses thinking and process skills, as well as problem-solving strategies. Subjects tested are reading, writing, and mathematics. Grades 1–12.
Riverside Publishing Company
425 Spring Lake Drive
Itasca, IL 60143-2079
Phone: 800-323-9540
<www.riverpub.com>

S

SAGES-2 *see* Screening Assessment for Gifted Elementary and Middle School Students, 2nd edition

SAT 9 *see* Stanford Achievement Test Series, 9th edition

SAT I
The College Board-sponsored SAT Program consists of the SAT I:

Reasoning Test and SAT II: Subject Tests. The SAT I measures verbal- and mathematical-reasoning abilities, including reading comprehension, vocabulary, mathematical problem solving, arithmetic reasoning, algebra, and geometry. (The SAT II: Subject Tests measure knowledge of particular subjects and the ability to apply that knowledge.) Grades 11 and 12.

The College Board/Educational Testing Service
45 Columbus Avenue
New York, NY 10023-6992
Phone: 212-713-8000
<www.collegeboard.com>

SAT II
These assessment exams are one-hour, mostly multiple-choice tests in specific subjects that measure knowledge of particular subjects and the ability to apply that knowledge. Many colleges require or recommend these tests for admission or placement purposes. Grades 11–12.

The College Board/Educational Testing Service
45 Columbus Avenue
New York, NY 10023-6992
Phone: 212-713-8000
<www.collegeboard.com>

SBIS *see* Stanford-Binet Intelligence Scale, 4th edition

Screening Assessment for Gifted Elementary and Middle School Students, 2nd edition (SAGES-2)
This exam identifies gifted students through aptitude and achievement tests. Aptitude is measured using a Reasoning subtest in which students solve problems by identifying relationships among pictures and figures. The other two subtests, Mathematics/Science and Language Arts/Social Studies, assess achievement. Grades K–8.

Psychological Assessment Resources, Inc.
16204 North Florida Avenue
Lutz, FL 33549
Phone: 800-331-8378
Fax: 800-727-9329
<www.parinc.com>

Secondary Level English Proficiency Test (SLEP)
This exam measures English language ability in terms of listening comprehension and reading comprehension. Grades 7–12 nonnative English language speakers; also used by community colleges as an assessment tool for screening or placing entering students into ESL programs.

Educational Testing Service (ETS)
664 Rosedale Road
Princeton, NJ 08541
Phone: 609-683-2057
Fax: 609-734-5410
<www.ets.org>

SLEP *see* Secondary Level English Proficiency Test

SSHSAT *see* New York City Specialized Science High Schools Admission Test

Stanford Achievement Test Series, 9th edition (SAT 9)
This assessment combines multiple-choice and open-ended subtests to help educators obtain a more complete picture of both the breadth and depth of students' educational achievement. Grades K–13.

Harcourt Brace Educational Measurement
19500 Bulverde Road
San Antonio, TX 78259
Phone: 800-211-8378
<www.hemweb.com/trophy/achvtest/sat9view.htm>

Stanford-Binet Intelligence Scale, 4th edition (SBIS)
This test assesses intelligence and cognitive abilities. Ages 2–adult.

Riverside Publishing Company
425 Spring Lake Drive
Itasca, IL 60143-2079
Phone: 800-323-9540
<www.riverpub.com>

STS High School Placement Test (HSPT)
This multiple-choice exam assesses academic achievement and aptitude. Often used as an entrance exam for parochial school, subjects tested include: verbal cognitive skills, quantitative skills, reading, mathematics, and language, as well as optional sections on Catholic religion, mechanical aptitude, and science. Grades 8.3–9.3.

Scholastic Testing Service, Inc.
Administrative & Editorial Division/Order Department
480 Meyer Road
Bensenville, IL 60106
Phone: 800-642-6787
<www.ststesting.com>

T

TABE *see* Test of Adult Basic Education

TCS/2 *see* Test of Cognitive Skills, 2nd edition

TEMA *see* Test for Early Mathematics Ability

TERA-2 *see* Test of Early Reading Ability, 2nd edition

TerraNova (CTB5-5)
This multiple-choice exam assesses academic achievement in reading, language arts, mathematics, science, and social studies. Grades K–12.

CTB/McGraw-Hill
20 Ryan Ranch Road
Monterey, CA 93940
Phone: 800-538-9547
Fax: 800-282-0266
<www.ctb.com>

Test for Early Mathematics Ability (TEMA)
This exam measures mathematics performance in early childhood. It can be used as a diagnostic instrument to determine specific strengths and weaknesses, to measure progress, evaluate programs, screen for readiness, and identify gifted students. Ages 3–8 years, 11 months.

PRO-ED, Inc.
8700 Shoal Creek Boulevard
Austin, TX 78757-6897
Phone: 800-897-3202
Fax: 800-397-7633
<www.proedinc.com>

Test for Mathematical Abilities, 2nd edition (TOMA-2)
This exam measures mathematical performance in two major skill areas in mathematics: word problems and computation, as well as attitude, vocabulary, and general application of mathematics concepts in real life. Grades 3–12.

PRO-ED, Inc.
8700 Shoal Creek Boulevard
Austin, TX 78757-6897
Phone: 800-897-3202
Fax: 800-397-7633
<www.proedinc.com>

Test of Adult Basic Education (TABE)
This multiple-choice exam measures adult-level proficiency in reading, mathematics, and language in order to identify strengths and weaknesses, establish level of instruction, and measure academic growth. Adults.

CTB/McGraw-Hill
20 Ryan Ranch Road
Monterey, CA 93940
Phone: 800-538-9547
Fax: 800-282-0266
<www.ctb.com>

Test of Children's Language (TOCL)
This exam identifies students' strengths and weaknesses in language components, and it recognizes young students who are at risk for failure in reading and writing. Ages 5–8 years, 11 months.

PRO-ED, Inc.
8700 Shoal Creek Boulevard
Austin, TX 78757-6897
Phone: 800-897-3202
Fax: 800-397-7633
<www.proedinc.com>

Test of Cognitive Skills, 2nd edition (TCS/2)
This test serves as a predictor of future academic achievement when given in conjunction with an achievement test. Skills assessed include sequences, analogies, memory, and verbal reasoning. This test can be used to identify students for special programs. Grades 2–12.

CTB/McGraw-Hill
20 Ryan Ranch Road
Monterey, CA 93940
Phone: 800-538-9547
Fax: 800-282-0266
<www.ctb.com>

Test of Early Reading Ability, 2nd edition (TERA-2)
This exam assesses mastery of early developing reading skills, specifically the ability for spoken language using two subtests: receptive language and expressive language. Ages 3 years, 6 months–8 years, 6 months.

PRO-ED, Inc.
8700 Shoal Creek Boulevard
Austin, TX 78757-6897
Phone: 800-897-3202
Fax: 800-397-7633
<www.proedinc.com>

Test of Early Written Language, 2nd edition (TEWL-2)
This exam assesses mastery of early developing writing skills, measured in two forms, each containing a basic writing and contextual writing component. Ages 3–10 years, 11 months.

PRO-ED, Inc.
8700 Shoal Creek Boulevard
Austin, TX 78757-6897
Phone: 800-897-3202
Fax: 800-397-7633
<www.proedinc.com>

Test of English as a Foreign Language (TOEFL)
This exam is for non-native English language speakers who are planning to study in a North American college or university. It includes grammar, writing, listening, and speaking sections. Age 16 and above.

TOEFL Services
Educational Testing Service (ETS)
P.O. Box 6151
Princeton, NJ 08541
Phone: 609-771-7100
Fax: 609-771-7500
<www.toefl.org>

Test of English for International Communication (TOEIC)
This exam assesses English language proficiency and communication skills in non-native English language speakers who are planning to work in North American corporations. Age 18 and above.

Educational Testing Service (ETS)
664 Rosedale Road
Princeton, NJ 08541
Phone: 609-921-9000
Fax: 609-720-6550
<www.ets.org>

Test of Phonological Awareness (TOPA)
This exam measures young children's awareness of individual sounds in words. Grades K–2.

PRO-ED, Inc.
8700 Shoal Creek Boulevard
Austin, TX 78757-6897
Phone: 800-897-3202
Fax: 800-397-7633
<www.proedinc.com>

Test of Reading Comprehension, 3rd edition (TORC-3)
This test assesses reading comprehension ability in terms of language and cognition. Areas tested include: vocabulary, syntax, paragraph reading, and sentence sequencing. Grades 2–12.

Stoelting Company
620 Wheat Lane
Wood Dale, IL 60191
Phone: 630-860-9700
Fax: 630-860-9775
<http://stoeltingco.com>

Test of Spoken English (TSE)
This oral exam assesses non-native English language speakers' ability to speak the English language. All answers to the test questions are recorded on tape and scored by language specialists. Age 16 and above.

Educational Testing Service (ETS)
664 Rosedale Road
Princeton, NJ 08541
Phone: 609-921-9000
Fax: 609-734-5410
<www.ets.org>

Test of Written English (TWE)
This exam is administered along with the Test of English as a Foreign Language (TOEFL) at paper-based TOEFL test administrations. The test involves writing an essay in English on a provided topic. The essay is read and scored by writing specialists. Age 16 and above.

Educational Testing Service (ETS)
664 Rosedale Road
Princeton, NJ 08541
Phone: 609-921-9000
Fax: 609-734-5410
<www.ets.org>

Test of Written Expression (TOWE)
This exam, consisting of two parts, is used to assess writing achievement. The first part uses 76 items related to writing, such as vocabulary and spelling, to determine skill. The second part consists of providing the student with a stimulus, such as a beginning of a story, and having the student finish the story in writing. Ages 6 years, 6 months–14 years, 11 months.

PRO-ED, Inc.
8700 Shoal Creek Boulevard
Austin, TX 78757-6897
Phone: 800-897-3202
Fax: 800-397-7633
<www.proedinc.com>

Test of Written Language, 3rd edition (TOWL-3)
This written test assesses written expression ability in students. The test involves writing a story on a given theme. Grades 2–12.

PRO-ED, Inc.
8700 Shoal Creek Boulevard
Austin, TX 78757-6897
Phone: 800-897-3202
Fax: 800-397-7633
<www.proedinc.com>

Test of Written Spelling, 3rd edition (TOWS-3)
This 100-item test assesses written spelling ability. Ages 6 years, 7 months–18 years, 6 months.
PRO-ED, Inc.
8700 Shoal Creek Boulevard
Austin, TX 78757-6897
Phone: 800-897-3202
Fax: 800-397-7633
<www.proedinc.com>

TEWL-2 *see* Test of Early Written Language, 2nd edition

TIMSS *see* International Association for the Evaluation of Educational Achievement

TIMSS-R *see* International Association for the Evaluation of Educational Achievement

TOCL *see* Test of Children's Language

TOEFL *see* Test of English as a Foreign Language

TOEIC *see* Test of English for International Communication

TOMA-2 *see* Test for Mathematical Abilities, 2nd edition

TOPA *see* Test of Phonological Awareness

TORC-3 *see* Test of Reading Comprehension, 3rd edition

TOWE *see* Test of Written Expression

TOWL-3 *see* Test of Written Language, 3rd edition

TOWS-3 *see* Test of Written Spelling, 3rd edition

Trends in Mathematics and Science Studies (TIMSS) and Third International Mathematics and Science Studies Repeat (TIMSS-R) *see* International Association for the Evaluation of Educational Achievement (IEA)

TSE *see* Test of Spoken English

TWE *see* Test of Written English

W

Watson-Glaser Critical Thinking Appraisal (WGCTA)
This exams measures the ability to think critically. The test requires a ninth grade reading level. Adults.
The Psychological Corporation
19500 Bulverde Road
San Antonio, TX 78259
Phone: 800-622-3231
<www.tpcweb.com>

WDRB *see* Woodcock Diagnostic Reading Battery

Wechsler Individual Achievement Test (WIAT)
Using eight subtests linked to diagnostic tests Wechsler Intelligence Scale for Children (WISC-III) and Wechsler Preschool and Primary Scale of Intelligence (WPPSI-R), this exam measures academic abilities in order to evaluate discrepancies between aptitude and achievement. Subjects include: reading, mathematics, spelling, reasoning, reading comprehension, oral expression, and written expression. Ages 5–19.
Harcourt Brace Educational Measurement
19500 Bulverde Road
San Antonio, TX 78259
Phone: 800-211-8378
<www.hemweb.com/trophy/achvtest/sat9view.htm>

WGCTA *see* Watson-Glaser Critical Thinking Appraisal

WIAT *see* Wechsler Individual Achievement Test

Woodcock Diagnostic Reading Battery (WDRB)
This is a comprehensive set of tests that measure reading achievement and related cognitive abilities and aptitudes, such as oral language capabilities. It is composed of ten tests selected from several parts of the Woodcock-Johnson Psycho-Educational Battery—Revised: letter-word identification, word attack, reading vocabulary, passage comprehension, incomplete words, sound blending, oral vocabulary, listening comprehension, memory for sentences, and visual matching. The tests determine the status of an individual's abilities and achievement in five areas of functioning: basic reading skills, reading comprehension, phonological awareness, oral language comprehension, and reading aptitude. Ages 4–90.

Riverside Publishing Company
425 Spring Lake Drive
Itasca, IL 60143-2079
Phone: 800-323-9540
<www.riverpub.com>

APPENDIX II

STATE-BY-STATE DIRECTORY OF DEPARTMENTS OF EDUCATION

This directory of state departments of education is provided as a resource for parents, teachers, administrators, and researchers interested in learning more about statewide education initiatives and assessment programs. Specific statewide assessment programs are not listed because many states are in the process of developing new, proprietary assessments to reflect national standards for 2004. The No Child Left Behind Act of 2001 is also expected to have an impact on state assessment tests. Up-to-date information on statewide assessment programs is available online through individual state departments of education.

A

Alabama Department of Education
P.O. Box 302101
Montgomery, AL 36130-2101
334-242-9935
<www.alsde.edu>

Alaska Department of Education and Early Development
801 West 10th Street, Suite 200
Juneau, AK 99801-1894
907-465-2800
<www.educ.state.ak.us>

Arizona Department of Education
1535 West Jefferson Street
Phoenix, AZ 85007
602-542-4361
<www.ade.state.az.us>

Arkansas Department of Education
4 Capitol Mall
Little Rock, AR 72201
501-682-4475
<http://arkedu.state.ar.us>

C

California Department of Education
P.O. Box 944272
Sacramento, California 94244-2720
916-319-0791
<www.cde.ca.gov>

Colorado Department of Education
201 East Colfax Avenue
Denver, CO 80203
303-866-6600
<www.cde.state.co.us>

Connecticut State Department of Education
165 Capitol Avenue
Hartford, CT 06145
860-713-6548
<www.state.ct.us/sde>

D

Delaware Department of Education
John G. Townsend Building
401 Federal Street
P.O. Box 1402
Dover, DE 19903-1402
302-739-4601
<www.doe.state.de.us>

F

Florida Department of Education
Turlington Building
325 West Gaines Street
Tallahassee, FL 32399-0400
904-488-3217
<www.firn.edu/doe>

G

Georgia Department of Education
205 Jesse Hill Jr. Drive, SE
Atlanta, GA 30334
404-656-2800
<www.doe.k12.ga.us>

H

Hawaii Department of Education
P.O. Box 2360
Honolulu, HI 96804
808-586-3230
<www.doe.k12.hi.us>

I

Idaho State Department of Education
650 West State Street
P.O. Box 83720
Boise, ID 83720-0027
208-332-6800
<www.sde.state.id.us/Dept>

Illinois State Board of Education
100 West Randolph, Suite 14-300
Chicago, IL 60601
312-814-2220
<www.isbe.state.il.us>

Indiana Department of Education
State House, Room 229
Indianapolis, IN 46204-2798
317-232-0808
<http://ideanet.doe.state.in.us>

Iowa Department of Education
Grimes State Office Building
Des Moines, IA 50319-0146
515-281-5294
<www.state.ia.us/educate>

K

Kansas State Department of Education
120 SE 10th Avenue
Topeka, KS 66612-1182
785-296-3201
<www.ksbe.state.ks.us>

Kentucky Department of Education
500 Mero Street
Frankfurt, KY 40601
502-564-4770
<www.kde.state.ky.us>

L

Louisiana Department of Education
P.O. Box 94064
Baton Rouge, LA 70804
504-342-3490
<www.doe.state.la.us/DOE/asps/home.asp>

M

Maine State Department of Education
23 State House Station
Augusta, ME 04333
207-287-5944
<www.state.me.us/education/homepage.htm>

Maryland State Department of Education
200 West Baltimore Street
Baltimore, MD 21201
410-767-0100
<www.msde.state.md.us>

Massachusetts Department of Education
350 Main Street
Malden, MA 02148
781-338-3000
<www.doe.mass.edu>

Michigan Department of Education
608 West Allegan Street
Lansing, MI 48933
517-373-3324
<www.michigan.gov/mde>

Minnesota Department of Children, Families, and Learning
1500 Highway 36 West
Roseville, MN 55113
651-582-8200
<www.educ.state.mn.us>

Mississippi Department of Education
Central High School
P.O. Box 771
359 North West Street
Jackson, MS 39205
601-359-3513
<www.mde.k12.ms.us>

Missouri Department of Elementary and Secondary Education
P.O. Box 480
Jefferson City, MO 65102
573-751-4212
<www.dese.state.mo.us>

Montana Office of Public Instruction
P.O. Box 202501
Helena, MT 59620-2501
406-444-3095
<www.opi.state.mt.us>

N

Nebraska Department of Education
301 Centennial Mall South
Lincoln, NE 68509
402-471-2295
<www.nde.state.ne.us>

Nevada Department of Education
700 East Fifth Street
Carson City, NV 89701
775-687-9200
<www.nde.state.nv.us>

New Hampshire Department of Education
101 Pleasant Street
Concord, NH 03301-3860
603-271-3494
<www.state.nh.us/doe>

New Jersey Department of Education
100 Riverview Plaza
Trenton, NJ 08625
609-292-0739
<www.state.nj.us/education>

New Mexico Department of Education
Education Building
300 Don Gaspar
Santa Fe, NM 87501-2786
505-827-6575
<http://sde.state.nm.us>

New York State Education Department
89 Washington Avenue
Albany, NY 12234
518-474-3852
<www.nysed.gov>

North Carolina Department of Public Instruction
301 North Wilmington Street
Raleigh, NC 27601
919-807-3300
<www.dpi.state.nc.us>

North Dakota Department of Public Instruction
600 East Boulevard Avenue
Department 201
Bismark, ND 58505-0440
701-328-2260
<www.dpi.state.nd.us>

O

Ohio Department of Education
25 South Front Street
Columbus, OH 43215-4183
877-644-6338
<www.ode.state.oh.us>

Oklahoma State Department of Education
2500 North Lincoln Boulevard
Oklahoma City, OK 73105-4599
405-521-3301
<http://sde.state.ok.us>

Oregon Department of Education
255 Capitol Street NE
Salem, OR 97310-0203
503-378-3569
<www.ode.state.or.us>

P

Pennsylvania Department of Education
333 Market Street
Harrisburg, PA 17126
717-783-6788
<www.pde.psu.edu>

R

Rhode Island Department of Elementary and Secondary Education
255 Westminster Street
Providence, RI 02903
401-222-4600
<www.ridoe.net>

S

South Carolina State Department of Education
1429 Senate Street
Columbia, SC 29201
803-734-8500
<www.sde.state.sc.us>

South Dakota Department of Education and Cultural Affairs
Kneip Building, 3rd Floor
700 Governors Drive
Pierre, SD 57501-2291
605-773-3134
<www.state.sd.us/deca>

T

Tennessee Department of Education
Andrew Johnson Tower, 6th Floor
710 James Robertson Parkway
Nashville, TN 37243-0375
615-741-2731
<www.state.tn.us/education>

Texas Education Agency
1701 North Congress Avenue
Austin, TX 78701-1494
512-463-9734
<www.tea.state.tx.us>

U

Utah State Office of Education
250 East 500 South
P.O. Box 144200
Salt Lake City, UT 84114-4200
801-538-7500
<www.usoe.k12.ut.us>

V

Vermont Department of Education
120 State Street
Montpelier, VT 05620-2501
802-828-3147
<www.state.vt.us/educ>

Virginia Department of Education
101 North 14th Street
Richmond, VA 23218
800-292-3820
<www.pen.k12.va.us>

W

Washington Office of Superintendent of Public Instruction
Old Capitol Building
P.O. Box 47200
Olympia, WA 98504-7200
360-725-6000
<www.k12.wa.us>

West Virginia Department of Education
1900 Kanawha Boulevard East
Charleston, WV 25305
304-558-2861
<http://wvde.state.wv.us>

Wisconsin Department of Public Instruction
125 South Webster Street
P.O. Box 7841
Madison, WI 53707-7841
800-441-4563
<www.dpi.state.wi.us>

Wyoming Department of Education
2300 Capitol Avenue
Hathaway Building, 2nd Floor
Cheyenne, WY 82002-0050
307-777-7675
<www.k12.wy.us>

APPENDIX III

COURT CASES, LEGISLATION, AND INTERNATIONAL AGREEMENTS

The documents included in this Appendix were selected by the editors of the Encyclopedia of Education, Second Edition to represent the essential primary sources relating to the field of education. The documents are divided into four sections as listed in the table of contents. The first section contains key court decisions that govern educational policy and practice in the United States. Footnotes have been omitted due to space limitations. For complete transcripts of U.S. Supreme Court cases including footnotes, please see United States Reports, published for the Court by the Reporter of Decisions and released by the Government Printing Office. The second and third sections contain legislation and reports of significance to American education. The final section is a compilation of significant treaties and other documents that influence education around the world. The documents are organized chronologically. For a topical guide to the documents listed below, please see Appendix VI: Outline of Contents.

Court Cases

Reports and Other Sources

State Constitutions and Public Education Governance (2000)

Legislation

Land Ordinance of 1785

Northwest Ordinance of 1787

Constitution of the United States (1787)

Morrill Land-Grant Act of 1862

Second Morrill Act of 1890

Elementary and Secondary Education Act of 1965

Title IX of the Education Amendments of 1972

Education for All Handicapped Children Act of 1975

Education of the Handicapped Act Amendments of 1990

Individuals with Disabilities Education Act Amendments of 1997

Head Start: Overview of Programs and Legislation (1999)

National Education Goals Panel: Goals 2000

No Child Left Behind Act of 2001

International Agreements, Charters, and Declarations

Charter of the United Nations, Article 1 (1945)

Constitution of the United Nations Educational, Scientific and Cultural Organization (1945)

Universal Declaration of Human Rights (1948)

European Convention on Human Rights and Its Five Protocols (1950)

Declaration of the Rights of the Child (1959)

Convention against Discrimination in Education (1960)

Declaration on Race and Racial Prejudice (1978)

Convention on the Rights of the Child (1989)

Document of the Copenhagen Meeting on the Human Dimension of the Conference on Security and Co-operation in Europe (1990)

World Declaration on Education for All (1990)

Declaration on the Rights of Persons Belonging to National or Ethnic, Religious and Linguistic Minorities (1992)

European Charter for Regional or Minority Languages (1992)

Council of Europe Framework Convention for the Protection of National Minorities (1995)

COURT CASES

CHARLES E. STUART V. SCHOOL DISTRICT NO. 1 OF THE VILLAGE OF KALAMAZOO (1874)

SUPREME COURT OF MICHIGAN
JULY 10, 1874; JULY 15, 1874, HEARD
JULY 21, 1874, DECIDED

OPINION:

Cooley, J.:

The bill in this case is filed to restrain the collection of such portion of the school taxes assessed against complainants for the year 1872, as have been voted for the support of the high school in that village, and for the payment of the salary of the superintendent. While, nominally, this is the end sought to be attained by the bill, the real purpose of the suit is wider and vastly more comprehensive than this brief statement would indicate, inasmuch as it seeks a judicial determination of the right of school authorities, in what are called union school districts of the state, to levy taxes upon the general public for the support of what in this state are known as high schools, and to make free by such taxation the instruction of children in other languages than the English. The bill is, consequently, of no small interest to all the people of the state; and to a large number of very flourishing schools, it is of the very highest interest, as their prosperity and usefulness, in a large degree, depend upon the method in which they are supported, so that a blow at this method seems a blow at the schools themselves. The suit, however, is not to be regarded as a blow purposely aimed at the schools. It can never be unimportant to know that taxation, even for the most useful or indispensable purposes, is warranted by the strict letter of the law; and whoever doubts its being so in any particular case, may well be justified by his doubts in asking a legal investigation, that, if errors or defects in the law are found to exist, there may be a review of the subject in legislation, and the whole matter be settled on legal grounds, in such manner and on such principles as the public will may indicate, and as the legislature may prescribe.

The complainants rely upon two objections to the taxes in question, one of which is general, and the other applies only to the authority or action of this particular district. The general objection has already been indicated; the particular objection is that, even conceding that other districts in the state may have authority under special charters or laws, or by the adoption of general statutes, to levy taxes for the support of high schools in which foreign and dead languages shall be taught, yet this district has no such power, because the special legislation for its benefit, which was had in 1859, was invalid for want of compliance with the constitution in the forms of enactment, and it has never adopted the general law (*Comp. L., ?3742*), by taking a vote of the district to establish a union school in accordance with its provisions, though ever since that law was enacted the district has sustained such a school, and proceeded in its action apparently on the assumption that the statutes in all respects were constitutional enactments, and had been complied with.

Whether this particular objection would have been worthy of serious consideration had it been made sooner, we must, after this lapse of time, wholly decline to consider. This district existed *de facto,* and we suppose *de jure,* also, for we are not informed to the contrary, when the legislation of 1859 was had, and from that time to the present it has assumed to possess and exercise all the franchises which are now brought in question, and there has since been a steady concurrence of action on the part of its people in the election of officers, in the levy of large taxes, and in the employment of teachers for the support of a high school. The state has acquiesced in this assumption of authority, and it has never, so far as we are advised, been questioned by any one until, after thirteen years user, three individual tax payers, out of some thousands, in a suit instituted on their own behalf, and to which the public authorities give no countenance, come forward in this collateral manner and ask us to annul the franchises. To require a municipal corporation, after so long an acquiescence, to defend, in a merely private suit, the irregularity, not only of its own action, but even of the legislation that permitted such action to be had, could not be justified by the principles of law, much less by those of public policy. We may justly take cognizance in these cases, of the notorious fact that municipal action is often exceedingly informal and irregular, when, after all, no wrong or illegality has been intended, and the real purpose of the law has been had in view and been accomplished; so that it may be said the spirit of the law has been kept while the letter has been disregarded. We may also find in the statutes many instances of careless legislation, under which municipalities have acted for many years, until important interests have sprung up, which might be crippled or destroyed, if then for the first time matters of form in legislative action were suffered to be questioned. If every municipality must be subject to be called into court at any time to defend its original organization and its franchises at the will of any dissatisfied citizen who may feel disposed to question them, and subject to dissolution, perhaps, or to be crippled in authority and powers if defects appear, however complete and formal may have been the recognition of its rights and privileges, on the part alike of the state and of its citizens, it may very justly be said that few of our municipalities can be entirely certain of the ground they stand upon, and that any single person, however honestly inclined, if disposed to be litigious, or over technical and precise, may have it in his power in many cases to cause infinite trouble, embarrassment and mischief.

It was remarked by Mr. Justice Campbell in *People v. Maynard,* 15 Mich. 463, that "in public affairs where the people have organized themselves under color of law into the ordinary municipal bodies, and have gone on year after year raising taxes, making improvements, and exercising their usual franchises, their rights are properly regarded as depending quite as much on the acquiescence as on the regularity of their origin, and no *ex post facto* inquiry can be permitted to undo their corporate existence. Whatever may be the rights of individuals before such general acquiescence, the corporate standing of the community can no longer be open to question." To this doctrine were cited *Rumsey v. People,* 19 N.Y. 41, and *Lanning v. Carpenter,* 20 N.Y. 447. The cases of *State v. Bunker,* 59 Me. 366; *People v. Salomon,* 54 Ill. 39, and *People v. Lothrop,* 24 Mich. 235, are in the same direction. The legislature has recognized this principle with special reference to school districts, and has not only deemed it important that their power should not be questioned after any considerable lapse of time, but has even established what is in effect a very short act of limitation for the purpose in declaring that "Every school district shall, in all cases, be presumed to have been legally organized, when it shall have exercised the franchises and privileges of a district for the term of two years:" *Comp. L. 1871,* ?3591. This is wise legislation, and short as the period is, we have held that even a less period is sufficient to justify us in refusing to interfere except on the application of the state itself: *School District v. Joint Board, etc.,* 27 Mich. 3.

It may be said that this doctrine is not applicable to this case because here the corporate organization is not questioned, but only the authority which the district asserts to establish a high school and levy taxes therefor. But we think that, though the statute may not in terms apply, in principle it is strictly applicable. The district claims and has long exercised powers which take it out of the class of ordinary school districts, and place it in another class altogether, whose organization is greatly different and whose authority is much greater. So far as the externals of corporate action are concerned, the two classes are quite distinct, and the one subserves purposes of a higher order than the other, and is permitted to levy much greater burdens. It is not very clear that the case is not strictly within the law: for the organization here claimed is that of a union school district, and nothing else, and it seems little less than an absurdity to say it may be presumed from its user of corporate power to be a school district, but not such a district as the user indicates, and as it has for so long a period claimed to be. But however that may be, we are clear that even if we might be allowed by the law to listen to the objection after the two years, we cannot in reason consent to do so after thirteen. It cannot be permitted that communities can be suffered to be annoyed, embarrassed and unsettled by having agitated in the courts after such a lapse of time questions which every consideration of fairness to the people concerned and of public policy require should be raised and disposed of immediately or never raised at all.

The more general question which the record presents we shall endeavor to state in our own language, but so as to make it stand out distinctly as a naked question of law, disconnected from all considerations of policy or expediency; in which light alone are we at liberty to consider it. It is, as we understand it, that there is no authority in this state to make the high schools free by taxation levied on the people at large. The argument is that while there may be no constitutional provision expressly prohibiting such taxation, the general course of legislation in the state and the general understanding of the people have been such as to require us to regard the instruction in the classics and in living modern languages in these schools as in the nature not of practical and therefore necessary instruction for the benefit of the people at large, but rather as accomplishments for the few, to be sought after in the main by those best able to pay for them, and to be paid for by those who seek them, and not by general tax. And not only has this been the general state policy, but this higher learning of itself, when supplied by the state, is so far a matter of private concern to those who receive it that the courts ought to declare it incompetent to supply it wholly at the public expense. This is in substance, as we understand it, the position of the complainants in this suit.

When this doctrine was broached to us, we must confess to no little surprise that the legislation and policy of our state were appealed to against the right of the state to furnish a liberal education to the youth of the state in schools brought within the reach of all classes. We supposed it had always been understood in this state that education, not merely in the rudiments. but in an enlarged sense, was regarded as an important practical advantage to be supplied at their option to rich and poor alike, and not as something pertaining merely to culture and accomplishment to be brought as such within the reach of those whose accumulated wealth enabled them to pay for it. As this, however, is now so seriously disputed, it may be necessary, perhaps, to take a brief survey of the legislation and general course, not only of the state, but of the antecedent territory, on the subject.

It is not disputed that the dissemination of knowledge by means of schools has been a prominent object from the first, and we allude to the provision of the ordinance of 1787 on that subject, and to the donation of lands by congress for the purpose, only as preliminary to what we may have to say regarding the action of the territorial authorities in the premises. Those authorities accepted in the most liberal spirit the requirement of the ordinance that "schools and the means of education shall forever be encouraged," and endeavored to make early provision therefor on a scale which shows they were fully up to the most advanced ideas that then prevailed on the subject. The earliest territorial legislation regarding education, though somewhat eccentric in form, was framed in this spirit. It was "an act to establish the Catholepistemiad, or University of Michigania," adopted August 26, 1817, which not only incorporated the institution named in the title, with its president and thirteen professors, appointed by the governor, but it provided that its board of instruction should have power "to regulate all the concerns of the institution, to enact laws for that purpose," "to establish colleges, academies, schools, libraries, museums, atheneums, botanic gardens, laboratories and other useful literary and scientific institutions, consonant to the laws of the United States of America, and of Michigan, and to appoint officers and instructors and instructrices, in, among, and throughout the various counties, cities, towns, townships and other geographical divisions of Michigan." To provide for the expense thereof the existing public taxes were increased fifteen per cent, and from the proceeds of all future taxes fifteen per cent was appropriated for the benefit of this corporation: *Territorial Laws, Vol, 2, p. 104; Sherman's School Laws, p. 4.* The act goes but little into details, as was to be expected of a law which proposed to put the whole educational system of the commonwealth into the hands and under the control of a body of learned men, created and made territorial officers for the purpose of planning and carrying it out; but the general purpose was apparent that throughout the territory a system of most liberal education should be supported at the public expense for the benefit of the whole people. The system indicated was prophetic of that which exists to-day, and is remarkable in this connection mainly, as being the very first law on the subject enacted in the territory, and as announcing a policy regarding liberal instruction which, though perhaps impracticable in view of the then limited and scattered population of the territory, has been steadily kept in view from that day to the present.

This act continued in force until 1821, when it was repealed to make way for one "for the establishment of an university," with more limited powers, and authorized only "to establish colleges, academies and schools depending upon the said university," and which, according to the general understanding at the time and afterwards, were to be schools intermediate the university and such common schools as might exist or be provided for: *Code of 1820, p. 443; Code of 1827, p. 445.* In 1827 the educational system was supplemented by "an act for the establishment of common schools," which is also worthy of special attention and reflection, as indicating what was understood at that day by the common schools which were proposed to be established.

The first section of that act provided "that every township within this territory, containing fifty families or householders, shall be provided with a good schoolmaster or schoolmasters, of good morals, to teach children to read and write, and to instruct them in the English or French language, as well as in arithmetic, orthography, and decent behavior, for such term of time as shall be equivalent to six months for one school in each year. And every township containing one hundred families or householders, shall be provided with such schoolmaster or teacher, for such term of time, as shall be equivalent to twelve months for one school in each year. And every township containing one hundred and fifty families or householders shall be provided with such schoolmaster or teacher for such term of time as shall be equivalent to six months in each year, and shall, in addition thereto, be provided with a schoolmaster or teacher, as above described, to instruct children in the English language for such term of time as shall be equivalent to twelve months for one school in each year. And every township containing two hundred families or householders shall be provided with a grammar schoolmaster, of good morals, *well instructed in the Latin, French and English languages,* and shall, in addition thereto, be provided with a schoolmaster or teacher, as above described, to instruct children in the English language, for such term of time as shall be equivalent to twelve months for each of said schools in each year." And the townships respectively were required under a heavy penalty, to be levied in case of default on the inhabitants generally, to keep and maintain the schools so provided for: *Code of 1827, p. 448; Territorial Laws, Vol, 2, p, 472.*

Here, then, was a general law, which, under the name of common schools, required not only schools for elementary instruction, but also grammar schools to be maintained. The qualifications required in teachers of grammar schools were such as to leave it open to no doubt that grammar schools in the sense understood in England and the Eastern States were intended, in which instruction in the classics should be given, as well as in such higher branches of learning as would not usually be taught in the schools of lowest grade. How is it possible, then, to say, as the exigencies of complainants' case require them to do, that the term common or primary schools, as made use of in our legislation, has a known and definite meaning which limits it to the ordinary district schools, and that consequently the legislative authority to levy taxes for the primary schools cannot be held to embrace taxation for the schools supported by village and city districts in which a higher grade of learning is imparted.

It is probable that this act, like that of 1817, was found in advance of the demands of the people of the territory, or of their ability to support high schools, and it was repealed in 1833, and another passed which did not expressly require the establishment or support of schools of secondary grade, but which provided only for school directors, who must maintain a district school at least three months in each year: *Code of 1833, p. 129.* The act contains no express limitations upon their powers, but it is not important now to consider whether or not they extended to the establishment of grammar schools as district schools, where, in their judgment, they might be required. Such schools would certainly not be out of harmony with any territorial policy that as yet had been developed or indicated.

Thus stood the law when the constitution of 1835 was adopted. The article on education in that instrument contained the following provisions:

"2. The legislature shall encourage by all suitable means the promotion of intellectual, scientifical and agricultural improvement. The proceeds of all lands that have been, or hereafter may be, granted by the United States to this state for the support of schools, which shall hereafter be sold or disposed of, shall be and remain a perpetual fund, the interest of which, together with the rents of all such unsold lands, shall be inviolably appropriated to the support of schools throughout the state.

"3. The legislature shall provide for a system of common schools, by which a school shall be kept up and supported in each school district at least three months in every year; and any school district neglecting to keep up and support such a school may be deprived of its equal proportion of the interest of the public fund."

The fifth section provided for the support of the university, "with such branches as the public convenience may hereafter demand for the promotion of literature, the arts and sciences," etc. Two things are specially noticeable in these provisions: *first,* that they contemplated provision by the state for a complete system of instruction, beginning with that of the primary school and ending with that of the university; *second,* that while the legislature was required to make provision for district schools for at least three months in each year, no restriction was imposed upon its power to establish schools intermediate the common district school and the university, and we find nothing to indicate an intent to limit their discretion as to the class or grade of schools to which the proceeds of school lands might be devoted, or as to the range of studies or grade of instruction which might be provided for in the district schools.

In the very first executive message after the constitution went into effect, the governor, in view of the fact that "our institutions have leveled the artificial distinctions existing in the societies of other countries, and have left open to every one the avenues to distinction and honor," admonished the legislature that it was their "imperious duty to secure to the state a general diffusion of knowledge," and that "this can in no wise be so certainly effected as by the perfect organization of a uniform and liberal system of common schools." Their "attention was therefore called to the effectuation of a perfect school system, open to all classes, as the surest basis of public happiness and prosperity." In his second message he repeated his admonitions, advising that provision be made for ample compensation to teachers, that those of the highest character, both moral and intellectual, might be secured, and urging that the "youth be taught the first principles in morals, in science, and in government, commencing their studies in the primary schools, elevating its grades as you approach the district seminary, and continue its progress till you arrive at the university." This message indicated no plan, but referred the legislature to the report of the superintendent, who would recommend a general system.

The system reported by superintendent Pierce contemplated a university, with branches in different parts of the state as preparatory schools, and district schools. This is the parent of our present system, and though its author did not find the legislature prepared to accept all his views, the result has demonstrated that he was only a few years in advance of his generation, and that the changes in our school system which have since been adopted have been in the direction of the views which he then held and urged upon the public. And an examination of his official report for 1837 will show that the free schools he then favored were schools which taught something more than the rudiments of a common education; which were to give to the poor the advantages of the rich, and enable both alike to obtain within the state an education broad and liberal, as well as practical.

It would be instructive to make liberal extracts from this report did time and space permit. The superintendent would have teachers thoroughly trained, and he would have the great object of common schools "to furnish good instruction in all the elementary and common branches of knowledge, for all classes of community, *as good, indeed, for the poorest boy of the state as the rich man can furnish for his children with all his wealth.*" The context shows that he had the systems of Prussia and of New England in view, and that he proposed by a free school system to fit the children of the poor as well as of the rich for the highest spheres of activity and influence.

It might also be useful in this connection to show that the Prussian system and that "of the Puritans," of which he speaks in such terms of praise, resemble in their main features, so far as bringing within the reach of all a regular gradation of schools is concerned, the system of public instruction as it prevails in this state to-day. But it is not necessary for the purposes of the present case to enter upon this subject. It must suffice to say that the law of 1827, which provided for grammar schools as a grade of common schools, was adopted from laws which from a very early period had been in existence in Massachusetts, and which in like manner, under heavy penalties, compelled the support of these grammar schools in every considerable town: See *Mass. Laws, 1789, p. 39;* compare *General Stat., 1860, p. 215, ? 2.*

The system adopted by the legislature, and which embraced a university and branches, and a common or primary school in every school district of the state, was put into successful operation, and so continued, with one important exception, until the adoption of the constitution of 1850. The exception relates to the branches of the university, which the funds of the university did not warrant keeping up, and which were consequently abandoned. Private schools to some extent took their place; but when the convention met to frame a constitution in 1850, there were already in existence, in a number of the leading towns, schools belonging to the general public system, which were furnishing instruction which fitted young men for the university. These schools for the most part had been organized under special laws, which, while leaving the primary school laws in general applicable, gave the districts a larger board of officers and larger powers of taxation for buildings and the payment of teachers. As the establishment and support of such schools were optional with the people, they encountered in some localities considerable opposition, which, however, is believed to have been always overcome, and the authority of the districts to provide instruction in the languages in these union schools was not, so far as we are aware, seriously contested. The superintendent of public instruction devotes a considerable portion of his annual report for 1848 to these schools, and in that of 1849 he says: "This class of institutions, which may be made to constitute a connecting link between the ordinary common school and the state university, is fast gaining upon the confidence of the public. Those already established have generally surpassed the expectations of their founders. Some of them have already attained a standing rarely equaled by the academical institutions of the older states. Large, commodious, and beautiful edifices have been erected in quite a number of villages for the accommodation of these schools. These school-houses frequently occupy the most eligible sites in the villages where they are located. I am happy in being able to state in this connection that the late capitol of our state, having been fitted up at much expense, was, in June last, opened as a *common school-house;* and that in that house is maintained a free school which constitutes the pride and ornament of the city of the straits." This *common* free school was a union school equivalent in its instruction to the ordinary high school in most matters, and the report furnishes very clear evidence that the superintendent believed schools of that grade to be entirely competent under the primary school law.

It now becomes important to see whether the constitutional convention and the people, in 1850, did any thing to undo what previously had been accomplished towards furnishing high schools as a part of the primary school system. The convention certainly did nothing to that end. On the contrary, they demonstrated in the most unmistakable manner that they cherished no such desire or purpose. The article on education as originally reported, while providing for free schools to be kept in each district at least three months in every year, added that "the English language and no other shall be taught in such schools." Attention was called to this provision, and it was amended so as to read that instruction should be "conducted in the English language." The reason for the change was fully given, that as it was reported it might be understood to prohibit the teaching of other languages than the English in the primary schools; a result that was not desired. Judge Whipple stated in the convention that, in the section from which he came, French and German were taught, and "it is a most valuable improvement of the common school system." The late superintendent Pierce said that in some schools Latin was taught, and that he himself had taught Latin in a common school. He would not adopt any provision by which any knowledge would be excluded. "All that we ought to do is this: we should say the legislature shall establish primary schools." This, in his opinion, would give full power, and the details could be left to legislation: See *Debates of the Convention, 269, 549.*

The instrument submitted by the convention to the people and adopted by them provided for the establishment of free schools in every school district for at least three months in each year, and for the university. By the aid of these we have every reason to believe the people expected a complete collegiate education might be obtained. The branches of the university had ceased to exist; the university had no preparatory department, and it must either have been understood that young men were to be prepared for the university in the common schools, or else that they should go abroad for the purpose, or be prepared in private schools. Private schools adapted to the purpose were almost unknown in the state, and comparatively a very few persons were at that time of sufficient pecuniary ability to educate their children abroad. The inference seems irresistible that the people expected the tendency towards the establishment of high schools in the primary school districts would continue until every locality capable of supporting one was supplied. And this inference is strengthened by the fact that a considerable number of our union schools date their establishment from the year 1850 and the two or three years following.

If these facts do not demonstrate clearly and conclusively a general state policy, beginning in 1817 and continuing until after the adoption of the present constitution, in the direction of free schools in which education, and at their option the elements, of classical education, might be brought within the reach of all the children of the state, then, as it seems to us, nothing can demonstrate it. We might follow the subject further, and show that the subsequent legislation has all concurred with this policy, but it would be a waste of time and labor. We content ourselves with the statement that neither in our state policy, in our constitution, or in our laws, do we find the primary school districts restricted in the branches of knowledge which their officers may cause to be taught, or the grade of instruction that may be given, if their voters consent in regular form to bear the expense and raise the taxes for the purpose.

Having reached this conclusion, we shall spend no time upon the objection that the district in question had no authority to appoint a superintendent of schools, and that the duties of superintendency should be performed by the district board. We think the power to make the appointment was incident to the full control which by law the board had over the schools of the district, and that the board and the people of the district have been wisely left by the legislature to follow their own judgment in the premises.

It follows that the decree dismissing the bill was right, and should be affirmed.

The other justices concurred.

PLESSY V. FERGUSON, 163 U.S. 537 (1896)

SUPREME COURT OF THE UNITED STATES
ERROR TO THE SUPREME COURT OF THE STATE OF LOUISIANA
ARGUED APRIL 18, 1896. DECIDED MAY 18, 1896.

Syllabus

The statute of Louisiana, acts of 1890, c. 111, requiring railway companies carrying passengers in their coaches in that State, to provide equal, but separate, accommodations for the white and colored races, by providing two or more passenger coaches for each passenger train, or by dividing the passenger coaches by a partition so as to secure separate accommodations; and providing that no person shall be permitted to occupy seats in coaches other than the ones assigned to them, on account of the race they belong to; and requiring the officer of the passenger train to assign each passenger to the coach or compartment assigned for the race to which he or she belong; and imposing fines or imprisonment upon passengers insisting on going into a coach or compartment other than the one set aide for the race to which he or she belongs; and conferring upon officers of the train power to refuse to carry on the train passengers refusing to occupy the coach or compartment assigned to them, and exempting the railway company from liability for such refusal, are not in conflict with the provisions either of the Thirteenth Amendment or of the Fourteenth Amendment to the Constitution of the United States.

This was a petition for writs of prohibition and certiorari, originally filed in the Supreme Court of the State by Plessy, the plaintiff in error, against the Hon. John H. Ferguson, judge of the criminal District Court for the parish of Orleans, and setting forth in substance the following facts:

That petitioner was a citizen of the United States and a resident of the State of Louisiana, of mixed descent, in the proportion of seven eighths Caucasian and one eighth African blood; that the mixture of colored blood was not discernible in him, and that he was entitled to every recognition, right, privilege and immunity secured to the citizens of the United States of the white race by its Constitution and laws; that, on June 7, 1892, he engaged and paid for a first class passage on the East Louisiana Railway from New Orleans to Covington, in the same State, and thereupon entered a passenger train, and took possession of a vacant seat in a coach where passengers of the white race were accommodated; that such railroad company was incorporated by the laws of Louisiana as a common carrier, and was not authorized to distinguish between citizens according to their race. But, notwithstanding this, petitioner was required by the conductor, under penalty of ejection from said train and imprisonment, to vacate said coach and occupy another seat in a coach assigned by said company for persons not of the white race, and for no other reason than that petitioner was of the colored race; that, upon petitioner's refusal to comply with such order, he was, with the aid of a police officer, forcibly ejected from said coach and hurried off to and imprisoned in the parish jail ofNew Orleans, and there held to answer a charge made by such officer to the effect that he was guilty of having criminally violated an act of the General Assembly of the State, approved July 10, 1890, in such case made and provided.

That petitioner was subsequently brought before the recorder of the city for preliminary examination and committed for trial to the criminal District Court for the parish of Orleans, where an information was filed against him in the matter above set forth, for a violation of the above act, which act the petitioner affirmed to be null and void, because in conflict with the Constitution of the United States; that petitioner interposed a plea to such information based upon the unconstitutionality of the act of the General Assembly, to which the district attorney, on behalf of the State, filed a demurrer; that, upon issue being joined upon such demurrer and plea, the court sustained the demurrer, overruled the plea, and ordered petitioner to plead over to the facts set forth in the information, and that, unless the judge of the said court be enjoined by a writ of prohibition from further proceeding in such case, the court will proceed to fine and sentence petitioner to imprisonment, and thus deprive him of his constitutional rights set forth in his said plea, notwithstanding the unconstitutionality of the act under which he was being prosecuted; that no appeal lay from such sentence, and petitioner was without relief or remedy except by writs of prohibition and certiorari. Copies of the information and other proceedings in the criminal District Court were annexed to the petition as an exhibit.

Upon the filing of this petition, an order was issued upon the respondent to show cause why a writ of prohibition should not issue and be made perpetual, and a further order that the record of the proceedings had in the criminal cause be certified and transmitted to the Supreme Court.

To this order the respondent made answer, transmitting a certified copy of the proceedings, asserting the constitutionality of the law, and averring that, instead of pleading or admitting that he belonged to the colored race, the said Plessy declined and refused, either by pleading or otherwise, to admit that he was in any sense or in any proportion a colored man.

The case coming on for a hearing before the Supreme Court, that court was of opinion that the law under which the prosecution was had was constitutional, and denied the relief prayed for by the petitioner. Ex parte Plessy. Whereupon petitioner prayed for a writ of error from this court, which was allowed by the Chief Justice of the Supreme Court of Louisiana.

Opinions

BROWN, Opinion of the Court

MR. JUSTICE BROWN, after stating the case, delivered the opinion of the court.

This case turns upon the constitutionality of an act of the General Assembly of the State of Louisiana, passed in 1890, providing for separate railway carriages for the white and colored races. Acts 1890, No. 111, p. 152.

The first section of the statute enacts

> that all railway companies carrying passengers in their coaches in this State shall provide equal but separate accommodations for the white and colored races by providing two or more passenger coaches for each passenger train, or by dividing the passenger coaches by a partition so as to secure separate accommodations: Provided, That this section shall not be construed to apply to street railroads. No person or persons, shall be admitted to occupy seats in coaches other than the ones assigned to them on account of the race they belong to.

By the second section, it was enacted

> that the officers of such passenger trains shall have power and are hereby required to assign each passenger to the coach or compartment used for the race to which such passenger belongs; any passenger insisting on going into a coach or compartment to which by race he does not belong shall be liable to a fine of twenty-five dollars, or in lieu thereof to imprisonment for a period of not more than twenty days in the parish prison, and any officer of any railroad insisting on assigning a passenger to a coach or compartment other than the one set aside for the race to which said passenger belongs shall be liable to a fine of twenty-five dollars, or in lieu thereof to imprisonment for a period of not more than twenty days in the parish prison; and should any passenger refuse to occupy the coach or compartment to which he or she is assigned by the officer of such railway, said officer shall have power to refuse to carry such passenger on his train, and for such refusal neither he nor the railway company which he represents shall be liable for damages in any of the courts of this State.

The third section provides penalties for the refusal or neglect of the officers, directors, conductors, and employees of railway companies to comply with the act, with a proviso that "nothing in this act shall be construed as applying to nurses attending children of the other race." The fourth section is immaterial.

The information filed in the criminal District Court charged in substance that Plessy, being a passenger between two stations within the State of Louisiana, was assigned by officers of the company to the coach used for the race to which he belonged, but he insisted upon going into a coach used by the race to which he did not belong. Neither in the information nor plea was his particular race or color averred. The petition for the writ of prohibition averred that petitioner was seven-eighths Caucasian and one eighth African blood; that the mixture of colored blood was not discernible in him, and that he was entitled to every right, privilege and immunity secured to citizens of the United States of the white race; and that, upon such theory, he took possession of a vacant seat in a coach where passengers of the white race were accommodated, and was ordered by the conductor to vacate said coach and take a seat in another assigned to persons of the colored race, and, having refused to comply with such demand, he was forcibly ejected with the aid of a police officer, and imprisoned in the parish jail to answer a charge of having violated the above act.

The constitutionality of this act is attacked upon the ground that it conflicts both with the Thirteenth Amendment of the Constitution, abolishing slavery, and the Fourteenth Amendment, which prohibits certain restrictive legislation on the part of the States.

1. That it does not conflict with the Thirteenth Amendment, which abolished slavery and involuntary servitude, except as a punishment for crime, is too clear for argument. Slavery implies involuntary servitude—a state of bondage; the ownership of mankind as a chattel, or at least the control of the labor and services of one man for the benefit of another, and the absence of a legal right to the disposal of his own person, property and services. This amendment was said in the Slaughterhouse Cases, to have been intended primarily to abolish slavery as it had been previously known in this country, and that it equally forbade Mexican peonage or the Chinese coolie trade when they amounted to slavery or involuntary servitude, and that the use of the word "servitude" was intended to prohibit the use of all forms of involuntary slavery, of whatever class or name. It was intimated, however, in that case that this amendment was regarded by the statesmen of that day as insufficient to protect the colored race from certain laws which had been enacted in the Southern States, imposing upon the colored race onerous disabilities and burdens and curtailing their rights in the pursuit of life, liberty and property to such an extent that their freedom was of little value; and that the Fourteenth Amendment was devised to meet this exigency.

So, too, in the Civil Rights Cases, it was said that the act of a mere individual, the owner of an inn, a public conveyance or place of amusement, refusing accommodations to colored people cannot be justly regarded as imposing any badge of slavery or servitude upon the applicant, but only as involving an ordinary civil injury, properly cognizable by the laws of the State and presumably subject to redress by those laws until the contrary appears. "It would be running the slavery argument into the ground," said Mr. Justice Bradley,

> to make it apply to every act of discrimination which a person may see fit to make as to the guests he will entertain, or as to the people he will take into his coach or cab or car, or admit to his concert or theatre, or deal with in other matters of intercourse or business.

A statute which implies merely a legal distinction between the white and colored races—a distinction which is founded in the color of the two races and which must always exist so long as white men are distinguished from the other race by color—has no tendency to destroy the legal equality of the two races, or reestablish a state of involuntary servitude. Indeed, we do not understand that the Thirteenth Amendment is strenuously relied upon by the plaintiff in error in this connection.

2. By the Fourteenth Amendment, all persons born or naturalized in the United States and subject to the jurisdiction thereof are made citizens of the United States and of the State wherein they reside, and the States are forbidden from making or enforcing any law which shall abridge the privileges or immunities of citizens of the United States, or shall deprive any person of life, liberty, or property without due process of law, or deny to any person within their jurisdiction the equal protection of the laws.

The proper construction of this amendment was first called to the attention of this court in the Slaughterhouse Cases, 16 Wall. 36, which involved, however, not a question of race, but one of exclusive privileges. The case did not call for any expression of opinion as to the exact rights it was intended to secure to the colored race, but it was said generally that its main purpose was to establish the citizenship of the negro, to give definitions of citizenship of the United States and of the States, and to protect from the hostile legislation of the States the privileges and immunities of citizens of the United States, as distinguished from those of citizens of the States.

The object of the amendment was undoubtedly to enforce the absolute equality of the two races before the law, but, in the nature of things, it could not have been intended to abolish distinctions based upon color, or to enforce social, as distinguished from political, equality, or a commingling of the two races upon terms unsatisfactory to either. Laws permitting, and even requiring, their separation in places where they are liable to be brought into contact do not necessarily imply the inferiority of either race to the other, and have been generally, if not universally, recognized as within the competency of the state legislatures in the exercise of their police power. The most common instance of this is connected with the establishment of separate schools for white and colored children, which has been held to be a valid exercise of the legislative power even by courts of States where the political rights of the colored race have been longest and most earnestly enforced.

One of the earliest of these cases is that of Roberts v. City of Boston, in which the Supreme Judicial Court of Massachusetts held that the general school committee of Boston had power to make provision for the instruction of colored children in separate schools established exclusively for them, and to prohibit their attendance upon the other schools. "The great principle," said Chief Justice Shaw, "advanced by the learned and eloquent advocate for the plaintiff" (Mr. Charles Sumner),

> is that, by the constitution and laws of Massachusetts, all persons without distinction of age or sex, birth or color, origin or condition, are equal before the law. . . . But when this great principle comes to be applied to the actual and various conditions of persons in society, it will not warrant the assertion that men and women are legally clothed with the same civil and political powers, and that children and adults are legally to have the same functions and be subject to the same treatment, but only that the rights of all, as they are settled and regulated by law, are equally entitled to the paternal consideration and protection of the law for their maintenance and security.

It was held that the powers of the committee extended to the establishment of separate schools for children of different ages, sexes and colors, and that they might also establish special schools for poor and neglected children, who have become too old to attend the primary school and yet have not acquired the rudiments of learning to enable them to enter the ordinary schools. Similar laws have been enacted by Congress under its general power of legislation over the District of Columbia, Rev.Stat.D.C. [Sections] 281, 282, 283, 310, 319, as well as by the legislatures of many of the States, and have been generally, if not uniformly, sustained by the courts. State v. McCann; Lehew v. Brummell; Ward v. Flood; Bertonneau v. School Directors; People v. Gallagher; Cory v. Carter; Dawson v. Lee.

Laws forbidding the intermarriage of the two races may be said in a technical sense to interfere with the freedom of contract, and yet have been universally recognized as within the police power of the State. State v. Gibson.

The distinction between laws interfering with the political equality of the negro and those requiring the separation of the two races in schools, theatres and railway carriages has been frequently drawn by this court. Thus, in Strauder v. West Virginia, it was held that a law of West Virginia limiting to white male persons, 21 years of age and citizens of the State, the right to sit upon juries was a discrimination which implied a legal inferiority in civil society, which lessened the security of the right of the colored race, and was a step toward reducing them to a condition of servility. Indeed, the right of a colored man that, in the selection of jurors to pass upon his life, liberty and property, there shall be no exclusion of his race and no discrimination against them because of color has been asserted in a number of cases. Virginia v. Rives; Neal v. Delaware; Bush v. Kentucky; Gibson v. Mississippi. So, where the laws of a particular locality or the charter of a particular railway corporation has provided that no person shall be excluded from the cars on account of color, we have held that this meant that persons of color should travel in the same car as white ones, and that the enactment was not satisfied by the company's providing cars assigned exclusively to people of color, though they were as good as those which they assigned exclusively to white persons. Railroad Company v. Brown.

Upon the other hand, where a statute of Louisiana required those engaged in the transportation of passengers among the States to give to all persons traveling within that State, upon vessels employed in that business, equal rights and privileges in all parts of the vessel, without distinction on account of race or color, and subjected to an action for damages the owner of such a vessel, who excluded colored passengers on account of their color from the cabin set aside by him for the use of whites, it was held to be, so far as it applied to interstate commerce, unconstitutional and void. Hall v. De Cuir. The court in this case, however, expressly disclaimed that it had anything whatever to do with the statute as a regulation of internal commerce, or affecting anything else than commerce among the States.

In the Civil Rights Case, it was held that an act of Congress entitling all persons within the jurisdiction of the United States to the full and equal enjoyment of the accommodations, advantages, facilities and privileges of inns, public conveyances, on land or water, theatres and other places of public amusement, and made applicable to citizens of every race and color, regardless of any previous condition of servitude, was unconstitutional and void upon the ground that the Fourteenth Amendment was prohibitory upon the States only, and the legislation authorized to be adopted by Congress for enforcing it was not direct legislation on matters respecting which the States were prohibited from making or enforcing certain laws, or doing certain acts, but was corrective legislation such as might be necessary or proper for counteracting and redressing the effect of such laws or acts. In delivering the opinion of the court, Mr. Justice Bradley observed that the Fourteenth Amendment

> does not invest Congress with power to legislate upon subjects that are within the domain of state legislation, but to provide modes of relief against state legislation or state action of the kind referred to. It does not authorize Congress to create a code of municipal law for the regulation of private rights, but to provide modes of redress against the operation of state laws and the action of state officers, executive or judicial, when these are subversive of the fundamental rights specified in the amendment. Positive rights and privileges are undoubtedly secured by the Fourteenth Amendment, but they are secured by way of prohibition against state laws and state proceedings affecting those rights and privileges, and by power given to Congress to legislate for the purpose of carrying such prohibition into effect, and such legislation must necessarily be predicated upon such supposed state laws or state proceedings, and be directed to the correction of their operation and effect.

Much nearer, and, indeed, almost directly in point is the case of the Louisville, New Orleans &c. Railway v. Mississippi, wherein the railway company was indicted for a violation of a statute of Mississippi enacting that all railroads carrying passengers should provide equal but separate accommodations for the white and colored races by providing two or more passenger cars for each passenger train, or by dividing the passenger cars by a partition so as to secure separate accommodations. The case was presented in a different aspect from the one under consideration, inasmuch as it was an indictment against the railway company for failing to provide the separate accommodations, but the question considered was the constitutionality of the law. In that case, the Supreme Court of Mississippi, had held that the statute applied solely to commerce within the State, and that, being the construction of the state statute by its highest court, was accepted as conclusive. "If it be a matter," said the court,

> respecting commerce wholly within a State, and not interfering with commerce between the States, then obviously there is no violation of the commerce clause of the Federal Constitution . . . . No question arises under this section as to the power of the State to separate in different compartments interstate passengers or affect in any manner the privileges and rights of such passengers. All that we can consider is whether the State has the power to require that railroad trains within her limits shall have separate accommodations for the two races; that affecting only commerce within the State is no invasion of the power given to Congress by the commerce clause.

A like course of reasoning applies to the case under consideration, since the Supreme Court of Louisiana in the case of the State ex rel. Abbott v. Hicks, Judge, et al., held that the statute in question did not apply to interstate passengers, but was confined in its application to passengers traveling exclusively within the borders of the State. The case was decided largely upon the authority of Railway Co. v. State, and affirmed by this court. In the present case, no question of interference with interstate commerce can possibly arise, since the East Louisiana Railway appears to have been purely a local line, with both its termini within the State of Louisiana. Similar statutes for the separation of the to races upon public conveyances were held to be constitutional in West Chester &c. Railroad v. Miles; Day v. Owen; Chicago &c. Railway v. Williams; Chesapeake &c. Railroad v. Wells; Memphis &c. Railroad v. Benson; The Sue; Logwood v. Memphis &c. Railroad; McGuinn v. Forbes; People v. King; Houck v. South Pac. Railway; Heard v. Georgia Railroad Co.

While we think the enforced separation of the races, as applied to the internal commerce of the State, neither abridges the privileges or immunities of the colored man, deprives him of his property without due process of law, nor denies him the equal protection of the laws within the meaning of the Fourteenth Amendment, we are not prepared to say that the conductor, in assigning passengers to the coaches according to their race, does not act at his peril, or that the provision of the second section of the act that denies to the passenger compensation in damages for a refusal to receive him into the coach in which he properly belongs is a valid exercise of the legislative power. Indeed, we understand it to be conceded by the State's Attorney that such part of the act as exempts from liability the railway company and its officers is unconstitutional. The power to assign to a particular coach obviously implies the power to determine to which race the passenger belongs, as well as the power to determine who, under the laws of the particular State, is to be deemed a white and who a colored person. This question, though indicated in the brief of the plaintiff in error, does not properly arise upon the record in this case, since the only issue made is as to the unconstitutionality of the act so far as it requires the railway to provide separate accommodations and the conductor to assign passengers according to their race.

It is claimed by the plaintiff in error that, in any mixed community, the reputation of belonging to the dominant race, in this instance the white race, is property in the same sense that a right of action or of inheritance is property. Conceding this to be so for the purposes of this case, we are unable to see how this statute deprives him of, or in any way affects his right to, such property. If he be a white man and assigned to a colored coach, he may have his action for damages against the company for being deprived of his so-called property. Upon the other hand, if he be a colored man and be so assigned, he has been deprived of no property, since he is not lawfully entitled to the reputation of being a white man.

In this connection, it is also suggested by the learned counsel for the plaintiff in error that the same argument that will justify the state legislature in requiring railways to provide separate accommodations for the two races will also authorize them to require separate cars to be provided for people whose hair is of a certain color, or who are aliens, or who belong to certain nationalities, or to enact laws requiring colored people to walk upon one side of the street and white people upon the other, or requiring white men's houses to be painted white and colored men's black, or their vehicles or business signs to be of different colors, upon the theory that one side of the street is as good as the other, or that a house or vehicle of one color is as good as one of another color. The reply to all this is that every exercise of the police power must be reasonable, and extend only to such laws as are enacted in good faith for the promotion for the public good, and not for the annoyance or oppression of a particular class. Thus, in Yick Wo v. Hopkins, it was held by this court that a municipal ordinance of the city of San Francisco to regulate the carrying on of public laundries within the limits of the municipality violated the provisions of the Constitution of the United States if it conferred upon the municipal authorities arbitrary power, at their own will and without regard to discretion, in the legal sense of the term, to give or withhold consent as to persons or places without regard to the competency of the persons applying or the propriety of the places selected for the carrying on of the business. It was held to be a covert attempt on the part of the municipality to make an arbitrary and unjust discrimination against the Chinese race. While this was the case of a municipal ordinance, a like principle has been held to apply to acts of a state legislature passed in the exercise of the police power. Railroad Company v. Husen; Louisville & Nashville Railroad v. Kentucky; Duggett v. Hudson; Capen v. Foster; State ex rel. Wood v. Baker; Monroe v. Collins; Hulseman v. Rems; Orman v. Riley.

So far, then, as a conflict with the Fourteenth Amendment is concerned, the case reduces itself to the question whether the statute of Louisiana is a reasonable regulation, and, with respect to this, there must necessarily be a large discretion on the part of the legislature. In determining the question of reasonableness, it is at liberty to act with reference to the established usages, customs, and traditions of the people, and with a view to the promotion of their comfort and the preservation of the public peace and good order. Gauged by this standard, we cannot say that a law which authorizes or even requires the separation of the two races in public conveyances is unreasonable, or more obnoxious to the Fourteenth Amendment than the acts of Congress requiring separate schools for colored children in the District of Columbia, the constitutionality of which does not seem to have been questioned, or the corresponding acts of state legislatures.

We consider the underlying fallacy of the plaintiff's argument to consist in the assumption that the enforced separation of the two races stamps the colored race with a badge of inferiority. If this be so, it is not by reason of anything found in the act, but solely because the colored race chooses to put that construction upon it. The argument necessarily assumes that if, as has been more than once the case and is not unlikely to be so again, the colored race should become the dominant power in the state legislature, and should enact a law in precisely similar terms, it would thereby relegate the white race to an inferior position. We imagine that the white race, at least, would not acquiesce in this assumption. The argument also assumes that social prejudices may be overcome by legislation, and that equal rights cannot be secured to the negro except by an enforced commingling of the two races. We cannot accept this proposition. If the two races are to meet upon terms of social equality, it must be the result of natural affinities, a mutual appreciation of each other's merits, and a voluntary consent of individuals. As was said by the Court of Appeals of New York in People v. Gallagher, this end can neither be accomplished nor promoted by laws which conflict with the general sentiment of the community upon whom they are designed to operate. When the government, therefore, has secured to each of its citizens equal rights before the law and equal opportunities for improvement and progress, it has accomplished the end for which it was organized, and performed all of the functions respecting social advantages with which it is endowed.

Legislation is powerless to eradicate racial instincts or to abolish distinctions based upon physical differences, and the attempt to do so can only result in accentuating the difficulties of the present situation. If the civil and political rights of both races be equal, one cannot be inferior to the other civilly or politically. If one race be inferior to the other socially, the Constitution of the United States cannot put them upon the same plane.

It is true that the question of the proportion of colored blood necessary to constitute a colored person, as distinguished from a white person, is one upon which there is a difference of opinion in the different States, some holding that any visible admixture of black blood stamps the person as belonging to the colored race (State v. Chaver); others that it depends upon the preponderance of blood (Gray v. State; Monroe v. Collins); and still others that the predominance of white blood must only be in the proportion of three-fourths. (People v. Dean; Jones v. Commonwealth). But these are questions to be determined under the laws of each State, and are not properly put in issue in this case. Under the allegations of his petition, it may undoubtedly become a question of importance whether, under the laws of Louisiana, the petitioner belongs to the white or colored race.

The judgment of the court below is, therefore, Affirmed.

HARLAN, Dissenting Opinion

MR. JUSTICE HARLAN, dissenting.

By the Louisiana statute the validity of which is here involved, all railway companies (other than street railroad companies) carrying passengers in that State are required to have separate but equal accommodations for white and colored persons

> by providing two or more passenger coaches for each passenger train, or by dividing the passenger coaches by a partition so as to secure separate accommodations.

Under this statute, no colored person is permitted to occupy a seat in a coach assigned to white persons, nor any white person to occupy a seat in a coach assigned to colored persons. The managers of the railroad are not allowed to exercise any discretion in the premises, but are required to assign each passenger to some coach or compartment set apart for the exclusive use of his race. If a passenger insists upon going into a coach or compartment not set apart for persons of his race, he is subject to be fined or to be imprisoned in the parish jail. Penalties are prescribed for the refusal or neglect of the officers, directors, conductors and employees of railroad companies to comply with the provisions of the act.

Only "nurses attending children of the other race" are excepted from the operation of the statute. No exception is made of colored attendants traveling with adults. A white man is not permitted to have his colored servant with him in the same coach, even if his condition of health requires the constant, personal assistance of such servant. If a colored maid insists upon riding in the same coach with a white woman whom she has been employed to serve, and who may need her personal attention while traveling, she is subject to be fined or imprisoned for such an exhibition of zeal in the discharge of duty.

While there may be in Louisiana persons of different races who are not citizens of the United States, the words in the act "white and colored races" necessarily include all citizens of the United States of both races residing in that State. So that we have before us a state enactment that compels, under penalties, the separation of the two races in railroad passenger coaches, and makes it a crime for a citizen of either race to enter a coach that has been assigned to citizens of the other race.

Thus, the State regulates the use of a public highway by citizens of the United States solely upon the basis of race.

However apparent the injustice of such legislation may be, we have only to consider whether it is consistent with the Constitution of the United States.

That a railroad is a public highway, and that the corporation which owns or operates it is in the exercise of public functions, is not, at this day, to be disputed. Mr. Justice Nelson, speaking for this court in New Jersey Steam Navigation Co. v. Merchants' Bank, said that a common carrier was in the exercise of a sort of public office, and has public duties to perform, from which he should not be permitted to exonerate himself without the assent of the parties concerned.

Mr. Justice Strong, delivering the judgment of this court in Olcott v. The Supervisors, said:

> That railroads, though constructed by private corporations and owned by them, are public highways has been the doctrine of nearly all the courts ever since such conveniences for passage and transportation have had any existence. Very early the question arose whether a State's right of eminent domain could be exercised by a private corporation created for the purpose of constructing a railroad. Clearly it could not unless taking land for such a purpose by such an agency is taking land for public use. The right of eminent domain nowhere justifies taking property for a private use. Yet it is a doctrine universally accepted that a state legislature may authorize a private corporation to take land for the construction of such a road, making compensation to the owner. What else does this doctrine mean if not that building a railroad, though it be built by a private corporation, is an act done for a public use.

So, in Township of Pine Grove v. Talcott: "Though the corporation [a railroad company] was private, its work was public, as much so as if it were to be constructed by the State." So, in Inhabitants of Worcester v. Western Railroad Corporation:

> The establishment of that great thoroughfare is regarded as a public work, established by public authority, intended for the public use and benefit, the use of which is secured to the whole community, and constitutes, therefore, like a canal, turnpike or highway, a public easement. It is true that the real and personal property necessary to the establishment and management of the railroad is vested in the corporation, but it is in trust for the public.

In respect of civil rights common to all citizens, the Constitution of the United States does not, I think, permit any public authority to know the race of those entitled to be protected in the enjoyment of such rights. Every true man has pride of race, and, under appropriate circumstances, when the rights of others, his equals before the law, are not to be affected, it is his privilege to express such pride and to take such action based upon it as to him seems proper. But I deny that any legislative body or judicial tribunal may have regard to the race of citizens when the civil rights of those citizens are involved. Indeed, such legislation as that here in question is inconsistent not only with that equality of rights which pertains to citizenship, National and State, but with the personal liberty enjoyed by everyone within the United States.

The Thirteenth Amendment does not permit the withholding or the deprivation of any right necessarily inhering in freedom. It not only struck down the institution of slavery as previously existing in the United States, but it prevents the imposition of any burdens or disabilities that constitute badges of slavery or servitude. It decreed universal civil freedom in this country. This court has so adjudged. But that amendment having been found inadequate to the protection of the rights of those who had been in slavery, it was followed by the Fourteenth Amendment, which added greatly to the dignity and glory of American citizenship and to the security of personal liberty by declaring that

> all persons born or naturalized in the United States, and subject to the jurisdiction thereof, are citizens of the United States and of the State wherein they reside,

and that

> no State shall make or enforce any law which shall abridge the privileges or immunities of citizens of the United States; nor shall any State deprive any person of life, liber-

> ty or property without due process of law, nor deny to any person within its jurisdiction the equal protection of the laws.

These two amendments, if enforced according to their true intent and meaning, will protect all the civil rights that pertain to freedom and citizenship. Finally, and to the end that no citizen should be denied, on account of his race, the privilege of participating in the political control of his country, it was declared by the Fifteenth Amendment that

> the right of citizens of the United States to vote shall not be denied or abridged by the United States or by any State on account of race, color or previous condition of servitude.

These notable additions to the fundamental law were welcomed by the friends of liberty throughout the world. They removed the race line from our governmental systems. They had, as this court has said, a common purpose, namely to secure to a race recently emancipated, a race that through many generations have been held in slavery, all the civil rights that the superior race enjoy.

They declared, in legal effect, this court has further said, that the law in the States shall be the same for the black as for the white; that all persons, whether colored or white, shall stand equal before the laws of the States, and, in regard to the colored race, for whose protection the amendment was primarily designed, that no discrimination shall be made against them by law because of their color.

We also said:

> The words of the amendment, it is true, are prohibitory, but they contain a necessary implication of a positive immunity, or right, most valuable to the colored race—the right to exemption from unfriendly legislation against them distinctively as colored—exemption from legal discriminations, implying inferiority in civil society, lessening the security of their enjoyment of the rights which others enjoy, and discriminations which are steps towards reducing them to the condition of a subject race.

It was, consequently, adjudged that a state law that excluded citizens of the colored race from juries, because of their race and however well qualified in other respects to discharge the duties of jurymen, was repugnant to the Fourteenth Amendment. Strauder v. West Virginia; Virginia v. Rives; Ex parte Virginia; Neal v. Delaware; Bush v. Kentucky. At the present term, referring to the previous adjudications, this court declared that

> underlying all of those decisions is the principle that the Constitution of the United States, in its present form, forbids, so far as civil and political rights are concerned, discrimination by the General Government or the States against any citizen because of his race. All citizens are equal before the law. Gibson v. Mississippi.

The decisions referred to show the scope of the recent amendments of the Constitution. They also show that it is not within the power of a State to prohibit colored citizens, because of their race, from participating as jurors in the administration of justice.

It was said in argument that the statute of Louisiana does not discriminate against either race, but prescribes a rule applicable alike to white and colored citizens. But this argument does not meet the difficulty. Everyone knows that the statute in question had its origin in the purpose not so much to exclude white persons from railroad cars occupied by blacks as to exclude colored people from coaches occupied by or assigned to white persons. Railroad corporations of Louisiana did not make discrimination among whites in the matter of accommodation for travelers. The thing to accomplish was, under the guise of giving equal accommodation for whites and blacks, to compel the latter to keep to themselves while traveling in railroad passenger coaches. No one would be so wanting in candor a to assert the contrary. The fundamental objection, therefore, to the statute is that it interferes with the personal freedom of citizens. "Personal liberty," it has been well said,

> consists in the power of locomotion, of changing situation, or removing one's person to whatsoever places one's own inclination may direct, without imprisonment or restraint unless by due course of law.

1 Bl.Com. 134. If a white man and a black man choose to occupy the same public conveyance on a public highway, it is their right to do so, and no government, proceeding alone on grounds of race, can prevent it without infringing the personal liberty of each.

It is one thing for railroad carriers to furnish, or to be required by law to furnish, equal accommodations for all whom they are under a legal duty to carry. It is quite another thing for government to forbid citizens of the white and black races from traveling in the same public conveyance, and to punish officers of railroad companies for permitting persons of the two races to occupy the same passenger coach. If a State can prescribe, as a rule of civil conduct, that whites and blacks shall not travel as passengers in the same railroad coach, why may it not so regulate the use of the streets of its cities and towns as to compel white citizens to keep on one side of a street and black citizens to keep on the other? Why may it not, upon like grounds, punish whites and blacks who ride together in streetcars or in open vehicles on a public road or street? Why may it not require sheriffs to assign whites to one side of a courtroom and blacks to the other? And why may it not also prohibit the commingling of the two races in the galleries of legislative halls or in public assemblages convened for the consideration of the political questions of the day? Further, if this statute of Louisiana is consistent with the personal liberty of citizens, why may not the State require the separation in railroad coaches of native and naturalized citizens of the United States, or of Protestants and Roman Catholics?

The answer given at the argument to these questions was that regulations of the kind they suggest would be unreasonable, and could not, therefore, stand before the law. Is it meant that the determination of questions of legislative power depends upon the inquiry whether the statute whose validity is questioned is, in the judgment of the courts, a reasonable one, taking all the circumstances into consideration? A statute may be unreasonable merely because a sound public policy forbade its enactment. But I do not understand that the courts have anything to do with the policy or expediency of legislation. A statute may be valid and yet, upon grounds of public policy, may well be characterized as unreasonable. Mr. Sedgwick correctly states the rule when he says that, the legislative intention being clearly ascertained,

> the courts have no other duty to perform than to execute the legislative will, without any regard to their views as to the wisdom or justice of the particular enactment.

Stat. & Const.Constr. 324. There is a dangerous tendency in these latter days to enlarge the functions of the courts by means of judicial interference with the will of the people as expressed by the legislature. Our institutions have the distinguishing characteristic that the three departments of government are coordinate and separate. Each must keep within the limits defined by the Constitution. And the courts best discharge their duty by executing the will of the lawmaking power, constitutionally expressed, leaving the results of legislation to be dealt with by the people through their representatives. Statutes must always have a reasonable construction. Sometimes they are to be construed strictly; sometimes liberally, in order to carry out the legislative will. But however construed, the intent of the legislature is to be respected, if the particular statute in question is valid, although the courts, looking at the public interests, may conceive the statute to be both unreasonable and impolitic. If the power exists to enact a statute, that ends the matter so far as the courts are concerned. The adjudged cases in which statutes have been held to be void because unreasonable are those in which the means employed by the legislature were not at all germane to the end to which the legislature was competent.

The white race deems itself to be the dominant race in this country. And so it is in prestige, in achievements, in education, in wealth and in power. So, I doubt not, it will continue to be for all time if it remains true to its great heritage and holds fast to the principles of constitutional liberty. But in view of the Constitution, in the eye of the law, there is in this country no superior, dominant, ruling class of citizens. There is no caste here. Our Constitution is color-blind, and neither knows nor tolerates classes among citizens. In respect of civil rights, all citizens are equal before the law. The humblest is the peer of the most powerful. The law regards man as man, and takes no account of his surroundings or of his color when his civil rights as guaranteed by the supreme law of the land are involved. It is therefore to be regretted that this high tribunal, the final expositor of the fundamental law of the land, has reached the conclusion that it is competent for a State to regulate the enjoyment by citizens of their civil rights solely upon the basis of race.

In my opinion, the judgment this day rendered will, in time, prove to be quite as pernicious as the decision made by this tribunal in the Dred Scott Case. It was adjudged in that case that the descendants of Africans who were imported into this country and sold as slaves were not included nor intended to be included under the word "citizens" in the Constitution, and could not claim any of the rights and privileges which that instrument provided for and secured to citizens of the United States; that, at the time of the adoption of the Constitution, they were considered as a subordinate and inferior class of beings, who had been subjugated by the dominant race, and, whether emancipated or not, yet remained subject to their authority, and had no rights or privileges but such as those who held the power and the government might choose to grant them. 19 How. 393, 404. The recent amendments of the Constitution, it was supposed, had eradicated these principles from our institutions. But it seems that we have yet, in some of the States, a dominant race—a superior class of citizens, which assumes to regulate the enjoyment of civil rights, common to all citizens, upon the basis of race. The present decision, it may well be apprehended, will not only stimulate aggressions, more or less brutal and irritating, upon the admitted rights of colored citizens, but will encourage the belief that it is possible, by means of state enactments, to defeat the beneficent purposes which the people of the United States had in view when they adopted the recent amendments of the Constitution, by one of which the blacks of this country were made citizens of the United States and of the States in which they respectively reside, and whose privileges and immunities, as citizens, the States are forbidden to abridge. Sixty millions of whites are in no danger from the presence here of eight millions of blacks. The destinies of the two races in this country are indissolubly linked together, and the interests of both require that the common government of all shall not permit the seeds of race hate to be planted under the sanction of law. What can more certainly arouse race hate, what more certainly create and perpetuate a feeling of distrust between these races, than state enactments which, in fact, proceed on the ground that colored citizens are so inferior and degraded that they cannot be allowed to sit in public coaches occupied by white citizens. That, as all will admit, is the real meaning of such legislation as was enacted in Louisiana.

The sure guarantee of the peace and security of each race is the clear, distinct, unconditional recognition by our governments, National and State, of every right that inheres in civil freedom, and of the equality before the law of all citizens of the United States, without regard to race. State enactments regulating the enjoyment of civil rights upon the basis of race, and cunningly devised to defeat legitimate results of the war under the pretence of recognizing equality of rights, can have no other result than to render permanent peace impossible and to keep alive a conflict of races the continuance of which must do harm to all concerned. This question is not met by the suggestion that social equality cannot exist between the white and black races in this country. That argument, if it can be properly regarded as one, is scarcely worthy of consideration, for social equality no more exists between two races when traveling in a passenger coach or a public highway than when members of the same races sit by each other in a street car or in the jury box, or stand or sit with each other in a political assembly, or when they use in common the street of a city or town, or when they are in the same room for the purpose of having their names placed on the registry of voters, or when they approach the ballot box in order to exercise the high privilege of voting.

There is a race so different from our own that we do not permit those belonging to it to become citizens of the United States. Persons belonging to it are, with few exceptions, absolutely excluded from our country. I allude to the Chinese race. But, by the statute in question, a Chinaman can ride in the same passenger coach with white citizens of the United States, while citizens of the black race in Louisiana, many of whom, perhaps, risked their lives for the preservation of the Union, who are entitled, by law, to participate in the political control of the State and nation, who are not excluded, by law or by reason of their race, from public stations of any kind, and who have all the legal rights that belong to white citizens, are yet declared to be criminals, liable to imprisonment, if they ride in a public coach occupied by citizens of the white race. It is scarcely just to say that a colored citizen should not object to occupying a public coach assigned to his own race. He does not object, nor, perhaps, would he object to separate coaches for his race if his rights under the law were recognized. But he is objecting, and ought never to cease objecting, to the proposition that citizens of the white and black race can be adjudged criminals because they sit, or claim the right to sit, in the same public coach on a public highway.

The arbitrary separation of citizens on the basis of race while they are on a public highway is a badge of servitude wholly inconsistent with the civil freedom and the equality before the law established by the Constitution. It cannot be justified upon any legal grounds.

If evils will result from the commingling of the two races upon public highways established for the benefit of all, they will be infinitely less than those that will surely come from state legislation regulating the enjoyment of civil rights upon the basis of race. We boast of the freedom enjoyed by our people above all other peoples. But it is difficult to reconcile that boast with a state of the law which, practically, puts the brand of servitude and degradation upon a large class of our fellow citizens, our equals before the law. The thin disguise of "equal" accommodations for passengers in railroad coaches will not mislead anyone, nor atone for the wrong this day done.

The result of the whole matter is that, while this court has frequently adjudged, and at the present term has recognized the doctrine, that a State cannot, consistently with the Constitution of the United States, prevent white and black citizens, having the required qualifications for jury service, from sitting in the same jury box, it is now solemnly held that a State may prohibit white and black citizens from sitting in the same passenger coach on a public highway, or may require that they be separated by a "partition," when in the same passenger coach. May it not now be reasonably expected that astute men of the dominant race, who affect to be disturbed at the possibility that the integrity of the white race may be corrupted, or that its supremacy will be imperiled, by contact on public highways with black people, will endeavor to procure statutes requiring white and black jurors to be separated in the jury box by a "partition," and that, upon retiring from the courtroom to consult as to their verdict, such partition, if it be a moveable one, shall be taken to their consultation room and set up in such way as to prevent black jurors from coming too close to their brother jurors of the white race. If the "partition" used in the courtroom happens to be stationary, provision could be made for screens with openings through which jurors of the two races could confer as to their verdict without coming into personal contact with each other. I cannot see but that, according to the principles this day announced, such state legislation, although conceived in hostility to, and enacted for the purpose of humiliating, citizens of the United States of a particular race, would be held to be consistent with the Constitution.

I do not deem it necessary to review the decisions of state courts to which reference was made in argument. Some, and the most important, of them are wholly inapplicable because rendered prior to the adoption of the last amendments of the Constitution, when colored people had very few rights which the dominant race felt obliged to respect. Others were made at a time when public opinion in many localities was dominated by the institution of slavery, when it would not have been safe to do justice to the black man, and when, so far as the rights of blacks were concerned, race prejudice was, practically, the supreme law of the land. Those decisions cannot be guides in the era introduced by the recent amendments of the supreme law, which established universal civil freedom, gave citizenship to all born or naturalized in the United States and residing here, obliterated the race line from our systems of governments, National and State, and placed our free institutions upon the broad and sure foundation of the equality of all men before the law.

I am of opinion that the statute of Louisiana is inconsistent with the personal liberty of citizens, white and black, in that State, and hostile to both the spirit and letter of the Constitution of the United States. If laws of like character should be enacted in the several States of the Union, the effect would be in the highest degree mischievous. Slavery, as an institution tolerated by law would, it is true, have disappeared from our country, but there would remain a power in the States, by sinister legislation, to interfere with the full enjoyment of the blessings of freedom to regulate civil rights, common to all citizens, upon the basis of race, and to place in a condition of legal inferiority a large body of American citizens now constituting a part of the political community called the People of the United States, for whom and by whom, through representatives, our government is administered. Such a system is inconsistent with the guarantee given by the Constitution to each State of a republican form of government, and may be stricken down by Congressional action, or by the courts in the discharge of their solemn duty to maintain the supreme law of the land, anything in the constitution or laws of any State to the contrary notwithstanding.

For the reasons stated, I am constrained to withhold my assent from the opinion and judgment of the majority.

MR. JUSTICE BREWER did not hear the argument or participate in the decision of this case.

PIERCE V. SOCIETY OF THE SISTERS OF THE HOLY NAMES OF JESUS AND MARY, 268 U.S. 510 (1925)

SUPREME COURT OF THE UNITED STATES
PIERCE, GOVERNOR OF OREGON, ET AL. V. SOCIETY OF THE SISTERS OF THE HOLY NAMES OF JESUS AND MARY.
SAME V. HILL MILITARY ACADEMY.
ARGUED MARCH 16 AND 17, 1925. DECIDED JUNE 1, 1925.

Mr. Willis S. Moore, of Salem, Or., for other appellants.

Messrs. Wm. D. Guthrie, of New York City for appellee.

Mr. J. P. Kavanaugh, of Portland, Or., for appellee Society of the Sisters of the Holy Names of Jesus and Mary.

Messrs. George E. Chamberlain, of Portland, Or., and Albert H. Putney, of Washington, D. C., for appellant Pierce.

Mr. John C. Veatch, of Portland, Or., for appellee Hill Military Academy.

Mr. Justice McREYNOLDS delivered the opinion of the Court.

These appeals are from decrees, based upon undenied allegations, which granted preliminary orders restraining appellants from threatening or attempting to enforce the Compulsory Education Act1 adopted November 7, 1922 (Laws Or. 1923, p. 9), under the initiative provision of her Constitution by the voters of Oregon. Judicial Code, 266 (Comp. St. 1243). They present the same points of law; there are no controverted questions of fact. Rights said to be guaranteed by the federal Constitution were specially set up, and appropriate prayers asked for their protection.

The challenged act, effective September 1, 1926, requires every parent, guardian, or other person having control or charge or custody of a child between 8 and 16 years to send him 'to a public school for the period of time a public school shall be held during the current year' in the district where the child resides; and failure so to do is declared a misdemeanor. There are exemptions—not specially important here—for children who are not normal, or who have completed the eighth grade, or whose parents or private teachers reside at considerable distances from any public school, or who hold special permits from the county superintendent. The manifest purpose is to compel general attendance at public schools by normal children, between 8 and 16, who have not completed the eight grade. And without doubt enforcement of the statute would seriously impair, perhaps destroy, the profitable features of appellees' business and greatly diminish the value of their property.

Appellee the Society of Sisters is an Oregon corporation, organized in 1880, with power to care for orphans, educate and instruct the youth, establish and maintain academies or schools, and acquire necessary real and personal property. It has long devoted its property and effort to the secular and religious education and care of children, and has acquired the valuable good will of many parents and guardians. It conducts interdependent primary and high schools and junior colleges, and maintains orphanages for the custody and control of children between 8 and 16. In its primary schools many children between those ages are taught the subjects usually pursued in Oregon public schools during the first eight years. Systematic religious instruction and moral training according to the tenets of the Roman Catholic Church are also regularly provided. All courses of study, both temporal and religious, contemplate continuity of training under appellee's charge; the primary schools are essential to the system and the most profitable. It owns valuable buildings, especially constructed and equipped for school purposes. The business is remunerative—the annual income from primary schools exceeds $30,000—and the successful conduct of this requires long time contracts with teachers and parents. The Compulsory Education Act of 1922 has already caused the withdrawal from its schools of children who would otherwise continue, and their income has steadily declined. The appellants, public officers, have proclaimed their purpose strictly to enforce the statute.

After setting out the above facts, the Society's bill alleges that the enactment conflicts with the right of parents to choose schools where their children will receive appropriate mental and religious training, the right of the child to influence the parents' choice of a school, the right of schools and teachers therein to engage in a useful business or profession, and is accordingly repugnant to the Constitution and void. And, further, that unless enforcement of the measure is enjoined the corporation's business and property will suffer irreparable injury.

Appellee Hill Military Academy is a private corporation organized in 1908 under the laws of Oregon, engaged in owning, operating, and conducting for profit an elementary, college preparatory, and military training school for boys between the ages of 5 and 21 years. The average attendance is 100, and the annual fees received for each student amount to some $800. The elementary department is divided into eight grades, as in the public schools; the college preparatory department has four grades, similar to those of the public high schools; the courses of study conform to the requirements of the state board of education. Military instruction and training are also given, under the supervision of an army officer. It owns considerable real and personal property, some useful only for school purposes. The business and incident good will are very valuable. In order to conduct its affairs, long time contracts must be made for supplies, equipment, teachers, and pupils. Appellants, law officers of the state and county, have publicly announced that the Act of November 7, 1922, is valid and have declared their intention to enforce it. By reason of the statute and threat of enforcement appellee's business is being destroyed and its property depreciated; parents and guardians are refusing to make contracts for the future instruction of their sons, and some are being withdrawn.

The Academy's bill states the foregoing facts and then alleges that the challenged act contravenes the corporation's rights guaranteed by the Fourteenth Amendment and that unless appellants are restrained from proclaiming its validity and threatening to enforce it irreparable injury will result. The prayer is for an appropriate injunction.

No answer was interposed in either cause, and after proper notices they were heard by three judges (Judicial Code, 266 [Comp. St. 1243]) on motions for preliminary injunctions upon the specifically alleged facts. The court ruled that the Fourteenth Amendment guaranteed appellees against the deprivation of their property without due process of law consequent upon the unlawful interference by appellants with the free choice of patrons, present and prospective. It declared the right to conduct schools was property and that parents and guardians, as a part of their liberty, might direct the education of children by selecting reputable teachers and places. Also, that appellees' schools were not unfit or harmful to the public, and that enforcement of the challenged statute would unlawfully deprive them of patronage and thereby destroy appellees' business and property. Finally, that the threats to enforce the act would continue to cause irreparable injury; and the suits were not premature.

No question is raised concerning the power of the state reasonably to regulate all schools, to inspect, supervise and examine them, their teachers and pupils; to require that all children of proper age attend some school, that teachers shall be of good moral character and patriotic disposition, that certain studies plainly essential to good citizenship must be taught, and that nothing be taught which is manifestly inimical to the public welfare.

The inevitable practical result of enforcing the act under consideration would be destruction of appellees' primary schools, and perhaps all other private primary schools for normal children within the state of Oregon. Appellees are engaged in a kind of undertaking not inherently harmful, but long regarded as useful and meritorious. Certainly there is nothing in the present records to indicate that they have failed to discharge their obligations to patrons, students, or the state. And there are no peculiar circumstances or present emergencies which demand extraordinary measures relative to primary education.

Under the doctrine of Meyer v. Nebraska, 43 S. Ct. 625, 29 A. L. R. 1146, we think it entirely plain that the Act of 1922 unreasonably interferes with the liberty of parents and guardians to direct the upbringing and education of children under their control. As often heretofore pointed out, rights guaranteed by the Constitution may not be abridged by legislation which has no reasonable relation to some purpose within the competency of the state. The fundamental theory of liberty upon which all governments in this Union repose excludes any general power of the state to standardize its children by forcing them to accept instruction from public teachers only. The child is not the mere creature of the state; those who nurture him and direct his destiny have the right, coupled with the high duty, to recognize and prepare him for additional obligations.

Appellees are corporations, and therefore, it is said, they cannot claim for themselves the liberty which the Fourteenth Amendment guarantees. Accepted in the proper sense, this is true. Northwestern Life Ins. Co. v. Riggs, 27 S. Ct. 126, 7 Ann. Cas. 1104; Western Turf Association v. Greenberg, 27 S. Ct. 384. But they have business and property for which they claim protection. These are threatened with destruction through the unwarranted compulsion which appellants are exercising over present and prospective patrons of their schools. And this court has gone very far to protect against loss threatened by such action. Truax v. Raich, 36 S. Ct. 7, L. R. A. 1916D, 543, Ann. Cas. 1917B, 283; Truax v. Corrigan, 42 S. Ct. 124, 27 A. L. R. 375; Terrace v. Thompson, 44 S. Ct. 15.

The courts of the state have not construed the act, and we must determine its meaning for ourselves. Evidently it was expected to have general application and cannot be construed as though merely intended to amend the charters of certain private corporations, as in Berea College v. Kentucky, 29 S. Ct. 33. No argument in favor of such view has been advanced.

Generally, it is entirely true, as urged by counsel, that no person in any business has such an interest in possible customers as to enable him to restrain exercise of proper power of the state upon the ground that he will be deprived of patronage. But the injunctions here sought are not against the exercise of any proper power. Appellees asked protection against arbitrary, unreasonable, and unlawful interference with their patrons and the consequent destruction of their business and property. Their interest is clear and immediate, within the rule approved in Truax v. Raich, Truax v. Corrigan, and Terrace v. Thompson, supra, and many other cases where injunctions have issued to protect business enterprises against interference with the freedom of patrons or customers. Hitchman Coal & Coke Co. v. Mitchell, 38 S. Ct. 65, L. R. A. 1918C, 497, Ann. Cas. 1918B, 461; Duplex Printing Press Co. v. Deering, 41 S. Ct. 172, 16 A. L. R. 196; American Steel Foundries v. Tri-City Central Trades Council, 42 S. Ct. 72, 27 A. L. R. 360; Nebraska District, etc., v. McKelvie, 43 S. Ct. 628; Truax v. Corrigan, supra, and cases there cited.

The suits were not premature. The injury to appellees was present and very real, not a mere possibility in the remote future. If no relief had been possible prior to the effective date of the act, the injury would have become irreparable. Prevention of impending injury by unlawful action is a well-recognized function of courts of equity.

The decrees below are affirmed.

Be it enacted by the people of the state of Oregon:

Section 1. That section 5259, Oregon Laws, be and the same is hereby amended so as to read as follows:

Sec. 5259. Children Between the Ages of Eight and Sixteen Years. Any parent, guardian or other person in the state of Oregon, having control or charge or custody of a child under the age of sixteen years and of the age of eight years or over at the commencement of a term of public school of the district in which said child resides, who shall fail or neglect or refuse to send such child to a public school for the period of time a public school shall be held during the current year in said district, shall be guilty of a misdemeanor and each day's failure to send such child to a public school shall constitute a separate offense; provided, that in the following cases, children shall not be required to attend public schools:

(a) Children Physically Unable. Any child who is abnormal, subnormal or physically unable to attend school.

(b) Children Who Have Completed the Eighth Grade. Any child who has completed the eighth grade, in accordance with the provisions of the state course of study.

(c) Distance from School. Children between the ages of eight and ten years, inclusive, whose place of residence is more than one and one-half miles, and children over ten years of age whose place of residence is more than three miles, by the nearest traveled road, from a public school; provided, however, that if transportation to and from school is furnished by the school district, this exemption shall not apply.

(d) Private Instruction. Any child who is being taught for a like period of time by the parent or private teacher such subjects as are usually taught in the first eight years in the public school; but before such child can be taught by a parent or a private teacher, such parent or private teacher must receive written permission from the county superintendent, and such permission shall not extend longer than the end of the current school year. Such child must report to the county school superintendent or some person designated by him at least once every three months and take an examination in the work covered. If, after such examination, the county superintendent shall determine that such child is not being properly taught, then the county superintendent shall order the parent, guardian or other person, to send such child to the public school the remainder of the school year.

If any parent, guardian or other person having control or charge or custody of any child between the ages of eight and sixteen years, shall fail to comply with any provision of this section, he shall be guilty of a misdemeanor, and shall, on conviction thereof, be subject to a fine of not less than $5, nor more than $100, or to imprisonment in the county jail not less than two nor more than thirty days, or by both such fine and imprisonment in the discretion of the court.

This act shall take effect and be and remain in force from and after the first day of September, 1926.

BROWN V. BOARD OF EDUCATION, 347 U.S. 483 (1954)

No. 1.

SUPREME COURT OF THE UNITED STATES

Argued December 9, 1952

Reargued December 8, 1953

Decided May 17, 1954

APPEAL FROM THE UNITED STATES DISTRICT COURT FOR THE DISTRICT OF KANSAS

Syllabus

Segregation of white and Negro children in the public schools of a State solely on the basis of race, pursuant to state laws permitting or requiring such segregation, denies to Negro children the equal protection of the laws guaranteed by the Fourteenth Amendment—even though the physical facilities and other "tangible" factors of white and Negro schools may be equal.

(a) The history of the Fourteenth Amendment is inconclusive as to its intended effect on public education.

(b) The question presented in these cases must be determined not on the basis of conditions existing when the Fourteenth Amendment was adopted, but in the light of the full development of public education and its present place in American life throughout the Nation.

(c) Where a State has undertaken to provide an opportunity for an education in its public schools, such an opportunity is a right which must be made available to all on equal terms.

(d) Segregation of children in public schools solely on the basis of race deprives children of the minority group of equal educational opportunities, even though the physical facilities and other "tangible" factors may be equal.

(e) The "separate but equal" doctrine adopted in *Plessy* v. *Ferguson* has no place in the field of public education.

(f) The cases are restored to the docket for further argument on specified questions relating to the forms of the decrees.

Opinions

WARREN, Opinion of the Court

MR. CHIEF JUSTICE WARREN delivered the opinion of the Court.

These cases come to us from the States of Kansas, South Carolina, Virginia, and Delaware. They are premised on different facts and different local conditions, but a common legal question justifies their consideration together in this consolidated opinion.

In each of the cases, minors of the Negro race, through their legal representatives, seek the aid of the courts in obtaining admission to the public schools of their community on a nonsegregated basis. In each instance, they had been denied admission to schools attended by white children under laws requiring or permitting segregation according to race. This segregation was alleged to deprive the plaintiffs of the equal protection of the laws under the Fourteenth Amendment. In each of the cases other than the Delaware case, a three-judge federal district court denied relief to the plaintiffs on the so-called "separate but equal" doctrine announced by this Court in *Plessy* v. *Ferguson*. Under that doctrine, equality of treatment is accorded when the races are provided substantially equal facilities, even though these facilities be separate. In the Delaware case, the Supreme Court of Delaware adhered to that doctrine, but ordered that the plaintiffs be admitted to the white schools because of their superiority to the Negro schools.

The plaintiffs contend that segregated public schools are not "equal" and cannot be made "equal," and that hence they are deprived of the equal protection of the laws. Because of the obvious importance of the question presented, the Court took jurisdiction. Argument was heard in the 1952 Term, and reargument was heard this Term on certain questions propounded by the Court.

Reargument was largely devoted to the circumstances surrounding the adoption of the Fourteenth Amendment in 1868. It covered exhaustively consideration of the Amendment in Congress, ratification by the states, then-existing practices in racial segregation, and the views of proponents and opponents of the Amendment. This discussion and our own investigation convince us that, although these sources cast some light, it is not enough to resolve the problem with which we are faced. At best, they are inconclusive. The most avid proponents of the post-War Amendments undoubtedly intended them to remove all legal distinctions among "all persons born or naturalized in the United States." Their opponents, just as certainly, were antagonistic to both the letter and the spirit of the Amendments and wished them to have the most limited effect. What others in Congress and the state legislatures had in mind cannot be determined with any degree of certainty. An additional reason for the inconclusive nature of the Amendment's history with respect to segregated schools is the status of public education at that time. In the South, the movement toward free common schools, supported by general taxation, had not yet taken hold. Education of white children was largely in the hands of private groups. Education of Negroes was almost nonexistent, and practically all of the race were illiterate. In fact, any education of Negroes was forbidden by law in some states. Today, in contrast, many Negroes have achieved outstanding success in the arts and sciences, as well as in the business and professional world. It is true that public school education at the time of the Amendment had advanced further in the North, but the effect of the Amendment on Northern States was generally ignored in the congressional debates. Even in the North, the conditions of public education did not approximate those existing today. The curriculum was usually rudimentary; ungraded schools were common in rural areas; the school term was but three months a year in many states, and compulsory school attendance was virtually unknown. As a consequence, it is not surprising that there should be so little in the history of the Fourteenth Amendment relating to its intended effect on public education.

In the first cases in this Court construing the Fourteenth Amendment, decided shortly after its adoption, the Court interpreted it as proscribing all state-imposed discriminations against the Negro race. The doctrine of "separate but equal" did not make its appearance in this Court until 1896 in the case of *Plessy* v. *Ferguson*, supra, involving not education but transportation. American courts have since labored with the doctrine for over half a century. In this Court, there have been six cases involving the "separate but equal" doctrine in the field of public education. In *Cumming* v. *County Board of Education*, and *Gong Lum* v. *Rice*, the validity of the doctrine itself was not challenged. In more recent cases, all on the graduate school level, inequality was found in that specific benefits enjoyed by white students were denied to Negro students of the same educational qualifications. *Missouri ex rel. Gaines* v. *Canada*; *Sipuel* v. *Oklahoma*; *Sweatt* v. *Painter*; *McLaurin* v. *Oklahoma State Regents*. In none of these cases was it necessary to reexamine the doctrine to grant relief to the Negro plaintiff. And in *Sweatt* v. *Painter*, supra, the Court expressly reserved decision on the question whether *Plessy* v. *Ferguson* should be held inapplicable to public education.

In the instant cases, that question is directly presented. Here, unlike *Sweatt* v. *Painter*, there are findings below that the Negro and white schools involved have been equalized, or are being equalized, with respect to buildings, curricula, qualifications and salaries of teachers, and other "tangible" factors. Our decision, therefore, cannot turn on merely a comparison of these tangible factors in the Negro and white schools involved in each of the cases. We must look instead to the effect of segregation itself on public education.

In approaching this problem, we cannot turn the clock back to 1868, when the Amendment was adopted, or even to 1896, when *Plessy* v. *Ferguson* was written. We must consider public education in the light of its full development and its present place in American life throughout the Nation. Only in this way can it be determined if segregation in public schools deprives these plaintiffs of the equal protection of the laws.

Today, education is perhaps the most important function of state and local governments. Compulsory school attendance laws and the great expenditures for education both demonstrate our recognition of the importance of education to our democratic society. It is required in the performance of our most basic public responsibilities, even service in the armed forces. It is the very foundation of good citizenship. Today it is a principal instrument in awakening the child to cultural values, in preparing him for later professional training, and in helping him to adjust normally to his environment. In these days, it is doubtful that any child may reasonably be expected to succeed in life if he is denied the opportunity of an education. Such an opportunity, where the state has undertaken to provide it, is a right which must be made available to all on equal terms.

We come then to the question presented: Does segregation of children in public schools solely on the basis of race, even though the physical facilities and other "tangible" factors may be equal, deprive the children of the minority group of equal educational opportunities? We believe that it does.

In *Sweatt* v. *Painter*, supra, in finding that a segregated law school for Negroes could not provide them equal educational opportunities, this Court relied in large part on "those qualities which are incapable of objective measurement but which make for greatness in a law school." In *McLaurin* v. *Oklahoma State Regents*, the Court, in requiring that a Negro admitted to a white graduate school be treated like all other students, again resorted to intangible considerations: " . . . his ability to study, to engage in discussions and exchange views with other students, and, in general, to learn his profession." Such considerations apply with added force to children in grade and high schools. To separate them from others of similar age and qualifications solely because of their race generates a feeling of inferiority as to their status in the community that may affect their hearts and minds in a way unlikely ever to be undone. The effect of this separation on their educational opportunities was well stated by a finding in the Kansas case by a court which nevertheless felt compelled to rule against the Negro plaintiffs:

Segregation of white and colored children in public schools has a detrimental effect upon the colored children. The impact is greater when it has the sanction of the law, for the policy of separating the races is usually interpreted as denoting the inferiority of the negro group.

A sense of inferiority affects the motivation of a child to learn. Segregation with the sanction of law, therefore, has a tendency to [retard] the educational and mental development of negro children and to deprive them of some of the benefits they would receive in a racial[ly] integrated school system.

Whatever may have been the extent of psychological knowledge at the time of *Plessy* v. *Ferguson*, this finding is amply supported by modern authority. Any language in *Plessy* v. *Ferguson* contrary to this finding is rejected.

We conclude that, in the field of public education, the doctrine of "separate but equal" has no place. Separate educational facilities are inherently unequal. Therefore, we hold that the plaintiffs and others similarly situated for whom the actions have been brought are, by reason of the segregation complained of, deprived of the equal protection of the laws guaranteed by the Fourteenth Amendment. This disposition makes unnecessary any discussion whether such segregation also violates the Due Process Clause of the Fourteenth Amendment.

Because these are class actions, because of the wide applicability of this decision, and because of the great variety of local conditions, the formulation of decrees in these cases presents problems of considerable complexity. On reargument, the consideration of appropriate relief was necessarily subordinated to the primary question—the constitutionality of segregation in public education. We have now announced that such segregation is a denial of the equal protection of the laws. In order that we may have the full assistance of the parties in formulating decrees, the cases will be restored to the docket, and the parties are requested to present further argument on Questions 4 and 5 previously propounded by the Court for the reargument this Term The Attorney General of the United States is again invited to participate. The Attorneys General of the states requiring or permitting segregation in public education will also be permitted to appear as amici curiae upon request to do so by September 15, 1954, and submission of briefs by October 1, 1954.

It is so ordered.

Brown v. *Board of Education*, 349 U.S. 294 (1955)
SUPREME COURT OF THE UNITED STATES
Reargued on the question of relief April 11–14, 1955
Opinion and judgments announced May 31, 1955

APPEAL FROM THE UNITED STATES DISTRICT COURT FOR THE DISTRICT OF KANSAS.

Syllabus

1. Racial discrimination in public education is unconstitutional, and all provisions of federal, state or local law requiring or permitting such discrimination must yield to this principle.
2. The judgments below (except that in the Delaware case) are reversed and the cases are remanded to the District Courts to take such proceedings and enter such orders and decrees consistent with this opinion as are necessary and proper to admit the parties to these cases to public schools on a racially nondiscriminatory basis with all deliberate speed.
   (a) School authorities have the primary responsibility for elucidating, assessing and solving the varied local school problems which may require solution in fully implementing the governing constitutional principles.
   (b) Courts will have to consider whether the action of school authorities constitutes good faith implementation of the governing constitutional principles.
   (c) Because of their proximity to local conditions and the possible need for further hearings, the courts which originally heard these cases can best perform this judicial appraisal.

(d) In fashioning and effectuating the decrees, the courts will be guided by equitable principles—characterized by a practical flexibility in shaping remedies and a facility for adjusting and reconciling public and private needs.

(e) At stake is the personal interest of the plaintiffs in admission to public schools as soon as practicable on a nondiscriminatory basis.

(f) Courts of equity may properly take into account the public interest in the elimination in a systematic and effective manner of a variety of obstacles in making the transition to school systems operated in accordance with the constitutional principles enunciated in [Brown I]; but the vitality of these constitutional principles cannot be allowed to yield simply because of disagreement with them.

(g) While giving weight to these public and private considerations, the courts will require that the defendants make a prompt and reasonable start toward full compliance with the ruling of this Court.

(h) Once such a start has been made, the courts may find that additional time is necessary to carry out the ruling in an effective manner.

(i) The burden rests on the defendants to establish that additional time is necessary in the public interest and is consistent with good faith compliance at the earliest practicable date.

(j) The courts may consider problems related to administration, arising from the physical condition of the school plant, the school transportation system, personnel, revision of school districts and attendance areas into compact units to achieve a system of determining admission to the public schools on a nonracial basis, and revision of local laws and regulations which may be necessary in solving the foregoing problems.

(k) The courts will also consider the adequacy of any plans the defendants may propose to meet these problems and to effectuate a transition to a racially nondiscriminatory school system.

(l) During the period of transition, the courts will retain jurisdiction of these cases.

3. The judgment in the Delaware case, ordering the immediate admission of the plaintiffs to schools previously attended only by white children, is affirmed on the basis of the principles stated by this Court in its opinion but the case is remanded to the Supreme Court of Delaware for such further proceedings as that Court may deem necessary in the light of this opinion.

98 F.Supp. 797, 103 F.Supp. 920, 103 F.Supp. 337 and judgment in No. 4, reversed and remanded.

91 A.2d 137, affirmed and remanded.

Opinions

WARREN, Opinion of the Court

MR. CHIEF JUSTICE WARREN delivered the opinion of the Court.

These cases were decided on May 17, 1954. The opinions of that date, declaring the fundamental principle that racial discrimination in public education is unconstitutional, are incorporated herein by reference. All provisions of federal, state, or local law requiring or permitting such discrimination must yield to this principle. There remains for consideration the manner in which relief is to be accorded.

Because these cases arose under different local conditions and their disposition will involve a variety of local problems, we requested further argument on the question of relief. In view of the nationwide importance of the decision, we invited the Attorney General of the United States and the Attorneys General of all states requiring or permitting racial discrimination in public education to present their views on that question. The parties, the United States, and the States of Florida, North Carolina, Arkansas, Oklahoma, Maryland, and Texas filed briefs and participated in the oral argument.

These presentations were informative and helpful to the Court in its consideration of the complexities arising from the transition to a system of public education freed of racial discrimination. The presentations also demonstrated that substantial steps to eliminate racial discrimination in public schools have already been taken, not only in some of the communities in which these cases arose, but in some of the states appearing as amici curiae, and in other states as well. Substantial progress has been made in the District of Columbia and in the communities in Kansas and Delaware involved in this litigation. The defendants in the cases coming to us from South Carolina and Virginia are awaiting the decision of this Court concerning relief.

Full implementation of these constitutional principles may require solution of varied local school problems. School authorities have the primary responsibility for elucidating, assessing, and solving these problems; courts will have to consider whether the action of school authorities constitutes good faith implementation of the governing constitutional principles. Because of their proximity to local conditions and the possible need for further hearings, the courts which originally heard these cases can best perform this judicial appraisal. Accordingly, we believe it appropriate to remand the cases to those courts.

In fashioning and effectuating the decrees, the courts will be guided by equitable principles. Traditionally, equity has been characterized by a practical flexibility in shaping its remedies and by a facility for adjusting and reconciling public and private needs. These cases call for the exercise of these traditional attributes of equity power. At stake is the personal interest of the plaintiffs in admission to public schools as soon as practicable on a nondiscriminatory basis. To effectuate this interest may call for elimination of a variety of obstacles in making the transition to school systems operated in accordance with the constitutional principles set forth in our May 17, 1954, decision. Courts of equity may properly take into account the public interest in the elimination of such obstacles in a systematic and effective manner. But it should go without saying that the vitality of these constitutional principles cannot be allowed to yield simply because of disagreement with them.

While giving weight to these public and private considerations, the courts will require that the defendants make a prompt and reasonable start toward full compliance with our May 17, 1954, ruling. Once such a start has been made, the courts may find that additional time is necessary to carry out the ruling in an effective manner. The burden rests upon the defendants to establish that such time is necessary in the public interest and is consistent with good faith compliance at the earliest practicable date. To that end, the courts may consider problems related to administration, arising from the physical condition of the school plant, the school transportation system, personnel, revision of school districts and attendance areas into compact units to achieve a system of determining admission to the public schools on a nonracial basis, and revision of local laws and regulations which may be necessary in solving the foregoing problems. They will also consider the adequacy of any plans the defendants may propose to meet these problems and to effectuate a transition to a racially nondiscriminatory school system. During this period of transition, the courts will retain jurisdiction of these cases.

The judgments below, except that, in the Delaware case, are accordingly reversed, and the cases are remanded to the District Courts to take such proceedings and enter such orders and decrees consistent with this opinion as are necessary and proper to admit to public schools on a racially nondiscriminatory basis with all deliberate speed the parties to these cases. The judgment in the Delaware case—ordering the immediate admission of the plaintiffs to schools previously attended only by white children—is affirmed on the basis of the principles stated in our May 17, 1954, opinion, but the case is remanded to the Supreme Court of Delaware for such further proceedings as that Court may deem necessary in light of this opinion.

It is so ordered.

ENGEL V. VITALE, 370 U.S. 421 (1962)

SUPREME COURT OF THE UNITED STATES
CERTIORARI TO THE COURT OF APPEALS OF NEW YORK
ARGUED APRIL 3, 1962. DECIDED JUNE 25, 1962.

Because of the prohibition of the First Amendment against the enactment of any law "respecting an establishment of religion," which is made applicable to the States by the Fourteenth Amendment, state officials may not compose an official state prayer and require that it be recited in the public schools of the State at the beginning of each school day—even if the prayer is denominationally neutral and pupils who wish to do so may remain silent or be excused from the room while the prayer is being recited.

10 N.Y.2d 174, 176 N.E.2d 579, reversed.

BLACK, Opinion of the Court

MR. JUSTICE BLACK delivered the opinion of the Court.

The respondent Board of Education of Union Free School District No. 9, New Hyde Park, New York, acting in its official capacity under state law, directed the School District's principal to cause the following prayer to be said aloud by each class in the presence of a teacher at the beginning of each school day:

> Almighty God, we acknowledge our dependence upon Thee, and we beg Thy blessings upon us, our parents, our teachers and our Country.

This daily procedure was adopted on the recommendation of the State Board of Regents, a governmental agency created by the State Constitution to which the New York Legislature has granted broad supervisory, executive, and legislative powers over the State's public school system. These state officials composed the prayer which they recommended and published as a part of their "Statement on Moral and Spiritual Training in the Schools," saying:

> We believe that this Statement will be subscribed to by all men and women of good will, and we call upon all of them to aid in giving life to our program.

Shortly after the practice of reciting the Regents' prayer was adopted by the School District, the parents of ten pupils brought this action in a New York State Court insisting that use of this official prayer in the public schools was contrary to the beliefs, religions, or religious practices of both themselves and their children. Among other things, these parents challenged the constitutionality of both the state law authorizing the School District to direct the use of prayer in public schools and the School District's regulation ordering the recitation of this particular prayer on the ground that these actions of official governmental agencies violate that part of the First Amendment of the Federal Constitution which commands that "Congress shall make no law respecting an establishment of religion"—a command which was "made applicable to the State of New York by the Fourteenth Amendment of the said Constitution." The New York Court of Appeals, over the dissents of Judges Dye and Fuld, sustained an order of the lower state courts which had upheld the power of New York to use the Regents' prayer as a part of the daily procedures of its public schools so long as the schools did not compel any pupil to join in the prayer over his or his parents' objection. We granted certiorari to review this important decision involving rights protected by the First and Fourteenth Amendments.

We think that, by using its public school system to encourage recitation of the Regents' prayer, the State of New York has adopted a practice wholly inconsistent with the Establishment Clause. There can, of course, be no doubt that New York's program of daily classroom invocation of God's blessings as prescribed in the Regents' prayer is a religious activity. It is a solemn avowal of divine faith and supplication for the blessings of the Almighty. The nature of such a prayer has always been religious, none of the respondents has denied this, and the trial court expressly so found:

The religious nature of prayer was recognized by Jefferson, and has been concurred in by theological writers, the United States Supreme Court, and State courts and administrative officials, including New York's Commissioner of Education. A committee of the New York Legislature has agreed.

The Board of Regents as amicus curiae, the respondents, and intervenors all concede the religious nature of prayer, but seek to distinguish this prayer because it is based on our spiritual heritage . . .

The petitioners contend, among other things, that the state laws requiring or permitting use of the Regents' prayer must be struck down as a violation of the Establishment Clause because that prayer was composed by governmental officials as a part of a governmental program to further religious beliefs. For this reason, petitioners argue, the State's use of the Regents' prayer in its public school system breaches the constitutional wall of separation between Church and State. We agree with that contention, since we think that the constitutional prohibition against laws respecting an establishment of religion must at least mean that, in this country, it is no part of the business of government to compose official prayers for any group of the American people to recite as a part of a religious program carried on by government.

It is a matter of history that this very practice of establishing governmentally composed prayers for religious services was one of the reasons which caused many of our early colonists to leave England and seek religious freedom in America. The Book of Common Prayer, which was created under governmental direction and which was approved by Acts of Parliament in 1548 and 1549, set out in minute detail the accepted form and content of prayer and other religious ceremonies to be used in the established, tax supported Church of England. The controversies over the Book and what should be its content repeatedly threatened to disrupt the peace of that country as the accepted forms of prayer in the established church changed with the views of the particular ruler that happened to be in control at the time. Powerful groups representing some of the varying religious views of the people struggled among themselves to impress their particular views upon the Government and obtain amendments of the Book more suitable to their respective notions of how religious services should be conducted in order that the official religious establishment would advance their particular religious beliefs. Other groups, lacking the necessary political power to influence the Government on the matter, decided to leave England and its established church and seek freedom in America from England's governmentally ordained and supported religion.

It is an unfortunate fact of history that, when some of the very groups which had most strenuously opposed the established Church of England found themselves sufficiently in control of colonial governments in this country to write their own prayers into law, they passed laws making their own religion the official religion of their respective colonies. Indeed, as late as the time of the Revolutionary War, there were established churches in at least eight of the thirteen former colonies and established religions in at least four of the other five. But the successful Revolution against English political domination was shortly followed by intense opposition to the practice of establishing religion by law. This opposition crystallized rapidly into an effective political force in Virginia, where the minority religious groups such as Presbyterians, Lutherans, Quakers and Baptists had gained such strength that the adherents to the established Episcopal Church were actually a minority themselves. In 1785-1786, those opposed to the established Church, led by James Madison and Thomas Jefferson, who, though themselves not members of any of these dissenting religious groups, opposed all religious establishments by law on grounds of principle, obtained the enactment of the famous "Virginia Bill for Religious Liberty" by which all religious groups were placed on an equal footing so far as the State was concerned. Similar though less far-reaching legislation was being considered and passed in other states.

By the time of the adoption of the Constitution, our history shows that there was a widespread awareness among many Americans of the dangers of a union of Church and State. These people knew, some of them from bitter personal experience, that one of the greatest dangers to the freedom of the individual to worship in his own way lay in the Government's placing its official stamp of approval upon one particular kind of prayer or one particular form of religious services. They knew the anguish, hardship and bitter strife that could come when zealous religious groups struggled with one another to obtain the Government's stamp of approval from each King, Queen, or Protector that came to temporary power. The Constitution was intended to avert a part of this danger by leaving the government of this country in the hands of the people, rather than in the hands of any monarch. But this safeguard was not enough. Our Founders were no more willing to let the content of their prayers and their privilege of praying whenever they pleased be influenced by the ballot box than they were to let these vital matters of personal conscience depend upon the succession of monarchs. The First Amendment was added to the Constitution to stand as a guarantee that neither the power nor the prestige of the Federal Government would be used to control, support or influence the kinds of prayer the American people can say—that the people's religions must not be subjected to the pressures of government for change each time a new political administration is elected to office. Under that Amendment's prohibition against governmental establishment of religion, as reinforced by the provisions of the Fourteenth Amendment, government in this country, be it state or federal, is without power to prescribe by law any particular form of prayer which is to be used as an official prayer in carrying on any program of governmentally sponsored religious activity.

There can be no doubt that New York's state prayer program officially establishes the religious beliefs embodied in the Regents' prayer. The respondents' argument to the contrary, which is largely based upon the contention that the Regents' prayer is "nondenominational" and the fact that the program, as modified and approved by state courts, does not require all pupils to recite the prayer, but permits those who wish to do so to remain silent or be excused from the room, ignores the essential nature of the program's constitutional defects. Neither the fact that the prayer may be denominationally neutral nor the fact that its observance on the part of the students is voluntary can serve to free it from the limitations of the Establishment Clause, as it might from the Free Exercise Clause, of the First Amendment, both of which are operative against the States by virtue of the Fourteenth Amendment. Although these two clauses may, in certain instances, overlap, they forbid two quite different kinds of governmental encroachment upon religious freedom. The Establishment Clause, unlike the Free Exercise Clause, does not depend upon any showing of direct governmental compulsion and is violated by the enactment of laws which establish an official religion whether those laws operate directly to coerce nonobserving individuals or not. This is not to say, of course, that laws officially prescribing a particular form of religious worship do not involve coercion of such individuals. When the power, prestige and financial support of government is placed behind a particular religious belief, the indirect coercive pressure upon religious minorities to conform to the prevailing officially approved religion is plain. But the purposes underlying the Establishment Clause go much further than that. Its first and most immediate purpose rested on the belief that a union of government and religion tends to destroy government and to degrade religion. The history of governmentally established religion, both in England and in this country, showed that whenever government had allied itself with one particular form of religion, the inevitable result had been that it had incurred the hatred, disrespect and even contempt of those who held contrary beliefs. That same history showed that many people had lost their respect for any religion that had relied upon the support of government to spread its faith. The Establishment Clause thus stands as an expression of principle on the part of the Founders of our Constitution that religion is too personal, too sacred, too holy, to permit its "unhallowed perversion" by a civil magistrate. Another purpose of the Establishment Clause rested upon an awareness of the historical fact that governmentally established religions and religious persecutions go hand in hand. The Founders knew that, only a few years after the Book of Common Prayer became the only accepted form of religious services in the established Church of England, an Act of Uniformity was passed to compel all Englishmen to attend those services and to make it a criminal offense to conduct or attend religious gatherings of any other kind—a law which was consistently flouted by dissenting religious groups in England and which contributed to widespread persecutions of people like John Bunyan who persisted in holding "unlawful [religious] meetings . . . to the great disturbance and distraction of the good subjects of this kingdom . . . ." And they knew that similar persecutions had received the sanction of law in several of the colonies in this country soon after the establishment of official religions in those colonies. It was in large part to get completely away from this sort of systematic religious persecution that the Founders brought into being our Nation, our Constitution, and our Bill of Rights, with its prohibition against any governmental establishment of religion. The New York laws officially prescribing the Regents' prayer are inconsistent both with the purposes of the Establishment Clause and with the Establishment Clause itself.

It has been argued that to apply the Constitution in such a way as to prohibit state laws respecting an establishment of religious services in public schools is to indicate a hostility toward religion or toward prayer. Nothing, of course, could be more wrong. The history of man is inseparable from the history of religion. And perhaps it is not too much to say that, since the beginning of that history, many people have devoutly believed that "More things are wrought by prayer than this world dreams of." It was doubtless largely due to men who believed this that there grew up a sentiment that caused men to leave the cross-currents of officially established state religions and religious persecution in Europe and come to this country filled with the hope that they could find a place in which they could pray when they pleased to the God of their faith in the language they chose. And there were men of this same faith in the power of prayer who led the fight for adoption of our Constitution and also for our Bill of Rights with the very guarantees of religious freedom that forbid the sort of governmental activity which New York has attempted here. These men knew that the First Amendment, which tried to put an end to governmental control of religion and of prayer, was not written to destroy either. They knew, rather, that it was written to quiet well justified fears which nearly all of them felt arising out of an awareness that governments of the past had shackled men's tongues to make them speak only the religious thoughts that government wanted them to speak and to pray only to the God that government wanted them to pray to. It is neither sacrilegious nor anti-religious to say that each separate government in this country should stay out of the business of writing or sanctioning official prayers and leave that purely religious function to the people themselves and to those the people choose to look to for religious guidance.

It is true that New York's establishment of its Regents' prayer as an officially approved religious doctrine of that State does not amount to a total establishment of one particular religious sect to the exclusion of all others—that, indeed, the governmental endorsement of that prayer seems relatively insignificant when compared to the governmental encroachments upon religion which were commonplace 200 years ago. To those who may subscribe to the view that, because the Regents' official prayer is so brief and general there can be no danger to religious freedom in its governmental establishment, however, it may be appropriate to say in the words of James Madison, the author of the First Amendment:

[I]t is proper to take alarm at the first experiment on our liberties. . . . Who does not see that the same authority which can establish Christianity, in exclusion of all other Religions, may establish with the same ease any particular sect of Christians, in exclusion of all other Sects? That the same authority which can force a citizen to contribute three pence only of his property for the support of any one establishment may force him to conform to any other establishment in all cases whatsoever?

The judgment of the Court of Appeals of New York is reversed, and the cause remanded for further proceedings not inconsistent with this opinion.

Reversed and remanded.

MR. JUSTICE FRANKFURTER took no part in the decision of this case.

MR. JUSTICE WHITE took no part in the consideration or decision of this case.

DOUGLAS, Concurring Opinion

MR. JUSTICE DOUGLAS, concurring.

It is customary in deciding a constitutional question to treat it in its narrowest form. Yet at times the setting of the question gives it a form and content which no abstract treatment could give. The point for decision is whether the Government can constitutionally finance a religious exercise. Our system at the federal and state levels is presently honeycombed with such financing. Nevertheless, I think it is an unconstitutional undertaking whatever form it takes.

First, a word as to what this case does not involve.

Plainly, our Bill of Rights would not permit a State or the Federal Government to adopt an official prayer and penalize anyone who would not utter it. This, however, is not that case, for there is no element of compulsion or coercion in New York's regulation requiring that public schools be opened each day with the following prayer:

> Almighty God, we acknowledge our dependence upon Thee, and we beg Thy blessings upon us, our parents, our teachers and our Country.

The prayer is said upon the commencement of the school day, immediately following the pledge of allegiance to the flag. The prayer is said aloud in the presence of a teacher, who either leads the recitation or selects a student to do so. No student, however, is compelled to take part. The respondents have adopted a regulation which provides that

> Neither teachers nor any school authority shall comment on participation or non-participation . . . , nor suggest or request that any posture or language be used or dress be worn or be not used or not worn.

Provision is also made for excusing children, upon written request of a parent or guardian, from the saying of the prayer or from the room in which the prayer is said. A letter implementing and explaining this regulation has been sent to each taxpayer and parent in the school district. As I read this regulation, a child is free to stand or not stand, to recite or not recite, without fear of reprisal or even comment by the teacher or any other school official.

In short, the only one who need utter the prayer is the teacher, and no teacher is complaining of it. Students can stand mute, or even leave the classroom, if they desire.

McCollum v. Board of Education, does not decide this case. It involved the use of public school facilities for religious education of students. Students either had to attend religious instruction or go to some other place in the school building for pursuit of their secular studies . . . . Reports of their presence or absence were to be made to their secular teachers.

Id. The influence of the teaching staff was therefore brought to bear on the student body to support the instilling of religious principles. In the present case, school facilities are used to say the prayer, and the teaching staff is employed to lead the pupils in it. There is, however, no effort at indoctrination, and no attempt at exposition. Prayers, of course, may be so long and of such a character as to amount to an attempt at the religious instruction that was denied the public schools by the McCollum case. But New York's prayer is of a character that does not involve any element of proselytizing, as in the McCollum case.

The question presented by this case is therefore an extremely narrow one.

It is whether New York oversteps the bounds when it finances a religious exercise.

What New York does on the opening of its public schools is what we do when we open court. Our Crier has from the beginning announced the convening of the Court and then added "God save the United States and this Honorable Court." That utterance is a supplication, a prayer in which we, the judges, are free to join, but which we need not recite any more than the students need recite the New York prayer.

What New York does on the opening of its public schools is what each House of Congress does at the opening of each day's business. Reverend Frederick B. Harris is Chaplain of the Senate; Reverend Bernard Braskamp is Chaplain of the House. Guest chaplains of various denominations also officiate.

In New York, the teacher who leads in prayer is on the public payroll, and the time she takes seems minuscule as compared with the salaries appropriated by state legislatures and Congress for chaplains to conduct prayers in the legislative halls. Only a bare fraction of the teacher's time is given to reciting this short 22-word prayer, about the same amount of time that our Crier spends announcing the opening of our sessions and offering a prayer for this Court. Yet, for me, the principle is the same, no matter how briefly the prayer is said, for, in each of the instances given, the person praying is a public official on the public payroll, performing a religious exercise in a governmental institution. It is said that the element of coercion is inherent in the giving of this prayer. If that is true here, it is also true of the prayer with which this Court is convened, and of those that open the Congress. Few adults, let alone children, would leave our courtroom or the Senate or the House while those prayers are being given. Every such audience is in a sense a "captive" audience.

At the same time, I cannot say that to authorize this prayer is to establish a religion in the strictly historic meaning of those words. A religion is not established in the usual sense merely by letting those who choose to do so say the prayer that the public school teacher leads. Yet once government finances a religious exercise, it inserts a divisive influence into our communities. The New York Court said that the prayer given does not conform to all of the tenets of the Jewish, Unitarian, and Ethical Culture groups. One of the petitioners is an agnostic.

"We are a religious people whose institutions presuppose a Supreme Being." Zorach v. Clauson. Under our Bill of Rights, free play is given for making religion an active force in our lives. But "if a religious leaven is to be worked into the affairs of our people, it is to be done by individuals and groups, not by the Government." McGowan v. Maryland (dissenting opinion). By reason of the First Amendment, government is commanded "to have no interest in theology or ritual" (id.), for on those matters "government must be neutral." Ibid. The First Amendment leaves the Government in a position not of hostility to religion, but of neutrality. The philosophy is that the atheist or agnostic—the nonbeliever—is entitled to go his own way. The philosophy is that, if government interferes in matters spiritual, it will be a divisive force. The First Amendment teaches that a government neutral in the field of religion better serves all religious interests.

My problem today would be uncomplicated but for Everson v. Board of Education, which allowed taxpayers' money to be used to pay "the bus fares of parochial school pupils as a part of a general program under which" the fares of pupils attending public and other schools were also paid. The Everson case seems in retrospect to be out of line with the First Amendment. Its result is appealing, as it allows aid to be given to needy children. Yet, by the same token, public funds could be used to satisfy other needs of children in parochial schools—lunches, books, and tuition being obvious examples. Mr. Justice Rutledge stated in dissent what I think is durable First Amendment philosophy:

> The reasons underlying the Amendment's policy have not vanished with time or diminished in force. Now, as when it was adopted, the price of religious freedom is dou-

> ble. It is that the church and religion shall live both within and upon that freedom. There cannot be freedom of religion, safeguarded by the state, and intervention by the church or its agencies in the state's domain or dependency on its largesse. Madison's Remonstrance, Par. 6, 8. The great condition of religious liberty is that it be maintained free from sustenance, as also from other interferences, by the state. For when it comes to rest upon that secular foundation, it vanishes with the resting. Id., Par. 7, 8. Public money devoted to payment of religious costs, educational or other, brings the quest for more. It brings too the struggle of sect against sect for the larger share or for any. Here one by numbers alone will benefit most, there another. That is precisely the history of societies which have had an established religion and dissident groups. Id. Par. 8, 11. It is the very thing Jefferson and Madison experienced and sought to guard against, whether in its blunt or in its more screened forms. Ibid. The end of such strife cannot be other than to destroy the cherished liberty. The dominating group will achieve the dominant benefit; or all will embroil the state in their dissensions. Id., Par. 11. Id. pp. 53-54.

What New York does with this prayer is a break with that tradition. I therefore join the Court in reversing the judgment below.

STEWART, Dissenting Opinion

MR. JUSTICE STEWART, dissenting.

A local school board in New York has provided that those pupils who wish to do so may join in a brief prayer at the beginning of each school day, acknowledging their dependence upon God and asking His blessing upon them and upon their parents, their teachers, and their country. The Court today decides that, in permitting this brief nondenominational prayer, the school board has violated the Constitution of the United States. I think this decision is wrong.

The Court does not hold, nor could it, that New York has interfered with the free exercise of anybody's religion. For the state courts have made clear that those who object to reciting the prayer must be entirely free of any compulsion to do so, including any "embarrassments and pressures." Cf. West Virginia State Board of Education v. Barnette. But the Court says that, in permitting school children to say this simple prayer, the New York authorities have established "an official religion."

With all respect, I think the Court has misapplied a great constitutional principle. I cannot see how an "official religion" is established by letting those who want to say a prayer say it. On the contrary, I think that to deny the wish of these school children to join in reciting this prayer is to deny them the opportunity of sharing in the spiritual heritage of our Nation.

The Court's historical review of the quarrels over the Book of Common Prayer in England throws no light for me on the issue before us in this case. England had then and has now an established church. Equally unenlightening, I think, is the history of the early establishment and later rejection of an official church in our own States. For we deal here not with the establishment of a state church, which would, of course, be constitutionally impermissible, but with whether school children who want to begin their day by joining in prayer must be prohibited from doing so. Moreover, I think that the Court's task, in this as in all areas of constitutional adjudication is not responsibly aided by the uncritical invocation of metaphors like the "wall of separation," a phrase nowhere to be found in the Constitution. What is relevant to the issue here is not the history of an established church in sixteenth century England or in eighteenth century America, but the history of the religious traditions of our people, reflected in countless practices of the institutions and officials of our government.

At the opening of each day's Session of this Court we stand, while one of our officials invokes the protection of God. Since the days of John Marshall, our Crier has said, "God save the United States and this Honorable Court." Both the Senate and the House of Representatives open their daily Sessions with prayer. Each of our Presidents, from George Washington to John F. Kennedy, has, upon assuming his Office, asked the protection and help of God.

The Court today says that the state and federal governments are without constitutional power to prescribe any particular form of words to be recited by any group of the American people on any subject touching religion. One of the stanzas of "The Star-Spangled Banner" made our National Anthem by Act of Congress in 1931, contains these verses:

> Blest with victory and peace, may the heav'n rescued land Praise the Pow'r that hath made and preserved us a nation, Then conquer we must, when our cause it is just. And this be our motto "In God is our Trust."

In 1954, Congress added a phrase to the Pledge of Allegiance to the Flag so that it now contains the words "one Nation under God, indivisible, with liberty and justice for all." In 1952, Congress enacted legislation calling upon the President each year to proclaim a National Day of Prayer. Since 1865, the words "IN GOD WE TRUST" have been impressed on our coins.

Countless similar examples could be listed, but there is no need to belabor the obvious. It was all summed up by this Court just ten years ago in a single sentence: "We are a religious people whose institutions presuppose a Supreme Being." Zorach v. Clauson.

I do not believe that this Court, or the Congress, or the President has, by the actions and practices I have mentioned, established an "official religion" in violation of the Constitution. And I do not believe the State of New York has done so in this case. What each has done has been to recognize and to follow the deeply entrenched and highly cherished spiritual traditions of our Nation—traditions which come down to us from those who almost two hundred years ago avowed their "firm Reliance on the Protection of divine Providence" when they proclaimed the freedom and independence of this brave new world.

I dissent.

ABINGTON SCHOOL DISTRICT V. SCHEMPP, 374 U.S. 203 (1963)

SUPREME COURT OF THE UNITED STATES
SCHOOL DISTRICT OF ABINGTON TOWNSHIP, PENNSYLVANIA, ET AL. V. SCHEMPP ET AL.
APPEAL FROM THE UNITED STATES DISTRICT COURT FOR THE EASTERN DISTRICT OF PENNSYLVANIA. NO. 142.
ARGUED FEBRUARY 27–28, 1963. DECIDED JUNE 17, 1963.

MR. JUSTICE CLARK delivered the opinion of the Court.

Once again we are called upon to consider the scope of the provision of the First Amendment to the United States Constitution which declares that "Congress shall make no law respecting an establishment of religion, or prohibiting the free exercise thereof. . . ." These companion cases present the issues in the context of state action requiring that schools begin each day with readings from the Bible. While raising the basic questions under slightly different factual situations, the cases permit of joint treatment. In light of the history of the First Amendment and of our cases interpreting and applying its requirements, we hold that the practices at issue and the laws requiring them are unconstitutional under the Establishment Clause, as applied to the States through the Fourteenth Amendment.

I.

The Facts in Each Case: No. 142. The Commonwealth of Pennsylvania by law, 24 Pa. Stat. 15-1516, as amended, Pub. Law 1928 (Supp. 1960) Dec. 17, 1959, requires that "At least ten verses from the Holy Bible shall be read, without comment, at the opening of each public school on each school day. Any child shall be excused from such Bible reading, or attending such Bible reading, upon the written request of his parent or guardian." The Schempp family, husband and wife and two of their three children, brought suit to enjoin enforcement of the statute, contending that their rights under the Fourteenth Amendment to the Constitution of the United States are, have been, and will continue to be violated unless this statute be declared unconstitutional as violative of these provisions of the First Amendment. They sought to enjoin the appellant school district, wherein the Schempp children attend school, and its officers and the Superintendent of Public Instruction of the Commonwealth from continuing to conduct such readings and recitation of the Lord's Prayer in the public schools of the district pursuant to the statute. A three-judge statutory District Court for the Eastern District of Pennsylvania held that the statute is violative of the Establishment Clause of the First Amendment as applied to the States by the Due Process Clause of the Fourteenth Amendment and directed that appropriate injunctive relief issue. 201 F. Supp. 815. On appeal by the District, its officials and the Superintendent, under 28 U.S.C. 1253, we noted probable jurisdiction.

The appellees Edward Lewis Schempp, his wife Sidney, and their children, Roger and Donna, are of the Unitarian faith and are members of the Unitarian church in Germantown, Philadelphia, Pennsylvania, where they, as well as another son, Ellory, regularly attend religious services. The latter was originally a party but having graduated from the school system pendente lite was voluntarily dismissed from the action. The other children attend the Abington Senior High School, which is a public school operated by appellant district.

On each school day at the Abington Senior High School between 8:15 and 8:30 a. m., while the pupils are attending their home rooms or advisory sections, opening exercises are conducted pursuant to the statute. The exercises are broadcast into each room in the school building through an intercommunications system and are conducted under the supervision of a teacher by students attending the school's radio and television workshop. Selected students from this course gather each morning in the school's workshop studio for the exercises, which include readings by one of the students of 10 verses of the Holy Bible, broadcast to each room in the building. This is followed by the recitation of the Lord's Prayer, likewise over the intercommunications system, but also by the students in the various classrooms, who are asked to stand and join in repeating the prayer in unison. The exercises are closed with the flag salute and such pertinent announcements as are of interest to the students. Participation in the opening exercises, as directed by the statute, is voluntary. The student reading the verses from the Bible may select the passages and read from any version he chooses, although the only copies furnished by the school are the King James version, copies of which were circulated to each teacher by the school district. During the period in which the exercises have been conducted the King James, the Douay and the Revised Standard versions of the Bible have been used, as well as the Jewish Holy Scriptures. There are no prefatory statements, no questions asked or solicited, no comments or explanations made and no interpretations given at or during the exercises. The students and parents are advised that the student may absent himself from the classroom or, should he elect to remain, not participate in the exercises.

It appears from the record that in schools not having an intercommunications system the Bible reading and the recitation of the Lord's Prayer were conducted by the home-room teacher, who chose the text of the verses and read them herself or had students read them in rotation or by volunteers. This was followed by a standing recitation of the Lord's Prayer, together with the Pledge of Allegiance to the Flag by the class in unison and a closing announcement of routine school items of interest.

At the first trial Edward Schempp and the children testified as to specific religious doctrines purveyed by a literal reading of the Bible "which were contrary to the religious beliefs which they held and to their familial teaching." 177 F. Supp. 398, 400. The children testified that all of the doctrines to which they referred were read to them at various times as part of the exercises. Edward Schempp testified at the second trial that he had considered having Roger and Donna excused from attendance at the exercises but decided against it for several reasons, including his belief that the children's relationships with their teachers and classmates would be adversely affected.

Expert testimony was introduced by both appellants and appellees at the first trial, which testimony was summarized by the trial court as follows:

> "Dr. Solomon Grayzel testified that there were marked differences between the Jewish Holy Scriptures and the Christian Holy Bible, the most obvious of which was the absence of the New Testament in the Jewish Holy Scriptures. Dr. Grayzel testified that portions of the New Testament were offensive to Jewish tradition and that, from the standpoint of Jewish faith, the concept of Jesus Christ as the Son of God was 'practically blasphemous.' He cited instances in the New Testament which, assertedly, were not only sectarian in nature but tended to bring the Jews into ridicule or scorn. Dr. Grayzel gave as his expert opinion that such material from the New Testament could be explained to Jewish children in such a way as to do no harm to them. But if portions of the New Testament were read without explanation, they could be, and in his specific experience with children Dr. Grayzel observed, had been, psychologically harmful to the child and had caused a divisive force within the social media of the school.
>
> "Dr. Grayzel also testified that there was significant difference in attitude with regard to the respective Books of the Jewish and Christian Religions in that Judaism attaches no special significance to the reading of the Bible per se and that the Jewish Holy Scriptures are source materials to be studied. But Dr. Grayzel did state that many portions of the New, as well as of the Old, Testament contained passages of great literary and moral value.
>
> "Dr. Luther A. Weigle, an expert witness for the defense, testified in some detail as to the reasons for and the methods employed in developing the King James and the Revised Standard Versions of the Bible. On direct examination, Dr. Weigle stated that the Bible was non-sectarian. He later stated that the phrase 'non-sectarian' meant to him non-sectarian within the Christian faiths. Dr. Weigle stated that his definition of the Holy Bible would include the Jewish Holy Scriptures, but also stated that the 'Holy Bible' would not be complete without the New Testament. He stated that the New Testament 'conveyed the message of Christians.' In his opinion, reading of the Holy Scriptures to the exclusion of the New Testament would be a sectarian practice. Dr. Weigle stated that the Bible was of great moral, historical and literary value. This is conceded by all the parties and is also the view of the court." 177 F. Supp. 398, 401-402.

The trial court, in striking down the practices and the statute requiring them, made specific findings of fact that the children's attendance at Abington Senior High School is compulsory and that the practice of reading 10 verses from the Bible is also compelled by law. It also found that:

> "The reading of the verses, even without comment, possesses a devotional and religious character and constitutes in effect a religious observance. The devotional and religious nature of the morning exercises is made all the more apparent by the fact that the Bible reading is followed immediately by a recital in unison by the pupils of the Lord's Prayer. The fact that some pupils, or theoretically all pupils, might be excused from attendance at the exercises does not mitigate the obligatory nature of the ceremony for . . . Section 1516 . . . unequivocally requires the exercises to be held every school day in every school in the Commonwealth. The exercises are held in the

> school buildings and perforce are conducted by and under the authority of the local school authorities and during school sessions. Since the statute requires the reading of the 'Holy Bible,' a Christian document, the practice . . . prefers the Christian religion. The record demonstrates that it was the intention of. . . the Commonwealth . . . to introduce a religious ceremony into the public schools of the Commonwealth." 201 F. Supp., at 819.

No. 119. In 1905 the Board of School Commissioners of Baltimore City adopted a rule pursuant to Art. 77, 202 of the Annotated Code of Maryland. The rule provided for the holding of opening exercises in the schools of the city, consisting primarily of the "reading, without comment, of a chapter in the Holy Bible and/or the use of the Lord's Prayer." The petitioners, Mrs. Madalyn Murray and her son, William J. Murray III, are both professed atheists. Following unsuccessful attempts to have the respondent school board rescind the rule, this suit was filed for mandamus to compel its rescission and cancellation. It was alleged that William was a student in a public school of the city and Mrs. Murray, his mother, was a taxpayer therein; that it was the practice under the rule to have a reading on each school morning from the King James version of the Bible; that at petitioners' insistence the rule was amended to permit children to be excused from the exercise on request of the parent and that William had been excused pursuant thereto; that nevertheless the rule as amended was in violation of the petitioners' rights "to freedom of religion under the First and Fourteenth Amendments" and in violation of "the principle of separation between church and state, contained therein . . . ." The petition particularized the petitioners' atheistic beliefs and stated that the rule, as practiced, violated their rights

> "in that it threatens their religious liberty by placing a premium on belief as against non-belief and subjects their freedom of conscience to the rule of the majority; it pronounces belief in God as the source of all moral and spiritual values, equating these values with religious values, and thereby renders sinister, alien and suspect the beliefs and ideals of your Petitioners, promoting doubt and question of their morality, good citizenship and good faith."

The respondents demurred and the trial court, recognizing that the demurrer admitted all facts well pleaded, sustained it without leave to amend. The Maryland Court of Appeals affirmed, the majority of four justices holding the exercise not in violation of the First and Fourteenth Amendments, with three justices dissenting. 228 Md. 239, 179 A. 2d 698. We granted certiorari.

II.

It is true that religion has been closely identified with our history and government. As we said in Engel v. Vitale, (1962), "The history of man is inseparable from the history of religion. And . . . since the beginning of that history many people have devoutly believed that 'More things are wrought by prayer than this world dreams of.'" In Zorach v. Clauson, (1952), we gave specific recognition to the proposition that "[w]e are a religious people whose institutions presuppose a Supreme Being." The fact that the Founding Fathers believed devotedly that there was a God and that the unalienable rights of man were rooted in Him is clearly evidenced in their writings, from the Mayflower Compact to the Constitution itself. This background is evidenced today in our public life through the continuance in our oaths of office from the Presidency to the Alderman of the final supplication, "So help me God." Likewise each House of the Congress provides through its Chaplain an opening prayer, and the sessions of this Court are declared open by the crier in a short ceremony, the final phrase of which invokes the grace of God. Again, there are such manifestations in our military forces, where those of our citizens who are under the restrictions of military service wish to engage in voluntary worship. Indeed, only last year an official survey of the country indicated that 64% of our people have church membership, Bureau of the Census, U.S. Department of Commerce, Statistical

Abstract of the United States (83d ed. 1962), 48, while less than 3% profess no religion whatever. Id., at p. 46. It can be truly said, therefore, that today, as in the beginning, our national life reflects a religious people who, in the words of Madison, are "earnestly praying, as . . . in duty bound, that the Supreme Lawgiver of the Universe . . . guide them into every measure which may be worthy of his [blessing . . . .]" Memorial and Remonstrance Against Religious Assessments, quoted in Everson v. Board of Education, (1947) (Appendix to dissenting opinion of Rutledge, J.).

This is not to say, however, that religion has been so identified with our history and government that religious freedom is not likewise as strongly imbedded in our public and private life. Nothing but the most telling of personal experiences in religious persecution suffered by our forebears, see Everson v. Board of Education, supra, at 8-11, could have planted our belief in liberty of religious opinion any more deeply in our heritage. It is true that this liberty frequently was not realized by the colonists, but this is readily accountable by their close ties to the Mother Country. However, the views of Madison and Jefferson, preceded by Roger Williams, came to be incorporated not only in the Federal Constitution but likewise in those of most of our States. This freedom to worship was indispensable in a country whose people came from the four quarters of the earth and brought with them a diversity of religious opinion. Today authorities list 83 separate religious bodies, each with membership exceeding 50,000, existing among our people, as well as innumerable smaller groups. Bureau of the Census. op. cit., supra, at 46-47.

III.

Almost a hundred years ago in Minor v. Board of Education of Cincinnati, Judge Alphonso Taft, father of the revered Chief Justice, in an unpublished opinion stated the ideal of our people as to religious freedom as one of "absolute equality before the law, of all religious opinions and sects . . . ." "The government is neutral, and, while protecting all, it prefers none, and it disparages none."

Before examining this "neutral" position in which the Establishment and Free Exercise Clauses of the First Amendment place our Government it is well that we discuss the reach of the Amendment under the cases of this Court.

First, this Court has decisively settled that the First Amendment's mandate that "Congress shall make no law respecting an establishment of religion, or prohibiting the free exercise thereof" has been made wholly applicable to the States by the Fourteenth Amendment. Twenty-three years ago in Cantwell v. Connecticut, (1940), this Court, through Mr. Justice Roberts, said:

> "The fundamental concept of liberty embodied in that [Fourteenth] Amendment embraces the liberties guaranteed by the First Amendment. The First Amendment declares that Congress shall make no law respecting an establishment of religion or prohibiting the free exercise thereof. The Fourteenth Amendment has rendered the legislatures of the states as incompetent as Congress to enact such laws . . . ."

In a series of cases since Cantwell the Court has repeatedly reaffirmed that doctrine, and we do so now. Murdock v. Pennsylvania, (1943); Everson v. Board of Education, supra; Illinois ex rel. McCollum v. Board of Education, (1948); Zorach v. Clauson, supra; McGowan v. Maryland, (1961); Torcaso v. Watkins, (1961); and Engel v. Vitale, supra.

Second, this Court has rejected unequivocally the contention that the Establishment Clause forbids only governmental preference of one religion over another. Almost 20 years ago in Everson, supra, at 15, the Court said that "[n]either a state nor the Federal Government can set up a church. Neither can pass laws which aid one religion, aid all religions, or prefer one religion over another." And Mr. Justice Jackson, dissenting, agreed:

> "There is no answer to the proposition . . . that the effect of the religious freedom Amendment to our Constitution was to take every form of propagation of religion

out of the realm of things which could directly or indirectly be made public business and thereby be supported in whole or in part at taxpayers' expense. . . . This freedom was first in the Bill of Rights because it was first in the forefathers' minds; it was set forth in absolute terms, and its strength is its rigidity." Id., at 26.

Further, Mr. Justice Rutledge, joined by Justices Frankfurter, Jackson and Burton, declared:

"The [First] Amendment's purpose was not to strike merely at the official establishment of a single sect, creed or religion, outlawing only a formal relation such as had prevailed in England and some of the colonies. Necessarily it was to uproot all such relationships. But the object was broader than separating church and state in this narrow sense. It was to create a complete and permanent separation of the spheres of religious activity and civil authority by comprehensively forbidding every form of public aid or support for religion." Id., at 31-32.

The same conclusion has been firmly maintained ever since that time, see Illinois ex rel. McCollum, supra, at pp. 210-211; McGowan v. Maryland, supra, at 442-443; Torcaso v. Watkins, supra, at 492-493, 495, and we reaffirm it now.

While none of the parties to either of these cases has questioned these basic conclusions of the Court, both of which have been long established, recognized and consistently reaffirmed, others continue to question their history, logic and efficacy. Such contentions, in the light of the consistent interpretation in cases of this Court, seem entirely untenable and of value only as academic exercises.

IV.

The interrelationship of the Establishment and the Free Exercise Clauses was first touched upon by Mr. Justice Roberts for the Court in Cantwell v. Connecticut, supra, at 303-304, where it was said that their "inhibition of legislation" had

"a double aspect. On the one hand, it forestalls compulsion by law of the acceptance of any creed or the practice of any form of worship. Freedom of conscience and freedom to adhere to such religious organization or form of worship as the individual may choose cannot be restricted by law. On the other hand, it safeguards the free exercise of the chosen form of religion. Thus the Amendment embraces two concepts—freedom to believe and freedom to act. The first is absolute but, in the nature of things, the second cannot be."

A half dozen years later in Everson v. Board of Education, supra, at 14-15, this Court, through MR. JUSTICE BLACK, stated that the "scope of the First Amendment . . . was designed forever to suppress" the establishment of religion or the prohibition of the free exercise thereof. In short, the Court held that the Amendment

"requires the state to be a neutral in its relations with groups of religious believers and non-believers; it does not require the state to be their adversary. State power is no more to be used so as to handicap religions than it is to favor them." Id., at 18.

And Mr. Justice Jackson, in dissent, declared that public schools are organized

"on the premise that secular education can be isolated from all religious teaching so that the school can inculcate all needed temporal knowledge and also maintain a strict and lofty neutrality as to religion. The assumption is that after the individual has been instructed in worldly wisdom he will be better fitted to choose his religion." Id., at 23-24.

Moreover, all of the four dissenters, speaking through Mr. Justice Rutledge, agreed that

"Our constitutional policy . . . does not deny the value or the necessity for religious training, teaching or observance. Rather it secures their free exercise. But to that end

> it does deny that the state can undertake or sustain them in any form or degree. For this reason the sphere of religious activity, as distinguished from the secular intellectual liberties, has been given the twofold protection and, as the state cannot forbid, neither can it perform or aid in performing the religious function. The dual prohibition makes that function altogether private." Id., at 52.

Only one year later the Court was asked to reconsider and repudiate the doctrine of these cases in McCollum v. Board of Education. It was argued that "historically the First Amendment was intended to forbid only government preference of one religion over another . . . . In addition they ask that we distinguish or overrule our holding in the Everson case that the Fourteenth Amendment made the 'establishment of religion' clause of the First Amendment applicable as a prohibition against the States." The Court, with Mr. Justice Reed alone dissenting, was unable to "accept either of these contentions." Ibid. Mr. Justice Frankfurter, joined by Justices Jackson, Rutledge and Burton, wrote a very comprehensive and scholarly concurrence in which he said that "[s]eparation is a requirement to abstain from fusing functions of Government and of religious sects, not merely to treat them all equally." Id., at 227. Continuing, he stated that:

> "the Constitution . . . prohibited the Government common to all from becoming embroiled, however innocently, in the destructive religious conflicts of which the history of even this country records some dark pages." Id., at 228.

In 1952 in Zorach v. Clauson, supra, MR. JUSTICE DOUGLAS for the Court reiterated:

> "There cannot be the slightest doubt that the First Amendment reflects the philosophy that Church and State should be separated. And so far as interference with the 'free exercise' of religion and an 'establishment' of religion are concerned, the separation must be complete and unequivocal. The First Amendment within the scope of its coverage permits no exception; the prohibition is absolute. The First Amendment, however, does not say that in every and all respects there shall be a separation of Church and State. Rather, it studiously defines the manner, the specific ways, in which there shall be no concert or union or dependency one on the other. That is the common sense of the matter."

And then in 1961 in McGowan v. Maryland and in Torcaso v. Watkins each of these cases was discussed and approved. CHIEF JUSTICE WARREN in McGowan, for a unanimous Court on this point, said:

> "But, the First Amendment, in its final form, did not simply bar a congressional enactment establishing a church; it forbade all laws respecting an establishment of religion. Thus, this Court has given the Amendment a 'broad interpretation . . . in the light of its history and the evils it was designed forever to suppress . . . .'"

And MR. JUSTICE BLACK for the Court in Torcaso, without dissent but with Justices Frankfurter and HARLAN concurring in the result, used this language:

> "We repeat and again reaffirm that neither a State nor the Federal Government can constitutionally force a person 'to profess a belief or disbelief in any religion.' Neither can constitutionally pass laws or impose requirements which aid all religions as against non-believers, and neither can aid those religions based on a belief in the existence of God as against those religions founded on different beliefs."

Finally, in Engel v. Vitale, only last year, these principles were so universally recognized that the Court, without the citation of a single case and over the sole dissent of MR. JUSTICE STEWART, reaffirmed them. The Court found the 22-word prayer used in "New York's program of daily classroom invocation of God's blessings as prescribed in the Regents' prayer . . . [to be] a religious activity." It held that "it is no part of the business of government to compose official prayers for any group of the American people to recite as a part of a religious program carried on by government." Id., at 425. In discussing the reach of the Establishment and Free Exercise Clauses of the First Amendment the Court said:

"Although these two clauses may in certain instances overlap, they forbid two quite different kinds of governmental encroachment upon religious freedom. The Establishment Clause, unlike the Free Exercise Clause, does not depend upon any showing of direct governmental compulsion and is violated by the enactment of laws which establish an official religion whether those laws operate directly to coerce non-observing individuals or not. This is not to say, of course, that laws officially prescribing a particular form of religious worship do not involve coercion of such individuals. When the power, prestige and financial support of government is placed behind a particular religious belief, the indirect coercive pressure upon religious minorities to conform to the prevailing officially approved religion is plain." Id., at 430-431.

And in further elaboration the Court found that the "first and most immediate purpose [of the Establishment Clause] rested on the belief that a union of government and religion tends to destroy government and to degrade religion." Id., at 431. When government, the Court said, allies itself with one particular form of religion, the inevitable result is that it incurs "the hatred, disrespect and even contempt of those who held contrary beliefs." Ibid.

V.

The wholesome "neutrality" of which this Court's cases speak thus stems from a recognition of the teachings of history that powerful sects or groups might bring about a fusion of governmental and religious functions or a concert or dependency of one upon the other to the end that official support of the State or Federal Government would be placed behind the tenets of one or of all orthodoxies. This the Establishment Clause prohibits. And a further reason for neutrality is found in the Free Exercise Clause, which recognizes the value of religious training, teaching and observance and, more particularly, the right of every person to freely choose his own course with reference thereto, free of any compulsion from the state. This the Free Exercise Clause guarantees. Thus, as we have seen, the two clauses may overlap. As we have indicated, the Establishment Clause has been directly considered by this Court eight times in the past score of years and, with only one Justice dissenting on the point, it has consistently held that the clause withdrew all legislative power respecting religious belief or the expression thereof. The test may be stated as follows: what are the purpose and the primary effect of the enactment? If either is the advancement or inhibition of religion then the enactment exceeds the scope of legislative power as circumscribed by the Constitution. That is to say that to withstand the strictures of the Establishment Clause there must be a secular legislative purpose and a primary effect that neither advances nor inhibits religion. Everson v. Board of Education, supra; McGowan v. Maryland, supra, at 442. The Free Exercise Clause, likewise considered many times here, withdraws from legislative power, state and federal, the exertion of any restraint on the free exercise of religion. Its purpose is to secure religious liberty in the individual by prohibiting any invasions thereof by civil authority. Hence it is necessary in a free exercise case for one to show the coercive effect of the enactment as it operates against him in the practice of his religion. The distinction between the two clauses is apparent—a violation of the Free Exercise Clause is predicated on coercion while the Establishment Clause violation need not be so attended.

Applying the Establishment Clause principles to the cases at bar we find that the States are requiring the selection and reading at the opening of the school day of verses from the Holy Bible and the recitation of the Lord's Prayer by the students in unison. These exercises are prescribed as part of the curricular activities of students who are required by law to attend school. They are held in the school buildings under the supervision and with the participation of teachers employed in those schools. None of these factors, other than compulsory school attendance, was present in the program upheld in Zorach v. Clauson. The trial court in No. 142 has found that such an opening exercise is a religious ceremony and was intended by the State to be so. We agree with the trial court's finding as to the religious character of the exercises. Given that finding, the exercises and the law requiring them are in violation of the Establishment Clause.

There is no such specific finding as to the religious character of the exercises in No. 119, and the State contends (as does the State in No. 142) that the program is an effort to extend its benefits to all public school children without regard to their religious belief. Included within its secular purposes, it says, are the promotion of moral values, the contradiction to the materialistic trends of our times, the perpetuation of our institutions and the teaching of literature. The case came up on demurrer, of course, to a petition which alleged that the uniform practice under the rule had been to read from the King James version of the Bible and that the exercise was sectarian. The short answer, therefore, is that the religious character of the exercise was admitted by the State. But even if its purpose is not strictly religious, it is sought to be accomplished through readings, without comment, from the Bible. Surely the place of the Bible as an instrument of religion cannot be gainsaid, and the State's recognition of the pervading religious character of the ceremony is evident from the rule's specific permission of the alternative use of the Catholic Douay version as well as the recent amendment permitting nonattendance at the exercises. None of these factors is consistent with the contention that the Bible is here used either as an instrument for nonreligious moral inspiration or as a reference for the teaching of secular subjects.

The conclusion follows that in both cases the laws require religious exercises and such exercises are being conducted in direct violation of the rights of the appellees and petitioners. Nor are these required exercises mitigated by the fact that individual students may absent themselves upon parental request, for that fact furnishes no defense to a claim of unconstitutionality under the Establishment Clause. See Engel v. Vitale, supra, at 430. Further, it is no defense to urge that the religious practices here may be relatively minor encroachments on the First Amendment. The breach of neutrality that is today a trickling stream may all too soon become a raging torrent and, in the words of Madison, "it is proper to take alarm at the first experiment on our liberties." Memorial and Remonstrance Against Religious Assessments, quoted in Everson, supra, at 65.

It is insisted that unless these religious exercises are permitted a "religion of secularism" is established in the schools. We agree of course that the State may not establish a "religion of secularism" in the sense of affirmatively opposing or showing hostility to religion, thus "preferring those who believe in no religion over those who do believe." Zorach v. Clauson, supra, at 314. We do not agree, however, that this decision in any sense has that effect. In addition, it might well be said that one's education is not complete without a study of comparative religion or the history of religion and its relationship to the advancement of civilization. It certainly may be said that the Bible is worthy of study for its literary and historic qualities. Nothing we have said here indicates that such study of the Bible or of religion, when presented objectively as part of a secular program of education, may not be effected consistently with the First Amendment. But the exercises here do not fall into those categories. They are religious exercises, required by the States in violation of the command of the First Amendment that the Government maintain strict neutrality, neither aiding nor opposing religion.

Finally, we cannot accept that the concept of neutrality, which does not permit a State to require a religious exercise even with the consent of the majority of those affected, collides with the majority's right to free exercise of religion. While the Free Exercise Clause clearly prohibits the use of state action to deny the rights of free exercise to anyone, it has never meant that a majority could use the machinery of the State to practice its beliefs. Such a contention was effectively answered by Mr. Justice Jackson for the Court in West Virginia Board of Education v. Barnette, (1943):

> "The very purpose of a Bill of Rights was to withdraw certain subjects from the vicissitudes of political controversy, to place them beyond the reach of majorities and offi-

cials and to establish them as legal principles to be applied by the courts. One's right to . . . freedom of worship . . . and other fundamental rights may not be submitted to vote; they depend on the outcome of no elections."

The place of religion in our society is an exalted one, achieved through a long tradition of reliance on the home, the church and the inviolable citadel of the individual heart and mind. We have come to recognize through bitter experience that it is not within the power of government to invade that citadel, whether its purpose or effect be to aid or oppose, to advance or retard. In the relationship between man and religion, the State is firmly committed to a position of neutrality. Though the application of that rule requires interpretation of a delicate sort, the rule itself is clearly and concisely stated in the words of the First Amendment. Applying that rule to the facts of these cases, we affirm the judgment in No. 142. In No. 119, the judgment is reversed and the cause remanded to the Maryland Court of Appeals for further proceedings consistent with this opinion.

It is so ordered.

MR. JUSTICE DOUGLAS, concurring.

I join the opinion of the Court and add a few words in explanation.

While the Free Exercise Clause of the First Amendment is written in terms of what the State may not require of the individual, the Establishment Clause, serving the same goal of individual religious freedom, is written in different terms.

Establishment of a religion can be achieved in several ways. The church and state can be one; the church may control the state or the state may control the church; or the relationship may take one of several possible forms of a working arrangement between the two bodies. Under all of these arrangements the church typically has a place in the state's budget, and church law usually governs such matters as baptism, marriage, divorce and separation, at least for its members and sometimes for the entire body politic. Education too, is usually high on the priority list of church interests. In the past schools were often made the exclusive responsibility of the church. Today in some state-church countries the state runs the public schools, but compulsory religious exercises are often required of some or all students. Thus, under the agreement Franco made with the Holy See when he came to power in Spain, "The Church regained its place in the national budget. It insists on baptizing all children and has made the catechism obligatory in state schools."

The vice of all such arrangements under the Establishment Clause is that the state is lending its assistance to a church's efforts to gain and keep adherents. Under the First Amendment it is strictly a matter for the individual and his church as to what church he will belong to and how much support, in the way of belief, time, activity or money, he will give to it. "This pure Religious Liberty" "declared . . . [all forms of church-state relationships] and their fundamental idea to be oppressions of conscience and abridgments of that liberty which God and nature had conferred on every living soul."

In these cases we have no coercive religious exercise aimed at making the students conform. The prayers announced are not compulsory, though some may think they have that indirect effect because the nonconformist student may be induced to participate for fear of being called an "oddball." But that coercion, if it be present, has not been shown; so the vices of the present regimes are different.

These regimes violate the Establishment Clause in two different ways. In each case the State is conducting a religious exercise; and, as the Court holds, that cannot be done without violating the "neutrality" required of the State by the balance of power between individual, church and state that has been struck by the First Amendment. But the Establishment Clause is not limited to precluding the State itself from conducting religious exercises. It also forbids the State to employ its facilities or funds in a way that gives any church, or all churches, greater strength in our society than it would have by relying on its members alone. Thus, the present regimes must fall under that clause for the additional reason that public funds, though small in amount, are being used to promote a religious exercise. Through the mechanism of the State, all of the people are being required to finance a religious exercise that only some of the people want and that violates the sensibilities of others.

The most effective way to establish any institution is to finance it; and this truth is reflected in the appeals by church groups for public funds to finance their religious schools. Financing a church either in its strictly religious activities or in its other activities is equally unconstitutional, as I understand the Establishment Clause. Budgets for one activity may be technically separable from budgets for others. But the institution is an inseparable whole, a living organism, which is strengthened in proselytizing when it is strengthened in any department by contributions from other than its own members.

Such contributions may not be made by the State even in a minor degree without violating the Establishment Clause. It is not the amount of public funds expended; as this case illustrates, it is the use to which public funds are put that is controlling. For the First Amendment does not say that some forms of establishment are allowed; it says that "no law respecting an establishment of religion" shall be made. What may not be done directly may not be done indirectly lest the Establishment Clause become a mockery.

MR. JUSTICE BRENNAN, concurring.

Almost a century and a half ago, John Marshall, in M'Culloch v. Maryland, enjoined: ". . . we must never forget, that it is a constitution we are expounding." 4 Wheat. 316, 407. The Court's historic duty to expound the meaning of the Constitution has encountered few issues more intricate or more demanding than that of the relationship between religion and the public schools. Since undoubtedly we are "a religious people whose institutions presuppose a Supreme Being," Zorach v. Clauson, deep feelings are aroused when aspects of that relationship are claimed to violate the injunction of the First Amendment that government may make "no law respecting an establishment of religion, or prohibiting the free exercise thereof. . . ." Americans regard the public schools as a most vital civic institution for the preservation of a democratic system of government. It is therefore understandable that the constitutional prohibitions encounter their severest test when they are sought to be applied in the school classroom. Nevertheless it is this Court's inescapable duty to declare whether exercises in the public schools of the States, such as those of Pennsylvania and Maryland questioned here, are involvements of religion in public institutions of a kind which offends the First and Fourteenth Amendments.

When John Locke ventured in 1689, "I esteem it above all things necessary to distinguish exactly the business of civil government from that of religion and to settle the just bounds that lie between the one and the other," he anticipated the necessity which would be thought by the Framers to require adoption of a First Amendment, but not the difficulty that would be experienced in defining those "just bounds." The fact is that the line which separates the secular from the sectarian in American life is elusive. The difficulty of defining the boundary with precision inheres in a paradox central to our scheme of liberty. While our institutions reflect a firm conviction that we are a religious people, those institutions by solemn constitutional injunction may not officially involve religion in such a way as to prefer, discriminate against, or oppress, a particular sect or religion. Equally the Constitution enjoins those involvements of religious with secular institutions which (a) serve the essentially religious activities of religious institutions; (b) employ the organs of government for essentially religious purposes; or (c) use essentially religious means to serve governmental ends where secular means would suffice. The constitutional mandate expresses a deliberate and considered judgment that such matters are to be left to the conscience of the citizen, and declares as a basic postulate of the relation between the citizen and his government that "the rights of conscience are, in their nature, of peculiar delicacy, and will little bear the gentlest touch of governmental hand . . . ."

I join fully in the opinion and the judgment of the Court. I see no escape from the conclusion that the exercises called in question in these two cases violate the constitutional mandate. The reasons we gave only last Term in Engle v. Vitale, for finding in the New York Regents' prayer an impermissible establishment of religion, compel the same judgment of the practices at bar. The involvement of the secular with the religious is no less intimate here; and it is constitutionally irrelevant that the State has not composed the material for the inspirational exercises presently involved. It should be unnecessary to observe that our holding does not declare that the First Amendment manifests hostility to the practice or teaching of religion, but only applies prohibitions incorporated in the Bill of Rights in recognition of historic needs shared by Church and State alike. While it is my view that not every involvement of religion in public life is unconstitutional, I consider the exercises at bar a form of involvement which clearly violates the Establishment Clause.

The importance of the issue and the deep conviction with which views on both sides are held seem to me to justify detailing at some length my reasons for joining the Court's judgment and opinion.

I.

The First Amendment forbids both the abridgment of the free exercise of religion and the enactment of laws "respecting an establishment of religion." The two clauses, although distinct in their objectives and their applicability, emerged together from a common panorama of history. The inclusion of both restraints upon the power of Congress to legislate concerning religious matters shows unmistakably that the Framers of the First Amendment were not content to rest the protection of religious liberty exclusively upon either clause. "In assuring the free exercise of religion," Mr. Justice Frankfurter has said, "the Framers of the First Amendment were sensitive to the then recent history of those persecutions and impositions of civil disability with which sectarian majorities in virtually all of the Colonies had visited deviation in the matter of conscience. This protection of unpopular creeds, however, was not to be the full extent of the Amendment's guarantee of freedom from governmental intrusion in matters of faith. The battle in Virginia, hardly four years won, where James Madison had led the forces of disestablishment in successful opposition to Patrick Henry's proposed Assessment Bill levying a general tax for the support of Christian teachers, was a vital and compelling memory in 1789." McGowan v. Maryland.

It is true that the Framers' immediate concern was to prevent the setting up of an official federal church of the kind which England and some of the Colonies had long supported. But nothing in the text of the Establishment Clause supports the view that the prevention of the setting up of an official church was meant to be the full extent of the prohibitions against official involvements in religion. It has rightly been said:

> "If the framers of the Amendment meant to prohibit Congress merely from the establishment of a 'church,' one may properly wonder why they didn't so state. That the words church and religion were regarded as synonymous seems highly improbable, particularly in view of the fact that the contemporary state constitutional provisions dealing with the subject of establishment used definite phrases such as 'religious sect,' 'sect,' or 'denomination.' . . . With such specific wording in contemporary state constitutions, why was not a similar wording adopted for the First Amendment if its framers intended to prohibit nothing more than what the States were prohibiting?" Lardner, How Far Does the Constitution Separate Church and State? 45 Am. Pol. Sci. Rev. 110, 112 (1951).

Plainly, the Establishment Clause, in the contemplation of the Framers, "did not limit the constitutional proscription to any particular, dated form of state-supported theological venture." "What Virginia had long practiced, and what Madison, Jefferson and others fought to end, was the extension of civil government's support to religion in a manner which made the two in some degree interdependent, and thus threatened the freedom of each. The purpose of the Establishment Clause was to assure that the national legislature would not exert its power in the service of any purely religious end; that it would not, as Virginia and virtually all of the Colonies had done, make of religion, as religion, an object of legislation. . . . The Establishment Clause withdrew from the sphere of legitimate legislative concern and competence a specific, but comprehensive, area of human conduct: man's belief or disbelief in the verity of some transcendental idea and man's expression in action of that belief or disbelief." McGowan v. Maryland, supra, at 465-466 (opinion of Frankfurter, J.).

In sum, the history which our prior decisions have summoned to aid interpretation of the Establishment Clause permits little doubt that its prohibition was designed comprehensively to prevent those official involvements of religion which would tend to foster or discourage religious worship or belief.

But an awareness of history and an appreciation of the aims of the Founding Fathers do not always resolve concrete problems. The specific question before us has, for example, aroused vigorous dispute whether the architects of the First Amendment—James Madison and Thomas Jefferson particularly—understood the prohibition against any "law respecting an establishment of religion" to reach devotional exercises in the public schools. It may be that Jefferson and Madison would have held such exercises to be permissible—although even in Jefferson's case serious doubt is suggested by his admonition against "putting the Bible and Testament into the hands of the children at an age when their judgments are not sufficiently matured for religious inquiries . . . ." But I doubt that their view, even if perfectly clear one way or the other, would supply a dispositive answer to the question presented by these cases. A more fruitful inquiry, it seems to me, is whether the practices here challenged threaten those consequences which the Framers deeply feared; whether, in short, they tend to promote that type of interdependence between religion and state which the First Amendment was designed to prevent. Our task is to translate "the majestic generalities of the Bill of Rights, conceived as part of the pattern of liberal government in the eighteenth century, into concrete restraints on officials dealing with the problems of the twentieth century . . . ." West Virginia State Board of Education v. Barnette.

A too literal quest for the advice of the Founding Fathers upon the issues of these cases seems to me futile and misdirected for several reasons: First, on our precise problem the historical record is at best ambiguous, and statements can readily be found to support either side of the proposition. The ambiguity of history is understandable if we recall the nature of the problems uppermost in the thinking of the statesmen who fashioned the religious guarantees; they were concerned with far more flagrant intrusions of government into the realm of religion than any that our century has witnessed. While it is clear to me that the Framers meant the Establishment Clause to prohibit more than the creation of an established federal church such as existed in England, I have no doubt that, in their preoccupation with the imminent question of established churches, they gave no distinct consideration to the particular question whether the clause also forbade devotional exercises in public institutions.

Second, the structure of American education has greatly changed since the First Amendment was adopted. In the context of our modern emphasis upon public education available to all citizens, any views of the eighteenth century as to whether the exercises at bar are an "establishment" offer little aid to decision. Education, as the Framers knew it, was in the main confined to private schools more often than not under strictly sectarian supervision. Only gradually did control of education pass largely to public officials. It would, therefore, hardly be significant if the fact was that the nearly universal devotional exercises in the schools of the young Republic did not provoke criticism; even today religious ceremonies in church-supported private schools are constitutionally unobjectionable.

Third, our religious composition makes us a vastly more diverse people than were our forefathers. They knew differences chiefly among Protestant sects. Today the Nation is far more heterogeneous religiously, including as it does substantial minorities not only of Catholics and Jews but as well of those who worship according to no version of the Bible and those who worship no God at all. See Torcaso v. Watkins. In the face of such profound changes, practices which may have been objectionable to no one in the time of Jefferson and Madison may today be highly offensive to many persons, the deeply devout and the nonbelievers alike.

Whatever Jefferson or Madison would have thought of Bible reading or the recital of the Lord's Prayer in what few public schools existed in their day, our use of the history of their time must limit itself to broad purposes, not specific practices. By such a standard, I am persuaded, as is the Court, that the devotional exercises carried on in the Baltimore and Abington schools offend the First Amendment because they sufficiently threaten in our day those substantive evils the fear of which called forth the Establishment Clause of the First Amendment. It is "a constitution we are expounding," and our interpretation of the First Amendment must necessarily be responsive to the much more highly charged nature of religious questions in contemporary society.

Fourth, the American experiment in free public education available to all children has been guided in large measure by the dramatic evolution of the religious diversity among the population which our public schools serve. The interaction of these two important forces in our national life has placed in bold relief certain positive values in the consistent application to public institutions generally, and public schools particularly, of the constitutional decree against official involvements of religion which might produce the evils the Framers meant the Establishment Clause to forestall. The public schools are supported entirely, in most communities, by public funds—funds exacted not only from parents, nor alone from those who hold particular religious views, nor indeed from those who subscribe to any creed at all. It is implicit in the history and character of American public education that the public schools serve a uniquely public function: the training of American citizens in an atmosphere free of parochial, divisive, or separatist influences of any sort—an atmosphere in which children may assimilate a heritage common to all American groups and religions. See Illinois ex rel. McCollum v. Board of Education. This is a heritage neither theistic nor atheistic, but simply civic and patriotic. See Meyer v. Nebraska.

Attendance at the public schools has never been compulsory; parents remain morally and constitutionally free to choose the academic environment in which they wish their children to be educated. The relationship of the Establishment Clause of the First Amendment to the public school system is preeminently that of reserving such a choice to the individual parent, rather than vesting it in the majority of voters of each State or school district. The choice which is thus preserved is between a public secular education with its uniquely democratic values, and some form of private or sectarian education, which offers values of its own. In my judgment the First Amendment forbids the State to inhibit that freedom of choice by diminishing the attractiveness of either alternative—either by restricting the liberty of the private schools to inculcate whatever values they wish, or by jeopardizing the freedom of the public schools from private or sectarian pressures. The choice between these very different forms of education is one—very much like the choice of whether or not to worship—which our Constitution leaves to the individual parent. It is no proper function of the state or local government to influence or restrict that election. The lesson of history—drawn more from the experiences of other countries than from our own—is that a system of free public education forfeits its unique contribution to the growth of democratic citizenship when that choice ceases to be freely available to each parent.

II.

The exposition by this Court of the religious guarantees of the First Amendment has consistently reflected and reaffirmed the concerns which impelled the Framers to write those guarantees into the Constitution. It would be neither possible nor appropriate to review here the entire course of our decisions on religious questions. There emerge from those decisions, however, three principles of particular relevance to the issue presented by the cases at bar, and some attention to those decisions is therefore appropriate.

First. One line of decisions derives from contests for control of a church property or other internal ecclesiastical disputes. This line has settled the proposition that in order to give effect to the First Amendment's purpose of requiring on the part of all organs of government a strict neutrality toward theological questions, courts should not undertake to decide such questions. These principles were first expounded in the case of Watson v. Jones, 13 Wall. 679, which declared that judicial intervention in such a controversy would open up "the whole subject of the doctrinal theology, the usages and customs, the written laws, and fundamental organization of every religious denomination . . . ." 13 Wall., at 733. Courts above all must be neutral, for "[t]he law knows no heresy, and is committed to the support of no dogma, the establishment of no sect." 13 Wall., at 728. This principle has recently been reaffirmed in Kedroff v. St. Nicholas Cathedral; and Kreshik v. St. Nicholas Cathedral.

The mandate of judicial neutrality in theological controversies met its severest test in United States v. Ballard. That decision put in sharp relief certain principles which bear directly upon the questions presented in these cases. Ballard was indicted for fraudulent use of the mails in the dissemination of religious literature. He requested that the trial court submit to the jury the question of the truthfulness of the religious views he championed. The requested charge was refused, and we upheld that refusal, reasoning that the First Amendment foreclosed any judicial inquiry into the truth or falsity of the defendant's religious beliefs. We said: "Man's relation to his God was made no concern of the state. He was granted the right to worship as he pleased and to answer to no man for the verity of his religious views." "Men may believe what they cannot prove. They may not be put to the proof of their religious doctrines or beliefs. . . . Many take their gospel from the New Testament. But it would hardly be supposed that they could be tried before a jury charged with the duty of determining whether those teachings contained false representations."

The dilemma presented by the case was severe. While the alleged truthfulness of nonreligious publications could ordinarily have been submitted to the jury, Ballard was deprived of that defense only because the First Amendment forbids governmental inquiry into the verity of religious beliefs. In dissent Mr. Justice Jackson expressed the concern that under this construction of the First Amendment "[p]rosecutions of this character easily could degenerate into religious persecution." The case shows how elusive is the line which enforces the Amendment's injunction of strict neutrality, while manifesting no official hostility toward religion—a line which must be considered in the cases now before us. Some might view the result of the Ballard case as a manifestation of hostility—in that the conviction stood because the defense could not be raised. To others it might represent merely strict adherence to the principle of neutrality already expounded in the cases involving doctrinal disputes. Inevitably, insistence upon neutrality, vital as it surely is for untrammeled religious liberty, may appear to border upon religious hostility. But in the long view the independence of both church and state in their respective spheres will be better served by close adherence to the neutrality principle. If the choice is often difficult, the difficulty is endemic to issues implicating the religious guarantees of the First Amendment. Freedom of religion will be seriously jeopardized if we admit exceptions for no better reason than the difficulty of delineating hostility from neutrality in the closest cases.

Second. It is only recently that our decisions have dealt with the question whether issues arising under the Establishment Clause may be isolated from problems implicating the Free Exercise Clause. Everson v. Board of Education, is in my view the first of our decisions which treats a problem of asserted unconstitutional involvement as raising questions purely under the Establishment Clause. A scrutiny of several earlier decisions said by some to have etched the contours of the clause shows that such cases neither raised nor decided any constitutional issues under the First Amendment. Bradfield v. Roberts, for example, involved challenges to a federal grant to a hospital administered by a Roman Catholic order. The Court rejected the claim for lack of evidence that any sectarian influence changed its character as a secular institution chartered as such by the Congress.

Quick Bear v. Leupp, is also illustrative. The immediate question there was one of statutory construction, although the issue had originally involved the constitutionality of the use of federal funds to support sectarian education on Indian reservations. Congress had already prohibited federal grants for that purpose, thereby removing the broader issue, leaving only the question whether the statute authorized the appropriation for religious teaching of Treaty funds held by the Government in trust for the Indians. Since these were the Indians' own funds, the Court held only that the Indians might direct their use for such educational purposes as they chose, and that the administration by the Treasury of the disbursement of the funds did not inject into the case any issue of the propriety of the use of federal moneys. Indeed, the Court expressly approved the reasoning of the Court of Appeals that to deny the Indians the right to spend their own moneys for religious purposes of their choice might well infringe the free exercise of their religion: "it seems inconceivable that Congress should have intended to prohibit them from receiving religious education at their own cost if they so desired it . . . ." This case forecast, however, an increasingly troublesome First Amendment paradox: that the logical interrelationship between the Establishment and Free Exercise Clauses may produce situations where an injunction against an apparent establishment must be withheld in order to avoid infringement of rights of free exercise. That paradox was not squarely presented in Quick Bear, but the care taken by the Court to avoid a constitutional confrontation discloses an awareness of possible conflicts between the two clauses. I shall come back to this problem later, infra, pp. 296-299.

A third case in this group is Cochran v. Louisiana State Board, which involved a challenge to a state statute providing public funds to support a loan of free textbooks to pupils of both public and private schools. The constitutional issues in this Court extended no further than the claim that this program amounted to a taking of private property for nonpublic use. The Court rejected the claim on the ground that no private use of property was involved; " . . . we can not doubt that the taxing power of the State is exerted for a public purpose." The case therefore raised no issue under the First Amendment.

In Pierce v. Society of Sisters, a Catholic parochial school and a private but nonsectarian military academy challenged a state law requiring all children between certain ages to attend the public schools. This Court held the law invalid as an arbitrary and unreasonable interference both with the rights of the schools and with the liberty of the parents of the children who attended them. The due process guarantee of the Fourteenth Amendment "excludes any general power of the State to standardize its children by forcing them to accept instruction from public teachers only." While one of the plaintiffs was indeed a parochial school, the case obviously decided no First Amendment question but recognized only the constitutional right to establish and patronize private schools—including parochial schools—which meet the state's reasonable minimum curricular requirements.

Third. It is true, as the Court says, that the "two clauses [Establishment and Free Exercise] may overlap." Because of the overlap, however, our decisions under the Free Exercise Clause bear considerable relevance to the problem now before us, and should be briefly reviewed. The early free exercise cases generally involved the objections of religious minorities to the application to them of general nonreligious legislation governing conduct. Reynolds v. United States, involved the claim that a belief in the sanctity of plural marriage precluded the conviction of members of a particular sect under nondiscriminatory legislation against such marriage. The Court rejected the claim, saying:

> "Laws are made for the government of actions, and while they cannot interfere with mere religious beliefs and opinions, they may with practices . . . . Can a man excuse

> his practices to the contrary because of his religious belief? To permit this would be to make the professed doctrines of religious belief superior to the law of the land, and in effect to permit every citizen to become a law unto himself. Government could exist only in name under such circumstances."

Davis v. Beason, similarly involved the claim that the First Amendment insulated from civil punishment certain practices inspired or motivated by religious beliefs. The claim was easily rejected: "It was never intended or supposed that the amendment could be invoked as a protection against legislation for the punishment of acts inimical to the peace, good order and morals of society." See also Mormon Church v. United States; Jacobson v. Massachusetts; Prince v. Massachusetts; Cleveland v. United States.

But we must not confuse the issue of governmental power to regulate or prohibit conduct motivated by religious beliefs with the quite different problem of governmental authority to compel behavior offensive to religious principles. In Hamilton v. Regents of the University of California, the question was that of the power of a State to compel students at the State University to participate in military training instruction against their religious convictions. The validity of the statute was sustained against claims based upon the First Amendment. But the decision rested on a very narrow principle: since there was neither a constitutional right nor a legal obligation to attend the State University, the obligation to participate in military training courses, reflecting a legitimate state interest, might properly be imposed upon those who chose to attend. Although the rights protected by the First and Fourteenth Amendments were presumed to include "the right to entertain the beliefs, to adhere to the principles and to teach the doctrines on which these students base their objections to the order prescribing military training," those Amendments were construed not to free such students from the military training obligations if they chose to attend the University. Justices Brandeis, Cardozo and Stone, concurring separately, agreed that the requirement infringed no constitutionally protected liberties. They added, however, that the case presented no question under the Establishment Clause. The military instruction program was not an establishment since it in no way involved "instruction in the practice or tenets of a religion." Since the only question was one of free exercise, they concluded, like the majority, that the strong state interest in training a citizen militia justified the restraints imposed, at least so long as attendance at the University was voluntary.

Hamilton has not been overruled, although United States v. Schwimmer, and United States v. Macintosh, upon which the Court in Hamilton relied, have since been overruled by Girouard v. United States. But if Hamilton retains any vitality with respect to higher education, we recognized its inapplicability to cognate questions in the public primary and secondary schools when we held in West Virginia Board of Education v. Barnette, supra, that a State had no power to expel from public schools students who refused on religious grounds to comply with a daily flag salute requirement. Of course, such a requirement was no more a law "respecting an establishment of religion" than the California law compelling the college students to take military training. The Barnette plaintiffs, moreover, did not ask that the whole exercise be enjoined, but only that an excuse or exemption be provided for those students whose religious beliefs forbade them to participate in the ceremony. The key to the holding that such a requirement abridged rights of free exercise lay in the fact that attendance at school was not voluntary but compulsory. The Court said:

> "This issue is not prejudiced by the Court's previous holding that where a State, without compelling attendance, extends college facilities to pupils who voluntarily enroll, it may prescribe military training as part of the course without offense to the Constitution. . . . Hamilton v. Regents. In the present case attendance is not optional."

The Barnette decision made another significant point. The Court held that the State must make participation in the exercise voluntary for all students and not alone for those who found participation obnoxious on religious grounds. In short, there was simply no need to "inquire whether non-conformist beliefs will exempt from the duty to salute" because the Court found no state "power to make the salute a legal duty."

The distinctions between Hamilton and Barnette are, I think, crucial to the resolution of the cases before us. The different results of those cases are attributable only in part to a difference in the strength of the particular state interests which the respective statutes were designed to serve. Far more significant is the fact that Hamilton dealt with the voluntary attendance at college of young adults, while Barnette involved the compelled attendance of young children at elementary and secondary schools. This distinction warrants a difference in constitutional results. And it is with the involuntary attendance of young school children that we are exclusively concerned in the cases now before the Court.

III.

No one questions that the Framers of the First Amendment intended to restrict exclusively the powers of the Federal Government. Whatever limitations that Amendment now imposes upon the States derive from the Fourteenth Amendment. The process of absorption of the religious guarantees of the First Amendment as protections against the States under the Fourteenth Amendment began with the Free Exercise Clause. In 1923 the Court held that the protections of the Fourteenth included at least a person's freedom "to worship God according to the dictates of his own conscience . . . ." Meyer v. Nebraska. See also Hamilton v. Regents, supra, at 262. Cantwell v. Connecticut, completed in 1940 the process of absorption of the Free Exercise Clause and recognized its dual aspect: the Court affirmed freedom of belief as an absolute liberty, but recognized that conduct, while it may also be comprehended by the Free Exercise Clause, "remains subject to regulation for the protection of society." This was a distinction already drawn by Reynolds v. United States, supra. From the beginning this Court has recognized that while government may regulate the behavioral manifestations of religious beliefs, it may not interfere at all with the beliefs themselves.

The absorption of the Establishment Clause has, however, come later and by a route less easily charted. It has been suggested, with some support in history, that absorption of the First Amendment's ban against congressional legislation "respecting an establishment of religion" is conceptually impossible because the Framers meant the Establishment Clause also to foreclose any attempt by Congress to disestablish the existing official state churches. Whether or not such was the understanding of the Framers and whether such a purpose would have inhibited the absorption of the Establishment Clause at the threshold of the Nineteenth Century are questions not dispositive of our present inquiry. For it is clear on the record of history that the last of the formal state establishments was dissolved more than three decades before the Fourteenth Amendment was ratified, and thus the problem of protecting official state churches from federal encroachments could hardly have been any concern of those who framed the post-Civil War Amendments. Any such objective of the First Amendment, having become historical anachronism by 1868, cannot be thought to have deterred the absorption of the Establishment Clause to any greater degree than it would, for example, have deterred the absorption of the Free Exercise Clause. That no organ of the Federal Government possessed in 1791 any power to restrain the interference of the States in religious matters is indisputable. See Permoli v. New Orleans, 3 How. 589. It is equally plain, on the other hand, that the Fourteenth Amendment created a panoply of new federal rights for the protection of citizens of the various States. And among those rights was freedom from such state governmental involvement in the affairs of religion as the Establishment Clause had originally foreclosed on the part of Congress.

It has also been suggested that the "liberty" guaranteed by the Fourteenth Amendment logically cannot absorb the Establishment Clause because that clause is not one of the provisions of the Bill of Rights which in terms protects a "freedom" of the individual. See Corwin,

A Constitution of Powers in a Secular State (1951), 113-116. The fallacy in this contention, I think, is that it underestimates the role of the Establishment Clause as co-guarantor, with the Free Exercise Clause, of religious liberty. The Framers did not entrust the liberty of religious beliefs to either clause alone. The Free Exercise Clause "was not to be the full extent of the Amendment's guarantee of freedom from governmental intrusion in matters of faith." McGowan v. Maryland, supra, at 464 (opinion of Frankfurter, J.).

Finally, it has been contended that absorption of the Establishment Clause is precluded by the absence of any intention on the part of the Framers of the Fourteenth Amendment to circumscribe the residual powers of the States to aid religious activities and institutions in ways which fell short of formal establishments. That argument relies in part upon the express terms of the abortive Blaine Amendment—proposed several years after the adoption of the Fourteenth Amendment—which would have added to the First Amendment a provision that "[n]o State shall make any law respecting an establishment of religion . . . ." Such a restriction would have been superfluous, it is said, if the Fourteenth Amendment had already made the Establishment Clause binding upon the States.

The argument proves too much, for the Fourteenth Amendment's protection of the free exercise of religion can hardly be questioned; yet the Blaine Amendment would also have added an explicit protection against state laws abridging that liberty. Even if we assume that the draftsmen of the Fourteenth Amendment saw no immediate connection between its protections against state action infringing personal liberty and the guarantees of the First Amendment, it is certainly too late in the day to suggest that their assumed inattention to the question dilutes the force of these constitutional guarantees in their application to the States. It is enough to conclude that the religious liberty embodied in the Fourteenth Amendment would not be viable if the Constitution were interpreted to forbid only establishments ordained by Congress.

The issue of what particular activities the Establishment Clause forbids the States to undertake is our more immediate concern. In Everson v. Board of Education, a careful study of the relevant history led the Court to the view, consistently recognized in decisions since Everson, that the Establishment Clause embodied the Framers' conclusion that government and religion have discrete interests which are mutually best served when each avoids too close a proximity to the other. It is not only the nonbeliever who fears the injection of sectarian doctrines and controversies into the civil polity, but in as high degree it is the devout believer who fears the secularization of a creed which becomes too deeply involved with and dependent upon the government. It has rightly been said of the history of the Establishment Clause that "our tradition of civil liberty rests not only on the secularism of a Thomas Jefferson but also on the fervent sectarianism . . . of a Roger Williams." Freund, The Supreme Court of the United States (1961), 84.

Our decisions on questions of religious education or exercises in the public schools have consistently reflected this dual aspect of the Establishment Clause. Engel v. Vitale unmistakably has its roots in three earlier cases which, on cognate issues, shaped the contours of the Establishment Clause. First, in Everson the Court held that reimbursement by the town of parents for the cost of transporting their children by public carrier to parochial (as well as public and private nonsectarian) schools did not offend the Establishment Clause. Such reimbursement, by easing the financial burden upon Catholic parents, may indirectly have fostered the operation of the Catholic schools, and may thereby indirectly have facilitated the teaching of Catholic principles, thus serving ultimately a religious goal. But this form of governmental assistance was difficult to distinguish from myriad other incidental if not insignificant government benefits enjoyed by religious institutions—fire and police protection, tax exemptions, and the pavement of streets and sidewalks, for example. "The State contributes no money to the schools. It does not support them. Its legislation, as applied, does no more than provide a general program to help parents get their children, regardless of their religion, safely and expeditiously to and from accredited schools." Yet even this form of assistance was thought by four Justices of the Everson Court to be barred by the Establishment Clause because too perilously close to that public support of religion forbidden by the First Amendment.

The other two cases, Illinois ex rel. McCollum v. Board of Education, and Zorach v. Clauson, can best be considered together. Both involved programs of released time for religious instruction of public school students. I reject the suggestion that Zorach overruled McCollum in silence. The distinction which the Court drew in Zorach between the two cases is, in my view, faithful to the function of the Establishment Clause.

I should first note, however, that McCollum and Zorach do not seem to me distinguishable in terms of the free exercise claims advanced in both cases. The nonparticipant in the McCollum program was given secular instruction in a separate room during the times his classmates had religious lessons; the nonparticipant in any Zorach program also received secular instruction, while his classmates repaired to a place outside the school for religious instruction.

The crucial difference, I think, was that the McCollum program offended the Establishment Clause while the Zorach program did not. This was not, in my view, because of the difference in public expenditures involved. True, the McCollum program involved the regular use of school facilities, classrooms, heat and light and time from the regular school day—even though the actual incremental cost may have been negligible. All religious instruction under the Zorach program, by contrast, was carried on entirely off the school premises, and the teacher's part was simply to facilitate the children's release to the churches. The deeper difference was that the McCollum program placed the religious instructor in the public school classroom in precisely the position of authority held by the regular teachers of secular subjects, while the Zorach program did not. The McCollum program, in lending to the support of sectarian instruction all the authority of the governmentally operated public school system, brought government and religion into that proximity which the Establishment Clause forbids. To be sure, a religious teacher presumably commands substantial respect and merits attention in his own right. But the Constitution does not permit that prestige and capacity for influence to be augmented by investiture of all the symbols of authority at the command of the lay teacher for the enhancement of secular instruction.

More recent decisions have further etched the contours of Establishment. In the Sunday Law Cases, we found in state laws compelling a uniform day of rest from worldly labor no violation of the Establishment Clause (McGowan v. Maryland). The basic ground of our decision was that, granted the Sunday Laws were first enacted for religious ends, they were continued in force for reasons wholly secular, namely, to provide a universal day of rest and ensure the health and tranquillity of the community. In other words, government may originally have decreed a Sunday day of rest for the impermissible purpose of supporting religion but abandoned that purpose and retained the laws for the permissible purpose of furthering overwhelmingly secular ends.

Such was the evolution of the contours of the Establishment Clause before Engel v. Vitale. There, a year ago, we held that the daily recital of the State-composed Regents' Prayer constituted an establishment of religion because, although the prayer itself revealed no sectarian content or purpose, its nature and meaning were quite clearly religious. New York, in authorizing its recitation, had not maintained that distance between the public and the religious sectors commanded by the Establishment Clause when it placed the "power, prestige and financial support of government" behind the prayer. In Engel, as in McCollum, it did not matter that the amount of time and expense allocated to the daily recitation was small so long as the exercise itself was manifestly religious. Nor did it matter that few children had complained of the practice, for the measure of the seriousness of a breach of the Establishment Clause has never been thought to be the number of people who complain of it.

We also held two Terms ago in Torcaso v. Watkins, supra, that a State may not constitutionally require an applicant for the office of Notary Public to swear or affirm that he believes in God. The problem of that case was strikingly similar to the issue presented 18 years before in the flag salute case, West Virginia Board of Education v. Barnette, supra. In neither case was there any claim of establishment of religion, but only of infringement of the individual's religious liberty—in the one case, that of the nonbeliever who could not attest to a belief in God; in the other, that of the child whose creed forbade him to salute the flag. But Torcaso added a new element not present in Barnette. The Maryland test oath involved an attempt to employ essentially religious (albeit nonsectarian) means to achieve a secular goal to which the means bore no reasonable relationship. No one doubted the State's interest in the integrity of its Notaries Public, but that interest did not warrant the screening of applicants by means of a religious test. The Sunday Law Cases were different in that respect. Even if Sunday Laws retain certain religious vestiges, they are enforced today for essentially secular objectives which cannot be effectively achieved in modern society except by designating Sunday as the universal day of rest. The Court's opinions cited very substantial problems in selecting or enforcing an alternative day of rest. But the teaching of both Torcaso and the Sunday Law Cases is that government may not employ religious means to serve secular interests, however legitimate they may be, at least without the clearest demonstration that nonreligious means will not suffice.

IV.

I turn now to the cases before us. The religious nature of the exercises here challenged seems plain. Unless Engel v. Vitale is to be overruled, or we are to engage in wholly disingenuous distinction, we cannot sustain these practices. Daily recital of the Lord's Prayer and the reading of passages of Scripture are quite as clearly breaches of the command of the Establishment Clause as was the daily use of the rather bland Regents' Prayer in the New York public schools. Indeed, I would suppose that, if anything, the Lord's Prayer and the Holy Bible are more clearly sectarian, and the present violations of the First Amendment consequently more serious. But the religious exercises challenged in these cases have a long history. And almost from the beginning, Bible reading and daily prayer in the schools have been the subject of debate, criticism by educators and other public officials, and proscription by courts and legislative councils. At the outset, then, we must carefully canvass both aspects of this history.

The use of prayers and Bible readings at the opening of the school day long antedates the founding of our Republic. The Rules of the New Haven Hopkins Grammar School required in 1684 "[t]hat the Scholars being called together, the Mr. shall every morning begin his work with a short prayer for a blessing on his Laboures and their learning . . . ." More rigorous was the provision in a 1682 contract with a Dutch schoolmaster in Flatbush, New York:

> "When the school begins, one of the children shall read the morning prayer, as it stands in the catechism, and close with the prayer before dinner; in the afternoon it shall begin with the prayer after dinner, and end with the evening prayer. The evening school shall begin with the Lord's prayer, and close by singing a psalm."

After the Revolution, the new States uniformly continued these long-established practices in the private and the few public grammar schools. The school committee of Boston in 1789, for example, required the city's several schoolmasters "daily to commence the duties of their office by prayer and reading a portion of the Sacred Scriptures . . . ." That requirement was mirrored throughout the original States, and exemplified the universal practice well into the nineteenth century. As the free public schools gradually supplanted the private academies and sectarian schools between 1800 and 1850, morning devotional exercises were retained with few alterations. Indeed, public pressures upon school administrators in many parts of the country would hardly have condoned abandonment of practices to which a century or more of private religious education had accustomed the American people. The controversy centered, in fact, principally about the elimination of plainly sectarian practices and textbooks, and led to the eventual substitution of nonsectarian, though still religious, exercises and materials.

Statutory provision for daily religious exercises is, however, of quite recent origin. At the turn of this century, there was but one State— Massachusetts—which had a law making morning prayer or Bible reading obligatory. Statutes elsewhere either permitted such practices or simply left the question to local option. It was not until after 1910 that 11 more States, within a few years, joined Massachusetts in making one or both exercises compulsory. The Pennsylvania law with which we are concerned in the Schempp case, for example, took effect in 1913; and even the Rule of the Baltimore School Board involved in the Murray case dates only from 1905. In no State has there ever been a constitutional or statutory prohibition against the recital of prayers or the reading of Scripture, although a number of States have outlawed these practices by judicial decision or administrative order. What is noteworthy about the panoply of state and local regulations from which these cases emerge is the relative recency of the statutory codification of practices which have ancient roots, and the rather small number of States which have ever prescribed compulsory religious exercises in the public schools.

The purposes underlying the adoption and perpetuation of these practices are somewhat complex. It is beyond question that the religious benefits and values realized from daily prayer and Bible reading have usually been considered paramount, and sufficient to justify the continuation of such practices. To Horace Mann, embroiled in an intense controversy over the role of sectarian instruction and textbooks in the Boston public schools, there was little question that the regular use of the Bible—which he thought essentially nonsectarian—would bear fruit in the spiritual enlightenment of his pupils. A contemporary of Mann's, the Commissioner of Education of a neighboring State, expressed a view which many enlightened educators of that day shared:

> "As a textbook of morals the Bible is pre-eminent, and should have a prominent place in our schools, either as a reading book or as a source of appeal and instruction. Sectarianism, indeed, should not be countenanced in the schools; but the Bible is not sectarian . . . . The Scriptures should at least be read at the opening of the school, if no more. Prayer may also be offered with the happiest effects."

Wisconsin's Superintendent of Public Instruction, writing a few years later in 1858, reflected the attitude of his eastern colleagues, in that he regarded "with special favor the use of the Bible in public schools, as pre-eminently first in importance among text-books for teaching the noblest principles of virtue, morality, patriotism, and good order—love and reverence for God—charity and good will to man."

Such statements reveal the understanding of educators that the daily religious exercises in the schools served broader goals than compelling formal worship of God or fostering church attendance. The religious aims of the educators who adopted and retained such exercises were comprehensive, and in many cases quite devoid of sectarian bias—but the crucial fact is that they were nonetheless religious. While it has been suggested, see pp. 278-281, infra, that daily prayer and reading of Scripture now serve secular goals as well, there can be no doubt that the origins of these practices were unambiguously religious, even where the educator's aim was not to win adherents to a particular creed or faith.

Almost from the beginning religious exercises in the public schools have been the subject of intense criticism, vigorous debate, and judicial or administrative prohibition. Significantly, educators and school boards early entertained doubts about both the legality and the soundness of opening the school day with compulsory prayer or Bible reading. Particularly in the large Eastern cities, where immigration had exposed the public schools to religious diversities and conflicts unknown to the homogeneous academies of the eighteenth century, local authorities found it necessary even before the Civil War to seek an accommodation. In 1843, the Philadelphia School Board adopted the following resolutions:

"RESOLVED, that no children be required to attend or unite in the reading of the Bible in the Public Schools, whose parents are conscientiously opposed thereto:

"RESOLVED, that those children whose parents conscientiously prefer and desire any particular version of the Bible, without note or comment, be furnished with same."

A decade later, the Superintendent of Schools of New York State issued an even bolder decree that prayers could no longer be required as part of public school activities, and that where the King James Bible was read, Catholic students could not be compelled to attend. This type of accommodation was not restricted to the East Coast; the Cincinnati Board of Education resolved in 1869 that "religious instruction and the reading of religious books, including the Holy Bible, are prohibited in the common schools of Cincinnati, it being the true object and intent of this rule to allow the children of the parents of all sects and opinions, in matters of faith and worship, to enjoy alike the benefit of the common-school fund." The Board repealed at the same time an earlier regulation which had required the singing of hymns and psalms to accompany the Bible reading at the start of the school day. And in 1889, one commentator ventured the view that "[t]here is not enough to be gained from Bible reading to justify the quarrel that has been raised over it."

Thus a great deal of controversy over religion in the public schools had preceded the debate over the Blaine Amendment, precipitated by President Grant's insistence that matters of religion should be left "to the family altar, the church, and the private school, supported entirely by private contributions." There was ample precedent, too, for Theodore Roosevelt's declaration that in the interest of "absolutely nonsectarian public schools" it was "not our business to have the Protestant Bible or the Catholic Vulgate or the Talmud read in those schools." The same principle appeared in the message of an Ohio Governor who vetoed a compulsory Bible-reading bill in 1925:

"It is my belief that religious teaching in our homes, Sunday schools, churches, by the good mothers, fathers, and ministers of Ohio is far preferable to compulsory teaching of religion by the state. The spirit of our federal and state constitutions from the beginning . . . [has] been to leave religious instruction to the discretion of parents."

The same theme has recurred in the opinions of the Attorneys General of several States holding religious exercises or instruction to be in violation of the state or federal constitutional command of separation of church and state. Thus the basic principle upon which our decision last year in Engel v. Vitale necessarily rested, and which we reaffirm today, can hardly be thought to be radical or novel.

Particularly relevant for our purposes are the decisions of the state courts on questions of religion in the public schools. Those decisions, while not, of course, authoritative in this Court, serve nevertheless to define the problem before us and to guide our inquiry. With the growth of religious diversity and the rise of vigorous dissent it was inevitable that the courts would be called upon to enjoin religious practices in the public schools which offended certain sects and groups. The earliest of such decisions declined to review the propriety of actions taken by school authorities, so long as those actions were within the purview of the administrators' powers. Thus, where the local school board required religious exercises, the courts would not enjoin them; and where, as in at least one case, the school officials forbade devotional practices, the court refused on similar grounds to overrule that decision. Thus, whichever way the early cases came up, the governing principle of nearly complete deference to administrative discretion effectively foreclosed any consideration of constitutional questions.

The last quarter of the nineteenth century found the courts beginning to question the constitutionality of public school religious exercises. The legal context was still, of course, that of the state constitutions, since the First Amendment had not yet been held applicable to state action. And the state constitutional prohibitions against church-state cooperation or governmental aid to religion were generally less rigorous than the Establishment Clause of the First Amendment. It is therefore remarkable that the courts of a half dozen States found compulsory religious exercises in the public schools in violation of their respective state constitutions. These courts attributed much significance to the clearly religious origins and content of the challenged practices, and to the impossibility of avoiding sectarian controversy in their conduct. The Illinois Supreme Court expressed in 1910 the principles which characterized these decisions:

> "The public school is supported by the taxes which each citizen, regardless of his religion or his lack of it, is compelled to pay. The school, like the government, is simply a civil institution. It is secular, and not religious, in its purposes. The truths of the Bible are the truths of religion, which do not come within the province of the public school. . . . No one denies that they should be taught to the youth of the State. The constitution and the law do not interfere with such teaching, but they do banish theological polemics from the schools and the school districts. This is done, not from any hostility to religion, but because it is no part of the duty of the State to teach religion—to take the money of all and apply it to teaching the children of all the religion of a part, only. Instruction in religion must be voluntary." People ex rel. Ring v. Board of Education, 245 Ill. 334, 349, 92 N. E. 251, 256 (1910).

The Supreme Court of South Dakota, in banning devotional exercises from the public schools of that State, also cautioned that "[t]he state as an educator must keep out of this field, and especially is this true in the common schools, where the child is immature, without fixed religious convictions . . . ." State ex rel. Finger v. Weedman, 55 S. D. 343, 357, 226 N. W. 348, 354 (1929).

Even those state courts which have sustained devotional exercises under state law have usually recognized the primarily religious character of prayers and Bible readings. If such practices were not for that reason unconstitutional, it was necessarily because the state constitution forbade only public expenditures for sectarian instruction, or for activities which made the school-house a "place of worship," but said nothing about the subtler question of laws "respecting an establishment of religion." Thus the panorama of history permits no other conclusion than that daily prayers and Bible readings in the public schools have always been designed to be, and have been regarded as, essentially religious exercises. Unlike the Sunday closing laws, these exercises appear neither to have been divorced from their religious origins nor deprived of their centrally religious character by the passage of time, cf. McGowan v. Maryland, supra, at 442-445. On this distinction alone we might well rest a constitutional decision. But three further contentions have been pressed in the argument of these cases. These contentions deserve careful consideration, for if the position of the school authorities were correct in respect to any of them, we would be misapplying the principles of Engel v. Vitale.

A.

First, it is argued that however clearly religious may have been the origins and early nature of daily prayer and Bible reading, these practices today serve so clearly secular educational purposes that their religious attributes may be overlooked. I do not doubt, for example, that morning devotional exercises may foster better discipline in the classroom, and elevate the spiritual level on which the school day opens. The Pennsylvania Superintendent of Public Instruction, testifying by deposition in the Schempp case, offered his view that daily Bible reading "places upon the children or those hearing the reading of this, and the atmosphere which goes on in the reading . . . one of the last vestiges of moral value that we have left in our school system." The exercise thus affords, the Superintendent concluded, "a strong contradiction to the materialistic trends of our time." Baltimore's Superintendent of Schools expressed a similar view of the practices challenged in the Murray case, to the effect that "[t]he acknowledgement of the existence of God as symbolized in the opening exercises establishes a discipline tone which tends to cause each individual pupil to constrain his overt acts and to consequently conform to accepted standards of behavior during his attendance at school." These views are by no means novel, see, e. g., Billard v. Board of Education, 69 Kan. 53, 57-58, 76 P. 422, 423 (1904).

It is not the business of this Court to gainsay the judgments of experts on matters of pedagogy. Such decisions must be left to the discretion of those administrators charged with the supervision of the Nation's public schools. The limited province of the courts is to determine whether the means which the educators have chosen to achieve legitimate pedagogical ends infringe the constitutional freedoms of the First Amendment. The secular purposes which devotional exercises are said to serve fall into two categories—those which depend upon an immediately religious experience shared by the participating children; and those which appear sufficiently divorced from the religious content of the devotional material that they can be served equally by nonreligious materials. With respect to the first objective, much has been written about the moral and spiritual values of infusing some religious influence or instruction into the public school classroom. To the extent that only religious materials will serve this purpose, it seems to me that the purpose as well as the means is so plainly religious that the exercise is necessarily forbidden by the Establishment Clause. The fact that purely secular benefits may eventually result does not seem to me to justify the exercises, for similar indirect nonreligious benefits could no doubt have been claimed for the released time program invalidated in McCollum.

The second justification assumes that religious exercises at the start of the school day may directly serve solely secular ends—for example, by fostering harmony and tolerance among the pupils, enhancing the authority of the teacher, and inspiring better discipline. To the extent that such benefits result not from the content of the readings and recitation, but simply from the holding of such a solemn exercise at the opening assembly or the first class of the day, it would seem that less sensitive materials might equally well serve the same purpose. I have previously suggested that Torcaso and the Sunday Law Cases forbid the use of religious means to achieve secular ends where nonreligious means will suffice. That principle is readily applied to these cases. It has not been shown that readings from the speeches and messages of great Americans, for example, or from the documents of our heritage of liberty, daily recitation of the Pledge of Allegiance, or even the observance of a moment of reverent silence at the opening of class, may not adequately serve the solely secular purposes of the devotional activities without jeopardizing either the religious liberties of any members of the community or the proper degree of separation between the spheres of religion and government. Such substitutes would, I think, be unsatisfactory or inadequate only to the extent that the present activities do in fact serve religious goals. While I do not question the judgment of experienced educators that the challenged practices may well achieve valuable secular ends, it seems to me that the State acts unconstitutionally if it either sets about to attain even indirectly religious ends by religious means, or if it uses religious means to serve secular ends where secular means would suffice.

B.

Second, it is argued that the particular practices involved in the two cases before us are unobjectionable because they prefer no particular sect or sects at the expense of others. Both the Baltimore and Abington procedures permit, for example, the reading of any of several versions of the Bible, and this flexibility is said to ensure neutrality sufficiently to avoid the constitutional prohibition. One answer, which might be dispositive, is that any version of the Bible is inherently sectarian, else there would be no need to offer a system of rotation or alternation of versions in the first place, that is, to allow different sectarian versions to be used on different days. The sectarian character of the Holy Bible has been at the core of the whole controversy over religious practices in the public schools throughout its long and often bitter history. To vary the version as the Abington and Baltimore schools have done may well be less offensive than to read from the King James version every day, as once was the practice. But the result even of this relatively benign procedure is that majority sects are preferred in approximate proportion to their representation in the community and in the student body, while the smaller sects suffer commensurate discrimination. So long as the subject matter of the exercise is sectarian in character, these consequences cannot be avoided.

The argument contains, however, a more basic flaw. There are persons in every community—often deeply devout—to whom any version of the Judaeo-Christian Bible is offensive. There are others whose reverence for the Holy Scriptures demands private study or reflection and to whom public reading or recitation is sacrilegious, as one of the expert witnesses at the trial of the Schempp case explained. To such persons it is not the fact of using the Bible in the public schools, nor the content of any particular version, that is offensive, but only the manner in which it is used. For such persons, the anathema of public communion is even more pronounced when prayer is involved. Many deeply devout persons have always regarded prayer as a necessarily private experience. One Protestant group recently commented, for example: "When one thinks of prayer as sincere outreach of a human soul to the Creator, 'required prayer' becomes an absurdity." There is a similar problem with respect to comment upon the passages of Scripture which are to be read. Most present statutes forbid comment, and this practice accords with the views of many religious groups as to the manner in which the Bible should be read. However, as a recent survey discloses, scriptural passages read without comment frequently convey no message to the younger children in the school. Thus there has developed a practice in some schools of bridging the gap between faith and understanding by means of "definitions," even where "comment" is forbidden by statute. The present practice therefore poses a difficult dilemma: While Bible reading is almost universally required to be without comment, since only by such a prohibition can sectarian interpretation be excluded from the classroom, the rule breaks down at the point at which rudimentary definitions of Biblical terms are necessary for comprehension if the exercise is to be meaningful at all.

It has been suggested that a tentative solution to these problems may lie in the fashioning of a "common core" of theology tolerable to all creeds but preferential to none. But as one commentator has recently observed, "[h]istory is not encouraging to" those who hope to fashion a "common denominator of religion detached from its manifestation in any organized church." Sutherland, Establishment According to Engel, 76 Harv. L. Rev. 25, 51 (1962). Thus, the notion of a "common core" litany or supplication offends many deeply devout worshippers who do not find clearly sectarian practices objectionable. Father Gustave Weigel has recently expressed a widely shared view: "The moral code held by each separate religious community can reductively be unified, but the consistent particular believer wants no such reduction." And, as the American Council on Education warned several years ago, "The notion of a common core suggests a watering down of the several faiths to the point where common essentials appear. This might easily lead to a new sect—a public school sect—which would take its place alongside the existing faiths and compete with them." Engel is surely authority that nonsectarian religious practices, equally with sectarian exercises, violate the Establishment Clause. Moreover, even if the Establishment Clause were oblivious to nonsectarian religious practices, I think it quite likely that the "common core" approach would be sufficiently objectionable to many groups to be foreclosed by the prohibitions of the Free Exercise Clause.

C.

A third element which is said to absolve the practices involved in these cases from the ban of the religious guarantees of the Constitution is the provision to excuse or exempt students who wish not to participate. Insofar as these practices are claimed to violate the Establishment Clause, I find the answer which the District Court gave after our remand of Schempp to be altogether dispositive:

> "The fact that some pupils, or theoretically all pupils, might be excused from attendance at the exercises does not mitigate the obligatory nature of the ceremony . . . .

> The exercises are held in the school buildings and perforce are conducted by and under the authority of the local school authorities and during school sessions. Since the statute requires the reading of the 'Holy Bible,' a Christian document, the practice, as we said in our first opinion, prefers the Christian religion. The record demonstrates that it was the intention of the General Assembly of the Commonwealth of Pennsylvania to introduce a religious ceremony into the public schools of the Commonwealth." 201 F. Supp., at 819.

Thus the short, and to me sufficient, answer is that the availability of excusal or exemption simply has no relevance to the establishment question, if it is once found that these practices are essentially religious exercises designed at least in part to achieve religious aims through the use of public school facilities during the school day.

The more difficult question, however, is whether the availability of excusal for the dissenting child serves to refute challenges to these practices under the Free Exercise Clause. While it is enough to decide these cases to dispose of the establishment questions, questions of free exercise are so inextricably interwoven into the history and present status of these practices as to justify disposition of this second aspect of the excusal issue. The answer is that the excusal procedure itself necessarily operates in such a way as to infringe the rights of free exercise of those children who wish to be excused. We have held in Barnette and Torcaso, respectively, that a State may require neither public school students nor candidates for an office of public trust to profess beliefs offensive to religious principles. By the same token the State could not constitutionally require a student to profess publicly his disbelief as the prerequisite to the exercise of his constitutional right of abstention. And apart from Torcaso and Barnette, I think Speiser v. Randall, suggests a further answer. We held there that a State may not condition the grant of a tax exemption upon the willingness of those entitled to the exemption to affirm their loyalty to the Government, even though the exemption was itself a matter of grace rather than of constitutional right. We concluded that to impose upon the eligible taxpayers the affirmative burden of proving their loyalty impermissibly jeopardized the freedom to engage in constitutionally protected activities close to the area to which the loyalty oath related. Speiser v. Randall seems to me to dispose of two aspects of the excusal or exemption procedure now before us. First, by requiring what is tantamount in the eyes of teachers and schoolmates to a profession of disbelief, or at least of nonconformity, the procedure may well deter those children who do not wish to participate for any reason based upon the dictates of conscience from exercising an indisputably constitutional right to be excused. Thus the excusal provision in its operation subjects them to a cruel dilemma. In consequence, even devout children may well avoid claiming their right and simply continue to participate in exercises distasteful to them because of an understandable reluctance to be stigmatized as atheists or nonconformists simply on the basis of their request.

Such reluctance to seek exemption seems all the more likely in view of the fact that children are disinclined at this age to step out of line or to flout "peer-group norms." Such is the widely held view of experts who have studied the behaviors and attitudes of children. This is also the basis of Mr. Justice Frankfurter's answer to a similar contention made in the McCollum case:

> "That a child is offered an alternative may reduce the constraint; it does not eliminate the operation of influence by the school in matters sacred to conscience and outside the school's domain. The law of imitation operates, and non-conformity is not an outstanding characteristic of children. The result is an obvious pressure upon children to attend."

Also apposite is the answer given more than 70 years ago by the Supreme Court of Wisconsin to the argument that an excusal provision saved a public school devotional exercise from constitutional invalidation:

> ". . . the excluded pupil loses caste with his fellows, and is liable to be regarded with aversion, and subjected to reproach and insult. But it is a sufficient refutation of the

> argument that the practice in question tends to destroy the equality of the pupils which the constitution seeks to establish and protect, and puts a portion of them to serious disadvantage in many ways with respect to the others." State ex rel. Weiss v. District Board of School District No. 8, 76 Wis. 177, 200, 44 N. W. 967, 975.

And 50 years ago a like answer was offered by the Louisiana Supreme Court:

> "Under such circumstances, the children would be excused from the opening exercises . . . because of their religious beliefs. And excusing such children on religious grounds, although the number excused might be very small, would be a distinct preference in favor of the religious beliefs of the majority, and would work a discrimination against those who were excused. The exclusion of a pupil under such circumstances puts him in a class by himself; it subjects him to a religious stigma; and all because of his religious belief. Equality in public education would be destroyed by such act, under a Constitution which seeks to establish equality and freedom in religious matters." Herold v. Parish Board of School Directors, 136 La. 1034, 1049-1050, 68 So. 116, 121. See also Tudor v. Board of Education, 14 N. J. 31, 48-52, 100 A. 2d 857, 867-868; Brown v. Orange County Board of Public Instruction, 128 So.2d 181, 185 (Fla. App.).

Speiser v. Randall also suggests the answer to a further argument based on the excusal procedure. It has been suggested by the School Board, in Schempp, that we ought not pass upon the appellees' constitutional challenge at least until the children have availed themselves of the excusal procedure and found it inadequate to redress their grievances. Were the right to be excused not itself of constitutional stature, I might have some doubt about this issue. But we held in Speiser that the constitutional vice of the loyalty oath procedure discharged any obligation to seek the exemption before challenging the constitutionality of the conditions upon which it might have been denied. Similarly, we have held that one need not apply for a permit to distribute constitutionally protected literature, Lovell v. Griffin, or to deliver a speech, Thomas v. Collins, before he may attack the constitutionality of a licensing system of which the defect is patent. Insofar as these cases implicate only questions of establishment, it seems to me that the availability of an excuse is constitutionally irrelevant. Moreover, the excusal procedure seems to me to operate in such a way as to discourage the free exercise of religion on the part of those who might wish to utilize it, thereby rendering it unconstitutional in an additional and quite distinct respect.

To summarize my views concerning the merits of these two cases: The history, the purpose and the operation of the daily prayer recital and Bible reading leave no doubt that these practices standing by themselves constitute an impermissible breach of the Establishment Clause. Such devotional exercises may well serve legitimate nonreligious purposes. To the extent, however, that such purposes are really without religious significance, it has never been demonstrated that secular means would not suffice. Indeed, I would suggest that patriotic or other nonreligious materials might provide adequate substitutes—inadequate only to the extent that the purposes now served are indeed directly or indirectly religious. Under such circumstances, the States may not employ religious means to reach a secular goal unless secular means are wholly unavailing. I therefore agree with the Court that the judgment in Schempp, No. 142, must be affirmed, and that in Murray, No. 119, must be reversed.

V.

These considerations bring me to a final contention of the school officials in these cases: that the invalidation of the exercises at bar permits this Court no alternative but to declare unconstitutional every vestige, however slight, of cooperation or accommodation between religion and government. I cannot accept that contention. While it is not, of course, appropriate for this Court to decide questions not presently before it, I venture to suggest that religious exercises in the public schools present a unique problem. For not every involvement of religion in public life violates the Establishment Clause. Our decision in these cases does not clearly forecast anything about the constitutionality of other types of interdependence between religious and other public institutions.

Specifically, I believe that the line we must draw between the permissible and the impermissible is one which accords with history and faithfully reflects the understanding of the Founding Fathers. It is a line which the Court has consistently sought to mark in its decisions expounding the religious guarantees of the First Amendment. What the Framers meant to foreclose, and what our decisions under the Establishment Clause have forbidden, are those involvements of religious with secular institutions which (a) serve the essentially religious activities of religious institutions; (b) employ the organs of government for essentially religious purposes; or (c) use essentially religious means to serve governmental ends, where secular means would suffice. When the secular and religious institutions become involved in such a manner, there inhere in the relationship precisely those dangers—as much to church as to state—which the Framers feared would subvert religious liberty and the strength of a system of secular government. On the other hand, there may be myriad forms of involvements of government with religion which do not import such dangers and therefore should not, in my judgment, be deemed to violate the Establishment Clause. Nothing in the Constitution compels the organs of government to be blind to what everyone else perceives—that religious differences among Americans have important and pervasive implications for our society. Likewise nothing in the Establishment Clause forbids the application of legislation having purely secular ends in such a way as to alleviate burdens upon the free exercise of an individual's religious beliefs. Surely the Framers would never have understood that such a construction sanctions that involvement which violates the Establishment Clause. Such a conclusion can be reached, I would suggest, only by using the words of the First Amendment to defeat its very purpose.

The line between permissible and impermissible forms of involvement between government and religion has already been considered by the lower federal and state courts. I think a brief survey of certain of these forms of accommodation will reveal that the First Amendment commands not official hostility toward religion, but only a strict neutrality in matters of religion. Moreover, it may serve to suggest that the scope of our holding today is to be measured by the special circumstances under which these cases have arisen, and by the particular dangers to church and state which religious exercises in the public schools present. It may be helpful for purposes of analysis to group these other practices and forms of accommodation into several rough categories.

A. The Conflict Between Establishment and Free Exercise.—There are certain practices, conceivably violative of the Establishment Clause, the striking down of which might seriously interfere with certain religious liberties also protected by the First Amendment. Provisions for churches and chaplains at military establishments for those in the armed services may afford one such example. The like provision by state and federal governments for chaplains in penal institutions may afford another example. It is argued that such provisions may be assumed to contravene the Establishment Clause, yet be sustained on constitutional grounds as necessary to secure to the members of the Armed Forces and prisoners those rights of worship guaranteed under the Free Exercise Clause. Since government has deprived such persons of the opportunity to practice their faith at places of their choice, the argument runs, government may, in order to avoid infringing the free exercise guarantees, provide substitutes where it requires such persons to be. Such a principle might support, for example, the constitutionality of draft exemptions for ministers and divinity students, cf. Selective Draft Law Cases; of the excusal of children from school on their respective religious holidays; and of the allowance by government of temporary use of public buildings by religious organizations when their own churches have become unavailable because of a disaster or emergency.

Such activities and practices seem distinguishable from the sponsorship of daily Bible reading and prayer recital. For one thing, there is no element of coercion present in the appointment of military or prison chaplains; the soldier or convict who declines the opportunities for worship would not ordinarily subject himself to the suspicion or obloquy of his peers. Of special significance to this distinction is the fact that we are here usually dealing with adults, not with impressionable children as in the public schools. Moreover, the school exercises are not designed to provide the pupils with general opportunities for worship denied them by the legal obligation to attend school. The student's compelled presence in school for five days a week in no way renders the regular religious facilities of the community less accessible to him than they are to others. The situation of the school child is therefore plainly unlike that of the isolated soldier or the prisoner.

The State must be steadfastly neutral in all matters of faith, and neither favor nor inhibit religion. In my view, government cannot sponsor religious exercises in the public schools without jeopardizing that neutrality. On the other hand, hostility, not neutrality, would characterize the refusal to provide chaplains and places of worship for prisoners and soldiers cut off by the State from all civilian opportunities for public communion, the withholding of draft exemptions for ministers and conscientious objectors, or the denial of the temporary use of an empty public building to a congregation whose place of worship has been destroyed by fire or flood. I do not say that government must provide chaplains or draft exemptions, or that the courts should intercede if it fails to do so.

B. Establishment and Exercises in Legislative Bodies.—The saying of invocational prayers in legislative chambers, state or federal, and the appointment of legislative chaplains, might well represent no involvements of the kind prohibited by the Establishment Clause. Legislators, federal and state, are mature adults who may presumably absent themselves from such public and ceremonial exercises without incurring any penalty, direct or indirect. It may also be significant that, at least in the case of the Congress, Art. I, 5, of the Constitution makes each House the monitor of the "Rules of its Proceedings" so that it is at least arguable whether such matters present "political questions" the resolution of which is exclusively confided to Congress. See Baker v. Carr. Finally, there is the difficult question of who may be heard to challenge such practices. See Elliott v. White, 23 F.2d 997.

C. Non-Devotional Use of the Bible in the Public Schools.—The holding of the Court today plainly does not foreclose teaching about the Holy Scriptures or about the differences between religious sects in classes in literature or history. Indeed, whether or not the Bible is involved, it would be impossible to teach meaningfully many subjects in the social sciences or the humanities without some mention of religion. To what extent, and at what points in the curriculum, religious materials should be cited are matters which the courts ought to entrust very largely to the experienced officials who superintend our Nation's public schools. They are experts in such matters, and we are not. We should heed Mr. Justice Jackson's caveat that any attempt by this Court to announce curricular standards would be "to decree a uniform, rigid and, if we are consistent, an unchanging standard for countless school boards representing and serving highly localized groups which not only differ from each other but which themselves from time to time change attitudes." Illinois ex rel. McCollum v. Board of Education, supra, at 237.

We do not, however, in my view usurp the jurisdiction of school administrators by holding as we do today that morning devotional exercises in any form are constitutionally invalid. But there is no occasion now to go further and anticipate problems we cannot judge with the material now before us. Any attempt to impose rigid limits upon the mention of God or references to the Bible in the classroom would be fraught with dangers. If it should sometime hereafter be shown that in fact religion can play no part in the teaching of a given subject without resurrecting the ghost of the practices we strike down today, it will then be time enough to consider questions we must now defer.

D. Uniform Tax Exemptions Incidentally Available to Religious Institutions.— Nothing we hold today questions the propriety of certain tax deductions or exemptions which incidentally benefit churches and religious institutions, along with many secular charities and nonprofit organizations. If religious institutions benefit, it is in spite of rather than because of their religious character. For religious institutions simply share benefits which government makes generally available to educational, charitable, and eleemosynary groups. There is no indication that taxing authorities have used such benefits in any way to subsidize worship or foster belief in God. And as among religious beneficiaries, the tax exemption or deduction can be truly nondiscriminatory, available on equal terms to small as well as large religious bodies, to popular and unpopular sects, and to those organizations which reject as well as those which accept a belief in God.

E. Religious Considerations in Public Welfare Programs.—Since government may not support or directly aid religious activities without violating the Establishment Clause, there might be some doubt whether nondiscriminatory programs of governmental aid may constitutionally include individuals who become eligible wholly or partially for religious reasons. For example, it might be suggested that where a State provides unemployment compensation generally to those who are unable to find suitable work, it may not extend such benefits to persons who are unemployed by reason of religious beliefs or practices without thereby establishing the religion to which those persons belong. Therefore, the argument runs, the State may avoid an establishment only by singling out and excluding such persons on the ground that religious beliefs or practices have made them potential beneficiaries. Such a construction would, it seems to me, require government to impose religious discriminations and disabilities, thereby jeopardizing the free exercise of religion, in order to avoid what is thought to constitute an establishment.

The inescapable flaw in the argument, I suggest, is its quite unrealistic view of the aims of the Establishment Clause. The Framers were not concerned with the effects of certain incidental aids to individual worshippers which come about as by-products of general and nondiscriminatory welfare programs. If such benefits serve to make easier or less expensive the practice of a particular creed, or of all religions, it can hardly be said that the purpose of the program is in any way religious, or that the consequence of its nondiscriminatory application is to create the forbidden degree of interdependence between secular and sectarian institutions. I cannot therefore accept the suggestion, which seems to me implicit in the argument outlined here, that every judicial or administrative construction which is designed to prevent a public welfare program from abridging the free exercise of religious beliefs, is for that reason ipso facto an establishment of religion.

F. Activities Which, Though Religious in Origin, Have Ceased to Have Religious Meaning.—As we noted in our Sunday Law decisions, nearly every criminal law on the books can be traced to some religious principle or inspiration. But that does not make the present enforcement of the criminal law in any sense an establishment of religion, simply because it accords with widely held religious principles. As we said in McGowan v. Maryland, "the 'Establishment' Clause does not ban federal or state regulation of conduct whose reason or effect merely happens to coincide or harmonize with the tenets of some or all religions." This rationale suggests that the use of the motto "In God We Trust" on currency, on documents and public buildings and the like may not offend the clause. It is not that the use of those four words can be dismissed as "de minimis"—for I suspect there would be intense opposition to the abandonment of that motto. The truth is that we have simply interwoven the motto so deeply into the fabric of our civil polity that its present use may well not present that type of involvement which the First Amendment prohibits.

This general principle might also serve to insulate the various patriotic exercises and activities used in the public schools and elsewhere which, whatever may have been their origins, no longer have a religious purpose or meaning. The reference to divinity in the revised pledge of allegiance, for example, may merely recognize the historical fact that our Nation was believed to have been founded "under God." Thus reciting the pledge may be no more of a religious exercise than the reading aloud of Lincoln's Gettysburg Address, which contains an allusion to the same historical fact.

The principles which we reaffirm and apply today can hardly be thought novel or radical. They are, in truth, as old as the Republic itself, and have always been as integral a part of the First Amendment as the very words of that charter of religious liberty. No less applicable today than they were when first pronounced a century ago, one year after the very first court decision involving religious exercises in the public schools, are the words of a distinguished Chief Justice of the Commonwealth of Pennsylvania, Jeremiah S. Black:

> "The manifest object of the men who framed the institutions of this country, was to have a State without religion, and a Church without politics— that is to say, they meant that one should never be used as an engine for any purpose of the other, and that no man's rights in one should be tested by his opinions about the other. As the Church takes no note of men's political differences, so the State looks with equal eye on all the modes of religious faith. . . . Our fathers seem to have been perfectly sincere in their belief that the members of the Church would be more patriotic, and the citizens of the State more religious, by keeping their respective functions entirely separate." Essay on Religious Liberty, in Black, ed., Essays and Speeches of Jeremiah S. Black (1886), 53.

MR. JUSTICE GOLDBERG, with whom MR. JUSTICE HARLAN joins, concurring.

As is apparent from the opinions filed today, delineation of the constitutionally permissible relationship between religion and government is a most difficult and sensitive task, calling for the careful exercise of both judicial and public judgment and restraint. The considerations which lead the Court today to interdict the clearly religious practices presented in these cases are to me wholly compelling; I have no doubt as to the propriety of the decision and therefore join the opinion and judgment of the Court. The singular sensitivity and concern which surround both the legal and practical judgments involved impel me, however, to add a few words in further explication, while at the same time avoiding repetition of the carefully and ably framed examination of history and authority by my Brethren.

The First Amendment's guarantees, as applied to the States through the Fourteenth Amendment, foreclose not only laws "respecting an establishment of religion" but also those "prohibiting the free exercise thereof." These two proscriptions are to be read together, and in light of the single end which they are designed to serve. The basic purpose of the religion clause of the First Amendment is to promote and assure the fullest possible scope of religious liberty and tolerance for all and to nurture the conditions which secure the best hope of attainment of that end.

The fullest realization of true religious liberty requires that government neither engage in nor compel religious practices, that it effect no favoritism among sects or between religion and nonreligion, and that it work deterrence of no religious belief. But devotion even to these simply stated objectives presents no easy course, for the unavoidable accommodations necessary to achieve the maximum enjoyment of each and all of them are often difficult of discernment. There is for me no simple and clear measure which by precise application can readily and invariably demark the permissible from the impermissible.

It is said, and I agree, that the attitude of government toward religion must be one of neutrality. But untutored devotion to the concept of neutrality can lead to invocation or approval of results which partake not simply of that noninterference and noninvolvement with the religious which the Constitution commands, but of a brooding and pervasive devotion to the secular and a passive, or even active, hostility to the religious. Such results are not only not compelled by the Constitution, but, it seems to me, are prohibited by it.

Neither government nor this Court can or should ignore the significance of the fact that a vast portion of our people believe in and worship God and that many of our legal, political and personal values derive historically from religious teachings. Government must inevitably take cognizance of the existence of religion and, indeed, under certain circumstances the First Amendment may require that it do so. And it seems clear to me from the opinions in the present and past cases that the Court would recognize the propriety of providing military chaplains and of the teaching about religion, as distinguished from the teaching of religion, in the public schools. The examples could readily be multiplied, for both the required and the permissible accommodations between state and church frame the relation as one free of hostility or favor and productive of religious and political harmony, but without undue involvement of one in the concerns or practices of the other. To be sure, the judgment in each case is a delicate one, but it must be made if we are to do loyal service as judges to the ultimate First Amendment objective of religious liberty.

The practices here involved do not fall within any sensible or acceptable concept of compelled or permitted accommodation and involve the state so significantly and directly in the realm of the sectarian as to give rise to those very divisive influences and inhibitions of freedom which both religion clauses of the First Amendment preclude. The state has ordained and has utilized its facilities to engage in unmistakably religious exercises—the devotional reading and recitation of the Holy Bible—in a manner having substantial and significant import and impact. That it has selected, rather than written, a particular devotional liturgy seems to me without constitutional import. The pervasive religiosity and direct governmental involvement inhering in the prescription of prayer and Bible reading in the public schools, during and as part of the curricular day, involving young impressionable children whose school attendance is statutorily compelled, and utilizing the prestige, power, and influence of school administration, staff, and authority, cannot realistically be termed simply accommodation, and must fall within the interdiction of the First Amendment. I find nothing in the opinion of the Court which says more than this. And, of course, today's decision does not mean that all incidents of government which import of the religious are therefore and without more banned by the strictures of the Establishment Clause. As the Court declared only last Term in Engel v. Vitale, n. 21:

> "There is of course nothing in the decision reached here that is inconsistent with the fact that school children and others are officially encouraged to express love for our country by reciting historical documents such as the Declaration of Independence which contain references to the Deity or by singing officially espoused anthems which include the composer's professions of faith in a Supreme Being, or with the fact that there are many manifestations in our public life of belief in God. Such patriotic or ceremonial occasions bear no true resemblance to the unquestioned religious exercise that the State . . . has sponsored in this instance."

The First Amendment does not prohibit practices which by any realistic measure create none of the dangers which it is designed to prevent and which do not so directly or substantially involve the state in religious exercises or in the favoring of religion as to have meaningful and practical impact. It is of course true that great consequences can grow from small beginnings, but the measure of constitutional adjudication is the ability and willingness to distinguish between real threat and mere shadow.

MR. JUSTICE STEWART, dissenting.

I think the records in the two cases before us are so fundamentally deficient as to make impossible an informed or responsible determination of the constitutional issues presented. Specifically, I cannot agree that on these records we can say that the Establishment Clause has necessarily been violated. But I think there exist serious questions under both that provision and the Free Exercise Clause—insofar as each is imbedded in the Fourteenth Amendment—which require the remand of these cases for the taking of additional evidence.

I.

The First Amendment declares that "Congress shall make no law respecting an establishment of religion, or prohibiting the free exercise thereof. . . ." It is, I think, a fallacious oversimplification to regard these two provisions as establishing a single constitutional standard of "separation of church and state," which can be mechanically applied in every case to delineate the required boundaries between government and religion. We err in the first place if we do not recognize, as a matter of history and as a matter of the imperatives of our free society, that religion and government must necessarily interact in countless ways. Secondly, the fact is that while in many contexts the Establishment Clause and the Free Exercise Clause fully complement each other, there are areas in which a doctrinaire reading of the Establishment Clause leads to irreconcilable conflict with the Free Exercise Clause.

A single obvious example should suffice to make the point. Spending federal funds to employ chaplains for the armed forces might be said to violate the Establishment Clause. Yet a lonely soldier stationed at some faraway outpost could surely complain that a government which did not provide him the opportunity for pastoral guidance was affirmatively prohibiting the free exercise of his religion. And such examples could readily be multiplied. The short of the matter is simply that the two relevant clauses of the First Amendment cannot accurately be reflected in a sterile metaphor which by its very nature may distort rather than illumine the problems involved in a particular case. Cf. Sherbert v. Verner, post, p. 398.

II.

As a matter of history, the First Amendment was adopted solely as a limitation upon the newly created National Government. The events leading to its adoption strongly suggest that the Establishment Clause was primarily an attempt to insure that Congress not only would be powerless to establish a national church, but would also be unable to interfere with existing state establishments. See McGowan v. Maryland. Each State was left free to go its own way and pursue its own policy with respect to religion. Thus Virginia from the beginning pursued a policy of disestablishmentarianism. Massachusetts, by contrast, had an established church until well into the nineteenth century.

So matters stood until the adoption of the Fourteenth Amendment, or more accurately, until this Court's decision in Cantwell v. Connecticut, in 1940. In that case the Court said: "The First Amendment declares that Congress shall make no law respecting an establishment of religion or prohibiting the free exercise thereof. The Fourteenth Amendment has rendered the legislatures of the states as incompetent as Congress to enact such laws."

I accept without question that the liberty guaranteed by the Fourteenth Amendment against impairment by the States embraces in full the right of free exercise of religion protected by the First Amendment, and I yield to no one in my conception of the breadth of that freedom. See Braunfeld v. Brown, (dissenting opinion). I accept too the proposition that the Fourteenth Amendment has somehow absorbed the Establishment Clause, although it is not without irony that a constitutional provision evidently designed to leave the States free to go their own way should now have become a restriction upon their autonomy. But I cannot agree with what seems to me the insensitive definition of the Establishment Clause contained in the Court's opinion, nor with the different but, I think, equally mechanistic definitions contained in the separate opinions which have been filed.

III.

Since the Cantwell pronouncement in 1940, this Court has only twice held invalid state laws on the ground that they were laws "respecting an establishment of religion" in violation of the Fourteenth Amendment. McCollum v. Board of Education; Engel v. Vitale. On the other hand, the Court has upheld against such a challenge laws establishing Sunday as a compulsory day of rest, McGowan v. Maryland, and a law authorizing reimbursement from public funds for the transportation of parochial school pupils. Everson v. Board of Education.

Unlike other First Amendment guarantees, there is an inherent limitation upon the applicability of the Establishment Clause's ban on state support to religion. That limitation was succinctly put in Everson v. Board of Education: "State power is no more to be used so as to handicap religions than it is to favor them." And in a later case, this Court recognized that the limitation was one which was itself compelled by the free exercise guarantee. "To hold that a state cannot consistently with the First and Fourteenth Amendments utilize its public school system to aid any or all religious faiths or sects in the dissemination of their doctrines and ideals does not . . . manifest a governmental hostility to religion or religious teachings. A manifestation of such hostility would be at war with our national tradition as embodied in the First Amendment's guaranty of the free exercise of religion." McCollum v. Board of Education.

That the central value embodied in the First Amendment—and, more particularly, in the guarantee of "liberty" contained in the Fourteenth—is the safeguarding of an individual's right to free exercise of his religion has been consistently recognized. Thus, in the case of Hamilton v. Regents, Mr. Justice Cardozo, concurring, assumed that it was ". . . the religious liberty protected by the First Amendment against invasion by the nation [which] is protected by the Fourteenth Amendment against invasion by the states." (Emphasis added.) And in Cantwell v. Connecticut, supra, the purpose of those guarantees was described in the following terms: "On the one hand, it forestalls compulsion by law of the acceptance of any creed or the practice of any form of worship. Freedom of conscience and freedom to adhere to such religious organization or form of worship as the individual may choose cannot be restricted by law. On the other hand, it safeguards the free exercise of the chosen form of religion."

It is this concept of constitutional protection embodied in our decisions which makes the cases before us such difficult ones for me. For there is involved in these cases a substantial free exercise claim on the part of those who affirmatively desire to have their children's school day open with the reading of passages from the Bible.

It has become accepted that the decision in Pierce v. Society of Sisters, upholding the right of parents to send their children to nonpublic schools, was ultimately based upon the recognition of the validity of the free exercise claim involved in that situation. It might be argued here that parents who wanted their children to be exposed to religious influences in school could, under Pierce, send their children to private or parochial schools. But the consideration which renders this contention too facile to be determinative has already been recognized by the Court: "Freedom of speech, freedom of the press, freedom of religion are available to all, not merely to those who can pay their own way." Murdock v. Pennsylvania.

It might also be argued that parents who want their children exposed to religious influences can adequately fulfill that wish off school property and outside school time. With all its surface persuasiveness, however, this argument seriously misconceives the basic constitutional justification for permitting the exercises at issue in these cases. For a compulsory state educational system so structures a child's life that if religious exercises are held to be an impermissible activity in schools, religion is placed at an artificial and state-created disadvantage. Viewed in this light, permission of such exercises for those who want them is necessary if the schools are truly to be neutral in the matter of religion. And a refusal to permit religious exercises thus is seen, not as the realization of state neutrality, but rather as the establishment of a religion of secularism, or at the least, as government support of the beliefs of those who think that religious exercises should be conducted only in private.

What seems to me to be of paramount importance, then, is recognition of the fact that the claim advanced here in favor of Bible reading is sufficiently substantial to make simple reference to the constitutional phrase "establishment of religion" as inadequate an analysis of the cases before us as the ritualistic invocation of the nonconstitutional phrase "separation of church and state." What these cases compel, rather, is an analysis of just what the "neutrality" is which is required by the interplay of the Establishment and Free Exercise Clauses of the First Amendment, as imbedded in the Fourteenth.

IV.

Our decisions make clear that there is no constitutional bar to the use of government property for religious purposes. On the contrary, this Court has consistently held that the discriminatory barring of religious groups from public property is itself a violation of First and Fourteenth Amendment guarantees. Fowler v. Rhode Island; Niemotko v. Maryland. A different standard has been applied to public school property, because of the coercive effect which the use by religious sects of a compulsory school system would necessarily have upon the children involved. McCollum v. Board of Education. But insofar as the McCollum decision rests on the Establishment rather than the Free Exercise Clause, it is clear that its effect is limited to religious instruction—to government support of proselytizing activities of religious sects by throwing the weight of secular authority behind the dissemination of religious tenets.

The dangers both to government and to religion inherent in official support of instruction in the tenets of various religious sects are absent in the present cases, which involve only a reading from the Bible unaccompanied by comments which might otherwise constitute instruction. Indeed, since, from all that appears in either record, any teacher who does not wish to do so is free not to participate, it cannot even be contended that some infinitesimal part of the salaries paid by the State are made contingent upon the performance of a religious function.

In the absence of evidence that the legislature or school board intended to prohibit local schools from substituting a different set of readings where parents requested such a change, we should not assume that the provisions before us—as actually administered—may not be construed simply as authorizing religious exercises, nor that the designations may not be treated simply as indications of the promulgating body's view as to the community's preference. We are under a duty to interpret these provisions so as to render them constitutional if reasonably possible. Compare Two Guys v. McGinley; Everson v. Board of Education, and n. 2. In the Schempp case there is evidence which indicates that variations were in fact permitted by the very school there involved, and that further variations were not introduced only because of the absence of requests from parents. And in the Murray case the Baltimore rule itself contains a provision permitting another version of the Bible to be substituted for the King James version.

If the provisions are not so construed, I think that their validity under the Establishment Clause would be extremely doubtful, because of the designation of a particular religious book and a denominational prayer. But since, even if the provisions are construed as I believe they must be, I think that the cases before us must be remanded for further evidence on other issues—thus affording the plaintiffs an opportunity to prove that local variations are not in fact permitted—I shall for the balance of this dissenting opinion treat the provisions before us as making the variety and content of the exercises, as well as a choice as to their implementation, matters which ultimately reflect the consensus of each local school community. In the absence of coercion upon those who do not wish to participate—because they hold less strong beliefs, other beliefs, or no beliefs at all—such provisions cannot, in my view, be held to represent the type of support of religion barred by the Establishment Clause. For the only support which such rules provide for religion is the withholding of state hostility—a simple acknowledgment on the part of secular authorities that the Constitution does not require extirpation of all expression of religious belief.

V.

I have said that these provisions authorizing religious exercises are properly to be regarded as measures making possible the free exercise of religion. But it is important to stress that, strictly speaking, what is at issue here is a privilege rather than a right. In other words, the question presented is not whether exercises such as those at issue here are constitutionally compelled, but rather whether they are constitutionally invalid. And that issue, in my view, turns on the question of coercion.

It is clear that the dangers of coercion involved in the holding of religious exercises in a schoolroom differ qualitatively from those presented by the use of similar exercises or affirmations in ceremonies attended by adults. Even as to children, however, the duty laid upon government in connection with religious exercises in the public schools is that of refraining from so structuring the school environment as to put any kind of pressure on a child to participate in those exercises; it is not that of providing an atmosphere in which children are kept scrupulously insulated from any awareness that some of their fellows may want to open the school day with prayer, or of the fact that there exist in our pluralistic society differences of religious belief.

These are not, it must be stressed, cases like Brown v. Board of Education, in which this Court held that, in the sphere of public education, the Fourteenth Amendment's guarantee of equal protection of the laws required that race not be treated as a relevant factor. A segregated school system is not invalid because its operation is coercive; it is invalid simply because our Constitution presupposes that men are created equal, and that therefore racial differences cannot provide a valid basis for governmental action. Accommodation of religious differences on the part of the State, however, is not only permitted but required by that same Constitution.

The governmental neutrality which the First and Fourteenth Amendments require in the cases before us, in other words, is the extension of evenhanded treatment to all who believe, doubt, or disbelieve—a refusal on the part of the State to weight the scales of private choice. In these cases, therefore, what is involved is not state action based on impermissible categories, but rather an attempt by the State to accommodate those differences which the existence in our society of a variety of religious beliefs makes inevitable. The Constitution requires that such efforts be struck down only if they are proven to entail the use of the secular authority of government to coerce a preference among such beliefs.

It may well be, as has been argued to us, that even the supposed benefits to be derived from noncoercive religious exercises in public schools are incommensurate with the administrative problems which they would create. The choice involved, however, is one for each local community and its school board, and not for this Court. For, as I have said, religious exercises are not constitutionally invalid if they simply reflect differences which exist in the society from which the school draws its pupils. They become constitutionally invalid only if their administration places the sanction of secular authority behind one or more particular religious or irreligious beliefs.

To be specific, it seems to me clear that certain types of exercises would present situations in which no possibility of coercion on the part of secular officials could be claimed to exist. Thus, if such exercises were held either before or after the official school day, or if the school schedule were such that participation were merely one among a number of desirable alternatives, it could hardly be contended that the exercises did anything more than to provide an opportunity for the voluntary expression of religious belief. On the other hand, a law which provided for religious exercises during the school day and which contained no excusal provision would obviously be unconstitutionally coercive upon those who did not wish to participate. And even under a law containing an excusal provision, if the exercises were held during the school day, and no equally desirable alternative were provided by the school authorities, the likelihood that children might be under at least some psychological compulsion to participate would be great. In a case such as the latter, however, I think we would err if we assumed such coercion in the absence of any evidence.

VI.

Viewed in this light, it seems to me clear that the records in both of the cases before us are wholly inadequate to support an informed or responsible decision. Both cases involve provisions which explicitly permit any student who wishes, to be excused from participation in the exercises. There is no evidence in either case as to whether there would exist any coercion of any kind upon a student who did not want to participate. No evidence at all was adduced in the Murray case, because it was decided upon a demurrer. All that we have in that case, therefore, is the conclusory language of a pleading. While such conclusory allegations are acceptable for procedural purposes, I think that the nature of the constitutional problem involved here clearly demands that no decision be made except upon evidence. In the Schempp case the record shows no more than a subjective prophecy by a parent of what he thought would happen if a request were made to be excused from participation in the exercises under the amended statute. No such request was ever made, and there is no evidence whatever as to what might or would actually happen, nor of what administrative arrangements the school actually might or could make to free from pressure of any kind those who do not want to participate in the exercises. There were no District Court findings on this issue, since the case under the amended statute was decided exclusively on Establishment Clause grounds. 201 F. Supp. 815.

What our Constitution indispensably protects is the freedom of each of us, be he Jew or Agnostic, Christian or Atheist, Buddhist or Freethinker, to believe or disbelieve, to worship or not worship, to pray or keep silent, according to his own conscience, uncoerced and unrestrained by government. It is conceivable that these school boards, or even all school boards, might eventually find it impossible to administer a system of religious exercises during school hours in such a way as to meet this constitutional standard—in such a way as completely to free from any kind of official coercion those who do not affirmatively want to participate. But I think we must not assume that school boards so lack the qualities of inventiveness and good will as to make impossible the achievement of that goal.

I would remand both cases for further hearings.

GREEN ET AL. V. COUNTY SCHOOL BOARD OF NEW KENT COUNTY ET AL., 391 U.S. 430 (1968)

SUPREME COURT OF THE UNITED STATES
CERTIORARI TO THE UNITED STATES COURT OF APPEALS FOR THE FOURTH CIRCUIT
ARGUED APRIL 3, 1968. DECIDED MAY 27, 1968.

Respondent School Board maintains two schools, one on the east side and one on the west side of New Kent County, Virginia. About one-half of the county's population are Negroes, who reside throughout the county since there is no residential segregation. Although this Court held in Brown v. Board of Education, (Brown I), that Virginia's constitutional and statutory provisions requiring racial segregation in schools were unconstitutional, the Board continued segregated operation of the schools, presumably pursuant to Virginia statutes enacted to resist that decision. In 1965, after this suit for injunctive relief against maintenance of allegedly segregated schools was filed, the Board, in order to remain eligible for federal financial aid, adopted a "freedom-of-choice" plan for desegregating the schools. The plan permits students, except those entering the first and eighth grades, to choose annually between the schools; those not choosing are assigned to the school previously attended; first and eighth graders must affirmatively choose a school. The District Court approved the plan, as amended, and the Court of Appeals approved the "freedom-of-choice" provisions although it remanded for a more specific and comprehensive order concerning teachers. During the plan's three years of operation no white student has chosen to attend the all-Negro school, and although 115 Negro pupils enrolled in the formerly all-white school, 85% of the Negro students in the system still attend the all-Negro school. Held:

1. In 1955 this Court, in Brown v. Board of Education, (Brown II), ordered school boards operating dual school systems, part "white" and part "Negro," to "effectuate a transition to a racially nondiscriminatory school system," and it is in light of that command that the effectiveness of the "freedom-of-choice" plan to achieve that end is to be measured. Pp. 435-438.
2. The burden is on a school board to provide a plan that promises realistically to work now, and a plan that at this late date fails to provide meaningful assurance of prompt and effective disestablishment of a dual system is intolerable. Pp. 438-439.
3. A district court's obligation is to assess the effectiveness of the plan in light of the facts at hand and any alternatives which may be feasible and more promising, and to retain jurisdiction until it is clear that state-imposed segregation has been completely removed. P. 439.
4. Where a "freedom-of-choice" plan offers real promise of achieving a unitary, nonracial system there might be no objection to allowing it to prove itself in operation, but where there are reasonably available other ways, such as zoning, promising speedier and more effective conversion to a unitary school system, "freedom of choice" is not acceptable. Pp. 439-441.
5. The New Kent "freedom-of-choice" plan is not acceptable; it has not dismantled the dual system, but has operated simply to burden students and their parents with a responsibility which Brown II placed squarely on the School Board. Pp. 441-442.

382 F.2d 338, vacated in part and remanded.

MR. JUSTICE BRENNAN delivered the opinion of the Court.

The question for decision is whether, under all the circumstances here, respondent School Board's adoption of a "freedom-of-choice" plan which allows a pupil to choose his own public school constitutes adequate compliance with the Board's responsibility "to achieve a system of determining admission to the public schools on a nonracial basis . . . ." Brown v. Board of Education, (Brown II).

Petitioners brought this action in March 1965 seeking injunctive relief against respondent's continued maintenance of an alleged racially segregated school system. New Kent County is a rural county in Eastern Virginia. About one-half of its population of some 4,500 are Negroes. There is no residential segregation in the county; persons of both races reside throughout. The school system has only two schools, the New Kent school on the east side of the county and the George W. Watkins school on the west side. In a memorandum filed May 17, 1966, the District Court found that the "school system serves approximately 1,300 pupils, of which 740 are Negro and 550 are White. The School Board operates one white combined elementary and high school [New Kent], and one Negro combined elementary and high school [George W. Watkins]. There are no attendance zones. Each school serves the entire county." The record indicates that 21 school buses—11 serving the Watkins school and 10 serving the New Kent school —travel overlapping routes throughout the county to transport pupils to and from the two schools.

The segregated system was initially established and maintained under the compulsion of Virginia constitutional and statutory provisions mandating racial segregation in public education, Va. Const., Art. IX, 140 (1902); Va. Code 22-221 (1950). These provisions were held to violate the Federal Constitution in Davis v. County School Board of Prince Edward County, decided with Brown v. Board of Education, (Brown I). The respondent School Board continued the segregated operation of the system after the Brown decisions, presumably on the authority of several statutes enacted by Virginia in resistance to those decisions. Some of these statutes were held to be unconstitutional on their face or as applied. One statute, the Pupil Placement Act, Va. Code 22-232.1 et seq. (1964), not repealed until 1966, divested local boards of authority to assign children to particular schools and placed that authority in a State Pupil Placement Board. Under that Act children were each year automatically reassigned to the school previously attended unless upon their application the State Board assigned them to another school; students seeking enrollment for the first time were also assigned at the discretion of the State Board. To September 1964, no Negro pupil had applied for admission to the New Kent school under this statute and no white pupil had applied for admission to the Watkins school.

The School Board initially sought dismissal of this suit on the ground that petitioners had failed to apply to the State Board for assignment to New Kent school. However on August 2, 1965, five months after the suit was brought, respondent School Board, in order to remain eligible for federal financial aid, adopted a "freedom-of-choice" plan for desegregating the schools. Under that plan, each pupil, except those entering the first and eighth grades, may annually choose between the New Kent and Watkins schools and pupils not making a choice are assigned to the school previously attended; first and eighth grade pupils must affirmatively choose a school. After the plan was filed the District Court denied petitioners' prayer for an injunction and granted respondent leave to submit an amendment to the plan with respect to employment and assignment of teachers and staff on a racially nondiscriminatory basis. The amendment was duly filed and on June 28, 1966, the District Court approved the "freedom-of-choice" plan as so amended. The Court of Appeals for the Fourth Circuit, en banc, 382 F.2d 338, affirmed the District Court's approval of the "freedom-of-choice" provisions of the plan but remanded the case to the District Court for entry of an order regarding faculty "which is much more specific and more comprehensive" and which would incorporate in addition to a "minimal, objective time table" some of the faculty provisions of the decree entered by the Court of Appeals for the Fifth Circuit in United States v. Jefferson County Board of Education, 372 F.2d 836, aff'd en banc, 380 F.2d 385 (1967). Judges Sobeloff and Winter concurred with the remand on the teacher issue but otherwise disagreed, expressing the view "that the District Court should be directed . . . also to set up procedures for periodically evaluating the effectiveness of the [Board's] 'freedom of choice' [plan] in the elimination of other features of a segregated school system." Bowman v. County School Board of Charles City County, 382 F.2d 326, at 330. We granted certiorari.

The pattern of separate "white" and "Negro" schools in the New Kent County school system established under compulsion of state laws is precisely the pattern of segregation to which Brown I and Brown II were particularly addressed, and which Brown I declared unconstitutionally denied Negro school children equal protection of the laws. Racial identification of the system's schools was complete, extending not just to the composition of student bodies at the two schools but to every facet of school operations—faculty, staff, transportation, extracurricular activities and facilities. In short, the State, acting through the local school board and school officials, organized and operated a dual system, part "white" and part "Negro."

It was such dual systems that 14 years ago Brown I held unconstitutional and a year later Brown II held must be abolished; school boards operating such school systems were required by Brown II "to effectuate a transition to a racially nondiscriminatory school system." It is of course true that for the time immediately after Brown II the concern was with making an initial break in a long-established pattern of excluding Negro children from schools attended by white children. The principal focus was on obtaining for those Negro children courageous enough to break with tradition a place in the "white" schools. See, e. g., Cooper v. Aaron. Under Brown II that immediate goal was only the first step, however. The transition to a unitary, nonracial system of public education was and is the ultimate end to be brought about;

it was because of the "complexities arising from the transition to a system of public education freed of racial discrimination" that we provided for "all deliberate speed" in the implementation of the principles of Brown I. Thus we recognized the task would necessarily involve solution of "varied local school problems." Id., at 299. In referring to the "personal interest of the plaintiffs in admission to public schools as soon as practicable on a nondiscriminatory basis," we also noted that "[t]o effectuate this interest may call for elimination of a variety of obstacles in making the transition . . . ." Id., at 300. Yet we emphasized that the constitutional rights of Negro children required school officials to bear the burden of establishing that additional time to carry out the ruling in an effective manner "is necessary in the public interest and is consistent with good faith compliance at the earliest practicable date." Ibid. We charged the district courts in their review of particular situations to

> "consider problems related to administration, arising from the physical condition of the school plant, the school transportation system, personnel, revision of school districts and attendance areas into compact units to achieve a system of determining admission to the public schools on a nonracial basis, and revision of local laws and regulations which may be necessary in solving the foregoing problems. They will also consider the adequacy of any plans the defendants may propose to meet these problems and to effectuate a transition to a racially nondiscriminatory school system." Id., at 300-301.

It is against this background that 13 years after Brown II commanded the abolition of dual systems we must measure the effectiveness of respondent School Board's "freedom-of-choice" plan to achieve that end. The School Board contends that it has fully discharged its obligation by adopting a plan by which every student, regardless of race, may "freely" choose the school he will attend. The Board attempts to cast the issue in its broadest form by arguing that its "freedom-of-choice" plan may be faulted only by reading the Fourteenth Amendment as universally requiring "compulsory integration," a reading it insists the wording of the Amendment will not support. But that argument ignores the thrust of Brown II. In the light of the command of that case, what is involved here is the question whether the Board has achieved the "racially nondiscriminatory school system" Brown II held must be effectuated in order to remedy the established unconstitutional deficiencies of its segregated system. In the context of the state-imposed segregated pattern of long standing, the fact that in 1965 the Board opened the doors of the former "white" school to Negro children and of the "Negro" school to white children merely begins, not ends, our inquiry whether the Board has taken steps adequate to abolish its dual, segregated system. Brown II was a call for the dismantling of well-entrenched dual systems tempered by an awareness that complex and multifaceted problems would arise which would require time and flexibility for a successful resolution. School boards such as the respondent then operating state-compelled dual systems were nevertheless clearly charged with the affirmative duty to take whatever steps might be necessary to convert to a unitary system in which racial discrimination would be eliminated root and branch. See Cooper v. Aaron, supra, at 7; Bradley v. School Board; cf. Watson v. City of Memphis. The constitutional rights of Negro school children articulated in Brown I permit no less than this; and it was to this end that Brown II commanded school boards to bend their efforts.

In determining whether respondent School Board met that command by adopting its "freedom-of-choice" plan, it is relevant that this first step did not come until some 11 years after Brown I was decided and 10 years after Brown II directed the making of a "prompt and reasonable start." This deliberate perpetuation of the unconstitutional dual system can only have compounded the harm of such a system. Such delays are no longer tolerable, for "the governing constitutional principles no longer bear the imprint of newly enunciated doctrine." Watson v. City of Memphis, supra, at 529; see Bradley v. School Board, supra; Rogers v. Paul. Moreover, a plan that at this late date fails to provide meaningful assurance of prompt and effective disestablishment of a dual system is also intolerable. "The time for mere 'deliberate speed' has run out," Griffin v. County School Board; "the context in which we must interpret and apply this language [of Brown II] to plans for desegregation has been significantly altered." Goss v. Board of Education. See Calhoun v. Latimer. The burden on a school board today is to come forward with a plan that promises realistically to work, and promises realistically to work now.

The obligation of the district courts, as it always has been, is to assess the effectiveness of a proposed plan in achieving desegregation. There is no universal answer to complex problems of desegregation; there is obviously no one plan that will do the job in every case. The matter must be assessed in light of the circumstances present and the options available in each instance. It is incumbent upon the school board to establish that its proposed plan promises meaningful and immediate progress toward disestablishing state-imposed segregation. It is incumbent upon the district court to weigh that claim in light of the facts at hand and in light of any alternatives which may be shown as feasible and more promising in their effectiveness. Where the court finds the board to be acting in good faith and the proposed plan to have real prospects for dismantling the state-imposed dual system "at the earliest practicable date," then the plan may be said to provide effective relief. Of course, the availability to the board of other more promising courses of action may indicate a lack of good faith; and at the least it places a heavy burden upon the board to explain its preference for an apparently less effective method. Moreover, whatever plan is adopted will require evaluation in practice, and the court should retain jurisdiction until it is clear that state-imposed segregation has been completely removed. See No. 805, Raney v. Board of Education, post, at 449.

We do not hold that "freedom of choice" can have no place in such a plan. We do not hold that a "freedom-of-choice" plan might of itself be unconstitutional, although that argument has been urged upon us. Rather, all we decide today is that in desegregating a dual system a plan utilizing "freedom of choice" is not an end in itself. As Judge Sobeloff has put it,

> "'Freedom of choice' is not a sacred talisman; it is only a means to a constitutionally required end—the abolition of the system of segregation and its effects. If the means prove effective, it is acceptable, but if it fails to undo segregation, other means must be used to achieve this end. The school officials have the continuing duty to take whatever action may be necessary to create a 'unitary, non-racial system.'" Bowman v. County School Board, 382 F.2d 326, 333 (C. A. 4th Cir. 1967) (concurring opinion).

Accord, Kemp v. Beasley, 389 F.2d 178 (C. A. 8th Cir. 1968); United States v. Jefferson County Board of Education, supra. Although the general experience under "freedom of choice" to date has been such as to indicate its ineffectiveness as a tool of desegregation, there may well be instances in which it can serve as an effective device. Where it offers real promise of aiding a desegregation program to effectuate conversion of a state-imposed dual system to a unitary, nonracial system there might be no objection to allowing such a device to prove itself in operation. On the other hand, if there are reasonably available other ways, such for illustration as zoning, promising speedier and more effective conversion to a unitary, nonracial school system, "freedom of choice" must be held unacceptable.

The New Kent School Board's "freedom-of-choice" plan cannot be accepted as a sufficient step to "effectuate a transition" to a unitary system. In three years of operation not a single white child has chosen to attend Watkins school and although 115 Negro children enrolled in New Kent school in 1967 (up from 35 in 1965 and 111 in 1966) 85% of the Negro children in the system still attend the all-Negro Watkins school. In other words, the school system remains a dual system. Rather than further the dismantling of the dual system, the plan has operated simply to burden children and their parents with a responsibility which Brown II placed squarely on the School Board. The Board must be required to formulate a new plan and, in light of other courses which appear open to the Board, such as zoning, fashion steps which promise realistically to convert promptly to a system without a "white" school and a "Negro" school, but just schools.

The judgment of the Court of Appeals is vacated insofar as it affirmed the District Court and the case is remanded to the District Court for further proceedings consistent with this opinion.

It is so ordered.

TINKER ET AL. V. DES MOINES INDEPENDENT COMMUNITY SCHOOL DISTRICT ET AL., 393 U.S. 503 (1969)

SUPREME COURT OF THE UNITED STATES
CERTIORARI TO THE UNITED STATES COURT OF APPEALS FOR THE EIGHTH CIRCUIT
ARGUED NOVEMBER 12, 1968. DECIDED FEBRUARY 24, 1969.

Petitioners, three public school pupils in Des Moines, Iowa, were suspended from school for wearing black armbands to protest the Government's policy in Vietnam. They sought nominal damages and an injunction against a regulation that the respondents had promulgated banning the wearing of armbands. The District Court dismissed the complaint on the ground that the regulation was within the Board's power, despite the absence of any finding of substantial interference with the conduct of school activities. The Court of Appeals, sitting en banc, affirmed by an equally divided court. Held:

1. In wearing armbands, the petitioners were quiet and passive. They were not disruptive and did not impinge upon the rights of others. In these circumstances, their conduct was within the protection of the Free Speech Clause of the First Amendment and the Due Process Clause of the Fourteenth. Pp. 505-506.
2. First Amendment rights are available to teachers and students, subject to application in light of the special characteristics of the school environment. Pp. 506-507.
3. A prohibition against expression of opinion, without any evidence that the rule is necessary to avoid substantial interference with school discipline or the rights of others, is not permissible under the First and Fourteenth Amendments. Pp. 507-514.

383 F.2d 988, reversed and remanded.

MR. JUSTICE FORTAS delivered the opinion of the Court.

Petitioner John F. Tinker, 15 years old, and petitioner Christopher Eckhardt, 16 years old, attended high schools in Des Moines, Iowa. Petitioner Mary Beth Tinker, John's sister, was a 13-year-old student in junior high school.

In December 1965, a group of adults and students in Des Moines held a meeting at the Eckhardt home. The group determined to publicize their objections to the hostilities in Vietnam and their support for a truce by wearing black armbands during the holiday season and by fasting on December 16 and New Year's Eve. Petitioners and their parents had previously engaged in similar activities, and they decided to participate in the program.

The principals of the Des Moines schools became aware of the plan to wear armbands. On December 14, 1965, they met and adopted a policy that any student wearing an armband to school would be asked to remove it, and if he refused he would be suspended until he returned without the armband. Petitioners were aware of the regulation that the school authorities adopted.

On December 16, Mary Beth and Christopher wore black armbands to their schools. John Tinker wore his armband the next day. They were all sent home and suspended from school until they would come back without their armbands. They did not return to school until after the planned period for wearing armbands had expired—that is, until after New Year's Day.

This complaint was filed in the United States District Court by petitioners, through their fathers, under 1983 of Title 42 of the United States Code. It prayed for an injunction restraining the respondent school officials and the respondent members of the board of directors of the school district from disciplining the petitioners, and it sought nominal damages. After an evidentiary hearing the District Court dismissed the complaint. It upheld the constitutionality of the school authorities' action on the ground that it was reasonable in order to prevent disturbance of school discipline. 258 F. Supp. 971 (1966). The court referred to but expressly declined to follow the Fifth Circuit's holding in a similar case that the wearing of symbols like the armbands cannot be prohibited unless it "materially and substantially interfere[s] with the requirements of appropriate discipline in the operation of the school." Burnside v. Byars, 363 F.2d 744, 749 (1966).

On appeal, the Court of Appeals for the Eighth Circuit considered the case en banc. The court was equally divided, and the District Court's decision was accordingly affirmed, without opinion. 383 F.2d 988 (1967). We granted certiorari. (1968).

I.

The District Court recognized that the wearing of an armband for the purpose of expressing certain views is the type of symbolic act that is within the Free Speech Clause of the First Amendment. See West Virginia v. Barnette, (1943); Stromberg v. California, (1931). Cf. Thornhill v. Alabama, (1940); Edwards v. South Carolina, (1963); Brown v. Louisiana, (1966). As we shall discuss, the wearing of armbands in the circumstances of this case was entirely divorced from actually or potentially disruptive conduct by those participating in it. It was closely akin to "pure speech" which, we have repeatedly held, is entitled to comprehensive protection under the First Amendment. Cf. Cox v. Louisiana, (1965); Adderley v. Florida, (1966).

First Amendment rights, applied in light of the special characteristics of the school environment, are available to teachers and students. It can hardly be argued that either students or teachers shed their constitutional rights to freedom of speech or expression at the schoolhouse gate. This has been the unmistakable holding of this Court for almost 50 years. In Meyer v. Nebraska, (1923), and Bartels v. Iowa, (1923), this Court, in opinions by Mr. Justice McReynolds, held that the Due Process Clause of the Fourteenth Amendment prevents States from forbidding the teaching of a foreign language to young students. Statutes to this effect, the Court held, unconstitutionally interfere with the liberty of teacher, student, and parent. See also Pierce v. Society of Sisters, (1925); West Virginia v. Barnette, (1943); McCollum v. Board of Education, (1948); Wieman v. Updegraff, (1952) (concurring opinion); Sweezy v. New Hampshire, (1957); Shelton v. Tucker, (1960); Engel v. Vitale, (1962); Keyishian v. Board of Regents, (1967); Epperson v. Arkansas, ante, p. 97 (1968).

In West Virginia v. Barnette, supra, this Court held that under the First Amendment, the student in public school may not be compelled to salute the flag. Speaking through Mr. Justice Jackson, the Court said:

> The Fourteenth Amendment, as now applied to the States, protects the citizen against the State itself and all of its creatures—Boards of Education not excepted. These have, of course, important, delicate, and highly discretionary functions, but none that they may not perform within the limits of the Bill of Rights. That they are educating the young for citizenship is reason for scrupulous protection of Constitutional freedoms of the individual, if we are not to strangle the free mind at its source and teach youth to discount important principles of our government as mere platitudes.

On the other hand, the Court has repeatedly emphasized the need for affirming the comprehensive authority of the States and of school officials, consistent with fundamental constitutional safeguards, to prescribe and control conduct in the schools. See Epperson v. Arkansas, supra, at 104; Meyer v. Nebraska, supra, at 402. Our problem lies in the area where students in the exercise of First Amendment rights collide with the rules of the school authorities.

II.

The problem posed by the present case does not relate to regulation of the length of skirts or the type of clothing, to hair style, or deportment. Cf. Ferrell v. Dallas Independent School District, 392 F.2d 697 (1968); Pugsley v. Sellmeyer, 158 Ark. 247, 250 S. W. 538 (1923). It does not concern aggressive, disruptive action or even group demonstrations. Our problem involves direct, primary First Amendment rights akin to "pure speech."

The school officials banned and sought to punish petitioners for a silent, passive expression of opinion, unaccompanied by any disorder or disturbance on the part of petitioners. There is here no evidence whatever of petitioners' interference, actual or nascent, with the schools' work or of collision with the rights of other students to be secure and to be let alone. Accordingly, this case does not concern speech or action that intrudes upon the work of the schools or the rights of other students.

Only a few of the 18,000 students in the school system wore the black armbands. Only five students were suspended for wearing them. There is no indication that the work of the schools or any class was disrupted. Outside the classrooms, a few students made hostile remarks to the children wearing armbands, but there were no threats or acts of violence on school premises.

The District Court concluded that the action of the school authorities was reasonable because it was based upon their fear of a disturbance from the wearing of the armbands. But, in our system, undifferentiated fear or apprehension of disturbance is not enough to overcome the right to freedom of expression. Any departure from absolute regimentation may cause trouble. Any variation from the majority's opinion may inspire fear. Any word spoken, in class, in the lunchroom, or on the campus, that deviates from the views of another person may start an argument or cause a disturbance. But our Constitution says we must take this risk, Terminiello v. Chicago, (1949); and our history says that it is this sort of hazardous freedom—this kind of openness—that is the basis of our national strength and of the independence and vigor of Americans who grow up and live in this relatively permissive, often disputatious, society.

In order for the State in the person of school officials to justify prohibition of a particular expression of opinion, it must be able to show that its action was caused by something more than a mere desire to avoid the discomfort and unpleasantness that always accompany an unpopular viewpoint. Certainly where there is no finding and no showing that engaging in the forbidden conduct would "materially and substantially interfere with the requirements of appropriate discipline in the operation of the school," the prohibition cannot be sustained. Burnside v. Byars, supra, at 749.

In the present case, the District Court made no such finding, and our independent examination of the record fails to yield evidence that the school authorities had reason to anticipate that the wearing of the armbands would substantially interfere with the work of the school or impinge upon the rights of other students. Even an official memorandum prepared after the suspension that listed the reasons for the ban on wearing the armbands made no reference to the anticipation of such disruption.

On the contrary, the action of the school authorities appears to have been based upon an urgent wish to avoid the controversy which might result from the expression, even by the silent symbol of armbands, of opposition to this Nation's part in the conflagration in Vietnam. It is revealing, in this respect, that the meeting at which the school principals decided to issue the contested regulation was called in response to a student's statement to the journalism teacher in one of the schools that he wanted to write an article on Vietnam and have it published in the school paper. (The student was dissuaded.)

It is also relevant that the school authorities did not purport to prohibit the wearing of all symbols of political or controversial significance. The record shows that students in some of the schools wore buttons relating to national political campaigns, and some even wore the Iron Cross, traditionally a symbol of Nazism. The order prohibiting the wearing of armbands did not extend to these. Instead, a particular symbol—black armbands worn to exhibit opposition to this Nation's involvement in Vietnam—was singled out for prohibition. Clearly, the prohibition of expression of one particular opinion, at least without evidence that it is necessary to avoid material and substantial interference with schoolwork or discipline, is not constitutionally permissible.

In our system, state-operated schools may not be enclaves of totalitarianism. School officials do not possess absolute authority over their students. Students in school as well as out of school are "persons" under our Constitution. They are possessed of fundamental rights which the State must respect, just as they themselves must respect their obligations to the State. In our system, students may not be regarded as closed-circuit recipients of only that which the State chooses to communicate. They may not be confined to the expression of those sentiments that are officially approved. In the absence of a specific showing of constitutionally valid reasons to regulate their speech, students are entitled to freedom of expression of their views. As Judge Gewin, speaking for the Fifth Circuit, said, school officials cannot suppress "expressions of feelings with which they do not wish to contend." Burnside v. Byars, supra, at 749.

In Meyer v. Nebraska, supra, at 402, Mr. Justice McReynolds expressed this Nation's repudiation of the principle that a State might so conduct its schools as to "foster a homogeneous people." He said:

> "In order to submerge the individual and develop ideal citizens, Sparta assembled the males at seven into barracks and intrusted their subsequent education and training to official guardians. Although such measures have been deliberately approved by men of great genius, their ideas touching the relation between individual and State were wholly different from those upon which our institutions rest; and it hardly will be affirmed that any legislature could impose such restrictions upon the people of a State without doing violence to both letter and spirit of the Constitution."

This principle has been repeated by this Court on numerous occasions during the intervening years. In Keyishian v. Board of Regents, MR. JUSTICE BRENNAN, speaking for the Court, said:

> "'The vigilant protection of constitutional freedoms is nowhere more vital than in the community of American schools.' Shelton v. Tucker, at 487. The classroom is peculiarly the 'marketplace of ideas.' The Nation's future depends upon leaders trained through wide exposure to that robust exchange of ideas which discovers truth 'out of a multitude of tongues, [rather] than through any kind of authoritative selection.'"

The principle of these cases is not confined to the supervised and ordained discussion which takes place in the classroom. The principal use to which the schools are dedicated is to accommodate students during prescribed hours for the purpose of certain types of activities. Among those activities is personal intercommunication among the students. This is not only an inevitable part of the process of attending school; it is also an important part of the educational process. A student's rights, therefore, do not embrace merely the classroom hours. When he is in the cafeteria, or on the playing field, or on the campus during the authorized hours, he may express his opinions, even on controversial subjects like the conflict in Vietnam, if he does so without "materially and substantially interfer[ing] with the requirements of appropriate discipline in the operation of the school" and without colliding with the rights of others. Burnside v. Byars, supra, at 749. But conduct by the student, in class or out of it, which for any reason—whether it stems from time, place, or type of behavior— materially disrupts classwork or involves substantial disorder or invasion of the rights of others is, of course, not immunized by the constitutional guarantee of freedom of speech. Cf. Blackwell v. Issaquena County Board of Education, 363 F.2d 749 (C. A. 5th Cir. 1966).

Under our Constitution, free speech is not a right that is given only to be so circumscribed that it exists in principle but not in fact. Freedom of expression would not truly exist if the right could be exercised only in an area that a benevolent government has provided as a safe haven for crackpots. The Constitution says that Congress (and the States) may not abridge the right to free speech. This provision means what it says. We properly read it to permit reasonable regulation of speech-connected activities in carefully restricted circumstances. But we do not confine the permissible exercise of First Amendment rights to a telephone booth or the four corners of a pamphlet, or to supervised and ordained discussion in a school classroom.

If a regulation were adopted by school officials forbidding discussion of the Vietnam conflict, or the expression by any student of opposition to it anywhere on school property except as part of a prescribed classroom exercise, it would be obvious that the regulation would violate the constitutional rights of students, at least if it could not be justified by a showing that the students' activities would materially and substantially disrupt the work and discipline of the school. Cf. Hammond v. South Carolina State College, 272 F. Supp. 947 (D.C. S. C. 1967) (orderly protest meeting on state college campus); Dickey v. Alabama State Board of Education, 273 F. Supp. 613 (D.C. M. D. Ala. 1967) (expulsion of student editor of college newspaper). In the circumstances of the present case, the prohibition of the silent, passive "witness of the armbands," as one of the children called it, is no less offensive to the Constitution's guarantees.

As we have discussed, the record does not demonstrate any facts which might reasonably have led school authorities to forecast substantial disruption of or material interference with school activities, and no disturbances or disorders on the school premises in fact occurred. These petitioners merely went about their ordained rounds in school. Their deviation consisted only in wearing on their sleeve a band of black cloth, not more than two inches wide. They wore it to exhibit their disapproval of the Vietnam hostilities and their advocacy of a truce, to make their views known, and, by their example, to influence others to adopt them. They neither interrupted school activities nor sought to intrude in the school affairs or the lives of others. They caused discussion outside of the classrooms, but no interference with work and no disorder. In the circumstances, our Constitution does not permit officials of the State to deny their form of expression.

We express no opinion as to the form of relief which should be granted, this being a matter for the lower courts to determine. We reverse and remand for further proceedings consistent with this opinion.

Reversed and remanded.

MR. JUSTICE STEWART, concurring.

Although I agree with much of what is said in the Court's opinion, and with its judgment in this case, I cannot share the Court's uncritical assumption that, school discipline aside, the First Amendment rights of children are co-extensive with those of adults. Indeed, I had thought the Court decided otherwise just last Term in Ginsberg v. New York. I continue to hold the view I expressed in that case: "[A] State may permissibly determine that, at least in some precisely delineated areas, a child—like someone in a captive audience—is not possessed of that full capacity for individual choice which is the presupposition of First Amendment guarantees." Id., at 649-650 (concurring in result). Cf. Prince v. Massachusetts.

MR. JUSTICE WHITE, concurring.

While I join the Court's opinion, I deem it appropriate to note, first, that the Court continues to recognize a distinction between communicating by words and communicating by acts or conduct which sufficiently impinges on some valid state interest; and, second, that I do not subscribe to everything the Court of Appeals said about free speech in its opinion in Burnside v. Byars, 363 F.2d 744, 748 (C. A. 5th Cir. 1966), a case relied upon by the Court in the matter now before us.

MR. JUSTICE BLACK, dissenting.

The Court's holding in this case ushers in what I deem to be an entirely new era in which the power to control pupils by the elected "officials of state supported public schools . . . " in the United States is in ultimate effect transferred to the Supreme Court. The Court brought this particular case here on a petition for certiorari urging that the First and Fourteenth Amendments protect the right of school pupils to express their political views all the way "from kindergarten through high school." Here the constitutional right to "political expression" asserted was a right to wear black armbands during school hours and at classes in order to demonstrate to the other students that the petitioners were mourning because of the death of United States soldiers in Vietnam and to protest that war which they were against. Ordered to refrain from wearing the armbands in school by the elected school officials and the teachers vested with state authority to do so, apparently only seven out of the school system's 18,000 pupils deliberately refused to obey the order. One defying pupil was Paul Tinker, 8 years old, who was in the second grade; another, Hope Tinker, was 11 years old and in the fifth grade; a third member of the Tinker family was 13, in the eighth grade; and a fourth member of the same family was John Tinker, 15 years old, an 11th grade high school pupil. Their father, a Methodist minister without a church, is paid a salary by the American Friends Service Committee. Another student who defied the school order and insisted on wearing an armband in school was Christopher Eckhardt, an 11th grade pupil and a petitioner in this case. His mother is an official in the Women's International League for Peace and Freedom.

As I read the Court's opinion it relies upon the following grounds for holding unconstitutional the judgment of the Des Moines school officials and the two courts below. First, the Court concludes that the wearing of armbands is "symbolic speech" which is "akin to 'pure speech'" and therefore protected by the First and Fourteenth Amendments. Secondly, the Court decides that the public schools are an appropriate place to exercise "symbolic speech" as long as normal school functions are not "unreasonably" disrupted. Finally, the Court arrogates to itself, rather than to the State's elected officials charged with running the schools, the decision as to which school disciplinary regulations are "reasonable."

Assuming that the Court is correct in holding that the conduct of wearing armbands for the purpose of conveying political ideas is protected by the First Amendment, cf., e. g., Giboney v. Empire Storage & Ice Co., (1949), the crucial remaining questions are whether students and teachers may use the schools at their whim as a platform for the exercise of free speech—"symbolic" or "pure"—and whether the courts will allocate to themselves the function of deciding how the pupils' school day will be spent. While I have always believed that under the First and Fourteenth Amendments neither the State nor the Federal Government has any authority to regulate or censor the content of speech, I have never believed that any person has a right to give speeches or engage in demonstrations where he pleases and when he pleases. This Court has already rejected such a notion. In Cox v. Louisiana, (1965), for example, the Court clearly stated that the rights of free speech and assembly "do not mean that everyone with opinions or beliefs to express may address a group at any public place and at any time."

While the record does not show that any of these armband students shouted, used profane language, or were violent in any manner, detailed testimony by some of them shows their armbands caused comments, warnings by other students, the poking of fun at them, and a warning by an older football player that other, nonprotesting students had better let them alone. There is also evidence that a teacher of mathematics had his lesson period practically "wrecked" chiefly by disputes with Mary Beth Tinker, who wore her armband for her "demonstration." Even a casual reading of the record shows that this armband did divert students' minds from their regular lessons, and that talk, comments, etc., made John Tinker "self-conscious" in attending school with his armband. While the absence of obscene remarks or boisterous and loud disorder perhaps justifies the Court's statement that the few armband students did not actually "disrupt" the classwork, I think the record overwhelmingly shows that the armbands did exactly what the elected school officials and principals foresaw they would, that is, took the students' minds off their classwork and diverted them to thoughts about the highly emotional subject of the Vietnam war. And I repeat that if the time has come when pupils of state-supported schools, kindergartens, grammar schools, or high schools, can defy and flout orders of school officials to keep their minds on their own schoolwork, it is the beginning of a new revolutionary era of permissiveness in this country fostered by the judiciary. The next logical step, it appears to me, would be to hold unconstitutional laws that bar pupils under 21 or 18 from voting, or from being elected members of the boards of education.

The United States District Court refused to hold that the state school order violated the First and Fourteenth Amendments. 258 F. Supp. 971. Holding that the protest was akin to speech, which is protected by the First and Fourteenth Amendments, that court held that the school order was "reasonable" and hence constitutional. There was at one time a line of cases holding "reasonableness" as the court saw it to be the test of a "due process" violation. Two cases upon which the Court today heavily relies for striking down this school order used this test of reasonableness, Meyer v. Nebraska, (1923), and Bartels v. Iowa, (1923). The opinions in both cases were written by Mr. Justice McReynolds; Mr. Justice Holmes, who opposed this reasonableness test, dissented from the holdings as did Mr. Justice Sutherland. This constitutional test of reasonableness prevailed in this Court for a season. It was this test that brought on President Franklin Roosevelt's well-known Court fight. His proposed legislation did not pass, but the fight left the "reasonableness" constitutional test dead on the battlefield, so much so that this Court in Ferguson v. Skrupa, 730, after a thorough review of the old cases, was able to conclude in 1963:

> "There was a time when the Due Process Clause was used by this Court to strike down laws which were thought unreasonable, that is, unwise or incompatible with some particular economic or social philosophy.
>
> . . . .
>
> "The doctrine that prevailed in Lochner, Coppage, Adkins, Burns, and like cases—that due process authorizes courts to hold laws unconstitutional when they believe the legislature has acted unwisely—has long since been discarded."

The Ferguson case totally repudiated the old reasonableness-due process test, the doctrine that judges have the power to hold laws unconstitutional upon the belief of judges that they "shock the conscience" or that they are "unreasonable," "arbitrary," "irrational," "contrary to fundamental 'decency,'" or some other such flexible term without precise boundaries. I have many times expressed my opposition to that concept on the ground that it gives judges power to strike down any law they do not like. If the majority of the Court today, by agreeing to the opinion of my Brother FORTAS, is resurrecting that old reasonableness-due process test, I think the constitutional change should be plainly, unequivocally, and forthrightly stated for the benefit of the bench and bar. It will be a sad day for the country, I believe, when the present-day Court returns to the McReynolds due process concept. Other cases cited by the Court do not, as implied, follow the McReynolds reasonableness doctrine. West Virginia v. Barnette, clearly rejecting the "reasonableness" test, held that the Fourteenth Amendment made the First applicable to the States, and that the two forbade a State to compel little schoolchildren to salute the United States flag when they had religious scruples against doing so. Neither Thornhill v. Alabama; Stromberg v. California; Edwards v. South Carolina; nor Brown v. Louisiana, related to schoolchildren at all, and none of these cases embraced Mr. Justice McReynolds' reasonableness test; and Thornhill, Edwards, and Brown relied on the vagueness of state statutes under scrutiny to hold them unconstitutional. Cox v. Louisiana, and Adderley v. Florida, cited by the Court as a "compare," indicating, I suppose, that these two cases are no longer the law, were not rested to the slightest extent on the Meyer and Bartels "reasonableness-due process-McReynolds" constitutional test.

I deny, therefore, that it has been the "unmistakable holding of this Court for almost 50 years" that "students" and "teachers" take with them into the "schoolhouse gate" constitutional rights to "freedom of speech or expression." Even Meyer did not hold that. It makes no reference to "symbolic speech" at all; what it did was to strike down as "unreasonable" and therefore unconstitutional a Nebraska law barring the teaching of the German language before the children reached the eighth grade. One can well agree with Mr. Justice Holmes and Mr. Justice Sutherland, as I do, that such a law was no more unreasonable than it would be to bar the teaching of Latin and Greek to pupils who have not reached the eighth grade. In fact, I think the majority's reason for invalidating the Nebraska law was that it did not like it or in legal jargon that it "shocked the Court's conscience," "offended its sense of justice," or was "contrary to fundamental concepts of the English-speaking world," as the Court has sometimes said. See, e. g., Rochin v. California, and Irvine v. California. The truth is that a teacher of kindergarten, grammar school, or high school pupils no more carries into a school with him a complete right to freedom of speech and expression than an anti-Catholic or anti-Semite carries with him a complete freedom of speech and religion into a Catholic church or Jewish synagogue. Nor does a person carry with him into the United States Senate or House, or into the Supreme Court, or any other court, a complete constitutional right to go into those places contrary to their rules and speak his mind on any subject he pleases. It is a myth to say that any person has a constitutional right to say what he pleases, where he pleases, and when he pleases. Our Court has decided precisely the opposite. See, e. g., Cox v. Louisiana; Adderley v. Florida.

In my view, teachers in state-controlled public schools are hired to teach there. Although Mr. Justice McReynolds may have intimated to the contrary in Meyer v. Nebraska, supra, certainly a teacher is not paid to go into school and teach subjects the State does not hire him to teach as a part of its selected curriculum. Nor are public school students sent to the schools at public expense to broadcast political or any other views to educate and inform the public. The original idea of schools, which I do not believe is yet abandoned as worthless or out of date, was that children had not yet reached the point of experience and wisdom which enabled them to teach all of their elders. It may be that the Nation has outworn the old-fashioned slogan that "children are to be seen not heard," but one may, I hope, be permitted to harbor the thought that taxpayers send children to school on the premise that at their age they need to learn, not teach.

The true principles on this whole subject were in my judgment spoken by Mr. Justice McKenna for the Court in Waugh v. Mississippi University. The State had there passed a law barring students from peaceably assembling in Greek letter fraternities and providing that students who joined them could be expelled from school. This law would appear on the surface to run afoul of the First Amendment's freedom of assembly clause. The law was attacked as violative of due process and of the privileges and immunities clause and as a deprivation of property and of liberty, under the Fourteenth Amendment. It was argued that the fraternity made its members more moral, taught discipline, and inspired its members to study harder and to obey better the rules of discipline and order. This Court rejected all the "fervid" pleas of the fraternities' advocates and decided unanimously against these Fourteenth Amendment arguments. The Court in its next to the last paragraph made this statement which has complete relevance for us today:

> "It is said that the fraternity to which complainant belongs is a moral and of itself a disciplinary force. This need not be denied. But whether such membership makes against discipline was for the State of Mississippi to determine. It is to be remembered that the University was established by the State and is under the control of the State, and the enactment of the statute may have been induced by the opinion that membership in the prohibited societies divided the attention of the students and distracted from that singleness of purpose which the State desired to exist in its public educational institutions. It is not for us to entertain conjectures in opposition to the views of the State and annul its regulations upon disputable considerations of their wisdom or necessity." (Emphasis supplied.)

It was on the foregoing argument that this Court sustained the power of Mississippi to curtail the First Amendment's right of peaceable assembly. And the same reasons are equally applicable to curtailing in the States' public schools the right to complete freedom of expression. Iowa's public schools, like Mississippi's university, are operated to give students an opportunity to learn, not to talk politics by actual speech, or by "symbolic" speech. And, as I have pointed out before, the record amply shows that public protest in the school classes against the Vietnam war "distracted from that singleness of purpose which the State [here Iowa] desired to exist in its public educational institutions." Here the Court should accord Iowa educational institutions the same right to determine for themselves to what extent free expression should be allowed in its schools as it accorded Mississippi with reference to freedom of assembly. But even if the record were silent as to protests against the Vietnam war distracting students from their assigned class work, members of this Court, like all other citizens, know, without being told, that the disputes over the wisdom of the Vietnam war have disrupted and divided this country as few other issues ever have. Of course students, like other people, cannot concentrate on lesser issues when black armbands are being ostentatiously displayed in their presence to call attention to the wounded and dead of the war, some of the wounded and the dead being their friends and neighbors. It was, of course, to distract the attention of other students that some students insisted up to the very point of their own suspension from school that they were determined to sit in school with their symbolic armbands.

Change has been said to be truly the law of life but sometimes the old and the tried and true are worth holding. The schools of this Nation have undoubtedly contributed to giving us tranquility and to making us a more law-abiding people. Uncontrolled and uncontrollable liberty is an enemy to domestic peace. We cannot close our eyes to the fact that some of the country's greatest problems are crimes committed by the youth, too many of school age. School discipline, like parental discipline, is an integral and important part of training our children to be good citizens—to be better citizens. Here a very small number of students have crisply and summarily refused to obey a school order designed to give pupils who want to learn the opportunity to do so. One does not need to be a prophet or the son of a prophet to know that after the Court's holding today some students in Iowa schools and indeed in all schools will be ready, able, and willing to defy their teachers on practically all orders. This is the more unfortunate for the schools since groups of students all over the land are already running loose, conducting break-ins, sit-ins, lie-ins, and smash-ins. Many of these student groups, as is all too familiar to all who read the newspapers and watch the television news programs, have already engaged in rioting, property seizures, and destruction. They have picketed schools to force students not to cross their picket lines and have too often violently attacked earnest but frightened students who wanted an education that the pickets did not want them to get. Students engaged in such activities are apparently confident that they know far more about how to operate public school systems than do their parents, teachers, and elected school officials. It is no answer to say that the particular students here have not yet reached such high points in their demands to attend classes in order to exercise their political pressures. Turned loose with lawsuits for damages and injunctions against their teachers as they are here, it is nothing but wishful thinking to imagine that young, immature students will not soon believe it is their right to control the schools rather than the right of the States that collect the taxes to hire the teachers for the benefit of the pupils. This case, therefore, wholly without constitutional reasons in my judgment, subjects all the public schools in the country to the whims and caprices of their loudest-mouthed, but maybe not their brightest, students. I, for one, am not fully persuaded that school pupils are wise enough, even with this Court's expert help from Washington, to run the 23,390 public school systems in our 50 States. I wish, therefore, wholly to disclaim any purpose on my part to hold that the Federal Constitution compels the teachers, parents, and elected school officials to surrender control of the American public school system to public school students. I dissent.

MR. JUSTICE HARLAN, dissenting.

I certainly agree that state public school authorities in the discharge of their responsibilities are not wholly exempt from the requirements of the Fourteenth Amendment respecting the freedoms of expression and association. At the same time I am reluctant to believe that there is any disagreement between the majority and myself on the proposition that school officials should be accorded the widest authority in maintaining discipline and good order in their institutions. To translate that proposition into a workable constitutional rule, I would, in cases like this, cast upon those complaining the burden of showing that a particular school measure was motivated by other than legitimate school concerns—for example, a desire to prohibit the expression of an unpopular point of view, while permitting expression of the dominant opinion.

Finding nothing in this record which impugns the good faith of respondents in promulgating the armband regulation, I would affirm the judgment below.

PENNSYLVANIA ASSOCIATION FOR RETARDED CHILDREN V. COMMONWEALTH OF PENNSYLVANIA, 334 F. SUPP. 12471 (1971)

UNITED STATES DISTRICT COURT FOR THE EASTERN DISTRICT OF PENNSYLVANIA
DECIDED OCTOBER 8, 1971

And now, this 7th day of October, 1971, the parties having consented through their counsel to certain findings and conclusions and to the relief to be provided to the named plaintiffs and to the members of their class, the provisions of the Consent Agreement between the parties set out below are hereby approved and adopted and it is hereby so ordered.

And for the reasons set out below it is ordered that defendants the Commonwealth of Pennsylvania, the Secretary of the Department of Education, the State Board of Education, the Secretary of the Department of Public Welfare, the named defendant school districts and intermediate units and each of the School Districts and Intermediate Units in the Commonwealth of Pennsylvania, their officers, employees, agents and successors be and they hereby are enjoined as follows:

(a) from applying Section 1304 of the Public School Code of 1949, 24 Purd. Stat. Sec. 13-1304, so as to postpone or in any way to deny to any mentally retarded child access to a free public program of education and training;

(b) from applying Section 1326 or Section 1330(2) of the School Code of 1949, 24 Purd. Stat. Secs. 13-1326, 13-1330(2) so as to postpone, to terminate or in any way to deny to any mentally retarded child access to a free public program of education and training;

(c) from applying Section 1371(1) of the School Code of 1949, 24 Purd. Stat. Sec. 13-1371(1) so as to deny to any mentally retarded child access to a free public program of education and training;

(d) from applying Section 1376 of the School Code of 1949, 24 Purd. Stat. Sec. 13-1376, so as to deny tuition or tuition and maintenance to any mentally retarded person except on the same terms as may be applied to other exceptional children, including brain damaged children generally;

(e) from denying homebound instruction under Section 1372(3) of the School Code of 1949, 24 Purd. Stat. Sec. 13-1372(3) to any mentally retarded child merely because no physical disability accompanies the retardation or because retardation is not a short-term disability.

(f) from applying Section 1375 of the School Code of 1949, 24 Purd. Stat. Sec. 13-1375, so as to deny to any mentally retarded child access to a free public program of education and training;

(g) to immediately re-evaluate the named plaintiffs, and to accord to each of them, as soon as possible but in no event later than October 13, 1971, access to a free public program of education and training appropriate to his learning capacities;

(h) to provide, as soon as possible but in no event later than September 1, 1972, to every retarded person between the ages of six and twenty-one years as of the date of this Order and thereafter, access to a free public program of education and training appropriate to his learning capacities;

(i) to provide, as soon as possible but in no event later than September 1, 1972, wherever defendants provide a preschool program of education and training for children aged less than six years of age, access to a free public program of education and training appropriate to his learning capacities to every mentally retarded child of the same age.

The above Orders are entered as interim Orders only and without prejudice, pending notice, as described in Paragraph 3 below, to the class of plaintiffs and to the class of defendants determined in Paragraphs 1 and 2 below.

Any member of the classes so notified who may wish to be heard before permanent Orders are entered shall enter his appearance and file a written statement of objections with the Clerk of this Court on or before October 20, 1971. Any objections so entered will be heard by the Court at 10 o'clock on October 22, 1971.

CONSENT AGREEMENT

The Complaint in this action having been filed on January 7, 1971, alleging the unconstitutionality of certain Pennsylvania statutes and practices under the Equal Protection Clause of the Fourteenth Amendment and certain pendent claims; a three-judge court having been constituted, after motion, briefing and argument thereon, on May 26, 1971; an Order and Stipulation having been entered on June 18, 1971, requiring notice and a due process hearing before the educational assignment of any retarded child may be changed; and evidence having been received at preliminary hearing on August 12, 1971;

Now, therefore, this 7th of October 1971, the parties being desirous of effecting an amicable settlement of this action, the parties by their counsel agree, subject to the approval and Order of this Court, as follows:

I.

1. This action may and hereby shall be maintained by plaintiffs as a class action on behalf of all mentally retarded persons, residents of the Commonwealth of

Pennsylvania, who have been, are being, or may be denied access to a free public program of education and training while they are, or were, less than twenty-one years of age.

It is expressly understood, subject to the provisions of Paragraph 44 below, that the immediate relief hereinafter provided shall be provided to those persons less than twenty-one years of age as of the date of the Order of the Court herein.

2. This action may and hereby shall be maintained against defendant school districts and intermediate units as a class action against all of the School Districts and Intermediate Units of the Commonwealth of Pennsylvania.

3. Pursuant to Rule 23, Fed. R. Civ. P., notice of the extent of the Consent Agreement and the proposed Order approving this Consent Agreement, in the form set out in Appendix A, shall be given as follows:

   (a) to the class of defendants, by the Secretary of Education, by mailing immediately a copy of this proposed Order and Consent Agreement to the Superintendent and the Director of Special Education of each School District and Intermediate Unit in the Commonwealth of Pennsylvania;

   (b) to the class of plaintiffs, (i) by the Pennsylvania Association for Retarded Children, by immediately mailing a copy of this proposed Order and Consent Agreement to each of its Chapters in fifty-four counties of Pennsylvania; (ii) by the Department of Justice, by causing an advertisement in the form set out in Appendix A, to be placed in one newspaper of general circulation in each County in the Commonwealth; and (iii) by delivery of a joint press release of the parties to the television and radio stations, newspapers, and wire services in the Commonwealth.

II.

4. Expert testimony in this action indicates that all mentally retarded persons are capable of benefiting from a program of education and training; that the greatest number of retarded persons, given such education and training, are capable of achieving self-sufficiency, and the remaining few, with such education and training, are capable of achieving some degree of self-care; that the earlier such education and training begins, the more thoroughly and the more efficiently a mentally retarded person will benefit from it; and, whether begun early or not, that a mentally retarded person can benefit at any point in his life and development from a program of education and training.

5. The Commonwealth of Pennsylvania has undertaken to provide a free public education to all of its children between the ages of six and twenty-one years, and, even more specifically, has undertaken to provide education and training for all of its exceptional children.

6. Having undertaken to provide a free public education to all of its children, including its exceptional children, the Commonwealth of Pennsylvania may not deny any mentally retarded child access to a free public program of education and training.

7. It is the Commonwealth's obligation to place each mentally retarded child in a free, public program of education and training appropriate to the child's capacity, within the context of a presumption that, among the alternative programs of education and training required by statute to be available, placement in a regular public school class is preferable to placement in a special public school class and placement in a special public school class is preferable to placement in any other type of program of education and training.

III.

Section 1304

8. Section 1304 of the School Code of 1949, as amended, 24 Purd. Stat. Sec. 13-1304, provides:

   "Admission of beginners

   The admission of beginners to the public schools shall be confined to the first two weeks of the annual school term in districts operating on an annual promotion basis, and to the first two weeks of either the first or the second semester of the school term to districts operating on a semi-annual promotion basis. Admission shall be limited to beginners who have attained the age of five years and seven months before the first day of September if they are to be admitted in the fall, and to those who have attained the age of five years and seven months before the first day of February if they are to be admitted at the beginning of the second semester. The board of school directors of any school district may admit beginners who are less than five years and seven months of age, in accordance with standards prescribed by the State Board of Education. The board of school directors may refuse to accept or retain beginners who have not attained a mental age of five years, as determined by the supervisor of special education or a properly certificated public school psychologist in accordance with standards prescribed by the State Board of Education.

   "The term 'beginners,' as used in this section, shall mean any child that should enter the lowest grade of the primary school or the lowest primary class above the kindergarten level."

9. The Secretary of Education, the State Board of Education, the named School Districts and Intermediate Units, on their own behalf and on behalf of all School Districts and Intermediate Units in the Commonwealth of Pennsylvania, each of them, for themselves, their officers, employees, agents, and successors agree that they shall cease and desist from applying Section 1304 so as to postpone or in any way to deny access to a free public program of education and training to any mentally retarded child.
10. The Attorney General of the Commonwealth of Pennsylvania (hereinafter "the Attorney General") agrees to issue an Opinion declaring that Section 1304 means only that a school district may refuse to accept into or to retain in the lowest grade of the regular primary school or the lowest regular primary class above the kindergarten level, any child who has not attained a mental age of five years.
11. The Attorney General of the Commonwealth of Pennsylvania shall issue an Opinion thus construing Section 1304, and the State Board of Education (hereinafter "the Board") shall issue regulations to implement said construction and to supersede Sections 5-200 of the Pupil Attendance Regulations, copies of which Opinion and Regulations shall be filed with the Court and delivered to counsel for plaintiffs on or before October 25, 1971, and they shall be issued and promulgated respectively on or before October 27, 1971.
12. The aforementioned Opinion and Regulations shall (a) provide for notice and an opportunity for a hearing as set out in this Court's Order of June 18, 1971, before a child's admission as a beginner in the lowest grade of a regular primary school, or the lowest regular primary class above kindergarten, may be postponed; (b) require the automatic re-evaluation every two years of any educational assignment other than to a regular class, and (c) provide for an annual re-evaluation at the request of the child's parent or guardian, and (d) provide upon each such re-evaluation for notice and an opportunity for a hearing as set out in this Court's Order of June 18, 1971.
13. The aforementioned Opinion and Regulations shall also require the timely placement of any child whose admission to regular primary school or to the lowest regular

primary class above kindergarten is postponed, or who is not retained in such school or class, in a free public program of education and training pursuant to Sections 1371 through 1382 of the School Code of 1949, as amended 24 Purd. Stat. Sec. 13-1371 through Sec. 13-1382.

Section 1326

14. Section 1326 of the School Code of 1949, as amended, 24 Purd. Stat. Sec. 13-1326, provides:

    "Definitions: The term 'compulsory school age,' as hereinafter used, shall mean the period of a child's life from the time the child's parents elect to have the child enter school, which shall be not later than at the age of eight (8) years, until the age of seventeen (17) years. The term shall not include any child who holds a certificate of graduation from a regularly accredited senior high school."

15. The Secretary of Education, the State Board of Education, the named School Districts and Intermediate Units, on their own behalf and on behalf of all School Districts and Intermediate Units in the Commonwealth of Pennsylvania, each of them, for themselves, their officers, employees, agents and successors agree that they shall cease and desist from applying Section 1326 so as to postpone, to terminate, or in any way to deny access to a free public program of education and training to any mentally retarded child.
16. The Attorney General agrees to issue an Opinion declaring that Section 1326 means only that parents of a child have a compulsory duty while the child is between eight and seventeen years of age to assure his attendance in a program of education and training; and Section 1326 does not limit the ages between which a child must be granted access to a free, public program of education and training. Defendants are bound by Section 1301 of the School Code of 1949, 24 Purd. Stat. Sec. 13-1301, to provide free public education to all children six to twenty-one years of age. In the event that a parent elects to exercise the right of a child six through eight years and/or seventeen through twenty-one years of age to a free public education, defendants may not deny such child access to a program of education and training. Furthermore, if a parent does not discharge the duty of compulsory attendance with regard to any mentally retarded child between eight and seventeen years of age, defendants must and shall take those steps necessary to compel the child's attendance pursuant to Section 1327 of the School Code of 1949, 24 Purd. Stat. Sec. 13-1327, and related provisions of the School Code, and to the relevant regulations with regard to compulsory attendance promulgated by the Board.
17. The Attorney General shall issue an Opinion thus construing Section 1326, and related Sections, and the Board shall promulgate Regulations to implement said construction, copies of which Opinion and Regulations shall be filed with the Court and delivered to plaintiffs' counsel on or before October 25, 1971, and they shall be issued and promulgated respectively on or before October 27, 1971.

Section 1330(2)

18. Section 1330(2) of the School Code of 1949, as amended, 24 Purd. Stat. Sec. 13-1330(2) provides:

    "Exceptions to compulsory attendance.

    The provisions of this act requiring regular attendance shall not apply to any child who:

    . . .

(2) Has been examined by an approved mental clinic or by a person certified as a public school psychologist or psychological examiner, and has been found to be unable to profit from fur-

ther public school attendance, and who has been reported to the board of school directors and excused, in accordance with regulations prescribed by the State Board of Education."

19. The Secretary of Education, the State Board of Education, the named School Districts and Intermediate Units, on their own behalf and on behalf of all School Districts and Intermediate Units, each of them, for themselves, their officers, employees, agents, and successors agree that they shall cease and desist from applying Section 1330(2) so as to terminate or in any way to deny access to a free public program of education and training to any mentally retarded child.
20. The Attorney General agrees to issue an Opinion declaring that Section 1330(2) means only that a parent may be excused from liability under the compulsory attendance provisions of the School Code when, with the approval of the local school board and the Secretary of Education and a finding by an approved clinic or public school psychologist or psychological examiner, the parent elects to withdraw the child from attendance. Section 1330(2) may not be invoked by defendants, contrary to the parents' wishes, to terminate or in any way to deny access to a free public program of education and training to any mentally retarded child. Furthermore, if a parent does not discharge the duty of compulsory attendance with regards to any mentally retarded child between eight and seventeen years of age, defendants must and shall take those steps necessary to compel the child's attendance pursuant to Section 1327 and related provisions of the School Code and to the relevant regulations with regard to compulsory attendance promulgated by the Board.
21. The Attorney General shall issue an Opinion so construing Section 1330(2) and related provisions and the Board shall promulgate Regulations to implement said construction and to supersede Section 5-400 of the Pupil Attendance Regulations, a copy of which Opinion and Regulations shall be filed with the Court and delivered to counsel for plaintiff on or before October 25, 1971, and they shall be issued and promulgated respectively on or before October 27, 1971.

Pre-School Education

22. Defendants, the Commonwealth of Pennsylvania, the Secretary of Education, the State Board of Education, the named School Districts and Intermediate Units, on their own behalf and on behalf of all School Districts and Intermediate Units in the Commonwealth of Pennsylvania, the Secretary of Public Welfare, each of them, for themselves, their officers, employees, agents and successors agree that they shall cease and desist from applying Section 1371(1) of the School Code of 1949, as amended, 24 Purd. Stat. Sec. 13-1371(1) so as to deny access to a free public program of education and training to any mentally retarded child, and they further agree that wherever the Department of Education through its instrumentalities, the School Districts and Intermediate Units, or the Department of Public Welfare through any of its instrumentalities provides a pre-school program of education and training to children below the age of six, they shall also provide a program of education and training appropriate to their learning capacities to all retarded children of the same age.
23. Section 1371(1) of the School Code of 1949, as amended, 24 Purd. Stat. Sec. 13-1371(1), provides:

"Definition of exceptional children; reports; examination

(1) The term 'exceptional children' shall mean children of school age who deviate from the average in physical, mental, emotional or social characteristics to such an extent that they require special educational facilities or services and shall include all children in detention homes."

24. The Attorney General agrees to issue an Opinion declaring that the phrase "children of school age" as used in Section 1371 means children aged six to twenty-one and

also, whenever the Department of Education through any of its instrumentalities, the local School District, Intermediate Unit, or the Department of Public Welfare, through any of its instrumentalities, provides a pre-school program of education or training for children below the age of six, whether kindergarten or however so called, means all mentally retarded children who have reached the age less than six at which pre-school programs are available to others.

25. The Attorney General shall issue an Opinion thus construing Section 1371 and the Board shall issue regulations to implement said construction, copies of which Opinion and Regulations shall be filed with the Court and delivered to counsel for plaintiffs on or before October 25, 1971, and they shall be issued and promulgated respectively on or before October 27, 1971.

Tuition and Tuition and Maintenance

26. The Secretary of Education, the State Board of Education, the named School Districts and Intermediate Units, on their own behalf and on behalf of all School Districts and Intermediate Units in the Commonwealth of Pennsylvania, each of them, for themselves, their officers, employees, agents and successors agree that they shall cease and desist from applying Section 1376 of the School Code of 1949, as amended, 24 Purd. Stat. Sec. 13-1376, so as to deny tuition or tuition and maintenance to any mentally retarded person.
27. The Attorney General agrees to issue an Opinion, and the Council of Basic Education of the State Board of Education agrees to promulgate Regulations, construing the term "brain damage" as used in Section 1376 and as defined in the Board's "Criteria for Approval . . . of Reimbursement" so as to include thereunder all mentally retarded persons, thereby making available to them tuition for day school and tuition and maintenance for residential school up to the maximum sum available for day school or residential school, whichever provides the more appropriate program of education and training. Copies of the aforesaid Opinion and Regulations shall be filed with the Court and delivered to counsel for plaintiff on or before October 25, 1971, and they shall be issued and promulgated respectively on or before October 27, 1971.
28. Defendants may deny or withdraw payments of tuition or tuition and maintenance whenever the school district or intermediate unit in which a mentally retarded child resides provides a program of special education and training appropriate to the child's learning capacities into which the child may be placed.
29. The decision of defendants to deny or withdraw payments of tuition or tuition and maintenance shall be deemed a change in educational assignment as to which notice shall be given and an opportunity for a hearing afforded as set out in this Court's order of June 18, 1971.

Homebound Instruction

30. Section 1372(3) of the School Code of 1949, as amended, 24 Purd. Stat. Sec. 13-1372(3), provides in relevant part:

    "Standards; plans; special classes or schools

    . . .

(3) Special Classes or Schools Established and Maintained by School Districts.

. . . If . . . it is not feasible to form a special class in any district or to provide such education for any [exceptional] child in the public schools of the district, the board of school directors of the district shall secure such proper education and training outside the public schools of the district or in special institutions, or by providing for teaching the child in his home. . . . "

31. The Secretary of Education, the State Board of Education, the named School Districts and Intermediate Units, on their own behalf and on behalf of all School Districts and

Intermediate Units in the Commonwealth of Pennsylvania, each of them, for themselves, their officials, employees, agents and successors agree that they shall cease and desist from denying homebound instruction under Section 1372(3) to mentally retarded children merely because no physical disability accompanies the retardation or because retardation is not a short-term disability.

32. The Attorney General agrees to issue an Opinion declaring that a mentally retarded child, whether or not physically disabled, may receive homebound instruction and the State Board of Education and/or the Secretary of Education agrees to promulgate revised Regulations and forms in accord therewith, superseding the "Homebound Instruction Manual" (1970) insofar as it concerns mentally retarded children.
33. The aforesaid Opinion and Regulations shall also provide:
    (a) that homebound instruction is the least preferable of the programs of education and training administered by the Department of Education and a mentally retarded child shall not be assigned to it unless it is the program most appropriate to the child's capacities;
    (b) that homebound instruction shall involve education and training for at least five hours a week;
    (c) that an assignment to homebound instruction shall be re-evaluated not less than every three months, and notice of the re-evaluation and an opportunity for a hearing thereon shall be accorded to the parent or guardian, as set out in the Order of this Court dated June 18, 1971;
34. Copies of the aforementioned Opinion and Regulations shall be filed with the Court and delivered to counsel for plaintiffs on or before October 25, 1971, and they shall be issued and promulgated respectively on or before October 27, 1971.

Section 1375

35. Section 1375 of the School Code of 1949, as amended, 24 Purd. Stat. Sec. 13-1375, provides:

    "Uneducable children provided for by Department of Public Welfare."

    "The State Board of Education shall establish standards for temporary or permanent exclusion from the public school of children who are found to be uneducable and untrainable in the public schools. Any child who is reported by a person who is certified as a public school psychologist as being uneducable and untrainable in the public schools, may be reported by the board of school directors to the Superintendent of Public Instruction and when approved by him, in accordance with the standards of the State Board of Education, shall be certified to the Department of Public Welfare as a child who is uneducable and untrainable in the public schools. When a child is thus certified, the public schools shall be relieved of the obligation of providing education or training for such child. The Department of Public Welfare shall thereupon arrange for the care, training and supervision of such child in a manner not inconsistent with the laws governing mentally defective individuals."
36. Defendants the Commonwealth of Pennsylvania, the Secretary of Education, the State Board of Education, the named School Districts and Intermediate Units, on their own behalf and on behalf of all School Districts and Intermediate Units in the Commonwealth of Pennsylvania, and the Secretary of Public Welfare, each of them, for themselves, their officers, employees, agents and successors agree that they shall cease and desist from applying Section 1375 so as to deny access to a free public program of education and training to any mentally retarded child.
37. The Attorney General agrees to issue an Opinion declaring that since all children are capable of benefiting from a program of education and training, Section 1375 means

that insofar as the Department of Public Welfare is charged to "arrange for the care, training and supervision" of a child certified to it, the Department of Public Welfare must provide a program of education and training appropriate to the capacities of that child.

38. The Attorney General agrees to issue an Opinion declaring that Section 1375 means that when it is found, on the recommendation of a public school psychologist and upon the approval of the local board of school directors and the Secretary of Education, as reviewed in the due process hearing as set out in the Order of this Court dated June 18, 1971, that a mentally retarded child would benefit more from placement in a program of education and training administered by the Department of Public Welfare than he would from any program of education and training administered by the Department of Education, he shall be certified to the Department of Public Welfare for placement in a program of education and training.

39. To assure that any program of education and training administered by the Department of Public Welfare shall provide education and training appropriate to a child's capacities the plan referred to in Paragraph 49 below shall specify, inter alia,
   (a) the standards for hours of instruction, pupil-teacher ratios, curriculum, facilities, and teacher qualifications that shall be met in programs administered by the Department of Public Welfare;
   (b) the standards which will qualify any mentally retarded person who completes a program administered by the Department of Public Welfare for a High School Certificate or a Certificate of Attendance as contemplated in Sections 8-132 and 8-133 of the Special Education Regulations;
   (c) the reports which will be required in the continuing discharge by the Department of Education of its duty under Section 1302(1) of the Administrative Code of 1929, as amended, 71 P.S. Sec. 352(1), to inspect and to require reports of programs of education and training administered by the Department of Public Welfare, which reports shall include, for each child in such programs an annual statement of educational strategy (as defined in Section 8-123 of the Special Education Regulations) for the coming year and at the close of the year an evaluation of that strategy;
   (d) that the Department of Education shall exercise the power under Section 1926 of the School Code of 1949, as amended, 24 Purd. Stat. Sec. 19-1926 to supervise the programs of education and training in all institutions wholly or partly supported by the Department of Public Welfare, and the procedures to be adopted therefor.

40. The Attorney General agrees to issue an Opinion so construing Section 1375 and the Board to promulgate Regulations implementing said construction, which Opinion and Regulations shall also provide:
   (a) that the Secretary of Education shall be responsible for assuring that every mentally retarded child is placed in a program of education and training appropriate to his learning capacities, and to that end, by Rules of Procedure requiring that reports of the annual census and evaluation, under Section 1371(2) of the School Code of 1949, as amended, 24 Purd. Stat. 13-1371(2), be made to him, he shall be informed as to the identity, condition, and educational status of every mentally retarded child within the various school districts.
   (b) that should it appear that the provisions of the School Code relating to the proper education and training of mentally retarded children have not been complied with or the needs of the mentally retarded child are not being adequately served in any program administered by the Department of Public Welfare, the Department of Education shall provide such education and training pursuant to Section 1372(5) of the School Code of 1949, as amended, 21 Purd. Stat. Sec. 13-1372(5).

(c) that the same right to notice and an opportunity for a hearing as is set out in the Order of this Court of June 18, 1971, shall be accorded on any change in educational assignment among the programs of education and training administered by the Department of Public Welfare.

(d) that not less than every two years the assignment of any mentally retarded child to a program of education and training administered by the Department of Public Welfare shall be re-evaluated by the Department of Education and upon such re-evaluation, notice and an opportunity to be heard shall be accorded as set out in the Order of this Court, dated June 18, 1971.

40. Copies of the aforesaid Opinion and Regulations shall be filed with the Court and delivered to counsel for plaintiffs on or before October 25, 1971, and they shall be issued and promulgated respectively on or before October 27, 1971.

IV.

41. Each of the named plaintiffs shall be immediately re-evaluated by defendants and, as soon as possible, but in no event later than October 13, 1971, shall be accorded access to a free public program of education and training appropriate to his learning capacities.

42. Every retarded person between the ages of six and twenty-one years as of the date of this Order and thereafter shall be provided access to a free public program of education and training appropriate to his capacities as soon as possible but in no event later than September 1, 1972.

43. Wherever defendants provide a pre-school program of education and training for children less than six years of age, whether kindergarten or howsoever called, every mentally retarded child of the same age as of the date of this Order and hereafter shall be provided access to a free public program of education and training appropriate to his capacities as soon as possible but in no event later than September 1, 1972.

44. The parties explicitly reserve their right to hearing and argument on the question of the obligation of defendants to accord compensatory educational opportunity to members of the plaintiff class of whatever age who were denied access to a free public program of education and training without notice and without a due process hearing while they were aged six years to twenty-one years, for a period equal to the period of such wrongful denial.

45. To implement the aforementioned relief and to assure that it is extended to all members of the class entitled to it, Dr. Herbert Goldstein and Dennis E. Haggerty, Esquire are appointed Masters for the purpose of overseeing a process of identification, evaluation, notification, and compliance hereinafter described.

46. Notice of this Order and of the Order of June 18, 1971, in form to be agreed upon by counsel for the parties, shall be given by defendants to the parents and guardian of every mentally retarded person, and of every person thought by defendants to be mentally retarded, of the ages specified in Paragraphs 42 and 43 above, now resident in the Commonwealth of Pennsylvania, who while he was aged four years to twenty-one years was not accorded access to a free public program of education and training, whether as a result of exclusion, postponement, excusal, or in any other fashion, formal or informal.

47. Within thirty days of the date of this Order, defendants shall formulate and shall submit to the Masters for their approval a satisfactory plan to identify, locate, evaluate and give notice of all the persons described in the foregoing paragraph, and to

identify all persons described in Paragraph 44, which plan shall include, but not be limited to, a search of the records of the local school districts, of the intermediate units, of County MH/MR units, of the State Schools and Hospitals, including the waiting lists for admission thereto, and of interim care facilities, and, to the extent necessary, publication in newspapers and the use of radio and television in a manner calculated to reach the persons described in the foregoing paragraph. A copy of the proposed plan shall be delivered to counsel for plaintiffs who shall be accorded a right to be heard thereon.

48. Within ninety days of the date of this Order, defendants shall identify and locate all persons described in paragraph 46 above, give them notice and provide for their evaluation, and shall report to the Masters the names, circumstances, the educational histories and the educational diagnosis of all persons so identified.
49. By February 1, 1972, defendants shall formulate and submit to the Masters for their approval a plan, to be effectuated by September 1, 1972, to commence or recommence a free public program of education and training for all mentally retarded persons described in Paragraph 46 above and aged between four and twenty-one years as of the date of this Order, and for all mentally retarded persons of such ages hereafter. The plan shall specify the range of programs of education and training, their kind and number, necessary to provide an appropriate program of education and training to all mentally retarded children, where they shall be conducted, arrangements for their financing, and, if additional teachers are found to be necessary, the plan shall specify recruitment, hiring, and training arrangements. The plan shall specify such additional standards and procedures, including but not limited to those specified in Paragraph 39 above, as may be consistent with this Order and necessary to its effectuation. A copy of the proposed plan will be delivered to counsel for plaintiffs who shall be accorded a right to be heard thereon.
50. If by September 1, 1972, any local school district or intermediate unit is not providing a free public education to all mentally retarded persons 4 to 21 years of age within its responsibility, the Secretary of Education, pursuant to Section 1372(5) of the Public School Code of 1949, 24 Purd. Stat. 1372(5) shall directly provide, maintain, administer, supervise, and operate programs for the education and training of these children.
51. The Masters shall hear any members of the plaintiff class who may be aggrieved in the implementation of this Order.
52. The Masters shall be compensated by defendants.
53. This Court shall retain jurisdiction of the matter until it has heard the final report of the Masters on or before October 15, 1972.

APPENDIX

NOTICE

The bracketed portions below will appear in the Notice but not in the newspaper advertisement.

To: (1) All parents and guardians of mentally retarded persons resident in the Commonwealth of Pennsylvania

[(2) All School Districts and Intermediate Units in the Commonwealth of Pennsylvania]

Notice is hereby given (1) that a proposed Order approving a Consent Agreement and issuing certain Injunctions in Pennsylvania Association for Retarded Children et al. v. Commonwealth of Pennsylvania, E.D. Pa., C.A. No. 71-42, is on file with the Clerk of the United

States District Court and available for inspection there and in the offices of the Superintendent of each School District and Intermediate Unit in the Commonwealth of Pennsylvania and of each County Chapter of the Pennsylvania Association for Retarded Children.

(2) That the above mentioned action, on behalf of all mentally retarded persons who have been denied access to a free, public program of education and training, was begun on January 7, 1971, raising certain procedural and substantive claims against the laws and practices of the Commonwealth of Pennsylvania, the Department of Education, the Department of Public Welfare, 12 named School Districts and Intermediate Units and the class of all School Districts and Intermediate Units in the Commonwealth, because of their failure to provide a free public education to all mentally retarded children.

(3) That the proposed Order would approve a Consent Agreement entered into by the named parties on October 7, 1971, providing that each mentally retarded child shall be accorded access to a program of education and training, that notice and an opportunity for a hearing shall be accorded before any change in the educational assignment of mentally retarded children, that certain sections of the Public School Code shall be so construed, and that certain Regulations so providing shall be promulgated thereunder, and that a Special Master shall be appointed to oversee the identification by defendants of all mentally retarded children who have been denied an education and the formulation and implementation by defendants of a plan to provide a free, public program of education and training to all mentally retarded children as soon as possible and no later than September 1, 1972, and would also issue certain Injunctions consistent with the Consent Agreement.

(4) That the parents or guardian of any mentally retarded child [or any school district or intermediate unit] who may wish to make an objection to the Proposed Order approving the Consent Agreement may do so by entering an appearance and filing a statement of objections with the Clerk of the United States District Court for the Eastern District of Pennsylvania, 9th and Chestnut Streets, Philadelphia, on or before October 20, 1971. Hearing thereon shall be held before the Court at 10:00 o'clock A.M., October 22, 1971.

SWANN V. CHARLOTTE-MECKLENBURG BOARD OF EDUCATION, 402 U.S. 1 (1971)

SUPREME COURT OF THE UNITED STATES
CERTIORARI TO THE UNITED STATES COURT OF APPEALS FOR THE FOURTH CIRCUIT
ARGUED OCTOBER 12, 1970. DECIDED APRIL 20, 1971.

Syllabus

The Charlotte-Mecklenburg school system, which includes the city of Charlotte, North Carolina, had more than 84,000 students in 107 schools in the 1968-1969 school year. Approximately 29 [percent] (24,000) of the pupils were Negro, about 14,000 of whom attended 21 schools that were at least 99 [percent] Negro. This resulted from a desegregation plan approved by the District Court in 1965, at the commencement of this litigation. In 1968, petitioner Swann moved for further relief based on Green v. County School Board, which required school boards to

> "come forward with a plan that promises realistically to work . . . now . . . until it is clear that state-imposed segregation has been completely removed."

The District Court ordered the school board in April 1969 to provide a plan for faculty and student desegregation. Finding the board's submission unsatisfactory, the District Court appointed an expert to submit a desegregation plan. In February 1970, the expert and the board presented plans, and the court adopted the board's plan, as modified, for the junior and senior high schools, and the expert's proposed plan for the elementary schools. The Court of Appeals affirmed the District Court's order as to faculty desegregation and the secondary school plans, but vacated the order respecting elementary schools, fearing that the provisions for pairing and grouping of elementary schools would unreasonably burden the pupils and the board. The case was remanded to the District Court for reconsideration and submission of further plans. This Court granted certiorari and directed reinstatement of the District Court's order pending further proceedings in that court. On remand the District Court received two new plans, and ordered the board to adopt a plan, or the expert's plan would remain in effect. After the board "acquiesced" in the expert's plan, the District Court directed that it remain in effect.

Held:

1. Today's objective is to eliminate from the public schools all vestiges of state-imposed segregation that was held violative of equal protection guarantees by Brown v. Board of Education, in 1954.
2. In default by the school authorities of their affirmative obligation to proffer acceptable remedies, the district courts have broad power to fashion remedies that will assure unitary school systems.
3. Title IV of the Civil Rights Act of 1964 does not restrict or withdraw from the federal courts their historic equitable remedial powers. The proviso in 42 U.S.C. [Section] 2000c-6 was designed simply to foreclose any interpretation of the Act as expanding the existing powers of the federal courts to enforce the Equal Protection Clause.
4. Policy and practice with regard to faculty, staff, transportation, extracurricular activities, and facilities are among the most important indicia of a segregated system, and the first remedial responsibility of school authorities is to eliminate invidious racial distinctions in those respects. Normal administrative practice should then produce schools of like quality, facilities, and staffs.
5. The Constitution does not prohibit district courts from using their equity power to order assignment of teachers to achieve a particular degree of faculty desegregation. United States v. Montgomery County Board of Education, was properly followed by the lower courts in this case.
6. In devising remedies to eliminate legally imposed segregation, local authorities and district courts must see to it that future school construction and abandonment are not used and do not serve to perpetuate or reestablish a dual system.
7. Four problem areas exist on the issue of student assignment:
   (1) Racial quotas. The constitutional command to desegregate schools does not mean that every school in the community must always reflect the racial composition of the system as a whole; here the District Court's very limited use of the racial ratio—not as an inflexible requirement, but as a starting point in shaping a remedy—was within its equitable discretion.
   (2) One-race schools. While the existence of a small number of one-race, or virtually one-race, schools does not, in itself, denote a system that still practices segregation by law, the court should scrutinize such schools and require the school authorities to satisfy the court that the racial composition does not result from present or past discriminatory action on their part. An optional majority-to-minority transfer provision has long been recognized as a useful part of a desegregation plan, and to be effective such arrangement must provide the transferring student free transportation and available space in the school to which he desires to move.
   (3) Attendance zones. The remedial altering of attendance zones is not, as an interim corrective measure, beyond the remedial powers of a district court. A student

assignment plan is not acceptable merely because it appears to be neutral, for such a plan may fail to counteract the continuing effects of past school segregation. The pairing and grouping of noncontiguous zones is a permissible tool; judicial steps going beyond contiguous zones should be examined in light of the objectives to be sought. No rigid rules can be laid down to govern conditions in different localities.

(4) Transportation. The District Court's conclusion that assignment of children to the school nearest their home serving their grade would not effectively dismantle the dual school system is supported by the record, and the remedial technique of requiring bus transportation as a tool of school desegregation was within that court's power to provide equitable relief. An objection to transportation of students may have validity when the time or distance of travel is so great as to risk either the health of the children or significantly impinge on the educational process; limits on travel time will vary with many factors, but probably with none more than the age of the students.

8. Neither school authorities nor district courts are constitutionally required to make year-by-year adjustments of the racial composition of student bodies once a unitary system has been achieved.

431 F.2d 138, affirmed as to those parts in which it affirmed the District Court's judgment. The District Court's order of August 7, 1970, is also affirmed.

Opinions

BURGER, C.J., delivered the opinion for a unanimous Court.

BURGER, Opinion of the Court

MR. CHIEF JUSTICE BURGER delivered the opinion of the Court.

We granted certiorari in this case to review important issues as to the duties of school authorities and the scope of powers of federal courts under this Court's mandates to eliminate racially separate public schools established and maintained by state action. Brown v. Board of Education (1954) (Brown I).

This case and those argued with it arose in States having a long history of maintaining two sets of schools in a single school system deliberately operated to carry out a governmental policy to separate pupils in schools solely on the basis of race. That was what Brown v. Board of Education was all about. These cases present us with the problem of defining in more precise terms than heretofore the scope of the duty of school authorities and district courts in implementing Brown I and the mandate to eliminate dual systems and establish unitary systems at once. Meanwhile, district courts and courts of appeals have struggled in hundreds of cases with a multitude and variety of problems under this Court's general directive. Understandably, in an area of evolving remedies, those courts had to improvise and experiment without detailed or specific guidelines. This Court, in Brown I, appropriately dealt with the large constitutional principles; other federal courts had to grapple with the flinty, intractable realities of day-to-day implementation of those constitutional commands. Their efforts, of necessity, embraced a process of "trial and error," and our effort to formulate guidelines must take into account their experience.

I

The Charlotte-Mecklenburg school system, the 43d largest in the Nation, encompasses the city of Charlotte and surrounding Mecklenburg County, North Carolina. The area is large—550 square miles—spanning roughly 22 miles east-west and 36 miles north-south. During the 1968-1969 school year, the system served more than 84,000 pupils in 107 schools. Approximately 71 [percent] of the pupils were found to be white, and 29 [percent] Negro. As of June,

1969, there were approximately 24,000 Negro students in the system, of whom 21,000 attended schools within the city of Charlotte. Two-thirds of those 21,000—approximately 14,000 Negro students—attended 21 schools which were either totally Negro or more than 99 [percent] Negro.

This situation came about under a desegregation plan approved by the District Court at the commencement of the present litigation in 1965, 243 F.Supp. 667 (WDNC), aff'd, 369 F.2d 29 (1966), based upon geographic zoning with a free transfer provision. The present proceedings were initiated in September, 1968, by petitioner Swann's motion for further relief based on Green v. County School Board (1968), and its companion cases. All parties now agree that in 1969 the system fell short of achieving the unitary school system that those cases require.

The District Court held numerous hearings and received voluminous evidence. In addition to finding certain actions of the school board to be discriminatory, the court also found that residential patterns in the city and county resulted in part from federal, state, and local government action other than school board decisions. School board action based on these patterns, for example, by locating schools in Negro residential areas and fixing the size of the schools to accommodate the needs of immediate neighborhoods, resulted in segregated education. These findings were subsequently accepted by the Court of Appeals.

In April, 1969, the District Court ordered the school board to come forward with a plan for both faculty and student desegregation. Proposed plans were accepted by the court in June and August, 1969, on an interim basis only, and the board was ordered to file a third plan by November, 1969. In November, the board moved for an extension of time until February, 1970, but when that was denied the board submitted a partially completed plan. In December, 1969, the District Court held that the board's submission was unacceptable and appointed an expert in education administration, Dr. John Finger, to prepare a desegregation plan. Thereafter in February, 1970, the District Court was presented with two alternative pupil assignment plans—the finalized "board plan" and the "Finger plan."

The Board Plan. As finally submitted, the school board plan closed seven schools and reassigned their pupils. It restructured school attendance zones to achieve greater racial balance but maintained existing grade structures and rejected techniques such as pairing and clustering as part of a desegregation effort. The plan created a single athletic league, eliminated the previously racial basis of the school bus system, provided racially mixed faculties and administrative staffs, and modified its free-transfer plan into an optional majority-to-minority transfer system.

The board plan proposed substantial assignment of Negroes to nine of the system's 10 high schools, producing 17 [percent] to 36 [percent] Negro population in each. The projected Negro attendance at the 10th school, Independence, was 2 [percent]. The proposed attendance zones for the high schools were typically shaped like wedges of a pie, extending outward from the center of the city to the suburban and rural areas of the county in order to afford residents of the center city area access to outlying schools.

As for junior high schools, the board plan rezoned the 21 school areas so that, in 20, the Negro attendance would range from 0 [percent] to 38 [percent]. The other school, located in the heart of the Negro residential area, was left with an enrollment of 90 [percent] Negro.

The board plan with respect to elementary schools relied entirely upon gerrymandering of geographic zones. More than half of the Negro elementary pupils were left in nine schools that were 86 [percent] to 100 [percent] Negro; approximately half of the white elementary pupils were assigned to schools 86 [percent] to 100 [percent] white.

The Finger Plan. The plan submitted by the court-appointed expert, Dr. Finger, adopted the school board zoning plan for senior high schools with one modification: it required that an additional 300 Negro students be transported from the Negro residential area of the city to the nearly all-white Independence High School.

The Finger plan for the junior high schools employed much of the rezoning plan of the board, combined with the creation of nine "satellite" zones. Under the satellite plan, inner-city Negro students were assigned by attendance zones to nine outlying predominantly white junior high schools, thereby substantially desegregating every junior high school in the system.

The Finger plan departed from the board plan chiefly in its handling of the system's 76 elementary schools. Rather than relying solely upon geographic zoning, Dr. Finger proposed use of zoning, pairing, and grouping techniques, with the result that student bodies throughout the system would range from 9 [percent] to 38 [percent] Negro.

The District Court described the plan thus:

Like the board plan, the Finger plan does as much by rezoning school attendance lines as can reasonably be accomplished. However, unlike the board plan, it does not stop there. It goes further and desegregates all the rest of the elementary schools by the technique of grouping two or three outlying schools with one black inner city school; by transporting black students from grades one through four to the outlying white schools; and by transporting white students from the fifth and sixth grades from the outlying white schools to the inner city black school.

Under the Finger plan, nine inner-city Negro schools were grouped in this manner with 24 suburban white schools.

On February 5, 1970, the District Court adopted the board plan, as modified by Dr. Finger, for the junior and senior high schools. The court rejected the board elementary school plan and adopted the Finger plan as presented. Implementation was partially stayed by the Court of Appeals for the Fourth Circuit on March 5, and this Court declined to disturb the Fourth Circuit's order (1970).

On appeal, the Court of Appeals affirmed the District Court's order as to faculty desegregation and the secondary school plans, but vacated the order respecting elementary schools. While agreeing that the District Court properly disapproved the board plan concerning these schools, the Court of Appeals feared that the pairing and grouping of elementary schools would place an unreasonable burden on the board and the system's pupils. The case was remanded to the District Court for reconsideration and submission of further plans. This Court granted certiorari, and directed reinstatement of the District Court's order pending further proceedings in that court.

On remand, the District Court received two new plans for the elementary schools: a plan prepared by the United States Department of Health, Education, and Welfare (the HEW plan) based on contiguous grouping and zoning of schools, and a plan prepared by four members of the nine-member school board (the minority plan) achieving substantially the same results as the Finger plan but apparently with slightly less transportation. A majority of the school board declined to amend its proposal. After a lengthy evidentiary hearing, the District Court concluded that its own plan (the Finger plan), the minority plan, and an earlier draft of the Finger plan were all reasonable and acceptable. It directed the board to adopt one of the three or, in the alternative, to come forward with a new, equally effective plan of its own; the court ordered that the Finger plan would remain in effect in the event the school board declined to adopt a new plan. On August 7, the board indicated it would "acquiesce" in the Finger plan, reiterating its view that the plan was unreasonable. The District Court, by order dated August 7, 1970, directed that the Finger plan remain in effect.

II

Nearly 17 years ago, this Court held, in explicit terms, that state-imposed segregation by race in public schools denies equal protection of the laws. At no time has the Court deviated in the slightest degree from that holding or its constitutional underpinnings. None of the parties before us challenges the Court's decision of May 17, 1954, that,

> in the field of public education, the doctrine of "separate but equal" has no place. Separate educational facilities are inherently unequal. Therefore, we hold that the plaintiffs and others similarly situated . . . are, by reason of the segregation complained of, deprived of the equal protection of the laws guaranteed by the Fourteenth Amendment. . . .

Because these are class actions, because of the wide applicability of this decision, and because of the great variety of local conditions, the formulation of decrees in these cases presents problems of considerable complexity.

Brown v. Board of Education. None of the parties before us questions the Court's 1955 holding in Brown II, that school authorities have the primary responsibility for elucidating, assessing, and solving these problems; courts will have to consider whether the action of school authorities constitutes good faith implementation of the governing constitutional principles. Because of their proximity to local conditions and the possible need for further hearings, the courts which originally heard these cases can best perform this judicial appraisal. Accordingly, we believe it appropriate to remand the cases to those courts.

In fashioning and effectuating the decrees, the courts will be guided by equitable principles. Traditionally, equity has been characterized by a practical flexibility in shaping its remedies and by a facility for adjusting and reconciling public and private needs. These cases call for the exercise of these traditional attributes of equity power. At stake is the personal interest of the plaintiffs in admission to public schools as soon as practicable on a nondiscriminatory basis. To effectuate this interest may call for elimination of a variety of obstacles in making the transition to school systems operated in accordance with the constitutional principles set forth in our May 17, 1954, decision. Courts of equity may properly take into account the public interest in the elimination of such obstacles in a systematic and effective manner. But it should go without saying that the vitality of these constitutional principles cannot be allowed to yield simply because of disagreement with them.

Brown v. Board of Education (1955). Over the 16 years since Brown II, many difficulties were encountered in implementation of the basic constitutional requirement that the State not discriminate between public school children on the basis of their race. Nothing in our national experience prior to 1955 prepared anyone for dealing with changes and adjustments of the magnitude and complexity encountered since then. Deliberate resistance of some to the Court's mandates has impeded the good faith efforts of others to bring school systems into compliance. The detail and nature of these dilatory tactics have been noted frequently by this Court and other courts. By the time the Court considered Green v. County School Board, in 1968, very little progress had been made in many areas where dual school systems had historically been maintained by operation of state laws. In Green, the Court was confronted with a record of a freedom of choice program that the District Court had found to operate, in fact, to preserve a dual system more than a decade after Brown II. While acknowledging that a freedom of choice concept could be a valid remedial measure in some circumstances, its failure to be effective in Green required that:

> The burden on a school board today is to come forward with a plan that promises realistically to work . . . now . . . until it is clear that state-imposed segregation has been completely removed.

Green. This was plain language, yet the 1969 Term of Court brought fresh evidence of the dilatory tactics of many school authorities. Alexander v. Holmes County Board of Education, restated the basic obligation asserted in Griffin v. School Board (1964), and Green, supra, that the remedy must be implemented forthwith.

The problems encountered by the district courts and courts of appeals make plain that we should now try to amplify guidelines, however incomplete and imperfect, for the assistance of school authorities and courts. The failure of local authorities to meet their constitutional obligations aggravated the massive problem of converting from the state-enforced discrimination of racially separate school systems. This process has been rendered more difficult by changes since 1954 in the structure and patterns of communities, the growth of student population, movement of families, and other changes, some of which had marked impact on school planning, sometimes neutralizing or negating remedial action before it was fully implemented. Rural areas accustomed for half a century to the consolidated school systems implemented by bus transportation could make adjustments more readily than metropolitan areas with dense and shifting population, numerous schools, congested and complex traffic patterns.

III

The objective today remains to eliminate from the public schools all vestiges of state-imposed segregation. Segregation was the evil struck down by Brown I as contrary to the equal protection guarantees of the Constitution. That was the violation sought to be corrected by the remedial measures of Brown II. That was the basis for the holding in Green that school authorities are clearly charged with the affirmative duty to take whatever steps might be necessary to convert to a unitary system in which racial discrimination would be eliminated root and branch.

If school authorities fail in their affirmative obligations under these holdings, judicial authority may be invoked. Once a right and a violation have been shown, the scope of a district court's equitable powers to remedy past wrongs is broad, for breadth and flexibility are inherent in equitable remedies.

The essence of equity jurisdiction has been the power of the Chancellor to do equity and to mould each decree to the necessities of the particular case. Flexibility, rather than rigidity, has distinguished it. The qualities of mercy and practicality have made equity the instrument for nice adjustment and reconciliation between the public interest and private needs as well as between competing private claims.

Hecht Co. v. Bowles (1944), cited in Brown II. This allocation of responsibility once made, the Court attempted from time to time to provide some guidelines for the exercise of the district judge's discretion and for the reviewing function of the courts of appeals. However, a school desegregation case does not differ fundamentally from other cases involving the framing of equitable remedies to repair the denial of a constitutional right. The task is to correct, by a balancing of the individual and collective interests, the condition that offends the Constitution.

In seeking to define even in broad and general terms how far this remedial power extends, it is important to remember that judicial powers may be exercised only on the basis of a constitutional violation. Remedial judicial authority does not put judges automatically in the shoes of school authorities whose powers are plenary. Judicial authority enters only when local authority defaults.

School authorities are traditionally charged with broad power to formulate and implement educational policy, and might well conclude, for example, that, in order to prepare students to live in a pluralistic society, each school should have a prescribed ratio of Negro to white students reflecting the proportion for the district as a whole. To do this as an educational policy is within the broad discretionary powers of school authorities; absent a finding of a constitutional violation, however, that would not be within the authority of a federal court. As with any equity case, the nature of the violation determines the scope of the remedy. In default by the school authorities of their obligation to proffer acceptable remedies, a district court has broad power to fashion a remedy that will assure a unitary school system.

The school authorities argue that the equity powers of federal district courts have been limited by Title IV of the Civil Rights Act of 1964, 42 U.S.C. [Section] 2000c. The language and the history of Title IV show that it was enacted not to limit, but to define, the role of the Federal Government in the implementation of the Brown I decision. It authorizes the Commissioner of Education to provide technical assistance to local boards in the preparation of desegregation plans, to arrange "training institutes" for school personnel involved in desegregation efforts, and to make grants directly to schools to ease the transition to unitary systems. It also authorizes the Attorney General, in specified circumstances, to initiate federal desegregation suits. Section 2000c(b) defines "desegregation" as it is used in Title IV:

> "Desegregation" means the assignment of students to public schools and within such schools without regard to their race, color, religion, or national origin, but "desegregation" shall not mean the assignment of students to public schools in order to overcome racial imbalance.

Section 2000c-6, authorizing the Attorney General to institute federal suits, contains the following proviso:

> nothing herein shall empower any official or court of the United States to issue any order seeking to achieve a racial balance in any school by requiring the transportation of pupils or students from one school to another or one school district to another in order to achieve such racial balance, or otherwise enlarge the existing power of the court to insure compliance with constitutional standard.

On their face, the sections quoted purport only to insure that the provisions of Title IV of the Civil Rights Act of 1964 will not be read as granting new powers. The proviso in [Section] 2000c-6 is, in terms, designed to foreclose any interpretation of the Act as expanding the existing powers of federal courts to enforce the Equal Protection Clause. There is no suggestion of an intention to restrict those powers or withdraw from courts their historic equitable remedial powers. The legislative history of Title IV indicates that Congress was concerned that the Act might be read as creating a right of action under the Fourteenth Amendment in the situation of so-called "de facto segregation," where racial imbalance exists in the schools but with no showing that this was brought about by discriminatory action of state authorities. In short, there is nothing in the Act that provides us material assistance in answering the question of remedy for state-imposed segregation in violation of Brown I. The basis of our decision must be the prohibition of the Fourteenth Amendment that no State shall "deny to any person within its jurisdiction the equal protection of the laws."

IV

We turn now to the problem of defining with more particularity the responsibilities of school authorities in desegregating a state-enforced dual school system in light of the Equal Protection Clause. Although the several related cases before us are primarily concerned with problems of student assignment, it may be helpful to begin with a brief discussion of other aspects of the process.

In Green, we pointed out that existing policy and practice with regard to faculty, staff, transportation, extracurricular activities, and facilities were among the most important indicia of a segregated system. Independent of student assignment, where it is possible to identify a "white school" or a "Negro school" simply by reference to the racial composition of teachers and staff, the quality of school buildings and equipment, or the organization of sports activities, a prima facie case of violation of substantive constitutional rights under the Equal Protection Clause is shown.

When a system has been dual in these respects, the first remedial responsibility of school authorities is to eliminate invidious racial distinctions. With respect to such matters as transportation, supporting personnel, and extracurricular activities, no more than this may be necessary. Similar corrective action must be taken with regard to the maintenance of buildings and the distribution of equipment. In these areas, normal administrative practice should produce schools of like quality, facilities, and staffs. Something more must be said, however, as to faculty assignment and new school construction.

In the companion Davis case, the Mobile school board has argued that the Constitution requires that teachers be assigned on a "color blind" basis. It also argues that the Constitution prohibits district courts from using their equity power to order assignment of teachers to achieve a particular degree of faculty desegregation. We reject that contention.

In United States v. Montgomery County Board of Education (1969), the District Court set as a goal a plan of faculty assignment in each school with a ratio of white to Negro faculty members substantially the same throughout the system. This order was predicated on the District Court finding that:

> The evidence does not reflect any real administrative problems involved in immediately desegregating the substitute teachers, the student teachers, the night school faculties, and in the evolvement of a really legally adequate program for the substantial desegregation of the faculties of all schools in the system commencing with the school year 1968-69.

Quoted at 395 U.S. at 232.

The District Court, in Montgomery, then proceeded to set an initial ratio for the whole system of at least two Negro teachers out of each 12 in any given school. The Court of Appeals modified the order by eliminating what it regarded as "fixed mathematical" ratios of faculty and substituted an initial requirement of "substantially or approximately" a five-to-one ratio. With respect to the future, the Court of Appeals held that the numerical ratio should be eliminated and that compliance should not be tested solely by the achievement of specified proportions. Id.

We reversed the Court of Appeals and restored the District Court's order in its entirety, holding that the order of the District Judge

> was adopted in the spirit of this Court's opinion in Green . . . in that his plan "promises realistically to work, and promises realistically to work now." The modifications ordered by the panel of the Court of Appeals, while of course not intended to do so, would, we think, take from the order some of its capacity to expedite, by means of specific commands, the day when a completely unified, unitary, nondiscriminatory school system becomes a reality instead of a hope. . . . We also believe that, under all the circumstances of this case, we follow the original plan outlined in Brown II . . . by accepting the more specific and expeditious order of [District] Judge Johnson . . .

395 U.S. at 235-236. The principles of Montgomery have been properly followed by the District Court and the Court of Appeals in this case.

The construction of new schools and the closing of old ones are two of the most important functions of local school authorities and also two of the most complex. They must decide questions of location and capacity in light of population growth, finances, land values, site availability, through an almost endless list of factors to be considered. The result of this will be a decision which, when combined with one technique or another of student assignment, will determine the racial composition of the student body in each school in the system. Over the long run, the consequences of the choices will be far-reaching. People gravitate toward school facilities, just as schools are located in response to the needs of people. The location of schools may thus influence the patterns of residential development of a metropolitan area and have important impact on composition of inner-city neighborhoods.

In the past, choices in this respect have been used as a potent weapon for creating or maintaining a state-segregated school system. In addition to the classic pattern of building schools specifically intended for Negro or white students, school authorities have sometimes, since Brown, closed schools which appeared likely to become racially mixed through changes in neighborhood residential patterns. This was sometimes accompanied by building new schools in the areas of white suburban expansion farthest from Negro population centers in order to maintain the separation of the races with a minimum departure from the formal principles of "neighborhood zoning." Such a policy does more than simply influence the short-run composition of the student body of a new school. It may well promote segregated residential patterns which, when combined with "neighborhood zoning," further lock the school system into the mold of separation of the races. Upon a proper showing, a district court may consider this in fashioning a remedy.

In ascertaining the existence of legally imposed school segregation, the existence of a pattern of school construction and abandonment is thus a factor of great weight. In devising remedies where legally imposed segregation has been established, it is the responsibility of local authorities and district courts to see to it that future school construction and abandonment are not used and do not serve to perpetuate or reestablish the dual system. When necessary, district courts should retain jurisdiction to assure that these responsibilities are carried out. Cf. United States v. Board of Public Instruction (1968); Brewer v. School Board (1968).

V

The central issue in this case is that of student assignment, and there are essentially four problem areas:

(1) to what extent racial balance or racial quotas may be used as an implement in a remedial order to correct a previously segregated system;

(2) whether every all-Negro and all-white school must be eliminated as an indispensable part of a remedial process of desegregation;

(3) what the limits are, if any, on the rearrangement of school districts and attendance zones, as a remedial measure; and

(4) what the limits are, if any, on the use of transportation facilities to correct state-enforced racial school segregation.

Racial Balances or Racial Quotas. The constant theme and thrust of every holding from Brown I to date is that state-enforced separation of races in public schools is discrimination that violates the Equal Protection Clause. The remedy commanded was to dismantle dual school systems.

We are concerned in these cases with the elimination of the discrimination inherent in the dual school systems, not with myriad factors of human existence which can cause discrimination in a multitude of ways on racial, religious, or ethnic grounds. The target of the cases from Brown I to the present was the dual school system. The elimination of racial discrimination in public schools is a large task, and one that should not be retarded by efforts to achieve broader purposes lying beyond the jurisdiction of school authorities. One vehicle can carry only a limited amount of baggage. It would not serve the important objective of Brown I to seek to use school desegregation cases for purposes beyond their scope, although desegregation of schools ultimately will have impact on other forms of discrimination. We do not reach in this case the question whether a showing that school segregation is a consequence of other types of state action, without any discriminatory action by the school authorities, is a constitutional violation requiring remedial action by a school desegregation decree. This case does not present that question and we therefore do not decide it.

Our objective in dealing with the issues presented by these cases is to see that school authorities exclude no pupil of a racial minority from any school, directly or indirectly, on account of race; it does not and cannot embrace all the problems of racial prejudice, even when those problems contribute to disproportionate racial concentrations in some schools.

In this case, it is urged that the District Court has imposed a racial balance requirement of 71 [percent]-29 [percent] on individual schools. The fact that no such objective was actually achieved—and would appear to be impossible—tends to blunt that claim, yet in the opinion and order of the District Court of December 1, 1969, we find that court directing that efforts should be made to reach a 71-29 ratio in the various schools so that there will be no basis for contending that one school is racially different from the others . . . , [t]hat no school [should] be operated with an all-black or predominantly black student body, [and] [t]hat pupils of all grades [should] be assigned in such a way that as nearly as practicable the various schools at various grade levels have about the same proportion of black and white students.

The District Judge went on to acknowledge that variation "from that norm may be unavoidable." This contains intimations that the "norm" is a fixed mathematical racial balance reflecting the pupil constituency of the system. If we were to read the holding of the District Court to require, as a matter of substantive constitutional right, any particular degree of racial balance or mixing, that approach would be disapproved and we would be obliged to reverse. The constitutional command to desegregate schools does not mean that every school in every community must always reflect the racial composition of the school system as a whole.

As the voluminous record in this case shows, the predicate for the District Court's use of the 71 [percent]-29 [percent] ratio was twofold: first, its express finding, approved by the Court of Appeals and not challenged here, that a dual school system had been maintained by the school authorities at least until 1969; second, its finding, also approved by the Court of Appeals, that the school board had totally defaulted in its acknowledged duty to come forward with an acceptable plan of its own, notwithstanding the patient efforts of the District Judge who, on at least three occasions, urged the board to submit plans. As the statement of facts shows, these findings are abundantly supported by the record. It was because of this total failure of the school board that the District Court was obliged to turn to other qualified sources, and Dr. Finger was designated to assist the District Court to do what the board should have done.

We see therefore that the use made of mathematical ratios was no more than a starting point in the process of shaping a remedy, rather than an inflexible requirement. From that starting point, the District Court proceeded to frame a decree that was within its discretionary powers, as an equitable remedy for the particular circumstances. As we said in Green, a school authority's remedial plan or a district court's remedial decree is to be judged by its effectiveness. Awareness of the racial composition of the whole school system is likely to be a useful starting point in shaping a remedy to correct past constitutional violations. In sum, the very limited use made of mathematical ratios was within the equitable remedial discretion of the District Court.

One-race Schools. The record in this case reveals the familiar phenomenon that, in metropolitan areas, minority groups are often found concentrated in one part of the city. In some circumstances, certain schools may remain all or largely of one race until new schools can be provided or neighborhood patterns change. Schools all or predominantly of one race in a district of mixed population will require close scrutiny to determine that school assignments are not part of state-enforced segregation.

In light of the above, it should be clear that the existence of some small number of one-race, or virtually one-race, schools within a district is not, in and of itself, the mark of a system that still practices segregation by law. The district judge or school authorities should make every effort to achieve the greatest possible degree of actual desegregation, and will thus necessarily be concerned with the elimination of one-race schools. No per se rule can adequately embrace all the difficulties of reconciling the competing interests involved; but, in a system with a history of segregation, the need for remedial criteria of sufficient specificity to assure a school authority's compliance with its constitutional duty warrants a presumption against schools that are substantially disproportionate in their racial composition. Where the school authority's proposed plan for conversion from a dual to a unitary system contemplates the continued existence of some schools that are all or predominantly of one race, they have the burden of showing that such school assignments are genuinely nondiscriminatory. The court should scrutinize such schools, and the burden upon the school authorities will be to satisfy the court that their racial composition is not the result of present or past discriminatory action on their part.

An optional majority-to-minority transfer provision has long been recognized as a useful part of every desegregation plan. Provision for optional transfer of those in the majority racial group of a particular school to other schools where they will be in the minority is an indispensable remedy for those students willing to transfer to other schools in order to lessen the impact on them of the state-imposed stigma of segregation. In order to be effective, such a transfer arrangement must grant the transferring student free transportation and space must be made available in the school to which he desires to move. Cf. Ellis v. Board of Public Instruction (1970). The court orders in this and the companion Davis case now provide such an option.

Remedial Altering of Attendance Zones. The maps submitted in these cases graphically demonstrate that one of the principal tools employed by school planners and by courts to break up the dual school system has been a frank—and sometimes drastic— gerrymandering of school districts and attendance zones. An additional step was pairing, "clustering," or "grouping" of schools with attendance assignments made deliberately to accomplish the transfer of Negro students out of formerly segregated Negro schools and transfer of white students to formerly all-Negro schools. More often than not, these zones are neither compact nor contiguous; indeed they may be on opposite ends of the city. As an interim corrective measure, this cannot be said to be beyond the broad remedial powers of a court.

Absent a constitutional violation, there would be no basis for judicially ordering assignment of students on a racial basis. All things being equal, with no history of discrimination, it might well be desirable to assign pupils to schools nearest their homes. But all things are not equal in a system that has been deliberately constructed and maintained to enforce racial segregation. The remedy for such segregation may be administratively awkward, inconvenient, and even bizarre in some situations, and may impose burdens on some; but all awkwardness and inconvenience cannot be avoided in the interim period when remedial adjustments are being made to eliminate the dual school systems.

No fixed or even substantially fixed guidelines can be established as to how far a court can go, but it must be recognized that there are limits. The objective is to dismantle the dual school system. "Racially neutral" assignment plans proposed by school authorities to a district court may be inadequate; such plans may fail to counteract the continuing effects of past school segregation resulting from discriminatory location of school sites or distortion of school size in order to achieve or maintain an artificial racial separation. When school authorities present a district court with a "loaded game board," affirmative action in the form of remedial altering of attendance zones is proper to achieve truly nondiscriminatory assignments. In short, an assignment plan is not acceptable simply because it appears to be neutral.

In this area, we must of necessity rely to a large extent, as this Court has for more than 16 years, on the informed judgment of the district courts in the first instance and on courts of appeals.

We hold that the pairing and grouping of noncontiguous school zones is a permissible tool, and such action is to be considered in light of the objectives sought. Judicial steps in shaping such zones going beyond combinations of contiguous areas should be examined in light of what is said in subdivisions (1), (2), and (3) of this opinion concerning the objectives to be sought. Maps do not tell the whole story, since noncontiguous school zones may be more accessible to each other in terms of the critical travel time, because of traffic patterns and good highways, than schools geographically closer together. Conditions in different localities will vary so widely that no rigid rules can be laid down to govern all situations.

Transportation of Students. The scope of permissible transportation of students as an implement of a remedial decree has never been defined by this Court, and, by the very nature of the problem, it cannot be defined with precision. No rigid guidelines as to student transportation can be given for application to the infinite variety of problems presented in thousands of situations. Bus transportation has been an integral part of the public education system for years, and was perhaps the single most important factor in the transition from the one-room schoolhouse to the consolidated school. Eighteen million of the Nation's public school children, approximately 39 [percent], were transported to their schools by bus in 1969-1970 in all parts of the country.

The importance of bus transportation as a normal and accepted tool of educational policy is readily discernible in this and the companion case, Davis, supra. The Charlotte school authorities did not purport to assign students on the basis of geographically drawn zones until 1965, and then they allowed almost unlimited transfer privileges. The District Court's conclusion that assignment of children to the school nearest their home serving their grade would not produce an effective dismantling of the dual system is supported by the record.

Thus, the remedial techniques used in the District Court's order were within that court's power to provide equitable relief; implementation of the decree is well within the capacity of the school authority.

The decree provided that the buses used to implement the plan would operate on direct routes. Students would be picked up at schools near their homes and transported to the schools they were to attend. The trips for elementary school pupils average about seven miles, and the District Court found that they would take "not over 35 minutes, at the most." This system compares favorably with the transportation plan previously operated in Charlotte, under which, each day, 23,600 students on all grade levels were transported an average of 15 miles one way for an average trip requiring over an hour. In these circumstances, we find no basis for holding that the local school authorities may not be required to employ bus transportation as one tool of school desegregation. Desegregation plans cannot be limited to the walk-in school.

An objection to transportation of students may have validity when the time or distance of travel is so great as to either risk the health of the children or significantly impinge on the educational process. District courts must weigh the soundness of any transportation plan in light of what is said in subdivisions (1), (2), and (3) above. It hardly needs stating that the limits on time of travel will vary with many factors, but probably with none more than the age of the students. The reconciliation of competing values in a desegregation case is, of course, a difficult task with many sensitive facets, but fundamentally no more so than remedial measures courts of equity have traditionally employed.

VI

The Court of Appeals, searching for a term to define the equitable remedial power of the district courts, used the term "reasonableness." In Green, supra, this Court used the term "feasible," and, by implication, "workable," "effective," and "realistic" in the mandate to develop "a plan that promises realistically to work, and . . . to work now." On the facts of this case, we are unable to conclude that the order of the District Court is not reasonable, feasible and workable. However, in seeking to define the scope of remedial power or the limits on remedial power of courts in an area as sensitive as we deal with here, words are poor instruments to convey the sense of basic fairness inherent in equity. Substance, not semantics, must govern, and we have sought to suggest the nature of limitations without frustrating the appropriate scope of equity.

At some point, these school authorities and others like them should have achieved full compliance with this Court's decision in Brown I. The systems would then be "unitary" in the sense required by our decisions in Green and Alexander.

It does not follow that the communities served by such systems will remain demographically stable, for, in a growing, mobile society, few will do so. Neither school authorities nor district courts are constitutionally required to make year-by-year adjustments of the racial composition of student bodies once the affirmative duty to desegregate has been accomplished and racial discrimination through official action is eliminated from the system. This does not mean that federal courts are without power to deal with future problems; but, in the absence of a showing that either the school authorities or some other agency of the State has deliberately attempted to fix or alter demographic patterns to affect the racial composition of the schools, further intervention by a district court should not be necessary.

For the reasons herein set forth, the judgment of the Court of Appeals is affirmed as to those parts in which it affirmed the judgment of the District Court. The order of the District Court, dated August 7, 1970, is also affirmed.

It is so ordered.

MILLS V. BOARD OF EDUCATION OF THE DISTRICT OF COLUMBIA, 348 F. SUPP. 866 (1972)

UNITED STATES DISTRICT COURT FOR THE DISTRICT OF COLUMBIA AUGUST 1, 1972

WADDY, District Judge.

MEMORANDUM OPINION, and JUDGMENT AND DECREE

This is a civil action brought on behalf of seven children of school age by their next friends in which they seek a declaration of rights and to enjoin the defendants from excluding them from the District of Columbia Public Schools and/or denying them publicly supported education and to compel the defendants to provide them with immediate and adequate education and educational facilities in the public schools or alternative placement at public expense. They also seek additional and ancillary relief to effectuate the primary relief. They allege that although they can profit from an education either in regular classrooms with supportive services or in special classes adopted to their needs, they have been labelled as behavioral problems, mentally retarded, emotionally disturbed or hyperactive, and denied admission to the public schools or excluded therefrom after admission, with no provision for alternative educational placement or periodic review. The action was certified as a class action under Rule 23(b)(1) and (2) of Federal Rules of Civil Procedure by order of the Court dated December 17, 1971.

The defendants are the Board of Education of the District of Columbia and its members, the Superintendent of Schools for the District of Columbia and subordinate school officials, the Commissioner of the District of Columbia and certain subordinate officials and the District of Columbia.

THE PROBLEM

The genesis of this case is found (1) in the failure of the District of Columbia to provide publicly supported education and training to plaintiffs and other "exceptional" children, members of their class, and (2) the excluding, suspending, expelling, reassigning and transferring of "exceptional" children from regular public school classes without affording them due process of law.

The problem of providing special education for "exceptional" children (mentally retarded, emotionally disturbed, physically handicapped, hyperactive and other children with behavioral problems) is one of major proportions in the District of Columbia. The precise number of such children cannot be stated because the District has continuously failed to comply with Section 31-208 of the District of Columbia Code which requires a census of all children aged

3 to 18 in the District to be taken. Plaintiffs estimate that there are ". . . 22,000 retarded, emotionally disturbed, blind, deaf, and speech or learning disabled children, and perhaps as many as 18,000 of these children are not being furnished with programs of specialized education." According to data prepared by the Board of Education, Division of Planning, Research and Evaluation, the District of Columbia provides publicly supported special education programs of various descriptions to at least 3880 school age children. However, in a 1971 report to the Department of Health, Education and Welfare, the District of Columbia Public Schools admitted that an estimated 12,340 handicapped children were not to be served in the 1971-72 school year.

Each of the minor plaintiffs in this case qualifies as an "exceptional" child.

Plaintiffs allege in their complaint and defendants admit as follows:

"PETER MILLS is twelve years old, black, and a committed dependent ward of the District of Columbia resident at Junior Village. He was excluded from the Brent Elementary School on March 23, 1971, at which time he was in the fourth grade. Peter allegedly was a 'behavior problem' and was recommended and approved for exclusion by the principal. Defendants have not provided him with a full hearing or with a timely and adequate review of his status. Furthermore, Defendants have failed to provide for his reenrollment in the District of Columbia Public Schools or enrollment in private school. On information and belief, numerous other dependent children of school attendance age at Junior Village are denied a publicly-supported education. Peter remains excluded from any publicly-supported education.

"DUANE BLACKSHEARE is thirteen years old, black, resident at Saint Elizabeth's Hospital, Washington, D.C., and a dependent committed child. He was excluded from the Giddings Elementary School in October, 1967, at which time he was in the third grade. Duane allegedly was a "behavior problem." Defendants have not provided him with a full hearing or with a timely and adequate review of his status. Despite repeated efforts by his mother, Duane remained largely excluded from all publicly-supported education until February, 1971. Education experts at the Child Study Center examined Duane and found him to be capable of returning to regular class if supportive services were provided. Following several articles in the Washington Post and Washington Star, Duane was placed in a regular seventh grade classroom on a two-hour a day basis without any catch-up assistance and without an evaluation or diagnostic interview of any kind. Duane has remained on a waiting list for a tuition grant and is now excluded from all publicly-supported education.

"GEORGE LIDDELL, JR., is eight years old, black, resident with his mother, Daisy Liddell, at 601 Morton Street, N.W., Washington, D.C., and an AFDC recipient. George has never attended public school because of the denial of his application to the Maury Elementary School on the ground that he required a special class. George allegedly was retarded. Defendants have not provided him with a full hearing or with a timely and adequate review of his status. George remains excluded from all publicly-supported education, despite a medical opinion that he is capable of profiting from schooling, and despite his mother's efforts to secure a tuition grant from Defendants.

"STEVEN GASTON is eight years old, black, resident with his mother, Ina Gaston, at 714 9th Street, N.E., Washington, D.C. and unable to afford private instruction. He has been excluded from the Taylor Elementary School since September, 1969, at which time he was in the first grade. Steven allegedly was slightly brain-damaged and hyperactive, and was excluded because he wandered around the classroom. Defendants have not provided him with a full hearing or with a timely and adequate review of his status. Steven was accepted in the Contemporary School, a private school, provided that tuition was paid in full in advance. Despite the efforts of his parents, Steven has remained on a waiting list for the requisite tuition grant from Defendant school system and excluded from all publicly-supported education.

"MICHAEL WILLIAMS is sixteen years old, black, resident at Saint Elizabeth's Hospital, Washington, D.C., and unable to afford private instruction. Michael is epileptic and allegedly slightly retarded. He has been excluded from the Sharpe Health School since October, 1969, at which time he was temporarily hospitalized. Thereafter Michael was excluded from school because of health problems and school absences. Defendants have not provided him with a full hearing or with a timely and adequate review of his status. Despite his mother's efforts, and his attending physician's medical opinion that he could attend school, Michael has remained on a waiting list for a tuition grant and excluded from all publicly-supported education.

"JANICE KING is thirteen years old, black, resident with her father, Andrew King, at 233 Anacostia Avenue, N.E., Washington, D.C., and unable to afford private instruction. She has been denied access to public schools since reaching compulsory school attendance age, as a result of the rejection of her application, based on the lack of an appropriate educational program. Janice is brain-damaged and retarded, with right hemiplegia, resulting from a childhood illness. Defendants have not provided her with a full hearing or with a timely and adequate review of her status. Despite repeated efforts by her parents, Janice has been excluded from all publicly-supported education.

"JEROME JAMES is twelve years old, black, resident with his mother, Mary James, at 2512 Ontario Avenue, N.W., Washington, D.C., and an AFDC recipient. Jerome is a retarded child and has been totally excluded from public school. Defendants have not given him a full hearing or a timely and adequate review of his status. Despite his mother's efforts to secure either public school placement or a tuition grant, Jerome has remained on a waiting list for a tuition grant and excluded from all publicly supported education."

Although all of the named minor plaintiffs are identified as Negroes the class they represent is not limited by their race. They sue on behalf of and represent all other District of Columbia residents of school age who are eligible for a free public education and who have been, or may be, excluded from such education or otherwise deprived by defendants of access to publicly supported education.

Minor plaintiffs are poor and without financial means to obtain private instruction. There has been no determination that they may not benefit from specialized instruction adapted to their needs. Prior to the beginning of the 1971-72 school year minor plaintiffs, through their representatives, sought to obtain publicly supported education and certain of them were assured by the school authorities that they would be placed in programs of publicly supported education and certain others would be recommended for special tuition grants at private schools. However, none of the plaintiff children were placed for the 1971 Fall term and they continued to be entirely excluded from all publicly supported education. After thus trying unsuccessfully to obtain relief from the Board of Education the plaintiffs filed this action on September 24, 1971.

THERE IS NO GENUINE ISSUE OF MATERIAL FACT

Congress has decreed a system of publicly supported education for the children of the District of Columbia. The Board of Education has the responsibility of administering that system in accordance with law and of providing such publicly supported education to all of the children of the District, including these "exceptional" children.

Defendants have admitted in these proceedings that they are under an affirmative duty to provide plaintiffs and their class with publicly supported education suited to each child's needs, including special education and tuition grants, and also, a constitutionally adequate prior hearing and periodic review. They have also admitted that they failed to supply plaintiffs with such publicly supported education and have failed to afford them adequate prior hearing and periodic review. On December 20, 1971 the plaintiffs and defendants agreed to and the Court signed an interim stipulation and order which provided in part as follows:

> "Upon consent and stipulation of the parties, it is hereby ORDERED that:
>
> "1. Defendants shall provide plaintiffs Peter Mills, Duane Blacksheare, Steven Gaston and Michael Williams with a publicly-supported education suited to their (plaintiffs') needs by January 3, 1972."
>
> "2. Defendants shall provide counsel for plaintiffs, by January 3, 1972, a list showing, for every child of school age then known not to be attending a publicly-supported educational program because of suspension, expulsion, exclusion, or any other denial of placement, the name of the child's parent or guardian, the child's name, age, address and telephone number, the date of his suspension, expulsion, exclusion or denial of placement and, without attributing a particular characteristic to any specific child, a breakdown of such list, showing the alleged causal characteristics for such nonattendance and the number of children possessing such alleged characteristics."
>
> "3. By January 3, 1972, defendants shall initiate efforts to identify remaining members of the class not presently known to them, and also by that date, shall notify counsel for plaintiffs of the nature and extent of such efforts. Such efforts shall include, at a minimum, a system-wide survey of elementary and secondary schools, use of the mass written and electronic media, and a survey of District of Columbia agencies who may have knowledge pertaining to such remaining members of the class. By February 1, 1972, defendants shall provide counsel for plaintiffs with the names, addresses and telephone numbers of such remaining members of the class then known to them."
>
> "4. Pending further action by the Court herein, the parties shall consider the selection and compensation of a master for determination of special questions arising out of this action with regard to the placement of children in a publicly-supported educational program suited to their needs."

On February 9, 1972, the Board of Education passed a Resolution which included the following:

Special Education

> "7. All vacant authorized special education positions, whether in the regular, Impact Aid, or other Federal budgets, shall be filled as rapidly as possible within the capability of the Special Education Department. Regardless of the capability of the Department to fill vacant positions, all funds presently appropriated or allotted for special education, whether in the regular, Impact Aid, or other Federal budgets, shall be spent solely for special education."
>
> "8. The Board requests the Corporation Counsel to ask the United States District Court for an extension of time within which to file a response to plaintiffs' motion for summary judgment in Mills v. Board of Education on the grounds that (a) the Board intends to enter into a consent judgment declaring the rights of children in the District of Columbia to a public education; and (b) the Board needs time (not in excess of 30 days) to obtain from the Associate Superintendent for Special Education a precise projection on a monthly basis the cost of fulfilling those budgets."
>
> "9. The Board directs the Rules Committee to devise as soon as possible for the purpose of Mills v. Board of Education rules defining and providing for due process and fair hearings; and requests the Corporation Counsel to lend such assistance to the Board as may be necessary in devising such rules in a form which will meet the requirements of Mills v. Board of Education."

"10. It is the intention of the Board to submit for approval by the Court in Mills v. Board of Education a Memorandum of Understanding setting forth a comprehensive plan for the education, treatment and care of physically or mentally impaired children in the age range from three to twenty-one years. It is hoped that the various other District of Columbia agencies concerned will join with the Board in the submission of this plan.

"It is the further intention of the Board to establish procedures to implement the finding that all children can benefit from education and, have a right to it, by providing for comprehensive health and psychological appraisal of children and the provision for each child of any special education which he may need. The Board will further require that no change in the kind of education provided for a child will be made against his wishes or the wishes of his parent or guardian unless he has been accorded a full hearing on the matter consistent with due process."

Defendants failed to comply with that consent order and there is now pending before the Court a motion of the plaintiffs to require defendants to show cause why they should not be held in contempt for such failure to comply.

On January 21, 1972 the plaintiffs filed a motion for summary judgment and a proposed order and decree for implementation of the proposed judgment and requested a hearing. On March 1, 1972 the defendants responded as follows:

"1. The District of Columbia and its officers who are named defendants to this complaint consent to the entrance of a judgment declaring the rights of the plaintiff class to the effect prayed for in the complaint, as specified below, such rights to be prospectively effective as of March 1, 1972:"

That no child eligible for a publicly supported education in the District of Columbia public schools shall be excluded from a regular public school assignment by a Rule, policy, or practice of the Board of Education of the District of Columbia or its agents unless such child is provided (a) adequate alternative educational services suited to the child's needs, which may include special education or tuition grants, and (b) a constitutionally adequate prior hearing and periodic review of the child's status, progress, and the adequacy of any educational alternative.

It is submitted that the entrance of a declaratory judgment to this effect renders plaintiffs' motion for summary judgment moot.

"2. For response to plaintiffs' motion for a hearing, defendants respectfully request that this Court hold a hearing as soon as practicable at which defendants will present a plan to implement the above declaratory judgment and at which the Court may decide whether further relief is appropriate."

The Court set the date of March 24, 1972, for the hearing that both parties had requested and specifically ordered the defendants to submit a copy of their proposed implementation plan no later than March 20, 1972.

On March 24, 1972, the date of the hearing, the defendants not only had failed to submit their implementation plan as ordered but were also continuing in their violation of the provisions of the Court's order of December 20, 1971. At the close of the hearing on March 24, 1972, the Court found that there existed no genuine issue of a material fact; orally granted plaintiffs' motion for summary judgment, and directed defendants to submit to the Court any proposed plan they might have on or before March 31, 1972. The defendants, other than Cassell, failed to file any proposal within the time directed. However, on April 7, 1972, there was sent to the Clerk of the Court on behalf of the Board of Education and its employees who are defendants in this case the following documents:

1. A proposed form of Order to be entered by the Court.

2. An abstract of a document titled "A District of Columbia Plan for Identification, Assessment, Evaluation, and Placement of Exceptional Children".

3. A document titled "A District of Columbia Plan for Identification, Assessment, Evaluation, and Placement of Exceptional Children".

4. Certain Attachments and Appendices to this Plan.

The letter accompanying the documents contained the following paragraph:

"These documents express the position of the Board of Education and its employees as to what should be done to implement the judgment of the Honorable Joseph C. Waddy, the District Judge presiding over this civil action. The contents of these documents have not been endorsed by the other defendants in this case."

None of the other defendants have filed a proposed order or plan. Nor has any of them adopted the proposal submitted by the Board of Education. Throughout these proceedings it has been obvious to the Court that the defendants have no common program or plan for the alleviation of the problems posed by this litigation and that this lack of communication, cooperation and plan is typical and contributes to the problem.

PLAINTIFFS ARE ENTITLED TO RELIEF

Plaintiffs' entitlement to relief in this case is clear. The applicable statutes and regulations and the Constitution of the United States require it.

Statutes and Regulations

Section 31-201 of the District of Columbia Code requires that:

"Every parent, guardian, or other person residing [permanently or temporarily] in the District of Columbia who has custody or control of a child between the ages of seven and sixteen years shall cause said child to be regularly instructed in a public school or in a private or parochial school or instructed privately during the period of each year in which the public schools of the District of Columbia are in session . . ."

Under Section 31-203, a child may be "excused" from attendance only when

". . . upon examination ordered by . . . [the Board of Education of the District of Columbia], [the child] is found to be unable mentally or physically to profit from attendance at school: Provided, however, That if such examination shows that such child may benefit from specialized instruction adapted to his needs, he shall attend upon such instruction."

Failure of a parent to comply with Section 31-201 constitutes a criminal offense. D.C. Code 31-207. The Court need not belabor the fact that requiring parents to see that their children attend school under pain of criminal penalties presupposes that an educational opportunity will be made available to the children. The Board of Education is required to make such opportunity available. It has adopted rules and regulations consonant with the statutory direction. Chapter XIII of the Board Rules contains the following:

1.1—All children of the ages hereinafter prescribed who are bona fide residents of the District of Columbia are entitled to admission and free tuition in the Public Schools of the District of Columbia, subject to the rules, regulations, and orders of the Board of Education and the applicable statutes.

14.1—Every parent, guardian, or other person residing permanently or temporarily in the District of Columbia who has custody or control of a child residing in the District of Columbia between the ages of seven and sixteen years shall cause said child to be regularly instructed in a public school or in a private or parochial school or instructed privately during the period of each year in which the Public Schools of the District of Columbia are in session, provided that instruction given in such private or parochial school, or privately, is deemed reasonably equivalent by the Board of Education to the instruction given in the Public Schools.

14.3—The Board of Education of the District of Columbia may, upon written recommendation of the Superintendent of Schools, issue a certificate excusing from attendance at school a child who, upon examination by the Department of Pupil Appraisal, Study and Attendance or by the Department of Public Health of the District of Columbia, is found to be unable mentally or physically to profit from attendance at school: Provided, however, that if such examination shows that such child may benefit from specialized instruction adapted to his needs, he shall be required to attend such classes.

Thus the Board of Education has an obligation to provide whatever specialized instruction that will benefit the child. By failing to provide plaintiffs and their class the publicly supported specialized education to which they are entitled, the Board of Education violates the above statutes and its own regulations.

The Constitution—Equal Protection and Due Process

The Supreme Court in Brown v. Board of Education, 347 U.S. 483, 493, 74 S. Ct. 686, 691, 98 L. Ed. 873 (1954) stated:

"Today, education is perhaps the most important function of state and local governments. Compulsory school attendance laws and the great expenditures for education both demonstrate our recognition of the importance of education to our democratic society. It is required in the performance of our most basic public responsibilities, even service in the armed forces. It is the very foundation of good citizenship. Today it is a principal instrument in awakening the child to cultural values, in preparing him for later professional training, and in helping him to adjust normally to his environment. In these days, it is doubtful that any child may reasonably be expected to succeed in life if he is denied the opportunity of an education. Such an opportunity, where the state has undertaken to provide it, is a right which must be made available to all on equal terms." (emphasis supplied)

Bolling v. Sharpe, 347 U.S. 497, 74 S. Ct. 693, 98 L. Ed. 884, Decided the same day as Brown, applied the Brown rationale to the District of Columbia public schools by finding that:

"Segregation in public education is not reasonably related to any proper governmental objective, and thus it imposes on Negro children of the District of Columbia a burden that constitutes an arbitrary deprivation of their liberty in violation of the Due Process Clause."

In Hobson v. Hansen, 269 F. Supp. 401 (D.C.D.C. 1967) Circuit Judge J. Skelly Wright considered the pronouncements of the Supreme Court in the intervening years and stated that " . . . the Court has found the due process clause of the Fourteenth Amendment elastic enough to embrace not only the First and Fourth Amendments, but the self-incrimination clause of the Fifth, the speedy trial, confrontation and assistance of counsel clauses of the Sixth, and the cruel and unusual clause of the Eighth." (269 F. Supp. 401 at 493, citations omitted). Judge Wright concluded "From these considerations the court draws the conclusion that the doctrine of equal educational opportunity—the equal protection clause in its application to public school education—is in its full sweep a component of due process binding on the District under the due process clause of the Fifth Amendment."

In Hobson v. Hansen, supra, Judge Wright found that denying poor public school children educational opportunities equal to that available to more affluent public school children was violative of the Due Process Clause of the Fifth Amendment. A fortiori, the defendants' conduct here, denying plaintiffs and their class not just an equal publicly supported education but all publicly supported education while providing such education to other children, is violative of the Due Process Clause.

Not only are plaintiffs and their class denied the publicly supported education to which they are entitled many are suspended or expelled from regular schooling or specialized instruction or reassigned without any prior hearing and are given no periodic review thereafter. Due process of law requires a hearing prior to exclusion, termination of classification into a special program.

Vought v. Van Buren Public Schools, 306 F. Supp. 1388 (E.D. Mich. 1969); Williams v. Dade County School Board, 441 F.2d 299 (5th Cir. 1971); Cf. Soglin v. Kauffman, 295 F. Supp. 978 (W.D. Wis. 1968); Dixon v. Alabama State Board of Education, 294 F.2d 150 (5th Cir. 1961), cert. den., 368 U.S. 930, 82 S. Ct. 368, 7 L. Ed. 2d 193 (1961); Goldberg v. Kelly, 397 U.S. 254, 90 S. Ct. 1011, 25 L. Ed. 2d 287 (1970).

The Defense

The Answer of the defendants to the Complaint contains the following:

> "These defendants say that it is impossible to afford plaintiffs the relief they request unless:
>
> (a) The Congress of the United States appropriates millions of dollars to improve special education services in the District of Columbia; or
>
> (b) These defendants divert millions of dollars from funds already specifically appropriated for other educational services in order to improve special educational services. These defendants suggest that to do so would violate an Act of Congress and would be inequitable to children outside the alleged plaintiff class."

This Court is not persuaded by that contention.

The defendants are required by the Constitution of the United States, the District of Columbia Code, and their own regulations to provide a publicly-supported education for these "exceptional" children. Their failure to fulfill this clear duty to include and retain these children in the public school system, or otherwise provide them with publicly-supported education, and their failure to afford them due process hearing and periodical review, cannot be excused by the claim that there are insufficient funds. In Goldberg v. Kelly, 397 U.S. 254, 90 S. Ct. 1011, 25 L. Ed. 2d 287 (1969) the Supreme Court, in a case that involved the right of a welfare recipient to a hearing before termination of his benefits, held that Constitutional rights must be afforded citizens despite the greater expense involved. The Court stated at page 266, 90 S. Ct. at page 1019, that "the State's interest that his [welfare recipient] payments not be erroneously terminated, clearly outweighs the State's competing concern to prevent any increase in its fiscal and administrative burdens." Similarly the District of Columbia's interest in educating the excluded children clearly must outweigh its interest in preserving its financial resources. If sufficient funds are not available to finance all of the services and programs that are needed and desirable in the system then the available funds must be expended equitably in such a manner that no child is entirely excluded from a publicly supported education consistent with his needs and ability to benefit therefrom. The inadequacies of the District of Columbia Public School System whether occasioned by insufficient funding or administrative inefficiency, certainly cannot be permitted to bear more heavily on the "exceptional" or handicapped child than on the normal child.

IMPLEMENTATION OF JUDGMENT

This Court has pointed out that Section 31-201 of the District of Columbia Code requires that every person residing in the District of Columbia ". . . who has custody or control of a child between the ages of seven and sixteen years shall cause said child to be regularly instructed in a public school or in a private or parochial school or instructed privately . . ." It is the responsibility of the Board of Education to provide the opportunities and facilities for such instruction.

The Court has determined that the Board likewise has the responsibility for implementation of the judgment and decree of this Court in this case. Section 31-103 of the District of Columbia Code clearly places this responsibility upon the Board. It provides:

> "The Board shall determine all questions of general policy relating to the schools, shall appoint the executive officers hereinafter provided for, define their duties, and direct expenditures."

The lack of communication and cooperation between the Board of Education and the other defendants in this action shall not be permitted to deprive plaintiffs and their class of publicly supported education. Section 31-104b of the District of Columbia Code dictates that the Board of Education and the District of Columbia Government must coordinate educational and municipal functions:

> "(a) The Board of Education and the Commissioner of the District of Columbia shall jointly develop procedures to assure the maximum coordination of educational and other municipal programs and services in achieving the most effective educational system and utilization of educational facilities and services to serve broad community needs. Such procedures shall cover such matters as—
>
> "(1) design and construction of educational facilities to accommodate civic and community activities such as recreation, adult and vocational education and training, and other community purposes;
>
> "(2) full utilization of educational facilities during nonschool hours for community purposes;
>
> "(3) utilization of municipal services such as police, sanitation, recreational, maintenance services to enhance the effectiveness and stature of the school in the community;
>
> "(4) arrangements for cost-sharing and reimbursements on school and community programs involving utilization of educational facilities and services; and
>
> "(5) other matters of mutual interest and concern.
>
> "(b) The Board of Education may invite the Commissioner of the District of Columbia or his designee to attend and participate in meetings of the Board on matters pertaining to co-ordination of educational and other municipal programs and services and on such other matters as may be of mutual interest." (Emphasis supplied).

If the District of Columbia Government and the Board of Education cannot jointly develop the procedures and programs necessary to implement this Court's order then it shall be the responsibility of the Board of Education to present the irresolvable issue to the Court for resolution in a timely manner so that plaintiffs and their class may be afforded their constitutional and statutory rights. If any dispute should arise between the defendants which requires for its resolution a degree of expertise in the field of education not possessed by the Court, the Court will appoint a special master pursuant to the provisions of Rule 53 of the Federal Rules of Civil Procedure to assist the Court in resolving the issue.

Inasmuch as the Board of Education has presented for adoption by the Court a proposed "Order and Decree" embodying its present plans for the identification of "exceptional" children and providing for their publicly supported education, including a time table, and further requiring the Board to formulate and file with the Court a more comprehensive plan, the Court will not now appoint a special master as was requested by plaintiffs. Despite the defendants' failure to abide by the provisions of the Court's previous orders in this case and despite the defendants' continuing failure to provide an education for these children, the Court is reluctant to arrogate to itself the responsibility of administering this or any other aspect of the Public School System of the District of Columbia through the vehicle of a special master. Nevertheless, inaction or delay on the part of the defendants, or failure by the defendants to implement the judgment and decree herein within the time specified therein will result in the immediate appointment of a special master to oversee and direct such implementation under the direction of this Court. The Court will include as a part of its judgment the proposed "Order and Decree" submitted by the Board of Education, as modified in minor part by the Court, and will retain jurisdiction of the cause to assure prompt implementation of the judgment. Plaintiffs' motion to require certain defendants to show cause why they should not be adjudged in contempt will be held in abeyance for 45 days.

JUDGMENT AND DECREE

Plaintiffs having filed their verified complaint seeking an injunction and declaration of rights as set forth more fully in the verified complaint and the prayer for relief contained therein; and having moved this Court for summary judgment pursuant to Rule 56 of the Federal Rules of Civil Procedure, and this Court having reviewed the record of this cause including plaintiffs' Motion, pleadings, affidavits, and evidence and arguments in support thereof, and defendants' affidavit, pleadings, and evidence and arguments in support thereof, and the proceedings of pre-trial conferences on December 17, 1971, and January 14, 1972, it is hereby ordered, adjudged and decreed that summary judgment in favor of plaintiffs and against defendants be, and hereby is, granted, and judgment is entered in this action as follows:

1. That no child eligible for a publicly supported education in the District of Columbia public schools shall be excluded from a regular public school assignment by a Rule, policy, or practice of the Board of Education of the District of Columbia or its agents unless such child is provided (a) adequate alternative educational services suited to the child's needs, which may include special education or tuition grants, and (b) a constitutionally adequate prior hearing and periodic review of the child's status, progress, and the adequacy of any educational alternative.

2. The defendants, their officers, agents, servants, employees, and attorneys and all those in active concert or participation with them are hereby enjoined from maintaining, enforcing or otherwise continuing in effect any and all rules, policies and practices which exclude plaintiffs and the members of the class they represent from a regular public school assignment without providing them at public expense (a) adequate and immediate alternative education or tuition grants, consistent with their needs, and (b) a constitutionally adequate prior hearing and periodic review of their status, progress and the adequacy of any educational alternatives; and it is further ORDERED that:

3. The District of Columbia shall provide to each child of school age a free and suitable publicly-supported education regardless of the degree of the child's mental, physical or emotional disability or impairment. Furthermore, defendants shall not exclude any child resident in the District of Columbia from such publicly-supported education on the basis of a claim of insufficient resources.

4. Defendants shall not suspend a child from the public schools for disciplinary reasons for any period in excess of two days without affording him a hearing pursuant to the provisions of Paragraph 13.f., below, and without providing for his education during the period of any such suspension.

5. Defendants shall provide each identified member of plaintiff class with a publicly-supported education suited to his needs within thirty (30) days of the entry of this order. With regard to children who later come to the attention of any defendant, within twenty (20) days

after he becomes known, the evaluation (case study approach) called for in paragraph 9 below shall be completed and within 30 days after completion of the evaluation, placement shall be made so as to provide the child with a publicly supported education suited to his needs.

> In either case, if the education to be provided is not of a kind generally available during the summer vacation, the thirty-day limit may be extended for children evaluated during summer months to allow their educational programs to begin at the opening of school in September.

6. Defendants shall cause announcements and notices to be placed in the Washington Post, Washington Star-Daily News, and the Afro-American, in all issues published for a three week period commencing within five (5) days of the entry of this order, and thereafter at quarterly intervals, and shall cause spot announcements to be made on television and radio stations for twenty (20) consecutive days, commencing within five (5) days of the entry of this order, and thereafter at quarterly intervals, advising residents of the District of Columbia that all children, regardless of any handicap or other disability, have a right to a publicly-supported education suited to their needs, and informing the parents or guardians of such children of the procedures required to enroll their children in an appropriate educational program. Such announcements should include the listing of a special answering service telephone number to be established by defendants in order to (a) compile the names, addresses, phone numbers of such children who are presently not attending school and (b) provide further information to their parents or guardians as to the procedures required to enroll their children in an appropriate educational program.

7. Within twenty-five (25) days of the entry of this order, defendants shall file with the Clerk of this Court, an up-to-date list showing, for every additional identified child, the name of the child's parent or guardian, the child's name, age, address and telephone number, the date of his suspension, expulsion, exclusion or denial of placement and, without attributing a particular characteristic to any specific child, a breakdown of such list, showing the alleged causal characteristics for such nonattendance (e.g., educable mentally retarded, trainable mentally retarded, emotionally disturbed, specific learning disability, crippled/other health impaired, hearing impaired, visually impaired, multiple handicapped) and the number of children possessing each such alleged characteristic.

8. Notice of this order shall be given by defendants to the parent or guardian of each child resident in the District of Columbia who is now, or was during the 1971-72 school year or the 1970-71 school year, excluded, suspended or expelled from publicly-supported educational programs or otherwise denied a full and suitable publicly-supported education for any period in excess of two days. Such notice shall include a statement that each such child has the right to receive a free educational assessment and to be placed in a publicly-supported educational program suited to his needs. Such notice shall be sent by registered mail within five (5) days of the entry of this order, or within five (5) days after such child first becomes known to any defendant. Provision of notification for non-reading parents or guardians will be made.

9. a. Defendants shall utilize public or private agencies to evaluate the educational needs of all identified "exceptional" children and, within twenty (20) days of the entry of this order, shall file with the Clerk of this Court their proposal for each individual placement in a suitable educational program, including the provision of compensatory educational services where required.

b. Defendants, within twenty (20) days of the entry of this order, shall, also submit such proposals to each parent or guardian of such child, respectively, along with a notification that if they object to such proposed placement within a period of time to be fixed by the parties or by the Court, they may have their objection heard by a Hearing Officer in accordance with procedures required in Paragraph 13.e., below.

10. a. Within forty-five (45) days of the entry of this order, defendants shall file with the Clerk of the Court, with copy to plaintiffs' counsel, a comprehensive plan which provides for

the identification, notification, assessment, and placement of class members. Such plan shall state the nature and extent of efforts which defendants have undertaken or propose to undertake to

(1) describe the curriculum, educational objectives, teacher qualifications, and ancillary services for the publicly-supported educational programs to be provided to class members; and,

(2) formulate general plans of compensatory education suitable to class members in order to overcome the present effects of prior educational deprivations,

(3) institute any additional steps and proposed modifications designed to implement the matters decreed in paragraph 5 through 7 hereof and other requirements of this judgment.

11. The defendants shall make an interim report to this Court on their performance within forty-five (45) days of the entry of this order. Such report shall show:

(1) The adequacy of Defendants' implementation of plans to identify, locate, evaluate and give notice to all members of the class.

(2) The number of class members who have been placed, and the nature of their placements.

(3) The number of contested hearings before the Hearing Officers, if any, and the findings and determinations resulting therefrom.

12. Within forty-five (45) days of the entry of this order, defendants shall file with this Court a report showing the expunction from or correction of all official records of any plaintiff with regard to past expulsions, suspensions, or exclusions effected in violation of the procedural rights set forth in Paragraph 13 together with a plan for procedures pursuant to which parents, guardians, or their counsel may attach to such students' records any clarifying or explanatory information which the parent, guardian or counsel may deem appropriate.

13. Hearing Procedures.

a. Each member of the plaintiff class is to be provided with a publicly-supported educational program suited to his needs, within the context of a presumption that among the alternative programs of education, placement in a regular public school class with appropriate ancillary services is preferable to placement in a special school class.

b. Before placing a member of the class in such a program, defendants shall notify his parent or guardian of the proposed educational placement, the reasons therefor, and the right to a hearing before a Hearing Officer if there is an objection to the placement proposed. Any such hearing shall be held in accordance with the provisions of Paragraph 13.e., below.

c. Hereinafter, children who are residents of the District of Columbia and are thought by any of the defendants, or by officials, parents or guardians, to be in need of a program of special education, shall neither be placed in, transferred from or to, nor denied placement in such a program unless defendants shall have first notified their parents or guardians of such proposed placement, transfer or denial, the reasons therefor, and of the right to a hearing before a Hearing Officer if there is an objection to the placement, transfer or denial of placement. Any such hearings shall be held in accordance with the provisions of Paragraph 13.e., below.

d. Defendants shall not, on grounds of discipline, cause the exclusion, suspension, expulsion, postponement, interschool transfer, or any other denial of access to regular instruction in the public schools to any child for more than two days without first notifying the child's parent or guardian of such proposed action, the reasons therefor, and of the hearing before a Hearing Officer in accordance with the provisions of Paragraph 13.f., below.

e. Whenever defendants take action regarding a child's placement, denial of placement, or transfer, as described in Paragraphs 13.b. or 13.c., above, the following procedures shall be followed.

(1) Notice required hereinbefore shall be given in writing by registered mail to the parent or guardian of the child.

(2) Such notice shall:

(a) describe the proposed action in detail;

(b) clearly state the specific and complete reasons for the proposed action, including the specification of any tests or reports upon which such action is proposed;

(c) describe any alternative educational opportunities available on a permanent or temporary basis;

(d) inform the parent or guardian of the right to object to the proposed action at a hearing before the Hearing Officer;

(e) inform the parent or guardian that the child is eligible to receive, at no charge, the services of a federally or locally funded diagnostic center for an independent medical, psychological and educational evaluation and shall specify the name, address and telephone number of an appropriate local diagnostic center;

(f) inform the parent or guardian of the right to be represented at the hearing by legal counsel; to examine the child's school records before the hearing, including any tests or reports upon which the proposed action may be based, to present evidence, including expert medical, psychological and educational testimony; and, to confront and cross-examine any school official, employee, or agent of the school district or public department who may have evidence upon which the proposed action was based.

(3) The hearing shall be at a time and place reasonably convenient to such parent or guardian.

(4) The hearing shall be scheduled not sooner than twenty (20) days waivable by parent or child, nor later than forty-five (45) days after receipt of a request from the parent or guardian.

(5) The hearing shall be a closed hearing unless the parent or guardian requests an open hearing.

(6) The child shall have the right to a representative of his own choosing, including legal counsel. If a child is unable, through financial inability, to retain counsel, defendants shall advise child's parents or guardians of available voluntary legal assistance including the Neighborhood Legal Services Organization, the Legal Aid Society, the Young Lawyers Section of the D.C. Bar Association, or from some other organization.

(7) The decision of the Hearing Officer shall be based solely upon the evidence presented at the hearing.

(8) Defendants shall bear the burden of proof as to all facts and as to the appropriateness of any placement, denial of placement or transfer.

(9) A tape recording or other record of the hearing shall be made and transcribed and, upon request, made available to the parent or guardian or his representative.

(10) At a reasonable time prior to the hearing, the parent or guardian, or his counsel, shall be given access to all public school system and other public office records pertaining to the child, including any tests or reports upon which the proposed action may be based.

(11) The independent Hearing Officer shall be an employee of the District of Columbia, but shall not be an officer, employee or agent of the Public School System.

(12) The parent or guardian, or his representative, shall have the right to have the attendance of any official, employee or agent of the public school system or any public employee

who may have evidence upon which the proposed action may be based and to confront, and to cross-examine any witness testifying for the public school system.

(13) The parent or guardian, or his representative, shall have the right to present evidence and testimony, including expert medical, psychological or educational testimony.

(14) Within thirty (30) days after the hearing, the Hearing Officer shall render a decision in writing. Such decision shall include findings of fact and conclusions of law and shall be filed with the Board of Education and the Department of Human Resources and sent by registered mail to the parent or guardian and his counsel.

(15) Pending a determination by the Hearing Officer, defendants shall take no action described in Paragraphs 13.b. or 13.c., above, if the child's parent or guardian objects to such action. Such objection must be in writing and postmarked within five (5) days of the date of receipt of notification hereinabove described.

f. Whenever defendants propose to take action described in Paragraph 13.d., above, the following procedures shall be followed.

(1) Notice required hereinabove shall be given in writing and shall be delivered in person or by registered mail to both the child and his parent or guardian.

(2) Such notice shall

(a) describe the proposed disciplinary action in detail, including the duration thereof;

(b) state specific, clear and full reasons for the proposed action, including the specification of the alleged act upon which the disciplinary action is to be based and the reference to the regulation subsection under which such action is proposed;

(c) describe alternative educational opportunities to be available to the child during the proposed suspension period;

(d) inform the child and the parent or guardian of the time and place at which the hearing shall take place;

(e) inform the parent or guardian that if the child is thought by the parent or guardian to require special education services, that such child is eligible to receive, at no charge, the services of a public or private agency for a diagnostic medical, psychological or educational evaluation;

(f) inform the child and his parent or guardian of the right to be represented at the hearing by legal counsel; to examine the child's school records before the hearing, including any tests or reports upon which the proposed action may be based; to present evidence of his own; and to confront and cross-examine any witnesses or any school officials, employees or agents who may have evidence upon which the proposed action may be based.

(3) The hearing shall be at a time and place reasonably convenient to such parent or guardian.

(4) The hearing shall take place within four (4) school days of the date upon which written notice is given, and may be postponed at the request of the child's parent or guardian for no more than five (5) additional school days where necessary for preparation.

(5) The hearing shall be a closed hearing unless the child, his parent or guardian requests an open hearing.

(6) The child is guaranteed the right to a representative of his own choosing, including legal counsel. If a child is unable, through financial inability, to retain counsel, defendants shall advise child's parents or guardians of available voluntary legal assistance including the Neighborhood Legal Services Organization, the Legal Aid Society, the Young Lawyers Section of the D.C. Bar Association, or from some other organization.

(7) The decision of the Hearing Officer shall be based solely upon the evidence presented at the hearing.

(8) Defendants shall bear the burden of proof as to all facts and as to the appropriateness of any disposition and of the alternative educational opportunity to be provided during any suspension.

(9) A tape recording or other record of the hearing shall be made and transcribed and, upon request, made available to the parent or guardian or his representative.

(10) At a reasonable time prior to the hearing, the parent or guardian, or the child's counsel or representative, shall be given access to all records of the public school system and any other public office pertaining to the child, including any tests or reports upon which the proposed action may be based.

(11) The independent Hearing Officer shall be an employee of the District of Columbia, but shall not be an officer, employee or agent of the Public School System.

(12) The parent or guardian, or the child's counsel or representative, shall have the right to have the attendance of any public employee who may have evidence upon which the proposed action may be based and to confront and to cross-examine any witness testifying for the public school system.

(13) The parent or guardian, or the child's counsel or representative, shall have the right to present evidence and testimony.

(14) Pending the hearing and receipt of notification of the decision, there shall be no change in the child's educational placement unless the principal (responsible to the Superintendent) shall warrant that the continued presence of the child in his current program would endanger the physical well-being of himself or others. In such exceptional cases, the principal shall be responsible for insuring that the child receives some form of educational assistance and/or diagnostic examination during the interim period prior to the hearing.

(15) No finding that disciplinary action is warranted shall be made unless the Hearing Officer first finds, by clear and convincing evidence, that the child committed a prohibited act upon which the proposed disciplinary action is based. After this finding has been made, the Hearing Officer shall take such disciplinary action as he shall deem appropriate. This action shall not be more severe than that recommended by the school official initiating the suspension proceedings.

(16) No suspension shall continue for longer than ten (10) school days after the date of the hearing, or until the end of the school year, whichever comes first. In such cases, the principal (responsible to the Superintendent) shall be responsible for insuring that the child receives some form of educational assistance and/or diagnostic examination during the suspension period.

(17) If the Hearing Officer determines that disciplinary action is not warranted, all school records of the proposed disciplinary action, including those relating to the incidents upon which such proposed action was predicated, shall be destroyed.

(18) If the Hearing Officer determines that disciplinary action is warranted, he shall give written notification of his findings and of the child's right to appeal his decision to the Board of Education, to the child, the parent or guardian, and the counsel or representative of the child, within three (3) days of such determination.

(19) An appeal from the decision of the Hearing Officer shall be heard by the Student Life and Community Involvement Committee of the Board of Education which shall provide the child and his parent or guardian with the opportunity for an oral hearing, at which the child may be represented by legal counsel, to review the findings of the Hearing Officer. At the conclusion of such hearing, the Committee shall determine the appropriateness of and may modify such decision. However, in no event may such Committee impose added or more severe restrictions on the child.

14. Whenever the foregoing provisions require notice to a parent or guardian, and the child in question has no parent or duly appointed guardian, notice is to be given to any adult

with whom the child is actually living, as well as to the child himself, and every effort will be made to assure that no child's rights are denied for lack of a parent or duly appointed guardian. Again provision for such notice to non-readers will be made.

15. Jurisdiction of this matter is retained to allow for implementation, modification and enforcement of this Judgment and Decree as may be required.

WISCONSIN V. YODER, 406 U.S. 205 (1972)

SUPREME COURT OF THE UNITED STATES
CERTIORARI TO THE SUPREME COURT OF WISCONSIN
ARGUED DECEMBER 8, 1971. DECIDED MAY 15, 1972.

Respondents, members of the Old Order Amish religion and the Conservative Amish Mennonite Church, were convicted of violating Wisconsin's compulsory school-attendance law (which requires a child's school attendance until age 16) by declining to send their children to public or private school after they had graduated from the eighth grade. The evidence showed that the Amish provide continuing informal vocational education to their children designed to prepare them for life in the rural Amish community. The evidence also showed that respondents sincerely believed that high school attendance was contrary to the Amish religion and way of life and that they would endanger their own salvation and that of their children by complying with the law. The State Supreme Court sustained respondents' claim that application of the compulsory school-attendance law to them violated their rights under the Free Exercise Clause of the First Amendment, made applicable to the States by the Fourteenth Amendment.

Held:

1. The State's interest in universal education is not totally free from a balancing process when it impinges on other fundamental rights, such as those specifically protected by the Free Exercise Clause of the First Amendment and the traditional interest of parents with respect to the religious upbringing of their children. Pp. 213–215.
2. Respondents have amply supported their claim that enforcement of the compulsory formal education requirement after the eighth grade would gravely endanger if not destroy the free exercise of their religious beliefs. Pp. 215–219.
3. Aided by a history of three centuries as an identifiable religious sect and a long history as a successful and self-sufficient segment of American society, the Amish have demonstrated the sincerity of their religious beliefs, the interrelationship of belief with their mode of life, the vital role that belief and daily conduct play in the continuing survival of Old Order Amish communities, and the hazards presented by the State's enforcement of a statute generally valid as to others. Beyond this, they have carried the difficult burden of demonstrating the adequacy of their alternative mode of continuing informal vocational education in terms of the overall interests that the State relies on in support of its program of compulsory high school education. In light of this showing, and weighing the minimal difference between what the State would require and what the Amish already accept, it was incumbent on the State to show with more particularity how its admittedly strong interest in compulsory education would be adversely affected by granting an exemption to the Amish. Pp. 219–229, 234–236.
4. The State's claim that it is empowered, as parens patriae, to extend the benefit of secondary education to children regardless of the wishes of their parents cannot be sustained against a free exercise claim of the nature revealed by this record, for the

Amish have introduced convincing evidence that accommodating their religious objections by forgoing one or two additional years of compulsory education will not impair the physical or mental health of the child, or result in an inability to be self-supporting or to discharge the duties and responsibilities of citizenship, or in any other way materially detract from the welfare of society. Pp. 229-234.

49 Wis. 2d 430, 182 N. W. 2d 539, affirmed.

BURGER, C. J., delivered the opinion of the Court, in which BRENNAN, STEWART, WHITE, MARSHALL, and BLACKMUN, JJ., joined. STEWART, J., filed a concurring opinion, in which BRENNAN, J., joined, post, p. 237. WHITE, J., filed a concurring opinion, in which BRENNAN and STEWART, JJ., joined, post, p. 237. DOUGLAS, J., filed an opinion dissenting in part, post, p. 241. POWELL and REHNQUIST, JJ., took no part in the consideration or decision of the case.

John W. Calhoun, Assistant Attorney General of Wisconsin, argued the cause for petitioner. With him on the briefs were Robert W. Warren, Attorney General, and William H. Wilker, Assistant Attorney General.

William B. Ball argued the cause for respondents. With him on the brief was Joseph G. Skelly.

Briefs of amici curiae urging affirmance were filed by Donald E. Showalter for the Mennonite Central Committee; by Boardman Noland and Lee Boothby for the General Conference of Seventh-Day Adventists; by William S. Ellis for the National Council of the Churches of Christ; by Nathan Lewin for the National Jewish Commission on Law and Public Affairs; and by Leo Pfeffer for the Synagogue Council of America et al.

MR. CHIEF JUSTICE BURGER delivered the opinion of the Court.

On petition of the State of Wisconsin, we granted the writ of certiorari in this case to review a decision of the Wisconsin Supreme Court holding that respondents' convictions of violating the State's compulsory school-attendance law were invalid under the Free Exercise Clause of the First Amendment to the United States Constitution made applicable to the States by the Fourteenth Amendment. For the reasons hereafter stated we affirm the judgment of the Supreme Court of Wisconsin.

Respondents Jonas Yoder and Wallace Miller are members of the Old Order Amish religion, and respondent Adin Yutzy is a member of the Conservative Amish Mennonite Church. They and their families are residents of Green County, Wisconsin. Wisconsin's compulsory school-attendance law required them to cause their children to attend public or private school until reaching age 16 but the respondents declined to send their children, ages 14 and 15, to public school after they completed the eighth grade. The children were not enrolled in any private school, or within any recognized exception to the compulsory-attendance law, and they are conceded to be subject to the Wisconsin statute.

On complaint of the school district administrator for the public schools, respondents were charged, tried, and convicted of violating the compulsory-attendance law in Green Country Court and were fined the sum of $5 each. Respondents defended on the ground that the application of the compulsory-attendance law violated their rights under the First and Fourteenth Amendments. The trial testimony showed that respondents believed, in accordance with the tenets of Old Order Amish communities generally, that their children's attendance at high school, public or private, was contrary to the Amish religion and way of life. They believed that by sending their children to high school, they would not only expose themselves to the danger of the censure of the church community, but, as found by the county court, also endanger their own salvation and that of their children. The State stipulated that respondents' religious beliefs were sincere.

In support of their position, respondents presented as expert witnesses scholars on religion and education whose testimony is uncontradicted. They expressed their opinions on the relationship of the Amish belief concerning school attendance to the more general tenets of their religion, and described the impact that compulsory high school attendance could have on the continued survival of Amish communities as they exist in the United States today. The history of the Amish sect was given in some detail, beginning with the Swiss Anabaptists of the 16th century who rejected institutionalized churches and sought to return to the early, simple, Christian life de-emphasizing material success, rejecting the competitive spirit, and seeking to insulate themselves from the modern world. As a result of their common heritage, Old Order Amish communities today are characterized by a fundamental belief that salvation requires life in a church community separate and apart from the world and worldly influence. This concept of life aloof from the world and its values is central to their faith.

A related feature of Old Order Amish communities is their devotion to a life in harmony with nature and the soil, as exemplified by the simple life of the early Christian era that continued in America during much of our early national life. Amish beliefs require members of the community to make their living by farming or closely related activities. Broadly speaking, the Old Order Amish religion pervades and determines the entire mode of life of its adherents. Their conduct is regulated in great detail by the Ordnung, or rules, of the church community. Adult baptism, which occurs in late adolescence, is the time at which Amish young people voluntarily undertake heavy obligations, not unlike the Bar Mitzvah of the Jews, to abide by the rules of the church community.

Amish objection to formal education beyond the eighth grade is firmly grounded in these central religious concepts. They object to the high school, and higher education generally, because the values they teach are in marked variance with Amish values and the Amish way of life; they view secondary school education as an impermissible exposure of their children to a "worldly" influence in conflict with their beliefs. The high school tends to emphasize intellectual and scientific accomplishments, self-distinction, competitiveness, worldly success, and social life with other students. Amish society emphasizes informal learning-through-doing; a life of "goodness," rather than a life of intellect; wisdom, rather than technical knowledge; community welfare, rather than competition; and separation from, rather than integration with, contemporary worldly society.

Formal high school education beyond the eighth grade is contrary to Amish beliefs, not only because it places Amish children in an environment hostile to Amish beliefs with increasing emphasis on competition in class work and sports and with pressure to conform to the styles, manners, and ways of the peer group, but also because it takes them away from their community, physically and emotionally, during the crucial and formative adolescent period of life. During this period, the children must acquire Amish attitudes favoring manual work and self-reliance and the specific skills needed to perform the adult role of an Amish farmer or housewife. They must learn to enjoy physical labor. Once a child has learned basic reading, writing, and elementary mathematics, these traits, skills, and attitudes admittedly fall within the category of those best learned through example and "doing" rather than in a classroom. And, at this time in life, the Amish child must also grow in his faith and his relationship to the Amish community if he is to be prepared to accept the heavy obligations imposed by adult baptism. In short, high school attendance with teachers who are not of the Amish faith—and may even be hostile to it—interposes a serious barrier to the integration of the Amish child into the Amish religious community. Dr. John Hostetler, one of the experts on Amish society, testified that the modern high school is not equipped, in curriculum or social environment, to impart the values promoted by Amish society.

The Amish do not object to elementary education through the first eight grades as a general proposition because they agree that their children must have basic skills in the "three R's" in order to read the Bible, to be good farmers and citizens, and to be able to deal with non-Amish people when necessary in the course of daily affairs. They view such a basic education as acceptable because it does not significantly expose their children to worldly values or interfere with their development in the Amish community during the crucial adolescent period. While Amish accept compulsory elementary education generally, wherever possible they have established their own elementary schools in many respects like the small local schools of the past. In the Amish belief higher learning tends to develop values they reject as influences that alienate man from God.

On the basis of such considerations, Dr. Hostetler testified that compulsory high school attendance could not only result in great psychological harm to Amish children, because of the conflicts it would produce, but would also, in his opinion, ultimately result in the destruction of the Old Order Amish church community as it exists in the United States today. The testimony of Dr. Donald A. Erickson, an expert witness on education, also showed that the Amish succeed in preparing their high school age children to be productive members of the Amish community. He described their system of learning through doing the skills directly relevant to their adult roles in the Amish community as "ideal" and perhaps superior to ordinary high school education. The evidence also showed that the Amish have an excellent record as law-abiding and generally self-sufficient members of society.

Although the trial court in its careful findings determined that the Wisconsin compulsory school-attendance law "does interfere with the freedom of the Defendants to act in accordance with their sincere religious belief" it also concluded that the requirement of high school attendance until age 16 was a "reasonable and constitutional" exercise of governmental power, and therefore denied the motion to dismiss the charges. The Wisconsin Circuit Court affirmed the convictions. The Wisconsin Supreme Court, however, sustained respondents' claim under the Free Exercise Clause of the First Amendment and reversed the convictions. A majority of the court was of the opinion that the State had failed to make an adequate showing that its interest in "establishing and maintaining an educational system overrides the defendants' right to the free exercise of their religion." 49 Wis. 2d 430, 447, 182 N. W. 2d 539, 547 (1971).

I

There is no doubt as to the power of a State, having a high responsibility for education of its citizens, to impose reasonable regulations for the control and duration of basic education. See, e. g., Pierce v. Society of Sisters, (1925). Providing public schools ranks at the very apex of the function of a State. Yet even this paramount responsibility was, in Pierce, made to yield to the right of parents to provide an equivalent education in a privately operated system. There the Court held that Oregon's statute compelling attendance in a public school from age eight to age 16 unreasonably interfered with the interest of parents in directing the rearing of their offspring, including their education in church-operated schools. As that case suggests, the values of parental direction of the religious upbringing and education of their children in their early and formative years have a high place in our society. See also Ginsberg v. New York, (1968); Meyer v. Nebraska, (1923); cf. Rowan v. Post Office Dept., (1970). Thus, a State's interest in universal education, however highly we rank it, is not totally free from a balancing process when it impinges on fundamental rights and interests, such as those specifically protected by the Free Exercise Clause of the First Amendment, and the traditional interest of parents with respect to the religious upbringing of their children so long as they, in the words of Pierce, "prepare [them] for additional obligations."

It follows that in order for Wisconsin to compel school attendance beyond the eighth grade against a claim that such attendance interferes with the practice of a legitimate religious belief, it must appear either that the State does not deny the free exercise of religious belief by its requirement, or that there is a state interest of sufficient magnitude to override the interest claiming protection under the Free Exercise Clause. Long before there was general acknowledgment of the need for universal formal education, the Religion Clauses had specifically and firmly fixed the right to free exercise of religious beliefs, and buttressing this fundamental right was an equally firm, even if less explicit, prohibition against the establishment of any religion by government. The values underlying these two provisions relating to religion have been zealously protected, sometimes even at the expense of other interests of admittedly high social importance. The invalidation of financial aid to parochial schools by government grants for a salary subsidy for teachers is but one example of the extent to which courts have gone in this regard, notwithstanding that such aid programs were legislatively determined to be in the public interest and the service of sound educational policy by States and by Congress. Lemon v. Kurtzman, (1971); Tilton v. Richardson, (1971). See also Everson v. Board of Education, (1947).

The essence of all that has been said and written on the subject is that only those interests of the highest order and those not otherwise served can overbalance legitimate claims to the free exercise of religion. We can accept it as settled, therefore, that, however strong the State's interest in universal compulsory education, it is by no means absolute to the exclusion or subordination of all other interests. E. g., Sherbert v. Verner, (1963); McGowan v. Maryland, (1961) (separate opinion of Frankfurter, J.); Prince v. Massachusetts, (1944).

II

We come then to the quality of the claims of the respondents concerning the alleged encroachment of Wisconsin's compulsory school-attendance statute on their rights and the rights of their children to the free exercise of the religious beliefs they and their forebears have adhered to for almost three centuries. In evaluating those claims we must be careful to determine whether the Amish religious faith and their mode of life are, as they claim, inseparable and interdependent. A way of life, however virtuous and admirable, may not be interposed as a barrier to reasonable state regulation of education if it is based on purely secular considerations; to have the protection of the Religion Clauses, the claims must be rooted in religious belief. Although a determination of what is a "religious" belief or practice entitled to constitutional protection may present a most delicate question, the very concept of ordered liberty precludes allowing every person to make his own standards on matters of conduct in which society as a whole has important interests. Thus, if the Amish asserted their claims because of their subjective evaluation and rejection of the contemporary secular values accepted by the majority, much as Thoreau rejected the social values of his time and isolated himself at Walden Pond, their claims would not rest on a religious basis. Thoreau's choice was philosophical and personal rather than religious, and such belief does not rise to the demands of the Religion Clauses.

Giving no weight to such secular considerations, however, we see that the record in this case abundantly supports the claim that the traditional way of life of the Amish is not merely a matter of personal preference, but one of deep religious conviction, shared by an organized group, and intimately related to daily living. That the Old Order Amish daily life and religious practice stem from their faith is shown by the fact that it is in response to their literal interpretation of the Biblical injunction from the Epistle of Paul to the Romans, "be not conformed to this world . . . ." This command is fundamental to the Amish faith. Moreover, for the Old Order Amish, religion is not simply a matter of theocratic belief. As the expert witnesses explained, the Old Order Amish religion pervades and determines virtually their entire way of life, regulating it with the detail of the Talmudic diet through the strictly enforced rules of the church community.

The record shows that the respondents' religious beliefs and attitude toward life, family, and home have remained constant—perhaps some would say static— in a period of unparalleled progress in human knowledge generally and great changes in education. The respondents freely concede, and indeed assert as an article of faith, that their religious beliefs and what we would today call "life style" have not altered in fundamentals for centuries. Their way of life in a church-oriented community, separated from the outside world and "worldly" influences, their attachment to nature and the soil, is a way inherently simple and uncomplicated, albeit difficult to preserve against the pressure to conform. Their rejection of telephones, automobiles, radios, and television, their mode of dress, of speech, their habits of manual work do indeed set them apart from much of contemporary society; these customs are both symbolic and practical.

As the society around the Amish has become more populous, urban, industrialized, and complex, particularly in this century, government regulation of human affairs has correspondingly become more detailed and pervasive. The Amish mode of life has thus come into conflict increasingly with requirements of contemporary society exerting a hydraulic insistence on conformity to majoritarian standards. So long as compulsory education laws were confined to eight grades of elementary basic education imparted in a nearby rural schoolhouse, with a large proportion of students of the Amish faith, the Old Order Amish had little basis to fear that school attendance would expose their children to the worldly influence they reject. But modern compulsory secondary education in rural areas is now largely carried on in a consolidated school, often remote from the student's home and alien to his daily home life. As the record so strongly shows, the values and programs of the modern secondary school are in sharp conflict with the fundamental mode of life mandated by the Amish religion; modern laws requiring compulsory secondary education have accordingly engendered great concern and conflict. The conclusion is inescapable that secondary schooling, by exposing Amish children to worldly influences in terms of attitudes, goals, and values contrary to beliefs, and by substantially interfering with the religious development of the Amish child and his integration into the way of life of the Amish faith community at the crucial adolescent stage of development, contravenes the basic religious tenets and practice of the Amish faith, both as to the parent and the child.

The impact of the compulsory-attendance law on respondents' practice of the Amish religion is not only severe, but inescapable, for the Wisconsin law affirmatively compels them, under threat of criminal sanction, to perform acts undeniably at odds with fundamental tenets of their religious beliefs. See Braunfeld v. Brown, (1961). Nor is the impact of the compulsory-attendance law confined to grave interference with important Amish religious tenets from a subjective point of view. It carries with it precisely the kind of objective danger to the free exercise of religion that the First Amendment was designed to prevent. As the record shows, compulsory school attendance to age 16 for Amish children carries with it a very real threat of undermining the Amish community and religious practice as they exist today; they must either abandon belief and be assimilated into society at large, or be forced to migrate to some other and more tolerant region.

In sum, the unchallenged testimony of acknowledged experts in education and religious history, almost 300 years of consistent practice, and strong evidence of a sustained faith pervading and regulating respondents' entire mode of life support the claim that enforcement of the State's requirement of compulsory formal education after the eighth grade would gravely endanger if not destroy the free exercise of respondents' religious beliefs.

III

Neither the findings of the trial court nor the Amish claims as to the nature of their faith are challenged in this Court by the State of Wisconsin. Its position is that the State's interest in universal compulsory formal secondary education to age 16 is so great that it is paramount to the undisputed claims of respondents that their mode of preparing their youth for Amish life, after the traditional elementary education, is an essential part of their religious belief and practice. Nor does the State undertake to meet the claim that the Amish mode of life and education is inseparable from and a part of the basic tenets of their religion—indeed, as much a part of their religious belief and practices as baptism, the confessional, or a sabbath may be for others.

Wisconsin concedes that under the Religion Clauses religious beliefs are absolutely free from the State's control, but it argues that "actions," even though religiously grounded, are outside the protection of the First Amendment. But our decisions have rejected the idea that religiously grounded conduct is always outside the protection of the Free Exercise Clause. It is true that activities of individuals, even when religiously based, are often subject to regulation by the States in the exercise of their undoubted power to promote the health, safety, and general welfare, or the Federal Government in the exercise of its delegated powers. See, e. g., Gillette v. United States, (1971); Braunfeld v. Brown, (1961); Prince v. Massachusetts, (1944); Reynolds v. United States, (1879). But to agree that religiously grounded conduct must often be subject to the broad police power of the State is not to deny that there are areas of conduct protected by the Free Exercise Clause of the First Amendment and thus beyond the power of the State to control, even under regulations of general applicability. E. g., Sherbert v. Verner, (1963); Murdock v. Pennsylvania, (1943); Cantwell v. Connecticut, (1940). This case, therefore, does not become easier because respondents were convicted for their "actions" in refusing to send their children to the public high school; in this context belief and action cannot be neatly confined in logic-tight compartments. Cf. Lemon v. Kurtzman.

Nor can this case be disposed of on the grounds that Wisconsin's requirement for school attendance to age 16 applies uniformly to all citizens of the State and does not, on its face, discriminate against religions or a particular religion, or that it is motivated by legitimate secular concerns. A regulation neutral on its face may, in its application, nonetheless offend the constitutional requirement for governmental neutrality if it unduly burdens the free exercise of religion. Sherbert v. Verner, supra; cf. Walz v. Tax Commission, (1970). The Court must not ignore the danger that an exception from a general obligation of citizenship on religious grounds may run afoul of the Establishment Clause, but that danger cannot be allowed to prevent any exception no matter how vital it may be to the protection of values promoted by the right of free exercise. By preserving doctrinal flexibility and recognizing the need for a sensible and realistic application of the Religion Clauses

> "we have been able to chart a course that preserved the autonomy and freedom of religious bodies while avoiding any semblance of established religion. This is a 'tight rope' and one we have successfully traversed." Walz v. Tax Commission, supra, at 672.

We turn, then, to the State's broader contention that its interest in its system of compulsory education is so compelling that even the established religious practices of the Amish must give way. Where fundamental claims of religious freedom are at stake, however, we cannot accept such a sweeping claim; despite its admitted validity in the generality of cases, we must searchingly examine the interests that the State seeks to promote by its requirement for compulsory education to age 16, and the impediment to those objectives that would flow from recognizing the claimed Amish exemption. See, e. g., Sherbert v. Verner, supra; Martin v. City of Struthers, (1943); Schneider v. State, (1939).

The State advances two primary arguments in support of its system of compulsory education. It notes, as Thomas Jefferson pointed out early in our history, that some degree of education is necessary to prepare citizens to participate effectively and intelligently in our open political system if we are to preserve freedom and independence. Further, education prepares individuals to be self-reliant and self-sufficient participants in society. We accept these propositions.

However, the evidence adduced by the Amish in this case is persuasively to the effect that an additional one or two years of formal high school for Amish children in place of their long-established program of informal vocational education would do little to serve those interests. Respondents' experts testified at trial, without challenge, that the value of all education must be assessed in terms of its capacity to prepare the child for life. It is one thing to say that compulsory education for a year or two beyond the eighth grade may be necessary when its goal is the preparation of the child for life in modern society as the majority live, but it is quite another if the goal of education be viewed as the preparation of the child for life in the separated agrarian community that is the keystone of the Amish faith. See Meyer v. Nebraska.

The State attacks respondents' position as one fostering "ignorance" from which the child must be protected by the State. No one can question the State's duty to protect children from ignorance but this argument does not square with the facts disclosed in the record. Whatever their idiosyncrasies as seen by the majority, this record strongly shows that the Amish community has been a highly successful social unit within our society, even if apart from the conventional "mainstream." Its members are productive and very law-abiding members of society; they reject public welfare in any of its usual modern forms. The Congress itself recognized their self-sufficiency by authorizing exemption of such groups as the Amish from the obligation to pay social security taxes.

It is neither fair nor correct to suggest that the Amish are opposed to education beyond the eighth grade level. What this record shows is that they are opposed to conventional formal education of the type provided by a certified high school because it comes at the child's crucial adolescent period of religious development. Dr. Donald Erickson, for example, testified that their system of learning-by-doing was an "ideal system" of education in terms of preparing Amish children for life as adults in the Amish community, and that "I would be inclined to say they do a better job in this than most of the rest of us do." As he put it, "These people aren't purporting to be learned people, and it seems to me the self-sufficiency of the community is the best evidence I can point to—whatever is being done seems to function well."

We must not forget that in the Middle Ages important values of the civilization of the Western World were preserved by members of religious orders who isolated themselves from all worldly influences against great obstacles. There can be no assumption that today's majority is "right" and the Amish and others like them are "wrong." A way of life that is odd or even erratic but interferes with no rights or interests of others is not to be condemned because it is different.

The State, however, supports its interest in providing an additional one or two years of compulsory high school education to Amish children because of the possibility that some such children will choose to leave the Amish community, and that if this occurs they will be ill-equipped for life. The State argues that if Amish children leave their church they should not be in the position of making their way in the world without the education available in the one or two additional years the State requires. However, on this record, that argument is highly speculative. There is no specific evidence of the loss of Amish adherents by attrition, nor is there any showing that upon leaving the Amish community Amish children, with their practical agricultural training and habits of industry and self-reliance, would become burdens on society because of educational short-comings. Indeed, this argument of the State appears to rest primarily on the State's mistaken assumption, already noted, that the Amish do not provide any education for their children beyond the eighth grade, but allow them to grow in "ignorance." To the contrary, not only do the Amish accept the necessity for formal schooling through the eighth grade level, but continue to provide what has been characterized by the undisputed testimony of expert educators as an "ideal" vocational education for their children in the adolescent years.

There is nothing in this record to suggest that the Amish qualities of reliability, self-reliance, and dedication to work would fail to find ready markets in today's society. Absent some contrary evidence supporting the State's position, we are unwilling to assume that persons possessing such valuable vocational skills and habits are doomed to become burdens on society should they determine to leave the Amish faith, nor is there any basis in the record to warrant a finding that an additional one or two years of formal school education beyond the eighth grade would serve to eliminate any such problem that might exist.

Insofar as the State's claim rests on the view that a brief additional period of formal education is imperative to enable the Amish to participate effectively and intelligently in our democratic process, it must fall. The Amish alternative to formal secondary school education has enabled them to function effectively in their day-to-day life under self-imposed limitations on relations with the world, and to survive and prosper in contemporary society as a separate, sharply identifiable and highly self-sufficient community for more than 200 years in this country. In itself this is strong evidence that they are capable of fulfilling the social and political responsibilities of citizenship without compelled attendance beyond the eighth grade at the price of jeopardizing their free exercise of religious belief. When Thomas Jefferson emphasized the need for education as a bulwark of a free people against tyranny, there is nothing to indicate he had in mind compulsory education through any fixed age beyond a basic education. Indeed, the Amish communities singularly parallel and reflect many of the virtues of Jefferson's ideal of the "sturdy yeoman" who would form the basis of what he considered as the ideal of a democratic society. Even their idiosyncratic separateness exemplifies the diversity we profess to admire and encourage.

The requirement for compulsory education beyond the eighth grade is a relatively recent development in our history. Less than 60 years ago, the educational requirements of almost all of the States were satisfied by completion of the elementary grades, at least where the child was regularly and lawfully employed. The independence and successful social functioning of the Amish community for a period approaching almost three centuries and more than 200 years in this country are strong evidence that there is at best a speculative gain, in terms of meeting the duties of citizenship, from an additional one or two years of compulsory formal education. Against this background it would require a more particularized showing from the State on this point to justify the severe interference with religious freedom such additional compulsory attendance would entail.

We should also note that compulsory education and child labor laws find their historical origin in common humanitarian instincts, and that the age limits of both laws have been coordinated to achieve their related objectives. In the context of this case, such considerations, if anything, support rather than detract from respondents' position. The origins of the requirement for school attendance to age 16, an age falling after the completion of elementary school but before completion of high school, are not entirely clear. But to some extent such laws reflected the movement to prohibit most child labor under age 16 that culminated in the provisions of the Federal Fair Labor Standards Act of 1938. It is true, then, that the 16-year child labor age limit may to some degree derive from a contemporary impression that children should be in school until that age. But at the same time, it cannot be denied that, conversely, the 16-year education limit reflects, in substantial measure, the concern that children under that age not be employed under conditions hazardous to their health, or in work that should be performed by adults.

The requirement of compulsory schooling to age 16 must therefore be viewed as aimed not merely at providing educational opportunities for children, but as an alternative to the equally undesirable consequence of unhealthful child labor displacing adult workers, or, on the other hand, forced idleness. The two kinds of statutes—compulsory school attendance and child labor laws—tend to keep children of certain ages off the labor market and in school; this regimen in turn provides opportunity to prepare for a livelihood of a higher order than that which children could pursue without education and protects their health in adolescence.

In these terms, Wisconsin's interest in compelling the school attendance of Amish children to age 16 emerges as somewhat less substantial than requiring such attendance for children generally. For, while agricultural employment is not totally outside the legitimate concerns of the child labor laws, employment of children under parental guidance and on the family farm from age 14 to age 16 is an ancient tradition that lies at the periphery of the objectives of such laws. There is no intimation that the Amish employment of their children on family farms is in any way deleterious to their health or that Amish parents exploit children at tender years. Any such inference would be contrary to the record before us. Moreover, employment of Amish children on the family farm does not present the undesirable economic aspects of eliminating jobs that might otherwise be held by adults.

IV

Finally, the State, on authority of Prince v. Massachusetts, argues that a decision exempting Amish children from the State's requirement fails to recognize the substantive right of the Amish child to a secondary education, and fails to give due regard to the power of the State as parens patriae to extend the benefit of secondary education to children regardless of the wishes of their parents. Taken at its broadest sweep, the Court's language in Prince, might be read to give support to the State's position. However, the Court was not confronted in Prince with a situation comparable to that of the Amish as revealed in this record; this is shown by the Court's severe characterization of the evils that it thought the legislature could legitimately associate with child labor, even when performed in the company of an adult. The Court later took great care to confine Prince to a narrow scope in Sherbert v. Verner, when it stated:

> "On the other hand, the Court has rejected challenges under the Free Exercise Clause to governmental regulation of certain overt acts prompted by religious beliefs or principles, for 'even when the action is in accord with one's religious convictions, [it] is not totally free from legislative restrictions.' Braunfeld v. Brown. The conduct or actions so regulated have invariably posed some substantial threat to public safety, peace or order. See, e. g., Reynolds v. United States; Jacobson v. Massachusetts; Prince v. Massachusetts.

This case, of course, is not one in which any harm to the physical or mental health of the child or to the public safety, peace, order, or welfare has been demonstrated or may be properly inferred. The record is to the contrary, and any reliance on that theory would find no support in the evidence.

Contrary to the suggestion of the dissenting opinion of MR. JUSTICE DOUGLAS, our holding today in no degree depends on the assertion of the religious interest of the child as contrasted with that of the parents. It is the parents who are subject to prosecution here for failing to cause their children to attend school, and it is their right of free exercise, not that of their children, that must determine Wisconsin's power to impose criminal penalties on the parent. The dissent argues that a child who expresses a desire to attend public high school in conflict with the wishes of his parents should not be prevented from doing so. There is no reason for the Court to consider that point since it is not an issue in the case. The children are not parties to this litigation. The State has at no point tried this case on the theory that respondents were preventing their children from attending school against their expressed desires, and indeed the record is to the contrary. The State's position from the outset has been that it is empowered to apply its compulsory-attendance law to Amish parents in the same manner as to other parents—that is, without regard to the wishes of the child. That is the claim we reject today.

Our holding in no way determines the proper resolution of possible competing interests of parents, children, and the State in an appropriate state court proceeding in which the power of the State is asserted on the theory that Amish parents are preventing their minor children from attending high school despite their expressed desires to the contrary. Recognition of the claim of the State in such a proceeding would, of course, call into question traditional concepts of parental control over the religious up-bringing and education of their minor children recognized in this Court's past decisions. It is clear that such an intrusion by a State into family decisions in the area of religious training would give rise to grave questions of religious freedom comparable to those raised here and those presented in Pierce v. Society of Sisters, (1925). On this record we neither reach nor decide those issues.

The State's argument proceeds without reliance on any actual conflict between the wishes of parents and children. It appears to rest on the potential that exemption of Amish parents from the requirements of the compulsory-education law might allow some parents to act contrary to the best interests of their children by foreclosing their opportunity to make an intelligent choice between the Amish way of life and that of the outside world. The same argument could, of course, be made with respect to all church schools short of college. There is nothing in the record or in the ordinary course of human experience to suggest that non-Amish parents generally consult with children of ages 14-16 if they are placed in a church school of the parents' faith.

Indeed it seems clear that if the State is empowered, as parens patriae, to "save" a child from himself or his Amish parents by requiring an additional two years of compulsory formal high school education, the State will in large measure influence, if not determine, the religious future of the child. Even more markedly than in Prince, therefore, this case involves the fundamental interest of parents, as contrasted with that of the State, to guide the religious future and education of their children. The history and culture of Western civilization reflect a strong tradition of parental concern for the nurture and upbringing of their children. This primary role of the parents in the upbringing of their children is now established beyond debate as an enduring American tradition. If not the first, perhaps the most significant statements of the Court in this area are found in Pierce v. Society of Sisters, in which the Court observed:

> "Under the doctrine of Meyer v. Nebraska, we think it entirely plain that the Act of 1922 unreasonably interferes with the liberty of parents and guardians to direct the upbringing and education of children under their control. As often heretofore pointed out, rights guaranteed by the Constitution may not be abridged by legislation which has no reasonable relation to some purpose within the competency of the State. The fundamental theory of liberty upon which all governments in this Union repose excludes any general power of the State to standardize its children by forcing them to accept instruction from public teachers only. The child is not the mere creature of the State; those who nurture him and direct his destiny have the right, coupled with the high duty, to recognize and prepare him for additional obligations."

The duty to prepare the child for "additional obligations," referred to by the Court, must be read to include the inculcation of moral standards, religious beliefs, and elements of good citizenship. Pierce, of course, recognized that where nothing more than the general interest of the parent in the nurture and education of his children is involved, it is beyond dispute that the State acts "reasonably" and constitutionally in requiring education to age 16 in some public or private school meeting the standards prescribed by the State.

However read, the Court's holding in Pierce stands as a charter of the rights of parents to direct the religious up-bringing of their children. And, when the interests of parenthood are combined with a free exercise claim of the nature revealed by this record, more than merely a "reasonable relation to some purpose within the competency of the State" is required to sustain the validity of the State's requirement under the First Amendment. To be sure, the power of the parent, even when linked to a free exercise claim, may be subject to limitation under Prince if it appears that parental decisions will jeopardize the health or safety of the child, or have a potential for significant social burdens. But in this case, the Amish have introduced persuasive evidence undermining the arguments the State has advanced to support its claims in terms of the welfare of the child and society as a whole. The record strongly indicates that accommodating the religious objections of the Amish by forgoing one, or at most two, additional years of compulsory education will not impair the physical or mental health of the child, or result in an inability to be self-supporting or to discharge the duties and responsibilities of citizenship, or in any other way materially detract from the welfare of society.

In the face of our consistent emphasis on the central values underlying the Religion Clauses in our constitutional scheme of government, we cannot accept a parens patriae claim of such all-encompassing scope and with such sweeping potential for broad and unforeseeable application as that urged by the State.

V

For the reasons stated we hold, with the Supreme Court of Wisconsin, that the First and Fourteenth Amendments prevent the State from compelling respondents to cause their children to attend formal high school to age 16. Our disposition of this case, however, in no way alters our recognition of the obvious fact that courts are not school boards or legislatures, and are ill-equipped to determine the "necessity" of discrete aspects of a State's program of compulsory education. This should suggest that courts must move with great circumspection in performing the sensitive and delicate task of weighing a State's legitimate social concern when faced with religious claims for exemption from generally applicable educational requirements. It cannot be overemphasized that we are not dealing with a way of life and mode of education by a group claiming to have recently discovered some "progressive" or more enlightened process for rearing children for modern life.

Aided by a history of three centuries as an identifiable religious sect and a long history as a successful and self-sufficient segment of American society, the Amish in this case have convincingly demonstrated the sincerity of their religious beliefs, the interrelationship of belief with their mode of life, the vital role that belief and daily conduct play in the continued survival of Old Order Amish communities and their religious organization, and the hazards presented by the State's enforcement of a statute generally valid as to others. Beyond this, they have carried the even more difficult burden of demonstrating the adequacy of their alternative mode of continuing informal vocational education in terms of precisely those overall interests that the State advances in support of its program of compulsory high school education. In light of this convincing showing, one that probably few other religious groups or sects could make, and weighing the minimal difference between what the State would require and what the Amish already accept, it was incumbent on the State to show with more particularity how its admittedly strong interest in compulsory education would be adversely affected by granting an exemption to the Amish. Sherbert v. Verner, supra.

Nothing we hold is intended to undermine the general applicability of the State's compulsory school-attendance statutes or to limit the power of the State to promulgate reasonable standards that, while not impairing the free exercise of religion, provide for continuing agricultural vocational education under parental and church guidance by the Old Order Amish or others similarly situated. The States have had a long history of amicable and effective relationships with church-sponsored schools, and there is no basis for assuming that, in this related context, reasonable standards cannot be established concerning the content of the continuing vocational education of Amish children under parental guidance, provided always that state regulations are not inconsistent with what we have said in this opinion.

Affirmed.

MR. JUSTICE POWELL and MR. JUSTICE REHNQUIST took no part in the consideration or decision of this case.

MR. JUSTICE STEWART, with whom MR. JUSTICE BRENNAN joins, concurring.

This case involves the constitutionality of imposing criminal punishment upon Amish parents for their religiously based refusal to compel their children to attend public high schools. Wisconsin has sought to brand these parents as criminals for following their religious beliefs, and the Court today rightly holds that Wisconsin cannot constitutionally do so.

This case in no way involves any questions regarding the right of the children of Amish parents to attend public high schools, or any other institutions of learning, if they wish to do so. As the Court points out, there is no suggestion whatever in the record that the religious beliefs of the children here concerned differ in any way from those of their parents. Only one of the children testified. The last two questions and answers on her cross-examination accurately sum up her testimony:

Q. "So I take it then, Frieda, the only reason you are not going to school, and did not go to school since last September, is because of your religion?"

A. "Yes."

Q. "That is the only reason?"

A. "Yes." (Emphasis supplied.)

It is clear to me, therefore, that this record simply does not present the interesting and important issue discussed in Part II of the dissenting opinion of MR. JUSTICE DOUGLAS. With this observation, I join the opinion and the judgment of the Court.

MR. JUSTICE WHITE, with whom MR. JUSTICE BRENNAN and MR. JUSTICE STEWART join, concurring.

Cases such as this one inevitably call for a delicate balancing of important but conflicting interests. I join the opinion and judgment of the Court because I cannot say that the State's interest in requiring two more years of compulsory education in the ninth and tenth grades outweighs the importance of the concededly sincere Amish religious practice to the survival of that sect.

This would be a very different case for me if respondent's claim were that their religion forbade their children from attending any school at any time and from complying in any way with the educational standards set by the State. Since the Amish children are permitted to acquire the basic tools of literacy to survive in modern society by attending grades one through eight and since the deviation from the State's compulsory-education law is relatively slight, I conclude that respondents' claim must prevail, largely because "religious freedom—the freedom to believe and to practice strange and, it may be, foreign creeds—has classically been one of the highest values of our society." Braunfeld v. Brown, (1961) (BRENNAN, J., concurring and dissenting).

The importance of the state interest asserted here cannot be denigrated, however:

> "Today, education is perhaps the most important function of state and local governments. Compulsory school attendance laws and the great expenditures for education both demonstrate our recognition of the importance of education to our democratic society. It is required in the performance of our most basic public responsibilities, even service in the armed forces. It is the very foundation of good citizenship. Today it is a principal instrument in awakening the child to cultural values, in preparing him for later professional training, and in helping him to adjust normally to his environment." Brown v. Board of Education, (1954).

As recently as last Term, the Court re-emphasized the legitimacy of the State's concern for enforcing minimal educational standards, Lemon v. Kurtzman, (1971). Pierce v. Society of Sisters, (1925), lends no support to the contention that parents may replace state educational requirements with their own idiosyncratic views of what knowledge a child needs to be a productive and happy member of society; in Pierce, both the parochial and military schools were in compliance with all the educational standards that the State had set, and the Court held simply that while a State may posit such standards, it may not pre-empt the educational process by requiring children to attend public schools. In the present case, the State is not concerned with the maintenance of an educational system as an end in itself, it is rather attempting to nurture and develop the human potential of its children, whether Amish or non-Amish: to expand their knowledge, broaden their sensibilities, kindle their imagination, foster a spirit of free inquiry, and increase their human understanding and tolerance. It is possible that most Amish children will wish to continue living the rural life of their parents, in which case their training at home will adequately equip them for their future role. Others, however, may wish to become nuclear physicists, ballet dancers, computer programmers, or historians, and for these occupations, formal training will be necessary. There is evidence in the record that many children desert the Amish faith when they come of age. A State has a legitimate interest not only in seeking to develop the latent talents of its children but also in seeking to prepare them for the life style that they may later choose, or at least to provide them with an option other than the life they have led in the past. In the circumstances of this case, although the question is close, I am unable to say that the State has demonstrated that Amish children who leave school in the eighth grade will be intellectually stultified or unable to acquire new academic skills later. The statutory minimum school attendance age set by the State is, after all, only 16.

Decision in cases such as this and the administration of an exemption for Old Order Amish from the State's compulsory school-attendance laws will inevitably involve the kind of close and perhaps repeated scrutiny of religious practices, as is exemplified in today's opinion, which the Court has heretofore been anxious to avoid. But such entanglement does not create a forbidden establishment of religion where it is essential to implement free exercise values threatened by an otherwise neutral program instituted to foster some permissible, nonreligious state objective. I join the Court because the sincerity of the Amish religious policy here is uncontested, because the potentially adverse impact of the state requirement is great, and because the State's valid interest in education has already been largely satisfied by the eight years the children have already spent in school.

MR. JUSTICE DOUGLAS, dissenting in part.

I

I agree with the Court that the religious scruples of the Amish are opposed to the education of their children beyond the grade schools, yet I disagree with the Court's conclusion that the matter is within the dispensation of parents alone. The Court's analysis assumes that the only interests at stake in the case are those of the Amish parents on the one hand, and those of the State on the other. The difficulty with this approach is that, despite the Court's claim, the parents are seeking to vindicate not only their own free exercise claims, but also those of their high-school-age children.

It is argued that the right of the Amish children to religious freedom is not presented by the facts of the case, as the issue before the Court involves only the Amish parents' religious freedom to defy a state criminal statute imposing upon them an affirmative duty to cause their children to attend high school.

First, respondents' motion to dismiss in the trial court expressly asserts, not only the religious liberty of the adults, but also that of the children, as a defense to the prosecutions. It is, of course, beyond question that the parents have standing as defendants in a criminal prosecution to assert the religious interests of their children as a defense. Although the lower courts and a majority of this Court assume an identity of interest between parent and child, it is clear that they have treated the religious interest of the child as a factor in the analysis.

Second, it is essential to reach the question to decide the case, not only because the question was squarely raised in the motion to dismiss, but also because no analysis of religious-liberty claims can take place in a vacuum. If the parents in this case are allowed a religious exemption, the inevitable effect is to impose the parents' notions of religious duty upon their children. Where the child is mature enough to express potentially conflicting desires, it would be an invasion of the child's rights to permit such an imposition without canvassing his views. As in Prince v. Massachusetts, it is an imposition resulting from this very litigation. As the child has no other effective forum, it is in this litigation that his rights should be considered. And, if an Amish child desires to attend high school, and is mature enough to have that desire respected, the State may well be able to override the parents' religiously motivated objections.

Religion is an individual experience. It is not necessary, nor even appropriate, for every Amish child to express his views on the subject in a prosecution of a single adult. Crucial, however, are the views of the child whose parent is the subject of the suit. Frieda Yoder has in fact testified that her own religious views are opposed to high-school education. I therefore join the judgment of the Court as to respondent Jonas Yoder. But Frieda Yoder's views may not be those of Vernon Yutzy or Barbara Miller. I must dissent, therefore, as to respondents Adin Yutzy and Wallace Miller as their motion to dismiss also raised the question of their children's religious liberty.

II

This issue has never been squarely presented before today. Our opinions are full of talk about the power of the parents over the child's education. See Pierce v. Society of Sisters; Meyer v. Nebraska. And we have in the past analyzed similar conflicts between parent and State with little regard for the views of the child. See Prince v. Massachusetts, supra. Recent cases, however, have clearly held that the children themselves have constitutionally protectible interests.

These children are "persons" within the meaning of the Bill of Rights. We have so held over and over again. In Haley v. Ohio, we extended the protection of the Fourteenth Amendment in a state trial of a 15-year-old boy. In In re Gault, we held that "neither the Fourteenth Amendment nor the Bill of Rights is for adults alone." In In re Winship, we held that a 12-year-old boy, when charged with an act which would be a crime if committed by an adult, was entitled to procedural safeguards contained in the Sixth Amendment.

In Tinker v. Des Moines School District, we dealt with 13-year-old, 15-year-old, and 16-year-old students who wore armbands to public schools and were disciplined for doing so. We gave them relief, saying that their First Amendment rights had been abridged.

> "Students in school as well as out of school are 'persons' under our Constitution. They are possessed of fundamental rights which the State must respect, just as they themselves must respect their obligations to the State." Id., at 511.

In Board of Education v. Barnette, we held that schoolchildren, whose religious beliefs collided with a school rule requiring them to salute the flag, could not be required to do so. While the sanction included expulsion of the students and prosecution of the parents, id., at 630, the vice of the regime was its interference with the child's free exercise of religion. We said: "Here . . . we are dealing with a compulsion of students to declare a belief." Id., at 631. In emphasizing the important and delicate task of boards of education we said:

> "That they are educating the young for citizenship is reason for scrupulous protection of Constitutional freedoms of the individual, if we are not to strangle the free mind at its source and teach youth to discount important principles of our government as mere platitudes." Id., at 637.

On this important and vital matter of education, I think the children should be entitled to be heard. While the parents, absent dissent, normally speak for the entire family, the education of the child is a matter on which the child will often have decided views. He may want to be a pianist or an astronaut or an oceanographer. To do so he will have to break from the Amish tradition.

It is the future of the student, not the future of the parents, that is imperiled by today's decision. If a parent keeps his child out of school beyond the grade school, then the child will be forever barred from entry into the new and amazing world of diversity that we have today. The child may decide that that is the preferred course, or he may rebel. It is the student's judgment, not his parents', that is essential if we are to give full meaning to what we have said about the Bill of Rights and of the right of students to be masters of their own destiny. If he is harnessed to the Amish way of life by those in authority over him and if his education is truncated, his entire life may be stunted and deformed. The child, therefore, should be given an opportunity to be heard before the State gives the exemption which we honor today.

The views of the two children in question were not canvassed by the Wisconsin courts. The matter should be explicitly reserved so that new hearings can be held on remand of the case.

III

I think the emphasis of the Court on the "law and order" record of this Amish group of people is quite irrelevant. A religion is a religion irrespective of what the misdemeanor or felony records of its members might be. I am not at all sure how the Catholics, Episcopalians, the Baptists, Jehovah's Witnesses, the Unitarians, and my own Presbyterians would make out if subjected to such a test. It is, of course, true that if a group or society was organized to perpetuate crime and if that is its motive, we would have rather startling problems akin to those that were raised when some years back a particular sect was challenged here as operating on a fraudulent basis. United States v. Ballard. But no such factors are present here, and the Amish, whether with a high or low criminal record, certainly qualify by all historic standards as a religion within the meaning of the First Amendment.

The Court rightly rejects the notion that actions, even though religiously grounded, are always outside the protection of the Free Exercise Clause of the First Amendment. In so ruling, the Court departs from the teaching of Reynolds v. United States, where it was said concerning the reach of the Free Exercise Clause of the First Amendment, "Congress was deprived of all legislative power over mere opinion, but was left free to reach actions which were in violation of social duties or subversive of good order." In that case it was conceded that polygamy was a part of the religion of the Mormons. Yet the Court said, "It matters not that his belief [in polygamy] was a part of his professed religion: it was still belief, and belief only." Id., at 167.

Action, which the Court deemed to be antisocial, could be punished even though it was grounded on deeply held and sincere religious convictions. What we do today, at least in this respect, opens the way to give organized religion a broader base than it has ever enjoyed; and it even promises that in time Reynolds will be overruled.

In another way, however, the Court retreats when in reference to Henry Thoreau it says his "choice was philosophical and personal rather than religious, and such belief does not rise to the demands of the Religion Clauses." That is contrary to what we held in United States v. Seeger, where we were concerned with the meaning of the words "religious training and belief" in the Selective Service Act, which were the basis of many conscientious objector claims. We said:

> "Within that phrase would come all sincere religious beliefs which are based upon a power or being, or upon a faith, to which all else is subordinate or upon which all else is ultimately dependent. The test might be stated in these words: A sincere and meaningful belief which occupies in the life of its possessor a place parallel to that filled by the God of those admittedly qualifying for the exemption comes within the statutory definition. This construction avoids imputing to Congress an intent to classify different religious beliefs, exempting some and excluding others, and is in accord with the well-established congressional policy of equal treatment for those whose opposition to service is grounded in their religious tenets." Id., at 176.

Welsh v. United States, was in the same vein, the Court saying:

> "In this case, Welsh's conscientious objection to war was undeniably based in part on his perception of world politics. In a letter to his local board, he wrote:
>
> "'I can only act according to what I am and what I see. And I see that the military complex wastes both human and material resources, that it fosters disregard for (what I consider a paramount concern) human needs and ends; I see that the means we employ to "defend" our "way of life" profoundly change that way of life. I see that in our failure to recognize the political, social, and economic realities of the world, we, as a nation, fail our responsibility as a nation.'" Id., at 342.

The essence of Welsh's philosophy, on the basis of which we held he was entitled to an exemption, was in these words:

> "'I believe that human life is valuable in and of itself; in its living; therefore I will not injure or kill another human being. This belief (and the corresponding "duty" to abstain from violence toward another person) is not "superior to those arising from any human relation." On the contrary: it is essential to every human relation. I cannot, therefore, conscientiously comply with the Government's insistence that I assume duties which I feel are immoral and totally repugnant.'" Id., at 343.

I adhere to these exalted views of "religion" and see no acceptable alternative to them now that we have become a Nation of many religions and sects, representing all of the diversities of the human race. United States v. Seeger, (concurring opinion).

SAN ANTONIO INDEPENDENT SCHOOL DISTRICT ET AL. V. RODRIGUEZ ET AL., 411 U.S. 1 (1973)

SUPREME COURT OF THE UNITED STATES
APPEAL FROM THE UNITED STATES DISTRICT COURT FOR THE WESTERN DISTRICT OF TEXAS
ARGUED OCTOBER 12, 1972. DECIDED MARCH 21, 1973.

The financing of public elementary and secondary schools in Texas is a product of state and local participation. Almost half of the revenues are derived from a largely state-funded program designed to provide a basic minimum educational offering in every school. Each district supplements state aid through an ad valorem tax on property within its jurisdiction. Appellees brought this class action on behalf of schoolchildren said to be members of poor families who reside in school districts having a low property tax base, making the claim that the Texas system's reliance on local property taxation favors the more affluent and violates equal protection requirements because of substantial interdistrict disparities in per-pupil expenditures resulting primarily from differences in the value of assessable property among the districts. The District Court, finding that wealth is a "suspect" classification and that education is a "fundamental" right, concluded that the system could be upheld only upon a showing, which appellants failed to make, that there was a compelling state interest for the system. The court also concluded that appellants failed even to demonstrate a reasonable or rational basis for the State's system. Held:

1. This is not a proper case in which to examine a State's laws under standards of strict judicial scrutiny, since that test is reserved for cases involving laws that operate to the disadvantage of suspect classes or interfere with the exercise of fundamental rights and liberties explicitly or implicitly protected by the Constitution.
   - (a) The Texas system does not disadvantage any suspect class. It has not been shown to discriminate against any definable class of "poor" people or to occasion discriminations depending on the relative wealth of the families in any district. And, insofar as the financing system disadvantages those who, disregarding their individual income characteristics, reside in comparatively poor school districts, the resulting class cannot be said to be suspect.
   - (b) Nor does the Texas school-financing system impermissibly interfere with the exercise of a "fundamental" right or liberty. Though education is one of the most important services performed by the State, it is not within the limited category of rights recognized by this Court as guaranteed by the Constitution. Even if some identifiable quantum of education is arguably entitled to constitutional protection

to make meaningful the exercise of other constitutional rights, here there is no showing that the Texas system fails to provide the basic minimal skills necessary for that purpose.

(c) Moreover, this is an inappropriate case in which to invoke strict scrutiny since it involves the most delicate and difficult questions of local taxation, fiscal planning, educational policy, and federalism, considerations counseling a more restrained form of review.

2. The Texas system does not violate the Equal Protection Clause of the Fourteenth Amendment. Though concededly imperfect, the system bears a rational relationship to a legitimate state purpose. While assuring a basic education for every child in the State, it permits and encourages participation in and significant control of each district's schools at the local level.

MR. JUSTICE POWELL delivered the opinion of the Court.

This suit attacking the Texas system of financing public education was initiated by Mexican-American parents whose children attend the elementary and secondary schools in the Edgewood Independent School District, an urban school district in San Antonio, Texas. They brought a class action on behalf of schoolchildren throughout the State who are members of minority groups or who are poor and reside in school districts having a low property tax base. Named as defendants were the State Board of Education, the Commissioner of Education, the State Attorney General, and the Bexar County (San Antonio) Board of Trustees. The complaint was filed in the summer of 1968 and a three-judge court was impaneled in January 1969. In December 1971 the panel rendered its judgment in a per curiam opinion holding the Texas school finance system unconstitutional under the Equal Protection Clause of the Fourteenth Amendment. The State appealed, and we noted probable jurisdiction to consider the far-reaching constitutional questions presented. (1972). For the reasons stated in this opinion, we reverse the decision of the District Court.

I

The first Texas State Constitution, promulgated upon Texas' entry into the Union in 1845, provided for the establishment of a system of free schools. Early in its history, Texas adopted a dual approach to the financing of its schools, relying on mutual participation by the local school districts and the State. As early as 1883, the state constitution was amended to provide for the creation of local school districts empowered to levy ad valorem taxes with the consent of local taxpayers for the "erection . . . of school buildings" and for the "further maintenance of public free schools." Such local funds as were raised were supplemented by funds distributed to each district from the State's Permanent and Available School Funds. The Permanent School Fund, its predecessor established in 1854 with $2,000,000 realized from an annexation settlement, was thereafter endowed with millions of acres of public land set aside to assure a continued source of income for school support. The Available School Fund, which received income from the Permanent School Fund as well as from a state ad valorem property tax and other designated taxes, served as the disbursing arm for most state educational funds throughout the late 1800's and first half of this century. Additionally, in 1918 an increase in state property taxes was used to finance a program providing free textbooks throughout the State.

Until recent times, Texas was a predominantly rural State and its population and property wealth were spread relatively evenly across the State. Sizable differences in the value of assessable property between local school districts became increasingly evident as the State became more industrialized and as rural-to-urban population shifts became more pronounced. The location of commercial and industrial property began to play a significant role in determining the amount of tax resources available to each school district. These growing disparities in population and taxable property between districts were responsible in part for increasingly notable differences in levels of local expenditure for education.

In due time it became apparent to those concerned with financing public education that contributions from the Available School Fund were not sufficient to ameliorate these disparities. Prior to 1939, the Available School Fund contributed money to every school district at a rate of $17.50 per school-age child. Although the amount was increased several times in the early 1940's, the Fund was providing only $46 per student by 1945.

Recognizing the need for increased state funding to help offset disparities in local spending and to meet Texas' changing educational requirements, the state legislature in the late 1940's undertook a thorough evaluation of public education with an eye toward major reform. In 1947, an 18-member committee, composed of educators and legislators, was appointed to explore alternative systems in other States and to propose a funding scheme that would guarantee a minimum or basic educational offering to each child and that would help overcome interdistrict disparities in taxable resources. The Committee's efforts led to the passage of the Gilmer-Aikin bills, named for the Committee's co-chairmen, establishing the Texas Minimum Foundation School Program. Today, this Program accounts for approximately half of the total educational expenditures in Texas.

The Program calls for state and local contributions to a fund earmarked specifically for teacher salaries, operating expenses, and transportation costs. The State, supplying funds from its general revenues, finances approximately 80% of the Program, and the school districts are responsible—as a unit—for providing the remaining 20%. The districts' share, known as the Local Fund Assignment, is apportioned among the school districts under a formula designed to reflect each district's relative taxpaying ability. The Assignment is first divided among Texas' 254 counties pursuant to a complicated economic index that takes into account the relative value of each county's contribution to the State's total income from manufacturing, mining, and agricultural activities. It also considers each county's relative share of all payrolls paid within the State and, to a lesser extent, considers each county's share of all property in the State. Each county's assignment is then divided among its school districts on the basis of each district's share of assessable property within the county. The district, in turn, finances its share of the Assignment out of revenues from local property taxation.

The design of this complex system was twofold. First, it was an attempt to assure that the Foundation Program would have an equalizing influence on expenditure levels between school districts by placing the heaviest burden on the school districts most capable of paying. Second, the Program's architects sought to establish a Local Fund Assignment that would force every school district to contribute to the education of its children but that would not by itself exhaust any district's resources. Today every school district does impose a property tax from which it derives locally expendable funds in excess of the amount necessary to satisfy its Local Fund Assignment under the Foundation Program.

In the years since this program went into operation in 1949, expenditures for education—from state as well as local sources—have increased steadily. Between 1949 and 1967, expenditures increased approximately 500%. In the last decade alone the total public school budget rose from $750 million to $2.1 billion and these increases have been reflected in consistently rising per-pupil expenditures throughout the State. Teacher salaries, by far the largest item in any school's budget, have increased dramatically—the state-supported minimum salary for teachers possessing college degrees has risen from $2,400 to $6,000 over the last 20 years.

The school district in which appellees reside, the Edgewood Independent School District, has been compared throughout this litigation with the Alamo Heights Independent School District. This comparison between the least and most affluent districts in the San Antonio area serves to illustrate the manner in which the dual system of finance operates and to indicate the extent to which substantial disparities exist despite the State's impressive progress in recent years. Edgewood is one of seven public school districts in the metropolitan area. Approximately 22,000 students are enrolled in its 25 elementary and secondary schools. The district is situated in the core-city sector of San Antonio in a residential neighborhood that has little commercial or industrial property. The residents are predominantly of Mexican-American descent: approximately 90% of the student population is Mexican-American and over 6% is Negro. The average assessed property value per pupil is $5,960—the lowest in the metropolitan area—and the median family income ($4,686) is also the lowest. At an equalized tax rate of $1.05 per $100 of assessed property —the highest in the metropolitan area—the district contributed $26 to the education of each child for the 1967-1968 school year above its Local Fund Assignment for the Minimum Foundation Program. The Foundation Program contributed $222 per pupil for a state-local total of $248. Federal funds added another $108 for a total of $356 per pupil.

Alamo Heights is the most affluent school district in San Antonio. Its six schools, housing approximately 5,000 students, are situated in a residential community quite unlike the Edgewood District. The school population is predominantly "Anglo," having only 18% Mexican-Americans and less than 1% Negroes. The assessed property value per pupil exceeds $49,000, and the median family income is $8,001. In 1967-1968 the local tax rate of $.85 per $100 of valuation yielded $333 per pupil over and above its contribution to the Foundation Program. Coupled with the $225 provided from that Program, the district was able to supply $558 per student. Supplemented by a $36 per-pupil grant from federal sources, Alamo Heights spent $594 per pupil.

Although the 1967–1968 school year figures provide the only complete statistical breakdown for each category of aid, more recent partial statistics indicate that the previously noted trend of increasing state aid has been significant. For the 1970-1971 school year, the Foundation School Program allotment for Edgewood was $356 per pupil, a 62% increase over the 1967–1968 school year. Indeed, state aid alone in 1970–1971 equaled Edgewood's entire 1967–1968 school budget from local, state, and federal sources. Alamo Heights enjoyed a similar increase under the Foundation Program, netting $491 per pupil in 1970-1971. These recent figures also reveal the extent to which these two districts' allotments were funded from their own required contributions to the Local Fund Assignment. Alamo Heights, because of its relative wealth, was required to contribute out of its local property tax collections approximately $100 per pupil, or about 20% of its Foundation grant. Edgewood, on the other hand, paid only $8.46 per pupil, which is about 2.4% of its grant. It appears then that, at least as to these two districts, the Local Fund Assignment does reflect a rough approximation of the relative taxpaying potential of each.

Despite these recent increases, substantial interdistrict disparities in school expenditures found by the District Court to prevail in San Antonio and in varying degrees throughout the State still exist. And it was these disparities, largely attributable to differences in the amounts of money collected through local property taxation, that led the District Court to conclude that Texas' dual system of public school financing violated the Equal Protection Clause. The District Court held that the Texas system discriminates on the basis of wealth in the manner in which education is provided for its people. 337 F. Supp., at 282. Finding that wealth is a "suspect" classification and that education is a "fundamental" interest, the District Court held that the Texas system could be sustained only if the State could show that it was premised upon some compelling state interest. Id., at 282-284. On this issue the court concluded that "[n]ot only are defendants unable to demonstrate compelling state interests . . . they fail even to establish a reasonable basis for these classifications." Id., at 284.

Texas virtually concedes that its historically rooted dual system of financing education could not withstand the strict judicial scrutiny that this Court has found appropriate in reviewing legislative judgments that interfere with fundamental constitutional rights or that involve suspect classifications. If, as previous decisions have indicated, strict scrutiny means that the State's system is not entitled to the usual presumption of validity, that the State rather than the complainants must carry a "heavy burden of justification," that the State must demonstrate that its educational system has been structured with "precision," and is "tailored" narrowly to serve legitimate objectives and that it has selected the "less drastic means" for effectuating its objectives, the Texas financing system and its counterpart in virtually every other State will not pass muster. The State candidly admits that "[n]o one familiar with the Texas system would contend that it has yet achieved perfection." Apart from its concession that educational financing in Texas has "defects" and "imperfections," the State defends the system's rationality with vigor and disputes the District Court's finding that it lacks a "reasonable basis."

This, then, establishes the framework for our analysis. We must decide, first, whether the Texas system of financing public education operates to the disadvantage of some suspect class or impinges upon a fundamental right explicitly or implicitly protected by the Constitution, thereby requiring strict judicial scrutiny. If so, the judgment of the District Court should be affirmed. If not, the Texas scheme must still be examined to determine whether it rationally furthers some legitimate, articulated state purpose and therefore does not constitute an invidious discrimination in violation of the Equal Protection Clause of the Fourteenth Amendment.

II

The District Court's opinion does not reflect the novelty and complexity of the constitutional questions posed by appellees' challenge to Texas' system of school financing. In concluding that strict judicial scrutiny was required, that court relied on decisions dealing with the rights of indigents to equal treatment in the criminal trial and appellate processes, and on cases disapproving wealth restrictions on the right to vote. Those cases, the District Court concluded, established wealth as a suspect classification. Finding that the local property tax system discriminated on the basis of wealth, it regarded those precedents as controlling. It then reasoned, based on decisions of this Court affirming the undeniable importance of education, that there is a fundamental right to education and that, absent some compelling state justification, the Texas system could not stand.

We are unable to agree that this case, which in significant aspects is sui generis, may be so neatly fitted into the conventional mosaic of constitutional analysis under the Equal Protection Clause. Indeed, for the several reasons that follow, we find neither the suspect-classification nor the fundamental-interest analysis persuasive.

A

The wealth discrimination discovered by the District Court in this case, and by several other courts that have recently struck down school-financing laws in other States, is quite unlike any of the forms of wealth discrimination heretofore reviewed by this Court. Rather than focusing on the unique features of the alleged discrimination, the courts in these cases have virtually assumed their findings of a suspect classification through a simplistic process of analysis: since, under the traditional systems of financing public schools, some poorer people receive less expensive educations than other more affluent people, these systems discriminate on the basis of wealth. This approach largely ignores the hard threshold questions, including whether it makes a difference for purposes of consideration under the Constitution that the class of disadvantaged "poor" cannot be identified or defined in customary equal protection terms, and whether the relative—rather than absolute—nature of the asserted deprivation is of significant consequence. Before a State's laws and the justifications for the classifications they create are subjected to strict judicial scrutiny, we think these threshold considerations must be analyzed more closely than they were in the court below.

The case comes to us with no definitive description of the classifying facts or delineation of the disfavored class. Examination of the District Court's opinion and of appellees' complaint, briefs, and contentions at oral argument suggests, however, at least three ways in which the discrimination claimed here might be described. The Texas system of school financing might be regarded as discriminating (1) against "poor" persons whose incomes fall below some identifiable level of poverty or who might be characterized as functionally "indigent," or (2) against those who are relatively poorer than others, or (3) against all those who, irrespective of their personal incomes, happen to reside in relatively poorer school districts. Our task must be to ascertain whether, in fact, the Texas system has been shown to discriminate on any of these possible bases and, if so, whether the resulting classification may be regarded as suspect.

The precedents of this Court provide the proper starting point. The individuals, or groups of individuals, who constituted the class discriminated against in our prior cases shared two distinguishing characteristics: because of their impecunity they were completely unable to pay for some desired benefit, and as a consequence, they sustained an absolute deprivation of a meaningful opportunity to enjoy that benefit. In Griffin v. Illinois, (1956), and its progeny, the Court invalidated state laws that prevented an indigent criminal defendant from acquiring a transcript, or an adequate substitute for a transcript, for use at several stages of the trial and appeal process. The payment requirements in each case were found to occasion de facto discrimination against those who, because of their indigency, were totally unable to pay for transcripts. And the Court in each case emphasized that no constitutional violation would have been shown if the State had provided some "adequate substitute" for a full stenographic transcript. Britt v. North Carolina, (1971); Gardner v. California, (1969); Draper v. Washington, (1963); Eskridge v. Washington Prison Board, (1958).

Likewise, in Douglas v. California, (1963), a decision establishing an indigent defendant's right to court-appointed counsel on direct appeal, the Court dealt only with defendants who could not pay for counsel from their own resources and who had no other way of gaining representation. Douglas provides no relief for those on whom the burdens of paying for a criminal defense are, relatively speaking, great but not insurmountable. Nor does it deal with relative differences in the quality of counsel acquired by the less wealthy.

Williams v. Illinois, (1970), and Tate v. Short, (1971), struck down criminal penalties that subjected indigents to incarceration simply because of their inability to pay a fine. Again, the disadvantaged class was composed only of persons who were totally unable to pay the demanded sum. Those cases do not touch on the question whether equal protection is denied to persons with relatively less money on whom designated fines impose heavier burdens. The Court has not held that fines must be structured to reflect each person's ability to pay in order to avoid disproportionate burdens. Sentencing judges may, and often do, consider the defendant's ability to pay, but in such circumstances they are guided by sound judicial discretion rather than by constitutional mandate.

Finally, in Bullock v. Carter, (1972), the Court invalidated the Texas filing-fee requirement for primary elections. Both of the relevant classifying facts found in the previous cases were present there. The size of the fee, often running into the thousands of dollars and, in at least one case, as high as $8,900, effectively barred all potential candidates who were unable to pay the required fee. As the system provided "no reasonable alternative means of access to the ballot" (id., at 149), inability to pay occasioned an absolute denial of a position on the primary ballot.

Only appellees' first possible basis for describing the class disadvantaged by the Texas school-financing system—discrimination against a class of definably "poor" persons—might arguably meet the criteria established in these prior cases. Even a cursory examination, however, demonstrates that neither of the two distinguishing characteristics of wealth classifications can be found here. First, in support of their charge that the system discriminates against the "poor," appellees have made no effort to demonstrate that it operates to the peculiar disadvantage of any class fairly definable as indigent, or as composed of persons whose incomes are beneath any designated poverty level. Indeed, there is reason to believe that the poorest families are not necessarily clustered in the poorest property districts. A recent and exhaustive study of school districts in Connecticut concluded that "[i]t is clearly incorrect . . . to contend that the 'poor' live in 'poor' districts . . . . Thus, the major factual assumption of Serrano—that the educational financing system discriminates against the 'poor'—is simply false in Connecticut." Defining "poor" families as those below the Bureau of the Census "poverty level," the Connecticut study found, not surprisingly, that the poor were clustered around commercial and industrial areas—those same areas that provide the most attractive sources of property tax income for school districts. Whether a similar pattern would be discovered in Texas is not known, but there is no basis on the record in this case for assuming that the poorest people—defined by reference to any level of absolute impecunity—are concentrated in the poorest districts.

Second, neither appellees nor the District Court addressed the fact that, unlike each of the foregoing cases, lack of personal resources has not occasioned an absolute deprivation of the desired benefit. The argument here is not that the children in districts having relatively low assessable property values are receiving no public education; rather, it is that they are receiving a poorer quality education than that available to children in districts having more assessable wealth. Apart from the unsettled and disputed question whether the quality of education may be determined by the amount of money expended for it, a sufficient answer to appellees' argument is that, at least where wealth is involved, the Equal Protection Clause does not require absolute equality or precisely equal advantages. Nor, indeed, in view of the infinite variables affecting the educational process, can any system assure equal quality of education except in the most relative sense. Texas asserts that the Minimum Foundation Program provides an "adequate" education for all children in the State. By providing 12 years of free public-school education, and by assuring teachers, books, transportation, and operating funds, the Texas Legislature has endeavored to "guarantee, for the welfare of the state as a whole, that all people shall have at least an adequate program of education. This is what is meant by 'A Minimum Foundation Program of Education.'" The State repeatedly asserted in its briefs in this Court that it has fulfilled this desire and that it now assures "every child in every school district an adequate education." No proof was offered at trial persuasively discrediting or refuting the State's assertion.

For these two reasons—the absence of any evidence that the financing system discriminates against any definable category of "poor" people or that it results in the absolute deprivation of education—the disadvantaged class is not susceptible of identification in traditional terms.

As suggested above, appellees and the District Court may have embraced a second or third approach, the second of which might be characterized as a theory of relative or comparative discrimination based on family income. Appellees sought to prove that a direct correlation exists between the wealth of families within each district and the expenditures therein for education. That is, along a continuum, the poorer the family the lower the dollar amount of education received by the family's children.

The principal evidence adduced in support of this comparative-discrimination claim is an affidavit submitted by Professor Joel S. Berke of Syracuse University's Educational Finance Policy Institute. The District Court, relying in major part upon this affidavit and apparently accepting the substance of appellees' theory, noted, first, a positive correlation between the wealth of school districts, measured in terms of assessable property per pupil, and their levels of per-pupil expenditures. Second, the court found a similar correlation between district wealth and the personal wealth of its residents, measured in terms of median family income. 337 F. Supp., at 282 n. 3.

If, in fact, these correlations could be sustained, then it might be argued that expenditures on education—equated by appellees to the quality of education—are dependent on personal wealth. Appellees' comparative-discrimination theory would still face serious unanswered questions, including whether a bare positive correlation or some higher degree of correlation is necessary to provide a basis for concluding that the financing system is designed to operate to the peculiar disadvantage of the comparatively poor, and whether a class of this size and diversity could ever claim the special protection accorded "suspect" classes. These questions need not be addressed in this case, however, since appellees' proof fails to support their allegations or the District Court's conclusions.

Professor Berke's affidavit is based on a survey of approximately 10% of the school districts in Texas. His findings, previously set out in the margin, show only that the wealthiest few districts in the sample have the highest median family incomes and spend the most on education, and that the several poorest districts have the lowest family incomes and devote the least amount of money to education. For the remainder of the districts—96 districts composing almost 90% of the sample—the correlation is inverted, i. e., the districts that spend next to the most money on education are populated by families having next to the lowest median family incomes while the districts spending the least have the highest median family incomes. It is evident that, even if the conceptual questions were answered favorably to appellees, no factual basis exists upon which to found a claim of comparative wealth discrimination.

This brings us, then, to the third way in which the classification scheme might be defined—district wealth discrimination. Since the only correlation indicated by the evidence is between district property wealth and expenditures, it may be argued that discrimination might be found without regard to the individual income characteristics of district residents. Assuming a perfect correlation between district property wealth and expenditures from top to bottom, the disadvantaged class might be viewed as encompassing every child in every district except the district that has the most assessable wealth and spends the most on education. Alternatively, as suggested in MR. JUSTICE MARSHALL'S dissenting opinion, post, at 96, the class might be defined more restrictively to include children in districts with assessable property which falls below the statewide average, or median, or below some other artificially defined level.

However described, it is clear that appellees' suit asks this Court to extend its most exacting scrutiny to review a system that allegedly discriminates against a large, diverse, and amorphous class, unified only by the common factor of residence in districts that happen to have less taxable wealth than other districts. The system of alleged discrimination and the class it defines have none of the traditional indicia of suspectness: the class is not saddled with such disabilities, or subjected to such a history of purposeful unequal treatment, or relegated to such a position of political powerlessness as to command extraordinary protection from the majoritarian political process.

We thus conclude that the Texas system does not operate to the peculiar disadvantage of any suspect class. But in recognition of the fact that this Court has never heretofore held that wealth discrimination alone provides an adequate basis for invoking strict scrutiny, appellees have not relied solely on this contention. They also assert that the State's system impermissibly interferes with the exercise of a "fundamental" right and that accordingly the prior decisions of this Court require the application of the strict standard of judicial review. Graham v. Richardson,(1971); Kramer v. Union School District, (1969); Shapiro v. Thompson, (1969). It is this question—whether education is a fundamental right, in the sense that it is among the rights and liberties protected by the Constitution—which has so consumed the attention of courts and commentators in recent years.

B

In Brown v. Board of Education, (1954), a unanimous Court recognized that "education is perhaps the most important function of state and local governments." Id., at 493. What was said there in the context of racial discrimination has lost none of its vitality with the passage of time:

> "Compulsory school attendance laws and the great expenditures for education both demonstrate our recognition of the importance of education to our democratic society. It is required in the performance of our most basic public responsibilities, even service in the armed forces. It is the very foundation of good citizenship. Today it is a principal instrument in awakening the child to cultural values, in preparing him for later professional training, and in helping him to adjust normally to his environment. In these days, it is doubtful that any child may reasonably be expected to succeed in life if he is denied the opportunity of an education. Such an opportunity, where the state has undertaken to provide it, is a right which must be made available to all on equal terms." Ibid.

This theme, expressing an abiding respect for the vital role of education in a free society, may be found in numerous opinions of Justices of this Court writing both before and after Brown was decided. Wisconsin v. Yoder, (BURGER, C. J.), 237, 238-239 (WHITE, J.), (1972); Abington School Dist. v. Schempp, (1963) (BRENNAN, J.); McCollum v. Board of Education, (1948) (Frankfurter, J.); Pierce v. Society of Sisters, (1925); Meyer v. Nebraska, (1923); Interstate Consolidated Street R. Co. v. Massachusetts, (1907).

Nothing this Court holds today in any way detracts from our historic dedication to public education. We are in complete agreement with the conclusion of the three-judge panel below that "the grave significance of education both to the individual and to our society" cannot be doubted. But the importance of a service performed by the State does not determine whether it must be regarded as fundamental for purposes of examination under the Equal Protection Clause. Mr. Justice Harlan, dissenting from the Court's application of strict scrutiny to a law impinging upon the right of interstate travel, admonished that "[v]irtually every state statute affects important rights." Shapiro v. Thompson, 661. In his view, if the degree of judicial scrutiny of state legislation fluctuated, depending on a majority's view of the importance of the interest affected, we would have gone "far toward making this Court a 'super-legislature.'" Ibid. We would, indeed, then be assuming a legislative role and one for which the Court lacks both authority and competence. But MR. JUSTICE STEWART'S response in Shapiro to Mr. Justice Harlan's concern correctly articulates the limits of the fundamental-rights rationale employed in the Court's equal protection decisions:

> "The Court today does not 'pick out particular human activities, characterize them as "fundamental," and give them added protection . . . .' To the contrary, the Court simply recognizes, as it must, an established constitutional right, and gives to that right no less protection than the Constitution itself demands." Id., at 642. (Emphasis in original.)

MR. JUSTICE STEWART'S statement serves to underline what the opinion of the Court in Shapiro makes clear. In subjecting to strict judicial scrutiny state welfare eligibility statutes that imposed a one-year durational residency requirement as a precondition to receiving AFDC benefits, the Court explained:

> "[I]n moving from State to State . . . appellees were exercising a constitutional right, and any classification which serves to penalize the exercise of that right, unless shown to be necessary to promote a compelling governmental interest, is unconstitutional." Id., at 634. (Emphasis in original.)

The right to interstate travel had long been recognized as a right of constitutional significance, and the Court's decision, therefore, did not require an ad hoc determination as to the social or economic importance of that right.

Lindsey v. Normet, (1972), decided only last Term, firmly reiterates that social importance is not the critical determinant for subjecting state legislation to strict scrutiny. The complainants in that case, involving a challenge to the procedural limitations imposed on tenants in suits brought by landlords under Oregon's Forcible Entry and Wrongful Detainer Law, urged the Court to examine the operation of the statute under "a more stringent standard than mere rationality." Id., at 73. The tenants argued that the statutory limitations implicated "fundamental interests which are particularly important to the poor," such as the "'need for decent shelter'" and the "'right to retain peaceful possession of one's home.'" Ibid. MR. JUSTICE WHITE'S analysis, in his opinion for the Court, is instructive:

> "We do not denigrate the importance of decent, safe, and sanitary housing. But the Constitution does not provide judicial remedies for every social and economic ill. We are unable to perceive in that document any constitutional guarantee of access to dwellings of a particular quality or any recognition of the right of a tenant to occupy the real property of his landlord beyond the term of his lease, without the payment of rent . . . . Absent constitutional mandate, the assurance of adequate housing and the definition of landlord-tenant relationships are legislative, not judicial, functions." Id., at 74. (Emphasis supplied.)

Similarly, in Dandridge v. Williams, (1970), the Court's explicit recognition of the fact that the "administration of public welfare assistance . . . involves the most basic economic needs of impoverished human beings," id., at 485, provided no basis for departing from the settled mode of constitutional analysis of legislative classifications involving questions of economic and social policy. As in the case of housing, the central importance of welfare benefits to the poor was not an adequate foundation for requiring the State to justify its law by showing some compelling state interest. See also Jefferson v. Hackney, (1972); Richardson v. Belcher, (1971).

The lesson of these cases in addressing the question now before the Court is plain. It is not the province of this Court to create substantive constitutional rights in the name of guaranteeing equal protection of the laws. Thus, the key to discovering whether education is "fundamental" is not to be found in comparisons of the relative societal significance of education as opposed to subsistence or housing. Nor is it to be found by weighing whether education is as important as the right to travel. Rather, the answer lies in assessing whether there is a right to education explicitly or implicitly guaranteed by the Constitution. Eisenstadt v. Baird, (1972); Dunn v. Blumstein, (1972); Police Dept. of Chicago v. Mosley, (1972); Skinner v. Oklahoma, (1942).

Education, of course, is not among the rights afforded explicit protection under our Federal Constitution. Nor do we find any basis for saying it is implicitly so protected. As we have said, the undisputed importance of education will not alone cause this Court to depart from the usual standard for reviewing a State's social and economic legislation. It is appellees' contention, however, that education is distinguishable from other services and benefits provided by the State because it bears a peculiarly close relationship to other rights and liberties accorded protection under the Constitution. Specifically, they insist that education is itself a fundamental personal right because it is essential to the effective exercise of First Amendment freedoms and to intelligent utilization of the right to vote. In asserting a nexus between speech and education, appellees urge that the right to speak is meaningless unless the speaker is capable of articulating his thoughts intelligently and persuasively. The "marketplace of ideas" is an empty forum for those lacking basic communicative tools. Likewise, they argue that the corollary right to receive information becomes little more than a hollow privilege when the recipient has not been taught to read, assimilate, and utilize available knowledge.

A similar line of reasoning is pursued with respect to the right to vote. Exercise of the franchise, it is contended, cannot be divorced from the educational foundation of the voter. The electoral process, if reality is to conform to the democratic ideal, depends on an informed electorate: a voter cannot cast his ballot intelligently unless his reading skills and thought processes have been adequately developed.

We need not dispute any of these propositions. The Court has long afforded zealous protection against unjustifiable governmental interference with the individual's rights to speak and to vote. Yet we have never presumed to possess either the ability or the authority to guarantee to the citizenry the most effective speech or the most informed electoral choice. That these may be desirable goals of a system of freedom of expression and of a representative form of government is not to be doubted. These are indeed goals to be pursued by a people whose thoughts and beliefs are freed from governmental interference. But they are not values to be pursued by a implemented by judicial intrusion into otherwise legitimate state activities.

Even if it were conceded that some identifiable quantum of education is a constitutionally protected prerequisite to the meaningful exercise of either right, we have no indication that the present levels of educational expenditures in Texas provide an education that falls short. Whatever merit appellees' argument might have if a State's financing system occasioned an absolute denial of educational opportunities to any of its children, that argument provides no basis for finding an interference with fundamental rights where only relative differences in spending levels are involved and where—as is true in the present case—no charge fairly could be made that the system fails to provide each child with an opportunity to acquire the basic minimal skills necessary for the enjoyment of the rights of speech and of full participation in the political process.

Furthermore, the logical limitations on appellees' nexus theory are difficult to perceive. How, for instance, is education to be distinguished from the significant personal interests in the basics of decent food and shelter? Empirical examination might well buttress an assumption that the ill-fed, ill-clothed, and ill-housed are among the most ineffective participants in the political process, and that they derive the least enjoyment from the benefits of the First Amendment. If so, appellees' thesis would cast serious doubt on the authority of Dandridge v. Williams, supra, and Lindsey v. Normet, supra.

We have carefully considered each of the arguments supportive of the District Court's finding that education is a fundamental right or liberty and have found those arguments unpersuasive. In one further respect we find this a particularly inappropriate case in which to subject state action to strict judicial scrutiny. The present case, in another basic sense, is significantly different from any of the cases in which the Court has applied strict scrutiny to state or federal legislation touching upon constitutionally protected rights. Each of our prior cases involved legislation which "deprived," "infringed," or "interfered" with the free exercise of some such fundamental personal right or liberty. See Skinner v. Oklahoma, supra, at 536; Shapiro v. Thompson, supra, at 634; Dunn v. Blumstein, supra, at 338-343. A critical distinction between those cases and the one now before us lies in what Texas is endeavoring to do with respect to education. MR. JUSTICE BRENNAN, writing for the Court in Katzenbach v. Morgan, (1966), expresses well the salient point:

> "This is not a complaint that Congress . . . has unconstitutionally denied or diluted anyone's right to vote but rather that Congress violated the Constitution by not extending the relief effected [to others similarly situated] . . . .
>
> "[The federal law in question] does not restrict or deny the franchise but in effect extends the franchise to persons who otherwise would be denied it by state law. . . . We need only decide whether the challenged limitation on the relief effected . . . was permissible. In deciding that question, the principle that calls for the closest scrutiny of distinctions in laws denying fundamental rights . . . is inapplicable; for the distinction challenged by appellees is presented only as a limitation on a reform measure aimed at eliminating an existing barrier to the exercise of the franchise. Rather, in deciding the constitutional propriety of the limitations in such a reform measure we are guided by the familiar principles that a 'statute is not invalid under the Constitution because it might have gone farther than it did,' . . . that a leg-

islature need not 'strike at all evils at the same time,' . . . and that 'reform may take one step at a time, addressing itself to the phase of the problem which seems most acute to the legislative mind . . . .'" Id., at 656-657. (Emphasis in original.)

The Texas system of school financing is not unlike the federal legislation involved in Katzenbach in this regard. Every step leading to the establishment of the system Texas utilizes today—including the decisions permitting localities to tax and expend locally, and creating and continuously expanding state aid—was implemented in an effort to extend public education and to improve its quality. Of course, every reform that benefits some more than others may be criticized for what it fails to accomplish. But we think it plain that, in substance, the thrust of the Texas system is affirmative and reformatory and, therefore, should be scrutinized under judicial principles sensitive to the nature of the State's efforts and to the rights reserved to the States under the Constitution.

C

It should be clear, for the reasons stated above and in accord with the prior decisions of this Court, that this is not a case in which the challenged state action must be subjected to the searching judicial scrutiny reserved for laws that create suspect classifications or impinge upon constitutionally protected rights.

We need not rest our decision, however, solely on the inappropriateness of the strict-scrutiny test. A century of Supreme Court adjudication under the Equal Protection Clause affirmatively supports the application of the traditional standard of review, which requires only that the State's system be shown to bear some rational relationship to legitimate state purposes. This case represents far more than a challenge to the manner in which Texas provides for the education of its children. We have here nothing less than a direct attack on the way in which Texas has chosen to raise and disburse state and local tax revenues. We are asked to condemn the State's judgment in conferring on political subdivisions the power to tax local property to supply revenues for local interests. In so doing, appellees would have the Court intrude in an area in which it has traditionally deferred to state legislatures. This Court has often admonished against such interferences with the State's fiscal policies under the Equal Protection Clause:

> "The broad discretion as to classification possessed by a legislature in the field of taxation has long been recognized. . . . [T]he passage of time has only served to underscore the wisdom of that recognition of the large area of discretion which is needed by a legislature in formulating sound tax policies. . . . It has . . . been pointed out that in taxation, even more than in other fields, legislatures possess the greatest freedom in classification. Since the members of a legislature necessarily enjoy a familiarity with local conditions which this Court cannot have, the presumption of constitutionality can be overcome only by the most explicit demonstration that a classification is a hostile and oppressive discrimination against particular persons and classes . . . ." Madden v. Kentucky, (1940).

See also Lehnhausen v. Lake Shore Auto Parts Co., (1973); Wisconsin v. J. C. Penney Co., (1940).

Thus, we stand on familiar ground when we continue to acknowledge that the Justices of this Court lack both the expertise and the familiarity with local problems so necessary to the making of wise decisions with respect to the raising and disposition of public revenues. Yet, we are urged to direct the States either to alter drastically the present system or to throw out the property tax altogether in favor of some other form of taxation. No scheme of taxation, whether the tax is imposed on property, income, or purchases of goods and services, has yet been devised which is free of all discriminatory impact. In such a complex arena in which no perfect alternatives exist, the Court does well not to impose too rigorous a standard of scrutiny lest all local fiscal schemes become subjects of criticism under the Equal Protection Clause.

In addition to matters of fiscal policy, this case also involves the most persistent and difficult questions of educational policy, another area in which this Court's lack of specialized knowledge and experience counsels against premature interference with the informed judgments made at the state and local levels. Education, perhaps even more than welfare assistance, presents a myriad of "intractable economic, social, and even philosophical problems." Dandridge v. Williams. The very complexity of the problems of financing and managing a statewide public school system suggests that "there will be more than one constitutionally permissible method of solving them," and that, within the limits of rationality, "the legislature's efforts to tackle the problems" should be entitled to respect. Jefferson v. Hackney. On even the most basic questions in this area the scholars and educational experts are divided. Indeed, one of the major sources of controversy concerns the extent to which there is a demonstrable correlation between educational expenditures and the quality of education an assumed correlation underlying virtually every legal conclusion drawn by the District Court in this case. Related to the questioned relationship between cost and quality is the equally unsettled controversy as to the proper goals of a system of public education. And the question regarding the most effective relationship between state boards of education and local school boards, in terms of their respective responsibilities and degrees of control, is now undergoing searching reexamination. The ultimate wisdom as to these and related problems of education is not likely to be divined for all time even by the scholars who now so earnestly debate the issues. In such circumstances, the judiciary is well advised to refrain from imposing on the States inflexible constitutional restraints that could circumscribe or handicap the continued research and experimentation so vital to finding even partial solutions to educational problems and to keeping abreast of ever-changing conditions.

It must be remembered, also, that every claim arising under the Equal Protection Clause has implications for the relationship between national and state power under our federal system. Questions of federalism are always inherent in the process of determining whether a State's laws are to be accorded the traditional presumption of constitutionality, or are to be subjected instead to rigorous judicial scrutiny. While "[t]he maintenance of the principles of federalism is a foremost consideration in interpreting any of the pertinent constitutional provisions under which this Court examines state action," it would be difficult to imagine a case having a greater potential impact on our federal system than the one now before us, in which we are urged to abrogate systems of financing public education presently in existence in virtually every State.

The foregoing considerations buttress our conclusion that Texas' system of public school finance is an inappropriate candidate for strict judicial scrutiny. These same considerations are relevant to the determination whether that system, with its conceded imperfections, nevertheless bears some rational relationship to a legitimate state purpose. It is to this question that we next turn our attention.

III

The basic contours of the Texas school finance system have been traced at the outset of this opinion. We will now describe in more detail that system and how it operates, as these facts bear directly upon the demands of the Equal Protection Clause.

Apart from federal assistance, each Texas school receives its funds from the State and from its local school district. On a statewide average, a roughly comparable amount of funds is derived from each source. The State's contribution, under the Minimum Foundation Program, was designed to provide an adequate minimum educational offering in every school in the State. Funds are distributed to assure that there will be one teacher— compensated at the state-supported minimum salary—for every 25 students. Each school district's other supportive personnel are provided for: one principal for every 30 teachers; one "special service" teacher—

librarian, nurse, doctor, etc.— for every 20 teachers; superintendents, vocational instructors, counselors, and educators for exceptional children are also provided. Additional funds are earmarked for current operating expenses, for student transportation, and for free textbooks.

The program is administered by the State Board of Education and by the Central Education Agency, which also have responsibility for school accreditation and for monitoring the statutory teacher-qualification standards. As reflected by the 62% increase in funds allotted to the Edgewood School District over the last three years, the State's financial contribution to education is steadily increasing. None of Texas' school districts, however, has been content to rely alone on funds from the Foundation Program.

By virtue of the obligation to fulfill its Local Fund Assignment, every district must impose an ad valorem tax on property located within its borders. The Fund Assignment was designed to remain sufficiently low to assure that each district would have some ability to provide a more enriched educational program. Every district supplements its Foundation grant in this manner. In some districts, the local property tax contribution is insubstantial, as in Edgewood where the supplement was only $26 per pupil in 1967. In other districts, the local share may far exceed even the total Foundation grant. In part, local differences are attributable to differences in the rates of taxation or in the degree to which the market value for any category of property varies from its assessed value. The greatest interdistrict disparities, however, are attributable to differences in the amount of assessable property available within any district. Those districts that have more property, or more valuable property, have a greater capability for supplementing state funds. In large measure, these additional local revenues are devoted to paying higher salaries to more teachers. Therefore, the primary distinguishing attributes of schools in property-affluent districts are lower pupil-teacher ratios and higher salary schedules.

This, then, is the basic outline of the Texas school financing structure. Because of differences in expenditure levels occasioned by disparities in property tax income, appellees claim that children in less affluent districts have been made the subject of invidious discrimination. The District Court found that the State had failed even "to establish a reasonable basis" for a system that results in different levels of per-pupil expenditure. 337 F. Supp., at 284. We disagree.

In its reliance on state as well as local resources, the Texas system is comparable to the systems employed in virtually every other State. The power to tax local property for educational purposes has been recognized in Texas at least since 1883. When the growth of commercial and industrial centers and accompanying shifts in population began to create disparities in local resources, Texas undertook a program calling for a considerable investment of state funds.

The "foundation grant" theory upon which Texas legislators and educators based the Gilmer-Aikin bills, was a product of the pioneering work of two New York educational reformers in the 1920's, George D. Strayer and Robert M. Haig. Their efforts were devoted to establishing a means of guaranteeing a minimum statewide educational program without sacrificing the vital element of local participation. The Strayer-Haig thesis represented an accommodation between these two competing forces. As articulated by Professor Coleman:

> "The history of education since the industrial revolution shows a continual struggle between two forces: the desire by members of society to have educational opportunity for all children, and the desire of each family to provide the best education it can afford for its own children."

The Texas system of school finance is responsive to these two forces. While assuring a basic education for every child in the State, it permits and encourages a large measure of participation in and control of each district's schools at the local level. In an era that has witnessed a consistent trend toward centralization of the functions of government, local sharing of responsibility for public education has survived. The merit of local control was recognized last Term in both the majority and dissenting opinions in Wright v. Council of the City of Emporia, (1972). MR. JUSTICE STEWART stated there that "[d]irect control over decisions vitally affecting the education of one's children is a need that is strongly felt in our society." Id., at 469. THE CHIEF JUSTICE, in his dissent, agreed that "[l]ocal control is not only vital to continued public support of the schools, but it is of overriding importance from an educational standpoint as well." Id., at 478.

The persistence of attachment to government at the lowest level where education is concerned reflects the depth of commitment of its supporters. In part, local control means, as Professor Coleman suggests, the freedom to devote more money to the education of one's children. Equally important, however, is the opportunity it offers for participation in the decisionmaking process that determines how those local tax dollars will be spent. Each locality is free to tailor local programs to local needs. Pluralism also affords some opportunity for experimentation, innovation, and a healthy competition for educational excellence. An analogy to the Nation-State relationship in our federal system seems uniquely appropriate. Mr. Justice Brandeis identified as one of the peculiar strengths of our form of government each State's freedom to "serve as a laboratory; and try novel social and economic experiments." No area of social concern stands to profit more from a multiplicity of viewpoints and from a diversity of approaches than does public education.

Appellees do not question the propriety of Texas' dedication to local control of education. To the contrary, they attack the school-financing system precisely because, in their view, it does not provide the same level of local control and fiscal flexibility in all districts. Appellees suggest that local control could be preserved and promoted under other financing systems that resulted in more equality in educational expenditures. While it is no doubt true that reliance on local property taxation for school revenues provides less freedom of choice with respect to expenditures for some districts than for others, the existence of "some inequality" in the manner in which the State's rationale is achieved is not alone a sufficient basis for striking down the entire system. McGowan v. Maryland, (1961). It may not be condemned simply because it imperfectly effectuates the State's goals. Dandridge v. Williams. Nor must the financing system fail because, as appellees suggest, other methods of satisfying the State's interest, which occasion "less drastic" disparities in expenditures, might be conceived. Only where state action impinges on the exercise of fundamental constitutional rights or liberties must it be found to have chosen the least restrictive alternative. Cf. Dunn v. Blumstein; Shelton v. Tucker, (1960). It is also well to remember that even those districts that have reduced ability to make free decisions with respect to how much they spend on education still retain under the present system a large measure of authority as to how available funds will be allocated. They further enjoy the power to make numerous other decisions with respect to the operation of the schools. The people of Texas may be justified in believing that other systems of school financing, which place more of the financial responsibility in the hands of the State, will result in a comparable lessening of desired local autonomy. That is, they may believe that along with increased control of the purse strings at the state level will go increased control over local policies.

Appellees further urge that the Texas system is unconstitutionally arbitrary because it allows the availability of local taxable resources to turn on "happenstance." They see no justification for a system that allows, as they contend, the quality of education to fluctuate on the basis of the fortuitous positioning of the boundary lines of political subdivisions and the location of valuable commercial and industrial property. But any scheme of local taxation—indeed the very existence of identifiable local governmental units— requires the establishment of jurisdictional boundaries that are inevitably arbitrary. It is equally inevitable that some localities are going to be blessed with more taxable assets than others. Nor is local wealth a static quantity. Changes in the level of taxable wealth within any district may result from any number of events, some of which local residents can and do influence. For instance, commercial and industrial enterprises may be encouraged to locate within a district by various actions—public and private.

Moreover, if local taxation for local expenditures were an unconstitutional method of providing for education then it might be an equally impermissible means of providing other necessary services customarily financed largely from local property taxes, including local police and fire protection, public health and hospitals, and public utility facilities of various kinds. We perceive no justification for such a severe denigration of local property taxation and control as would follow from appellees' contentions. It has simply never been within the constitutional prerogative of this Court to nullify statewide measures for financing public services merely because the burdens or benefits thereof fall unevenly depending upon the relative wealth of the political subdivisions in which citizens live.

In sum, to the extent that the Texas system of school financing results in unequal expenditures between children who happen to reside in different districts, we cannot say that such disparities are the product of a system that is so irrational as to be invidiously discriminatory. Texas has acknowledged its shortcomings and has persistently endeavored—not without some success—to ameliorate the differences in levels of expenditures without sacrificing the benefits of local participation. The Texas plan is not the result of hurried, ill-conceived legislation. It certainly is not the product of purposeful discrimination against any group or class. On the contrary, it is rooted in decades of experience in Texas and elsewhere, and in major part is the product of responsible studies by qualified people. In giving substance to the presumption of validity to which the Texas system is entitled, Lindsley v. Natural Carbonic Gas Co., (1911), it is important to remember that at every stage of its development it has constituted a "rough accommodation" of interests in an effort to arrive at practical and workable solutions. Metropolis Theatre Co. v. City of Chicago, (1913). One also must remember that the system here challenged is not peculiar to Texas or to any other State. In its essential characteristics, the Texas plan for financing public education reflects what many educators for a half century have thought was an enlightened approach to a problem for which there is no perfect solution. We are unwilling to assume for ourselves a level of wisdom superior to that of legislators, scholars, and educational authorities in 50 States, especially where the alternatives proposed are only recently conceived and nowhere yet tested. The constitutional standard under the Equal Protection Clause is whether the challenged state action rationally furthers a legitimate state purpose or interest. McGinnis v. Royster, (1973). We hold that the Texas plan abundantly satisfies this standard.

IV

In light of the considerable attention that has focused on the District Court opinion in this case and on its California predecessor, Serrano v. Priest, 5 Cal. 3d 584, 487 P.2d 1241 (1971), a cautionary postscript seems appropriate. It cannot be questioned that the constitutional judgment reached by the District Court and approved by our dissenting Brothers today would occasion in Texas and elsewhere an unprecedented upheaval in public education. Some commentators have concluded that, whatever the contours of the alternative financing programs that might be devised and approved, the result could not avoid being a beneficial one. But, just as there is nothing simple about the constitutional issues involved in these cases, there is nothing simple or certain about predicting the consequences of massive change in the financing and control of public education. Those who have devoted the most thoughtful attention to the practical ramifications of these cases have found no clear or dependable answers and their scholarship reflects no such unqualified confidence in the desirability of completely uprooting the existing system.

The complexity of these problems is demonstrated by the lack of consensus with respect to whether it may be said with any assurance that the poor, the racial minorities, or the children in overburdened core-city school districts would be benefited by abrogation of traditional modes of financing education. Unless there is to be a substantial increase in state expenditures on education across the board—an event the likelihood of which is open to considerable question—these groups stand to realize gains in terms of increased per-pupil expenditures only if they reside in districts that presently spend at relatively low levels, i. e., in those districts that would benefit from the redistribution of existing resources. Yet, recent studies have indicated that the poorest families are not invariably clustered in the most impecunious school districts. Nor does it now appear that there is any more than a random chance that racial minorities are concentrated in property-poor districts. Additionally, several research projects have concluded that any financing alternative designed to achieve a greater equality of expenditures is likely to lead to higher taxation and lower educational expenditures in the major urban centers, a result that would exacerbate rather than ameliorate existing conditions in those areas.

These practical considerations, of course, play no role in the adjudication of the constitutional issues presented here. But they serve to highlight the wisdom of the traditional limitations on this Court's function. The consideration and initiation of fundamental reforms with respect to state taxation and education are matters reserved for the legislative processes of the various States, and we do no violence to the values of federalism and separation of powers by staying our hand. We hardly need add that this Court's action today is not to be viewed as placing its judicial imprimatur on the status quo. The need is apparent for reform in tax systems which may well have relied too long and too heavily on the local property tax. And certainly innovative thinking as to public education, its methods, and its funding is necessary to assure both a higher level of quality and greater uniformity of opportunity. These matters merit the continued attention of the scholars who already have contributed much by their challenges. But the ultimate solutions must come from the lawmakers and from the democratic pressures of those who elect them.

Reversed.

MR. JUSTICE STEWART, concurring.

The method of financing public schools in Texas, as in almost every other State, has resulted in a system of public education that can fairly be described as chaotic and unjust. It does not follow, however, and I cannot find, that this system violates the Constitution of the United States. I join the opinion and judgment of the Court because I am convinced that any other course would mark an extraordinary departure from principled adjudication under the Equal Protection Clause of the Fourteenth Amendment. The uncharted directions of such a departure are suggested, I think, by the imaginative dissenting opinion my Brother MARSHALL has filed today.

Unlike other provisions of the Constitution, the Equal Protection Clause confers no substantive rights and creates no substantive liberties. The function of the Equal Protection Clause, rather, is simply to measure the validity of classifications created by state laws.

There is hardly a law on the books that does not affect some people differently from others. But the basic concern of the Equal Protection Clause is with state legislation whose purpose or effect is to create discrete and objectively identifiable classes. And with respect to such legislation, it has long been settled that the Equal Protection Clause is offended only by laws that are invidiously discriminatory—only by classifications that are wholly arbitrary or capricious. See, e. g., Rinaldi v. Yeager. This settled principle of constitutional law was compendiously stated in Mr. Chief Justice Warren's opinion for the Court in McGowan v. Maryland, in the following words:

> "Although no precise formula has been developed, the Court has held that the Fourteenth Amendment permits the States a wide scope of discretion in enacting laws which affect some groups of citizens differently than others. The constitutional safeguard is offended only if the classification rests on grounds wholly irrelevant to the

> achievement of the State's objective. State legislatures are presumed to have acted within their constitutional power despite the fact that, in practice, their laws result in some inequality. A statutory discrimination will not be set aside if any state of facts reasonably may be conceived to justify it."

This doctrine is no more than a specific application of one of the first principles of constitutional adjudication—the basic presumption of the constitutional validity of a duly enacted state or federal law. See Thayer, The Origin and Scope of the American Doctrine of Constitutional Law, 7 Harv. L. Rev. 129 (1893).

Under the Equal Protection Clause, this presumption of constitutional validity disappears when a State has enacted legislation whose purpose or effect is to create classes based upon criteria that, in a constitutional sense, are inherently "suspect." Because of the historic purpose of the Fourteenth Amendment, the prime example of such a "suspect" classification is one that is based upon race. See, e. g., Brown v. Board of Education; McLaughlin v. Florida. But there are other classifications that, at least in some settings, are also "suspect"—for example, those based upon national origin, alienage, indigency, or illegitimacy.

Moreover, quite apart from the Equal Protection Clause, a state law that impinges upon a substantive right or liberty created or conferred by the Constitution is, of course, presumptively invalid, whether or not the law's purpose or effect is to create any classifications. For example, a law that provided that newspapers could be published only by people who had resided in the State for five years could be superficially viewed as invidiously discriminating against an identifiable class in violation of the Equal Protection Clause. But, more basically, such a law would be invalid simply because it abridged the freedom of the press. Numerous cases in this Court illustrate this principle.

In refusing to invalidate the Texas system of financing its public schools, the Court today applies with thoughtfulness and understanding the basic principles I have so sketchily summarized. First, as the Court points out, the Texas system has hardly created the kind of objectively identifiable classes that are cognizable under the Equal Protection Clause. Second, even assuming the existence of such discernible categories, the classifications are in no sense based upon constitutionally "suspect" criteria. Third, the Texas system does not rest "on grounds wholly irrelevant to the achievement of the State's objective." Finally, the Texas system impinges upon no substantive constitutional rights or liberties. It follows, therefore, under the established principle reaffirmed in Mr. Chief Justice Warren's opinion for the Court in McGowan v. Maryland, supra, that the judgment of the District Court must be reversed.

MR. JUSTICE BRENNAN, dissenting.

Although I agree with my Brother WHITE that the Texas statutory scheme is devoid of any rational basis, and for that reason is violative of the Equal Protection Clause, I also record my disagreement with the Court's rather distressing assertion that a right may be deemed "fundamental" for the purposes of equal protection analysis only if it is "explicitly or implicitly guaranteed by the Constitution." Ante, at 33-34. As my Brother MARSHALL convincingly demonstrates, our prior cases stand for the proposition that "fundamentality" is, in large measure, a function of the right's importance in terms of the effectuation of those rights which are in fact constitutionally guaranteed. Thus, "[a]s the nexus between the specific constitutional guarantee and the non-constitutional interest draws closer, the nonconstitutional interest becomes more fundamental and the degree of judicial scrutiny applied when the interest is infringed on a discriminatory basis must be adjusted accordingly." Post, at 102-103.

Here, there can be no doubt that education is inextricably linked to the right to participate in the electoral process and to the rights of free speech and association guaranteed by the First Amendment. See post, at 111-115. This being so, any classification affecting education must be subjected to strict judicial scrutiny, and since even the State concedes that the statutory scheme now before us cannot pass constitutional muster under this stricter standard of review, I can only conclude that the Texas school-financing scheme is constitutionally invalid.

MR. JUSTICE WHITE, with whom MR. JUSTICE DOUGLAS and MR. JUSTICE BRENNAN join, dissenting.

The Texas public schools are financed through a combination of state funding, local property tax revenue, and some federal funds. Concededly, the system yields wide disparity in per-pupil revenue among the various districts. In a typical year, for example, the Alamo Heights district had total revenues of $594 per pupil, while the Edgewood district had only $356 per pupil. The majority and the State concede, as they must, the existence of major disparities in spendable funds. But the State contends that the disparities do not invidiously discriminate against children and families in districts such as Edgewood, because the Texas scheme is designed "to provide an adequate education for all, with local autonomy to go beyond that as individual school districts desire and are able . . . . It leaves to the people of each district the choice whether to go beyond the minimum and, if so, by how much." The majority advances this rationalization: "While assuring a basic education for every child in the State, it permits and encourages a large measure of participation in and control of each district's schools at the local level."

I cannot disagree with the proposition that local control and local decisionmaking play an important part in our democratic system of government. Cf. James v. Valtierra, (1971). Much may be left to local option, and this case would be quite different if it were true that the Texas system, while insuring minimum educational expenditures in every district through state funding, extended a meaningful option to all local districts to increase their per-pupil expenditures and so to improve their children's education to the extent that increased funding would achieve that goal. The system would then arguably provide a rational and sensible method of achieving the stated aim of preserving an area for local initiative and decision.

The difficulty with the Texas system, however, is that it provides a meaningful option to Alamo Heights and like school districts but almost none to Edgewood and those other districts with a low per-pupil real estate tax base. In these latter districts, no matter how desirous parents are of supporting their schools with greater revenues, it is impossible to do so through the use of the real estate property tax. In these districts, the Texas system utterly fails to extend a realistic choice to parents because the property tax, which is the only revenue-raising mechanism extended to school districts, is practically and legally unavailable. That this is the situation may be readily demonstrated.

Local school districts in Texas raise their portion of the Foundation School Program—the Local Fund Assignment—by levying ad valorem taxes on the property located within their boundaries. In addition, the districts are authorized, by the state constitution and by statute, to levy ad valorem property taxes in order to raise revenues to support educational spending over and above the expenditure of Foundation School Program funds.

Both the Edgewood and Alamo Heights districts are located in Bexar County, Texas. Student enrollment in Alamo Heights is 5,432, in Edgewood 22,862. The per-pupil market value of the taxable property in Alamo Heights is $49,078, in Edgewood $5,960. In a typical, relevant year, Alamo Heights had a maintenance tax rate of $1.20 and a debt service (bond) tax rate of 20 cents per $100 assessed evaluation, while Edgewood had a maintenance rate of 52 cents and a bond rate of 67 cents. These rates, when applied to the respective tax bases, yielded Alamo Heights $1,433,473 in maintenance dollars and $236,074 in bond dollars, and Edgewood $223,034 in maintenance dollars and $279,023 in bond dollars. As is readily apparent, because of the variance in tax bases between the districts, results, in terms of revenues, do not correlate with effort, in terms of tax rate. Thus, Alamo Heights, with a tax base approximately twice the size of Edgewood's base, realized approximately six times as many maintenance dollars as Edgewood by using a tax rate only approximately two and one-half times larger. Similarly, Alamo Heights realized slightly fewer bond dollars by using a bond tax rate less than one-third of that used by Edgewood.

Nor is Edgewood's revenue-raising potential only deficient when compared with Alamo Heights. North East District has taxable property with a per-pupil market value of approximately $31,000, but total taxable property approximately four and one-half times that of Edgewood. Applying a maintenance rate of $1, North East yielded $2,818,148. Thus, because of its superior tax base, North East was able to apply a tax rate slightly less than twice that applied by Edgewood and yield more than 10 times the maintenance dollars. Similarly, North East, with a bond rate of 45 cents, yielded $1,249,159—more than four times Edgewood's yield with two-thirds the rate.

Plainly, were Alamo Heights or North East to apply the Edgewood tax rate to its tax base, it would yield far greater revenues than Edgewood is able to yield applying those same rates to its base. Conversely, were Edgewood to apply the Alamo Heights or North East rates to its base, the yield would be far smaller than the Alamo Heights or North East yields. The disparity is, therefore, currently operative and its impact on Edgewood is undeniably serious. It is evident from statistics in the record that show that, applying an equalized tax rate of 85 cents per $100 assessed valuation, Alamo Heights was able to provide approximately $330 per pupil in local revenues over and above the Local Fund Assignment. In Edgewood, on the other hand, with an equalized tax rate of $1.05 per $100 of assessed valuation, $26 per pupil was raised beyond the Local Fund Assignment. As previously noted, in Alamo Heights, total per-pupil revenues from local, state, and federal funds was $594 per pupil, in Edgewood $356.

In order to equal the highest yield in any other Bexar County district, Alamo Heights would be required to tax at the rate of 68 cents per $100 of assessed valuation. Edgewood would be required to tax at the prohibitive rate of $5.76 per $100. But state law places a $1.50 per $100 ceiling on the maintenance tax rate, a limit that would surely be reached long before Edgewood attained an equal yield. Edgewood is thus precluded in law, as well as in fact, from achieving a yield even close to that of some other districts.

The Equal Protection Clause permits discriminations between classes but requires that the classification bear some rational relationship to a permissible object sought to be attained by the statute. It is not enough that the Texas system before us seeks to achieve the valid, rational purpose of maximizing local initiative; the means chosen by the State must also be rationally related to the end sought to be achieved. As the Court stated just last Term in Weber v. Aetna Casualty & Surety Co., (1972):

> "The tests to determine the validity of state statutes under the Equal Protection Clause have been variously expressed, but this Court requires, at a minimum, that a statutory classification bear some rational relationship to a legitimate state purpose. Morey v. Doud, (1957); Williamson v. Lee Optical Co., (1955); Gulf, Colorado & Santa Fe R. Co. v. Ellis, (1897); Yick Wo v. Hopkins, (1886)."

Neither Texas nor the majority heeds this rule. If the State aims at maximizing local initiative and local choice, by permitting school districts to resort to the real property tax if they choose to do so, it utterly fails in achieving its purpose in districts with property tax bases so low that there is little if any opportunity for interested parents, rich or poor, to augment school district revenues. Requiring the State to establish only that unequal treatment is in furtherance of a permissible goal, without also requiring the State to show that the means chosen to effectuate that goal are rationally related to its achievement, makes equal protection analysis no more than an empty gesture. In my view, the parents and children in Edgewood, and in like districts, suffer from an invidious discrimination violative of the Equal Protection Clause.

This does not, of course, mean that local control may not be a legitimate goal of a school-financing system. Nor does it mean that the State must guarantee each district an equal per-pupil revenue from the state school-financing system. Nor does it mean, as the majority appears to believe, that, by affirming the decision below, this Court would be "imposing on the States inflexible constitutional restraints that could circumscribe or handicap the continued research and experimentation so vital to finding even partial solutions to educational problems and to keeping abreast of ever-changing conditions." On the contrary, it would merely mean that the State must fashion a financing scheme which provides a rational basis for the maximization of local control, if local control is to remain a goal of the system, and not a scheme with "different treatment be[ing] accorded to persons placed by a statute into different classes on the basis of criteria wholly unrelated to the objective of that statute." Reed v. Reed, (1971).

Perhaps the majority believes that the major disparity in revenues provided and permitted by the Texas system is inconsequential. I cannot agree, however, that the difference of the magnitude appearing in this case can sensibly be ignored, particularly since the State itself considers it so important to provide opportunities to exceed the minimum state educational expenditures.

There is no difficulty in identifying the class that is subject to the alleged discrimination and that is entitled to the benefits of the Equal Protection Clause. I need go no farther than the parents and children in the Edgewood district, who are plaintiffs here and who assert that they are entitled to the same choice as Alamo Heights to augment local expenditures for schools but are denied that choice by state law. This group constitutes a class sufficiently definite to invoke the protection of the Constitution. They are as entitled to the protection of the Equal Protection Clause as were the voters in allegedly under represented counties in the reapportionment cases. See, e. g., Baker v. Carr, (1962); Gray v. Sanders, (1963); Reynolds v. Sims, (1964). And in Bullock v. Carter, (1972), where a challenge to the Texas candidate filing fee on equal protection grounds was upheld, we noted that the victims of alleged discrimination wrought by the filing fee "cannot be described by reference to discrete and precisely defined segments of the community as is typical of inequities challenged under the Equal Protection Clause," but concluded that "we would ignore reality were we not to recognize that this system falls with unequal weight on voters, as well as candidates, according to their economic status." Id., at 144. Similarly, in the present case we would blink reality to ignore the fact that school districts, and students in the end, are differentially affected by the Texas school-financing scheme with respect to their capability to supplement the Minimum Foundation School Program. At the very least, the law discriminates against those children and their parents who live in districts where the per-pupil tax base is sufficiently low to make impossible the provision of comparable school revenues by resort to the real property tax which is the only device the State extends for this purpose.

MR. JUSTICE MARSHALL, with whom MR. JUSTICE DOUGLAS concurs, dissenting.

The Court today decides, in effect, that a State may constitutionally vary the quality of education which it offers its children in accordance with the amount of taxable wealth located in the school districts within which they reside. The majority's decision represents an abrupt departure from the mainstream of recent state and federal court decisions concerning the unconstitutionality of state educational financing schemes dependent upon taxable local wealth. More unfortunately, though, the majority's holding can only be seen as a retreat from our historic commitment to equality of educational opportunity and as unsupportable acquiescence in a system which deprives children in their earliest years of the chance to reach their full potential as citizens. The Court does this despite the absence of any substantial justification for a scheme which arbitrarily channels educational resources in accordance with the fortuity of the amount of taxable wealth within each district.

In my judgment, the right of every American to an equal start in life, so far as the provision of a state service as important as education is concerned, is far too vital to permit state discrimination on grounds as tenuous as those presented by this record. Nor can I accept the notion that it is sufficient to remit these appellees to the vagaries of the political process which, contrary to the majority's suggestion, has proved singularly unsuited to the task of providing a remedy for this discrimination. I, for one, am unsatisfied with the hope of an ultimate "political" solution sometime in the indefinite future while, in the meantime, countless children unjustifiably receive inferior educations that "may affect their hearts and minds in a way unlikely ever to be undone." Brown v. Board of Education, (1954). I must therefore respectfully dissent.

I

The Court acknowledges that "substantial interdistrict disparities in school expenditures" exist in Texas, ante, at 15, and that these disparities are "largely attributable to differences in the amounts of money collected through local property taxation," ante, at 16. But instead of closely examining the seriousness of these disparities and the invidiousness of the Texas financing scheme, the Court undertakes an elaborate exploration of the efforts Texas has purportedly made to close the gaps between its districts in terms of levels of district wealth and resulting educational funding. Yet, however praiseworthy Texas' equalizing efforts, the issue in this case is not whether Texas is doing its best to ameliorate the worst features of a discriminatory scheme but, rather, whether the scheme itself is in fact unconstitutionally discriminatory in the face of the Fourteenth Amendment's guarantee of equal protection of the laws. When the Texas financing scheme is taken as a whole, I do not think it can be doubted that it produces a discriminatory impact on substantial numbers of the school-age children of the State of Texas.

A

Funds to support public education in Texas are derived from three sources: local ad valorem property taxes; the Federal Government; and the state government. It is enlightening to consider these in order.

Under Texas law, the only mechanism provided the local school district for raising new, unencumbered revenues is the power to tax property located within its boundaries. At the same time, the Texas financing scheme effectively restricts the use of monies raised by local property taxation to the support of public education within the boundaries of the district in which they are raised, since any such taxes must be approved by a majority of the property-taxpaying voters of the district.

The significance of the local property tax element of the Texas financing scheme is apparent from the fact that it provides the funds to meet some 40% of the cost of public education for Texas as a whole. Yet the amount of revenue that any particular Texas district can raise is dependent on two factors—its tax rate and its amount of taxable property. The first factor is determined by the property-taxpaying voters of the district. But, regardless of the enthusiasm of the local voters for public education, the second factor—the taxable property wealth of the district—necessarily restricts the district's ability to raise funds to support public education. Thus, even though the voters of two Texas districts may be willing to make the same tax effort, the results for the districts will be substantially different if one is property rich while the other is property poor. The necessary effect of the Texas local property tax is, in short, to favor property-rich districts and to disfavor property-poor ones.

The seriously disparate consequences of the Texas local property tax, when that tax is considered alone, are amply illustrated by data presented to the District Court by appellees. These data included a detailed study of a sample of 110 Texas school districts for the 1967-1968 school year conducted by Professor Joel S. Berke of Syracuse University's Educational Finance Policy Institute. Among other things, this study revealed that the 10 richest districts examined, each of which had more than $100,000 in taxable property per pupil, raised through local effort an average of $610 per pupil, whereas the four poorest districts studied, each of which had less than $10,000 in taxable property per pupil, were able to raise only an average of $63 per pupil. And, as the Court effectively recognizes, ante, at 27, this correlation between the amount of taxable property per pupil and the amount of local revenues per pupil holds true for the 96 districts in between the richest and poorest districts.

It is clear, moreover, that the disparity of per-pupil revenues cannot be dismissed as the result of lack of local effort—that is, lower tax rates—by property-poor districts. To the contrary, the data presented below indicate that the poorest districts tend to have the highest tax rates and the richest districts tend to have the lowest tax rates. Yet, despite the apparent extra effort being made by the poorest districts, they are unable even to begin to match the richest districts in terms of the production of local revenues. For example, the 10 richest districts studied by Professor Berke were able to produce $585 per pupil with an equalized tax rate of 31 cents on $100 of equalized valuation, but the four poorest districts studied, with an equalized rate of 70 cents on $100 of equalized valuation, were able to produce only $60 per pupil. Without more, this state-imposed system of educational funding presents a serious picture of widely varying treatment of Texas school districts, and thereby of Texas schoolchildren, in terms of the amount of funds available for public education.

Nor are these funding variations corrected by the other aspects of the Texas financing scheme. The Federal Government provides funds sufficient to cover only some 10% of the total cost of public education in Texas. Furthermore, while these federal funds are not distributed in Texas solely on a per-pupil basis, appellants do not here contend that they are used in such a way as to ameliorate significantly the widely varying consequences for Texas school districts and schoolchildren of the local property tax element of the state financing scheme.

State funds provide the remaining some 50% of the monies spent on public education in Texas. Technically, they are distributed under two programs. The first is the Available School Fund, for which provision is made in the Texas Constitution. The Available School Fund is composed of revenues obtained from a number of sources, including receipts from the state ad valorem property tax, one-fourth of all monies collected by the occupation tax, annual contributions by the legislature from general revenues, and the revenues derived from the Permanent School Fund. For the 1970-1971 school year the Available School Fund contained $296,000,000. The Texas Constitution requires that this money be distributed annually on a per capita basis to the local school districts. Obviously, such a flat grant could not alone eradicate the funding differentials attributable to the local property tax. Moreover, today the Available School Fund is in reality simply one facet of the second state financing program, the Minimum Foundation School Program, since each district's annual share of the Fund is deducted from the sum to which the district is entitled under the Foundation Program.

The Minimum Foundation School Program provides funds for three specific purposes: professional salaries, current operating expenses, and transportation expenses. The State pays, on an overall basis, for approximately 80% of the cost of the Program; the remaining 20% is distributed among the local school districts under the Local Fund Assignment. Each district's share of the Local Fund Assignment is determined by a complex "economic index" which is designed to allocate a larger share of the costs to property-rich districts than to property-poor districts. Each district pays its share with revenues derived from local property taxation.

The stated purpose of the Minimum Foundation School Program is to provide certain basic funding for each local Texas school district. At the same time, the Program was apparently intended to improve, to some degree, the financial position of property-poor districts relative to property-rich districts, since—through the use of the economic index—an effort is made to charge a disproportionate share of the costs of the Program to rich districts. It bears noting, however, that substantial criticism has been leveled at the practical effectiveness of the economic index system of local cost allocation. In theory, the index is designed to ascertain the relative ability of each district to contribute to the Local Fund Assignment from local property taxes. Yet the index is not developed simply on the basis of each district's taxable wealth. It also takes into account the district's relative income from manufacturing, mining, and agriculture, its payrolls, and its scholastic population. It is difficult to discern precisely how these latter factors are predictive of a district's relative ability to raise revenues through local property taxes. Thus, in 1966, one of the consultants who originally participated in the development of the Texas economic index adopted in 1949 told the Governor's Committee on Public School Education: "The Economic Index approach to evaluating local ability offers a little better measure than sheer chance, but not much."

Moreover, even putting aside these criticisms of the economic index as a device for achieving meaningful district wealth equalization through cost allocation, poor districts still do not necessarily receive more state aid than property-rich districts. For the standards which currently determine the amount received from the Foundation School Program by any particular district favor property-rich districts. Thus, focusing on the same Edgewood Independent and Alamo Heights School Districts which the majority uses for purposes of illustration, we find that in 1967-1968 property-rich Alamo Heights, which raised $333 per pupil on an equalized tax rate of 85 cents per $100 valuation, received $225 per pupil from the Foundation School Program, while property-poor Edgewood, which raised only $26 per pupil with an equalized tax rate of $1.05 per $100 valuation, received only $222 per pupil from the Foundation School Program. And, more recent data, which indicate that for the 1970-1971 school year Alamo Heights received $491 per pupil from the Program while Edgewood received only $356 per pupil, hardly suggest that the wealth gap between the districts is being narrowed by the State Program. To the contrary, whereas in 1967-1968 Alamo Heights received only $3 per pupil, or about 1%, more than Edgewood in state aid, by 1970-1971 the gap had widened to a difference of $135 per pupil, or about 38%. It was data of this character that prompted the District Court to observe that "the current [state aid] system tends to subsidize the rich at the expense of the poor, rather than the other way around." 337 F. Supp. 280, 282. And even the appellants go no further here than to venture that the Minimum Foundation School Program has "a mildly equalizing effect."

Despite these facts, the majority continually emphasizes how much state aid has, in recent years, been given to property-poor Texas school districts. What the Court fails to emphasize is the cruel irony of how much more state aid is being given to property-rich Texas school districts on top of their already substantial local property tax revenues. Under any view, then, it is apparent that the state aid provided by the Foundation School Program fails to compensate for the large funding variations attributable to the local property tax element of the Texas financing scheme. And it is these stark differences in the treatment of Texas school districts and school children inherent in the Texas financing scheme, not the absolute amount of state aid provided to any particular school district, that are the crux of this case. There can, moreover, be no escaping the conclusion that the local property tax which is dependent upon taxable district property wealth is an essential feature of the Texas scheme for financing public education.

B

The appellants do not deny the disparities in educational funding caused by variations in taxable district property wealth. They do contend, however, that whatever the differences in per-pupil spending among Texas districts, there are no discriminatory consequences for the children of the disadvantaged districts. They recognize that what is at stake in this case is the quality of the public education provided Texas children in the districts in which they live. But appellants reject the suggestion that the quality of education in any particular district is determined by money—beyond some minimal level of funding which they believe to be assured every Texas district by the Minimum Foundation School Program. In their view, there is simply no denial of equal educational opportunity to any Texas schoolchildren as a result of the widely varying per-pupil spending power provided districts under the current financing scheme.

In my view, though, even an unadorned restatement of this contention is sufficient to reveal its absurdity. Authorities concerned with educational quality no doubt disagree as to the significance of variations in per-pupil spending. Indeed, conflicting expert testimony was presented to the District Court in this case concerning the effect of spending variations on educational achievement. We sit, however, not to resolve disputes over educational theory but to enforce our Constitution. It is an inescapable fact that if one district has more funds available per pupil than another district, the former will have greater choice in educational planning than will the latter. In this regard, I believe the question of discrimination in educational quality must be deemed to be an objective one that looks to what the State provides its children, not to what the children are able to do with what they receive. That a child forced to attend an underfunded school with poorer physical facilities, less experienced teachers, larger classes, and a narrower range of courses than a school with substantially more funds—and thus with greater choice in educational planning—may nevertheless excel is to the credit of the child, not the State, cf. Missouri ex rel. Gaines v. Canada, (1938). Indeed, who can ever measure for such a child the opportunities lost and the talents wasted for want of a broader, more enriched education? Discrimination in the opportunity to learn that is afforded a child must be our standard.

Hence, even before this Court recognized its duty to tear down the barriers of state-enforced racial segregation in public education, it acknowledged that inequality in the educational facilities provided to students may be discriminatory state action as contemplated by the Equal Protection Clause. As a basis for striking down state-enforced segregation of a law school, the Court in Sweatt v. Painter, (1950), stated:

> "[W]e cannot find substantial equality in the educational opportunities offered white and Negro law students by the State. In terms of number of the faculty, variety of courses and opportunity for specialization, size of the student body, scope of the library, availability of law review and similar activities, the [whites-only] Law School is superior. . . . It is difficult to believe that one who had a free choice between these law schools would consider the question close."

See also McLaurin v. Oklahoma State Regents for Higher Education, (1950). Likewise, it is difficult to believe that if the children of Texas had a free choice, they would choose to be educated in districts with fewer resources, and hence with more antiquated plants, less experienced teachers, and a less diversified curriculum. In fact, if financing variations are so insignificant to educational quality, it is difficult to understand why a number of our country's wealthiest school districts, which have no legal obligation to argue in support of the constitutionality of the Texas legislation, have nevertheless zealously pursued its cause before this Court.

The consequences, in terms of objective educational input, of the variations in district funding caused by the Texas financing scheme are apparent from the data introduced before the District Court. For example, in 1968-1969, 100% of the teachers in the property-rich Alamo Heights School District had college degrees. By contrast, during the same school year only 80.02% of the teachers had college degrees in the property poor Edgewood Independent School District. Also, in 1968-1969, approximately 47% of the teachers in the Edgewood District were on emergency teaching permits, whereas only 11% of the teachers in Alamo Heights were on such permits. This is undoubtedly a reflection of the fact that the top of Edgewood's teacher salary scale was approximately 80% of Alamo Heights'. And, not surprisingly, the teacher-student ratio varies significantly between the two districts. In other words, as might be expected, a difference in the funds available to districts results in a difference in educational inputs available for a child's public education in Texas. For constitutional purposes, I believe this situation, which is directly attributable to the Texas financing scheme, raises a grave question of state-created discrimination in the provision of public education. Cf. Gaston County v. United States, (1969).

At the very least, in view of the substantial interdistrict disparities in funding and in resulting educational inputs shown by appellees to exist under the Texas financing scheme, the burden of proving that these disparities do not in fact affect the quality of children's education must fall upon the appellants. Cf. Hobson v. Hansen, 327 F. Supp. 844, 860-861 (DC 1971). Yet appellants made no effort in the District Court to demonstrate that educational quality is not affected by variations in funding and in resulting inputs. And, in this Court, they have argued no more than that the relationship is ambiguous. This is hardly sufficient to overcome appellees' prima facie showing of state-created discrimination between the schoolchildren of Texas with respect to objective educational opportunity.

Nor can I accept the appellants' apparent suggestion that the Texas Minimum Foundation School Program effectively eradicates any discriminatory effects otherwise resulting from the local property tax element of the Texas financing scheme. Appellants assert that, despite its imperfections, the Program "does guarantee an adequate education to every child." The majority, in considering the constitutionality of the Texas financing scheme, seems to find substantial merit in this contention, for it tells us that the Foundation Program "was designed to provide an adequate minimum educational offering in every school in the State," ante, at 45, and that the Program "assur[es] a basic education for every child," ante, at 49. But I fail to understand how the constitutional problems inherent in the financing scheme are eased by the Foundation Program. Indeed, the precise thrust of the appellants' and the Court's remarks are not altogether clear to me.

The suggestion may be that the state aid received via the Foundation Program sufficiently improves the position of property-poor districts vis-a-vis property-rich districts—in terms of educational funds—to eliminate any claim of interdistrict discrimination in available educational resources which might otherwise exist if educational funding were dependent solely upon local property taxation. Certainly the Court has recognized that to demand precise equality of treatment is normally unrealistic, and thus minor differences inherent in any practical context usually will not make out a substantial equal protection claim. See, e. g., Mayer v. City of Chicago, (1971); Draper v. Washington, (1963); Bain Peanut Co. v. Pinson, (1931). But, as has already been seen, we are hardly presented here with some de minimis claim of discrimination resulting from the play necessary in any functioning system; to the contrary, it is clear that the Foundation Program utterly fails to ameliorate the seriously discriminatory effects of the local property tax.

Alternatively, the appellants and the majority may believe that the Equal Protection Clause cannot be offended by substantially unequal state treatment of persons who are similarly situated so long as the State provides everyone with some unspecified amount of education which evidently is "enough." The basis for such a novel view is far from clear. It is, of course, true that the Constitution does not require precise equality in the treatment of all persons. As Mr. Justice Frankfurter explained:

> "The equality at which the 'equal protection' clause aims is not a disembodied equality. The Fourteenth Amendment enjoins 'the equal protection of the laws,' and laws are not abstract propositions. . . . The Constitution does not require things which are different in fact or opinion to be treated in law as though they were the same." Tigner v. Texas, (1940). See also Douglas v. California, (1963); Goesaert v. Cleary, (1948).

But this Court has never suggested that because some "adequate" level of benefits is provided to all, discrimination in the provision of services is therefore constitutionally excusable.

The Equal Protection Clause is not addressed to the minimal sufficiency but rather to the unjustifiable inequalities of state action. It mandates nothing less than that "all persons similarly circumstanced shall be treated alike." F. S. Royster Guano Co. v. Virginia, (1920).

Even if the Equal Protection Clause encompassed some theory of constitutional adequacy, discrimination in the provision of educational opportunity would certainly seem to be a poor candidate for its application. Neither the majority nor appellants inform us how judicially manageable standards are to be derived for determining how much education is "enough" to excuse constitutional discrimination. One would think that the majority would heed its own fervent affirmation of judicial self-restraint before undertaking the complex task of determining at large what level of education is constitutionally sufficient. Indeed, the majority's apparent reliance upon the adequacy of the educational opportunity assured by the Texas Minimum Foundation School Program seems fundamentally inconsistent with its own recognition that educational authorities are unable to agree upon what makes for educational quality, see ante, at 42-43 and n. 86 and at 47 n. 101. If, as the majority stresses, such authorities are uncertain as to the impact of various levels of funding on educational quality, I fail to see where it finds the expertise to divine that the particular levels of funding provided by the Program assure an adequate educational opportunity—much less an education substantially equivalent in quality to that which a higher level of funding might provide. Certainly appellants' mere assertion before this Court of the adequacy of the education guaranteed by the Minimum Foundation School Program cannot obscure the constitutional implications of the discrimination in educational funding and objective educational inputs resulting from the local property tax—particularly since the appellees offered substantial uncontroverted evidence before the District Court impugning the now much-touted "adequacy" of the education guaranteed by the Foundation Program.

In my view, then, it is inequality—not some notion of gross inadequacy—of educational opportunity that raises a question of denial of equal protection of the laws. I find any other approach to the issue unintelligible and without directing principle. Here, appellees have made a substantial showing of wide variations in educational funding and the resulting educational opportunity afforded to the schoolchildren of Texas. This discrimination is, in large measure, attributable to significant disparities in the taxable wealth of local Texas school districts. This is a sufficient showing to raise a substantial question of discriminatory state action in violation of the Equal Protection Clause.

C

Despite the evident discriminatory effect of the Texas financing scheme, both the appellants and the majority raise substantial questions concerning the precise character of the disadvantaged class in this case. The District Court concluded that the Texas financing scheme draws "distinction between groups of citizens depending upon the wealth of the district in which they live" and thus creates a disadvantaged class composed of persons living in property-poor districts. See 337 F. Supp., at 282. See also id., at 281. In light of the data introduced before the District Court, the conclusion that the schoolchildren of property-poor districts constitute a sufficient class for our purposes seems indisputable to me.

Appellants contend, however, that in constitutional terms this case involves nothing more than discrimination against local school districts, not against individuals, since on its face the state scheme is concerned only with the provision of funds to local districts. The result of the Texas financing scheme, appellants suggest, is merely that some local districts have more available revenues for education; others have less. In that respect, they point out, the States have broad discretion in drawing reasonable distinctions between their political subdivisions. See Griffin v. County School Board of Prince Edward County, (1964); McGowan v. Maryland, (1961); Salsburg v. Maryland, (1954).

But this Court has consistently recognized that where there is in fact discrimination against individual interests, the constitutional guarantee of equal protection of the laws is not inapplicable simply because the discrimination is based upon some group characteristic such as geographic location. See Gordon v. Lance, (1971); Reynolds v. Sims, (1964); Gray v. Sanders (1963). Texas has chosen to provide free public education for all its citizens, and it has embodied that decision in its constitution. Yet, having established public education for its citizens, the State, as a direct consequence of the variations in local property wealth endemic to Texas' financing scheme, has provided some Texas schoolchildren with substantially less resources for their education than others. Thus, while on its face the Texas scheme may merely discriminate between local districts, the impact of that discrimination falls directly upon the children whose educational opportunity is dependent upon where they happen to live. Consequently, the District Court correctly concluded that the Texas financing scheme discriminates, from a constitutional perspective, between schoolchildren on the basis of the amount of taxable property located within their local districts.

In my Brother STEWART'S view, however, such a description of the discrimination inherent in this case is apparently not sufficient, for it fails to define the "kind of objectively identifiable classes" that he evidently perceives to be necessary for a claim to be "cognizable under the Equal Protection Clause," ante, at 62. He asserts that this is also the view of the majority, but he is unable to cite, nor have I been able to find, any portion of the Court's opinion which remotely suggests that there is no objectively identifiable or definable class in this case. In any event, if he means to suggest that an essential predicate to equal protection analysis is the precise identification of the particular individuals who compose the disadvantaged class, I fail to find the source from which he derives such a requirement. Certainly such precision is not analytically necessary. So long as the basis of the discrimination is clearly identified, it is possible to test it against the State's purpose for such discrimination—whatever the standard of equal protection analysis employed. This is clear from our decision only last Term in Bullock v. Carter, (1972), where the Court, in striking down Texas' primary filing fees as violative of equal protection, found no impediment to equal protection analysis in the fact that the members of the disadvantaged class could not be readily identified. The Court recognized that the filing-fee system tended "to deny some voters the opportunity to vote for a candidate of their choosing; at the same time it gives the affluent the power to place on the ballot their own names or the names of persons they favor." Id., at 144. The Court also recognized that "[t]his disparity in voting power based on wealth cannot be described by reference to discrete and precisely defined segments of the community as is typical of inequities challenged under the Equal Protection Clause . . . ." Ibid. Nevertheless, it concluded that "we would ignore reality were we not to recognize that this system falls with unequal weight on voters . . . according to their economic status." Ibid. The nature of the classification in Bullock was clear, although the precise membership of the disadvantaged class was not. This was enough in Bullock for purposes of equal protection analysis. It is enough here.

It may be, though, that my Brother STEWART is not in fact demanding precise identification of the membership of the disadvantaged class for purposes of equal protection analysis, but is merely unable to discern with sufficient clarity the nature of the discrimination charged in this case. Indeed, the Court itself displays some uncertainty as to the exact nature of the discrimination and the resulting disadvantaged class alleged to exist in this case. See ante, at 19-20. It is, of course, essential to equal protection analysis to have a firm grasp upon the nature of the discrimination at issue. In fact, the absence of such a clear, articulable understanding of the nature of alleged discrimination in a particular instance may well suggest the absence of any real discrimination. But such is hardly the case here.

A number of theories of discrimination have, to be sure, been considered in the course of this litigation. Thus, the District Court found that in Texas the poor and minority group members tend to live in property-poor districts, suggesting discrimination on the basis of both personal wealth and race. See 337 F. Supp., at 282 and n. 3. The Court goes to great lengths to discredit the data upon which the District Court relied, and thereby its conclusion that poor people live in property-poor districts. Although I have serious doubts as to the correctness of the Court's analysis in rejecting the data submitted below, I have no need to join issue on these factual disputes.

I believe it is sufficient that the overarching form of discrimination in this case is between the schoolchildren of Texas on the basis of the taxable property wealth of the districts in which they happen to live. To understand both the precise nature of this discrimination and the parameters of the disadvantaged class it is sufficient to consider the constitutional principle which appellees contend is controlling in the context of educational financing. In their complaint appellees asserted that the Constitution does not permit local district wealth to be determinative of educational opportunity. This is simply another way of saying, as the District Court concluded, that consistent with the guarantee of equal protection of the laws, "the quality of public education may not be a function of wealth, other than the wealth of the state as a whole." 337 F. Supp., at 284. Under such a principle, the children of a district are excessively advantaged if that district has more taxable property per pupil than the average amount of taxable property per pupil considering the State as a whole. By contrast, the children of a district are disadvantaged if that district has less taxable property per pupil than the state average. The majority attempts to disparage such a definition of the disadvantaged class as the product of an "artificially defined level" of district wealth. Ante. at 28. But such is clearly not the case, for this is the definition unmistakably dictated by the constitutional principle for which appellees have argued throughout the course of this litigation. And I do not believe that a clearer definition of either the disadvantaged class of Texas schoolchildren or the allegedly unconstitutional discrimination suffered by the members of that class under the present Texas financing scheme could be asked for, much less needed. Whether this discrimination, against the schoolchildren of property-poor districts, inherent in the Texas financing scheme, is violative of the Equal Protection Clause is the question to which we must now turn.

II

To avoid having the Texas financing scheme struck down because of the interdistrict variations in taxable property wealth, the District Court determined that it was insufficient for appellants to show merely that the State's scheme was rationally related to some legitimate state purpose; rather, the discrimination inherent in the scheme had to be shown necessary to promote a "compelling state interest" in order to withstand constitutional scrutiny. The basis for this determination was twofold: first, the financing scheme divides citizens on a wealth basis, a classification which the District Court viewed as highly suspect; and second, the discriminatory scheme directly affects what it considered to be a "fundamental interest," namely, education.

This Court has repeatedly held that state discrimination which either adversely affects a "fundamental interest," see, e. g., Dunn v. Blumstein, (1972); Shapiro v. Thompson, (1969), or is based on a distinction of a suspect character, see, e. g., Graham v. Richardson, (1971); McLaughlin v. Florida, (1964), must be carefully scrutinized to ensure that the scheme is necessary to promote a substantial, legitimate state interest. See, e. g., Dunn v. Blumstein, supra, at 342-343; Shapiro v. Thompson, supra, at 634. The majority today concludes, however, that the Texas scheme is not subject to such a strict standard of review under the Equal Protection Clause. Instead, in its view, the Texas scheme must be tested by nothing more than that lenient standard of rationality which we have traditionally applied to discriminatory state action in the context of economic and commercial matters. See, e. g., McGowan, v. Maryland; Morey v. Doud, (1957); F. S. Royster Guano Co. v. Virginia; Lindsley v. Natural Carbonic Gas Co., (1911). By so doing, the Court avoids the telling task of searching for a substantial state interest which the Texas financing scheme, with its variations in taxable district property wealth, is necessary to further. I cannot accept such an emasculation of the Equal Protection Clause in the context of this case.

A

To begin, I must once more voice my disagreement with the Court's rigidified approach to equal protection analysis. See Dandridge v. Williams, (1970) (dissenting opinion); Richardson v. Belcher, (1971) (dissenting opinion). The Court apparently seeks to establish today that equal protection cases fall into one of two neat categories which dictate the appropriate standard of review—strict scrutiny or mere rationality. But this Court's decisions in the field of equal protection defy such easy categorization. A principled reading of what this Court has done reveals that it has applied a spectrum of standards in reviewing discrimination allegedly violative of the Equal Protection Clause. This spectrum clearly comprehends variations in the degree of care with which the Court will scrutinize particular classifications, depending, I believe, on the constitutional and societal importance of the interest adversely affected and the recognized invidiousness of the basis upon which the particular classification is drawn. I find in fact that many of the Court's recent decisions embody the very sort of reasoned approach to equal protection analysis for which I previously argued—that is, an approach in which "concentration [is] placed upon the character of the classification in question, the relative importance to individuals in the class discriminated against of the governmental benefits that they do not receive, and the asserted state interests in support of the classification." Dandridge v. Williams, supra, at 520-521 (dissenting opinion).

I therefore cannot accept the majority's labored efforts to demonstrate that fundamental interests, which call for strict scrutiny of the challenged classification, encompass only established rights which we are somehow bound to recognize from the text of the Constitution itself. To be sure, some interests which the Court has deemed to be fundamental for purposes of equal protection analysis are themselves constitutionally protected rights. Thus, discrimination against the guaranteed right of freedom of speech has called for strict judicial scrutiny. See Police Dept. of Chicago v. Mosley, (1972). Further, every citizen's right to travel interstate, although nowhere expressly mentioned in the Constitution, has long been recognized as implicit in the premises underlying that document: the right "was conceived from the beginning to be a necessary concomitant of the stronger Union the Constitution created." United States v. Guest, (1966). See also Crandall v. Nevada, 6 Wall. 35, 48 (1868). Consequently, the Court has required that a state classification affecting the constitutionally protected right to travel must be "shown to be necessary to promote a compelling governmental interest." Shapiro v. Thompson. But it will not do to suggest that the "answer" to whether an interest is fundamental for purposes of equal protection analysis is always determined by whether that interest "is a right . . . explicitly or implicitly guaranteed by the Constitution," ante, at 33-34.

I would like to know where the Constitution guarantees the right to procreate, Skinner v. Oklahoma, (1942), or the right to vote in state elections, e. g., Reynolds v. Sims, (1964), or the right to an appeal from a criminal conviction, e. g., Griffin v. Illinois, (1956). These are instances in which, due to the importance of the interests at stake, the Court has displayed a strong concern with the existence of discriminatory state treatment. But the Court has never said or indicated that these are interests which independently enjoy full-blown constitutional protection.

Thus, in Buck v. Bell, (1927), the Court refused to recognize a substantive constitutional guarantee of the right to procreate. Nevertheless, in Skinner v. Oklahoma, supra, at 541, the Court, without impugning the continuing validity of Buck v. Bell, held that "strict scrutiny" of state discrimination affecting procreation "is essential," for "[m]arriage and procreation are fundamental to the very existence and survival of the race." Recently, in Roe v. Wade, (1973), the importance of procreation has, indeed, been explained on the basis of its intimate relationship with the constitutional right of privacy which we have recognized. Yet the limited stature thereby accorded any "right" to procreate is evident from the fact that at the same time the Court reaffirmed its initial decision in Buck v. Bell. See Roe v. Wade, supra, at 154.

Similarly, the right to vote in state elections has been recognized as a "fundamental political right," because the Court concluded very early that it is "preservative of all rights." Yick

Wo v. Hopkins, (1886); see, e. g., Reynolds v. Sims, supra, at 561-562. For this reason, "this Court has made clear that a citizen has a constitutionally protected right to participate in elections on an equal basis with other citizens in the jurisdiction." Dunn v. Blumstein (emphasis added). The final source of such protection from inequality in the provision of the state franchise is, of course, the Equal Protection Clause. Yet it is clear that whatever degree of importance has been attached to the state electoral process when unequally distributed, the right to vote in state elections has itself never been accorded the stature of an independent constitutional guarantee. See Oregon v. Mitchell, (1970); Kramer v. Union School District, (1969); Harper v. Virginia Bd. of Elections, (1966).

Finally, it is likewise "true that a State is not required by the Federal Constitution to provide appellate courts or a right to appellate review at all." Griffin v. Illinois. Nevertheless, discrimination adversely affecting access to an appellate process which a State has chosen to provide has been considered to require close judicial scrutiny. See, e. g., Griffin v. Illinois, supra; Douglas v. California, (1963).

The majority is, of course, correct when it suggests that the process of determining which interests are fundamental is a difficult one. But I do not think the problem is insurmountable. And I certainly do not accept the view that the process need necessarily degenerate into an unprincipled, subjective "picking-and-choosing" between various interests or that it must involve this Court in creating "substantive constitutional rights in the name of guaranteeing equal protection of the laws," ante, at 33. Although not all fundamental interests are constitutionally guaranteed, the determination of which interests are fundamental should be firmly rooted in the text of the Constitution. The task in every case should be to determine the extent to which constitutionally guaranteed rights are dependent on interests not mentioned in the Constitution. As the nexus between the specific constitutional guarantee and the nonconstitutional interest draws closer, the nonconstitutional interest becomes more fundamental and the degree of judicial scrutiny applied when the interest is infringed on a discriminatory basis must be adjusted accordingly. Thus, it cannot be denied that interests such as procreation, the exercise of the state franchise, and access to criminal appellate processes are not fully guaranteed to the citizen by our Constitution. But these interests have nonetheless been afforded special judicial consideration in the face of discrimination because they are, to some extent, interrelated with constitutional guarantees. Procreation is now understood to be important because of its interaction with the established constitutional right of privacy. The exercise of the state franchise is closely tied to basic civil and political rights inherent in the First Amendment. And access to criminal appellate processes enhances the integrity of the range of rights implicit in the Fourteenth Amendment guarantee of due process of law. Only if we closely protect the related interests from state discrimination do we ultimately ensure the integrity of the constitutional guarantee itself. This is the real lesson that must be taken from our previous decisions involving interests deemed to be fundamental.

The effect of the interaction of individual interests with established constitutional guarantees upon the degree of care exercised by this Court in reviewing state discrimination affecting such interests is amply illustrated by our decision last Term in Eisenstadt v. Baird, (1972). In Baird, the Court struck down as violative of the Equal Protection Clause a state statute which denied unmarried persons access to contraceptive devices on the same basis as married persons. The Court purported to test the statute under its traditional standard whether there is some rational basis for the discrimination effected. Id., at 446-447. In the context of commercial regulation, the Court has indicated that the Equal Protection Clause "is offended only if the classification rests on grounds wholly irrelevant to the achievement of the State's objective." See, e. g., McGowan v. Maryland; Kotch v. Board of River Port Pilot Comm'rs, (1947). And this lenient standard is further weighted in the State's favor by the fact that "[a] statutory discrimination will not be set aside if any state of facts reasonably may be conceived [by the Court] to justify it." McGowan v. Maryland, supra, at 426. But in Baird the Court clearly did not adhere to these highly tolerant standards of traditional rational review. For although there were conceivable state interests intended to be advanced by the statute—e. g., deterrence of premarital sexual activity and regulation of the dissemination of potentially dangerous articles—the Court was not prepared to accept these interests on their face, but instead proceeded to test their substantiality by independent analysis. Such close scrutiny of the State's interests was hardly characteristic of the deference shown state classifications in the context of economic interests. See, e. g., Goesaert v. Cleary, (1948); Kotch v. Board of River Port Pilot Comm'rs, supra. Yet I think the Court's action was entirely appropriate, for access to and use of contraceptives bears a close relationship to the individual's constitutional right of privacy. See also Roe v. Wade.

A similar process of analysis with respect to the invidiousness of the basis on which a particular classification is drawn has also influenced the Court as to the appropriate degree of scrutiny to be accorded any particular case. The highly suspect character of classifications based on race, nationality, or alienage is well established. The reasons why such classifications call for close judicial scrutiny are manifold. Certain racial and ethnic groups have frequently been recognized as "discrete and insular minorities" who are relatively powerless to protect their interests in the political process. See Graham, v. Richardson; cf. United States v. Carolene Products Co., n. 4 (1938). Moreover, race, nationality, or alienage is "'in most circumstances irrelevant' to any constitutionally acceptable legislative purpose, Hirabayashi v. United States." McLaughlin v. Florida. Instead, lines drawn on such bases are frequently the reflection of historic prejudices rather than legislative rationality. It may be that all of these considerations, which make for particular judicial solicitude in the face of discrimination on the basis of race, nationality, or alienage, do not coalesce—or at least not to the same degree—in other forms of discrimination. Nevertheless, these considerations have undoubtedly influenced the care with which the Court has scrutinized other forms of discrimination.

In James v. Strange, (1972), the Court held unconstitutional a state statute which provided for recoupment from indigent convicts of legal defense fees paid by the State. The Court found that the statute impermissibly differentiated between indigent criminals in debt to the State and civil judgment debtors, since criminal debtors were denied various protective exemptions afforded civil judgment debtors. The Court suggested that in reviewing the statute under the Equal Protection Clause, it was merely applying the traditional requirement that there be "'some rationality'" in the line drawn between the different types of debtors. Id., at 140. Yet it then proceeded to scrutinize the statute with less than traditional deference and restraint. Thus, the Court recognized "that state recoupment statutes may betoken legitimate state interests" in recovering expenses and discouraging fraud. Nevertheless, MR. JUSTICE POWELL, speaking for the Court, concluded that:

> "these interests are not thwarted by requiring more even treatment of indigent criminal defendants with other classes of debtors to whom the statute itself repeatedly makes reference. State recoupment laws, notwithstanding the state interests they may serve, need not blight in such discriminatory fashion the hopes of indigents for self-sufficiency and self-respect." Id., at 141-142.

The Court, in short, clearly did not consider the problems of fraud and collection that the state legislature might have concluded were peculiar to indigent criminal defendants to be either sufficiently important or at least sufficiently substantiated to justify denial of the protective exemptions afforded to all civil judgment debtors, to a class composed exclusively of indigent criminal debtors.

Similarly, in Reed v. Reed, (1971), the Court, in striking down a state statute which gave men preference over women when persons of equal entitlement apply for assignment as an administrator of a particular estate, resorted to a more stringent standard of equal protection review than that employed in cases involving commercial matters. The Court indicated that it was testing the claim of sex discrimination by nothing more than whether the line drawn bore "a rational relationship to a state objective," which it recognized as a legitimate effort to reduce the work of probate courts in choosing between competing applications for letters of administration. Id., at 76. Accepting such a purpose, the Idaho Supreme Court had thought the classification to be sustainable on the basis that the legislature might have reasonably concluded that, as a rule, men have more experience than women in business matters relevant to the administration of an estate. 93 Idaho 511, 514, 465 P.2d 635, 638 (1970). This Court, however, concluded that "[t]o give a mandatory preference to members of either sex over members of the other, merely to accomplish the elimination of hearings on the merits, is to make the very kind of arbitrary legislative choice forbidden by the Equal Protection Clause of the Fourteenth Amendment. . . ." This Court, in other words, was unwilling to consider a theoretical and unsubstantiated basis for distinction—however reasonable it might appear—sufficient to sustain a statute discriminating on the basis of sex.

James and Reed can only be understood as instances in which the particularly invidious character of the classification caused the Court to pause and scrutinize with more than traditional care the rationality of state discrimination. Discrimination on the basis of past criminality and on the basis of sex posed for the Court the specter of forms of discrimination which it implicitly recognized to have deep social and legal roots without necessarily having any basis in actual differences. Still, the Court's sensitivity to the invidiousness of the basis for discrimination is perhaps most apparent in its decisions protecting the interests of children born out of wedlock from discriminatory state action. See Weber v. Aetna Casualty & Surety Co., (1972); Levy v. Louisiana, (1968).

In Weber, the Court struck down a portion of a state workmen's compensation statute that relegated unacknowledged illegitimate children of the deceased to a lesser status with respect to benefits than that occupied by legitimate children of the deceased. The Court acknowledged the true nature of its inquiry in cases such as these: "What legitimate state interest does the classification promote? What fundamental personal rights might the classification endanger?" Id., at 173. Embarking upon a determination of the relative substantiality of the State's justifications for the classification, the Court rejected the contention that the classifications reflected what might be presumed to have been the deceased's preference of beneficiaries as "not compelling . . . where dependency on the deceased is a prerequisite to anyone's recovery. . . ." Ibid. Likewise, it deemed the relationship between the State's interest in encouraging legitimate family relationships and the burden placed on the illegitimates too tenuous to permit the classification to stand. Ibid. A clear insight into the basis of the Court's action is provided by its conclusion:

> "[I]mposing disabilities on the illegitimate child is contrary to the basic concept of our system that legal burdens should bear some relationship to individual responsibility or wrongdoing. Obviously, no child is responsible for his birth and penalizing the illegitimate child is an ineffectual—as well as an unjust—way of deterring the parent. Courts are powerless to prevent the social opprobrium suffered by these hapless children, but the Equal Protection Clause does enable us to strike down discriminatory laws relating to status of birth . . . ." Id., at 175-176.

Status of birth, like the color of one's skin, is something which the individual cannot control, and should generally be irrelevant in legislative considerations. Yet illegitimacy has long been stigmatized by our society. Hence, discrimination on the basis of birth—particularly when it affects innocent children—warrants special judicial consideration.

In summary, it seems to me inescapably clear that this Court has consistently adjusted the care with which it will review state discrimination in light of the constitutional significance of the interests affected and the invidiousness of the particular classification. In the context of economic interests, we find that discriminatory state action is almost always sustained, for such interests are generally far removed from constitutional guarantees. Moreover, "[t]he extremes to which the Court has gone in dreaming up rational bases for state regulation in that area may in many instances be ascribed to a healthy revulsion from the Court's earlier excesses in using the Constitution to protect interests that have more than enough power to protect themselves in the legislative halls." Dandridge v. Williams, (dissenting opinion). But the situation differs markedly when discrimination against important individual interests with constitutional implications and against particularly disadvantaged or powerless classes is involved. The majority suggests, however, that a variable standard of review would give this Court the appearance of a "superlegislature." Ante, at 31. I cannot agree. Such an approach seems to me a part of the guarantees of our Constitution and of the historic experiences with oppression of and discrimination against discrete, powerless minorities which underlie that document. In truth, the Court itself will be open to the criticism raised by the majority so long as it continues on its present course of effectively selecting in private which cases will be afforded special consideration without acknowledging the true basis of its action. Opinions such as those in Reed and James seem drawn more as efforts to shield rather than to reveal the true basis of the Court's decisions. Such obfuscated action may be appropriate to a political body such as a legislature, but it is not appropriate to this Court. Open debate of the bases for the Court's action is essential to the rationality and consistency of our decisionmaking process. Only in this way can we avoid the label of legislature and ensure the integrity of the judicial process.

Nevertheless, the majority today attempts to force this case into the same category for purposes of equal protection analysis as decisions involving discrimination affecting commercial interests. By so doing, the majority singles this case out for analytic treatment at odds with what seems to me to be the clear trend of recent decisions in this Court, and thereby ignores the constitutional importance of the interest at stake and the invidiousness of the particular classification, factors that call for far more than the lenient scrutiny of the Texas financing scheme which the majority pursues. Yet if the discrimination inherent in the Texas scheme is scrutinized with the care demanded by the interest and classification present in this case, the unconstitutionality of that scheme is unmistakable.

B

Since the Court now suggests that only interests guaranteed by the Constitution are fundamental for purposes of equal protection analysis, and since it rejects the contention that public education is fundamental, it follows that the Court concludes that public education is not constitutionally guaranteed. It is true that this Court has never deemed the provision of free public education to be required by the Constitution. Indeed, it has on occasion suggested that state-supported education is a privilege bestowed by a State on its citizens. See Missouri ex rel. Gaines v. Canada. Nevertheless, the fundamental importance of education is amply indicated by the prior decisions of this Court, by the unique status accorded public education by our society, and by the close relationship between education and some of our most basic constitutional values.

The special concern of this Court with the educational process of our country is a matter of common knowledge. Undoubtedly, this Court's most famous statement on the subject is that contained in Brown v. Board of Education:

> "Today, education is perhaps the most important function of state and local governments. Compulsory school attendance laws and the great expenditures for education both demonstrate our recognition of the importance of education to our democratic society. It is required in the performance of our most basic public responsibilities, even service in the armed forces. It is the very foundation of good citizenship. Today it is a principal instrument in awakening the child to cultural values, in preparing him for later professional training, and in helping him to adjust normally to his environment . . . ."

Only last Term, the Court recognized that "[p]roviding public schools ranks at the very apex of the function of a State." Wisconsin v. Yoder, (1972). This is clearly borne out by the fact that in 48 of our 50 States the provision of public education is mandated by the state constitution. No other state function is so uniformly recognized as an essential element of our society's well-being. In large measure, the explanation for the special importance attached to education must rest, as the Court recognized in Yoder, id., at 221, on the facts that "some degree of education is necessary to prepare citizens to participate effectively and intelligently in our open political system . . . ," and that "education prepares individuals to be self-reliant and self-sufficient participants in society." Both facets of this observation are suggestive of the substantial relationship which education bears to guarantees of our Constitution.

Education directly affects the ability of a child to exercise his First Amendment rights, both as a source and as a receiver of information and ideas, whatever interests he may pursue in life. This Court's decision in Sweezy v. New Hampshire, (1957), speaks of the right of students "to inquire, to study and to evaluate, to gain new maturity and understanding . . . ." Thus, we have not casually described the classroom as the "'marketplace of ideas.'" Keyishian v. Board of Regents, (1967). The opportunity for formal education may not necessarily be the essential determinant of an individual's ability to enjoy throughout his life the rights of free speech and association guaranteed to him by the First Amendment. But such an opportunity may enhance the individual's enjoyment of those rights, not only during but also following school attendance. Thus, in the final analysis, "the pivotal position of education to success in American society and its essential role in opening up to the individual the central experiences of our culture lend it an importance that is undeniable."

Of particular importance is the relationship between education and the political process. "Americans regard the public schools as a most vital civic institution for the preservation of a democratic system of government." Abington School Dist. v. Schempp, (1963) (BRENNAN, J., concurring). Education serves the essential function of instilling in our young an understanding of and appreciation for the principles and operation of our governmental processes. Education may instill the interest and provide the tools necessary for political discourse and debate. Indeed, it has frequently been suggested that education is the dominant factor affecting political consciousness and participation. A system of "[c]ompetition in ideas and governmental policies is at the core of our electoral process and of the First Amendment freedoms." Williams v. Rhodes, (1968). But of most immediate and direct concern must be the demonstrated effect of education on the exercise of the franchise by the electorate. The right to vote in federal elections is conferred by Art. I, 2, and the Seventeenth Amendment of the Constitution, and access to the state franchise has been afforded special protection because it is "preservative of other basic civil and political rights," Reynolds v. Sims. Data from the Presidential Election of 1968 clearly demonstrate a direct relationship between participation in the electoral process and level of educational attainment; and, as this Court recognized in Gaston County v. United States, (1969), the quality of education offered may influence a child's decision to "enter or remain in school." It is this very sort of intimate relationship between a particular personal interest and specific constitutional guarantees that has heretofore caused the Court to attach special significance, for purposes of equal protection analysis, to individual interests such as procreation and the exercise of the state franchise.

While ultimately disputing little of this, the majority seeks refuge in the fact that the Court has "never presumed to possess either the ability or the authority to guarantee to the citizenry the most effective speech or the most informed electoral choice." Ante, at 36. This serves only to blur what is in fact at stake. With due respect, the issue is neither provision of the most effective speech nor of the most informed vote. Appellees do not now seek the best education Texas might provide. They do seek, however, an end to state discrimination resulting from the unequal distribution of taxable district property wealth that directly impairs the ability of some districts to provide the same educational opportunity that other districts can provide with the same or even substantially less tax effort. The issue is, in other words, one of discrimination that affects the quality of the education which Texas has chosen to provide its children;

and, the precise question here is what importance should attach to education for purposes of equal protection analysis of that discrimination. As this Court held in Brown v. Board of Education, the opportunity of education, "where the state has undertaken to provide it, is a right which must be made available to all on equal terms." The factors just considered, including the relationship between education and the social and political interests enshrined within the Constitution, compel us to recognize the fundamentality of education and to scrutinize with appropriate care the bases for state discrimination affecting equality of educational opportunity in Texas' school districts—a conclusion which is only strengthened when we consider the character of the classification in this case.

C

The District Court found that in discriminating between Texas schoolchildren on the basis of the amount of taxable property wealth located in the district in which they live, the Texas financing scheme created a form of wealth discrimination. This Court has frequently recognized that discrimination on the basis of wealth may create a classification of a suspect character and thereby call for exacting judicial scrutiny. See e. g., Griffin v. Illinois, (1956); Douglas v. California, (1963); McDonald v. Board of Election Comm'rs of Chicago, (1969). The majority, however, considers any wealth classification in this case to lack certain essential characteristics which it contends are common to the instances of wealth discrimination that this Court has heretofore recognized. We are told that in every prior case involving a wealth classification, the members of the disadvantaged class have "shared two distinguishing characteristics: because of their impecunity they were completely unable to pay for some desired benefit, and as a consequence, they sustained an absolute deprivation of a meaningful opportunity to enjoy that benefit." Ante, at 20. I cannot agree. The Court's distinctions may be sufficient to explain the decisions in Williams v. Illinois, (1970); Tate v. Short, (1971); and even Bullock v. Carter, (1972). But they are not in fact consistent with the decisions in Harper v. Virginia Bd. of Elections, (1966), or Griffin v. Illinois, supra, or Douglas v. California, supra.

In Harper, the Court struck down as violative of the Equal Protection Clause an annual Virginia poll tax of $1.50, payment of which by persons over the age of 21 was a prerequisite to voting in Virginia elections. In part, the Court relied on the fact that the poll tax interfered with a fundamental interest— the exercise of the state franchise. In addition, though, the Court emphasized that "[l]ines drawn on the basis of wealth or property . . . are traditionally disfavored." Under the first part of the theory announced by the majority, the disadvantaged class in Harper, in terms of a wealth analysis, should have consisted only of those too poor to afford the $1.50 necessary to vote. But the Harper Court did not see it that way. In its view, the Equal Protection Clause "bars a system which excludes [from the franchise] those unable to pay a fee to vote or who fail to pay." Ibid. (Emphasis added.) So far as the Court was concerned, the "degree of the discrimination [was] irrelevant." Ibid. Thus, the Court struck down the poll tax in toto; it did not order merely that those too poor to pay the tax be exempted; complete impecunity clearly was not determinative of the limits of the disadvantaged class, nor was it essential to make an equal protection claim.

Similarly, Griffin and Douglas refute the majority's contention that we have in the past required an absolute deprivation before subjecting wealth classifications to strict scrutiny. The Court characterizes Griffin as a case concerned simply with the denial of a transcript or an adequate substitute therefore, and Douglas as involving the denial of counsel. But in both cases the question was in fact whether "a State that [grants] appellate review can do so in a way that discriminates against some convicted defendants on account of their poverty." Griffin v. Illinois, supra, at 18 (emphasis added). In that regard, the Court concluded that inability to purchase a transcript denies "the poor an adequate appellate review accorded to all who have money enough to pay the costs in advance," ibid. (emphasis added), and that "the type of an appeal a person is afforded . . . hinges upon whether or not he can pay for the assistance of counsel," Douglas v. California, supra, at 355-356 (emphasis added). The right of appeal itself was not absolutely denied to those too poor to pay; but because of the cost of a transcript and of counsel, the appeal was a substantially less meaningful right for the poor than for the rich. It was on these terms that the Court found a denial of equal protection, and those terms clearly encompassed degrees of discrimination on the basis of wealth which do not amount to outright denial of the affected right or interest.

This is not to say that the form of wealth classification in this case does not differ significantly from those recognized in the previous decisions of this Court. Our prior cases have dealt essentially with discrimination on the basis of personal wealth. Here, by contrast, the children of the disadvantaged Texas school districts are being discriminated against not necessarily because of their personal wealth or the wealth of their families, but because of the taxable property wealth of the residents of the district in which they happen to live. The appropriate question, then, is whether the same degree of judicial solicitude and scrutiny that has previously been afforded wealth classifications is warranted here.

As the Court points out, ante, at 28-29, no previous decision has deemed the presence of just a wealth classification to be sufficient basis to call forth rigorous judicial scrutiny of allegedly discriminatory state action. Compare, e. g., Harper v. Virginia Bd. of Elections, supra, with, e. g., James v. Valtierra, (1971). That wealth classifications alone have not necessarily been considered to bear the same high degree of suspectness as have classifications based on, for instance, race or alienage may be explainable on a number of grounds. The "poor" may not be seen as politically powerless as certain discrete and insular minority groups. Personal poverty may entail much the same social stigma as historically attached to certain racial or ethnic groups. But personal poverty is not a permanent disability; its shackles may be escaped. Perhaps most importantly, though, personal wealth may not necessarily share the general irrelevance as a basis for legislative action that race or nationality is recognized to have. While the "poor" have frequently been a legally disadvantaged group, it cannot be ignored that social legislation must frequently take cognizance of the economic status of our citizens. Thus, we have generally gauged the invidiousness of wealth classifications with an awareness of the importance of the interests being affected and the relevance of personal wealth to those interests. See Harper v. Virginia Bd. of Elections, supra.

When evaluated with these considerations in mind, it seems to me that discrimination on the basis of group wealth in this case likewise calls for careful judicial scrutiny. First, it must be recognized that while local district wealth may serve other interests, it bears no relationship whatsoever to the interest of Texas schoolchildren in the educational opportunity afforded them by the State of Texas. Given the importance of that interest, we must be particularly sensitive to the invidious characteristics of any form of discrimination that is not clearly intended to serve it, as opposed to some other distinct state interest. Discrimination on the basis of group wealth may not, to be sure, reflect the social stigma frequently attached to personal poverty. Nevertheless, insofar as group wealth discrimination involves wealth over which the disadvantaged individual has no significant control, it represents in fact a more serious basis of discrimination than does personal wealth. For such discrimination is no reflection of the individual's characteristics or his abilities. And thus—particularly in the context of a disadvantaged class composed of children—we have previously treated discrimination on a basis which the individual cannot control as constitutionally disfavored. Cf. Weber v. Aetna Casualty & Surety Co., (1972); Levy v. Louisiana, (1968).

The disability of the disadvantaged class in this case extends as well into the political processes upon which we ordinarily rely as adequate for the protection and promotion of all interests. Here legislative reallocation of the State's property wealth must be sought in the face of inevitable opposition from significantly advantaged districts that have a strong vested interest in the preservation of the status quo, a problem not completely dissimilar to that faced by underrepresented districts prior to the Court's intervention in the process of reapportionment, see Baker v. Carr, (1962).

Nor can we ignore the extent to which, in contrast to our prior decisions, the State is responsible for the wealth discrimination in this instance. Griffin, Douglas, Williams, Tate, and our other prior cases have dealt with discrimination on the basis of indigency which was attributable to the operation of the private sector. But we have no such simple de facto wealth discrimination here. The means for financing public education in Texas are selected and specified by the State. It is the State that has created local school districts, and tied educational funding to the local property tax and thereby to local district wealth. At the same time, governmentally imposed land use controls have undoubtedly encouraged and rigidified natural trends in the allocation of particular areas for residential or commercial use, and thus determined each district's amount of taxable property wealth. In short, this case, in contrast to the Court's previous wealth discrimination decisions, can only be seen as "unusual in the extent to which governmental action is the cause of the wealth classification."

In the final analysis, then, the invidious characteristics of the group wealth classification present in this case merely serve to emphasize the need for careful judicial scrutiny of the State's justifications for the resulting interdistrict discrimination in the educational opportunity afforded to the schoolchildren of Texas.

D

The nature of our inquiry into the justification for state discrimination is essentially the same in all equal protection cases: We must consider the substantiality of the state interests sought to be served, and we must scrutinize the reasonableness of the means by which the State has sought to advance its interest. See Police Dept. of Chicago v. Mosley. Differences in the application of this test are, in my view, a function of the constitutional importance of the interests at stake and the invidiousness of the particular classification. In terms of the asserted state interests, the Court has indicated that it will require, for instance, a "compelling," Shapiro v. Thompson, or a "substantial" or "important," Dunn v. Blumstein, state interest to justify discrimination affecting individual interests of constitutional significance. Whatever the differences, if any, in these descriptions of the character of the state interest necessary to sustain such discrimination, basic to each is, I believe, a concern with the legitimacy and the reality of the asserted state interests. Thus, when interests of constitutional importance are at stake, the Court does not stand ready to credit the State's classification with any conceivable legitimate purpose, but demands a clear showing that there are legitimate state interests which the classification was in fact intended to serve. Beyond the question of the adequacy of the State's purpose for the classification, the Court traditionally has become increasingly sensitive to the means by which a State chooses to act as its action affects more directly interests of constitutional significance. See, e. g., United States v. Robel, (1967); Shelton v. Tucker, (1960). Thus, by now, "less restrictive alternatives" analysis is firmly established in equal protection jurisprudence. See Dunn v. Blumstein, supra at 343; Kramer v. Union School District. It seems to me that the range of choice we are willing to accord the State in selecting the means by which it will act, and the care with which we scrutinize the effectiveness of the means which the State selects, also must reflect the constitutional importance of the interest affected and the invidiousness of the particular classification. Here, both the nature of the interest and the classification dictate close judicial scrutiny of the purposes which Texas seeks to serve with its present educational financing scheme and of the means it has selected to serve that purpose.

The only justification offered by appellants to sustain the discrimination in educational opportunity caused by the Texas financing scheme is local educational control. Presented with this justification, the District Court concluded that "[n]ot only are defendants unable to demonstrate compelling state interests for their classifications based upon wealth, they fail even to establish a reasonable basis for these classifications." 337 F. Supp., at 284. I must agree with this conclusion.

At the outset, I do not question that local control of public education, as an abstract matter, constitutes a very substantial state interest. We observed only last Term that "[d]irect control over decisions vitally affecting the education of one's children is a need that is strongly felt in our society." Wright v. Council of the City of Emporia, (1972). See also id., at 477-478 (BURGER, C. J., dissenting). The State's interest in local educational control—which certainly includes questions of educational funding—has deep roots in the inherent benefits of community support for public education. Consequently, true state dedication to local control would present, I think, a substantial justification to weigh against simply interdistrict variations in the treatment of a State's schoolchildren. But I need not now decide how I might ultimately strike the balance were we confronted with a situation where the State's sincere concern for local control inevitably produced educational inequality. For, on this record, it is apparent that the State's purported concern with local control is offered primarily as an excuse rather than as a justification for interdistrict inequality.

In Texas, statewide laws regulate in fact the most minute details of local public education. For example, the State prescribes required courses. All textbooks must be submitted for state approval, and only approved textbooks may be used. The State has established the qualifications necessary for teaching in Texas public schools and the procedures for obtaining certification. The State has even legislated on the length of the school day. Texas' own courts have said:

> "As a result of the acts of the Legislature our school system is not of mere local concern but it is statewide. While a school district is local in territorial limits, it is an integral part of the vast school system which is coextensive with the confines of the State of Texas." (Treadaway v. Whitney Independent School District, 205 S. W. 2d 97, 99 Tex. Ct. Civ. App. 1947).

See also El Dorado Independent School District v. Tisdale, 3 S. W. 2d 420, 422 (Tex. Comm'n App. 1928).

Moreover, even if we accept Texas' general dedication to local control in educational matters, it is difficult to find any evidence of such dedication with respect to fiscal matters. It ignores reality to suggest—as the Court does, ante, at 49-50—that the local property tax element of the Texas financing scheme reflects a conscious legislative effort to provide school districts with local fiscal control. If Texas had a system truly dedicated to local fiscal control, one would expect the quality of the educational opportunity provided in each district to vary with the decision of the voters in that district as to the level of sacrifice they wish to make for public education. In fact, the Texas scheme produces precisely the opposite result. Local school districts cannot choose to have the best education in the State by imposing the highest tax rate. Instead, the quality of the educational opportunity offered by any particular district is largely determined by the amount of taxable property located in the district—a factor over which local voters can exercise no control.

The study introduced in the District Court showed a direct inverse relationship between equalized taxable district property wealth and district tax effort with the result that the property-poor districts making the highest tax effort obtained the lowest per-pupil yield. The implications of this situation for local choice are illustrated by again comparing the Edgewood and Alamo Heights School Districts. In 1967-1968, Edgewood, after contributing its share to the Local Fund Assignment, raised only $26 per pupil through its local property tax, whereas Alamo Heights was able to raise $333 per pupil. Since the funds received through the Minimum Foundation School Program are to be used only for minimum professional salaries, transportation costs, and operating expenses, it is not hard to see the lack of local choice—with respect to higher teacher salaries to attract more and better teachers, physical facilities, library books, and facilities, special courses, or participation in special state and federal matching funds programs—under which a property-poor district such as Edgewood is forced to labor. In fact, because of the difference in taxable local property wealth, Edgewood would have to tax itself almost nine times as heavily to obtain the same yield as Alamo Heights. At present, then, local control is a myth for many of the local school districts in Texas. As one district court has observed, "rather than reposing in each school district the economic power to fix its own level of per pupil expenditure, the State has so arranged the structure as to guarantee that some districts will spend low (with high taxes) while others will spend high (with low taxes)." Van Dusartz v. Hatfield, 334 F. Supp. 870, 876 (Minn. 1971).

In my judgment, any substantial degree of scrutiny of the operation of the Texas financing scheme reveals that the State has selected means wholly inappropriate to secure its purported interest in assuring its school districts local fiscal control. At the same time, appellees have pointed out a variety of alternative financing schemes which may serve the State's purported interest in local control as well as, if not better than, the present scheme without the current impairment of the educational opportunity of vast numbers of Texas schoolchildren. I see no need, however, to explore the practical or constitutional merits of those suggested alternatives at this time for, whatever their positive or negative features, experience with the present financing scheme impugns any suggestion that it constitutes a serious effort to provide local fiscal control. If, for the sake of local education control, this Court is to sustain interdistrict discrimination in the educational opportunity afforded Texas school children, it should require that the State present something more than the mere sham now before us.

III

In conclusion, it is essential to recognize that an end to the wide variations in taxable district property wealth inherent in the Texas financing scheme would entail none of the untoward consequences suggested by the Court or by the appellants.

First, affirmance of the District Court's decisions would hardly sound the death knell for local control of education. It would mean neither centralized decisionmaking nor federal court intervention in the operation of public schools. Clearly, this suit has nothing to do with local decisionmaking with respect to educational policy or even educational spending. It involves only a narrow aspect of local control—namely, local control over the raising of educational funds. In fact, in striking down interdistrict disparities in taxable local wealth, the District Court took the course which is most likely to make true local control over educational decisionmaking a reality for all Texas school districts.

Nor does the District Court's decision even necessarily eliminate local control of educational funding. The District Court struck down nothing more than the continued interdistrict wealth discrimination inherent in the present property tax. Both centralized and decentralized plans for educational funding not involving such interdistrict discrimination have been put forward. The choice among these or other alternatives would remain with the State, not with the federal courts. In this regard, it should be evident that the degree of federal intervention in matters of local concern would be substantially less in this context than in previous decisions in which we have been asked effectively to impose a particular scheme upon the States under the guise of the Equal Protection Clause. See, e. g., Dandridge v. Williams, (1970); cf. Richardson v. Belcher, (1971).

Still, we are told that this case requires us "to condemn the State's judgment in conferring on political subdivisions the power to tax local property to supply revenues for local interest." Ante, at 40. Yet no one in the course of this entire litigation has ever questioned the constitutionality of the local property tax as a device for raising educational funds. The District Court's decision, at most, restricts the power of the State to make educational funding dependent exclusively upon local property taxation so long as there exists interdistrict disparities in taxable property wealth. But it hardly eliminates the local property tax as a source of educational funding or as a means of providing local fiscal control.

The Court seeks solace for its action today in the possibility of legislative reform. The Court's suggestions of legislative redress and experimentation will doubtless be of great comfort to the schoolchildren of Texas' disadvantaged districts, but considering the vested interests of wealthy school districts in the preservation of the status quo, they are worth little more. The possibility of legislative action is, in all events, no answer to this Court's duty under the Constitution to eliminate unjustified state discrimination. In this case we have been presented with an instance of such discrimination, in a particularly invidious form, against an individual interest of large constitutional and practical importance. To support the demonstrated discrimination in the provision of educational opportunity the State has offered a justification which, on analysis, takes on at best an ephemeral character. Thus, I believe that the wide disparities in taxable district property wealth inherent in the local property tax element of the Texas financing scheme render that scheme violative of the Equal Protection Clause.

I would therefore affirm the judgment of the District Court.

LAU ET AL. V. NICHOLS ET AL., 414 U.S. 563 (1974)

SUPREME COURT OF THE UNITED STATES
CERTIORARI TO THE UNITED STATES COURT OF APPEALS FOR THE NINTH CIRCUIT
ARGUED DECEMBER 10, 1973. DECIDED JANUARY 21, 1974.

The failure of the San Francisco school system to provide English language instruction to approximately 1,800 students of Chinese ancestry who do not speak English, or to provide them with other adequate instructional procedures, denies them a meaningful opportunity to participate in the public educational program and thus violates 601 of the Civil Rights Act of 1964, which bans discrimination based "on the ground of race, color, or national origin," in "any program or activity receiving Federal financial assistance," and the implementing regulations of the Department of Health, Education, and Welfare.

MR. JUSTICE DOUGLAS delivered the opinion of the Court.

The San Francisco, California, school system was integrated in 1971 as a result of a federal court decree, 339 F. Supp. 1315. See Lee v. Johnson. The District Court found that there are 2,856 students of Chinese ancestry in the school system who do not speak English. Of those who have that language deficiency, about 1,000 are given supplemental courses in the English language. About 1,800, however, do not receive that instruction.

This class suit brought by non-English-speaking Chinese students against officials responsible for the operation of the San Francisco Unified School District seeks relief against the unequal educational opportunities, which are alleged to violate, inter alia, the Fourteenth Amendment. No specific remedy is urged upon us. Teaching English to the students of Chinese ancestry who do not speak the language is one choice. Giving instructions to this group in Chinese is another. There may be others. Petitioners ask only that the Board of Education be directed to apply its expertise to the problem and rectify the situation.

The District Court denied relief. The Court of Appeals affirmed, holding that there was no violation of the Equal Protection Clause of the Fourteenth Amendment or of 601 of the Civil Rights Act of 1964, 78 Stat. 252, 42 U.S.C. 2000d, which excludes from participation in federal financial assistance, recipients of aid which discriminate against racial groups, 483 F.2d 791. One judge dissented. A hearing en banc was denied, two judges dissenting. Id., at 805.

We granted the petition for certiorari because of the public importance of the question presented.

The Court of Appeals reasoned that "[e]very student brings to the starting line of his educational career different advantages and disadvantages caused in part by social, economic and cultural background, created and continued completely apart from any contribution by the school system," 483 F.2d, at 797. Yet in our view the case may not be so easily decided. This is a public school system of California and 71 of the California Education Code states that "English shall be the basic language of instruction in all schools." That section permits a school district to determine "when and under what circumstances instruction may be given bilingually." That section also states as "the policy of the state" to insure "the mastery of English by all pupils in the schools." And bilingual instruction is authorized "to the extent that it does not interfere with the systematic, sequential, and regular instruction of all pupils in the English language."

Moreover, 8573 of the Education Code provides that no pupil shall receive a diploma of graduation from grade 12 who has not met the standards of proficiency in "English," as well as other prescribed subjects. Moreover, by 12101 of the Education Code (Supp. 1973) children between the ages of six and 16 years are (with exceptions not material here) "subject to compulsory full-time education."

Under these state-imposed standards there is no equality of treatment merely by providing students with the same facilities, textbooks, teachers, and curriculum; for students who do not understand English are effectively foreclosed from any meaningful education.

Basic English skills are at the very core of what these public schools teach. Imposition of a requirement that, before a child can effectively participate in the educational program, he must already have acquired those basic skills is to make a mockery of public education. We know that those who do not understand English are certain to find their classroom experiences wholly incomprehensible and in no way meaningful.

We do not reach the Equal Protection Clause argument which has been advanced but rely solely on 601 of the Civil Rights Act of 1964, 42 U.S.C. 2000d, to reverse the Court of Appeals.

That section bans discrimination based "on the ground of race, color, or national origin," in "any program or activity receiving Federal financial assistance." The school district involved in this litigation receives large amounts of federal financial assistance. The Department of Health, Education, and Welfare (HEW), which has authority to promulgate regulations prohibiting discrimination in federally assisted school systems, 42 U.S.C. 2000d-1, in 1968 issued one guideline that "[s]chool systems are responsible for assuring that students of a particular race, color, or national origin are not denied the opportunity to obtain the education generally obtained by other students in the system." 33 Fed. Reg. 4956. In 1970 HEW made the guidelines more specific, requiring school districts that were federally funded "to rectify the language deficiency in order to open" the instruction to students who had "linguistic deficiencies," 35 Fed. Reg. 11595.

By 602 of the Act HEW is authorized to issue rules, regulations, and orders to make sure that recipients of federal aid under its jurisdiction conduct any federally financed projects consistently with 601. HEW's regulations, 45 CFR 80.3 (b) (1), specify that the recipients may not

"(ii) Provide any service, financial aid, or other benefit to an individual which is different, or is provided in a different manner, from that provided to others under the program;

. . . .

"(iv) Restrict an individual in any way in the enjoyment of any advantage or privilege enjoyed by others receiving any service, financial aid, or other benefit under the program."

Discrimination among students on account of race or national origin that is prohibited includes "discrimination . . . in the availability or use of any academic . . . or other facilities of the grantee or other recipient." Id., 80.5 (b).

Discrimination is barred which has that effect even though no purposeful design is present: a recipient "may not . . . utilize criteria or methods of administration which have the effect of subjecting individuals to discrimination" or have "the effect of defeating or substantially impairing accomplishment of the objectives of the program as respect individuals of a particular race, color, or national origin." Id., 80.3 (b) (2).

It seems obvious that the Chinese-speaking minority receive fewer benefits than the English-speaking majority from respondents' school system which denies them a meaningful opportunity to participate in the educational program—all earmarks of the discrimination banned by the regulations. In 1970 HEW issued clarifying guidelines, 35 Fed. Reg. 11595, which include the following:

> "Where inability to speak and understand the English language excludes national origin-minority group children from effective participation in the educational program offered by a school district, the district must take affirmative steps to rectify the language deficiency in order to open its instructional program to these students."
>
> "Any ability grouping or tracking system employed by the school system to deal with the special language skill needs of national origin-minority group children must be designed to meet such language skill needs as soon as possible and must not operate as an educational deadend or permanent track."

Respondent school district contractually agreed to "comply with title VI of the Civil Rights Act of 1964 . . . and all requirements imposed by or pursuant to the Regulation" of HEW (45 CFR pt. 80) which are "issued pursuant to that title . . . " and also immediately to "take any measures necessary to effectuate this agreement." The Federal Government has power to fix the terms on which its money allotments to the States shall be disbursed. Oklahoma v. CSC. Whatever may be the limits of that power, Steward Machine Co. v. Davis, et seq., they have not been reached here. Senator Humphrey, during the floor debates on the Civil Rights Act of 1964, said:

> "Simple justice requires that public funds, to which all taxpayers of all races contribute, not be spent in any fashion which encourages, entrenches, subsidizes, or results in racial discrimination."

We accordingly reverse the judgment of the Court of Appeals and remand the case for the fashioning of appropriate relief.

Reversed and remanded.

MR. JUSTICE WHITE concurs in the result.

MR. JUSTICE STEWART, with whom THE CHIEF JUSTICE and MR. JUSTICE BLACKMUN join, concurring in the result.

It is uncontested that more than 2,800 schoolchildren of Chinese ancestry attend school in the San Francisco Unified School District system even though they do not speak, understand, read, or write the English language, and that as to some 1,800 of these pupils the respondent school authorities have taken no significant steps to deal with this language deficiency. The petitioners do not contend, however, that the respondents have affirmatively or intentionally contributed to this inadequacy, but only that they have failed to act in the face of changing social and linguistic patterns. Because of this laissezfaire attitude on the part of the school administrators, it is not entirely clear that 601 of the Civil Rights Act of 1964, 42 U.S.C. 2000d, standing alone, would render illegal the expenditure of federal funds on these schools. For that section provides that "[n]o person in the United States shall, on the ground of race, color, or national origin, be excluded from participation in, be denied the benefits of, or be subjected to discrimination under any program or activity receiving Federal financial assistance."

On the other hand, the interpretive guidelines published by the Office for Civil Rights of the Department of Health, Education, and Welfare in 1970, 35 Fed. Reg. 11595, clearly indicate that affirmative efforts to give special training for non-English-speaking pupils are required by Tit. VI as a condition to receipt of federal aid to public schools:

> "Where inability to speak and understand the English language excludes national origin-minority group children from effective participation in the educational program offered by a school district, the district must take affirmative steps to rectify the language deficiency in order to open its instructional program to these students."

The critical question is, therefore, whether the regulations and guidelines promulgated by HEW go beyond the authority of 601. Last Term, in Mourning v. Family Publications Service, Inc., we held that the validity of a regulation promulgated under a general authorization provision such as 602 of Tit. VI "will be sustained so long as it is 'reasonably related to the purposes of the enabling legislation.' Thorpe v. Housing Authority of the City of Durham, (1969)." I think the guidelines here fairly meet that test. Moreover, in assessing the purposes of remedial legislation we have found that departmental regulations and "consistent administrative construction" are "entitled to great weight." Trafficante v. Metropolitan Life Insurance Co.; Griggs v. Duke Power Co.; Udall v. Tallman. The Department has reasonably and consistently interpreted 601 to require affirmative remedial efforts to give special attention to linguistically deprived children.

For these reasons I concur in the result reached by the Court.

MR. JUSTICE BLACKMUN, with whom THE CHIEF JUSTICE joins, concurring in the result.

I join MR. JUSTICE STEWART'S opinion and thus I, too, concur in the result. Against the possibility that the Court's judgment may be interpreted too broadly, I stress the fact that the children with whom we are concerned here number about 1,800. This is a very substantial group that is being deprived of any meaningful schooling because the children cannot understand the language of the classroom. We may only guess as to why they have had no exposure to English in their preschool years. Earlier generations of American ethnic groups have overcome the language barrier by earnest parental endeavor or by the hard fact of being pushed out of the family or community nest and into the realities of broader experience.

I merely wish to make plain that when, in another case, we are concerned with a very few youngsters, or with just a single child who speaks only German or Polish or Spanish or any language other than English, I would not regard today's decision, or the separate concurrence, as conclusive upon the issue whether the statute and the guidelines require the funded school district to provide special instruction. For me, numbers are at the heart of this case and my concurrence is to be understood accordingly.

UNIVERSITY OF CALIFORNIA REGENTS V. BAKKE, 438 U.S. 265 (1978)

SUPREME COURT OF THE UNITED STATES ARGUED OCTOBER 12, 1977. DECIDED JUNE 28, 1978.

The Medical School of the University of California at Davis (hereinafter Davis) had two admissions programs for the entering class of 100 students—the regular admissions program and the special admissions program. Under the regular procedure, candidates whose overall under-graduate grade point averages fell below 2.5 on a scale of 4.0 were summarily rejected. About one out of six applicants was then given an interview, following which he was rated on a scale of 1 to 100 by each of the committee members (five in 1973 and six in 1974), his rating being based on the interviewers' summaries, his overall grade point average, his science courses grade point average, his Medical College Admissions Test (MCAT) scores, letters of recommendation, extracurricular activities, and other biographical data, all of which resulted in a total "benchmark score." The full admissions committee then made offers of admission on the basis of their review of the applicant's file and his score, considering and acting upon applications as they were received. The committee chairman was responsible for placing names on the waiting list and had discretion to include persons with "special skills." A separate committee, a majority of whom were members of minority groups, operated the special admissions program. The 1973 and 1974 application forms, respectively, asked candidates whether they wished to be considered as "economically and/or educationally disadvantaged" applicants and members of a "minority group" (blacks, Chicanos, Asians, American Indians). If an applicant of a minority group was found to be "disadvantaged," he would be rated in a manner similar to the one employed by the general admissions committee. Special candidates, however, did not have to meet the 2.5 grade point cutoff and were not ranked against candidates in the general admissions process. About one-fifth of the special applicants were invited for interviews in 1973 and 1974, following which they were given benchmark scores, and the top choices were then given to the general admissions committee, which could reject special candidates for failure to meet course requirements or other specific deficiencies. The special committee continued to recommend candidates until 16 special admission selections had been made. During a four-year period 63 minority students were admitted to Davis under the special program and 44 under the general program. No disadvantaged whites were admitted under the special program, though many applied. Respondent, a white male, applied to Davis in 1973 and 1974, in both years being considered only under the general admissions program. Though he had a 468 out of 500 score in 1973, he was rejected since no general applicants with scores less than 470 were being accepted after respondent's application, which was filed late in the year, had been processed and completed. At that time four special admission slots were still unfilled. In 1974 respondent applied early, and though he had a total score of 549 out of 600, he was again rejected. In neither year was his name placed on the discretionary waiting list. In both years special applicants were admitted with significantly lower scores than respondent's. After his second rejection, respondent filed this action in state court for mandatory, injunctive, and declaratory relief to compel his admission to Davis, alleging that the special admissions program operated to exclude him on the basis of his race in violation of the Equal Protection Clause of the Fourteenth Amendment, a provision of the California Constitution, and 601 of Title VI of the Civil Rights Act of 1964, which provides, inter alia, that no person shall on the ground of race or color be excluded from participating in any program receiving federal financial assistance. Petitioner cross-claimed for a declaration that its special admissions program was lawful. The trial court found that the special program operated as a racial quota, because minority applicants in that program were rated only against one another, and 16 places in the class of 100 were reserved for them. Declaring that petitioner could not take race into account in making admissions decisions, the program was held to violate the Federal and State Constitutions and Title VI. Respondent's admission was not ordered, however, for lack of proof that he would have been admitted but for the special program. The California Supreme Court, applying a strict-scrutiny standard, concluded that the special admissions program was not the least intrusive means of achieving the goals of the admittedly compelling state interests of integrating the medical profession and increasing the number of doctors willing to serve minority patients. Without passing on the state constitutional or federal statutory grounds the court held that petitioner's special admissions program violated the Equal Protection Clause. Since petitioner could not satisfy its burden of demonstrating that respondent, absent the special program, would not have been admitted, the court ordered his admission to Davis.

> Held: The judgment below is affirmed insofar as it orders respondent's admission to Davis and invalidates petitioner's special admissions program, but is reversed insofar as it prohibits petitioner from taking race into account as a factor in its future admissions decisions.

18 Cal. 3d 34, 553 P.2d 1152, affirmed in part and reversed in part.

MR. JUSTICE POWELL, concluded:

1. Title VI proscribes only those racial classifications that would violate the Equal Protection Clause if employed by a State or its agencies.
2. Racial and ethnic classifications of any sort are inherently suspect and call for the most exacting judicial scrutiny. While the goal of achieving a diverse student body is sufficiently compelling to justify consideration of race in admissions decisions under some circumstances, petitioner's special admissions program, which forecloses consideration to persons like respondent, is unnecessary to the achievement of this compelling goal and therefore invalid under the Equal Protection Clause.
3. Since petitioner could not satisfy its burden of proving that respondent would not have been admitted even if there had been no special admissions program, he must be admitted.

MR. JUSTICE BRENNAN, MR. JUSTICE WHITE, MR. JUSTICE MARSHALL, and MR. JUSTICE BLACKMUN concluded:

1. Title VI proscribes only those racial classifications that would violate the Equal Protection Clause if employed by a State or its agencies.
2. Racial classifications call for strict judicial scrutiny. Nonetheless, the purpose of overcoming substantial, chronic minority underrepresentation in the medical profession is sufficiently important to justify petitioner's remedial use of race. Thus, the judgment below must be reversed in that it prohibits race from being used as a factor in university admissions.

MR. JUSTICE STEVENS, joined by THE CHIEF JUSTICE, MR. JUSTICE STEWART, and MR. JUSTICE REHNQUIST, being of the view that whether race can ever be a factor in an admissions policy is not an issue here; that Title VI applies; and that respondent was excluded from Davis in violation of Title VI, concurs in the Court's judgment insofar as it affirms the judgment of the court below ordering respondent admitted to Davis.

POWELL, J., announced the Court's judgment and filed an opinion expressing his views of the case, in Parts I, III-A, and V-C of which WHITE, J., joined; and in Parts I and V-C of which BRENNAN, MARSHALL, and BLACKMUN, JJ., joined. BRENNAN, WHITE, MARSHALL, and BLACKMUN, JJ., filed an opinion concurring in the judgment in part and dissenting in part, post, p. 324. WHITE, J., post, p. 379, MARSHALL, J., post, p. 387, and BLACKMUN, J., post, p. 402, filed separate opinions. STEVENS, J., filed an opinion concurring in the judgment in part and dissenting in part, in which BURGER, C. J., and STEWART and REHNQUIST, JJ., joined, post, p. 408.

Archibald Cox argued the cause for petitioner. With him on the briefs were Paul J. Mishkin, Jack B. Owens, and Donald L. Reidhaar.

Reynold H. Colvin argued the cause and filed briefs for respondent.

Solicitor General McCree argued the cause for the United States as amicus curiae. With him on the briefs were Attorney General Bell, Assistant Attorney General Days, Deputy Solicitor General Wallace, Brian K. Landsberg, Jessica Dunsay Silver, Miriam R. Eisenstein, and Vincent F. O'Rourke.

MR. JUSTICE POWELL announced the judgment of the Court.

This case presents a challenge to the special admissions program of the petitioner, the Medical School of the University of California at Davis, which is designed to assure the admission of a specified number of students from certain minority groups. The Superior Court of California sustained respondent's challenge, holding that petitioner's program violated the California Constitution, Title VI of the Civil Rights Act of 1964, 42 U.S.C. 2000d et seq., and the Equal Protection Clause of the Fourteenth Amendment. The court enjoined petitioner from considering respondent's race or the race of any other applicant in making admissions decisions. It refused, however, to order respondent's admission to the Medical School, holding that he had not carried his burden of proving that he would have been admitted but for the constitutional and statutory violations. The Supreme Court of California affirmed those portions of the trial court's judgment declaring the special admissions program unlawful and enjoining petitioner from considering the race of any applicant. It modified that portion of the judgment denying respondent's requested injunction and directed the trial court to order his admission.

For the reasons stated in the following opinion, I believe that so much of the judgment of the California court as holds petitioner's special admissions program unlawful and directs that respondent be admitted to the Medical School must be affirmed. For the reasons expressed in a separate opinion, my Brothers THE CHIEF JUSTICE, MR. JUSTICE STEWART, MR. JUSTICE REHNQUIST, and MR. JUSTICE STEVENS concur in this judgment.

I also conclude for the reasons stated in the following opinion that the portion of the court's judgment enjoining petitioner from according any consideration to race in its admissions process must be reversed. For reasons expressed in separate opinions, my Brothers MR. JUSTICE BRENNAN, MR. JUSTICE WHITE, MR. JUSTICE MARSHALL, and MR. JUSTICE BLACKMUN concur in this judgment.

Affirmed in part and reversed in part.

I

The Medical School of the University of California at Davis opened in 1968 with an entering class of 50 students. In 1971, the size of the entering class was increased to 100 students, a level at which it remains. No admissions program for disadvantaged or minority students existed when the school opened, and the first class contained three Asians but no blacks, no Mexican-Americans, and no American Indians. Over the next two years, the faculty devised a special admissions program to increase the representation of "disadvantaged" students in each Medical School class. The special program consisted of a separate admissions system operating in coordination with the regular admissions process.

Under the regular admissions procedure, a candidate could submit his application to the Medical School beginning in July of the year preceding the academic year for which admission was sought. Record 149. Because of the large number of applications, the admissions committee screened each one to select candidates for further consideration. Candidates whose overall undergraduate grade point averages fell below 2.5 on a scale of 4.0 were summarily rejected. Id., at 63. About one out of six applicants was invited for a personal interview. Ibid. Following the interviews, each candidate was rated on a scale of 1 to 100 by his interviewers and four other members of the admissions committee. The rating embraced the interviewers' summaries, the candidate's overall grade point average, grade point average in science courses, scores on the Medical College Admissions Test (MCAT), letters of recommendation, extracurricular activities, and other biographical data. Id., at 62. The ratings were added together to arrive at each candidate's "benchmark" score. Since five committee members rated each candidate in 1973, a perfect score was 500; in 1974, six members rated each candidate, so that a perfect score was 600. The full committee then reviewed the file and scores of each applicant and made offers of admission on a "rolling" basis. The chairman was responsible for placing names on the waiting list. They were not placed in strict numerical order; instead, the chairman had discretion to include persons with "special skills." Id., at 63-64.

The special admissions program operated with a separate committee, a majority of whom were members of minority groups. Id., at 163. On the 1973 application form, candidates were asked to indicate whether they wished to be considered as "economically and/or educationally disadvantaged" applicants; on the 1974 form the question was whether they wished to be considered as members of a "minority group," which the Medical School apparently viewed as "Blacks," "Chicanos," "Asians," and "American Indians." Id., at 65-66, 146, 197, 203-205, 216-218. If these questions were answered affirmatively, the application was forwarded to the special admissions committee. No formal definition of "disadvantaged" was ever produced, id., at 163-164, but the chairman of the special committee screened each application to see whether it reflected economic or educational deprivation. Having passed this initial hurdle, the applications then were rated by the special committee in a fashion similar to that used by the general admissions committee, except that special candidates did not have to meet the 2.5 grade point average cutoff applied to regular applicants. About one-fifth of the total number of special applicants were invited for interviews in 1973 and 1974. Following each interview, the special committee assigned each special applicant a benchmark score. The special committee then presented its top choices to the general admissions committee. The latter did not rate or compare the special candidates against the general applicants, id., at 388, but could reject recommended special candidates for failure to meet course requirements or other specific deficiencies. Id., at 171-172. The special committee continued to recommend special applicants until a number prescribed by faculty vote were admitted. While the overall class size was still 50, the prescribed number was 8; in 1973 and 1974, when the class size had doubled to 100, the prescribed number of special admissions also doubled, to 16. Id., at 164, 166.

From the year of the increase in class size—1971—through 1974, the special program resulted in the admission of 21 black students, 30 Mexican-Americans, and 12 Asians, for a total of 63 minority students. Over the same period, the regular admissions program produced 1 black, 6 Mexican-Americans, and 37 Asians, for a total of 44 minority students. Although disadvantaged whites applied to the special program in large numbers, see n. 5, supra, none received an offer of admission through that process. Indeed, in 1974, at least, the special committee explicitly considered only "disadvantaged" special applicants who were members of one of the designated minority groups. Record 171.

Allan Bakke is a white male who applied to the Davis Medical School in both 1973 and 1974. In both years Bakke's application was considered under the general admissions program, and he received an interview. His 1973 interview was with Dr. Theodore C. West, who considered Bakke "a very desirable applicant to [the] medical school." Id., at 225. Despite a strong benchmark score of 468 out of 500, Bakke was rejected. His application had come late in the year, and no applicants in the general admissions process with scores below 470 were accepted after Bakke's application was completed. Id., at 69. There were four special admissions slots unfilled at that time, however, for which Bakke was not considered. Id., at 70. After his 1973 rejection, Bakke wrote to Dr. George H. Lowrey, Associate Dean and Chairman of the Admissions Committee, protesting that the special admissions program operated as a racial and ethnic quota. Id., at 259.

Bakke's 1974 application was completed early in the year. Id., at 70. His student interviewer gave him an overall rating of 94, finding him "friendly, well tempered, conscientious and delightful to speak with." Id., at 229. His faculty interviewer was, by coincidence, the same Dr. Lowrey to whom he had written in protest of the special admissions program. Dr. Lowrey found Bakke "rather limited in his approach" to the problems of the medical profession and found disturbing Bakke's "very definite opinions which were based more on his personal viewpoints than upon a study of the total problem." Id., at 226. Dr. Lowrey gave Bakke the lowest of his six ratings, an 86; his total was 549 out of 600. Id., at 230. Again, Bakke's application was rejected. In neither year did the chairman of the admissions committee, Dr. Lowrey, exercise his discretion to place Bakke on the waiting list. Id., at 64. In both years, applicants were admitted under the special program with grade point averages, MCAT scores, and benchmark scores significantly lower than Bakke's.

After the second rejection, Bakke filed the instant suit in the Superior Court of California. He sought mandatory, injunctive, and declaratory relief compelling his admission to the Medical School. He alleged that the Medical School's special admissions program operated to exclude him from the school on the basis of his race, in violation of his rights under the Equal Protection Clause of the Fourteenth Amendment, Art. I, 21, of the California Constitution, and 601 of Title VI of the Civil Rights Act of 1964, 78 Stat. 252, 42 U.S.C. 2000d. The University cross-complained for a declaration that its special admissions program was lawful. The trial court found that the special program operated as a racial quota, because minority applicants in the special program were rated only against one another, Record 388, and 16 places in the class of 100 were reserved for them. Id., at 295-296. Declaring that the University could not take race into account in making admissions decisions, the trial court held the challenged program violative of the Federal Constitution, the State Constitution, and Title VI. The court refused to order Bakke's admission, however, holding that he had failed to carry his burden of proving that he would have been admitted but for the existence of the special program.

Bakke appealed from the portion of the trial court judgment denying him admission, and the University appealed from the decision that its special admissions program was unlawful and the order enjoining it from considering race in the processing of applications. The Supreme Court of California transferred the case directly from the trial court, "because of the importance of the issues involved." 18 Cal. 3d 34, 39, 553 P.2d 1152, 1156 (1976). The California court accepted the findings of the trial court with respect to the University's program. Because the special admissions program involved a racial classification, the Supreme Court held itself bound to apply strict scrutiny. Id., at 49, 553 P.2d, at 1162-1163. It then turned to the goals the University presented as justifying the special program. Although the court agreed that the goals of integrating the medical profession and increasing the number of physicians willing to serve members of minority groups were compelling state interests, id., at 53, 553 P.2d, at 1165, it concluded that the special admissions program was not the least intrusive means of achieving those goals. Without passing on the state constitutional or the federal statutory grounds cited in the trial court's judgment, the California court held that the Equal Protection Clause of the Fourteenth Amendment required that "no applicant may be rejected because of his race, in favor of another who is less qualified, as measured by standards applied without regard to race." Id., at 55, 553 P.2d, at 1166.

Turning to Bakke's appeal, the court ruled that since Bakke had established that the University had discriminated against him on the basis of his race, the burden of proof shifted to the University to demonstrate that he would not have been admitted even in the absence of the special admissions program. Id., at 63-64, 553 P.2d, at 1172. The court analogized Bakke's situation to that of a plaintiff under Title VII of the Civil Rights Act of 1964, 42 U.S.C. 2000e-17 (1970 ed., Supp. V), see, e. g., Franks v. Bowman Transportation Co., (1976). 18 Cal. 3d, at 63-64, 553 P.2d, at 1172. On this basis, the court initially ordered a remand for the purpose of determining whether, under the newly allocated burden of proof, Bakke would have been admitted to either the 1973 or the 1974 entering class in the absence of the special admissions program. App. A to Application for Stay 48. In its petition for rehearing below, however, the University conceded its inability to carry that burden. App. B to Application for Stay A19-A20. The California court thereupon amended its opinion to direct that the trial court enter judgment ordering Bakke's admission to the Medical School. 18 Cal. 3d, at 64, 553 P.2d, at 1172. That order was stayed pending review in this Court. We granted certiorari to consider the important constitutional issue.

II

In this Court the parties neither briefed nor argued the applicability of Title VI of the Civil Rights Act of 1964. Rather, as had the California court, they focused exclusively upon the validity of the special admissions program under the Equal Protection Clause. Because it was possible, however, that a decision on Title VI might obviate resort to constitutional interpretation, see Ashwander v. TVA, (1936) (concurring opinion), we requested supplementary briefing on the statutory issue.

A

At the outset we face the question whether a right of action for private parties exists under Title VI. Respondent argues that there is a private right of action, invoking the test set forth in Cort v. Ash, (1975). He contends that the statute creates a federal right in his favor, that legislative history reveals an intent to permit private actions, that such actions would further the remedial purposes of the statute, and that enforcement of federal rights under the Civil Rights Act generally is not relegated to the States. In addition, he cites several lower court decisions which have recognized or assumed the existence of a private right of action. Petitioner denies the existence of a private right of action, arguing that the sole function of 601, see n. 11, supra, was to establish a predicate for administrative action under 602, 78 Stat. 252, 42 U.S.C. 2000d-1. In its view, administrative curtailment of federal funds under that section was the only sanction to be imposed upon recipients that violated 601. Petitioner also points out that Title VI contains no explicit grant of a private right of action, in contrast to Titles II, III, IV, and VII, of the same statute, 42 U.S.C. 2000a-3 (a), 2000b-2, 2000c-8, and 2000e-5 (f) (1970 ed. and Supp. V).

We find it unnecessary to resolve this question in the instant case. The question of respondent's right to bring an action under Title VI was neither argued nor decided in either of the courts below, and this Court has been hesitant to review questions not addressed below. McGoldrick v. Compagnie Generale Transatlantique, (1940). See also Massachusetts v. Westcott, (1977); Cardinale v. Louisiana, (1969). Cf. Singleton v. Wulff, (1976). We therefore do not address this difficult issue. Similarly, we need not pass upon petitioner's claim that private plaintiffs under Title VI must exhaust administrative remedies. We assume, only for the purposes of this case, that respondent has a right of action under Title VI. See Lau v. Nichols, n. 2 (1974) (STEWART, J., concurring in result).

B

The language of 601, 78 Stat. 252, like that of the Equal Protection Clause, is majestic in its sweep:

> "No person in the United States shall, on the ground of race, color, or national origin, be excluded from participation in, be denied the benefits of, or be subjected to discrimination under any program or activity receiving Federal financial assistance."

The concept of "discrimination," like the phrase "equal protection of the laws," is susceptible of varying interpretations, for as Mr. Justice Holmes declared, "[a] word is not a crystal, transparent and unchanged, it is the skin of a living thought and may vary greatly in color and content according to the circumstances and the time in which it is used." Towne v. Eisner, (1918). We must, therefore, seek whatever aid is available in determining the precise meaning of the statute before us. Train v. Colorado Public Interest Research Group, (1976), quoting United States v. American Trucking Assns., (1940). Examination of the voluminous legislative history of Title VI reveals a congressional intent to halt federal funding of entities that violate a prohibition of racial discrimination similar to that of the Constitution. Although isolated statements of various legislators, taken out of context, can be marshaled in support of the proposition that 601 enacted a purely color-blind scheme, without regard to the reach of the Equal Protection Clause, these comments must be read against the background of both the problem that Congress was addressing and the broader view of the statute that emerges from a full examination of the legislative debates.

The problem confronting Congress was discrimination against Negro citizens at the hands of recipients of federal moneys. Indeed, the color blindness pronouncements cited in the margin at n. 19, generally occur in the midst of extended remarks dealing with the evils of segregation in federally funded programs. Over and over again, proponents of the bill detailed the plight of Negroes seeking equal treatment in such programs. There simply was no reason for Congress to consider the validity of hypothetical preferences that might be accorded minority citizens; the legislators were dealing with the real and pressing problem of how to guarantee those citizens equal treatment.

In addressing that problem, supporters of Title VI repeatedly declared that the bill enacted constitutional principles. For example, Representative Celler, the Chairman of the House Judiciary Committee and floor manager of the legislation in the House, emphasized this in introducing the bill:

> "The bill would offer assurance that hospitals financed by Federal money would not deny adequate care to Negroes. It would prevent abuse of food distribution programs whereby Negroes have been known to be denied surplus supplies when white persons were given such food. It would assure Negroes the benefits now accorded only white students in programs of high[er] education financed by Federal funds. It would, in short, assure the existing right to equal treatment in the enjoyment of Federal funds. It would not destroy any rights of private property or freedom of association." 110 Cong. Rec. 1519 (1964) (emphasis added).

Other sponsors shared Representative Celler's view that Title VI embodied constitutional principles.

In the Senate, Senator Humphrey declared that the purpose of Title VI was "to insure that Federal funds are spent in accordance with the Constitution and the moral sense of the Nation." Id., at 6544. Senator Ribicoff agreed that Title VI embraced the constitutional standard: "Basically, there is a constitutional restriction against discrimination in the use of federal funds; and title VI simply spells out the procedure to be used in enforcing that restriction." Id., at 13333. Other Senators expressed similar views.

Further evidence of the incorporation of a constitutional standard into Title VI appears in the repeated refusals of the legislation's supporters precisely to define the term "discrimination." Opponents sharply criticized this failure, but proponents of the bill merely replied that the meaning of "discrimination" would be made clear by reference to the Constitution or other existing law. For example, Senator Humphrey noted the relevance of the Constitution:

> "As I have said, the bill has a simple purpose. That purpose is to give fellow citizens—Negroes—the same rights and opportunities that white people take for granted. This is no more than what was preached by the prophets, and by Christ Himself. It is no more than what our Constitution guarantees." Id., at 6553.

In view of the clear legislative intent, Title VI must be held to proscribe only those racial classifications that would violate the Equal Protection Clause or the Fifth Amendment.

III

A

Petitioner does not deny that decisions based on race or ethnic origin by faculties and administrations of state universities are reviewable under the Fourteenth Amendment. See, e. g., Missouri ex rel. Gaines v. Canada, (1938); Sipuel v. Board of Regents, (1948); Sweatt v. Painter, (1950); McLaurin v. Oklahoma State Regents, (1950). For his part, respondent does not argue that all racial or ethnic classifications are per se invalid. See, e. g., Hirabayashi v. United States, (1943); Korematsu v. United States, (1944); Lee v. Washington, (1968) (Black, Harlan, and STEWART, JJ., concurring); United Jewish Organizations v. Carey, (1977). The parties do disagree as to the level of judicial scrutiny to be applied to the special admissions program. Petitioner argues that the court below erred in applying strict scrutiny, as this inexact term has been applied in our cases. That level of review, petitioner asserts, should be reserved for classifications that disadvantage "discrete and insular minorities." See United States v. Carolene Products Co., n. 4 (1938). Respondent, on the other hand, contends that the California court correctly rejected the notion that the degree of judicial scrutiny accorded a particular racial or ethnic classification hinges upon membership in a discrete and insular minority and duly recognized that the "rights established [by the Fourteenth Amendment] are personal rights." Shelley v. Kraemer, (1948).

En route to this crucial battle over the scope of judicial review, the parties fight a sharp preliminary action over the proper characterization of the special admissions program. Petitioner prefers to view it as establishing a "goal" of minority representation in the Medical School. Respondent, echoing the courts below, labels it a racial quota.

This semantic distinction is beside the point: The special admissions program is undeniably a classification based on race and ethnic background. To the extent that there existed a pool of at least minimally qualified minority applicants to fill the 16 special admissions seats, white applicants could compete only for 84 seats in the entering class, rather than the 100 open to minority applicants. Whether this limitation is described as a quota or a goal, it is a line drawn on the basis of race and ethnic status.

The guarantees of the Fourteenth Amendment extend to all persons. Its language is explicit: "No State shall . . . deny to any person within its jurisdiction the equal protection of the laws." It is settled beyond question that the "rights created by the first section of the Fourteenth Amendment are, by its terms, guaranteed to the individual. The rights established are personal rights," Shelley v. Kraemer, supra, at 22. Accord, Missouri ex rel. Gaines v. Canada, supra, at 351; McCabe v. Atchison, T. & S. F. R. Co., (1914). The guarantee of equal protection cannot mean one thing when applied to one individual and something else when applied to a person of another color. If both are not accorded the same protection, then it is not equal.

Nevertheless, petitioner argues that the court below erred in applying strict scrutiny to the special admissions program because white males, such as respondent, are not a "discrete and insular minority" requiring extraordinary protection from the majoritarian political process. Carolene Products Co., supra, at 152-153, n. 4. This rationale, however, has never been invoked in our decisions as a prerequisite to subjecting racial or ethnic distinctions to strict scrutiny. Nor has this Court held that discreteness and insularity constitute necessary preconditions to a holding that a particular classification is invidious. See, e. g., Skinner v. Oklahoma ex rel. Williamson, (1942); Carrington v. Rash, (1965). These characteristics may be relevant in deciding whether or not to add new types of classifications to the list of "suspect" categories or whether a particular classification survives close examination. See, e. g., Massachusetts Board of Retirement v. Murgia, (1976) (age); San Antonio Independent School Dist. v. Rodriguez, (1973) (wealth); Graham v. Richardson, (1971) (aliens). Racial and ethnic classifications, however, are subject to stringent examination without regard to these additional characteristics. We declared as much in the first cases explicitly to recognize racial distinctions as suspect:

> "Distinctions between citizens solely because of their ancestry are by their very nature odious to a free people whose institutions are founded upon the doctrine of equality." Hirabayashi.

> "[A]ll legal restrictions which curtail the civil rights of a single racial group are immediately suspect. That is not to say that all such restrictions are unconstitutional. It is to say that courts must subject them to the most rigid scrutiny." Korematsu.

The Court has never questioned the validity of those pronouncements. Racial and ethnic distinctions of any sort are inherently suspect and thus call for the most exacting judicial examination.

B

This perception of racial and ethnic distinctions is rooted in our Nation's constitutional and demographic history. The Court's initial view of the Fourteenth Amendment was that its "one pervading purpose" was "the freedom of the slave race, the security and firm establishment of that freedom, and the protection of the newly-made freeman and citizen from the oppressions of those who had formerly exercised dominion over him." Slaughter-House Cases, 16 Wall. 36, 71 (1873). The Equal Protection Clause, however, was "[v]irtually strangled in infancy by post-civil-war judicial reactionism." It was relegated to decades of relative desuetude while the Due Process Clause of the Fourteenth Amendment, after a short germinal period, flourished as a cornerstone in the Court's defense of property and liberty of contract. See, e. g., Mugler v. Kansas, (1887); Allgeyer v. Louisiana, (1897); Lochner v. New York, (1905). In that cause, the Fourteenth Amendment's "one pervading purpose" was displaced. See, e. g., Plessy v. Ferguson, (1896). It was only as the era of substantive due process came to a close, see, e. g., Nebbia v. New York, (1934); West Coast Hotel Co. v. Parrish, (1937), that the Equal Protection Clause began to attain a genuine measure of vitality, see, e. g., United States v. Carolene Products, (1938); Skinner v. Oklahoma ex rel. Williamson, supra.

By that time it was no longer possible to peg the guarantees of the Fourteenth Amendment to the struggle for equality of one racial minority. During the dormancy of the Equal Protection Clause, the United States had become a Nation of minorities. Each had to struggle—and to some extent struggles still—to overcome the prejudices not of a monolithic majority, but of a "majority" composed of various minority groups of whom it was said— perhaps unfairly in many cases—that a shared characteristic was a willingness to disadvantage other groups. As the Nation filled with the stock of many lands, the reach of the Clause was gradually extended to all ethnic groups seeking protection from official discrimination. See Strauder v. West Virginia, (1880) (Celtic Irishmen) (dictum); Yick Wo v. Hopkins, (1886) (Chinese); Truax v. Raich, (1915) (Austrian resident aliens); Korematsu, supra (Japanese); Hernandez v. Texas, (1954) (Mexican-Americans). The guarantees of equal protection, said the Court in Yick Wo, "are universal in their application, to all persons within the territorial jurisdiction, without regard to any differences of race, of color, or of nationality; and the equal protection of the laws is a pledge of the protection of equal laws."

Although many of the Framers of the Fourteenth Amendment conceived of its primary function as bridging the vast distance between members of the Negro race and the white "majority," Slaughter-House Cases, supra, the Amendment itself was framed in universal terms, without reference to color, ethnic origin, or condition of prior servitude. As this Court recently remarked in interpreting the 1866 Civil Rights Act to extend to claims of racial discrimination against white persons, "the 39th Congress was intent upon establishing in the federal law a broader principle than would have been necessary simply to meet the particular and immediate plight of the newly freed Negro slaves." McDonald v. Santa Fe Trail Transportation Co., (1976). And that legislation was specifically broadened in 1870 to ensure that "all persons," not merely "citizens," would enjoy equal rights under the law. See Runyon v. McCrary, (1976) (WHITE, J., dissenting). Indeed, it is not unlikely that among the Framers were many who would have applauded a reading of the Equal Protection Clause that states a principle of universal application and is responsive to the racial, ethnic, and cultural diversity of the Nation. See, e. g., Cong. Globe, 39th Cong., 1st Sess., 1056 (1866) (remarks of Rep. Niblack); id., at 2891-2892 (remarks of Sen. Conness); id., 40th Cong., 2d Sess., 883 (1868) (remarks of Sen. Howe) (Fourteenth Amendment "protect[s] classes from class legislation"). See also Bickel, The Original Understanding and the Segregation Decision, 69 Harv. L. Rev. 1, 60-63 (1955).

Over the past 30 years, this Court has embarked upon the crucial mission of interpreting the Equal Protection Clause with the view of assuring to all persons "the protection of equal laws," Yick Wo, supra, at 369, in a Nation confronting a legacy of slavery and racial discrimination. See, e. g., Shelley v. Kraemer, (1948); Brown v. Board of Education, (1954); Hills v. Gautreaux, (1976). Because the landmark decisions in this area arose in response to the continued exclusion of Negroes from the mainstream of American society, they could be characterized as involving discrimination by the "majority" white race against the Negro minority. But they need not be read as depending upon that characterization for their results. It suffices to say that "[o]ver the years, this Court has consistently repudiated '[d]istinctions between citizens solely because of their ancestry' as being 'odious to a free people whose institutions are founded upon the doctrine of equality.'" Loving v. Virginia, (1967), quoting Hirabayashi.

Petitioner urges us to adopt for the first time a more restrictive view of the Equal Protection Clause and hold that discrimination against members of the white "majority" cannot be suspect if its purpose can be characterized as "benign." The clock of our liberties, however, cannot be turned back to 1868. Brown v. Board of Education, supra, at 492; accord, Loving v. Virginia, supra, at 9. It is far too late to argue that the guarantee of equal protection to all persons permits the recognition of special wards entitled to a degree of protection greater than that accorded others. "The Fourteenth Amendment is not directed solely against discrimination due to a 'two-class theory'—that is, based upon differences between 'white' and Negro." Hernandez.

Once the artificial line of a "two-class theory" of the Fourteenth Amendment is put aside, the difficulties entailed in varying the level of judicial review according to a perceived "preferred" status of a particular racial or ethnic minority are intractable. The concepts of "majority" and "minority" necessarily reflect temporary arrangements and political judgments. As observed above, the white "majority" itself is composed of various minority groups, most of which can lay claim to a history of prior discrimination at the hands of the State and private individuals. Not all of these groups can receive preferential treatment and corresponding judicial tolerance of distinctions drawn in terms of race and nationality, for then the only "majority" left would be a new minority of white Anglo-Saxon Protestants. There is no principled basis for deciding which groups would merit "heightened judicial solicitude" and which would not. Courts would be asked to evaluate the extent of the prejudice and consequent harm suffered by various minority groups. Those whose societal injury is thought to exceed some arbitrary level of tolerability then would be entitled to preferential classifications at the expense of individuals belonging to other groups. Those classifications would be free from exacting judicial scrutiny. As these preferences began to have their desired effect, and the consequences of past discrimination were undone, new judicial rankings would be necessary. The kind of variable sociological and political analysis necessary to produce such rankings simply does not lie within the judicial competence—even if they otherwise were politically feasible and socially desirable.

Moreover, there are serious problems of justice connected with the idea of preference itself. First, it may not always be clear that a so-called preference is in fact benign. Courts may be asked to validate burdens imposed upon individual members of a particular group in order to advance the group's general interest. See United Jewish Organizations v. Carey, (BRENNAN, J., concurring in part). Nothing in the Constitution supports the notion that individuals may be asked to suffer otherwise impermissible burdens in order to enhance the societal standing of their ethnic groups. Second, preferential programs may only reinforce common stereotypes holding that certain groups are unable to achieve success without special protection based on a factor having no relationship to individual worth. See DeFunis v. Odegaard, (1974) (Douglas, J., dissenting). Third, there is a measure of inequity in forcing innocent persons in respondent's position to bear the burdens of redressing grievances not of their making.

By hitching the meaning of the Equal Protection Clause to these transitory considerations, we would be holding, as a constitutional principle, that judicial scrutiny of classifications touching on racial and ethnic background may vary with the ebb and flow of political forces. Disparate constitutional tolerance of such classifications well may serve to exacerbate racial and ethnic antagonisms rather than alleviate them. United Jewish Organizations, supra, at 173-174 (BRENNAN, J., concurring in part). Also, the mutability of a constitutional principle, based upon shifting political and social judgments, undermines the chances for consistent application of the Constitution from one generation to the next, a critical feature of its coherent interpretation. Pollock v. Farmers' Loan & Trust Co., (1895) (White, J., dissenting). In expounding the Constitution, the Court's role is to discern "principles sufficiently absolute to give them roots throughout the community and continuity over significant periods of time, and to lift them above the level of the pragmatic political judgments of a particular time and place." A. Cox, The Role of the Supreme Court in American Government 114 (1976).

If it is the individual who is entitled to judicial protection against classifications based upon his racial or ethnic background because such distinctions impinge upon personal rights, rather than the individual only because of his membership in a particular group, then constitutional standards may be applied consistently. Political judgments regarding the necessity for the particular classification may be weighed in the constitutional balance, Korematsu v. United States, (1944), but the standard of justification will remain constant. This is as it should be, since those political judgments are the product of rough compromise struck by contending groups within the democratic process. When they touch upon an individual's race or ethnic background, he is entitled to a judicial determination that the burden he is asked to bear on that basis is precisely tailored to serve a compelling governmental interest. The Constitution guarantees that right to every person regardless of his background. Shelley v. Kraemer; Missouri ex rel. Gaines v. Canada.

C

Petitioner contends that on several occasions this Court has approved preferential classifications without applying the most exacting scrutiny. Most of the cases upon which petitioner relies are drawn from three areas: school desegregation, employment discrimination, and sex discrimination. Each of the cases cited presented a situation materially different from the facts of this case.

The school desegregation cases are inapposite. Each involved remedies for clearly determined constitutional violations. E. g., Swann v. Charlotte-Mecklenburg Board of Education, (1971); McDaniel v. Barresi, (1971); Green v. County School Board, (1968). Racial classifications thus were designed as remedies for the vindication of constitutional entitlement. Moreover, the scope of the remedies was not permitted to exceed the extent of the violations. E. g., Dayton Board of Education v. Brinkman, (1977); Milliken v. Bradley, (1974); see Pasadena City Board of Education v. Spangler, (1976). See also Austin Independent School Dist. v. United States, (1976) (POWELL, J., concurring). Here, there was no judicial determination of constitutional violation as a predicate for the formulation of a remedial classification.

The employment discrimination cases also do not advance petitioner's cause. For example, in Franks v. Bowman Transportation Co., (1976), we approved a retroactive award of seniority to a class of Negro truckdrivers who had been the victims of discrimination—not just by society at large, but by the respondent in that case. While this relief imposed some burdens on other employees, it was held necessary "'to make [the victims] whole for injuries suffered on account of unlawful employment discrimination.'" Id., at 763, quoting Albemarle Paper Co. v. Moody, (1975). The Courts of Appeals have fashioned various types of racial preferences as remedies for constitutional or statutory violations resulting in identified, race-based injuries to individuals held entitled to the preference. E. g., Bridgeport Guardians, Inc. v. Bridgeport Civil Service Commission, 482 F.2d 1333 (CA2 1973); Carter v. Gallagher, 452 F.2d 315 (CA8 1972), modified on rehearing en banc, id., at 327. Such preferences also have been upheld where a legislative or administrative body charged with the responsibility made determinations of past discrimination by the industries affected, and fashioned remedies deemed appropriate to rectify the discrimination. E. g., Contractors Association of Eastern Pennsylvania v. Secretary of Labor, 442 F.2d 159 (CA3), cert. denied, (1971); Associated General Contractors of Massachusetts, Inc. v. Altshuler, 490 F.2d 9 (CA1 1973), cert. denied, (1974); cf. Katzenbach

v. Morgan, (1966). But we have never approved preferential classifications in the absence of proved constitutional or statutory violations.

Nor is petitioner's view as to the applicable standard supported by the fact that gender-based classifications are not subjected to this level of scrutiny. E. g., Califano v. Webster, (1977); Craig v. Boren, n. (1976) (POWELL, J., concurring). Gender-based distinctions are less likely to create the analytical and practical problems present in preferential programs premised on racial or ethnic criteria. With respect to gender there are only two possible classifications. The incidence of the burdens imposed by preferential classifications is clear. There are no rival groups which can claim that they, too, are entitled to preferential treatment. Classwide questions as to the group suffering previous injury and groups which fairly can be burdened are relatively manageable for reviewing courts. See, e. g., Califano v. Goldfarb, (1977); Weinberger v. Wiesenfeld, (1975). The resolution of these same questions in the context of racial and ethnic preferences presents far more complex and intractable problems than gender-based classifications. More importantly, the perception of racial classifications as inherently odious stems from a lengthy and tragic history that gender-based classifications do not share. In sum, the Court has never viewed such classification as inherently suspect or as comparable to racial or ethnic classifications for the purpose of equal protection analysis.

Petitioner also cites Lau v. Nichols, (1974), in support of the proposition that discrimination favoring racial or ethnic minorities has received judicial approval without the exacting inquiry ordinarily accorded "suspect" classifications. In Lau, we held that the failure of the San Francisco school system to provide remedial English instruction for some 1,800 students of oriental ancestry who spoke no English amounted to a violation of Title VI of the Civil Rights Act of 1964, 42 U.S.C. 2000d, and the regulations promulgated thereunder. Those regulations required remedial instruction where inability to understand English excluded children of foreign ancestry from participation in educational programs. Because we found that the students in Lau were denied "a meaningful opportunity to participate in the educational program," ibid., we remanded for the fashioning of a remedial order.

Lau provides little support for petitioner's argument. The decision rested solely on the statute, which had been construed by the responsible administrative agency to reach educational practices "which have the effect of subjecting individuals to discrimination," ibid. We stated: "Under these state-imposed standards there is no equality of treatment merely by providing students with the same facilities, textbooks, teachers, and curriculum; for students who do not understand English are effectively foreclosed from any meaningful education." Id., at 566. Moreover, the "preference" approved did not result in the denial of the relevant benefit—"meaningful opportunity to participate in the educational program"—to anyone else. No other student was deprived by that preference of the ability to participate in San Francisco's school system, and the applicable regulations required similar assistance for all students who suffered similar linguistic deficiencies. Id., at 570-571 (STEWART, J., concurring in result).

In a similar vein, petitioner contends that our recent decision in United Jewish Organizations v. Carey, (1977), indicates a willingness to approve racial classifications designed to benefit certain minorities, without denominating the classifications as "suspect." The State of New York had redrawn its reapportionment plan to meet objections of the Department of Justice under 5 of the Voting Rights Act of 1965, 42 U.S.C. 1973c (1970 ed., Supp. V). Specifically, voting districts were redrawn to enhance the electoral power of certain "nonwhite" voters found to have been the victims of unlawful "dilution" under the original reapportionment plan. United Jewish Organizations, like Lau, properly is viewed as a case in which the remedy for an administrative finding of discrimination encompassed measures to improve the previously disadvantaged group's ability to participate, without excluding individuals belonging to any other group from enjoyment of the relevant opportunity—meaningful participation in the electoral process.

In this case, unlike Lau and United Jewish Organizations, there has been no determination by the legislature or a responsible administrative agency that the University engaged in a discriminatory practice requiring remedial efforts. Moreover, the operation of petitioner's special admissions program is quite different from the remedial measures approved in those cases. It prefers the designated minority groups at the expense of other individuals who are totally foreclosed from competition for the 16 special admissions seats in every Medical School class. Because of that foreclosure, some individuals are excluded from enjoyment of a state-provided benefit—admission to the Medical School—they otherwise would receive. When a classification denies an individual opportunities or benefits enjoyed by others solely because of his race or ethnic background, it must be regarded as suspect. E. g., McLaurin v. Oklahoma State Regents.

IV

We have held that in "order to justify the use of a suspect classification, a State must show that its purpose or interest is both constitutionally permissible and substantial, and that its use of the classification is 'necessary . . . to the accomplishment' of its purpose or the safeguarding of its interest." In re Griffiths, (1973) (footnotes omitted); Loving v. Virginia; McLaughlin v. Florida, (1964). The special admissions program purports to serve the purposes of: (i) "reducing the historic deficit of traditionally disfavored minorities in medical schools and in the medical profession," Brief for Petitioner 32; (ii) countering the effects of societal discrimination; (iii) increasing the number of physicians who will practice in communities currently underserved; and (iv) obtaining the educational benefits that flow from an ethnically diverse student body. It is necessary to decide which, if any, of these purposes is substantial enough to support the use of a suspect classification.

A

If petitioner's purpose is to assure within its student body some specified percentage of a particular group merely because of its race or ethnic origin, such a preferential purpose must be rejected not as insubstantial but as facially invalid. Preferring members of any one group for no reason other than race or ethnic origin is discrimination for its own sake. This the Constitution forbids. E. g., Loving v. Virginia, supra, at 11; McLaughlin v. Florida, supra, at 196; Brown v. Board of Education, (1954).

B

The State certainly has a legitimate and substantial interest in ameliorating, or eliminating where feasible, the disabling effects of identified discrimination. The line of school desegregation cases, commencing with Brown, attests to the importance of this state goal and the commitment of the judiciary to affirm all lawful means toward its attainment. In the school cases, the States were required by court order to redress the wrongs worked by specific instances of racial discrimination. That goal was far more focused than the remedying of the effects of "societal discrimination," an amorphous concept of injury that may be ageless in its reach into the past.

We have never approved a classification that aids persons perceived as members of relatively victimized groups at the expense of other innocent individuals in the absence of judicial, legislative, or administrative findings of constitutional or statutory violations. See, e. g., Teamsters v. United States, (1977); United Jewish Organizations; South Carolina v. Katzenbach, (1966). After such findings have been made, the governmental interest in preferring members of the injured groups at the expense of others is substantial, since the legal rights of the victims must be vindicated. In such a case, the extent of the injury and the consequent remedy will have been judicially, legislatively, or administrative defined. Also, the remedial action usually remains subject to continuing oversight to assure that it will work the least harm possible to other innocent persons competing for the benefit. Without such findings of constitutional or statutory violations, it cannot be said that the government has any greater interest in helping one individual than in refraining from harming another. Thus, the government has no compelling justification for inflicting such harm.

Petitioner does not purport to have made, and is in no position to make, such findings. Its broad mission is education, not the formulation of any legislative policy or the adjudication of particular claims of illegality. For reasons similar to those stated in Part III of this opinion, isolated segments of our vast governmental structures are not competent to make those decisions, at least in the absence of legislative mandates and legislatively determined criteria. Cf. Hampton v. Mow Sun Wong, (1976); n. 41, supra. Before relying upon these sorts of findings in establishing a racial classification, a governmental body must have the authority and capability to establish, in the record, that the classification is responsive to identified discrimination. See, e. g., Califano v. Webster; Califano v. Goldfarb. Lacking this capability, petitioner has not carried its burden of justification on this issue.

Hence, the purpose of helping certain groups whom the faculty of the Davis Medical School perceived as victims of "societal discrimination" does not justify a classification that imposes disadvantages upon persons like respondent, who bear no responsibility for whatever harm the beneficiaries of the special admissions program are thought to have suffered. To hold otherwise would be to convert a remedy heretofore reserved for violations of legal rights into a privilege that all institutions throughout the Nation could grant at their pleasure to whatever groups are perceived as victims of societal discrimination. That is a step we have never approved. Cf. Pasadena City Board of Education v. Spangler, (1976).

C

Petitioner identifies, as another purpose of its program, improving the delivery of health-care services to communities currently underserved. It may be assumed that in some situations a State's interest in facilitating the health care of its citizens is sufficiently compelling to support the use of a suspect classification. But there is virtually no evidence in the record indicating that petitioner's special admissions program is either needed or geared to promote that goal. The court below addressed this failure of proof:

> "The University concedes it cannot assure that minority doctors who entered under the program, all of whom expressed an 'interest' in practicing in a disadvantaged community, will actually do so. It may be correct to assume that some of them will carry out this intention, and that it is more likely they will practice in minority communities than the average white doctor. (See Sandalow, Racial Preferences in Higher Education: Political Responsibility and the Judicial Role (1975) 42 U. Chi. L. Rev. 653, 688.) Nevertheless, there are more precise and reliable ways to identify applicants who are genuinely interested in the medical problems of minorities than by race. An applicant of whatever race who has demonstrated his concern for disadvantaged minorities in the past and who declares that practice in such a community is his primary professional goal would be more likely to contribute to alleviation of the medical shortage than one who is chosen entirely on the basis of race and disadvantage. In short, there is no empirical data to demonstrate that any one race is more selflessly socially oriented or by contrast that another is more selfishly acquisitive." 18 Cal. 3d, at 56, 553 P.2d, at 1167.

Petitioner simply has not carried its burden of demonstrating that it must prefer members of particular ethnic groups over all other individuals in order to promote better health-care delivery to deprived citizens. Indeed, petitioner has not shown that its preferential classification is likely to have any significant effect on the problem.

D

The fourth goal asserted by petitioner is the attainment of a diverse student body. This clearly is a constitutionally permissible goal for an institution of higher education. Academic freedom, though not a specifically enumerated constitutional right, long has been viewed as a special concern of the First Amendment. The freedom of a university to make its own judgments as to education includes the selection of its student body. Mr. Justice Frankfurter summarized the "four essential freedoms" that constitute academic freedom:

> "'It is the business of a university to provide that atmosphere which is most conducive to speculation, experiment and creation. It is an atmosphere in which there prevail "the four essential freedoms" of a university—to determine for itself on academic grounds who may teach, what may be taught, how it shall be taught, and who may be admitted to study.'" Sweezy v. New Hampshire, (1957) (concurring in result).

Our national commitment to the safeguarding of these freedoms within university communities was emphasized in Keyishian v. Board of Regents, (1967):

> "Our Nation is deeply committed to safeguarding academic freedom which is of transcendent value to all of us and not merely to the teachers concerned. That freedom is therefore a special concern of the First Amendment . . . . The Nation's future depends upon leaders trained through wide exposure to that robust exchange of ideas which discovers truth 'out of a multitude of tongues, [rather] than through any kind of authoritative selection.' United States v. Associated Press, 52 F. Supp. 362, 372."

The atmosphere of "speculation, experiment and creation"—so essential to the quality of higher education—is widely believed to be promoted by a diverse student body. As the Court noted in Keyishian, it is not too much to say that the "nation's future depends upon leaders trained through wide exposure" to the ideas and mores of students as diverse as this Nation of many peoples.

Thus, in arguing that its universities must be accorded the right to select those students who will contribute the most to the "robust exchange of ideas," petitioner invokes a countervailing constitutional interest, that of the First Amendment. In this light, petitioner must be viewed as seeking to achieve a goal that is of paramount importance in the fulfillment of its mission.

It may be argued that there is greater force to these views at the undergraduate level than in a medical school where the training is centered primarily on professional competency. But even at the graduate level, our tradition and experience lend support to the view that the contribution of diversity is substantial. In Sweatt v. Painter, the Court made a similar point with specific reference to legal education:

> "The law school, the proving ground for legal learning and practice, cannot be effective in isolation from the individuals and institutions with which the law interacts. Few students and no one who has practiced law would choose to study in an academic vacuum, removed from the interplay of ideas and the exchange of views with which the law is concerned."

Physicians serve a heterogeneous population. An otherwise qualified medical student with a particular background—whether it be ethnic, geographic, culturally advantaged or disadvantaged—may bring to a professional school of medicine experiences, outlooks, and ideas that enrich the training of its student body and better equip its graduates to render with understanding their vital service to humanity.

Ethnic diversity, however, is only one element in a range of factors a university properly may consider in attaining the goal of a heterogeneous student body. Although a university must have wide discretion in making the sensitive judgments as to who should be admitted, constitutional limitations protecting individual rights may not be disregarded. Respondent urges—and the courts below have held—that petitioner's dual admissions program is a racial classification that impermissibly infringes his rights under the Fourteenth Amendment. As the interest of diversity is compelling in the context of a university's admissions program, the question remains whether the program's racial classification is necessary to promote this interest. In re Griffiths.

V

A

It may be assumed that the reservation of a specified number of seats in each class for individuals from the preferred ethnic groups would contribute to the attainment of considerable ethnic diversity in the student body. But petitioner's argument that this is the only effective means of serving the interest of diversity is seriously flawed. In a most fundamental sense the argument misconceives the nature of the state interest that would justify consideration of race or ethnic background. It is not an interest in simple ethnic diversity, in which a specified percentage of the student body is in effect guaranteed to be members of selected ethnic groups, with the remaining percentage an undifferentiated aggregation of students. The diversity that furthers a compelling state interest encompasses a far broader array of qualifications and characteristics of which racial or ethnic origin is but a single though important element. Petitioner's special admissions program, focused solely on ethnic diversity, would hinder rather than further attainment of genuine diversity.

Nor would the state interest in genuine diversity be served by expanding petitioner's two-track system into a multitrack program with a prescribed number of seats set aside for each identifiable category of applicants. Indeed, it is inconceivable that a university would thus pursue the logic of petitioner's two-track program to the illogical end of insulating each category of applicants with certain desired qualifications from competition with all other applicants.

The experience of other university admissions programs, which take race into account in achieving the educational diversity valued by the First Amendment, demonstrates that the assignment of a fixed number of places to a minority group is not a necessary means toward that end. An illuminating example is found in the Harvard College program:

> "In recent years Harvard College has expanded the concept of diversity to include students from disadvantaged economic, racial and ethnic groups. Harvard College now recruits not only Californians or Louisianans but also blacks and Chicanos and other minority students. . . . "
>
> "In practice, this new definition of diversity has meant that race has been a factor in some admission decisions. When the Committee on Admissions reviews the large middle group of applicants who are 'admissible' and deemed capable of doing good work in their courses, the race of an applicant may tip the balance in his favor just as geographic origin or a life spent on a farm may tip the balance in other candidates' cases. A farm boy from Idaho can bring something to Harvard College that a Bostonian cannot offer. Similarly, a black student can usually bring something that a white person cannot offer. . . . "
>
> "In Harvard College admissions the Committee has not set target-quotas for the number of blacks, or of musicians, football players, physicists or Californians to be admitted in a given year. . . . But that awareness [of the necessity of including more than a token number of black students] does not mean that the Committee sets a minimum number of blacks or of people from west of the Mississippi who are to be admitted. It means only that in choosing among thousands of applicants who are not only 'admissible' academically but have other strong qualities, the Committee, with a number of criteria in mind, pays some attention to distribution among many types and categories of students." App. to Brief for Columbia University, Harvard University, Stanford University, and the University of Pennsylvania, as Amici Curiae 2-3.

In such an admissions program, race or ethnic background may be deemed a "plus" in a particular applicant's file, yet it does not insulate the individual from comparison with all other candidates for the available seats. The file of a particular black applicant may be examined for his potential contribution to diversity without the factor of race being decisive when compared, for example, with that of an applicant identified as an Italian-American if the latter is thought to exhibit qualities more likely to promote beneficial educational pluralism. Such qualities could include exceptional personal talents, unique work or service experience, leadership potential, maturity, demonstrated compassion, a history of overcoming disadvantage, ability to communicate with the poor, or other qualifications deemed important. In short, an admissions program operated in this way is flexible enough to consider all pertinent elements of diversity in light of the particular qualifications of each applicant, and to place them on the same footing for consideration, although not necessarily according them the same weight. Indeed, the weight attributed to a particular quality may vary from year to year depending upon the "mix" both of the student body and the applicants for the incoming class.

This kind of program treats each applicant as an individual in the admissions process. The applicant who loses out on the last available seat to another candidate receiving a "plus" on the basis of ethnic background will not have been foreclosed from all consideration for that seat simply because he was not the right color or had the wrong surname. It would mean only that his combined qualifications, which may have included similar nonobjective factors, did not outweigh those of the other applicant. His qualifications would have been weighed fairly and competitively, and he would have no basis to complain of unequal treatment under the Fourteenth Amendment.

It has been suggested that an admissions program which considers race only as one factor is simply a subtle and more sophisticated—but no less effective— means of according racial preference than the Davis program. A facial intent to discriminate, however, is evident in petitioner's preference program and not denied in this case. No such facial infirmity exists in an admissions program where race or ethnic background is simply one element—to be weighed fairly against other elements—in the selection process. "A boundary line," as Mr. Justice Frankfurter remarked in another connection, "is none the worse for being narrow." McLeod v. Dilworth, (1944). And a court would not assume that a university, professing to employ a facially nondiscriminatory admissions policy, would operate it as a cover for the functional equivalent of a quota system. In short, good faith would be presumed in the absence of a showing to the contrary in the manner permitted by our cases. See, e. g., Arlington Heights v. Metropolitan Housing Dev. Corp., (1977); Washington v. Davis, (1976); Swain v. Alabama, (1965).

B

In summary, it is evident that the Davis special admissions program involves the use of an explicit racial classification never before countenanced by this Court. It tells applicants who are not Negro, Asian, or Chicano that they are totally excluded from a specific percentage of the seats in an entering class. No matter how strong their qualifications, quantitative and extracurricular, including their own potential for contribution to educational diversity, they are never afforded the chance to compete with applicants from the preferred groups for the special admissions seats. At the same time, the preferred applicants have the opportunity to compete for every seat in the class.

The fatal flaw in petitioner's preferential program is its disregard of individual rights as guaranteed by the Fourteenth Amendment. Shelley v. Kraemer. Such rights are not absolute. But when a State's distribution of benefits or imposition of burdens hinges on ancestry or the color of a person's skin, that individual is entitled to a demonstration that the challenged classification is necessary to promote a substantial state interest. Petitioner has failed to carry this burden. For this reason, that portion of the California court's judgment holding petitioner's special admissions program invalid under the Fourteenth Amendment must be affirmed.

C

In enjoining petitioner from ever considering the race of any applicant, however, the courts below failed to recognize that the State has a substantial interest that legitimately may be served by a properly devised admissions program involving the competitive consideration of race and ethnic origin. For this reason, so much of the California court's judgment as enjoins petitioner from any consideration of the race of any applicant must be reversed.

VI

With respect to respondent's entitlement to an injunction directing his admission to the Medical School, petitioner has conceded that it could not carry its burden of proving that, but for the existence of its unlawful special admissions program, respondent still would not have been admitted. Hence, respondent is entitled to the injunction, and that portion of the judgment must be affirmed.

APPENDIX TO OPINION OF POWELL, J.

Harvard College Admissions Program

For the past 30 years Harvard College has received each year applications for admission that greatly exceed the number of places in the freshman class. The number of applicants who are deemed to be not "qualified" is comparatively small. The vast majority of applicants demonstrate through test scores, high school records and teachers' recommendations that they have the academic ability to do adequate work at Harvard, and perhaps to do it with distinction. Faced with the dilemma of choosing among a large number of "qualified" candidates, the Committee on Admissions could use the single criterion of scholarly excellence and attempt to determine who among the candidates were likely to perform best academically. But for the past 30 years the Committee on Admissions has never adopted this approach. The belief has been that if scholarly excellence were the sole or even predominant criterion, Harvard College would lose a great deal of its vitality and intellectual excellence and that the quality of the educational experience offered to all students would suffer. Final Report of W. J. Bender, Chairman of the Admission and Scholarship Committee and Dean of Admissions and Financial Aid, pp. 20 et seq. (Cambridge, 1960). Consequently, after selecting those students whose intellectual potential will seem extraordinary to the faculty—perhaps 150 or so out of an entering class of over 1,100—the Committee seeks—

> variety in making its choices. This has seemed important . . . in part because it adds a critical ingredient to the effectiveness of the educational experience [in Harvard College]. . . . The effectiveness of our students' educational experience has seemed to the Committee to be affected as importantly by a wide variety of interests, talents, backgrounds and career goals as it is by a fine faculty and our libraries, laboratories and housing arrangements. (Dean of Admissions Fred L. Glimp, Final Report to the Faculty of Arts and Sciences, 65 Official Register of Harvard University No. 25, 93, 104-105 (1968) (emphasis supplied).

The belief that diversity adds an essential ingredient to the educational process has long been a tenet of Harvard College admissions. Fifteen or twenty years ago, however, diversity meant students from California, New York, and Massachusetts; city dwellers and farm boys; violinists, painters and football players; biologists, historians and classicists; potential stockbrokers, academics and politicians. The result was that very few ethnic or racial minorities attended Harvard College. In recent years Harvard College has expanded the concept of diversity to include students from disadvantaged economic, racial and ethnic groups. Harvard College now recruits not only Californians or Louisianans but also blacks and Chicanos and other minority students. Contemporary conditions in the United States mean that if Harvard College is to continue to offer a first-rate education to its students, minority representation in the undergraduate body cannot be ignored by the Committee on Admissions.

In practice, this new definition of diversity has meant that race has been a factor in some admission decisions. When the Committee on Admissions reviews the large middle group of applicants who are "admissible" and deemed capable of doing good work in their courses, the race of an applicant may tip the balance in his favor just as geographic origin or a life spent on a farm may tip the balance in other candidates' cases. A farm boy from Idaho can bring something to Harvard College that a Bostonian cannot offer. Similarly, a black student can usually bring something that a white person cannot offer. The quality of the educational experience of all the students in Harvard College depends in part on these differences in the background and outlook that students bring with them.

In Harvard College admissions the Committee has not set target-quotas for the number of blacks, or of musicians, football players, physicists or Californians to be admitted in a given year. At the same time the Committee is aware that if Harvard College is to provide a truly heterogen[e]ous environment that reflects the rich diversity of the United States, it cannot be provided without some attention to numbers. It would not make sense, for example, to have 10 or 20 students out of 1,100 whose homes are west of the Mississippi. Comparably, 10 or 20 black students could not begin to bring to their classmates and to each other the variety of points of view, backgrounds and experiences of blacks in the United States. Their small numbers might also create a sense of isolation among the black students themselves and thus make it more difficult for them to develop and achieve their potential. Consequently, when making its decisions, the Committee on Admissions is aware that there is some relationship between numbers and achieving the benefits to be derived from a diverse student body, and between numbers and providing a reasonable environment for those students admitted. But that awareness does not mean that the Committee sets a minimum number of blacks or of people from west of the Mississippi who are to be admitted. It means only that in choosing among thousands of applicants who are not only "admissible" academically but have other strong qualities, the Committee, with a number of criteria in mind, pays some attention to distribution among many types and categories of students.

The further refinements sometimes required help to illustrate the kind of significance attached to race. The Admissions Committee, with only a few places left to fill, might find itself forced to choose between A, the child of a successful black physician in an academic community with promise of superior academic performance, and B, a black who grew up in an inner-city ghetto of semi-literate parents whose academic achievement was lower but who had demonstrated energy and leadership as well as an apparently-abiding interest in black power. If a good number of black students much like A but few like B had already been admitted, the Committee might prefer B; and vice versa. If C, a white student with extraordinary artistic talent, were also seeking one of the remaining places, his unique quality might give him an edge over both A and B. Thus, the critical criteria are often individual qualities or experience not dependent upon race but sometimes associated with it.

2 MR. JUSTICE BRENNAN, MR. JUSTICE WHITE, MR. JUSTICE MARSHALL, and MR. JUSTICE BLACKMUN join Parts I and V-C of this opinion. MR. JUSTICE WHITE also joins Part III-A of this opinion.

Opinion of MR. JUSTICE BRENNAN, MR. JUSTICE WHITE, MR. JUSTICE MARSHALL, and MR. JUSTICE BLACKMUN, concurring in the judgment in part and dissenting in part.

The Court today, in reversing in part the judgment of the Supreme Court of California, affirms the constitutional power of Federal and State Governments to act affirmatively to achieve equal opportunity for all. The difficulty of the issue presented—whether government may use race-conscious programs to redress the continuing effects of past discrimination—and the mature consideration which each of our Brethren has brought to it have resulted in many opinions, no single one speaking for the Court. But this should not and must not mask the central meaning of today's opinions: Government may take race into account when it acts not to demean or insult any racial group, but to remedy disadvantages cast on minorities by past racial prejudice, at least when appropriate findings have been made by judicial, legislative, or administrative bodies with competence to act in this area.

THE CHIEF JUSTICE and our Brothers STEWART, REHNQUIST, and STEVENS, have concluded that Title VI of the Civil Rights Act of 1964, 78 Stat. 252, as amended, 42 U.S.C. 2000d et seq., prohibits programs such as that at the Davis Medical School. On this statutory theory alone, they would hold that respondent Allan Bakke's rights have been violated and that he must, therefore, be admitted to the Medical School. Our Brother POWELL, reaching the Constitution, concludes that, although race may be taken into account in university admissions, the particular special admissions program used by petitioner, which resulted in the exclusion of respondent Bakke, was not shown to be necessary to achieve petitioner's stated goals. Accordingly, these Members of the Court form a majority of five affirming the judgment of the Supreme Court of California insofar as it holds that respondent Bakke "is entitled to an order that he be admitted to the University." 18 Cal. 3d 34, 64, 553 P.2d 1152, 1172 (1976).

We agree with MR. JUSTICE POWELL that, as applied to the case before us, Title VI goes no further in prohibiting the use of race than the Equal Protection Clause of the Fourteenth Amendment itself. We also agree that the effect of the California Supreme Court's affirmance of the judgment of the Superior Court of California would be to prohibit the University from establishing in the future affirmative-action programs that take race into account. See ante, at 271 n. Since we conclude that the affirmative admissions program at the Davis Medical School is constitutional, we would reverse the judgment below in all respects. MR. JUSTICE POWELL agrees that some uses of race in university admissions are permissible and, therefore, he joins with us to make five votes reversing the judgment below insofar as it prohibits the University from establishing race-conscious programs in the future.

I

Our Nation was founded on the principle that "all Men are created equal." Yet candor requires acknowledgment that the Framers of our Constitution, to forge the 13 Colonies into one Nation, openly compromised this principle of equality with its antithesis: slavery. The consequences of this compromise are well known and have aptly been called our "American Dilemma." Still, it is well to recount how recent the time has been, if it has yet come, when the promise of our principles has flowered into the actuality of equal opportunity for all regardless of race or color.

The Fourteenth Amendment, the embodiment in the Constitution of our abiding belief in human equality, has been the law of our land for only slightly more than half its 200 years. And for half of that half, the Equal Protection Clause of the Amendment was largely moribund so that, as late as 1927, Mr. Justice Holmes could sum up the importance of that Clause by remarking that it was the "last resort of constitutional arguments." Buck v. Bell, (1927). Worse than desuetude, the Clause was early turned against those whom it was intended to set free, condemning them to a "separate but equal" status before the law, a status always separate but seldom equal. Not until 1954—only 24 years ago—was this odious doctrine interred by our decision in Brown v. Board of Education, (Brown I), and its progeny, which proclaimed that separate schools and public facilities of all sorts were inherently unequal and forbidden under our Constitution. Even then inequality was not eliminated with "all deliberate speed." Brown v. Board of Education, (1955). In 1968 and again in 1971, for example, we were forced to remind school boards of their obligation to eliminate racial discrimination root and branch. And a glance at our docket and at dockets of lower courts will show that even today officially sanctioned discrimination is not a thing of the past.

Against this background, claims that law must be "color-blind" or that the datum of race is no longer relevant to public policy must be seen as aspiration rather than as description of reality. This is not to denigrate aspiration; for reality rebukes us that race has too often been used by those who would stigmatize and oppress minorities. Yet we cannot—and, as we shall demonstrate, need not under our Constitution or Title VI, which merely extends the constraints of the Fourteenth Amendment to private parties who receive federal funds—let color blindness become myopia which masks the reality that many "created equal" have been treated within our lifetimes as inferior both by the law and by their fellow citizens.

II

The threshold question we must decide is whether Title VI of the Civil Rights Act of 1964 bars recipients of federal funds from giving preferential consideration to disadvantaged members of racial minorities as part of a program designed to enable such individuals to surmount the obstacles imposed by racial discrimination. We join Parts I and V-C of our Brother POWELL'S opinion and three of us agree with his conclusion in Part II that this case does not require us to resolve the question whether there is a private right of action under Title VI.

In our view, Title VI prohibits only those uses of racial criteria that would violate the Fourteenth Amendment if employed by a State or its agencies; it does not bar the preferential treatment of racial minorities as a means of remedying past societal discrimination to the extent that such action is consistent with the Fourteenth Amendment. The legislative history of Title VI, administrative regulations interpreting the statute, subsequent congressional and executive action, and the prior decisions of this Court compel this conclusion. None of these sources lends support to the proposition that Congress intended to bar all race-conscious efforts to extend the benefits of federally financed programs to minorities who have been historically excluded from the full benefits of American life.

A

The history of Title VI—from President Kennedy's request that Congress grant executive departments and agencies authority to cut off federal funds to programs that discriminate against Negroes through final enactment of legislation incorporating his proposals—reveals one fixed purpose: to give the Executive Branch of Government clear authority to terminate federal funding of private programs that use race as a means of disadvantaging minorities in a manner that would be prohibited by the Constitution if engaged in by government.

This purpose was first expressed in President Kennedy's June 19, 1963, message to Congress proposing the legislation that subsequently became the Civil Rights Act of 1964. Representative Celler, the Chairman of the House Judiciary Committee, and the floor manager of the legislation in the House, introduced Title VI in words unequivocally expressing the intent to provide the Federal Government with the means of assuring that its funds were not used to subsidize racial discrimination inconsistent with the standards imposed by the Fourteenth and Fifth Amendments upon state and federal action.

> "The bill would offer assurance that hospitals financed by Federal money would not deny adequate care to Negroes. It would prevent abuse of food distribution programs whereby Negroes have been known to be denied food surplus supplies when white persons were given such food. It would assure Negroes the benefits now accorded only white students in programs of high[er] education financed by Federal funds. It would, in short, assure the existing right to equal treatment in the enjoyment of Federal funds. It would not destroy any rights of private property or freedom of association." 110 Cong. Rec. 1519 (1964).

It was clear to Representative Celler that Title VI, apart from the fact that it reached all federally funded activities even in the absence of sufficient state or federal control to invoke the Fourteenth or Fifth Amendments, was not placing new substantive limitations upon the use of racial criteria, but rather was designed to extend to such activities "the existing right to equal treatment" enjoyed by Negroes under those Amendments, and he later specifically defined the purpose of Title VI in this way:

"In general, it seems rather anomalous that the Federal Government should aid and abet discrimination on the basis of race, color, or national origin by granting money and other kinds of financial aid. It seems rather shocking, moreover, that while we have on the one hand the 14th amendment, which is supposed to do away with discrimination since it provides for equal protection of the laws, on the other hand, we have the Federal Government aiding and abetting those who persist in practicing racial discrimination.

"It is for these reasons that we bring forth title VI. The enactment of title VI will serve to override specific provisions of law which contemplate Federal assistance to racially segregated institutions." Id., at 2467.

Representative Celler also filed a memorandum setting forth the legal basis for the enactment of Title VI which reiterated the theme of his oral remarks: "In exercising its authority to fix the terms on which Federal funds will be disbursed . . . , Congress clearly has power to legislate so as to insure that the Federal Government does not become involved in a violation of the Constitution." Id., at 1528.

Other sponsors of the legislation agreed with Representative Celler that the function of Title VI was to end the Federal Government's complicity in conduct, particularly the segregation or exclusion of Negroes, inconsistent with the standards to be found in the antidiscrimination provisions of the Constitution. Representative Lindsay, also a member of the Judiciary Committee, candidly acknowledged, in the course of explaining why Title VI was necessary, that it did not create any new standard of equal treatment beyond that contained in the Constitution:

"Both the Federal Government and the States are under constitutional mandates not to discriminate. Many have raised the question as to whether legislation is required at all. Does not the Executive already have the power in the distribution of Federal funds to apply those conditions which will enable the Federal Government itself to live up to the mandate of the Constitution and to require States and local government entities to live up to the Constitution, most especially the 5th and 14th amendments?" Id., at 2467.

He then explained that legislation was needed to authorize the termination of funding by the Executive Branch because existing legislation seemed to contemplate the expenditure of funds to support racially segregated institutions. Ibid. The views of Representatives Celler and Lindsay concerning the purpose and function of Title VI were shared by other sponsors and proponents of the legislation in the House. Nowhere is there any suggestion that Title VI was intended to terminate federal funding for any reason other than consideration of race or national origin by the recipient institution in a manner inconsistent with the standards incorporated in the Constitution.

The Senate's consideration of Title VI reveals an identical understanding concerning the purpose and scope of the legislation. Senator Humphrey, the Senate floor manager, opened the Senate debate with a section-by-section analysis of the Civil Rights Act in which he succinctly stated the purpose of Title VI:

"The purpose of title VI is to make sure that funds of the United States are not used to support racial discrimination. In many instances the practices of segregation or discrimination, which title VI seeks to end, are unconstitutional. This is clearly so wherever Federal funds go to a State agency which engages in racial discrimination. It may also be so where Federal funds go to support private, segregated institutions, under the decision in Simkins v. Moses H. Cone Memorial Hospital, 323 F.2d 959 (C. A. 4, 1963), [cert. denied, (1964)]. In all cases, such discrimination is contrary to national policy, and to the moral sense of the Nation. Thus, title VI is simply designed to insure that Federal funds are spent in accordance with the Constitution and the moral sense of the Nation." Id., at 6544.

Senator Humphrey, in words echoing statements in the House, explained that legislation was needed to accomplish this objective because it was necessary to eliminate uncertainty concerning the power of federal agencies to terminate financial assistance to programs engaging in racial discrimination in the face of various federal statutes which appeared to authorize grants to racially segregated institutions. Ibid. Although Senator Humphrey realized that Title VI reached conduct which, because of insufficient governmental action, might be beyond the reach of the Constitution, it was clear to him that the substantive standard imposed by the statute was that of the Fifth and Fourteenth Amendments.

Senate supporters of Title VI repeatedly expressed agreement with Senator Humphrey's description of the legislation as providing the explicit authority and obligation to apply the standards of the Constitution to all recipients of federal funds. Senator Ribicoff described the limited function of Title VI:

> "Basically, there is a constitutional restriction against discrimination in the use of Federal funds; and title VI simply spells out the procedure to be used in enforcing that restriction." Id., at 13333.

Other strong proponents of the legislation in the Senate repeatedly expressed their intent to assure that federal funds would only be spent in accordance with constitutional standards. See remarks of Senator Pastore, id., at 7057, 7062; Senator Clark, id., at 5243; Senator Allott, id., at 12675, 12677.

Respondent's contention that Congress intended Title VI to bar affirmative-action programs designed to enable minorities disadvantaged by the effects of discrimination to participate in federally financed programs is also refuted by an examination of the type of conduct which Congress thought it was prohibiting by means of Title VI. The debates reveal that the legislation was motivated primarily by a desire to eradicate a very specific evil: federal financial support of programs which disadvantaged Negroes by excluding them from participation or providing them with separate facilities. Again and again supporters of Title VI emphasized that the purpose of the statute was to end segregation in federally funded activities and to end other discriminatory uses of race disadvantaging Negroes. Senator Humphrey set the theme in his speech presenting Title VI to the Senate:

> "Large sums of money are contributed by the United States each year for the construction, operation, and maintenance of segregated schools.
>
> . . . .
>
> "Similarly, under the Hill-Burton Act, Federal grants are made to hospitals which admit whites only or Negroes only . . . .
>
> "In higher education also, a substantial part of the Federal grants to colleges, medical schools and so forth, in the South is still going to segregated institutions.
>
> "Nor is this all. In several States, agricultural extension services, supported by Federal funds, maintain racially segregated offices for Negroes and whites . . . .
>
> " . . . Vocational training courses, supported with Federal funds, are given in segregated schools and institutions and often limit Negroes to training in less skilled occupations. In particular localities it is reported that Negroes have been cut off from relief rolls, or denied surplus agricultural commodities, or otherwise deprived of the benefit of federally assisted programs, in retaliation for their participation in voter registration drives, sit-in demonstrations and the like." Id., at 6543-6544.

See also the remarks of Senator Pastore (id., at 7054-7055); Senator Ribicoff (id., at 7064-7065); Senator Clark (id., at 5243, 9086); Senator Javits (id., at 6050, 7102).

The conclusion to be drawn from the foregoing is clear. Congress recognized that Negroes, in some cases with congressional acquiescence, were being discriminated against in the administration of programs and denied the full benefits of activities receiving federal financial support. It was aware that there were many federally funded programs and institutions which discriminated against minorities in a manner inconsistent with the standards of the Fifth and Fourteenth Amendments but whose activities might not involve sufficient state or federal action so as to be in violation of these Amendments. Moreover, Congress believed that it was questionable whether the Executive Branch possessed legal authority to terminate the funding of activities on the ground that they discriminated racially against Negroes in a manner violative of the standards contained in the Fourteenth and Fifth Amendments. Congress' solution was to end the Government's complicity in constitutionally forbidden racial discrimination by providing the Executive Branch with the authority and the obligation to terminate its financial support of any activity which employed racial criteria in a manner condemned by the Constitution.

Of course, it might be argued that the Congress which enacted Title VI understood the Constitution to require strict racial neutrality or color blindness, and then enshrined that concept as a rule of statutory law. Later interpretation and clarification of the Constitution to permit remedial use of race would then not dislodge Title VI's prohibition of race-conscious action. But there are three compelling reasons to reject such a hypothesis.

First, no decision of this Court has ever adopted the proposition that the Constitution must be colorblind. See infra, at 355-356.

Second, even if it could be argued in 1964 that the Constitution might conceivably require color blindness, Congress surely would not have chosen to codify such a view unless the Constitution clearly required it. The legislative history of Title VI, as well as the statute itself, reveals a desire to induce voluntary compliance with the requirement of nondiscriminatory treatment. See 602 of the Act, 42 U.S.C. 2000d-1 (no funds shall be terminated unless and until it has been "determined that compliance cannot be secured by voluntary means"); H. R. Rep. No. 914, 88th Cong., 1st Sess., pt. 1, p. 25 (1963); 110 Cong Rec. 13700 (1964) (Sen. Pastore); id., at 6546 (Sen. Humphrey). It is inconceivable that Congress intended to encourage voluntary efforts to eliminate the evil of racial discrimination while at the same time forbidding the voluntary use of race-conscious remedies to cure acknowledged or obvious statutory violations. Yet a reading of Title VI as prohibiting all action predicated upon race which adversely affects any individual would require recipients guilty of discrimination to await the imposition of such remedies by the Executive Branch. Indeed, such an interpretation of Title VI would prevent recipients of federal funds from taking race into account even when necessary to bring their programs into compliance with federal constitutional requirements. This would be a remarkable reading of a statute designed to eliminate constitutional violations, especially in light of judicial decisions holding that under certain circumstances the remedial use of racial criteria is not only permissible but is constitutionally required to eradicate constitutional violations. For example, in Board of Education v. Swann, (1971), the Court held that a statute forbidding the assignment of students on the basis of race was unconstitutional because it would hinder the implementation of remedies necessary to accomplish the desegregation of a school system: "Just as the race of students must be considered in determining whether a constitutional violation has occurred, so also must race be considered in formulating a remedy." Id., at 46. Surely Congress did not intend to prohibit the use of racial criteria when constitutionally required or to terminate the funding of any entity which implemented such a remedy. It clearly desired to encourage all remedies, including the use of race, necessary to eliminate racial discrimination in violation of the Constitution rather than requiring the recipient to await a judicial adjudication of unconstitutionality and the judicial imposition of a racially oriented remedy.

Third, the legislative history shows that Congress specifically eschewed any static definition of discrimination in favor of broad language that could be shaped by experience, administrative necessity, and evolving judicial doctrine. Although it is clear from the debates that the supporters of Title VI intended to ban uses of race prohibited by the Constitution and, more specifically, the maintenance of segregated facilities, they never precisely defined the term "discrimination," or what constituted an exclusion from participation or a denial of benefits on the ground of race. This failure was not lost upon its opponents. Senator Ervin complained:

> "The word 'discrimination,' as used in this reference, has no contextual explanation whatever, other than the provision that the discrimination 'is to be against' individuals participating in or benefiting from federally assisted programs and activities on the ground specified. With this context, the discrimination condemned by this reference occurs only when an individual is treated unequally or unfairly because of his race, color, religion, or national origin. What constitutes unequal or unfair treatment? Section 601 and section 602 of title VI do not say. They leave the determination of that question to the executive department or agencies administering each program, without any guideline whatever to point out what is the congressional intent." 110 Cong. Rec. 5612 (1964).

See also remarks of Representative Abernethy (id., at 1619); Representative Dowdy (id., at 1632); Senator Talmadge (id., at 5251); Senator Sparkman (id., at 6052). Despite these criticisms, the legislation's supporters refused to include in the statute or even provide in debate a more explicit definition of what Title VI prohibited.

The explanation for this failure is clear. Specific definitions were undesirable, in the views of the legislation's principal backers, because Title VI's standard was that of the Constitution and one that could and should be administratively and judicially applied. See remarks of Senator Humphrey (id., at 5253, 6553); Senator Ribicoff (id., at 7057, 13333); Senator Pastore (id., at 7057); Senator Javits (id., at 5606-5607, 6050). Indeed, there was a strong emphasis throughout Congress' consideration of Title VI on providing the Executive Branch with considerable flexibility in interpreting and applying the prohibition against racial discrimination. Attorney General Robert Kennedy testified that regulations had not been written into the legislation itself because the rules and regulations defining discrimination might differ from one program to another so that the term would assume different meanings in different contexts. This determination to preserve flexibility in the administration of Title VI was shared by the legislation's supporters. When Senator Johnston offered an amendment that would have expressly authorized federal grantees to take race into account in placing children in adoptive and foster homes, Senator Pastore opposed the amendment, which was ultimately defeated by a 56-29 vote, on the ground that federal administrators could be trusted to act reasonably and that there was no danger that they would prohibit the use of racial criteria under such circumstances. Id., at 13695.

Congress' resolve not to incorporate a static definition of discrimination into Title VI is not surprising. In 1963 and 1964, when Title VI was drafted and debated, the courts had only recently applied the Equal Protection Clause to strike down public racial discrimination in America, and the scope of that Clause's nondiscrimination principle was in a state of flux and rapid evolution. Many questions, such as whether the Fourteenth Amendment barred only de jure discrimination or in at least some circumstances reached de facto discrimination, had not yet received an authoritative judicial resolution. The congressional debate reflects an awareness of the evolutionary change that constitutional law in the area of racial discrimination was undergoing in 1964.

In sum, Congress' equating of Title VI's prohibition with the commands of the Fifth and Fourteenth Amendments, its refusal precisely to define that racial discrimination which it intended to prohibit, and its expectation that the statute would be administered in a flexible manner, compel the conclusion that Congress intended the meaning of the statute's prohibition to evolve with the interpretation of the commands of the Constitution. Thus, any claim that the use of racial criteria is barred by the plain language of the statute must fail in light of the remedial purpose of Title VI and its legislative history. The cryptic nature of the language employed in Title VI merely reflects Congress' concern with the then-prevalent use of racial standards as a means of excluding or disadvantaging Negroes and its determination to prohibit absolutely such discrimination. We have recently held that "[w]hen aid to construction of the meaning of words, as used in the statute, is available, there certainly can be no 'rule of law' which forbids its use, however clear the words may appear on 'superficial examination.'" Train v. Colorado Public Interest Research Group, (1976), quoting United States v. American Trucking Assns., (1940). This is especially so when, as is the case here, the literal application of what is believed to be the plain language of the statute, assuming that it is so plain, would lead to results in direct conflict with Congress' unequivocally expressed legislative purpose.

B

Section 602 of Title VI, 42 U.S.C. 2000d-1, instructs federal agencies to promulgate regulations interpreting Title VI. These regulations, which, under the terms of the statute, require Presidential approval, are entitled to considerable deference in construing Title VI. See, e. g., Lau v. Nichols, (1974); Mourning v. Family Publications Service, Inc., (1973); Red Lion Broadcasting Co. v. FCC, (1969). Consequently, it is most significant that the Department of Health, Education, and Welfare (HEW), which provides much of the federal assistance to institutions of higher education, has adopted regulations requiring affirmative measures designed to enable racial minorities which have been previously discriminated against by a federally funded institution or program to overcome the effects of such actions and authorizing the voluntary undertaking of affirmative-action programs by federally funded institutions that have not been guilty of prior discrimination in order to overcome the effects of conditions which have adversely affected the degree of participation by persons of a particular race.

Title 45 CFR 80.3 (b) (6) (i) (1977) provides:

> "In administering a program regarding which the recipient has previously discriminated against persons on the ground of race, color, or national origin, the recipient must take affirmative action to overcome the effects of prior discrimination."

Title 45 CFR 80.5 (i) (1977) elaborates upon this requirement:

> "In some situations, even though past discriminatory practices attributable to a recipient or applicant have been abandoned, the consequences of such practices continue to impede the full availability of a benefit. If the efforts required of the applicant or recipient under 80.6 (d), to provide information as to the availability of the program or activity and the rights of beneficiaries under this regulation, have failed to overcome these consequences, it will become necessary under the requirement stated in (i) of 80.3 (b) (6) for such applicant or recipient to take additional steps to make the benefits fully available to racial and nationality groups previously subject to discrimination. This action might take the form, for example, of special arrangements for obtaining referrals or making selections which will insure that groups previously subjected to discrimination are adequately served."

These regulations clearly establish that where there is a need to overcome the effects of past racially discriminatory or exclusionary practices engaged in by a federally funded institution, race-conscious action is not only permitted but required to accomplish the remedial objectives of Title VI. Of course, there is no evidence that the Medical School has been guilty of past discrimination and consequently these regulations would not compel it to employ a program of preferential admissions in behalf of racial minorities. It would be difficult to explain from the language of Title VI, however, much less from its legislative history, why the statute compels race-conscious remedies where a recipient institution has engaged in past discrimination but prohibits such remedial action where racial minorities, as a result of the effects of past discrimination imposed by entities other than the recipient, are excluded from the benefits of federally funded programs. HEW was fully aware of the incongruous nature of such an interpretation of Title VI.

Title 45 CFR 80.3 (b) (6) (ii) (1977) provides:

> "Even in the absence of such prior discrimination, a recipient in administering a program may take affirmative action to overcome the effects of conditions which resulted in limiting participation by persons of a particular race, color, or national origin."

An explanatory regulation explicitly states that the affirmative action which 80.3 (b) (6) (ii) contemplates includes the use of racial preferences:

> "Even though an applicant or recipient has never used discriminatory policies, the services and benefits of the program or activity it administers may not in fact be equally available to some racial or nationality groups. In such circumstances, an applicant or recipient may properly give special consideration to race, color, or national origin to make the benefits of its program more widely available to such groups, not then being adequately served. For example, where a university is not adequately serving members of a particular racial or nationality group, it may establish special recruitment policies to make its program better known and more readily available to such group, and take other steps to provide that group with more adequate service." 45 CFR 80.5 (j) (1977).

This interpretation of Title VI is fully consistent with the statute's emphasis upon voluntary remedial action and reflects the views of an agency responsible for achieving its objectives.

The Court has recognized that the construction of a statute by those charged with its execution is particularly deserving of respect where Congress has directed its attention to the administrative construction and left it unaltered. Cf. Red Lion Broadcasting Co. v. FCC; Zemel v. Rusk, (1965). Congress recently took just this kind of action when it considered an amendment to the Departments of Labor and Health, Education, and Welfare appropriation bill for 1978, which would have restricted significantly the remedial use of race in programs funded by the appropriation. The amendment, as originally submitted by Representative Ashbrook, provided that "[n]one of the funds appropriated in this Act may be used to initiate, carry out or enforce any program of affirmative action or any other system of quotas or goals in regard to admission policies or employment practices which encourage or require any discrimination on the basis of race, creed, religion, sex or age." 123 Cong. Rec. 19715 (1977). In support of the measure, Representative Ashbrook argued that the 1964 Civil Rights Act never authorized the imposition of affirmative action and that this was a creation of the bureaucracy. Id., at 19722. He explicitly stated, however, that he favored permitting universities to adopt affirmative-action programs giving consideration to racial identity but opposed the imposition of such programs by the Government. Id., at 19715. His amendment was itself amended to reflect this position by only barring the imposition of race-conscious remedies by HEW:

> "None of the funds appropriated in this Act may be obligated or expended in connection with the issuance, implementation, or enforcement of any rule, regulation, standard, guideline, recommendation, or order issued by the Secretary of Health, Education, and Welfare which for purposes of compliance with any ratio, quota, or other numerical requirement related to race, creed, color, national origin, or sex requires any individual or entity to take any action with respect to (1) the hiring or promotion policies or practices of such individual or entity, or (2) the admissions policies or practices of such individual or entity." Id., at 19722.

This amendment was adopted by the House. Ibid. The Senate bill, however, contained no such restriction upon HEW's authority to impose race-conscious remedies and the Conference Committee, upon the urging of the Secretary of HEW, deleted the House provision from the bill. More significant for present purposes, however, is the fact that even the proponents of imposing limitations upon HEW's implementation of Title VI did not challenge the right of federally funded educational institutions voluntarily to extend preferences to racial minorities.

Finally, congressional action subsequent to the passage of Title VI eliminates any possible doubt about Congress' views concerning the permissibility of racial preferences for the purpose of assisting disadvantaged racial minorities. It confirms that Congress did not intend to prohibit and does not now believe that Title VI prohibits the consideration of race as part of a remedy for societal discrimination even where there is no showing that the institution extending the preference has been guilty of past discrimination nor any judicial finding that the particular beneficiaries of the racial preference have been adversely affected by societal discrimination.

Just last year Congress enacted legislation explicitly requiring that no grants shall be made "for any local public works project unless the applicant gives satisfactory assurance to the Secretary [of Commerce] that at least 10 per centum of the amount of each grant shall be expended for minority business enterprises." The statute defines the term "minority business enterprise" as "a business, at least 50 per centum of which is owned by minority group members or, in case of a publicly owned business, at least 51 per centum of the stock of which is owned by minority group members." The term "minority group members" is defined in explicitly racial terms: "citizens of the United States who are Negroes, Spanish-speaking, Orientals, Indians, Eskimos, and Aleuts." Although the statute contains an exemption from this requirement "to the extent that the Secretary determines otherwise," this escape clause was provided only to deal with the possibility that certain areas of the country might not contain sufficient qualified "minority business enterprises" to permit compliance with the quota provisions of the legislation.

The legislative history of this race-conscious legislation reveals that it represents a deliberate attempt to deal with the excessive rate of unemployment among minority citizens and to encourage the development of viable minority controlled enterprises. It was believed that such a "set-aside" was required in order to enable minorities, still "new on the scene" and "relatively small," to compete with larger and more established companies which would always be successful in underbidding minority enterprises. 123 Cong. Rec. 5327 (1977) (Rep. Mitchell). What is most significant about the congressional consideration of the measure is that although the use of a racial quota or "set-aside" by a recipient of federal funds would constitute a direct violation of Title VI if that statute were read to prohibit race-conscious action, no mention was made during the debates in either the House or the Senate of even the possibility that the quota provisions for minority contractors might in any way conflict with or modify Title VI. It is inconceivable that such a purported conflict would have escaped congressional attention through an inadvertent failure to recognize the relevance of Title VI. Indeed, the Act of which this affirmative-action provision is a part also contains a provision barring discrimination on the basis of sex which states that this prohibition "will be enforced through agency provisions and rules similar to those already established, with respect to racial and other discrimination under Title VI of the Civil Rights Act of 1964." 42 U.S.C. 6709 (1976 ed.). Thus Congress was fully aware of the applicability of Title VI to the funding of public works projects. Under these circumstances, the enactment of the 10% "set-aside" for minority enterprises reflects a congressional judgment that the remedial use of race is permissible under Title VI. We have repeatedly recognized that subsequent legislation reflecting an interpretation of an earlier Act is entitled to great weight in determining the meaning of the earlier statute. Red Lion Broadcasting Co. v. FCC; Erlenbaugh v. United States, (1972). See also United States v. Stewart, (1940).

C

Prior decisions of this Court also strongly suggest that Title VI does not prohibit the remedial use of race where such action is constitutionally permissible. In Lau v. Nichols, (1974), the

Court held that the failure of the San Francisco school system to provide English-language instruction to students of Chinese ancestry who do not speak English, or to provide them with instruction in Chinese, constituted a violation of Title VI. The Court relied upon an HEW regulation which stipulates that a recipient of federal funds "may not . . . utilize criteria or methods of administration which have the effect of subjecting individuals to discrimination" or have "the effect of defeating or substantially impairing accomplishment of the objectives of the program as respect individuals of a particular race, color, or national origin." 45 CFR 80.3 (b) (2) (1977). It interpreted this regulation as requiring San Francisco to extend the same educational benefits to Chinese-speaking students as to English-speaking students, even though there was no finding or allegation that the city's failure to do so was a result of a purposeful design to discriminate on the basis of race.

Lau is significant in two related respects. First, it indicates that in at least some circumstances agencies responsible for the administration of Title VI may require recipients who have not been guilty of any constitutional violations to depart from a policy of color blindness and to be cognizant of the impact of their actions upon racial minorities. Secondly, Lau clearly requires that institutions receiving federal funds be accorded considerable latitude in voluntarily undertaking race-conscious action designed to remedy the exclusion of significant numbers of minorities from the benefits of federally funded programs. Although this Court has not yet considered the question, presumably, by analogy to our decisions construing Title VII, a medical school would not be in violation of Title VI under Lau because of the serious under representation of racial minorities in its student body as long as it could demonstrate that its entrance requirements correlated sufficiently with the performance of minority students in medical school and the medical profession. It would be inconsistent with Lau and the emphasis of Title VI and the HEW regulations on voluntary action, however, to require that an institution wait to be adjudicated to be in violation of the law before being permitted to voluntarily undertake corrective action based upon a good-faith and reasonable belief that the failure of certain racial minorities to satisfy entrance requirements is not a measure of their ultimate performance as doctors but a result of the lingering effects of past societal discrimination.

We recognize that Lau, especially when read in light of our subsequent decision in Washington v. Davis, (1976), which rejected the general proposition that governmental action is unconstitutional solely because it has a racially disproportionate impact, may be read as being predicated upon the view that, at least under some circumstances, Title VI proscribes conduct which might not be prohibited by the Constitution. Since we are now of the opinion, for the reasons set forth above, that Title VI's standard, applicable alike to public and private recipients of federal funds, is no broader than the Constitution's, we have serious doubts concerning the correctness of what appears to be the premise of that decision. However, even accepting Lau's implication that impact alone is in some contexts sufficient to establish a prima facie violation of Title VI, contrary to our view that Title VI's definition of racial discrimination is absolutely coextensive with the Constitution's, this would not assist the respondent in the least. First, for the reasons discussed supra, at 336-350, regardless of whether Title VI's prohibitions extend beyond the Constitution's the evidence fails to establish, and, indeed, compels the rejection of, the proposition that Congress intended to prohibit recipients of federal funds from voluntarily employing race-conscious measures to eliminate the effects of past societal discrimination against racial minorities such as Negroes. Secondly, Lau itself, for the reasons set forth in the immediately preceding paragraph, strongly supports the view that voluntary race-conscious remedial action is permissible under Title VI. If discriminatory racial impact alone is enough to demonstrate at least a prima facie Title VI violation, it is difficult to believe that the Title would forbid the Medical School from attempting to correct the racially exclusionary effects of its initial admissions policy during the first two years of the School's operation.

The Court has also declined to adopt a "colorblind" interpretation of other statutes containing nondiscrimination provisions similar to that contained in Title VI. We have held under

Title VII that where employment requirements have a disproportionate impact upon racial minorities they constitute a statutory violation, even in the absence of discriminatory intent, unless the employer is able to demonstrate that the requirements are sufficiently related to the needs of the job. More significantly, the Court has required that preferences be given by employers to members of racial minorities as a remedy for past violations of Title VII, even where there has been no finding that the employer has acted with a discriminatory intent. Finally, we have construed the Voting Rights Act of 1965, 42 U.S.C. 1973 et seq. (1970 ed. and Supp. V), which contains a provision barring any voting procedure or qualification that denies or abridges "the right of any citizen of the United States to vote on account of race or color," as permitting States to voluntarily take race into account in a way that fairly represents the voting strengths of different racial groups in order to comply with the commands of the statute, even where the result is a gain for one racial group at the expense of others.

These prior decisions are indicative of the Court's unwillingness to construe remedial statutes designed to eliminate discrimination against racial minorities in a manner which would impede efforts to attain this objective. There is no justification for departing from this course in the case of Title VI and frustrating the clear judgment of Congress that race-conscious remedial action is permissible.

We turn, therefore, to our analysis of the Equal Protection Clause of the Fourteenth Amendment.

III

A

The assertion of human equality is closely associated with the proposition that differences in color or creed, birth or status, are neither significant nor relevant to the way in which persons should be treated. Nonetheless, the position that such factors must be "constitutionally an irrelevance," Edwards v. California, (1941) (Jackson, J., concurring), summed up by the shorthand phrase "[o]ur Constitution is color-blind," Plessy v. Ferguson, (1896) (Harlan, J., dissenting), has never been adopted by this Court as the proper meaning of the Equal Protection Clause. Indeed, we have expressly rejected this proposition on a number of occasions.

Our cases have always implied that an "overriding statutory purpose," McLaughlin v. Florida, (1964), could be found that would justify racial classifications. See, e. g., ibid.; Loving v. Virginia, (1967); Korematsu v. United States, (1944); Hirabayashi v. United States, (1943). More recently, in McDaniel v. Barresi, (1971), this Court unanimously reversed the Georgia Supreme Court which had held that a desegregation plan voluntarily adopted by a local school board, which assigned students on the basis of race, was per se invalid because it was not colorblind. And in North Carolina Board of Education v. Swann we held, again unanimously, that a statute mandating colorblind school-assignment plans could not stand "against the background of segregation," since such a limit on remedies would "render illusory the promise of Brown [I]."

We conclude, therefore, that racial classifications are not per se invalid under the Fourteenth Amendment. Accordingly, we turn to the problem of articulating what our role should be in reviewing state action that expressly classifies by race.

B

Respondent argues that racial classifications are always suspect and, consequently, that this Court should weigh the importance of the objectives served by Davis' special admissions program to see if they are compelling. In addition, he asserts that this Court must inquire whether, in its judgment, there are alternatives to racial classifications which would suit Davis' purposes. Petitioner, on the other hand, states that our proper role is simply to accept petitioner's determination that the racial classifications used by its program are reasonably related to what it tells us are its benign purposes. We reject petitioner's view, but, because our prior cases are in many respects in apposite to that before us now, we find it necessary to define with precision the meaning of that inexact term, "strict scrutiny."

Unquestionably we have held that a government practice or statute which restricts "fundamental rights" or which contains "suspect classifications" is to be subjected to "strict scrutiny" and can be justified only if it furthers a compelling government purpose and, even then, only if no less restrictive alternative is available. See, e. g., San Antonio Independent School District v. Rodriguez, (1973); Dunn v. Blumstein, (1972). But no fundamental right is involved here. See San Antonio, supra, at 29-36. Nor do whites as a class have any of the "traditional indicia of suspectness: the class is not saddled with such disabilities, or subjected to such a history of purposeful unequal treatment, or relegated to such a position of political powerlessness as to command extraordinary protection from the majoritarian political process." Id., at 28; see United States v. Carolene Products Co., n. 4 (1938).

Moreover, if the University's representations are credited, this is not a case where racial classifications are "irrelevant and therefore prohibited." Hirabayashi, supra, at 100. Nor has anyone suggested that the University's purposes contravene the cardinal principle that racial classifications that stigmatize—because they are drawn on the presumption that one race is inferior to another or because they put the weight of government behind racial hatred and separatism—are invalid without more. See Yick Wo v. Hopkins, (1886); accord, Strauder v. West Virginia, (1880); Korematsu v. United States, supra, at 223; Oyama v. California, (1948) (Murphy, J., concurring); Brown I, (1954); McLaughlin v. Florida, supra, at 191-192; Loving v. Virginia, supra, at 11-12; Reitman v. Mulkey, (1967); United Jewish Organizations v. Carey, (1977) (UJO) (opinion of WHITE, J., joined by REHNQUIST and STEVENS, JJ.); id., at 169 (opinion concurring in part).

On the other hand, the fact that this case does not fit neatly into our prior analytic framework for race cases does not mean that it should be analyzed by applying the very loose rational-basis standard of review that is the very least that is always applied in equal protection cases. "'[T]he mere recitation of a benign, compensatory purpose is not an automatic shield which protects against any inquiry into the actual purposes underlying a statutory scheme.'" Califano v. Webster, (1977), quoting Weinberger v. Wiesenfeld, (1975). Instead, a number of considerations—developed in gender-discrimination cases but which carry even more force when applied to racial classifications—lead us to conclude that racial classifications designed to further remedial purposes "'must serve important governmental objectives and must be substantially related to achievement of those objectives.'" Califano v. Webster, supra, at 317, quoting Craig v. Boren, (1976).

First, race, like, "gender-based classifications too often [has] been inexcusably utilized to stereotype and stigmatize politically powerless segments of society." Kahn v. Shevin, (1974) (dissenting opinion). While a carefully tailored statute designed to remedy past discrimination could avoid these vices, see Califano v. Webster, supra; Schlesinger v. Ballard, (1975); Kahn v. Shevin, supra, we nonetheless have recognized that the line between honest and thoughtful appraisal of the effects of past discrimination and paternalistic stereotyping is not so clear and that a statute based on the latter is patently capable of stigmatizing all women with a badge of inferiority. Cf. Schlesinger v. Ballard, supra, at 508; UJO, supra, at 174, and n. 3 (opinion concurring in part); Califano v. Goldfarb, (1977) (STEVENS, J., concurring in judgment). See also Stanton v. Stanton, (1975). State programs designed ostensibly to ameliorate the effects of past racial discrimination obviously create the same hazard of stigma, since they may promote racial separatism and reinforce the views of those who believe that members of racial minorities are inherently incapable of succeeding on their own. See UJO, supra, at 172 (opinion concurring in part); ante, at 298 (opinion of POWELL, J.).

Second, race, like gender and illegitimacy, see Weber v. Aetna Casualty & Surety Co., (1972), is an immutable characteristic which its possessors are powerless to escape or set aside.

While a classification is not per se invalid because it divides classes on the basis of an immutable characteristic, see supra, at 355-356, it is nevertheless true that such divisions are contrary to our deep belief that "legal burdens should bear some relationship to individual responsibility or wrongdoing," Weber, supra, at 175; Frontiero v. Richardson, (1973) (opinion of BRENNAN, WHITE, and MARSHALL, JJ.), and that advancement sanctioned, sponsored, or approved by the State should ideally be based on individual merit or achievement, or at the least on factors within the control of an individual. See UJO, (opinion concurring in part); Kotch v. Board of River Port Pilot Comm'rs, (1947) (Rutledge, J., dissenting).

Because this principle is so deeply rooted it might be supposed that it would be considered in the legislative process and weighed against the benefits of programs preferring individuals because of their race. But this is not necessarily so: The "natural consequence of our governing processes [may well be] that the most 'discrete and insular' of whites . . . will be called upon to bear the immediate, direct costs of benign discrimination." UJO, supra, at 174 (opinion concurring in part). Moreover, it is clear from our cases that there are limits beyond which majorities may not go when they classify on the basis of immutable characteristics. See, e. g., Weber, supra. Thus, even if the concern for individualism is weighed by the political process, that weighing cannot waive the personal rights of individuals under the Fourteenth Amendment. See Lucas v. Colorado General Assembly, (1964).

In sum, because of the significant risk that racial classifications established for ostensibly benign purposes can be misused, causing effects not unlike those created by invidious classifications, it is inappropriate to inquire only whether there is any conceivable basis that might sustain such a classification. Instead, to justify such a classification an important and articulated purpose for its use must be shown. In addition, any statute must be stricken that stigmatizes any group or that singles out those least well represented in the political process to bear the brunt of a benign program. Thus, our review under the Fourteenth Amendment should be strict—not "'strict' in theory and fatal in fact," because it is stigma that causes fatality—but strict and searching nonetheless.

IV

Davis' articulated purpose of remedying the effects of past societal discrimination is, under our cases, sufficiently important to justify the use of race-conscious admissions programs where there is a sound basis for concluding that minority underrepresentation is substantial and chronic, and that the handicap of past discrimination is impeding access of minorities to the Medical School.

A

At least since Green v. County School Board, (1968), it has been clear that a public body which has itself been adjudged to have engaged in racial discrimination cannot bring itself into compliance with the Equal Protection Clause simply by ending its unlawful acts and adopting a neutral stance. Three years later, Swann v. Charlotte-Mecklenburg Board of Education, (1971), and its companion cases, Davis v. School Comm'rs of Mobile County, (1971); McDaniel v. Barresi, (1971); and North Carolina Board of Education v. Swann, (1971), reiterated that racially neutral remedies for past discrimination were inadequate where consequences of past discriminatory acts influence or control present decisions. See, e. g., Charlotte-Mecklenburg, supra, at 28. And the Court further held both that courts could enter desegregation orders which assigned students and faculty by reference to race, Charlotte-Mecklenburg, supra; Davis, supra; United States v. Montgomery County Board of Ed., (1969), and that local school boards could voluntarily adopt desegregation plans which made express reference to race if this was necessary to remedy the effects of past discrimination. McDaniel v. Barresi, supra. Moreover, we stated that school boards, even in the absence of a judicial finding of past discrimination, could voluntarily adopt plans which assigned students with the end of creating racial pluralism by establishing fixed ratios of black and white students in each school. Charlotte-Mecklenburg, supra, at 16. In each instance, the creation of unitary school systems, in which the effects of past discrimination had been "eliminated root and branch," Green, supra, at 438, was recognized as a compelling social goal justifying the overt use of race.

Finally, the conclusion that state educational institutions may constitutionally adopt admissions programs designed to avoid exclusion of historically disadvantaged minorities, even when such programs explicitly take race into account, finds direct support in our cases construing congressional legislation designed to overcome the present effects of past discrimination. Congress can and has outlawed actions which have a disproportionately adverse and unjustified impact upon members of racial minorities and has required or authorized race-conscious action to put individuals disadvantaged by such impact in the position they otherwise might have enjoyed. See Franks v. Bowman Transportation Co., (1976); Teamsters v. United States, (1977). Such relief does not require as a predicate proof that recipients of preferential advancement have been individually discriminated against; it is enough that each recipient is within a general class of persons likely to have been the victims of discrimination. See id., at 357-362. Nor is it an objection to such relief that preference for minorities will upset the settled expectations of nonminorities. See Franks, supra. In addition, we have held that Congress, to remove barriers to equal opportunity, can and has required employers to use test criteria that fairly reflect the qualifications of minority applicants vis-a-vis nonminority applicants, even if this means interpreting the qualifications of an applicant in light of his race. See Albemarle Paper Co. v. Moody, (1975).

These cases cannot be distinguished simply by the presence of judicial findings of discrimination, for race-conscious remedies have been approved where such findings have not been made. McDaniel v. Barresi, supra; UJO; see Califano v. Webster, (1977); Schlesinger v. Ballard, (1975); Kahn v. Shevin, (1974). See also Katzenbach v. Morgan, (1966). Indeed, the requirement of a judicial determination of a constitutional or statutory violation as a predicate for race-conscious remedial actions would be self-defeating. Such a requirement would severely undermine efforts to achieve voluntary compliance with the requirements of law. And our society and jurisprudence have always stressed the value of voluntary efforts to further the objectives of the law. Judicial intervention is a last resort to achieve cessation of illegal conduct or the remedying of its effects rather than a prerequisite to action.

Nor can our cases be distinguished on the ground that the entity using explicit racial classifications itself had violated 1 of the Fourteenth Amendment or an antidiscrimination regulation, for again race-conscious remedies have been approved where this is not the case. See UJO, (opinion of WHITE, J., joined by BRENNAN, BLACKMUN, and STEVENS, JJ.); id., at 167 (opinion of WHITE, J., joined by REHNQUIST and STEVENS, JJ.); cf. Califano v. Webster, supra, at 317; Kahn v. Shevin, supra. Moreover, the presence or absence of past discrimination by universities or employers is largely irrelevant to resolving respondent's constitutional claims. The claims of those burdened by the race-conscious actions of a university or employer who has never been adjudged in violation of an antidiscrimination law are not any more or less entitled to deference than the claims of the burdened nonminority workers in Franks v. Bowman Transportation Co., supra, in which the employer had violated Title VII, for in each case the employees are innocent of past discrimination. And, although it might be argued that, where an employer has violated an antidiscrimination law, the expectations of nonminority workers are themselves products of discrimination and hence "tainted," see Franks, supra, at 776, and therefore more easily upset, the same argument can be made with respect to respondent. If it was reasonable to conclude—as we hold that it was—that the failure of minorities to qualify for admission at Davis under regular procedures was due principally to the effects of past discrimination, than there is a reasonable likelihood that, but for pervasive racial discrimination, respondent would have failed to qualify for admission even in the absence of Davis' special admissions program.

Thus, our cases under Title VII of the Civil Rights Act have held that, in order to achieve minority participation in previously segregated areas of public life, Congress may require or authorize preferential treatment for those likely disadvantaged by societal racial discrimination. Such legislation has been sustained even without a requirement of findings of intentional racial discrimination by those required or authorized to accord preferential treatment, or a case-by-case determination that those to be benefited suffered from racial discrimination. These decisions compel the conclusion that States also may adopt race-conscious programs designed to overcome substantial, chronic minority under representation where there is reason to believe that the evil addressed is a product of past racial discrimination.

Title VII was enacted pursuant to Congress' power under the Commerce Clause and 5 of the Fourteenth Amendment. To the extent that Congress acted under the Commerce Clause power, it was restricted in the use of race in governmental decisionmaking by the equal protection component of the Due Process Clause of the Fifth Amendment precisely to the same extent as are the States by 1 of the Fourteenth Amendment. Therefore, to the extent that Title VII rests on the Commerce Clause power, our decisions such as Franks and Teamsters v. United States, (1977), implicitly recognize that the affirmative use of race is consistent with the equal protection component of the Fifth Amendment and therefore with the Fourteenth Amendment. To the extent that Congress acted pursuant to 5 of the Fourteenth Amendment, those cases impliedly recognize that Congress was empowered under that provision to accord preferential treatment to victims of past discrimination in order to overcome the effects of segregation, and we see no reason to conclude that the States cannot voluntarily accomplish under 1 of the Fourteenth Amendment what Congress under 5 of the Fourteenth Amendment validly may authorize or compel either the States or private persons to do. A contrary position would conflict with the traditional understanding recognizing the competence of the States to initiate measures consistent with federal policy in the absence of congressional pre-emption of the subject matter. Nothing whatever in the legislative history of either the Fourteenth Amendment or the Civil Rights Acts even remotely suggests that the States are foreclosed from furthering the fundamental purpose of equal opportunity to which the Amendment and those Acts are addressed. Indeed, voluntary initiatives by the States to achieve the national goal of equal opportunity have been recognized to be essential to its attainment. "To use the Fourteenth Amendment as a sword against such State power would stultify that Amendment." Railway Mail Assn. v. Corsi, (1945) (Frankfurter, J., concurring). We therefore conclude that Davis' goal of admitting minority students disadvantaged by the effects of past discrimination is sufficiently important to justify use of race-conscious admissions criteria.

B

Properly construed, therefore, our prior cases unequivocally show that a state government may adopt race-conscious programs if the purpose of such programs is to remove the disparate racial impact its actions might otherwise have and if there is reason to believe that the disparate impact is itself the product of past discrimination, whether its own or that of society at large. There is no question that Davis' program is valid under this test.

Certainly, on the basis of the undisputed factual submissions before this Court, Davis had a sound basis for believing that the problem of under representation of minorities was substantial and chronic and that the problem was attributable to handicaps imposed on minority applicants by past and present racial discrimination. Until at least 1973, the practice of medicine in this country was, in fact, if not in law, largely the prerogative of whites. In 1950, for example, while Negroes constituted 10% of the total population, Negro physicians constituted only 2.2% of the total number of physicians. The overwhelming majority of these, moreover, were educated in two predominantly Negro medical schools, Howard and Meharry. By 1970, the gap between the proportion of Negroes in medicine and their proportion in the population had widened: The number of Negroes employed in medicine remained frozen at 2.2% while the Negro population had increased to 11.1%. The number of Negro admittees to predominantly white medical schools, moreover, had declined in absolute numbers during the years 1955 to 1964. Odegaard 19.

Moreover, Davis had very good reason to believe that the national pattern of underrepresentation of minorities in medicine would be perpetuated if it retained a single admissions standard. For example, the entering classes in 1968 and 1969, the years in which such a standard was used, included only 1 Chicano and 2 Negroes out of the 50 admittees for each year. Nor is there any relief from this pattern of underrepresentation in the statistics for the regular admissions program in later years.

Davis clearly could conclude that the serious and persistent underrepresentation of minorities in medicine depicted by these statistics is the result of handicaps under which minority applicants labor as a consequence of a background of deliberate, purposeful discrimination against minorities in education and in society generally, as well as in the medical profession. From the inception of our national life, Negroes have been subjected to unique legal disabilities impairing access to equal educational opportunity. Under slavery, penal sanctions were imposed upon anyone attempting to educate Negroes. After enactment of the Fourteenth Amendment the States continued to deny Negroes equal educational opportunity, enforcing a strict policy of segregation that itself stamped Negroes as inferior, Brown I, (1954), that relegated minorities to inferior educational institutions, and that denied them intercourse in the mainstream of professional life necessary to advancement. See Sweatt v. Painter, (1950). Segregation was not limited to public facilities, moreover, but was enforced by criminal penalties against private action as well. Thus, as late as 1908, this Court enforced a state criminal conviction against a private college for teaching Negroes together with whites. Berea College v. Kentucky. See also Plessy v. Ferguson, (1896).

Green v. County School Board, (1968), gave explicit recognition to the fact that the habit of discrimination and the cultural tradition of race prejudice cultivated by centuries of legal slavery and segregation were not immediately dissipated when Brown I, supra, announced the constitutional principle that equal educational opportunity and participation in all aspects of American life could not be denied on the basis of race. Rather, massive official and private resistance prevented, and to a lesser extent still prevents, attainment of equal opportunity in education at all levels and in the professions. The generation of minority students applying to Davis Medical School since it opened in 1968— most of whom were born before or about the time Brown I was decided— clearly have been victims of this discrimination. Judicial decrees recognizing discrimination in public education in California testify to the fact of widespread discrimination suffered by California-born minority applicants; many minority group members living in California, moreover, were born and reared in school districts in Southern States segregated by law. Since separation of schoolchildren by race "generates a feeling of inferiority as to their status in the community that may affect their hearts and minds in a way unlikely ever to be undone," Brown I, supra, at 494, the conclusion is inescapable that applicants to medical school must be few indeed who endured the effects of de jure segregation, the resistance to Brown I, or the equally debilitating pervasive private discrimination fostered by our long history of official discrimination, cf. Reitman v. Mulkey, (1967), and yet come to the starting line with an education equal to whites.

Moreover, we need not rest solely on our own conclusion that Davis had sound reason to believe that the effects of past discrimination were handicapping minority applicants to the Medical School, because the Department of Health, Education, and Welfare, the expert agency charged by Congress with promulgating regulations enforcing Title VI of the Civil Rights Act of 1964, see supra, at 341-343, has also reached the conclusion that race may be taken into account in situations where a failure to do so would limit participation by minorities in federally funded programs, and regulations promulgated by the Department expressly contemplate that appropriate race-conscious programs may be adopted by universities to remedy unequal access to university programs caused by their own or by past societal discrimination. See supra, at 344-345, discussing 45 CFR 80.3 (b) (6) (ii) and 80.5 (j) (1977). It cannot be questioned that, in the absence of the special admissions program, access of minority students to the Medical School would be severely limited and, accordingly, race-conscious admissions would be deemed an appropriate response under these federal regulations. Moreover, the Department's regulatory policy is not one that has gone unnoticed by Congress. See supra, at 346-347. Indeed, although an amendment to an appropriations bill was introduced just last year that would have prevented the Secretary of Health, Education, and Welfare from mandating race-conscious programs in university admissions, proponents of this measure, significantly, did not question the validity of voluntary implementation of race-conscious admissions criteria. See ibid. In these circumstances, the conclusion implicit in the regulations—that the lingering effects of past discrimination continue to make race-conscious remedial programs appropriate means for ensuring equal educational opportunity in universities—deserves considerable judicial deference. See, e. g., Katzenbach v. Morgan, (1966); UJO, (opinion concurring in part).

C

The second prong of our test—whether the Davis program stigmatizes any discrete group or individual and whether race is reasonably used in light of the program's objectives—is clearly satisfied by the Davis program.

It is not even claimed that Davis' program in any way operates to stigmatize or single out any discrete and insular, or even any identifiable, nonminority group. Nor will harm comparable to that imposed upon racial minorities by exclusion or separation on grounds of race be the likely result of the program. It does not, for example, establish an exclusive preserve for minority students apart from and exclusive of whites. Rather, its purpose is to overcome the effects of segregation by bringing the races together. True, whites are excluded from participation in the special admissions program, but this fact only operates to reduce the number of whites to be admitted in the regular admissions program in order to permit admission of a reasonable percentage—less than their proportion of the California population—of otherwise underrepresented qualified minority applicants.

Nor was Bakke in any sense stamped as inferior by the Medical School's rejection of him. Indeed, it is conceded by all that he satisfied those criteria regarded by the school as generally relevant to academic performance better than most of the minority members who were admitted. Moreover, there is absolutely no basis for concluding that Bakke's rejection as a result of Davis' use of racial preference will affect him throughout his life in the same way as the segregation of the Negro school children in Brown I would have affected them. Unlike discrimination against racial minorities, the use of racial preferences for remedial purposes does not inflict a pervasive injury upon individual whites in the sense that wherever they go or whatever they do there is a significant likelihood that they will be treated as second-class citizens because of their color. This distinction does not mean that the exclusion of a white resulting from the preferential use of race is not sufficiently serious to require justification; but it does mean that the injury inflicted by such a policy is not distinguishable from disadvantages caused by a wide range of government actions, none of which has ever been thought impermissible for that reason alone.

In addition, there is simply no evidence that the Davis program discriminates intentionally or unintentionally against any minority group which it purports to benefit. The program does not establish a quota in the invidious sense of a ceiling on the number of minority applicants to be admitted. Nor can the program reasonably be regarded as stigmatizing the program's beneficiaries or their race as inferior. The Davis program does not simply advance less qualified applicants; rather, it compensates applicants, who it is uncontested are fully qualified to study medicine, for educational disadvantages which it was reasonable to conclude were a product of state-fostered discrimination. Once admitted, these students must satisfy the same degree requirements as regularly admitted students; they are taught by the same faculty in the same classes; and their performance is evaluated by the same standards by which regularly admitted students are judged. Under these circumstances, their performance and degrees must be regarded equally with the regularly admitted students with whom they compete for standing. Since minority graduates cannot justifiably be regarded as less well qualified than nonminority graduates by virtue of the special admissions program, there is no reasonable basis to conclude that minority graduates at schools using such programs would be stigmatized as inferior by the existence of such programs.

D

We disagree with the lower courts' conclusion that the Davis program's use of race was unreasonable in light of its objectives. First, as petitioner argues, there are no practical means by which it could achieve its ends in the foreseeable future without the use of race-conscious measures. With respect to any factor (such as poverty or family educational background) that may be used as a substitute for race as an indicator of past discrimination, whites greatly outnumber racial minorities simply because whites make up a far larger percentage of the total population and therefore far outnumber minorities in absolute terms at every socio-economic level. For example, of a class of recent medical school applicants from families with less than $10,000 income, at least 71% were white. Of all 1970 families headed by a person not a high school graduate which included related children under 18, 80% were white and 20% were racial minorities. Moreover, while race is positively correlated with differences in GPA and MCAT scores, economic disadvantage is not. Thus, it appears that economically disadvantaged whites do not score less well than economically advantaged whites, while economically advantaged blacks score less well than do disadvantaged whites. These statistics graphically illustrate that the University's purpose to integrate its classes by compensating for past discrimination could not be achieved by a general preference for the economically disadvantaged or the children of parents of limited education unless such groups were to make up the entire class.

Second, the Davis admissions program does not simply equate minority status with disadvantage. Rather, Davis considers on an individual basis each applicant's personal history to determine whether he or she has likely been disadvantaged by racial discrimination. The record makes clear that only minority applicants likely to have been isolated from the mainstream of American life are considered in the special program; other minority applicants are eligible only through the regular admissions program. True, the procedure by which disadvantage is detected is informal, but we have never insisted that educators conduct their affairs through adjudicatory proceedings, and such insistence here is misplaced. A case-by-case inquiry into the extent to which each individual applicant has been affected, either directly or indirectly, by racial discrimination, would seem to be, as a practical matter, virtually impossible, despite the fact that there are excellent reasons for concluding that such effects generally exist. When individual measurement is impossible or extremely impractical, there is nothing to prevent a State from using categorical means to achieve its ends, at least where the category is closely related to the goal. Cf. Gaston County v. United States, (1969); Katzenbach v. Morgan, (1966). And it is clear from our cases that specific proof that a person has been victimized by discrimination is not a necessary predicate to offering him relief where the probability of victimization is great. See Teamsters v. United States, (1977).

E

Finally, Davis' special admissions program cannot be said to violate the Constitution simply because it has set aside a predetermined number of places for qualified minority applicants rather than using minority status as a positive factor to be considered in evaluating the applications of disadvantaged minority applicants. For purposes of constitutional adjudication, there is no difference between the two approaches. In any admissions program which accords special consideration to disadvantaged racial minorities, a determination of the degree of preference to be given is unavoidable, and any given preference that results in the exclusion of a white candidate is no more or less constitutionally acceptable than a program such as that at Davis. Furthermore, the extent of the preference inevitably depends on how many minority applicants the particular school is seeking to admit in any particular year so long as the number of qualified minority applicants exceeds that number. There is no sensible, and certainly no constitutional, distinction between, for example, adding a set number of points to the admissions rating of disadvantaged minority applicants as an expression of the preference with the expectation that this will result in the admission of an approximately determined number of qualified minority applicants and setting a fixed number of places for such applicants as was done here.

The "Harvard" program, see ante, at 316-318, as those employing it readily concede, openly and successfully employs a racial criterion for the purpose of ensuring that some of the scarce places in institutions of higher education are allocated to disadvantaged minority students. That the Harvard approach does not also make public the extent of the preference and the precise workings of the system while the Davis program employs a specific, openly stated number, does not condemn the latter plan for purposes of Fourteenth Amendment adjudication. It may be that the Harvard plan is more acceptable to the public than is the Davis "quota." If it is, any State, including California, is free to adopt it in preference to a less acceptable alternative, just as it is generally free, as far as the Constitution is concerned, to abjure granting any racial preferences in its admissions program. But there is no basis for preferring a particular preference program simply because in achieving the same goals that the Davis Medical School is pursuing, it proceeds in a manner that is not immediately apparent to the public.

V

Accordingly, we would reverse the judgment of the Supreme Court of California holding the Medical School's special admissions program unconstitutional and directing respondent's admission, as well as that portion of the judgment enjoining the Medical School from according any consideration to race in the admissions process.

MR. JUSTICE WHITE.

I write separately concerning the question of whether Title VI of the Civil Rights Act of 1964, 42 U.S.C. 2000d et seq., provides for a private cause of action. Four Justices are apparently of the view that such a private cause of action exists, and four Justices assume it for purposes of this case. I am unwilling merely to assume an affirmative answer. If in fact no private cause of action exists, this Court and the lower Courts as well are without jurisdiction to consider respondent's Title VI claim. As I see it, if we are not obliged to do so, it is at least advisable to address this threshold jurisdictional issue. See United States v. Griffin, (1938). Furthermore, just as it is inappropriate to address constitutional issues without determining whether statutory grounds urged before us are dispositive, it is at least questionable practice to adjudicate a novel and difficult statutory issue without first considering whether we have jurisdiction to decide it. Consequently, I address the question of whether respondent may bring suit under Title VI.

A private cause of action under Title VI, in terms both of the Civil Rights Act as a whole and that Title, would not be "consistent with the underlying purposes of the legislative scheme" and would be contrary to the legislative intent. Cort v. Ash, (1975). Title II, 42 U.S.C. 2000a et seq., dealing with public accommodations, and Title VII, 42 U.S.C. 2000e et seq. (1970 ed. and Supp. V), dealing with employment, proscribe private discriminatory conduct that as of 1964 neither the Constitution nor other federal statutes had been construed to forbid. Both Titles carefully provided for private actions as well as for official participation in enforcement. Title III, 42 U.S.C. 2000b et seq., and Title IV, 42 U.S.C. 2000c et seq. (1970 ed. and Supp. V), dealing with public facilities and public education, respectively, authorize suits by the Attorney General to eliminate racial discrimination in these areas. Because suits to end discrimination in public facilities and public education were already available under 42 U.S.C. 1983, it was, of course, unnecessary to provide for private actions under Titles III and IV. But each Title carefully provided that its provisions for public actions would not adversely affect pre-existing private remedies. 2000b-2 and 2000c-8.

The role of Title VI was to terminate federal financial support for public and private institutions or programs that discriminated on the basis of race. Section 601, 42 U.S.C. 2000d, imposed the proscription that no person, on the grounds of race, color, or national origin, was to be excluded from or discriminated against under any program or activity receiving federal financial assistance. But there is no express provision for private actions to enforce Title VI, and it would be quite incredible if Congress, after so carefully attending to the matter of private actions in other Titles of the Act, intended silently to create a private cause of action to enforce Title VI.

It is also evident from the face of 602, 42 U.S.C. 2000d-1, that Congress intended the departments and agencies to define and to refine, by rule or regulation, the general proscription of 601, subject only to judicial review of agency action in accordance with established procedures. Section 602 provides for enforcement: Every federal department or agency furnishing financial support is to implement the proscription by appropriate rule or regulation, each of which requires approval by the President. Termination of funding as a sanction for noncompliance is authorized, but only after a hearing and after the failure of voluntary means to secure compliance. Moreover, termination may not take place until the department or agency involved files with the appropriate committees of the House and Senate a full written report of the circumstances and the grounds for such action and 30 days have elapsed thereafter. Judicial review was provided, at least for actions terminating financial assistance.

Termination of funding was regarded by Congress as a serious enforcement step, and the legislative history is replete with assurances that it would not occur until every possibility for conciliation had been exhausted. To allow a private individual to sue to cut off funds under Title VI would compromise these assurances and short circuit the procedural preconditions provided in Title VI. If the Federal Government may not cut off funds except pursuant to an agency rule, approved by the President, and presented to the appropriate committee of Congress for a layover period, and after voluntary means to achieve compliance have failed, it is inconceivable that Congress intended to permit individuals to circumvent these administrative prerequisites themselves.

Furthermore, although Congress intended Title VI to end federal financial support for racially discriminatory policies of not only public but also private institutions and programs, it is extremely unlikely that Congress, without a word indicating that it intended to do so, contemplated creating an independent, private statutory cause of action against all private as well as public agencies that might be in violation of the section. There is no doubt that Congress regarded private litigation as an important tool to attack discriminatory practices. It does not at all follow, however, that Congress anticipated new private actions under Title VI itself. Wherever a discriminatory program was a public undertaking, such as a public school, private remedies were already available under other statutes, and a private remedy under Title VI was unnecessary. Congress was well aware of this fact. Significantly, there was frequent reference to Simkins v. Moses H. Cone Memorial Hospital, 323 F.2d 959 (CA4 1963), cert. denied, (1964), throughout the congressional deliberations. See, e. g., 110 Cong. Rec. 6544 (1964) (Sen. Humphrey). Simkins held that under appropriate circumstances, the operation of a private hospital with "massive use of public funds and extensive state-federal sharing in the common plan" constituted "state action" for the purposes of the Fourteenth Amendment. 323

F.2d, at 967. It was unnecessary, of course, to create a Title VI private action against private discriminators where they were already within the reach of existing private remedies. But when they were not—and Simkins carefully disclaimed holding that "every subvention by the federal or state government automatically involves the beneficiary in 'state action,'" ibid.—it is difficult to believe that Congress silently created a private remedy to terminate conduct that previously had been entirely beyond the reach of federal law.

For those who believe, contrary to my views, that Title VI was intended to create a stricter standard of color blindness than the Constitution itself requires, the result of no private cause of action follows even more readily. In that case Congress must be seen to have banned degrees of discrimination, as well as types of discriminators, not previously reached by law. A Congress careful enough to provide that existing private causes of action would be preserved (in Titles III and IV) would not leave for inference a vast new extension of private enforcement power. And a Congress so exceptionally concerned with the satisfaction of procedural preliminaries before confronting fund recipients with the choice of a cutoff or of stopping discriminating would not permit private parties to pose precisely that same dilemma in a greatly widened category of cases with no procedural requirements whatsoever.

Significantly, in at least three instances legislators who played a major role in the passage of Title VI explicitly stated that a private right of action under Title VI does not exist. As an "indication of legislative intent, explicit or implicit, either to create such a remedy or to deny one," Cort v. Ash, clearer statements cannot be imagined, and under Cort, "an explicit purpose to deny such cause of action [is] controlling." Id., at 82. Senator Keating, for example, proposed a private "right to sue" for the "person suffering from discrimination"; but the Department of Justice refused to include it, and the Senator acquiesced. These are not neutral, ambiguous statements. They indicate the absence of a legislative intent to create a private remedy. Nor do any of these statements make nice distinctions between a private cause of action to enjoin discrimination and one to cut off funds, as MR. JUSTICE STEVENS and the three Justices who join his opinion apparently would. See post, at 419-420, n. 26. Indeed, it would be odd if they did, since the practical effect of either type of private cause of action would be identical. If private suits to enjoin conduct allegedly violative of 601 were permitted, recipients of federal funds would be presented with the choice of either ending what the court, rather than the agency, determined to be a discriminatory practice within the meaning of Title VI or refusing federal funds and thereby escaping from the statute's jurisdictional predicate. This is precisely the same choice as would confront recipients if suit were brought to cut off funds. Both types of actions would equally jeopardize the administrative processes so carefully structured into the law.

This Court has always required "that the inference of such a private cause of action not otherwise authorized by the statute must be consistent with the evident legislative intent and, of course, with the effectuation of the purposes intended to be served by the Act." National Railroad Passenger Corp. v. National Association of Railroad Passengers, (1974). See also Securities Investor Protection Corp. v. Barbour, (1975). A private cause of action under Title VI is unable to satisfy either prong of this test.

Because each of my colleagues either has a different view or assumes a private cause of action, however, the merits of the Title VI issue must be addressed. My views in that regard, as well as my views with respect to the equal protection issue, are included in the joint opinion that my Brothers BRENNAN, MARSHALL, and BLACKMUN and I have filed.

MR. JUSTICE MARSHALL.

I agree with the judgment of the Court only insofar as it permits a university to consider the race of an applicant in making admissions decisions. I do not agree that petitioner's admissions program violates the Constitution. For it must be remembered that, during most of the past 200 years, the Constitution as interpreted by this Court did not prohibit the most ingenious and pervasive forms of discrimination against the Negro. Now, when a state acts to remedy the effects of that legacy of discrimination, I cannot believe that this same Constitution stands as a barrier.

I

A

Three hundred and fifty years ago, the Negro was dragged to this country in chains to be sold into slavery. Uprooted from his homeland and thrust into bondage for forced labor, the slave was deprived of all legal rights. It was unlawful to teach him to read; he could be sold away from his family and friends at the whim of his master; and killing or maiming him was not a crime. The system of slavery brutalized and dehumanized both master and slave.

The denial of human rights was etched into the American Colonies' first attempts at establishing self-government. When the colonists determined to seek their independence from England, they drafted a unique document cataloguing their grievances against the King and proclaiming as "self-evident" that "all men are created equal" and are endowed "with certain unalienable Rights," including those to "Life, Liberty and the pursuit of Happiness." The self-evident truths and the unalienable rights were intended, however, to apply only to white men. An earlier draft of the Declaration of Independence, submitted by Thomas Jefferson to the Continental Congress, had included among the charges against the King that

> "[h]e has waged cruel war against human nature itself, violating its most sacred rights of life and liberty in the persons of a distant people who never offended him, captivating and carrying them into slavery in another hemisphere, or to incur miserable death in their transportation thither." Franklin 88.

The Southern delegation insisted that the charge be deleted; the colonists themselves were implicated in the slave trade, and inclusion of this claim might have made it more difficult to justify the continuation of slavery once the ties to England were severed. Thus, even as the colonists embarked on a course to secure their own freedom and equality, they ensured perpetuation of the system that deprived a whole race of those rights.

The implicit protection of slavery embodied in the Declaration of Independence was made explicit in the Constitution, which treated a slave as being equivalent to three-fifths of a person for purposes of apportioning representatives and taxes among the States. Art. I, 2. The Constitution also contained a clause ensuring that the "Migration or Importation" of slaves into the existing States would be legal until at least 1808, Art. I, 9, and a fugitive slave clause requiring that when a slave escaped to another State, he must be returned on the claim of the master, Art. IV, 2. In their declaration of the principles that were to provide the cornerstone of the new Nation, therefore, the Framers made it plain that "we the people," for whose protection the Constitution was designed, did not include those whose skins were the wrong color. As Professor John Hope Franklin has observed, Americans "proudly accepted the challenge and responsibility of their new political freedom by establishing the machinery and safeguards that insured the continued enslavement of blacks." Franklin 100.

The individual States likewise established the machinery to protect the system of slavery through the promulgation of the Slave Codes, which were designed primarily to defend the property interest of the owner in his slave. The position of the Negro slave as mere property was confirmed by this Court in Dred Scott v. Sandford, 19 How. 393 (1857), holding that the Missouri Compromise —which prohibited slavery in the portion of the Louisiana Purchase Territory north of Missouri—was unconstitutional because it deprived slave owners of their property without due process. The Court declared that under the Constitution a slave was property, and "[t]he right to traffic in it, like an ordinary article of merchandise and property, was guarantied to the citizens of the United States . . . ." Id., at 451. The Court further concluded that Negroes were not intended to be included as citizens under the Constitution but were "regarded as beings of an inferior order . . . altogether unfit to associate with the white race, either in social or political relations; and so far inferior, that they had no rights which the white man was bound to respect . . . ." Id., at 407.

B

The status of the Negro as property was officially erased by his emancipation at the end of the Civil War. But the long-awaited emancipation, while freeing the Negro from slavery, did not bring him citizenship or equality in any meaningful way. Slavery was replaced by a system of "laws which imposed upon the colored race onerous disabilities and burdens, and curtailed their rights in the pursuit of life, liberty, and property to such an extent that their freedom was of little value." Slaughter-House Cases, 16 Wall. 36, 70 (1873). Despite the passage of the Thirteenth, Fourteenth, and Fifteenth Amendments, the Negro was systematically denied the rights those Amendments were supposed to secure. The combined actions and inactions of the State and Federal Governments maintained Negroes in a position of legal inferiority for another century after the Civil War.

The Southern States took the first steps to re-enslave the Negroes. Immediately following the end of the Civil War, many of the provisional legislatures passed Black Codes, similar to the Slave Codes, which, among other things, limited the rights of Negroes to own or rent property and permitted imprisonment for breach of employment contracts. Over the next several decades, the South managed to disenfranchise the Negroes in spite of the Fifteenth Amendment by various techniques, including poll taxes, deliberately complicated balloting processes, property and literacy qualifications, and finally the white primary.

Congress responded to the legal disabilities being imposed in the Southern States by passing the Reconstruction Acts and the Civil Rights Acts. Congress also responded to the needs of the Negroes at the end of the Civil War by establishing the Bureau of Refugees, Freedmen, and Abandoned Lands, better known as the Freedmen's Bureau, to supply food, hospitals, land, and education to the newly freed slaves. Thus, for a time it seemed as if the Negro might be protected from the continued denial of his civil rights and might be relieved of the disabilities that prevented him from taking his place as a free and equal citizen.

That time, however, was short-lived. Reconstruction came to a close, and, with the assistance of this Court, the Negro was rapidly stripped of his new civil rights. In the words of C. Vann Woodward: "By narrow and ingenious interpretation [the Supreme Court's] decisions over a period of years had whittled away a great part of the authority presumably given the government for protection of civil rights." Woodward 139.

The Court began by interpreting the Civil War Amendments in a manner that sharply curtailed their substantive protections. See, e. g., Slaughter-House Cases, supra; United States v. Reese, (1876); United States v. Cruikshank, (1876). Then in the notorious Civil Rights Cases, (1883), the Court strangled Congress' efforts to use its power to promote racial equality. In those cases the Court invalidated sections of the Civil Rights Act of 1875 that made it a crime to deny equal access to "inns, public conveyances, theaters and other places of public amusement." Id., at 10. According to the Court, the Fourteenth Amendment gave Congress the power to proscribe only discriminatory action by the State. The Court ruled that the Negroes who were excluded from public places suffered only an invasion of their social rights at the hands of private individuals, and Congress had no power to remedy that. Id., at 24-25. "When a man has emerged from slavery, and by the aid of beneficent legislation has shaken off the inseparable concomitants of that state," the Court concluded, "there must be some stage in the progress of his elevation when he takes the rank of a mere citizen, and ceases to be the special favorite of the laws . . . ." Id., at 25. As Mr. Justice Harlan noted in dissent, however, the Civil War Amendments and Civil Rights Acts did not make the Negroes the "special favorite" of the laws but instead "sought to accomplish in reference to that race . . . —what had already been done in every State of the Union for the white race—to secure and protect rights belonging to them as freemen and citizens; nothing more." Id., at 61.

The Court's ultimate blow to the Civil War Amendments and to the equality of Negroes came in Plessy v. Ferguson, (1896). In upholding a Louisiana law that required railway companies to provide "equal but separate" accommodations for whites and Negroes, the Court held that the Fourteenth Amendment was not intended "to abolish distinctions based upon color, or to enforce social, as distinguished from political equality, or a commingling of the two races upon terms unsatisfactory to either." Id., at 544. Ignoring totally the realities of the positions of the two races, the Court remarked:

> "We consider the underlying fallacy of the plaintiff's argument to consist in the assumption that the enforced separation of the two races stamps the colored race with a badge of inferiority. If this be so, it is not by reason of anything found in the act, but solely because the colored race chooses to put that construction upon it." Id., at 551.

Mr. Justice Harlan's dissenting opinion recognized the bankruptcy of the Court's reasoning. He noted that the "real meaning" of the legislation was "that colored citizens are so inferior and degraded that they cannot be allowed to sit in public coaches occupied by white citizens." Id., at 560. He expressed his fear that if like laws were enacted in other States, "the effect would be in the highest degree mischievous." Id., at 563. Although slavery would have disappeared, the States would retain the power "to interfere with the full enjoyment of the blessings of freedom; to regulate civil rights, common to all citizens, upon the basis of race; and to place in a condition of legal inferiority a large body of American citizens . . . ." Ibid.

The fears of Mr. Justice Harlan were soon to be realized. In the wake of Plessy, many States expanded their Jim Crow laws, which had up until that time been limited primarily to passenger trains and schools. The segregation of the races was extended to residential areas, parks, hospitals, theaters, waiting rooms, and bathrooms. There were even statutes and ordinances which authorized separate phone booths for Negroes and whites, which required that textbooks used by children of one race be kept separate from those used by the other, and which required that Negro and white prostitutes be kept in separate districts. In 1898, after Plessy, the Charlestown News and Courier printed a parody of Jim Crow laws:

> "'If there must be Jim Crow cars on the railroads, there should be Jim Crow cars on the street railways. Also on all passenger boats. . . . If there are to be Jim Crow cars, moreover, there should be Jim Crow waiting saloons at all stations, and Jim Crow eating houses. . . . There should be Jim Crow sections of the jury box, and a separate Jim Crow dock and witness stand in every court—and a Jim Crow Bible for colored witnesses to kiss.'" Woodward 68.

The irony is that before many years had passed, with the exception of the Jim Crow witness stand, "all the improbable applications of the principle suggested by the editor in derision had been put into practice—down to and including the Jim Crow Bible." Id., at 69.

Nor were the laws restricting the rights of Negroes limited solely to the Southern States. In many of the Northern States, the Negro was denied the right to vote, prevented from serving on juries, and excluded from theaters, restaurants, hotels, and inns. Under President Wilson, the Federal Government began to require segregation in Government buildings; desks of Negro employees were curtained off; separate bathrooms and separate tables in the cafeterias were provided; and even the galleries of the Congress were segregated. When his segregationist policies were attacked, President Wilson responded that segregation was "'not humiliating but a benefit'" and that he was "'rendering [the Negroes] more safe in their possession of office and less likely to be discriminated against.'" Kluger 91.

The enforced segregation of the races continued into the middle of the 20th century. In both World Wars, Negroes were for the most part confined to separate military units; it was not until 1948 that an end to segregation in the military was ordered by President Truman. And the history of the exclusion of Negro children from white public schools is too well known and recent to require repeating here. That Negroes were deliberately excluded from public graduate and professional schools—and thereby denied the opportunity to become doctors, lawyers, engineers, and the like—is also well established. It is of course true that some of the Jim Crow laws (which the decisions of this Court had helped to foster) were struck down by this Court in a series of decisions leading up to Brown v. Board of Education, (1954). See, e. g., Morgan v. Virginia, (1946); Sweatt v. Painter, (1950); McLaurin v. Oklahoma State Regents, (1950). Those decisions, however, did not automatically end segregation, nor did they move Negroes from a position of legal inferiority to one of equality. The legacy of years of slavery and of years of second-class citizenship in the wake of emancipation could not be so easily eliminated.

II

The position of the Negro today in America is the tragic but inevitable consequence of centuries of unequal treatment. Measured by any benchmark of comfort or achievement, meaningful equality remains a distant dream for the Negro.

A Negro child today has a life expectancy which is shorter by more than five years than that of a white child. The Negro child's mother is over three times more likely to die of complications in childbirth, and the infant mortality rate for Negroes is nearly twice that for whites. The median income of the Negro family is only 60% that of the median of a white family, and the percentage of Negroes who live in families with incomes below the poverty line is nearly four times greater than that of whites.

When the Negro child reaches working age, he finds that America offers him significantly less than it offers his white counterpart. For Negro adults, the unemployment rate is twice that of whites, and the unemployment rate for Negro teenagers is nearly three times that of white teenagers. A Negro male who completes four years of college can expect a median annual income of merely $110 more than a white male who has only a high school diploma. Although Negroes represent 11.5% of the population, they are only 1.2% of the lawyers and judges, 2% of the physicians, 2.3% of the dentists, 1.1% of the engineers and 2.6% of the college and university professors.

The relationship between those figures and the history of unequal treatment afforded to the Negro cannot be denied. At every point from birth to death the impact of the past is reflected in the still disfavored position of the Negro.

In light of the sorry history of discrimination and its devastating impact on the lives of Negroes, bringing the Negro into the mainstream of American life should be a state interest of the highest order. To fail to do so is to ensure that America will forever remain a divided society.

III

I do not believe that the Fourteenth Amendment requires us to accept that fate. Neither its history nor our past cases lend any support to the conclusion that a university may not remedy the cumulative effects of society's discrimination by giving consideration to race in an effort to increase the number and percentage of Negro doctors.

A

This Court long ago remarked that

> "in any fair and just construction of any section or phrase of these [Civil War] amendments, it is necessary to look to the purpose which we have said was the pervading spirit of them all, the evil which they were designed to remedy . . . ." Slaughter-House Cases, 16 Wall., at 72.

It is plain that the Fourteenth Amendment was not intended to prohibit measures designed to remedy the effects of the Nation's past treatment of Negroes. The Congress that passed the Fourteenth Amendment is the same Congress that passed the 1866 Freedmen's Bureau Act, an Act that provided many of its benefits only to Negroes. Act of July 16, 1866, ch. 200, 14 Stat. 173; see supra, at 391. Although the Freedmen's Bureau legislation provided aid for refugees, thereby including white persons within some of the relief measures, 14 Stat. 174; see also Act of Mar. 3, 1865, ch. 90, 13 Stat. 507, the bill was regarded, to the dismay of many Congressmen, as "solely and entirely for the freedmen, and to the exclusion of all other persons. . . ." Cong. Globe, 39th Cong., 1st Sess., 544 (1866) (remarks of Rep. Taylor). See also id., at 634-635 (remarks of Rep. Ritter); id., at App. 78, 80-81 (remarks of Rep. Chanler). Indeed, the bill was bitterly opposed on the ground that it "undertakes to make the negro in some respects . . . superior . . . and gives them favors that the poor white boy in the North cannot get." Id., at 401 (remarks of Sen. McDougall). See also id., at 319 (remarks of Sen. Hendricks); id., at 362 (remarks of Sen. Saulsbury); id., at 397 (remarks of Sen. Willey); id., at 544 (remarks of Rep. Taylor). The bill's supporters defended it—not by rebutting the claim of special treatment—but by pointing to the need for such treatment:

> "The very discrimination it makes between 'destitute and suffering' negroes, and destitute and suffering white paupers, proceeds upon the distinction that, in the omitted case, civil rights and immunities are already sufficiently protected by the possession of political power, the absence of which in the case provided for necessitates governmental protection." Id., at App. 75 (remarks of Rep. Phelps).

Despite the objection to the special treatment the bill would provide for Negroes, it was passed by Congress. Id., at 421, 688. President Johnson vetoed this bill and also a subsequent bill that contained some modifications; one of his principal objections to both bills was that they gave special benefits to Negroes. 8 Messages and Papers of the Presidents 3596, 3599, 3620, 3623 (1897). Rejecting the concerns of the President and the bill's opponents, Congress overrode the President's second veto. Cong. Globe, 39th Cong., 1st Sess., 3842, 3850 (1866).

Since the Congress that considered and rejected the objections to the 1866 Freedmen's Bureau Act concerning special relief to Negroes also proposed the Fourteenth Amendment, it is inconceivable that the Fourteenth Amendment was intended to prohibit all race-conscious relief measures. It "would be a distortion of the policy manifested in that amendment, which was adopted to prevent state legislation designed to perpetuate discrimination on the basis of race or color," Railway Mail Assn. v. Corsi, (1945), to hold that it barred state action to remedy the effects of that discrimination. Such a result would pervert the intent of the Framers by substituting abstract equality for the genuine equality the Amendment was intended to achieve.

B

As has been demonstrated in our joint opinion, this Court's past cases establish the constitutionality of race-conscious remedial measures. Beginning with the school desegregation cases, we recognized that even absent a judicial or legislative finding of constitutional violation, a school board constitutionally could consider the race of students in making school-assignment decisions. See Swann v. Charlotte-Mecklenburg Board of Education, (1971); McDaniel v. Barresi, (1971). We noted, moreover, that a

> "flat prohibition against assignment of students for the purpose of creating a racial balance must inevitably conflict with the duty of school authorities to disestablish dual school systems. As we have held in Swann, the Constitution does not compel any particular degree of racial balance or mixing, but when past and continuing constitutional violations are found, some ratios are likely to be useful as starting points in shaping a remedy. An absolute prohibition against use of such a device—even as a starting point—contravenes the implicit command of Green v. Country School

> Board, (1968), that all reasonable methods be available to formulate an effective remedy." Board of Education v. Swann, (1971).

As we have observed, "[a]ny other approach would freeze the status quo that is the very target of all desegregation processes." McDaniel v. Barresi, supra, at 41.

Only last Term, in United Jewish Organizations v. Carey, (1977), we upheld a New York reapportionment plan that was deliberately drawn on the basis of race to enhance the electoral power of Negroes and Puerto Ricans; the plan had the effect of diluting the electoral strength of the Hasidic Jewish community. We were willing in UJO to sanction the remedial use of a racial classification even though it disadvantaged otherwise "innocent" individuals. In another case last Term, Califano v. Webster, (1977), the Court upheld a provision in the Social Security laws that discriminated against men because its purpose was "'the permissible one of redressing our society's longstanding disparate treatment of women.'" Id., at 317, quoting Califano v. Goldfarb, n. 8 (1977) (plurality opinion). We thus recognized the permissibility of remedying past societal discrimination through the use of otherwise disfavored classifications.

Nothing in those cases suggests that a university cannot similarly act to remedy past discrimination. It is true that in both UJO and Webster the use of the disfavored classification was predicated on legislative or administrative action, but in neither case had those bodies made findings that there had been constitutional violations or that the specific individuals to be benefited had actually been the victims of discrimination. Rather, the classification in each of those cases was based on a determination that the group was in need of the remedy because of some type of past discrimination. There is thus ample support for the conclusion that a university can employ race-conscious measures to remedy past societal discrimination, without the need for a finding that those benefited were actually victims of that discrimination.

IV

While I applaud the judgment of the Court that a university may consider race in its admissions process, it is more than a little ironic that, after several hundred years of class-based discrimination against Negroes, the Court is unwilling to hold that a class-based remedy for that discrimination is permissible. In declining to so hold, today's judgment ignores the fact that for several hundred years Negroes have been discriminated against, not as individuals, but rather solely because of the color of their skins. It is unnecessary in 20th-century America to have individual Negroes demonstrate that they have been victims of racial discrimination; the racism of our society has been so pervasive that none, regardless of wealth or position, has managed to escape its impact. The experience of Negroes in America has been different in kind, not just in degree, from that of other ethnic groups. It is not merely the history of slavery alone but also that a whole people were marked as inferior by the law. And that mark has endured. The dream of America as the great melting pot has not been realized for the Negro; because of his skin color he never even made it into the pot.

These differences in the experience of the Negro make it difficult for me to accept that Negroes cannot be afforded greater protection under the Fourteenth Amendment where it is necessary to remedy the effects of past discrimination. In the Civil Rights Cases, supra, the Court wrote that the Negro emerging from slavery must cease "to be the special favorite of the laws." See supra, at 392. We cannot in light of the history of the last century yield to that view. Had the Court in that decision and others been willing to "do for human liberty and the fundamental rights of American citizenship, what it did . . . for the protection of slavery and the rights of the masters of fugitive slaves," (Harlan, J., dissenting), we would not need now to permit the recognition of any "special wards."

Most importantly, had the Court been willing in 1896, in Plessy v. Ferguson, to hold that the Equal Protection Clause forbids differences in treatment based on race, we would not be faced with this dilemma in 1978. We must remember, however, that the principle that the

"Constitution is color-blind" appeared only in the opinion of the lone dissenter. The majority of the Court rejected the principle of color blindness, and for the next 60 years, from Plessy to Brown v. Board of Education, ours was a Nation where, by law, an individual could be given "special" treatment based on the color of his skin.

It is because of a legacy of unequal treatment that we now must permit the institutions of this society to give consideration to race in making decisions about who will hold the positions of influence, affluence, and prestige in America. For far too long, the doors to those positions have been shut to Negroes. If we are ever to become a fully integrated society, one in which the color of a person's skin will not determine the opportunities available to him or her, we must be willing to take steps to open those doors. I do not believe that anyone can truly look into America's past and still find that a remedy for the effects of that past is impermissible.

It has been said that this case involves only the individual, Bakke, and this University. I doubt, however, that there is a computer capable of determining the number of persons and institutions that may be affected by the decision in this case. For example, we are told by the Attorney General of the United States that at least 27 federal agencies have adopted regulations requiring recipients of federal funds to take "'affirmative action to overcome the effects of conditions which resulted in limiting participation . . . by persons of a particular race, color, or national origin.'" Supplemental Brief for United States as Amicus Curiae 16 (emphasis added). I cannot even guess the number of state and local governments that have set up affirmative-action programs, which may be affected by today's decision.

I fear that we have come full circle. After the Civil War our Government started several "affirmative action" programs. This Court in the Civil Rights Cases and Plessy v. Ferguson destroyed the movement toward complete equality. For almost a century no action was taken, and this nonaction was with the tacit approval of the courts. Then we had Brown v. Board of Education and the Civil Rights Acts of Congress, followed by numerous affirmative-action programs. Now, we have this Court again stepping in, this time to stop affirmative-action programs of the type used by the University of California.

MR. JUSTICE BLACKMUN.

I participate fully, of course, in the opinion, ante, p. 324, that bears the names of my Brothers BRENNAN, WHITE, MARSHALL, and myself. I add only some general observations that hold particular significance for me, and then a few comments on equal protection.

I

At least until the early 1970's, apparently only a very small number, less than 2%, of the physicians, attorneys, and medical and law students in the United States were members of what we now refer to as minority groups. In addition, approximately three-fourths of our Negro physicians were trained at only two medical schools. If ways are not found to remedy that situation, the country can never achieve its professed goal of a society that is not race conscious.

I yield to no one in my earnest hope that the time will come when an "affirmative action" program is unnecessary and is, in truth, only a relic of the past. I would hope that we could reach this stage within a decade at the most. But the story of Brown v. Board of Education, (1954), decided almost a quarter of a century ago, suggests that that hope is a slim one. At some time, however, beyond any period of what some would claim is only transitional inequality, the United States must and will reach a stage of maturity where action along this line is no longer necessary. Then persons will be regarded as persons, and discrimination of the type we address today will be an ugly feature of history that is instructive but that is behind us.

The number of qualified, indeed highly qualified, applicants for admission to existing medical schools in the United States far exceeds the number of places available. Wholly apart from racial and ethnic considerations, therefore, the selection process inevitably results in the denial of admission to many qualified persons, indeed, to far more than the number of those who are granted admission. Obviously, it is a denial to the deserving. This inescapable fact is brought into sharp focus here because Allan Bakke is not himself charged with discrimination and yet is the one who is disadvantaged, and because the Medical School of the University of California at Davis itself is not charged with historical discrimination.

One theoretical solution to the need for more minority members in higher education would be to enlarge our graduate schools. Then all who desired and were qualified could enter, and talk of discrimination would vanish. Unfortunately, this is neither feasible nor realistic. The vast resources that apparently would be required simply are not available. And the need for more professional graduates, in the strict numerical sense, perhaps has not been demonstrated at all.

There is no particular or real significance in the 84-16 division at Davis. The same theoretical, philosophical, social, legal, and constitutional considerations would necessarily apply to the case if Davis' special admissions program had focused on any lesser number, that is, on 12 or 8 or 4 places or, indeed, on only 1.

It is somewhat ironic to have us so deeply disturbed over a program where race is an element of consciousness, and yet to be aware of the fact, as we are, that institutions of higher learning, albeit more on the undergraduate than the graduate level, have given conceded preferences up to a point to those possessed of athletic skills, to the children of alumni, to the affluent who may bestow their largess on the institutions, and to those having connections with celebrities, the famous, and the powerful.

Programs of admission to institutions of higher learning are basically a responsibility for academicians and for administrators and the specialists they employ. The judiciary, in contrast, is ill-equipped and poorly trained for this. The administration and management of educational institutions are beyond the competence of judges and are within the special competence of educators, provided always that the educators perform within legal and constitutional bounds. For me, therefore, interference by the judiciary must be the rare exception and not the rule.

II

I, of course, accept the propositions that (a) Fourteenth Amendment rights are personal; (b) racial and ethnic distinctions where they are stereotypes are inherently suspect and call for exacting judicial scrutiny; (c) academic freedom is a special concern of the First Amendment; and (d) the Fourteenth Amendment has expanded beyond its original 1868 concept and now is recognized to have reached a point where, as MR. JUSTICE POWELL states, ante, at 293, quoting from the Court's opinion in McDonald v. Santa Fe Trail Transp. Co., (1976), it embraces a "broader principle."

This enlargement does not mean for me, however, that the Fourteenth Amendment has broken away from its moorings and its original intended purposes. Those original aims persist. And that, in a distinct sense, is what "affirmative action," in the face of proper facts, is all about. If this conflicts with idealistic equality, that tension is original Fourteenth Amendment tension, constitutionally conceived and constitutionally imposed, and it is part of the Amendment's very nature until complete equality is achieved in the area. In this sense, constitutional equal protection is a shield.

I emphasize in particular that the decided cases are not easily to be brushed aside. Many, of course, are not precisely on point, but neither are they off point. Racial factors have been given consideration in the school desegregation cases, in the employment cases, in Lau v. Nichols, (1974), and in United Jewish Organizations v. Carey, (1977). To be sure, some of these may be "distinguished" on the ground that victimization was directly present. But who is to say that victimization is not present for some members of today's minority groups, although it is of a lesser and perhaps different degree. The petitioners in United Jewish Organizations certainly complained bitterly of their reapportionment treatment, and I rather doubt that they regard the "remedy" there imposed as one that was "to improve" the group's ability to participate, as MR. JUSTICE POWELL describes it, ante, at 305. And surely in Lau v. Nichols we looked to ethnicity.

I am not convinced, as MR. JUSTICE POWELL seems to be, that the difference between the Davis program and the one employed by Harvard is very profound or constitutionally significant. The line between the two is a thin and indistinct one. In each, subjective application is at work. Because of my conviction that admission programs are primarily for the educators, I am willing to accept the representation that the Harvard program is one where good faith in its administration is practiced as well as professed. I agree that such a program, where race or ethnic background is only one of many factors, is a program better formulated than Davis' two-track system. The cynical, of course, may say that under a program such as Harvard's one may accomplish covertly what Davis concedes it does openly. I need not go that far, for despite its two-track aspect, the Davis program, for me, is within constitutional bounds, though perhaps barely so. It is surely free of stigma, and, as in United Jewish Organizations, I am not willing to infer a constitutional violation.

It is worth noting, perhaps, that governmental preference has not been a stranger to our legal life. We see it in veterans' preferences. We see it in the aid-to-the-handicapped programs. We see it in the progressive income tax. We see it in the Indian programs. We may excuse some of these on the ground that they have specific constitutional protection or, as with Indians, that those benefited are wards of the Government. Nevertheless, these preferences exist and may not be ignored. And in the admissions field, as I have indicated, educational institutions have always used geography, athletic ability, anticipated financial largess, alumni pressure, and other factors of that kind.

I add these only as additional components on the edges of the central question as to which I join my Brothers BRENNAN, WHITE, and MARSHALL in our more general approach. It is gratifying to know that the Court at least finds it constitutional for an academic institution to take race and ethnic background into consideration as one factor, among many, in the administration of its admissions program. I presume that that factor always has been there, though perhaps not conceded or even admitted. It is a fact of life, however, and a part of the real world of which we are all a part. The sooner we get down the road toward accepting and being a part of the real world, and not shutting it out and away from us, the sooner will these difficulties vanish from the scene.

I suspect that it would be impossible to arrange an affirmative-action program in a racially neutral way and have it successful. To ask that this be so is to demand the impossible. In order to get beyond racism, we must first take account of race. There is no other way. And in order to treat some persons equally, we must treat them differently. We cannot—we dare not—let the Equal Protection Clause perpetuate racial supremacy.

So the ultimate question, as it was at the beginning of this litigation, is: Among the qualified, how does one choose?

A long time ago, as time is measured for this Nation, a Chief Justice, both wise and farsighted, said:

> "In considering this question, then, we must never forget, that it is a constitution we are expounding." McCulloch v. Maryland, 4 Wheat. 316, 407 (1819) (emphasis in original).

In the same opinion, the Great Chief Justice further observed:

> "Let the end be legitimate, let it be within the scope of the constitution, and all means which are appropriate, which are plainly adapted to that end, which are not prohibit-

ed, but consist with the letter and spirit of the constitution, are constitutional." Id., at 421.

More recently, one destined to become a Justice of this Court observed:

"The great generalities of the constitution have a content and a significance that vary from age to age." B. Cardozo, The Nature of the Judicial Process 17 (1921).

And an educator who became a President of the United States said:

"But the Constitution of the United States is not a mere lawyers' document: it is a vehicle of life, and its spirit is always the spirit of the age." W. Wilson, Constitutional Government in the United States 69 (1911).

These percepts of breadth and flexibility and ever-present modernity are basic to our constitutional law. Today, again, we are expounding a Constitution. The same principles that governed McCulloch's case in 1819 govern Bakke's case in 1978. There can be no other answer.

MR. JUSTICE STEVENS, with whom THE CHIEF JUSTICE, MR. JUSTICE STEWART, and MR. JUSTICE REHNQUIST join, concurring in the judgment in part and dissenting in part.

It is always important at the outset to focus precisely on the controversy before the Court. It is particularly important to do so in this case because correct identification of the issues will determine whether it is necessary or appropriate to express any opinion about the legal status of any admissions program other than petitioner's.

I

This is not a class action. The controversy is between two specific litigants. Allan Bakke challenged petitioner's special admissions program, claiming that it denied him a place in medical school because of his race in violation of the Federal and California Constitutions and of Title VI of the Civil Rights Act of 1964, 42 U.S.C. 2000d et seq. The California Supreme Court upheld his challenge and ordered him admitted. If the state court was correct in its view that the University's special program was illegal, and that Bakke was therefore unlawfully excluded from the Medical School because of his race, we should affirm its judgment, regardless of our views about the legality of admissions programs that are not now before the Court.

The judgment as originally entered by the trial court contained four separate paragraphs, two of which are of critical importance. Paragraph 3 declared that the University's special admissions program violated the Fourteenth Amendment, the State Constitution, and Title VI. The trial court did not order the University to admit Bakke because it concluded that Bakke had not shown that he would have been admitted if there had been no special program. Instead, in paragraph 2 of its judgment it ordered the University to consider Bakke's application for admission without regard to his race or the race of any other applicant. The order did not include any broad prohibition against any use of race in the admissions process; its terms were clearly limited to the University's consideration of Bakke's application. Because the University has since been ordered to admit Bakke, paragraph 2 of the trial court's order no longer has any significance.

The California Supreme Court, in a holding that is not challenged, ruled that the trial court incorrectly placed the burden on Bakke of showing that he would have been admitted in the absence of discrimination. The University then conceded "that it [could] not meet the burden of proving that the special admissions program did not result in Mr. Bakke's failure to be admitted." Accordingly, the California Supreme Court directed the trial court to enter judgment ordering Bakke's admission. Since that order superseded paragraph 2 of the trial court's judgment, there is no outstanding injunction forbidding any consideration of racial criteria in processing applications.

It is therefore perfectly clear that the question whether race can ever be used as a factor in an admissions decision is not an issue in this case, and that discussion of that issue is inappropriate.

II

Both petitioner and respondent have asked us to determine the legality of the University's special admissions program by reference to the Constitution. Our settled practice, however, is to avoid the decision of a constitutional issue if a case can be fairly decided on a statutory ground. "If there is one doctrine more deeply rooted than any other in the process of constitutional adjudication, it is that we ought not to pass on questions of constitutionality . . . unless such adjudication is unavoidable." Spector Motor Co. v. McLaughlin, The more important the issue, the more force there is to this doctrine. In this case, we are presented with a constitutional question of undoubted and unusual importance. Since, however, a dispositive statutory claim was raised at the very inception of this case, and squarely decided in the portion of the trial court judgment affirmed by the California Supreme Court, it is our plain duty to confront it. Only if petitioner should prevail on the statutory issue would it be necessary to decide whether the University's admissions program violated the Equal Protection Clause of the Fourteenth Amendment.

III

Section 601 of the Civil Rights Act of 1964, 78 Stat. 252, 42 U.S.C. 2000d, provides:

> "No person in the United States shall, on the ground of race, color, or national origin, be excluded from participation in, be denied the benefits of, or be subjected to discrimination under any program or activity receiving Federal financial assistance."

The University, through its special admissions policy, excluded Bakke from participation in its program of medical education because of his race. The University also acknowledges that it was, and still is, receiving federal financial assistance. The plain language of the statute therefore requires affirmance of the judgment below. A different result cannot be justified unless that language misstates the actual intent of the Congress that enacted the statute or the statute is not enforceable in a private action. Neither conclusion is warranted.

Title VI is an integral part of the far-reaching Civil Rights Act of 1964. No doubt, when this legislation was being debated, Congress was not directly concerned with the legality of "reverse discrimination" or "affirmative action" programs. Its attention was focused on the problem at hand, the "glaring . . . discrimination against Negroes which exists throughout our Nation," and, with respect to Title VI, the federal funding of segregated facilities. The genesis of the legislation, however, did not limit the breadth of the solution adopted. Just as Congress responded to the problem of employment discrimination by enacting a provision that protects all races, see McDonald v. Santa Fe Trail Transp. Co., so, too, its answer to the problem of federally funding of segregated facilities stands as a broad prohibition against the exclusion of any individual from a federally funded program "on the ground of race." In the words of the House Report, Title VI stands for "the general principle that no person . . . be excluded from participation . . . on the ground of race, color, or national origin under any program or activity receiving Federal financial assistance." H. R. Rep. No. 914, 88th Cong., 1st Sess., pt. 1, p. 25 (1963) (emphasis added). This same broad view of Title VI and 601 was echoed throughout the congressional debate and was stressed by every one of the major spokesmen for the Act.

Petitioner contends, however, that exclusion of applicants on the basis of race does not violate Title VI if the exclusion carries with it no racial stigma. No such qualification or limitation of 601's categorical prohibition of "exclusion" is justified by the statute or its history. The language of the entire section is perfectly clear; the words that follow "excluded from" do not modify or qualify the explicit outlawing of any exclusion on the stated grounds.

The legislative history reinforces this reading. The only suggestion that 601 would allow exclusion of non minority applicants came from opponents of the legislation and then only by way of a discussion of the meaning of the word "discrimination." The opponents feared that the term "discrimination" would be read as mandating racial quotas and "racially balanced" colleges and universities, and they pressed for a specific definition of the term in order to avoid this possibility. In response, the proponents of the legislation gave repeated assurances that the Act would be "colorblind" in its application. Senator Humphrey, the Senate floor manager for the Act, expressed this position as follows:

> "[T]he word 'discrimination' has been used in many a court case. What it really means in the bill is a distinction in treatment . . . given to different individuals because of their different race, religion or national origin . . . .
>
> "The answer to this question [what was meant by 'discrimination'] is that if race is not a factor, we do not have to worry about discrimination because of race. . . . The Internal Revenue Code does not provide that colored people do not have to pay taxes, or that they can pay their taxes 6 months later than everyone else." 110 Cong. Rec. 5864 (1964).
>
> "[I]f we started to treat Americans as Americans, not as fat ones, thin ones, short ones, tall ones, brown ones, green ones, yellow ones, or white ones, but as Americans. If we did that we would not need to worry about discrimination." Id., at 5866.

In giving answers such as these, it seems clear that the proponents of Title VI assumed that the Constitution itself required a colorblind standard on the part of government, but that does not mean that the legislation only codifies an existing constitutional prohibition. The statutory prohibition against discrimination in federally funded projects contained in 601 is more than a simple paraphrasing of what the Fifth or Fourteenth Amendment would require. The Act's proponents plainly considered Title VI consistent with their view of the Constitution and they sought to provide an effective weapon to implement that view. As a distillation of what the supporters of the Act believed the Constitution demanded of State and Federal Governments, 601 has independent force, with language and emphasis in addition to that found in the Constitution.

As with other provisions of the Civil Rights Act, Congress' expression of its policy to end racial discrimination may independently proscribe conduct that the Constitution does not. However, we need not decide the Congruence—or lack of congruence—of the controlling statute and the Constitution since the meaning of the Title VI ban on exclusion is crystal clear: Race cannot be the basis of excluding anyone from participation in a federally funded program.

In short, nothing in the legislative history justifies the conclusion that the broad language of 601 should not be given its natural meaning. We are dealing with a distinct statutory prohibition, enacted at a particular time with particular concerns in mind; neither its language nor any prior interpretation suggests that its place in the Civil Rights Act, won after long debate, is simply that of a constitutional appendage. In unmistakable terms the Act prohibits the exclusion of individuals from federally funded programs because of their race. As succinctly phrased during the Senate debate, under Title VI it is not "permissible to say 'yes' to one person; but to say 'no' to another person, only because of the color of his skin."

Belatedly, however, petitioner argues that Title VI cannot be enforced by a private litigant. The claim is unpersuasive in the context of this case. Bakke requested injunctive and declaratory relief under Title VI; petitioner itself then joined issue on the question of the legality of its program under Title VI by asking for a declaratory judgment that it was in compliance with the statute. Its view during state-court litigation was that a private cause of action does exist under Title VI. Because petitioner questions the availability of a private cause of action for the first time in this Court, the question is not properly before us. See McGoldrick v. Compagnie Generale Transatlantique. Even if it were, petitioner's original assumption is in accord with the federal courts' consistent interpretation of the Act. To date, the courts, including this Court, have unanimously concluded or assumed that a private action may be maintained under Title VI. The United States has taken the same position; in its amicus curiae brief directed to this specific issue, it concluded that such a remedy is clearly available, and Congress has repeatedly enacted legislation predicated on the assumption that Title VI may be enforced in a private action. The conclusion that an individual may maintain a private cause of action is amply supported in the legislative history of Title VI itself. In short, a fair consideration of petitioner's tardy attack on the propriety of Bakke's suit under Title VI requires that it be rejected.

The University's special admissions program violated Title VI of the Civil Rights Act of 1964 by excluding Bakke from the Medical School because of his race. It is therefore our duty to affirm the judgment ordering Bakke admitted to the University.

Accordingly, I concur in the Court's judgment insofar as it affirms the judgment of the Supreme Court of California. To the extent that it purports to do anything else, I respectfully dissent.

REPORTS AND OTHER SOURCES

MY PEDAGOGIC CREED

BY JOHN DEWEY (1897)

ARTICLE ONE. WHAT EDUCATION IS

I believe that all education proceeds by the participation of the individual in the social consciousness of the race. This process begins unconsciously almost at birth, and is continually shaping the individual's powers, saturating his consciousness, forming his habits, training his ideas, and arousing his feelings and emotions. Through this unconscious education the individual gradually comes to share in the intellectual and moral resources which humanity has succeeded in getting together. He becomes an inheritor of the funded capital of civilization. The most formal and technical education in the world cannot safely depart from this general process. It can only organize it; or differentiate it in some particular direction.

I believe that the only true education comes through the stimulation of the child's powers by the demands of the social situations in which he finds himself. Through these demands he is stimulated to act as a member of a unity, to emerge from his original narrowness of action and feeling and to conceive of himself from the standpoint of the welfare of the group to which he belongs. Through the responses which others make to his own activities he comes to know what these mean in social terms. The value which they have is reflected back into them. For instance, through the response which is made to the child's instinctive babblings the child comes to know what those babblings mean; they are transformed into articulate language and thus the child is introduced into the consolidated wealth of ideas and emotions which are now summed up in language.

I believe that this educational process has two sides—one psychological and one sociological; and that neither can be subordinated to the other or neglected without evil results following. Of these two sides, the psychological is the basis. The child's own instincts and powers furnish the material and give the starting point for all education. Save as the efforts of the educator connect with some activity which the child is carrying on of his own initiative independent of the educator, education becomes reduced to a pressure from without. It may, indeed, give certain external results but cannot truly be called educative. Without insight into the psychological structure and activities of the individual, the educative process will, therefore, be haphazard and arbitrary. If it chances to coincide with the child's activity it will get a leverage; if it does not, it will result in friction, or disintegration, or arrest of the child nature.

I believe that knowledge of social conditions, of the present state of civilization, is necessary in order properly to interpret the child's powers. The child has his own instincts and tendencies, but we do not know what these mean until we can translate them into their social equivalents. We must be able to carry them back into a social past and see them as the inheritance of previous race activities. We must also be able to project them into the future to see what their outcome and end will be. In the illustration just used, it is the ability to see in the child's babblings the promise and potency of a future social intercourse and conversation which enables one to deal in the proper way with that instinct.

I believe that the psychological and social sides are organically related and that education cannot be regarded as a compromise between the two, or a superimposition of one upon the other. We are told that the psychological definition of education is barren and formal—that it gives us only the idea of a development of all the mental powers without giving us any idea of the use to which these powers are put. On the other hand, it is urged that the social definition of education, as getting adjusted to civilization, makes of it a forced and external process, and results in subordinating the freedom of the individual to a preconceived social and political status.

I believe each of these objections is true when urged against one side isolated from the other. In order to know what a power really is we must know what its end, use, or function is; and this we cannot know save as we conceive of the individual as active in social relationships. But, on the other hand, the only possible adjustment which we can give to the child under existing conditions, is that which arises through putting him in complete possession of all his powers. With the advent of democracy and modern industrial conditions, it is impossible to foretell definitely just what civilization will be twenty years from now. Hence it is impossible to prepare the child for any precise set of conditions. To prepare him for the future life means to give him command of himself; it means so to train him that he will have the full and ready use of all his capacities; that his eye and ear and hand may be tools ready to command, that his judgment may be capable of grasping the conditions under which it has to work, and the executive forces be trained to act economically and efficiently. It is impossible to reach this sort of adjustment save as constant regard is had to the individual's own powers, tastes, and interests—say, that is, as education is continually converted into psychological terms. In sum, I believe that the individual who is to be educated is a social individual and that society is an organic union of individuals. If we eliminate the social factor from the child we are left only with an abstraction; if we eliminate the individual factor from society, we are left only with an inert and lifeless mass. Education, therefore, must begin with a psychological insight into the child's capacities, interests, and habits. It must be controlled at every point by reference to these same considerations. These powers, interests, and habits must be continually interpreted—we must know what they mean. They must be translated into terms of their social equivalents—into terms of what they are capable of in the way of social service.

ARTICLE TWO. WHAT THE SCHOOL IS

I believe that the school is primarily a social institution. Education being a social process, the school is simply that form of community life in which all those agencies are concentrated that will be most effective in bringing the child to share in the inherited resources of the race, and to use his own powers for social ends.

I believe that education, therefore, is a process of living and not a preparation for future living.

I believe that the school must represent present life—life as real and vital to the child as that which he carries on in the home, in the neighborhood, or on the play-ground.

I believe that education which does not occur through forms of life, forms that are worth living for their own sake, is always a poor substitute for the genuine reality and tends to cramp and to deaden.

I believe that the school, as an institution, should simplify existing social life; should reduce it, as it were, to an embryonic form. Existing life is so complex that the child cannot be brought into contact with it without either confusion or distraction; he is either overwhelmed by multiplicity of activities which are going on, so that he loses his own power of orderly reaction, or he is so stimulated by these various activities that his powers are prematurely called into play and he becomes either unduly specialized or else disintegrated.

I believe that, as such simplified social life, the school life should grow gradually out of the home life; that it should take up and continue the activities with which the child is already familiar in the home.

I believe that it should exhibit these activities to the child, and reproduce them in such ways that the child will gradually learn the meaning of them, and be capable of playing his own part in relation to them.

I believe that this is a psychological necessity, because it is the only way of securing continuity in the child's growth, the only way of giving a background of past experience to the new ideas given in school.

I believe it is also a social necessity because the home is the form of social life in which the child has been nurtured and in connection with which he has had his moral training. It is the business of the school to deepen and extend his sense of the values bound up in his home life.

I believe that much of present education fails because it neglects this fundamental principle of the school as a form of community life. It conceives the school as a place where certain information is to be given, where certain lessons are to be learned, or where certain habits are to be formed. The value of these is conceived as lying largely in the remote future; the child must do these things for the sake of something else he is to do; they are mere preparation. As a result they do not become a part of the life experience of the child and so are not truly educative.

I believe that moral education centres about this conception of the school as a mode of social life, that the best and deepest moral training is precisely that which one gets through having to enter into proper relations with others in a unity of work and thought. The present educational systems, so far as they destroy or neglect this unity, render it difficult or impossible to get any genuine, regular moral training.

I believe that the child should be stimulated and controlled in his work through the life of the community.

I believe that under existing conditions far too much of the stimulus and control proceeds from the teacher, because of neglect of the idea of the school as a form of social life.

I believe that the teacher's place and work in the school is to be interpreted from this same basis. The teacher is not in the school to impose certain ideas or to form certain habits in the child, but is there as a member of the community to select the influences which shall affect the child and to assist him in properly responding to these influences.

I believe that the discipline of the school should proceed from the life of the school as a whole and not directly from the teacher.

I believe that the teacher's business is simply to determine on the basis of larger experience and riper wisdom, how the discipline of life shall come to the child.

I believe that all questions of the grading of the child and his promotion should be determined by reference to the same standard. Examinations are of use only so far as they test the child's fitness for social life and reveal the place in which he can be of most service and where he can receive the most help.

ARTICLE THREE. THE SUBJECT-MATTER OF EDUCATION

I believe that the social life of the child is the basis of concentration, or correlation, in all his training or growth. The social life gives the unconscious unity and the background of all his efforts and of all his attainments.

I believe that the subject-matter of the school curriculum should mark a gradual differentiation out of the primitive unconscious unity of social life.

I believe that we violate the child's nature and render difficult the best ethical results, by introducing the child too abruptly to a number of special studies, of reading, writing, geography, etc., out of relation to this social life.

I believe, therefore, that the true centre of correlation of the school subjects is not science, nor literature, nor history, nor geography, but the child's own social activities.

I believe that education cannot be unified in the study of science, or so-called nature study, because apart from human activity, nature itself is not a unity; nature in itself is a number of diverse objects in space and time, and to attempt to make it the centre of work by itself, is to introduce a principle of radiation rather than one of concentration.

I believe that literature is the reflex expression and interpretation of social experience; that hence it must follow upon and not precede such experience. It, therefore, cannot be made the basis, although it may be made the summary of unification.

I believe once more that history is of educative value in so far as it presents phases of social life and growth. It must be controlled by reference to social life. When taken simply as history it is thrown into the distant past and becomes dead and inert. Taken as the record of man's social life and progress it becomes full of meaning. I believe, however, that it cannot be so taken excepting as the child is also introduced directly into social life.

I believe accordingly that the primary basis of education is in the child's powers at work along the same general constructive lines as those which have brought civilization into being.

I believe that the only way to make the child conscious of his social heritage is to enable him to perform those fundamental types of activity which makes civilization what it is.

I believe, therefore, in the so-called expressive or constructive activities as the centre of correlation.

I believe that this gives the standard for the place of cooking, sewing, manual training, etc., in the school.

I believe that they are not special studies which are to be introduced over and above a lot of others in the way of relaxation or relief, or as additional accomplishments. I believe rather that they represent, as types, fundamental forms of social activity; and that it is possible and desirable that the child's introduction into the more formal subjects of the curriculum be through the medium of these activities.

I believe that the study of science is educational in so far as it brings out the materials and processes which make social life what it is.

I believe that one of the greatest difficulties in the present teaching of science is that the material is presented in purely objective form, or is treated as a new peculiar kind of experience which the child can add to that which he has already had. In reality, science is of value because it gives the ability to interpret and control the experience already had. It should be introduced, not as so much new subject- matter, but as showing the factors already involved in previous experience and as furnishing tools by which that experience can be more easily and effectively regulated.

I believe that at present we lose much of the value of literature and language studies because of our elimination of the social element. Language is almost always treated in the books of pedagogy simply as the expression of thought. It is true that language is a logical instrument, but it is fundamentally and primarily a social instrument. Language is the device for communication; it is the tool through which one individual comes to share the ideas and feelings of others. When treated simply as a way of getting individual information, or as a means of showing off what one has learned, it loses its social motive and end.

I believe that there is, therefore, no succession of studies in the ideal school curriculum. If education is life, all life has, from the outset, a scientific aspect; an aspect of art and culture and an aspect of communication. It cannot, therefore, be true that the proper studies for one grade are mere reading and writing, and that at a later grade, reading, or literature, or science, may be introduced. The progress is not in the succession of studies but in the development of new attitudes towards, and new interests in, experience.

I believe finally, that education must be conceived as a continuing reconstruction of experience; that the process and the goal of education are one and the same thing.

I believe that to set up any end outside of education, as furnishing its goal and standard, is to deprive the educational process of much of its meaning and tends to make us rely upon false and external stimuli in dealing with the child.

ARTICLE FOUR. THE NATURE OF METHOD

I believe that the question of method is ultimately reducible to the question of the order of development of the child's powers and interests. The law for presenting and treating material is the law implicit within the child's own nature. Because this is so I believe the following statements are of supreme importance as determining the spirit in which education is carried on:

1. I believe that the active side precedes the passive in the development of the child nature; that expression comes before conscious impression; that the muscular development precedes the sensory; that movements come before conscious sensations; I believe that consciousness is essentially motor or impulsive; that conscious states tend to project themselves in action.

I believe that the neglect of this principle is the cause of a large part of the waste of time and strength in school work. The child is thrown into a passive, receptive or absorbing attitude. The conditions are such that he is not permitted to follow the law of his nature; the result is friction and waste.

I believe that ideas (intellectual and rational processes) also result from action and devolve for the sake of the better control of action. What we term reason is primarily the law of orderly or effective action. To attempt to develop the reasoning powers, the powers of judgment, without reference to the selection and arrangement of means in action, is the fundamental fallacy in our present methods of dealing with this matter. As a result we present the child with arbitrary symbols. Symbols are a necessity in mental development, but they have their place as tools for economizing effort; presented by themselves they are a mass of meaningless and arbitrary ideas imposed from without.

2. I believe that the image is the great instrument of instruction. What a child gets out of any subject presented to him is simply the images which he himself forms with regard to it.

I believe that if nine-tenths of the energy at present directed towards making the child learn certain things, were spent in seeing to it that the child was forming proper images, the work of instruction would be indefinitely facilitated.

I believe that much of the time and attention now given to the preparation and presentation of lessons might be more wisely and profitably expended in training the child's power of imagery and in seeing to it that he was continually forming definite, vivid, and growing images of the various subjects with which he comes in contact in his experience.

3. I believe that interests are the signs and symptoms of growing power. I believe that they represent dawning capacities. Accordingly the constant and careful observation of interests is of the utmost importance for the educator.

I believe that these interests are to be observed as showing the state of development which the child has reached.

I believe that they prophesy the stage upon which he is about to enter.

I believe that only through the continual and sympathetic observation of childhood's interests can the adult enter into the child's life and see what it is ready for, and upon what material it could work most readily and fruitfully.

I believe that these interests are neither to be humored nor repressed. To repress interest is to substitute the adult for the child, and so to weaken intellectual curiosity and alertness, to suppress initiative, and to deaden interest. To humor the interests is to substitute the transient for the permanent. The interest is always the sign of some power below; the important thing is to discover this power. To humor the interest is to fail to penetrate below the surface and its sure result is to substitute caprice and whim for genuine interest.

4. I believe that the emotions are the reflex of actions.

I believe that to endeavor to stimulate or arouse the emotions apart from their corresponding activities, is to introduce an unhealthy and morbid state of mind.

I believe that if we can only secure right habits of action and thought, with reference to the good, the true, and the beautiful, the emotions will for the most part take care of themselves.

I believe that next to deadness and dullness, formalism and routine, our education is threatened with no greater evil than sentimentalism.

I believe that this sentimentalism is the necessary result of the attempt to divorce feeling from action.

ARTICLE FIVE. THE SCHOOL AND SOCIAL PROGRESS

I believe that education is the fundamental method of social progress and reform.

I believe that all reforms which rest simply upon the enactment of law, or the threatening of certain penalties, or upon changes in mechanical or outward arrangements, are transitory and futile.

I believe that education is a regulation of the process of coming to share in the social consciousness; and that the adjustment of individual activity on the basis of this social consciousness is the only sure method of social reconstruction.

I believe that this conception has due regard for both the individualistic and socialistic ideals. It is duly individual because it recognizes the formation of a certain character as the only genuine basis of right living. It is socialistic because it recognizes that this right character is not to be formed by merely individual precept, example, or exhortation, but rather by the influence of a certain form of institutional or community life upon the individual, and that the social organism through the school, as its organ, may determine ethical results.

I believe that in the ideal school we have the reconciliation of the individualistic and the institutional ideals.

I believe that the community's duty to education is, therefore, its paramount moral duty. By law and punishment, by social agitation and discussion, society can regulate and form itself in a more or less haphazard and chance way. But through education society can formulate its own purposes, can organize its own means and resources, and thus shape itself with definiteness and economy in the direction in which it wishes to move.

I believe that when society once recognizes the possibilities in this direction, and the obligations which these possibilities impose, it is impossible to conceive of the resources of time, attention, and money which will be put at the disposal of the educator.

I believe it is the business of every one interested in education to insist upon the school as the primary and most effective instrument of social progress and reform in order that society may be awakened to realize what the school stands for, and aroused to the necessity of endowing the educator with sufficient equipment properly to perform his task.

I believe that education thus conceived marks the most perfect and intimate union of science and art conceivable in human experience.

I believe that the art of thus giving shape to human powers and adapting them to social service, is the supreme art; one calling into its service the best of artists; that no insight, sympathy, tact, executive power is too great for such service.

I believe that with the growth of psychological science, giving added insight into individual structure and laws of growth; and with growth of social science, adding to our knowledge of the right organization of individuals, all scientific resources can be utilized for the purposes of education.

I believe that when science and art thus join hands the most commanding motive for human action will be reached; the most genuine springs of human conduct aroused and the best service that human nature is capable of guaranteed.

I believe, finally, that the teacher is engaged, not simply in the training of individuals, but in the formation of the proper social life.

I believe that every teacher should realize the dignity of his calling; that he is a social servant set apart for the maintenance of proper social order and the securing of the right social growth.

I believe that in this way the teacher always is the prophet of the true God and the usherer in of the true kingdom of God.

A NATION AT RISK: THE IMPERATIVE FOR EDUCATIONAL REFORM (ABBREVIATED) (1983)

All, regardless of race or class or economic status, are entitled to a fair chance and to the tools for developing their individual powers of mind and spirit to the utmost. This promise means that all children by virtue of their own efforts, competently guided, can hope to attain the mature and informed judgement needed to secure gainful employment, and to manage their own lives, thereby serving not only their own interests but also the progress of society itself.

Our Nation is at risk. Our once unchallenged preeminence in commerce, industry, science, and technological innovation is being overtaken by competitors throughout the world. This report is concerned with only one of the many causes and dimensions of the problem, but it is the one that undergirds American prosperity, security, and civility. We report to the American people that while we can take justifiable pride in what our schools and colleges have historically accomplished and contributed to the United States and the well-being of its people, the educational foundations of our society are presently being eroded by a rising tide of mediocrity that threatens our very future as a Nation and a people. What was unimaginable a generation ago has begun to occur—others are matching and surpassing our educational attainments.

If an unfriendly foreign power had attempted to impose on America the mediocre educational performance that exists today, we might well have viewed it as an act of war. As it stands, we have allowed this to happen to ourselves. We have even squandered the gains in student achievement made in the wake of the Sputnik challenge. Moreover, we have dismantled essential support systems which helped make those gains possible. We have, in effect, been committing an act of unthinking, unilateral educational disarmament.

Our society and its educational institutions seem to have lost sight of the basic purposes of schooling, and of the high expectations and disciplined effort needed to attain them. This report, the result of 18 months of study, seeks to generate reform of our educational system in fundamental ways and to renew the Nation's commitment to schools and colleges of high quality throughout the length and breadth of our land.

That we have compromised this commitment is, upon reflection, hardly surprising, given the multitude of often conflicting demands we have placed on our Nation's schools and colleges. They are routinely called on to provide solutions to personal, social, and political problems that the home and other institutions either will not or cannot resolve. We must understand that these demands on our schools and colleges often exact an educational cost as well as a financial one.

On the occasion of the Commission's first meeting, President Reagan noted the central importance of education in American life when he said: "Certainly there are few areas of American life as important to our society, to our people, and to our families as our schools and colleges." This report, therefore, is as much an open letter to the American people as it is a report to the Secretary of Education. We are confident that the American people, properly informed, will do what is right for their children and for the generations to come.

The Risk

History is not kind to idlers. The time is long past when America's destiny was assured simply by an abundance of natural resources and inexhaustible human enthusiasm, and by our relative isolation from the malignant problems of older civilizations. The world is indeed one global village. We live among determined, well-educated, and strongly motivated competitors. We compete with them for international standing and markets, not only with products but also with the ideas of our laboratories and neighborhood workshops. America's position in the world may once have been reasonably secure with only a few exceptionally well-trained men and women. It is no longer.

The risk is not only that the Japanese make automobiles more efficiently than Americans and have government subsidies for development and export. It is not just that the South Koreans recently built the world's most efficient steel mill, or that American machine tools, once the pride of the world, are being displaced by German products. It is also that these developments signify a redistribution of trained capability throughout the globe. Knowledge, learning, information, and skilled intelligence are the new raw materials of international commerce and are today spreading throughout the world as vigorously as miracle drugs, synthetic fertilizers, and blue jeans did earlier. If only to keep and improve on the slim competitive edge we still retain in world markets, we must dedicate ourselves to the reform of our educational system for the benefit of all—old and young alike, affluent and poor, majority and minority. Learning is the indispensable investment required for success in the "information age" we are entering.

Our concern, however, goes well beyond matters such as industry and commerce. It also includes the intellectual, moral, and spiritual strengths of our people which knit together the very fabric of our society. The people of the United States need to know that individuals in our society who do not possess the levels of skill, literacy, and training essential to this new era will be effectively disenfranchised, not simply from the material rewards that accompany competent performance, but also from the chance to participate fully in our national life. A high level of shared education is essential to a free, democratic society and to the fostering of a common culture, especially in a country that prides itself on pluralism and individual freedom.

For our country to function, citizens must be able to reach some common understandings on complex issues, often on short notice and on the basis of conflicting or incomplete evidence. Education helps form these common understandings, a point Thomas Jefferson made long ago in his justly famous dictum:

> I know no safe depository of the ultimate powers of the society but the people themselves; and if we think them not enlightened enough to exercise their control with

a wholesome discretion, the remedy is not to take it from them but to inform their discretion.

Part of what is at risk is the promise first made on this continent: All, regardless of race or class or economic status, are entitled to a fair chance and to the tools for developing their individual powers of mind and spirit to the utmost. This promise means that all children by virtue of their own efforts, competently guided, can hope to attain the mature and informed judgment needed to secure gainful employment, and to manage their own lives, thereby serving not only their own interests but also the progress of society itself.

Indicators of the Risk

The educational dimensions of the risk before us have been amply documented in testimony received by the Commission. For example:

- International comparisons of student achievement, completed a decade ago, reveal that on 19 academic tests American students were never first or second and, in comparison with other industrialized nations, were last seven times.
- Some 23 million American adults are functionally illiterate by the simplest tests of everyday reading, writing, and comprehension.
- About 13 percent of all 17-year-olds in the United States can be considered functionally illiterate. Functional illiteracy among minority youth may run as high as 40 percent.
- Average achievement of high school students on most standardized tests is now lower than 26 years ago when Sputnik was launched.
- Over half the population of gifted students do not match their tested ability with comparable achievement in school.
- The College Board's Scholastic Aptitude Tests (SAT) demonstrate a virtually unbroken decline from 1963 to 1980. Average verbal scores fell over 50 points and average mathematics scores dropped nearly 40 points.
- College Board achievement tests also reveal consistent declines in recent years in such subjects as physics and English.
- Both the number and proportion of students demonstrating superior achievement on the SATs (i.e., those with scores of 650 or higher) have also dramatically declined.
- Many 17-year-olds do not possess the "higher order" intellectual skills we should expect of them. Nearly 40 percent cannot draw inferences from written material; only one-fifth can write a persuasive essay; and only one-third can solve a mathematics problem requiring several steps.
- There was a steady decline in science achievement scores of U.S. 17-year-olds as measured by national assessments of science in 1969, 1973, and 1977.
- Between 1975 and 1980, remedial mathematics courses in public 4-year colleges increased by 72 percent and now constitute one-quarter of all mathematics courses taught in those institutions.
- Average tested achievement of students graduating from college is also lower.
- Business and military leaders complain that they are required to spend millions of dollars on costly remedial education and training programs in such basic skills as reading, writing, spelling, and computation. The Department of the Navy, for example, reported to the Commission that one-quarter of its recent recruits cannot read at the ninth grade level, the minimum needed simply to understand written safety instructions. Without remedial work they cannot even begin, much less complete, the sophisticated training essential in much of the modern military.

These deficiencies come at a time when the demand for highly skilled workers in new fields is accelerating rapidly. For example:

- Computers and computer-controlled equipment are penetrating every aspect of our lives—homes, factories, and offices.
- One estimate indicates that by the turn of the century millions of jobs will involve laser technology and robotics.
- Technology is radically transforming a host of other occupations. They include health care, medical science, energy production, food processing, construction, and the building, repair, and maintenance of sophisticated scientific, educational, military, and industrial equipment.

Analysts examining these indicators of student performance and the demands for new skills have made some chilling observations. Educational researcher Paul Hurd concluded at the end of a thorough national survey of student achievement that within the context of the modern scientific revolution, "We are raising a new generation of Americans that is scientifically and technologically illiterate." In a similar vein, John Slaughter, a former Director of the National Science Foundation, warned of "a growing chasm between a small scientific and technological elite and a citizenry ill-informed, indeed uninformed, on issues with a science component."

But the problem does not stop there, nor do all observers see it the same way. Some worry that schools may emphasize such rudiments as reading and computation at the expense of other essential skills such as comprehension, analysis, solving problems, and drawing conclusions. Still others are concerned that an over-emphasis on technical and occupational skills will leave little time for studying the arts and humanities that so enrich daily life, help maintain civility, and develop a sense of community. Knowledge of the humanities, they maintain, must be harnessed to science and technology if the latter are to remain creative and humane, just as the humanities need to be informed by science and technology if they are to remain relevant to the human condition. Another analyst, Paul Copperman, has drawn a sobering conclusion. Until now, he has noted:

> Each generation of Americans has outstripped its parents in education, in literacy, and in economic attainment. For the first time in the history of our country, the educational skills of one generation will not surpass, will not equal, will not even approach, those of their parents.

It is important, of course, to recognize that *the average citizen* today is better educated and more knowledgeable than the average citizen of a generation ago—more literate, and exposed to more mathematics, literature, and science. The positive impact of this fact on the well-being of our country and the lives of our people cannot be overstated. Nevertheless, *the average graduate* of our schools and colleges today is not as well-educated as the average graduate of 25 or 35 years ago, when a much smaller proportion of our population completed high school and college. The negative impact of this fact likewise cannot be overstated.

Hope and Frustration

Statistics and their interpretation by experts show only the surface dimension of the difficulties we face. Beneath them lies a tension between hope and frustration that characterizes current attitudes about education at every level.

We have heard the voices of high school and college students, school board members, and teachers; of leaders of industry, minority groups, and higher education; of parents and State officials. We could hear the hope evident in their commitment to quality education and in their descriptions of outstanding programs and schools. We could also hear the intensity of their frustration, a growing impatience with shoddiness in many walks of American life, and the complaint that this shoddiness is too often reflected in our schools and colleges. Their frustration threatens to overwhelm their hope.

What lies behind this emerging national sense of frustration can be described as both a dimming of personal expectations and the fear of losing a shared vision for America.

On the personal level the student, the parent, and the caring teacher all perceive that a basic promise is not being kept. More and more young people emerge from high school ready neither for college nor for work. This predicament becomes more acute as the knowledge base continues its rapid expansion, the number of traditional jobs shrinks, and new jobs demand greater sophistication and preparation.

On a broader scale, we sense that this undertone of frustration has significant political implications, for it cuts across ages, generations, races, and political and economic groups. We have come to understand that the public will demand that educational and political leaders act forcefully and effectively on these issues. Indeed, such demands have already appeared and could well become a unifying national preoccupation. This unity, however, can be achieved only if we avoid the unproductive tendency of some to search for scapegoats among the victims, such as the beleaguered teachers.

On the positive side is the significant movement by political and educational leaders to search for solutions—so far centering largely on the nearly desperate need for increased support for the teaching of mathematics and science. This movement is but a start on what we believe is a larger and more educationally encompassing need to improve teaching and learning in fields such as English, history, geography, economics, and foreign languages. We believe this movement must be broadened and directed toward reform and excellence throughout education.

Excellence in Education

We define "excellence" to mean several related things. At the level of the *individual learner*, it means performing on the boundary of individual ability in ways that test and push back personal limits, in school and in the workplace. Excellence characterizes a *school or college* that sets high expectations and goals for all learners, then tries in every way possible to help students reach them. Excellence characterizes a *society* that has adopted these policies, for it will then be prepared through the education and skill of its people to respond to the challenges of a rapidly changing world. Our Nation's people and its schools and colleges must be committed to achieving excellence in all these senses.

We do not believe that a public commitment to excellence and educational reform must be made at the expense of a strong public commitment to the equitable treatment of our diverse population. The twin goals of equity and high-quality schooling have profound and practical meaning for our economy and society, and we cannot permit one to yield to the other either in principle or in practice. To do so would deny young people their chance to learn and live according to their aspirations and abilities. It also would lead to a generalized accommodation to mediocrity in our society on the one hand or the creation of an undemocratic elitism on the other.

Our goal must be to develop the talents of all to their fullest. Attaining that goal requires that we expect and assist all students to work to the limits of their capabilities. We should expect schools to have genuinely high standards rather than minimum ones, and parents to support and encourage their children to make the most of their talents and abilities.

The search for solutions to our educational problems must also include a commitment to life-long learning. The task of rebuilding our system of learning is enormous and must be properly understood and taken seriously: Although a million and a half new workers enter the economy each year from our schools and colleges, the adults working today will still make up about 75 percent of the workforce in the year 2000. These workers, and new entrants into the workforce, will need further education and retraining if they—and we as a Nation—are to thrive and prosper.

The Learning Society

In a world of ever-accelerating competition and change in the conditions of the workplace, of ever-greater danger, and of ever-larger opportunities for those prepared to meet them, educational reform should focus on the goal of creating a Learning Society. At the heart of such a society is the commitment to a set of values and to a system of education that affords all members the opportunity to stretch their minds to full capacity, from early childhood through adulthood, learning more as the world itself changes. Such a society has as a basic foundation the idea that education is important not only because of what it contributes to one's career goals but also because of the value it adds to the general quality of one's life. Also at the heart of the Learning Society are educational opportunities extending far beyond the traditional institutions of learning, our schools and colleges. They extend into homes and workplaces; into libraries, art galleries, museums, and science centers; indeed, into every place where the individual can develop and mature in work and life. In our view, formal schooling in youth is the essential foundation for learning throughout one's life. But without life-long learning, one's skills will become rapidly dated.

In contrast to the ideal of the Learning Society, however, we find that for too many people education means doing the minimum work necessary for the moment, then coasting through life on what may have been learned in its first quarter. But this should not surprise us because we tend to express our educational standards and expectations largely in terms of "minimum requirements." And where there should be a coherent continuum of learning, we have none, but instead an often incoherent, outdated patchwork quilt. Many individual, sometimes heroic, examples of schools and colleges of great merit do exist. Our findings and testimony confirm the vitality of a number of notable schools and programs, but their very distinction stands out against a vast mass shaped by tensions and pressures that inhibit systematic academic and vocational achievement for the majority of students. In some metropolitan areas basic literacy has become the goal rather than the starting point. In some colleges maintaining enrollments is of greater day-to-day concern than maintaining rigorous academic standards. And the ideal of academic excellence as the primary goal of schooling seems to be fading across the board in American education.

Thus, we issue this call to all who care about America and its future: to parents and students; to teachers, administrators, and school board members; to colleges and industry; to union members and military leaders; to governors and State legislators; to the President; to members of Congress and other public officials; to members of learned and scientific societies; to the print and electronic media; to concerned citizens everywhere. America is at risk.

We are confident that America can address this risk. If the tasks we set forth are initiated now and our recommendations are fully realized over the next several years, we can expect reform of our Nation's schools, colleges, and universities. This would also reverse the current declining trend—a trend that stems more from weakness of purpose, confusion of vision, underuse of talent, and lack of leadership, than from conditions beyond our control.

The Tools at Hand

It is our conviction that the essential raw materials needed to reform our educational system are waiting to be mobilized through effective leadership:

- the natural abilities of the young that cry out to be developed and the undiminished concern of parents for the well-being of their children;
- the commitment of the Nation to high retention rates in schools and colleges and to full access to education for all;
- the persistent and authentic American dream that superior performance can raise one's state in life and shape one's own future;
- the dedication, against all odds, that keeps teachers serving in schools and colleges, even as the rewards diminish;
- our better understanding of learning and teaching and the implications of this knowledge for school practice, and the numerous examples of local success as a result of superior effort and effective dissemination;

- the ingenuity of our policymakers, scientists, State and local educators, and scholars in formulating solutions once problems are better understood;
- the traditional belief that paying for education is an investment in ever-renewable human resources that are more durable and flexible than capital plant and equipment, and the availability in this country of sufficient financial means to invest in education;
- the equally sound tradition, from the Northwest Ordinance of 1787 until today, that the Federal Government should supplement State, local, and other resources to foster key national educational goals; and
- the voluntary efforts of individuals, businesses, and parent and civic groups to cooperate in strengthening educational programs.

These raw materials, combined with the unparalleled array of educational organizations in America, offer us the possibility to create a Learning Society, in which public, private, and parochial schools; colleges and universities; vocational and technical schools and institutes; libraries; science centers, museums, and other cultural institutions; and corporate training and retraining programs offer opportunities and choices for all to learn throughout life.

The Public's Commitment

Of all the tools at hand, the public's support for education is the most powerful. In a message to a National Academy of Sciences meeting in May 1982, President Reagan commented on this fact when he said:

> This public awareness—and I hope public action—is long overdue . . . . This country was built on American respect for education . . . . Our challenge now is to create a resurgence of that thirst for education that typifies our Nation's history.

The most recent (1982) Gallup Poll of the *Public's Attitudes Toward the Public Schools* strongly supported a theme heard during our hearings: People are steadfast in their belief that education is the major foundation for the future strength of this country. They even considered education more important than developing the best industrial system or the strongest military force, perhaps because they understood education as the cornerstone of both. They also held that education is "extremely important" to one's future success, and that public education should be the top priority for additional Federal funds. Education occupied first place among 12 funding categories considered in the survey—above health care, welfare, and military defense, with 55 percent selecting public education as one of their first three choices. Very clearly, the public understands the primary importance of education as the foundation for a satisfying life, an enlightened and civil society, a strong economy, and a secure Nation.

At the same time, the public has no patience with undemanding and superfluous high school offerings. In another survey, more than 75 percent of all those questioned believed every student planning to go to college should take 4 years of mathematics, English, history/U.S. government, and science, with more than 50 percent adding 2 years each of a foreign language and economics or business. The public even supports requiring much of this curriculum for students who do not plan to go to college. These standards far exceed the strictest high school graduation requirements of any State today, and they also exceed the admission standards of all but a handful of our most selective colleges and universities.

Another dimension of the public's support offers the prospect of constructive reform. The best term to characterize it may simply be the honorable word "patriotism." Citizens know intuitively what some of the best economists have shown in their research, that education is one of the chief engines of a society's material well-being. They know, too, that education is the common bond of a pluralistic society and helps tie us to other cultures around the globe. Citizens also know in their bones that the safety of the United States depends principally on the wit, skill, and spirit of a self-confident people, today and tomorrow. It is, therefore, essential—especially in a period of long-term decline in educational achievement—for government at all levels to affirm its responsibility for nurturing the Nation's intellectual capital.

And perhaps most important, citizens know and believe that the meaning of America to the rest of the world must be something better than it seems to many today. Americans like to think of this Nation as the preeminent country for generating the great ideas and material benefits for all mankind. The citizen is dismayed at a steady 15-year decline in industrial productivity, as one great American industry after another falls to world competition. The citizen wants the country to act on the belief, expressed in our hearings and by the large majority in the Gallup Poll, that education should be at the top of the Nation's agenda.

National Commission on Excellence in Education

April 1983

JOINT STATEMENT ON THE EDUCATION SUMMIT WITH THE NATION'S GOVERNORS IN CHARLOTTESVILLE, VIRGINIA

SEPTEMBER 28, 1989

The President and the nation's Governors agree that a better educated citizenry is the key to the continued growth and prosperity of the United States. Education has historically been, and should remain, a state responsibility and a local function, which works best when there is also strong parental involvement in the schools. And, as [a] Nation we must have an educated workforce, second to none, in order to succeed in an increasingly competitive world economy.

Education has always been important, but never this important because the stakes have changed: Our competitors for opportunity are also working to educate their people. As they continue to improve, they make the future a moving target. We believe that the time has come, for the first time in U.S. history, to establish clear, national performance goals, goals that will make us internationally competitive.

The President and the nation's Governors have agreed at this summit to:

- establish a process for setting national educational goals;
- to seek greater flexibility and enhanced accountability in the use of Federal resources to meet the goals, through both regulatory and legislative changes;
- to undertake a major state-by-state effort to restructure our education system; and
- to report annually on progress in achieving our goals.

This agreement represents the first step in a long-term commitment to reorient the education system and to marshal widespread support for the needed reforms.

National Education Goals

The first step in restructuring our education system is to build a broad-based consensus around a defined set of national education goals. The National Governors Association Task Force on Education will work with the President's designees to recommend goals to the President and the Nation's Governors. The process to develop the goals will involve teachers, parents, local school administrators, school board members, elected officials, business and labor communities, and the public at large. The overriding objective is to develop an ambitious, realistic set of performance goals that reflect the views of those with a stake in the performance of our education system. To succeed we need a common understanding and a common mission. National goals will allow us to plan effectively, to set priorities, and to establish clear lines of accountability and authority. These goals will lead to the development of detailed strategies that will allow us to meet these objectives.

The process for establishing these goals should be completed and the goals announced in early 1990.

By performance we mean goals that will, if achieved, guarantee that we are internationally competitive, such as goals related to:

- the readiness of children to start school;
- the performance of students on international achievement tests, especially in math and science;
- the reduction of the dropout rate and the improvement of academic performance, especially among at-risk students;
- the functional literacy of adult Americans;
- the level of training necessary to guarantee a competitive workforce;
- the supply of qualified teachers and up-to-date technology; and
- the establishment of safe, disciplined, and drug-free schools.

THE FEDERAL/STATE PARTNERSHIP

Flexibility and Accountability

The President and the Governors are committed to achieving the maximum return possible from our investments in the Nation's education system. We define maximum return as the following: significant and sustained educational improvement for all children. Nothing less will meet the Nation's needs for a strong, competitive workforce; nothing less will meet our children's needs for successful citizenship and economic opportunity.

Federal funds, which represent only a small part of total education spending, are directed particularly toward services for young people most at risk. Federal laws and regulations control where and for whom states and localities spend this money. State and local laws and regulations control what is taught, and how, for all students.

At present, neither Federal nor State and local laws and regulations focus sufficiently on results, or on real educational improvement for all children. Federal and State executives need authority to waive statutory and regulatory provisions in return for greater accountability for results.

The President and the Governors have agreed:

- to examine Federal regulations under current law and to move in the direction of greater flexibility;
- to take parallel steps in each state with respect to State laws and administrative rules;
- to submit legislation to Congress early next year that would provide State and local recipients greater flexibility in the use of Federal funds, in return for firm commitments to improved levels of education and skill training.

The President and the Governors have agreed to establish a working group of Governors and the President's designees to begin work immediately to accomplish these tasks.

We know that other voices need to be heard in this discussion — voices of educators, parents, and those whose primary interest is the protection of the disadvantaged, minorities, and the handicapped. We need to work with the Congress. The processes we will set up immediately following this conference will involve all parties.

The urgent need for flexibility in using Federal funds can best be illustrated by a few examples.

First, the Federal Vocational Education Act, which mandates specific set-asides that often result in individual awards that are too small to be meaningful and that prohibit the money from being spent to achieve its purpose. One state reported being required to divide $300,000 in aid among far too many categories and set-asides.

Second, similarly, the Chapter 1 program requires that equipment purchased to provide remedial education services cannot be used for non-Chapter 1 institutions in areas such as adult education. Several States report that large numbers of computers purchased by Federal funds are idle at night, while adult education classes that need them either do without or use scarce tax dollars to buy other equipment.

Third, the requirements that children who benefit from Federal funds for compensatory and special education be taught separately often undermines their achievement. Waivers that permit these students to return to regular classes and receive extra help have produced large increases in their test scores. This option should be available for all school districts.

These commitments are historic steps toward ensuring that young people with the greatest needs receive the best our schools and training programs can give them, and that all children reach their highest educational potential.

In a phrase, we want to swap redtape for results.

The Federal Government's Financial Role

State and local Governments provide more than 90 percent of education funding. They should continue to bear that lion's share of the load. The Federal financial role is limited and has even declined, but it is still important. That role is:

- to promote National education equity by helping our poor children get off to a good start in school, giving disadvantaged and handicapped children extra help to assist them in their school years, ensuring accessibility to a college education, and preparing the workforce for jobs;
- and second, to provide research and development for programs that work, good information on the real performance of students, schools, and states, and assistance in replicating successful state and local initiatives all across the United States.

We understand the limits imposed on new spending by the Federal deficit and the budget process. However, we urge that priority for any further funding increases be given to prepare young children to succeed in school. This is consistent with the President's recommendation for an increase in the number of children served by Head Start in this year's budget. If we are ever to develop a system that ensures that our children are healthy and succeed in school, the Federal Government will have to play a leading role.

Further, we urge that the Congress not impose new Federal mandates that are unrelated to children, but that require States to spend state tax money that could otherwise go to education.

Commitment to Restructuring

Virtually every State has substantially increased its investment in education, increased standards, and improved learning. Real gains have occurred. However, we still have a long way to go. We must make dramatic improvements in our education system. This cannot be done without a genuine, National, Bipartisan commitment to excellence and without a willingness to dramatically alter our system of education.

The President and the Nation's Governors agree that significant steps must be taken to restructure education in all states. We share the view that simply more of the same will not achieve the results we need. We must find ways to deploy the resources we commit to education more effectively.

A similar process has been going on in American manufacturing industry over the last decade with astonishing results: An increase in productivity of nearly 4 percent a year.

There are many promising new ideas and strategies for restructuring education. These include greater choice for parents and students, greater authority and accountability for teachers and principals, alternative certification programs for teachers, and programs that systematically reward excellence and performance. Most successful restructuring efforts seem to have certain common characteristics:

- a system of accountability that focuses on results, rather than on compliance with rules and regulations;
- decentralization of authority and decision-making responsibility to the school site, so that educators are empowered to determine the means for achieving the goals and to be held accountable for accomplishing them;
- a rigorous program of instruction designed to ensure that every child can acquire the knowledge and skills required in an economy in which our citizens must be able to think for a living;
- an education system that develops first-rate teachers and creates a professional environment that provides real rewards for success with students, real consequences for failure, and the tools and flexibility required to get the job done; and
- active, sustained parental and business community involvement.

Restructuring efforts are now underway in many states. The Nation's Governors are committed to a major restructuring effort in every state. The Governors will give this task high priority and will report on their programs in one year.

Assuring Accountability

As elected chief executives, we expect to be held accountable for progress in meeting the new additional goals and we expect to hold others accountable as well.

When goals are set and strategies for achieving them are adopted, we must establish clear measures of performance and then issue annual Report Cards on the progress of students, schools, the states, and the Federal Government.

Over the last few days we have humbly walked in the footsteps of Thomas Jefferson. We have started down a promising path. We have entered into a compact—a Jeffersonian compact to enlighten our children and the children of generations to come.

The time for rhetoric is past; the time for performance is now.

STATE CONSTITUTIONS AND PUBLIC EDUCATION GOVERNANCE

FIRST COMPLETED IN OCTOBER 1998
LAST UPDATED IN OCTOBER 2000

Introduction

Each state constitution articulates, to varying degrees of detail, the state's responsibilities for providing an education to its citizens. This *ECS StateNote* outlines and compares the provisions in each state's constitution that concern public education governance.

For the purposes of this *ECS StateNote,* governance is defined as who makes what decisions, and in what manner. In public education, the "who" part of this definition is everybody from state legislators to parents. The "what" part of this definition covers everything from standards to professional development. The "in what manner" or "how" part of this definition is everything from decisions made autonomously to decisions made within a framework established by others.

Summary

Each state constitution contain at least one of the following provisions:

- Establishing and maintaining a free system of public schools open to all children of the state

- Financing schools (in varying degrees of detail)
- Separating church and state, often in at least one of the following two ways:
  - Forbidding any public funds to be appropriated to or used for the support of any sectarian school
  - Requiring public schools to be free from sectarian control
- Creating certain decisionmaking entities (e.g., state board of education, state superintendent of education, local board of education, local superintendent of education); although most state constitutions require at least some of these entities to be in place, they usually do not specify their qualifications, powers and duties.

State-by-State Review

This section presents some of the details within each state constitution that relate to public education governance.

Alabama

- Requires the legislature to establish, organize and maintain a liberal system of public schools throughout the state for the benefit of the children of the state between the ages of 7 and 21 years.
- Prohibits any money raised for the support of public schools to be appropriated to or used for the support of any sectarian or denominational school.
- Provides that no religion be established by law; that no preference be given by law to any religious sect, society, denomination, or mode of worship; and that no one be compelled by law to attend any place of worship, nor to pay any tithes, taxes, or other rate for building or repairing any place of worship, or for maintaining any minister or ministry.
- Forbids any more than 4% of all moneys raised or appropriated for the support of public schools to be used for the payment of teachers. Allows the legislature, by a vote of two-thirds of each house, to suspend this provision.
- Vests general supervision of the state's public schools in a state board of education. Charges the legislature with establishing the method of state board member election. Charges the state board with appointing the state superintendent of education, who shall be the chief state school officer.
- Allows the legislature to provide for the election of local board of education members in certain counties.
- Provides for the election of the superintendent of education in a certain county.

Alaska

- Requires the legislature to establish and maintain a system of public schools open to all children of the state.
- Prohibits any money to be paid from public funds for the direct benefit of any religious or other private education institution.
- Requires that no law be made respecting an establishment of religion, or prohibiting the free exercise thereof.
- Requires that public schools be free from sectarian control.

Arizona

- Requires the legislature to provide for the establishment and maintenance of a general and uniform public school system, which includes kindergarten schools, common schools, high schools, normal schools, industrial schools and a university.
- Requires the legislature to provide for a system of common schools by which a free school is established and maintained in every school district for at least six months in each year and is open to all pupils between the ages of 6 and 21 years.

- Requires that public schools be free from sectarian instruction.
- Requires that no public money or property be appropriated for or applied to any religious worship, exercise, or instruction, or to the support of any religious establishment.
- Vests general conduct and supervision of the state's public schools in an appointed state board of education, a state superintendent of public instruction and county school superintendents.
- Establishes the composition and method of appointment of the state board.
- Requires that the state superintendent be a member, and secretary, of the state board.

Arkansas

- Requires the state to maintain a general, suitable and efficient system of free public schools.
- Forbids any money or property belonging to the public school fund, or to the state for the benefit of schools or universities, to be used for any other than for the respective purposes for which it belongs.
- Provides that no man can, of right, be compelled to attend, erect or support any place of worship; or to maintain any ministry against his consent. Requires that no preference ever be given, by law, to any religious establishment, denomination or mode of worship above any other.

California

- Requires the legislature to provide for a system of common schools by which a free school is kept up and supported in each district at least six months in every year.
- Prohibits any public money to ever be appropriated for the support of any sectarian or denominational school or any school not under the exclusive control of the officers of the public schools.
- Forbids any sectarian or denominational doctrine to be taught, or instruction to be permitted (directly or indirectly), in any common schools.
- Provides that free exercise and enjoyment of religion without discrimination or preference are guaranteed. Prohibits the legislature from making any laws respecting an establishment of religion.
- Charges the legislature with providing for the appointment or election of a state board of education and a board of education for each county or for the election of a joint county board of education in two or more counties.
- Creates an elected state superintendent of public instruction. Establishes the method of election and the terms of office for the state superintendent of public instruction.
- Charges the state board of education, on nomination from the superintendent, with appointing one deputy superintendent and three associate superintendents.
- Authorizes the legislature to provide for the incorporation and organization of school districts and high school districts.
- Allows the legislature to authorize the governing boards of all school districts to initiate and carry on any programs or activities which are not in conflict with the laws and purposes for which school districts are established.
- Allows each county to decide how to choose its local superintendent, either through voter election or county school board appointment.
- Requires the county board of education to fix the salary of the county superintendent.
- Allows two or more counties to unite and establish one joint board of education and one joint county superintendent of schools.
- Requires the state board of education to adopt textbooks for use in grades 1 through 8 throughout the state, to be furnished without cost.

Colorado

- Requires the legislature to provide for the establishment and maintenance of a thorough and uniform system of free public schools throughout the state, so that all state residents, between the ages of 6 and 21 years, may be educated gratuitously.
- Forbids any appropriation or payment from any public fund in aid of any church or sectarian society, for any sectarian purpose or to help support or sustain any school, academy, seminary, college, university or other literary or scientific institution controlled by any church or sectarian denomination. Forbids any grant or donation of land, money or other personal property to be made by the state to any church or for any sectarian purpose.
- Requires public schools to be free from sectarian instruction.
- Provides that the free exercise and enjoyment of religious profession and worship, without discrimination, are guaranteed; that no person be required to attend or support any ministry or place of worship, religious sect or denomination against his consent; and that no preference be given by law to any religious denomination or mode of worship.
- Vests general supervision of the public schools in an elected board of education. Specifies the composition of the state board. Charges the state board with appointing a state commissioner of education.
- Charges the legislature with providing for the organization of school districts, in each of which shall be established a board of education to consist of three or more elected directors, who will have control of instruction in the public schools of their respective districts.
- Requires one or more public schools to be maintained in each school district for at least three months in each year. Allows the legislature to require that every child of sufficient mental and physical ability between the ages of 6 and 18 attend the public school for a time equivalent to three years, unless educated by other means.
- Allows for a superintendent of schools in each county. Establishes the terms of office for county superintendents of schools. Allows each county's electors to abolish this office.
- Forbids the legislature or the state board from prescribing textbooks to be used in the public schools.

Connecticut

- Requires the legislature to provide free public elementary and secondary schools.
- Prohibits any laws to ever be made which authorize the school fund to be diverted to any other use than the encouragement and support of public schools.
- Requires that no person by law be compelled to join or support, be classed or associated with, any congregation, church or religious association; that no preference be given by law to any religious society or denomination in the state; and that each religious society or denomination has and enjoys the same and equal powers, rights and privileges, and may support and maintain the ministers or teachers of its society or denomination, and may build and repair houses for public worship.

Delaware

- Requires the legislature to provide for the establishment and maintenance of a general and efficient system of free public schools.
- Prohibits any property tax receipts received by a public school district as a result of a property tax levied for a particular purpose to be used for any other purpose except upon the favorable vote of a majority of the eligible voters in the district voting on the question.
- Forbids any funds raised for educational purposes to be appropriated to or used by or in aid of any sectarian, church or denominational school.
- Requires that no man be compelled to attend any religious worship, to contribute to the erection or support of any place of worship, or to the maintenance of any ministry, against

his own free will and consent; that no power be vested in or assumed by any magistrate that interferes with, or in any manner controls the rights of conscience, in the free exercise of religious worship; and that no preference be given by law to any religious societies, denominations or modes of worship.

- Allows the legislature to provide for the transportation of students of nonpublic, nonprofit elementary and high schools.
- Allows the legislature to require that every child attend public school, unless educated by other means.

Florida

- Provides that a paramount duty of the state is to make adequate provision for the education of all children residing within its borders, and that adequate provision be made by law for a uniform, efficient, safe, secure and high-quality system of free public schools that allows students to obtain a high-quality education and for the establishment, maintenance, and operation of institutions of higher learning and other public education programs that the needs of the people may require.
- Provides that the income derived from the state school fund, and the principal of the fund, be appropriated but only to the support and maintenance of free public schools.
- Provides that there be no law respecting the establishment of religion or prohibiting or penalizing the free exercise thereof, and that no revenue of the state or any political subdivision or agency thereof ever be taken from the public treasury directly or indirectly in aid of any church, sect, or religious denomination, or in aid of any sectarian institution.
- Provides that the governor and the members of his or her cabinet constitute the state board of education, which shall be a body corporate and have supervision of the system of public education. As of January 7, 2003, requires that the state board of education be a body corporate and have such supervision of the system of free public education as is provided by law, and that the state board of education consist of seven members appointed by the governor to staggered 4-year terms, subject to confirmation by the senate.
- Creates an elected state commissioner of education, who shall supervise the public education system and be a member of the governor's cabinet. As of January 7, 2003, requires that the state board of education appoint the commissioner of education.
- Provides that each county constitutes a school district. Allows two or more contiguous counties, upon vote of the electors of each county, to be combined into one school district.
- Requires that there be, in each school district, a school board composed of five or more members chosen by vote of the electors for appropriately staggered terms of four years. Charges the school board with operating, controlling and supervising all free public schools within the school district and determining the rate of school district taxes within prescribed limits. Allows two or more school districts to operate and finance joint educational programs.
- Provides for an elected superintendent of schools in each school district. Allows a school district, either through a district school board resolution, special law or vote of the electors, to change from an elected superintendent to an appointed superintendent. Establishes the terms of office for the district school superintendents.

Georgia

- Requires that the provision of an adequate public education for the state's citizens be a primary obligation of the state, free and provided for by taxation.
- Requires that school tax funds be expended only for the support and maintenance of public schools, public vocational-technical schools and public education.
- Provides that no money ever be taken from the public treasury, directly or indirectly, in aid of any church, sect or denomination of religionists, or of any sectarian institution.

- Provides for a state board of education, to be appointed by the governor and confirmed by the senate. Establishes the terms of office for state board members.
- Provides for an elected state school superintendent, who shall be the executive officer of the state board.
- Requires each school system to be under the management and control of an elected board of education. Charges each local board of education with appointing a school superintendent, who shall be the executive officer of the local board of education.
- Grants authority to county and area boards of education to establish and maintain public schools within their limits.
- Allows the legislature to provide for the consolidation of two or more school systems, although no consolidation becomes effective until a majority of voters in each school system approves it.
- Allows two or more boards of education to contract with each other for the care, education and transportation of pupils.
- Allows the legislature to provide for the sharing of facilities or services by and between local boards of education under such joint administrative authority as may be authorized.
- Allows the legislature to provide for special schools and the participation of local boards of education in the establishment of such schools, although a majority of the voters must approve any bonded indebtedness or school tax levy.

Hawaii

- Requires the state to provide for the establishment, support and control of a statewide system of public schools.
- Prohibits public funds to be appropriated for the support or benefit of any sectarian or private educational institution, with certain exceptions.
- Requires that public schools be free from sectarian control.
- Provides that no law be enacted respecting an establishment of religion or prohibiting the free exercise thereof.
- Creates an elected state board of education. Specifies the composition and the method of election of the state board. Charges the state board with formulating statewide educational policy and appointing the state superintendent of education, who shall be the chief executive officer of the public school system.
- Requires the state to provide for a Hawaiian education program consisting of language, culture and history in the public schools. Encourages the use of community expertise as a suitable and essential means in furtherance of the Hawaiian education program.

Idaho

- Requires the legislature to establish and maintain a general, uniform and thorough system of public, free common schools.
- Forbids any appropriation or payment from any public fund in aid of any church or sectarian or religious society, for any sectarian or religious purpose or to help support or sustain any school, academy, seminary, college, university or other literary or scientific institution controlled by any church, sectarian or religious denomination. Forbids any grant or donation of land, money or other personal property by the state to any church or for any sectarian or religious purpose.
- Requires that public schools be free from sectarian instruction.
- Provides that the exercise and enjoyment of religious faith and worship forever be guaranteed; that no person be required to attend or support any ministry or place of worship, religious sect or denomination, or pay tithes against his consent; and that no preference be given by law to any religious denomination or mode of worship.

- Vests general supervision of state educational institutions and the public school system in a state board of education. Requires that the state superintendent of public instruction be an ex officio member of the state board.
- Allows the legislature to require that every child attend the public schools throughout the period between the ages of 6 and 18, unless educated by other means.

Illinois

- Requires the state to provide for an efficient system of high-quality public educational institutions and services, and a free education in public schools through the secondary level.
- Provides that the state has the primary responsibility for financing the system of public education.
- Forbids any appropriation or payment from any public fund in aid of any church or sectarian purpose or to help support or sustain any school, academy, seminary, college, university or other literary or scientific institution controlled by any church or sectarian denomination. Forbids any grant or donation of land, money or other personal property by the state to any church or for any sectarian purpose.
- Provides that the free exercise and enjoyment of religious profession and worship, without discrimination, forever be guaranteed; that no person be required to attend or support any ministry or place of worship against his consent; and that no preference be given by law to any religious denomination or mode of worship.
- Creates a state board of education. Allows the state board to establish goals, determine policies, provide for planning and evaluating education programs and recommend financing. Charges the state board with appointing the chief state educational officer.

Indiana

- Requires the legislature to provide for a general and uniform system of common schools, which shall be free and equally open to all.
- Requires that the income of the common school fund be inviolably appropriated to the support of common schools and to no other purpose whatever.
- Provides that no law, in any case whatever, control the free exercise and enjoyment of religious opinions, or interfere with the rights of conscience; that no preference be given, by law, to any creed, religious society or mode of worship; that no person be compelled to attend, erect or support any place of worship, or to maintain any ministry, against his consent; and that no money be drawn from the treasury, for the benefit of any religious or theological institution.
- Creates a state superintendent of public instruction.

Iowa

- Provides that the general assembly make no law respecting an establishment of religion or prohibiting the free exercise thereof, and that no person be compelled to attend any place of worship, pay tithes, taxes or other rates for building, or repairing places of worship, or the maintenance of any minister or ministry.
- According to an official at the Iowa Department of Education, the state of Iowa removed the education section from the Iowa Constitution and placed it in the Iowa statutes in 1864.

Kansas

- Requires the legislature to establish and maintain public schools, educational institutions and related activities.
- Forbids any religious sect or sects from controlling any part of the public educational funds.

- Provides that the right to worship God according to the dictates of conscience never be infringed; that no person be compelled to attend or support any form of worship; that no control of or interference with the rights of conscience be permitted; and that no preference be given by law to any religious establishment or mode of worship.
- Charges the legislature with providing for an elected state board of education, which shall have general supervision of public schools, educational institutions and all the educational interests of the state. Establishes the number of state board members. Charges the state board with appointing a state superintendent of public instruction, who shall be the state board's executive officer.
- Requires that local public schools under the general supervision of the state board of education be maintained, developed and operated by locally elected boards. Allows these local boards, under certain conditions, to make and carry out agreements for cooperative operation and administration of educational programs.
- Prohibits any state superintendent of public instruction or county superintendent of public instruction to be elected.

Kentucky

- Requires the legislature to provide for an efficient system of common schools throughout the state.
- Forbids any monies raised or levied for educational purposes to be appropriated to or used by or in aid of any church, sectarian or denominational school.
- Provides that no preference ever be given by law to any religious sect, society or denomination, nor to any particular creed, mode of worship or system of ecclesiastical polity; that no person be compelled to attend any place of worship, to contribute to the erection or maintenance of any such place, or to the salary or support of any minister of religion; that no man be compelled to send his child to any school to which he may be conscientiously opposed; and that no human authority, in any case whatever, control or interfere with the rights of conscience.

Louisiana

- Requires the legislature to provide for the education of the people of the state, and establish and maintain a public educational system.
- Provides that no law be enacted respecting an establishment of religion or prohibiting the free exercise thereof.
- Creates a state board of elementary and secondary education to supervise and control the public elementary and secondary schools, vocational technical training and other special schools. Establishes the terms of office, and the methods for appointing and electing state board members.
- Provides that the state board shall have no control over the business affairs of a parish or city school board, or the selection or removal of its officers and employees.
- Allows the state board to approve a private school with a sustained curriculum or specialized course of study of quality at least equal to that prescribed for similar public schools. Provides that a certificate issued by an approved private school carries the same privileges as one issued by a state public school.
- Provides for an elected state superintendent of education for public elementary and secondary education.
- Requires the legislature to create parish school boards and provide for the election of their members. Charges each parish board with electing a superintendent of parish schools.
- Allows any two or more school systems to be consolidated, subject to approval by a majority of the voting electors in each system affected.

- Requires the legislature to appropriate funds to supply free school books and other materials of instruction prescribed by the state board.

Maine

- Authorizes the legislature to require towns to make suitable provision, at their own expense, for the support and maintenance of public schools.
- Authorizes the legislature to encourage and suitably endow all academies, colleges and seminaries of learning within the state.
- Provides that all persons demeaning themselves peaceably, as good members of the state, be equally under the protection of the laws, and no subordination nor preference of any one sect or denomination to another ever be established by law, nor any religious test be required as a qualification for any office or trust, under this state; and that all religious societies in this state, whether incorporate or unincorporate, at all times have the exclusive right of electing their public teachers, and contracting with them for their support and maintenance.

Maryland

- Requires the legislature to provide for the establishment of a thorough and efficient system of free public schools, and to provide by taxation for their maintenance.
- Provides that the school fund be kept inviolate and appropriated only to the purposes of education.
- Provides that all persons are equally entitled to protection in their religious liberty, and that no person be compelled to frequent, maintain or contribute, unless on contract, to maintain any place of worship or any ministry.

Massachusetts

- Requires the legislatures and magistrates to cherish the interests of literature and the sciences and all seminaries of them, especially the University at Cambridge, public schools and grammar schools in the towns. Requires the legislatures and magistrates to encourage private societies and public institutions for the promotion of agriculture, arts, sciences, commerce, trades, manufactures and a natural history of the country.
- Forbids any grant, appropriation or use of public money or property or loan of credit to be made or authorized by the commonwealth for the purpose of founding, maintaining or aiding any infirmary, hospital, institution, primary or secondary school or charitable or religious undertaking which is not publicly owned and under the exclusive control, order and supervision of public officers or public agents authorized by the commonwealth or federal authority or both. Prohibits any such grant, appropriation or use of public money or property or loan of public credit to be made or authorized for the purpose of founding, maintaining or aiding any church, religious denomination or society.
- Provides that all religious sects and denominations, demeaning themselves peaceably and as good citizens of the commonwealth, be equally under the protection of the law; that no subordination of any one sect or denomination to another ever be established by law; and that no law be passed prohibiting the free exercise of religion.

Michigan

- Requires the legislature to maintain and support a system of free public elementary and secondary schools.
- Forbids any public monies or property to be appropriated or paid or any public credit utilized by the legislature or any other political subdivision or agency directly or indirectly to aid or maintain any private, denominational or other nonpublic pre-elementary, elementary or secondary school.
- Prohibits any payment, credit, tax benefit, exemption or deduction, tuition voucher, subsidy, grant or loan of public monies or property to be provided, directly or indirectly, to

support the attendance of any student or the employment of any person at any nonpublic school or at any location or institution where instruction is offered in whole or in part to nonpublic school systems.

- Provides that no person be compelled to attend or, against his consent, to contribute to the erection or support of any place of religious worship, or to pay tithes, taxes or other rates for the support of any minister of the gospel or teacher of religion; that no money be appropriated or drawn from the treasury for the benefit of any religious sect or society, theological or religious seminary; and that no property belonging to the state be appropriated for any such purpose.
- Vests leadership and general supervision over all public education in an elected state board of education. Establishes the number, method of election and terms of office of state board members. Charges the state board with appointing a state superintendent of public instruction, who shall be the chairman of the state board, the principal executive officer of a state department of education and responsible for the execution of the state board's policies.
- Allows the legislature to provide for the transportation of students to and from any school.

Minnesota

- Requires the legislature to establish a general and uniform system of public schools and make such provisions by taxation or otherwise as will secure a thorough and efficient system of public schools throughout the state.
- Forbids any public money or property to be appropriated or used for the support of schools wherein the distinctive doctrines, creeds or tenets of any particular Christian or other religious sect are promulgated or taught.
- Provides that no man be compelled to attend, erect or support any place of worship, or to maintain any religious or ecclesiastical ministry, against his consent; that no preference be given by law to any religious establishment or mode of worship; and that no money be drawn from the treasury for the benefit of any religious societies or religious or theological seminaries.

Mississippi

- Requires the legislature to provide for the establishment, maintenance and support of free public schools.
- Prohibits any funds to be appropriated toward the support of any sectarian school or to any school that at the time of receiving such appropriation is not conducted as a free school.
- Requires that public schools be free from sectarian control.
- Provides that no preference be given by law to any religious sect or mode of worship, but that the free enjoyment of all religious sentiments and the different modes of worship be held sacred.
- Creates an appointed state board of education. Establishes the method of appointment and terms of office for state board members. Delineates the state board's responsibilities. Charges the state board, with the advice and consent of the senate, with appointing a state superintendent of public education and a superintendent of public education in each county.
- Allows the legislature to make the office of county school superintendent elective, discharge the duties of county superintendent or abolish the office of county school superintendent.

Missouri

- Requires the legislature to establish and maintain free public schools for the gratuitous instruction of all persons in the state within ages not in excess of 21 years.

- Forbids any appropriation or payment from any public fund in aid of any religious creed, church or sectarian purpose or to help support or sustain any private or public school, academy, seminary, college, university or other institution of learning controlled by any religious creed, church or sectarian denomination. Forbids any grant or donation of personal property or real estate by the state for any religious creed, church or sectarian purpose.
- Provides that no person be compelled to erect, support or attend any place or system of worship, or to maintain or support any priest, minister, preacher or teacher of any sect, church, creed or denomination of religion, but if any person voluntarily makes a contract for any such object, he shall be held to the performance of the same; that no money ever be taken from the public treasury, directly or indirectly, in aid of any church, sect or denomination of religion, or in aid of any priest, preacher, minister or teacher thereof, as such; and that no preference be given to nor any discrimination made against any church, sect or creed of religion, or any form of religious faith or worship.
- Vests the supervision of instruction in the public schools in a state board of education, with its members appointed by the governor by and with the advice and consent of the senate. Sets the terms of office for state board members. Requires that there are never more than four members of the same political party on the state board. Charges the state board with selecting and appointing a commissioner of education.

Montana

- Requires the legislature to provide a basic system of free quality public elementary and secondary schools.
- Disallows any direct or indirect appropriation or payment from any public fund or monies or any grant of lands or other property for any sectarian purpose or to aid any church, school, academy, seminary, college, university or other literary or scientific institution controlled in whole or in part by any church, sect or denomination.
- Requires that public schools be free from sectarian instruction.
- Requires that the state make no law respecting an establishment of religion or prohibiting the free exercise thereof.
- Creates a state board of education, to be composed of the board of regents of higher education and the board of public education. Holds the state board responsible for long-range planning, and for coordinating and evaluating policies and programs for the state's educational systems.
- Creates a board of public education to exercise general supervision over the public school system, to be composed of the governor, the commissioner of higher education, the state superintendent of public instruction and seven members appointed by the governor and confirmed by the senate.
- Requires that the supervision and control of schools in each school district be vested in an elected board of trustees.

Nebraska

- Requires the legislature to provide for the free instruction in the state's common schools of all persons between the ages of 5 and 21 years.
- Forbids the appropriation of public funds to any school or institution of learning not owned or exclusively controlled by the state. Prohibits the state from accepting money or property to be used for sectarian purposes.
- Allows the legislature to authorize the state to contract with institutions not wholly owned or controlled by the state for the provision of educational or other services for the benefit of children under the age of 21 years who are handicapped, if such services are nonsectarian in nature.

- Requires that public schools be free from sectarian instruction.
- Provides that no person be compelled to attend, erect or support any place of worship against his consent, and no preference be given by law to any religious society.
- Creates the state department of education, to be composed of the state board of education and the commissioner of education. Provides that the state department has general supervision and administration of the school system of the state.
- Creates an elected state board of education, to be composed of eight members. Establishes the terms of office for state board members. Charges the state board with appointing the commissioner of education, who shall be the executive officer of the state board and the administrative head of the state department of education.

Nevada

- Requires the legislature to provide for a uniform system of common schools, by which a school shall be established and maintained in each school district at least six months in every year.
- Prohibits public funds of any kind or character to be used for sectarian purposes.
- Forbids any sectarian instruction to be imparted or tolerated in any school or university that is established under the state's constitution.
- Provides that any school district which allows instruction of a sectarian character may be deprived of its proportion of the interest of the public school fund during such neglect or infraction.
- Provides that the free exercise and enjoyment of religious profession and worship without discrimination or preference forever be allowed in the state.
- Requires the legislature to provide for a superintendent of public instruction.
- Allows the legislature to pass such laws as will secure a general attendance of the children at the public schools in each school district.

New Hampshire

- Requires the legislature to cherish all seminaries and public schools, and to encourage private and public institutions for the promotion of agriculture, arts, sciences, commerce, trades, manufactures and the natural history of the country.
- Forbids the state from mandating or assigning any new, expanded or modified programs or responsibilities to any political subdivision in such a way as to necessitate additional local expenditures by the political subdivision unless such programs or responsibilities are fully funded by the state or unless such programs or responsibilities are approved for funding by a vote of the local legislative body of the political subdivision.
- Prohibits any money raised by taxation to ever be granted or applied for the use of the schools or institutions of any religious sect or denomination.
- Provides that the several parishes, bodies, corporate or religious societies at all times have the right of electing their own teachers and of contracting with them for their support or maintenance, or both; that no person ever be compelled to pay towards the support of the schools of any sect or denomination; and that every person, denomination or sect be equally under the protection of the law, and no subordination of any one sect, denomination or persuasion to another ever be established.

New Jersey

- Requires the legislature to provide for the maintenance and support of a thorough and efficient system of free public schools for the instruction of all the children in the state between the ages of 5 and 18 years.
- Forbids the legislature from diverting the public school fund from the support of the public schools.

- Provides that no person be obliged to pay tithes, taxes or other rates for building or repairing any church or churches, place or places of worship, or for the maintenance of any minister or ministry, contrary to what he believes to be right or has deliberately and voluntarily engaged to perform, and that there be no establishment of one religious sect in preference to another.
- Allows the legislature to provide for the transportation of children between the ages of 5 to 18 years, inclusive, to and from any school.
- Provides that no person be denied the enjoyment of any civil or military right, nor be discriminated against in the exercise of any civil or military right, nor be segregated in the militia or in the public schools because of religious principles, race, color, ancestry or national origin.

New Mexico

- Requires that a uniform system of free public schools sufficient for the education of, and open to, all children of school age in the state be established and maintained.
- Forbids any money appropriated, levied or collected for educational purposes to be used for the support of any sectarian, denominational or private school.
- Provides that no person be required to attend any place of worship or support any religious sect or denomination, and that no preference be given by law to any religious denomination or mode of worship.
- Creates a state board of education to determine, control, manage and direct public school policy and vocational educational policy. Sets the terms of office for state board members, some of whom are elected and some of whom are appointed by the governor with the consent of the senate. Charges the state board with appointing a superintendent of public instruction to direct the state department of public education.
- Requires the legislature to provide for the training of teachers in the normal schools or otherwise so they become proficient in both the English and Spanish languages and are able to teach Spanish-speaking pupils and students in the public schools and educational institutions of the state. Requires the legislature to provide proper means and methods to facilitate the teaching of the English language and other branches of learning to such pupils and teachers.
- Allows those local school districts having a population of more than 200,000 to choose to have a local school board composed of seven members, who must be residents of and elected from single member districts.
- Provides for the recall of any elected local school board member by the voters of a local school district.
- Provides that every child of school age and of sufficient physical and mental ability be required to attend a public or other school.

New York

- Requires the legislature to provide for the maintenance and support of a system of free common schools, wherein all the state's children may be educated.
- Forbids the state from using its property or credit or any public money, or authorizing or permitting either to be used directly or indirectly in aid or maintenance of any school or institution of learning wholly or in part under the control or direction of any religious denomination, or in which any denominational tenet or doctrine is taught.
- Provides that the free exercise and enjoyment of religious profession and worship, without discrimination or preference, forever be allowed in New York to all mankind.
- Allows the legislature to provide for the transportation of children to and from any school or institution of learning.

North Carolina

- Provides that the people have a right to the privilege of education, and it is the duty of the state to guard and maintain that right.
- Requires the legislature to provide by taxation and otherwise for a general and uniform system of free public schools, which shall be maintained at least nine months in every year and wherein equal opportunities shall be provided for all students.
- Requires that the state school fund and the county school funds be faithfully appropriated and used exclusively for establishing and maintaining a uniform system of free public schools.
- Provides that no human authority, in any case whatever, control or interfere with the rights of conscience; that no person be denied the equal protection of the laws; and that no person be subjected to discrimination by the state because of race, color, religion or national origin.
- Creates a state board of education to supervise and administer the free public school system and the educational funds provided for its support. Requires that the state board consist of the lieutenant governor, the treasurer and eleven members appointed by the governor, and subject to confirmation by the legislature in a joint session. Establishes the methods of appointment and terms of office for state board members.
- Creates a state superintendent of public instruction, who shall be the secretary and chief administrative officer of the state board.

North Dakota

- Requires the legislature to make provision for the establishment and maintenance of a system of public schools, which shall be open to all the state's children.
- Requires the legislature to provide for a uniform system of free public schools throughout the state.
- Prohibits any money raised for the support of public schools to be appropriated to or used for the support of any sectarian school.
- Requires that public schools be free from sectarian control.
- Provides that the free exercise and enjoyment of religious profession and worship, without discrimination or preference, be forever guaranteed in North Dakota.

Ohio

- Requires the legislature to make such provision, by taxation or otherwise, as will secure a thorough and efficient system of common schools throughout the state.
- Requires that provisions be made by law for the organization, administration and control of the public school system of the state supported by public funds.
- Forbids any religious or other sect from having any exclusive right to, or control of, any part of the school funds of the state.
- Provides that no person be compelled to attend, erect or support any place of worship, or maintain any form of worship, against his consent; that no preference be given, by law, to any religious society; that no interference with the rights of conscience be permitted; and that it is the duty of the general assembly to pass suitable laws to protect every religious denomination in the peaceable enjoyment of its own mode of public worship, and to encourage schools and the means of instruction.
- Creates a state board of education. Charges the legislature with establishing the method of selection and terms of office for state board members. Charges the state board with appointing a state superintendent of public instruction.
- Authorizes each school district to determine by referendum vote the number of members and the organization of the district board of education.

Oklahoma

- Requires the legislature to establish and maintain a system of free public schools, which shall be open to all the children of the state and free from sectarian control; said schools shall always be conducted in English, although the teaching of other languages in said public schools is not precluded.
- Provides that no public money or property ever be appropriated, applied, donated or used, directly or indirectly, for the use, benefit or support of any sect, church, denomination, or system of religion, or for the use, benefit or support of any priest, preacher, minister, or other religious teacher or dignitary, or sectarian institution as such.
- Vests the supervision of instruction in the public schools in a state board of education. Requires the state superintendent of public instruction to be the president of the state board.
- Requires the legislature to provide for a system of textbooks for the common schools. Requires the state to furnish such textbooks free of cost for use by all the pupils of the common schools. Requires the legislature to authorize the governor to appoint a committee composed of active educators of the state, whose duty it shall be to prepare official multiple textbook lists from which textbooks for use in common schools shall be selected by committees composed of active educators in the local school districts in a manner to be designated by the legislature.
- Requires the legislature to provide for the teaching of the elements of agriculture, horticulture, stock feeding and domestic science in the common schools.
- Requires that the legislature provide for the compulsory attendance at some public or other school of all the children between the ages of 8 and 16 years for at least three months in each year.

Oregon

- Requires the legislature to provide for the establishment of a uniform and general system of common schools.
- Provides that no law in any case whatever control the free exercise and enjoyment of religious opinions, or interfere with the rights of conscience, that no money be drawn from the treasury for the benefit of any religious, or theological institution; and that no money be appropriated for the payment of any religious services in either house of the legislature.
- Charges the legislature with providing for the election of a state superintendent of public instruction.

Pennsylvania

- Requires the legislature to provide for the maintenance and support of a thorough and efficient system of public education to serve the needs of the commonwealth.
- Forbids any money raised for the support of the public schools to be appropriated to or used for the support of any sectarian school.
- Provides that no man can of right be compelled to attend, erect or support any place of worship, or to maintain any ministry against his consent; and that no preference ever be given by law to any religious establishments or modes of worship.

Rhode Island

- Requires the legislature to promote public schools and to adopt all means which it may deem necessary and proper to secure to the people the advantages and opportunities of education.
- Forbids the legislature from diverting the school fund from the support of the public schools.
- Provides that no person be compelled to frequent or to support any religious worship, place or ministry whatever, except in fulfillment of such person's voluntary contract.

South Carolina

- Requires the legislature to provide for the maintenance and support of a system of free public schools open to all children.
- Forbids any money to be paid from public funds for the direct benefit of any religious or other private educational institution.
- Provides that the legislature make no law respecting an establishment of religion or prohibiting the free exercise thereof.
- Creates a state board of education, all of whose members are elected (except a member appointed by the governor).
- Creates a state superintendent of education, who shall be the chief administrative officer of the public education system.

South Dakota

- Requires the legislature to establish and maintain a general and uniform system of public schools, equally open to all and wherein tuition shall be without charge.
- Disallows any appropriation of lands, money or other property or credits to aid any sectarian school by the state. Forbids the state to accept any grant, conveyance, gift or bequest of lands, money or other property to be used for sectarian purposes.
- Requires that public schools be free from sectarian instruction.
- Allows the legislature to authorize the loaning of nonsectarian textbooks to all children of school age.
- Provides that no person be compelled to attend or support any ministry or place of worship against his consent; that no preference be given by law to any religious establishment or mode of worship; and that no money or property of the state be given or appropriated for the benefit of any sectarian or religious society or institution.

Tennessee

- Requires the legislature to provide for the maintenance, support and eligibility standards of a system of free public schools.
- Provides that no man be compelled to attend, erect or support any place of worship, or to maintain any minister against his consent; and that no preference ever be given, by law, to any religious establishment or mode of worship.

Texas

- Requires the legislature to establish and make suitable provision for the support and maintenance of an efficient system of free public schools.
- Prohibits any part of the public school fund to ever be appropriated to or used for the support of any sectarian school.
- Provides that no man be compelled to attend, erect or support any place of worship, or to maintain any ministry against his consent; that no preference ever be given by law to any religious society or mode of worship; that it is the duty of the legislature to pass such laws as may be necessary to protect equally every religious denomination in the peaceable enjoyment of its own mode of public worship; that no money be appropriated, or drawn from the treasury for the benefit of any sect or religious society, theological or religious seminary; and that no property belonging to the state be appropriated for any such purposes.
- Provides for the support of public schools for not less than six months in each year.
- Requires the legislature to provide for a state board of education and establish the terms of office for each board member.
- Requires the legislature to set the terms of all offices of the public school system not to exceed six years.

- Charges the state board with providing free textbooks for children attending the public schools.

Utah

- Requires the legislature to provide for the establishment and maintenance of a public education system, which shall include all public elementary and secondary schools, be open to all children of the state and free, except that the legislature may authorize the imposition of fees in secondary schools.
- Prohibits any appropriations for the direct support of any school or educational institution controlled by any religious organization.
- Requires that the public education system be free of sectarian control.
- Provides that the state make no law respecting an establishment of religion or prohibiting the free exercise thereof; that there be no union of church and state; that no church dominate the state or interfere with its functions; and that no public money or property be appropriated for or applied to any religious worship, exercise or instruction, or for the support of any ecclesiastical establishment.
- Vests the general control and supervision of public education in an elected state board of education. Charges the state board with appointing a state superintendent of public instruction.

Vermont

- Provides that a competent number of schools ought to be maintained in each town unless the general assembly permits other provisions for the convenient instruction of youth.
- Provides that no person ought to, or of right be compelled to attend any religious worship, or erect or support any place of worship, or maintain any minister, contrary to the dictates of conscience, and that no authority can, or ought to be vested in, or assumed by, any power whatever, that in any case interferes with, or in any manner control the rights of conscience, in the free exercise of religious worship.

Virginia

- Requires the legislature to provide for a system of free public elementary and secondary schools for all children of school age and to seek to ensure that an educational program of high quality is established and maintained.
- Allows the legislature to provide for the establishment, maintenance and operation of any educational institutions which are desirable for the intellectual, cultural and occupational development of the people.
- Prohibits any appropriation of public funds to any school or institution of learning not owned or exclusively controlled by the state or some political subdivision. Allows the state to appropriate funds for educational purposes in public and nonsectarian private schools and institutions of learning.
- Provides that no man be compelled to frequent or support any religious worship, place or ministry whatsoever; that the legislature not prescribe any religious test whatever, or confer any peculiar privileges or advantages on any sect or denomination, or pass any law requiring or authorizing any religious society, or the people of any district within the commonwealth, to levy on themselves or others, any tax for the erection or repair of any house of public worship, or for the support of any church or ministry; but it shall be left free to every person to select his religious instructor, and to make for his support such private contract as he shall please.
- Vests the general supervision of the public school system in a state board of education, to be composed of nine members appointed by the governor and subject to confirmation by the legislature. Establishes the terms of office for state board members. Prescribes the powers and duties of the state board.

- Creates a state superintendent of public instruction, who shall be an experienced educator, appointed by the governor and subject to confirmation by the legislature. Allows the legislature to alter the method of selection and term of office for the state superintendent of public instruction.
- Vests the supervision of schools in each school division in a school board.
- Requires the state board to certify to the school board of each division a list of qualified persons for the office of division superintendent of schools, one of whom shall be selected to fill the post by the division school board. Charges the state board with appointing a division superintendent if a division school board fails to select a division superintendent within the time prescribed by law.
- Requires the state board to periodically determine and prescribe standards of quality for school divisions, subject to revision only by the legislature.
- Authorizes the state board to approve textbooks and instructional aids and materials for use in courses in the public schools.
- Requires the legislature to ensure that textbooks are provided at no cost to each child attending public school whose parent or guardian is financially unable to furnish them.
- Charges the legislature with providing for the compulsory elementary and secondary education of every eligible child of appropriate age.

Washington

- Requires the legislature to provide for a general and uniform system of public schools.
- Requires that the entire revenue derived from the common school fund and the state tax for common schools be exclusively applied to the support of the common schools.
- Requires that all schools maintained or supported wholly or in part by public funds be forever free from sectarian control or influence.
- Provides that no public money or property be appropriated for or applied to any religious worship, exercise or instruction, or the support of any religious establishment.

West Virginia

- Requires the legislature to provide for a thorough and efficient system of free schools.
- Provides that no man be compelled to frequent or support any religious worship, place or ministry whatsoever; that the legislature not prescribe any religious test whatever, or confer any peculiar privileges or advantages on any sect or denomination, or pass any law requiring or authorizing any religious society, or the people of any district within the state, to levy on themselves, or others, any tax for the erection or repair of any house for public worship, or for the support of any church or ministry, but it shall be left free for every person to select his religious instructor, and to make for his support, such private contracts as he shall please.
- Requires public schools to provide a designated brief time at the beginning of each school day for any student desiring to exercise their right to personal and private contemplation, meditation or prayer; that no student of a public school be denied the right to personal and private contemplation, meditation or prayer; and that no student be required or encouraged to engage in any given contemplation, meditation or prayer as a part of the school curriculum.
- Vests the general supervision of the free schools in the state board of education, to be composed of nine members appointed by the governor by and with the advice and consent of the senate. Forbids any more than five members of the state board from belonging to the same political party. Establishes the terms of office and the grounds for removal from office for state board members. Charges the state board with selecting the state superintendent of free schools, who shall be the chief school officer of the state.

- Allows the legislature to provide for county superintendents and such other officers as may be necessary.

Wisconsin

- Requires the legislature to provide for the establishment of district schools, which shall be as nearly uniform as practicable and free and without charge for tuition for all children between the ages of 4 and 20 years.
- Forbids any money to be drawn from the treasury for the benefit of religious societies or religious or theological seminaries.
- Prohibits any sectarian instruction in district schools. Allows the legislature, for the purpose of religious instruction outside the district schools, to authorize the release of students during regular school hours.
- Allows the legislature to provide for the transportation of children to and from any parochial or private school or institution of learning.
- Allows the legislature to authorize, by law, the use of public school buildings by civic, religious or charitable organizations during nonschool hours upon payment by the organization to the school district of reasonable compensation for such use.
- Provides that no man be compelled to attend, erect or support any place of worship, or to maintain any ministry, against his consent; that no control of, or interference with, the rights of conscience be permitted, or any preference be given by law to any religious establishments or modes of worship; and that no money be drawn from the treasury for the benefit of religious societies, or religious or theological seminaries.
- Vests the supervision of public instruction in an elected state superintendent of public instruction. Prescribes the method of election and the term of office for the state superintendent of public instruction.

Wyoming

- Provides that the right of the citizens to opportunities for education have practical recognition, and requires the legislature to suitably encourage means and agencies calculated to advance the sciences and liberal arts.
- Requires the legislature to provide for the establishment and maintenance of a complete and uniform system of public instruction.
- Requires the legislature to create and maintain a thorough and efficient system of public schools, adequate to the proper instruction of all youth of the state between the ages of 6 and 21 years, and free of charge.
- Forbids any portion of any public school fund to ever be used to support or assist any private school or any school, academy, seminary, college or other institution of learning controlled by any church or sectarian organization or religious denomination.
- Requires that public schools be free from sectarian instruction.
- Provides that the free exercise and enjoyment of religious profession and worship without discrimination or preference be forever guaranteed in the state, and that no money of the state ever be given or appropriated to any sectarian or religious society or institution.
- Provides for the support of public schools for not less than three months in each year.
- Entrusts the general supervision of the public schools to the state superintendent of public instruction.
- Charges the legislature with requiring every child of sufficient physical and mental ability to attend a public school during the period between 6 and 18 years for a time equivalent to three years, unless educated by other means.
- Forbids the legislature and the state superintendent of public instruction from prescribing textbooks to be used in the public schools.

This *ECS StateNote* was compiled by Todd Ziebarth, policy analyst, ECS National Center for Innovation in Governing American Education, with financial support from the Joyce Foundation.

Reprinted with permission of the Education Commission of the States, *ECS StateNote* "State Constitutions and Public Education Governance," 2000.

LEGISLATION

LAND ORDINANCE OF 1785

An Ordinance for ascertaining the mode of disposing of Lands in the Western Territory.

Be it ordained by the United States in Congress assembled, that the territory ceded by individual States to the United States, which has been purchased of the Indian inhabitants, shall be disposed of in the following manner:

A surveyor from each state shall be appointed by Congress, or a committee of the States, who shall take an Oath for the faithful discharge of his duty, before the Geographer of the United States, who is hereby empowered and directed to administer the same; and the like oath shall be administered to each chain carrier, by the surveyor under whom he acts.

The Geographer, under whose direction the surveyors shall act, shall occasionally form such regulations for their conduct, as he shall deem necessary; and shall have authority to suspend them for misconduct in Office, and shall make report of the same to Congress, or to the Committee of the States; and he shall make report in case of sickness, death, or resignation of any surveyor.

The Surveyors, as they are respectively qualified, shall proceed to divide the said territory into townships of six miles square, by lines running due north and south, and others crossing these at right angles, as near as may be, unless where the boundaries of the late Indian purchases may render the same impracticable, and then they shall depart from this rule no farther than such particular circumstances may require; and each surveyor shall be allowed and paid at the rate of two dollars for every mile, in length, he shall run, including the wages of chain carriers, markers, and every other expense attending the same.

The first line, running north and south as aforesaid, shall begin on the river Ohio, at a point that shall be found to be due north from the western termination of a line, which has been run as the southern boundary of the state of Pennsylvania; and the first line, running east and west, shall begin at the same point, and shall extend throughout the whole territory. Provided, that nothing herein shall be construed, as fixing the western boundary of the state of Pennsylvania. The geographer shall designate the townships, or fractional parts of townships, by numbers progressively from south to north; always beginning each range with number one; and the ranges shall be distinguished by their progressive numbers to the westward. The first range, extending from the Ohio to the lake Erie, being marked number one. The Geographer shall personally attend to the running of the first east and west line; and shall take the latitude of the extremes of the first north and south line, and of the mouths of the principal rivers.

The lines shall be measured with a chain; shall be plainly marked by chaps on the trees, and exactly described on a plat; whereon shall be noted by the surveyor, at their proper distances, all mines, salt springs, salt licks and mill seats, that shall come to his knowledge, and all water courses, mountains and other remarkable and permanent things, over and near which such lines shall pass, and also the quality of the lands.

The plats of the townships respectively, shall be marked by subdivisions into lots of one mile square, or 640 acres, in the same direction as the external lines, and numbered from 1 to 36; always beginning the succeeding range of the lots with the number next to that with which the preceding one concluded. And where, from the causes before mentioned, only a fractional part of a township shall be surveyed, the lots, protracted thereon, shall bear the same numbers as if the township had been entire. And the surveyors, in running the external lines of the townships, shall, at the interval of every mile, mark corners for the lots which are adjacent, always designating the same in a different manner from those of the townships.

The geographer and surveyors shall pay the utmost attention to the variation of the magnetic needle; and shall run and note all lines by the true meridian, certifying, with every plat, what was the variation at the times of running the lines thereon noted.

As soon as seven ranges of townships, and fractional parts of townships, in the direction from south to north, shall have been surveyed, the geographer shall transmit plats thereof to the board of treasury, who shall record the same, with the report, in well bound books to be kept for that purpose. And the geographer shall make similar returns, from time to time, of every seven ranges as they may be surveyed. The Secretary at War shall have recourse thereto, and shall take by lot therefrom, a number of townships, and fractional parts of townships, as well from those to be sold entire as from those to be sold in lots, as will be equal to one seventh part of the whole of such seven ranges, as nearly as may be, for the use of the late continental army; and he shall make a similar draught, from time to time, until a sufficient quantity is drawn to satisfy the same, to be applied in manner hereinafter directed. The board of treasury shall, from time to time, cause the remaining numbers, as well those to be sold entire, as those to be sold in lots, to be drawn for, in the name of the thirteen states respectively, according to the quotas in the last preceding requisition on all the states; provided, that in case more land than its proportion is allotted for sale, in any state, at any distribution, a deduction be made therefor at the next.

The board of treasury shall transmit a copy of the original plats, previously noting thereon, the townships, and fractional parts of townships, which shall have fallen to the several states, by the distribution aforesaid, to the Commissioners of the loan office of the several states, who, after giving notice of not less than two nor more than six months, by causing advertisements to be posted up at the court houses, or other noted places in every county, and to be inserted in one newspaper, published in the states of their residence respectively, shall proceed to sell the townships, or fractional parts of townships, at public venue, in the following manner, viz: The township, or fractional part of a township, N 1, in the first range, shall be sold entire; and N 2, in the same range, by lots; and thus in alternate order through the whole of the first range. The township, or fractional part of a township, N 1, in the second range, shall be sold by lots; and N 2, in the same range, entire; and so in alternate order through the whole of the second range; and the third range shall be sold in the same manner as the first, and the fourth in the same manner as the second, and thus alternately throughout all the ranges; provided, that none of the lands, within the said territory, be sold under the price of one dollar the acre, to be paid in specie, or loan office certificates, reduced to specie value, by the scale of depreciation, or certificates of liquidated debts of the United States, including interest, besides the expense of the survey and other charges thereon, which are hereby rated at thirty six dollars the township, in specie, or certificates as aforesaid, and so in the same proportion for a fractional part of a township, or of a lot, to be paid at the time of sales; on failure of which payment, the said lands shall again be offered for sale.

There shall be reserved for the United States out of every township, the four lots, being numbered 8, 11, 26, 29, and out of every fractional part of a township, so many lots of the same numbers as shall be found thereon, for future sale. There shall be reserved the lot N 16, of every township, for the maintenance of public schools, within the said township; also one third part of all gold, silver, lead and copper mines, to be sold, or otherwise disposed of as Congress shall hereafter direct.

When any township, or fractional part of a township, shall have been sold as aforesaid, and the money or certificates received therefor, the loan officer shall deliver a deed in the following terms:

The United States of America, to all to whom these presents shall come, greeting:

Know ye, That for the consideration of dollars, we have granted, and hereby do grant and confirm unto the township, (or fractional part of a township, as the case may be) numbered in the range excepting therefrom, and reserving one third part of all gold, silver, lead and copper mines within the same; and the lots Ns 8, 11, 26, and 29, for future sale or disposition, and the lot N 16, for the maintenance of public schools. To have to the said his heirs and assigns for ever; (or if more than one purchaser, to the said their heirs and assigns forever as tenants in Common.) In witness whereof, (A. B.) Commissioner of the loan office, in the State of hath, in conformity to the Ordinance passed by the United States in Congress assembled, the twentieth day of May, in the year of our Lord one thousand seven hundred and eighty five, hereunto set his hand, and affixed his seal, this day of in the year of our Lord and of the independence of the United States of America

And when any township, or fractional part of a township, shall be sold by lots as aforesaid, the Commissioner of the loan office shall deliver a deed therefor in the following form:

The United States of America, to all to whom these presents shall come, Greeting:

Know ye, That for the consideration of dollars, we have granted, and hereby do grant and confirm unto the lot (or lots, as the case may be, in the township or fractional part of the township, as the case may be) numbered in the range excepting and reserving one third part of all gold, silver, lead and copper mines within the same, for future sale or disposition. To have to the said his heirs and assigns for ever; (or if more than one purchaser, to the said their heirs and assigns for ever as tenants in common.) In witness whereof, (A. B.) Commissioner of the continental loan office in the state of hath, in conformity to the Ordinance passed by the United States in Congress assembled, the twentieth day of May, in the year of our Lord 1785, hereunto set his hand, and affixed his seal, this day of in the year of our Lord and of the independence of the United States of America

Which deeds shall be recorded in proper books, by the commissioner of the loan office, and shall be certified to have been recorded, previous to their being delivered to the purchaser, and shall be good and valid to convey the lands in the same described.

The commissioners of the loan offices respectively, shall transmit to the board of treasury every three months, an account of the townships, fractional parts of townships, and lots committed to their charge; specifying therein the names of the persons to whom sold, and the sums of money or certificates received for the same; and shall cause all certificates by them received, to be struck through with a circular punch; and they shall be duly charged in the books of the treasury, with the amount of the moneys or certificates, distinguishing the same, by them received as aforesaid.

If any township, or fractional part of a township or lot, remains unsold for eighteen months after the plat shall have been received, by the commissioners of the loan office, the same shall be returned to the board of treasury, and shall be sold in such manner as Congress may hereafter direct.

And whereas Congress, by their resolutions of September 16 and 18 in the year 1776, and the 12th of August, 1780, stipulated grants of land to certain officers and soldiers of the late continental army, and by the resolution of the 22d September, 1780, stipulated grants of land to certain officers in the hospital department of the late continental army; for complying therefore with such engagements, Be it ordained, That the secretary at war, from the returns in his office, or such other sufficient evidence as the nature of the case may admit, determine who are the objects of the above resolutions and engagements, and the quantity of land to which such persons or their representatives are respectively entitled, and cause the townships, or fractional parts of townships, hereinbefore reserved for the use of the late continental army, to be drawn for in such manner as he shall deem expedient, to answer the purpose of an impartial distribution. He shall, from time to time, transmit certificates to the commissioners of the loan offices of the different states, to the lines of which the military claimants have respectively belonged, specifying the name and rank of the party, the terms of his engagement and time of his service, and the division, brigade, regiment or company to which he belonged, the quantity of land he is entitled to, and the township, or fractional part of a township, and range out of which his portion is to be taken.

The commissioners of the loan offices shall execute deeds for such undivided proportions in manner and form herein before-mentioned, varying only in such a degree as to make the same conformable to the certificate from the Secretary at War.

Where any military claimants of bounty in lands shall not have belonged to the line of any particular state, similar certificates shall be sent to the board of treasury, who shall execute deeds to the parties for the same.

The Secretary at War, from the proper returns, shall transmit to the board of treasury, a certificate, specifying the name and rank of the several claimants of the hospital department of the late continental army, together with the quantity of land each claimant is entitled to, and the township, or fractional part of a township, and range out of which his portion is to be taken; and thereupon the board of treasury shall proceed to execute deeds to such claimants.

The board of treasury, and the commissioners of the loan offices in the states, shall, within 18 months, return receipts to the secretary at war, for all deeds which have been delivered, as also all the original deeds which remain in their hands for want of applicants, having been first recorded; which deeds so returned, shall be preserved in the office, until the parties or their representatives require the same.

And be it further Ordained, That three townships adjacent to lake Erie be reserved, to be hereafter disposed of by Congress, for the use of the officers, men, and others, refugees from Canada, and the refugees from Nova Scotia, who are or may be entitled to grants of land under resolutions of Congress now existing, or which may hereafter be made respecting them, and for such other purposes as Congress may hereafter direct.

And be it further Ordained, That the towns of Gnadenhutten, Schoenbrun and Salem, on the Muskingum, and so much of the lands adjoining to the said towns, with the buildings and improvements thereon, shall be reserved for the sole use of the Christian Indians, who were formerly settled there, or the remains of that society, as may, in the judgment of the Geographer, be sufficient for them to cultivate.

Saving and reserving always, to all officers and soldiers entitled to lands on the northwest side of the Ohio, by donation or bounty from the commonwealth of Virginia, and to all persons claiming under them, all rights to which they are so entitled, under the deed of cession executed by the delegates for the state of Virginia, on the first day of March, 1784, and the act of Congress accepting the same: and to the end, that the said rights may be fully and effectually secured, according to the true intent and meaning of the said deed of cession and act aforesaid, Be it Ordained, that no part of the land included between the rivers called little Miami and Sciota, on the northwest side of the river Ohio, be sold, or in any manner alienated, until there shall first have been laid off and appropriated for the said Officers and Soldiers, and persons claiming under them, the lands they are entitled to, agreeably to the said deed of cession and act of Congress accepting the same.

Done by the United States in Congress assembled, the 20th day of

May, in the year of our Lord 1785, and of our sovereignty and independence the ninth.

Charles Thomson, Secretary.

Richard H. Lee, President.

NORTHWEST ORDINANCE OF 1787

An Ordinance for the government of the Territory of the United States northwest of the River Ohio.

Section 1. Be it ordained by the United States in Congress assembled, That the said territory, for the purposes of temporary government, be one district, subject, however, to be divided into two districts, as future circumstances may, in the opinion of Congress, make it expedient.

Sec. 2. Be it ordained by the authority aforesaid, That the estates, both of resident and non-resident proprietors in the said territory, dying intestate, shall descend to, and be distributed among their children, and the descendants of a deceased child, in equal parts; the descendants of a deceased child or grandchild to take the share of their deceased parent in equal parts among them: And where there shall be no children or descendants, then in equal parts to the next of kin in equal degree; and among collaterals, the children of a deceased brother or sister of the intestate shall have, in equal parts among them, their deceased parents' share; and there shall in no case be a distinction between kindred of the whole and half-blood; saving, in all cases, to the widow of the intestate her third part of the real estate for life, and one-third part of the personal estate; and this law relative to descents and dower, shall remain in full force until altered by the legislature of the district. And until the governor and judges shall adopt laws as hereinafter mentioned, estates in the said territory may be devised or bequeathed by wills in writing, signed and sealed by him or her in whom the estate may be (being of full age), and attested by three witnesses; and real estates may be conveyed by lease and release, or bargain and sale, signed sealed and delivered by the person, being of full age, in whom the estate may be, and attested by two witnesses, provided such wills be duly proved, and such conveyances be acknowledged, or the execution thereof duly proved, and be recorded within one year after proper magistrates, courts, and registers shall be appointed for that purpose; and personal property may be transferred by delivery; saving, however to the French and Canadian inhabitants, and other settlers of the Kaskaskies, St. Vincents and the neighboring villages who have heretofore professed themselves citizens of Virginia, their laws and customs now in force among them, relative to the descent and conveyance, of property.

Sec. 3. Be it ordained by the authority aforesaid, That there shall be appointed from time to time by Congress, a governor, whose commission shall continue in force for the term of three years, unless sooner revoked by Congress; he shall reside in the district, and have a freehold estate therein in 1,000 acres of land, while in the exercise of his office.

Sec. 4. There shall be appointed from time to time by Congress, a secretary, whose commission shall continue in force for four years unless sooner revoked; he shall reside in the district, and have a freehold estate therein in 500 acres of land, while in the exercise of his office. It shall be his duty to keep and preserve the acts and laws passed by the legislature, and the public records of the district, and the proceedings of the governor in his executive department, and transmit authentic copies of such acts and proceedings, every six months, to the Secretary of Congress: There shall also be appointed a court to consist of three judges, any two of whom to form a court, who shall have a common law jurisdiction, and reside in the district, and have each therein a freehold estate in 500 acres of land while in the exercise of their offices; and their commissions shall continue in force during good behavior.

Sec. 5. The governor and judges, or a majority of them, shall adopt and publish in the district such laws of the original States, criminal and civil, as may be necessary and best suited to the circumstances of the district, and report them to Congress from time to time: which laws shall be in force in the district until the organization of the General Assembly therein, unless disapproved of by Congress; but afterwards the Legislature shall have authority to alter them as they shall think fit.

Sec. 6. The governor, for the time being, shall be commander-in-chief of the militia, appoint and commission all officers in the same below the rank of general officers; all general officers shall be appointed and commissioned by Congress.

Sec. 7. Previous to the organization of the general assembly, the governor shall appoint such magistrates and other civil officers in each county or township, as he shall find necessary for the preservation of the peace and good order in the same: After the general assembly shall be organized, the powers and duties of the magistrates and other civil officers shall be regulated and defined by the said assembly; but all magistrates and other civil officers not herein otherwise directed, shall, during the continuance of this temporary government, be appointed by the governor.

Sec. 8. For the prevention of crimes and injuries, the laws to be adopted or made shall have force in all parts of the district, and for the execution of process, criminal and civil, the governor shall make proper divisions thereof; and he shall proceed from time to time as circumstances may require, to lay out the parts of the district in which the Indian titles shall have been extinguished, into counties and townships, subject however to such alterations as may thereafter be made by the legislature.

Sec. 9. So soon as there shall be five thousand free male inhabitants of full age in the district, upon giving proof thereof to the governor, they shall receive authority, with time and place, to elect representatives from their counties or townships to represent them in the general assembly: Provided, That, for every five hundred free male inhabitants, there shall be one representative, and so on progressively with the number of free male inhabitants shall the right of representation increase, until the number of representatives shall amount to twenty-five; after which, the number and proportion of representatives shall be regulated by the legislature: Provided, That no person be eligible or qualified to act as a representative unless he shall have been a citizen of one of the United States three years, and be a resident in the district, or unless he shall have resided in the district three years; and, in either case, shall likewise hold in his own right, in fee simple, two hundred acres of land within the same: Provided, also, That a freehold in fifty acres of land in the district, having been a citizen of one of the states, and being resident in the district, or the like freehold and two years residence in the district, shall be necessary to qualify a man as an elector of a representative.

Sec. 10. The representatives thus elected, shall serve for the term of two years; and, in case of the death of a representative, or removal from office, the governor shall issue a writ to the county or township for which he was a member, to elect another in his stead, to serve for the residue of the term.

Sec. 11. The general assembly or legislature shall consist of the governor, legislative council, and a house of representatives. The Legislative Council shall consist of five members, to continue in office five years, unless sooner removed by Congress; any three of whom to be a quorum: and the members of the Council shall be nominated and appointed in the following manner, to wit: As soon as representatives shall be elected, the Governor shall appoint a time and place for them to meet together; and, when met, they shall nominate ten persons, residents in the district, and each possessed of a freehold in five hundred acres of land, and return their names to Congress; five of whom Congress shall appoint and commission to serve as aforesaid; and, whenever a vacancy shall happen in the council, by death or removal from office, the house of representatives shall nominate two persons, qualified as aforesaid, for each vacancy, and return their names to Congress; one of whom Congress shall appoint and commission for the residue of the term. And every five years, four months at least before the expiration of the time of service of the members of council, the said house shall nominate ten persons, qualified as aforesaid, and return their names to Congress; five of whom Congress shall appoint and commission to serve as members of the council five years, unless sooner removed. And the governor, legislative council, and house of representatives shall have authority to make laws in all cases, for the good government of the district, not repugnant to the principles and articles in this ordinance established and declared. And all bills, having passed by a majority in the house, and by a majority in the council, shall be referred to the governor for his assent; but no bill, or legislative act whatever, shall be of any force without his assent. The governor shall have power to convene, prorogue, and dissolve the general assembly, when, in his opinion, it shall be expedient.

Sec. 12. The governor, judges, legislative council, secretary, and such other officers as Congress shall appoint in the district, shall take an oath or affirmation of fidelity and of office; the governor before the president of congress, and all other officers before the Governor. As soon as a legislature shall be formed in the district, the council and house assembled in one room, shall have authority, by joint ballot, to elect a delegate to Congress, who shall have a seat in Congress, with a right of debating but not of voting during this temporary government.

Sec. 13. And, for extending the fundamental principles of civil and religious liberty, which form the basis whereon these republics, their laws and constitutions are erected; to fix and establish those principles as the basis of all laws, constitutions, and governments, which forever hereafter shall be formed in the said territory: to provide also for the establishment of States, and permanent government therein, and for their admission to a share in the federal councils on an equal footing with the original States, at as early periods as may be consistent with the general interest:

Sec. 14. It is hereby ordained and declared by the authority aforesaid, That the following articles shall be considered as articles of compact between the original States and the people and States in the said territory and forever remain unalterable, unless by common consent, to wit:

Art. 1. No person, demeaning himself in a peaceable and orderly manner, shall ever be molested on account of his mode of worship or religious sentiments, in the said territory.

Art. 2. The inhabitants of the said territory shall always be entitled to the benefits of the writ of habeas corpus, and of the trial by jury; of a proportionate representation of the people in the legislature; and of judicial proceedings according to the course of the common law. All persons shall be bailable, unless for capital offences, where the proof shall be evident or the presumption great. All fines shall be moderate; and no cruel or unusual punishments shall be inflicted. No man shall be deprived of his liberty or property, but by the judgment of his peers or the law of the land; and, should the public exigencies make it necessary, for the common preservation, to take any person's property, or to demand his particular services, full compensation shall be made for the same. And, in the just preservation of rights and property, it is understood and declared, that no law ought ever to be made, or have force in the said territory, that shall, in any manner whatever, interfere with or affect private contracts or engagements, bona fide, and without fraud, previously formed.

Art. 3. Religion, morality, and knowledge, being necessary to good government and the happiness of mankind, schools and the means of education shall forever be encouraged. The utmost good faith shall always be observed towards the Indians; their lands and property shall never be taken from them without their consent; and, in their property, rights, and liberty, they shall never be invaded or disturbed, unless in just and lawful wars authorized by Congress; but laws founded in justice and humanity, shall from time to time be made for preventing wrongs being done to them, and for preserving peace and friendship with them.

Art. 4. The said territory, and the States which may be formed therein, shall forever remain a part of this Confederacy of the United States of America, subject to the Articles of Confederation, and to such alterations therein as shall be constitutionally made; and to all the acts and ordinances of the United States in Congress assembled, conformable thereto. The inhabitants and settlers in the said territory shall be subject to pay a part of the federal debts contracted or to be contracted, and a proportional part of the expenses of government, to be apportioned on them by Congress according to the same common rule and measure by which apportionments thereof shall be made on the other States; and the taxes for paying their proportion shall be laid and levied by the authority and direction of the legislatures of the district or districts, or new States, as in the original States, within the time agreed upon by the United States in Congress assembled. The legislatures of those districts or new States, shall never interfere with the primary disposal of the soil by the United States in Congress assembled, nor with any regulations Congress may find necessary for securing the title in such soil to the bona fide purchasers. No tax shall be imposed on lands the property of the United States; and, in no case, shall non-resident proprietors be taxed higher than residents. The navigable waters leading into the Mississippi and St. Lawrence, and the carrying places between the same, shall be common highways and forever free, as well to the inhabitants of the said territory as to the citizens of the United States, and those of any other States that may be admitted into the confederacy, without any tax, impost, or duty therefor.

Art. 5. There shall be formed in the said territory, not less than three nor more than five States; and the boundaries of the States, as soon as Virginia shall alter her act of cession, and consent to the same, shall become fixed and established as follows, to wit: The western State in the said territory, shall be bounded by the Mississippi, the Ohio, and Wabash Rivers; a direct line drawn from the Wabash and Post Vincents, due North, to the territorial line between the United States and Canada; and, by the said territorial line, to the Lake of the Woods and Mississippi. The middle State shall be bounded by the said direct line, the Wabash from Post Vincents to the Ohio, by the Ohio, by a direct line, drawn due north from the mouth of the Great Miami, to the said territorial line, and by the said territorial line. The eastern State shall be bounded by the last mentioned direct line, the Ohio, Pennsylvania, and the said territorial line: Provided, however, and it is further understood and declared, that the boundaries of these three States shall be subject so far to be altered, that, if Congress shall hereafter find it expedient, they shall have authority to form one or two States in that part of the said territory which lies north of an east and west line drawn through the southerly bend or extreme of lake Michigan. And, whenever any of the said States shall have sixty thousand free inhabitants therein, such State shall be admitted, by its delegates, into the Congress of the United States, on an equal footing with the original States in all respects whatever, and shall be at liberty to form a permanent constitution and State government: Provided, the constitution and government so to be formed, shall be republican, and in conformity to the principles contained in these articles; and, so far as it can be consistent with the general interest of the confederacy, such admission shall be allowed at an earlier period, and when there may be a less number of free inhabitants in the State than sixty thousand.

Art. 6. There shall be neither slavery nor involuntary servitude in the said territory, otherwise than in the punishment of crimes whereof the party shall have been duly convicted: Provided, always, That any person escaping into the same, from whom labor or service is lawfully claimed in any one of the original States, such fugitive may be lawfully reclaimed and conveyed to the person claiming his or her labor or service as aforesaid.

Be it ordained by the authority aforesaid, That the resolutions of the 23rd of April 1784, relative to the subject of this ordinance, be, and the same are hereby repealed and declared null and void.

CONSTITUTION OF THE UNITED STATES (1787)

PREAMBLE

WE THE PEOPLE of the United States, in Order to form a more perfect Union, establish Justice, insure domestic Tranquility, provide for the common defence, promote the general Welfare, and secure the Blessings of Liberty to ourselves and our Posterity, do ordain and establish this Constitution for the United States of America.

ARTICLE I

Section 1. All legislative Powers herein granted shall be vested in a Congress of the United States, which shall consist of a Senate and House of Representatives.

Section 2. The House of Representatives shall be composed of Members chosen every second Year by the People of the several States, and the Electors in each State shall have the qualifications requisite for Electors of the most numerous Branch of the State Legislature. No Person shall be a Representative who shall not have attained to the age of twenty five Years, and been seven Years a Citizen of the United States, and who shall not, when elected, be an Inhabitant of that State in which he shall be chosen.

Representatives and direct Taxes shall be apportioned among the several States which may be included within this Union, according to their respective Numbers, which shall be determined by adding to the whole Number of free Persons, including those bound to Service for a Term of Years, and excluding Indians not taxed, three fifths of all other Persons. The actual Enumeration shall be made within three Years after the first Meeting of the Congress of the United States, and within every subsequent Term of ten Years, in such Manner as they shall by Law direct. The Number of Representatives shall not exceed one for every thirty Thousand, but each State shall have at Least one Representative; and until such enumeration shall be made, the State of New Hampshire shall be entitled to chuse three, Massachusetts eight, Rhode Island and Providence Plantations one, Connecticut five, New York six, New Jersey four, Pennsylvania eight, Delaware one, Maryland six, Virginia ten, North Carolina five, South Carolina five and Georgia three.

When vacancies happen in the Representation from any State, the Executive Authority thereof shall issue Writs of Election to fill such Vacancies.

The House of Representatives shall chuse their Speaker and other officers; and shall have the sole Power of Impeachment.

Section 3. The Senate of the United States shall be composed of two Senators from each State, chosen by the Legislature thereof, for six Years; and each Senator shall have one Vote.

Immediately after they shall be assembled in Consequence of the first Election, they shall be divided as equally as may be into three Classes. The Seats of the Senators of the first class shall be vacated at the Expiration of the second Year, of the second Class at the Expiration of the fourth Year, and of the third Class at the Expiration of the sixth Year, so that one third may be chosen every second Year; and if Vacancies happen by Resignation, or otherwise, during the Recess of the Legislature of any State, the Executive thereof may make temporary Appointments until the next Meeting of the Legislature, which shall then fill such Vacancies.

No Person shall be a Senator who shall not have attained to the Age of thirty Years, and been nine Years a Citizen of the United States, and who shall not, when elected, be an Inhabitant of that State for which he shall be chosen.

The Vice President of the United States shall be President of the Senate, but shall have no Vote, unless they be equally divided.

The Senate shall chuse their other Officers, and also a President pro tempore, in the Absence of the Vice President, or when he shall exercise the Office of President of the United States.

The Senate shall have the sole Power to try all Impeachments. When sitting for that Purpose, they shall be on Oath or Affirmation. When the President of the United States is tried, the Chief Justice shall preside: and no Person shall be convicted without the Concurrence of two thirds of the Members present.

Judgment in Cases of Impeachment shall not extend further than to removal from Office, and disqualification to hold and enjoy any Office of honor, Trust or Profit under the United

States: but the Party convicted shall nevertheless be liable and subject to Indictment, Trial, Judgment and Punishment, according to Law.

Section 4. The Times, Places and Manner of holding Elections for Senators and Representatives, shall be prescribed in each State by the Legislature thereof; but the Congress may at any time by Law make or alter such Regulations, except as to the Places of chusing Senators.

The Congress shall assemble at least once in every Year, and such Meeting shall be on the first Monday in December, unless they shall by Law appoint a different Day.

Section 5. Each House shall be the Judge of the Elections, returns and Qualifications of its own Members, and a Majority of each shall constitute a Quorum to do Business; but a smaller Number may adjourn from day to day, and may be authorized to compel the Attendance of absent Members, in such Manner, and under such Penalties as each House may provide.

Each House may determine the Rules of its Proceedings, punish its Members for disorderly Behavior, and, with the Concurrence of two thirds, expel a Member.

Each House shall keep a Journal of its Proceedings, and from time to time publish the same, excepting such Parts as may in their Judgment require Secrecy; and the Yeas and Nays of the Members of either House on any question shall, at the Desire of one-fifth of those Present, be entered on the Journal.

Neither House, during the Session of Congress, shall, without the Consent of the other, adjourn for more than three days, nor to any other Place than that in which the two Houses shall be sitting.

Section 6. The Senators and Representatives shall receive a Compensation for their Services, to be ascertained by Law, and paid out of the Treasury of the United States. They shall in all Cases, except Treason, Felony and Breach of the Peace, be privileged from Arrest during their Attendance at the Session of their respective Houses, and in going to and returning from the same; and for any Speech or Debate in either House, they shall not be questioned in any other Place.

No Senator or Representative shall, during the Time for which he was elected, be appointed to any civil Office under the Authority of the United States which shall have been created, or the Emoluments whereof shall have been increased during such time; and no Person holding any Office under the United States, shall be a member of either House during his Continuance in Office.

Section 7. All Bills for raising Revenue shall originate in the House of Representatives; but the Senate may propose or concur with Amendments as on other Bills.

Every Bill which shall have passed the House of Representatives and the Senate, shall, before it become a Law, be presented to the President of the United States; if he approve he shall sign it, but if not he shall return it, with his Objections to that House in which it shall have originated, who shall enter the Objections at large on their Journal, and proceed to reconsider it. If after such Reconsideration two thirds of that House shall agree to pass the Bill, it shall be sent, together with the Objections, to the other House, by which it shall likewise be reconsidered, and if approved by two thirds of that House, it shall become a Law. But in all such Cases the Votes of both Houses shall be determined by yeas and Nays, and the Names of the Persons voting for and against the Bill shall be entered on the Journal of each House respectively. If any Bill shall not be returned by the President within ten Days (Sundays excepted) after it shall have been presented to him, the Same shall be a Law, in like Manner as if he had signed it, unless the Congress by their Adjournment prevent its Return, in which Case it shall not be a Law.

Every Order, resolution, or Vote to which the Concurrence of the Senate and House of Representatives may be necessary (except on a question of Adjournment) shall be presented to the President of the United States; and before the Same shall take Effect, shall be approved by him, or being disapproved by him, shall be repassed by two thirds of the Senate and House of Representatives, according to the Rules and Limitations prescribed in the Case of a Bill.

Section 8. The Congress shall have Power To lay and collect Taxes, Duties, Imposts and Excises, to pay the Debts and provide for the common Defence and general Welfare of the United States; but all Duties, Imposts and Excises shall be uniform throughout the United States;

To borrow Money on the credit of the United States;

To regulate Commerce with foreign Nations, and among the several States, and with the Indian Tribes;

To establish a uniform Rule of Naturalization, and uniform Laws on the subject of Bankruptcies throughout the United States;

To coin Money, regulate the Value thereof, and of foreign coin, and fix the Standard of Weights and Measures;

To provide for the Punishment of counterfeiting the Securities and current Coin of the United States;

To establish Post-Offices and post-Roads;

To promote the Progress of Science and useful Arts, by securing for limited Times to Authors and Inventors the exclusive Right to their respective Writings and Discoveries;

To constitute Tribunals inferior to the Supreme Court;

To define and punish Piracies and Felonies committed on the high Seas, and Offenses against the Law of Nations;

To declare War, grant Letters of Marque and Reprisal, and make Rules concerning Captures on Land and Water;

To raise and support Armies, but no Appropriation of Money to that Use shall be for a longer Term than two Years;

To provide and maintain a Navy;

To make Rules for the Government and Regulation of the land and naval Forces;

To provide for calling forth the Militia to execute the Laws of the Union, suppress insurrections and repel invasions;

To provide for organizing, arming, and disciplining, the Militia, and for governing such Part of them as may be employed in the Service of the United States, reserving to the States respectively, the Appointment of the Officers, and the Authority of training the Militia according to the discipline prescribed by Congress;

To exercise exclusive Legislation in all Cases whatsoever, over such District (not exceeding ten Miles square) as may, by Cession of particular States, and the Acceptance of Congress, become the Seat of the Government of the United States, and to exercise like Authority over all Places purchased by the Consent of the Legislature of the State in which the Same shall be, for the erection of Forts, Magazines, arsenals, dock-Yards, and other needful Buildings; and

To make all Laws which shall be necessary and proper for carrying into Execution the foregoing Powers, and all other Powers vested by this Constitution in the Government of the United States, or in any Department or Officer thereof.

Section 9. The Migration or Importation of such Persons as any of the States now existing shall think proper to admit, shall not be prohibited by the Congress prior to the Year one thousand eight hundred and eight, but a Tax or duty may be imposed on such Importation, not exceeding ten dollars for each Person.

The Privilege of the Writ of Habeas Corpus shall not be suspended, unless when in Cases of Rebellion or Invasion the public Safety may require it.

No bill of Attainder or ex post facto Law shall be passed.

No Capitation, or other direct Tax shall be laid, unless in Proportion to the Census or Enumeration herein before directed to be taken.

No Tax or Duty shall be laid on Articles exported from any State.

No Preference shall be given by any Regulation of Commerce or Revenue to the Ports of one State over those of another: nor shall Vessels bound to, or from, one State, be obliged to enter, clear, or pay Duties in another.

No Money shall be drawn from the Treasury, but in Consequence of Appropriations made by Law; and a regular Statement and Account of the Receipts and Expenditures of all public Money shall be published from time to time.

No Title of Nobility shall be granted by the United States: And no Person holding any Office of Profit or Trust under them, shall, without the Consent of the Congress, accept of any present, Emolument, Office, or Title, of any kind whatever, from any King, Prince or Foreign State.

Section 10. No State shall enter into any Treaty, Alliance, or Confederation; grant Letters of Marque and Reprisal; coin Money; emit Bills of Credit; make any Thing but gold and silver Coin a Tender in Payment of Debts; pass any Bill of Attainder, ex post facto Law, or Law impairing the Obligation of Contracts, or grant any Title of Nobility.

No State shall, without the Consent of the Congress, lay any Imposts or Duties on Imports or Exports, except what may be absolutely necessary for executing it's inspection Laws: and the net Produce of all Duties and Imposts, laid by any State on Imports or Exports, shall be for the use of the Treasury of the United States; and all such Laws shall be subject to the Revision and Controul of the Congress.

No State shall, without the Consent of Congress, lay any Duty of Tonnage, keep Troops, or Ships of War in time of Peace, enter into any Agreement or Compact with another State, or with a foreign Power, or engage in War, unless actually invaded, or in such imminent Danger as will not admit of delay.

ARTICLE II

Section 1. The executive Power shall be vested in a President of the United States of America. He shall hold his Office during the Term of four Years, and, together with the Vice President chosen for the same Term, be elected, as follows:

Each State shall appoint, in such Manner as the Legislature thereof may direct, a Number of Electors, equal to the whole Number of Senators and Representatives to which the State may be entitled in the Congress: but no Senator or Representative, or person holding an Office of Trust or Profit under the United States, shall be appointed an elector.

The Electors shall meet in their respective States, and vote by Ballot for two Persons, of whom one at least shall not be an Inhabitant of the same State with themselves. And they shall make a List of all the persons voted for, and of the Number of Votes for each; which List they shall sign and certify, and transmit sealed to the Seat of the Government of the United States, directed to the President of the Senate. The President of the Senate shall, in the Presence of the Senate and House of Representatives, open all the Certificates, and the Votes shall then be counted. The Person having the greatest Number of Votes shall be the President, if such Number be a Majority of the whole Number of Electors appointed; and if there be more than one who have such Majority, and have an equal Number of Votes, then the House of Representatives shall immediately chuse by Ballot one of them for President; and if no person have a Majority, then from the five highest on the List the said House shall in like Manner chuse the President. But in chusing the President, the Votes shall be taken by States, the representation from each State having one Vote; a quorum for this Purpose shall consist of a Member or Members from two thirds of the States, and a Majority of all the States shall be necessary to a Choice. In every Case, after the Choice of the President, the Person having the greatest number of votes of the electors shall be the Vice President. But if there should remain two or more who have equal Votes, the Senate shall chuse from them by Ballot the Vice President.

The Congress may determine the time of chusing the Electors, and the Day on which they shall give their Votes; which Day shall be the same throughout the United States.

No Person except a natural born Citizen, or a Citizen of the United States, at the time of the Adoption of this Constitution, shall be eligible to the Office of President; neither shall any person be eligible to that Office who shall not have attained to the Age of thirty five Years, and been fourteen Years a Resident within the United States.

In Case of the Removal of the President from Office, or of his Death, Resignation, or Inability to discharge the Powers and Duties of the said Office, the Same shall devolve on the Vice President, and the Congress may by Law provide for the Case of Removal, Death, Resignation or Inability, both of the President and Vice President, declaring what Officer shall then act as President, and such Officer shall act accordingly, until the Disability be removed, or a President shall be elected.

The President shall, at stated Times, receive for his Services, a Compensation, which shall neither be increased nor diminished during the Period for which he shall have been elected, and he shall not receive within that Period any other Emolument from the United States, or any of them.

Before he enter on the Execution of his Office, he shall take the following Oath or Affirmation:—"I do solemnly swear (or affirm) that I will faithfully execute the Office of President of the United States, and will to the best of my Ability, preserve, protect and defend the Constitution of the United States."

Section 2. The President shall be Commander in Chief of the Army and Navy of the United States, and of the Militia of the several States, when called into the actual service of the United States; he may require the Opinion, in writing, of the principal Officer in each of the executive Departments, upon any Subject relating to the Duties of their respective Offices, and he shall have Power to grant Reprieves and Pardons for Offenses against the United States, except in Cases of Impeachment.

He shall have Power, by and with the Advice and Consent of the Senate, to make Treaties, provided two thirds of the Senators present concur; and he shall nominate, and by and with the Advice and Consent of the Senate, shall appoint Ambassadors, other public Ministers and Consuls, Judges of the supreme Court, and all other Officers of the United States, whose appointments are not herein otherwise provided for, and which shall be established by law: but the Congress may by law vest the appointment of such inferior officers, as they think proper, in the President alone, in the Courts of Law, or in the Heads of Departments.

The President shall have Power to fill up all Vacancies that may happen during the Recess of the Senate, by granting Commissions which shall expire at the End of their next session.

Section 3. He shall from time to time give to the Congress Information of the State of the Union, and recommend to their consideration such Measures as he shall judge necessary and expedient; he may, on extraordinary Occasions, convene both Houses, or either of them, and in Case of Disagreement between them, with Respect to the Time of Adjournment, he may adjourn them to such Time as he shall think proper; he shall receive Ambassadors and other public Ministers; he shall take Care that the Laws be faithfully executed, and shall Commission all the Officers of the United States.

Section 4. The President, Vice President and all civil Officers of the United States, shall be removed from Office on Impeachment for, and Conviction of, Treason, Bribery, or other high Crimes and Misdemeanors.

ARTICLE III

Section 1. The judicial Power of the United States, shall be vested in one supreme Court, and in such inferior Courts as the Congress may from time to time ordain and establish. The Judges, both of the supreme and inferior courts, shall hold their Offices during good Behavior, and shall, at stated times, receive for their Services, a Compensation, which shall not be diminished during their Continuance in Office.

Section 2. The judicial Power shall extend to all Cases, in Law and Equity, arising under this Constitution, the Laws of the United States, and Treaties made, or which shall be made, under their Authority; to all Cases affecting Ambassadors, other public Ministers and Consuls; to all Cases of admiralty and maritime Jurisdiction; to Controversies to which the United States shall be a Party; to Controversies between two or more States; between a State and Citizens of another State; between Citizens of different States; between Citizens of the same State claiming Lands under Grants of different States, and between a State, or the Citizens thereof, and foreign States, Citizens or Subjects.

In all Cases affecting Ambassadors, other public Ministers and Consuls, and those in which a State shall be party, the supreme Court shall have original Jurisdiction. In all the other Cases before mentioned, the supreme Court shall have appellate Jurisdiction, both as to Law and Fact, with such Exceptions, and under such Regulations as the Congress shall make.

The trial of all Crimes, except in Cases of Impeachment, shall be by Jury; and such trial shall be held in the State where the said Crimes shall have been committed; but when not committed within any State, the Trial shall be at such Place or Places as the Congress may by Law have directed.

Section 3. Treason against the United States, shall consist only in levying War against them, or in adhering to their Enemies, giving them Aid and Comfort. No Person shall be convicted of Treason unless on the Testimony of two Witnesses to the same overt Act, or on Confession in open court.

The Congress shall have Power to declare the Punishment of Treason, but no Attainder of Treason shall work Corruption of Blood, or Forfeiture except during the Life of the Person attainted.

ARTICLE IV

Section 1. Full Faith and Credit shall be given in each State to the public Acts, Records, and judicial Proceedings of every other State. And the Congress may by general Laws prescribe the Manner in which such Acts, Records and Proceedings shall be proved, and the Effect thereof.

Section 2. The Citizens of each State shall be entitled to all Privileges and Immunities of Citizens in the several States.

A person charged in any State with Treason, Felony, or other Crime, who shall flee from Justice, and be found in another State, shall on Demand of the Executive Authority of the State from which he fled, be delivered up, to be removed to the State having Jurisdiction of the Crime.

No Person held to Service or Labour in one State, under the Laws thereof, escaping into another, shall, in Consequence of any Law or Regulation therein, be discharged from such Service or Labour, but shall be delivered up on Claim of the Party to whom such Service or Labour may be due.

Section 3. New States may be admitted by the Congress into this Union; but no new States shall be formed or erected within the Jurisdiction of any other State; nor any State be formed by the Junction of two or more States, or Parts of States, without the Consent of the Legislatures of the States concerned as well as of the Congress.

The Congress shall have Power to dispose of and make all needful Rules and Regulations respecting the Territory or other Property belonging to the United States; and nothing in this

Constitution shall be so construed as to Prejudice any Claims of the United States, or of any particular State.

Section 4. The United States shall guarantee to every State in this Union a Republican Form of government, and shall protect each of them against Invasion; and on Application of the Legislature, or of the Executive (when the legislature cannot be convened) against domestic Violence.

ARTICLE V

The Congress, whenever two thirds of both Houses shall deem it necessary, shall propose Amendments to this Constitution, or, on the Application of the Legislatures of two thirds of the several States, shall call a Convention for proposing Amendments, which, in either Case, shall be valid to all intents and purposes, as part of this Constitution, when ratified by the Legislatures of three fourths of the several States, or by Conventions in three fourths thereof, as the one or the other Mode of Ratification may be proposed by the Congress; Provided that no Amendment which may be made prior to the Year One thousand eight hundred and eight shall in any Manner affect the first and fourth Clauses in the Ninth Section of the first Article; and that no State, without its Consent, shall be deprived of its equal Suffrage in the Senate.

ARTICLE VI

All Debts contracted and Engagements entered into, before the Adoption of this Constitution, shall be as valid against the United States under this Constitution, as under the Confederation.

This Constitution, and the Laws of the United States which shall be made in Pursuance thereof; and all Treaties made, or which shall be made, under the Authority of the United States, shall be the supreme Law of the Land; and the Judges in every State shall be bound thereby, any Thing in the Constitution or Laws of any State to the Contrary notwithstanding.

The Senators and Representatives before mentioned, and the Members of the several State Legislatures, and all executive and judicial Officers, both of the United States and of the several States, shall be bound by Oath or Affirmation, to support this Constitution; but no religious Test shall ever be required as a Qualification to any Office or public Trust under the United States

ARTICLE VII

The Ratification of the Conventions of nine States, shall be sufficient for the establishment of this Constitution between the States so ratifying the Same.

Done in Convention by the Unanimous Consent of the States present the assistant Seventeenth day of September in the Year of our Lord one thousand seven hundred and Eighty-seven and of the Independence of the United States of America the Twelfth, In witness whereof We have hereunto subscribed our Names,

George Washington

President and deputy from Virginia

NEW HAMPSHIRE.

John Langdon

Nicholas Gilman

GEORGIA.

William Few

Abraham Baldwin

MASSACHUSETTS.

Nathaniel Gorham
Rufus King
CONNECTICUT.
William Samuel Johnson
Roger Sherman
NEW JERSEY.
William Livingston
David Brearley
William Paterson
Jonathan Dayton
NEW YORK.
Alexander Hamilton
MARYLAND.
James McHenry
Daniel Carrol
Daniel of St. Thomas Jenifer
PENNSYLVANIA.
Benjamin Franklin
Robert Morris
Thomas FitzSimons
James Wilson
Thomas Mifflin
George Clymer
Jared Ingersoll
Gouverneur Morris
VIRGINIA.
John Blair
James Madison Jr.
NORTH CAROLINA.
William Blount
Hugh Williamson
Richard Dobbs Spaight
DELAWARE.
George Read
John Dickinson
Jacob Broom
Gunning Bedford Jr.
Richard Bassett
SOUTH CAROLINA.
John Ruttledge
Charles Pinckney

Charles Cotesworth Pinckney

Pierce Butler

Attest:

William Jackson, Secretary

AMENDMENTS

(The first ten Amendments were ratified December 15, 1791, and form what is known as the Bill of Rights.)

AMENDMENT ONE

Congress shall make no law respecting an establishment of religion, or prohibiting the free exercise thereof; or abridging the freedom of speech, or of the press; or the right of the people peaceably to assemble, and to petition the government for a redress of grievances.

AMENDMENT TWO

A well regulated militia, being necessary to the security of a free State, the right of the people to keep and bear arms, shall not be infringed.

AMENDMENT THREE

No soldier shall, in time of peace, be quartered in any house, without the consent of the owner, nor in time of war, but in a manner to be prescribed by law.

AMENDMENT FOUR

The right of the people to be secure in their persons, houses, papers, and effects, against unreasonable searches and seizures, shall not be violated, and no warrants shall issue, but upon probable cause, supported by Oath or affirmation, and particularly describing the place to be searched, and the persons or things to be seized.

AMENDMENT FIVE

No person shall be held to answer for a capital, or otherwise infamous crime, unless on a presentment or indictment of a Grand Jury, except in cases arising in the land or naval forces, or in the militia, when in actual service in time of war or public danger; nor shall any person be subject for the same offence to be twice put in jeopardy of life or limb; nor shall be compelled in any criminal case to be a witness against himself, nor be deprived of life, liberty, or property, without due process of law; nor shall private property be taken for public use, without just compensation.

AMENDMENT SIX

In all criminal prosecutions, the accused shall enjoy the right to a speedy and public trial, by an impartial jury of the State and district wherein the crime shall have been committed, which district shall have been previously ascertained by law, and to be informed of the nature and cause of the accusation; to be confronted with the witnesses against him; to have compulsory process for obtaining witnesses in his favor, and to have the assistance of counsel for his defence.

AMENDMENT SEVEN

In suits at common law, where the value in controversy shall exceed twenty dollars, the right of trial by jury shall be preserved, and no fact tried by a jury, shall be otherwise re-examined in any court of the United States, than according to the rules of the common law.

AMENDMENT EIGHT

Excessive bail shall not lie required, nor excessive fines imposed, nor cruel and unusual punishments inflicted.

AMENDMENT NINE

The enumeration in the Constitution, of certain rights, shall not be construed to deny or disparage others retained by the people.

AMENDMENT TEN

The powers not delegated to the United States by the Constitution, nor prohibited by it to the States, are reserved to the States respectively, or to the people.

AMENDMENT ELEVEN

(Ratified February 7, 1795)

The judicial power of the United States shall not be construed to extend to any suit in law or equity, commenced or prosecuted against one of the United States by Citizens of another State, or by citizens or subjects of any foreign State.

AMENDMENT TWELVE

(Ratified June 15, 1804)

The Electors shall meet in their respective States, and vote by ballot for President and Vice President, one of whom at least, shall not be an inhabitant of the same State with themselves; they shall name in their ballots the person voted for as President, and in distinct ballots the person voted for as Vice President, and they shall make distinct lists of all persons voted for as President, and of all persons voted for as Vice President, and of the number of votes for each, which lists they shall sign and certify, and transmit sealed to the seat of the Government of the United States, directed to the President of the Senate; the President of the Senate shall, in the presence of the Senate and House of Representatives, open all the certificates and the votes shall then be counted; the person having the greatest number of votes for President, shall be the President, if such number be a majority of the whole number of Electors appointed; and if no person have such majority, then from the persons having the highest numbers not exceeding three on the list of those voted for as President, the House of Representatives shall choose immediately, by ballot, the President. But in choosing the President, the votes shall be taken by States, the representation from each State having one vote; a quorum for this purpose shall consist of a member or members from two-thirds of the States, and a majority of all the States shall be necessary to a choice. And if the House of Representatives shall not choose a President whenever the right of choice shall devolve upon them, before the fourth day of March next following, then the Vice President shall act as President, as in the case of the death or other constitutional disability of the President. The person having the greatest number of votes as Vice President, shall be the Vice President, if such number be a majority of the whole number of Electors appointed, and if no person have a majority, then from the two highest numbers on the list, the Senate shall choose the Vice President; a quorum for the purpose shall consist of two-thirds of the whole number of Senators, and a majority of the whole number shall be necessary to a choice. But no person constitutionally ineligible to the office of President shall be eligible to that of Vice-President of the United States.

AMENDMENT THIRTEEN

(Ratified December 6, 1865)

Section 1. Neither slavery nor involuntary servitude, except as a punishment for crime whereof the party shall have been duly convicted, shall exist within the United States, or any place subject to their jurisdiction.

Section 2. Congress shall have power to enforce this article by appropriate legislation.

AMENDMENT FOURTEEN

(Ratified July 9, 1868)

Section 1. All persons born or naturalized in the United States, and subject to the jurisdiction thereof, are citizens of the United States and of the State wherein they reside. No State shall make or enforce any law which shall abridge the privileges or immunities of citizens of the United States; nor shall any State deprive any person of life, liberty, or property, without due process of law; nor deny to any person within its jurisdiction the equal protection of the laws.

Section 2. Representatives shall be apportioned among the several States according to their respective numbers, counting the whole number of persons in each State, excluding Indians not taxed. But when the right to vote at any election for the choice of Electors for President and Vice President of the United States, Representatives in Congress, the executive and judicial officers of a State, or the members of the Legislature thereof, is denied to any of the male inhabitants of such State, being twenty-one years of age, and citizens of the United States, or in any way abridged, except for participation in rebellion, or other crime, the basis of representation therein shall be reduced in the proportion which the number of such male citizens shall bear to the whole number of male citizens twenty-one years of age in such State.

Section 3. No person shall be a Senator or Representative in Congress, or Elector of President and Vice-President, or hold any office, civil or military, under the United States, or under any State, who, having previously taken an oath, as a member of Congress, or as an officer of the United States, or as a member of any State Legislature, or as an executive or judicial officer of any State, to support the Constitution of the United States, shall have engaged in insurrection or rebellion against the same, or given aid or comfort to the enemies thereof, but Congress may by a vote of two-thirds of each House, remove such disability.

Section 4. The validity of the public debt of the United States, authorized by law, including debts incurred for payment of pensions and bounties for services in suppressing insurrection or rebellion, shall not be questioned. But neither the United States nor any State shall assume or pay any debt or obligation incurred in aid of insurrection or rebellion against the United States, or any claim for the loss or emancipation of any slave; but all such debts, obligations and claims shall be held illegal and void.

Section 5. The Congress shall have power to enforce, by appropriate legislation, the provisions of this article.

AMENDMENT FIFTEEN

(Ratified February 3, 1870)

Section 1. The right of citizens of the United States to vote shall not be denied or abridged by the United States or by any State on account of race, color, or previous condition of servitude.

Section 2. The Congress shall have power to enforce this article by appropriate legislation.

AMENDMENT SIXTEEN

(Ratified February 3, 1913)

The Congress shall have power to lay and collect taxes on incomes, from whatever source derived, without apportionment among the several States and without regard to any census or enumeration.

AMENDMENT SEVENTEEN

(Ratified April 8, 1913)

The Senate of the United States shall be composed of two Senators from each State, elected by the people thereof, for six years; and each Senator shall have one vote. The electors in each State shall have the qualifications requisite for electors of the most numerous branch of the State legislature.

When vacancies happen in the representation of any State in the Senate, the executive authority of such State shall issue writs of election to fill such vacancies: Provided, That the legislature of any State may empower the Executive thereof to make temporary appointments until the people fill the vacancies by election as the legislature may direct.

This amendment shall not be so construed as to affect the election or term of any senator chosen before it becomes valid as part of the Constitution.

AMENDMENT EIGHTEEN

(Ratified January 16, 1919. Repealed December 5, 1933 by Amendment 21)

Section 1. After one year from the ratification of this article, the manufacture, sale, or transportation of intoxicating liquors within, the importation thereof into, or the exportation thereof from the United States and all territory subject to the jurisdiction thereof for beverage purposes is hereby prohibited.

Section 2. The Congress and the several States shall have concurrent power to enforce this article by appropriate legislation.

Section 3. This article shall be inoperative unless it shall have been ratified as an amendment to the Constitution by the Legislatures of the several States, as provided in the Constitution, within seven years from the date of the submission hereof to the States by Congress.

AMENDMENT NINETEEN

(Ratified August 18, 1920)

The right of citizens of the United States to vote shall not be denied or abridged by the United States or by any State on account of sex.

The Congress shall have power by appropriate legislation to enforce the provisions of this article.

AMENDMENT TWENTY

(Ratified January 23, 1933)

Section 1. The terms of the President and Vice-President shall end at noon on the twentieth day of January, and the terms of Senators and Representatives at noon on the third day of January, of the years in which such terms would have ended if this article had not been ratified; and the terms of their successors shall then begin.

Section 2. The Congress shall assemble at least once in every year, and such meeting shall begin at noon on the third day of January, unless they shall by law appoint a different day.

Section 3. If, at the time fixed for the beginning of the term of the President, the President-elect shall have died, the Vice-President-elect shall become President. If a President shall not have been chosen before the time fixed for the beginning of his term, or if the President-elect shall have failed to qualify, then the Vice-President-elect shall act as President until a President shall have qualified; and the Congress may by law provide for the case wherein neither a President-elect nor a Vice-President-elect shall have qualified, declaring who shall then act as President, or the manner in which one who is to act shall be selected, and such person shall act accordingly until a President or Vice-President shall have qualified.

Section 4. The Congress may by law provide for the case of the death of any of the persons from whom the House of Representatives may choose a President whenever the right of choice shall have devolved upon them, and for the case of the death of any of the persons from whom the Senate may choose a Vice-President whenever the right of choice shall have devolved upon them.

Section 5. Sections 1 and 2 shall take effect on the 15th day of October following the ratification of this article.

Section 6. This article shall be inoperative unless it shall have been ratified as an amendment to the Constitution by the Legislatures of three-fourths of the several States within seven years from the date of its submission.

AMENDMENT TWENTY-ONE

(Ratified December 5, 1933)

Section 1. The eighteenth article of amendment to the Constitution of the United States is hereby repealed.

Section 2. The transportation or importation into any State, Territory, or Possession of the United States for delivery or use therein of intoxicating liquors, in violation of the laws thereof, is hereby prohibited.

Section 3. The article shall be inoperative unless it shall have been ratified as an amendment to the Constitution by conventions in the several States, as provided in the Constitution, within seven years from the date of the submission hereof to the States by the Congress.

AMENDMENT TWENTY-TWO

(Ratified February 27, 1951)

Section 1. No person shall be elected to the office of the President more than twice, and no person who has held the office of President, or acted as President for more than two years of a term to which some other person was elected President shall be elected to the office of the President more than once. But this Article shall not apply to any person holding the office of President when this Article was proposed by the Congress, and shall not prevent any person who may be holding the office of President, or acting as President, during the term within which this Article becomes operative from holding the office of President or acting as President during the remainder of such term.

Section 2. This article shall be inoperative unless it shall have been ratified as an amendment to the Constitution by the Legislatures of three-fourths of the several States within seven years from the date of its submission to the States by the Congress.

AMENDMENT TWENTY-THREE

(Ratified March 29, 1961)

Section 1. The District constituting the seat of government of the United States shall appoint in such manner as the Congress may direct:

A number of electors of President and Vice-President equal to the whole number of Senators and Representatives in Congress to which the District would be entitled if it were a State, but in no event more than the least populous State; they shall be in addition to those appointed by the States, but they shall be considered, for the purposes of the election of President and Vice-President, to be electors appointed by a State; and they shall meet in the District and perform such duties as provided by the twelfth article of amendment.

Section 2. The Congress shall have power to enforce this article by appropriate legislation.

AMENDMENT TWENTY-FOUR

(Ratified January 23, 1964)

Section 1. The right of citizens of the United States to vote in any primary or other election for President or Vice-President, for electors for President or Vice-President, or for Senator or Representative in Congress, shall not be denied or abridged by the United States or any State by reason of failure to pay any poll tax or other tax.

Section 2. The Congress shall have power to enforce this article by appropriate legislation.

AMENDMENT TWENTY-FIVE

(Ratified February 10, 1967)

Section 1. In case of the removal of the President from office or of his death or resignation, the Vice-President shall become President.

Section 2. Whenever there is a vacancy in the office of the Vice-President, the President shall nominate a Vice-President who shall take office upon confirmation by a majority vote of both Houses of Congress.

Section 3. Whenever the President transmits to the President pro tempore of the Senate and the Speaker of the House of Representatives his written declaration that he is unable to discharge the powers and duties of his office, and until he transmits to them a written declaration to the contrary, such powers and duties shall be discharged by the Vice-President as Acting President.

Section 4. Whenever the Vice-President and a majority of either the principal officers of the executive departments or of such other body as Congress may by law provide, transmit to the President pro tempore of the Senate and the Speaker of the House of Representatives their written declaration that the President is unable to discharge the powers and duties of his office, the Vice-President shall immediately assume the powers and duties of the office as Acting President.

Thereafter, when the President transmits to the President pro tempore of the Senate and the Speaker of the House of Representatives his written declaration that no inability exists, he shall resume the powers and duties of his office unless the Vice-President and a majority of either the principal officers of the executive department or of such other body as Congress may by law provide, transmit within four days to the President pro tempore of the Senate and the Speaker of the House of Representatives their written declaration that the President is unable to discharge the powers and duties of his office. Thereupon Congress shall decide the issue, assembling within forty-eight hours for that purpose if not in session. If the Congress, within twenty-one days after receipt of the latter written declaration, or, if Congress is not in session, within twenty-one days after Congress is required to assemble, determines by two-thirds vote of both Houses that the President is unable to discharge the powers and duties of his office, the Vice-President shall continue to discharge the same as Acting President; otherwise, the President shall resume the powers and duties of his office.

AMENDMENT TWENTY-SIX

(Ratified July 1, 1971)

Section 1. The right of citizens of the United States, who are eighteen years of age or older, to vote shall not be denied or abridged by the United States or by any State on account of age.

Section 2. The Congress shall have power to enforce this article by appropriate legislation.

MORRILL LAND-GRANT ACT OF 1862

An Act donating Public Lands to the several States and Territories which may provide Colleges for the Benefit of Agriculture and the Mechanic Arts.

Be it enacted by the Senate and House of Representatives of the United States of America in Congress assembled, That there be granted to the several States, for the purposes hereinafter mentioned, an amount of public land, to be apportioned to each State a quantity equal to thirty thousand acres for each senator and representative in Congress to which the States are respectively entitled by the apportionment under the census of eighteen hundred and sixty: Provided, That no mineral lands shall be selected or purchased under the provisions of this act.

Sec. 2. And be it further enacted, That the land aforesaid, after being surveyed, shall be apportioned to the several States in sections or subdivisions of sections, not less than one quarter of a section; and whenever there are public lands in a State subject to sale at private entry at one dollar and twenty-five cents per acre, the quantity to which said State shall be entitled shall be selected from such lands within the limits of such State, and the Secretary of the Interior is hereby directed to issue to each of the States in which there is not the quantity of public lands subject to sale at private entry at one dollar and twenty-five cents per acre, to which said State may be entitled under the provisions of this act, land scrip to the amount in acres for the deficiency of its distributive share: said scrip to be sold by said States and the proceeds thereof applied to the uses and purposes prescribed in this act, and for no other use or purpose whatsoever: Provided, That in no case shall any State to which land scrip may thus be issued be allowed to locate the same within the limits of any other State, or of any Territory of the United States, but their assignees may thus locate said land scrip upon any of the unappropriated lands of the United States subject to sale at private entry at one dollar and twenty-five cents, or less, per acre: And provided, further, That not more than one million acres shall be located by such assignees in any one of the States: And provided, further, That no such location shall be made before one year from the passage of this act.

Sec. 3. And be it further enacted, That all the expenses of management, superintendence, and taxes from date of selection of said lands, previous to their sales, and all expenses incurred in the management and disbursement of the moneys which may be received therefrom, shall be paid by the States to which they may belong, out of the treasury of said States, so that the entire proceeds of the sale of said lands shall be applied without any diminution whatever to the purposes hereinafter mentioned.

Sec. 4. And be it further enacted, That all moneys derived from the sale of the lands aforesaid by the States to which the lands are apportioned, and from the sales of land scrip hereinbefore provided for, shall be invested in stocks of the United States, or of the States, or some other safe stocks, yielding not less than five per centum upon the par value of said stocks; and that the moneys so invested shall constitute a perpetual fund, the capital of which shall remain forever undiminished, (except so far as may be provided in section fifth of this act,) and the interest of which shall be inviolably appropriated, by each State which may take and claim the benefit of this act, to the endowment, support, and maintenance of at least one college where the leading object shall be, without excluding other scientific and classical studies, and including military tactics, to teach such branches of learning as are related to agriculture and the mechanic arts, in such manner as the legislatures of the States may respectively prescribe, in order to promote the liberal and practical education of the industrial classes in the several pursuits and professions in life.

Sec. 5. And be it further enacted, That the grant of land and land scrip hereby authorized shall be made on the following conditions, to which, as well as to the provisions hereinbefore contained, the previous assent of the several States shall be signified by legislative acts:

First. If any portion of the fund invested as provided by the foregoing section, or any portion of the interest thereon, shall, by any action or contingency, be diminished or lost, it shall be replaced by the State to which it belongs, so that the capital of the fund shall remain forever undiminished; and the annual interest shall be regularly applied without diminution to the purposes mentioned in the fourth section of this act, except that a sum, not exceeding ten per centum upon the amount received by any State under the provisions of this act, may be expended for the purchase of lands for sites or experimental farms, whenever authorized by the respective legislatures of said States.

Second. No portion of said fund, nor the interest thereon, shall be applied, directly or indirectly, under any pretence whatever, to the purchase, erection, preservation, or repair of any building or buildings.

Third. Any State which may take and claim the benefit of the provisions of this act shall provide, within five years, at least not less than one college, as described in the fourth section of this act, or the grant to such State shall cease; and said State shall be bound to pay the United States the amount received of any lands previously sold, and that the title to purchasers under the State shall be valid.

Fourth. An annual report shall be made regarding the progress of each college, recording any improvements and experiments made, with their cost and results, and such other matters, including State industrial and economical statistics, as may be supposed useful; one copy of which shall be transmitted by mail free, by each, to all the other colleges which may be endowed under the provisions of this act, and also one copy to the Secretary of the Interior.

Fifth. When lands shall be selected from those which have been raised to double the minimum price, in consequence of railroad grants, they shall be computed to the States at the maximum price, and the number of acres proportionally diminished.

Sixth. No State while in a condition of rebellion or insurrection against the government of the United States shall be entitled to the benefit of this act.

Seventh. No State shall be entitled to the benefits of this act unless it shall express its acceptance thereof by its legislature within two years from the date of its approval by the President.

Sec. 6. And be it further enacted, That land scrip issued under the provisions of this act shall not be subject to location until after the first day of January, one thousand eight hundred and sixty-three.

Sec. 7. And be it further enacted, That the land officers shall receive the same fees for locating land scrip issued under the provisions of this act as is now allowed for the location of military bounty land warrants under existing laws; Provided, their maximum compensation shall not be thereby increased.

Sec. 8. And be it further enacted, That the Governors of the several States to which scrip shall be issued under this act shall be required to report annually to Congress all sales made of such scrip until the whole shall be disposed of, the amount received for the same, and what appropriation has been made of the proceeds.

Approved, July 2, 1862.

SECOND MORRILL ACT OF AUGUST 30, 1890

Providing for the further endowment and support of colleges of agriculture and mechanic arts

[An act to apply a portion of the proceeds of the public lands to the more complete endowment and support of the colleges for the benefit of agriculture and the mechanic arts established under the provisions of an act of Congress approved July second, eighteen hundred and sixty-two]

Be it enacted by the Senate and House of Representatives of the United States of America in Congress assembled, That there shall be, and hereby is, annually appropriated, out of any money in the Treasury not otherwise appropriated, arising from the sale of public lands, to be paid as hereinafter provided, to each State and Territory for the more complete endowment and maintenance of colleges for the benefit of agriculture and the mechanic arts now established, or which may be hereafter established, in accordance with an act of Congress approved July second, eighteen hundred and sixty-two, the sum of fifteen thousand dollars for the year ending June thirtieth, eighteen hundred and ninety, and an annual increase of the amount of such appropriation thereafter for ten years by an additional sum of one thousand dollars over the preceding year and the annual amount of be paid thereafter to each State and Territory shall be twenty-five thousands dollars to be applied only to instruction in agriculture, the mechanic arts, the English language and the various branches of mathematical, physical, natural, and economic science, with special reference to their applications in the industries of life, and to the facilities for such instruction: *Provided*, That no money shall be paid out under this act to all State and Territory for the support and maintenance of a college where a distinction of race or color is made in the admission of students, but the establishment and maintenance of such colleges separately for white and colored students shall be held to be a compliance with the provisions of this act if the funds received in such State or Territory be equitably divided as hereinafter set forth: *Provided*, That in any State in which there has been one college established in pursuance of the act of July second, eighteen hundred and sixty-two, and also in which an educational institution of like character has been established, or may be hereafter established, and is now aided by such State from its own revenue for the education of colored students in agriculture and the mechanic arts, however named or styled, or whether or not it has received money heretofore under the act to which this act is an amendment, the legislature of such a State may propose and report to the Secretary of the Interior a just and equitable division of the fund to be received under this act between one college for white students and one institution for colored students established as aforesaid, which shall be divided into two parts and paid accordingly, and thereupon such institution for colored students shall be entitled to the benefits of this act and subject to its provisions, as much as it would have been if it had been included under the act of eighteen hundred and sixty-two, and the fulfillment of the foregoing provisions shall be taken as a compliance with the provision in reference to separate colleges for white and colored students.

Section 2

That the sums hereby appropriated to the States and Territories for the further endowment and support of colleges shall be annually paid on or before the thirty-first day of July of each year, by the Secretary of the Treasury, upon the warrant of the Secretary of the Interior, out of the Treasury of the United States, to the State or Territorial treasurer, or to such officer as shall be designated by the laws of such State or Territory to receive the same, who shall, upon the order of the trustees of the college, or the institution for colored students, immediately pay over said sums to the treasurers of the respective colleges or other institutions entitled to receive the same, and such treasurer shall be required to report to the Secretary of Agriculture and to the Secretary of the Interior, on or before the first day of September of each year, a detailed statement of the amount so received and of its disbursement. The grants of moneys authorized by this act are made subject to the legislative assent of the several States and Territories to the purpose of said grants: *Provided*, That payments of such installments of the appropriation herein made as shall become due to any State before the adjournment of the regular session of legislature meeting next after the passage of this act shall be made upon the assent of the governor thereof, duly certified to the Secretary of the Treasury.

Section 3

That if any portion of the moneys received by the designated officer of the State or Territory for the further and more complete endowment, support, and maintenance of colleges, or of institutions for colored students, as provided in this act, shall, by any action or contingency, be diminished or lost, or be misapplied, it shall be replaced by the State or Territory to which it belongs, and until so replaced no subsequent appropriation shall be apportioned or paid to such State or Territory; and no portion of said moneys shall be applied, directly or indirectly, under any pretense whatever, to the purchase, erection, preservation, or repair of any building or buildings. An annual report by the president of each of said colleges shall be made to the Secretary of Agriculture, as well as to the Secretary of the Interior, regarding the condition and progress of each college, including statistical information in relation to its receipts and expenditures, its library, the number of its students and professors, and also as to any improvements and experiments made under the direction of any experiment stations attached to said colleges, with their costs and results, and such other industrial and economical statistics as may be regarded as useful, one copy of which shall be transmitted by mail free to all other colleges further endowed under this act.

Section 4

That on or before the first day of July in each year, after the passage of this act, the Secretary of the Interior shall ascertain and certify to the Secretary of the Treasury as to each State and Territory whether it is entitled to receive its share of the annual appropriation for colleges, or of institutions for colored students, under this act, and the amount which thereupon each is entitled, respectively, to receive. If the Secretary of the Interior shall withhold a certificate from any State or Territory of its appropriation, the facts and reasons therefor shall be reported to the President, and the amount involved shall be kept separate in the Treasury until the close of the next Congress, in order that the State or Territory may, if it should so desire, appeal to Congress from the determination of the Secretary of the Interior. If the next Congress shall not direct such sum to be paid, it shall be covered into the Treasury. And the Secretary of the Interior is hereby charged with the proper administration of this law.

Section 5

That the Secretary of the Interior shall annually report to Congress the disbursements which have been made in all the States and Territories, and also whether the appropriation of any State or Territory has been withheld, and if so, the reasons therefor.

Section 6

Congress may at any time amend, suspend, or repeal any or all of the provisions of this act.
Approved, August 30, 1890. (26 Stat. 417.)

ELEMENTARY AND SECONDARY EDUCATION ACT OF 1965

PUBLIC LAW 89-10

Be it enacted by the Senate and House of Representatives of the United States of America in Congress assembled, That this Act may be cited as the "Elementary and Secondary Education Act of 1965".

TITLE I—FINANCIAL ASSISTANCE TO LOCAL EDUCATIONAL AGENCIES FOR THE EDUCATION OF CHILDREN OF LOW-INCOME FAMILIES AND EXTENSION OF PUBLIC LAW 874, EIGHTY-FIRST CONGRESS

Sec. 2. The Act of September 30, 1950, Public Law 874, Eighty-first Congress, as amended (20 U.S.C. 236-244), is amended by inserting:

"TITLE I—FINANCIAL ASSISTANCE FOR LOCAL EDUCATIONAL AGENCIES IN AREAS AFFECTED BY FEDERAL ACTIVITY"

immediately above the heading of section 1, by striking out "this Act" wherever it appears in sections 1 through 6, inclusive (other than where it appears in clause (B) of section 4(a)), and inserting in lieu thereof "this title", and by adding immediately after section 6 the following new title:

"TITLE II—FINANCIAL ASSISTANCE FOR LOCAL EDUCATIONAL AGENCIES FOR THE EDUCATION OF CHILDREN OF LOW-INCOME FAMILIES

"Declaration of Policy

"Sec. 201. In recognition of the special educational needs of children of low-income families and the impact that concentrations of low-income families have on the ability of local educational agencies to support adequate educational programs, the Congress hereby declares it to be the policy of the United States to provide financial assistance (as set forth in this title) to local educational agencies serving areas with concentrations of children from low-income families to expand and improve their educational programs by various means (including preschool programs) which contribute particularly to meeting the special educational needs of educationally deprived children.

"Kinds and Duration of Grants

"Sec. 202. The Commissioner shall, in accordance with the provisions of this title, make payments to State educational agencies for basic grants to local educational agencies for the period beginning July 1, 1965, and ending June 30, 1968, and he shall make payments to State educational agencies for special incentive grants to local educational agencies for the period beginning July 1, 1966, and ending June 30, 1968.

"Basic Grants—Amount and Eligibility

"Sec. 203. (a) (1) From the sums appropriated for making basic grants under this title for a fiscal year, the Commissioner shall reserve such amount, but not in excess of 2 per centum thereof, as he may determine and shall allot such amount among Puerto Rico, Guam, American Samoa, the Virgin Islands, and the Trust Territory of the Pacific Islands according to their respective need for such grants. The maximum basic grant which a local educational agency in Puerto Rico, Guam, American Samoa, the Virgin Islands, and the Trust Territory of the Pacific Islands shall be eligible to receive shall be determined pursuant to such criteria as the Commissioner determines will best carry out the purposes of this title.

"(2) In any case in which the Commissioner determines that satisfactory data for that purpose are available, the maximum basic grant which a local educational agency in a State shall be eligible to receive under this title for any fiscal year shall be (except as provided in paragraph (3)) an amount equal to the Federal percentage (established pursuant to subsection (c)) of the average per pupil expenditure in that State multiplied by the sum of (A) the number of children aged five to seventeen, inclusive, in the school district of such agency, of families having an annual income of less than the low-income factor (established pursuant to subsection (c)), and (B) the number of children of such ages in such school district of families receiving an annual income in excess of the low-income factor (as established pursuant to subsection (c)) from payments under the program of aid to families with dependent children under a State plan approved under title IV of the Social Security Act. In any other case, the maximum basic grant for any local educational agency in a State shall be determined on the basis of the aggregate maximum amount of such grants for all such agencies in the county or counties in which the school district of the particular agency is located, which aggregate maximum amount shall be equal to the Federal percentage of such per pupil expenditure multiplied by the number of children of such ages and families in such county or counties be allocated among those agencies upon such equitable basis as may be determined by the State educational agency in accordance with basic criteria prescribed by the Commissioner. For purposes of this subsection the 'average per pupil expenditure' in a State shall be the aggregate current expenditures, during the second fiscal year preceding the fiscal year for which the computation is made, of all local educational agencies in the State (without regard to the sources of funds from which such expenditures are made), divided by the aggregate number of children in average daily attendance to whom such agencies provided free public education during such preceding year. In determining the maximum amount of a basic grant and the eligibility of a local educational agency for a basic grant for any fiscal year, the number of children determined under the first two sentences of this subsection or under subsection (b) shall be reduced by the number of children aged five to seventeen, inclusive, of families having an annual income of less than the low-income factor (as established pursuant to subsection (c)) for whom a payment was made under title I for the previous fiscal year.

"(3) If the maximum amount of the basic grant determined pursuant to paragraph (1) or (2) for any local educational agency for the fiscal year ending June 30, 1966, is greater than 30 per centum of the sum budgeted by that agency for current expenditures for that year (as determined pursuant to regulations of the Commissioner), such maximum amount shall be reduced to 30 per centum of such budgeted sum.

"(4) For purposes of this subsection, the term 'State' does not include Puerto Rico, Guam, American Samoa, the Virgin Islands, and the Trust Territory of the Pacific Islands.

"(b) A local educational agency shall be eligible for a basic grant for a fiscal year under this title only if it meets the following requirements with respect to the number of children aged five to seventeen, inclusive, of families having an annual income of less than the low-income factor (as established pursuant to subsection (c)):

"(1) In any case (except as provided in paragraph (3)) in which the Commissioner determines that satisfactory data for the purpose of this subsection as to the number of such children of such families are available on a school district basis, the number of such children of such families in the school district of such local educational agency shall be—

"(A) at least one hundred, or

"(B) equal to 3 per centum or more of the total number of all children aged five to seventeen, inclusive, in such district,

whichever is less, except that it shall in no case be less than ten.

"(2) In any other case, except as provided in paragraph (3), the number of children of such ages of families with such income in the county which includes such local educational agency's school district shall be one hundred or more.

"(3) In any case in which a county includes a part of the school district of the local educational agency concerned and the Commissioner has not determined that satisfactory data for the purpose of this subsection are available on a school district basis for all the local educational agencies for all the counties into which the school district of the local educational agency concerned extends, the eligibility requirement with respect to the number of children of such ages of families of such income for such local educational agency shall be determined in accordance with regulations prescribed by the Commissioner for the purposes of this subsection.

"(c) For the purposes of this section, the 'Federal percentage' and the 'low-income factor' for the fiscal year ending June 30, 1966, shall be 50 per centum and $2,000, respectively. For each of the two succeeding fiscal years the Federal percentage and the low-income factor shall be established by the Congress by law.

"(d) For the purposes of this section, the Commissioner shall determine the number of children aged five to seventeen, inclusive, of families having an annual income of less than the low-income factor (as established pursuant to subsection (c)) on the basis of the most recent satisfactory data available from the Department of Commerce. At any time such data for a county are available in the Department of Commerce, such data shall be used in making calculations under this section. The Secretary of Health, Education, and Welfare shall determine the number of children of such ages from families receiving an annual income in excess of the low-income factor (established pursuant to subsection (c)) from payments under the program of aid to families with dependent children under a State plan approved under title IV of the Social Security Act on the basis of the best available data for the period most nearly comparable to those which are used by the Commissioner under the first two sentences of this subsection in making determinations for the purposes of subsections (a) and (b). When requested by the Commissioner, the Secretary of Commerce shall make a special estimate of the number of children of such ages who are from families having an annual income less than the low income factor (established pursuant to subsection (c)) in each county or school district, and the Commissioner is authorized to pay (either in advance or by way of reimbursement) the Secretary of Commerce the cost of making this special estimate. The Secretary of Commerce shall give consideration to any request of the chief executive of a State for the collection of additional census information.

"Special Incentive Grants

"Sec. 204. Each local educational agency which is eligible to receive a basic grant for the fiscal year ending June 30, 1967, shall be eligible to receive in addition a special incentive grant which does not exceed the product of (a) the aggregate number of children in average daily attendance to whom such agency provided free public education during the fiscal year ending June 30, 1965, and (b) the amount by which the average per pupil expenditure of that agency for the fiscal year ending June 30, 1965, exceeded 105 per centum of such expenditure for the fiscal year ending June 30, 1964. Each local educational agency which is eligible to receive a basic grant for the fiscal year ending June 30, 1968, shall be eligible to receive in addition a special incentive grant which does not exceed the product of (c) the aggregate number of children in average daily attendance to whom such agency provided free public education during the fiscal year ending June 30, 1966, and (d) the amount by which the average per pupil expenditure of that agency for the fiscal year ending June 30, 1966, exceeded 110 per centum of such expenditure for the fiscal year ending June 30, 1964. For the purpose of this section the 'average per pupil expenditure' of a local educational agency for any year shall be the aggregate expenditures (without regard to the sources of funds from which such expenditures are made, except that funds derived from Federal sources shall not be used in computing such expenditures) from current revenues made by that agency during that year for free public education, divided by the aggregate number of children in average daily attendance to whom such agency provided free public education during that year.

"Application

"Sec. 205. (a) A local educational agency may receive a basic grant or a special incentive grant under this title for any fiscal year only upon application therefor approved by the appropriate State educational agency, upon its determination (consistent with such basic criteria as the Commissioner may establish)—

"(1) that payments under this title will be used for programs and projects (including the acquisition of equipment and where necessary the construction of school facilities) (A) which are designed to meet the special educational needs of educationally deprived children in school attendance areas having high concentrations of children from low-income families and (B) which are of sufficient size, scope, and quality to give reasonable promise of substantial progress toward meeting those needs, and nothing herein shall be deemed to preclude two or more local educational agencies from entering into agreements, at their option, for carrying out jointly operated programs and projects under this title;

"(2) that, to the extent consistent with the number of educationally deprived children in the school district of the local educational agency who are enrolled in private elementary and secondary schools, such agency has made provision for including special educational services and arrangements (such as dual enrollment, educational radio and television, and mobile educational services and equipment) in which such children can participate;

"(3) that the local educational agency has provided satisfactory assurance that the control of funds provided under this title, and title to property derived therefrom, shall be in a public agency for the uses and purposes provided in this title, and that a public agency will administer such funds and property;

"(4) in the case of any project for construction of school facilities, that the project is not inconsistent with overall State plans for the construction of school facilities and that the requirements of section 209 will be complied with on all such construction projects;

"(5) that effective procedures, including provision for appropriate objective measurements of educational achievement, will be adopted for evaluating at least annually the effectiveness of the programs in meeting the special educational needs of educationally deprived children;

"(6) that the local educational agency will make an annual report and such other reports to the State educational agency, in such form and containing such information, as may be reasonably necessary to enable the State educational agency to perform its duties under this title, including information relating to the educational achievement of students participating in programs carried out under this title, and will keep such records and afford such access thereto as the State educational agency may find necessary to assure the correctness and verification of such reports;

"(7) that wherever there is, in the area served by the local educational agency, a community action program approved pursuant to title II of the Economic Opportunity Act of 1964 (Public Law 88-452), the programs and projects have been developed in cooperation with the public or private nonprofit agency responsible for the community action program; and

"(8) that effective procedures will be adopted for acquiring and disseminating to teachers and administrators significant information derived from educational research, demonstration, and similar projects, and for adopting, where appropriate, promising educational practices developed through such projects.

"(b) The State educational agency shall not finally disapprove in whole or in part any application for funds under this title without first affording the local educational agency submitting the application reasonable notice and opportunity for a hearing.

"Assurance from States

"Sec. 206. (a) Any State desiring to participate in the program of this title shall submit through its State educational agency to the Commissioner an application, in such detail as the Commissioner deems necessary, which provides satisfactory assurance—

"(1) that, except as provided in section 207 (b), payments under this title will be used only for programs and projects which have been approved by the State educational agency pursuant to section 205 (a) and which meet the requirements of that section, and that such agency will in all other respects comply with the provisions of this title, including the enforcement of any obligations imposed upon a local educational agency under section 205 (a);

"(2) that such fiscal control and fund accounting procedures will be adopted as may be necessary to assure proper disbursement of, and accounting for, Federal funds paid to the State (including such funds paid by the State to local educational agencies) under this title; and

"(3) that the State educational agency will make to the Commissioner (A) periodic reports (including the results of objective measurements required by section 205(a) (5)) evaluating the effectiveness of payments under this title and of particular programs assisted under it in improving the educational attainment of educationally deprived children, and (B) such other reports as may be reasonably necessary to enable the Commissioner to perform his duties under this title (including such reports as he may require to determine the amounts which the local educational agencies of that State are eligible to receive for any fiscal year), and assurance that such agency will keep such records and afford such access thereto as the Commissioner may find necessary to assure the correctness and verification of such reports.

"(b) The Commissioner shall approve an application which meets the requirements specified in subsection (a), and he shall not finally disapprove an application except after reasonable notice and opportunity for a hearing to the State educational agency.

"Payment

"Sec. 207. (a) (1) The Commissioner shall, subject to the provisions of section 208, from time to time pay to each State, in advance or otherwise, the amount which the local educational agencies of that State are eligible to receive under this title. Such payments shall take into account the extent (if any) to which any previous payment to such State educational agency under this title (whether or not in the same fiscal year) was greater or less than the amount which should have been paid to it.

"(2) From the funds paid to it pursuant to paragraph (1) each State educational agency shall distribute to each local educational agency of the State which is not ineligible by reason of section 203 (b) and which has submitted an application approved pursuant to section 205(a) the amount for which such application has been approved, except that this amount shall not exceed an amount equal to the total of the maximum amount of the basic grant plus the maximum amount of the special incentive grant as determined for that agency pursuant to sections 203 and 204, respectively.

"(b) The Commissioner is authorized to pay to each State amounts equal to the amounts expended by it for the proper and efficient performance of its duties under this title (including technical assistance for the measurements and evaluations required by section 205 (a) (5)), except that the total of such payments in any fiscal year shall not exceed 1 per centum of the total of the amount of the basic grants paid under this title for that year to the local educational agencies of the State.

"(c) (1) No payments shall be made under this title for any fiscal year to a State which has taken into consideration payments under this title in determining the eligibility of any local educational agency in that State for State aid, or the amount of that aid, with respect to the free public education of children during that year or the preceding fiscal year.

"(2) No payments shall be made under this title to any local educational agency for any fiscal year unless the State educational agency finds that the combined fiscal effort (as determined in accordance with regulations of the Commissioner) of that agency and the State with respect to the provision of free public education by that agency for the preceding fiscal year was not less than such combined fiscal effort for that purpose for the fiscal year ending June 30, 1964.

"Adjustments where Necessitated by Appropriations

"Sec. 208. If the sums appropriated for the fiscal year ending June 30, 1966, for making the payments provided in this title are not sufficient to pay in full the total amounts which all local and State educational agencies are eligible to receive under this title for such year, such amounts shall be reduced ratably. In case additional funds become available for making payments under this title for that year, such reduced amounts shall be increased on the same basis that they were reduced.

"Labor Standards

"Sec. 209. All laborers and mechanics employed by contractors or subcontractors on all construction projects assisted under this title shall be paid wages at rates not less than those prevailing on similar construction in the locality as determined by the Secretary of Labor in accordance with the Davis-Bacon Act, as amended (40 U.S.C. 276a—276a-5). The Secretary of Labor shall have with respect to the labor standards specified in this section the authority and functions set forth in Reorganization Plan Numbered 14 of 1950 (15 F.R. 3176; 5 U.S.C. 133z-15) and section 2 of the Act of June 13, 1934, as amended (40 U.S.C. 276c).

"Withholding

"Sec. 210. Whenever the Commissioner, after reasonable notice and opportunity for hearing to any State educational agency, finds that there has been a failure to comply substantially with any assurance set forth in the application of that State approved under section 206 (b), the Commissioner shall notify the agency that further payments will not be made to the State under this title (or, in his discretion, that the State educational agency shall not make further payments under this title to specified local educational agencies affected by the failure) until he is satisfied that there is no longer any such failure to comply. Until he is so satisfied, no further payments shall be made to the State under this title, or payments by the State educational agency under this title shall be limited to local educational agencies not affected by the failure, as the case may be.

"Judicial Review

"Sec. 211. (a) If any State is dissatisfied with the Commissioner's final action with respect to the approval of its application submitted under section 206 (a) or with his final action under section 210, such State may, within sixty days after notice of such action, file with the United States court of appeals for the circuit in which such State is located a petition for review of that action. A copy of the petition shall be forthwith transmitted by the clerk of the court to the Commissioner. The Commissioner thereupon shall file in the court the record of the proceedings on which he based his action, as provided in section 2112 of title 28, United States Code.

"(b) The findings of fact by the Commissioner, if supported by substantial evidence, shall be conclusive; but the court, for good cause shown, may remand the case to the Commissioner to take further evidence, and the Commissioner may thereupon make new or modified findings of fact and may modify his previous action, and shall file in the court the record of the further proceedings. Such new or modified findings of fact shall likewise be conclusive if supported by substantial evidence.

"(c) Upon the filing of such petition, the court shall have jurisdiction to affirm the action of the Commissioner or to set it aside, in whole or in part. The judgment of the court shall be subject to review by the Supreme Court of the United States upon certiorari or certification as provided in section 1254 of title 28, United States Code.

"National Advisory Council

"Sec. 212. (a) The President shall, within ninety days after the enactment of this title, appoint a National Advisory Council on the Education of Disadvantaged Children for the purpose of reviewing the administration and operation of this title, including its effectiveness in improving the educational attainment of educationally deprived children, and making recommendations for the improvement of this title and its administration and operation. These recommendations shall take into consideration experience gained under this and other Federal educational programs for disadvantaged children and, to the extent appropriate, experience gained under other public and private educational programs for disadvantaged children.

"(b) The Council shall be appointed by the President without regard to the civil service laws and shall consist of twelve persons. When requested by the President, the Secretary of Health,

Education, and Welfare shall engage such technical assistance as may be required to carry out the functions of the Council, and the Secretary shall make available to the Council such secretarial, clerical, and other assistance and such pertinent data prepared by the Department of Health, Education, and Welfare as it may require to carry out such functions.

"(c) The Council shall make an annual report of its findings and recommendations (including recommendations for changes in the provisions of this title) to the President not later than March 31 of each calendar year beginning after the enactment of this title. The President shall transmit each such report to the Congress together with his comments and recommendations.

"(d) Members of the Council who are not regular full-time employees of the United States shall, while serving on business of the Council, be entitled to receive compensation at rates fixed by the President, but not exceeding $100 per day, including travel time; and while so serving away from their homes or regular places of business, they may be allowed travel expenses, including per diem in lieu of subsistence, as authorized by section 5 of the Administrative Expenses Act of 1946 (5 U.S.C. 73b-2) for persons in Government service employed intermittently."

Technical and Conforming Amendments

Sec. 3. (a) Clause (A) of section 3 (c) (4) of the Act of September 30, 1950, Public Law 874, Eighty-first Congress, as amended (20 U.S.C. 238 (c) (4)(A)) is amended by striking out ") is," and inserting ", but excluding funds available under title II) is,".

(b) The sentence which immediately follows clause (B) of section 4 (a) of such Act (20 U.S.C. 239(a) (B)) is amended by inserting "(exclusive of funds available under title II)" immediately after "Federal funds".

(c) (1) Such Act is further amended by inserting "TITLE III—GENERAL" above the heading for section 7, and by redesignating sections 7, 8, and 9, and references thereto, as sections 301, 302, and 303, respectively.

(2) Subsections (b) and (c) of the section of such Act redesignated as section 302 are amended by striking out "this Act" wherever it appears and inserting in lieu thereof "title I".

Definitions

Sec. 4. (a) Paragraph (2) of the section of the Act of September 30, 1950, Public Law 874, Eighty-first Congress, as amended, redesignated by section 3 of this Act as section 303, is amended to read as follows:

"(2) The term 'child', except as used in title II, means any child who is within the age limits for which the applicable State provides free public education."

(b) Paragraph (4) of such section 303 is amended by inserting before the period at the end thereof ", except that for the purposes of title II such term does not include any education provided beyond grade 12".

(c) Paragraph (5) of such section 303 is amended by inserting immediately before the period at the end thereof the following: ", or any expenditures made from funds granted under title II of this Act or titles II or III of the Elementary and Secondary Education Act of 1965".

(d) (1) Paragraph (8) of such section 303 is amended by inserting "American Samoa," after "the District of Columbia,", and by inserting after "the Virgin Islands" the following: ", and for purposes of title II, such term includes the Trust Territory of the Pacific Islands".

(2) Sections 3(d) and 6(c) of such Act (20 U.S.C. 238 (d), 241 (c)) are each amended by inserting "American Samoa," after "Guam," each time that it appears.

(e) Such section 303 is further amended by adding at the end thereof the following new paragraphs:

"(11) The term 'county' means those divisions of a State utilized by the Secretary of Commerce in compiling and reporting data regarding counties.

"(12) The term 'construction' includes the preparation of drawings and specifications for school facilities; erecting, building, acquiring, altering, remodeling, improving, or extending school facilities; and the inspection and supervision of the construction of school facilities.

"(13) The term 'school facilities' means classrooms and related facilities (including initial equipment) for free public education and interests in land (including site, grading, and improvements) on which such facilities are constructed, except that such term does not include those gymnasiums and similar facilities intended primarily for exhibitions for which admission is to be charged to the general public.

"(14) The term 'equipment' includes machinery, utilities, and built-in equipment and any necessary enclosures or structures to house them, and includes all other items necessary for the functioning of a particular facility as a facility for the provision of educational services, including items such as instructional equipment and necessary furniture, printed, published, and audio-visual instructional materials, and books, periodicals, documents, and other related materials.

"(15) For the purpose of title II, the term 'elementary school' means a day or residential school which provides elementary education, as determined under State law, and the term 'secondary school' means a day or residential school which provides secondary education, as determined under State law, except that it does not include any education provided beyond grade 12."

TITLE IX OF THE EDUCATION AMENDMENTS OF 1972

PUBLIC LAW 92-318
20 U.S.C. SECS. 1681–1688
TITLE 20—EDUCATION
CHAPTER 38—DISCRIMINATION BASED ON SEX OR BLINDNESS

Sec. 1681. Sex

(a) Prohibition against discrimination; exceptions

No person in the United States shall, on the basis of sex, be excluded from participation in, be denied the benefits of, or be subjected to discrimination under any education program or activity receiving Federal financial assistance, except that:

(1) Classes of educational institutions subject to prohibition

in regard to admissions to educational institutions, this section shall apply only to institutions of vocational education, professional education, and graduate higher education, and to public institutions of undergraduate higher education;

(2) Educational institutions commencing planned change in admissions

in regard to admissions to educational institutions, this section shall not apply

(A) for one year from June 23, 1972, nor for six years after June 23, 1972, in the case of an educational institution which has begun the process of changing from being an institution which admits only students of one sex to being an institution which admits students of both sexes, but only if it is carrying out a plan for such a change which is approved by the Secretary of Education or

(B) for seven years from the date an educational institution begins the process of changing from being an institution which admits only students of only one sex to being an institution which admits students of both sexes, but only if it is carrying out a plan for such a change which is approved by the Secretary of Education, whichever is the later;

(3) Educational institutions of religious organizations with contrary religious tenets

this section shall not apply to an educational institution which is controlled by a religious organization if the application of this subsection would not be consistent with the religious tenets of such organization;

(4) Educational institutions training individuals for military services or merchant marine

this section shall not apply to an educational institution whose primary purpose is the training of individuals for the military services of the United States, or the merchant marine;

(5) Public educational institutions with traditional and continuing admissions policy

in regard to admissions this section shall not apply to any public institution of undergraduate higher education which is an institution that traditionally and continually from its establishment has had a policy of admitting only students of one sex;

(6) Social fraternities or sororities; voluntary youth service organizations

this section shall not apply to membership practices

(A) of a social fraternity or social sorority which is exempt from taxation under section 501(a) of title 26, the active membership of which consists primarily of students in attendance at an institution of higher education, or

(B) of the Young Men's Christian Association, Young Women's Christian Association, Girl Scouts, Boy Scouts, Camp Fire Girls, and voluntary youth service organizations which are so exempt, the membership of which has traditionally been limited to persons of one sex and principally to persons of less than nineteen years of age;

(7) Boy or Girl conferences

this section shall not apply to

(A) any program or activity of the American Legion undertaken in connection with the organization or operation of any Boys State conference, Boys Nation conference, Girls State conference, or Girls Nation conference; or

(B) any program or activity of any secondary school or educational institution specifically for

(i) the promotion of any Boys State conference, Boys Nation conference, Girls State conference, or Girls Nation conference; or

(ii) the selection of students to attend any such conference;

(8) Father-son or mother-daughter activities at educational institutions

this section shall not preclude father-son or mother-daughter activities at an educational institution, but if such activities are provided for students of one sex, opportunities for reasonably comparable activities shall be provided for students of the other sex; and

(9) Institution of higher education scholarship awards in "beauty" pageants

this section shall not apply with respect to any scholarship or other financial assistance awarded by an institution of higher education to any individual because such individual has received such award in any pageant in which the attainment of such award is based upon a combination of factors related to the personal appearance, poise, and talent of such individual and in which participation is limited to individuals of one sex only, so long as such pageant is in compliance with other nondiscrimination provisions of Federal law.

(b) Preferential or disparate treatment because of imbalance in participation or receipt of Federal benefits; statistical evidence of imbalance

Nothing contained in subsection (a) of this section shall be interpreted to require any educational institution to grant preferential or disparate treatment to the members of one sex on account of an imbalance which may exist with respect to the total number or percentage of persons of that sex participating in or receiving the benefits of any federally supported program or activity, in comparison with the total number or percentage of persons of that sex in any community, State, section, or other area: *Provided*, That this subsection shall not be construed to prevent the consideration in any hearing or proceeding under this chapter of statistical evidence tending to show that such an imbalance exists with respect to the participation in, or receipt of the benefits of, any such program or activity by the members of one sex.

(c)"Educational institution" defined

For purposes of this chapter an educational institution means any public or private preschool, elementary, or secondary school, or any institution of vocational, professional, or higher education, except that in the case of an educational institution composed of more than one school, college, or department which are administratively separate units, such term means each such school, college, or department.

(Pub. L. 92-318, title IX, Sec. 901, June 23, 1972, 86 Stat. 373; Pub. L. 93-568, Sec. 3(a), Dec. 31, 1974, 88 Stat. 1862; Pub. L. 94-482, title IV, Sec. 412(a), Oct. 12, 1976, 90 Stat. 2234; Pub. L. 96-88, title III, Sec. 301(a)(1), title V, Sec. 507, Oct. 17, 1979, 93 Stat. 677, 692; Pub. L. 99-514, Sec. 2, Oct. 22, 1986, 100 Stat. 2095.)

REFERENCES IN TEXT

This chapter, referred to in subsecs. (b) and (c), was in the original "this title", meaning title IX of Pub. L. 92-318 which enacted this chapter and amended sections 203 and 213 of Title 29, Labor, and sections 2000c, 2000c-6, 2000c-9, and 2000h-2 of Title 42, The Public Health and Welfare. For complete classification of title IX to the Code, see Tables.

AMENDMENTS

1986 - Subsec. (a)(6)(A). Pub. L. 99-514 substituted "Internal Revenue Code of 1986" for "Internal Revenue Code of 1954", which for purposes of codification was translated as "title 26" thus requiring no change in text.

1976 - Subsec. (a)(6) to (9). Pub. L. 94-482 substituted "this" for "This" in par. (6) and added pars. (7) to (9).

1974 - Subsec. (a)(6). Pub. L. 93-568 added par. (6).

EFFECTIVE DATE OF 1976 AMENDMENT

Section 412(b) of Pub. L. 94-482 provided that: "The amendment made by subsection (a) [amending this section] shall take effect upon the date of enactment of this Act [Oct. 12, 1976]."

EFFECTIVE DATE OF 1974 AMENDMENT

Section 3(b) of Pub. L. 93-568 provided that: "The provisions of the amendment made by subsection (a) [amending this section] shall be effective on, and retroactive to, July 1, 1972."

SHORT TITLE OF 1988 AMENDMENT

Pub. L. 100-259, Sec. 1, Mar. 22, 1988, 102 Stat. 28, provided that: "This Act [enacting sections 1687 and 1688 of this title and section 2000d-4a of Title 42, The Public Health and Welfare, amending sections 706 and 794 of Title 29, Labor, and section 6107 of Title 42, and enacting provisions set out as notes under sections 1687 and 1688 of this title] may be cited as the 'Civil Rights Restoration Act of 1987'."

TRANSFER OF FUNCTIONS

"Secretary" substituted for "Commissioner" in subsec. (a)(2) pursuant to sections 301(a)(1) and 507 of Pub. L. 96-88, which are classified to sections 3441(a)(1) and 3507 of this title and which transferred all functions of Commissioner of Education to the Secretary of Education.

COORDINATION OF IMPLEMENTATION AND ENFORCEMENT OF PROVISIONS

For provisions relating to the coordination of implementation and enforcement of the provisions of this chapter by the Attorney General, see section 1-201(b) of Ex. Ord. No. 12250, Nov. 2, 1980, 45 F.R. 72995, set out as a note under section 2000d-1 of Title 42, The Public Health and Welfare.

REGULATIONS; NATURE OF PARTICULAR SPORTS: INTERCOLLEGIATE ATHLETIC ACTIVITIES

Pub. L. 93-380, title VIII, Sec. 844, Aug. 21, 1974, 88 Stat. 612, provided that the Secretary prepare and publish, not more than 30 days after Aug. 21, 1974, proposed regulations implementing the provisions of this chapter regarding prohibition of sex discrimination in federally assisted programs, including reasonable regulations for intercollegiate athletic activities considering the nature of the particular sports.

SECTION REFERRED TO IN OTHER SECTIONS

This section is referred to in sections 1682, 1687 of this title.

EDUCATION FOR ALL HANDICAPPED CHILDREN ACT OF 1975

PUBLIC LAW 94-142

SUMMARY AS OF:

(REVISED AS OF 11/14/75—Conference report filed in Senate, S. Rept. 94-455)

Education for All Handicapped Children Act—Extends the provisions of the Education of the Handicapped Act through fiscal year 1977 and authorizes appropriations for such years.

States the findings of the Congress, including that: (1) the special educational needs of handicapped children are not being fully met; (2) one million of the handicapped children in the United States are excluded entirely from the public school system and will not go through the educational process with their peers; and (3) it is in the national interest that the Federal Government assist State and local efforts to provide programs to meet the educational needs of handicapped children in order to assure equal protection of the laws.

Describes the purposes of this Act, including to insure that all handicapped children have available to them special education and related services designed to meet their unique needs. Defines the terms used in this Act.

States that the maximum amount of the grant to which a State is entitled under such Act shall equal the number of handicapped children aged three to twenty-one, who are receiving special education in such State, multiplied by a percentage of the average per pupil expenditure in public elementary and secondary schools in the United States. Increases such percentage from 5 to 40 percent by 1982.

Requires States to distribute portions of such grants to local education agencies and intermediate educational units, to spend for administration, and to match Federal grants for specified expenditures for support services and direct services.

Sets forth provisions relating to extension of grants to Territories and to Indian children.

Sets forth requirements for eligibility including the following which a State must demonstrate to the Commissioner: (1) the State has in effect a policy that assures all handicapped children the right to a free appropriate public education; and (2) the State has developed a plan which requires it to assure that a free appropriate public education will be available for all handicapped children between the ages of three and eighteen within the State not later than September 1, 1978, and for all handicapped children between the ages of three and twenty-four within the State not later than September 1, 1980; and (3) each local educational agency in the State will maintain records of the individualized education program for each handicapped child and such program shall be established, reviewed, and revised.

Requires applications for assistance under this Act to: (1) set forth a description of programs and procedures for the development and implementation of a comprehensive system of personnel development which shall include the in-service training of general and special educational instructional and support personnel; (2) set forth policies and procedures to assure that to the extent consistent with the number and location of handicapped children in the State who are enrolled in private elementary and secondary schools, provision is made for the participation of such children in the program assisted or carried out under this part by providing for such children special education and related services; (3) provide satisfaction assurance that Federal funds made available will not be commingled with State funds, and will be so used as to supplement and increase the level of State and local funds expended for the education of handicapped children and not to supplant such State and local funds; and (4) provide that the State has an advisory panel, appointed by the Governor or any other official authorized under State law to make such appointments, composed of individuals involved in or concerned with the education of handicapped children, including handicapped individuals, teachers, parents or guardians of handicapped children, State and local education officials, and administrators of programs for handicapped children.

States that a local educational agency or an intermediate educational unit which desires to receive payments under this Act shall submit an application to the appropriate State educational agency, and such application shall: (1) provide satisfactory assurance that payments under this part will be used for excess costs directly attributable to programs which provide that all children residing within the jurisdiction of the local educational agency or the intermediate educational unit who are handicapped, regardless of the severity of their handicap, and are in need of special education and related services will be identified, located, and evaluated; and (2) provide assurances that the local educational agency or intermediate educational unit will establish, or revise, whichever is appropriate, an individualized education program of each handicapped child at the beginning of each school year and will then review and, if appropriate revise, its provisions periodically, but not less than annually.

Provides that whenever a State educational agency finds that a local educational agency or an intermediate educational unit, in the administration of an application approved by the State educational agency, has failed to comply with any requirement set forth in such application, the State educational agency, after giving appropriate notice to the local educational agency or the intermediate educational unit, shall make no further payments to such local educational agency or such intermediate educational unit until the State educational agency is satisfied that there is no longer any failure to comply with the requirement involved.

States that whenever a State educational agency determines that a local educational agency is unable or unwilling to establish and maintain programs of free appropriate public education; is unable or unwilling to be consolidated with other local educational agencies in order to establish and maintain such programs; or has one or more handicapped children who can best be served by a regional or State center designed to meet the needs of such children; the State educational agency shall use the payments which would have been available to such local educational agency to provide special education and related services directly to handicapped children residing in the area by such local educational agency.

Requires any State educational agency, any local educational agency, and any intermediate educational unit which receives assistance under this part to establish and maintain procedures to assure that handicapped children and their parents or guardians are guaranteed procedural safeguards with respect to the provision of free appropriate public education by such agencies and units, which procedures shall include, but shall not be limited to, an opportunity for the parents or guardian of a handicapped child to examine all relevant records with respect to the identification, evaluation, and educational placement of the child.

Provides that whenever a complaint has been received under this Act the parents or guardian shall have an opportunity for an impartial due process hearing, and a right of appeal therefrom to State or Federal court.

Provides that whenever the Commissioner, after reasonable notice and opportunity for hearing to the State educational agency involved, finds that there has been a failure to comply substantially with specified provisions of this Act, or that in the administration of the State plan there is a failure to comply or with any requirements set forth in the application of a local educational agency or intermediate educational unit the Commissioner of Education shall, after notifying the State educational agency, withhold any further payments to the State under this Act.

Permits an appeal to United States circuit court of appeals from any such action by the Commissioner.

Directs the Commissioner to conduct, directly or by grant or contract, such studies, investigations, and evaluations as are necessary to assure effective implementation of this Act, and through the National Center for Education Statistics, to provide to the appropriate committees of each House of the Congress and to the general public at least annually, programmatic information concerning programs and projects assisted under this Act and other Federal programs supporting the education of handicapped children.

Requires that, not later than 120 days after the close of each fiscal year, the Commissioner shall transmit to the appropriate committees of each House of the Congress a report on the progress being made toward the provisions of free appropriate public education to all handicapped children, including a detailed description of all evaluation activities conducted.

Authorizes grants to States which have met the eligibility requirements of this Act and have an approved State plan, to be used for the provision of special education and related services to the handicapped aged three to five. Sets a maximum for such grants of $300 per child.

Sets forth provisions relating to the procedures of payments under this Act to State education agencies, and to local and intermediate educational agencies.

Requires any proposed changes in the definition of "children with specific learning disabilities" to be submitted to the Congress. Defines such term presently to mean those children who have a disorder in one or more of the basic psychological processes involved in understanding or in using language, spoken or written, which disorder may manifest itself in imperfect ability to listen, think, speak, read, write, spell, or do mathematical calculations.

Directs the Secretary of Health, Education, and Welfare to assure that each recipient of assistance under this Act shall make positive efforts to employ and advance in employment qualified handicapped individuals in programs assisted under this Act.

Authorizes, upon application by any State or local educational agency or intermediate educational unit, the Commissioner to make grants to pay part or all of the cost of altering existing buildings and equipment to remove architectural barriers.

Authorizes the Secretary to enter into agreements with institutions of higher education, State and local educational agencies, or other appropriate nonprofit agencies, for the establishment and operation of centers on educational media and materials for the handicapped.

EDUCATION OF THE HANDICAPPED ACT AMENDMENTS OF 1990

PUBLIC LAW 101-476
OCTOBER 30, 1990

An Act

To amend the Education of the Handicaps Act to revise and extend the programs established in parts C through G of such Act, and for other purposes.

Be it enacted by the Senate and House of Representatives of the United States of America in Congress assembled,

SECTION 1. SHORT TITLE; REFERENCE.

(a) Short Title. — This Act may be cited as the "Education of the Handicapped Act Amendments of 1990".

(b) REFERENCE. — Except as otherwise provided in section 901, whenever in this Act an amendment or repeal is expressed in terms of an amendment to, or repeal of, a section or other provision, the reference shall be considered to be made to a section or other provision of the Education of the Handicapped Act.

TITLE I—GENERAL PROVISIONS

SEC. 101. DEFINITIONS.

(a) HANDICAPPED CHILDREN. — Section 602(a)(1) (20 U.S.C. 1401(a)(1)) is amended to read as follows:

"(1) The term 'children with disabilities' means children —

"(A) with mental retardation, hearing impairments including deafness, speech or language impairments, visual impairments including blindness, serious emotional disturbance, orthopedic impairments, autism, traumatic brain injury, other health impairments, or specific learning disabilities; and

"(B) who, by reason thereof need special education and related services.".

(b) SPECIAL EDUCATION. — Section 602(a)(16) (20 U.S.C. 1401(a)(16)) is amended by striking "including classroom instruction" and all that follows and inserting the following: "including —

"(A) instruction conducted in the classroom, in the home, in hospitals and institutions, and in other settings; and

"(B) instruction in physical education.".

(c) RELATED SERVICES. — Section 602(a)(17) (20 U.S.C. 1401(a)(17)) is amended —

(1) by striking "recreation," and inserting "recreation, including therapeutic recreation and social work services,"; and

(2) by inserting ", including rehabilitation counseling," after counseling services,".

(d) TRANSITION SERVICES. — Section 602(a) (20 U.S.C. 1401(a)) is amended by redesignating paragraphs (19) through (23) as paragraphs (20) through (24), respectively, and by inserting after paragraph (18) the following new paragraph:

"(19) The term 'transition services' means a coordinated set of activities for a student, designed within an outcome-oriented process, which promotes movement from school to post-school activities; including post-secondary education, vocational training, integrated employment (including supported employment), continuing and adult education, adult services, independent living, or community participation. The coordinated set of activities shall be based upon the individual student's needs, taking into account the student's preferences and interests, and shall include instruction, community experiences, the development of employment and other post-school adult living objectives, and, when appropriate, acquisition of daily living skills and functional vocational evaluation.".

(e) INDIVIDUALIZED EDUCATION PROGRAM. — Section 602(a)(20), as redesignated by subsection (d) of this section, is amended —

(1) by redesignating subparagraphs (D) and (E) as subparagraphs (E) and (F), respectively, and by inserting after subparagraph (C) the following new subparagraph:

"(D) a statement of the needed transition services for students beginning no later than age 16 and annually thereafter (and, when determined appropriate for the individual, beginning at age 14 or younger), including, when appropriate, a statement of the interagency reponsibilities or linkages (or both) before the student leaves the school setting,", and

(2) by inserting after subparagraph (F) (as so redesignated) the following: "In the case where a participating agency, other than the educational agency, fails to provide agreed upon services, the educational agency shall reconvene the IEP team to identify alternative strategies to meet the transition objectives.".

(f) PUBLIC OR PRIVATE NONPROFIT AGENCY OR ORGANIZATION. — Section 602(a)(24)(A), as redesignated by subsection (d) of this section, is amended by inserting before the period the following: "and the Bureau of Indian Affairs of the Department of the Interior (when acting on behalf of schools operated by the Bureau for children and students on Indian reservations) and tribally controlled schools funded by the Department of the Interior".

(g) ASSISTIVE TECHNOLOGY DEVICE. — Section 602(a), as amended by subsection (d) of this section, is amended by adding at the end the following new paragraph:

"(25) The term 'assistive technology device' means any item, piece of equipment, or product system, whether acquired commercially off the shelf, modified, or customized, that is used to increase, maintain, or improve functional capabilities of individuals with disabilities.".

(h) ASSISTIVE TECHNOLOGY SERVICE. — Section 602(a), as amended by subsection (g) of this section, is amended by adding at the end the following new paragraph:

"(26) The term 'assistive technology service' means any service that directly assists an individual with a disability in the selection, acquisition, or use of an assistive technology device. Such term includes —

"(A) the evaluation of the needs of an individual with a disability, including a functional evaluation of the individual in the individual's customary environment;

"(B) purchasing, leasing, or otherwise providing for the acquisition of assistive technology devices by individuals with disabilities;

"(C) selecting, designing, fitting, customizing, adapting, applying, maintaining, repairing, or replacing of assistive technology devices;

"(D) coordinating and using other therapies, interventions, or services with assistive technology devices, such as those associated with existing education and rehabilitation plans and programs;

"(E) training or technical assistance for an individual with disabilities, or, where appropriate, the family of an individual with disabilities; and

"(F) training or technical assistance for professionals (including individuals providing education and rehabilitation services), employers, or other individuals who provide services to, employ, or are otherwise substantially involved in the major life functions of individuals with disabilities.".

(i) UNDERREPRESENTED. — Section 602(a), as amended by subsection (h) of this section, is amended by adding at the end the following new paragraph:

"(27) The term 'underrepresented' means populations such as minorities, the poor, the limited English proficient, and individuals with disabilities.".

SEC. 102. NOTICE OF INQUIRY.

(a) PUBLICATION. — Not later than 30 days after the date of the enactment of the Education of the Handicapped Act Amendments of 1990, the Secretary shall publish a Notice of Inquiry in the Federal Register for the purpose of soliciting public comments regarding the appropriate components of an operational definition under such Act for the term "attention deficit disorder" (hereinafter referred to in this section as the "disorder") in accordance with subsection (b)(2).

(b) PUBLIC COMMENT. —

(1) The Notice of Inquiry published under subsection (a) shall provide for a 120-day period for public comment.

(2) The Notice of Inquiry shall request comments concerning the following issues:

(A) How should the disorder be described operationally for purposes of qualifying a child for special education and related services under part B of the Education of the Handicapped Act.

(B) What criteria should be included in the definition to qualify children with the disorder whose disability is comparable in severity to other children with disabilities currently determined to be eligible for special education and related services under part B of the Education of the Handicapped Act.

(C) What specific manifestations of the disorder, if any, should be included in the definition.

(D) Whether the definition should include references to characteristics or circumstances that produce transient inattentive behaviors that, in and of themselves, would not make a child eligible for special education and related services under the definition of the disorder.

(E) Whether the definition should address the concurrence of this disorder with other disabilities such as specific learning disabilities or serious emotional disturbance, and if so addressed, the manner in which such is to be accomplished.

(F) Whether guidelines should be provided to State and local educational agencies regarding their obligation to conduct an evaluation of a child suspected of having this disorder, and a description of such guidelines.

(G) Who should be authorized to conduct an assessment of a child having or suspected of having the disorder and whether the assessment should be conducted by more than one individual (such as a teacher and a psychologist).

(H) What provisions should be included in the definition and what additional steps, if any, not currently required by the regulations implementing part B of the Education of the Handicapped Act, should be included to ensure that racial, ethnic, and linguistic minorities are not misclassified under this definition.

(c) REPORT TO COMMITTEES. — Not later than 30 days after the close of the comment period referred to in subsection (b)(1), the Secretary shall transmit the public comments received in response to the Notice of Inquiry in a usable form, accompanied by a document summarizing such comments, to the Committee on Labor and Human Resources of the Senate and the Committee on Education and Labor of the House of Representatives.

INDIVIDUALS WITH DISABILITIES EDUCATION ACT AMENDMENTS OF 1997

PUBLIC LAW 105-17

Due to their length, the 1997 amendments to the Individuals with Disabilities Act are not reprinted in this volume. A complete text of the amendments is available from the U.S. Department of Education IDEA website: <www.ed.gov/offices/OSERS/Policy/IDEA>.

HEAD START REAUTHORIZATION OF 1998: OVERVIEW OF PROGRAMS AND LEGISLATION

PUBLIC LAW 105-285

Head Start is a national program which provides comprehensive developmental services for America's low-income, pre-school children ages three to five and social services for their families. Approximately 1,400 community-based non-profit organizations and school systems develop unique and innovative programs to meet specific needs.

Head Start began in 1965 in the Office of Economic Opportunity and is now administered by the Administration for Children and Families. In FY 1999, $4.66 billion was available for Head Start services.

Major Components of Head Start

Head Start provides diverse services to meet the goals of the following four components:

- **Education.** Head Start's educational program is designed to meet the needs of each child, the community served, and its ethnic and cultural characteristics. Every child receives a variety of learning experiences to foster intellectual, social, and emotional growth.
- **Health.** Head Start emphasizes the importance of the early identification of health problems. Every child is involved in a comprehensive health program, which includes immunizations, medical, dental, and mental health, and nutritional services.
- **Parent Involvement.** An essential part of Head Start is the involvement of parents in parent education, program planning, and operating activities. Many parents serve as members of policy councils and committees and have a voice in administrative and managerial decisions. Participation in classes and workshops on child development and staff visits to the home allow parents to learn about the needs of their children and about educational activities that can take place at home.
- **Social Services.** Specific services are geared to each family after its needs are determined. They include: community outreach; referrals; family need assessments; recruitment and enrollment of children; and emergency assistance and/or crisis intervention.

Grants are awarded to local public or private non-profit agencies. Twenty percent of the total cost of a Head Start program must be contributed by the community. Head Start programs operate in all 50 states, the District of Columbia, Puerto Rico, and the U.S. territories.

Most of the Head Start program's appropriation funds local Head Start projects. The remainder is used for: training and technical assistance to assist local projects in meeting the Head Start Program Performance Standards and in maintaining and improving the quality of local programs; research, demonstration, and evaluation activities to test innovative program models and to assess program effectiveness; and required monitoring activities. Head Start provides training to staff at all levels and in all program areas. The Child Development Associate (CDA) program gives professional and non-professional employees the opportunity to pursue academic degrees or certification in early childhood education.

Volunteers are an important part of all Head Start programs. High school and college students, homemakers, parents of Head Start children, retired senior citizens—all kinds of people—have offered critical help to local Head Start programs. Volunteers assist with: indoor creative play; transportation; parent education; renovation of centers; and recruiting and instructing other volunteers. Approximately 1,315,000 individuals volunteer, and community organizations provide a wide array of services to Head Start, including the donation of classroom space, educational materials, and equipment for children with disabilities.

Since 1965, Head Start has served over 15.3 million children and their families. Head Start plays a major role in focusing attention on the importance of early childhood development.

The program also has an impact on: child development and day care services; the expansion of state and local activities for children; the range and quality of services offered to young children and their families; and the design of training programs for those who staff such programs. Outreach and training activities also assist parents in increasing their parenting skills and knowledge of child development.

American Indian Head Start Program

American Indian Head Start supports a rich, diverse and unique Indian language, heritage and legacy. Programs are encouraged to integrate language and culture into their curriculum and program goals. There are more than 84 different Indian languages spoken in Head Start.

As of May 1997, the American Indian Head Start Programs network has 131 funded grantees. These grantees are located in 25 states and represent the following tribes, villages and towns:

- 112 federally recognized Tribes who directly operate programs;
- 3 Inter-Tribal consortia representing 26 reservations, 12 colonies and 14 rancherias;
- 8 Native Alaskan Regional Corporations serving 35 villages and cities.

In FY 1997, 18,550 children are enrolled in American Indian Head Start programs and 320 children are enrolled in Parent Child Centers. The Head Start Bureau provides resources to 4 Tribal Governments to operate Parent Child Centers and to 7 Tribal Governments to operate Early Childhood Centers that serve pregnant women, infants, and toddlers (ages birth to three years). These programs offer a wide range of services to families living on the reservations.

Some 83 percent of Indian Head Start programs are center-based services, and 17 percent feature both center-based and home-based options. The Indian network has 487 centers and 919 classrooms. American Indian and Native Alaskan Head Start programs are typically located in remote areas and are usually small.

The Navajo Nation holds a major grant from the Head Start Bureau to facilitate the transition of Head Start children to the Bureau of Indian Affairs and public schools. Other transition activities are funded with the Crow Tribe, Turtle Mountain Band of Chippewa Indians and the Seminole Tribe of Oklahoma.

Migrant Head Start Program

Services provided by the Migrant Head Start program are identical to those of regular Head Start, but Migrant grantees modify delivery to meet the specific needs of migrant farmworker families. However, the Migrant Head Start program has a unique emphasis on serving infants and toddlers as well as pre-school age children, so that they will not have to be cared for in the fields or left in the care of very young siblings while parents are working. Infants as young as 6 weeks of age are served in Migrant centers.

Making service available to all pre-schoolers (including infants and toddlers) means that both parents can work to maximize the meager earnings from farmwork. Migrant Head Start families earn more than half their annual income from agricultural work and move at least once within each 2-year period in search of farm work. Preference is given to those who must move more often. Families must also meet the annual Head Start poverty income guidelines.

There are two types of Migrant Head Start grantees: Home-Based Grantees are located in the southern part of the United States (generally in California, Arizona, New Mexico, Texas, and Florida), and provide services to mobile migrant farmworker families from October through May. Upstream Grantees (generally in Washington, Idaho, Michigan, Illinois, Maine, Indiana, Wisconsin, Nebraska, and Minnesota) provide services to families as they move northward in search of agricultural work during the spring, summer and fall months.

Families who are in an upstream location working crops rarely have family members who can provide child care outside traditional center hours. Therefore, Migrant centers provide extended day services, usually up to 12 hours a day and up to 7 days a week during the height of the harvest season. Some grantees open and operate centers for as little as six weeks.

Migrant Head Start parents serve on Policy Councils and share decisionmaking with grantees. They volunteer to work at the centers and they attend literacy, ESL, GED, parenting, and safety and health classes.

A total of 25 grantees and 41 delegate agencies provide services in 33 States and serve over 30,000 migrant children.

Improving Head Start

Funding for Head Start has increased by 68 percent, increasing from $2.2 billion in 1992 to $4.66 billion in FY 1999. These additional funds have enabled Head Start to increase enrollment by over 200,000 children, enhance the quality of Head Start services, launch a new initiative to serve infants and toddlers, and improve program research. In FY 1998, Head Start served an estimated 830,000 children and their families.

On January 12, 1994, the Advisory Committee on Head Start Quality and Expansion, appointed by HHS Secretary Donna E. Shalala, presented recommendations that called for improved staff training and career development, including better salaries for Head Start workers, improving management of local Head Start centers, reengineering federal oversight, and providing for better facilities. Bipartisan legislation was soon introduced to reauthorize and strengthen the Head Start program. The reauthorization bill, which reflected the Administration's commitment to strengthening the quality of all Head Start programs, was signed on May 18, 1994. It included tough new provisions to ensure that no Head Start grantee will be funded if it falls below a minimum quality level and fails to correct deficiencies promptly.

Acting on the committee's recommendation, HHS offered technical assistance, partnership and support to Head Start programs that are ready to pursue excellence—and terminated the grants of those programs that were not delivering quality services. HHS has helped turn around approximately 120 grantees identified as deficient. Since October 1993, approximately 100 grantees have been terminated or have relinquished their Head Start grants.

New Performance Standards

A cornerstone of the bipartisan 1994 legislation was the requirement to develop a major revision of the Head Start Program Performance Standards—key regulations that set the guidelines and standards for quality in Head Start programs nationwide.

In the spirit of the Administration's reinvention goals, the revised Head Start Program Performance Standards were developed based on communication with Head Start and early childhood program practitioners. This new version focuses on quality services for children, including infants and toddlers, and their families. It was published as a final rule in the Federal Register on November 5, 1996.

The new guidelines integrate new standards for infants and toddlers, reform the structure of the earlier standards for increased ease of use, incorporate emerging research knowledge and expertise of health professionals, and highlight the importance of collaboration between Head Start programs and the broader community.

Early Head Start

The Head Start Act Amendments of 1994 also established the Early Head Start program, which expands the benefits of early childhood development to low income families with children under three and to pregnant women.

The purpose of this program is to:

- enhance children's physical, social, emotional and cognitive development;
- enable parents to be better caregivers of and teachers to their children; and

- help parents meet their own goals, including that of economic independence.

The services provided by Early Head Start programs are designed to reinforce and respond to the unique strengths and needs of each child and family. Services include quality early education in and out of the home; home visits; parent education, including parent-child activities; comprehensive health services, including services to women before, during and after pregnancy; nutrition; and case management and peer support groups for parents.

Early Head Start focuses on four cornerstones essential to quality programs: child development, family development, community building and staff development. Projects must coordinate with local Head Start programs to ensure continuity of services for children and families.

In FY 1998, funding for Early Head Start totaled $279 million, or more than 5 percent of the total Head Start budget, which served approximately 39,000 children and their families. In FY 1999, funding for Early Head Start totalled nearly $340 million. Head Start proposes to more than double the number of children in Early Head Start over 5 years.

New Investments

From 1992 through 1998, HHS will have invested more than $600 million in quality improvements to ensure that every Head Start program works. Head Start programs across the country have used these quality resources to fix leaky roofs, make sure facilities are healthy and safe for children, and hire more teachers to reduce class size and eliminate double-session classes.

Head Start plays an important role as a national laboratory for early childhood development programs. Head Start is now taking up the challenge to focus on measurable results for social competence and school-readiness in young children. To initiate this effort, four major academic institutions and Head Start grantees around the country have formed Head Start Quality Research Centers which are piloting new approaches to measuring and collecting data.

Head Start is also increasing investment in research that follows children and families over time and is collaborating with the National Academy of Sciences and the National Institutes of Health to develop strong scientific research on young children.

January 1999

U.S. Department of Health and Human Services

Administration for Children and Families

Phone: 202-401-9215

Website: <www.acf.dhhs.gov>

NATIONAL EDUCATION GOALS PANEL: GOALS 2000

In September 1989, President Bush and 50 Governors convened a historic Education Summit at Charlottesville, Virginia, and agree to set education goals for the nation.

The National Education Goals Panel was thus established as an independent executive branch agency of the federal government charged with monitoring national and state progress toward the National Education Goals. Under the legislation, the Panel was charged with a variety of responsibilities to support systemwide reform, including:

- Reporting on national and state progress toward the Goals over a 10-year period;
- Working to establish a system of high academic standards and assessments;
- Identifying actions for federal, state, and local governments to take; and
- Building a nationwide, bipartisan consensus to achieve the Goals.

Goal 1: Ready to Learn

By the year 2000, all children will start school ready to learn.

Objectives:

- Children will receive the nutrition, physical activity experiences, and health care needed to arrive at school with healthy minds and bodies, and to maintain the mental alertness necessary to be prepared to learn, and the number of low-birthweight babies will be significantly reduced through enhanced prenatal health systems.
- Every parent in the United States will be a child's first teacher and devote time each day to helping such parent's preschool child learn, and parents will have access to the training and support parents need.
- All children will have access to high-quality and developmentally appropriate preschool programs that help prepare children for school.

Goal 2: School Completion

By the year 2000, the high school graduation rate will increase to at least 90 percent.

Objectives:

- The Nation must dramatically reduce its school dropout rate, and 75 percent of the students who do drop out will successfully complete a high school degree or its equivalent.
- The gap in high school graduation rates between American students from minority backgrounds and their non-minority counterparts will be eliminated.

Goal 3: Student Achievement and Citizenship

By the year 2000, all students will leave grades 4, 8, and 12 having demonstrated competency over challenging subject matter including English, mathematics, science, foreign languages, civics and government, economics, arts, history, and geography, and every school in America will ensure that all students learn to use their minds well, so they may be prepared for responsible citizenship, further learning, and productive employment in our Nation's modern economy.

Objectives:

- The academic performance of all students at the elementary and secondary level will increase significantly in every quartile, and the distribution of minority students in each quartile will more closely reflect the student population as a whole.
- The percentage of all students who demonstrate the ability to reason, solve problems, apply knowledge, and write and communicate effectively will increase substantially.
- All students will be involved in activities that promote and demonstrate good citizenship, good health, community service, and personal responsibility.
- All students will have access to physical education and health education to ensure they are healthy and fit.
- The percentage of all students who are competent in more than one language will substantially increase.
- All students will be knowledgeable about the diverse cultural heritage of this Nation and about the world community.

Goal 4: Teacher Education and Professional Development

By the year 2000, the Nation's teaching force will have access to programs for the continued improvement of their professional skills and the opportunity to acquire the knowledge and skills needed to instruct and prepare all American students for the next century.

Objectives:

- All teachers will have access to preservice teacher education and continuing professional development activities that will provide such teachers with the knowledge and skills needed to teach to an increasingly diverse student population with a variety of educational, social, and health needs.
- All teachers will have continuing opportunities to acquire additional knowledge and skills needed to teach challenging subject matter and to use emerging new methods, forms of assessment, and technologies.
- States and school districts will create integrated strategies to attract, recruit, prepare, retrain, and support the continued professional development of teachers, administrators, and other educators, so that there is a highly talented work force of professional educators to teach challenging subject matter.
- Partnerships will be established, whenever possible, among local educational agencies, institutions of higher education, parents, and local labor, business, and professional associations to provide and support programs for the professional development of educators.

Goal 5: Mathematics and Science

By the year 2000, United States students will be the first in the world in mathematics and science achievement.

Objectives:

- Mathematics and science education, including the metric system of measurement, will be strengthened throughout the system, especially in the early grades.
- The number of teachers with a substantive background in mathematics and science, including the metric system of measurement, will increase by 50 percent.
- The number of United States undergraduate and graduate students, especially women and minorities, who complete degrees in mathematics, science, and engineering will increase significantly.

Goal 6: Adult Literacy and Lifelong Learning

By the year 2000, every adult American will be literate and will possess the knowledge and skills necessary to compete in a global economy and exercise the rights and responsibilities of citizenship.

Objectives:

- Every major American business will be involved in strengthening the connection between education and work.
- All workers will have the opportunity to acquire the knowledge and skills, from basic to highly technical, needed to adapt to emerging new technologies, work methods, and markets through public and private educational, vocational, technical, workplace, or other programs.
- Schools, in implementing comprehensive parent involvement programs, will offer more adult literacy, parent training and lifelong learning opportunities to improve the ties between home and school, and enhance parents' work and home lives.
- The number of quality programs, including those at libraries, that are designed to serve more effectively the needs of the growing number of part-time and midcareer students will increase substantially.
- The proportion of qualified students, especially minorities, who enter college, who complete at least two years, and who complete their degree programs will increase substantially.
- The proportion of college graduates who demonstrate an advanced ability to think critically, communicate effectively, and solve problems will increase substantially.

Goal 7: Safe, Disciplined, and Alcohol- and Drug-Free Schools

By the year 2000, every school in the United States will be free of drugs, violence and the unauthorized presence of firearms and alcohol and will offer a disciplined environment conducive to learning.

Objectives:

- Every school will implement a firm and fair policy on use, possession, and distribution of drugs and alcohol.
- Parents, businesses, governmental and community organizations will work together to ensure the rights of students to study in a safe and secure environment that is free of drugs and crime, and that schools provide a healthy environment and are a safe haven for all children.
- Every local educational agency will develop and implement a policy to ensure that all schools are free of violence and the unauthorized presence of weapons.
- Every local educational agency will develop a sequential, comprehensive kindergarten through twelfth grade drug and alcohol prevention education program. Drug and alcohol curriculum should be taught as an integral part of sequential, comprehensive health education.
- Community-based teams should be organized to provide students and teachers with needed support.
- Every school should work to eliminate sexual harassment.

Goal 8: Parental Participation

By the year 2000, every school will promote partnerships that will increase parental involvement and participation in promoting the social, emotional, and academic growth of children.

Objectives:

- Every State will develop policies to assist local schools and local educational agencies to establish programs for increasing partnerships that respond to the varying needs of parents and the home, including parents of children who are disadvantaged or bilingual, or parents of children with disabilities.
- Every school will actively engage parents and families in a partnership which supports the academic work of children at home and shared educational decision making at school.
- Parents and families will help to ensure that schools are adequately supported and will hold schools and teachers to high standards of accountability.

NO CHILD LEFT BEHIND ACT OF 2001

PUBLIC LAW 107-110

Executive Summary

Three days after taking office in January 2001 as the 43rd President of the United States, George W. Bush announced *No Child Left Behind*, his framework for bipartisan education reform that he described as "the cornerstone of my Administration." President Bush emphasized his deep belief in our public schools, but an even greater concern that "too many of our neediest children are being left behind," despite the nearly $200 billion in Federal spending since the passage of the Elementary and Secondary Education Act of 1965 (ESEA). The President called for bipartisan solutions based on accountability, choice, and flexibility in Federal education programs.

Less than a year later, despite the unprecedented challenges of engineering an economic recovery while leading the Nation in the war on terrorism following the events of September 11, President Bush secured passage of the landmark *No Child Left Behind Act* of 2001 (NCLB Act). The new law reflects a remarkable consensus—first articulated in the President's *No Child Left Behind* framework—on how to improve the performance of America's elementary and secondary schools while at the same time ensuring that no child is trapped in a failing school.

The NCLB Act, which reauthorizes the ESEA, incorporates the principles and strategies proposed by President Bush. These include increased accountability for States, school districts, and schools; greater choice for parents and students, particularly those attending low-performing schools; more flexibility for States and local educational agencies (LEAs) in the use of Federal education dollars; and a stronger emphasis on reading, especially for our youngest children.

Increased Accountability

The NCLB Act will strengthen Title I accountability by requiring States to implement statewide accountability systems covering all public schools and students. These systems must be based on challenging State standards in reading and mathematics, annual testing for all students in grades 3–8, and annual statewide progress objectives ensuring that all groups of students reach proficiency within 12 years. Assessment results and State progress objectives must be broken out by poverty, race, ethnicity, disability, and limited English proficiency to ensure that no group is left behind. School districts and schools that fail to make adequate yearly progress (AYP) toward statewide proficiency goals will, over time, be subject to improvement, corrective action, and restructuring measures aimed at getting them back on course to meet State standards. Schools that meet or exceed AYP objectives or close achievement gaps will be eligible for State Academic Achievement Awards.

More Choices for Parents and Students

The NCLB Act significantly increases the choices available to the parents of students attending Title I schools that fail to meet State standards, including immediate relief—beginning with the 2002–03 school year—for students in schools that were previously identified for improvement or corrective action under the 1994 ESEA reauthorization.

LEAs must give students attending schools identified for improvement, corrective action, or restructuring the opportunity to attend a better public school, which may include a public charter school, within the school district. The district must provide transportation to the new school, and must use at least 5 percent of its Title I funds for this purpose, if needed.

For students attending persistently failing schools (those that have failed to meet State standards for at least 3 of the 4 preceding years), LEAs must permit low-income students to use Title I funds to obtain supplemental educational services from the public- or private-sector provider selected by the students and their parents. Providers must meet State standards and offer services tailored to help participating students meet challenging State academic standards.

To help ensure that LEAs offer meaningful choices, the new law requires school districts to spend up to 20 percent of their Title I allocations to provide school choice and supplemental educational services to eligible students.

In addition to helping ensure that no child loses the opportunity for a quality education because he or she is trapped in a failing school, the choice and supplemental service requirements provide a substantial incentive for low-performing schools to improve. Schools that want to avoid losing students—along with the portion of their annual budgets typically associated with those students—will have to improve or, if they fail to make AYP for 5 years, run the risk of reconstitution under a restructuring plan.

Greater Flexibility for States, School Districts, and Schools

One important goal of *No Child Left Behind* was to breathe new life into the "flexibility for accountability" bargain with States first struck by President George H.W. Bush during his historic 1989 education summit with the Nation's Governors at Charlottesville, Virginia. Prior flexibility efforts have focused on the waiver of program requirements; the NCLB Act moves beyond this limited approach to give States and school districts unprecedented flexibility in the use of Federal education funds in exchange for strong accountability for results.

New flexibility provisions in the NCLB Act include authority for States and LEAs to transfer up to 50 percent of the funding they receive under 4 major State grant programs to any one of the programs, or to Title I. The covered programs include Teacher Quality State Grants, Educational Technology, Innovative Programs, and Safe and Drug-Free Schools.

The new law also includes a competitive State Flexibility Demonstration Program that permits up to 7 States to consolidate the State share of nearly all Federal State grant programs—including Title I, Part A Grants to Local Educational Agencies—while providing additional flexibility in their use of Title V Innovation funds. Participating States must enter into 5-year performance agreements with the Secretary covering the use of the consolidated funds, which may be used for any educational purpose authorized under the ESEA. As part of their plans, States also must enter into up to 10 local performance agreements with LEAs, which will enjoy the same level of flexibility granted under the separate Local Flexibility Demonstration Program.

The new competitive Local Flexibility Demonstration Program would allow up to 80 LEAs, in addition to the 70 LEAs under the State Flexibility Demonstration Program, to consolidate funds received under Teacher Quality State Grants, Educational Technology State Grants, Innovative Programs, and Safe and Drug-Free Schools programs. Participating LEAs would enter into performance agreements with the Secretary of Education, and would be able to use the consolidated funds for any ESEA-authorized purpose.

Putting Reading First

No Child Left Behind stated President Bush's unequivocal commitment to ensuring that every child can read by the end of third grade. To accomplish this goal, the new Reading First initiative would significantly increase the Federal investment in scientifically based reading instruction programs in the early grades. One major benefit of this approach would be reduced identification of children for special education services due to a lack of appropriate reading instruction in their early years.

The NCLB Act fully implements the President's Reading First initiative. The new Reading First State Grant program will make 6-year grants to States, which will make competitive subgrants to local communities. Local recipients will administer screening and diagnostic assessments to determine which students in grades K–3 are at risk of reading failure, and provide professional development for K–3 teachers in the essential components of reading instruction.

The new Early Reading First program will make competitive 6-year awards to LEAs to support early language, literacy, and pre-reading development of preschool-age children, particularly those from low-income families. Recipients will use instructional strategies and professional development drawn from scientifically based reading research to help young children to attain the fundamental knowledge and skills they will need for optimal reading development in kindergarten and beyond.

Other Major Program Changes

The *No Child Left Behind* Act of 2001 also put the principles of accountability, choice, and flexibility to work in its reauthorization of other major ESEA programs. For example, the new law combines the Eisenhower Professional Development and Class Size Reduction programs into a new Improving Teacher Quality State Grants program that focuses on using practices grounded in scientifically based research to prepare, train, and recruit high-quality teachers. The new program gives States and LEAs flexibility to select the strategies that best meet their particular needs for improved teaching that will help them raise student achievement in the core academic subjects. In return for this flexibility, LEAs are required to demonstrate annual progress in ensuring that all teachers teaching in core academic subjects within the State are highly qualified.

The NCLB Act also simplified Federal support for English language instruction by combining categorical bilingual and immigrant education grants that benefited a small percentage of limited English proficient students in relatively few schools into a State formula program. The new formula program will facilitate the comprehensive planning by States and school districts needed to ensure implementation of programs that benefit all limited English proficient students by helping them learn English and meet the same high academic standards as other students.

Other changes will support State and local efforts to keep our schools safe and drug-free, while at the same time ensuring that students—particularly those who have been victims of violent crimes on school grounds—are not trapped in persistently dangerous schools. As proposed in No Child Left Behind, States must allow students who attend a persistently dangerous school, or who are victims of violent crime at school, to transfer to a safe school. States also must report school safety statistics to the public on a school-by-school basis, and LEAs must use Federal Safe and Drug-Free Schools and Communities funding to implement drug and violence prevention programs of demonstrated effectiveness.

Internet Resource: <www.nochildleftbehind.gov>

INTERNATIONAL AGREEMENTS, CHARTERS, AND DECLARATIONS

CHARTER OF THE UNITED NATIONS, ARTICLE 1: JUNE 26, 1945

In its charter, which was adopted on June 25, 1945, the United Nations recognized the necessity of the preservation of human rights, and made states legally responsible for the promotion of those rights in order to ensure worldwide peace.

Preamble

WE THE PEOPLES OF THE UNITED NATIONS DETERMINED to save succeeding generations from the scourge of war, which twice in our lifetime has brought untold sorrow to mankind, and to reaffirm faith in fundamental human rights, in the dignity and worth of the human person, in the equal rights of men and women and of nations large and small, and to establish conditions under which justice and respect for the obligations arising from treaties and other sources of international law can be maintained, and to promote social progress and better standards of life in larger freedom,

AND FOR THESE ENDS to practice tolerance and live together in peace with one another as good neighbors, and to unite our strength to maintain international peace and security, and to ensure by the acceptance of principles and the institution of methods, that armed force shall not be used, save in the common interest, and to employ international machinery for the promotion of the economic and social advancement of all peoples,

HAVE RESOLVED TO COMBINE OUR EFFORTS TO ACCOMPLISH THESE AIMS Accordingly, our respective Governments, through representatives assembled in the city of San

Francisco, who have exhibited their full powers found to be in good and due form, have agreed to the present Charter of the United Nations and do hereby establish an international organization to be known as the United Nations.

CHAPTER I: PURPOSES AND PRINCIPLES

Article 1

The Purposes of the United Nations are:

1. To maintain international peace and security, and to that end: to take effective collective measures for the prevention and removal of threats to the peace, and for the suppression of acts of aggression or other breaches of the peace, and to bring about by peaceful means, and in conformity with the principles of justice and international law, adjustment or settlement of international disputes or situations which might lead to a breach of the peace;
2. To develop friendly relations among nations based on respect for the principle of equal rights and self-determination of peoples, and to take other appropriate measures to strengthen universal peace;
3. To achieve international cooperation in solving international problems of an economic, social, cultural, or humanitarian character, and in promoting and encouraging respect for human rights and for fundamental freedoms for all without distinction as to race, sex, language, or religion; and
4. To be a center for harmonizing the actions of nations in the attainment of these common ends.

CONSTITUTION OF THE UNITED NATIONS EDUCATIONAL, SCIENTIFIC AND CULTURAL ORGANIZATION

Adopted in London on 16 November 1945 and amended by the General Conference at its second, third, fourth, fifth, sixth, seventh, eighth, ninth, tenth, twelfth, fifteenth, seventeenth, nineteenth, twentieth, twenty-first, twenty-fourth, and twenty-fifth sessions.

The Governments of the States Parties to this Constitution on behalf of their peoples declare:

That since wars begin in the minds of men, it is in the minds of men that the defenses of peace must be constructed;

That ignorance of each other's ways and lives has been a common cause, throughout the history of mankind, of that suspicion and mistrust between the peoples of the world through which their differences have all too often broken into war;

That the great and terrible war which has now ended was a war made possible by the denial of the democratic principles of the dignity, equality and mutual respect of men, and by the propagation, in their place, through ignorance and prejudice, of the doctrine of the inequality of men and races;

That the wide diffusion of culture, and the education of humanity for justice and liberty and peace are indispensable to the dignity of man and constitute a sacred duty which all the nations must fulfil in a spirit of mutual assistance and concern;

That a peace based exclusively upon the political and economic arrangements of governments would not be a peace which could secure the unanimous, lasting and sincere support of the peoples of the world, and that the peace must therefore be founded, if it is not to fail, upon the intellectual and moral solidarity of mankind.

For these reasons, the States Parties to this Constitution, believing in full and equal opportunities for education for all, in the unrestricted pursuit of objective truth, and in the free exchange of ideas and knowledge, are agreed and determined to develop and to increase the means of communication between their peoples and to employ these means for the purposes of mutual understanding and a truer and more perfect knowledge of each other's lives;

In consequence whereof they do hereby create the United Nations Educational, Scientific and Cultural Organization for the purpose of advancing, through the educational and scientific and cultural relations of the peoples of the world, the objectives of international peace and of the common welfare of mankind for which the United Nations Organization was established and which its Charter proclaims.

ARTICLE I

Purposes and Functions

1. The purpose of the Organization is to contribute to peace and security by promoting collaboration among the nations through education, science and culture in order to further universal respect for justice, for the rule of law and for the human rights and fundamental freedoms which are affirmed for the peoples of the world, without distinction of race, sex, language or religion, by the Charter of the United Nations.
2. To realize this purpose the Organization will:
    a. Collaborate in the work of advancing the mutual knowledge and understanding of peoples, through all means of mass communication and to that end recommend such international agreements as may be necessary to promote the free flow of ideas by word and image;
    b. Give fresh impulse to popular education and to the spread of culture; By collaborating with Members, at their request, in the development of educational activities; By instituting collaboration among the nations to advance the ideal of equality of educational opportunity without regard to race, sex or any distinctions, economic or social; By suggesting educational methods best suited to prepare the children of the world for the responsibilities of freedom;
    c. Maintain, increase and diffuse knowledge; By assuring the conservation and protection of the world's inheritance of books, works of art and monuments of history and science, and recommending to the nations concerned the necessary international conventions; By encouraging co-operation among the nations in all branches of intellectual activity, including the international exchange of persons active in the fields of education, science and culture and the exchange of publications, objects of artistic and scientific interest and other materials of information; By initiating methods of international co-operation calculated to give the people of all countries access to the printed and published materials produced by any of them.
3. With a view to preserving the independence, integrity and fruitful diversity of the cultures and educational systems of the States members of this Organization, the Organization is prohibited from intervening in matters which are essentially within their domestic jurisdiction.

ARTICLE II

Membership

1. Membership of the United Nations Organization shall carry with it the right to membership of the United Nations Educational, Scientific and Cultural Organization.
2. Subject to the conditions of the Agreement between this Organization and the United Nations Organization, approved pursuant to Article X of this Constitution, States not

members of the United Nations Organization may be admitted to membership of the Organization, upon recommendation of the Executive Board, by a two-thirds majority vote of the General Conference.

3. Territories or groups of territories which are not responsible for the conduct of their international relations may be admitted as Associate Members by the General Conference by a two-thirds majority of Members present and voting, upon application made on behalf of such territory or group of territories by the Member or other authority having responsibility for their international relations. The nature and extent of the rights and obligations of Associate Members shall be determined by the General Conference.
4. Members of the Organization which are suspended from the exercise of the rights and privileges of membership of the United Nations Organization shall, upon the request of the latter, be suspended from the rights and privileges of this Organization.
5. Members of the Organization which are expelled from the United Nations Organization shall automatically cease to be members of this Organization.
6. Any Member State or Associate Member of the Organization may withdraw from the Organization by notice addressed to the Director-General. Such notice shall take effect on 31 December of the year following that during which the notice was given. No such withdrawal shall affect the financial obligations owed to the Organization on the date the withdrawal takes effect. Notice of withdrawal by an Associate Member shall be given on its behalf by the Member State or other authority having responsibility for its international relations.

ARTICLE III

Organs

The Organization shall include a General Conference, an Executive Board and a Secretariat.

ARTICLE IV

The General Conference

A. Composition

1. The General Conference shall consist of the representatives of the States members of the Organization. The Government of each Member State shall appoint not more than five delegates, who shall be selected after consultation with the National Commission if established, or with educational, scientific and cultural bodies.

B. Functions

2. The General Conference shall determine the policies and the main lines of work of the Organization. It shall take decisions on programmes submitted to it by the Executive Board.
3. The General Conference shall, when it deems desirable and in accordance with the regulations to be made by it, summon international conferences of States on education, the sciences and humanities or the dissemination of knowledge; non-governmental conferences on the same subjects may be summoned by the General Conference or by the Executive Board in accordance with such regulations.
4. The General Conference shall, in adopting proposals for submission to the Member States, distinguish between recommendations and international conventions submitted for their approval. In the former case a majority vote shall suffice; in the latter case a two-thirds majority shall be required. Each of the

Member States shall submit recommendations or conventions to its competent authorities within a period of one year from the close of the session of the General Conference at which they were adopted.

5. Subject to the provisions of Article V, paragraph 5(c), the General Conference shall advise the United Nations Organization on the educational, scientific and cultural aspects of matters of concern to the latter; in accordance with the terms and procedure agreed upon between the appropriate authorities of the two Organizations.
6. The General Conference shall receive and consider the reports sent to the Organization by Member States on the action taken upon the recommendations and conventions referred to in paragraph 4 above or, if it so decides, analytical summaries of these reports.
7. The General Conference shall elect the members of the Executive Board and, on the recommendation of the Board, shall appoint the Director-General.

C. Voting

8.
   a. Each Member State shall have one vote in the General Conference. Decisions shall be made by a simple majority except in cases in which a two-thirds majority is required by the provisions of this Constitution, or of the Rules of Procedure of the General Conference. A majority shall be a majority of the Members present and voting.
   b. A Member State shall have no vote in the General Conference if the total amount of contributions due from it exceeds the total amount of contributions payable by it for the current year and the immediately preceding calendar year.
   c. The General Conference may nevertheless permit such a Member State to vote, if it is satisfied that failure to pay is due to conditions beyond the control of the Member State.

D. Procedure

9.
   a. The General Conference shall meet in ordinary session every two years. It may meet in extraordinary session if it decides to do so itself or if summoned by the Executive Board, or on the demand of at least one-third of the Member States.
   b. At each session the location of its next ordinary session shall be designated by the General Conference. The location of an extraordinary session shall be decided by the General Conference if the session is summoned by it, or otherwise by the Executive Board.

10. The General Conference shall adopt its own rules of procedure. It shall at each session elect a President and other officers.
11. The General Conference shall set up special and technical committees and such other subordinate organs as may be necessary for its purposes.
12. The General Conference shall cause arrangements to be made for public access to meetings, subject to such regulations as it shall prescribe.

E. Observers

13. The General Conference, on the recommendation of the Executive Board and by a two-thirds majority may, subject to its rules of procedure, invite as observers at specified sessions of the Conference or of its Commissions representatives of international organizations, such as those referred to in Article XI, paragraph 4.

14. When consultative arrangements have been approved by the Executive Board for such international non-governmental or semi-governmental organizations in the manner provided in Article XI, paragraph 4, those organizations shall be invited to send observers to sessions of the General Conference and its Commissions.

ARTICLE V

Executive Board

A. Composition

1. The Executive Board shall be elected by the General Conference from among the delegates appointed by the Member States and shall consist of fifty-one members each of whom shall represent the Government of the Member State of which he is a national. The President of the General Conference shall sit ex officio in an advisory capacity on the Executive Board.
2. In electing the members of the Executive Board the General Conference shall endeavour to include persons competent in the arts, the humanities, the sciences, education and the diffusion of ideas, and qualified by their experience and capacity to fulfil the administrative and executive duties of the Board. It shall also have regard to the diversity of cultures and a balanced geographical distribution. Not more than one national of any Member State shall serve on the Board at any one time, the President of the Conference excepted.
3. Members of the Board shall serve from the close of the session of the General Conference which elected them until the close of the second ordinary session of the General Conference following that election. They shall not be immediately eligible for a second term. The General Conference shall, at each of its ordinary sessions, elect the number of members required to fill vacancies occurring at the end of the session.
4.
   a. In the event of the death or resignation of a member of the Executive Board, his replacement for the remainder of his term shall be appointed by the Executive Board on the nomination of the Government of the Member State the former member of the Board represented.
   b. The Government making the nomination and the Executive Board shall have regard to the factors set forth in paragraph 2 of this Article.
   c. When exceptional circumstances arise, which, in the considered opinion of the represented State, make it indispensable for its representative to be replaced, even if he does not tender his resignation, measures shall be taken in accordance with the provisions of sub-paragraph (a) above.
   d. In the event of the withdrawal from the Organization of a Member State a national of which is a member of the Executive Board, that member's term of office shall be terminated on the date the withdrawal becomes effective.

B. Functions

5.
   a. The Executive Board shall prepare the agenda for the General Conference. It shall examine the programme of work for the Organization and corresponding budget estimates submitted to it by the Director-General in accordance with paragraph 3 of Article VI and shall submit them with such recommendations as it considers desirable to the General Conference.
   b. The Executive Board, acting under the authority of the General Conference, shall be responsible for the execution of the programme adopted by the

Conference. In accordance with the decisions of the General Conference and having regard to circumstances arising between two ordinary sessions, the Executive Board shall take all necessary measures to ensure the effective and rational execution of the programme by the Director-General.

c. Between ordinary sessions of the General Conference, the Board may discharge the functions of adviser to the United Nations, set forth in Article IV, paragraph 5, whenever the problem upon which advice is sought has already been dealt with in principle by the Conference, or when the solution is implicit in decisions of the Conference.

6. The Executive Board shall recommend to the General Conference the admission of new Members to the Organization.
7. Subject to decisions of the General Conference, the Executive Board shall adopt its own rules of procedure. It shall elect its officers from among its members.
8. The Executive Board shall meet in regular session at least twice a year and may meet in special session if convoked by the Chairman on his own initiative or upon the request of six members of the Board.
9. The Chairman of the Executive Board shall present, on behalf of the Board, to each ordinary session of the General Conference, with or without comments, the reports on the activities of the Organization which the Director-General is required to prepare in accordance with the provisions of Article VI.3(b).
10. The Executive Board shall make all necessary arrangements to consult the representatives of international organizations or qualified persons concerned with questions within its competence.
11. Between sessions of the General Conference, the Executive Board may request advisory opinions from the International Court of Justice on legal questions arising within the field of the Organization's activities.
12. Although the members of the Executive Board are representative of their respective Governments they shall exercise the powers delegated to them by the General Conference on behalf of the Conference as a whole.

ARTICLE VI

Secretariat

1. The Secretariat shall consist of a Director-General and such staff as may be required.
2. The Director-General shall be nominated by the Executive Board and appointed by the General Conference for a period of six years, under such conditions as the Conference may approve. The Director-General may be appointed for a further term of six years but shall not be eligible for reappointment for a subsequent term. The Director-General shall be the chief administrative officer of the Organization.
3.
   a. The Director-General, or a deputy designated by him, shall participate, without the right to vote, in all meetings of the General Conference, of the Executive Board, and of the Committees of the Organization. He shall formulate proposals for appropriate action by the Conference and the Board, and shall prepare for submission to the Board a draft programme of work for the Organization with corresponding budget estimates.
   b. The Director-General shall prepare and communicate to Member States and to the Executive Board periodical reports on the activities of the Organization. The General Conference shall determine the periods to be covered by these reports.

4. The Director-General shall appoint the staff of the Secretariat in accordance with staff regulations to be approved by the General Conference. Subject to the paramount consideration of securing the highest standards of integrity, efficiency and technical competence, appointment to the staff shall be on as wide a geographical basis as possible.
5. The responsibilities of the Director-General and of the staff shall be exclusively international in character. In the discharge of their duties they shall not seek or receive instructions from any Government or from any authority external to the Organization. They shall refrain from any action which might prejudice their position as international officials. Each State member of the Organization undertakes to respect the international character of the responsibilities of the Director-General and the staff, and not to seek to influence them in the discharge of their duties.
6. Nothing in this Article shall preclude the Organization from entering into special arrangements within the United Nations Organization for common services and staff and for the interchange of personnel.

ARTICLE VII

National Co-operating Bodies

1. Each Member State shall make such arrangements as suit its particular conditions for the purpose of associating its principal bodies interested in educational, scientific and cultural matters with the work of the Organization, preferably by the formation of a National Commission broadly representative of the Government and such bodies.
2. National Commissions or National Co-operating Bodies, where they exist, shall act in an advisory capacity to their respective delegations to the General Conference and to their Governments in matters relating to the Organization and shall function as agencies of liaison in all matters of interest to it.
3. The Organization may, on the request of a Member State, delegate, either temporarily or permanently, a member of its Secretariat to serve on the National Commission of that State, in order to assist in the development of its work.

ARTICLE VIII

Reports by Member States

Each Member State shall submit to the Organization, at such times and in such manner as shall be determined by the General Conference, reports on the laws, regulations and statistics relating to its educational, scientific and cultural institutions and activities, and on the action taken upon the recommendations and conventions referred to in Article IV, paragraph 4.

ARTICLE IX

Budget

1. The Budget shall be administered by the Organization.
2. The General Conference shall approve and give final effect to the budget and to the apportionment of financial responsibility among the States members of the Organization subject to such arrangement with the United Nations as may be provided in the agreement to be entered into pursuant to Article X.
3. The Director-General may accept voluntary contributions, gifts, bequests, and subventions directly from Governments, public and private institutions, associations and private persons, subject to the conditions specified in the Financial Regulations.

ARTICLE X

Relations with the United Nations Organization

This Organization shall be brought into relation with the United Nations Organization, as soon as practicable, as one of the Specialized Agencies referred to in Article 57 of the Charter of the United Nations. This relationship shall be effected through an agreement with the United Nations Organization under Article 63 of the Charter, which agreement shall be subject to the approval of the General Conference of this Organization. The agreement shall provide for effective co-operation between the two Organizations in the pursuit of their common purposes, and at the same time shall recognize the autonomy of this Organization, within the fields of its competence as defined in this Constitution. Such agreement may, among other matters, provide for the approval and financing of the budget of the Organization by the General Assembly of the United Nations.

ARTICLE XI

Relations with other Specialized International Organizations and Agencies

1. This Organization may cooperate with other specialized intergovernmental organizations and agencies whose interests and activities are related to its purposes. To this end the Director-General, acting under the general authority of the Executive Board, may establish effective working relationships with such organizations and agencies and establish such joint committees as may be necessary to assure effective co-operation. Any formal arrangements entered into with such organizations or agencies shall be subject to the approval of the Executive Board.
2. Whenever the General Conference of this Organization and the competent authorities of any other specialized intergovernmental organizations or agencies whose purpose and functions lie within the competence of this Organization, deem it desirable to effect a transfer of their resources and activities to this Organization, the Director-General, subject to the approval of the Conference, may enter into mutually acceptable arrangements for this purpose.
3. This Organization may make appropriate arrangements with other intergovernmental organizations for reciprocal representation at meetings.
4. The United Nations Educational, Scientific and Cultural Organization may make suitable arrangements for consultation and co-operation with non-governmental international organizations concerned with matters within its competence, and may invite them to undertake specific tasks. Such co-operation may also include appropriate participation by representatives of such organizations on advisory committees set up by the General Conference.

ARTICLE XII

Legal status of the Organization

The provisions of Articles 104 and 105 of the Charter of the United Nations Organization concerning the legal status of that Organization, its privileges and immunities, shall apply in the same way to this Organization.

ARTICLE XIII

Amendments

1. Proposals for amendments to this Constitution shall become effective upon receiving the approval of the General Conference by a two-thirds majority; provided, however,

that those amendments which involve fundamental alterations in the aims of the Organization or new obligations for the Member States shall require subsequent acceptance on the part of two-thirds of the Member States before they come into force. The draft texts of proposed amendments shall be communicated by the Director-General to the Member States at least six months in advance of their consideration by the General Conference.

2. The General Conference shall have power to adopt by a two-thirds majority rules of procedure for carrying out the provisions of this Article.

ARTICLE XIV

Interpretation

1. The English and French texts of this Constitution shall be regarded as equally authoritative.
2. Any question or dispute concerning the interpretation of this Constitution shall be referred for determination to the International Court of Justice or to an arbitral tribunal, as the General Conference may determine under its rules of procedure.

ARTICLE XV

Entry into Force

1. This Constitution shall be subject to acceptance. The instrument of acceptance shall be deposited with the Government of the United Kingdom.
2. This Constitution shall remain open for signature in the archives of the Government of the United Kingdom. Signature may take place either before or after the deposit of the instrument of acceptance. No acceptance shall be valid unless preceded or followed by signature. However, a State that has withdrawn from the Organization shall simply deposit a new instrument of acceptance in order to resume membership.
3. This Constitution shall come into force when it has been accepted by twenty of its signatories. Subsequent acceptances shall take effect immediately.

The Government of the United Kingdom will inform all Members of the United Nations of the receipt of all instruments of acceptance and of the date on which the Constitution comes into force in accordance with the preceding paragraph.

In faith whereof, the undersigned, duly authorized to that effect, have signed this Constitution in the English and French languages, both texts being equally authentic.

Done in London the sixteenth day of November, one thousand nine hundred and forty-five, in a single copy, in the English and French languages, of which certified copies will be communicated by the Government of the United Kingdom to the Governments of all the Members of the United Nations.

UNIVERSAL DECLARATION OF HUMAN RIGHTS

Adopted and proclaimed by General Assembly resolution 217 A (III) of 10 December 1948

On December 10, 1948 the General Assembly of the United Nations adopted and proclaimed the Universal Declaration of Human Rights the full text of which appears in the following pages. Following this historic act the Assembly called upon all Member countries to publicize the text of the Declaration and "to cause it to be disseminated, displayed, read and expounded principally in schools and other educational institutions, without distinction based on the political status of countries or territories."

PREAMBLE

Whereas recognition of the inherent dignity and of the equal and inalienable rights of all members of the human family is the foundation of freedom, justice and peace in the world,

Whereas disregard and contempt for human rights have resulted in barbarous acts which have outraged the conscience of mankind, and the advent of a world in which human beings shall enjoy freedom of speech and belief and freedom from fear and want has been proclaimed as the highest aspiration of the common people,

Whereas it is essential, if man is not to be compelled to have recourse, as a last resort, to rebellion against tyranny and oppression, that human rights should be protected by the rule of law,

Whereas it is essential to promote the development of friendly relations between nations,

Whereas the peoples of the United Nations have in the Charter reaffirmed their faith in fundamental human rights, in the dignity and worth of the human person and in the equal rights of men and women and have determined to promote social progress and better standards of life in larger freedom,

Whereas Member States have pledged themselves to achieve, in co-operation with the United Nations, the promotion of universal respect for and observance of human rights and fundamental freedoms,

Whereas a common understanding of these rights and freedoms is of the greatest importance for the full realization of this pledge,

Now, Therefore THE GENERAL ASSEMBLY proclaims THIS UNIVERSAL DECLARATION OF HUMAN RIGHTS as a common standard of achievement for all peoples and all nations, to the end that every individual and every organ of society, keeping this Declaration constantly in mind, shall strive by teaching and education to promote respect for these rights and freedoms and by progressive measures, national and international, to secure their universal and effective recognition and observance, both among the peoples of Member States themselves and among the peoples of territories under their jurisdiction.

Article 1.

All human beings are born free and equal in dignity and rights. They are endowed with reason and conscience and should act towards one another in a spirit of brotherhood.

Article 2.

Everyone is entitled to all the rights and freedoms set forth in this Declaration, without distinction of any kind, such as race, colour, sex, language, religion, political or other opinion, national or social origin, property, birth or other status. Furthermore, no distinction shall be made on the basis of the political, jurisdictional or international status of the country or territory to which a person belongs, whether it be independent, trust, non-self-governing or under any other limitation of sovereignty.

Article 3.

Everyone has the right to life, liberty and security of person.

Article 4.

No one shall be held in slavery or servitude; slavery and the slave trade shall be prohibited in all their forms.

Article 5.

No one shall be subjected to torture or to cruel, inhuman or degrading treatment or punishment.

Article 6.

Everyone has the right to recognition everywhere as a person before the law.

Article 7.

All are equal before the law and are entitled without any discrimination to equal protection of the law. All are entitled to equal protection against any discrimination in violation of this Declaration and against any incitement to such discrimination.

Article 8.

Everyone has the right to an effective remedy by the competent national tribunals for acts violating the fundamental rights granted him by the constitution or by law.

Article 9.

No one shall be subjected to arbitrary arrest, detention or exile.

Article 10.

Everyone is entitled in full equality to a fair and public hearing by an independent and impartial tribunal, in the determination of his rights and obligations and of any criminal charge against him.

Article 11.

(1) Everyone charged with a penal offence has the right to be presumed innocent until proved guilty according to law in a public trial at which he has had all the guarantees necessary for his defence.

(2) No one shall be held guilty of any penal offence on account of any act or omission which did not constitute a penal offence, under national or international law, at the time when it was committed. Nor shall a heavier penalty be imposed than the one that was applicable at the time the penal offence was committed.

Article 12.

No one shall be subjected to arbitrary interference with his privacy, family, home or correspondence, nor to attacks upon his honour and reputation. Everyone has the right to the protection of the law against such interference or attacks.

Article 13.

(1) Everyone has the right to freedom of movement and residence within the borders of each state.

(2) Everyone has the right to leave any country, including his own, and to return to his country.

Article 14.

(1) Everyone has the right to seek and to enjoy in other countries asylum from persecution.

(2) This right may not be invoked in the case of prosecutions genuinely arising from non-political crimes or from acts contrary to the purposes and principles of the United Nations.

Article 15.

(1) Everyone has the right to a nationality.

(2) No one shall be arbitrarily deprived of his nationality nor denied the right to change his nationality.

Article 16.

(1) Men and women of full age, without any limitation due to race, nationality or religion, have the right to marry and to found a family. They are entitled to equal rights as to marriage, during marriage and at its dissolution.

(2) Marriage shall be entered into only with the free and full consent of the intending spouses.

(3) The family is the natural and fundamental group unit of society and is entitled to protection by society and the State.

Article 17.

(1) Everyone has the right to own property alone as well as in association with others.

(2) No one shall be arbitrarily deprived of his property.

Article 18.

Everyone has the right to freedom of thought, conscience and religion; this right includes freedom to change his religion or belief, and freedom, either alone or in community with others and in public or private, to manifest his religion or belief in teaching, practice, worship and observance.

Article 19.

Everyone has the right to freedom of opinion and expression; this right includes freedom to hold opinions without interference and to seek, receive and impart information and ideas through any media and regardless of frontiers.

Article 20.

(1) Everyone has the right to freedom of peaceful assembly and association.

(2) No one may be compelled to belong to an association.

Article 21.

(1) Everyone has the right to take part in the government of his country, directly or through freely chosen representatives.

(2) Everyone has the right of equal access to public service in his country.

(3) The will of the people shall be the basis of the authority of government; this will shall be expressed in periodic and genuine elections which shall be by universal and equal suffrage and shall be held by secret vote or by equivalent free voting procedures.

Article 22.

Everyone, as a member of society, has the right to social security and is entitled to realization, through national effort and international co-operation and in accordance with the organization and resources of each State, of the economic, social and cultural rights indispensable for his dignity and the free development of his personality.

Article 23.

(1) Everyone has the right to work, to free choice of employment, to just and favourable conditions of work and to protection against unemployment.

(2) Everyone, without any discrimination, has the right to equal pay for equal work.

(3) Everyone who works has the right to just and favourable remuneration ensuring for himself and his family an existence worthy of human dignity, and supplemented, if necessary, by other means of social protection.

(4) Everyone has the right to form and to join trade unions for the protection of his interests.

Article 24.

Everyone has the right to rest and leisure, including reasonable limitation of working hours and periodic holidays with pay.

Article 25.

(1) Everyone has the right to a standard of living adequate for the health and well-being of himself and of his family, including food, clothing, housing and medical care and necessary social services, and the right to security in the event of unemployment, sickness, disability, widowhood, old age or other lack of livelihood in circumstances beyond his control.

(2) Motherhood and childhood are entitled to special care and assistance. All children, whether born in or out of wedlock, shall enjoy the same social protection.

Article 26.

(1) Everyone has the right to education. Education shall be free, at least in the elementary and fundamental stages. Elementary education shall be compulsory. Technical and professional education shall be made generally available and higher education shall be equally accessible to all on the basis of merit.

(2) Education shall be directed to the full development of the human personality and to the strengthening of respect for human rights and fundamental freedoms. It shall promote understanding, tolerance and friendship among all nations, racial or religious groups, and shall further the activities of the United Nations for the maintenance of peace.

(3) Parents have a prior right to choose the kind of education that shall be given to their children.

Article 27.

(1) Everyone has the right freely to participate in the cultural life of the community, to enjoy the arts and to share in scientific advancement and its benefits.

(2) Everyone has the right to the protection of the moral and material interests resulting from any scientific, literary or artistic production of which he is the author.

Article 28.

Everyone is entitled to a social and international order in which the rights and freedoms set forth in this Declaration can be fully realized.

Article 29.

(1) Everyone has duties to the community in which alone the free and full development of his personality is possible.

(2) In the exercise of his rights and freedoms, everyone shall be subject only to such limitations as are determined by law solely for the purpose of securing due recognition and respect for the rights and freedoms of others and of meeting the just requirements of morality, public order and the general welfare in a democratic society.

(3) These rights and freedoms may in no case be exercised contrary to the purposes and principles of the United Nations.

Article 30.

Nothing in this Declaration may be interpreted as implying for any State, group or person any right to engage in any activity or to perform any act aimed at the destruction of any of the rights and freedoms set forth herein.

EUROPEAN CONVENTION ON HUMAN RIGHTS AND ITS FIVE PROTOCOLS

ROME 4 NOVEMBER 1950
PARIS 20 MARCH 1952
STRASBOURG 6 MAY 1963
STRASBOURG 16 SEPTEMBER 1963
STRASBOURG 20 JANUARY 1966

THE EUROPEAN CONVENTION ON HUMAN RIGHTS

The Governments signatory hereto, being Members of the Council of Europe,

Considering the Universal Declaration of Human Rights proclaimed by the General Assembly of the United Nations on 10 December 1948;

Considering that this Declaration aims at securing the universal and effective recognition and observance of the Rights therein declared;

Considering that the aim of the Council of Europe is the achievement of greater unity between its Members and that one of the methods by which the aim is to be pursued is the maintenance and further realization of Human Rights and Fundamental Freedoms;

Reaffirming their profound belief in those Fundamental Freedoms which are the foundation of justice and peace in the world and are best maintained on the one hand by an effective political democracy and on the other by a common understanding and observance of the Human Rights upon which they depend;

Being resolved, as the Governments of European countries which are like-minded and have a common heritage of political traditions, ideals, freedom and the rule of law to take the first steps for the collective enforcement of certain of the Rights stated in the Universal Declaration;

Have agreed as follows:

ARTICLE 1

The High Contracting Parties shall secure to everyone within their jurisdiction the rights and freedoms defined in Section I of this Convention.

SECTION I

ARTICLE 2

1. Everyone's right to life shall be protected by law. No one shall be deprived of his life intentionally save in the execution of a sentence of a court following his conviction of a crime for which this penalty is provided by law.
2. Deprivation of life shall not be regarded as inflicted in contravention of this article when it results from the use of force which is no more than absolutely necessary:
   (a) in defence of any person from unlawful violence;
   (b) in order to effect a lawful arrest or to prevent escape of a person lawfully detained;
   (c) in action lawfully taken for the purpose of quelling a riot or insurrection.

ARTICLE 3

No one shall be subjected to torture or to inhuman or degrading treatment or punishment.

ARTICLE 4

1. No one shall be held in slavery or servitude.
2. No one shall be required to perform forced or compulsory labour.
3. For the purpose of this article the term forced or compulsory labour shall not include:
   (a) any work required to be done in the ordinary course of detention imposed according to the provisions of Article 5 of this Convention or during conditional release from such detention;
   (b) any service of a military character or, in case of conscientious objectors in countries where they are recognized, service exacted instead of compulsory military service;
   (c) any service exacted in case of an emergency or calamity threatening the life or well-being of the community;
   (d) any work or service which forms part of normal civic obligations.

ARTICLE 5

1. Everyone has the right to liberty and security of person.

No one shall be deprived of his liberty save in the following cases and in accordance with a procedure prescribed by law:

   (a) the lawful detention of a person after conviction by a competent court;
   (b) the lawful arrest or detention of a person for non-compliance with the lawful order of a court or in order to secure the fulfilment of any obligation prescribed by law;
   (c) the lawful arrest or detention of a person effected for the purpose of bringing him before the competent legal authority of reasonable suspicion of having committed and offence or when it is reasonably considered necessary to prevent his committing an offence or fleeing after having done so;
   (d) the detention of a minor by lawful order for the purpose of educational supervision or his lawful detention for the purpose of bringing him before the competent legal authority;
   (e) the lawful detention of persons for the prevention of the spreading of infectious diseases, of persons of unsound mind, alcoholics or drug addicts, or vagrants;
   (f) the lawful arrest or detention of a person to prevent his effecting an unauthorized entry into the country or of a person against whom action is being taken with a view to deportation or extradition.

2. Everyone who is arrested shall be informed promptly, in a language which he understands, of the reasons for his arrest and the charge against him.
3. Everyone arrested or detained in accordance with the provisions of paragraph 1(c) of this article shall be brought promptly before a judge or other officer authorized by law to exercise judicial power and shall be entitled to trial within a reasonable time or to release pending trial. Release may be conditioned by guarantees to appear for trial.
4. Everyone who is deprived of his liberty by arrest or detention shall be entitled to take proceedings by which the lawfulness of his detention shall be decided speedily by a court and his release ordered if the detention is not lawful.

Everyone who has been the victim of arrest or detention in contravention of the provisions of this article shall have an enforceable right to compensation.

ARTICLE 6

1. In the determination of his civil rights and obligations or of any criminal charge against him, everyone is entitled to a fair and public hearing within a reasonable time by an independent and impartial tribunal established by law. Judgement shall be pronounced publicly by the press and public may be excluded from all or part of the trial in the interest of morals, public order or national security in a democratic society, where the interests of juveniles or the protection of the private life of the parties so require, or the extent strictly necessary in the opinion of the court in special circumstances where publicity would prejudice the interests of justice.
2. Everyone charged with a criminal offence shall be presumed innocent until proved guilty according to law.
3. Everyone charged with a criminal offence has the following minimum rights:
   (a) to be informed promptly, in a language which he understands and in detail, of the nature and cause of the accusation against him;
   (b) to have adequate time and the facilities for the preparation of his defence;
   (c) to defend himself in person or through legal assistance of his own choosing or, if he has not sufficient means to pay for legal assistance, to be given it free when the interests of justice so require;
   (d) to examine or have examined witnesses against him and to obtain the attendance and examination of witnesses on his behalf under the same conditions as witnesses against him;
   (e) to have the free assistance of an interpreter if he cannot understand or speak the language used in court.

ARTICLE 7

1. No one shall be held guilty of any criminal offence on account of any act or omission which did not constitute a criminal offence under national or international law at the time when it was committed. Nor shall a heavier penalty be imposed than the one that was applicable at the time the criminal offence was committed.
2. This article shall not prejudice the trial and punishment of any person for any act or omission which, at the time when it was committed, was criminal according the general principles of law recognized by civilized nations.

ARTICLE 8

1. Everyone has the right to respect for his private and family life, his home and his correspondence.
2. There shall be no interference by a public authority with the exercise of this right except such as is in accordance with the law and is necessary in a democratic society in the interests of national security, public safety or the economic well-being of the country, for the prevention of disorder or crime, for the protection of health or morals, or for the protection of the rights and freedoms of others.

ARTICLE 9

1. Everyone has the right to freedom of thought, conscience and religion; this right includes freedom to change his religion or belief, and freedom, either alone or in community with others and in public or private, to manifest his religion or belief, in worship, teaching, practice and observance.

2. Freedom to manifest one's religion or beliefs shall be subject only to such limitations as are prescribed by law and are necessary in a democratic society in the interests of public safety, for the protection of public order, health or morals, or the protection of the rights and freedoms of others.

ARTICLE 10

1. Everyone has the right to freedom of expression. This right shall include freedom to hold opinions and to receive and impart information an ideas without interference by public authority and regardless of frontiers. This article shall not prevent States from requiring the licensing of broadcasting, television or cinema enterprises.
2. The exercise of these freedoms, since it carries with it duties and responsibilities, may be subject to such formalities, conditions, restrictions or penalties as are prescribed by law and are necessary in a democratic society, in the interests of national security, territorial integrity or public safety, for the prevention of disorder or crime, for the protection of health or morals, for the protection of the reputation or the rights of others, for preventing the disclosure of information received in confidence, or for maintaining the authority and impartiality of the judiciary.

ARTICLE 11

1. Everyone has the right to freedom of peaceful assembly and to freedom of association with others, including the right to form and to join trade unions for the protection of his interests.
2. No restrictions shall be placed on the exercise of these rights other than such as are prescribed by law and are necessary in a democratic society in the interests of national security or public safety, for the prevention of disorder or crime, for the protection of health or morals or for the protection of the rights and freedoms of others. This article shall not prevent the imposition of lawful restrictions on the exercise of these rights by members of the armed forces, of the police or of the administration of the State.

ARTICLE 12

Men and women of marriageable age have the right to marry and to found a family, according to the national laws governing the exercise of this right.

ARTICLE 13

Everyone whose rights and freedoms as set forth in this Convention are violated shall have an effective remedy before a national authority notwithstanding that the violation has been committed by persons acting in an official capacity.

ARTICLE 14

The enjoyment of the rights and freedoms set forth in this Convention shall be secured without discrimination on any ground such as sex, race, colour, language, religion, political or other opinion, national or social origin, association with a national minority, property, birth or other status.

ARTICLE 15

1. In time of war or other public emergency threatening the life of the nation any High Contracting Party may take measures derogating from its obligations under this Convention to the extent strictly required by the exigencies of the situation, provided that such measures are not inconsistent with its other obligations under international law.

2. No derogation from Article 2, except in respect of deaths resulting from lawful acts of war, or from Articles 3, 4 (paragraph 1) and 7 shall be made under this provision.
3. Any High Contracting Party availing itself of this right of derogation shall keep the Secretary-General of the Council of Europe fully informed of the measures which it has taken and the reasons therefor. It shall also inform the Secretary-General of the Council of Europe when such measures have ceased to operate and the provisions of the Convention are again being fully executed.

ARTICLE 16

Nothing in Articles 10, 11, and 14 shall be regarded as preventing the High Contracting Parties from imposing restrictions on the political activity of aliens.

ARTICLE 17

Nothing in this Convention may be interpreted as implying for any State, group or person any right to engage in any activity or perform any act aimed at the destruction on any of the rights and freedoms set forth herein or at their limitation to a greater extent than is provided for in the Convention.

ARTICLE 18

The restrictions permitted under this Convention to the said rights and freedoms shall not be applied for any purpose other than those for which they have been prescribed.

SECTION II

ARTICLE 19

To ensure the observance of the engagements undertaken by the High Contracting Parties in the present Convention, there shall be set up:

1. A European Commission of Human Rights hereinafter referred to as 'the Commission';
2. A European Court of Human Rights, hereinafter referred to as 'the Court'.

SECTION III

ARTICLE 20

The Commission shall consist of a number of members equal to that of the High Contracting Parties. No two members of the Commission may be nationals of the same state.

ARTICLE 21

1. The members of the Commission shall be elected by the Committee of Ministers by an absolute majority of votes, from a list of names drawn up by the Bureau of the Consultative Assembly; each group of the Representatives of the High Contracting Parties in the Consultative Assembly shall put forward three candidates, of whom two at least shall be its nationals.
2. As far as applicable, the same procedure shall be followed to complete the Commission in the event of other States subsequently becoming Parties to this Convention, and in filing casual vacancies.

ARTICLE 22

1. The members of the Commission shall be elected for a period of six years. They may be re-elected. However, of the members elected at the first election, the terms of seven members shall expire at the end of three years.

2. The members whose terms are to expire at the end of the initial period of three years shall be chosen by lot by the Secretary-General of the Council of Europe immediately after the first election has been completed.
3. A member of the Commission elected to replace a member whose term of office has not expired shall hold office for the remainder of his predecessor's term.
4. The members of the Commission shall hold office until replaced. After having been replaced, they shall continue to deal with such cases as they already have under consideration.

ARTICLE 23

The members of the Commission shall sit on the Commission in their individual capacity.

ARTICLE 24

Any High Contracting Party may refer to the Commission, through the Secretary-General of the Council of Europe, any alleged breach of the provisions of the Convention by another High Contracting Party.

ARTICLE 25

1. The Commission may receive petitions addressed to the Secretary-General of the Council of Europe from any person, non-governmental organization or group of individuals claiming to the victim of a violation by one of the High Contracting Parties of the rights set forth in this Convention, provided that the High Contracting Party against which the complaint has been lodged has declared that it recognizes the competence of the Commission to receive such petitions. Those of the High Contracting Parties who made such a declaration undertake not to hinder in any way the effective exercise of this right.
2. Such declarations may be made for a specific period.
3. The declarations shall be deposited with the Secretary-General of the Council of Europe who shall transmit copies thereof to the High Contracting Parties and publish them.
4. The Commission shall only exercise the powers provided for in this article when at least six High Contracting Parties are bound by declarations made in accordance with the preceding paragraphs.

ARTICLE 26

The Commission may only deal with the matter after all domestic remedies have been exhausted, according to the generally recognized rules of international law, and within a period of six months from the date on which the final decision was taken.

ARTICLE 27

1. The Commission shall not deal with any petition submitted under Article 25 which
   (a) is anonymous, or
   (b) is substantially the same as a matter which has already been examined by the Commission or has already been submitted to another procedure or international investigation or settlement and if it contains no relevant new information.
2. The Commission shall consider inadmissible any petition submitted under Article 25 which it considers incompatible with the provisions of the present Convention, manifestly ill-founded, or an abuse of the right of petition.
3. The Commission shall reject any petition referred to it which it considers inadmissible under Article 26.

ARTICLE 28

In the event of the Commission accepting a petition referred to it:

- (a) it shall, with a view to ascertaining the facts undertake together with the representatives of the parties and examination of the petition and, if need be, an investigation, for the effective conduct of which the States concerned shall furnish all necessary facilities, after an exchange of views with the Commission;
- (b) it shall place itself at the disposal of the parties concerned with a view to securing a friendly settlement of the matter on the basis of respect for Human Rights as defined in this Convention.

ARTICLE 29

1. The Commission shall perform the functions set out in Article 28 by means of a Sub-Commission consisting of seven members of the Commission.
2. Each of the parties concerned may appoint as members of this Sub-Commission a person of its choice.
3. The remaining members shall be chosen by lot in accordance with arrangements prescribed in the Rules of Procedure of the Commission.

ARTICLE 30

If the Sub-Commission succeeds in effecting a friendly settlement in accordance with Article 28, it shall draw up a Report which shall be sent to the States concerned, to the Committee of Ministers and to the Secretary-General of the Council of Europe for publication. This Report shall be confined to a brief statement of the facts and of the solution reached.

ARTICLE 31

1. If a solution is not reached, the Commission shall draw up a Report on the facts and state its opinion as to whether the facts found disclose a breach by the State concerned of its obligations under the Convention. The opinions of all the members of the Commission on this point may be stated in the Report.
2. The Report shall be transmitted to the Committee of Ministers. It shall also be transmitted to the States concerned, who shall not be at liberty to publish it.
3. In transmitting the Report to the Committee of Ministers the Commission may make such proposals as it thinks fit.

ARTICLE 32

1. If the question is not referred to the Court in accordance with Article 48 of this Convention within a period of three months from the date of the transmission of the Report to the Committee of Ministers, the Committee of Ministers shall decide by a majority of two-thirds of the members entitled to sit on the Committee whether there has been a violation of the Convention.
2. In the affirmative case the Committee of Ministers shall prescribe a period during which the Contracting Party concerned must take the measures required by the decision of the Committee of Ministers.
3. If the High Contracting Party concerned has not taken satisfactory measures within the prescribed period, the Committee of Ministers shall decide by the majority provided for in paragraph 1 above what effect shall be given to its original decision and shall publish the Report.
4. The High Contracting Parties undertake to regard as binding on them any decision which the Committee of Ministers may take in application of the preceding paragraphs.

ARTICLE 33

The Commission shall meet 'in camera'.

ARTICLE 34

The Commission shall take its decision by a majority of the Members present and voting; the Sub-Commission shall take its decisions by a majority of its members.

ARTICLE 35

The Commission shall meet as the circumstances require. The meetings shall be convened by the Secretary-General of the Council of Europe.

ARTICLE 36

The Commission shall draw up its own rules of procedure.

ARTICLE 37

The secretariat of The Commission shall be provided by the Secretary-General of the Council of Europe.

SECTION IV

ARTICLE 38

The European Court of Human Rights shall consist of a number of judges equal to that of the Members of the Council of Europe. No two judges may be nationals of the State.

ARTICLE 39

1. The members of the Court shall be elected by the Consultative Assembly by a majority of the votes cast from a list of persons nominated by Members of the Council of Europe; each Member shall nominate three candidates, of whom two at least shall be its nationals.
2. As far as applicable, the same procedure shall be followed to complete the Court in the event of the admission of new members of the Council of Europe, and in filling casual vacancies.
3. The candidates shall be of high moral character and must either possess the qualifications required for appointment to high judicial office or be jurisconsults of recognized competence.

ARTICLE 40

1. The members of the Court shall be elected for a period of nine years. They may be re-elected. However, of the members elected at the first election the terms of four members shall expire at the end of three years, and the terms of four more members shall expire at the end of six years.
2. The members whose terms are to expire at the end of the initial periods of three and six years shall be chosen by lot by the Secretary-General immediately after the first election has been completed.
3. A member of the Court elected to replace a member whose term of office has not expired shall hold office for the remainder of his predecessor's term.
4. The members of the Court shall hold office until replaced. After having been replaced, they shall continue to deal with such cases as they already have under consideration.

ARTICLE 41

The Court shall elect the President and Vice-President for a period of three years. They may be re-elected.

ARTICLE 42

The members of the Court shall receive for each day of duty a compensation to be determined by the Committee of Ministers.

ARTICLE 43

For the consideration of each case brought before it the Court shall consist of a Chamber composed of seven judges. There shall sit as an 'ex officio' member of the Chamber the judge who is a national of any State party concerned, or, if there is none, a person of its choice who shall sit in the capacity of judge; the names of the other judges shall be chosen by lot by the President before the opening of the case.

ARTICLE 44

Only the High Contracting Parties and the Commission shall have the right to bring a case before the Court.

ARTICLE 45

The jurisdiction of the Court shall extend to all cases concerning the interpretation and application of the present Convention which the High Contracting Parties or the Commission shall refer to it in accordance with Article 48.

ARTICLE 46

1. Any of the High Contracting Parties may at any time declare that it recognizes as compulsory 'ipso facto' and without special agreement the jurisdiction of the Court in all matters concerning the interpretation and application of the present Convention.
2. The declarations referred to above may be made unconditionally or on condition of reciprocity on the part of several or certain other High Contracting Parties or for a specified period.
3. These declarations shall be deposited with the Secretary-General of the Council of Europe who shall transmit copies thereof to the High Contracting Parties.

ARTICLE 47

The Court may only deal with a case after the Commission has acknowledged the failure of efforts for a friendly settlement and within the period of three months provided for in Article 32.

ARTICLE 48

The following may bring a case before the Court, provided that the High Contracting Party concerned, if there is only one, or the High Contracting Parties concerned, if there is more than one, are subject to the compulsory jurisdiction of the Court, or failing that, with the consent of the High Contracting Party concerned, if there is only one, or of the High Contracting Parties concerned if there is more than one:

(a) the Commission;

(b) a High Contracting Party whose national is alleged to be a victim;

(c) a High Contracting Party which referred the case to the Commission;

(d) a High Contracting Party against which the complaint has been lodged.

ARTICLE 49

In the event of dispute as to whither the Court has the jurisdiction, the matter shall be settled by the decision of the Court.

ARTICLE 50

If the Court finds that a decision or a measure taken by a legal authority or any other authority of a High Contracting Party, is completely or partially in conflict with the obligations arising from the present convention, and if the internal law of the said Party allows only partial reparation to be made for the consequences of this decision or measure, the decision of the Court shall, if necessary, afford just satisfaction to the injured party.

ARTICLE 51

1. Reasons shall be given for the judgement of the Court.
2. If the judgement does not represent in whole or in part the unanimous opinion of the judges, any judges shall be entitled to deliver a separate opinion.

ARTICLE 52

The judgement of the Court shall be final.

ARTICLE 53

The High Contracting Parties undertake to abide by the decision of the Court in any case to which they are parties.

ARTICLE 54

The judgement of the Court shall be transmitted to the Committee of Ministers which shall supervise its execution.

ARTICLE 55

The Court shall draw up its own rules and shall determine its own procedure.

ARTICLE 56

1. The first election of the members of the Court shall take place after the declarations by the High Contracting Parties mentioned in Article 46 have reached a total of eight.

No case can be brought before the Court before this election.

SECTION V

ARTICLE 57

On receipt of a request from the Secretary-General of the Council of Europe any High Contracting Party shall furnish an explanation of the manner in which its internal law ensures the effective implementation of any of the provisions of this Convention.

ARTICLE 58

The expenses of the Commission and the Court shall be borne by the Council of Europe.

ARTICLE 59

The members of the Commission and of the Court shall be entitled, during the discharge of their functions, to the privileges and immunities provided for in Article 40 of the Statute of the Council of Europe and in the agreements made thereunder.

ARTICLE 60

Nothing in this Convention shall be construed as limiting or derogating from any of the human rights and fundamental freedoms which may be ensured under the laws of any High Contracting Party or under any other agreement to which it is a Party.

ARTICLE 61

Nothing in this Convention shall prejudice the powers conferred on the Committee of Ministers by the Statute of the Council of Europe.

ARTICLE 62

The High Contracting Parties agree that, except by special agreement, they will not avail themselves of treaties, conventions or declarations in force between them for the purpose of submitting, by way of petition, a dispute arising out of the interpretation or application of this Convention to a means of settlement other than those provided for in this Convention.

ARTICLE 63

1. Any State may at the time of its ratification or at any time thereafter declare by notification addressed to the Secretary-General of the Council of Europe that the present Convention shall extend to all or any of the territories for whose international relations it is responsible.
2. The Convention shall extend to the territory or territories named in the notification as from the thirtieth day after the receipt of this notification by the Secretary-General of the Council of Europe.
3. The provisions of this Convention shall be applied in such territories with due regard, however, to local requirements. Any State which has made a declaration in accordance with paragraph 1 of this article may at any time thereafter declare on behalf of one or more of the territories to which the declaration relates that it accepts the competence of the Commission to receive petitions from individuals, non-governmental organizations or groups of individuals in accordance with Article 25 of the present Convention.

ARTICLE 64

1. Any State may, when signing this Convention or when depositing its instrument of ratification, make a reservation in respect of any particular provision of the Convention to the extent that any law then in force in its territory is not in conformity with the provision. Reservations of a general character shall not be permitted under this article.
2. Any reservation made under this article shall contain a brief statement of the law concerned.

ARTICLE 65

1. A High Contracting Party may denounce the present Convention only after the expiry of five years from the date of which it became a Party to it and after six months' notice contained in a notification addressed to the Secretary-General of the Council of Europe, who shall inform the other High Contracting Parties.
2. Such a denunciation shall not have the effect of releasing the High Contracting Party concerned from its obligations under this Convention in respect of any act which, being capable of constituting a violation of such obligations, may have been performed by it before the date at which the denunciation became effective.
3. Any High Contracting Party which shall cease to be a Member of the Council of Europe shall cease to be a Party to this Convention under the same conditions.

4. The Convention may be denounced in accordance with the provisions of the preceding paragraphs in respect of any territory to which it has been declared to extend under the terms Article 63.

ARTICLE 66

1. This Convention shall be open to the signature of the Members of the Council of Europe. It shall be ratified. Ratifications shall be deposited with the Secretary-General of the Council of Europe.
2. The present Convention shall come into force after the deposit of ten instruments of ratification.
3. As regards any signatory ratifying subsequently, the Convention shall come into force at the date of the deposit of all instruments of ratification.
4. The Secretary-General of the Council of Europe shall notify all the Members of the Council of Europe of the entry into force of the Convention, the names of the High Contracting Parties who have ratified it, and the deposit of all instruments of ratification which may be effected subsequently.

Done at Rome this 4th day of November, 1950, in English and French, both text being equally authentic, in a single copy which shall remain deposited in the archives of the Council of Europe. The Secretary-General shall transmit certified copies to each of the signatories.

PROTOCOLS

1. Enforcement of certain Rights and Freedoms not included in Section I of the Convention

The Governments signatory hereto, being Members of the Council of Europe,

Being resolved to take steps to ensure the collective enforcement of certain rights and freedoms other than those already included in Section I of the Convention for the Protection of Human Rights and Fundamental Freedoms signed at Rome on 4th November, 1950 (hereinafter referred to as 'the Convention'),

Have agreed as follows:

ARTICLE 1

Every natural or legal person is entitled to the peaceful enjoyment of his possessions. No one shall be deprived of his possessions except in the public interest and subject to the conditions provided for by law and by the general principles of international law.

The preceding provisions shall not, however, in any way impair the right of a State to enforce such laws as it deems necessary to control the use of property in accordance with the general interest or to secure the payment of taxes or other contributions or penalties.

ARTICLE 2

No person shall be denied the right to education. In the exercise of any functions which it assumes in relation to education and to teaching, the State shall respect the right of parents to ensure such education and teaching in conformity with their own religions and philosophical convictions.

ARTICLE 3

The High Contracting Parties undertake to hold free elections at reasonable intervals by secret ballot, under conditions which will ensure the free expression of the opinion of the people in the choice of the legislature.

ARTICLE 4

Any High Contracting Party may at the time of signature or ratification or at any time thereafter communicate to the Secretary-General of the Council of Europe a declaration stating the extent to which it undertakes that the provisions of the present Protocol shall apply to such of the territories for the international relations of which it is responsible as are named therein.

Any High Contracting Party which has communicated a declaration in virtue of the preceding paragraph may from time to time communicate a further declaration modifying the terms of any former declaration or terminating the application of the provisions of this Protocol in respect of any territory.

A declaration made in accordance with this article shall be deemed to have been made in accordance with paragraph 1 of Article 63 of the Convention.

ARTICLE 5

As between the High Contracting Parties the provisions of Articles 1, 2, 3 and 4 of this Protocol shall be regarded as additional articles to the convention and all the provisions of the Convention shall apply accordingly.

ARTICLE 6

This Protocol shall be open for signature by the Members of the Council of Europe, who are the signatories of the Convention; it shall be ratified at the same time as or after the ratification of the Convention. It shall enter into force after the deposit of ten instruments of ratification. As regards any signatory ratifying subsequently, the Protocol shall enter into force at the date of the deposit of its instrument of ratification.

The instruments of ratification shall be deposited with the Secretary-General of the Council of Europe, who will notify all the Members of the names of those who have ratified.

Done at Paris on the 20th day of March 1952, In English and French, both text being equally authentic, in a single copy which shall remain deposited in the archives of the Council of Europe. The Secretary-General shall transmit certified copies to each of the signatory Governments.

2. Conferring upon the European Court of Human Rights Competence to give Advisory Opinions

The Member States of the Council of Europe signatory hereto:

Having regard to the provisions of the Convention for the Protection of Human Rights and Fundamental Freedoms signed at Rome on 4 November 1950 (hereinafter referred to as 'the Convention'), and in particular Article 19 instituting, among other bodies, a European Court of Human Rights (hereinafter referred to as 'the Court');

Considering that it is expedient to confer upon the Court competence to give advisory opinions subject to certain conditions;

Have agreed as follows:

ARTICLE 1

1. The Court may, at the request of the Committee of Ministers, give advisory opinions on legal questions concerning the interpretation of the Convention and the Protocols thereto.
2. Such opinions shall not deal with any question relating to the content or scope of the rights or freedoms defined in Section I of the convention and in the Protocols thereto, or with any other question which the Commission, the Court, or the committee of Ministers might have to consider in consequence of any such proceedings as could be instituted in accordance with the Convention.

3. Decisions of the Committee of Ministers to request an advisory opinion of the Court shall require a two-thirds majority vote of the representatives entitled to sit on the Committee.

ARTICLE 2

The Court shall decide whether a request for an advisory opinion submitted by the Committee of Ministers is within its consultative competence as defined in Article 1 of this Protocol.

ARTICLE 3

1. For the consideration of requests for an advisory opinion, the Court shall sit in plenary session.
2. Reasons shall be given for advisory opinions of the Court.
3. If the advisory opinion does not represent in whole or in part the unanimous opinion of the judges, any judge shall be entitled to deliver a separate opinion.
4. Advisory opinions of the Court shall be communicated to the Committee of Ministers.

ARTICLE 4

The powers of the Court under Article 55 of the Convention shall extend to the drawing up of such rules and the determination of such procedure as the Court may think necessary for the purposes of this Protocol.

ARTICLE 5

1. This Protocol shall be open to signature by member States of the Council of Europe, signatories to the Convention, who may become Parties to it by:
   (a) signature without reservation in respect of ratification or acceptance;
   (b) signature with reservation in respect of ratification or acceptance, followed by ratification or acceptance. Instruments of ratification or acceptance shall be deposited with the Secretary-General of the Council of Europe.
2. This Protocol shall enter into force as soon as all the States Parties to the Convention shall have become Parties to the Protocol in accordance with the Provisions of paragraph 1 of this article.
3. From the date of the entry into force of this Protocol, Articles 1 to 4 shall be considered an integral part of the Convention.
4. The Secretary-General of the Council of Europe shall notify the Member States of the Council of:
   (a) any signature without reservation in respect of ratification or acceptance;
   (b) any signature with reservation in respect of ratification or acceptance;
   (c) the deposit of any instrument of ratification or acceptance;
   (d) the date of entry into force of this Protocol in accordance with paragraph 2 of this article.

In witness whereof the undersigned, being duly authorized thereto, have signed this Protocol.

Done at Strasbourg, this 6th day of May 1963, in English and French, both text being equally authentic, in a single copy which shall remain deposited in the archives of the Council of Europe. The Secretary-General shall transmit certified copies to each of the signatory States.

3. Amending Articles 29, 30, and 94 of the Convention

The member States of the Council, signatories to this Protocol,

Considering that it is advisable to amend certain provisions of the Convention for the Protection of Human Rights and Fundamental Freedoms signed at Rome on 4 November 1950 (hereinafter referred to as 'the Convention') concerning the procedure of the European Commission of Human Rights,

Have agreed as follows:

ARTICLE 1

1. Article 29 of the Convention is deleted.
2. The following provision shall be inserted in the Convention:

"ARTICLE 29

After it has accepted a petition submitted under Article 25, the Commission may nevertheless decide unanimously to reject the petition if, in the course of its examination, it finds that the existence of one of the grounds for non-acceptance provided for in Article 27 has been established.

In such a case, the decision shall be communicated to the parties."

ARTICLE 2

1. At the beginning of Article 34 of the Convention, the following shall be inserted: "Subject to the provisions of Article 29 . . . "

At the end of the same article, the sentence "the Sub-commission shall take its decisions by a majority of its members" shall be deleted.

ARTICLE 4

1. The Protocol shall be open to signature by the member States of the Council of Europe, who may become Parties to it either by:
   (a) signature without reservation in respect of ratification or acceptance, or
   (b) signature with reservation in respect of ratification or acceptance, followed by ratification or acceptance. Instruments of ratification shall be deposited with the Secretary-General of the Council of Europe.
2. This Protocol shall enter force as soon as all States Parties to the Convention shall have become Parties to the Protocol, in accordance with paragraph 1 of this article.
3. The Secretary-General of the Council of Europe shall notify the Member States of the Council of:
   (a) any signature without reservation in respect of ratification or acceptance;
   (b) any signature with reservation in respect of ratification or acceptance;
   (c) the deposit of any instrument of ratification or acceptance;
   (d) the date of entry into force of this Protocol in accordance with paragraph 2 of this article.

In witness whereof the undersigned, being duly authorized thereto, have signed this Protocol.

Done at Strasbourg, this 6th day of May 1963, in English and French, both text being equally authentic, in a single copy which shall remain deposited in the archives of the Council of Europe. The Secretary-General shall transmit certified copies to each of the signatory States.

4. Protecting certain Additional Rights

The Governments signatory hereto, being Members of the Council of Europe,

Being resolved to take steps to ensure the collective enforcement of certain rights and freedoms other than those already included in Section 1 of the Convention for the Protection of Human Rights and Fundamental Freedoms signed at Rome on 4 November 1950 (hereinafter referred to as 'the Convention') and in Articles 1 to 3 of the First Protocol to the Convention, signed at Paris on 20 March 1952,

Have agreed as follows:

ARTICLE 1

No one shall be deprived of his liberty merely on the ground of inability to fulfil a contractual obligation.

ARTICLE 2

1. Everyone lawfully within the territory of a State shall, within that territory, have the right to liberty of movement and freedom to choose his residence.
2. Everyone shall be free to leave any country, including his own.
3. No restrictions shall be placed on the exercise of these rights other than such as are in accordance with law and are necessary in a democratic society in the interests of national security or public safety for the maintenance of 'ordre public', for the prevention of crime, for the protection of rights and freedoms of others.
4. The rights set forth in paragraph 1 may also be subject, in particular areas, to restrictions imposes in accordance with law and justified by the public interest in a democratic society.

ARTICLE 3

1. No one shall be expelled, by means either of an individual or of a collective measure, from the territory of the State of which he is a national.
2. No one shall be deprived of the right to enter the territory of the State of which he is a national.

ARTICLE 4

Collective expulsion of aliens is prohibited.

ARTICLE 5

1. Any High Contracting Party may, at the time of signature or ratification of this Protocol, or at any time thereafter, communicate to the Secretary-General of the Council of Europe a declaration stating the extent to which it undertakes that the provisions of this Protocol shall apply to such of the territories for the international relations of which it is responsible as are named therein.
2. Any High Contracting Party which has communicated a declaration in virtue of the preceding paragraph may, from time to time, communicate a further declaration modifying the terms of any former declaration or terminating the application of the provisions of this Protocol in respect of territory.
3. A declaration made in accordance with this article shall be deemed to have been made in accordance with paragraph 1 of Article 63 of the Convention.
4. The territory of any State to which this Protocol applies by virtue of the ratification or acceptance by that State, and each territory to which this Protocol is applied by virtue of a declaration by that State under this article, shall be treated as separate territories for the purpose of the references in Articles 2 and 3 to the territory of a State.

ARTICLE 6

1. As between the High Contracting Parties the provisions of Articles 1 to 5 of this Protocol shall be regarded as additional articles to the convention, and all the provisions of the Convention shall apply accordingly.

2. Nevertheless, the right of individual recourse recognized by a declaration made under Article 25 of the convention, or the acceptance of the compulsory jurisdiction of the court by a declaration made under Article 46 of the convention, shall not be effective in relation to this Protocol unless the High Contracting Party concerned has made a statement recognizing such a right, or accepting such jurisdiction, in respect of all or any of Articles 1 to 4 of the Protocol.

ARTICLE 7

1. This Protocol shall be open for signature by the members of the Council of Europe who are the signatories of the Convention; it shall be ratified at the same time as or after the ratification of the Convention. It shall enter into force after the deposit of five instruments of ratification. As regards any signatory ratifying subsequently, the Protocol shall enter into force at the date of the deposit of its instrument of ratification.

The instruments of ratification shall be deposited with the Secretary-General of the Council of Europe, who will notify all members of the names of those who have ratified.

In witness thereof, the undersigned, being duly authorized thereto, have signed this Protocol.

Done at Strasbourg, this 16th day of September 1963, in English and French, both texts being equally authentic, in a single copy which shall remain deposited in the archives of the Council of Europe. The Secretary-General shall transmit certified copies to each of the signatory States.

5. Amending Articles 22 and 40 of the Convention

The Governments signatory hereto, being Members of the Council of Europe,

Considering that certain inconveniences have arisen in the application of the provisions of Articles 22 and 40 of the Convention for the Protection of Human Rights and fundamental Freedoms signed at Rome of 4th November 1950 (hereinafter referred to as 'the Convention') relating to the length of the terms of office of the members of the European Commission of Human Rights (hereinafter referred to as 'the Commission') and of the European Court of Human Rights (hereinafter referred to as 'the Court');

Considering that it is desirable to ensure as far as possible an election every three years of one half of the members of the Commission and of one third of the members of the Court;

Considering therefore that it is desirable to amend certain provisions of the Convention,

Have agreed as follows:

ARTICLE 1

In Article 22 of the Convention, the following two paragraphs shall be inserted after paragraph (2):

"(3) In order to ensure that, as far as possible, one half of the membership of the Commission shall be renewed every three years, the Committee of Ministers may decide, before proceeding to any subsequent election, that the term or terms of office of one or more members to be elected shall be for a period other than six years but not more than nine and not less than three years.

(4) In cases where more than one term of office is involved and the Committee of Ministers applies the preceding paragraph, the allocation of the terms of office shall be effected by the drawing of lots by the Secretary-General, immediately after the election."

ARTICLE 2

In Article 22 of the Convention, the former paragraphs (3) and (4) shall become respectively paragraphs (5) and (6).

ARTICLE 3

In Article 40 of the Convention, the following two paragraphs shall be inserted after paragraph (2):

"(3) In order to ensure that, as far as possible, one half of the membership of the Court shall be renewed every three years, the Consultative Assembly may decide, before proceeding to any subsequent election, that the term or terms of office of one or more members to be elected shall be for a period other than nine years but not more than twelve and not less than six years.

(4) In cases where more than one term of office is involved and the Consultative Assembly applies the preceding paragraph, the allocation of the terms of office shall be effected by the drawing of lots by the Secretary-General, immediately after the election."

ARTICLE 4

In Article 40 of the Convention, the former paragraphs (3) and (4) shall become respectively paragraphs (5) and (6).

ARTICLE 5

1. This Protocol shall be open to signature by Members of the Council of Europe, signatories to the Convention, who may become Parties to it by;
   (a) signature without reservation in respect of ratification or acceptance;
   (b) signature with reservation in respect of ratification or acceptance, followed by ratification or acceptance.

Instruments of ratification or acceptance shall be deposited with the Secretary-General of the Council of Europe.

2. This Protocol shall enter into force as soon as all Contracting Parties to the Convention shall have become Parties to the Protocol, in accordance with the provisions of paragraph 1 of this article.
3. The Secretary-General of the Council of Europe shall notify the Members of the Council of:
   (a) any signature without reservation in respect of ratification or acceptance;
   (b) any signature with reservation in respect of ratification or acceptance;
   (c) the deposit of any instrument of ratification or acceptance;
   (d) the date of entry into force of this Protocol in accordance with paragraph 2 of this article.

In witness whereof the undersigned, being duly authorized thereto, have signed this Protocol.

Done at Strasbourg, this 20th day of January 1966, in English and French, both texts being equally authentic, in a single copy which shall remain deposited in the archives of the Council of Europe. The Secretary-General shall transmit certified copies to each of the signatory Governments.

DECLARATION OF THE RIGHTS OF THE CHILD

Proclaimed by General Assembly resolution 1386(XIV) of 20 November 1959

Preamble

Whereas the peoples of the United Nations have, in the *Charter*, reaffirmed their faith in fundamental human rights and in the dignity and worth of the human person, and have determined to promote social progress and better standards of life in larger freedom,

Whereas the United Nations has, in the *Universal Declaration of Human Rights*, proclaimed that everyone is entitled to all the rights and freedoms set forth therein, without distinction of any kind, such as race, colour, sex, language, religion, political or other opinion, national or social origin, property, birth or other status,

Whereas the child, by reason of his physical and mental immaturity, needs special safeguards and care, including appropriate legal protection, before as well as after birth,

Whereas the need for such special safeguards has been stated in the *Geneva Declaration of the Rights of the Child* of 1924, and recognized in the *Universal Declaration of Human Rights* and in the statutes of specialized agencies and international organizations concerned with the welfare of children,

Whereas mankind owes to the child the best it has to give,

Now therefore,

The General Assembly

Proclaims this *Declaration of the Rights of the Child* to the end that he may have a happy childhood and enjoy for his own good and for the good of society the rights and freedoms herein set forth, and calls upon parents, upon men and women as individuals, and upon voluntary organizations, local authorities and national Governments to recognize these rights and strive for their observance by legislative and other measures progressively taken in accordance with the following principles:

Principle 1

The child shall enjoy all the rights set forth in this Declaration. Every child, without any exception whatsoever, shall be entitled to these rights, without distinction or discrimination on account of race, colour, sex, language, religion, political or other opinion, national or social origin, property, birth or other status, whether of himself or of his family.

Principle 2

The child shall enjoy special protection, and shall be given opportunities and facilities, by law and by other means, to enable him to develop physically, mentally, morally, spiritually and socially in a healthy and normal manner and in conditions of freedom and dignity. In the enactment of laws for this purpose, the best interests of the child shall be the paramount consideration.

Principle 3

The child shall be entitled from his birth to a name and a nationality.

Principle 4

The child shall enjoy the benefits of social security. He shall be entitled to grow and develop in health; to this end, special care and protection shall be provided both to him and to his mother, including adequate pre-natal and post-natal care. The child shall have the right to adequate nutrition, housing, recreation and medical services.

Principle 5

The child who is physically, mentally or socially handicapped shall be given the special treatment, education and care required by his particular condition.

Principle 6

The child, for the full and harmonious development of his personality, needs love and understanding. He shall, wherever possible, grow up in the care and under the responsibility of his parents, and, in any case, in an atmosphere of affection and of moral and material security; a child of tender years shall not, save in exceptional circumstances, be separated from his mother. Society and the public authorities shall have the duty to extend particular care to children without a family and to those without adequate means of support. Payment of State and other assistance towards the maintenance of children of large families is desirable.

Principle 7

The child is entitled to receive education, which shall be free and compulsory, at least in the elementary stages. He shall be given an education which will promote his general culture and enable him, on a basis of equal opportunity, to develop his abilities, his individual judgement, and his sense of moral and social responsibility, and to become a useful member of society.

The best interests of the child shall be the guiding principle of those responsible for his education and guidance; that responsibility lies in the first place with his parents.

The child shall have full opportunity for play and recreation, which should be directed to the same purposes as education; society and the public authorities shall endeavour to promote the enjoyment of this right.

Principle 8

The child shall in all circumstances be among the first to receive protection and relief.

Principle 9

The child shall be protected against all forms of neglect, cruelty and exploitation. He shall not be the subject of traffic, in any form.

The child shall not be admitted to employment before an appropriate minimum age; he shall in no case be caused or permitted to engage in any occupation or employment which would prejudice his health or education, or interfere with his physical, mental or moral development.

Principle 10

The child shall be protected from practices which may foster racial, religious and any other form of discrimination. He shall be brought up in a spirit of understanding, tolerance, friendship among peoples, peace and universal brotherhood, and in full consciousness that his energy and talents should be devoted to the service of his fellow men.

CONVENTION AGAINST DISCRIMINATION IN EDUCATION

Adopted by the General Conference of the United Nations Educational, Scientific and Cultural Organization on 14 December 1960

The General Conference of the United Nations Educational, Scientific and Cultural Organization, meeting in Paris from 14 November to 15 December 1960, at its eleventh session,

Recalling that the Universal Declaration of Human Rights asserts the principle of non-discrimination and proclaims that every person has the right to education,

Considering that discrimination in education is a violation of rights enunciated in that Declaration,

Considering that, under the terms of its Constitution, the United Nations Educational, Scientific and Cultural Organization has the purpose of instituting collaboration among the nations with a view to furthering for all universal respect for human rights and equality of educational opportunity,

Recognizing that, consequently, the United Nations Educational, Scientific and Cultural Organization, while respecting the diversity of national educational systems, has the duty not only to proscribe any form of discrimination in education but also to promote equality of opportunity and treatment for all in education,

Having before it proposals concerning the different aspects of discrimination in education, constituting item 17.1.4 of the agenda of the session,

Having decided at its tenth session that this question should be made the subject of an international convention as well as of recommendations to Member States,

Adopts this Convention on the fourteenth day of December 1960.

Article 1

1. For the purpose of this Convention, the term "discrimination" includes any distinction, exclusion, limitation or preference which, being based on race, colour, sex, language, religion, political or other opinion, national or social origin, economic condition or birth, has the purpose or effect of nullifying or impairing equality of treatment in education and in particular:

   (a) Of depriving any person or group of persons of access to education of any type or at any level;

   (b) Of limiting any person or group of persons to education of an inferior standard;

   (c) Subject to the provisions of article 2 of this Convention, of establishing or maintaining separate educational systems or institutions for persons or groups of persons; or

   (d) Of inflicting on any person or group of persons conditions which are incompatible with the dignity of man.

2. For the purposes of this Convention, the term "education" refers to all types and levels of education, and includes access to education, the standard and quality of education, and the conditions under which it is given.

Article 2

When permitted in a State, the following situations shall not be deemed to constitute discrimination, within the meaning of article 1 of this Convention:

(a) The establishment or maintenance of separate educational systems or institutions for pupils of the two sexes, if these systems or institutions offer equivalent access to education, provide a teaching staff with qualifications of the same standard as well as school premises and equipment of the same quality, and afford the opportunity to take the same or equivalent courses of study;

(b) The establishment or maintenance, for religious or linguistic reasons, of separate educational systems or institutions offering an education which is in keeping with the wishes of the pupil's parents or legal guardians, if participation in such systems or attendance at such institutions is optional and if the education provided conforms to such standards as may be laid down or approved by the competent authorities, in particular for education of the same level;

(c) The establishment or maintenance of private educational institutions, if the object of the institutions is not to secure the exclusion of any group but to provide educational facilities in addition to those provided by the public authorities, if the institutions are conducted in accordance with that object, and if the education provided conforms with such standards as may be laid down or approved by the competent authorities, in particular for education of the same level.

Article 3

In order to eliminate and prevent discrimination within the meaning of this Convention, the States Parties thereto undertake:

(a) To abrogate any statutory provisions and any administrative instructions and to discontinue any administrative practices which involve discrimination in education;

(b) To ensure, by legislation where necessary, that there is no discrimination in the admission of pupils to educational institutions;

(c) Not to allow any differences of treatment by the public authorities between nationals, except on the basis of merit or need, in the matter of school fees and the grant of scholarships or other forms of assistance to pupils and necessary permits and facilities for the pursuit of studies in foreign countries;

(d) Not to allow, in any form of assistance granted by the public authorities to educational institutions, any restrictions or preference based solely on the ground that pupils belong to a particular group;

(e) To give foreign nationals resident within their territory the same access to education as that given to their own nationals.

Article 4

The States Parties to this Convention undertake furthermore to formulate, develop and apply a national policy which, by methods appropriate to the circumstances and to national usage, will tend to promote equality of opportunity and of treatment in the matter of education and in particular:

(a) To make primary education free and compulsory; make secondary education in its different forms generally available and accessible to all; make higher education equally accessible to all on the basis of individual capacity; assure compliance by all with the obligation to attend school prescribed by law;

(b) To ensure that the standards of education are equivalent in all public education institutions of the same level, and that the conditions relating to the quality of education provided are also equivalent;

(c) To encourage and intensify by appropriate methods the education of persons who have not received any primary education or who have not completed the entire primary education course and the continuation of their education on the basis of individual capacity;

(d) To provide training for the teaching profession without discrimination.

Article 5

1. The States Parties to this Convention agree that:

   (a) Education shall be directed to the full development of the human personality and to the strengthening of respect for human rights and fundamental freedoms; it shall promote understanding, tolerance and friendship among all nations, racial or religious groups, and shall further the activities of the United Nations for the maintenance of peace;

   (b) It is essential to respect the liberty of parents and, where applicable, of legal guardians, firstly to choose for their children institutions other than those maintained by the public authorities but conforming to such minimum educational standards as may be laid down or approved by the competent authorities and, secondly, to ensure in a manner consistent with the procedures followed in the State for the application of its legislation, the religious and moral education of the children in conformity with their own convictions; and no person or group of persons should be compelled to receive religious instruction inconsistent with his or their conviction;

(c) It is essential to recognize the right of members of national minorities to carry on their own educational activities, including the maintenance of schools and, depending on the educational policy of each State, the use or the teaching of their own language, provided however:

(i) That this right is not exercised in a manner which prevents the members of these minorities from understanding the culture and language of the community as a whole and from participating in its—activities, or which prejudices national sovereignty;

(ii) That the standard of education is not lower than the general standard laid down or approved by the competent authorities; and

(iii) That attendance at such schools is optional.

2. The States Parties to this Convention undertake to take all necessary measures to ensure the application of the principles enunciated in paragraph 1 of this article.

Article 6

In the application of this Convention, the States Parties to it undertake to pay the greatest attention to any recommendations hereafter adopted by the General Conference of the United Nations Educational, Scientific and Cultural Organization defining the measures to be taken against the different forms of discrimination in education and for the purpose of ensuring equality of opportunity and treatment in education.

Article 7

The States Parties to this Convention shall in their periodic reports submitted to the General Conference of the United Nations Educational, Scientific and Cultural Organization on dates and in a manner to be determined by it, give information on the legislative and administrative provisions which they have adopted and other action which they have taken for the application of this Convention, including that taken for the formulation and the development of the national policy defined in article 4 as well as the results achieved and the obstacles encountered in the application of that policy.

Article 8

Any dispute which may arise between any two or more States Parties to this Convention concerning the interpretation or application of this Convention which is not settled by negotiations shall at the request of the parties to the dispute be referred, failing other means of settling the dispute, to the International Court of Justice for decision.

Article 9

Reservations to this Convention shall not be permitted.

Article 10

This Convention shall not have the effect of diminishing the rights which individuals or groups may enjoy by virtue of agreements concluded between two or more States, where such rights are not contrary to the letter or spirit of this Convention.

Article 11

This Convention is drawn up in English, French, Russian and Spanish, the four texts being equally authoritative.

Article 12

1. This Convention shall be subject to ratification or acceptance by States Members of the United Nations Educational, Scientific and Cultural Organization in accordance with their respective constitutional procedures.
2. The instruments of ratification or acceptance shall be deposited with the Director-General of the United Nations Educational, Scientific and Cultural Organization.

Article 13

1. This Convention shall be open to accession by all States not Members of the United Nations Educational, Scientific and Cultural Organization which are invited to do so by the Executive Board of the Organization.
2. Accession shall be effected by the deposit of an instrument of accession with the Director-General of the United Nations Educational, Scientific and Cultural Organization.

Article 14

This Convention shall enter into force three months after the date of the deposit of the third instrument of ratification, acceptance or accession, but only with respect to those States which have deposited their respective instruments on or before that date. It shall enter into force with respect to any other State three months after the deposit of its instrument of ratification, acceptance or accession.

Article 15

The States Parties to this Convention recognize that the Convention is applicable not only to their metropolitan territory but also to all non-self-governing, trust, colonial and other territories for the international relations of which they are responsible; they undertake to consult, if necessary, the governments or other competent authorities of these territories on or before ratification, acceptance or accession with a view to securing the application of the Convention to those territories, and to notify the Director-General of the United Nations Educational, Scientific and Cultural Organization of the territories to which it is accordingly applied, the notification to take effect three months after the date of its receipt.

Article 16

1. Each State Party to this Convention may denounce the Convention on its own behalf or on behalf of any territory for whose international relations it is responsible.
2. The denunciation shall be notified by an instrument in writing, deposited with the Director-General of the United Nations Educational, Scientific and Cultural Organization.
3. The denunciation shall take effect twelve months after the receipt of the instrument of denunciation.

Article 17

The Director-General of the United Nations Educational, Scientific and Cultural Organization shall inform the States Members of the Organization, the States not members of the Organization which are referred to in article 13, as well as the United Nations, of the deposit of all the instruments of ratification, acceptance and accession provided for in articles 12 and 13, and of notifications and denunciations provided for in articles 15 and 16 respectively.

Article 18

1. This Convention may be revised by the General Conference of the United Nations Educational, Scientific and Cultural Organization. Any such revision shall, however, bind only the States which shall become Parties to the revising convention.

2. If the General Conference should adopt a new convention revising this Convention in whole or in part, then, unless the new convention otherwise provides, this Convention shall cease to be open to ratification, acceptance or accession as from the date on which the new revising convention enters into force.

Article 19

In conformity with Article 102 of the Charter of the United Nations, this Convention shall be registered with the Secretariat of the United Nations at the request of the Director-General of the United Nations Educational, Scientific and Cultural Organization.

DONE in Paris, this fifteenth day of December 1960, in two authentic copies bearing the signatures of the President of the eleventh session of the General Conference and of the Director-General of the United Nations Educational, Scientific and Cultural Organization, which shall be deposited in the archives of the United Nations Educational, Scientific and Cultural Organization, and certified true copies of which shall be delivered to all the States referred to in articles 12 and 13 as well as to the United Nations.

The foregoing is the authentic text of the Convention duly adopted by the General Conference of the United Nations Educational, Scientific and Cultural Organization during its eleventh session, which was held in Paris and declared closed the fifteenth day of December 1960.

IN FAITH WHEREOF we have appended our signatures this fifteenth day of December 1960.

DECLARATION ON RACE AND RACIAL PREJUDICE

Adopted and proclaimed by the General Conference of the United Nations Educational, Scientific and Cultural Organization at its twentieth session, on 27 November 1978

Preamble

The General Conference of the United Nations Educational, Scientific and Cultural Organization, meeting at Paris at its twentieth session, from 24 October to 28 November 1978,

Whereas it is stated in the Preamble to the Constitution of UNESCO, adopted on 16 November 1945, that "the great and terrible war which has now ended was a war made possible by the denial of the democratic principles of the dignity, equality and mutual respect of men, and by the propagation, in their place, through ignorance and prejudice, of the doctrine of the inequality of men and races", and whereas, according to Article I of the said Constitution, the purpose of UNESCO "is to contribute to peace and security by promoting collaboration among the nations through education, science and culture in order to further universal respect for justice, for the rule of law and for the human rights and fundamental freedoms which are affirmed for the peoples of the world, without distinction of race, sex, language or religion, by the Charter of the United Nations",

Recognizing that, more than three decades after the founding of UNESCO, these principles are just as significant as they were when they were embodied in its Constitution,

Mindful of the process of decolonization and other historical changes which have led most of the peoples formerly under foreign rule to recover their sovereignty, making the international community a universal and diversified whole and creating new opportunities of eradicating the scourge of racism and of putting an end to its odious manifestations in all aspects of social and political life, both nationally and internationally,

Convinced that the essential unity of the human race and consequently the fundamental equality of all human beings and all peoples, recognized in the loftiest expressions of philosophy, morality and religion, reflect an ideal towards which ethics and science are converging today,

Convinced that all peoples and all human groups, whatever their composition or ethnic origin, contribute according to their own genius to the progress of the civilizations and cultures which, in their plurality and as a result of their interpenetration, constitute the common heritage of mankind,

Confirming its attachment to the principles proclaimed in the United Nations Charter and the Universal Declaration of Human Rights and its determination to promote the implementation of the International Covenants on Human Rights as well as the Declaration on the Establishment of a New International Economic Order,

Determined also to promote the implementation of the United Nations Declaration and the International Convention on the Elimination of All Forms of Racial Discrimination,

Noting the Convention on the Prevention and Punishment of the Crime of Genocide, the International Convention on the Suppression and Punishment of the Crime of Apartheid and the Convention on the Non-Applicability of Statutory Limitations to War Crimes and Crimes against Humanity,

Recalling also the international instruments already adopted by UNESCO, including in particular the Convention and Recommendation against Discrimination in Education, the Recommendation concerning the Status of Teachers, the Declaration of the Principles of International Cultural Co-operation, the Recommendation concerning Education for International Understanding, Co-operation and Peace and Education relating to Human Rights and Fundamental Freedoms, the Recommendations on the Status of Scientific Researchers, and the Recommendation on participation by the people at large in cultural life and their contribution to it,

Bearing in mind the four statements on the race question adopted by experts convened by UNESCO,

Reaffirming its desire to play a vigorous and constructive part in the implementation of the programme of the Decade for Action to Combat Racism and Racial Discrimination, as defined by the General Assembly of the United Nations at its twenty-eighth session,

Noting with the gravest concern that racism, racial discrimination, colonialism and apartheid continue to afflict the world in ever-changing forms, as a result both of the continuation of legislative provisions and government and administrative practices contrary to the principles of human rights and also of the continued existence of political and social structures, and of relationships and attitudes, characterized by injustice and contempt for human beings and leading to the exclusion, humiliation and exploitation, or to the forced assimilation, of the members of disadvantaged groups,

Expressing its indignation at these offences against human dignity, deploring the obstacles they place in the way of mutual understanding between peoples and alarmed at the danger of their seriously disturbing international peace and security,

Adopts and solemnly proclaims this Declaration on Race and Racial Prejudice:

Article 1

1. All human beings belong to a single species and are descended from a common stock. They are born equal in dignity and rights and all form an integral part of humanity.
2. All individuals and groups have the right to be different, to consider themselves as different and to be regarded as such. However, the diversity of life styles and the right to be different may not, in any circumstances, serve as a pretext for racial prejudice; they may not justify either in law or in fact any discriminatory practice whatsoever, nor provide a ground for the policy of apartheid, which is the extreme form of racism.

3. Identity of origin in no way affects the fact that human beings can and may live differently, nor does it preclude the existence of differences based on cultural, environmental and historical diversity nor the right to maintain cultural identity.
4. All peoples of the world possess equal faculties for attaining the highest level in intellectual, technical, social, economic, cultural and political development.
5. The differences between the achievements of the different peoples are entirely attributable to geographical, historical, political, economic, social and cultural factors. Such differences can in no case serve as a pretext for any rank-ordered classification of nations or peoples.

Article 2

1. Any theory which involves the claim that racial or ethnic groups are inherently superior or inferior, thus implying that some would be entitled to dominate or eliminate others, presumed to be inferior, or which bases value judgements on racial differentiation, has no scientific foundation and is contrary to the moral and ethical principles of humanity.
2. Racism includes racist ideologies, prejudiced attitudes, discriminatory behaviour, structural arrangements and institutionalized practices resulting in racial inequality as well as the fallacious notion that discriminatory relations between groups are morally and scientifically justifiable; it is reflected in discriminatory provisions in legislation or regulations and discriminatory practices as well as in anti-social beliefs and acts; it hinders the development of its victims, perverts those who practise it, divides nations internally, impedes international co-operation and gives rise to political tensions between peoples; it is contrary to the fundamental principles of international law and, consequently, seriously disturbs international peace and security.
3. Racial prejudice, historically linked with inequalities in power, reinforced by economic and social differences between individuals and groups, and still seeking today to justify such inequalities, is totally without justification.

Article 3

Any distinction, exclusion, restriction or preference based on race, colour, ethnic or national origin or religious intolerance motivated by racist considerations, which destroys or compromises the sovereign equality of States and the right of peoples to self-determination, or which limits in an arbitrary or discriminatory manner the right of every human being and group to full development is incompatible with the requirements of an international order which is just and guarantees respect for human rights; the right to full development implies equal access to the means of personal and collective advancement and fulfilment in a climate of respect for the values of civilizations and cultures, both national and world-wide.

Article 4

1. Any restriction on the complete self-fulfilment of human beings and free communication between them which is based on racial or ethnic considerations is contrary to the principle of equality in dignity and rights; it cannot be admitted.
2. One of the most serious violations of this principle is represented by apartheid, which, like genocide, is a crime against humanity, and gravely disturbs international peace and security.
3. Other policies and practices of racial segregation and discrimination constitute crimes against the conscience and dignity of mankind and may lead to political tensions and gravely endanger international peace and security.

Article 5

1. Culture, as a product of all human beings and a common heritage of mankind, and education in its broadest sense, offer men and women increasingly effective means of adaptation, enabling them not only to affirm that they are born equal in dignity and rights, but also to recognize that they should respect the right of all groups to their own cultural identity and the development of their distinctive cultural life within the national and international contexts, it being understood that it rests with each group to decide in complete freedom on the maintenance, and, if appropriate, the adaptation or enrichment of the values which it regards as essential to its identity.
2. States, in accordance with their constitutional principles and procedures, as well as all other competent authorities and the entire teaching profession, have a responsibility to see that the educational resources of all countries are used to combat racism, more especially by ensuring that curricula and textbooks include scientific and ethical considerations concerning human unity and diversity and that no invidious distinctions are made with regard to any people; by training teachers to achieve these ends; by making the resources of the educational system available to all groups of the population without racial restriction or discrimination; and by taking appropriate steps to remedy the handicaps from which certain racial or ethnic groups suffer with regard to their level of education and standard of living and in particular to prevent such handicaps from being passed on to children.
3. The mass media and those who control or serve them, as well as all organized groups within national communities, are urged-with due regard to the principles embodied in the Universal Declaration of Human Rights, particulary the principle of freedom of expression-to promote understanding, tolerance and friendship among individuals and groups and to contribute to the eradication of racism, racial discrimination and racial prejudice, in particular by refraining from presenting a stereotyped, partial, unilateral or tendentious picture of individuals and of various human groups. Communication between racial and ethnic groups must be a reciprocal process, enabling them to express themselves and to be fully heard without let or hindrance. The mass media should therefore be freely receptive to ideas of individuals and groups which facilitate such communication.

Article 6

1. The State has prime responsibility for ensuring human rights and fundamental freedoms on an entirely equal footing in dignity and rights for all individuals and all groups.
2. So far as its competence extends and in accordance with its constitutional principles and procedures, the State should take all appropriate steps, inter alia by legislation, particularly in the spheres of education, culture and communication, to prevent, prohibit and eradicate racism, racist propaganda, racial segregation and apartheid and to encourage the dissemination of knowledge and the findings of appropriate research in natural and social sciences on the causes and prevention of racial prejudice and racist attitudes with due regard to the principles embodied in the Universal Declaration of Human Rights and in the International Covenant on Civil and Political Rights.
3. Since laws proscribing racial discrimination are not in themselves sufficient, it is also incumbent on States to supplement them by administrative machinery for the systematic investigation of instances of racial discrimination, by a comprehensive framework of legal remedies against acts of racial discrimination, by broadly based education and research programmes designed to combat racial prejudice and racial

discrimination and by programmes of positive political, social, educational and cultural measures calculated to promote genuine mutual respect among groups. Where circumstances warrant, special programmes should be undertaken to promote the advancement of disadvantaged groups and, in the case of nationals, to ensure their effective participation in the decision-making processes of the community.

Article 7

In addition to political, economic and social measures, law is one of the principal means of ensuring equality in dignity and rights among individuals, and of curbing any propaganda, any form of organization or any practice which is based on ideas or theories referring to the alleged superiority of racial or ethnic groups or which seeks to justify or encourage racial hatred and discrimination in any form. States should adopt such legislation as is appropriate to this end and see that it is given effect and applied by all their services, with due regard to the principles embodied in the Universal Declaration of Human Rights. Such legislation should form part of a political, economic and social framework conducive to its implementation. Individuals and other legal entities, both public and private, must conform with such legislation and use all appropriate means to help the population as a whole to understand and apply it.

Article 8

1. Individuals, being entitled to an economic, social, cultural and legal order, on the national and international planes, such as to allow them to exercise all their capabilities on a basis of entire equality of rights and opportunities, have corresponding duties towards their fellows, towards the society in which they live and towards the international community. They are accordingly under an obligation to promote harmony among the peoples, to combat racism and racial prejudice and to assist by every means available to them in eradicating racial discrimination in all its forms.
2. In the field of racial prejudice and racist attitudes and practices, specialists in natural and social sciences and cultural studies, as well as scientific organizations and associations, are called upon to undertake objective research on a wide interdisciplinary basis; all States should encourage them to this end.
3. It is, in particular, incumbent upon such specialists to ensure, by all means available to them, that their research findings are not misinterpreted, and also that they assist the public in understanding such findings.

Article 9

1. The principle of the equality in dignity and rights of all human beings and all peoples, irrespective of race, colour and origin, is a generally accepted and recognized principle of international law. Consequently any form of racial discrimination practised by a State constitutes a violation of international law giving rise to its international responsibility.
2. Special measures must be taken to ensure equality in dignity and rights for individuals and groups wherever necessary, while ensuring that they are not such as to appear racially discriminatory. In this respect, particular attention should be paid to racial or ethnic groups which are socially or economically disadvantaged, so as to afford them, on a completely equal footing and without discrimination or restriction, the protection of the laws and regulations and the advantages of the social measures in force, in particular in regard to housing, employment and health; to respect the authenticity of their culture and values; and to facilitate their social and occupational advancement, especially through education.
3. Population groups of foreign origin, particularly migrant workers and their families who contribute to the development of the host country, should benefit from

appropriate measures designed to afford them security and respect for their dignity and cultural values and to facilitate their adaptation to the host environment and their professional advancement with a view to their subsequent reintegration in their country of origin and their contribution to its development; steps should be taken to make it possible for their children to be taught their mother tongue.

4. Existing disequilibria in international economic relations contribute to the exacerbation of racism and racial prejudice; all States should consequently endeavour to contribute to the restructuring of the international economy on a more equitable basis.

Article 10

International organizations, whether universal or regional, governmental or non-governmental, are called upon to co-operate and assist, so far as their respective fields of competence and means allow, in the full and complete implementation of the principles set out in this Declaration, thus contributing to the legitimate struggle of all men, born equal in dignity and rights, against the tyranny and oppression of racism, racial segregation, apartheid and genocide, so that all the peoples of the world may be forever delivered from these scourges.

CONVENTION ON THE RIGHTS OF THE CHILD

Adopted and opened for signature, ratification and accession by General Assembly resolution 44/25 of 20 November 1989

Entry into force 2 September 1990, in accordance with article 49

Preamble

The States Parties to the present Convention,

Considering that, in accordance with the principles proclaimed in the Charter of the United Nations, recognition of the inherent dignity and of the equal and inalienable rights of all members of the human family is the foundation of freedom, justice and peace in the world,

Bearing in mind that the peoples of the United Nations have, in the Charter, reaffirmed their faith in fundamental human rights and in the dignity and worth of the human person, and have determined to promote social progress and better standards of life in larger freedom,

Recognizing that the United Nations has, in the Universal Declaration of Human Rights and in the International Covenants on Human Rights, proclaimed and agreed that everyone is entitled to all the rights and freedoms set forth therein, without distinction of any kind, such as race, colour, sex, language, religion, political or other opinion, national or social origin, property, birth or other status,

Recalling that, in the Universal Declaration of Human Rights, the United Nations has proclaimed that childhood is entitled to special care and assistance,

Convinced that the family, as the fundamental group of society and the natural environment for the growth and well-being of all its members and particularly children, should be afforded the necessary protection and assistance so that it can fully assume its responsibilities within the community,

Recognizing that the child, for the full and harmonious development of his or her personality, should grow up in a family environment, in an atmosphere of happiness, love and understanding,

Considering that the child should be fully prepared to live an individual life in society, and brought up in the spirit of the ideals proclaimed in the Charter of the United Nations, and in particular in the spirit of peace, dignity, tolerance, freedom, equality and solidarity,

Bearing in mind that the need to extend particular care to the child has been stated in the Geneva Declaration of the Rights of the Child of 1924 and in the Declaration of the Rights of the Child adopted by the General Assembly on 20 November 1959 and recognized in the Universal Declaration of Human Rights, in the International Covenant on Civil and Political Rights (in particular in articles 23 and 24), in the International Covenant on Economic, Social and Cultural Rights (in particular in article 10) and in the statutes and relevant instruments of specialized agencies and international organizations concerned with the welfare of children,

Bearing in mind that, as indicated in the Declaration of the Rights of the Child, "the child, by reason of his physical and mental immaturity, needs special safeguards and care, including appropriate legal protection, before as well as after birth,"

Recalling the provisions of the Declaration on Social and Legal Principles relating to the Protection and Welfare of Children, with Special Reference to Foster Placement and Adoption Nationally and Internationally; the United Nations Standard Minimum Rules for the Administration of Juvenile Justice (The Beijing Rules); and the Declaration on the Protection of Women and Children in Emergency and Armed Conflict,

Recognizing that, in all countries in the world, there are children living in exceptionally difficult conditions, and that such children need special consideration,

Taking due account of the importance of the traditions and cultural values of each people for the protection and harmonious development of the child,

Recognizing the importance of international co-operation for improving the living conditions of children in every country, in particular in the developing countries, Have agreed as follows:

PART I

Article 1

For the purposes of the present Convention, a child means every human being below the age of eighteen years unless under the law applicable to the child, majority is attained earlier.

Article 2

1. States Parties shall respect and ensure the rights set forth in the present Convention to each child within their jurisdiction without discrimination of any kind, irrespective of the child's or his or her parent's or legal guardian's race, colour, sex, language, religion, political or other opinion, national, ethnic or social origin, property, disability, birth or other status.
2. States Parties shall take all appropriate measures to ensure that the child is protected against all forms of discrimination or punishment on the basis of the status, activities, expressed opinions, or beliefs of the child's parents, legal guardians, or family members.

Article 3

1. In all actions concerning children, whether undertaken by public or private social welfare institutions, courts of law, administrative authorities or legislative bodies, the best interests of the child shall be a primary consideration.
2. States Parties undertake to ensure the child such protection and care as is necessary for his or her well-being, taking into account the rights and duties of his or her parents, legal guardians, or other individuals legally responsible for him or her, and, to this end, shall take all appropriate legislative and administrative measures.
3. States Parties shall ensure that the institutions, services and facilities responsible for the care or protection of children shall conform with the standards established by

competent authorities, particularly in the areas of safety, health, in the number and suitability of their staff, as well as competent supervision.

Article 4

States Parties shall undertake all appropriate legislative, administrative, and other measures for the implementation of the rights recognized in the present Convention. With regard to economic, social and cultural rights, States Parties shall undertake such measures to the maximum extent of their available resources and, where needed, within the framework of international co-operation.

Article 5

States Parties shall respect the responsibilities, rights and duties of parents or, where applicable, the members of the extended family or community as provided for by local custom, legal guardians or other persons legally responsible for the child, to provide, in a manner consistent with the evolving capacities of the child, appropriate direction and guidance in the exercise by the child of the rights recognized in the present Convention.

Article 6

1. States Parties recognize that every child has the inherent right to life.
2. States Parties shall ensure to the maximum extent possible the survival and development of the child.

Article 7

1. The child shall be registered immediately after birth and shall have the right from birth to a name, the right to acquire a nationality and, as far as possible, the right to know and be cared for by his or her parents.
2. States Parties shall ensure the implementation of these rights in accordance with their national law and their obligations under the relevant international instruments in this field, in particular where the child would otherwise be stateless.

Article 8

1. States Parties undertake to respect the right of the child to preserve his or her identity, including nationality, name and family relations as recognized by law without unlawful interference.
2. Where a child is illegally deprived of some or all of the elements of his or her identity, States Parties shall provide appropriate assistance and protection, with a view to re-establishing speedily his or her identity.

Article 9

1. States Parties shall ensure that a child shall not be separated from his or her parents against their will, except when competent authorities subject to judicial review determine, in accordance with applicable law and procedures, that such separation is necessary for the best interests of the child. Such determination may be necessary in a particular case such as one involving abuse or neglect of the child by the parents, or one where the parents are living separately and a decision must be made as to the child's place of residence.
2. In any proceedings pursuant to paragraph 1 of the present article, all interested parties shall be given an opportunity to participate in the proceedings and make their views known.
3. States Parties shall respect the right of the child who is separated from one or both parents to maintain personal relations and direct contact with both parents on a regular basis, except if it is contrary to the child's best interests.

4. Where such separation results from any action initiated by a State Party, such as the detention, imprisonment, exile, deportation or death (including death arising from any cause while the person is in the custody of the State) of one or both parents or of the child, that State Party shall, upon request, provide the parents, the child or, if appropriate, another member of the family with the essential information concerning the whereabouts of the absent member(s) of the family unless the provision of the information would be detrimental to the well-being of the child. States Parties shall further ensure that the submission of such a request shall of itself entail no adverse consequences for the person(s) concerned.

Article 10

1. In accordance with the obligation of States Parties under article 9, paragraph 1, applications by a child or his or her parents to enter or leave a State Party for the purpose of family reunification shall be dealt with by States Parties in a positive, humane and expeditious manner. States Parties shall further ensure that the submission of such a request shall entail no adverse consequences for the applicants and for the members of their family.
2. A child whose parents reside in different States shall have the right to maintain on a regular basis, save in exceptional circumstances personal relations and direct contacts with both parents. Towards that end and in accordance with the obligation of States Parties under article 9, paragraph 1, States Parties shall respect the right of the child and his or her parents to leave any country, including their own, and to enter their own country. The right to leave any country shall be subject only to such restrictions as are prescribed by law and which are necessary to protect the national security, public order (ordre public), public health or morals or the rights and freedoms of others and are consistent with the other rights recognized in the present Convention.

Article 11

1. States Parties shall take measures to combat the illicit transfer and non-return of children abroad.
2. To this end, States Parties shall promote the conclusion of bilateral or multilateral agreements or accession to existing agreements.

Article 12

1. States Parties shall assure to the child who is capable of forming his or her own views the right to express those views freely in all matters affecting the child, the views of the child being given due weight in accordance with the age and maturity of the child.
2. For this purpose, the child shall in particular be provided the opportunity to be heard in any judicial and administrative proceedings affecting the child, either directly, or through a representative or an appropriate body, in a manner consistent with the procedural rules of national law.

Article 13

1. The child shall have the right to freedom of expression; this right shall include freedom to seek, receive and impart information and ideas of all kinds, regardless of frontiers, either orally, in writing or in print, in the form of art, or through any other media of the child's choice.
2. The exercise of this right may be subject to certain restrictions, but these shall only be such as are provided by law and are necessary:
   (a) For respect of the rights or reputations of others; or

(b) For the protection of national security or of public order (ordre public), or of public health or morals.

Article 14

1. States Parties shall respect the right of the child to freedom of thought, conscience and religion.
2. States Parties shall respect the rights and duties of the parents and, when applicable, legal guardians, to provide direction to the child in the exercise of his or her right in a manner consistent with the evolving capacities of the child.
3. Freedom to manifest one's religion or beliefs may be subject only to such limitations as are prescribed by law and are necessary to protect public safety, order, health or morals, or the fundamental rights and freedoms of others.

Article 15

1. States Parties recognize the rights of the child to freedom of association and to freedom of peaceful assembly.
2. No restrictions may be placed on the exercise of these rights other than those imposed in conformity with the law and which are necessary in a democratic society in the interests of national security or public safety, public order (ordre public), the protection of public health or morals or the protection of the rights and freedoms of others.

Article 16

1. No child shall be subjected to arbitrary or unlawful interference with his or her privacy, family, home or correspondence, nor to unlawful attacks on his or her honour and reputation.
2. The child has the right to the protection of the law against such interference or attacks.

Article 17

States Parties recognize the important function performed by the mass media and shall ensure that the child has access to information and material from a diversity of national and international sources, especially those aimed at the promotion of his or her social, spiritual and moral well-being and physical and mental health. To this end, States Parties shall:

(a) Encourage the mass media to disseminate information and material of social and cultural benefit to the child and in accordance with the spirit of article 29;

(b) Encourage international co-operation in the production, exchange and dissemination of such information and material from a diversity of cultural, national and international sources;

(c) Encourage the production and dissemination of children's books;

(d) Encourage the mass media to have particular regard to the linguistic needs of the child who belongs to a minority group or who is indigenous;

(e) Encourage the development of appropriate guidelines for the protection of the child from information and material injurious to his or her well-being, bearing in mind the provisions of articles 13 and 18.

Article 18

1. States Parties shall use their best efforts to ensure recognition of the principle that both parents have common responsibilities for the upbringing and development of

the child. Parents or, as the case may be, legal guardians, have the primary responsibility for the upbringing and development of the child. The best interests of the child will be their basic concern.

2. For the purpose of guaranteeing and promoting the rights set forth in the present Convention, States Parties shall render appropriate assistance to parents and legal guardians in the performance of their child-rearing responsibilities and shall ensure the development of institutions, facilities and services for the care of children.
3. States Parties shall take all appropriate measures to ensure that children of working parents have the right to benefit from child-care services and facilities for which they are eligible.

Article 19

1. States Parties shall take all appropriate legislative, administrative, social and educational measures to protect the child from all forms of physical or mental violence, injury or abuse, neglect or negligent treatment, maltreatment or exploitation, including sexual abuse, while in the care of parent(s), legal guardian(s) or any other person who has the care of the child.
2. Such protective measures should, as appropriate, include effective procedures for the establishment of social programmes to provide necessary support for the child and for those who have the care of the child, as well as for other forms of prevention and for identification, reporting, referral, investigation, treatment and follow-up of instances of child maltreatment described heretofore, and, as appropriate, for judicial involvement.

Article 20

1. A child temporarily or permanently deprived of his or her family environment, or in whose own best interests cannot be allowed to remain in that environment, shall be entitled to special protection and assistance provided by the State.
2. States Parties shall in accordance with their national laws ensure alternative care for such a child.
3. Such care could include, inter alia, foster placement, kafalah of Islamic law, adoption or if necessary placement in suitable institutions for the care of children. When considering solutions, due regard shall be paid to the desirability of continuity in a child's upbringing and to the child's ethnic, religious, cultural and linguistic background.

Article 21

States Parties that recognize and/or permit the system of adoption shall ensure that the best interests of the child shall be the paramount consideration and they shall:

(a) Ensure that the adoption of a child is authorized only by competent authorities who determine, in accordance with applicable law and procedures and on the basis of all pertinent and reliable information, that the adoption is permissible in view of the child's status concerning parents, relatives and legal guardians and that, if required, the persons concerned have given their informed consent to the adoption on the basis of such counselling as may be necessary;

(b) Recognize that inter-country adoption may be considered as an alternative means of child's care, if the child cannot be placed in a foster or an adoptive family or cannot in any suitable manner be cared for in the child's country of origin;

(c) Ensure that the child concerned by inter-country adoption enjoys safeguards and standards equivalent to those existing in the case of national adoption;

(d) Take all appropriate measures to ensure that, in inter-country adoption, the placement does not result in improper financial gain for those involved in it;

(e) Promote, where appropriate, the objectives of the present article by concluding bilateral or multilateral arrangements or agreements, and endeavour, within this framework, to ensure that the placement of the child in another country is carried out by competent authorities or organs.

Article 22

1. States Parties shall take appropriate measures to ensure that a child who is seeking refugee status or who is considered a refugee in accordance with applicable international or domestic law and procedures shall, whether unaccompanied or accompanied by his or her parents or by any other person, receive appropriate protection and humanitarian assistance in the enjoyment of applicable rights set forth in the present Convention and in other international human rights or humanitarian instruments to which the said States are Parties.
2. For this purpose, States Parties shall provide, as they consider appropriate, co-operation in any efforts by the United Nations and other competent intergovernmental organizations or non-governmental organizations co-operating with the United Nations to protect and assist such a child and to trace the parents or other members of the family of any refugee child in order to obtain information necessary for reunification with his or her family. In cases where no parents or other members of the family can be found, the child shall be accorded the same protection as any other child permanently or temporarily deprived of his or her family environment for any reason, as set forth in the present Convention.

Article 23

1. States Parties recognize that a mentally or physically disabled child should enjoy a full and decent life, in conditions which ensure dignity, promote self-reliance and facilitate the child's active participation in the community.
2. States Parties recognize the right of the disabled child to special care and shall encourage and ensure the extension, subject to available resources, to the eligible child and those responsible for his or her care, of assistance for which application is made and which is appropriate to the child's condition and to the circumstances of the parents or others caring for the child.
3. Recognizing the special needs of a disabled child, assistance extended in accordance with paragraph 2 of the present article shall be provided free of charge, whenever possible, taking into account the financial resources of the parents or others caring for the child, and shall be designed to ensure that the disabled child has effective access to and receives education, training, health care services, rehabilitation services, preparation for employment and recreation opportunities in a manner conducive to the child's achieving the fullest possible social integration and individual development, including his or her cultural and spiritual development.
4. States Parties shall promote, in the spirit of international cooperation, the exchange of appropriate information in the field of preventive health care and of medical, psychological and functional treatment of disabled children, including dissemination of and access to information concerning methods of rehabilitation, education and vocational services, with the aim of enabling States Parties to improve their capabilities and skills and to widen their experience in these areas. In this regard, particular account shall be taken of the needs of developing countries.

Article 24

1. States Parties recognize the right of the child to the enjoyment of the highest attainable standard of health and to facilities for the treatment of illness and rehabilitation of health. States Parties shall strive to ensure that no child is deprived of his or her right of access to such health care services.
2. States Parties shall pursue full implementation of this right and, in particular, shall take appropriate measures:
   (a) To diminish infant and child mortality;
   (b) To ensure the provision of necessary medical assistance and health care to all children with emphasis on the development of primary health care;
   (c) To combat disease and malnutrition, including within the framework of primary health care, through, inter alia, the application of readily available technology and through the provision of adequate nutritious foods and clean drinking-water, taking into consideration the dangers and risks of environmental pollution;
   (d) To ensure appropriate pre-natal and post-natal health care for mothers;
   (e) To ensure that all segments of society, in particular parents and children, are informed, have access to education and are supported in the use of basic knowledge of child health and nutrition, the advantages of breastfeeding, hygiene and environmental sanitation and the prevention of accidents;
   (f) To develop preventive health care, guidance for parents and family planning education and services.
3. States Parties shall take all effective and appropriate measures with a view to abolishing traditional practices prejudicial to the health of children.
4. States Parties undertake to promote and encourage international co-operation with a view to achieving progressively the full realization of the right recognized in the present article. In this regard, particular account shall be taken of the needs of developing countries.

Article 25

States Parties recognize the right of a child who has been placed by the competent authorities for the purposes of care, protection or treatment of his or her physical or mental health, to a periodic review of the treatment provided to the child and all other circumstances relevant to his or her placement.

Article 26

1. States Parties shall recognize for every child the right to benefit from social security, including social insurance, and shall take the necessary measures to achieve the full realization of this right in accordance with their national law.
2. The benefits should, where appropriate, be granted, taking into account the resources and the circumstances of the child and persons having responsibility for the maintenance of the child, as well as any other consideration relevant to an application for benefits made by or on behalf of the child.

Article 27

1. States Parties recognize the right of every child to a standard of living adequate for the child's physical, mental, spiritual, moral and social development.
2. The parent(s) or others responsible for the child have the primary responsibility to secure, within their abilities and financial capacities, the conditions of living necessary for the child's development.

3. States Parties, in accordance with national conditions and within their means, shall take appropriate measures to assist parents and others responsible for the child to implement this right and shall in case of need provide material assistance and support programmes, particularly with regard to nutrition, clothing and housing.
4. States Parties shall take all appropriate measures to secure the recovery of maintenance for the child from the parents or other persons having financial responsibility for the child, both within the State Party and from abroad. In particular, where the person having financial responsibility for the child lives in a State different from that of the child, States Parties shall promote the accession to international agreements or the conclusion of such agreements, as well as the making of other appropriate arrangements.

Article 28

1. States Parties recognize the right of the child to education, and with a view to achieving this right progressively and on the basis of equal opportunity, they shall, in particular:
   (a) Make primary education compulsory and available free to all;
   (b) Encourage the development of different forms of secondary education, including general and vocational education, make them available and accessible to every child, and take appropriate measures such as the introduction of free education and offering financial assistance in case of need;
   (c) Make higher education accessible to all on the basis of capacity by every appropriate means;
   (d) Make educational and vocational information and guidance available and accessible to all children;
   (e) Take measures to encourage regular attendance at schools and the reduction of drop-out rates.
2. States Parties shall take all appropriate measures to ensure that school discipline is administered in a manner consistent with the child's human dignity and in conformity with the present Convention.
3. States Parties shall promote and encourage international cooperation in matters relating to education, in particular with a view to contributing to the elimination of ignorance and illiteracy throughout the world and facilitating access to scientific and technical knowledge and modern teaching methods. In this regard, particular account shall be taken of the needs of developing countries.

Article 29

1. States Parties agree that the education of the child shall be directed to:
   (a) The development of the child's personality, talents and mental and physical abilities to their fullest potential;
   (b) The development of respect for human rights and fundamental freedoms, and for the principles enshrined in the Charter of the United Nations;
   (c) The development of respect for the child's parents, his or her own cultural identity, language and values, for the national values of the country in which the child is living, the country from which he or she may originate, and for civilizations different from his or her own;
   (d) The preparation of the child for responsible life in a free society, in the spirit of understanding, peace, tolerance, equality of sexes, and friendship among all peoples, ethnic, national and religious groups and persons of indigenous origin;

(e) The development of respect for the natural environment.

2. No part of the present article or article 28 shall be construed so as to interfere with the liberty of individuals and bodies to establish and direct educational institutions, subject always to the observance of the principle set forth in paragraph 1 of the present article and to the requirements that the education given in such institutions shall conform to such minimum standards as may be laid down by the State.

Article 30

In those States in which ethnic, religious or linguistic minorities or persons of indigenous origin exist, a child belonging to such a minority or who is indigenous shall not be denied the right, in community with other members of his or her group, to enjoy his or her own culture, to profess and practise his or her own religion, or to use his or her own language.

Article 31

1. States Parties recognize the right of the child to rest and leisure, to engage in play and recreational activities appropriate to the age of the child and to participate freely in cultural life and the arts.
2. States Parties shall respect and promote the right of the child to participate fully in cultural and artistic life and shall encourage the provision of appropriate and equal opportunities for cultural, artistic, recreational and leisure activity.

Article 32

States Parties recognize the right of the child to be protected from economic exploitation and from performing any work that is likely to be hazardous or to interfere with the child's education, or to be harmful to the child's health or physical, mental, spiritual, moral or social development.

States Parties shall take legislative, administrative, social and educational measures to ensure the implementation of the present article. To this end, and having regard to the relevant provisions of other international instruments, States Parties shall in particular:

(a) Provide for a minimum age or minimum ages for admission to employment;

(b) Provide for appropriate regulation of the hours and conditions of employment;

(c) Provide for appropriate penalties or other sanctions to ensure the effective enforcement of the present article.

Article 33

States Parties shall take all appropriate measures, including legislative, administrative, social and educational measures, to protect children from the illicit use of narcotic drugs and psychotropic substances as defined in the relevant international treaties, and to prevent the use of children in the illicit production and trafficking of such substances.

Article 34

States Parties undertake to protect the child from all forms of sexual exploitation and sexual abuse. For these purposes, States Parties shall in particular take all appropriate national, bilateral and multilateral measures to prevent:

(a) The inducement or coercion of a child to engage in any unlawful sexual activity;

(b) The exploitative use of children in prostitution or other unlawful sexual practices;

(c) The exploitative use of children in pornographic performances and materials.

Article 35

States Parties shall take all appropriate national, bilateral and multilateral measures to prevent the abduction of, the sale of or traffic in children for any purpose or in any form.

Article 36

States Parties shall protect the child against all other forms of exploitation prejudicial to any aspects of the child's welfare.

Article 37

States Parties shall ensure that:

(a) No child shall be subjected to torture or other cruel, inhuman or degrading treatment or punishment. Neither capital punishment nor life imprisonment without possibility of release shall be imposed for offences committed by persons below eighteen years of age;

(b) No child shall be deprived of his or her liberty unlawfully or arbitrarily. The arrest, detention or imprisonment of a child shall be in conformity with the law and shall be used only as a measure of last resort and for the shortest appropriate period of time;

(c) Every child deprived of liberty shall be treated with humanity and respect for the inherent dignity of the human person, and in a manner which takes into account the needs of persons of his or her age. In particular, every child deprived of liberty shall be separated from adults unless it is considered in the child's best interest not to do so and shall have the right to maintain contact with his or her family through correspondence and visits, save in exceptional circumstances;

(d) Every child deprived of his or her liberty shall have the right to prompt access to legal and other appropriate assistance, as well as the right to challenge the legality of the deprivation of his or her liberty before a court or other competent, independent and impartial authority, and to a prompt decision on any such action.

Article 38

1. States Parties undertake to respect and to ensure respect for rules of international humanitarian law applicable to them in armed conflicts which are relevant to the child.
2. States Parties shall take all feasible measures to ensure that persons who have not attained the age of fifteen years do not take a direct part in hostilities.
3. States Parties shall refrain from recruiting any person who has not attained the age of fifteen years into their armed forces. In recruiting among those persons who have attained the age of fifteen years but who have not attained the age of eighteen years, States Parties shall endeavour to give priority to those who are oldest.
4. In accordance with their obligations under international humanitarian law to protect the civilian population in armed conflicts, States Parties shall take all feasible measures to ensure protection and care of children who are affected by an armed conflict.

Article 39

States Parties shall take all appropriate measures to promote physical and psychological recovery and social reintegration of a child victim of: any form of neglect, exploitation, or abuse; torture or any other form of cruel, inhuman or degrading treatment or punishment; or armed conflicts. Such recovery and reintegration shall take place in an environment which fosters the health, self-respect and dignity of the child.

Article 40

1. States Parties recognize the right of every child alleged as, accused of, or recognized as having infringed the penal law to be treated in a manner consistent with the promotion of the child's sense of dignity and worth, which reinforces the child's respect for the human rights and fundamental freedoms of others and which takes into account the child's age and the desirability of promoting the child's reintegration and the child's assuming a constructive role in society.
2. To this end, and having regard to the relevant provisions of international instruments, States Parties shall, in particular, ensure that:
   - (a) No child shall be alleged as, be accused of, or recognized as having infringed the penal law by reason of acts or omissions that were not prohibited by national or international law at the time they were committed;
   - (b) Every child alleged as or accused of having infringed the penal law has at least the following guarantees:
     - (i) To be presumed innocent until proven guilty according to law;
     - (ii) To be informed promptly and directly of the charges against him or her, and, if appropriate, through his or her parents or legal guardians, and to have legal or other appropriate assistance in the preparation and presentation of his or her defence;
     - (iii) To have the matter determined without delay by a competent, independent and impartial authority or judicial body in a fair hearing according to law, in the presence of legal or other appropriate assistance and, unless it is considered not to be in the best interest of the child, in particular, taking into account his or her age or situation, his or her parents or legal guardians;
     - (iv) Not to be compelled to give testimony or to confess guilt; to examine or have examined adverse witnesses and to obtain the participation and examination of witnesses on his or her behalf under conditions of equality;
     - (v) If considered to have infringed the penal law, to have this decision and any measures imposed in consequence thereof reviewed by a higher competent, independent and impartial authority or judicial body according to law;
     - (vi) To have the free assistance of an interpreter if the child cannot understand or speak the language used;
     - (vii) To have his or her privacy fully respected at all stages of the proceedings.
3. States Parties shall seek to promote the establishment of laws, procedures, authorities and institutions specifically applicable to children alleged as, accused of, or recognized as having infringed the penal law, and, in particular:
   - (a) The establishment of a minimum age below which children shall be presumed not to have the capacity to infringe the penal law;
   - (b) Whenever appropriate and desirable, measures for dealing with such children without resorting to judicial proceedings, providing that human rights and legal safeguards are fully respected.
4. A variety of dispositions, such as care, guidance and supervision orders; counselling; probation; foster care; education and vocational training programmes and other alternatives to institutional care shall be available to ensure that children are dealt with in a manner appropriate to their well-being and proportionate both to their circumstances and the offence.

Article 41

Nothing in the present Convention shall affect any provisions which are more conducive to the realization of the rights of the child and which may be contained in:

(a) The law of a State party; or

(b) International law in force for that State.

PART II

Article 42

States Parties undertake to make the principles and provisions of the Convention widely known, by appropriate and active means, to adults and children alike.

Article 43

1. For the purpose of examining the progress made by States Parties in achieving the realization of the obligations undertaken in the present Convention, there shall be established a Committee on the Rights of the Child, which shall carry out the functions hereinafter provided.
2. The Committee shall consist of ten experts of high moral standing and recognized competence in the field covered by this Convention. The members of the Committee shall be elected by States Parties from among their nationals and shall serve in their personal capacity, consideration being given to equitable geographical distribution, as well as to the principal legal systems.
3. The members of the Committee shall be elected by secret ballot from a list of persons nominated by States Parties. Each State Party may nominate one person from among its own nationals.
4. The initial election to the Committee shall be held no later than six months after the date of the entry into force of the present Convention and thereafter every second year. At least four months before the date of each election, the Secretary-General of the United Nations shall address a letter to States Parties inviting them to submit their nominations within two months. The Secretary-General shall subsequently prepare a list in alphabetical order of all persons thus nominated, indicating States Parties which have nominated them, and shall submit it to the States Parties to the present Convention.
5. The elections shall be held at meetings of States Parties convened by the Secretary-General at United Nations Headquarters. At those meetings, for which two thirds of States Parties shall constitute a quorum, the persons elected to the Committee shall be those who obtain the largest number of votes and an absolute majority of the votes of the representatives of States Parties present and voting.
6. The members of the Committee shall be elected for a term of four years. They shall be eligible for re-election if renominated. The term of five of the members elected at the first election shall expire at the end of two years; immediately after the first election, the names of these five members shall be chosen by lot by the Chairman of the meeting.
7. If a member of the Committee dies or resigns or declares that for any other cause he or she can no longer perform the duties of the Committee, the State Party which nominated the member shall appoint another expert from among its nationals to serve for the remainder of the term, subject to the approval of the Committee.
8. The Committee shall establish its own rules of procedure.
9. The Committee shall elect its officers for a period of two years.

10. The meetings of the Committee shall normally be held at United Nations Headquarters or at any other convenient place as determined by the Committee. The Committee shall normally meet annually. The duration of the meetings of the Committee shall be determined, and reviewed, if necessary, by a meeting of the States Parties to the present Convention, subject to the approval of the General Assembly.
11. The Secretary-General of the United Nations shall provide the necessary staff and facilities for the effective performance of the functions of the Committee under the present Convention.
12. With the approval of the General Assembly, the members of the Committee established under the present Convention shall receive emoluments from United Nations resources on such terms and conditions as the Assembly may decide.

Article 44

1. States Parties undertake to submit to the Committee, through the Secretary-General of the United Nations, reports on the measures they have adopted which give effect to the rights recognized herein and on the progress made on the enjoyment of those rights:
   (a) Within two years of the entry into force of the Convention for the State Party concerned;
   (b) Thereafter every five years.
2. Reports made under the present article shall indicate factors and difficulties, if any, affecting the degree of fulfilment of the obligations under the present Convention. Reports shall also contain sufficient information to provide the Committee with a comprehensive understanding of the implementation of the Convention in the country concerned.
3. A State Party which has submitted a comprehensive initial report to the Committee need not, in its subsequent reports submitted in accordance with paragraph 1 (b) of the present article, repeat basic information previously provided.
4. The Committee may request from States Parties further information relevant to the implementation of the Convention.
5. The Committee shall submit to the General Assembly, through the Economic and Social Council, every two years, reports on its activities.
6. States Parties shall make their reports widely available to the public in their own countries.

Article 45

In order to foster the effective implementation of the Convention and to encourage international co-operation in the field covered by the Convention:

(a) The specialized agencies, the United Nations Children's Fund, and other United Nations organs shall be entitled to be represented at the consideration of the implementation of such provisions of the present Convention as fall within the scope of their mandate. The Committee may invite the specialized agencies, the United Nations Children's Fund and other competent bodies as it may consider appropriate to provide expert advice on the implementation of the Convention in areas falling within the scope of their respective mandates. The Committee may invite the specialized agencies, the United Nations Children's Fund, and other United Nations organs to submit reports on the implementation of the Convention in areas falling within the scope of their activities;

(b) The Committee shall transmit, as it may consider appropriate, to the specialized agencies, the United Nations Children's Fund and other competent bodies, any reports from States Parties that contain a request, or indicate a need, for technical advice or assistance, along with the Committee's observations and suggestions, if any, on these requests or indications;

(c) The Committee may recommend to the General Assembly to request the Secretary-General to undertake on its behalf studies on specific issues relating to the rights of the child;

(d) The Committee may make suggestions and general recommendations based on information received pursuant to articles 44 and 45 of the present Convention. Such suggestions and general recommendations shall be transmitted to any State Party concerned and reported to the General Assembly, together with comments, if any, from States Parties.

PART III

Article 46

The present Convention shall be open for signature by all States.

Article 47

The present Convention is subject to ratification. Instruments of ratification shall be deposited with the Secretary-General of the United Nations.

Article 48

The present Convention shall remain open for accession by any State. The instruments of accession shall be deposited with the Secretary-General of the United Nations.

Article 49

1. The present Convention shall enter into force on the thirtieth day following the date of deposit with the Secretary-General of the United Nations of the twentieth instrument of ratification or accession.
2. For each State ratifying or acceding to the Convention after the deposit of the twentieth instrument of ratification or accession, the Convention shall enter into force on the thirtieth day after the deposit by such State of its instrument of ratification or accession.

Article 50

1. Any State Party may propose an amendment and file it with the Secretary-General of the United Nations. The Secretary-General shall thereupon communicate the proposed amendment to States Parties, with a request that they indicate whether they favour a conference of States Parties for the purpose of considering and voting upon the proposals. In the event that, within four months from the date of such communication, at least one third of the States Parties favour such a conference, the Secretary-General shall convene the conference under the auspices of the United Nations. Any amendment adopted by a majority of States Parties present and voting at the conference shall be submitted to the General Assembly for approval.
2. An amendment adopted in accordance with paragraph 1 of the present article shall enter into force when it has been approved by the General Assembly of the United Nations and accepted by a two-thirds majority of States Parties.
3. When an amendment enters into force, it shall be binding on those States Parties which have accepted it, other States Parties still being bound by the provisions of the present Convention and any earlier amendments which they have accepted.

Article 51

1. The Secretary-General of the United Nations shall receive and circulate to all States the text of reservations made by States at the time of ratification or accession.
2. A reservation incompatible with the object and purpose of the present Convention shall not be permitted.
3. Reservations may be withdrawn at any time by notification to that effect addressed to the Secretary-General of the United Nations, who shall then inform all States. Such notification shall take effect on the date on which it is received by the Secretary-General.

Article 52

A State Party may denounce the present Convention by written notification to the Secretary-General of the United Nations. Denunciation becomes effective one year after the date of receipt of the notification by the Secretary-General.

Article 53

The Secretary-General of the United Nations is designated as the depositary of the present Convention.

Article 54

The original of the present Convention, of which the Arabic, Chinese, English, French, Russian and Spanish texts are equally authentic, shall be deposited with the Secretary-General of the United Nations.

IN WITNESS THEREOF the undersigned plenipotentiaries, being duly authorized thereto by their respective governments, have signed the present Convention.

DOCUMENT OF THE COPENHAGEN MEETING OF THE CONFERENCE ON THE HUMAN DIMENSION OF THE CONFERENCE ON SECURITY AND CO-OPERATION IN EUROPE

COPENHAGEN 1990

The representatives of the participating States of the Conference on Security and Co-operation in Europe (CSCE), Austria, Belgium, Bulgaria, Canada, Cyprus, Czechoslovakia, Denmark, Finland, France, the German Democratic Republic, the Federal Republic of Germany, Greece, the Holy See, Hungary, Iceland, Ireland, Italy, Liechtenstein, Luxembourg, Malta, Monaco, the Netherlands, Norway, Poland, Portugal, Romania, San Marino, Spain, Sweden, Switzerland, Turkey, the Union of Soviet Socialist Republics, the United Kingdom, the United States of America and Yugoslavia, met in Copenhagen from 5 to 29 June 1990, in accordance with the provisions relating to the Conference on the Human Dimension of the CSCE contained in the Concluding Document of the Vienna Follow-up Meeting of the CSCE.

The representative of eting was opened and closed by the Minister for Foreign Affairs of Denmark Albania attended the Copenhagen Meeting as observer.

The first Meeting of the Conference was held in Paris from 30 May to 23 June 1989.

The Copenhagen Meeting was opened and closed by the Minister for Foreign Affairs of Denmark.

The formal opening of the Copenhagen Meeting was attended by Her Majesty the Queen of Denmark and His Royal Highness the Prince Consort.

Opening statements were made by Ministers and Deputy Ministers of the participating States.

At a special meeting of the Ministers for Foreign Affairs of the participating States of the CSCE on 5 June 1990, convened on the invitation of the Minister for Foreign Affairs of Denmark, it was agreed to convene a Preparatory Committee in Vienna on 10 July 1990 to prepare a Summit Meeting in Paris of their Heads of State or Government.

The participating States welcome with great satisfaction the fundamental political changes that have occurred in Europe since the first Meeting of the Conference on the Human Dimension of the CSCE in Paris in 1989. They note that the CSCE process has contributed significantly to bringing about these changes and that these developments in turn have greatly advanced the implementation of the provisions of the Final Act and of the other CSCE documents.

They recognize that pluralistic democracy and the rule of law are essential for ensuring respect for all human rights and fundamental freedoms, the development of human contacts and the resolution of other issues of a related humanitarian character. They therefore welcome the commitment expressed by all participating States to the ideals of democracy and political pluralism as well as their common determination to build democratic societies based on free elections and the rule of law.

At the Copenhagen Meeting the participating States held a review of the implementation of their commitments in the field of the human dimension. They considered that the degree of compliance with the commitments contained in the relevant provisions of the CSCE documents had shown a fundamental improvement since the Paris Meeting. They also expressed the view, however, that further steps are required for the full realization of their commitments relating to the human dimension.

The participating States express their conviction that full respect for human rights and fundamental freedoms and the development of societies based on pluralistic democracy and the rule of law are prerequisites for progress in setting up the lasting order of peace, security, justice and co-operation that they seek to establish in Europe. They therefore reaffirm their commitment to implement fully all provisions of the Final Act and of the other CSCE documents relating to the human dimension and undertake to build on the progress they have made.

They recognize that co-operation among themselves, as well as the active involvement of persons, groups, organizations and institutions, will be essential to ensure continuing progress towards their shared objectives.

In order to strengthen respect for, and enjoyment of, human rights and fundamental freedoms, to develop human contacts and to resolve issues of a related humanitarian character, the participating States agree on the following:

I

(1). The participating States express their conviction that the protection and promotion of human rights and fundamental freedoms is one of the basic purposes of government, and reaffirm that the recognition of these rights and freedoms constitutes the foundation of freedom, justice and peace.

(2). They are determined to support and advance those principles of justice which form the basis of the rule of law. They consider that the rule of law does not mean merely a formal legality which assures regularity and consistency in the achievement and enforcement of democratic order, but justice based on the recognition and full acceptance of the supreme value of the human personality and guaranteed by institutions providing a framework for its fullest expression.

(3). They reaffirm that democracy is an inherent element of the rule of law. They recognize the importance of pluralism with regard to political organizations.

(4). They confirm that they will respect each others right freely to choose and develop, in accordance with international human rights standards, their political, social, economic and cultural systems. In exercising this right, they will ensure that their laws, regulations, practices and policies conform with their obligations under international law and are brought into harmony with the provisions of the Declaration on Principles and other CSCE commitments.

(5). They solemnly declare that among those elements of justice which are essential to the full expression of the inherent dignity and of the equal and inalienable rights of all human beings are the following:

(5.1). free elections that will be held at reasonable intervals by secret ballot or by equivalent free voting procedure, under conditions which ensure in practice the free expression of the opinion of the electors in the choice of their representatives;

(5.2). a form of government that is representative in character, in which the executive is accountable to the elected legislature or the electorate;

(5.3). the duty of the government and public authorities to comply with the constitution and to act in a manner consistent with law;

(5.4). a clear separation between the State and political parties; in particular, political parties will not be merged with the State;

(5.5). the activity of the government and the administration as well as that of the judiciary will be exercised in accordance with the system established by law. Respect for that system must be ensured;

(5.6). military forces and the police will be under the control of, and accountable to, the civil authorities;

(5.7). human rights and fundamental freedoms will be guaranteed by law and in accordance with their obligations under international law;

(5.8). legislation, adopted at the end of a public procedure, and regulations will be published, that being the condition for their applicability. Those texts will be accessible to everyone;

(5.9). all persons are equal before the law and are entitled without any discrimination to the equal protection of the law. In this respect, the law will prohibit any discrimination and guarantee to all persons equal and effective protection against discrimination on any ground;

(5.10). everyone will have an effective means of redress against administrative decisions, so as to guarantee respect for fundamental rights and ensure legal integrity;

(5.11). administrative decisions against a person must be fully justifiable and must as a rule indicate the usual remedies available;

(5.12). the independence of judges and the impartial operation of the public judicial service will be ensured;

(5.13). the independence of legal practitioners will be recognized and protected, in particular as regards conditions for recruitment and practice;

(5.14). the rules relating to criminal procedure will contain a clear definition of powers in relation to prosecution and the measures preceding and accompanying prosecution;

(5.15). any person arrested or detained on a criminal charge will have the right, so that the lawfulness of his arrest or detention can be decided, to be brought promptly before a judge or other officer authorized by law to exercise this function;

(5.16). in the determination of any criminal charge against him, or of his rights and obligations in a suit at law, everyone will be entitled to a fair and public hearing by a competent, independent and impartial tribunal established by law;

(5.17). any person prosecuted will have the right to defend himself in person or through prompt legal assistance of his own choosing or, if he does not have sufficient means to pay for legal assistance, to be given it free when the interests of justice so require;

(5.18). no one will be charged with, tried for or convicted of any criminal offence unless the offence is provided for by a law which defines the elements of the offence with clarity and precision;

(5.19). everyone will be presumed innocent until proved guilty according to law;

(5.20). considering the important contribution of international instruments in the field of human rights to the rule of law at a national level, the participating States reaffirm that they will consider acceding to the International Covenant on Civil and Political Rights, the International Covenant on Economic, Social and Cultural Rights and other relevant international instruments, if they have not yet done so;

(5.21). in order to supplement domestic remedies and better to ensure that the participating States respect the international obligations they have undertaken, the participating States will consider acceding to a regional or global international convention concerning the protection of human rights, such as the European Convention on Human Rights or the Optional Protocol to the International Covenant on Civil and Political Rights, which provide for procedures of individual recourse to international bodies.

(6). The participating States declare that the will of the people, freely and fairly expressed through periodic and genuine elections, is the basis of the authority and legitimacy of all government. The participating States will accordingly respect the right of their citizens to take part in the governing of their country, either directly or through representatives freely chosen by them through fair electoral processes. They recognize their responsibility to defend and protect, in accordance with their laws, their international human rights obligations and their international commitments, the democratic order freely established through the will of the people against the activities of persons, groups or organizations that engage in or refuse to renounce terrorism or violence aimed at the overthrow of that order or of that of another participating State.

(7). To ensure that the will of the people serves as the basis of the authority of government, the participating States will

(7.1). hold free elections at reasonable intervals, as established by law;

(7.2). permit all seats in at least one chamber of the national legislature to be freely contested in a popular vote;

(7.3). guarantee universal and equal suffrage to adult citizens;

(7.4). ensure that votes are cast by secret ballot or by equivalent free voting procedure, and that they are counted and reported honestly with the official results made public;

(7.5). respect the right of citizens to seek political or public office, individually or as representatives of political parties or organizations, without discrimination;

(7.6). respect the right of individuals and groups to establish, in full freedom, their own political parties or other political organizations and provide such political parties and organizations with the necessary legal guarantees to enable them to compete with each other on a basis of equal treatment before the law and by the authorities;

(7.7). ensure that law and public policy work to permit political campaigning to be conducted in a fair and free atmosphere in which neither administrative action, violence nor intimidation bars the parties and the candidates from freely presenting their views and qualifications, or prevents the voters from learning and discussing them or from casting their vote free of fear of retribution;

(7.8). provide that no legal or administrative obstacle stands in the way of unimpeded access to the media on a non-discriminatory basis for all political groupings and individuals wishing to participate in the electoral process;

(7.9). ensure that candidates who obtain the necessary number of votes required by law are duly installed in office and are permitted to remain in office until their term expires or is otherwise brought to an end in a manner that is regulated by law in conformity with democratic parliamentary and constitutional procedures.

(8). The participating States consider that the presence of observers, both foreign and domestic, can enhance the electoral process for States in which elections are taking place. They therefore invite observers from any other CSCE participating States and any appropriate private institutions and organizations who may wish to do so to observe the course of their national election proceedings, to the extent permitted by law. They will also endeavour to facilitate similar access for election proceedings held below the national level. Such observers will undertake not to interfere in the electoral proceedings.

II

(9). The participating States reaffirm that

(9.1). everyone will have the right to freedom of expression including the right to communication. This right will include freedom to hold opinions and to receive and impart information and ideas without interference by public authority and regardless of frontiers. The exercise of this right may be subject only to such restrictions as are prescribed by law and are consistent with international standards. In particular, no limitation will be imposed on access to, and use of, means of reproducing documents of any kind, while respecting, however, rights relating to intellectual property, including copyright;

(9.2). everyone will have the right of peaceful assembly and demonstration. Any restrictions which may be placed on the exercise of these rights will be prescribed by law and consistent with international standards;

(9.3). the right of association will be guaranteed. The right to form and subject to the general right of a trade union to determine its own membership freely to join a trade union will be guaranteed. These rights will exclude any prior control. Freedom of association for workers, including the freedom to strike, will be guaranteed, subject to limitations prescribed by law and consistent with international standards;

(9.4). everyone will have the right to freedom of thought, conscience and religion. This right includes freedom to change ones religion or belief and freedom to manifest ones religion or belief, either alone or in community with others, in public or in private, through worship, teaching, practice and observance. The exercise of these rights may be subject only to such restrictions as are prescribed by law and are consistent with international standards;

(9.5). they will respect the right of everyone to leave any country, including his own, and to return to his country, consistent with a States international obligations and CSCE commitments. Restrictions on this right will have the character of very rare exceptions, will be considered necessary only if they respond to a specific public need, pursue a legitimate aim and are proportionate to that aim, and will not be abused or applied in an arbitrary manner;

(9.6). everyone has the right peacefully to enjoy his property either on his own or in common with others. No one may be deprived of his property except in the public interest and subject to the conditions provided for by law and consistent with international commitments and obligations.

(10). In reaffirming their commitment to ensure effectively the rights of the individual to know and act upon human rights and fundamental freedoms, and to contribute actively, individually or in association with others, to their promotion and protection, the participating States express their commitment to

(10.1). respect the right of everyone, individually or in association with others, to seek, receive and impart freely views and information on human rights and fundamental freedoms, including the rights to disseminate and publish such views and information;

(10.2). respect the rights of everyone, individually or in association with others, to study and discuss the observance of human rights and fundamental freedoms and to develop and discuss ideas for improved protection of human rights and better means for ensuring compliance with international human rights standards;

(10.3). ensure that individuals are permitted to exercise the right to association, including the right to form, join and participate effectively in non-governmental organizations which seek the promotion and protection of human rights and fundamental freedoms, including trade unions and human rights monitoring groups;

(10.4). allow members of such groups and organizations to have unhindered access to and communication with similar bodies within and outside their countries and with international organizations, to engage in exchanges, contacts and co-operation with such groups and organizations and to solicit, receive and utilize for the purpose of promoting and protecting human rights and fundamental freedoms voluntary financial contributions from national and international sources as provided for by law.

(11). The participating States further affirm that, where violations of human rights and fundamental freedoms are alleged to have occurred, the effective remedies available include

(11.1). the right of the individual to seek and receive adequate legal assistance;

(11.2). the right of the individual to seek and receive assistance from others in defending human rights and fundamental freedoms, and to assist others in defending human rights and fundamental freedoms;

(11.3). the right of individuals or groups acting on their behalf to communicate with international bodies with competence to receive and consider information concerning allegations of human rights abuses.

(12). The participating States, wishing to ensure greater transparency in the implementation of the commitments undertaken in the Vienna Concluding Document under the heading of the human dimension of the CSCE, decide to accept as a confidence-building measure the presence of observers sent by participating States and representatives of non-governmental organizations and other interested persons at proceedings before courts as provided for in national legislation and international law; it is understood that proceedings may only be held *in camera* in the circumstances prescribed by law and consistent with obligations under international law and international commitments.

(13). The participating States decide to accord particular attention to the recognition of the rights of the child, his civil rights and his individual freedoms, his economic, social and cultural rights, and his right to special protection against all forms of violence and exploitation. They will consider acceding to the Convention on the Rights of the Child, if they have not yet done so, which was opened for signature by States on 26 January 1990. They will recognize in their domestic legislation the rights of the child as affirmed in the international agreements to which they are Parties.

(14). The participating States agree to encourage the creation, within their countries, of conditions for the training of students and trainees from other participating States, including persons taking vocational and technical courses. They also agree to promote travel by young people from their countries for the purpose of obtaining education in other participating States and to that end to encourage the conclusion, where appropriate, of bilateral and multilateral agreements between their relevant governmental institutions, organizations and educational establishments.

(15). The participating States will act in such a way as to facilitate the transfer of sentenced persons and encourage those participating States which are not Parties to the Convention on the Transfer of Sentenced Persons, signed at Strasbourg on 21 November 1983, to consider acceding to the Convention.

(16). The participating States

(16.1). reaffirm their commitment to prohibit torture and other cruel, inhuman or degrading treatment or punishment, to take effective legislative, administrative, judicial and other measures to prevent and punish such practices, to protect individuals from any psychiatric or other medical practices that violate human rights and fundamental freedoms and to take effective measures to prevent and punish such practices;

(16.2). intend, as a matter of urgency, to consider acceding to the Convention against Torture and Other Cruel, Inhuman or Degrading Treatment or Punishment, if they have not yet done so, and recognizing the competences of the Committee against Torture under articles 21 and 22 of the Convention and withdrawing reservations regarding the competence of the Committee under article 20;

(16.3). stress that no exceptional circumstances whatsoever, whether a state of war or a threat of war, internal political instability or any other public emergency, may be invoked as a justification of torture;

(16.4). will ensure that education and information regarding the prohibition against torture are fully included in the training of law enforcement personnel, civil or military, medical personnel, public officials and other persons who may be involved in the custody, interrogation or treatment of any individual subjected to any form of arrest, detention or imprisonment;

(16.5). will keep under systematic review interrogation rules, instructions, methods and practices as well as arrangements for the custody and treatment of persons subjected to any form of arrest, detention or imprisonment in any territory under their jurisdiction, with a view to preventing any cases of torture;

(16.6). will take up with priority for consideration and for appropriate action, in accordance with the agreed measures and procedures for the effective implementation of the commitments relating to the human dimension of the CSCE, any cases of torture and other inhuman or degrading treatment or punishment made known to them through official channels or coming from any other reliable source of information;

(16.7). will act upon the understanding that preserving and guaranteeing the life and security of any individual subjected to any form of torture and other inhuman or degrading treatment or punishment will be the sole criterion in determining the urgency and priorities to be accorded in taking appropriate remedial action; and, therefore, the consideration of any cases of torture and other inhuman or degrading treatment or punishment within the framework of any other international body or mechanism may not be invoked as a reason for refraining from consideration and appropriate action in accordance with the agreed measures and procedures for the effective implementation of the commitments relating to the human dimension of the CSCE.

(17). The participating States

(17.1). recall the commitment undertaken in the Vienna Concluding Document to keep the question of capital punishment under consideration and to co-operate within relevant international organizations;

(17.2). recall, in this context, the adoption by the General Assembly of the United Nations, on 15 December 1989, of the Second Optional Protocol to the International Covenant on Civil and Political Rights, aiming at the abolition of the death penalty;

(17.3). note the restrictions and safeguards regarding the use of the death penalty which have been adopted by the international community, in particular article 6 of the International Covenant on Civil and Political Rights;

(17.4). note the provisions of the Sixth Protocol to the European Convention for the Protection of Human Rights and Fundamental Freedoms, concerning the abolition of the death penalty;

(17.5). note recent measures taken by a number of participating States towards the abolition of capital punishment;

(17.6). note the activities of several non-governmental organizations on the question of the death penalty;

(17.7). will exchange information within the framework of the Conference on the Human Dimension on the question of the abolition of the death penalty and keep that question under consideration;

(17.8). will make available to the public information regarding the use of the death penalty.

(18). The participating States

(18.1). note that the United Nations Commission on Human Rights has recognized the right of everyone to have conscientious objections to military service;

(18.2). note recent measures taken by a number of participating States to permit exemption from compulsory military service on the basis of conscientious objections;

(18.3). note the activities of several non-governmental organizations on the question of conscientious objections to compulsory military service;

(18.4). agree to consider introducing, where this has not yet been done, various forms of alternative service, which are compatible with the reasons for conscientious objection, such forms of alternative service being in principle of a non-combatant or civilian nature, in the public interest and of a non-punitive nature;

(18.5). will make available to the public information on this issue;

(18.6). keep under consideration, within the framework of the Conference on the Human Dimension, the relevant questions related to the exemption from compulsory military service, where it exists, of individuals on the basis of conscientious objections to armed service, and will exchange information on these questions.

(19). The participating States affirm that freer movement and contacts among their citizens are important in the context of the protection and promotion of human rights and fundamental freedoms. They will ensure that their policies concerning entry into their territories are fully consistent with the aims set out in the relevant provisions of the Final Act, the Madrid Concluding Document and the Vienna Concluding Document. While reaffirming their determination not to recede from the commitments contained in CSCE documents, they undertake to implement fully and improve present commitments in the field of human contacts, including on a bilateral and multilateral basis. In this context they will

(19.1). strive to implement the procedures for entry into their territories, including the issuing of visas and passport and customs control, in good faith and without unjustified delay. Where necessary, they will shorten the waiting time for visa decisions, as well as simplify practices and reduce administrative requirements for visa applications;

(19.2). ensure, in dealing with visa applications, that these are processed as expeditiously as possible in order, *inter alia*, to take due account of important family, personal or professional considerations, especially in cases of an urgent, humanitarian nature;

(19.3). endeavour, where necessary, to reduce fees charged in connection with visa applications to the lowest possible level.

(20). The participating States concerned will consult and, where appropriate, cooperate in dealing with problems that might emerge as a result of the increased movement of persons.

(21). The participating States recommend the consideration, at the next CSCE Follow-up Meeting in Helsinki, of the advisability of holding a meeting of experts on consular matters.

(22). The participating States reaffirm that the protection and promotion of the rights of migrant workers have their human dimension. In this context, they

(22.1). agree that the protection and promotion of the rights of migrant workers are the concern of all participating States and that as such they should be addressed within the CSCE process;

(22.2). reaffirm their commitment to implement fully in their domestic legislation the rights of migrant workers provided for in international agreements to which they are parties;

(22.3). consider that, in future international instruments concerning the rights of migrant workers, they should take into account the fact that this issue is of importance for all of them;

(22.4). express their readiness to examine, at future CSCE meetings, the relevant aspects of the further promotion of the rights of migrant workers and their families.

(23). The participating States reaffirm their conviction expressed in the Vienna Concluding Document that the promotion of economic, social and cultural rights as well as of civil and political rights is of paramount importance for human dignity and for the attainment of the legitimate aspirations of every individual. They also reaffirm their commitment taken in the Document of the Bonn Conference on Economic Co-operation in Europe to the promotion of social justice and the improvement of living and working conditions. In the context of continuing their efforts with a view to achieving progressively the full realization of economic, social and cultural rights by all appropriate means, they will pay special attention to problems in the areas of employment, housing, social security, health, education and culture.

(24). The participating States will ensure that the exercise of all the human rights and fundamental freedoms set out above will not be subject to any restrictions except those which are provided by law and are consistent with their obligations under international law, in particular the International Covenant on Civil and Political Rights, and with their international commitments, in particular the Universal Declaration of Human Rights. These restrictions have the character of exceptions. The participating States will ensure that these restrictions are not abused and are not applied in an arbitrary manner, but in such a way that the effective exercise of these rights is ensured.

Any restriction on rights and freedoms must, in a democratic society, relate to one of the objectives of the applicable law and be strictly proportionate to the aim of that law.

(25). The participating States confirm that any derogations from obligations relating to human rights and fundamental freedoms during a state of public emergency must remain strictly within the limits provided for by international law, in particular the relevant international instruments by which they are bound, especially with respect to rights from which there can be no derogation. They also reaffirm that

(25.1). measures derogating from such obligations must be taken in strict conformity with the procedural requirements laid down in those instruments;

(25.2). the imposition of a state of public emergency must be proclaimed officially, publicly, and in accordance with the provisions laid down by law;

(25.3). measures derogating from obligations will be limited to the extent strictly required by the exigencies of the situation;

(25.4). such measures will not discriminate solely on the grounds of race, colour, sex, language, religion, social origin or of belonging to a minority.

III

(26). The participating States recognize that vigorous democracy depends on the existence as an integral part of national life of democratic values and practices as well as an extensive range of democratic institutions. They will therefore encourage, facilitate and, where appropriate, support practical co-operative endeavours and the sharing of information, ideas and expertise among themselves and by direct contacts and co-operation between individuals, groups and organizations in areas including the following:

- constitutional law, reform and development,
- electoral legislation, administration and observation,
- establishment and management of courts and legal systems,
- the development of an impartial and effective public service where recruitment and advancement are based on a merit system,
- law enforcement,
- local government and decentralization,
- access to information and protection of privacy,
- developing political parties and their role in pluralistic societies,
- free and independent trade unions,
- co-operative movements,
- developing other forms of free associations and public interest groups,
- journalism, independent media, and intellectual and cultural life,
- the teaching of democratic values, institutions and practices in educational institutions and the fostering of an atmosphere of free enquiry.

Such endeavours may cover the range of co-operation encompassed in the human dimension of the CSCE, including training, exchange of information, books and instructional materials, co-operative programmes and projects, academic and professional exchanges and conferences, scholarships, research grants, provision of expertise and advice, business and scientific contacts and programmes.

(27). The participating States will also facilitate the establishment and strengthening of independent national institutions in the area of human rights and the rule of law, which may also serve as focal points for co-ordination and collaboration between such institutions in the participating States. They propose that co-operation be encouraged between parliamentarians from participating States, including through existing inter-parliamentary associations and, *inter alia*, through joint commissions, television debates involving parliamentarians, meetings and round-table discussions. They will also encourage existing institutions, such as organizations within the United Nations system and the Council of Europe, to continue and expand the work they have begun in this area.

(28). The participating States recognize the important expertise of the Council of Europe in the field of human rights and fundamental freedoms and agree to consider further ways and means to enable the Council of Europe to make a contribution to the human dimension of the CSCE. They agree that the nature of this contribution could be examined further in a future CSCE forum.

(29). The participating States will consider the idea of convening a meeting or seminar of experts to review and discuss co-operative measures designed to promote and sustain viable democratic institutions in participating States, including comparative studies of legislation in participating States in the area of human rights and fundamental freedoms, *inter alia* drawing upon the experience acquired in this area by the Council of Europe and the activities of the Commission "Democracy through Law".

IV

(30). The participating States recognize that the questions relating to national minorities can only be satisfactorily resolved in a democratic political framework based on the rule of law, with a functioning independent judiciary. This framework guarantees full respect for human rights and fundamental freedoms, equal rights and status for all citizens, the free expression of all their legitimate interests and aspirations, political pluralism, social tolerance and the implementation of legal rules that place effective restraints on the abuse of governmental power.

They also recognize the important role of non-governmental organizations, including political parties, trade unions, human rights organizations and religious groups, in the promotion of tolerance, cultural diversity and the resolution of questions relating to national minorities.

They further reaffirm that respect for the rights of persons belonging to national minorities as part of universally recognized human rights is an essential factor for peace, justice, stability and democracy in the participating States.

(31). Persons belonging to national minorities have the right to exercise fully and effectively their human rights and fundamental freedoms without any discrimination and in full equality before the law.

The participating States will adopt, where necessary, special measures for the purpose of ensuring to persons belonging to national minorities full equality with the other citizens in the exercise and enjoyment of human rights and fundamental freedoms.

(32). To belong to a national minority is a matter of a persons individual choice and no disadvantage may arise from the exercise of such choice.

Persons belonging to national minorities have the right freely to express, preserve and develop their ethnic, cultural, linguistic or religious identity and to maintain and develop their culture in all its aspects, free of any attempts at assimilation against their will. In particular, they have the right

(32.1). to use freely their mother tongue in private as well as in public;

(32.2). to establish and maintain their own educational, cultural and religious institutions, organizations or associations, which can seek voluntary financial and other contributions as well as public assistance, in conformity with national legislation;

(32.3). to profess and practise their religion, including the acquisition, possession and use of religious materials, and to conduct religious educational activities in their mother tongue;

(32.4). to establish and maintain unimpeded contacts among themselves within their country as well as contacts across frontiers with citizens of other States with whom they share a common ethnic or national origin, cultural heritage or religious beliefs;

(32.5). to disseminate, have access to and exchange information in their mother tongue;

(32.6). to establish and maintain organizations or associations within their country and to participate in international non-governmental organizations.

Persons belonging to national minorities can exercise and enjoy their rights individually as well as in community with other members of their group. No disadvantage may arise for a person belonging to a national minority on account of the exercise or non-exercise of any such rights.

(33). The participating States will protect the ethnic, cultural, linguistic and religious identity of national minorities on their territory and create conditions for the promotion of that identity. They will take the necessary measures to that effect after due consultations, including contacts with organizations or associations of such minorities, in accordance with the decision-making procedures of each State.

Any such measures will be in conformity with the principles of equality and non-discrimination with respect to the other citizens of the participating State concerned.

(34). The participating States will endeavour to ensure that persons belonging to national minorities, notwithstanding the need to learn the official language or languages of the State concerned, have adequate opportunities for instruction of their mother tongue or in their mother tongue, as well as, wherever possible and necessary, for its use before public authorities, in conformity with applicable national legislation.

In the context of the teaching of history and culture in educational establishments, they will also take account of the history and culture of national minorities.

(35). The participating States will respect the right of persons belonging to national minorities to effective participation in public affairs, including participation in the affairs relating to the protection and promotion of the identity of such minorities.

The participating States note the efforts undertaken to protect and create conditions for the promotion of the ethnic, cultural, linguistic and religious identity of certain national minorities by establishing, as one of the possible means to achieve these aims, appropriate local or autonomous administrations corresponding to the specific historical and territorial circumstances of such minorities and in accordance with the policies of the State concerned.

(36). The participating States recognize the particular importance of increasing constructive co-operation among themselves on questions relating to national minorities. Such co-operation seeks to promote mutual understanding and confidence, friendly and good-neighbourly relations, international peace, security and justice.

Every participating State will promote a climate of mutual respect, understanding, co-operation and solidarity among all persons living on its territory, without distinction as to ethnic or national origin or religion, and will encourage the solution of problems through dialogue based on the principles of the rule of law.

(37). None of these commitments may be interpreted as implying any right to engage in any activity or perform any action in contravention of the purposes and principles of the Charter of the United Nations, other obligations under international law or the provisions of the Final Act, including the principle of territorial integrity of States.

(38). The participating States, in their efforts to protect and promote the rights of persons belonging to national minorities, will fully respect their undertakings under existing human rights conventions and other relevant international instruments and consider adhering to the relevant conventions, if they have not yet done so, including those providing for a right of complaint by individuals.

(39). The participating States will co-operate closely in the competent international organizations to which they belong, including the United Nations and, as appropriate, the Council of Europe, bearing in mind their on-going work with respect to questions relating to national minorities.

They will consider convening a meeting of experts for a thorough discussion of the issue of national minorities.

(40). The participating States clearly and unequivocally condemn totalitarianism, racial and ethnic hatred, anti-semitism, xenophobia and discrimination against anyone as well as persecution on religious and ideological grounds. In this context, they also recognize the particular problems of Roma (gypsies).

They declare their firm intention to intensify the efforts to combat these phenomena in all their forms and therefore will

(40.1). take effective measures, including the adoption, in conformity with their constitutional systems and their international obligations, of such laws as may be necessary, to provide protection against any acts that constitute incitement to violence against persons or groups based on national, racial, ethnic or religious discrimination, hostility or hatred, including anti-semitism;

(40.2). commit themselves to take appropriate and proportionate measures to protect persons or groups who may be subject to threats or acts of discrimination, hostility or violence as a result of their racial, ethnic, cultural, linguistic or religious identity, and to protect their property;

(40.3). take effective measures, in conformity with their constitutional systems, at the national, regional and local levels to promote understanding and tolerance, particularly in the fields of education, culture and information;

(40.4). endeavour to ensure that the objectives of education include special attention to the problem of racial prejudice and hatred and to the development of respect for different civilizations and cultures;

(40.5). recognize the right of the individual to effective remedies and endeavour to recognize, in conformity with national legislation, the right of interested persons and groups to initiate and support complaints against acts of discrimination, including racist and xenophobic acts;

(40.6). consider adhering, if they have not yet done so, to the international instruments which address the problem of discrimination and ensure full compliance with the obligations therein, including those relating to the submission of periodic reports;

(40.7). consider, also, accepting those international mechanisms which allow States and individuals to bring communications relating to discrimination before international bodies.

V

(41). The participating States reaffirm their commitment to the human dimension of the CSCE and emphasize its importance as an integral part of a balanced approach to security and co-operation in Europe. They agree that the Conference on the Human Dimension of the CSCE and the human dimension mechanism described in the section on the human dimension of the CSCE of the Vienna Concluding Document have demonstrated their value as methods of furthering their dialogue and co-operation and assisting in the resolution of relevant specific questions. They express their conviction that these should be continued and developed as part of an expanding CSCE process.

(42). The participating States recognize the need to enhance further the effectiveness of the procedures described in paragraphs 1 to 4 of the section on the human dimension of the CSCE of the Vienna Concluding Document and with this aim decide

(42.1). to provide in as short a time as possible, but no later than four weeks, a written response to requests for information and to representations made to them in writing by other participating States under paragraph 1;

(42.2). that the bilateral meetings, as contained in paragraph 2, will take place as soon as possible, as a rule within three weeks of the date of the request;

(42.3). to refrain, in the course of a bilateral meeting held under paragraph 2, from raising situations and cases not connected with the subject of the meeting, unless both sides have agreed to do so.

(43). The participating States examined practical proposals for new measures aimed at improving the implementation of the commitments relating to the human dimension of the CSCE. In this regard, they considered proposals related to the sending of observers to examine situations and specific cases, the appointment of rapporteurs to investigate and suggest appropriate solutions, the setting up of a Committee on the Human Dimension of the CSCE, greater involvement of persons, organizations and institutions in the human dimension mechanism and further bilateral and multilateral efforts to promote the resolution of relevant issues.

They decide to continue to discuss thoroughly in subsequent relevant CSCE fora these and other proposals designed to strengthen the human dimension mechanism, and to consider adopting, in the context of the further development of the CSCE process, appropriate new measures. They agree that these measures should contribute to achieving further effective progress, enhance conflict prevention and confidence in the field of the human dimension of the CSCE.

* * *

(44). The representatives of the participating States express their profound gratitude to the people and Government of Denmark for the excellent organization of the Copenhagen Meeting and the warm hospitality extended to the delegations which participated in the Meeting.

(45). In accordance with the provisions relating to the Conference on the Human Dimension of the CSCE contained in the Concluding Document of the Vienna Follow-up Meeting of the CSCE, the third Meeting of the Conference will take place in Moscow from 10 September to 4 October 1991.

Copenhagen, 29 June 1990

CHAIRMAN'S STATEMENT ON THE ACCESS OF NON-GOVERNMENTAL ORGANIZATIONS AND THE MEDIA TO MEETINGS OF THE CONFERENCE ON THE HUMAN DIMENSION

The Chairman notes that the practices of openness and access to the Meetings of the Conference on the Human Dimension, as they were applied at the Vienna Meeting and as contained in Annex XI of the Concluding Document of that Meeting, are of importance to all participating States. In order to follow and build upon those practices at forthcoming CSCE meetings of the Conference on the Human Dimension, the participating States agree that the following practices of openness and access should be respected:

- free movement by members of interested non-governmental organizations (NGOs) in the Conference premises, except for the areas restricted to delegations and to the services of the Executive Secretariat. Accordingly, badges will be issued to them, at their request, by the Executive Secretariat;
- unimpeded contacts between members of interested NGOs and delegates, as well as with accredited representatives of the media;
- access to official documents of the Conference in all the working languages and also to any document that delegates might wish to communicate to members of interested NGOs;
- the opportunity for members of interested NGOs to transmit to delegates communications relating to the human dimension of the CSCE. Mailboxes for each delegation will be accessible to them for this purpose;
- free access for delegates to all documents emanating from interested NGOs and addressed to the Executive Secretariat for the information of the Conference. Accordingly, the Executive Secretariat will make available to delegates a regularly updated collection of such documents.

They further undertake to guarantee to representatives of the media

- free movement in the Conference premises, except for the areas restricted to delegations and to the services of the Executive Secretariat. Accordingly, badges will be issued to them by the Executive Secretariat upon presentation of the requisite credentials;
- unimpeded contacts with delegates and with members of interested NGOs;

- access to official documents of the Conference in all the working languages.

The Chairman notes further that this statement will be an Annex to the Document of the Copenhagen Meeting and will be published with it.

WORLD DECLARATION ON EDUCATION FOR ALL

MEETING BASIC LEARNING NEEDS

PREAMBLE

More than 40 years ago, the nations of the world, speaking through the *Universal Declaration of Human Rights*, asserted that "everyone has a right to education".

Despite notable efforts by countries around the globe to ensure the right to education for all, the following realities persist:

More than 100 million children, including at least 60 million girls, have no access to primary schooling;

More than 960 million adults, two-thirds of whom are women, are illiterate, and functional illiteracy is a significant problem in all countries, industrialized and developing;

More than one-third of the world's adults have no access to the printed knowledge, new skills and technologies that could improve the quality of their lives and help them shape, and adapt to, social and cultural change; and

More than 100 million children and countless adults fail to complete basic education programmes; millions more satisfy the attendance requirements but do not acquire essential knowledge and skills;

At the same time, the world faces daunting problems: notably mounting debt burdens, the threat of economic stagnation and decline, rapid population growth, widening economic disparities among and within nations, war, occupation, civil strife, violent crime, the preventable deaths of millions of children and widespread environmental degradation. These problems constrain efforts to meet basic learning needs, while the lack of basic education among a significant proportion of the population prevents societies from addressing such problems with strength and purpose.

These problems have led to major setbacks in basic education in the 1980s in many of the least developed countries. In some other countries, economic growth has been available to finance education expansion, but even so, many millions remain in poverty and unschooled or illiterate. In certain industrialized countries too, cutbacks in government expenditure over the 1980s have led to the deterioration of education

Yet the world is also at the threshold of a new century, with all its promise and possibilities. Today, there is genuine progress toward peaceful detente and greater cooperation among nations. Today, the essential rights and capacities of women are being realized. Today, there are many useful scientific and cultural developments. Today, the sheer quantity of information available in the world—much of it relevant to survival and basic well-being—is exponentially greater than that available only a few years ago, and the rate of its growth is accelerating. This includes information about obtaining more life-enhancing knowledge—or learning how to learn. A synergistic effect occurs when important information is coupled with another modern advance—our new capacity to communicate. These new forces, when combined with the cumulative experience of reform, innovation, research and the remarkable educational progress of many countries, make the goal of basic education for all—for the first time in history—an attainable goal.

Therefore, we participants in the World Conference on Education for All, assembled in Jomtien, Thailand, from 5 to 9 March, 1990:

- Recalling that education is a fundamental right for all people, women and men, of all ages, throughout our world;
- Understanding that education can help ensure a safer, healthier, more prosperous and environmentally sound world, while simultaneously contributing to social, economic, and cultural progress, tolerance, and international cooperation;
- Knowing that education is an indispensable key to, though not a sufficient condition for, personal and social improvement;
- Recognizing that traditional knowledge and indigenous cultural heritage have a value and validity in their own right and a capacity to both define and promote development;
- Acknowledging that, overall, the current provision of education is seriously deficient and that it must be made more relevant and qualitatively improved, and made universally available;
- Recognizing that sound basic education is fundamental to the strengthening of higher levels of education and of scientific and technological literacy and capacity and thus to self-reliant development; and
- Recognizing the necessity to give to present and coming generations an expanded vision of, and a renewed commitment to, basic education to address the scale and complexity of the challenge; proclaim the following

EDUCATION FOR ALL: THE PURPOSE

ARTICLE I—MEETING BASIC LEARNING NEEDS

1. Every person—child, youth and adult—shall be able to benefit from educational opportunities designed to meet their basic learning needs. These needs comprise both essential learning tools (such as literacy, oral expression, numeracy, and problem solving) and the basic learning content (such as knowledge, skills, values, and attitudes) required by human beings to be able to survive, to develop their full capacities, to live and work in dignity, to participate fully in development, to improve the quality of their lives, to make informed decisions, and to continue learning. The scope of basic learning needs and how they should be met varies with individual countries and cultures, and inevitably, changes with the passage of time.
2. The satisfaction of these needs empowers individuals in any society and confers upon them a responsibility to respect and build upon their collective cultural, linguistic and spiritual heritage, to promote the education of others, to further the cause of social justice, to achieve environmental protection, to be tolerant towards social, political and religious systems which differ from their own, ensuring that commonly accepted humanistic values and human rights are upheld, and to work for international peace and solidarity in an interdependent world.
3. Another and no less fundamental aim of educational development is the transmission and enrichment of common cultural and moral values. It is in these values that the individual and society find their identity and worth.
4. Basic education is more than an end in itself. It is the foundation for lifelong learning and human development on which countries may build, systematically, further levels and types of education and training.

EDUCATION FOR ALL: AN EXPANDED VISION AND A RENEWED COMMITMENT

ARTICLE II—SHAPING THE VISION

To serve the basic learning needs of all requires more than a recommitment to basic education as it now exists. What is needed is an "expanded vision" that surpasses present resource levels, institutional structures, curricula, and conventional delivery systems while building on the best in current practices. New possibilities exist today which result from the convergence of the increase in information and the unprecedented capacity to communicate. We must seize them with creativity and a determination for increased effectiveness. As elaborated in Articles III-VII, the expanded vision encompasses:

Universalizing access and promoting equity;

Focussing on learning;

Broadening the means and scope of basic education;

Enhancing the environment for learning;

Strengthening partnerships.

The realization of an enormous potential for human progress and empowerment is contingent upon whether people can be enabled to acquire the education and the start needed to tap into the ever-expanding pool of relevant knowledge and the new means for sharing this knowledge.

ARTICLE III—UNIVERSALIZING ACCESS AND PROMOTING EQUITY

1. Basic education should be provided to all children, youth and adults. To this end, basic education services of quality should be expanded and consistent measures must be taken to reduce disparities.
2. For basic education to be equitable, all children, youth and adults must be given the opportunity to achieve and maintain an acceptable level of learning.
3. The most urgent priority is to ensure access to, and improve the quality of, education for girls and women, and to remove every obstacle that hampers their active participation. All gender stereotyping in education should be eliminated.
4. An active commitment must be made to removing educational disparities. Underserved groups: the poor; street and working children; rural and remote populations; nomads and migrant workers; indigenous peoples; ethnic, racial, and linguistic minorities; refugees; those displaced by war; and people under occupation, should not suffer any discrimination in access to learning opportunities.
5. The learning needs of the disabled demand special attention. Steps need to be taken to provide equal access to education to every category of disabled persons as an integral part of the education system.

ARTICLE IV—FOCUSING ON LEARNING

Whether or not expanded educational opportunities will translate into meaningful development—for an individual or for society— depends ultimately on whether people actually learn as a result of those opportunities, i.e., whether they incorporate useful knowledge, reasoning ability, skills, and values. The focus of basic education must, therefore, be on actual learning acquisition and outcome, rather than exclusively upon enrolment, continued participation in organized programmes and completion of certification requirements. Active and participatory approaches are particularly valuable in assuring learning acquisition and allowing learners to reach their fullest potential. It is, therefore, necessary to define acceptable levels of learning acquisition for educational programmes and to improve and apply systems of assessing learning achievement.

ARTICLE V—BROADENING THE MEANS AND SCOPE OF BASIC EDUCATION

The diversity, complexity, and changing nature of basic learning needs of children, youth and adults necessitates broadening and constantly redefining the scope of basic education to include the following components:

Learning begins at birth. This calls for early childhood care and initial education. These can be provided through arrangements involving families, communities, or institutional programmes, as appropriate.

The main delivery system for the basic education of children outside the family is primary schooling. Primary education must be universal, ensure that the basic learning needs of all children are satisfied, and take into account the culture, needs, and opportunities of the community. Supplementary alternative programmes can help meet the basic learning needs of children with limited or no access to formal schooling, provided that they share the same standards of learning applied to schools, and are adequately supported.

The basic learning needs of youth and adults are diverse and should be met through a variety of delivery systems. Literacy programmes are indispensable because literacy is a necessary skill in itself and the foundation of other life skills. Literacy in the mother-tongue strengthens cultural identity and heritage. Other needs can be served by: skills training, apprenticeships, and formal and non-formal education programmes in health, nutrition, population, agricultural techniques, the environment, science, technology, family life, including fertility awareness, and other societal issues.

All available instruments and channels of information, communications, and social action could be used to help convey essential knowledge and inform and educate people on social issues. In addition to the traditional means, libraries, television, radio and other media can be mobilized to realize their potential towards meeting basic education needs of all.

These components should constitute an integrated system—complementary, mutually reinforcing, and of comparable standards, and they should contribute to creating and developing possibilities for lifelong learning.

ARTICLE VI—ENHANCING THE ENVIRONMENT FOR LEARNING

Learning does not take place in isolation. Societies, therefore, must ensure that all learners receive the nutrition, health care, and general physical and emotional support they need in order to participate actively in and benefit from their education. Knowledge and skills that will enhance the learning environment of children should be integrated into community learning programmes for adults. The education of children and their parents or other caretakers is mutually supportive and this interaction should be used to create, for all, a learning environment of vibrancy and warmth.

ARTICLE VII—STRENGTHENING PARTNERSHIPS

National, regional, and local educational authorities have a unique obligation to provide basic education for all, but they cannot be expected to supply every human, financial or organizational requirement for this task. New and revitalized partnerships at all levels will be necessary: partnerships among all sub-sectors and forms of education, recognizing the special role of teachers and that of administrators and other educational personnel; partnerships between education and other government departments, including planning, finance, labour, communications, and other social sectors; partnerships between government and non-governmental organizations, the private sector, local communities, religious groups, and families. The recognition of the vital role of both families and teachers is particularly important. In this context, the terms and conditions of service of teachers and their status, which constitute a determining factor in the implementation of education for all, must be urgently improved in all countries in line with the joint ILO/UNESCO Recommendation Concerning the Status of Teachers (1966). Genuine partnerships contribute to the planning, implementing, managing and evaluating of basic education programmes. When we speak of "an expanded vision and a renewed commitment", partnerships are at the heart of it.

EDUCATION FOR ALL: THE REQUIREMENTS

ARTICLE VIII—DEVELOPING A SUPPORTIVE POLICY CONTEXT

1. Supportive policies in the social, cultural, and economic sectors are required in order to realize the full provision and utitlization of basic education for individual and societal improvement. The provision of basic education for all depends on political commitment and political will backed by appropriate fiscal measures and reinforced by educational policy reforms and institutional strengthening. Suitable economic, trade, labour, employment and health policies will enhance learners' incentives and contributions to societal development.
2. Societies should also insure a strong intellectual and scientific environment for basic education. This implies improving higher education and developing scientific research. Close contact with contemporary technological and scientific knowledge should be possible at every level of education.

ARTICLE IX—MOBILIZING RESOURCES

1. If the basic learning needs of all are to be met through a much broader scope of action than in the past, it will be essential to mobilize existing and new financial and human resources, public, private and voluntary. All of society has a contribution to make, recognizing that time, energy and funding directed to basic education are perhaps the most profound investment in people and in the future of a country which can be made.
2. Enlarged public-sector support means drawing on the resources of all the government agencies responsible for human development, through increased absolute and proportional allocations to basic education services with the clear recognition of competing claims on national resources of which education is an important one, but not the only one. Serious attention to improving the efficiency of existing educational resources and programmes will not only produce more, it can also be expected to attract new resources. The urgent task of meeting basic learning needs may require a reallocation between sectors, as, for example, a transfer from military to educational expenditure. Above all, special protection for basic education will be required in countries undergoing structural adjustment and facing severe external debt burdens. Today, more than ever, education must be seen as a fundamental dimension of any social, cultural, and economic design.

ARTICLE X—STRENGTHENING INTERNATIONAL SOLIDARITY

1. Meeting basic learning needs constitutes a common and universal human responsibility. It requires international solidarity and equitable and fair economic relations in order to redress existing economic disparities. All nations have valuable knowledge and experiences to share for designing effective educational policies and programmes.
2. Substantial and long-term increases in resources for basic education will be needed. The world community, including intergovernmental agencies and institutions, has an

urgent responsibility to alleviate the constraints that prevent some countries from achieving the goal of education for all. It will mean the adoption of measures that augment the national budgets of the poorest countries or serve to relieve heavy debt burdens. Creditors and debtors must seek innovative and equitable formulae to resolve these burdens, since the capacity of many developing countries to respond effectively to education and other basic needs will be greatly helped by finding solutions to the debt problem.

3. Basic learning needs of adults and children must be addressed wherever they exist. Least developed and low-income countries have special needs which require priority in international support for basic education in the 1990s.
4. All nations must also work together to resolve conflicts and strife, to end military occupations, and to settle displaced populations, or to facilitate their return to their countries of origin, and ensure that their basic learning needs are met. Only a stable and peaceful environment can create the conditions in which every human being, child and adult alike, may benefit from the goals of this Declaration.

We, the participants in the World Conference on Education for All, reaffirm the right of all people to education. This is the foundation of our determination, singly and together, to ensure education for all.

We commit ourselves to act cooperatively through our own spheres of responsibility, taking all necessary steps to achieve the goals of education for all. Together we call on governments, concerned organizations and individuals to join in this urgent undertaking.

The basic learning needs of all can and must be met. There can be no more meaningful way to begin the International Literacy Year, to move forward the goals of the United Nations Decade of Disabled Persons (1983–92), the World Decade for Cultural Development (1988–97), the Fourth United Nations Development Decade (1991–2000), of the Convention on the Elimination of Discrimination against Women and the Forward Looking Strategies for the Advancement of Women, and of the Convention on the Rights of the Child. There has never been a more propitious time to commit ourselves to providing basic learning opportunities for all the people of the world.

We adopt, therefore, this World Declaration on Education for All: Meeting Basic Learning Needs and agree on the *Framework for Action to Meet Basic Learning Needs*, to achieve the goals set forth in this *Declaration.*

DECLARATION ON THE RIGHTS OF PERSONS BELONGING TO NATIONAL OR ETHNIC, RELIGIOUS AND LINGUISTIC MINORITIES

Adopted by General Assembly resolution 47/135 of 18 December 1992

The General Assembly,

Reaffirming that one of the basic aims of the United Nations, as proclaimed in the Charter, is to promote and encourage respect for human rights and for fundamental freedoms for all, without distinction as to race, sex, language or religion,

Reaffirming faith in fundamental human rights, in the dignity and worth of the human person, in the equal rights of men and women and of nations large and small,

Desiring to promote the realization of the principles contained in the Charter, the Universal Declaration of Human Rights, the Convention on the Prevention and Punishment of the

Crime of Genocide, the International Convention on the Elimination of All Forms of Racial Discrimination, the International Covenant on Civil and Political Rights, the International Covenant on Economic, Social and Cultural Rights, the Declaration on the Elimination of All Forms of Intolerance and of Discrimination Based on Religion or Belief, and the Convention on the Rights of the Child, as well as other relevant international instruments that have been adopted at the universal or regional level and those concluded between individual States Members of the United Nations,

Inspired by the provisions of article 27 of the International Covenant on Civil and Political Rights concerning the rights of persons belonging to ethnic, religious and linguistic minorities,

Considering that the promotion and protection of the rights of persons belonging to national or ethnic, religious and linguistic minorities contribute to the political and social stability of States in which they live,

Emphasizing that the constant promotion and realization of the rights of persons belonging to national or ethnic, religious and linguistic minorities, as an integral part of the development of society as a whole and within a democratic framework based on the rule of law, would contribute to the strengthening of friendship and cooperation among peoples and States,

Considering that the United Nations has an important role to play regarding the protection of minorities,

Bearing in mind the work done so far within the United Nations system, in particular by the Commission on Human Rights, the Subcommission on Prevention of Discrimination and Protection of Minorities and the bodies established pursuant to the International Covenants on Human Rights and other relevant international human rights instruments in promoting and protecting the rights of persons belonging to national or ethnic, religious and linguistic minorities,

Taking into account the important work which is done by intergovernmental and non-governmental organizations in protecting minorities and in promoting and protecting the rights of persons belonging to national or ethnic, religious and linguistic minorities,

Recognizing the need to ensure even more effective implementation of international human rights instruments with regard to the rights of persons belonging to national or ethnic, religious and linguistic minorities,

Proclaims this Declaration on the Rights of Persons Belonging to National or Ethnic, Religious and Linguistic Minorities:

Article 1

1. States shall protect the existence and the national or ethnic, cultural, religious and linguistic identity of minorities within their respective territories and shall encourage conditions for the promotion of that identity.
2. States shall adopt appropriate legislative and other measures to achieve those ends.

Article 2

1. Persons belonging to national or ethnic, religious and linguistic minorities (hereinafter referred to as persons belonging to minorities) have the right to enjoy their own culture, to profess and practise their own religion, and to use their own language, in private and in public, freely and without interference or any form of discrimination.
2. Persons belonging to minorities have the right to participate effectively in cultural, religious, social, economic and public life.
3. Persons belonging to minorities have the right to participate effectively in decisions on the national and, where appropriate, regional level concerning the minority to which they belong or the regions in which they live, in a manner not incompatible with national legislation.

4. Persons belonging to minorities have the right to establish and maintain their own associations.
5. Persons belonging to minorities have the right to establish and maintain, without any discrimination, free and peaceful contacts with other members of their group and with persons belonging to other minorities, as well as contacts across frontiers with citizens of other States to whom they are related by national or ethnic, religious or linguistic ties.

Article 3

1. Persons belonging to minorities may exercise their rights, including those set forth in the present Declaration, individually as well as in community with other members of their group, without any discrimination.
2. No disadvantage shall result for any person belonging to a minority as the consequence of the exercise or non-exercise of the rights set forth in the present Declaration.

Article 4

1. States shall take measures where required to ensure that persons belonging to minorities may exercise fully and effectively all their human rights and fundamental freedoms without any discrimination and in full equality before the law.
2. States shall take measures to create favourable conditions to enable persons belonging to minorities to express their characteristics and to develop their culture, language, religion, traditions and customs, except where specific practices are in violation of national law and contrary to international standards.
3. States should take appropriate measures so that, wherever possible, persons belonging to minorities may have adequate opportunities to learn their mother tongue or to have instruction in their mother tongue.
4. States should, where appropriate, take measures in the field of education, in order to encourage knowledge of the history, traditions, language and culture of the minorities existing within their territory. Persons belonging to minorities should have adequate opportunities to gain knowledge of the society as a whole.
5. States should consider appropriate measures so that persons belonging to minorities may participate fully in the economic progress and development in their country.

Article 5

1. National policies and programmes shall be planned and implemented with due regard for the legitimate interests of persons belonging to minorities.
2. Programmes of cooperation and assistance among States should be planned and implemented with due regard for the legitimate interests of persons belonging to minorities.

Article 6

States should cooperate on questions relating to persons belonging to minorities, inter alia, exchanging information and experiences, in order to promote mutual understanding and confidence.

Article 7

States should cooperate in order to promote respect for the rights set forth in the present Declaration.

Article 8

1. Nothing in the present Declaration shall prevent the fulfillment of international obligations of States in relation to persons belonging to minorities. In particular, States shall fulfil in good faith the obligations and commitments they have assumed under international treaties and agreements to which they are parties.
2. The exercise of the rights set forth in the present Declaration shall not prejudice the enjoyment by all persons of universally recognized human rights and fundamental freedoms.
3. Measures taken by States to ensure the effective enjoyment of the rights set forth in the present Declaration shall not prima facie be considered contrary to the principle of equality contained in the Universal Declaration of Human Rights.
4. Nothing in the present Declaration may be construed as permitting any activity contrary to the purposes and principles of the United Nations, including sovereign equality, territorial integrity and political independence of States.

Article 9

The specialized agencies and other organizations of the United Nations system shall contribute to the full realization of the rights and principles set forth in the present Declaration, within their respective fields of competence.

EUROPEAN CHARTER FOR REGIONAL OR MINORITY LANGUAGES

Strasbourg, 5.XI.1992

PREAMBLE

The member States of the Council of Europe signatory hereto, Considering that the aim of the Council of Europe is to achieve a greater unity between its members, particularly for the purpose of safeguarding and realising the ideals and principles which are their common heritage; Considering that the protection of the historical regional or minority languages of Europe, some of which are in danger of eventual extinction, contributes to the maintenance and development of Europe's cultural wealth and traditions; Considering that the right to use a regional or minority language in private and public life is an inalienable right conforming to the principles embodied in the United Nations International Covenant on Civil and Political Rights, and according to the spirit of the Council of Europe Convention for the Protection of Human Rights and Fundamental Freedoms; Having regard to the work carried out within the CSCE and in particular to the Helsinki Final Act of 1975 and the document of the Copenhagen Meeting of 1990; Stressing the value of interculturalism and multilingualism and considering that the protection and encouragement of regional or minority languages should not be to the detriment of the official languages and the need to learn them; Realising that the protection and promotion of regional or minority languages in the different countries and regions of Europe represent an important contribution to the building of a Europe based on the principles of democracy and cultural diversity within the framework of national sovereignty and territorial integrity; Taking into consideration the specific conditions and historical traditions in the different regions of the European States, Have agreed as follows:

PART I—GENERAL PROVISIONS

Article 1—Definitions

For the purposes of this Charter:

a. "regional or minority languages" means languages that are:

i. traditionally used within a given territory of a State by nationals of that State who form a group numerically smaller than the rest of the State's population; and

ii. different from the official language(s) of that State;

it does not include either dialects of the official language(s) of the State or the languages of migrants;

a. "territory in which the regional or minority language is used" means the geographical area in which the said language is the mode of expression of a number of people justifying the adoption of the various protective and promotional measures provided for in this Charter;

b. "non-territorial languages" means languages used by nationals of the State which differ from the language or languages used by the rest of the State's population but which, although traditionally used within the territory of the State, cannot be identified with a particular area thereof.

Article 2—Undertakings

1. Each Party undertakes to apply the provisions of Part II to all the regional or minority languages spoken within its territory and which comply with the definition in Article 1.
2. In respect of each language specified at the time of ratification, acceptance or approval, in accordance with Article 3, each Party undertakes to apply a minimum of thirty-five paragraphs or sub-paragraphs chosen from among the provisions of Part III of the Charter, including at least three chosen from each of the Articles 8 and 12 and one from each of the Articles 9, 10, 11 and 13.

Article 3—Practical arrangements

1. Each Contracting State shall specify in its instrument of ratification, acceptance or approval, each regional or minority language, or official language which is less widely used on the whole or part of its territory, to which the paragraphs chosen in accordance with Article 2, paragraph 2, shall apply.
2. Any Party may, at any subsequent time, notify the Secretary General that it accepts the obligations arising out of the provisions of any other paragraph of the Charter not already specified in its instrument of ratification, acceptance or approval, or that it will apply paragraph 1 of the present article to other regional or minority languages, or to other official languages which are less widely used on the whole or part of its territory.
3. The undertakings referred to in the foregoing paragraph shall be deemed to form an integral part of the ratification, acceptance or approval and will have the same effect as from their date of notification.

Article 4—Existing regimes of protection

1. Nothing in this Charter shall be construed as limiting or derogating from any of the rights guaranteed by the European Convention on Human Rights.
2. The provisions of this Charter shall not affect any more favourable provisions concerning the status of regional or minority languages, or the legal regime of persons

belonging to minorities which may exist in a Party or are provided for by relevant bilateral or multilateral international agreements.

Article 5—Existing obligations

Nothing in this Charter may be interpreted as implying any right to engage in any activity or perform any action in contravention of the purposes of the Charter of the United Nations or other obligations under international law, including the principle of the sovereignty and territorial integrity of States.

Article 6—Information

The Parties undertake to see to it that the authorities, organisations and persons concerned are informed of the rights and duties established by this Charter.

PART II—OBJECTIVES AND PRINCIPLES PURSUED IN ACCORDANCE WITH ARTICLE 2, PARAGRAPH 1

Article 7—Objectives and principles

1. In respect of regional or minority languages, within the territories in which such languages are used and according to the situation of each language, the Parties shall base their policies, legislation and practice on the following objectives and principles:
   a. the recognition of the regional or minority languages as an expression of cultural wealth;
   b. the respect of the geographical area of each regional or minority language in order to ensure that existing or new administrative divisions do not constitute an obstacle to the promotion of the regional or minority language in question;
   c. the need for resolute action to promote regional or minority languages in order to safeguard them;
   d. the facilitation and/or encouragement of the use of regional or minority languages, in speech and writing, in public and private life;
   e. the maintenance and development of links, in the fields covered by this Charter, between groups using a regional or minority language and other groups in the State employing a language used in identical or similar form, as well as the establishment of cultural relations with other groups in the State using different languages;
   f. the provision of appropriate forms and means for the teaching and study of regional or minority languages at all appropriate stages;
   g. the provision of facilities enabling non-speakers of a regional or minority language living in the area where it is used to learn it if they so desire;
   h. the promotion of study and research on regional or minority languages at universities or equivalent institutions;
   i. the promotion of appropriate types of transnational exchanges, in the fields covered by this Charter, for regional or minority languages used in identical or similar form in two or more States.
2. The Parties undertake to eliminate, if they have not yet done so, any unjustified distinction, exclusion, restriction or preference relating to the use of a regional or minority language and intended to discourage or endanger the maintenance or development of it. The adoption of special measures in favour of regional or minority languages aimed at promoting equality between the users of these languages and the rest of the population or which take due account of their specific conditions is not considered to be an act of discrimination against the users of more widely-used languages.

3. The Parties undertake to promote, by appropriate measures, mutual understanding between all the linguistic groups of the country and in particular the inclusion of respect, understanding and tolerance in relation to regional or minority languages among the objectives of education and training provided within their countries and encouragement of the mass media to pursue the same objective.
4. In determining their policy with regard to regional or minority languages, the Parties shall take into consideration the needs and wishes expressed by the groups which use such languages. They are encouraged to establish bodies, if necessary, for the purpose of advising the authorities on all matters pertaining to regional or minority languages.
5. The Parties undertake to apply, *mutatis mutandis*, the principles listed in paragraphs 1 to 4 above to non-territorial languages. However, as far as these languages are concerned, the nature and scope of the measures to be taken to give effect to this Charter shall be determined in a flexible manner, bearing in mind the needs and wishes, and respecting the traditions and characteristics, of the groups which use the languages concerned.

PART III—MEASURES TO PROMOTE THE USE OF REGIONAL OR MINORITY LANGUAGES IN PUBLIC LIFE IN ACCORDANCE WITH THE UNDERTAKINGS ENTERED INTO UNDER ARTICLE 2, PARAGRAPH 2

Article 8—Education

1. With regard to education, the Parties undertake, within the territory in which such languages are used, according to the situation of each of these languages, and without prejudice to the teaching of the official language(s) of the State:

   a.

      i. to make available pre-school education in the relevant regional or minority languages; or

      ii. to make available a substantial part of pre-school education in the relevant regional or minority languages; or

      iii. to apply one of the measures provided for under i and ii above at least to those pupils whose families so request and whose number is considered sufficient; or

      iv. if the public authorities have no direct competence in the field of pre-school education, to favour and/or encourage the application of the measures referred to under i to iii above;

   b.

      i. to make available primary education in the relevant regional or minority languages; or

      ii. to make available a substantial part of primary education in the relevant regional or minority languages; or

      iii. to provide, within primary education, for the teaching of the relevant regional or minority languages as an integral part of the curriculum; or

      iv. to apply one of the measures provided for under i to iii above at least to those pupils whose families so request and whose number is considered sufficient;

   c.

      i. to make available secondary education in the relevant regional or minority languages; or

      ii. to make available a substantial part of secondary education in the relevant regional or minority languages; or

   iii. to provide, within secondary education, for the teaching of the relevant regional or minority languages as an integral part of the curriculum; or
   iv. to apply one of the measures provided for under i to iii above at least to those pupils who, or where appropriate whose families, so wish in a number considered sufficient;

d.
   i. to make available technical and vocational education in the relevant regional or minority languages; or
   ii. to make available a substantial part of technical and vocational education in the relevant regional or minority languages; or
   iii. to provide, within technical and vocational education, for the teaching of the relevant regional or minority languages as an integral part of the curriculum; or
   iv. to apply one of the measures provided for under i to iii above at least to those pupils who, or where appropriate whose families, so wish in a number considered sufficient;

e.
   i. to make available university and other higher education in regional or minority languages; or
   ii. to provide facilities for the study of these languages as university and higher education subjects; or
   iii. if, by reason of the role of the State in relation to higher education institutions, sub-paragraphs i and ii cannot be applied, to encourage and/or allow the provision of university or other forms of higher education in regional or minority languages or of facilities for the study of these languages as university or higher education subjects;

f.
   i. to arrange for the provision of adult and continuing education courses which are taught mainly or wholly in the regional or minority languages; or
   ii. to offer such languages as subjects of adult and continuing education; or
   iii. if the public authorities have no direct competence in the field of adult education, to favour and/or encourage the offering of such languages as subjects of adult and continuing education;

g. to make arrangements to ensure the teaching of the history and the culture which is reflected by the regional or minority language;

h. to provide the basic and further training of the teachers required to implement those of paragraphs a to g accepted by the Party;

i. to set up a supervisory body or bodies responsible for monitoring the measures taken and progress achieved in establishing or developing the teaching of regional or minority languages and for drawing up periodic reports of their findings, which will be made public.

2. With regard to education and in respect of territories other than those in which the regional or minority languages are traditionally used, the Parties undertake, if the number of users of a regional or minority language justifies it, to allow, encourage or provide teaching in or of the regional or minority language at all the appropriate stages of education.

Article 9—Judicial authorities

1. The Parties undertake, in respect of those judicial districts in which the number of residents using the regional or minority languages justifies the measures specified

below, according to the situation of each of these languages and on condition that the use of the facilities afforded by the present paragraph is not considered by the judge to hamper the proper administration of justice:

a. in criminal proceedings:
   i. to provide that the courts, at the request of one of the parties, shall conduct the proceedings in the regional or minority languages; and/or
   ii. to guarantee the accused the right to use his/her regional or minority language; and/or
   iii. to provide that requests and evidence, whether written or oral, shall not be considered inadmissible solely because they are formulated in a regional or minority language; and/or
   iv. to produce, on request, documents connected with legal proceedings in the relevant regional or minority language, if necessary by the use of interpreters and translations involving no extra expense for the persons concerned;
b. in civil proceedings:
   i. to provide that the courts, at the request of one of the parties, shall conduct the proceedings in the regional or minority languages; and/or
   ii. to allow, whenever a litigant has to appear in person before a court, that he or she may use his or her regional or minority language without thereby incurring additional expense; and/or
   iii. to allow documents and evidence to be produced in the regional or minority languages, if necessary by the use of interpreters and translations;
c. in proceedings before courts concerning administrative matters:
   i. to provide that the courts, at the request of one of the parties, shall conduct the proceedings in the regional or minority languages; and/or
   ii. to allow, whenever a litigant has to appear in person before a court, that he or she may use his or her regional or minority language without thereby incurring additional expense; and/or
   iii. to allow documents and evidence to be produced in the regional or minority languages, if necessary by the use of interpreters and translations;
d. to take steps to ensure that the application of sub-paragraphs i and iii of paragraphs b and c above and any necessary use of interpreters and translations does not involve extra expense for the persons concerned.

2. The Parties undertake:
   a. not to deny the validity of legal documents drawn up within the State solely because they are drafted in a regional or minority language; or
   b. not to deny the validity, as between the parties, of legal documents drawn up within the country solely because they are drafted in a regional or minority language, and to provide that they can be invoked against interested third parties who are not users of these languages on condition that the contents of the document are made known to them by the person(s) who invoke(s) it; or
   c. not to deny the validity, as between the parties, of legal documents drawn up within the country solely because they are drafted in a regional or minority language.
3. The Parties undertake to make available in the regional or minority languages the most important national statutory texts and those relating particularly to users of these languages, unless they are otherwise provided.

Article 10—Administrative authorities and public services

1. Within the administrative districts of the State in which the number of residents who are users of regional or minority languages justifies the measures specified below and according to the situation of each language, the Parties undertake, as far as this is reasonably possible:
   a.
      i. to ensure that the administrative authorities use the regional or minority languages; or
      ii. to ensure that such of their officers as are in contact with the public use the regional or minority languages in their relations with persons applying to them in these languages; or
      iii. to ensure that users of regional or minority languages may submit oral or written applications and receive a reply in these languages; or
      iv. to ensure that users of regional or minority languages may submit oral or written applications in these languages; or
      v. to ensure that users of regional or minority languages may validly submit a document in these languages;
   b. to make available widely used administrative texts and forms for the population in the regional or minority languages or in bilingual versions;
   c. to allow the administrative authorities to draft documents in a regional or minority language.
2. In respect of the local and regional authorities on whose territory the number of residents who are users of regional or minority languages is such as to justify the measures specified below, the Parties undertake to allow and/or encourage:
   a. the use of regional or minority languages within the framework of the regional or local authority;
   b. the possibility for users of regional or minority languages to submit oral or written applications in these languages;
   c. the publication by regional authorities of their official documents also in the relevant regional or minority languages;
   d. the publication by local authorities of their official documents also in the relevant regional or minority languages;
   e. the use by regional authorities of regional or minority languages in debates in their assemblies, without excluding, however, the use of the official language(s) of the State;
   f. the use by local authorities of regional or minority languages in debates in their assemblies, without excluding, however, the use of the official language(s) of the State;
   g. the use or adoption, if necessary in conjunction with the name in the official language(s), of traditional and correct forms of place-names in regional or minority languages.
3. With regard to public services provided by the administrative authorities or other persons acting on their behalf, the Parties undertake, within the territory in which regional or minority languages are used, in accordance with the situation of each language and as far as this is reasonably possible:
   a. to ensure that the regional or minority languages are used in the provision of the service; or

b. to allow users of regional or minority languages to submit a request and receive a reply in these languages; or

c. to allow users of regional or minority languages to submit a request in these languages.

4. With a view to putting into effect those provisions of paragraphs 1, 2 and 3 accepted by them, the Parties undertake to take one or more of the following measures:

a. translation or interpretation as may be required;

b. recruitment and, where necessary, training of the officials and other public service employees required;

c. compliance as far as possible with requests from public service employees having a knowledge of a regional or minority language to be appointed in the territory in which that language is used.

5. The Parties undertake to allow the use or adoption of family names in the regional or minority languages, at the request of those concerned.

Article 11—Media

1. The Parties undertake, for the users of the regional or minority languages within the territories in which those languages are spoken, according to the situation of each language, to the extent that the public authorities, directly or indirectly, are competent, have power or play a role in this field, and respecting the principle of the independence and autonomy of the media:

a. to the extent that radio and television carry out a public service mission:

i. to ensure the creation of at least one radio station and one television channel in the regional or minority languages; or

ii. to encourage and/or facilitate the creation of at least one radio station and one television channel in the regional or minority languages; or

iii. to make adequate provision so that broadcasters offer programmes in the regional or minority languages;

b.

i. to encourage and/or facilitate the creation of at least one radio station in the regional or minority languages; or

ii. to encourage and/or facilitate the broadcasting of radio programmes in the regional or minority languages on a regular basis;

c.

i. to encourage and/or facilitate the creation of at least one television channel in the regional or minority languages; or

ii. to encourage and/or facilitate the broadcasting of television programmes in the regional or minority languages on a regular basis;

d. to encourage and/or facilitate the production and distribution of audio and audiovisual works in the regional or minority languages;

e.

i. to encourage and/or facilitate the creation and/or maintenance of at least one newspaper in the regional or minority languages; or

ii. to encourage and/or facilitate the publication of newspaper articles in the regional or minority languages on a regular basis;

f.
   i. to cover the additional costs of those media which use regional or minority languages, wherever the law provides for financial assistance in general for the media; or
   ii. to apply existing measures for financial assistance also to audiovisual productions in the regional or minority languages;

g. to support the training of journalists and other staff for media using regional or minority languages.

2. The Parties undertake to guarantee freedom of direct reception of radio and television broadcasts from neighbouring countries in a language used in identical or similar form to a regional or minority language, and not to oppose the retransmission of radio and television broadcasts from neighbouring countries in such a language. They further undertake to ensure that no restrictions will be placed on the freedom of expression and free circulation of information in the written press in a language used in identical or similar form to a regional or minority language. The exercise of the above-mentioned freedoms, since it carries with it duties and responsibilities, may be subject to such formalities, conditions, restrictions or penalties as are prescribed by law and are necessary in a democratic society, in the interests of national security, territorial integrity or public safety, for the prevention of disorder or crime, for the protection of health or morals, for the protection of the reputation or rights of others, for preventing disclosure of information received in confidence, or for maintaining the authority and impartiality of the judiciary.
3. The Parties undertake to ensure that the interests of the users of regional or minority languages are represented or taken into account within such bodies as may be established in accordance with the law with responsibility for guaranteeing the freedom and pluralism of the media.

Article 12—Cultural activities and facilities

1. With regard to cultural activities and facilities—especially libraries, video libraries, cultural centres, museums, archives, academies, theatres and cinemas, as well as literary work and film production, vernacular forms of cultural expression, festivals and the culture industries, including *inter alia* the use of new technologies—the Parties undertake, within the territory in which such languages are used and to the extent that the public authorities are competent, have power or play a role in this field:
   a. to encourage types of expression and initiative specific to regional or minority languages and foster the different means of access to works produced in these languages;
   b. to foster the different means of access in other languages to works produced in regional or minority languages by aiding and developing translation, dubbing, post-synchronisation and subtitling activities;
   c. to foster access in regional or minority languages to works produced in other languages by aiding and developing translation, dubbing, post-synchronisation and subtitling activities;
   d. to ensure that the bodies responsible for organising or supporting cultural activities of various kinds make appropriate allowance for incorporating the knowledge and use of regional or minority languages and cultures in the undertakings which they initiate or for which they provide backing;
   e. to promote measures to ensure that the bodies responsible for organising or supporting cultural activities have at their disposal staff who have a full command

of the regional or minority language concerned, as well as of the language(s) of the rest of the population;

f. to encourage direct participation by representatives of the users of a given regional or minority language in providing facilities and planning cultural activities;

g. to encourage and/or facilitate the creation of a body or bodies responsible for collecting, keeping a copy of and presenting or publishing works produced in the regional or minority languages;

h. if necessary, to create and/or promote and finance translation and terminological research services, particularly with a view to maintaining and developing appropriate administrative, commercial, economic, social, technical or legal terminology in each regional or minority language.

2. In respect of territories other than those in which the regional or minority languages are traditionally used, the Parties undertake, if the number of users of a regional or minority language justifies it, to allow, encourage and/or provide appropriate cultural activities and facilities in accordance with the preceding paragraph.

3. The Parties undertake to make appropriate provision, in pursuing their cultural policy abroad, for regional or minority languages and the cultures they reflect.

Article 13—Economic and social life

1. With regard to economic and social activities, the Parties undertake, within the whole country:

   a. to eliminate from their legislation any provision prohibiting or limiting without justifiable reasons the use of regional or minority languages in documents relating to economic or social life, particularly contracts of employment, and in technical documents such as instructions for the use of products or installations;

   b. to prohibit the insertion in internal regulations of companies and private documents of any clauses excluding or restricting the use of regional or minority languages, at least between users of the same language;

   c. to oppose practices designed to discourage the use of regional or minority languages in connection with economic or social activities;

   d. to facilitate and/or encourage the use of regional or minority languages by means other than those specified in the above sub-paragraphs.

2. With regard to economic and social activities, the Parties undertake, in so far as the public authorities are competent, within the territory in which the regional or minority languages are used, and as far as this is reasonably possible:

   a. to include in their financial and banking regulations provisions which allow, by means of procedures compatible with commercial practice, the use of regional or minority languages in drawing up payment orders (cheques, drafts, etc.) or other financial documents, or, where appropriate, to ensure the implementation of such provisions;

   b. in the economic and social sectors directly under their control (public sector), to organise activities to promote the use of regional or minority languages;

   c. to ensure that social care facilities such as hospitals, retirement homes and hostels offer the possibility of receiving and treating in their own language persons using a regional or minority language who are in need of care on grounds of ill-health, old age or for other reasons;

   d. to ensure by appropriate means that safety instructions are also drawn up in regional or minority languages;

e. to arrange for information provided by the competent public authorities concerning the rights of consumers to be made available in regional or minority languages.

Article 14—Transfrontier exchanges

The Parties undertake:

a. to apply existing bilateral and multilateral agreements which bind them with the States in which the same language is used in identical or similar form, or if necessary to seek to conclude such agreements, in such a way as to foster contacts between the users of the same language in the States concerned in the fields of culture, education, information, vocational training and permanent education;

b. for the benefit of regional or minority languages, to facilitate and/ or promote co-operation across borders, in particular between regional or local authorities in whose territory the same language is used in identical or similar form.

PART IV—APPLICATION OF THE CHARTER

Article 15—Periodical reports

1. The Parties shall present periodically to the Secretary General of the Council of Europe, in a form to be prescribed by the Committee of Ministers, a report on their policy pursued in accordance with Part II of this Charter and on the measures taken in application of those provisions of Part III which they have accepted. The first report shall be presented within the year following the entry into force of the Charter with respect to the Party concerned, the other reports at three-yearly intervals after the first report.
2. The Parties shall make their reports public.

Article 16—Examination of the reports

1. The reports presented to the Secretary General of the Council of Europe under Article 15 shall be examined by a committee of experts constituted in accordance with Article 17.
2. Bodies or associations legally established in a Party may draw the attention of the committee of experts to matters relating to the undertakings entered into by that Party under Part III of this Charter. After consulting the Party concerned, the committee of experts may take account of this information in the preparation of the report specified in paragraph 3 below. These bodies or associations can furthermore submit statements concerning the policy pursued by a Party in accordance with Part II.
3. On the basis of the reports specified in paragraph 1 and the information mentioned in paragraph 2, the committee of experts shall prepare a report for the Committee of Ministers. This report shall be accompanied by the comments which the Parties have been requested to make and may be made public by the Committee of Ministers.
4. The report specified in paragraph 3 shall contain in particular the proposals of the committee of experts to the Committee of Ministers for the preparation of such recommendations of the latter body to one or more of the Parties as may be required.
5. The Secretary General of the Council of Europe shall make a two-yearly detailed report to the Parliamentary Assembly on the application of the Charter.

Article 17—Committee of experts

1. The committee of experts shall be composed of one member per Party, appointed by the Committee of Ministers from a list of individuals of the highest integrity and

recognised competence in the matters dealt with in the Charter, who shall be nominated by the Party concerned.

2. Members of the committee shall be appointed for a period of six years and shall be eligible for reappointment. A member who is unable to complete a term of office shall be replaced in accordance with the procedure laid down in paragraph 1, and the replacing member shall complete his predecessor's term of office.
3. The committee of experts shall adopt rules of procedure. Its secretarial services shall be provided by the Secretary General of the Council of Europe.

PART V—FINAL PROVISIONS

Article 18

This Charter shall be open for signature by the member States of the Council of Europe. It is subject to ratification, acceptance or approval. Instruments of ratification, acceptance or approval shall be deposited with the Secretary General of the Council of Europe.

Article 19

1. This Charter shall enter into force on the first day of the month following the expiration of a period of three months after the date on which five member States of the Council of Europe have expressed their consent to be bound by the Charter in accordance with the provisions of Article 18.
2. In respect of any member State which subsequently expresses its consent to be bound by it, the Charter shall enter into force on the first day of the month following the expiration of a period of three months after the date of the deposit of the instrument of ratification, acceptance or approval.

Article 20

1. After the entry into force of this Charter, the Committee of Ministers of the Council of Europe may invite any State not a member of the Council of Europe to accede to this Charter.
2. In respect of any acceding State, the Charter shall enter into force on the first day of the month following the expiration of a period of three months after the date of deposit of the instrument of accession with the Secretary General of the Council of Europe.

Article 21

1. Any State may, at the time of signature or when depositing its instrument of ratification, acceptance, approval or accession, make one or more reservations to paragraphs 2 to 5 of Article 7 of this Charter. No other reservation may be made.
2. Any Contracting State which has made a reservation under the preceding paragraph may wholly or partly withdraw it by means of a notification addressed to the Secretary General of the Council of Europe. The withdrawal shall take effect on the date of receipt of such notification by the Secretary General.

Article 22

1. Any Party may at any time denounce this Charter by means of a notification addressed to the Secretary General of the Council of Europe.
2. Such denunciation shall become effective on the first day of the month following the expiration of a period of six months after the date of receipt of the notification by the Secretary General.

Article 23

The Secretary General of the Council of Europe shall notify the member States of the Council and any State which has acceded to this Charter of:

a. any signature;

b. the deposit of any instrument of ratification, acceptance, approval or accession;

c. any date of entry into force of this Charter in accordance with Articles 19 and 20;

d. any notification received in application of the provisions of Article 3, paragraph 2;

e. any other act, notification or communication relating to this Charter.

In witness whereof the undersigned, being duly authorised thereto, have signed this Charter.

Done at Strasbourg, this 5th day of November 1992, in English and French, both texts being equally authentic, in a single copy which shall be deposited in the archives of the Council of Europe. The Secretary General of the Council of Europe shall transmit certified copies to each member State of the Council of Europe and to any State invited to accede to this Charter.

COUNCIL OF EUROPE FRAMEWORK CONVENTION FOR THE PROTECTION OF NATIONAL MINORITIES

Strasbourg, 1.II.1995

The member States of the Council of Europe and the other States, signatories to the present framework Convention,

Considering that the aim of the Council of Europe is to achieve greater unity between its members for the purpose of safeguarding and realising the ideals and principles which are their common heritage;

Considering that one of the methods by which that aim is to be pursued is the maintenance and further realisation of human rights and fundamental freedoms;

Wishing to follow-up the Declaration of the Heads of State and Government of the member States of the Council of Europe adopted in Vienna on 9 October 1993;

Being resolved to protect within their respective territories the existence of national minorities;

Considering that the upheavals of European history have shown that the protection of national minorities is essential to stability, democratic security and peace in this continent;

Considering that a pluralist and genuinely democratic society should not only respect the ethnic, cultural, linguistic and religious identity of each person belonging to a national minority, but also create appropriate conditions enabling them to express, preserve and develop this identity;

Considering that the creation of a climate of tolerance and dialogue is necessary to enable cultural diversity to be a source and a factor, not of division, but of enrichment for each society;

Considering that the realisation of a tolerant and prosperous Europe does not depend solely on co-operation between States but also requires transfrontier co-operation between local and regional authorities without prejudice to the constitution and territorial integrity of each State;

Having regard to the Convention for the Protection of Human Rights and Fundamental Freedoms and the Protocols thereto;

Having regard to the commitments concerning the protection of national minorities in United Nations conventions and declarations and in the documents of the Conference on Security and Co-operation in Europe, particularly the Copenhagen Document of 29 June 1990;

Being resolved to define the principles to be respected and the obligations which flow from them, in order to ensure, in the member States and such other States as may become Parties to the present instrument, the effective protection of national minorities and of the rights and freedoms of persons belonging to those minorities, within the rule of law, respecting the territorial integrity and national sovereignty of states;

Being determined to implement the principles set out in this framework Convention through national legislation and appropriate governmental policies,

Have agreed as follows:

SECTION I

Article 1

The protection of national minorities and of the rights and freedoms of persons belonging to those minorities forms an integral part of the international protection of human rights, and as such falls within the scope of international co-operation.

Article 2

The provisions of this framework Convention shall be applied in good faith, in a spirit of understanding and tolerance and in conformity with the principles of good neighbourliness, friendly relations and co-operation between States.

Article 3

1. Every person belonging to a national minority shall have the right freely to choose to be treated or not to be treated as such and no disadvantage shall result from this choice or from the exercise of the rights which are connected to that choice.
2. Persons belonging to national minorities may exercise the rights and enjoy the freedoms flowing from the principles enshrined in the present framework Convention individually as well as in community with others.

SECTION II

Article 4

1. The Parties undertake to guarantee to persons belonging to national minorities the right of equality before the law and of equal protection of the law. In this respect, any discrimination based on belonging to a national minority shall be prohibited.
2. The Parties undertake to adopt, where necessary, adequate measures in order to promote, in all areas of economic, social, political and cultural life, full and effective equality between persons belonging to a national minority and those belonging to the majority. In this respect, they shall take due account of the specific conditions of the persons belonging to national minorities.
3. The measures adopted in accordance with paragraph 2 shall not be considered to be an act of discrimination.

Article 5

1. The Parties undertake to promote the conditions necessary for persons belonging to national minorities to maintain and develop their culture, and to preserve the essential elements of their identity, namely their religion, language, traditions and cultural heritage.
2. Without prejudice to measures taken in pursuance of their general integration policy, the Parties shall refrain from policies or practices aimed at assimilation of persons belonging to national minorities against their will and shall protect these persons from any action aimed at such assimilation.

Article 6

1. The Parties shall encourage a spirit of tolerance and intercultural dialogue and take effective measures to promote mutual respect and understanding and co-operation among all persons living on their territory, irrespective of those persons' ethnic, cultural, linguistic or religious identity, in particular in the fields of education, culture and the media.
2. The Parties undertake to take appropriate measures to protect persons who may be subject to threats or acts of discrimination, hostility or violence as a result of their ethnic, cultural, linguistic or religious identity.

Article 7

The Parties shall ensure respect for the right of every person belonging to a national minority to freedom of peaceful assembly, freedom of association, freedom of expression, and freedom of thought, conscience and religion.

Article 8

The Parties undertake to recognise that every person belonging to a national minority has the right to manifest his or her religion or belief and to establish religious institutions, organisations and associations.

Article 9

1. The Parties undertake to recognise that the right to freedom of expression of every person belonging to a national minority includes freedom to hold opinions and to receive and impart information and ideas in the minority language, without interference by public authorities and regardless of frontiers. The Parties shall ensure, within the framework of their legal systems, that persons belonging to a national minority are not discriminated against in their access to the media.
2. Paragraph 1 shall not prevent Parties from requiring the licensing, without discrimination and based on objective criteria, of sound radio and television broadcasting, or cinema enterprises.
3. The Parties shall not hinder the creation and the use of printed media by persons belonging to national minorities. In the legal framework of sound radio and television broadcasting, they shall ensure, as far as possible, and taking into account the provisions of paragraph 1, that persons belonging to national minorities are granted the possibility of creating and using their own media.
4. In the framework of their legal systems, the Parties shall adopt adequate measures in order to facilitate access to the media for persons belonging to national minorities and in order to promote tolerance and permit cultural pluralism.

Article 10

1. The Parties undertake to recognise that every person belonging to a national minority has the right to use freely and without interference his or her minority language, in private and in public, orally and in writing.
2. In areas inhabited by persons belonging to national minorities traditionally or in substantial numbers, if those persons so request and where such a request corresponds to a real need, the Parties shall endeavour to ensure, as far as possible, the conditions which would make it possible to use the minority language in relations between those persons and the administrative authorities.
3. The Parties undertake to guarantee the right of every person belonging to a national minority to be informed promptly, in a language which he or she understands, of the

reasons for his or her arrest, and of the nature and cause of any accusation against him or her, and to defend himself or herself in this language, if necessary with the free assistance of an interpreter.

Article 11

1. The Parties undertake to recognise that every person belonging to a national minority has the right to use his or her surname (patronym) and first names in the minority language and the right to official recognition of them, according to modalities provided for in their legal system.
2. The Parties undertake to recognise that every person belonging to a national minority has the right to display in his or her minority language signs, inscriptions and other information of a private nature visible to the public.
3. In areas traditionally inhabited by substantial numbers of persons belonging to a national minority, the Parties shall endeavour, in the framework of their legal system, including, where appropriate, agreements with other States, and taking into account their specific conditions, to display traditional local names, street names and other topographical indications intended for the public also in the minority language when there is a sufficient demand for such indications.

Article 12

1. The Parties shall, where appropriate, take measures in the fields of education and research to foster knowledge of the culture, history, language and religion of their national minorities and of the majority.
2. In this context the Parties shall *inter alia* provide adequate opportunities for teacher training and access to textbooks, and facilitate contacts among students and teachers of different communities.
3. The Parties undertake to promote equal opportunities for access to education at all levels for persons belonging to national minorities.

Article 13

1. Within the framework of their education systems, the Parties shall recognise that persons belonging to a national minority have the right to set up and to manage their own private educational and training establishments.

The exercise of this right shall not entail any financial obligation for the Parties.

Article 14

1. The Parties undertake to recognise that every person belonging to a national minority has the right to learn his or her minority language.
2. In areas inhabited by persons belonging to national minorities traditionally or in substantial numbers, if there is sufficient demand, the Parties shall endeavour to ensure, as far as possible and within the framework of their education systems, that persons belonging to those minorities have adequate opportunities for being taught the minority language or for receiving instruction in this language.
3. Paragraph 2 of this article shall be implemented without prejudice to the learning of the official language or the teaching in this language.

Article 15

The Parties shall create the conditions necessary for the effective participation of persons belonging to national minorities in cultural, social and economic life and in public affairs, in particular those affecting them.

Article 16

The Parties shall refrain from measures which alter the proportions of the population in areas inhabited by persons belonging to national minorities and are aimed at restricting the rights and freedoms flowing from the principles enshrined in the present framework Convention.

Article 17

1. The Parties undertake not to interfere with the right of persons belonging to national minorities to establish and maintain free and peaceful contacts across frontiers with persons lawfully staying in other States, in particular those with whom they share an ethnic, cultural, linguistic or religious identity, or a common cultural heritage.
2. The Parties undertake not to interfere with the right of persons belonging to national minorities to participate in the activities of non-governmental organisations, both at the national and international levels.

Article 18

1. The Parties shall endeavour to conclude, where necessary, bilateral and multilateral agreements with other States, in particular neighbouring States, in order to ensure the protection of persons belonging to the national minorities concerned.
2. Where relevant, the Parties shall take measures to encourage transfrontier co-operation.

Article 19

The Parties undertake to respect and implement the principles enshrined in the present framework Convention making, where necessary, only those limitations, restrictions or derogations which are provided for in international legal instruments, in particular the Convention for the Protection of Human Rights and Fundamental Freedoms, in so far as they are relevant to the rights and freedoms flowing from the said principles.

SECTION III

Article 20

In the exercise of the rights and freedoms flowing from the principles enshrined in the present framework Convention, any person belonging to a national minority shall respect the national legislation and the rights of others, in particular those of persons belonging to the majority or to other national minorities.

Article 21

Nothing in the present framework Convention shall be interpreted as implying any right to engage in any activity or perform any act contrary to the fundamental principles of international law and in particular of the sovereign equality, territorial integrity and political independence of States.

Article 22

Nothing in the present framework Convention shall be construed as limiting or derogating from any of the human rights and fundamental freedoms which may be ensured under the laws of any Contracting Party or under any other agreement to which it is a Party.

Article 23

The rights and freedoms flowing from the principles enshrined in the present framework Convention, in so far as they are the subject of a corresponding provision in the Convention for the Protection of Human Rights and Fundamental Freedoms or in the Protocols thereto, shall be understood so as to conform to the latter provisions.

SECTION IV

Article 24

1. The Committee of Ministers of the Council of Europe shall monitor the implementation of this framework Convention by the Contracting Parties.
2. The Parties which are not members of the Council of Europe shall participate in the implementation mechanism, according to modalities to be determined.

Article 25

1. Within a period of one year following the entry into force of this framework Convention in respect of a Contracting Party, the latter shall transmit to the Secretary General of the Council of Europe full information on the legislative and other measures taken to give effect to the principles set out in this framework Convention.
2. Thereafter, each Party shall transmit to the Secretary General on a periodical basis and whenever the Committee of Ministers so requests any further information of relevance to the implementation of this framework Convention.
3. The Secretary General shall forward to the Committee of Ministers the information transmitted under the terms of this article.

Article 26

1. In evaluating the adequacy of the measures taken by the Parties to give effect to the principles set out in this framework Convention the Committee of Ministers shall be assisted by an advisory committee, the members of which shall have recognised expertise in the field of the protection of national minorities.
2. The composition of this advisory committee and its procedure shall be determined by the Committee of Ministers within a period of one year following the entry into force of this framework Convention.

SECTION V

Article 27

This framework Convention shall be open for signature by the member States of the Council of Europe. Up until the date when the Convention enters into force, it shall also be open for signature by any other State so invited by the Committee of Ministers. It is subject to ratification, acceptance or approval. Instruments of ratification, acceptance or approval shall be deposited with the Secretary General of the Council of Europe.

Article 28

1. This framework Convention shall enter into force on the first day of the month following the expiration of a period of three months after the date on which twelve member States of the Council of Europe have expressed their consent to be bound by the Convention in accordance with the provisions of Article 27.
2. In respect of any member State which subsequently expresses its consent to be bound by it, the framework Convention shall enter into force on the first day of the month following the expiration of a period of three months after the date of the deposit of the instrument of ratification, acceptance or approval.

Article 29

1. After the entry into force of this framework Convention and after consulting the Contracting States, the Committee of Ministers of the Council of Europe may invite

to accede to the Convention, by a decision taken by the majority provided for in Article 20.d of the Statute of the Council of Europe, any non-member State of the Council of Europe which, invited to sign in accordance with the provisions of Article 27, has not yet done so, and any other non-member State.

2. In respect of any acceding State, the framework Convention shall enter into force on the first day of the month following the expiration of a period of three months after the date of the deposit of the instrument of accession with the Secretary General of the Council of Europe.

Article 30

1. Any State may at the time of signature or when depositing its instrument of ratification, acceptance, approval or accession, specify the territory or territories for whose international relations it is responsible to which this framework Convention shall apply.
2. Any State may at any later date, by a declaration addressed to the Secretary General of the Council of Europe, extend the application of this framework Convention to any other territory specified in the declaration. In respect of such territory the framework Convention shall enter into force on the first day of the month following the expiration of a period of three months after the date of receipt of such declaration by the Secretary General.
3. Any declaration made under the two preceding paragraphs may, in respect of any territory specified in such declaration, be withdrawn by a notification addressed to the Secretary General. The withdrawal shall become effective on the first day of the month following the expiration of a period of three months after the date of receipt of such notification by the Secretary General.

Article 31

1. Any Party may at any time denounce this framework Convention by means of a notification addressed to the Secretary General of the Council of Europe.
2. Such denunciation shall become effective on the first day of the month following the expiration of a period of six months after the date of receipt of the notification by the Secretary General.

Article 32

The Secretary General of the Council of Europe shall notify the member States of the Council, other signatory States and any State which has acceded to this framework Convention, of:

a. any signature;

b. the deposit of any instrument of ratification, acceptance, approval or accession;

c. any date of entry into force of this framework Convention in accordance with Articles 28, 29 and 30;

d. any other act, notification or communication relating to this framework Convention.

In witness whereof the undersigned, being duly authorised thereto, have signed this framework Convention. Done at Strasbourg, this 1st day of February 1995, in English and French, both texts being equally authentic, in a single copy which shall be deposited in the archives of the Council of Europe. The Secretary General of the Council of Europe shall transmit certified copies to each member State of the Council of Europe and to any State invited to sign or accede to this framework Convention.

APPENDIX IV

INTERNET RESOURCES

EDUCATION WEBSITES—INTERNATIONAL

MULTILATERAL INSTITUTIONS

African Development Bank Group <www.afdb.org>

Asian Development Bank <www.adb.org>

Food and Agriculture Organization of the United Nations (FAO) <www.fao.org>

Inter-American Development Bank <www.iadb.org>

International Labour Organization (ILO) <www.ilo.org/public/english/dialogue/sector/sectors/educat.htm>

United Nations Children's Fund (UNICEF) <www.unicef.org>

United Nations Development Programme (UNDP) <www.undp.org>

United Nations Educational, Scientific and Cultural Organization (UNESCO) <www.unesco.org>

- Mid-Decade Meeting on Education for All, 1996 <www.unesco.org/education/efa/ed_for_all/background/mid_decade_amman.shtml>
- UNESCO Institute for Education (UIE) <www.unesco.org/education/uie>
- UNESCO Institute for Statistics (UIS) <www.uis.unesco.org>
- UNESCO International Bureau of Education (IBE) <www.ibe.unesco.org>
- UNESCO International Institute for Educational Planning (IIEP) <www.unesco.org/iiep>
- UNESCO International Institute for Higher Education in Latin America and the Caribbean (IESALC) <www.iesalc.unesco.org.ve>
- UNESCO World Education Report 2000 <www.unesco.org/education/information/wer>
- United Nations General Assembly Resolution <www.unesco.org/education/efa/ed_for_all/background/un_resolution_1997.shtml>
- United Nations Resolution on a UN Literacy Decade <www.unesco.org/education/efa/ed_for_all/background/un_draft_literacy.shtml>
- The World Conference on Education for All, Jomtien, Thailand <www.unesco.org/education/efa/ed_for_all/background/background_documents.shtml>
- World Education Forum (Dakar, Senegal, April 2000) <www.unesco.org/education/efa/wef_2000/index.shtml>

United Nations Population Fund (UNFPA) <www.unfpa.org>

World Bank Group <www.worldbank.org>

- Schools (for students and teachers) <www.worldbank.org/html/schools>
- Statistical databases <www.worldbank.org/data>

World Health Organization, School Health and Youth Health Promotion <www.who.int/hpr/gshi/docs/index.html>

BILATERAL INSTITUTIONS

Canadian International Development Agency (CIDA) <www.acdi-cida.gc.ca/index.htm>

Danish Ministry of Foreign Affairs <www.um.dk/english>

Department for International Development (DFID), United Kingdom <www.dfid.gov.uk>

Federal Ministry for Economic Cooperation and Development (BMZ), Germany <www.bmz.de>

Finnish International Development Cooperation (FINNIDA) <http://global.finland.fi/index.php?kieli=3>

Ministry of Development Cooperation, France <www.france.diplomatie.fr/index.html>

Ministry of Foreign Affairs, Italy <www.esteri.it/eng/index.htm>

Ministry of Foreign Affairs, Japan <www.mofa.go.jp/policy/oda>

Ministry of Foreign Affairs, the Netherlands <www.bz.minbuza.nl/homepage.asp>

Norwegian Agency for Development Cooperation (NORAD) <www.norad.no>

Swedish International Development Agency (SIDA) <www.sida.se>

United States Agency for International Development (USAID) <www.usaid.gov>

INTERGOVERNMENTAL ORGANIZATIONS

European Commission DG Development <http://europa.eu.int/comm/development/index_en.htm>

G8-Summit <www.g7.utoronto.ca>

Inter-Parliamentary Union (IPU) <www.ipu.org>

Islamic Educational, Scientific and Cultural Organization (ISESCO) <www.isesco.org.ma>

Organisation for Economic Co-operation and Development (OECD) <www.oecd.org>

OECD Development Assistance Committee (DAC) <www.oecd.org/oecd/pages/home/displaygeneral/0,3380,EN-home-notheme-2-no-no-no,FF.html>

Organization of American States (OAS) <www.oas.org>

South East Asian Ministers of Education Organization <www.seameo.org>

CIVIL SOCIETY ORGANIZATIONS AND NONGOVERNMENTAL ORGANIZATIONS

Academy for Educational Development <www.aed.org>

ActionAid <www.actionaid.org>

Civitas International <www.civnet.org>

Dhaka Ahsania Mission <www.ahsania.org>

Education International <www.ei-ie.org>

Enda Third World <www.enda.sn>

Global Campaign for Education <www.campaignforeducation.org>

International Association of Universities <www.unesco.org/iau>

International Dance Council <www.unesco.org/ngo/cid>

International Federation of University Women <www.ifuw.org>

International Reading Association (IRA) <www.reading.org>

International Save the Children Alliance <www.savethechildren.net>

Oxfam International <www.oxfam.org>

Summer Institute of Linguistics (SIL International) <www.sil.org/sil>

Tamer Institute for Community Education <www.tamerinst.org>

World Education <www.worlded.org>

World Learning <www.worldlearning.org>

MISCELLANEOUS

Center for Higher Education Policy Studies <www.utwente.nl/cheps>

Educational Testing Service (ETS) Global Institute <www.ets.org/etsglobal>

Institute of International Education <www.iie.org>

Inter-American Dialogue <www.iadialog.org>

Open Learning Agency <www.ola.bc.ca>

EDUCATION WEBSITES—UNITED STATES

FEDERAL

U.S. Department of Education <www.ed.gov>

U.S. Department of Education publications <www.ed.gov/about/ordering.jsp>

MIDWESTERN UNITED STATES

Coordinating Commission for Postsecondary Education—Nebraska <www.ccpe.state.ne.us/PublicDoc/CCPE/Default.asp>

Illinois Board of Higher Education <www.ibhe.state.il.us>

Kansas Board of Regents <www.kansasregents.org>

Midwestern Higher Education Commission <www.mhec.org>

Missouri Coordinating Board for Higher Education <www.mocbhe.gov>

North Dakota University System <www.ndus.edu>

Ohio Board of Regents <www.regents.state.oh.us>

South Dakota Board of Regents <www.ris.sdbor.edu>

University of Wisconsin System Administration <www.uwsa.edu>

NORTHEASTERN UNITED STATES

Center for the Study of Higher Education, the Pennsylvania State University College of Education <www.ed.psu.edu/cshe>

Massachusetts Board of Higher Education <www.mass.edu>

New England Board of Higher Education <www.nebhe.org>

New Jersey Commission on Higher Education <www.state.nj.us/highereducation>

Office of Higher Education—New York <www.highered.nysed.gov>

Rhode Island Board of Governors for Higher Education <www.ribghe.org>

State of Connecticut Department of Higher Education <www.ctdhe.org>

University of Maine System <www.maine.edu>

University System of Maryland <www.usmd.edu/IndexNB.html>

University System of New Hampshire <http://usnh.unh.edu>

SOUTHERN UNITED STATES

Board of Regents of the University System of Georgia <www.usg.edu>

Florida Board of Education <www.flboe.org>

Kentucky Council on Postsecondary Education <www.che.state.ky.us/index/index.asp>

Lousiana Board of Regents <www.regents.state.la.us>

Mississippi Board of Trustees of State Institutions of Higher Learning <www.ihl.state.ms.us>

Oklahoma Higher Education <www.okhighered.org>

Southern Regional Education Board <www.sreb.org>

State Council of Higher Education for Virginia <www.schev.edu/main.asp>

Tennessee Higher Education Commission <www.state.tn.us/thec>

Texas Higher Education Coordinating Board <www.thecb.state.tx.us>

University of North Carolina General Administration <www.ga.unc.edu/UNCGA>

WESTERN UNITED STATES

Access Washington List of Education Resources <http://access.wa.gov/education/awedu.asp>

Arizona Board of Regents <www.abor.asu.edu>

California Postsecondary Education Commission <www.cpec.ca.gov>

Center for Studies in Higher Education, University of California, Berkeley <http://ishi.lib.berkeley.edu/cshe>

Colorado Commission on Higher Education <www.state.co.us/cche_dir/hecche.html>

Idaho State Board of Education <www.sde.state.id.us/osbe/board.htm>

Montana Board of Regents of Higher Education <www.montana.edu/wwwbor>

New Mexico Commission on Higher Education <www.nmche.org>

Oregon State Board of Higher Education <www.ous.edu/board>

University and Community College System of Nevada <www.nevada.edu>

University of Alaska Board of Regents <http://gemini.atspg.alaska.edu/bor>

University of Hawaii Board of Regents <www.hawaii.edu/admin/bor>

Utah System of Higher Education <www.utahsbr.edu>

Western Governors University <www.wgu.edu/wgu/index.html>

Western Interstate Commission for Higher Education <www.wiche.edu>

Wyoming Postsecondary Education <www.k12.wy.us/higher_ed>

MISCELLANEOUS

American Association of State Colleges and Universities <www.aascu.org>

American Council on Education Internet Sources for Higher Education Policy and Research Topics <www.acenet.edu/resources/policy-research/home.cfm>

American Institutes for Research <www.air.org>

Association of American Universities <www.aau.edu>

Brookings Institution <www.brookings.org>

Carnegie Foundation for the Advancement of Teaching <www.carnegiefoundation.org>

Center on Juvenile and Criminal Justice <www.cjcj.org>

The Century Foundation <www.tcf.org>

Chronicle of Higher Education <http://chronicle.com>

College Board <www.collegeboard.com>

College Savings Plans Network <www.collegesavings.org>

Consortium for Policy Research in Education <www.wcer.wisc.edu/cpre>

Council for Adult and Experiential Learning <www.cael.org/index.asp>

Council for Aid to Education <www.cae.org>

Council for Basic Education <www.c-b-e.org>

Council of Chief State School Officers <www.ccsso.org>

Educational Resources Information Center (ERIC) <www.eric.ed.gov>

ERIC Clearinghouse on Assessment and Education <http://ericae.net>

Educational Testing Service <www.ets.org>

Education Commission of the States <www.ecs.org>

Education Development Center <www.edc.org>

The Education Trust <www.edtrust.org/main/main/index.asp>

Education Week <www.edweek.com>

FinAid <www.finaid.org>

Ford Foundation <www.fordfound.org>

The Futures Project <www.futuresproject.org>

Grapevine: National Database of Tax Support for Higher Education <www.coe.ilstu.edu/grapevine>

Hechinger Institute on Education and the Media <www.teacherscollege.edu/hechinger>

Higher Education Abstracts <www.cgu.edu/inst/hea/hea.html>

Institute for Educational Leadership <www.iel.org>

Institute for Higher Education Policy <www.ihep.com>

James Irvine Foundation <www.irvine.org>

National Association for College Admission Counseling <www.nacac.com/index.html>

National Association of College and University Business Officers <www.nacubo.org>

National Association of Independent Colleges and Universities <www.naicu.edu>

National Association of State Budget Officers <www.nasbo.org>

National Association of State Student Grant and Aid Programs <www.nassgap.org>

National Association of State Universities and Land-Grant Colleges <www.nasulgc.org>

National Center for Higher Education Management Systems <www.nchems.org>

National Center for Postsecondary Improvement <www.stanford.edu/group/ncpi>

National Center for Public Policy and Higher Education <www.highereducation.org>

National Center on Education and the Economy <www.ncee.org>

National Conference of States Legislatures <www.ncsl.org>

National Education Association <www.nea.org>

National Governors Association <www.nga.org>

National School Boards Association <www.nsba.org>

Public Agenda <www.publicagenda.org>

RAND <www.rand.org>

State Higher Education Executive Officers <www.sheeo.org>

Urban Institute <www.urban.org>

U.S. Department of Commerce, Bureau of Economic Analysis <www.bea.doc.gov>

U.S. Department of Education, Individuals with Disabilities Education Act Amendments of 1997 <www.ed.gov/offices/OSERS/Policy/IDEA>

U.S. Department of Labor, Bureau of Labor Statistics <www.bls.gov>

DATA SOURCES

American Legislative Exchange Council Report Card on American Education <www.alec.org/meSWFiles/pdf/education2000.pdf>

College Board Advanced Placement Library: 2000 State and National Summary Reports <www.collegeboard.org/ap/library/state_nat_rpts_00.html>

Digest of Education Statistics 2000 www.nces.ed.gov/pubs2001/digest>

Education Commission of the States Selected State Policies 1990–2000 <www.ecs.org/clearinghouse/19/04/1904.pdf>

Education Week Special Reports <www.edweek.com/sreports>

Kids Count Databook <www.aecf.org/kidscount/kc2001/index.htm>

National Assessment of Educational Progress <www.nces.ed.gov/nationsreportcard>

National Center for Education Statistics <http://nces.ed.gov>

- National Center for Education Statistics Common Core of Data <http://nces.ed.gov/ccd>
- National Center for Education Statistics Education Finance Statistical Center <http://nces.ed.gov/edfin>

National Education Goals Panel Interactive Data Center <www.negp.gov/datasystemlinks.html>

Regional Educational Laboratories <www.lab.brown.edu/public/national/national.shtml>

U.S. Department of Commerce, U.S. Census Bureau <www.census.gov>

- U.S. Census Bureau Educational Attainment <www.census.gov/population/www/socdemo/educ-attn.html>

U.S. Department of Education <www.ed.gov>

- U.S. Department of Education Office of Education Research and Improvement <www.ed.gov/offices/OERI>
- U.S. Department of Education Research and Statistics <www.ed.gov/topics/topics.jsp?&top=Research+%26+Stats>

APPENDIX V

BIBLIOGRAPHY

ELEMENTARY AND SECONDARY EDUCATION

Bobbitt, John Franklin. 1924. *How to Make a Curriculum.* Boston: Houghton Mifflin.

Bowles, Samuel, and **Gintis, Herbert.** 1976. *Schooling in Capitalist America: Educational Reform and the Contradictions of Economic Life.* New York: Basic Books.

Boyer, Ernest L., and **Carnegie Foundation for the Advancement of Teaching.** 1983. *High School: A Report on Secondary Education in America.* New York: Harper and Row.

Bruner, Jerome S. 1960. *The Process of Education.* Cambridge, MA: Harvard University Press.

Callahan, Raymond E. 1962. *Education and the Cult of Efficiency; a Study of the Social Forces That Have Shaped the Administration of the Public Schools.* Chicago: University of Chicago Press.

Charters, Werrett Wallace. 1923. *Curriculum Construction.* New York: Macmillan.

Chubb, John E., and **Moe, Terry M.** 1990. *Politics, Markets, and America's Schools.* Washington, DC: Brookings Institution.

Coleman, James S., et al. 1966. *Equality of Educational Opportunity.* Washington, DC: U.S. Dept. of Health, Education, and Welfare, Office of Education.

Conant, James Bryant. 1959. *The American High School Today: A First Report to Interested Citizens.* New York: McGraw-Hill.

Goodlad, John I. 1984. *A Place Called School: Prospects for the Future.* New York: McGraw-Hill.

Krug, Edward A. 1964. *The Shaping of the American High School.* New York: Harper and Row.

National Education Association of the United States. Commission on the Reorganization of Secondary Education. 1918. *Cardinal Principles of Secondary Education. A Report of the Commission on the Reorganization of Secondary Education.* Washington, DC: Government Printing Office.

National Education Association of the United States. Committee of Fifteen on Elementary Education. 1895. *Report of the Committee of Fifteen on Elementary Education, with the Reports of the Sub-Committees.* New York: American Book Company.

The New-England Primer. 1810. Haverhill, MA: Printed by Wm. B. Allen.

The New-England Primer, Improved for the More Easy Attaining the True Reading of English. 1807. Springfield: Printed for Isaiah Thomas, Jr. Worcester: Henry Brewer Printer.

Sizer, Theodore R. 1992. *Horace's Compromise: The Dilemma of the American High School.* Boston: Houghton Mifflin.

POSTSECONDARY EDUCATION

Birnbaum, Robert. 1988. *How Colleges Work: The Cybernetics of Academic Organization and Leadership.* San Francisco: Jossey-Bass.

Gaff, Jeffrey G., and **Ratcliff, James L.** 1997. *Handbook of the Undergraduate Curriculum: A Comprehensive Guide to Purposes, Structures, Practices, and Change.* San Francisco: Jossey-Bass.

Hossler, Don; Schmit, Jack L.; and **Vesper, Nick.** 1999. *Going to College: How Social, Economic, and Educational Factors Influence the Decisions Students Make.* Baltimore: Johns Hopkins University Press.

Pascarella, Ernest T., and **Terenzini, Patrick T.** 1991. *How College Affects Students: Findings and Insights from Twenty Years of Research.* San Francisco: Jossey-Bass.

Smart, John C. 1985–2002. *Higher Education: A Handbook of Theory and Research.* Vols. I–XVII. New York: Agathon Press.

Tinto, Vincent. 1993. *Leaving College: Rethinking the Causes and Cures of Student Attrition,* 2nd edition. Chicago: University of Chicago Press.

HISTORY AND BIOGRAPHY

Aikin, Wilford Merton. 1942. *The Story of the Eight Year Study.* New York: Harper and Brothers.

Cremin, Lawrence Arthur. 1970. *American Education; the Colonial Experience, 1607–1783.* New York: Harper and Row.

Cremin, Lawrence Arthur. 1980. *American Education, the National Experience, 1783–1876.* New York: Harper and Row.

Cremin, Lawrence Arthur. 1988. *American Education, the Metropolitan Experience, 1876–1980.* New York: Harper and Row.

Cuban, Larry. 1993. *How Teachers Taught: Constancy and Change in American Classrooms, 1890–1990.* New York: Longman.

Dewey, John. 1899. *The School and Society; Being Three Lectures by John Dewey Supplemented by a Statement of the University Elementary School.* Chicago: University of Chicago Press.

Dewey, John. 1916. *Democracy and Education: An Introduction to the Philosophy of Education.* New York: Macmillan.

Du Bois, W. E. B. 1903. *The Souls of Black Folk; Essays and Sketches.* Chicago: McClurg.

Kaestle, Carl F., and **Foner, Eric..** 1983. *Pillars of the Republic: Common Schools and American Society, 1780–1860.* New York: Hill and Wang.

Kliebard, Herbert M. 1995. *The Struggle for the American Curriculum, 1893–1958,* 2nd edition. New York: Routledge and Kegan Paul.

Mann, Horace. 1840. *Lecture on Education.* Boston: Marsh, Capen, Lyon and Webb.

Mann, Horace. 1841. *A Lecture on the Best Mode of Preparing and Using Spelling-Books: Delivered before the American Institute of Instruction, August, 1841.* Boston: S. D. Ticknor.

Mann, Horace. 1848. *Speech of Hon. Horace Mann, on the Right of Congress to Legislate for the Territories of the United States, and Its Duty to Exclude Slavery Therefrom: Delivered in the House of Representatives, in Committee of the Whole, June 30, 1848. To Which is Added, a Letter from Hon. Martin Van Buren, and Rev. Joshua Leavitt.* Boston: J. Howe, Printer.

Mann, Horace. 1850. *Lectures on Education.* Boston: L. N. Ide.

Mann, Horace. 1902. *The Ground of the Free School System.* Boston: Directors of the Old South Work.

Mann, Horace. 1903. *Education and Prosperity.* Boston: Directors of the Old South Work.

Mann, Horace. 1983. *Horace Mann on the Crisis in Education,* ed. Louis Filler. Lanham, MD: University Press of America.

Mann, Horace, and **Committee on the Horace Mann Centennial.** 1937. *Go Forth and Teach; An Oration Delivered before the Authorities of the City of Boston, July 4, 1842.* Centennial ed. Washington, DC: Committee on the Horace Mann Centennial, National Education Association.

Mann, Mary T. P., and **Peabody, Elizabeth P.** 1863. *Moral Culture of Infancy, and Kindergarten Guide.* Boston: T. O. H. P. Burnham.

McGuffey, William Holmes. 1884. *List of New Words by Lessons of the Primer and First Four McGuffey Readers.* n.p.

McGuffey, William Holmes. 1936. *Old Favorites from the McGuffey Readers.* New York; Cincinnati, OH: American Book Company.

McGuffey, William Holmes, and **Gorn, Elliot J.** 1998. *The McGuffey Readers: Selections from the 1879 Edition.* Boston: Bedford Books.

McGuffey, William Holmes, and **Minnich, Harvey C.** 1969. *Old Favorites from the McGuffey Readers.* 1836–1936. Detroit, MI: Singing Tree Press.

Montessori, Maria; George, Anne E.; and **Holmes, Henry W.** 1912. *The Montessori Method; Scientific Pedagogy as Applied to Child Education in "The Children's Houses" with Additions and Revisions by the Author.* New York: Frederick A. Stokes.

Montessori, Maria; Simmonds, Florence; and **Livingston, Arthur.** 1917. *The Advanced Montessori Method.* New York: Frederick A. Stokes.

Payne, Joseph. 1877. *Pestalozzi: The Influence of his Principles and Practice on Elementary Education; A Lecture Delivered at the College of Preceptors, February 20, 1875.* New York: E. Steiger.

Pestalozzi, Johann Heinrich, and **Riedel, K.** 1877. *Wie Gertrud ihre Kinder lehrt: mit einer Einleitung, Johann Heinrich Pestalozzi's Leben, Werke und Grundsatze.* Vienna, Austria: A. Pichler's Witwe and Sohn.

Tyack, David B. 1974. *The One Best System: A History of American Urban Education.* Cambridge, MA: Harvard University Press.

Tyack, David B., and **Hansot, Elisabeth.** 1982. *Managers of Virtue: Public School Leadership in America, 1820–1980.* New York: Basic Books.

Webster, Noah. 1788. *The American Spelling Book: Containing, an Easy Standard of Pronunciation. Being the First Part of a Grammatical Institute of the English Language.* In three parts. By Noah Webster, Jun'r. Esquire The eleventh edition. Hartford: Printed by Hudson and Goodwin.

Willis, G. 1993. *The American Curriculum: A Documentary History.* Westport, CT: Greenwood Press.

COMMUNITY AND SOCIAL CONTEXT

Freire, Paulo. 1993. *Pedagogy of the Oppressed.* 20th Anniversary Edition. New York: Continuum.

Freire, Paulo. 1998. *Pedagogy of Freedom: Ethics, Democracy, and Civic Courage.* Lanham, MD: Rowman and Littlefield.

Hollingshead, August de Belmont. 1949. *Elmtown's Youth, the Impact of Social Classes on Adolescents.* New York: J. Wiley.

Peshkin, Alan. 1978. *Growing Up American: Schooling and the Survival of Community.* Chicago: University of Chicago Press.

MISCELLANEOUS

Fullan, Michael G., and Stiegelbauer, Suzanne. 1991. *The Meaning of Educational Change.* New York: Teachers College, Columbia University.

Gardner, Howard. 1993. *Frames of Mind: The Theory of Multiple Intelligences.* New York: Basic Books.

Ginsberg, Rick, and **Plank, David N.,** eds. 1995. *Commissions, Reports, Reforms, and Educational Policy.*Westport, CT: Praeger.

Illich, Ivan. 1971. *Deschooling Society.* New York: Harper and Row.

Jencks, Christopher. 1972. *Inequality: A Reassessment of the Effect of Family and Schooling in America.* New York: Basic Books.

Kluger, Richard. 1976. *Simple Justice: The History of Brown v. Board of Education and Black America's Struggle for Equality.* New York: Knopf.

Maddox, Taddy, ed. 1997. *Tests: A Comprehensive Reference for Assessments in Psychology, Education, and Business,* 4th edition. Austin, TX: Pro-Ed.

McCall, William Anderson. 1922. *How to Measure in Education.* New York: Macmillan.

Myrdal, Gunnar; Sterner, Richard M. E.; and **Rose, Arnold M.** 1944. *An American Dilemma; the Negro Problem and Modern Democracy.* New York: Harper and Brothers.

National Center for Education Statistics. 1966. *Equality of Educational Opportunity Summary Report.* Washington, DC: U.S. Government Printing Office.

Noddings, Nel. 1984. *Caring, a Feminine Approach to Ethics and Moral Education.* Berkeley: University of California Press.

Silberman, Charles E. 1970. *Crisis in the Classroom: The Remaking of American Education.* New York: Random House.

Thorndike, Edward Lee. 1913. *Educational Psychology.* New York: Teachers College, Columbia University.

Tyler, Ralph W. 1950. *Basic Principles of Curriculum and Instruction, Syllabus for Education 360.* Chicago: University of Chicago Press.

Washington, Booker T. 1901. *Up from Slavery; An Autobiography.* New York: A. L. Burt.

APPENDIX VI

OUTLINE OF CONTENTS

The systematic outline in this Appendix is designed to provide a general overview of the conceptual scheme of the Encyclopedia, listing entries or subentries found in the main body of the text along with primary source documents from Appendix III: Court Cases, Legislation, and International Agreements. The outline is divided into sixteen parts: Curriculum; Learning and Instruction; Assessment, Measurement, and Methods; Elementary and Secondary Education; Postsecondary Education; History of Education; Philosophy of Education; Educational Policy and Governance; International Education; Social Context of Education; Out-of-School Influences on Academic Success; Exceptional Students and Special Education; Teacher Education; Administration; Professional Education; and Education and Commerce. Most parts are divided into several sections. Because the section headings are not mutually exclusive, certain entries from the main text and documents from Appendix III are listed more than once.

I. CURRICULUM

A. SCHOOL

Advanced Placement Courses/Exams

Agricultural Education

Art Education: School

Bilingual Education

Business Education: School

Civics and Citizenship Education

Curriculum, School: Core Knowledge Curriculum

Curriculum, School: Hidden Curriculum

Curriculum, School: Overview

Driver Education

English Education: Teaching of

Family and Consumer Sciences Education

Foreign Language Education

Geography, Teaching of

Handwriting, Teaching of

Health Education, School

History: Learning

History: Teaching of

Journalism, Teaching of

Language Arts, Teaching of

Latin in Schools, Teaching of

Mathematics Learning: Algebra

Mathematics Learning: Complex Problem Solving

Mathematics Learning: Geometry

Mathematics Learning: Learning Tools

Mathematics Learning: Myths, Mysteries, and Realities

Mathematics Learning: Number Sense

Mathematics Learning: Numeracy and Culture

Mathematics Learning: Word-Problem Solving

Multicultural Education

Music Education: Overview

Outdoor and Environmental Education

Physical Education: Overview

Physical Education: Preparation of Teachers

Reading: Teaching of

Science Education: Overview

Science Learning: Explanation and Argumentation

Science Learning: Knowledge Organization and Understanding

Science Learning: Standards

Science Learning: Tools

Service Learning: School

Sexuality Education
Social Studies Education: Overview
Speech and Theater Education
Spelling, Teaching of
Student Activities: Overview
Technology Education
Vocational and Technical Education: Current Trends
Vocational and Technical Education: History of
Writing, Teaching of

B. HIGHER EDUCATION
Academic Calendars
Academic Major, The
African-American Studies
Berea College
Bethune, Mary McLeod
Buchanan, Scott
Capstone Courses in Higher Education
College Seminars for First-Year Students
Curriculum, Higher Education: Innovations in the Undergraduate Curriculum
Curriculum, Higher Education: National Reports on the Undergraduate Curriculum
Curriculum, Higher Education: Traditional and Contemporary Perspectives
Eliot, Charles
Gay and Lesbian Studies
General Education in Higher Education
Honors Programs in Higher Education
Hutchins, Robert
Interdisciplinary Courses and Majors in Higher Education
Internships in Higher Education
Learning Communities and the Undergraduate Curriculum
Life Experience for College Credit
Lifelong Learning
Mieklejohn, Alexander
Multiculturalism in Higher Education
Rice, John A.
Service Learning: Higher Education
Study Abroad
Taylor, Harold
Women's Studies

C. INTERNATIONAL
Curriculum, International
Elementary Education: Current Trends
Freire, Paulo
Froebel, Friedrich
Herbart, Johann
Montessori, Maria
Neill, A. S.
Pestalozzi, Johann
Secondary Education: International Issues
Steiner, Rudolf
Vocational and Technical Education: International Context

II. LEARNING AND INSTRUCTION
Pressey, Sidney L.
Rogers, Carl
Skinner, B. F.
Teaching and Learning: International Perspective
Vygotsky, Lev
Watson, John B.

A. AFFECTIVE AND SOCIAL PROCESSES IN LEARNING AND DEVELOPMENT

1. Affective and Social Processes
Aggressive Behavior
Character Development
Cooperative and Collaborative Learning
Educational Psychology
Instructional Design: Learning Communities
Moral Development
Peace Education
Peer Relations and Learning

2. Motivation
Motivation: Instruction
Motivation: Overview
Motivation: Self-Regulated Learning

3. Effort and Interest
Effort and Interest
Motivation: Self-Regulated Learning
Reading: Interest

B. THEORIES OF DEVELOPMENT AND LEARNING
Bloom, B. S.
Developmental Theory: Cognitive and Information Processing
Developmental Theory: Evolutionary Approach
Developmental Theory: Historical Overview
Developmental Theory: Vygotskian Theory

Educational Psychology
Learning Theory: Constructivist Approach
Learning Theory: Historical Overview
Learning Theory: Schema Theory
Motor Learning
Piaget, Jean

1. Processes of Human Development
Affect and Emotional Development
Aggressive Behavior
Character Development
Child Development, Stages of Growth
Creativity
Erikson, Erik
Havighurst, Robert J.
Kohlberg, Lawrence
Memory: Development of
Moral Development
Peer Relations and Learning

C. LEARNING PROCESSES
Teaching and Learning: International Perspective

1. Biological Bases of Behavior
Brain-Based Education
Learning: Neurological Foundation

2. Individual Differences
Individual Differences: Abilities and Aptitudes
Individual Differences: Affective and Conative Processes
Individual Differences: Ethnicity
Individual Differences: Gender Equity and Schooling

3. Intelligence
Intelligence: Emotional Intelligence
Intelligence: Measurement
Intelligence: Multiple Intelligences
Intelligence: Myths, Mysteries, and Realities
Intelligence: Triarchic Theory of Intelligence

4. Attention, Memory, and Perception
Attention
Learning: Perceptual Processes
Memory: Autobiographical Memory
Memory: Development of
Memory: Graphics, Diagrams, and Videos
Memory: Implicit Memory
Memory: Mental Models
Memory: Metamemory
Memory: Myths, Mysteries, and Realities
Memory: Structures and Functions
Mnemonic Strategies and Techniques

5. Knowledge Acquisition and Expertise
Expertise: Adaptive Expertise
Expertise: Domain Expertise
Knowledge Building
Knowledge Management
Learning to Learn and Metacognition
Learning: Conceptual Change
Learning: Knowledge Acquisition, Representation, and Organization
Reading: Comprehension
Reading: Learning from Text
Reading: Prior Knowledge, Beliefs, and Learning
Science Learning: Knowledge Organization and Understanding

6. Problem Solving and Reasoning
Creativity
Instructional Design: Problem-Based Learning
Learning: Analogical Reasoning
Learning: Causal Reasoning
Learning: Problem Solving
Learning: Reasoning
Learning: Transfer of Learning
Learning to Learn and Metacognition

7. Technology, Media, and Learning
Computer-Supported Collaborative Learning
International Assessments: IEA Study of Technology in the Classroom
International Gap in Technology, The
Literacy: Learning from Multimedia Sources
Literacy: Multimedia Literacy
Mathematics Learning: Learning Tools
Media and Learning
Media, Influence on Children
School-Linked Services: Outcomes
School-Linked Services: Types of Services and Organizational Forms
Science Learning: Tools
Sexual Orientation
Summer Enrichment Programs
Technology Education
Technology in Education: Current Trends

Technology in Education: Higher Education
Technology in Education: School
Vocational and Technical Education: International Context

D. LITERACY, LITERACY STUDIES, AND READING

Bilingualism, Second Language Learning, and English as a Second Language
Chall, Jeanne
Discourse: Classroom Discourse
Discourse: Cognitive Perspective
Gray, William Scott
International Assessments: IEA and OECD Studies of Reading Literacy
Language Acquisition
Language Arts, Teaching of
Literacy: Emergent Literacy
Literacy: Intertextuality
Literacy: Learning from Multimedia Sources
Literacy: Multimedia Literacy
Literacy: Narrative Comprehension and Production
Literacy: Vocabulary and Vocabulary Learning
Literacy: Writing and Composition
Literacy and Culture
Literacy and Reading
Readability Indices
Reading: Beginning Reading
Reading: Comprehension
Reading: Content Areas
Reading: Interest
Reading: Learning from Text
Reading: Prior Knowledge, Beliefs, and Learning
Reading: Value of Reading Engagement for Children

E. CONTENT AREA LEARNING

1. Mathematics

International Assessments: IEA Third International Mathematics and Science Study
Mathematics Learning: Algebra
Mathematics Learning: Complex Problem Solving
Mathematics Learning: Geometry
Mathematics Learning: Learning Tools
Mathematics Learning: Myths, Mysteries, and Realities
Mathematics Learning: Number Sense
Mathematics Learning: Numeracy and Culture
Mathematics Learning: Word-Problem Solving

2. Science

International Assessments: IEA Third International Mathematics and Science Study
Science Education: Overview
Science Learning: Explanation and Argumentation
Science Learning: Knowledge Organization and Understanding
Science Learning: Standards
Science Learning: Tools

3. Social Studies

Character Development
History: Learning
History: Teaching of
International Assessments: Political Democracy and the IEA Study of Civic Education
Social Studies Education: Overview

4. Language Arts

Chall, Jeanne
Children's Literature
Gray, William Scott
Handwriting, Teaching of
International Assessments: IEA and OECD Studies of Reading Literacy
Language Acquisition
Language Arts, Teaching of
Literacy: Emergent Literacy
Literacy: Intertextuality
Literacy: Learning from Multimedia Sources
Literacy: Multimedia Literacy
Literacy: Narrative Comprehension and Production
Literacy: Vocabulary and Vocabulary Learning
Literacy: Writing and Composition
Literacy and Reading
Readability Indices
Reading: Beginning Reading
Reading: Comprehension
Reading: Content Areas
Reading: Interest
Reading: Learning from Text

Reading: Prior Knowledge, Beliefs, and Learning

Reading: Value of Reading Engagement for Children

Spelling, Teaching of

Writing, Teaching of

5. Visual and Performing Arts

Art Education: Preparation of Teachers

Art Education: School

Barkan, Manuel

National Art Education Association

National Association of Schools of Art and Design

Speech and Theater Education

6. Vocational and Technical Education

State Departments of Education: Vocational Education

Vocational and Technical Education: Current Trends

Vocational and Technical Education: History of

Vocational and Technical Education: International Context

Vocational and Technical Education: Preparation of Teachers

Vocational School Fallacy

F. INSTRUCTIONAL PROCESSES AND INSTRUCTIONAL DESIGN

Discourse: Classroom Discourse

Discourse: Cognitive Perspective

Instructional Design: Anchored Instruction

Instructional Design: Case-Based Reasoning

Instructional Design: Direct Instruction

Instructional Design: Learning Communities

Instructional Design: Learning through Design

Instructional Design: Overview

Instructional Design: Pedagogical Agents and Tutors

Instructional Design: Problem-Based Learning

Motivation: Instruction

G. INTELLIGENCE

Binet, Alfred

Gifted and Talented, Education of

Intelligence: Emotional Intelligence

Intelligence: Measurement

Intelligence: Multiple Intelligences

Intelligence: Myths, Mysteries, and Realities

Intelligence: Triarchic Theory of Intelligence

III. ASSESSMENT, MEASUREMENT, AND METHODS

Assessment: Classroom Assessment

Assessment: Dynamic Assessment

Assessment: National Assessment of Educational Progress

Assessment: Performance Assessment

Assessment: Portfolio Assessment

Binet, Alfred

Buros, Oscar Krisen

Charters, W. W.

Educational Testing Service

General Educational Development Test

Goddard, Henry H.

Intelligence: Measurement

International Assessments: IEA and OECD Studies of Reading Literacy

International Assessments: IEA Third International Mathematics and Science Study

International Assessments: International Association for Educational Assessment

International Assessments: Political Democracy and the IEA Study of Civic Education

International Education Statistics: Overview

International Education Statistics: The Use of Indicators to Evaluate the Condition of Education Systems

Lindquist, E. F.

McCall, William A.

Research Methods: Overview

Research Methods: Qualitative and Ethnographic

Research Methods: School and Program Evaluation

Research Methods: Verbal Protocols

Rice, Joseph Mayer

Taxonomies of Educational Objectives

Terman, Lewis

Testing: International Standards of Test Development

Testing: Standardized Tests and Educational Policy

Testing: Standardized Tests and High-Stakes Assessment

Testing: Statewide Testing Programs

Testing: Test Preparation Programs, Impact of

Thorndike, Edward L.

A. TOOLS FOR ASSESSMENT

Assessment Tools: Psychometric and Statistical

Assessment Tools: Technology Based

International Assessments: Overview

B. STANDARDS FOR ASSESSMENT
Science Learning: Standards
Social Promotion
Standards for Student Learning
Standards Movement in American Education
Testing: International Standards of Test Development
Testing: Standardized Tests and Educational Policy

C. ASSESSMENT ORGANIZATIONS
Assessment: National Assessment of Educational Progress
Educational Testing Service
International Assessments: International Association for Educational Assessment
International Assessments: International Association for the Evaluation of Educational Achievement
Nongovernmental Organizations and Foundations
Testing: Test Preparation Programs, Impact of

IV. ELEMENTARY AND SECONDARY EDUCATION

A. TYPES OF SCHOOLS/SCHOOLING
Accelerated Schools
Alternative Schooling
American Overseas Schools
Catholic Schools
Common School Movement
Community Education
Early Childhood Education: Overview
Elementary Education: Current Trends
Elementary Education: History of
Home Schooling
Immigrant Education: United States
Independent Study, Schools
Infant Schools in England
International Baccalaureate Diploma
Magnet Schools
Middle Schools
Migrants, Education of
Mississippi Freedom Schools
Nongraded Schools
Open Classroom Schools
Outdoor and Environmental Education
Private Schooling
Professional Development Schools
Progressive Education
Protestant School Systems
Rural Education: Overview
Secondary Education: Current Trends
Secondary Education: History of
Summer School
Urban Education

B. SCHOOL SERVICES AND POLICIES
Abington School District v. Schempp (1963) *Appendix III*
Brown v. Board of Education (1954 and 1955) *Appendix III*
Commencement
Compulsory School Attendance
Engel v. Vitale (1962) *Appendix III*
Full-Service Schools
Guidance and Counseling, School
Head Start: Overview of Programs and Legislation (1999) *Appendix III*
Health Services: School
Parental Involvement in Education
Plessy v. Ferguson (1896) *Appendix III*
Psychologist, School
Records and Reports, School
Recreation Programs in the Schools
School Libraries
School-Linked Services: Outcomes
School-Linked Services: Types of Services and Organizational Forms
Special Education: International Context
Sports, School: Overview
Sports, School: Role in Student's Social and Emotional Development
Swann v. Charlotte-Mecklenburg Board of Education (1971) *Appendix III*
Textbooks: Overview
Tinker et al. v. Des Moines Independent Community School District et al. (1969) *Appendix III*
Title IX of the Education Amendments of 1972 *Appendix III*

C. INSTRUCTIONAL METHODS
Class Size and Student Learning
Classroom Management
Classroom Observation
Classroom Questions

Discourse: Classroom Discourse
Discourse: Cognitive Perspective
Grading Systems: School
Group Processes in the Classroom
Homework
Individualized Instruction
Instructional Design: Anchored Instruction
Instructional Design: Case-Based Reasoning
Instructional Design: Direct Instruction
Instructional Design: Learning through Design
Instructional Design: Overview
Instructional Design: Pedagogical Agents and Tutors
Instructional Design: Problem-Based Learning
Instructional Objectives
Instructional Strategies
Language and Education
Microteaching
Motivation: Instruction
Open Classroom Schools
Scheduling
Technology in Education: School
Textbooks: Overview
Textbooks: School Textbooks in the United States

V. POSTSECONDARY EDUCATION
Federal Schools and Colleges
Harvard University
Higher Education in Context
Higher Education in the United States: Historical Development
Higher Education, International Issues
International Students: The Global Commerce of Higher Education
Johns Hopkins University
Military Academies: U.S. Air Force Academy
Military Academies: U.S. Coast Guard Academy
Military Academies: U.S. Merchant Marine Academy
Military Academies: U.S. Military Academy
Military Academies: U.S. Naval Academy
Military Professional Education System
St. John's College
Student Loans in an International Context
University of Chicago
University of Virginia
U.S. War Colleges
Yale University

A. FACULTY
Academic Disciplines
Academic Freedom and Tenure
Academic Labor Markets
American Association of University Professors
Centers for Teaching Improvement in Colleges and Universities
College Teaching
Faculty as Entrepreneurs
Faculty Consulting
Faculty Diversity
Faculty Members, Part Time
Faculty Performance of Research and Scholarship
Faculty Research and Scholarship, Assessment of
Faculty Roles and Responsibilities
Faculty Service Role, The
Faculty Teaching, Assessment of
Future Faculty Preparation Programs
Grading Systems: Higher Education
Graduate School Training
Teaching and Learning: Higher Education
University-Industrial Research Collaboration

B. RESEARCH
Bowen, Howard
Ethics: Higher Education
Faculty as Entrepreneurs
Faculty Performance of Research and Scholarship
Federal Funding for Academic Research
Human Subjects, Protection of
Intellectual Property Rights
Postdoctoral Education
Research Grants and Indirect Costs
Research Misconduct
Research Universities
Teaching and Research, The Relationship between
Technology Transfer
University-Industrial Research Collaboration

C. STUDENTS
1. College Search and Selection
College Admissions

College Admissions Tests
College Entrance Examination Board, The
College Financial Aid
College Recruitment Practices
College Search and Selection
Enrollment Management in Higher Education
National Merit Scholarships

2. Types of Students
Commuter Students
International Students: U.S. Colleges and Universities
Nontraditional Students in Higher Education
Race, Ethnicity, and Culture: Racial and Ethnic Minority Students in Higher Education

3. Student Affairs
Adjustment to College
College and University Residence Halls
College Extracurricular Activities
College Student Retention
Drug and Alcohol Abuse: College
Living and Learning Center Residence Halls
Residential Colleges
Student Orientation Programs
Student Services: Colleges and Universities
Student Services: Community Colleges

4. Student Organizations
Honor Societies: Alpha Chi
Honor Societies: Alpha Mu Gamma
Honor Societies: Alpha Omega Alpha
Honor Societies: Association for Women in Communications
Honor Societies: Association of College Honor Societies
Honor Societies: Beta Phi Mu
Honor Societies: Delta Kappa Gamma Society
Honor Societies: Delta Sigma Rho–Tau Kappa Alpha
Honor Societies: Kappa Delta Pi
Honor Societies: Kappa Omicron Nu
Honor Societies: Lambda Iota Tau
Honor Societies: Phi Beta Kappa
Honor Societies: Phi Delta Kappa International
Honor Societies: Pi Kappa Lambda
Honor Societies: Pi Sigma Alpha
Honor Societies: Rho Chi
Honor Societies: Sigma Xi
Honor Societies: Tau Beta Pi
Honors Programs in Higher Education
Social Fraternities and Sororities

5. Student Services
Career Counseling in Higher Education
College Students with Disabilities: Accommodating
College Students with Disabilities: Special Learning Needs
Health Services: Colleges and Universities
Personal and Psychological Counseling at Colleges and Universities
Personal and Psychological Problems of College Students
Student Services: Colleges and Universities
Student Services: Community Colleges

6. Academic Performance
Grading Systems: Higher Education
Honor Societies: Alpha Chi
Honor Societies: Phi Beta Kappa
Honor Societies: Sigma Xi
Honor Societies: Tau Beta Pi
Tutoring: Higher Education

7. Affective Development
College and Its Effect on Students

D. ORGANIZATIONAL STRUCTURE OF COLLEGES AND UNIVERSITIES
Boyer, Ernest
Butler, Nicholas M.
Harper, William Rainey
Palmer, Alice Freeman

1. Governance and Decision-Making
Board of Trustees, College and University
Colleges and Universities, Organizational Structure of
Faculty Senates, College and University
Governance and Decision-Making in Colleges and Universities

2. Administrative Officers of Colleges and Universities
Academic Dean, The
Chief Academic Affairs Officers, College and University
Department Chairperson, The
Presidency, College and University

3. Functional Areas
Accounting Systems in Higher Education

Enrollment Management in Higher Education

Institutional Advancement in Higher Education

Institutional Research in Higher Education

University Presses

4. Administrative Issues

Affirmative Action Compliance in Higher Education

Risk Management in Higher Education

Strategic and Long-Range Planning in Higher Education

Technology in Education: Higher Education

E. ACADEMIC ORGANIZATIONS

American Association for Higher Education

American Association of Community Colleges

American Association of State Colleges and Universities

American Association of University Professors

American Council on Education

Association of American Colleges and Universities

Association of American Universities

Honor Societies: Alpha Chi

Honor Societies: Alpha Mu Gamma

Honor Societies: Alpha Omega Alpha

Honor Societies: Association for Women in Communications

Honor Societies: Association of College Honor Societies

Honor Societies: Beta Phi Mu

Honor Societies: Delta Kappa Gamma Society

Honor Societies: Delta Sigma Rho–Tau Kappa Alpha

Honor Societies: Kappa Delta Pi

Honor Societies: Kappa Omicron Nu

Honor Societies: Lambda Iota Tau

Honor Societies: Phi Beta Kappa

Honor Societies: Phi Delta Kappa International

Honor Societies: Pi Kappa Lambda

Honor Societies: Pi Sigma Alpha

Honor Societies: Rho Chi

Honor Societies: Sigma Xi

Honor Societies: Tau Beta Pi

Honors Programs in Higher Education

International Reading Association

National Association of Independent Colleges and Universities

National Association of Independent Schools

National Association of State Universities and Land-Grant Colleges

F. CURRICULUM

Academic Calendars

Academic Major, The

African-American Studies

Capstone Courses in Higher Education

College Seminars for First-Year Students

Curriculum, Higher Education: Innovations in the Undergraduate Curriculum

Curriculum, Higher Education: National Reports on the Undergraduate Curriculum

Curriculum, Higher Education: Traditional and Contemporary Perspectives

Curriculum, International

Gay and Lesbian Studies

General Education in Higher Education

Honors Programs in Higher Education

Interdisciplinary Courses and Majors in Higher Education

Internships in Higher Education

Islam

Learning Communities and the Undergraduate Curriculum

Life Experience for College Credit

Lifelong Learning

Multiculturalism in Higher Education

Service Learning: Higher Education

Study Abroad

Women's Studies

G. ATHLETICS

College Athletics: Academic Support Systems for Athletes

College Athletics: Athletic Scholarships

College Athletics: College Students as Athletes

College Athletics: History of Athletics in U.S. Colleges and Universities

College Athletics: Intramural Athletics in U.S. Colleges and Universities

College Athletics: NCAA Rules and Regulations

College Athletics: The National Collegiate Athletic Association

College Athletics: The Role and Scope of Intercollegiate Athletics in U.S. Colleges and Universities

Title IX: Intercollegiate Athletics

H. COMMUNITY COLLEGES
American Association of Community Colleges
Community Colleges
Koos, Leonard
Student Services: Community Colleges

I. SYSTEM OF HIGHER EDUCATION AND TYPES OF INSTITUTIONS
Accreditation in an International Context, Higher Education
Accreditation in the United States: Higher Education
Carnegie Classification System, The
College Rankings
Colleges and Universities with Religious Affiliations
Consortia in Higher Education
Corporate Colleges
Higher Education in Context
Higher Education in the United States: System
Hispanic-Serving Colleges and Universities
Historically Black Colleges and Universities
Land-Grant Colleges and Universities
Liberal Arts Colleges
Research Universities
Single-Sex Institutions
Tribal Colleges and Universities

J. DISTANCE LEARNING AND POSTSECONDARY EDUCATION
Distance Learning in Higher Education
Globalization of Education
International Trade in Education Programs, Goods, and Services
Student Loans in an International Context

K. GRADUATE EDUCATION
Business Education: College and Graduate Study
Dentistry Education
Divinity Studies
Doctoral Degree, The
Engineering Education
Flexner, Abraham
Graduate Record Examination
Graduate School Training
Graduate Study in Education
Law Education
Law School Admission Test
Master's Degree, The
Medical College Admission Test
Medical Education
Nursing Education
Postdoctoral Education

VI. HISTORY OF EDUCATION

A. COLONIAL PERIOD
Harvard University
Land Ordinance of 1785 *Appendix III*
Northwest Ordinance of 1787 *Appendix III*
Textbooks: School Textbooks in the United States

B. COMMON SCHOOL PERIOD
Common School Movement
Mann, Horace
Morrill Land-Grant Act of 1862 *Appendix III*
Second Morrill Act of 1890 *Appendix III*
Stuart et al. v. School District No. 1 of the Village of Kalamazoo et al. (1874) *Appendix III*
Webster, Noah

C. LATE NINETEENTH CENTURY
Hall, G. Stanley
McMurry, Charles

D. PROGRESSIVE ERA
Bode, Boyd H.
Childs, John L.
Clapp, Elsie Ripley
Counts, George S.
Dalton School
Gary Schools
Johnson, Marietta Pierce
Kilpatrick, William H.
Lincoln School
My Pedagogic Creed by John Dewey (1897) *Appendix III*
Plessy v. Ferguson (1896) *Appendix III*
Progressive Education
Rugg, Harold

E. GENERAL CURRICULUM AND INSTRUCTION
Alberty, H. B.
Benjamin, H. R. W.
Bestor, A. E., Jr.
Bobbitt, Franklin

Broudy, Harry S.
Curriculum, Higher Education: Traditional and Contemporary Perspectives
Curriculum, International
Curriculum, School: Overview
Kandel, Isaac L.
Macdonald, James
Miel, Alice
Taba, Hilda
Teacher Education: Historical Overview
Vocational and Technical Education: History of
Vocational and Technical Education: International Context
Vocational School Fallacy

F. EARLY CHILDHOOD EDUCATION
Blow, Susan
Early Childhood Education: International Context
Early Childhood Education: Overview
Froebel, Friedrich
Montessori, Maria
Putnam, Alice

G. ELEMENTARY EDUCATION
Barkan, Manuel
De Lima, Agnes
Elementary Education: History of
Hopkins, L. Thomas
Infant Schools in England
Lowenfeld, Viktor
Washburne, Carleton
Zirbes, Laura

H. SECONDARY EDUCATION
Carnegie Units
Eight-Year Study
Fawcett, Harold P.
Hanna, Paul
LaBrant, Lou L.
Morrison, Henry C.
Prosser, Charles
Secondary Education: History of
Secondary Education: International Issues
Smith, David Eugene
Snedden, David
Zacharias, Jerrold

I. HIGHER EDUCATION
Conant, J. B.
Harvard University
Higher Education in the United States: Historical Development
Historically Black Colleges and Universities
Johns Hopkins University
St. John's College
University of Chicago
University of Virginia
Yale University

VII. PHILOSOPHY OF EDUCATION
Aristotle
Augustine, St.
Bagley, William C.
Comenius, Johann
Dewey, John
Educational Change
Government and Education, The Changing Role of
Islam
James, William
Misconduct in Education
Philosophy of Education: Current Trends
Plato
Rousseau, Jean-Jacques
Vocational and Technical Education: International Context
Vocational School Fallacy
Whitehead, Alfred North

VIII. EDUCATIONAL POLICY AND GOVERNANCE
Conant, J. B.
Decentralization and Education
Educational Policy
Efficiency in Education
Intergovernmental Relations in Education
Public Education, Criticism of
Tyler, Ralph W.
Young, Ella Flagg

A. FEDERAL GOVERNMENT
Compensatory Education: United States
Constitutional Requirements Governing American Education
Constitution of the United States (1787) *Appendix III*
Educational Resources Information Center
Federal Educational Activities: History

Federal Educational Activities: Summary by Agency

Federal Interagency Committee on Education

Federal Schools and Colleges

G.I. Bill of Rights

Impact Aid, Public Laws 815 and 874

Military Training Doctrine, Philosophy and Practice

No Child Left Behind Act of 2001 *Appendix III*

People with Disabilities, Federal Programs to Assist

School Food Programs

Title IX: School Sports

Upward Bound

U.S. Department of Education: International Role

U.S. Department of Education: Overview

White House Fellows

B. STATE GOVERNMENT

State Constitutions and Public Education Governance (2000) *Appendix III*

State Departments of Education: Role and Function

State Departments of Education: Vocational Education

State Educational Systems

States and Education: Legal Basis of State Relations to Nonpublic Schools

States and Education: State Administrative Services in Education

States and Education: State Boards of Education

States and Education: State Governments in Higher Education

U.S. Department of Education: Overview

C. LOCAL GOVERNMENT

Liability of School Districts and School Personnel for Negligence

School Board Relations: Control of the Schools

School Board Relations: Relation of School Board to the Community

School Board Relations: Relation of School Board to the Superintendent

School Boards: Duties, Responsibilities, Decision-Making, and Legal Basis for Local School Board Powers

School Boards: Selection and Education of Members

School Facilities: Maintenance and Modernization of

Superintendent of Large-City School Systems

Superintendent of Schools

Transportation and School Busing

D. ECONOMIC DEVELOPMENT

Economic Benefits of Education Investment, Measurement

Education Development Projects

Social Capital and Education

Social Cohesion and Education

Vocational and Technical Education: International Context

Vocational School Fallacy

E. FINANCING

Cost Effectiveness in Education

Decision-Making in Schools, Applying Economic Analysis to

Educational Broadcasting, Federal Support

Educational Expenditures, Projecting

Financial Support of Schools: History

Financial Support of Schools: State Support

Student Activities: Financing

1. Elementary and Secondary Education

Financial Support of Schools: Capital Outlay in Local School Systems

Public School Budgeting, Accounting, and Auditing

San Antonio Independent School District et al. v. Rodriguez et al. (1973) *Appendix III*

Stuart et al. v. School District No. 1 of the Village of Kalamazoo et al. (1874) *Appendix III*

2. Postsecondary Education

Federal Funds for Higher Education

Finance, Higher Education: Community and Junior Colleges

Finance, Higher Education: Overview

Resource Allocation in Higher Education

Student Loans in an International Context

F. EDUCATION REFORM

A Nation at Risk (abbreviated)(1983) *Appendix III*

Accelerated Schools

Coalition of Essential Schools' Common Principles

Coleman, James S.

Educational Accountability

Educational Change

Education Reform: Overview

Education Reform: Reports of Historical Significance
Experiential Education
Government and Education, The Changing Role of
Joint Statement on the Education Summit with the Nation's Governors in Charlottesville, Virginia (1989) *Appendix III*
Looping
Outcome Based Education
National Education Goals Panel: Goals 2000 *Appendix III*
No Child Left Behind Act of 2001 *Appendix III*
Paideia Program
School-Based Decision-Making
School Reform
Science Learning: Standards
Standards for Student Learning
Standards Movement in American Education
Student Loans in an International Context
Success for All Programs
Vocational and Technical Education: International Context
Vocational School Fallacy
Year-Round Education

G. PRIVATIZATION
Beacon Education Management, Inc.
Business Involvement in Education
Catholic Schools
Modern Red Schoolhouse
New American Schools
Private Schooling
Protestant School Systems
Student Loans in an International Context

H. EDUCATION ECONOMICS
Economic Benefits of Education Investment, Measurement
Education Development Projects
International Gap in Technology, The
International Issues of Social Mobility of Underprivileged Groups
International Trade in Education Programs, Goods, and Services
Misconduct in Education
Social Capital and Education
Social Cohesion and Education
Student Loans in an International Context
Vocational and Technical Education: International Context
Vocational School Fallacy

I. STATISTICS
International Education Statistics: Overview
International Education Statistics: The Use of Indicators to Evaluate the Condition of Education Systems
National Center for Education Statistics
Youth Demographic Trends

J. EDUCATIONAL LAWS AND TREATIES
Abington School District v. Schempp (1963) *Appendix III*
Brown v. Board of Education (1954 and 1955) *Appendix III*
Charter of the United Nations, Article 1 (1945) *Appendix III*
Constitutional Requirements Governing American Education
Constitution of the United Nations Educational, Scientific and Cultural Organization (1945) *Appendix III*
Constitution of the United States (1787) *Appendix III*
Convention against Discrimination in Education (1960) *Appendix III*
Convention on the Rights of the Child (1989) *Appendix III*
Council of Europe Framework Convention for the Protection of National Minorities (1995) *Appendix III*
Declaration of the Rights of the Child (1959) *Appendix III*
Declaration on Race and Racial Prejudice (1978) *Appendix III*
Declaration on the Rights of Persons Belonging to National or Ethnic, Religious and Linguistic Minorities (1992) *Appendix III*
Document of the Copenhagen Meeting on the Human Dimension of the Conference on Security and Co-operation in Europe (1990) *Appendix III*
Education for All Handicapped Children Act of 1975 *Appendix III*
Education of the Handicapped Act Amendments of 1990 *Appendix III*
Elementary and Secondary Education Act of 1965 *Appendix III*
Engel v. Vitale (1962) *Appendix III*
European Charter for Regional or Minority Languages (1992) *Appendix III*
European Convention on Human Rights and Its Five Protocols (1950) *Appendix III*
Green et al. v. County School Board of New Kent County et al. (1968) *Appendix III*

Head Start: Overview of Programs and Legislation (1999) *Appendix III*

Impact Aid, Public Laws 815 and 874

International Development Agencies and Education: Bilateral Agencies

International Development Agencies and Education: Regional Institutions

International Development Agencies and Education: United Nations and International Agencies

International Education Agreements

Land Ordinance of 1785 *Appendix III*

Lau et al. v. Nichols et al. (1974) *Appendix III*

Mills v. Board of Education of the District of Columbia (1972) *Appendix III*

Misconduct in Education

Morrill Land-Grant Act of 1862 *Appendix III*

National Education Goals Panel: Goals 2000 *Appendix III*

No Child Left Behind Act of 2001 *Appendix III*

Northwest Ordinance of 1787 *Appendix III*

Pennsylvania Association of Retarded Children v. Commonwealth of Pennsylvania (1971) *Appendix III*

Pierce v. Society of the Sisters of the Holy Names of Jesus and Mary (1925) *Appendix III*

Plessy v. Ferguson (1896) *Appendix III*

San Antonio Independent School District et al. v. Rodriguez et al. (1973) *Appendix III*

Second Morrill Act of 1890 *Appendix III*

Segregation, Legal Aspects

Stuart et al. v. School District No. 1 of the Village of Kalamazoo et al. (1874) *Appendix III*

Supreme Court of the United States and Education, The

Swann v. Charlotte-Mecklenburg Board of Education (1971) *Appendix III*

Tinker et al. v. Des Moines Independent Community School District et al. (1969) *Appendix III*

Title IX of the Education Amendments of 1972 *Appendix III*

Universal Declaration of Human Rights (1948) *Appendix III*

University of California Regents v. Bakke (1978) *Appendix III*

U.S. Department of Education: International Role

Wisconsin v. Yoder (1972) *Appendix III*

World Declaration on Education for All (1990) *Appendix III*

K. PROFESSIONAL AND POLICY ORGANIZATIONS AND PHILANTHROPIC ORGANIZATIONS

Brookings Institution

Education Commission of the States

Institute of International Education

Journalism Education Association

Modern Language Association of America

National Academy of Sciences

National Archives and Records Administration

National Board for Professional Teaching Standards

National Center for Education Statistics

National Conference of State Legislatures

National Council for Accreditation of Teacher Education

National Council for the Social Studies

National Council of Teachers of English

National Council of Teachers of Mathematics

National Endowment for the Arts

National Endowment for the Humanities

National Governors Association

National Merit Scholarships

National School Boards Association

National Science Foundation

NTL Institute for Applied Behavioral Science

Regional Laboratories and Research and Development Centers

Sea Grant Program

Smithsonian Institution, Education Programs

University Council for Educational Administration

Urban Institute

L. ASSOCIATIONS AND INTEREST GROUPS

AACSB International

Accreditation in the United States: School

Accrediting Commission of Career Schools and Colleges of Technology

American Academy of Arts and Sciences

American Alliance for Health, Physical Education, Recreation, and Dance

American Association for the Advancement of Science

American Association of Colleges for Teacher Education

American Association of Colleges of Pharmacy

American Association of Physics Teachers
American Association of School Administrators
American Association of University Women
American Council of Learned Societies
Council for Basic Education
Council for Exceptional Children
Educational Interest Groups
International Society for Performance Improvement
National Art Education Association
National Association for the Education of Young Children
National Association of Biology Teachers
National Association of Elementary School Principals
National Association of Schools of Art and Design
National Association of Secondary School Principals
National Association of State Boards of Education
National Business Education Association
National Catholic Educational Association
National Committee for Children and Youth
National Communication Association
National Honor Society
National PTA
National School Public Relations Association
National Science Teachers Association
Nongovernmental Organizations and Foundations
Youth Organizations: American Field Service
Youth Organizations: Big Brothers Big Sisters of America
Youth Organizations: B'nai B'rith Youth Organization
Youth Organizations: Boys and Girls Clubs of America
Youth Organizations: Boys and Girls States
Youth Organizations: Boy Scouts of America
Youth Organizations: Camp Fire USA
Youth Organizations: Distributive Education Clubs of America
Youth Organizations: Four-H Programs
Youth Organizations: Future Business Leaders of America–Phi Beta Lambda
Youth Organizations: Future Scientists and Engineers of America
Youth Organizations: Girl Scouts of the USA
Youth Organizations: Hostelling International–American Youth Hostels
Youth Organizations: National Forensic League
Youth Organizations: National Future Farmers of America Organization
Youth Organizations: Quill and Scroll
Youth Organizations: SkillsUSA–VICA
Youth Organizations: Young Men's Christian Association
Youth Organizations: Young Men's Hebrew Association and Young Women's Hebrew Association
Youth Organizations: Young Women's Christian Association

M. INTERNATIONAL ORGANIZATIONS
Charter of the United Nations, Article 1 (1945) *Appendix III*
Constitution of the United Nations Educational, Scientific and Cultural Organization (1945) *Appendix III*
International Development Agencies and Education: Bilateral Agencies
International Development Agencies and Education: Regional Institutions
International Development Agencies and Education: United Nations and International Agencies
Nongovernmental Organizations and Foundations

N. TEACHER UNIONS
American Federation of Teachers
Haley, Margaret
International Teachers Associations
National Education Association
Shanker, Albert
Teacher Unions: Influence on Instruction and Other Educational Practices
Teacher Unions: Overview

O. FACILITIES
School Facilities: Maintenance and Modernization of
School Facilities: Overview
School Libraries

IX. INTERNATIONAL EDUCATION
Decision-Making in Developing Nations, Applying Economic Analysis to

A. COMPARATIVE EDUCATION
Convention against Discrimination in Education (1960) *Appendix III*
Convention on the Rights of the Child (1989) *Appendix III*

Council of Europe Framework Convention for the Protection of National Minorities (1995) *Appendix III*

Curriculum, International

Declaration of the Rights of the Child (1959) *Appendix III*

Declaration on Race and Racial Prejudice (1978) *Appendix III*

Declaration on the Rights of Persons Belonging to National or Ethnic, Religious and Linguistic Minorities (1992) *Appendix III*

Document of the Copenhagen Meeting on the Human Dimension of the Conference on Security and Co-operation in Europe (1990) *Appendix III*

Early Childhood Education: International Context

Economic Benefits of Education Investment, Measurement

Educational Change

Education Development Projects

European Charter for Regional or Minority Languages (1992) *Appendix III*

European Convention on Human Rights and Its Five Protocols (1950) *Appendix III*

Gender Issues, International

Globalization of Education

Government and Education, The Changing Role of

Health and Education

Higher Education, International Issues

Immigrant Education: International

International Aspects of Education Commerce

International Assessments: IEA and OECD Studies of Reading Literacy

International Assessments: IEA Study of Technology in the Classroom

International Assessments: IEA Third International Mathematics and Science Study

International Assessments: International Association for Educational Assessment

International Assessments: International Association for the Evaluation of Educational Achievement

International Assessments: Political Democracy and the IEA Study of Civic Education

International Development Agencies and Education: Bilateral Agencies

International Development Agencies and Education: Regional Institutions

International Development Agencies and Education: United Nations and International Agencies

International Education

International Education Agreements

International Education Statistics: Overview

International Education Statistics: The Use of Indicators to Evaluate the Condition of Education Systems

International Gap in Technology, The

International Issues of Social Mobility of Underprivileged Groups

International Students: The Global Commerce of Higher Education

International Teachers Associations

International Trade in Education Programs, Goods, and Services

Islam

Misconduct in Education

Nongovernmental Organizations and Foundations

Population and Education

Rural Education: International Context

Secondary Education: International Issues

Social Capital and Education

Social Cohesion and Education

Special Education: International Context

Student Loans in an International Context

Teacher Preparation, International Perspective

Teaching and Learning: International Perspective

Testing: International Standards of Test Development

Testing: Standardized Tests and Educational Policy

Textbooks: Overview

Tutoring: International Trends

Universal Declaration of Human Rights (1948) *Appendix III*

U.S. Department of Education: International Role

Vocational and Technical Education: International Context

Vocational School Fallacy

World Declaration on Education for All (1990) *Appendix III*

B. DEVELOPMENT

Education Development Projects

Gender Issues, International

Health and Education

Higher Education, International Issues
Immigrant Education: International
International Aspects of Education Commerce
International Development Agencies and Education: Bilateral Agencies
International Development Agencies and Education: Regional Institutions
International Development Agencies and Education: United Nations and International Agencies
International Education
International Education Agreements
International Education Statistics: Overview
International Education Statistics: The Use of Indicators to Evaluate the Condition of Education Systems
International Gap in Technology, The
International Issues of Social Mobility of Underprivileged Groups
International Students: The Global Commerce of Higher Education
International Teachers Associations
International Trade in Education Programs, Goods, and Services
Islam
Language and Education
Misconduct in Education
Nongovernmental Organizations and Foundations
Population and Education
Rural Education: International Context
Secondary Education: International Issues
Social Capital and Education
Social Cohesion and Education
Textbooks: Overview
Tutoring: International Trends
Vocational and Technical Education: International Context
Vocational School Fallacy

C. GLOBAL REGIONS
Canada
Compensatory Education: Policies and Programs in Latin America
East Asia and the Pacific
Eastern Europe and Central Asia
Islam
Language and Education
Latin America and the Caribbean
Middle East and North Africa
South Asia
Sub-Saharan Africa
Western Europe

X. SOCIAL CONTEXT OF EDUCATION
Benne, Kenneth D.
Brameld, Theodore
Curti, Merle
Goodman, Paul
School Climate
Schwab, Joseph
Social Organization of Schools

A. MULTICULTURAL EDUCATION
African-American Studies
Bilingualism, Second Language Learning, and English as a Second Language
Bond, Horace Mann
Brown v. Board of Education (1954 and 1955) *Appendix III*
Clark, Septima Poinsette
Collier, John, Jr.
Du Bois, W. E. B.
Gay and Lesbian Studies
Green et al. v. County School Board of New Kent County et al. (1968) *Appendix III*
Individual Differences: Ethnicity
Jeanes Teachers
Language and Education
Language Minority Students: Impact on Education
Language Minority Students: Scope
Lau et al. v. Nichols et al. (1974) *Appendix III*
Literacy and Culture
Mays, Benjamin
Multiculturalism in Higher Education
Plessy v. Ferguson (1896) *Appendix III*
Race, Ethnicity, and Culture: Cultural Expectations and Student Learning
Race, Ethnicity, and Culture: Latino Growth
Race, Ethnicity, and Culture: Racial and Ethnic Minority Students in Higher Education
Sanchez, George I.
Service Learning: Higher Education
Service Learning: Schools
Swann v. Charlotte-Mecklenburg Board of Education (1971) *Appendix III*
Taba, Hilda

Washington, Booker T.
Women's Studies
Woodson, Carter Godwin

B. AFFIRMATIVE ACTION
Affirmative Action Compliance in Higher Education
Gender Issues, International
Immigrant Education: International
Multicultural Education
Supreme Court of the United States and Education, The
University of California Regents v. Bakke (1978) *Appendix III*

C. GENDER
Gender Issues, International
Faculty Diversity
Individual Differences: Gender Equity and Schooling
Single-Sex Institutions
Title IX of the Education Amendments of 1972 *Appendix III*
Women's Studies

D. EDUCATION AND RELIGION
Abington School District v. Schempp (1963) *Appendix III*
Catholic Schools
Colleges and Universities with Religious Affiliations
Engel v. Vitale (1962) *Appendix III*
Higher Education in Context
Islam
Jewish Education, United States
Private Schooling
Protestant School Systems
Wisconsin v. Yoder (1972) *Appendix III*

XI. OUT-OF-SCHOOL INFLUENCES ON ACADEMIC SUCCESS
Out-of-School Influences and Academic Success

A. DEMOGRAPHIC TRENDS
Population and Education
Rural Education: International Context
Youth Demographic Trends

B. RACE, ETHNICITY, AND CULTURE
Gender Issues, International
Individual Differences: Ethnicity
Islam
Language and Education
Language Minority Students: Impact on Education
Language Minority Students: Scope
Lau et al. v. Nichols et al. (1974) *Appendix III*
Literacy and Culture
Multicultural Education
Multiculturalism in Higher Education
Race, Ethnicity, and Culture: Cultural Expectations and Student Learning
Race, Ethnicity, and Culture: Latino Growth
Race, Ethnicity, and Culture: Racial and Ethnic Minority Students in Higher Education
Rural Education: International Context

C. FAMILY CIRCUMSTANCE AND INFLUENCE
Adolescent Peer Culture: Parents' Role
Child Care: Availability and Quality
Child Care: Cost and Financing
Family Composition and Circumstance: Adoption
Family Composition and Circumstance: Alcohol, Tobacco, and Other Drugs
Family Composition and Circumstance: Foster Care
Family Composition and Circumstance: Overview
Family Support Services: Income Support Services for Children and Families
Family Support Services: Overview
Immigrant Education: International
International Assessments: IEA and OECD Studies of Reading Literacy
International Assessments: IEA Study of Technology in the Classroom
International Assessments: IEA Third International Mathematics and Science Study
International Assessments: Political Democracy and the IEA Study of Civic Education
International Issues of Social Mobility of Underprivileged Groups
Language and Education
Latchkey Children
Nongovernmental Organizations and Foundations
Parental Involvement in Education

Parenting: High-Risk Neighborhoods
Parenting: Influence of Parents' Level of Education
Parenting: Influence on Child's Educational Aspirations and Attainment
Parenting: Overview
Population and Education
Poverty and Education: Children and Adolescents
Poverty and Education: Overview
Rural Education: International Context
School Readiness
Special Education: International Context
Student Mobility
Tutoring: International Trends
Violence, Children's Exposure to: Domestic Violence
Violence, Children's Exposure to: General Effects
Welfare Reform: Effects on Families and Children
Welfare Reform: Moving Mothers from Welfare to Work

D. COMMUNITY INFLUENCE
Community-Based Organizations, Agencies, and Groups
Community Education
Family, School, and Community Connections
Neighborhoods
Violence, Children's Exposure to: Community Violence
Violence, Children's Exposure to: General Effects

E. CHILDREN'S HEALTH AND HEALTH CARE
Dental Health and Children
Health and Education
Health Care and Children
Immunization and Children's Physical Health
Managed Care and Children
Mental Health Services and Children
Nutrition and Children's Physical Health
Population and Education
Risk Behaviors: Drug Use Among Teens
Risk Behaviors: HIV/AIDS and Its Impact on Adolescents
Risk Behaviors: Sexual Activity among Teens and Teen Pregnancy Trends
Risk Behaviors: Sexually Transmitted Diseases
Risk Behaviors: Smoking and Its Effect on Children's Health
Risk Behaviors: Suicide
Risk Behaviors: Teen Pregnancy
Sleep and Children's Physical Health
Special Education: International Context

F. OUT-OF-SCHOOL ACTIVITIES
Adolescent Peer Culture: Gangs
Adolescent Peer Culture: Overview
Adolescent Peer Culture: Parents' Role
Child Abuse and Neglect
Child Protective Services: Current System
Child Protective Services: Historical Overview
Clubs
Dropouts, School
Drug and Alcohol Abuse: School
Employment: Employers' Perceptions of Employment Readiness
Employment: General Impact on Students
Employment: Reasons Students Work
Health and Education
Juvenile Justice System: Contemporary Juvenile Justice System and Juvenile Detention Alternatives
Juvenile Justice System: History of Juvenile Courts
Juvenile Justice System: Juvenile Crime and Violence
Language and Education
Media, Influence on Children
Museum as an Educational Institution, The
Population and Education
Rural Education: International Context
Testing: Test Preparation Programs, Impact of
Tutoring: International Trends
Tutoring: School
Violence, Children's Exposure to: Community Violence
Violence, Children's Exposure to: Domestic Violence
Violence, Children's Exposure to: General Effects
Volunteer Work
Youth Development Programs

G. INCOME AND ECONOMIC CHANGE
Compensatory Education: Policies and Programs in Latin America
Family Support Services: Income Support Services for Children and Families

Globalization of Education
Head Start: Overview of Programs and Legislation (1999) *Appendix III*
International Assessments: IEA Study of Technology in the Classroom
International Gap in Technology, The
Population and Education
Poverty and Education

H. VIOLENCE
Adolescent Peer Culture: Gangs
Aggressive Behavior
Child Abuse and Neglect
Child Protective Services: Current System
Child Protective Services: Historical Overview
Juvenile Justice System: History of Juvenile Courts
Juvenile Justice System: Juvenile Crime and Violence
Violence, Children's Exposure to: Community Violence
Violence, Children's Exposure to: Domestic Violence
Violence, Children's Exposure to: General Effects

XII. EXCEPTIONAL STUDENTS AND SPECIAL EDUCATION
Adapted Physical Education
Assistive Technology
Attention Deficit Hyperactivity Disorder
Autism, Education of Individuals with
College Students with Disabilities: Accommodating
College Students with Disabilities: Special Learning Needs
Compensatory Education: Policies and Programs in Latin America
Compensatory Education: United States
Education for All Handicapped Children Act of 1975 *Appendix III*
Education of the Handicapped Act Amendments of 1990 *Appendix III*
Emotionally Disturbed, Education of
Gifted and Talented, Education of
Hearing Impairment: School Programs
Hearing Impairment: Teaching Methods
Language and Education
Learning Disabilities, Education of Individuals with
Mental Retardation, Education of Individuals with
Mills v. Board of Education of the District of Columbia (1972) *Appendix III*
People with Disabilities, Special Programs to Assist
Pennsylvania Association of Retarded Children v. Commonwealth of Pennsylvania (1971) *Appendix III*
Physical Disabilities, Education of Individuals with
Reading Disabilities
Severe and Multiple Disabilities, Education of Individuals with
Special Education: Current Trends
Special Education: History of
Special Education: International Context
Special Education: Preparation of Teachers
Speech and Language Impairment, Education of Individuals with
Visual Impairments, Education of Individuals with

XIII. TEACHER EDUCATION
Ethics: School Teaching
Hunter, Madeline Cheek
Motivation: Instruction
National Board for Professional Teaching Standards
Sheldon, Edward
Stratemeyer, Florence
Teacher
Teacher Employment
Teacher Evaluation: Methods
Teacher Evaluation: Overview
Teacher Learning Communities
Teaching: Knowledge Bases of
Teaching: Learning to Teach
Teaching: Methods for Studying
Team Teaching
Waller, Willard W.

A. ELEMENTARY AND SECONDARY EDUCATION
Art Education: Preparation of Teachers
Business Education: Preparation of Teachers
Coalition of Essential Schools
Early Childhood Education: Preparation of Teachers
Elementary Education: Preparation of Teachers
English Education: Preparation of Teachers

- Mathematics Education, Teacher Preparation
- Mentoring
- Music Education: Preparation of Teachers
- Physical Education: Preparation of Teachers
- Science Education: Preparation of Teachers
- Secondary Education: International Issues
- Social Studies Education: Preparation of Teachers
- Special Education: Preparation of Teachers
- Teacher Education: Historical Overview
- Vocational and Technical Education: Preparation of Teachers

B. POSTSECONDARY EDUCATION

- Centers for Teaching Improvement in Colleges and Universities
- College Teaching
- Faculty Roles and Responsibilities
- Faculty Teaching, Assessment of
- Future Faculty Preparation Programs
- Grading Systems: Higher Education
- Teaching and Learning: Higher Education

C. INTERNATIONAL EDUCATION

- Decentralization and Education
- International Students: The Global Commerce of Higher Education
- International Teachers Associations
- Teacher Education: International Perspective
- Teacher Preparation, International Perspective
- Teaching and Learning: International Perspective

XIV. ADMINISTRATION

- Campbell, Roald F.
- Cubberley, Ellwood
- Decentralization and Education
- Educational Leadership
- Goslin, Willard E.
- Harris, William T.
- Newlon, Jesse
- Principal, School
- Scheduling
- School-Based Decision-Making
- School Board Relations: Relation of School Board to the Superintendent
- Superintendent of Large-City School Systems
- Superintendent of Schools
- Supervision of Instruction

XV. PROFESSIONAL EDUCATION

A. CONTINUING EDUCATION

- Continuing Professional Education: International Corporations
- Continuing Professional Education: United States
- Corporate Colleges
- Distance Learning in Higher Education
- Life Experience for College Credit
- Lifelong Learning

B. GRADUATE TRAINING

- Business Education: College and Graduate Study
- Dentistry Education
- Divinity Studies
- Graduate Record Examination
- Graduate School Training
- Graduate Study in Education
- Engineering Education
- Higher Education, International Issues
- Law Education
- Law School Admission Test
- Medical College Admission Test
- Medical Education
- Nursing Education
- Student Loans in an International Context

XVI. EDUCATION AND COMMERCE

- Commerce of Education
- Continuing Professional Education: International Corporations
- Globalization of Education
- International Aspects of Education Commerce
- International Education
- International Gap in Technology, The
- International Students: The Global Commerce of Higher Education
- International Trade in Education Programs, Goods, and Services
- Nongovernmental Organizations and Foundations
- Student Loans in an International Context
- Textbooks: Overview
- Tutoring: International Trends

INDEX

Page references to entire articles are in ***boldface.*** *References to figures and tables are denoted by italics.*

A

AAALF (American Association for Active Lifestyles and Fitness), 89

AAAS. *See* American Association for the Advancement of Science (AAAS)

AAC. *See* Association of American Colleges (AAC)

AACC (American Association of Community Colleges), **95–97,** 101

AACC Letter, 96

AACJC (American Association of Junior and Community Colleges), 96–97

AACP (American Association of Colleges of Pharmacy), **94–95**

AACRO study of academic calendars, 5–6

AACSB International, **1–2**

AACTE (American Association of Colleges for Teacher Education), **93–94,** 2442

AAC&U (Association of American Colleges and Universities), **151–153,** 1711–1712

AADT (Advanced Assessment and Delivery Technologies) Division, Educational Testing Services, 685

AAE (American Association of Educators), 2478

AAHE (American Association for Health Education), 89

AAHE (American Association for Higher Education), **90–91,** 255, 415

AAHPERD (American Alliance for Health, Physical Education, Recreation, and Dance), **88–90,** 1888

AAIE (Association for the Advancement of International Education), 115

AAJC (American Association of Junior Colleges), 96

AALR (American Association for Leisure and Recreation), 89

AAMC (American Association of Medical Colleges), 1586

AAPT (American Association of Physics Teachers), **97–98**

AAPT Distinguished Service Citation, 98

AARs (After Action Reviews), 1658

AASA (American Association of School Administrators), **99–100**

AAS (Association of Alumni Secretaries), 1140

AASCU (American Association of State Colleges and Universities), **100–101**

AAU (Association of American Universities), **153–155**

AAUP. *See* American Association of University Professors (AAUP)

AAUW (American Association of University Women), **103–105**

AAUW Recognition Award for Emerging Scholars, 104

ABC reading method, 1999

Abelson, Robert, 1468

ABET (Accreditation Board of Engineering and Technology), 737

Abilities and aptitudes, **1112–1118**
- Alpha and Beta tests, Army, 1113, 1195, 1201, 2566–2567
- Armed Services Vocational Aptitude Battery (ASVAB), 1113
- assessment, 1112–1116, 1208
- attribution theory, 1692–1693
- beliefs, 1692–1693, 1696
- creativity, 506
- emotional intelligence tests, 1192
- General Aptitude Test Battery (GATB), 1113
- grouping, 681
- multiple cognitive abilities, 680–681
- primary and secondary abilities, 572–573
- vocational aptitude tests, 1113

Abington School District v. Schempp, **2802–2839**

Abolition of slavery, 63

Absenteeism. *See* Compulsory education attendance; Truancy and attendance problems

Abstinence-based sex education programs, 2062, 2072–2073

Abstract conceptual knowledge, 247

Academic achievement
- adolescent peer culture, 49–50
- aggressive behavior, 71
- child care, 273, 275, 1836
- classroom assessment, 124–125
- club participation, 318–319
- college counseling services, 1870
- cooperative and collaborative learning, 491–492
- cultural expectations, 1964
- disruptive behavior, 70
- dropout rates, 600
- employment's effect, 729–730, 736, 1838
- ethnicity and achievement gaps, 1122–1124
- extra-school influences, 693
- foster care children, 819
- full-service schools, 908
- health and nutrition, 1003, 1836–1837
- insufficient sleep, 2233
- learning communities, 1455–1456
- levels, 134
- as measure of teacher effectiveness, 2453–2454, 2457–2458
- media, 1582
- multiculturalism, 1962
- National Education Association strategy, 1769–1770
- out-of-school influences, **1835–1839**
- parental involvement, 1844–1846, 1854–1855, 1858–1859
- parents' education level, 1856–1857
- physical fitness, 1888
- public schools, 1949–1950
- reform results, 693
- school factors *vs.* socioeconomic factors, 547
- secondary school students, 2192
- self care students, 1405–1406
- service learning, 2204, 2209
- social capital, 2243
- social promotion, 2262–2264
- stress and depression, 2372
- structural inequality, 1963–1964
- student athletes, 360–361
- Success for All programs, *2406*
- targets, 125–126, *126*
- tests, 116, 2533, **2545–2550,** 2609
- values, 1693–1694, 1697
- *See also* Achievement tests

Academic activities, 2375

Academic advising, higher education, **2–5**
- *See also* Adjustment to college; Career counseling; Counseling; Guidance and counseling

Academic affairs committees, 192

Academic calendars, **5–8**
- *See also* Year-round education

Academic clubs, 318–319
- *See also* Extracurricular activities; Student activities; Youth organizations and clubs

Academic consortia, 475–476, **475–478**

Academic deans, **8–9**
- *See also* Chief academic affairs officers

Academic demands, college students', 43

Academic departments
- curriculum, 520
- department chairpersons, **559–561**
- involvement in athletics, 345
- majors, 20–21
- *See also* Disciplines; Majors, academic

Academic disciplines. *See* Disciplines

Academic freedom
- American Association of University Professors (AAUP), 101–103, 756
- Eliot, Charles, 723–724
- part-time faculty, 781
- tenure, **14–16**
- textbooks, 2556
- university research, 2042

Academic integration, 404

Academic labor market, **17–19,** 1031–1032
- *See also* Teacher supply and demand

Academic majors, **19–23**
- African-American studies, **65–69,** *68, 69,* 2691–2693
- business education, 220–222
- classics, 1414
- curriculum, 523
- engineering, 737–740
- evaluation, 22
- exponential, 1087
- interdisciplinary, **1210–1215**
- U.S. Air Force Academy, 1644–1645
- *See also* Degree programs; Disciplines; Interdisciplinarity

Academic organizations, college, 375

Academic performance. *See* Academic achievement

Academic Preparation for College (report), 697

Academic research. *See* Faculty research; Research universities

Academic residential programs, 2044

Academic rigor of secondary school courses, 2193

Academic standards, **2315–2323**
- arts content, 1720
- art teacher education, 121–122
- business education, 218
- Carnegie units, 246
- classroom assessment, 125–126
- content, 2001, 2315
- core competencies, 227
- defining, 2174
- development, 216, 218, 2316–2317
- elementary education, 714, 717–718
- English education, 741–742
- Europe, 2532
- foreign language education, 894
- geometry, 1548
- health education, 1005, 1009
- higher education, 1037
- instructional design, 1164
- international issues, 1216
- internships, 1326
- journalism education, 1348
- language arts, 1394–1395
- Latin, 1415–1416
- leadership, 667–668
- mathematics, 717–718, 1541, 1545, 1547, 1767, 2174
- performance standards, 133, 2315–2316
- principals, 1921
- private *vs.* public schools, 950–951
- problems with, 1301
- professional development schools, 1931
- professional testing standards, 2536–2537
- public school organization, 2259–2260
- rural schools, 2085–2086

school counseling programs, 976, 977
science education, 1729, **2173–2177,** *2176*
secondary education, 2188, 2190
social studies education, 1764
special education, 500, 2285
states, 227, 654–655, 700–701, 1216, 2320–2321
teacher education, 498, 1009, 1763, 1770
technology education, 2176
test development, **2550–2551**
testing, 2531–2532
vocational education, 2329, 2644, 2645, 2649
world-class, 526–529
writing education, 2694–2695
See also Education reform; School reform; Standards-based education

Academic support centers, 354, 357

Academic vice presidents. *See* Chief academic affairs officers

Academy of Natural Sciences, 93

Accelerated learning, 932

Accelerated Schools, **23–25**

Accelerated Schools Project (ASP), 24

Access, health care, 1531–1532

Access to education
African Americans, 618, 671
community colleges, 876–880
compensatory education, 459
disabled children, 1868–1869
early childhood education, 618
gender, 919
girls, 1301
higher education, 1030–1031
Hispanic Americans, 618
international issues, 919, 1030–1031, 1300–1304
Latin America, 1408
See also Equality in education; Equity

Access to student records and reports, 2014–2015

Accidents, school bus, 2573

Accolade, Sega Enterprises Ltd. v., 1190

Accommodation and intelligence, 1896

Accountability, **651–656**
Canadian education, 237
Carnegie Units, 246
Coleman, James S., 326
college education, 414
community colleges, 883
Eastern Europe and Central Asia region education systems, 645
educational change, 658
efficiency, 673–674
federal funds, 2341
guidance and counseling, 977
international higher education, 1031
international issues, 951–952
public schools, 951–952, 1950
school, 551
school boards, 2105–2106
secondary education, 2190–2191
standards-based reform model, 2319, 2321–2322
state boards of education, 2357–2358
statewide testing programs, 2538
teacher evaluation, 2455–2456, 2458
teachers, 652–655, 2319, 2321–2322
urban schools, 2607
See also Education reform; School reform; Standards-based education

Accountancy standards, 2

Accounting, school. *See* Finance

Accounting education, 1–2
See also Business education

Account systems, higher education, **25–26**
See also Finance

Accreditation
American overseas schools, 114
art and design schools, 1744
business schools, 1, 2
career schools and colleges of technology, 35–37
continuing professional education (CPE), 485–486
corporate colleges, 493
corruption, 1660–1661
early childhood programs, 1737
engineering, 737–738
federal financial aid, 33–34
history, 31–32
international aspects, **27–28,** 30
master's degree programs, 1539
National Collegiate Athletic Association (NCAA), 366, 369–370
nursing programs, 1820
physical education teachers, 1890–1891
private schools, 30, 1926–1927
private sector, 1220
regional *vs.* specialized, 32–33
Revised Standards and Policies for Accrediting Colleges for Teacher Education (American Association of Colleges for Teacher Education), 2442
school improvement programs and, 30
secondary education, 28–31, 2185
teacher education, 1762–1763, 2442
tribal colleges, 2579
United States, **28–37**
U.S. Coast Guard Academy, 1645
voluntary, 27
See also Certification and licensure

Accreditation Board of Engineering and Technology (ABET), 737, 738

Accrediting agencies
AACSB International, 1, 2
Accreditation Board of Engineering and Technology (ABET), 737, 738
Accrediting Commission for Business Schools, 36
Accrediting Commission of Career Schools and Colleges of Technology (ACCSCT), **35–37**
Association of American Universities (AAU), 154
Council for Higher Education Accreditation (CHEA), 32
Council of Arts Accrediting Associations, 121
Federation of Regional Accrediting Commissions in Higher Education (FRACHE), 32
International Council of School Accreditation Commissions, Inc. (ICSAC), 29–30
Montessori Accreditation Council for Teacher Education (MACTE), 1679–1680
National Association of Schools of Art and Design, 1744

National Council for Accreditation of Teacher Education (NCATE), 1009, **1762–1763,** *1763,* 1931, 2442
National Council for Private School Accreditation (NCPSA), 30
Accrediting Commission for Business Schools, 36
Accrediting Commission of Career Schools and Colleges of Technology (ACCSCT), **35–37**
ACCSCT (Accrediting Commission of Career Schools and Colleges of Technology), **35–37**
ACE. *See* American Council on Education (ACE)
ACEI (Association for Childhood Education International), 624
ACF (Administration for Children and Families), 844
Achievement, academic. *See* Academic achievement
Achievement tests
national, **2545–2550**
policy, 2533
urban schools, 2609
vs. basic ability tests, 1116
See also Academic achievement; Assessment; Standardized tests; Testing
Achievement values, 1693–1694, 1697
Achieve (organization), 227
ACHS (Association of College Honor Societies), **1070–1071**
ACHS Handbook (Association of College Honor Societies), 1070
Acknowledgment of contributions, 757
ACTE (Association for Career and Technical Education), 2508
ACTFL (American Council on the Teaching of Foreign Languages), 893, 895
Action Research Group (ARG), 2466
Action Teams for Partnerships, 826
Active listening, 1979
Active modification of child's disabilities, 127
Activism
Highlander Folk School, 1090
student protests, 67, 1039
women's studies, 2690
Activities, student, **2374–2377**
academic, 2375
community colleges, 2393
financing, **2376–2377**
overview, **2374–2376**
See also Extracurricular activities; Youth organizations and clubs
Activity based physical education curriculum, 1888
ACT model, 1611
ACT tests
admissions, 329, 330, 331
test preparation programs, 2543–2546
See also Admissions tests; Application process
ACUHO-I (Association of College and University Housing Officers-International), 342
ADA. *See* Americans with Disabilities Act (ADA)
Adams, Abby, 1978
Adams, James, 1702
Adams, John, 87, 2074, 2439
Adams, Raymond, 141
Adams, Samuel, 87
Adams v. Richardson, 776
Adapted physical education (APE), **37–40**
Adaptive expertise, **763–765**
Adaptive teaching, 1120
Adarand Constructors, Inc. v. Pena, 2424
ADB (Asian Development Bank), 1256–1257
Addams, Jane, **40–42,** 829
Adding It Up: Helping Children Learn Mathematics (National Research Council), 1729
ADELE (Agent for Distance Learning-Light Edition), 1169, 1170
ADEPT Program, 2713
Adequacy
constitutional right, 479, 481–482
school funding, 672
Aderhold, Omer, 76
ADHD (attention deficit hyperactivity disorder), **157–159,** 1615, 2287
Adjudication of disputes, 2245
Adjustment problems of adoptive children, 814
Adjustment to college, **42–45**
Adler, Mortimer, 84, 697
Administration, educational
academic deans, **8–9**
administrative Progressives, 1935–1937
alternative school, 85
American Association of School Administrators (AASA), **99–100**
Bowen, Howard, 198–199
business schools, 1
Campbell, Roald F., 233–234
Chief academic affairs officers, **265–267**
college enrollment management, 749–750
Cubberley, Ellwood, 508–509
faculty consulting policy, 773–774
international higher education, 1031
large-city superintendents, **2411–2415**
leadership, **664–668**
National Policy Board for Educational Administration (NPBEA), 99–100, 1920–1921
principals, 665–668, **1919–1922,** 2192
Progressive education, 1935–1937
residence halls, 341
school boards, 2114–2115
staff, college and university, 387
state services, **2335–2364**
superintendents, 666–668, **2411–2418**
supervision of instruction, **2418–2422**
University Council for Educational Administration (UCEA), **2591–2592**
urban schools, 2606
See also Decentralization; Decision-making; Governance
Administration for Children and Families (ACF), 844
Administration on Aging (AOA), 844
Administrative Progressives, 1935–1937
Administrative services, state, **2338–2350**
Admissions
affirmative action, **61–65,** 397, 2424

American Association of Collegiate Registrars and Admissions Officers (AACRAO), 5
business school, 221–222
college and university, 58, **327–330,** 396–397, 724
community colleges, 2390–2391
dental school, 557–558
diploma admission, 2185
divinity school, 593–594
education graduate programs, 968–969
engineering departments, 738
enrollment management, **748–751,** 1145
Graduate Record Examination (GRE), 962–964
graduate school, 963–964
Harvard University, 724
international students, 1311–1312, 2707
law school, 1417–1418, 1419–1420
medical school, 1584, 1585–1586
minorities, 1968–1969
National Association of College Admission Counseling (NACAC), 383
nursing programs, 1819–1820
offices, 749
process, 328
race/ethnicity, 64–65, 1968–1969
rates, 2706, 2707
standardization of high school curriculum, 2184–2185
student athletes, 359–361, *360*
U.S. Air Force Academy, 1643
U.S. Coast Guard Academy, 1646
U.S. Merchant Marine Academy, 1648
U.S. Military Academy, 1650
See also Application process; College search and selection; Enrollment management; Recruitment

Admissions tests, **330–332**
higher education history, 1039
law school, **1419–1420**
Medical College Admission Test (MCAT), 1584
standardized testing, 2530–2531
test preparation programs, 2543–2544
See also ACT tests; College Entrance Examination Board; SAT

Adolescent peer culture, **45–56**
gangs, **51–54**
overview, **45–51**
parents' role, **54–56**
peer pressure, 812
stages of growth, 279
See also Youth

Adopt-a-Grandparent Program, 2720

Adopt-a-Ship, 851

Adoption, **813–815**
child abuse and neglect, 269
child protective services, 282, 284
See also Foster care

Adoption and Safe Families Act
adoption, 282, 284
child abuse and neglect, 269

Adoption Assistance and Child Welfare Act, 282, 284

ADTSEA (American Driver and Traffic Safety Education Association), 597

Adult education
American Council on Education (ACE), **107–110**
Empire State College, 199
Jewish study, 1342
People's Institute, 212
rural, 2088
See also Nontraditional students

Adult literacy
Eastern Europe and Central Asia, 642
Gray, William S., 971
international comparisons, 1289, 1299
pedagogy, 901–902
tutoring, 2581
See also Literacy

Adult students. *See* Adult education; Nontraditional students

Adult-to-child ratios in child care, 273

Advanced Assessment and Delivery Technologies (AADT), Educational Testing Service, 685

Advanced placement courses/exams, **56–58**
College Entrance Examination Board, 373
foreign language, 898
subject areas, *57*

Adventures in Learning (report), 708

Adventures of Ideas (Whitehead), 2686

The Adventures of Jasper Woodbury (middle school mathematics series), 1151–1153, 2510

Advertising
children, influence on, 1580
tobacco products, 2067–2068

Advising. *See* Academic advising, higher education

Advising, academic, **2–5**
See also Adjustment to college; Career counseling; Counseling; Guidance and counseling

Aerospace engineering, 739

Aesthetic Education in a Technological Society (Broudy), 211

Aesthetic studies, 210, 211

AfDB (African Development Bank), 1258

AFDC (Aid to Families with Dependent Children), 834, 2677

AFD (French Agency for Development), 1244–1245

Affect and emotional development, **58–61**

Affective and conative processes, **1118–1121**

Affective domain of self-regulation, 1699

Affective objectives, 1177

Affective questions, 312

Affinity groups, AACSB, 1

Affirmative action, **61–65,** 397, 2424

Affordability, college, 378, 1035–1036

Afghanistan. *See* South Asia

AFI (American Film Institute), 1773

AFL (American Federation of Labor), 2637

AFL-CIO, 110, 111

Africa. *See* Middle East and North Africa; Sub-Saharan Africa

African Americans
access to education, 618, 671
affirmative action, **61–65,** 397, 2424

African-American Language, 1391–1392
American Federation of Teachers, 111–112
Berea College, admission to, 171
Bethune, Mary McLeod, **173–175**
Bethune-Cookman College, 174
Bond, Horace Julian, 197
Bond, Horace Mann, **196–197**
children's literature award, Coretta Scott King, 289
Clark, Septima Poinsette, **298–299**
Coleman Report, 324–325, 326
college athletics, 350
community violence exposure, 2627–26390
A Comparative Study of Intramural Programs in Negro Colleges (Wasson), 362
Coretta Scott King Fund, 104
Day Law, 171
Daytona Normal and Industrial Institute for Negro Girls, 174
desegregation and the Constitution, 478–479
dropout rates, 599
Du Bois, W. E. B., 66, 174, **609–613,** 2636
early childhood education access, 618
Ebonics, 1391–1392
elementary education, 712
faculty, 18–19, 776–778
foster care, 284
gang members, 52
Gary schools, 915–916
graduation test requirements, 2541
group rights politics, 663
Harvard University, 724
higher education, 1036
Highlander Research and Education Center, 1090
Homemakers Clubs, 1338
Howard University, 867, 868
inequitable instruction, 305–306
Jeanes teachers, **1337–1339**
Laney, Lucy Craft, 174
literacy and culture, 1510–1512
magnet schools, 1526–1527
Mays, Benjamin, **1569–1572**
Mississippi Freedom Schools, **1668–1669**
National Achievement Scholarship, 1781
National Board Certification, 1752
National PTA, 1783
Negro History Week, 66
number sense and culture, 1564–1565
Office for the Advancement of Public Black Colleges (OAPBC), 100
public schools, 2186–2187, 2199–2202
role of the black church, 1570, 1571
Rosenwald schools, 1338–1339
school boards, 2106
school effectiveness, 305
school responsiveness to, 663
student athletes, 359
student employment, 728
teachers of, 2449
teachers' pay equity, 298–299
textbooks, 1704
vocational education, 2636
Washington, Booker T., 610, 2636, **2664–2668**
Woodson, Carter Godwin, 66, 1704, **2691–2693**
See also African-American studies; Historically black colleges and universities (HBCUs); Multiculturalism; Race/ethnicity; Segregation

African-American studies, **65–69**
basic objective, *68*
relevance, *69*
Woodson, Carter Godwin, 2691–2693
See also African Americans

African Development Bank (AfDB), 1258

AFT (American Federation of Teachers). *See* American Federation of Teachers (AFT)

After Action Reviews (AARs), 1658

After-school programs, 2713–2714

After-School Snack Program, 2135

Agassiz, Louis, 93

Age and intelligence, 1204–1205

Agencies, government. *See* Government agencies and offices, U.S.

Agent for Distance Learning-Light Edition (ADELE), 1169, 1170

Age segregation and peer culture, 46, 47

Aggregation and general intelligence, 1194

Aggression. *See* Behavior problems

Aging, study of, 1918

Aging schools, 2128

Agne, Russell, 2441

Agostini v. Felton, 2423

Agreement crafters, educational leaders as, 667–668

Agricultural education, **72–80**
land-grant colleges and universities, 1381, 1383
United Nations Food and Agriculture Organization (FAO), 1264

Agricultural engineering, 739–740

Aguillard, Edwards v., 2423

AIAA (American Industrial Arts Association), 2506

AI (anchored instruction), **1151–1154**

AI (artificial intelligence), 1546

AIAW (Association for Intercollegiate Athletics for Women), 351

AIDS and HIV, **2058–2060**
international aspects, 627
risk behaviors, 2066, 2072–2073
school health services, 1015
sub-Saharan Africa, 2398
See also Sexually transmitted diseases (STDs)

Aid to Families with Dependent Children (AFDC), 834, 2677

AIHEC (American Indian Higher Education Consortium), 2579

Aiken Commission, 707–708, 2427–2428

Aims of Education (Whitehead), 2684

AIP (American Institute of Physics), 98

Aircrib, 2229–2230

Air Force Academy, U.S., **1642–1645**

Airport and Airway Development Act, 849

Air University (AU), 2621

ALA (American Library Association), 288

Alaskan Eskimo Education: A Film Analysis of Cultural Confrontation in the Schools (Collier), 418

Albania. *See* Eastern Europe and Central Asia
Alberty, H. B., **80–82**
Alcohol abuse. *See* Substance abuse
Alcuin, 160
Alexander, Patricia, 1468, 1985
Alexander, William, 1631
Alexander v. Holmes County Board of Education, 2201
Algebra, **1542–1545,** *1544*
  See also Mathematics education
Algeria. *See* Middle East and North Africa
ALI, 1169
Allen, Board of Education v., 2423
Allen, Dwight W., 1620
Allen, Joseph P., 2073
Allen, Mueller v., 2423
Allensworth, Diane, 1013
Alliance for Higher Education, Dallas, Texas, 476
Allington, Richard L., 2001
Allocation
  average daily attendance (ADA), 2258, 2260
  cost/benefit analysis, 702
  decision-making, 551–553
  higher education resources, **2047–2052**
  state revenue services, 2340–2342
  See also Budgeting; Economics of education; Finance
Allport, Gordon, 1705, 1862
Allred, Keith, 733
Alpha and Beta tests, Army
  history of intelligence measurement, 1195, 1201
  individual differences, 1113
  Thorndike, Edward L., 2566–2567
Alphabetical writing systems (AWS), 1488–1489
Alphabetics, 2000
Alpha Chi, **1065–1067**
Alpha Mu Gamma, **1067**
Alpha Omega Alpha, **1067–1068**
ALSC (Association of Library Services to Children), 288
Alternative education, **82–86**
  independent study, 1110–1112
  international issues, 2500–2501
Alternative Public Schools, Inc. *See* Beacon Education Management, Inc.
Alternative Spring Break program, 375, 2207
Altman, Janice, 2517
Alumni
  Association of Alumni Secretaries (AAS), 1140
  Association of Collegiate Alumnae, 105
  as career resources, 242
  relations, 1140–1141
AMA (American Medical Association), 33
The Ambitious Generation (Schneider and Stevenson), 736
AMCAS (American Medical College Application Service), 1585
America 2000 (initiative), 717, 2154
American Academy of Arts and Sciences, **86–87**
American Alliance for Health, Physical Education, Recreation, and Dance (AAHPERD), **88–90,** 1888
American Assembly of Collegiate Schools of Business. *See* AACSB International
American Association for Active Lifestyles and Fitness (AAALF), 89
American Association for Health Education (AAHE), 89
American Association for Higher Education (AAHE), **90–91**
  college teacher improvement programs, 255
  scholarship of teaching, 415
American Association for Leisure and Recreation (AALR), 89
American Association for the Advancement of Physical Education, 89
American Association for the Advancement of Science (AAAS), **91–93**
  federal support for science research, 854
  science education standards, 2174–2175
American Association of Business Schools, 36
American Association of Colleges for Teacher Education (AACTE), **93–94,** 2442
American Association of Colleges of Nursing, 1818–1819
American Association of Colleges of Pharmacy (AACP), **94–95**
American Association of Collegiate Registrars and Admissions Officers (AACRAO), 5
American Association of Community Colleges (AACC), **95–97,** 101
American Association of Educators (AAE), 2478
American Association of Family and Consumer Sciences, 803–804
American Association of Junior and Community Colleges (AACJC), 96–97
American Association of Junior Colleges (AAJC), 96
American Association of Medical Colleges (AAMC), 1586
American Association of Physics Teachers (AAPT), **97–98**
American Association of School Administrators (AASA), **99–100**
American Association of State Colleges and Universities (AASCU), **100–101,** 1750
American Association of University Professors (AAUP), **101–103**
  academic freedom, 14–16
  areas of interest, 387
  ethics, 756–758
  higher education governance, 794
American Association of University Women (AAUW), **103–105**
American Chemical Society, 759
The American College: A Criticism (Flexner), 892
American College Athletics (Savage), 350
American College Test. *See* ACT tests
American Council of Learned Societies, **105–107**
American Council on Education (ACE), **107–110**
  General Educational Development Test (GED), 921–922
  life experience for college credit, 1478, 1479
  Statement on College and University Government, 102

Student Personnel Point of View, 2388
See also Association of American Universities (AAU); College Entrance Examination Board
American Council on Pharmaceutical Education, 94–95
American Council on the Teaching of Foreign Languages (ACTFL), 893, 895
American Driver and Traffic Safety Education Association (ADTSEA), 597
American Education under Fire: The Story of the Phony Three-R Fight (Melby), 944
American Federation of Labor (AFL), 2637
American Federation of Teachers (AFT), **110–112**
academic freedom and tenure, 15
Childs, John L., 293
Haley, Margaret, 984
in history of teacher unions, 2476, 2477–2478, 2479–2481
National Education Association (NEA), 1771
rise of unionism, 1320
Shanker, Albert, 2222–2223
American Field Service, **2717–2718**
American Film Institute (AFI), 1773
American Heart Association, 88
The American High School Today (Conant), 473, 697
American Home Economics Association. *See* American Association of Family and Consumer Sciences
An American Imperative: Higher Expectations for Higher Education (report), 518
American Indian Head Start program, 844
American Indian Higher Education Consortium (AIHEC), 2579
American Industrial Arts Association (AIAA), 2506
American Institute of Physics (AIP), 98
Americanization of immigrants, 1099
American Library Association (ALA), 288
American Medical Association (AMA), 33
American Medical College Application Service (AMCAS), 1585
American Men of Science (Cattell), 378
American National Biography, 106
American Negro Academy, 66
American overseas schools, **112–115**
American Overseas Schools Historical Society (AOSHS), 115
American Physical Education Association, 89–90
American Political Science Association, 296
American pragmatism, 194–196
American Pragmatism and Education (Childs), 293–294
American Psychological Association (APA)
higher education ethics, 758
in history of educational psychology, 677
strengths-based youth interventions, 438
American Public Health Association (APHA), 1003–1004
Americans Abroad Program, 2718
American School Board Journal, 1785
American School Counselors Association (ASCA), 976, 977
American Scientist, 1084
American Sign Language, 1018, 1020
American Society for African Culture (AMSAC), 196
American Sociological Association, 757–758, 759
American Spelling Book (Webster), 1998, 2303, 2554, 2670, 2671
Americans with Disabilities Act (ADA)
assistive technology, 149
disabled college students, 409
federal assistance programs, 1868–1869
See also Disabled students; Individuals with Disabilities Education Act (IDEA); Special education
The American University (Barzun), 414
America's Choice: High Skills or Low Wages! (National Center on Education and Economy), 2319
America's Competitive Challenge (report), 697
Ames, Carole, 1854
Amherst College, 348
Amish education
compulsory attendance, 466
court cases, 1943–1944
state relations to private schools, 2336
Ammons, Johan, 1019–1020
Amnesics and recall, 1596–1597, *1597*
AMSAC (American Society for African Culture), 196
Analogical reasoning, **1421–1424**
case-based reasoning, 1154
conceptual learning, 1492
transfer of learning, 1450
Analysis in Bloom's taxonomy, 311
Analytical impulse and the philosophy of education, 1882, 1883
Analytical intelligence, 1207
Analytical philosophy of education, 1877, 1880
Anatomy of attention, 155
Anchored instruction (AI), **1151–1154**
constructivism, 1464
educational psychology, 681
Anderson, John, 1466
Anderson, Lorin, 2430–2432
Anderson, Richard, 1468
Anderson, Robert, 2418
Anderson, William Gilbert, 89
Andorra. *See* Western Europe
Andrew W. Mellon Foundation, 106
Anemia, 1822
Angell, James, 725
Angelo, Thomas, 255, 2497
Angola. *See* Sub-Saharan Africa
Animal Intelligence (Thorndike), 2564–2565
Animal studies
attention, 156
intelligence, 2564–2565
Animated learning aids
criticisms, 1494–1495

display problems, 1577
overview, 1169–1170
See also Educational technology; Software
Ann Arbor school system (Michigan), 1391
Annie Jump Cannon Award in Astronomy, 104
Annual funds, college and university, 1141
A-not-B task, 1592
Anschauung principle, 1875–1876
Anthropology, visual, 417–419
Anti-Communism and academic freedom, 102
Antigua & Barbuda. *See* Latin America and the Caribbean
Antioch College, 1537
AOA (Administration on Aging), 844
AOSHS (American Overseas Schools Historical Society), 115
APA. *See* American Psychological Association (APA)
APE (adapted physical education), **37–40**
APEC (Asia-Pacific Economic Corporation), 27
APEC Education Dialogue and Knowledge Sharing Network, 27
APHA (American Public Health Association), 1003–1004
Appalachia, 171–172, 298
Application in Bloom's taxonomy, 311
Application process
business schools, 221–222
college, 328–329
dental school, 557, 558
divinity school, 593–594
education graduate programs, 968–969
engineering programs, 738
financial aid, 376–377
Graduate Record Examination (GRE), 962–964
law school, 1418, 1419–1420
medical college, 1584, 1585–1586
nursing programs, 1819–1820
U.S. Air Force Academy, 1643
U.S. Coast Guard Academy, 1646
U.S. Merchant Marine Academy, 1648
U.S. Military Academy, 1650
See also Admissions; Admissions tests; College search and selection
Appointments
academic deans, 8
research university faculty, 17
school board, 2118–2119
Apprenticeship
international issues, 487–488
in vocational education history, 2636, 2641
Aptitudes and abilities, **1112–1118**
Alpha and Beta tests, Army, 1113, 1195, 1201, 2566–2567
Armed Services Vocational Aptitude Battery (ASVAB), 1113
assessment, 1112–1116, 1208
attribution theory, 1692–1693
beliefs, 1692–1693, 1696
creativity, 506
emotional intelligence tests, 1192
General Aptitude Test Battery (GATB), 1113
grouping, 681
multiple cognitive abilities, 680–681
primary and secondary abilities, 572–573
vocational aptitude tests, 1113
Arab countries. *See* Middle East and North Africa
Arabic language, 1625
Architecture
full-service schools, 909
new facilities, 2125
open classrooms, 1823
residence hall design, 343
residential colleges, 2045
school, 1678, 1813
See also Facilities
Archival Information Locator, National Archives and Records Administration, 1734
Arcuri, Kathleen, 819
Area learning centers, 84
Area studies, 106
ARG (Action Research Group), 2466
Argentina. *See* Latin America and the Caribbean
Argument
formal reasoning, 1444–1445
text structure, 1994, 1996–1997
Aristotle, **115–117**
history of educational psychology, 676
history of education theory, 1878
Arithmetic, 569
See also Mathematics education
Arizona, 82
Arkansas, Eperson v., 2422
Armed forces. *See* Department of Defense, U.S.; Military; Specific branches
Armed Services Vocational Aptitude Battery (ASVAB), 1113
Armenia. *See* Eastern Europe and Central Asia
Armstrong, Samuel Chapman
vocational education, 2636
Washington, Booker T., 2664, 2666–2667, 2668
Army, U.S.
Alpha and Beta tests, 1113, 1195, 1201, 2566–2567
Army Training and Evaluation Programs (ARTEP), 1657, 1658
Army War College (AWC), 2621
intelligence testing, 1195
professional education, 1653–1655
training doctrine, 1656–1658
Arnold, John, 734
Aronson, Pamela, 730
Arousal, 155
Arreola, Raoul, 415
Art education, **117–123**
Art Education (periodical), 1735
Arts Education Partnership, 121, 123
Barkan, Manuel, 165–167
community arts programs, 1720–1721
Consortium of National Arts Education Associations, 121
content standards, 1720
Council of Arts Accrediting Associations, 121
Henry Luce Foundation/ACLS Dissertation Fellowship in American Art, 106
International Council of Fine Arts Deans (ICFAD), 121–122
Lowenfeld, Viktor, 1522–1523

National Art Education Association (NAEA), 118, 121, 122, **1734–1736**
National Association of Schools of Art and Design (NASAD), **1743–1745**
National Endowment for the Arts (NEA), **1771–1773**
schools, **117–121**
teacher preparation, **121–123**
technological advances, 120
youth art programs, 318–319

Art Education (periodical), 1735

ARTEP (Army Training and Evaluation Programs), 1657, 1658

Arthurdale School, 297–298

Artifacts and educational research, 2028

Artificial intelligence (AI), 1546

Arts activities, collegiate, 375

Arts and Humanities Act of 1965, 1771

Arts content standards, 1720

Arts Education Partnership, 121, 123

Aruba. *See* Latin America and the Caribbean

Asabati, Elias, 2038

Asante, Molefi, 1963

ASCA (American School Counselors Association), 976, 977

Aschner, Mary Jane, 311

ASEAN (Association of Southeast Asian Nations)
accreditation, 27

Asia
Asian Development Bank (ADB), 1256–1257
Southeast Asian Ministers of Education Organization (SEAMEO), 1255
tutoring, 2585–2587
See also East Asia and the Pacific; Eastern Europe and Central Asia; South Asia

Asian Americans
academic achievement, 1122
faculty, 18
gang members, 52

Asian Development Bank (ADB), 631, 1256–1257

Asia-Pacific Economic Corporation (APEC)
accreditation, 27

AskERIC, 683

ASP (Accelerated Schools Project), 24

Aspiring principals program, 666

Assessment, **123–139**
abilities and aptitudes, 1112–1116, 1208
anchored instruction, 1152–1153
assessment triangle, 139–140, *140*
case-based learning, 1158
civics, 295, 296
classroom assessment, **123–127**
Classroom Assessment and the National Science Education Standards (National Research Council), 1729
Classroom Assessment Techniques (Angelo and Cross), 2497
Cognitive Assessment System (CAS), 570
cognitive development, 141–143, 570
computer technology, 2512
constructivist, 1465
Core Knowledge Sequence, 536–537
curriculum, 719
dynamic assessment, **127–131**
efficiency, 701, 703–704
experiential learning, 761–762, 1478–1479
faculty research, **786–789**
faculty teaching, **798–802**
first-year seminars, 401
foreign language proficiency, 894
full-service schools, 908–909
geographic learning, 927–928
gifted and talented program evaluation, 932–933
higher education, 90, 2497–2498
high-stakes tests, 2533–2537
history learning, 1057–1058
infant schools (England), 1135
information processing skills, 570
internships, 1326
Interstate New Teacher Assessment and Support Consortium (INTASC), 121, 122
learning, 761–762
life experience for college credit, 1478–1479
mathematics education, 1557
mentoring programs, 1619–1620
moral education, 1687–1688
multiple intelligences, 1200
National Assessment Governing Board (NAGB), 133, 134
National Research Council studies, 1730
open education, 1826
performance assessment, **134–137,** 654–655, 787–788
principals, 1920–1921
problem-solving, 147
psychoeducational, 1945
public school organization and, 2259–2260
purposes of, 2534–2535
school-based service outcomes, 2145–2147
school performance, 2539
secondary education, 2190
state-level educational progress assessment, 132, 133
state standards, 654–655
student self-assessment, 125
studies of, 1730
teacher certification, 1751–1752
of testing, 654
undergraduate learning, 512–513
working memory, 1591–1592
writing and composition, 147–148, 963, 2694–2695
See also Assessment tools; Comparative assessment; Educational Testing Service (ETS); Evaluation; Grading systems; National Assessment of Educational Progress (NAEP); Portfolio assessment; Standardized tests; Teacher evaluation; Testing

Assessment Forum, American Association for Higher Education, 90

Assessment tools, **139–148**
faculty research and scholarship, 788
psychometric and statistical, **139–145**
technology based, **145–148**
See also Standardized tests; Testing

Assimilation
ethnically minority groups, 2255–2256
immigrant children, 1099

intelligence and, 1895–1896
Assistive technology, **149–151,** 2517–2518
Associate degree programs
business education, 220, 222
Carnegie Classification, 244, 245
See also Community colleges
Association for Career and Technical Education (ACTE), 2508
Association for Childhood Education International (ACEI), 624
Association for Intercollegiate Athletics for Women (AIAW), 351
Association for the Advancement of International Education (AAIE), 115
Association for the Study of Afro-American Life and History. *See* Association for the Study of Negro Life and History (ASNLH)
Association for the Study of Negro Life and History (ASNLH)
in development of African American studies, 66
multiculturalism, 1704
Woodson, Carter Godwin, 2692–2693
Association for Women in Communications, **1068–1069**
Associationist principle of pedagogy, 1333
Association of Advanced Rabbinical and Talmudic Schools, 390
Association of Alumni Secretaries (AAS), 1140
Association of American Agricultural Colleges and Experiment Stations, 1381, 1383
Association of American Colleges (AAC)
academic freedom, 16
American Association of University Professors (AAUP), 102
history, 1741–1742
as predecessor to Association of American Colleges and Universities (AAC&U), 152
undergraduate curriculum reports, 515–516
See also Association of American Colleges and Universities (AAC&U)
Association of American Colleges and Universities (AAC&U), **151–153,** 1711–1712
Association of American Geologists and Naturalists, 93
Association of American Medical Colleges, 2037
Association of American Universities (AAU), **153–155,** 1036–1037, 2037
Association of College and University Housing Officers-International (ACUHO-I), 342
Association of College Honor Societies (ACHS), **1070–1071**
Association of Colleges of Jewish Studies, 390
Association of Collegiate Alumnae, 105
Association of Library Services to Children (ALSC), 288
Association of Southeast Asian Nations (ASEAN), 27
Association of Test Publishers (ATP), 2550
Association of Theological Schools, 593
Associations, educational
AACSB International, **1–2**
Achieve, 227
American Alliance for Health, Physical Education, Recreation, and Dance (AAHPERD), **88–90,** 1888
American Association for Health Education (AAHE), 89
American Association for Higher Education (AAHE), **90–91,** 255
American Association for the Advancement of Physical Education, 89
American Association for the Advancement of Science (AAAS), **91–93,** 854, 2174–2175
American Association of Colleges for Teacher Education (AACTE), **93–94,** 2442
American Association of Colleges of Nursing, 1818–1819
American Association of Colleges of Pharmacy (AACP), **94–95**
American Association of Collegiate Registrars and Admissions Officers (AACRAO), 5
American Association of Community Colleges (AACC), **95–97,** 101
American Association of Educators (AAE), 2478
American Association of Family and Consumer Sciences, 803–804
American Association of Junior and Community Colleges (AACJC), 96–97
American Association of Junior Colleges (AAJC), 96
American Association of Medical Colleges (AAMC), 1586
American Association of Physics Teachers (AAPT), **97–98**
American Association of School Administrators (AASA), **99–100**
American Association of State Colleges and Universities (AASCU), **100–101,** 1750
American Association of University Professors (AAUP), 14–15, **101–103,** 387, 757, 758, 794
American Association of University Women (AAUW), **103–105**
American Council of Learned Societies, **105–107**
American Council on the Teaching of Foreign Languages (ACTFL), 893, 895
American Driver and Traffic Safety Education Association (ADTSEA), 597
American Negro Academy, 66
American Physical Education Association, 89–90
American School Counselors Association (ASCA), 976, 977
Association for Career and Technical Education (ACTE), 2508
Association for Childhood Education International (ACEI), 624

Association for Intercollegiate Athletics for Women (AIAW), 351
Association for the Advancement of International Education (AAIE), 115
Association for the Study of Negro Life and History (ASNLH), 66, 1704, 2692–2693
Association of Advanced Rabbinical and Talmudic Schools, 390
Association of Alumni Secretaries (AAS), 1140
Association of American Agricultural Colleges and Experiment Stations, 1381, 1383
Association of American Colleges (AAC), 102, 152, 515–516, 1741–1742
Association of American Colleges and Universities (AAC&U), **151–153,** 1711–1712
Association of American Medical Colleges, 2037
Association of American Universities (AAU), **153–155,** 1036–1037, 2037
Association of College and University Housing Officers-International (ACUHO-I), 342
Association of College Honor Societies (ACHS), **1070–1071**
Association of Colleges of Jewish Studies, 390
Association of Collegiate Alumnae, 105
Association of Test Publishers (ATP), 2550
Association of Theological Schools, 593
The Big Six, 108, 109
Business Coalition for Excellence in Education (BCEE), 228
Catholic Education Association, 251
Center for Civic Education, 296
Character Education Partnership (CEP), 260
Chicago Froebel Association, 1957–1958
Coalition of Essential Schools (CES), **321–322,** 323
Collaborative to Advance Social and Emotional Learning (CASEL), 1193
Committee on East European Studies, ACLS, 106
Comparative and International Education Society, 1266
Consortium of National Arts Education Associations, 121
Council for Basic Education (CBE), **498–499**
Council for Christian Colleges and Universities, 392
Council for Exceptional Children (CEC), **499–500**
Council for Higher Education Accreditation (CHEA), 32
Council of Arts Accrediting Associations, 121
Council of Chief State School Officers (CCSSO), 121, 122, **501–503,** 1921, 2324
Council of Regional School Accrediting Commissions (CORSAC), 29
Emergency Council on Education, 108
Federation of Regional Accrediting Commissions in Higher Education (FRACHE), 32
Hispanic Association of Colleges and Universities (HACU), 1046, 1047
Independent Education Associations (IEA), 2478
Intercollegiate Athletic Association of the United States (IAAUS), 364–365
International Academy of Educational Accreditors (IAEA), 30
International Association for Educational Assessment (IAEA), **1225**
International Association for the Evaluation of Educational Achievement (IEA), 296, 1222–1223, **1225–1238,** 1288, 1293, 1409
International Baccalaureate Organization (IBO), 1239
International Council of Fine Arts Deans (ICFAD), 121–122
International Council of School Accreditation Commissions, Inc. (ICSAC), 29–30
International Federation of University Women, 105
International Kindergarten Union, 190
International Reading Association (IRA), 741, **1307–1309,** 1394–1395
International Schools Association (ISA), 1238
International Schools Services (ISS), 115
International Society for Business Education, 219
International Society for Performance Improvement (ISPI), **1309–1310**
international teacher associations, **1318–1321**
International Technology Education Association (ITEA), 2506–2507
Interstate New Teacher Assessment and Support Consortium (INTASC), 121, 122
Interstate School Leaders Licensure Consortium (ISLLC), 1921
Journalism Education Association (JEA), **1346–1347**
Magnet Schools of America (MSA), 1528
MENC: The National Association for Music Education, 1720
Middle States Association of Colleges and Schools (MSA), 28
Modern Language Association of America (MLA), **1672–1674**
National Academy of Education, 133
National Academy of Sciences, 133, 854, **1727–1731,** 2038
National Alliance for Civic Education, 296
National Art Education Association (NAEA), 118, 121, 122, **1734–1736**
National Assessment Governing Board (NAGB), 133, 134
National Association for Business Teacher Education (NABTE), 224
National Association for Sport and Physical Education (NASPE), 89, 1006, 1889, 1890–1891

National Association for the Education of Young Children (NAEYC), 273, 623, 624, 625, **1736–1737**
National Association of Biology Teachers (NABT), **1737–1739**
National Association of College Admission Counseling (NACAC), 383
National Association of College and University Residence Halls (NACURH), 342
National Association of Elementary School Principals (NAESP), **1739–1741**
National Association of Independent Colleges and Universities (NAICU), 152, **1741–1742**
National Association of Independent Schools (NAIS), **1742–1743**
National Association of Scholars (NAS), 517
National Association of Schools of Art and Design (NASAD), **1743–1745**
National Association of School Superintendents, 100
National Association of Secondary School Principals (NASSP), **1745–1747,** 1778–1780, 1920, 2193–2194
National Association of State Boards of Education (NASBE), **1747–1749**
National Association of State Universities and Land-Grant Colleges (NASULGC), 100, 101, **1749–1750**
National Association of Student Councils (NASC), 1747
National Association of Trade and Technical Schools, 36
National Business Education Association (NBEA), 215–216, 218, 224, **1753–1754**
National Catholic Educational Association (NCEA), **1754–1756**
National Catholic Forensic League, 2300–2301
National Center for Higher Education, 108
National Coalition for Education in the Arts, 118
National Collegiate Honors Council (NCHC), 1086–1087
National Committee on Nursery Schools, 623
National Consortium for Physical Education and Recreation for Individuals with Disabilities (NCPERID), 38
National Council for Accreditation of Teacher Education (NCATE), 1009, **1762–1763,** *1763,* 1931, 2442
National Council for Private School Accreditation (NSPSA), 30
National Council for the Social Studies (NCSS), **1764–1765,** 2265, 2266, 2269–2270
National Council of Teachers of English (NCTE), 741, 1394–1395, **1765–1767**
National Council of Teachers of Mathematics (NCTM), 717–718, 1541, 1545, 1565, **1767–1768**
National Council on Education Standards and Testing (NCEST), 2154–2155
National Forensic League, 2300–2301, **2733–2734**
National Intramural Association (NIA), 362
National Intramural-Recreational Sports Association (NIRSA), 362
National Mental Health and Special Education Coalition, 726
National Middle School Association, 1631
National Policy Board for Educational Administration (NPBEA), 99–100, 1920–1921
National PTA, **1782–1784**
National School Boards Association (NSBA), **1784–1786**
National School Public Relations Association (NSPRA), **1786–1788**
National Science Teachers Association (NSTA), **1791–1792,** 2174–2175
National Society for the Promotion of Industrial Education, 73
National Vocational Guidance Association, 975
Network of Outcome Based Schools (NOBS), 1829
New England Association of Schools and Colleges (NEASC), 28, 32, 2185
North Central Association of Colleges and Schools (NCA), 28
Northwest Association of Schools and Colleges (NASC), 28
Office for the Advancement of Public Black Colleges (OAPBC), 100
Professional and Organizational Development Network for Higher Education (POD), 255, 256
professional organizations, 375
Progressive Education Association, 80–81, 696–697, 707–708
REFORMA, 289
regional school accrediting commissions, 28–29, 32
social studies teachers, 2271
The Society for Educational Reconstruction (SER), 208
Society for the Study of the Child, 186
Southern Association of Colleges and Schools (SACS), 28
Southern Association of College Women, 105
student personnel workers, 2388
Western Association of Schools and Colleges (WASC), 28
World Council on Curriculum and Instruction (WCCI), 1637
Zero to Three, 273
See also American Council on Education (ACE); Honor societies; National Collegiate Athletic Association (NCAA); National Education Association (NEA); Youth organizations and clubs

Association to Advance Collegiate Schools of Business (AACSB), **1–2**

Associative function of schooling, 211

Assumption of risk, 1474

"Assuring Education Success for All" (Council of Chief State School Officers), 502

Astin, Alexander
college impact research, 334–335
college rankings, 379, 380
Astronomy, 104
Asynchronous communication, 592
Atherton, George W., 1381, 1383
Athletics, college, **344–372**
academic support for athletes, **353–356,** 356–357
athletic scholarships, 2309
community colleges, 2390
intercollegiate athletics, **344–347,** 1037
intramural athletics, **361–364**
NCAA rules and regulations, **368–371**
scholarships, 351–352, **356–358,** 2309
students as athletes, **358–361**
students' social and emotional development, 2313
Title IX, 351–352, 673, 837, **2570–2573**
Yale University, 2697
See also Intramural athletics; Sports; Student Athletes
Atkin, J. Myron, 1164
Atkinson, John, 1691–1692
Atkinson, Robert, 1170
Atlanta University, 197
Atlanta University Conferences, 1898-1914, 66
ATLAS Communities Project, 323
Atlas of Science Literacy (AAAS), 2175
Atomic bomb development, 473
Atomic Energy Commission, 855
ATP (Association of Test Publishers), 2550
ATP Guidelines for Computer-Based Testing (Association of Test Publishers), 2550–2551
At-risk children
Accelerated Schools, 23–24
early childhood education, 629–630
preschool initiatives, 617
Success for All programs, **2405–2407,** *2406*
See also Youth development programs
At-risk neighborhoods, **1851–1856,** 1907
At-risk schools, 719
Attachment
adoption, 814
developmental theory, 565, 566
evolutionary theory, 571
foster care, 818–819
international early childhood education, 631
stage of growth, 277, 565, 566
See also Child development; Developmental theory
Attainment, educational
earnings, 339
Hispanic Americans, 1966
international statistics, *1305*
parents', **1856–1858**
reasoning skills, 1447
South Asia, 2273–2274
students' educational aspirations and attainment, 1858–1859
Attendance. *See* Compulsory education attendance; Truancy and attendance problems
Attention, **155–157**
learning, 1334
perception and, 1438
Attention deficit hyperactivity disorder (ADHD), **157–159**
behavior problems, 70
mental health services, 1615
special education, 2287
Attitudes of college students, 338
Attribution theory of ability, 1692–1693
Attrition, college. *See* Retention, college
Au, Kathryn H., 2002
AU (Air University), 2621
Audiotapes, 592
Audio-tutorial instruction, 1130–1131
Audiovisual education, 264
Audit committees, 192
Auditing, public school, 1955
Auditory processing, 1385–1386
Augustine, St., **159–161**
Au Pair Program, ECA, 848
Au pairs, 271, 848
Aural learning aids, 1577
Austin, Mary C., 1999
Australia, 1316
Austria. *See* Western Europe
Ausubel, David, 678
Authoritarian education, 901–903
Authoritarian *vs.* authoritative parenting
characterizations, 55, 1849–1851
Authority, democratic, 170
Autism, **161–162,** 2287
Autobiographical memory, **1588–1591**
Automatization of information processing, 568
Autonomous power centers, 663
AutoTutor, 1169–1170
Auxiliary budget, 2048
Average annual expenditure increases, 659–660
Average daily attendance (ADA) allocations, 2258, 2260
Aviation Education Program, FAA, 849
Award for International Scientific Cooperation, 92
Award for Public Understanding of Science and Technology, 92
Awards
AAPT Distinguished Service Citation, 98
AAUW Recognition Award for Emerging Scholars, 104
American Association for the Advancement of Science, 92
American Association of Physics Teachers, 98
American Association of University Women, 104
Annie Jump Cannon Award in Astronomy, 104
Association for Women in Communications, 1069
Award for International Scientific Cooperation, 92
Award for Public Understanding of Science and Technology, 92
Batchelder Award, 288–289
Caldecott Medal, 288
children's literature, 288–292
Coretta Scott King Awards, 289
Excellence in Pre-College Physics Teaching Award, 98
Founders Distinguished Senior Scholar Award, 104
Hans Christian Andersen prize, 289
journalism, 1349
Journalism Education Association (JEA), 1347
Klopsteg Memorial Lecture, 98

Laura Ingalls Wilder Award, 288
Mentor Prize, 92
Millikan Medal, 98
National Art Education Association, 1735
National Association of Biology Teachers, 1738
National Catholic Educational Association, 1755
National Communication Association, 1759
National Council of Teachers of English, 1766
National Council of Teachers of Mathematics, 1768
National Endowment for the Humanities, 1775
National Future Farmers of America, 2735
National Merit Scholarship Corporation, 1781
Newbery Medal, 288
Newcomb Cleveland Prize, 92
Oersted Medal, 98
Phi Beta Kappa book awards, 1078
Philip Hauge Abelson Prize, 92
Pura Belpré Award, 289
Quill and Scroll Society, 2736
Robert F. Sibert Informational Book Award, 288
Scientific Freedom and Responsibility Award, 92
Student Speaker of the Year, 1074
AWC (Army War College), 2621
AWS (alphabetical writing systems), 1488–1489
Aydelotte, Frank, 1086
Aymes v. Bonnelli, 1188
Azerbaijan. *See* Eastern Europe and Central Asia

B

Baby-tenders, 2229–2230
Baccalaureate degrees. *See* Bachelor's degree programs
Bachelor's degree programs
AAC Project on Redefining the Meaning and Purpose of a Baccalaureate Degree, 515
business, 220, 222
Carnegie Classification, 244, 245
early childhood education, 624
engineering, 738
majors, 20–21
nontraditional students, 2706
nursing, 220, 1818–1819
teacher education, 721
Backwoods Utopias (Bestor), 172
Bacon, Francis, 420
Bagley, William Chandler, **163–165,** 194, 195, 2555
Bahamas. *See* Latin America and the Caribbean
Bahrain. *See* Middle East and North Africa
Bahrick, Harry P., 1607
Bailey, Liberty Hyde, 74, 75
Bailey, State v., 465
Baillargeon, Renee, 564
Baird's Manual of American College Fraternities (ACHS), 1070
Baker, Eva L., 733
Bakke v. Regents of the University of California, 62–63, 64, 2424
Bakutes, Arlene, 256
Bales, Ruby J., 1979
Ball, Samuel, 1707, 2024
Ball, Stephen, 949
Baltimore, David, 2039
Band programs, 1722
Bandura, Albert, 1692–1693, 1865
Bangladesh. *See* South Asia
Banking education, 901
Banks, Cherry A. McGee, 1963
Banks, James A., 1705, 1963
Barbados. *See* Latin America and the Caribbean
Barber, Bonnie, 318
Barenblatt v. United States, 102
Barkan, Manuel, **165–167**
Barker, Roger, 433–434
Barkley, Russell A., 157, 158
Barnard, Frederick A. P., 229, 230
Barnard, Henry, 695, 905, 1876, 2614–2615
Barnett, Ronald, 2502
Barnette, West Virginia Board of Education v., 2425
Bar-On Emotional Quotient Inventory (EQ-i), 1191
Barr, Donald, 541–542
Barr, Stringfellow, 212, 2366
Barrick, R. Kirby, 78
Barriers, educational, 591
Barsalou, Lawrence W., 247
Bartlett, Frederic, 1467
Barzun, Jacques, 414
Basic education
Basic School Network, 201
Catholic schools, 253
Council for Basic Education (CBE), **498–499**
international issues, 2196
South Asia, 2275–2276
Basic elements ability tests, 1113
Basic interpersonal communication skills (BICS), 176
Basic Learning Materials Initiative (UNESCO), 1262
Basic Principles of Curriculum and Instruction (Tyler), 520–521, 1994, 2589
The Basic School: A Community for Learning (report), 201
Basic School Network, 201
Basketball, 359–360, 366
Batchelder Award, 288–289
Bateman, Helen, 50
Battered child syndrome, 268
See also Child abuse and neglect
Battle Command Training Programs (BCTPs), 1658
Baumann, James F., 2000
Baumrind, Diana, 55, 1849
Baxter, Frank, 592
Bayes Nets, 142
Bayh-Dole Act, 856
BCEE (Business Coalition for Excellence in Education), 228
BCTPs (Battle Command Training Programs), 1658
BEA (Bureau of Economic Analysis), 841
Beach v. the University of Utah, 2075
Beacon Education Management, Inc., **167–168**
Beacons. *See* Full-service schools
Bean, John, 404–405, 748
Bean, Thomas W., 1981
Beard, Charles, 539
Beard, Joseph, 2454
Beaumis, Henri, 186
Becher, Tony, 12
Beck, Isabel L., 1980
Becoming Adult: How Teenagers Prepare for the World of Work (Csikszentmihalyi and Schneider), 736
Be Cool. Follow the Rules (initiative), 1783
Bednar, Anne K., 1149

Beecher, Catharine
common schools, 430
family and consumer sciences, 803
physical education, 1887
Behavior, classroom, 300–301
Behavioral objectives. *See* Instruction, objectives
Behavioral settings, 434
Behavior control, 1699
Behaviorism
behavior modification, 1695
learning theory, 563, 678–679, 680, 1458–1461, 2493
motivation and peer relations, 1865
technology and, 2516
vocational education, 649
Watson, John B., 2668–2669
See also Skinner, B. F.
The Behavior of Organisms (Skinner), 2229
Behavior problems
aggressive behavior, **69–72**
children of welfare-to-work parents, 2675
classroom management, 302
community violence exposure, 2629
domestic violence exposure, 2632–2633
family support services, 832
insufficient sleep and, 2233
media violence, 1582
poverty, 1911–1912
stress and depression, 2372–2373
violence exposure, 2625–2626
Zero Tolerance (initiative), 110
Belarus. *See* Eastern Europe and Central Asia
Belgium. *See* Western Europe
Beliefs, reading and learning, 1997–1998
Belize. *See* Latin America and the Caribbean
Bell, Andrew, 711
Bell, Carl C., 2628
Bell, Terrell H., 838, 2152, 2616
See also A Nation at Risk: The Imperative for Educational Reform (report)
The Bell Curve (Herrnstein and Murray), 1962
Belmont, John M., 1470
Belmont Report (National Commission for the Protection of Human Subjects of Biomedical and Behavioral Research), 1091
Benchmarking, 526–527
Benchmarks for Science Literacy (American Association for the Advancement of Science), 2174, 2175
Bencraft, C. Edwin, 1888
Benin. *See* Sub-Saharan Africa
Benjamin, Harold R. W., **168–169**
Benjamin A. Gilman International Scholarship Program, 1138
Benne, Kenneth D., **169–171**
Bennet, Melissa, 320
Bennett, William, 514–515, 2154
Bennett Law (Wisconsin), 1924, 1942
Bennis, Warren, 170
Bensimon, Estela M., 793
Benson, Thomas C., 1211
Berea College, **171–172**
Bereiter, Carl, 1466
Bergquist, William H., 521
Berkowitz, Marvin, 260–261
Berman, Paul, 2031
Berman, Summer M., 1873
Bernhardt, Elizabeth, 1516
Bernstein, Basil, 1511
Berry, Jeffrey, 664
Bess, James, 415
Bestor, A. E., Jr., **172–173,** 1937
Best practices
Center for Best Practices, National Governors Association, 1777
early childhood education, international aspects of, 630
teacher unions and, 2481
Beta Phi Mu, **1071–1072**
Bethel School District No. 403 v. Frazer, 2425
Bethune, Mary McLeod, **173–175**
Bethune-Cookman College, 174
Betrayers of the Truth: Fraud and Deceit in the Hall of Science (Broad and Wade), 2039
Beveridge, Andrew, 1846
Beyer, Janice, 10
Beyond Freedom and Dignity (Skinner), 2231
Beyond the Classroom (Steinberg), 49
Bhutan. *See* South Asia
BIA. *See* Bureau of Indian Affairs, U.S. (BIA)
Bias
academic freedom and tenure, 15
gender, 1126–1128
grading and teacher bias, 957
Graduate Record Examination (GRE), 964
standardized tests, 1204
See also Discrimination; Gender; Race/ethnicity
Bickel, Robert D., 2075
BICS (basic interpersonal communication skills), 176
Bicultural education, 1102
Bidding process, construction, 2125–2126
Bielaczyc, Katerine, 1465
Big Brothers Big Sisters of America, 2713, **2718–2719**
Biglan, Anthony, 11
Biglan Model of academic disciplines, 11, *12*
The Big Six, 108, 109, 155
Big Ten Conference, 349
Bilateral international development agencies, **1241–1249**
Bilingual education, **175–181**
Bilingual Education Act, 178, 182
bilingualism and, 182–183
dual immersion, 180, 182, 896
elementary schools, 713
English language learners (ELLs), 182–183, 1516
immigrants, 1099–1103
international issues, 1105
language immersion, 1102
literacy and culture, 1510–1512
multilingual English, 743
Office of Bilingual Education and Minority Languages Affairs (OBEMLA), Department of Education, 2618
reading, 1516
typology, *176*
See also English as a second language (ESL); Language; Language acquisition; Language minority students
Bilingual Education Act, 178, 182
Bilingualism, **181–185**

Bill and Melinda Gates Foundation, 1807–1808
A Bill for the More General Diffusion of Knowledge (Jefferson), 428
Binet, Alfred, **185–187**
  Binet-Simon scale, 1112–1113
  educational psychology, 677–678
  intelligence measurement, 1194
Biographies, 106
  See also Educator's biographies; Progressive educator's biographies
Biological-maturationist theory of development, 563
Biological models of intellectual development, 1895–1896
Biology, folk, 572
Biology and general intelligence. *See* Genetics
Biomedical engineering, 740
Biomedical research fraud, 2037
Biotech development, 2595–2596
Bipolar disorder, 810
Birnbaum, Robert, 795
Bisexuality. *See* Sexual orientation
Bishop, Roosevelt v., 888
BizEd (periodical), 2
Black, Paul, 124, 1164
Black, Ruby, 1069
Black Alliance for Educational Options, 1928
Black colleges. *See* Historically black colleges and universities (HBCUs)
Black history. *See* African-American studies
Black Mountain College, 2052–2053
"Black Papers" (report), 1826
Black Power movement, 67
Black's Law Dictionary, 1472
Black Student Union, San Francisco State University, 67
Black studies. *See* African-American studies
Blackwell, Jacqueline, 1707
Blackwell, Peggy, 1751
Blanton, Annie Webb, 1073
Blended sentences, 1351, 1356
Blimling, Gregory, 2046
Blind students. *See* Visually impaired students
Block scheduling
  alternate day, *2098*
  Carnegie units, 246
  explained, 2096, 2097–2098
Bloom, Benjamin S., **188–189**
  classroom assessment, 124
  classroom questions, 311
  domain expertise, 766
  educational psychology, 678
  outcome-based education, 1829, 2429–2430
  See also Taxonomies of educational objectives
Blow, Susan, **189–191,** 622, 905
Blue-Backed Speller (Webster), 1998, 2303, 2554, 2670, 2671
Blueprints for Reform (AAAS), 2175
B'nai B'rith Youth Organization, **2720–2721**
Board certified teachers, 1750–1752, 2450–2451, 2458–2460
Boarding schools, Native American, 712, 2187
Board of Curators of the University of Missouri v. Horowitz, 2425
Board of Education, Everson v., 2423
Board of Education, King v., 1391
Board of Education Island Trees Union Free School District No. 26 v. Pico, 2425
Board of Education of Kiryas Joel v. Grumet, 2423
Board of Education of Oklahoma City Public Schools v. Dowell, 2202, 2424
Board of Education of the District of Columbia, Mills v., 672, 1868
Board of Education of the Hendrick Hudson Central School District v. Rowley, 2281
Board of Education of Topeka, Kansas, Brown v. See Brown v. Board of Education of Topeka, Kansas
Board of Education of Westside Community Schools v. Mergens, 2423
Board of Education v. Allen, 2423
Board of regents. *See* Board of trustees
Board of Regents, Sipuel v., 64
Board of Regents of the University of California, Tarasoff v., 2075
Board of trustees, **191–192**
  in college organization, 385–386
  decision-making, 946
  state government, 2360–2362
Board of visitors. *See* Board of trustees
Boards of education, state, 1747–1749, **2350–2359,** *2352–2356*
Bobbitt, Franklin, **192–194**
Bode, Boyd H., 80, **194–196,** 293
Bodily-kinesthetic intelligence, 1199
Bodrova, Elena, 576
Body image, 1582
Boelte, Maria Kraus, 189
Bogatz, Gerry, 1707, 2024
Boggs, George R., 96
Bogue, E. Grady, 378
Bogue, Jesse, 96
Bohen, D. B., 1751
Bolam, Raymond, 2444
Bolivia. *See* Latin America and the Caribbean
Bollinger, Gratz v. See Gratz v. Bollinger
Bollinger, Grutter v. See Grutter v. Bollinger
Bologna Process, 27
Bond, Horace Julian, 197
Bond, Horace Mann, **196–197**
Bonds, 2340–2341
Bonet, Juan Pablo, 1019
Bonnelli, Aymes v., 1188
Bonser, Frederick, 2506
Boodt, Gloria, 1979
Book Flood (Fiji), 2091
Bookkeeping, 215
  See also Finance
Book proposals, 2601–2602
Booster colleges, 442
Borderline personality disorder, 268
Bork, Alfred, 1578
Borkowski, John G., 1470
Boruch, Robert, 2031
Borzak, Lenore, 1326
Bosnia and Herzegovina, 2247–2248
  See also Eastern Europe and Central Asia
Boston Girls High and Normal School, 2184
Boston public high schools, 2184
Boston Vocation Bureau, 975
Botswana. *See* Sub-Saharan Africa
Botvin, Gill, 2056
Boud, David, 762
Boundaries and expectations for children, 811

Bourne, Randolph, 553
Bowdoin, John, 87
Bowen, Howard, **197–199,** 334
Bowen, William G., 352–353
Bower, Eli M., 726
Boyd, William, 2141
Boyer, Ernest L., **199–201**
college teaching, 415
on the definition of research, 2502
teacher improvement programs, 255
undergraduate curriculum, 516
See also Scholarship Reconsidered: Priorities of the Professoriate (Boyer)
Boyer Center at Messiah College, 201
Boys
education of, 985–986
fertility and education, 1903
See also Gender
Boys and Girls Clubs of America, 319, **2721–2722**
Boy Scouts of America, 1688, **2724–2725**
Boys State and Girls State programs, **2722–2723**
Brace, Charles Loring, 2709
Bradley, Lynette, 569
Bradley, Milliken v., 2424
Bradley Home, 2279
Bradstreet v. Sobol, 1062
Braille, 2635
Brain-based education, **202–206**
Brain drain, 2397
Brain gym, 1702
Brain imaging, 205
Brameld, Theodore, **206–208**
Brand, Christopher, 1196
Bransford, John D., 1148
Braskamp, Larry, 786
Brassie, P. Stanley, 1892
Braunwald, Eugene, 2039
Braverman, Harry, 733
Braxton, John, 12, 405
Brazil, 461
See also Latin America and the Caribbean
Breach of duty, 1473
Bread Loaf Teacher Network, 2467
Breakfast Program, School
average daily participation, *2135*
federal costs, *2136*
health and, 1006
overview, 2134
Breaking Ranks: Changing an American Institution (report), 1746, 1778, 2191
Brennan, Robert, 140
Brenner, Mary, 1564
Bridges to Success (initiative), 2711
"Bridging the Gap between Neuroscience and Education" (meeting), 203, 205
Briggs, Derek, 729
Brighouse, Harry, 949
Broad, William, 2039
Broadcasting, educational, 592, **656–658**
Broadcast stations, student, 1349
Broad Foundation, 1806
Brodzinsky, David, 814
Brooke-Gunn, Jeanne, 1905
Brookings, Robert Somers, 209
Brookings Institution, **208–210**
Brookings Institution Press, 209
Brookings Review (newsletter), 209
Brookline Teacher Researcher Seminar, 2467
Brophy, Jere, 305, 306, 312, 2454
Broudy, Harry S., **210–212**
Brown, Ann, 1451, 1464, 1604, 1978, 1982
Brown, Bradford, 48, 55–56, 1859
Brown, David, 2525
Brown, Rachel, 1978, 1982
Brown, William, 1194
Brown University, 322, 323
Brown v. Board of Education of Topeka, Kansas, **2789–2795**
affirmative action, 61
American Federation of Teachers (AFT), 112
constitutional requirements of state education, 478–479
disabled students, rights of, 1868
historically black colleges and universities (HBCUs), 1049
history of secondary education, 2186
overview, 2423
policy, 671
school board authority, 2113
segregation, legal aspects, 430, 2200–2201
sociology of education, 326
in timeline of affirmative action, 64
white flight, 2151
BRT (Business Roundtable), 226
Bruer, John, 203, 204, 565
Bruffee, Kenneth A., 521
Brunei Darussalam. *See* East Asia and the Pacific
Bruner, Jerome, 166, 678
Bruning, Roger, 1604
Bryan, Anna, 190, 622
Bryant, Peter E., 569
Bryk, Anthony, 999
Buchanan, Scott, **212–213,** 2366
Buckley Amendment, 2013–2015
Budgeting
public schools, 1952–1954, 2258–2259
school-based decision-making, 2100
state administrative services, 2342–2343
See also Allocation; Finance
Building America (textbook series), 2556
Building a Presence for Science (initiative), 1792
Buildings and grounds committees, 192
See also Facilities
Building Successful Partnerships: A Guide for Developing Parent and Family Involvement Programs (National PTA), 1783
Bulgaria. *See* Eastern Europe and Central Asia
Bulletin 54 (report), 539
Bulletin (National Association of Secondary School Principals), 1746
Bullying, 1355, 1359
Bureaucracy
accountability, 652
public schools, 1949, 2256
urban schools, 2606–2607
See also Administration, educational; Governance
Bureau of Census, U.S., 841
Bureau of Economic Analysis, U.S. (BEA), 841
Bureau of Education, U.S., 2615
Bureau of Educational and Cultural Affairs, U.S. (ECA), 113, 847–848
Bureau of Export Administration, U.S. (BXA), 841

Bureau of Indian Affairs, U.S. (BIA)
educational activities, 845
elementary education, 712
federal schools, 866
secondary education, 2187
See also Native Americans; Tribal colleges and universities
Bureau of Labor Statistics, U.S., 847
Bureau of Transportation Statistics, U.S., 851
Burk, Frederic, 2662–2663
Burkina Faso. *See* Sub-Saharan Africa
Burks, Virginia, 47
Buros, Luella, 214
Buros, Oscar Krisen, **213–215**
Burrow, John, 223
Burt, Cyril L., 1202
Burundi. *See* Sub-Saharan Africa
Bush, George H. W.
business involvement in education, 226
education reform, 691
federal involvement in education, 838
Bush, George W.
business involvement in education, 227–228
reform "blueprint," 2546
school reform, 2156
standards movement, 714
Bush, Robert, 1620
Bush, Vannevar, 855, 1038
Business
Business Coalition for Excellence in Education (BCEE), 228
Canadian education, 237
child care issues, 275
consortia development, 476
continuing professional education (CPE), **483–489**
corporate colleges and universities, **492–494,** 1482
corporate sponsorship of intercollegiate athletics, 346
educational involvement, **226–229,** 425, 1030
faculty consulting, **772–775,** *774*
lifelong learning, 1481–1482
overseas corporate schools, 113
school involvement, 824
tutoring, 2581
See also Industry-university research collaboration
Business Coalition for Excellence in Education (BCEE), 228
Business education
AACSB International, **1–2**
accreditation, 1, 2
college and graduate study, **220–222**
Distributive Education Clubs of America (DECA), **2726–2727**
Future Business Leaders of America-Phi Beta Lambda (FBLA-PBL), **2729–2730**
Global Forum on Management Education, 1
National Business Education Association (NBEA), **1753–1754**
school, **215–220**
teacher preparation, **222–226**
Whitehead, Alfred North, 2685–2686
Business models
schools, 2256
standards-based reform, 2319, 2322
Business Roundtable (BRT), 226
Business School Development Conference, AACSB, 1
Busing for racial integration, 325, 326, 480
See also Segregation
Butler, Nicholas M., **229–231,** 1138
Butterfield, Earl C., 1470
BXA (Bureau of Export Administration), 841

C

Cable television, 657–658
CAEL (Council for Adult and Experiential Learning), 1478, 1479
Cafeteria-style course selection, 925
CAI (computer-aided instruction), 2582–2583
Caine, Geoffrey, 202–203, 204
Caine, Renate Nummela, 202–203, 204
Calculus Reform, 512
Caldecott Medal, 288
Caldwell, Otis W., 1484
Calendars, academic, **5–8**
See also Year-round education
Calexico School District, California, 179–180
California
Calexico School District, 179–180
class-size reduction, 315
Department of Education, 2326
Health Start Initiative, 832
higher education, 1025, 1038
immigrant education, 100–1102
language minority students, 1402
Policy Analysis for California Education (PACE), 82
Proposition 209, 63, 64
Proposition 227, 179, 182
statewide testing programs, 2540
textbooks, 2558
California Civil Rights Initiative. *See* Proposition 209 (California)
California Institute of Technology
intramural/recreation programs, *364*
Callahan, Raymond E., 673
Callan, Eamonn, 754
CALP (Cognitive academic language proficiency), 176
Cambodia, 639
See also East Asia and the Pacific
Cameroon. *See* Sub-Saharan Africa
Camp, Walter, 349
Campbell, Doak S., 96
Campbell, Donald, 2031
Campbell, John, 1196
Campbell, Roald F., **233–234**
Campbell County School District, State of Wyoming v., 888
Campbell Donald, 2032
Camp Fire USA, **2725–2726**
Camping, 1833
Campione, Joseph, 1464
Campus-based services for minority students, 1969–1970
Campus communities, 200
Campus Compact, 2207
Campus crime, 2075–2076
See also Gangs; Juvenile justice system; Violence
Campus Life: In Search of Community (Boyer), 200
Campus senates, 946–947
Canada, **234–239**
adolescent peer culture, 48

Canadian International Development Agency (CIDA), 1242–1243
Canada, Missouri ex rel Gaines v., 2423
Canadian International Development Agency (CIDA), 1242–1243
Canady, Robert, 2097–2098
Cantor, Nancy, 1191
Caperton, Gaston, 373
Cape Verde. *See* Sub-Saharan Africa
Capital assets, 26
Capital campaigns, college and university, 1142
Capitalism, 539–540
Capital outlay
college and university, 870, 2340
local school system, **886–889**
Capstone courses, **239–241**
CAPTA (Child Abuse Prevention and Treatment Act), 267
Captains Career Course, U.S. Army, 1654
Captive Voices: The Report of the Commission of Inquiry into High School Journalism (Robert F. Kennedy Commission), 1349
Cardinal Principles of Secondary Education (National Education Association), 193, 696, 2185–2186
CARE (Cooperative for Assistance and Relief Everywhere), 1803–1804
Career clusters, vocational education, 2643–2644, 2649–2650
Career counseling, **241–243**
Career development
capstone courses, 240
career choice, 339
career education courses, 805–806
community colleges, 2390
counseling, **241–243,** 1870
resource libraries, 241–242
service learning, 2204, 2207, 2208–2209
services, 241–242
See also Employment
Career paths
academic deans, 9
chief academic affairs officers, 265
college and university presidents, 1915–1916
vocational education teachers, 2650
Career school accreditation, 35–37
Career technical education. *See* Vocational and technical education
Carey, Susan, 248–249
Caribbean countries. *See* Latin America and the Caribbean
Caring Communities (initiative), 830
Carini, Patricia, 2467
Carl D. Perkins Vocational Education acts
business education, 216–217
federal participation in education, 838
state departments of education, 2329
vocational education, 2638–2639
Carl Rogers on Encounter Groups (Rogers), 2078
Carnegie Classification System, **243–245**
chart showing, *244*
overview, 1041–1042
research universities, 783, 2042–2043
Carnegie Commission on Higher Education, 1041
Carnegie Corporation
American Council of Learned Societies, 106
child care, 273, 274
education reform reports, 697
overview, 1806–1807
Carnegie Council on Policy Studies in Higher Education, 239
Carnegie Forum on Education, 2154
Carnegie Foundation for the Advancement of Teaching
American College Athletics (Savage), 350
Boyer, Ernest, 200
Higher Education and the American Resurgence (report), 517–518
profile, 1807
scholarship of teaching, 415
The Undergraduate Experience in America (report), 516
Carnegie units, **246–247,** 2185
Carpinteria Preschool Program, 183
Carr, Edward G., 158
Carrera program (initiative), 2073
Carroll, J. M., 442
Carroll, John, 1115, 1195, 1829
Carskadon, Mary, 2232
Carter, Heather, 2441
Carter, James G., 1535
Carter, Jimmy, 715, 2616
CAS (Cognitive Assessment System), 570
Case, Robbie, 1560
Case-based reasoning, **1154–1159**
CASE (Council for the Advancement and Support of Education), 1140
CASEL (Collaborative to Advance Social and Emotional Learning), 1193
Case libraries, instructional, 1155–1157
Case Studies for the Foundations of American Education (Broudy), 211
Case studies in study of teaching, 2489–2490
Cassiodorus, 160
Casteen, John T., III, 2599–2600
Catalina Foothills School District, Zobrest v., 2423
Categorical grants, 890–891
Categorization and concept learning, **247–250**
concept mapping, 145–146, *146*, 2491
conceptual change, 248–249, **1427–1431**
differentiation, 1428
knowledge, 247, 764
memory tests, 1598–1599
Piaget, Jean, 1896
teaching, 1183
Catholic Education Association, 251
Catholic schools, **250–254**
Catholic Education Association, 251
common schools and, 430
history, 1924
immigrants, 1098–1099
integration and performance of students, 325–326
minority students, 1925–1926

National Catholic Educational Association (NCEA), **1754–1756**
National Catholic Forensic League, 2300–2301
public *vs.*, 1926
See also Private schools; Religiously affiliated schools; Voucher programs
CATM (Children's Analogical Thinking Modifiability) test, 128
Catsambis, Sophia, 1846
CATs (classroom assessment techniques), 255
Cattell, James, 378
Cattell, Raymond, 1202, 1205
Causal maps, 146–147
Causal reasoning, 1053, **1425–1427**
Causation in negligence liability, 1474
Cayman Islands. *See* Latin America and the Caribbean
Cazden, Courtney, 1510
CBE (Council for Basic Education), **498–499**
CBR (case-based reasoning), **1154–1159**
CBTE (competency-based teacher education), 2441–2442, 2447
CCAF (Community College of the Air Force), 843
CCDF (Child Care and Development Fund), 616–617, 2673–2674
CCSSO. *See* Council of Chief State School Officers (CCSSO)
CDA (Child development associate), 618
CDC (Centers for Disease Control and Prevention), 1004, 1013–1014
CDP (Character Development Project), 1687–1688
CD-ROMs, 592
CEC (Council for Exceptional Children), **499–500**
CEFEB (Center for Finance, Business, and Banking Studies, France), 1244–1245
Celio, Mary Beth, 692
Censorship, textbook, 2556–2557
Censured colleges and universities, 101–102
Census Bureau, 841
Center for Applied Linguistics, 895
Center for Best Practices, National Governors Association, 1777
Center for Civic Education, 296
Center for Coordination of Research on Social Indicators, Social Science Research Council, 1291–1292
Center for Ethics in Government, National Conference of State Legislatures, 1761
Center for Evidence-Based Education, 1799
Center for Finance, Business, and Banking Studies (France), 1244–1245
Center for Global Development (CGD), 1137
Center for Lesbian and Gay Studies (CLAGS), 917
Centers for Disease Control and Prevention (CDC)
health education, 1004
health services, 1013–1014
sexually transmitted diseases, 2065–2066
youth smoking, 2068
See also Youth Risk Behavior Survey (YRBS)
Central African Republic. *See* Sub-Saharan Africa
Central America. *See* Latin America and the Caribbean
Central Park East Secondary School, 321
Centre College, 350
Centre for Educational Research and Innovation (CERI), Organisation for Economic Co-operation and Development, 1250–1251, 1266–1267
CEP (Character Education Partnership), 260
CERI (Centre for Educational Research and Innovation), Organisation for Economic Co-operation and Development, 1250, 1266–1267
Certification and licensure
advanced graduate studies, 221, 222
alternative teacher licensing, 2608
board certified teachers, 2450–2451, 2458–2460
business education teachers, 217, 219, 223, 224
child-care, 272, 273
coaches, 2308–2309
computer technology, 219
dentistry, 558–559
early childhood education, 618, 624, 625
education study programs, 968
examinations, 2530–2531
family day homes, 271
guidance and counseling, 977
health education, 1009
international issues, 2472
journalism teachers, 1347
middle school teachers, 1634
nursing, 1819
pharmacy education, 94–95
physical education teachers, 1893
preschool teachers, 618
principals, 1920–1921
private schools, 1926
reciprocity licensing, 2436
sexuality education teachers, 2216
social studies teachers, 2271
special education teachers, 2288, 2291
state education agencies and, 2346–2347
teacher, 1751–1752, 2436, 2450
teacher accountability, 652
teacher evaluation methods, 2459
technology, 2527
urban school teachers, 2607–2608
vocational education teachers, 2649
See also Credentials
CES (Coalition of Essential Schools), **321–322, 322–324**
CES University, 321
CGD (Center for Global Development), 1137
Chad. *See* Sub-Saharan Africa
Chairpersons, department, **559–561,** 800–801
Chall, Jeanne, **257–259**
The Challenges of Connecting Learning (report), 517
Chambers, Jay G., 1954
Champion, Tempii, 1510
CHAMPS/Life Skills program, 357, 367

Chancellor Beacon Academies, Inc. *See* Beacon Education Management, Inc.
Change agents, 1817, 2031
Changing Concepts of Education (Cubberley), 508
Chapman, Laura, 166
Chapman, Saul, 313
Character development, **259–263**
  Character Development Project (CDP), 1687–1688
  Character Education Partnership (CEP), 260
  college students, 338
  elementary school, 716–717
  See Also Civics and citizenship education; Moral development; Moral education
Character Education Partnership (CEP), 260
Charcot, Jean-Martin, 185
Chard, David J., 1457
Charitable organizations, 432
  See also Nongovernmental Organizations (NGOs) and foundations
Charles A. Ryskamp Fellowship Program, 106
Charles Stewart Mott Foundation, 1808
Charlotte-Mecklenburg Board of Education, Swann v., 480, 2424
Chartered universities, federally, 867
Charter of the United Nations, Article 1, **3090–3091**
Charters, W. W., **263–265,** 2588
Charter schools
  accountability, 653
  alternative education, 82–85
  Beacon Education Management, Inc., **167–168**
  district reorganization, 2344–2345
  market-based reform, 552
  policy, 675
  public school criticism, 1950
  social organization, 2260
  See also School choice
Chase, William G., 765
Chaskin, Richard, 1853
CHEA (Council for Higher Education Accreditation), 32
Chemical engineering, 739
Cheney, Lynne, 515
Chi, Michelene, 1426
Chicago Child-Parent Center (CPC), 619
Chicago Froebel Association, 1957–1958
Chicago Kindergarten and Training School, 622
Chicago Public Schools
  Keppel, Francis C., 1366
  Young, Ella Flagg, 2702
Chicago School Board
  accountability, 2105–2106
  Addams, Jane, 42
Chicago School of Business, 221
Chicago Teachers Federation, 983–985
Chicago youth gang study, 51
Chickenpox, 1107
Chickering, Arthur, 43, 415, 2495
Chief academic affairs officers, **265–267**
Chief state school officers, 501–503
  See also Departments of education, state
Child abuse and neglect, **267–270**
  family circumstance, 809
  foster care, 284–285, 819
  school counselors, 978
  school/police partnership, 1355
  See also Child protective services; Domestic violence
Child Abuse Prevention and Treatment Act (CAPTA), 267
Child advocacy, 1784
The Child and the Curriculum (Dewey), 578
Child art, 1523
Child care, **270–276**
  academic performance, influence on, 1836
  availability and quality, **270–274,** 275
  centers, 271–273, 616–617
  cost and financing, **274–276**
  early education integration, 619–620
  Jewish community centers, 2740
  poverty and quality of, 1907
Child Care and Development Fund (CCDF), 616–617, 2673–2674
Child-centered education
  infant schools, 1134
  Johnson, Marietta Pierce, 1344
  Kandel, Isaac L., 1364
  Kilpatrick, William H., 1369
  Progressive education, 1934
  Rugg, Harold, 2082, 2494
  See also Progressive education
The Child-Centered School (Rugg), 2082
Child development
  Binet, Alfred, 186
  developmental delays identification, 277
  neighborhoods, 1794–1795
  peer relations, 47, 1864–1865
  stages of growth, **276–280**
  violence exposure, 2624
  working memory, 1592–1593
  See also Cognitive development; Developmental theory; Early childhood
Child development associate (CDA), 618, 623
Child Development Project, 1405, 1406
Child labor, 1625
Child mortality, 998–999
Child neglect. *See* Child abuse and neglect
Child Nutrition Act of 1966, 2134
Child Parent Education Centers, 623
Child protective services, **280–285**
  child abuse and neglect, 269–270
  current system, **283–285**
  families, 809–810
  historical overview, **280–283**
  See also Foster care
Children and Their Primary Schools (report, England), 1134, 1825–1826
Children in Need (report), 698
Children of Immigration, 1396
Children's Aid Society, 2073
Children's Analogical Thinking Modifiability (CATM) test, 128
Children's Bureau, U.S., 2676
Children's House, 1676–1678
Children's Inferential Thinking Modifiability (CITM) test, 129
Children's literature, **285–292**
Children's rights
  history, 281–282
  international agreements, 1281
  international issues, 631, 632
Children's Seriational Thinking Modifiability (CSTM) test, 129
Childs, John L., 195, **292–294**

Child welfare. *See* Child protective services
Child Welfare League of America, 268
Chile
compensatory education, 459, 461–462
education access, 1408
elementary education, 716
privatization, 547
See also Latin America and the Caribbean
Chin, Robert, 170
China
Du Bois, W. E. B., 612
early childhood education, 634–635
educational testing, 1573–1574
gross enrollment rates, 638
higher education, 1027, 1028
secondary education, 2188
See also East Asia and the Pacific
China Hong Kong, 978–979
See also East Asia and the Pacific
Chinese immigrants, 1100–1101
Chira, Susan, 2629
Chlamydia, 2065
Chomsky, Carol, 1487
Chomsky, Noam, 1384, 1387, 1415
Chopack, Joanne, 2062
Christiaansen, Robert E., 1606, 1608
Christian day schools, 1944
Christian Democrats, 1319
Christian Schools International (CSI), 1943
Christian teaching, 159–160
Chronology of school libraries, 2137–2138
Chronometric information processing measuring methods, 568–569
Chubb, John, 1927, 2105
Church related institutions. *See* Religiously affiliated colleges and universities; Religiously affiliated schools
Church schools, American overseas, 114
Church-state issues
Catholic schools, 252–253
prayer at commencement exercises, 423
school prayer, 2423
Supreme Court cases, 2422–2423
See also Court cases; Religion; Religiously affiliated schools
CIDA (Canadian International Development Agency), 1242–1243
CIES (Council for the International Exchange of Scholars), 1137
Cincinnati school district, 2450
Circumvention of technological copyright protection measures, 1189–1190
CIRP (Cooperative Institutional Research Program), 334–335
CITA, Inc., 30
CITM (Children's Inferential Thinking Modifiability) test, 129
City of Boston, Roberts v., 2200
City University of New York Graduate School, Center for Lesbian and Gay Studies (CLAGS), 917
Civic capacity, 2143
Civic dispositions, 295
Civics and citizenship education, **294–297**
Civic Education Study, 1288
civic ethic, 754–755
Clark, Septima Poinsette, 299
Eastern Europe and Central Asia region, 642
international comparative studies, **1236–1238**
Jefferson, Thomas, 428
minorities, 2255–2256
Organization for Security and Cooperation in Europe, 1254
race/ethnicity, 2255–2256
service learning, 2209
social cohesion, 2245–2249
social studies, 2265
See also Character development; Democracy and education; Moral development; Moral education
Civil engineering, 739
Civil rights
Civil Rights acts, 62
Civil Rights Restoration Act, 2571
Clark, Septima Poinsette, 298–299
Covenant of Civil and Political Rights, 1280
Du Bois, W. E. B., 610–612
Office for Civil Rights, Department of Education, 2619
superintendents, 2410, 2417
See also Affirmative action; Constitution, U.S.; Court cases; Discrimination; Minorities; Race/ethnicity; Supreme Court, U.S.; Specific minority groups
Civil Rights acts
affirmative action, 62, 64
bilingual education, 178
court cases, 2424
disabled individuals, 1868
Civil Rights Restoration Act, 2571
Civil servants, 544
Civil War, U.S., 854
CLAGS (Center for Lesbian and Gay Studies), 917
Clandinin, D. Jean, 2491
Clapp, Elsie Ripley, **297–298**
Clark, Burton R., 797–798
Clark, Richard, 1576, 2515
Clark, Septima Poinsette, **298–299**
Clark, Terry, 664
Clarke, Kenneth, 2446
Classical conditioning, 1459–1460
See also Behaviorism
Classical Investigation (American Classical League), 1415
Classics majors, 1414
Classification of disciplines, 10–11
Classification of Institutions (Carnegie Foundation for the Advancement of Teaching), 2043
Class periods. *See* Scheduling
Classroom assessment, **123–127**
Classroom Assessment and the National Science Education Standards (National Research Council), 1729
Classroom Assessment Techniques (Angelo and Cross), 2497
techniques, 255, 2497
Classroom behavior, 300–301
Classroom curriculum, 532
Classroom design, 2126–2127
Classroom discourse, **582–586**
Classroom dynamics of peer relations, 1866
Classroom environment
civics education, 1237

classroom management, 300
group processes, 973–974
Montessori, Maria, 1678
peer relations and learning, 1868
Classroom freedom of college faculty, 14
Classroom management, **299–303**
Classroom observation, **303–310**
Classroom questions, **310–314**
classroom discourse, 583
cognitive perspective, 588
language, 1390
Class rushes, 348
Class size, **314–317,** *315,* 888
Claxton, Philander, 96
Clay, Mary, 1487
Clayton, Thomas, 938
Clearinghouse on Higher Education, ERIC, 91
Clearinghouse on Languages and Linguistics, ERIC, 895
Clearinghouse on Teaching and Teacher Education, ERIC, 94
Clearinghouses, ERIC, 683–684
Clerc, Laurent, 1020
Client-Centered Therapy: Its Current Practice, Implications, and Theory (Rogers), 976, 2077–2078
Clifford, Richard, 271
Clifton, Rodney, 235
Climate, school. *See* Classroom environment; School climate
Clinical psychology, 2077–2079
Clinical research, 2039
Clinical Treatment of the Problem Child (Rogers), 2077
Clinton, Bill, 691, 838
Cliques, 48–50
See also Peer culture, adolescent; Peer relations
Closed-circuit technology, 592–593
Cloward, Richard, 2710
Clubs. *See* Youth organizations and clubs
CM (Cultural Modeling), 1512
Coaches
athletic scholarships, 357–358
earnings, 346
school sports, 2308–2309
Coalescence, 1428
Coalition of English Associations Conference, 1394
Coalition of Essential Schools (CES), 246, **321–322, 322–324**
Coast Guard, U.S., 849
Coast Guard Academy, U.S., 849, **1645–1646**
Cobb, Charles, 1668
Cobb, Paul, 1560–1561
Cochlear implants, 1019
Code of Ethics for the Education Profession (National Education Association), 753–754
Code of Fair Testing Practices in Education, 2550
Code of Federal Regulations, 840, 1732
Codification and academic disciplines, 10
COE. *See* Council of Europe (COE)
Coeducational colleges and universities, 2226–2227
Coeducational residence halls, 342
Cogan, Morris, 2418–2419
Cognition and Technology Group, Vanderbilt University, 681
Cognitive academic language proficiency (CALP), 176
Cognitive Assessment System (CAS), 570
Cognitive development
adolescence, 278–279
assessment, 141–143, 570
attention, 156–157
cognitive and information processing, **567–571**
cognitive architecture, 568
culture, 1511
dynamic assessment, 127–130
emotions, 59, 60
evolutionary approach, 571–572
intelligence, 1203
low-income children, 808
middle childhood, 278
moral education, 1685
motivation, 1698
science learning, 2169–2172
service learning, 2209
verbal techniques in assessing, 2034
violence exposure and, 2624–2625
Vygotskian theory, 575
See also Abilities and aptitudes; Child development; Developmental theory; Learning theory
Cognitive disequilibrium, 588
Cognitive dissonance, 1428–1429
Cognitive domain of self-regulation, 1699
Cognitive education programs, 129
Cognitive engagement, 1119
Cognitive incongruity, 764
Cognitive neuroscience, 203–205
Cognitive objectives, 1177
Cognitive processes
higher education, 336–337, 2495
motivation, 1696
problem solving, 1441–1444
Cognitive sciences, 133
Cohen, Donald, 2628
Cohen, Elizabeth, 491
Cohen, Leslie, 1425
Cohen, Michael, 2042
Colbeck, Carol L., 2503
Cold war era
federal R&D spending, 855–856, 863, 1038
international teachers associations, 1320
policy, 669
secondary education and, 2187–2188
textbooks, 2556
Cole, Ardra L., 2491
Cole, Michael, 576, 1464
Coleman, James S., **324–327**
Coleman Report, 673, 728
peer culture, 47–48
public *vs.* private education, 950
school reform, 2152
social capital, 2243
Collaboration. *See* Industry-university research collaboration; Team teaching
Collaborative and cooperative learning, **489–492**
computer-supported collaborative learning, **468–471**
design-based learning, 1165–1166
full-service schools, 907
higher education, 2494
instructional strategies, 1184–1185
Internet, 2511–2512
mathematics learning, 1550
peace education, 1863
problem-based learning, 1174

reading comprehension, 1982–1983
teacher learning communities, **2461–2469**
Vygotsky, Lev, 2659–2660
See also Learning communities
Collaborative to Advance Social and Emotional Learning (CASEL), 1193
Colleagues and teaching evaluation, 800–801
Collective bargaining
faculty roles, 793
policy, 672–673
Shanker, Albert, 2222
See also Unions
Collective faculty, 792–793
Collective knowledge, 1162–1163
College: The Undergraduate Experience in America (report), 200
College athletics, **344–372**
academic support for athletes, **353–356,** 356–357
athletic scholarships, 351–352, **356–358,** 2309
community colleges, 2390
intercollegiate athletics, **344–347,** 1037
intramural athletics, **361–364**
NCAA rules and regulations, **368–371**
students as athletes, **358–361**
students' social and emotional development, 2313
Title IX, 351–352, 673, 837, **2570–2573**
Yale University, 2697
See also Intramural athletics; Sports; Student Athletes
College Board. *See* College Entrance Examination Board
College credit
academic calendar conversion and credit value, 6–7
life experience, **1477–1480**
transfer of, 2683
College Curriculum and Student Protest (Schwab), 2157
College Entrance Examination Board, **372–373**
advanced placement courses/exams, 57
Butler, Nicholas M., 230
Educational Testing Service (ETS), 684
Harvard University, 724
See also ACT tests; Admissions tests; SAT
College faculty. *See* Faculty
College of the Atlantic, 1214
Colleges and Classrooms: State Strategies for Redesigning Teacher Preparation Policies (initiative), 1777
Colleges and universities
academic departments, 20–21, 345, 520, **559–561**
academic organizations, 375
accountability, 414
accreditation, 32–33
admissions, 58, **327–330,** 396–397, 724
affirmative action, **61–65,** 397, 2424
affordability, 378, 1035–1036
annual funds, 1141
application process, 328–329
architecture, 2045
Association of American Colleges (AAC), 16, 102, 152, 515–516, 1741–1742
Association of American Colleges and Universities (AAC&U), **151–153,** 1711–1712
Association of American Universities (AAU), 154
boards of trustees, **191–192,** 385–386
Canada, 235
capital campaigns, 1142
capital outlay, 870, 2340
career and technical education programs, 2648
Carnegie Classification System, **243–245,** *244,* 783, 1041–1042, 2042–2043
censured, 101–102
chartered universities, federally, 867
chief academic affairs officers, **265–267**
coeducational, 2226–2227
College Curriculum and Student Protest (Schwab), 2157
Colonial America, 340, 2225
commuter students, **451–453**
computer technology and college teaching, 416
coordinate colleges, 2226
corporate, **492–494,** 1482
corporate relations departments, 1143
counseling, personal and psychological, **1869–1871,** 1873–1874
credit, 607, **1477–1480,** 2683
decision-making, **945–949**
demographics, 1024–1025, 1709–1710
department chairpersons, **559–561**
development offices, 1141–1143
diploma admission, 2185
disciplines and structure, 10
dropouts, 402
effect on students, **332–340**
elective system, 723–724, 995
English proficiency requirements, 925
enrollment, 235–236, 328, 406, 1037–1039
enrollment management, 406, 749–750, 1145
evaluation, 32
expenditures, 26, 870
facilities, 1145–1146
fact books, 1145
financial aid, **376–378**
free-school movement, 1536–1537
funding, 1023–1024
fundraising, 386
future faculty preparation programs, **909–913**
general education, 995
governance, 102, **945–949**
health services, **1016–1017**
Hispanic-serving institutions, 776, 1044, **1045–1048**
home schooled students, 1062
honor system, 759, 1651, 1653
How to Change Colleges: Notes on Radical Reform (Taylor), 2434
institutional aid, 377–378
institutional cultures, 783
Integrity in the College Curriculum: A Report to the Academic Community (report), 152, 515–516
interdisciplinary, 1213–1214
international admissions rates, 2707
international recognition of credentials, 1247, 1252–1253
international students in the U.S., *1270, 1272, 1273, 1275,* **1310–1314,** 1314–1317
Jewish, 390
labor market, **17–19**

land-grand, **1380–1384,** *1382–1383*
liberal arts colleges, **1475–1477**
living and learning centers, **1518–1520**
low income students' attendance encouragement, 395–396
major gifts, 1141–1142
National Association of College Admission Counseling (NACAC), 383
National Association of Independent Colleges and Universities (NAICU), 152, **1741–1742**
National Association of State Universities and Land-Grant Colleges (NASULGC), 100, 101, **1749–1750**
National Commission on the Role and Future of State Colleges and Universities, 518
nursery schools, 623
Office for the Advancement of Public Black Colleges (OAPBC), 100
offices of institutional research, 1144–1146
organizational structure, **384–389,** 749–750
planned giving, 1142
policy, alcohol and drug abuse, 607–608
presidency, 386, 946, **1915–1917**
program initiatives, alcohol and drug abuse, 607–608
publications offices, 1140
rankings, **378–381,** 397, 1024, 1644
recruitment practices, **382–384,** 396, 397–398
religiously affiliated, **389–393**
reputational diversity, 1044
residence halls, **340–344**
residential colleges, **2043–2047**
retention, **401–407,** 452
revenue, 25–26, 2340–2341
safety and institution liability, 2075–2076
sea-grant program, 2181–2183
seminars, 399
Seven Sisters, 2226, 2227
Shaping the College Curriculum: Academic Plans in Action (Stark and Lattuca), 521
single-sex, 1037, 1044, **2225–2228**
Statement on College and University Government (American Association of University Professors), 102, 794
stewardship offices, college and university, 1143
stopouts, 402
The Strategic Management of College Enrollments (Hossler and Bean), 406
student services, **2387–2389**
study abroad programs, **2394–2396**
substance abuse, 607, 2056
teacher education programs, 2439–2440
teaching, **413–417,** 790–791
teaching assistants, 910–912
Title IX, **2570–2573**
tribal, 868, **2578–2580**
tuition, *880*
women's colleges, 1037, 1044, 2225–2228
See also Administration, educational; Admissions tests; College athletics; College students; Community colleges; Faculty; Financial aid; Higher education; Historically black colleges and universities (HBCUs); Nontraditional students; Public colleges and universities; Research universities; Tribal colleges and universities; Specific colleges and universities

College Scholarship Service, 373, 376

College search and selection, **394–399**

College students, **332–340**
academic demands, 43
academic majors, 21–22
adjustment to college, **42–45**
adviser/student relationship, 4
attitudes and values, 338
commuter, **451–453**
demographics, 1024–1025, 1709–1710
departure, 403–405
disabled, 44, **407–413**
ethics, 758–759
exploitation, 771, 772
extracurricular activities, **373–376**
fair treatment, 758
first-year seminars, **399–401**
freshmen interest groups, 44
governance involvement, 946
honor codes, 759, 1651, 1653
How College Affects Students (Pascarella and Terenzini), 335–340, 2494–2496
learning communities, 1455–1456
minorities, 1969–1971
in organizational structure of colleges and universities, 387–388
orientation programs, 44, 749, **2385–2387,** 2391
peer group influence, 335
personal and psychological problems and counseling, **1869–1871, 1871–1874,** 1970
relationships, 43
retention, **401–407,** 452
roles, 43
safety and institution liability, 2075–2076
search and selection process, **394–399**
service learning, 518, 2205–2209
sexual orientation, 44
socialization, 43
student government, 374–375
subject-matter competence, 336
subpopulations, 44
substance abuse, **606–609,** 1872–1873, 2056
teaching evaluation, 254, 414, 415–416, 788
See also Honor societies; International students; Nontraditional students

Collier, John, Jr., **417–419**

Collier, Virginia, 179

Collins, Allan, 1149, 1465

Collins, Valerie, 794

Colombia
compensatory education, 462–463
private *vs.* public schools, 950
student loans, 2380
See also Latin America and the Caribbean

Colonial America
child criminals, 1350
child protection policies, 281–282
colleges, 340, 2225
compulsory education laws, 465
elementary education, 710

faculty research and scholarship, 782–783
higher education, **1034–1035**
immigrants and education, 1098
literacy education, 740
moral education, 1683–1684
New England Primer, 713
New England town schools, 427
Protestant schools, 1941
school funding, 884–885
school organization, 2331–2332
teacher education, 2439
teachers, 720
vocational education, 2636

Colonialism
Du Bois, W. E. B., 611–612
South Asia, 2272–2273

Columbia Institution for the Instruction of the Deaf, Dumb, and Blind. *See* Gallaudet University

Columbia University, 230

Columbia University, Teachers College. *See* Teachers College of Columbia University

Combined Arms and Services Staff School, U.S. Army, 1654

Comenius, Johann, **419–422,** 677, 1833

Comer, James, 1854

Command General Staff College, U.S. Army, 1654–1655

Commencement, **422–423**

Commentaries and study of teaching, 2490–2491

Commerce of education, **423–426, 1218–1221**
corruption, 1661–1663
international higher education, **1314–1318**
international trade in education goods and services, **1321–1324**
See also Economics of education; Finance

Commercialization, knowledge, 769

Commissioner of Education, U.S., 199–200

Commission on Higher Education, 96

Commission on Human Relations, PEA, 708

Commission on International and Trans-Regional Accreditation (CITA), 30

Commission on Secondary School Curriculum, PEA, 708, 2561

Commission on the Future of Intercollegiate Athletics, 352

Commission on the Orientation of Secondary Education, NEA, 696

Commission on the Relation of School and College, 707–708, 2427–2428

Committee for Public Education v. Nyquist, 2423

Committee for the Study of Research-Doctoral Programs, National Research Council, 379

Committee of Nineteen, International Kindergarten Union, 190

Committee of Ten
Eliot, Charles, 725
middle schools, 1630
Report of the Committee of Ten, 696
secondary education history, 2184–2185
writing instruction, 2693

Committee on East European Studies, ACLS, 106

Committee on Science, Engineering, and Public Policy, 759

Committee on the Reorganization of Secondary Education, NEA, 696

Committees, board, 192

Committees on Trustees, 192

Common Core of Data (National Center for Education Statistics), 2084

Common Principles of the Coalition of Essential Schools, **322–324**

Commons, John R., 1099

Common School Journal, 905

Common schools, **427–431**
elementary education history, 711–712
Mann, Horace, 1535–1536, 2245–2256
Protestant schools and, 1941–1942
school funding, 885
vs. private schools, 1923–1924
See also Public schools

Common underlying proficiency model of bilingualism, 175–176

Commonwealth of Pennsylvania, Pennsylvania Association for Retarded Children v., 672, 1868

Communicable diseases, 1014–1015

Communication
home/school, 822, 1402, 1845
home/school/community, 450
superintendent/school board, 2109–2111

Communication and public speaking. *See* Speech and theater education

Communication disorders. *See* Speech and language impairment

Communications and Public Affairs Division, ETS, 685

Communicative language teaching, 899

Communist Party membership, 15

Communitarian socialism, 172

Communities
Accelerated Schools involvement, 24
arts programs, 1720–1721
community-based language, 1510–1511
community-based organizations, **431–441**
community capacity, 1853–1854
community education, **448–451**
ecological aspects, 433–435
educational control, 675
education and, 1377–1378
education/community integration, 297–298, 580–581
family support services, 829–830
full-service schools, 907
functional, 1926
gang prevention and intervention, 53–54
health education involvement, 1007, 1014
juvenile justice programs, 1356
recreation programs, 2016, 2017
school board relation to, **2104–2107**
school-community family support partnerships, 828–832
school control, 2259
school involvement, 548, **821–828**

school-linked services, 2141–2147
service-learning, 437–438
social capital, 2243
teacher learning communities, **2461–2469**
violence, 2623, **2627–2631**
youth development programs, 2714
See also Neighborhoods
Community-based learning. *See* Service learning
Community-based organizations, **431–441**
Community College Journal, 96
Community College of the Air Force (CCAF), 843
Community colleges, **441–448**
academic calendars, 5, 6
academic labor market, 17
accountability, 883
American Association of Community Colleges (AACC), **95–97,** 101
American Association of Junior and Community Colleges (AACJC), 96–97
American Association of Junior Colleges (AAJC), 96
athletics, 2390
curricula offerings, 97
finance, **875–885,** 2393
financial aid, 2392
honors programs, 1087
lifelong learning, 1481
local unit reorganization, 2343
part-time faculty, 779
post–World War II expansion, 1038–1039
retention rates, 402, 2391
rural education, 2088
student orientation, 2391
student services, **2389–2394**
tribal colleges, 2579
See also Colleges and universities; Higher education
Community development
Bill and Melinda Gates Foundation, 1807
neighborhoods, 1794
organizations, 435
Community education, **448–451**
See also Extension services
Community for Creative Non-Violence (CCNV) v. Reid, 1188
Community of Scholars (Goodman), 942
Community psychology, 433–435
Community Relations Service, Department of Justice, 846
Community schools, 113, 2711–2722
Community service, **2656–2658**
Boyer, Ernest, 200
civics education, 295–296
as extracurricular activity, 375
See also Service learning; Volunteers
Community services
community colleges, 445–446
school-linked services, 2141–2147
Commuter students, **451–453**
Comoros. *See* Sub-Saharan Africa
Comparative assessment
Comparative and International Education Society, 1266
Comparative Education (Kandel), 1364
International Association for Educational Assessment (IAEA), **1225**
International Association for the Evaluation of Educational Achievement (IEA), 1222–1223, **1225–1238**
international education, 169, **1221–1238,** 1626
international statistics comparability, 1286–1287
Kandel, Isaac L., 1363–1364
national achievement tests, 2548
National Research Council, 1730
Rice, Joseph Mayer, 2054–2055
science education, 2161
secondary students, 2192
student loans, 2379–2380
vocational school fallacy, **2654–2656**
See also International issues; Third International Mathematics and Science Study (TIMSS)
Comparative Education (Kandel), 1364
Comparative negligence, 1475
A Comparative Study of Intramural Programs in Negro Colleges (Wasson), 362
CompEd study, **1229–1233**
Compensatory education, **453–464**
Latin America, **458–464**
United States, **453–458**
Competency
competency-based teacher education (CBTE), 2441–2442, 2447
core competencies, 227
global competencies, 511
knowledge management competencies, 1232, *1233*
measuring, 2523
minimum competency testing, 2535
model of language arts instruction, 1393–1394
social, 812
social studies, 2266
subject-matter, 336
substance abuse education, 604–605
testing, 2532
undergraduate education, 510–511, 515–516
Competition in higher education, 1024
Compliance, affirmative action, 62
Composition. *See* Writing and composition
Comprehension
in Bloom's taxonomy, 311
calibration, 588
discourse, 586–588
language, 1385
literacy, 1515
mental models, 1600–1601
monitoring, 1604, 1979
problems, 2008
See also Reading; Reading comprehension
Comprehensive high schools, 2185–2186, 2187–2188
Comprehensive School Reform Demonstration (CSRD) programs, 1798–1800, 2018
Compulsory education
attendance, **464–468**
Amish children, 2336
Canada, 235
Europe, 716
home schooling, 1061
Japan, 716
Middle East and North Africa, 1629
South Asia, 2276
state departments of education, 2324
western Europe, 2680–2681
See also Truancy and attendance problems

Compulsory Mis-Education (Goodman), 942

Computers in Education Study, **1229–1233**

Computer technology
- algebra, 1544
- art education, 120
- assessment tools, **145–148**
- business education, 215–216
- capital outlay, 888–889
- career services field, 242–243
- certification, 219
- children's access, 1580
- classroom use, 305, 1578, 2518
- collaborative learning, computer-supported, **468–471**
- college teaching, 416
- computer-aided instruction (CAI), 1131–1132, 2582–2583
- computer literacy, 714, 743, 2518
- Computers in Education Study, **1229–1233**
- consortia, 477
- constructivism, 1465
- demographics, 2706–2707
- digital divide, **1296–1299,** 2519–2520
- distance learning, 593
- elementary education, 714, 718–719
- engineering, 740
- foreign language education, 894–895
- gender equity, 1127
- geometry education, 1549
- global economics and, 424–425
- graphics, 286
- independent study, 1111
- instructional use, 2512
- international aspects, 1297–1298
- journalism education, 1348–1349
- learning and, 1577–1578, 2515–2516
- low income families, 1122
- mathematics learning tools, 1550–1551
- migrant students, 1641
- military training, 1657–1658
- music education, 1725
- reading instruction, 2002
- rural schools, 2086
- school libraries, 2139
- science education tools, 2177–2181
- smart buildings, 2127, 2129–2131
- social studies education, 2268, 2271
- student athletes, 354
- teachers and, 2436
- teaching centers and, 255
- textbooks and, 2555–2556
- urban schools, 2610
- violence and children, 1581
- writing instruction, 2695
- as a writing tool, 1507–1509
- *See also* Educational technology; Information and communications technology; Software

Conant, J. B., **471–474**
- appointment of Keppel as Dean of Harvard's Graduate School of Education, 1365
- Harvard University, 995
- Progressive education, 1937
- secondary education, 2187–2188

Conative processes. *See* Affective and conative processes

Concept learning and categorization, **247–250**
- concept mapping, 145–146, *146,* 2491
- conceptual change, 248–249, **1427–1431**
- differentiation, 1428
- knowledge, 247, 764
- memory tests, 1598–1599
- Piaget, Jean, 1896
- teaching, 1183

Concrete operations, 1897

Condition of Education (Department of Education, U.S.), 843

The Conditions of Children in California (Kirst), 2141

A Confederacy of Dunces (Toole), 2602

Conference Board of Associated Research Councils, 379

Conference of Allied Ministers of Education, 1279

Conference on Faculty Roles and Rewards, 90

Conferences and conventions
- 1990 World Conference on Education for All, 626, 687
- AACSB, 1
- Alpha Mu Gamma, 1067
- American Alliance for Health, Physical Education, Recreation, and Dance, 89
- American Association for Higher Education, 90, 91
- American Association of State Colleges and Universities, 100–101
- American Federation of Teachers, 111
- Association for Women in Communications, 1069
- Future Business Leaders of America-Phi Beta Lambda, 2729
- Global Forum on Management education, 1
- International Reading Association, 1308
- Journalism Education Association, 1347
- Kappa Delta Pi, 1075
- Modern Language Association of America, 1673
- National Art Education Association, 1734
- National Association of Biology Teachers, 1738
- National Association of Elementary School Principals, 1739
- National Association of Schools of Art and Design, 1744
- National Association of Secondary School Principals, 1747
- National Communication Association, 1759
- National Conference on Education, 99
- National Conference on Higher Education, 90
- National Honor Society, 1780
- National PTA, 1784
- National School Public Relations Association, 1787
- progressive education, 1278–1279

Conferences on Students in Transition, 239

Conferences on the Senior Year Experience, 239

Conference Statement on Academic Freedom and Tenure (American Association of University Professors), 101, 102

The Confessions (Augustine, St.), 160

Confidentiality and health services, 1017

Configurations, parenting, 1848–1849
Conflict
  classroom, 974
  peace education, 1862
  superintendent/school board, 2109–2111
Conflicting Psychologies of Learning (Bode), 195
Conflict of interest, 757, 771, 791
Conger, Rand, 1907
Congressional Office of the Budget, 210
Connecticut, 2451
Conrad, Clifton, 521
Conscientiousness in employment, 734
Consensus. *See* Paradigm development and academic disciplines
Conservation and intellectual development, 1896–1987
Conservation education, 1833
Consolidation, school, 2259
Consortia, higher education, **475–478**
Consortium of National Arts Education Associations, 121
Constituent diversity in higher education, 1043–1044
Constitution, NCAA, 368–369
Constitution, U.S., **3046–3060**
  affirmative action related amendments, 63–64
  child protection laws and, 282
  education and constitutional rights, **478–483**
  state sand education, 2331, 2350
  states' responsibility for education, 710, 712
  See also Civil rights; Court cases; Equal protection clause; Supreme Court, U.S.
Constitution Act (Canada), 234
Constitution of the United Nations Educational, Scientific and Cultural Organization, **3091–3099**
Constructed-response tasks, 135
Constructing Physics Understanding, 2179
Construction, new school, 2124–2126
The Construction Zone: Working for Cognitive Change in School (Cole et al.), 576
Constructive activities, 811
Constructivism, **1463–1467**
  anchored instruction, 1152
  art education, 118
  classroom, 584, 585, 1465–1466
  deep *vs.* shallow, 1371
  developmental theory, 563
  mathematics, 1553
  teacher education, 2470
  technology, 2516
  theory, 679–680
Construct maps, 141, *142*
Consultation services, teacher improvement, 255–256
Consultative Committee on the Primary School (England), 1825
Consulting, faculty, **772–775,** *774*
Consumerism and higher education, 1024
Consumer price index, 659, *660*
Consumer sciences education. *See* Family and consumer sciences education
Contact hypothesis, 1862–1863
Content
  arts, 1720
  curriculum, 521–522, 524–525
  customizing, 1129–1130
  knowledge, 414, 1179
  multiculturalism, 1705
  National Assessment of Educational Progress (NAEP), 131
  packaging, 6
  reading in content areas, **1985–1989**
  science education, 2170
  standards, 2001, 2315
  teachers' knowledge, 2483–2484, 2485–2486
"The Contents of Children's Minds" (Hall), 985
Context
  contextual planning, 2368
  contextual teaching and learning, 2649, 2652
  cultural-context theory of development, 563
  dependency of memory, 1449
  inference and motor learning, 1702
  reading instruction, 2001
  vocabulary learning, 1504–1505
Continental soldiers, 1656
Contingent faculty. *See* Part-time faculty
Continuing education
  community colleges, 445–446
  school board members, 2120–2121
  Smithsonian Institution programs, 2240–2241
Continuing professional education (CPE), **483–489**
  elementary school teachers, 721–722
  International corporations, **486–489**
  United States, **483–486**
  See also Professional development
Contraceptives, 2061–2062, 2071–2072
Contracting out reform, 953
Contracts
  educational services, 2341
  facility building, 2125–2126
  faculty consulting, 772
  government, 209–210
  industry-university research collaboration, 2595
  research, 770
Contract schools, 84
Contributory negligence, 1474–1475
Control and coupling, 2257–2258
Controversies
  ability grouping, 681
  African-American Language, 1391–1392
  autistic students, 162
  bilingual education, 178–179, 718
  college rankings, 379–381
  culture and literacy, 1510–1511
  disabled students, education of, 1886
  early childhood education teacher preparation, 624–625
  educational psychology, 680–682
  educational testing, 681
  elementary education, 717, 718–719
  emotionally disturbed, education of, 727
  family and consumer sciences education, 804–805
  full-service schools, 908
  gifted and talented education, 933–935

Goddard's intelligence studies, 941
guidance and counseling, school, 977–978
hearing impaired students, teaching methods for, 1020
independent study, 1111
individual abilities and aptitudes, 1115–1116
instructional design, 1148–1150
intelligence, 680–681
intelligence testing, 1197, 1204
learning disabled students, placement of, 1458
mathematics education teacher preparation, 1541
mentally retarded students, education of, 1617
moral development research, 1682–1683
moral education, 1687
multiculturalism in higher education, 1709–1711
new teacher mentoring, 1619–1620
open education, 1826–1827
parental involvement in education, 1846
physical education, 1889
physical education teacher education, 1892–1893
private schools, 1926–1928
privatization, 1927
professional development schools, 1932
reading instruction, 681, 1516–1517, 2001–2002
school-based decision making, 2101–2102
school choice, 1927–1928
school climate, 2123
science education, 2161–2162
science education teacher preparation, 2165
severe and multiple disabilities, education of students with, 2212–2213
sexual orientation, 2220–2221
social studies education, 2267–2268
social studies textbooks, 2556
special education, 2282–2283
standardized tests, 719
summer school, 2411
supervision of instruction, 2420–2421
teacher evaluation, 2455–2456
tenure, 16
textbooks, 2555–2556
vouchers, 1927–1928
Convention against Discrimination in Education, 1282, **3123–3128**
Conventional moral development level, 1681
Convention on Technical and Vocational Education, 1283
Convention on the Elimination of All Forms of Discrimination Against Women, 1280–1281
Convention on the Rights of the Child, 1281, **3133–3148**
Conversion, calendar, 5–6
Cook, Glen, 75
Cook Islands. *See* East Asia and the Pacific
Cooney, Joan Ganz, 1580
Coons, John, 1927
Cooper, Bruce, 663
Cooperative Agricultural Extension Service, 2088
Cooperative and collaborative learning, **489–492**
computer-supported collaborative learning, **468–471**
design-based learning, 1165–1166
full-service schools, 907
higher education, 2494
instructional strategies, 1184–1185
Internet, 2511–2512
mathematics learning, 1550
peace education, 1863
problem-based learning, 1174
reading comprehension, 1982–1983
teacher learning communities, **2461–2469**
Vygotsky, Lev, 2659–2660
See also Learning communities
Cooperative Assessment of Experiential Learning (CAEL). *See* Council for Adult and Experiential Learning (CAEL)
Cooperative education, 242, 2641
Cooperative Extension, 806
Cooperative for Assistance and Relief Everywhere (CARE), 1803–1804
Cooperative Institutional Research Program (CIRP), 334–335
Cooperative Research Program in First Grade Reading Instruction, 2000
Coordinate colleges, 2226
Coordinated-services, 2141–2147
Copple, Carol, 2141
COPS (Office of Community Oriented Policing Services), 846
Copyright, 1186–1190
Corbett, Robert, 1165
Corcellis v. Corcellis No. 1 (England), 280–281
Core competencies, 227, 2266
Core curriculum
Alberty, H. B., 81
Core Knowledge Sequence, **535–537**
diversity requirements, 1711–1713
language minority students, 1402
See also General education
Coretta Scott King Awards, 289
Coretta Scott King Fund, 104
Cornell University
college athletics, 348
college rankings, 380
university presses, 2600
Corporate colleges and universities, **492–494,** 1482
Corporate gangs, 52
Corporate relations departments, college and university, 1143
Corporate schools, American overseas, 113
Corporate sponsorship of intercollegiate athletics, 346
Corporation for National Service, 2207
Corporation for Public Broadcasting (CPB), 657
Correlated curriculum, 741, 1575
Correspondence study, 590
See also Distance education
Corruption
accreditation, 34
college athletics, 349, 351
education, **1659–1668**
See also Misconduct
CORSAC (Council of Regional School Accrediting Commissions), 29
Corsaro, William, 46
Cosmo, 1169
Costa Rica. *See* Latin America and the Caribbean
Cost/benefit analysis, **495–497, 647–651**
college athletics, 345–347

developing countries' investment in education, 546–549
early childhood education programs, 274–276, 619, 620
efficiency, 701
media selection, 1576–1577
methodological limitations, 648–649
private rates of return, 647, 648
resource allocation, 702
selected countries, *649, 650*
social rate of return, 647–648, 649–650
See also Costs; Economics of education; Finance

Costs
capital, 887
child care, **274–276**
dynamic assessment, 130
geographic differences and school funding, 891
health care, 1532–1533
higher education, 1303, 2523
performance assessment, 134–135
school facilities, 2127, 2128–2129
smoking, 2068
technology, 2523
Upward Bound (UB) programs, 2604
See also Cost/benefit analysis; Economics of education; Finance

Côte d'Ivoire. *See* Sub-Saharan Africa

Coulmas, Florian, 1488

Coulson, Andrew, 949

Council for Adult and Experiential Learning (CAEL), 1478, 1479

Council for Basic Education (CBE), **498–499**

Council for Better Education, Kentucky v., 672

Council for Christian Colleges and Universities, 392

Council for Exceptional Children (CEC), **499–500**

Council for Higher Education Accreditation (CHEA), 32

Council for the Advancement and Support of Education (CASE), 1140

Council for the International Exchange of Scholars (CIES), 1137

Council of Arts Accrediting Associations, 121

Council of Chief State School Officers (CCSSO), **501–503**
art education, 121, 122
civics education, 296
school principals, 1921
state departments of education, 2324

Council of Europe (COE)
accreditation, 27
higher education, 1253–1254
lifelong learning, 1481

Council of Europe Framework Convention for the Protection of National Minorities, **3182–3188**

Council of Regional School Accrediting Commissions (CORSAC), 29

Council of School Attorneys, 1785

Council of Urban Boards of Education, 1785

Council on Medical Education and Hospitals, AMA, 32–33

Counseling
athletic counselors, 354–355, 357
career, **241–243**
colleges and universities, **1869–1871,** 1873–1874, 1970
community colleges, 2391
Rogers, Carl, 2077–2079
school, 976, 977, 978, 1014
See also Guidance and counseling

Counseling and Psychotherapy (Rogers), 976

The Counselor in a Changing World (Wrenn), 976

Country Life Commission, 74

Counts, George S., 195, 206, **503–505**

County School Board, Green v., 2424

County School Board, Griffin v., 2424

Coupling and school control, 2257–2258

Course credit. *See* Carnegie units

Courses
academic majors, 21
academic rigor of, 2193
advanced placement, **56–58,** *57,* 373, 898
art, secondary school, 119–120
capstone courses, **239–241**
career education courses, 805–806
distance education, 590
diversity requirements, 1711–1713
family and consumer sciences, 805–806
general education, 924–925, 1458, 1711–1714
information technology, 224
microteaching, 1622
public schools, 84
remedial/developmental, 44
required, 517, 2203–2204, 2298–2299
service learning, 2203–2204
telecourses, 592
See also Interdisciplinarity; Specific disciplines

Court cases, **2422–2425**
Adams v. Richardson, 776
Adarand Constructors, Inc. v. Pena, 2424
affirmative action, 62–65
Agostini v. Felton, 2423
Alexander v. Holmes County Board of Education, 2201
Aymes v. Bonnelli, 1188
Bakke v. Regents of the University of California, 62–63, 64, 2424
Barenblatt v. United States, 102
Beach v. the University of Utah, 2075
Bethel School District No. 403 v. Frazer, 2425
Board of Curators of the University of Missouri v. Horowitz, 2425
Board of Education Island Trees Union Free School District No. 26 v. Pico, 2425
Board of Education of Kiryas Joel v. Grumet, 2423
Board of Education of Oklahoma City Public Schools v. Dowell, 2202, 2424
Board of Education of the Hendrick Hudson Central School District v. Rowley, 2281
Board of Education of Westside Community Schools v. Mergens, 2423

Board of Education v. Allen, 2423
Bradstreet v. Sobol, 1062
Brown v. Board of Education of Topeka, Kansas, 61, 112, 326, 430, 478–479, 671, 1049, 1868, 2113, 2151, 2186, 2200–2201, 2423
Committee for Public Education v. Nyquist, 2423
Community for Creative Non-Violence (CCNV) v. Reid, 1188
Corcellis v. Corcellis No. 1 (England), 280–281
Cumming v. Richmond Board of Education, 2186, 2200
Delgado v. Gracy, 2094
DeRonde v. Regents of the University, 64
Dred Scott v. Sanford, 2199
Edwards v. Aguillard, 2423
Engel v. Vitale, 2422
Epperson v. Arkansas, 2422
Everson v. Board of Education, 2423
Ex parte Crouse, 1350
Farrington v. Tokushige, 1925, 2336
Freeman v. Pits, 2202
Furek v. University of Delaware, 2075
Giardino v. State Board of Education, 887–888
Gong Lum v. Rice, 1100
Goss v. Lopez, 2425
Gratz v. Bollinger, 63, 65, 397
Green v. School Board of New Kent County, 480, 2201, 2424
Griffin v. County School Board, 2424
Grutter v. Bollinger, 63, 65, 397
Hazelwood School District v. Kuhlmeier, 2425
Hernandez v. Texas, 2094
higher education, 1025–1026
Hopwood v. State of Texas, 63, 64, 397
Ingraham v. Wright, 2425
Jenkins v. Missouri, 480
Kalamazoo case, 2184
Kent v. United States, 1350–1351
Keyes v. School District No. 1, 2201, 2424
King v. Board of Education, 1391
Kirwan v. Podberesky, 63, 64
Knox v. O'Brien, 1062
Lassiter v. Department of Social Services, 282
Lau v. Nichols, 177–178, 672, 1101, 1102
Lee v. Weisman, 2423
Lemon v. Kurtzman, 2337, 2423
McKiever v. Pennsylvania, 1351
McLaurin v. Oklahoma State Regents, 64
Meyer v. State of Nebraska, 282, 464, 1061, 1100, 1924–1925, 2335–2336, 2422
Milliken v. Bradley, 2424
Mills v. Board of Education of the District of Columbia, 672, 1868
Missouri ex rel Gaines v. Canada, 2423
Missouri v. Jenkins, 2202, 2424
Mueller v. Allen, 2423
Mullins v. Pine Manor College, 2075
Murphy v. State of Arkansas, 1061
Nero v. Kansas State University, 2075
New Jersey v. T.L.O., 2425
Norwood v. Harrison, 2424
Pennsylvania Association for Retarded Children v. Commonwealth of Pennsylvania, 672, 1868
Peter W. v. San Francisco Unified School District, 1475
Pierce v. Society of Sisters, 466, 1061, 1925, 1942, 2336, 2422
Plessy v. Ferguson, 63, 1049, 2186, 2200, 2423
Prince v. Massachusetts, 465
In re Gault, 1351
In re Winship, 1351
Roberts v. City of Boston, 2200
Roosevelt v. Bishop, 888
Rosenberger v. University of Virginia, 2423
Rose v. Council for Better Education, 672
Runyon v. McCrary, 2424
San Antonio Independent School District v. Rodriquez, 481, 2113
Santa Fe Independent School District v. Doe, 2423
Santosky v. Kramer, 282
School District v. Schempp, 2422
Sega Enterprises Ltd. v. Accolade, 1190
Serrano v. Priest, 481, 889
Shaftsbury v. Hannam (England), 280–281
Stanley v. Darlington School District, 479–480
State of Wyoming v. Campbell County School District, 888
State v. Bailey, 465
State v. Edgington, 1062
State v. Scopes, 2556
State v. Whisner, 2336–2337
Stell v. Savannah-Chatham County Board of Education, 480
Swann v. Charlotte-Mecklenburg Board of Education, 480, 2424
Swanson v. Guthrie Independent School District, 1062
Sweatt v. Painter, 64
Tarasoff v. Board of Regents of the University of California, 2075
Timothy W. v. Rochester, New Hampshire, School District, 2212
United States v. Fordice, 2202
United States v. Lopez, 478
United States v. Virginia, 2202
Wallace v. Jaffree, 2423
Walz v. Tax Commission, 2423
West Virginia Board of Education v. Barnette, 2425
Widmar v. Vincent, 2423
Wisconsin v. Yoder, 466, 1061, 2336
Witters v. Washington Department of Services for the Blind, 2423
Wygant v. Jackson Board of Education, 63, 64
Zobrest v. Catalina Foothills School District, 2423
See also Civil rights; Constitution, U.S.; Specific court cases; Supreme Court, U.S.

Court of Chancery (England), 281
Cousin, Victor, 695
Covenant of Civil and Political Rights, 1280
CPB (Corporation for Public Broadcasting), 657
CPC (Chicago Child-Parent Center), 619
CPE (continuing professional education). *See* Continuing professional education (CPE)
Craik, Fergus I., 1606
Cram schools, 2585–2586

Crawford, Clarence, 346
Creating Citizens (Callan), 754
Creative activities, 811
Creative and Mental Growth (Lowenfield), 1522–1523
Creativity, **505–507,** 1207
Credentialism, 237
Credentials
  college admissions, 329–330
  guidance and counseling, 977
  international recognition of college and university, 1247, 1252–1253
  school psychologists, 1946, 1947
  See also Certification and licensure
Credit, college
  academic calendar conversion and credit value, 6–7
  life experience, **1477–1480**
  transfer of, 2683
Cremin, Lawrence, 553–554
Crewdson, John, 2039
Crime, campus, 2075–2076
  See also Gangs; Juvenile justice system; Violence
Crisis (periodical), 610–611
Criterion Zones, 141
Critical developmental periods, 562, 564–566
Critical impulse and the philosophy of education, 1882–1884
Critical literacy, 2002
Critical pedagogy, 1124
Critical theory, 1124
Criticisms and concerns
  achievement-based outcomes, 1949–1950
  animated learning aids, 1494–1495
  brain-based education, 204
  charter schools, 1950
  child protective services, 284
  civics education, 296
  classroom observation, 307–309
  class size, 316
  college search and selection, 397–398
  driver education, 598
  education, 942–943
  education reform, 691, 1951
  federal research and development funding, 859–860
  Freire's educational theory, 903
  guidance and counseling, school, 977–978
  history education, 1057–1058
  inequality of opportunity, 1948–1949
  interdisciplinary courses and majors, 1211
  learning from multimedia sources, 1494–1495
  National Assessment of Educational Progress (NAEP), 133–134
  national reports on the undergraduate curriculum, 518
  open education, 1826–1827
  open enrollment, 1951
  performance assessment, 135–136
  privatization, school, 547
  Progressive education, 172–173, 994, 1364
  project method, 1939
  public school budgeting, 1954
  public schools, 172–173, 1059, **1948–1952**
  school bureaucracy, 1949
  school choice, 1950–1951
  school reform, 168–169
  tax credits, 1951
  teacher education, 2447
  undergraduate curriculum, 510
  vouchers, 1950–1951
  youth development programs, 2714–2715
Croatia. *See* Eastern Europe and Central Asia
Crockett, Lisa, 2062
Croft, Don, 2122
Cronbach, Lee, 1114
Crooks, Terry, 124
Crookston, Burns B., 2
Cross, K. Patricia, 255, 2497
CROSS (Coordination Dutch-Russian Cooperation in Education) program, 1267
Cross-cultural education, 418–419, 2395
Cross-cultural research, 1121–1122
Crowds, adolescent. *See* Peer culture, adolescent
Crowson, Robert, 2141
Cruickshank, William, 158
Crystallized intelligence, 1202, 1205
CSC Writing programs, 469
CSI (Christian Schools International), 1943
Csikszentmihalyi, Mihaly
  affective processes, 1119
  peer culture, 46
  student employment, 730, 736
  students' sports participation, 2313–2314
CSILE/Knowledge Forum, 1372
CSRD (Comprehensive School Reform Demonstration) programs, 1798–1800, 2018
CSTM (Children's Seriational Thinking Modifiability) test, 129
CTT (classical test theory), 140
Cuba. *See* Latin America and the Caribbean
Cuban, Larry
  Carnegie units, 246
  education reform, 691
  family support services, 829
Cuban immigrants, 1102
Cubberley, Ellwood, **507–509**
  educational psychology, 677
  immigrant education, 1099
  school funding, 886
  urban education, 2412–2413
The Cult of Uncertainty (Kandel), 1364
Cultural Foundations of Education: An Interdisciplinary Exploration (Brameld), 207
Culture
  bicultural education, 1102
  Brameld, Theodore, 207
  cross-cultural education, 418–419, 2395
  cross-cultural research, 1121–1122
  cultural adaptation of international students, 1313
  cultural capital, 1301–1302
  cultural-context theory of development, 563
  cultural deprivation, 129, 1123, 1962
  cultural difference, 1123–1124, 1962
  cultural ecological theory, 1859
  cultural expectations and learning, **1961–1966**
  cultural-historical theory, 574–575, 2658–2660
  cultural literacy, 717
  culturally responsive pedagogy, 1511–1512

Cultural Modeling (CM), 1512
cultural-process educational research, 1121–1122
culture circle, 901
development and, 564
Hispanic Americans, **1967–1968**
learning and, 2499
literacy and, **1509–1513**
narratives, 1502–1503
number sense and, **1563–1566**
parenting and, 1850–1851
pedagogy, culturally responsive, 1124, 1511–1512
race/ethnicity and, **1961–1971**
school, 537–538, 1706
sociocultural theory, 574–575, 2658–2660
See also Minorities; Multiculturalism; Pluralism; Race/ethnicity
Culture Wars, 522
Cumbo, Kathryn, 762
Cumming v. Richmond Board of Education, 2186, 2200
Cummins, Jim, 175–176
Cunningham, Anne, 2005
Cunningham, James W., 1978
Cunningham, Joan, 2067
Cureton, Jeanette, 1711
Curie, Marie, 104
Current Index to Journals in Education (Educational Resources Information Center), 683
Current trends
academic achievement, 2192
accountability, 2190–2191
adapted physical education, 38–40
assessment, 2190, 2545–2546
business education, 219
business teacher education, 224–225
career counseling, 242
character development, 261
community organizing for youth, 437–438
comparative assessment, 2192
continuing professional education (CPE), 486
decentralization, 1269
demographics, 1707–1708, **2703–2708**
disabled students, education of, 1886
doctoral degrees, 596
driver education, 597–598
early childhood education, 628
early childhood education teacher preparation, 624–625
educational technology, **2509–2513**
education development programs, 688
education of autistic students, 162
elementary education, **715–720,** 718–719
English education, 742–743
facilities, 2192
family and consumer sciences education, 804–805
gay and lesbian studies, 917–918
gifted and talented education, 933–935
governance, 947–948
graduation rates, 2191–2192
guidance and counseling, school, 977–978
health services, school, 1015
hearing impairment programs, 1019
higher education, 1030–1033
home schooling legal trends, 1062
independent study, 1111
individual abilities and aptitudes, 1116
instructional design, 1148
language, 1399–1400
leadership shortages, 2192
mathematics education teacher preparation, 1541
mentally retarded students, education of, 1617
migrant students, education of, 1641–1642
moral education, 1685–1687
museums, 1718
national standards, 2531–2532
outdoor and environmental education, 1834
parental involvement in education research, 1846
part-time faculty, 781
philosophy of education, **1880–1885**
physical education, 1889
physical education teacher education, 1892–1893
private schools, 1926–1928
privatization, 1927
professional development schools, 1931–1932
program evaluation, 2033
reading instruction, 2001–2002
recreation programs, 2016–
school choice, 1927–1928
school climate, 2123
school facilities, 2126–2127
science education, 2161–2162
science education teacher preparation, 2165
secondary education, 2189, **2190–2195**
severe and multiple disabilities, education of students with, 2212–2213
social studies education teacher preparation, 2271
special education, 2281–2282, **2284–2290**
standards, 2190
student services, 2388–2389
summer school, 2410–2411
supervision of instruction, 2420–2421
teacher education, 2439–2440
teacher evaluation, 2455–2456
teacher supply and demand, 2192
technology education, 2508
tutoring, **2585–2587**
undergraduate curriculum, 510–511
vocational and technical education, 2639–2640, **2642–2647**
vocational education teacher preparation, 2649–2650
vouchers, 1927–1928
Western Europe, education reform in, 2682–2683
writing instruction, 2694–2695
Curriculum
50 Hours: A Core Curriculum for College Students (report), 515
academic subject matter *vs.* needs of students, 164
academic/vocational curriculum, 2640–2641
activity analysis, 264
Alberty, H. B., 80–81
alternative public schools, 83
art education, 118–119
assessment, 719
Basic Principles of Curriculum and Instruction (Tyler), 520–521, 2589
Bobbitt, Franklin, 193–194
business education, 217–218
calendar use and conversion, effect of, 6–7

character education, 1686
Charters, W. W., 263–264
The Child and the Curriculum (Dewey), 578
children's literature, 288
classroom, 532
College Curriculum and Student Protest (Schwab), 2157
Commission on Secondary School Curriculum, PEA, 708, 2561
Committee of Ten, 696, 725, 2184–2185, 2693
community colleges, 97
constructivist, 1464–1465
content, 521–522, 524–525
core, 81, 1402, 1711–1713
core knowledge, **535–537**
correlated, 741, 1575
curricular knowledge, 414
Curriculum and Evaluation Standards for School Mathematics (National Council of Teachers of Mathematics), 1547, 1548, 1559, 2174, 2320
The Curriculum (Bobbitt), 193
Curriculum Development: Theory and Practice (Taba), 521
Denver Plan, 1800–1801
design-based, 1164
Developing a Curriculum for Modern Living (Stratemeyer), 2370
differentiation, 1936, 2185–2186, 2187–2188
educational change, 658
elementary school, 535–537, 713–714, 717–718
engineering, 738–739
English education, 741, 746, 747
evaluation, 719
gender and, 919–920
globalization, 525–528
Hanna, Paul R., 990–992
Harvard University, 995
health education, 1005
hidden curriculum, **537–539**
higher education, **509–524**
history, 1055–1057
Hopkins, L. Thomas, 1088–1089
How to Make a Curriculum (Bobbitt), 193
identification of objectives, 193
institutional nature, 534–535
integration, 511–512
Integrity in the College Curriculum: A Report to the Academic Community (report), 152, 515–516
intended, 524
interdisciplinary, 1210–1214
international, **524–529**
journalism, 1347–1348
kindergarten, 905
language arts, 1394
law school, 1418
learning communities, **1452–1457,** *1454*
Learning for Life Curriculum, 1688
liberal education, 522–523
Macdonald, James, 1525–1526
mathematics, 1547, 2237
Miel, Alice, 1636–1637
Mississippi Freedom Schools, 1668
multiculturalism, 1704–1708, 1710–1714
multiple intelligences, 1199–1200
national reports on undergraduate, **514–519**
The Overcrowded Curriculum (International Center for Leadership in Education), 2644–2645
overview, **529–535**
Paideia Program, **1841–1842**
physical education, 1888–1889
The Practical (Schwab), 2157–2158
as preparation for adulthood, 193
problem-centered and discipline centered, 166
programmatic, 531
Progressive education, 707–708
reading instruction within the, 2000–2001
reform, 532, 2153
Reorganizing the High School Curriculum (Alberty), 81
Rugg, Harold, 2082
The Saber Tooth Curriculum (Benjamin), 168–169
school, **529–539**
school-based decision-making, 2100–2101
Schwab, Joseph, 2157–2158
science, 2159–2162
science education reform, 2745–2746
scientific curriculum-making, 2242
scope and sequence, 717
secondary education, 80–81, 172–173, 532–535, 707–708, 2184–2186, 2195–2198
self-paced learning, 2662–2663
Shaping the College Curriculum: Academic Plans in Action (Stark and Lattuca), 521
social studies, 2265–2268
societal influences, 1026
speech education, 2299
Sputnik and reform of, 118, 166, 173, 1826, 2030, 2196
standardization, 2184–2185
state administrative services, 2345–2346
study abroad programs, 2396
study of, 80–81
subject centered, 993–994
Taba, Hilda, 2427–2428
teacher education, 2370–2371, 2446–2447
technology education, 2507–2508
Thayer, V. T., 2561
Tyler, Ralph W., 2588–2589
undergraduate innovations, **509–514**
undergraduate learning communities, **1452–1457,** *1454*
urban schools, 2608–2609, 2610
U.S. Merchant Marine Academy, 1647–1648
U.S. Military Academy, 1649–1650
vocational and technical education, 193–194
vocationalism, 2640–2641
western Europe, 2681
World Council on Curriculum and Instruction (WCCI), 1637
See also Eight-Year Study; General education; Instructional design
Curriculum and Evaluation Standards for School Mathematics (National Council of Teachers of Mathematics), 1547, 1548, 1559, 2174, 2320
The Curriculum (Bobbitt), 193
Curriculum Development: Theory and Practice (Taba), 521
Cursive *vs.* manuscript handwriting, 988–989
Curti, Merle, **539–540**
Cuseo, Joseph, 239

Custody of Infants Act (England), 281
Cybernetics, 1182
Czech Republic. *See* Eastern Europe and Central Asia

D

Dade, Chris, 1495
Dade County school system (Florida), 1102
Daedalus (periodical), 86, 87
Dahl, Robert, 663
Dale, Edgar, 257–258, 1497
Dale-Chall Formula for Predicting Readability (Dale and Chall), 258
Dalton School, **541–542**
Dance, 89, 90
Danish Folk Schools, 1090
Dansereau, Donald, 490
Danzberger, Jacqueline, 2105
DARE (Drug Abuse Resistance Education) program, 604, 718
Darling, Nancy, 1848, 1849
Darling-Hammond, Linda, 2471
Darlington School District, Stanley v., 479–480
Darsee, John, 2039
D'Arusmont, William, 1876
Das, Jagannath P., 570
DASH (Division of Adolescent and School Health), 1004, 1008
Database, ERIC, 683
Data collection and analysis
program evaluation, 2032
science education technology tools, 2179, 2180
technology, 2511
university research, 757, 2021, 2027–2029, 2034–2036
DAT (Dental Admissions Test), 557–558
DATSCH (Germany), 487
Dauber, Susan L., 1845
Davey, Kate Mackenzie, 734
Davis, Gayle, 1633
Davis, James R., 1210
Davis, Meredith, 1164
Dawkins, Karen, 1751
Day, Jeannie D., 1982
Day Law (Kentucky), 171
Day schools, Jewish, 1340–1341, 1342
Daytona Normal and Industrial Institute for Negro Girls, 174
DBAE (Discipline-based art education), 118, 119
DDESS (Domestic Dependent Elementary and Secondary Schools), 838, 843, 866
Deaf education, 469, 867, **1017–1021**
Gallaudet University, 469, 867
school programs, **1017–1019**
teaching methods, **1019–1021**
See also Disabled students
Deans, academic, **8–9**
Dean's Conference, AACSB, 1
Deans of men and deans of women, 2387–2388
Deary, Ian J., 1114, 1195
Deaths, school sports, 2308
Debate, 1448, 2300–2301
DeBello, Louis, 142
DeBlock, Alfred, 2433
DECA (Distributive Education Clubs of America), **2726–2727**
Decentralization, **542–546**
Canadian education, 237
Catholic schools, 253
Decentralizing Power (Stoehr), 942
East Asia and the Pacific, 637
gap between rich and poor, 1302
gender issues, 920
intergovernmental relations, 1215–1216
public school organization, 2259
school-based decision-making, 2099–2100
South Asia, 2276
trend towards, 1269
western Europe, 2681–2682
See also Administration, educational; Governance
Decentralizing Power (Stoehr), 942
DeChiara, Edith, 1707
Decision-making
academic deans, 8
college and university, **945–949**
cost-effectiveness analysis, 495–497
decentralization, 543–544
economic analysis, **546–550**
parent involvement with schools, 823–824
school-based, **550–553, 2099–2102**
school boards, 2116
state discretion, 675
"Declaration of Principles." *See General Declaration of Principles and Practical Proposals* (American Association of University Professors)
Declaration of the Rights on the Child, **3121–3123**
Declaration on Race and Racial Prejudice, **3128–3133**
Declaration on the Rights of Persons Belonging to National or Ethnic, Religious and Linguistic Minorities, **3167–3170**
Declarative component of metamemory, 1603
Declarative knowledge, 1432
Declarative memory, 1436–1437
Decoding and reading, 1975
Deconcentration, 542
Deductive reasoning, 678
DEELSA (Directorate of Education, Employment, Labor, and Social Affairs), 1250
Deep comprehension, 586–588
Deep constructivism, 1371
De facto segregation, 2201
Defense Department. *See* Department of Defense, U.S.; Military; Specific branches
Defenses, negligence, 1474–1475
Definitions *vs.* examples in teaching new concepts, 248
DeGarmo, Charles, 1022
De Glopper, Kees, 1504
Degree programs, **1537–1539**
business, 220–221
Child Development Associate (CDA) degree, 623–624
divinity, 594–595
doctoral, **595–596,** 966–967
education, 967–970
joint, 221
law, 1418
nursing science, 1818–1819
teacher education, 721, 968–970
See also Associate degree programs; Bachelor's degree programs; Doctoral degree programs; Graduate education; Master's degree programs; Undergraduate education
De Groot, Adrian, 765
Dehaene, Stanislas, 1559, 1660

Delamont, Sara, 307
De Lauretis, Teresa, 918
Delcourt, Marcia, 933
Delgado v. Gracy, 2094
De Lima, Agnes, **553–554**
Delinquency, 2710
See also Gangs; Juvenile justice system
Delta Kappa Gamma Society, **1072–1073**
Delta Pi Epsilon, 224
Delta Sigma Rho-Tau Kappa Alpha, **1073–1074**
Demandingness, parental, 55
Dementia, 810
Democracy and education
Addams, Jane, 41
Brameld, Theodore, 206–207
Broudy, Harry S., 210–21
civics education, 1236–1237
Curti, Merle, 539–540
decentralization, 544
Democracy and Education (Dewey), 195
Dewey, John, 41, 195, 581–582, 1933–1934
elementary education, 715
ethics, 754
globalization, 938
Harvard University, 724–725
international, 1269
just communities, 1377–1378
Miel, Alice, 1636–1637
open education, 1825
school leadership, 80
Young, Ella Flagg, 2702–2703
Democracy and Education (Dewey), 195
Democracy as a Way of Life (Bode), 195
Democratic authority, 170
Democratic Education (Gutmann), 754
Democratic Republic of Congon. *See* Sub-Saharan Africa
Democrats, 2476–2477
Demographics
faculty, 18–19, *777*, 777–778, *778*
graduate study in education, 967
higher education, 1024–1025, 1709–1710
juvenile crime, 1353–1354
multiculturalism, 1707–1708
nontraditional students, 1815
nursery school enrollment, 618
population trends, 1901–1903, 2703–2707
principals, 1921–1922
suicide, 2069
teacher education faculty, 2441
teachers, 2437
teaching-support leaders, 256
See also Enrollment; Statistics
Denison University, 1711
Denmark, 953, 1090
See also Western Europe
Dennison, Paul and Gail, 1702
Dennison, R. S., 1990
Dental Admissions Test (DAT), 557–558
Dental health, **554–557**
Dentistry education, **557–559**
Denver Plan, 1800–1801
Department-based capstone courses, 240
Department chairpersons, **559–561,** 800–801
Department for International Development (Great Britain), 1244
Department of Agriculture, U.S.
educational activities, 840–841
food service programs, 2131–2136
research funding, 857–858
Department of Agriculture Graduate School, 868
Department of Commerce, U.S., 841–842
Department of Defense, U.S.
academic R&D support, 858
Department of Defense Dependent Schools (DoDDS), 112–114, 838, 843, 866
educational activities, 842–843
See also Military; Specific branches
Department of Education, U.S., **2614–2620**
accreditation process, 33–34
activities, 843–844
Department of Education Organization Act, 2616–2617
educational reform, 2152
Educational Resources Information Center (ERIC), **683–684,** 843, 1832
establishment of, 839
Higher Education Center for Alcohol and Other Drug Prevention, 608
international role, **2619–2620**
Office of Civil Rights, 2571
overview, **2614–2619**
Safe and Drug-Free Schools Program, 603
Salish I and II studies, 2164
TRIO Programs, 1971, 2603
Upward Bound (UB) program, 1970–1971, **2603–2605**
See also Office of Educational Research and Improvement (OERI)
Department of Energy, U.S., 844, 858
Department of Health, Education, and Welfare (HEW), 839, 2615
Department of Health and Human Services, U.S., 844–845
Department of Housing and Urban Development, U.S., 845
Department of Justice, U.S., 846
Department of Labor, U.S., 729, 846–847
Department of School Superintendence, 100
Department of Social Services, Lassiter v., 282
Department of State, U.S.
Benjamin A. Gilman International Scholarship Program, 1138
educational programs, 847–849
schools, 113–114
Department of the Interior, U.S., 845
Department of the Treasury, U.S., 852
Department of Transportation, U.S., 849–851
Department of Veterans Affairs, U.S., 852
Departments, academic
curriculum, 520
department chairpersons, **559–561**
involvement in athletics, 345
majors, 20–21
See also Disciplines; Majors, academic
Departments of education, state, **2323–2331**
administrative services, 2339
role and function, **2323–2328**
vocational education, **2328–2331**
Departure, student, 403–405

Depression
college students, 1872
parents and family, 810
stress and, **2371–2374**
DeRonde v. Regents of the University, 64
Descartes, René, 421
Description, research for, 2022
Desegregation. *See* Segregation
Design, facility, 2125, 2126–2127, 2577
Design and Analysis of Experiments in Psychology and Education (Lindquist), 1486
Design-A-Plant, 1169, 1170
Designated School Officials (DSOs), 1313–1314
Design-based learning, **1163–1169**
Design Discussions (software), 1157–1158
Design experiments, 1149
Designing Undergraduate Education (Bergquist et al.), 521
Desocialization, college students', 43
Des Peres School, 190
Determinism in Education: A Series of Papers on the Relative Influence of Inherited and Acquired Traits (Bagley), 164
Detroit gang study, 51–52
Deutsche Gesselschaft fur Technische Zusammenarbeit (GTZ, Germany), 1248
Developing a Curriculum for Modern Living (Stratemeyer), 2370
Developing nations
alternative schooling models, 2500–2501
college faculty, 1031–1032
digital divide, 1296–1299
economic analysis of decision-making, **546–550**
education development projects, **686–689**
gender and access to education, 919–921
higher education enrollment, 1027–1028
penetration of dominant ideology, 938–939
private higher education, 1218–1219
privatization, school, 547
productivity, 549
public *vs.* private schools, 950–953
rate of return on investment in education, 648–650
rural education, 2090–2091
school funding, 547
secondary education, 600–601, 2195, 2196–2198
student loans, 2378–2380
textbooks, 2552–2554
vocational education, 2198
See also International development agencies; International issues; Specific countries; Specific regions
Developmental academic advising, 2–3
Developmental education, 576
Developmental task, 997
Developmental theory, **561–577**
cognitive and information processing, **567–571**
constructivism, 1464
dynamic assessment, 130
evolutionary theory, **571–574**
historical overview, **561–567**
interdependence, 175
peer relations and learning, 1865
Piaget, Jean, 678, 1825, 1894–1898
Vygotskian theory, **574–577,** 585, 2659–2660
See also Child development; Cognitive development; Zone of proximal development (ZPD)
Development offices, college and university, 1141–1143
Devolution, 542–543
Dewey, John, **577–582**
Addams, Jane and, 41
Bode, Boyd H. and, 194–195
Childs, John L. and, 293, 294
Clapp, Elsie Ripley and, 297
constructivist theory, 679
curriculum reform, 532
Curti's analysis of, 539–540
effort and interest, 704
environment ideal, 75
experiential education, 85, 760–761
on growth, 344
philosophy of education, 1879–1880
problem solving experiences, 1464
Progressive education, 1933–1935
school as miniature democracy, 1825
as student of G. Stanley Hall, 677
values and morals education, 259
Dewey in the Library of Living Philosophers (Schilpp), 294
DeYoung, Alan J., 2088
DFID (Department for International Development), 1244
Dhillon, Amarjit S., 569
Diagnosis
mental health, 157, 161, 1613
severe and multiple disabilities, 2210–2211
Diagnostic and Statistical Manual of Mental Disorders (American Psychiatric Association), 157, 161
Diagrams. *See* Visual media
Dialect and multilingual English, 743
Dialectical teaching method, 1899–1900
"Dick and Jane" readers, 971, 1999
Dictionaries, 2671
Didactic teaching, 2438–2439
Diez, Mary, 1751
Differential item functioning (DIF) parameters in psychometric models, 142
Differentiation, curricular, 1936, 2185–2186, 2187–2188
Difficulty parameters in standard psychometric models, 140–141
Digest of Education Statistics (Department of Education, U.S.), 843
Digital Classroom, National Archives and Records Administration, 1734
Digital divide, **1296–1299,** 2519–2520
Digital Millennium Copyright Act (DMCA), 1189–1190
Digit-symbol mnemonic method, 1671–1672
Dijkstra, Sanne, 1160
Dimensions of college teaching, 415–416

Dimensions of Multicultural Education (Banks), 1705
Dimensions of parenting, 1848
Diné College, 868
Dingell, John, 2039
Diplomas
high school, 422
international baccalaureate (IB) diploma, 898, **1238–1241**
recognition, 2683–2684
Diptheria, 1106–1107
Direct instruction, **1159–1162,** 1180–1181
Direct mail recruiting practices, 383
Directorate of Education, Employment, Labor, and Social Affairs (DEELSA), 1250
Directory information, 2014
Disabled students
accommodating, **407–409,** 411–412
active modification of child's disabilities, 127
adapted physical education, **37–40**
assistive technology, **149–151,** 2517–2518
classifications, 2286–2288
college, 44, **407–413**
Collier, John, Jr., 418
community college services, 2391–2392
Council for Exceptional Children (CEC), 499–500
cultural-historical theory, 2660
disability services, 2391–2392
Educating One and All: Students with Disabilities and Standards-Based Reform (National Research Council), 1730
elementary education, 719
equality of education, 672
extended-year programs, 2409–2410
Federal assistance programs, **1867–1869**
Gallaudet University, 469, 867
hearing impaired, 867, **1017–1021**
Individualized Education Program (IEP), 37, 161, 2281
institutionalization, 2278–2279, 2281
least restrictive environment (LRE), 37, 39
mental retardation, 186–187, **1616–1618,** 2210, 2211
Montessori's work with, 1675–1676
moral treatment, 2278–2279
Office of Special Education and Rehabilitative Services, Department of Education, 2619
physically, **1885–1886**
placement in physical education programs, 39–40
Regular Education Initiative (REI), 2281–2282
school sports, 2310–2311
severe and multiple disabilities, students with, **2210–2213**
special learning needs, **410–413**
speech and language impairment, **2295–2297**
transportation issues, 2575
urban education, 2608–2609
visually impaired students, **2634–2635**
vocational education, 2638
See also Education for All Handicapped Children Act; Emotionally disturbed students; Individuals with Disabilities Education Act (IDEA); Learning disabilities; Special education
Disadvantaged students
compensatory education, U.S., 453–463
dynamic assessment, 128–129
See also Low income families; Minorities; Poverty; Socioeconomic status
Disciplinary Path to Outcome Based Education, 1829–1830
Discipline, student, 2436, 2575–2576
Discipline-based art education (DBAE), 118, 119
Discipline-based capstone courses, 240
Disciplines, **9–14**
codification, 10
disciplinary variation, 12
earnings, 19
faculty scholarship and research, 783–785
higher education, 21–22
standards generation, 2316–2317
See also Academic majors; Interdisciplinarity; Specific disciplines
Discourse, **582–589**
classroom discourse, **582–586**
cognitive perspective, **586–589**
coherence, 587–588
instructional strategies, 1183–1184
learning communities, 1162–1163
processing, 586–589
science education, 2171–2172
threaded, 1371–1372
Discourse on Inequality (Rousseau), 2079
Discourse on the Arts and Sciences (Rousseau), 2079
Discreet state theory of emotions, 59
Discrepancy models of learning disabilities, 2008–2009
Discrimination
Convention against Discrimination in Education, 1282
Convention on the Elimination of All Forms of Discrimination Against Women, 1280–1281
peace education and, 1861–1862
sex discrimination, 104
Young Women's Christian Association's fight against, 2742
See also Bias; Civil rights; Minorities; Race/ethnicity; Specific minority groups
Dismissal of college faculty, 16
Disposition of juvenile justice cases, 1355–1356
Disruptive behavior. *See* Behavior problems
Dissertations, 595–596, 966
The Dissolution of General Education (report), 517
Dissonance, cognitive, 1428–1429
Distance education, **589–593**
adult learning, 2498
business education, 224–225
college teaching, 416
consortia, 476
continuing professional education (CPE), 485
copyright, 1188–1189

The Distance Learner's Guide (Western Cooperative for Educational Telecommunications), 590
Empire State College, 199
foreign language education, 895
globalism, 425
individualized instruction, 1132
information and communication technology, 2511–2512
Statement on Distance Education (American Association of University Professors), 590
teacher education, 2445
teaching centers, 255
western Europe, 2683
See also Correspondence study; Online education; Virtual universities
The Distance Learner's Guide (Western Cooperative for Educational Telecommunications), 590
Distinguished Lectureship program, Sigma Xi, 1084
"Distinguished Teaching Professor" rank, 199
Distributed education, 590
Distributive Education Clubs of America (DECA), **2726–2727**
Divergent questions, 312
Diversity
academic advising, 3, 4
American Association for Higher Education initiative, 90
constitutional issues, 480–481
faculty, **775–779**
international higher education, 1032
learning, 511
school counselors role, 978
undergraduate curricular content, 521–522
See also Multiculturalism; Pluralism
Divinity studies, **593–595**
Division of Adolescent and School Health (DASH), 1004, 1008
Division of Behavioral and Social Sciences and Education, NRC, 1728
Divisions, NCAA, 365
Dix, Dorothea, 2278
Dixon, John, 740, 742
Djibouti. *See* Sub-Saharan Africa
DMCA (Digital Millennium Copyright Act), 1189–1190
DNA general intelligence markers, 1196–1197
Doctoral degree programs, **595–596**
academic labor market, 17–18
business, 221, 222
Carnegie Classification, 243–245
divinity, 594–595
education, 968, 969–970
engineering, 739
nursing, 1820
overview, 966–967
pharmacy education, 94–95
See also Graduate education
Document of the Copenhagen Meeting on the Human Dimension of the Conference on Security and Co-operation in Europe, **3148–3162**
DoDDS (Department of Defense Dependent Schools), 112–114, 838, 843, 866
Dodge, Kenneth, 47, 70
Doe, Santa Fe Independent School District v., 2423
Does School Quality Matter, Beyond Rhetoric: A New American Agenda for Children and Families (report), 698
Domain expertise, **765–767,** 1114
Domain-references teacher evaluation, 2454
Domain theory of moral development, 1682
Domestic Dependent Elementary and Secondary Schools (DDESS), 838, 843, 866
Domestic economy. *See* Family and consumer sciences education
Domestic science. *See* Family and consumer sciences education
Domestic violence, **2631–2634**
academic achievement, 1837
exposure to, children's, 2628
family circumstance, 809
foster care, 818
See also Child abuse and neglect
Dominica. *See* Latin America and the Caribbean
Dominican Republic, 950
See also Latin America and the Caribbean
Dominie series (Neill), 1797
Donor organizations, educational aid, 686–688
Dooling, D. James, 1606, 1608
Dormitories. *See* Residence halls
Dornbusch, Sanford, 1859
Dossier, teaching, 414–415
Double immersion bilingual education. *See* Dual immersion bilingual education
Dove, Linda A., 2446
Dowell, Board of Education of Oklahoma City Public Schools v., 2202, 2424
Dow Jones Newspaper Fund, 1348
Doyle, Walter, 531
Draney, Karen, 142
Dred Scott v. Sanford, 2199
Dressel, Paul, 521, 523
Drexel Institute, 223
Driscoll, Amy, 797
Driscoll, Mary, 2141
Driver, Rosalind, 1464
Driver education, **596–599**
Drivers, school bus, 2576–2577
Drive theory of motivation, 1691
Dropouts
college, 402
graduation test requirements, 2541
high school, **599–602,** 921–922
mentoring and dropout prevention, 2581
prevention, 978
South Asia, 2274
Drug abuse. *See* Substance abuse
Drug Abuse Resistance Education (DARE) program, 604, 718
Drug trafficking, 52–53
Dryfoos, Joy, 906, 2062
Dual immersion bilingual education, 180, 182, 896
Du Bois, W. E. B., **609–613**
African-American studies, 66
Bethune, Mary McLeod, 174
vocational education, 2636
Ducharme, Edward, 2441
Duderstadt, James J., 2048, 2051, 2526
Due care, 1473
Due process, 1351, 1352–1353
Duffy, Gerald G., 1978, 1983
Duggan, Stephen, 1138
Dugoni, Bernard, 966
Dugresne, Annette, 1471
Duke, Alex, 2046

Duke, Daniel, L., 2455
Dumaret, Annick, 819
Dunlap, Caroline, 622
Dunnan, Gardner, 542
DuPuy, William, 1657
Durham, Charlotte, 541
Durkheim, Émile, 404
Durkin, Dolores, 1977–1978, 1999
Durkin, Mary, 2428
Dvorak, Jack, 1347
Dweck, Carol, 705, 1693
Dyadic interaction, 490–491
Dykstra, Robert, 1999
Dynamic assessment, **127–131**
The Dynamics of Education (Taba), 2427
Dyslexia, 989–990, 2008

E

Eager to Learn: Educating Our Preschoolers (National Research Council), 1730
Early action admissions, 328
Early childhood
 analogical reasoning, 1422
 causal reasoning, 1425–1426
 development, 272, 276–277, 562, 565–566, 629
 domestic violence exposure, 2632–3633
 health and nutrition, 626–627
 international issues, 626–634
 language development, 1974
 literacy experiences, 1974
 phonological awareness, 1974–1975
 poverty and cognitive ability, 1905–1906
 print concepts, 1974
 working memory, 1592
 See also Child development; Developmental theory
Early childhood education, **615–634**
 Eager to Learn: Educating Our Preschoolers (National Research Council), 1730
 Montessori, Maria, 84, 1676–1680
 Montessori Accreditation Council for Teacher Education (MACTE), 1679–1680
 music, 1721–1722
 National Association for the Education of Young Children (NAEYC), 623, 624, 652, **1736–1737**
 nursery school enrollment demographics, 618
 overview, **615–621**
 school readiness, 277, 716, 831–832, **2148–2151**
 studies, 1730
 Success for All programs, 2405
 teacher certification, 618, 624, 625
 teacher preparation, **621–626,** 632
 Tools of the Mind (Bodrova and Leong), 576
 See also Head Start program; Kindergarten; Preschool
Early decision admissions, 328
Early Head Start program, 844
Early national period
 elementary education, 710–711
 higher education, 1035–1036
 See also History, educational
Early reform period school funding, 885–886
Early semester calendar. *See* Academic calendars
Early warning systems, 44–45
Earmarking, 2342
Earned Income Tax Credit (EITC), 834
Earnings
 accountability, 652
 benefits of education investment, 647, 648
 college faculty, 18–19, 102, 346–347
 college graduates, 339–340
 early childhood education teachers, 618
 equity in teachers' pay, 298–299
 faculty consulting, 774, 775
 gender and ethnicity differentiation, 18–19
 intercollegiate athletics faculty, 346–347
 part-time faculty, 781
 performance-based teachers' pay, 2480
 Professional Education Data System, 94
 school psychologists, 1947
 students, 729
 teachers, 2437, 2448–2449, 2450–2451
 White House Fellows, 2687
East Asia and the Pacific, **634–640**
 American Council of Learned Societies, 106
 early childhood education, 627, 628
 educational data, *636*
 higher education, 1028
 See also Specific countries
Eastern Europe and Central Asia, **640–647**
 American Council of Learned Societies, 106
 early childhood education, 627, 628
 See also Specific countries
Eating disorders, 1872
Eaton, John, 2615
Eaton, Susan, 663
Eaton, Theodore, 74–75
Ebbinghaus, Herman, 1607
Ebonics, 1391–1392
ECA (Bureau of Educational and Cultural Affairs), 847–848
ECA (Economic Commission for Africa), 1257–1258
Eccles, Jacquelynne, 318, 1694
Echo in My Soul (Clark), 299
Ecker, David, 166
Ecology of community, 434–435
Economic and Statistics Administration (ESA), 841
Economic Commission for Africa (ECA), 1257–1258
Economic development
 fertility, 1902
 higher education, 2359–2360
 Middle East and North Africa, 1623–1624
 programs, 2596
 secondary education, 2187
 small nations, 2235
 social cohesion, 2241
 standards movement, 2317, 2318–2319
 success and education reform, 690
 See also International development agencies
Economic Development Administration (EDA), 841
Economic Opportunity Act of 1964, 2677
Economic recession, 883
Economics of education
 Bowen, Howard, 197–199
 college athletics, 345–348
 commerce, **423–426**

cost effectiveness, **495–497**
decentralization, 542–543, 545–546
decision-making in developing nations, **546–550**
decision-making in schools, **550–553**
Eastern Europe and Central Asia region, 643–644
education investment benefits, **647–651**
expenditures, international, *1662, 1663*
faculty entrepreneurship, 770, 797–798
funds allocation, 551–553
growth with equity, 549
higher education, 198–199, 1023–1024
human capital theory, 549
industry-university research collaboration, 2594–2595
intergovernmental relations, 1216–1217
international issues, 1032–1033
international students, 1314–1317
media benefits, 1576–1577
part-time faculty, 780
poverty reduction, 549
projecting expenditures, **659–662,** *660, 661*
school boards, 2105
South Asia, 2275
student retention, 405
technology and higher education, 2523
tribal college funding, 2579
See also Allocation; Commerce of education; Cost/benefit analysis; Costs; Expenditures; Finance; Funding

ECS (Education Commission of the States), **685–686**

ECTS (European Credit Transfer System), 2683

Ecuador. *See* Latin America and the Caribbean

EDA (Economic Development Administration), 841

Edgerton, Russell, 800

Edgington, State v., 1062

Edison Company, 1926

Educating Americans for the 21st Century (report), 697

Educating One and All: Students with Disabilities and Standards-Based Reform (National Research Council), 1730

Educating Teachers of Science, Mathematics, and Technology: New Practices for a New Millennium (National Research Council), 1729

Education, graduate study in, **967–970**

Education Act of 1944 (England), 1134

Educational access
African Americans, 618, 671
community colleges, 876–880
compensatory education, 459
disabled children, 1868–1869
early childhood education, 618
gender, 919
girls, 1301
higher education, 1030–1031
Hispanic Americans, 618
international issues, 919, 1030–1031, 1300–1304
Latin America, 1408
See also Equality in education; Equity

Educational administration. *See* Administration, educational

Educational aid, international, 686–688

Educational and Corporate Services, IIE, 1137

Educational associations. *See* Associations, educational

Educational attainment
earnings, 339
Hispanic Americans, 1966
international statistics, *1305*
parents', **1856–1858**
reasoning skills, 1447
South Asia, 2273–2274

Educational broadcasting, 592, **656–658**

Educational change, **658–659**
See also Education reform

Educational companions, 1618

Educational Foundation, AAUW, 104

The Educational Frontier (Kilpatrick ed.), 293

Educational Information and Resources Branch, ECA, 847–848

Educational intervention and brain imaging, 205

Educational malpractice, 1475

Educational Measurement (Lindquist), 1486

Educational objectives, taxonomies of. *See* Bloom, Benjamin S.; Taxonomies of educational objectives

Educational philosophy. *See* Philosophy of education

Educational Policies Commission (EPC), 696

Educational psychology, **676–683**
Bagley, William Chandler, 163–164
Binet, Alfred, 185–187
Bloom, Benjamin S., 188–189
Educational Psychology (Thorndike), 2566
James, William, 1331–1337
Journal of Educational Psychology, 164
McCall, William A., 1572–1574
Piaget, Jean, 1894–1898
Thorndike, Edward L., 2562–2568
See also Cognitive development; Developmental theory; Psychology

Educational Psychology (Thorndike), 2566

Educational radio, 656, 657

Educational research
analogical reasoning, 1421–1423
bilingual education, 179–180, 182–183
Binet, Alfred, 186
Bloom, Benjamin S., 188–189
brain-based education, 202–205
causal reasoning, 1425–1427
child care effects, 273, 275
classroom discourse, 582–589
classroom observation limitations, 307–309
classroom questions, 312–313
class size, 314–316
college impact, 332–340
comprehension, 1515
computer-supported collaborative learning, 469–470
conceptual change, 1427–1430
cost effectiveness studies, 496–497
cross-cultural *vs.* cultural-process, 1121–1122
design-based learning, 1165–1166
documents, 2028

Educational Research and Dissemination Program (professional development program), 110, 2481
Educational Resources Information Center (ERIC), **683–684,** 843, 1832
experiential education, 761–762
grading systems, 956–958
group processes, 973–974
instructional design, 1148–1150
interest and reading, 1989–1991
international, **1265–1276**
international education statistics, **1285–1296**
knowledge acquisition, 1431–1435
Latin America, 1411–1412
living and learning centers, 1519
mathematics learning, 1546–1547
methodology, 1486
motor learning, 1701–1702
multicultural education, 1706–1707
multimedia literacy, 1498–1499
National Academy of Sciences, 1730
National Education Association, 1771
National Research Council (NRC), 1728–1730
neighborhood risk and parenting, 1854–1855
numeracy and culture, 1564–1565
Office of Educational Research and Improvement (OERI), Department of Education, 2618
poverty, 1905–1908, 1910–1914
reading comprehension, 1977–1983
reading instruction, 1999–2000, 2002
regional laboratories and research and development centers, **2017–2019**
rural education, 2088
studies of, 1730
teacher evaluation, 2454–2456
teaching, 413–415
teaching, methods for studying, **2488–2492**
urban education, 2609–2610
Urban Institute, 2613
vocational education, 2646
writing instruction, 2695–2696
See also Comparative assessment; Learning theory; Measurement; Reports and publications; Research methods; Studies
Educational Research and Dissemination Program, 110, 2481
Educational Resources Information Center (ERIC), **683–684,** 843, 1832
Clearinghouse on Higher Education, 91
Clearinghouse on Languages and Linguistics, 895
Clearinghouse on Teaching and Teacher Education, 94
Educational Review, 230
Educational service, 424–425
Educational service agencies (ESAs), 2087
Educational Sociology (Snedden), 2242
Educational technology, **2509–2526**
community colleges, 2393
developing nations, 547–548
higher education, **2521–2526**
international commerce, 424–425
overview, **2509–2513**
school, **2513–2521**
textbooks and, 2555–2556
See also Animated learning aids; Software
Educational television
children and media influence, 1580
distance education, 592
government involvement, 656–658
Educational Television Facilities Act, 657
Educational Testing Service (ETS), **684–685**
Advanced Assessment and Delivery Technologies (AADT), 685
advanced placement courses/exams, 57
Communications and Public Affairs Division, 685
Council for Adult and Experiential Learning (CAEL), 1478, 1479
Graduate and Professional Education Division, 685
Graduate Record Examination (GRE), **962–965,** 968
Information Systems and Technology Division, 685
School and College Services Division, 684
Statistics and Research Division, 684
Teaching and Learning Division, 685
See also National Assessment of Educational Progress (NAEP)
Educational Wastelands (Bestor), 172, 173
Education and Emergent Man: A Theory of Education With Particular Application to Public Education in the United States (Bagley), 164
Education and Morals (Childs), 293
Education and the Cult of Efficiency (Callahan), 673
"Education and the Philosophy of Experimentalism" (Childs), 293
Education and the State (West), 949
Education as Power (Brameld), 207
Education at a Glance: OECD Indicators (OECD), 1287, 1291, 1293
Education Commission of the States (ECS), 518, **685–686**
Education Department. *See* Department of Education, U.S.
Education development projects, **686–689**
Education Entrepreneurs Fund, 1799
Education for All American Youth (report), 697, 2187
Education for All Handicapped Children Act, **3075–3077**; **3077–3080**
adaptive physical education, 40
elementary education, 719
emotionally disturbed students, 726
federal involvement in education, 838
mentally retarded students, 1617
See also Individuals with Disabilities Education Act (IDEA)

Education for All (initiative), 920, 2275–2276
Education for Self-Reliance (Nyerere), 2091
Education Foundation, AAUW, 104
Education goods and services, **1321–1324**
Education International (EI), 1318, 1804
Education materials. *See* Instructional materials
Education of Man (Froebel), 904
Education Performance Network (EPN), 1799
Education policy. *See* Policy, education
Education quality
  child care, 273
  decentralization, 544
  Education Quality Institute, 1798–1799
  Latin America, 1408–1410
  school-parent-community partnerships, 825–826
  teacher quality, 1770
  texts, 1997
Education Quality Institute, 1798–1799
Education reform, **658–659, 689–700**
  Boyer, Ernest, 200
  character education, 1685
  Coalition of Essential Schools (CES), **321–322, 322–324**
  cold war, 669
  college athletics, 350–351
  decentralization, 544–545
  Education Reform Act (England), 1134–1135
  elementary education, 718–719
  Eliot, Charles, 725
  England, 1134–1135
  family support services, 829, 830–831
  Gray, William Scott, 970–971
  higher education curriculum, 510, 512, 524–525
  international higher education, 1029–1030
  international issues, 1301–1302
  James, William, 1333–1334
  Johnson, Marietta Pierce, **1344–1346**
  junior colleges, 443
  Latin America, 1409–1410
  medical schools, 892–893
  middle schools, 1632–1634
  Modern Red Schoolhouse (MRSh), **1674–1675**
  New American Schools, **1798–1800**
  overview, **689–695**
  Paideia Program, 84, **1841–1842**
  policy, 669
  public schools, 1951, 2259–2260
  reports, historically significant, **695–700**
  restructuring, 2104
  school-based decision-making, **2099–2102**
  school boards, 2105–2107
  secondary education, 2190–2194
  Skinner, B. F., 2230–2231
  teacher education, 722
  teacher evaluation and, 2455–2456
  vocational education, 2637–2639
  western Europe, 2680–2681, 2681–2683
  See also Academic standards; Accountability; School reform; Standards-based education
Education Reform Act (England), 1134–1135
Education Sector Policy Paper (African Development Bank), 1258
Education services, NCAA, 367
Education summits
  Council for Basic Education, 498
  education reform, 691
  federal involvement in education, 838
  National Assessment of Educational Progress (NAEP), 132
  school reform, 2154, 2155
  statewide testing, 2538
Education theory. *See* Theory of education
Education Trust, 1804
Educative Process (Bagley), 163
Educator's biographies
  Addams, Jane, **40–42**
  Alberty, H. B., **80–82**
  Aristotle, **115–117**
  Augustine, St., **159–161**
  Bagley, William Chandler, **163–165**
  Barkan, Manuel, **165–167**
  Benjamin, Harold R. W., **168–169**
  Benne, Kenneth D., **169–171**
  Bestor, A. E., Jr., **172–173**
  Bethune, Mary McLeod, **173–175**
  Binet, Alfred, **185–187**
  Bloom, Benjamin S., **188–189**
  Blow, Susan, **189–191**
  Bobbitt, Franklin, **192–194**
  Bode, Boyd H., **194–196**
  Bond, Horace Mann, **196–197**
  Bowen, Howard, **197–199**
  Boyer, Ernest L., **199–201**
  Brameld, Theodore, **206–208**
  Broudy, Harry S., **210–212**
  Buchanan, Scott, **212–213**
  Buros, Oscar Krisen, **213–215**
  Butler, Nicholas M., **229–231**
  Campbell, Roald F., **233–234**
  Chall, Jeanne, **257–259**
  Charters, W. W., **263–265**
  Childs, John L., **292–294**
  Clapp, Elsie Ripley, **297–298**
  Clark, Septima Poinsette, **298–299**
  Coleman, James S., **324–327**
  Collier, John, Jr., **417–419**
  Comenius, Johann, **419–422**
  Conant, J. B., **471–474**
  Counts, George S., **503–505**
  Cubberley, Ellwood, **507–509**
  Curti, Merle, **539–540**
  De Lima, Agnes, **553–554**
  Dewey, John, **572–582**
  Du Bois, W. E. B., **609–613**
  Eliot, Charles, **722–725**
  Erikson, Erik, **751–752**
  Fawcett, Harold P., **835–836**
  Flexner, Abraham, **891–893**
  Freire, Paulo, **900–903**
  Froebel, Friedrich, **903–906**
  Goddard, Henry H., **940–942**
  Goodman, Paul, **942–943**
  Goslin, Willard E., **943–945**
  Gray, William S., **970–971**
  Hahn, Kurt, 761, **981–982**
  Haley, Margaret, **982–985**
  Hall, G. Stanley, **985–987**
  Hanna, Paul R., **990–991**
  Harper, William Rainey, **991–993**
  Harris, William T., **993–994**
  Havighurst, Robert J., **996–998**
  Herbart, Johann, **1021–1023**
  Holt, John, **1059–1060**
  Hopkins, L. Thomas, **1088–1089**
  Horton, Myles, **1089–1091**

Hunter, Madeline Cheek, **1093–1094**
Hutchins, Robert, **1094–1096**
James, William, **1331–1337**
Johnson, Marietta Pierce, **1344–1346**
Kandel, Isaac L., **1363–1365**
Keppel, Francis C., **1365–1367**
Kerschensteiner, Georg, **1367–1369**
Kilpatrick, William H., **1368–1369**
Kohlberg, Lawrence, **1376–1378**
Labrant, Lou L., **1379–1380**
Lindquist, E. F., **1485–1487**
Lowenfeld, Viktor, **1522–1524**
Macdonald, James, **1525–1526**
Mann, Horace, **1534–1537**
Mays, Benjamin, **1569–1572**
McCall, William A., **1572–1574**
McMurry, Charles, **1574–1575**
Meiklejohn, Alexander, **1587–1588**
Miel, Alice, **1635–1638**
Montessori, Maria, **1675–1680**
Morrison, Henry C., **1688–1690**
Neill, A. S., **1796–198**
Palmer, Alice Freeman, **1842–1844**
Pestalozzi, Johann, **1874–1876**
Piaget, Jean, **1894–1898**
Plato, **1898–1901**
Pressey, Sidney L., **1917–1919**
Prosser, Charles, **1940–1941**
Putnam, Alice, **1957–1959**
Rice, John A., **2052–2053**
Rice, Joseph Mayer, **2053–2055**
Rogers, Carl, **2076–2079**
Rousseau, Jean-Jacques, **2079–2081**
Rugg, Harold, **2081–2083**
Schwab, Joseph, **2156–2158**
Shanker, Albert, **2221–2223**
Sheldon, Edward, **2223–2225**
Skinner, B. F., **2228–2231**
Smith, David Eugene, **2236–2238**
Snedden, David, **2241–2242**
Steiner, Rudolf, **2364–2366**
Stratemeyer, Florence, **2369–2371**
Taba, Hilda, **2427–2429**
Taylor, Harold, **2433–2435**
Terman, Lewis, **2528–2529**
Thayer, V. T., **2560–2562**
Thorndike, Edward L., **2562–2569**
Tyler, Ralph W., **2587–2590**
Vygotsky, Lev, **2658–2660**
Waller, Willard W., **2661–2662**
Washburne, Carleton, **2662–2664**
Washington, Booker T., **2664–2668**
Watson, John B., **2668–2670**
Webster, Noah, **2670–2673**
Whitehead, Alfred North, **2684–2686**
Woodson, Carter Godwin, **2691–2693**
Young, Ella Flagg, **2701–2703**
Zacharias, Jerrold, **2745–2747**
Zirbes, Laura, **2747–2748**

EduFrance, 1316
Edwards v. Aguillard, 2423
Eells, Walter Crosby, 96
EEOC (Equal Employment Opportunity Commission), 62
EFC (Expected Family Contribution), 376
Efficiency, **700–704**
- accountability, 673–674
- decentralization and, 544
- educational policy, 669, 670
- internal, 546–548
- public schools *vs.* private schools, 950–951

Effort and interest, **704–707**
Effortful control, 156
Eggert, Leona, 2056
Egocentrism, 1895
Egypt. *See* Middle East and North Africa
Ehman, Lee, 538
Eichorn, Donald, 1631
EI (Education International), 1318, 1804
Eight-Year Study, **707–709**
- accreditation, 29
- Alberty, H. B., 80
- as landmark education reform study, 696–697
- Taba, Hilda, 2427–2428
- Tyler, Ralph W., 2588

Einstein, Albert, 93
Eisenhower, Dwight D., 1758, 2538
Eisenhower, Milton S., 1343–1344
EITC (Earned Income Tax Credit), 834
Elbow, Peter, 745
Elder, Donna, 46
Elderly, 2704
Eleanor Roosevelt Fund Award, 104
Eleanor Roosevelt Teacher Fellowships, 104
E-learning. *See* Online education
Elections
- National Education Association, 1770
- school board members, 2118–2119

Electives, college, 723–724, 995
Electoral organizing, 435
Electrical engineering, 739
Electronic Access Project, National Archives and Records Administration, 1733–1734
Electronic media and art education, 120
Electronic probes, 2179, 2180
Electronic publishing, 2602
Elementary and Secondary Education Act (ESEA), **3064–3072**
- bilingual education, 177
- class size, 314
- elementary education, 715
- enforcement, 1801–1802
- equality of opportunity, 1948–1949
- history of federal participation in education, 837–838, 886
- impact aid, 1108
- Keppel, Francis C., 1365–1366
- reauthorization, 502
- standardized testing, 2545
- Title I, 454–456, 457–458, 837–838, 2581
- Title IV, 2017
- Title V, 2325
- Title VI, 1868

Elementary education, **709–722**
- art education, 119
- bilingual education, 713
- children's literature, 288
- Core Knowledge Sequence, 535–537
- current trends, **715–720**
- curriculum, 535–537
- dental health, 556
- developmentalist approach, 2747–2748
- entrance age, 563
- federal, 866
- foreign language programs, 895–897
- geometry, 1548–1549
- guidance and counseling, 976–977
- history, **709–715**
- independent study, 1110–1111

infant schools' influence, 1136
Inner-City Private Elementary Schools (report), 1925–1926
Jasper Project, 1165
mathematics teachers, 1539
music, 1719–1720
National Association of Elementary School Principals (NAESP), **1739–1741**
Office of Elementary and Secondary Education, Department of Education, 2618
physical education, 1888
scheduling, 2096
school readiness, 277, 716, 831–832, **2148–2151**
science, 2160
Smithsonian Institution programs, 2239–2240
social studies, 2266
South Asia, *2275*
standards movement, 714
student mobility, 2382
sub-Saharan Africa, 2398–2400
teacher preparation, **720–722**
volunteerism, 2656–2657
western Europe, 2681
Zirbes, Laura, 2747–2748
See also Infant schools (England)

Elementary Spelling Book (Webster), 2670, 2671, 2672

Eliot, Charles, **722–725,** 995, 1484

Elkonin, Daniel, 576

Ellickson, Phyllis, 2056

Elliott, Clark, 1169

ELLs (English language learners). *See* Bilingual education; English as a second language (ESL); Language minority students

Elmira Female College, 2225

Elmore, Richard, 324

ELOs (extra learning opportunities), 1777

El Salvador. *See* Latin America and the Caribbean

Elson-Gray Basic Readers, 971

Emancipated slaves, 867, 2665–2666

Emancipation Proclamation, 63

Embassy schools, 113

Embedded assessment, 1116

Embretson, Susan, 141, 1114

Emergency Council on Education, 108

Emergency health care, 1014

Emergent literacy, **1487–1489**

Emergent theory of language acquisition, 1387

Emerging Self in School and Home (Hopkins), 1088–1089

Émile (Rousseau), 2080–2081

Emotional abuse. *See* Child abuse and neglect

Emotional development
affect, **58–61**
emotional intelligence, 1199
emotional memory, 1436
school readiness, 2148
sports participation, **2312–2315**

Emotional intelligence, **1191–1194,** 1199

Emotionally disturbed students, **726–728**
mental health services, 1613–1616
special education, 2287
violence exposure, 2624
See also Behavior problems; Disabled students; Mental health

Emotions
discreet state theory, 59
fictional emotions, 1502
functionalist approach, 59
learning, 60–61
milestones, 60
pedagogical agents, 1169–1170
process viewpoint, 59–60
See also Affective and conative processes

Empathy, 60

Empire State College, 199

Empiricism, 1439

Employment, **728–737**
academic performance and student employment, 1838
readiness, **732–735**
reasons students work, **735–737**
school psychologists, 1947
students, impact on, **728–732**
teacher, **2448–2453**
teacher job placement, 76
See also Academic labor market; Career development; Earnings; Job skills; Teacher supply and demand; Workforce training

Employment and Training Act (Great Britain), 487

Employment and Training Administration, 847

Empowerment, 811

Encoding
knowledge, 1433–1435
memory, 1605, 1606–1607

Encounter groups, 2078

Endowments, 26

Ends and Means in Education: A Midcentury Appraisal (Brameld), 206

ENFL project, 469

Engel v. Vitale, 2422, **2795–2802**

Engineering education, **737–740**
career choice, 18
National Science Foundation (NSF), 1790
Sigma Xi, **1083–1085**
Tau Beta Pi, **1085–1086**
undergraduate curriculum reform, 512

England
children's rights, 281
common law, 280–281, 1349–1350
continuing professional education (CPE), 487
Court of Chancery, 281
Department for International Development (DFID), 1244
English common law, 1349–1350
government's role in education, 949
higher education reform, 1029
history teaching, 1055–1056
infant schools, **1133–1136**
international student recruitment, 1316
language arts instruction, 1395–1396
monitorialism, 711
open education, 1825–1826
Royal Agricultural Society (England), 72
secondary education standards, 2188
standards and testing, 2531–2532
technology education, 2507–2508
workforce development, 487
writing instruction, 2693
See also Europe; Western Europe

England, Robert E., 1964

English as a second language (ESL), **181–185**
  See also Bilingual education; Language; Language acquisition; Language minority students
English common law
  child guardianship, 280–281
  juvenile justice, 1349–1350
English education, **740–748**
  National Council of Teachers of English (NCTE), 741, 1394–1395, **1765–1767**
  proficiency requirements, college, 925
  teacher preparation, **745–748**
  teaching of, **740–745**
  See also Literature; Writing and composition
English High School, 2184
English language learners (ELLs). *See* Bilingual education; English as a second language (ESL); Language; Language minority students
Enlightened Cherishing: An Essay in Aesthetic Education (Broudy), 211
Enochs, Larry G., 2164
Enrichment programs, 932, **2407–2409**
Enrollment
  American overseas schools, 112–113
  calendar use and conversion by, 5
  Canadian college, 235–236
  Catholic schools, 250, 253
  China, 638
  college, 235–236, 328, 406, 1037–1039
  community colleges, 441, 875
  drivers education courses, 597
  East Asia and the Pacific, *636*
  Eastern Europe and Central Asia region, 627, 643, *643*
  governance and enrollment shortages, 795
  international early childhood education trends, 627–629
  international higher education, 1027–1028
  Jewish day schools, 1341
  kindergarten, 615
  Latin courses, 1413–1414
  nursery school, 618
  open, 84, 1951, 2260
  private schools, 1922–1923, 1927
  programs, 1969
  Protestant schools, 1942–1944
  public alternative schools, 83
  public schools, 887
  secondary school, 2192
  South Asia schools, 2273–2274, *2276*
  The Strategic Management of College Enrollments (Hossler and Bean), 406
  Sub-Saharan Africa, 2397, 2398, *2399,* 2400
  vocational education, 2640
  wait lists, 328
  See also Statistics
Enrollment management, 406, **748–751,** 1145
Entertainment, violence in, 1360, 1581–1582
Entrance age, elementary school, 563
Entrance examinations. *See* Admissions tests
Entrepreneurship, faculty, **769–772,** 797–798
Enumeration systems, 1563
Environmental education. *See* Outdoor and environmental education
Environmental engineering, 740
Environmental learning, 563
Environmental model of special education, 2293
Environmental quality of school facilities, 2126
Environmental tobacco smoke (ETS), 2067, 2068
Environment control, 1699
EPC (Educational Policies Commission), 696
Episcopal schools, 1943
Episodic memory, 1610
Epistemologies
  discipline differences, 12
  Piaget, Jean, 1895–1898, 2168, 2171
  science learning, 2168, 2171
EPN (Education Performance Network), 1799
Epperson v. Arkansas, 2422
Epstein, Debbie, 2220
Epstein, Erwin H., 938–939
Epstein, Joyce L., 1845
EQ-I (Bar-On Emotional Quotient Inventory), 1191
Equal Access Act, 2375–2376
Equal Educational Opportunities Act of 1974, 178
Equal Employment Opportunity Commission (EEOC), 62, 64
Equality in education, 669–673, 2245
Equality of Education Opportunity (Coleman et al.), 697, 1835
Equal protection clause, U.S. Constitution
  "adequacy," 479, 481–482, 672
  affirmative action, 61–63
  segregation cases, 478–480, 2199, 2423–2424, 2425
  U.S. Constitution, 63
  vocational education, 2637
  See also Equity
Equatorial Guinea. *See* Sub-Saharan Africa
Equipotentiality, 1459
Equity
  Equity in Athletics Disclosure Act of 1996, 2571
  gender, 920–921, **1125–1129**
  gifted and talented programs, 933
  international issues, 951–952
  Latin America, 1409
  Mexican-American education, 2094
  Middle East and North Africa, 1625
  multiculturalism, 1705–1706
  pedagogy, 1705–1706
  public schools, 951, 1948–1949
  See also Discrimination; Equal protection clause
Erasmus program (European Union), 160, 1251–1252, 2682, 2683
Eraut, Michael, 1892
ERIC. *See* Educational Resources Information Center (ERIC)
ERIC Digests (research syntheses), 683
Erickson, Judith, 2712
ERIC Review (periodical), 683
Ericsson, K. Anders, 765, 766, 2035
Erikson, Erik, **751–752**
Eritrea. *See* Sub-Saharan Africa
Error, reasoning, 1445
Ertmer, Peggy, 1149

ESA (Economic and Statistics Administration), 841
ESAs (Educational service agencies), 2087
Escoffier, Jeffrey, 917
Escuela Nueva (initiative, Colombia), 462–463, 1409
ESEA. *See* Elementary and Secondary Education Act (ESEA)
ESL (English as a second language), **181–185**
Essay questions and assessment, 135
Essays, college application, 329
Essentialism
  Bagley, William C., 164–165
  Brameld, Theodore, 207
  Kandel, Isaac L., 1364
Essentialist's Platform (Bagley), 164
The Essential Profession (report), 698
Estonia. *See* Eastern Europe and Central Asia
Ethical Culture Schools, 2561–2562
Ethics, **753–760**
  Aristotle, 116–117
  college recruitment, 383
  government, 1761
  higher education, **756–760**
  inquiry, 754
  journalism, 1349
  politics, 116–117
  school teaching, **753–756**
  technology and, 2519–2520
  See also Character development; Moral development
Ethiopia. *See* Sub-Saharan Africa
Ethnic Catholic schools, 251
Ethnicity. *See* Minorities; Race/ethnicity
Ethnic studies. *See* African-American studies; Multiculturalism; Pluralism
Ethnography, **2026–2030,** 2489–2490
ETS. *See* Educational Testing Service (ETS)
ETS (environmental tobacco smoke), 2067, 2068
EU. *See* European Union (EU); Western Europe
Euclid, 572
Eugenics, 941
Eurocentrism, 1710
Europe
  Council of Europe (COE), 27, 1253–1254, 1481
  early childhood education, 620
  elementary education, 716
  foreign language instruction, 899
  higher education, 1027
  higher education enrollment, 1027
  higher education reform, 1029
  infant schools, 1135
  international development agencies, 1251–1255
  international education, 1267
  lifelong learning, 1481
  school counseling, 979
  secondary education, 2188, 2195
  standards and testing, 2532
  university restructuring, 1029
  See also Eastern Europe and Central Asia; European Union (EU); Western Europe; Specific countries
European Charter for Regional or Minority Languages, **3170–3182**
European Convention on Human Rights and Its Five Protocols, **3104–3121**
European Credit Transfer System (ECTS), 2683
European Union (EU)
  economic development, 1251–1253
  student loans, 2380
  See also Eastern Europe and Central Asia; Europe; Western Europe
Evaluation
  academic advising, 3
  academic programs and majors, 22
  accelerated schools, 24
  in Bloom's taxonomy, 311
  career schools, 35
  case-based reasoning, 1158
  colleges and universities, 32
  compensatory education effectiveness, 457–458
  elementary curriculum, 719
  family support services, 832
  foreign transcripts, 1311–1312
  full-service schools, 908–909
  geographic learning, 927–928
  Graduate Record Examination (GRE), 964
  guidance and counseling, school, 977
  higher education, 2497–2498
  military training methods, 1657–1658
  moral education, 1687–1688
  of National Assessment of Educational Progress (NAEP), 132–133
  Paideia program, 1842
  research for, 2022
  school and program evaluation research methods, **2030–2034**
  school-based service outcomes, 2145–2147
  technology in higher education, 2525–2526
  testing as, 2588
  Upward Bound program, 2604
  youth development programs, 2713–2715
  See also Assessment; Teacher evaluation
Evan B. Donaldson Adoption Institute, 813
Evans, Norman, 762
Evergreen State College, 1214
Everson v. Board of Education, 2423
Every Child a Scientist (National Research Council), 2162
Evidence
  informal reasoning, 1446–1448
  research, 2021
  tradeoffs scoring guide, *143*
Evocative teaching, 2438–2439
Evolutionary theory of development, **571–574**
Examples *vs.* definitions in teaching new concepts, 248
Excellence and Equity, 1717–1718
Excellence educational reform movement, 173, 690–691
Excellence in Pre-College Physics Teaching Award, 98
Exceptional changers, 332
Exchange programs
  American Abroad Program, 2718
  Department of Education, U.S., 2619–2620
  Exchange Programs and Regional Services, IIE, 1137
  exchange students, 1136–1138
  western Europe, 2682, 2683
  See also International students; Study abroad

Exchange Programs and Regional Services, IIE, 1137
Executive committees, 192
Executive educational programs, 220
Executive Management Committee, Department of Education, 2617
Executive Order 11246, 64
Executive Order 11375, 64
Exemplars, handwriting, 987–988
Exemptions, copyright, 1188–1189
Exhibitions. *See* Museums
Expanding communities approach to social studies, 2266
Expansion, higher education, 1027–1029
Ex parte Crouse, 1350
Expectancy-value theory of motivation, 1691–1692, 1696, 1865
Expectations
  classroom management, 300–301
  student/teacher, 974
  undergraduate education, 518
Expectations of Excellence: Curriculum Standards for Social Studies (National Council for the Social Studies), 2266
Expected Family Contribution (EFC), 376
Expeditionary Learning, 85
Expenditures
  community colleges, 880–883, *881, 882*
  higher education, 26, 870, 2048
  international comparisons, 1288
  projecting, **659–660**
  state level, *660, 661*
  state services, 2342–2343
  See also Budgeting; Economics of education; Finance
Experience and Education (Dewey), 579, 760–761
The Experienced Hand: A Student Manual for Making the Most of an Internship (Stanton and Ali), 1326
Experiential learning, **760–763**
  alternative education, 85
  career development, 242
  Dewey, John, 579–580
  English education, 741
  Experiential Learning: Experience as the Source of Learning (Kolb), 762
  Hahn, Kurt, 981–982
  undergraduate education, 518
  See also Internships; Service learning
Experiential Learning: Experience as the Source of Learning (Kolb), 762
Experimental and Quasi-Experimental Designs for Generalized Causal Inference (Shadish, Cook and Campbell), 2024
Experimental College, University of Wisconsin, 1587–1588
Experimentalism, 1380
Experimental research, 2023–2024, 2031, 2229
Expertise, **763–767**
  adaptive, **763–765**
  anchored instruction, 1151
  domain, **765–767**
  history learning, 1052–1053
  knowledge and, 1114
  problem solving, 569
  See also Mastery learning
Explanation in texts, 1994
Explicit memory, 1596–1599, 1606, 1609–1610
Exploration, research for, 2022
Exploratory architectures, 1160
Exponential majors, 1087
Exports, educational services, 423–424
Expository texts, 1996
Exposure to alcohol, tobacco and other drugs, children's, 815–816, *816*
Extended-year programs, 2409–2411
Extension services
  faculty role, 792
  family and consumer sciences, 804, 806
  4-H programs, 2728
  rural education, 2088
External accountability, 655
External audits, 1955
Externalities, 648, 649, 950
Externalizing behavior problems, 1912
Extracurricular activities, **373–376,** 1127–1128
  See also Student activities; Youth organizations and clubs
Extra learning opportunities (ELOs), 1777
Extrinsic reinforcers, 1695
Eyler, Janet, 2204, 2207

F

FAA (Federal Aviation Administration), 849
Face-name mnemonic technique, 1670–1671
Facilitators, problem-based learning, 1173–1174
Facilities, **2124–2131**
  capital outlay, 887
  data, college and university, 1145–1146
  design, 2125, 2126–2127, 2577
  maintenance and modernization, **2128–2131**
  overview, **2124–2128**
  residence halls, 343
  rural, 2086
  secondary schools, 2192
  See also Architecture
Facing the Challenge: The Report of the Twentieth Century Task Force on School Governance (report), 2105, 2115
Fact books, college and university, 1145
Factor analysis model, 141
Faculty
  advisers, 354
  assessment, **798–802**
  behavioral patterns and academic disciplines, 11, *13*
  career and technical education, 2648
  college teaching, **413–417**
  commuter students/faculty interaction, 452
  consulting, **772–775,** *774*
  deans, 3–4, 8–9
  demographics, 18–19, 777–778
  department chairpersons, **559–561**
  developers, 254–255
  developing nations, 1031–1032
  development, 560
  dismissal, grounds for, 14–16
  diversity, **775–779**
  entrepreneurship, **769–772,** 797–798
  ethics, 757–758
  faculty senates, 793, **794–796**
  first-year seminars, 400
  future faculty preparation programs, **909–913**
  gender, *777, 778*

harassment, 758
Harvard, 723
international issues, 1031–1032
labor market, **17–19**
Latin America, 1411
learning communities, 1455
living and learning centers, 1519
networking, 560
nondiscrimination, 758
non-tenure track, 19
as part of organizational structure, 386–387
part-time, 19, *777*, *778*, **779–782**
practitioner instructors, 1538–1539
race/ethnicity, *778*
recognition and rewarding, 560
reinforcement, 560
residential colleges, 2045, 2046
roles and responsibilities, 414–415, 417, **789–794, 796–798**
salaries, 18–19, 102, 346–347, 781
selection, 560
service role, **796–798**
sexual harassment, 758
social connectedness, 11
student evaluation of, 254, 414, 415–416, 788
teacher education faculty, 2441
teaching assessment, 414, 415–416, **798–802**
teaching improvement programs, **254–257**
team teaching, 1212–1213
technology and professors' roles, 2524
technology training, 2525
union movement, 103
unions, 110
See also Academic freedom; American Association of University Professors (AAUP); Faculty research

Faculty research, **782–789, 1144–1146**
academic freedom, 14
assessment, **786–789**
business involvement, 154, 791
consulting, impact of, 775
contractual, 770
doctoral, 595–596
earmarking, 154
entrepreneurship, 769–771, 797–798
ethics, 757–758, 759, 771
federal funding, 154, **853–861,** 862, 863–864, 1038
international issues, 1031
misconduct, 758, 1664
reporting findings, 2029
responsible conduct of research, 2039–2040
role of faculty, 791–792, 796–797
social connectedness, 11
teaching and, **2501–2504**
See also Industry-university research collaboration; Research methods; Research universities

Failure
families, 813
learning from, 1154–1155, 1158
See also Grade retention

Fairhope community, 1344–1345

Fairness, Access, Multiculturalism, and Equity (FAME) Initiative, 685

Fair use, 1188–1189, 2519

FAME (Fairness, Access, Multiculturalism, and Equity) Initiative, 685

Families
academic performance, influence on, 1835–1836
adoption, **813–815**
alcohol, tobacco, and other drug use, **815–817**
children's literature at home, 287
college students and family dynamics, 1871–1872
dropout rates, 600
family composition and circumstance, **807–820**
family day homes, 271
family preservation, 269, 282, 284, 818
foster care, **817–820**
health education involvement, 1007, 1014
income support, **833–836**
interaction, 808–809
poverty and home environment, 1907
school involvement with, **821–828**
social capital, 2242–2243
See also Family support services; Low income families; Parents and parenting

Families and Schools in a Pluralistic Society (Dauber and Epstein), 1845
Family, Career and Community Leaders of America (FCCLA), 804
Family and consumer sciences education, **802–807**
Family Day Care Rating Scale, 271
Family Education Rights and Privacy Act (FERPA), 2013–2015
Family planning services, 2072
Family Preservation and Support Initiative, 269
Family Resource Coalition. *See* Family Support America
Family Stress Model, 1912–1913
Family Support Act of 1988 (FSA), 2677
Family Support America, 831
Family support services, **828–835**
academic achievement, 1838
child abuse and neglect, 269
family composition and circumstance, 811
foster care, 818
full-service schools, 906–909
poverty, 1913–1914
school-linked, 2142
Family Violence Prevention and Services Act, 2633
Fancher, Raymond, 186
Fantuzzo, John, 490
FAO (Food and Agriculture Organization), 1264
Farivar, Sydney, 491
Farm and Foreign Agricultural Services (FFAS), 840
Farrington, David, 1360
Farrington v. Tokushige, 1925, 2336
Faure Report (UNESCO), 1481
Fawcett, Harold P., **835–836**
FBI National Academy, 846
FBLA (Future Business Leaders of America), 218–219, **2729–2730**
FCC (Federal Communications Commission), 656
FCCLA (Family, Career and Community Leaders of America), 804
FDA (Food and Drug Administration), 845

FD (Fifth Dimension Project), 1512
Feder, Ned, 2039
Federal Aviation Administration (FAA), 849
Federal Board for Vocational Education, 73
Federal Bureau of Prisons, 846
Federal Communications Commission (FCC), 656–657
Federal government. *See* Government, U.S.
Federal government (Canada), 235–237
Federal Highway Administration (FHWA), 849–850
Federal Highway Safety Act, 598
Federal Interagency Committee on Education (FICE), **864–865**
Federal Law Enforcement Center, 852
Federal Methodology for defining financial aid need, 376, 378
Federal Motor Carrier Safety Administration (FMCSA), 851
Federal Motor Vehicle Safety Standards, 2574
Federal Railroad Administration (FRA), 850
The Federal Register, 1732, 2038
Federal Relations Network, National School Boards Association, 1785
Federal Republic of Yugoslavia. *See* Eastern Europe and Central Asia
Federal Transit Administration (FTA), 850
Federal Vocational Education Act. *See* Smith-Hughes Act
Federation of Regional Accrediting Commissions in Higher Education (FRACHE), 32
Fee, John G., 171
Feiman-Nemser, Sharon, 1891
Feldman, Kenneth, 332–333, 416, 2502
Felig, Philip, 20399
Fellowships
- American Association of University Women (AAUW), 104
- American Council of Learned Societies, 105–106
- Beta Phi Mu, 1071
- Bureau of Educational and Cultural Affairs (ECA), 847–848
- International Fellowships Program, 1138
- Kappa Omicron Nu, 1076
- National Endowment for the Arts, 1772
- Senior Research Fellow Program, 847
- Smithsonian Institution, 2240
- Spencer Foundation, 1811
- Tau Beta Pi, 1085
- teaching improvement, 256
- White House Fellows program, **2686–2688**
- *See also* Grants; Nongovernmental organizations (NGOs) and foundations; Scholarships

Felner, Robert, 1633
Felton, Agostini v., 2423
Fennema, Elizabeth, 305
Fenske, Robert, 2389
Ferguson, Plessy v. See Plessy v. Ferguson
FERPA (Family Educational Rights and Privacy Act of 1974), 2013–2015
Fertility and education, 1901–1903
Feuerstein, Reuben, 128
FFA (Future Farmers of America), **2734–2736**
FFAS (Farm and Foreign Agricultural Services), 840
FHA (Future Homemakers of America), 804
FHWA (Federal Highway Administration), 849–850
Fichte, Gottlieb, 1876
Fidler, William P., 102
Field experience
- educational research, 2027–2028
- physical education teacher education, 1893
- teacher education, 2440–2441
- *See also* In-service training

Fields of study. *See* Academic majors; Disciplines
Fifth Dimension Project (FD), 469, 1512
50 Hours: A Core Curriculum for College Students (report), 515
FIGs (freshmen interest groups), 44
Figurative thought, 1897–1898
Fillmore, Millard, 93
Filter-effect theory, 938–939
Final Regulations for Misconduct in Science and Engineering Research (National Science Foundation), 2037
Finance
- account systems, higher education, **25–26**
- capital assets, 26
- capital campaigns, 1142
- capital outlay, 870, **886–889,** 2340
- child care, **274–276**
- colleges and universities, 1023–1024
- committees, 192
- community colleges, **875–885,** 2393
- cost-reimbursement, research grants, 2019–2020
- decentralization, 542–543, 545–546
- decision-making, 547
- educational expenditures, college and university, 870
- educational policy, 671–672
- enrollment management and, 749
- financial compliance audits, 1955
- financial statements, 26
- health services, college and university, 1017
- higher education, **869–885,** 2360–2361
- institutional advancement, **1139–1144**
- institutional research, 1145
- intergovernmental relations, 1216–1217
- international higher education, 1032–1033
- public schools, **1952–1957,** 1954–1955
- research, 2019–2020
- resource allocation in higher education, **2047–2052**
- school facility costs, 2127, 2128–2129
- student activities, **2376–2377**
- *See also* Allocation; Commerce of education; Cost/benefit analysis; Costs; Economics of education; Expenditures; Funding

Financial Accounting for Local and State Schools Systems (Fowler), 1952
Financial aid
accreditation and, 33–34
college, **376–378**
College Scholarship Service, 373, 376
community colleges, 2392
dental schools, 558
Department of Education programs, 843
Department of Veterans Affairs programs, 852
federal, 862–863, 868, 1039
graduate study in education, 969
independent schools, 1743
merit *vs.* need-based, 398
need-based, 872
offices, 749
preschool, 616–617
student recruitment, 383–384, 397–398
See also Scholarships; Student loans
Findings, research, 2029
Finkelstein, Martin, 777
Finland, 2395
See also Western Europe
Finn, Chester, Jr., 1057
First amendment rights, 15, 2422–2423, 2425
First-year seminars, **399–401**
Fischer, Gerhard, 141
FISE (World Federation of Teachers' Unions), 1319–1321
Fish, Stanley, 2462
Fisher, Laura, 190
Fishman, Sylvia, 1340
Fitness. *See* Physical education
Fitzgerald, Jill, 1981
Five windows of the soul, 994
Fixed capital outlay, 2048
Flag of Learning and Liberty, 1787
Flanagan, Ann, 2536
Flanders, Ned, 2489
Flat grants, 890
Flavell, John H., 1470
Fleisch, Brahm, 727
Flesch, Rudolf, 258
FLES (foreign languages in elementary schools) programs, 896–897
Fletcher-Janzen, Elaine, 2294
FLEX (foreign language exploration or experience) programs, 897
Flexible production, 641
Flexner, Abraham, **891–893**
Florida, 2541
Florida State University, 2048
Flower, Linda, 2695
Fluency, reading, 1514–1515
Fluid block scheduling, 2096
Fluid intelligence, 1205
Flunking. *See* Failure; Grade retention
Fluoride, 555
FMCSA (Federal Motor Carrier Safety Administration), 851
FNCS (Food, Nutrition, and Consumer Service), 840
Foley, Douglas E., 938
Folk psychology, biology and physics, 572
Follow-up study, Aiken Commission, 708
Food, Nutrition, and Consumer Service (FNCS), 840–841
Food and Agriculture Organization (FAO), United Nations, 1264
Food and Drug Administration (FDA), 845
Food and Nutrition Service, USDA
National School Lunch Program, 2131–2136
School Breakfast Program, 2134
Food Safety and Inspection Service (FSIS), 841
Food service programs, 1006, **2131–2136**
Foorman, Barbara, 2009
Football, college, 359–361
Forced busing, 325, 326, 480
See also Segregation
Ford Foundation, 1138, 1807
Fordice, United States v., 2202
Foreign Assistance Act, 1242
Foreign language education, **893–900**
Alpha Mu Gamma, 1067
Latin, **1413–1417**
Lingua program (European Union), 1252
Modern Language Association of America (MLA), **1672–1674**
western Europe, 2682
Foreign Service Act, 113
Foreign Service Institute, 848–849
Foreign student advisers, 1313–1314
Foreign students. *See* International students
Forensics, 2299–2301, 2733–2734
Forkner, Hamden L., 2729
Formalism, 740–741
Formal operations, 1897
Formal reasoning, 1444–1445
Formative research, 1149
Formative teacher evaluation, 2454
Former Soviet Union, 627
Formula-based allocation, 2049
For-profit degree- and certificate-granting institutions, 1482
For-profit private schools, international, 1219
Forum (periodical), 2054–2055
Forum Series, Sigma Xi, 1084
Foshay, Arthur, 166
Foster, B. F., 988
Foster, Henry, 2062
Foster, Philip, 2655
Foster care, **817–820**
child protective services, 281–282, 284–285
family circumstance, 813–814, 814
See also Adoption; Child protective services
Fostering Communities of Learners (initiative), 1464–1465
A Foundation for Art Education (Barkan), 166
Foundation programs, 890
Foundations. *See* Nongovernmental Organizations (NGOs) and foundations
Founders Distinguished Senior Scholar Award, 104
Four Critical Years (Astin), 334–335
4-H programs, 320, 806, **2727–2728**
Fourteenth amendment
"adequacy," 479, 481–482, 672
affirmative action, 61–63
segregation cases, 478–480, 2199, 2423–2424, 2425
U.S. Constitution, 63
vocational education, 2637
See also Equity

4-youth program, 2088
Fox, Mary, 819
Foxfire, 85
FRACHE (Federation of Regional Accrediting Commissions in Higher Education), 32
FRA (Federal Railroad Administration), 850
Fraga, Luis, 663
Frames of Mind (Gardner), 1191
Frame theory, 1467
Frameworks of academic disciplines, 10–11
France
  Center for Finance, Business, and Banking Studies (CEFEB), 1244–1245
  elementary education, 711
  French Agency for Development (AFD), 1244–1245
  immigrant education, 1105
  international student recruitment, 1316
  Promotion and Participation for Economic Cooperation (Proparco), 1244
  school counseling, 978
  See also Europe; Western Europe
Francke, August Hermann, 1022
Frank, Lawrence, 623
Franklin, Benjamin, 1098
Fraternities and sororities
  drug and alcohol abuse, 607
  social, **2250–2253**
Frazer, Bethel School District No. 403 v., 2425
Frederick Burkhardt Residential Fellowships for Recently Tenured Scholars, 106
Free Application for Federal Student Aid (FAFSA), 376
Freedman, Sarah Warshauer, 2695
Freedman's Aid Society, 389
Freedmen's Bureau, 712, 2665
Freedom, academic. *See* Academic freedom
Freedom Schools, Mississippi, **1668–1669**
Freedom to Learn: A View of What Education Might Become (Rogers), 2078
Freeman, Howard, 2030
Freeman v. Pits, 2202
Free schools, 84
Free speech of students, 2425
Freire, Paulo, **900–903**
  Benne, Kenneth D., 170
  English education, 742
  reading instruction, 2002
French Agency for Development (AFD), 1244–1245
French Guiana. *See* Latin America and the Caribbean
Freshman seminars, **399–401**
Freshman-to-senior changes, 332–334
Freshman Year Experience housing, 2044
Freshmen interest groups (FIGs), 44
Fretageot, Marie Duclos, 1876
Freud, Sigmund, 277–278
Frick, Otto, 1022
Frick, Theodore, 1149
Friedman, Milton, 1927
Friesen, David, 48
Froebel, Friedrich, **903–906**
  Blow, Susan, 189–190
  early childhood education teacher preparation, 621
  Progressive education, 1934
  view on childhood, 2709
Froebel, Luise, 621, 622
Frost, William, 171
FSA (Family Support Act) of 1988, 2677
FSEA (Future Scientists and Engineers of America), **2730**
FSIS (Food Safety and Inspection Service), 841
FTA (Federal Transit Administration), 850
Fuchs, Doug, 2008
Fuchs, Ralph F., 102
Fulbright-Hays Act, 113, 2619–2620
Fulbright Scholar Program, 847, 1137
Fulbright Teacher Exchange program, 847
Fuller, Howard, 1928
Full-service schools, **906–909**
  health education, 1007
  youth development programs, 2711
Full-Service Schools: A Revolution in Health and Services for Children, Youth, and Families (Dryfoos), 906
Functional areas and decision-making, *543*
Functional communities, 1854, 1926
Functionalist theory of emotions, 59
Function/object budgeting, 1953
Functions, memory, **1609–1613**
Functions of Secondary Education (report), 696
Fundamentals of Education (Bode), 195
Fund for the Republic, 1095
Funding, school, **884–891**
  accountability, 653–654
  American Association of University Women (AAUW), 104
  average daily attendance (ADA) allocations, 2258, 2260
  Canada, 237
  capital outlay in local school systems, **886–889**
  Catholic schools, 251–252
  constitutional issues, 479, 481–482
  decentralization, 542–543, 545–546
  developing nations, 547
  disparities, 671–672
  early childhood education, international aspects of, 629, 631, 632
  East Asia and the Pacific, 635–637, *636*
  Eastern Europe and Central Asia region, 644
  educational technology, 2520
  equity, 692
  history, **884–886**
  intergovernmental relations, 1216–1217
  kindergarten, 615–616
  Magnet School Assistance Program, 1528–1529
  Middle East and North Africa, 1629
  modernization of facilities, 2130
  No Child Left Behind Act of 2001, 1802
  preschool, 616–617
  privatization of public schools, 1956
  public funding of private schools, 2337–2338
  public school organization and, 2256–2257, 2258–2259
  reform, 692

rural schools, 2085
Safe and Drug-Free Schools Program, 603
South Asia, 2275, *2277*
special education, 2288–2289
state administrative services, 2340–2342
state funded private schools, 953
state support, **889–891**
student activities, 2376–2377
Sub-Saharan Africa, 2402–2403, *2403*
summer school, 2410
Title I, Elementary and Secondary Education Act (ESEA), 454–456, 457–458
tribal colleges, 2579
tutoring, 2581
urban schools, 2608
vocational education, 2330
See also Economics of education; Finance; Revenue

Fundraising
academic deans, 8
organizational structure of colleges and universities, 386
student activities, 2377

Funds of Knowledge project, 1564

Furek v. University of Delaware, 2075

Future Business Leaders of America (FBLA), 218–219, **2729–2730**

Future directions
accreditation, 34
agricultural education, 79
brain-based education, 204–205
business education, 219
business teacher education, 225
capstone courses, 241
Catholic schools, 252
chief academic affairs officers' roles, 266
classroom observation, 309
college recruitment, 384
college teaching, 416
community colleges, 884
cultural expectations and learning research, 1964–1965
disabled college students, 412
distance learning, 593
dynamic assessment, 130
East Asia and the Pacific, 637–638
educational broadcasting, 657–658
educational technology, 2512
full-service schools, 909
future faculty preparation programs, 912
health services, school, 1015
home schooling, 1062
individual abilities and aptitudes, 1116
instructional design, 1150
intelligence testing, 1205
international baccalaureate (IB) diploma, 1240
international education, 1273
Latin in schools, 1416
Middle East and North Africa, education in, 1628–1629
motivation theory, 1694–1695
music education teacher preparation, 1724–1725
organizational structure of colleges and universities, 388
Outcome Based Education, 1830–1831
part-time faculty, 782
reading comprehension strategy instruction, 1983
religiously-affiliated colleges and universities, 392
research misconduct policy, 2040
service learning programs, 2205
standards movement, 2322
state boards of education, 2359
student services, 2393
study abroad, 2396
Sub-Saharan Africa, education in, 2402–2403
technology in the social studies, 2268
Western Europe, education in, 2683–2684

Future Farmers of America (FFA), **2734–2736**

Future-focused approach to Outcome Based Education, 1830

Future Homemakers of America (FHA), 804

Future Scientists and Engineers of America (FSEA), **2730**

G

GAAP (Generally Accepted Accounting Principles), 1954–1955

Gabelnick, Faith, 1453

Gabon. *See* Sub-Saharan Africa

Gabric, Daniela, 733, 734

Gadsden, Vivian, 2001

Gaff, Jerry G., 256

Gage, Nathaniel, 2442, 2482

Gagné, Robert, 1160, 1177

Gaining Early Awareness and Readiness for Undergraduate Programs (GEAR UP), 837

Galambos, Nancy, 1405

Gallagher, James, 311

Gallagher, Margaret C., 1978

Gallagher, Shelagh, 1174

Gallaudet, Thomas Hopkins, 1018

Gallaudet University, 469, 867

Gallimore, Ronald, 576

Gallo, Robert, 2039

Gal'perin, Piotr, 576

Galton, Francis, 1113, 1194, 1201

The Gambia. *See* Sub-Saharan Africa

Gambrell, Linda B., 1979

The Game of Life: College Sports and Educational Values (Bowen and Shulman), 352

Gamson, Zelda, 415, 2495

Gandhi's Truth: On the Origins of Militant Nonviolence (Erikson), 752

Gang Resistance Education and Training (GREAT), 54

Gangs, **51–54**
academic performance, 1837
appeal of, 53
crime and, 52–53
definition and characteristics, 51–52
increase in, 51
prevention and intervention, 53–54, 978
statistics, 1354
See also Peer culture, adolescent

Garcia, Paul, 895

Gardner, Howard
alternative schooling, 84
art education, 119
educational psychology, 680–681
emotional intelligence, 1191
multiple intelligences, 1115, 1198–1199
naturalist intelligence, 1834
triarchic theory of intelligence, 1209

Gardner, John W., 2017

Garner, Ruth, 1494, 1499

Garrett, Jimmy, 67

Gary Plan, **915–916**
De Lima, Agnes, 553
Progressive education, 1935
Gasaway, Laura, 1187
GASB (General Accounting Standards Board), 1954, 1955
Gas warfare, 471–472
GATB (General Aptitude Test Battery), 1113
The Gate of Languages Unlocked (Comenius), 420
Gates Millennium Scholars program, 1808
Gathercole, Susan E., 568
GATS (General Agreement on Trade in Services), 423–424, 1322–1323
Gault, In re, 1351
Gay, Geneva, 1963
Gay Academic Union, 917
Gay and lesbian students. *See* Sexual orientation
Gay and lesbian studies, **916–919**
Gay/Straight Alliances (GSAs), 2220
Gearhart, Maryl, 138
GEAR UP (Gaining Early Awareness and Readiness for Undergraduate Programs), 837
GED. *See* General Educational Development Test (GED)
Gee, James, 1510
Geiger, Philip E., 2128
Gelles, Richard, 2628
Gelsinger, Jesse, 2039
Gender
academic fields, 18
academic freedom and tenure, 15
academic labor market, 18
American Association of University Women (AAUW), **103–105**
Canadian college enrollment, 236
chief academic affairs officers, 265
coeducational residence halls, 342
earnings differences, 18–19
economic benefits of education investment, 648
equity, 104, **1125–1129**
faculty, 18–19, 775–778, *777*
faculty consulting, 774
family and consumer sciences education, 804
gangs, 52
graduate study in education, 967
health and education, 998–999
inequitable instruction, 305–306
intercollegiate athletics participation, 2571–2572
international early childhood education enrollment trends, 628–629
international issues, **919–921**
multicultural English, 743
part-time faculty, *778,* 779
Rousseau, Jean-Jacques, 2081
salaries, faculty, 18–19
school sports, 2306–2307, *2307, 2308, 2309,* 2569–2572
sex-based segregation, 2202
sexual orientation and, 2218
student employment, 728–729
teacher salary, 2437
technology, 2519
technology education, 2508
Terman's standardized personality tests, 2529
women's studies, **2686–2688**
See also Boys; Girls; Title IX, Higher Education Act; Women
Genealogical intelligence studies. *See* Intelligence, genetics
General Accounting Office, U.S., 2639
General Accounting Standards Board (GASB), 1954, 1955
General Agreement on Trade in Services (GATS), 423–424, 1322
General aid to schools, 890
General Aptitude Test Battery (GATB), 1113
General assistance programs, 834
General Declaration of Principles and Practical Proposals (American Association of University Professors), 101, 102, 789–790
General education
college, 995
common curriculum for democratic society, 210–211
in curriculum development, 193–194
curriculum requirements, 522
curriculum study, 80–81
democratic society, 211
The Dissolution of General Education, 517
higher education, **923–925**
Hutchins, Robert, 1094–1095
inclusion of learning disabled students, 1458
interdisciplinarity, 1211–1212
multiculturalism, 1711–1714
special education and, 2282, 2285–2286
specialization *vs.,* 74–78
teacher education, 2446
undergraduate, 516–517, 522
General Educational Development Test (GED), **921–923**
lifelong learning, 1481
Lindquist, E. F., 1841
General Education Board, Rockefeller Foundation, 996–997
General expenditures, college and university, 870
General fraternities and sororities. *See* Social fraternities and sororities
General honors, 1087
General intelligence, 1194–1197, 1202
"'General Intelligence': Objectively Determined and Measured" (Spearman), 1194, 1195
Generalist approaches to psychometric modeling, 142
Generalizability and comparability, assessment
performance assessment, 135
portfolio assessment, 138
Generalizability theory (GT), 140, 1486
Generalizable *vs.* local knowledge, 1149–1150
General knowledge and school readiness, 2150
Generally Accepted Accounting Principles (GAAP), 1954–1955
General Motors Institute (GMI), 493
Genetic epistemology, 1895–1898
Genetics
behavior problems, 71
development, 563
intelligence, 941, 1115, 1196–1197, 1204, 2567
race/ethnicity and academic achievement, 1962
Gentner, Dedre, 1421
Geographic cost differences and school funding, 891
Geography education, **926–928**

Geometry education, **1548–1550**
  design approach, 1165
  Fawcett, Harold P., 835–836
George, Paul S., 1521
George-Barden Act, 2647
George-Deen Act, 976, 2647
Georgia
  ESFL model programs, 897
  Sabbath schools, 2665
Georgia Female College, 2225
German immigrants, 1098–1099
German Organization for Technical Cooperation, 1248
Germany
  academic freedom, 20
  continuing professional education (CPE), 487–488
  desegregation, 1105
  faculty research and scholarship, 783
  Froebel, Friedrich, 904–905
  German Organization for Technical Cooperation, 1248
  higher education model, 10
  higher education reform, 1029
  immigrant education, 1105
  kindergarten movement, 189–190, 622, 904–905
  Progressive education movement, 1367–1368
  roots of academic freedom, 14
  Waldorf School, 2365–2366
  See also Europe; Western Europe
Gersten, Russell, 1457
Getty Center for Education in the Arts, 118, 1722
"The g Factor" (Jensen), 1196
Ghana, 612, 2655–2656
  See also Sub-Saharan Africa
G.I. Bill. *See* Servicemen's Readjustment Act
Giardino v. State Board of Education, 887–888
Gibson, Eleanor, 1437, 1439
Gibson, James, 1439
Gick, Mary, 1450
Gifted and talented students, **930–936**
  Council for Exceptional Children (CEC), 499–500
  intelligence measurement, 1195
  special education, 2287
  summer enrichment programs, **2407–2409**
  Terman's study of, 2529
  See also Special education
Giles, Dwight, 2204, 2207
Gilligan, Carol, 755, 1682
Gillingham, Mark G., 1499
Gilman, Daniel Coit, 725, 1343, 2042
Gimmestad, Beverly, 1707
Gingiss, Phyllis, 1008–1009
Girls
  access to schooling, 1301
  Daytona Normal and Industrial Institute for Negro Girls, 174
  dropout rates, 600
  gang members, 52
  inequity in schooling, 1126–1128
  secondary schools, 2184
  teenage pregnancy, 978, 2061–2064, 2067, 2071–2074
  See also Gender
Girl Scouts of the USA, **2731**
Gitomer, Drew, 142
Glass, Gene, 314
Glassick, Charles, 786, 787–788
Gleazer, Edmund J., Jr., 96, 445
Glenn, Charles, 1927
Global Campaign for Education, 1804
Global Educators Program, 2718
Global Forum on Management Education, 1
Globalization, **936–940**
  accreditation, 27
  commerce, educational, 425–426
  curriculum and, 525–528
  Eastern Europe and Central Asia, 641
  educational policy, 669
  small nations, 2236
  See also International issues
Global Learning and Observations to Benefit the Environment (GLOBE) project, 2180
Global Perspectives for Local Action: Using TIMSS to Improve U.S. Mathematics and Science Education (National Research Council), 1730
Global studies. *See* International education
GLOBE (Global Learning and Observations to Benefit the Environment) project, 2180
GMI (General Motors Institute), 493
Goal-based scenarios, 1155–1156
Goal-free program evaluation, 2032
Goals 2000: Educate America Act
  art education, 118
  business education, 216, 217
  civic education, 294–295
  Council of Chief State School Officers, 502
  federal involvement in education, 838
  national achievement tests, 2546
  school readiness, 277
  school reform, 2155
  science education standards, 2174
  Title IX, 2017
Goddard, Henry H., **940–942**
Goethe Institute, 899
Goggin, Catharine, 983, 984, 985
Golden Anniversary White House Conference on Children and Youth, 1758
Goldhammer, Robert, 2418–2419
Goldman, Susan R., 1995
Goldstein, Alice, 1340
Goleman, Daniel, 1199
Gompers, Samuel, 111
Gong Lum v. Rice, 1100
Gonorrhea, 2065
Good, Mary L., 93
Good, Thomas
  classroom observation, 304, 305, 306
  classroom questions, 312
  teacher evaluation, 2454
Goodlad, John, 761, 2555
Goodman, Paul, **942–943**
Goodwich, Samuel Griswold, 1178
Gorman-Smith, Deborah, 2529
Goslin, Willard E., **943–945**
Goss v. Lopez, 2425
Gould, Stephen Jay, 93
Governance
  Accelerated Schools, 24
  alternative school, 85
  American overseas schools, 114
  Board of trustees, **191–192**
  colleges and universities, 102, **945–949**
  democracy's influence, 1269
  Eastern Europe and Central Asia region education systems, 644–645
  faculty involvement, 797
  faculty roles and responsibilities, 793

faculty senates, 793, **794–796**
higher education, 2360–2363
integrated, 2106
international higher education, 1030, 1031
public schools, 1949, 2254
religiously affiliated colleges and universities, 391–392
residential colleges, 2044–2045
school-based decision-making, **2099–2102**
school boards, **2102–2121**
state boards of education, **2350–2359,** *2352–2356*
state educational systems, **2331–2334**
Statement on College and University Government (American Association of University Professors), 102, 794
student participation, 295
superintendents, **2411–2418**
U.S. Air Force Academy, 1643
U.S. Coast Guard Academy, 1646
vocational education, 2329–2330
See also Administration, educational; Decentralization; Decision-making

Governing boards, college and university. *See* Board of trustees

Government, U.S.
academic research funding, **853–861,** 862, 863–864, 1038
agency educational activities, **840–853**
Association of American Universities' relationship with, 154
capital outlay support, 888
child care funding, 275
child protection statutes, 282–283, 283–284
compensatory programs, 453–458, 1948
consortia, 477
continuing professional education (CPE), 484
contracts, 209–210
Country Life Commission, 74
disabled persons, assistance programs for, **1867–1869**
early childhood education initiatives, 623
earmarking research dollars, 154
educational activities, **836–853**
educational broadcasting, **656–658**
education policy, 227–228
financial aid and accreditation, 33–34
financial aid to states, 2324–2325, 2333–2334, 2341–2342
financial support for higher education, **861–865**
Gallaudet University, 867
grants, 871–872
higher education funding, 871–872, *873,* 1025
history of participation in education, **836–840**
Howard University, 867, 868
Magnet School Assistance Program, 1528–1529
Migrant Education Program (MEP), 1640–1641
minority student programs, 1970–1971
National School Lunch Program, 2131–2134
National Telecommunications and Information Administration (NTIA), 657
Office of Civil Rights, Department of Education, 2571
Office of Economic Opportunity, 2677
overseas schools, 112–115
partnership with states, 2324–2325
preschool initiatives, 616–617
regional laboratories and research and development centers, **2017–2019**
reinventing government, 691
research and development funding, *854, 856, 857, 858, 859,* 862, 863–864
research funding, 1091–1092, 1789
research grants, **2019–2020**
research misconduct policy, 2037–2038
role in college choice, 395–396
rural education programs, 2088
school boards and policy, 2113
School Breakfast Program (SBP), 2134
school funding, 886
schools and colleges, **865–869**
secondary school programs, 2192–2193
secondary schools and funds, 2191
special education funding, 2288
special education teacher education, 2290
student financial aid, 376–377, 2392
substance abuse education programs, 608
tribal colleges funding, 2579
TRIO programs, 1971, 2603
Upward Bound (UB) program, 1970–1971, **2603–2605**
Veteran's Upward Bound (VUB) program, 2604
vocational education funding, 73, 2330
welfare policy, 2676–2677
welfare reform, 2673–2674
White House Fellows program, **2686–2688**
See also Head Start program

Government agencies and offices, U.S.
Bureau of Education, 2615
Bureau of Educational and Cultural Affairs (ECA), 113, 847–848
Bureau of Export Administration (BXA), 841
Bureau of Indian Affairs (BIA), 712, 2187
Bureau of Labor Statistics, 847
Bureau of Transportation Statistics, 851
Centers for Disease Control and Prevention (CDC), 1004, 1013–1014, 2065–2066, 2068
Children's Bureau, 2676
Coast Guard, U.S., 849
Combined Arms and Services Staff School, U.S. Army, 1654
Command General Staff College, U.S. Army, 1654–1655
Commissioner of Education, 199–200
Commission on Higher Education, 96
Congressional Office of the Budget, 210
Corporation for National Service, 2207
Country Life Commission, 74
Department of Agriculture, 840–841, 857–858, 2131–2136
Department of Agriculture Graduate School, 868

Department of Defense, 842–843, 858
Department of Defense Dependent Schools (DoDDS), 112–114, 838, 843, 866
Department of Education, 33–34, 715, 839, 843–844, 2152, **2614–2619, 2614–2620, 2619–2620**
Department of Energy, 858
Department of Energy, U.S., 844
Department of Health, Education, and Welfare (HEW), 839, 2615
Department of Health and Human Services, 844–845
Department of Housing and Urban Development, 845
Department of Justice, 846
Department of Labor, 729, 846–847
Department of State, 113–114, 847–849, 1138
Department of the Interior, 845
Department of the Treasury, 852
Department of Transportation, 849–851
Department of Veterans Affairs, 852
Educational Resources Information Center (ERIC), **683–684,** 843, 1832
Equal Employment Opportunity Commission (EEOC), 62, 64
Federal Board for Vocational Education, 73
Federal Communications Commission (FCC), 656–658
Federal Interagency Committee on Education, **864–865**
Federal Law Enforcement Center, 852
Federal Motor Carrier Safety Administration (FMCSA), 851
Federal Railroad Administration (FRA), 850
Federal Transit Administration (FTA), 850
General Accounting Office, U.S., 2639
Higher Education Center for Alcohol and Other Drug Prevention, 608
Immigration and Naturalization Service (INS), 1312
National Archives and Records Administration (NARA), **1731–1734**
National Cancer Institute, 1092
National Center for Education Statistics (NCES), **1756–1757**
National Highway Traffic Safety Administration (NHTSA), 598, 2575
National Institute of Child Health and Human Development (NICHD), 183
National Institute of Education (NIE), 2017
National Institutes of Health, 845, 855, 857, 2039–2040
National Telecommunications and Information Administration (NTIA), 657
National Training Center (NTC), U.S. Army, 1657–1658
Office of Civil Rights, Department of Education, 2571
Office of Economic Opportunity, 2677
Office of Education, 838–839, 2614–2615
Office of Educational Research and Improvement (OERI), 183, 838, 2017–2018, 2088
Office of Elementary and Secondary Education, Department of Education, 2618
Office of Federal Contract Compliance Programs (OFCCP), 62, 64
Office of Global Education Programs, 847
Office of Indian Education Programs (OIEP), 866
Office of Justice Programs, 846
Office of Juvenile Justice and Delinquency Prevention, DOJ, 1354–1355
Office of Legislative and Congressional Affairs, Department of Education, 2618
Office of Management, Department of Education, 2617–2618
Office of Naval Research (ONR), 855
Office of Overseas Schools (OOS), 112
Office of Overseas Schools (OOS), State Department, 112, 113
Office of Postsecondary Education, Department of Education, 2618
Office of Presidential Libraries, National Archives and Records Administration, 1733
Office of Records Services, National Archives and Records Administration, 1732
Office of Science and Technology Policy (OSTP), 2038
Office of Scientific Research and Development (OSRD), 855
Office of Special Education and Rehabilitative Services, Department of Education, 2619
Office of the Chief Financial Officer, Department of Education, 2618
Office of the Chief Information Officer, Department of Education, 2618
Office of the Federal Register, 1732
Office of the General Counsel, Department of Education, 2617
Office of the Inspector General, Department of Commerce, 842
Office of the Inspector General, Department of Education, 2617
Office of Vocational and Adult Education, Department of Education, 2619
Office of Vocational Rehabilitation and Employment, VA, 852
Public Health Service (PHS), 2037, 2038
Regional Educational Laboratories, 2088
Training and Doctrine Command (TRADOC), U.S. Army, 1657
United States Agency for International Development (USAID), 113, 1241–1242
Works Progress Administration (WPA), 623

See also Military, U.S.; National Science Foundation (NSF)
Government Employee Training Act, 840
Governments, international
educational spending, 547, 548, 629, 631, 632
higher education regulation, 27
role in education, **949–954**
See also Decentralization; Developing nations; International issues
Governors and state boards of education, 2358
Goyette-Ewing, Michele, 1405
GPA. *See* Grade point average (GPA)
Gracy, Delgado v., 2094
GradeMap software, *142, 144*
Grade point average (GPA)
college admissions, 329, 331
higher education, 960–961
student athletes, *360,* 360–361
Grade retention, 2262–2264
Grade structure, 1631–1633
Grading systems, **954–962**
advanced placement examinations, 57–58
higher education, **960–962**
school, **954–959**
See also Assessment; Nongraded schools; Tests
Gradual exit model of secondary language acquisition, 177
Graduate and Professional Education Division, ETS, 685
Graduate education, **965–967**
academic calendars, 5, 6
academic labor market, 17–18
admissions, 963–964, 968–969
Brookings Institution, 208
business, 220–221, 222
doctoral degrees, **595–596**
education degrees, 967–970
engineering, 738–739
future faculty preparation programs, **909–913**
Harvard, 723
joint degrees, 221
medical education, 1586
nursing, 1819–1820
physical education teacher education, 1891
rankings, 378–379
student services programs, 2388
teaching assistants, 910–912
U.S. Air Force Academy, 1644
women's studies, 2689
Yale University, 2697
See also Doctoral degree programs; Higher education; Master's degree programs
Graduate Record Examination (GRE), **962–965,** 968
Graduation
accountability, 654
commencement exercises, **422–423**
service learning, 2203–2204
test requirements, 2539–2540, 2541
volunteer service, 2657
Graduation rates
college athletes, 359–360
secondary education, 2191–2192, 2706, 2707, *2708*
Graff, Harvey, 1516
Graham, Amy, 380
Grammar, 1385, 1391
A Grammatical Institute of the English Language (Webster), 2670, 2671, 2672
Grand teaching style, 160
Grant, Carl, 1963
Grant, Gerald, 2246
Grants
Administration for Children and Families (ACF), 844
American Association of University Women (AAUW), 104
arts programs, 1772–1773
Carnegie Corporation of New York, 1806–1807
categorical, 890–891
Charles Stewart Mott Foundation, 1808
federal, 837
Ford Foundation, 1807
humanities programs, 1774
Japan International Cooperation Agency, 1245
Kappa Omicron Nu, 1076
Lilly Endowment, 1808
magnet schools, 1528–1529
migrant students, 1640–1641
National Association of Secondary School Principals, 1747
National Council of Teachers of Mathematics, 1768
National Endowment for the Arts, 1772
National Endowment for the Humanities, 1774–1775
research, **2019–2020**
Sigma Xi, 1084
Smith Richardson Foundation, 1809
state programs for school districts, 890–891
student aid, 377
teaching improvement, 256
Trust to Reach Education Excellence (TREE), 1747
See also Fellowships; Nongovernmental organizations (NGOs) and foundations; Scholarships
Graphic organizers and reading comprehension, 1980
Graphics. *See* Multimedia; Visual media
Graphing calculators, 1551
Graphs, 1595
Gratz v. Bollinger
affirmative action, 63, 65
college search and selection, 397
Gray, Asa, 93
Gray, Charlene, 2204, 2207
Gray, Eddie, 1561
Gray, Marianne J., 2207
Gray, William S., **970–971,** 1999
Great Books program
Buchanan, Scott, 212
interdisciplinarity, 1213–1214
St. John's College, 2366–2367
Great Britain. *See* England
Great Depression
college enrollment, 1037
secondary education, 2187
social welfare programs, 2676–2677
Great Didactic (Comenius), 420
GREAT (Gang Resistance Education and Training), 54
"Great Transformation," 235
Greece. *See* Western Europe
Green, Burt, 1194
Green, Kenneth, 2522
Green, Thomas F., 261
Green, William J., 1210
Greenberg, James, 1564
Greene, Jay, 1927
Greeno, James, 1149, 1559, 1561
Green v. School Board of New Kent County, **2839–2844**
constitutional issues, 480
segregation, 2201
Supreme Court cases, 2424

Gregg, Robert, 215
GRE (Graduate Record Examination), **962–965,** 968
Grenada. *See* Latin America and the Caribbean
Griffin, Sharon, 1560
Griffin v. County School Board, 2424
Grimshaw, William, 663
Grissmer, David, 2536
Grobstein, Paul, 203
Grolnick, Wendy S., 1844
Groneman, Nancy, 223
Gross enrollment ratio, 627–629
Grossman, Pamela, 746
Grouping, abilities, 681, 932
Group processes in the classroom, **971–975**
Groups
collaborative learning, 490–492
intergroup relations, 1861–1863
rights, 662–663
Groves, Betsy, 2628
Growing Up Absurd (Goodman), 942
"Growing Without Schooling" (newsletter), 1059–1060
Growth, physical
adolescence, 278
early childhood, 276–277
middle childhood, 278
The Growth of American Thought (Curti), 540
Growth Through English (Dixon), 740–741
Gruener, Anton, 904
Grumet, Board of Education of Kiryas Joel v., 2423
Grutter v. Bollinger
affirmative action, 63, 65
college search and selection, 397
Grzondziel, Harriet, 1494
GSAs (Gay/Straight Alliances), 2220
GT (generalizability theory), 140
GTZ (Deutsche Gesselschaft fur Technische Zusammenarbeit, Germany), 1248
Guadeloupe. *See* Latin America and the Caribbean
Guaranteed yield programs, 890
Guatemala. *See* Latin America and the Caribbean
Guidance and counseling, 826, **975–980**
See also Academic advising, higher education; Counseling
Guided discovery, 1160
Guided peer questioning, 490
Guided reading, 2005
Guidelines for Art Instruction through Television for the Elementary School (Barkan and Chapman), 166
Guidelines for Comprehensive Sexuality Education: Kindergarten-Twelfth Grade (Sexuality Information and Education Council of the United States), 2214
Guidelines for Preparation of Early Childhood Professionals (National Association for the Education of Young Children), 625
Guidelines for School and Community Programs (report), 1888
Guide to the Evaluation of Educational Experiences in the Armed Services (ACE), 1478, 1479
Guilford, Joy Paul, 680
Guinea-Bissau. *See* Sub-Saharan Africa
Guizot, Francois, 711
Gump, Paul, 301
Gumperz, John, 2462
Guskey, Thomas, 2471
Gustafsson, Jan-Eric, 1114–1115
Guthrie, John, 1513
Guthrie Independent School District, Swanson v., 1062
Gutmann, Amy, 754
Guyana. *See* Latin America and the Caribbean

H

Haberman, Martin, 2609
Habermas, Jurgen, 170
Habit, 1335–1336
HACU (Hispanic Association of Colleges and Universities), 1046, 1047
Hadow Report (England), 1825
Haemophilus influenzae, 1107
Haertel, Edward, 141, 142
The Hague Recommendations, 2248
Hahn, Kurt, 761, **981–982**
Haimson, Joshua, 731
Haiti. *See* Latin America and the Caribbean
Haley, Margaret, **982–985**
Hall, G. Stanley, **985–987**
educational psychology, 677
Putnam, Alice, 1958
research universities, 2042
view on adolescents, 2709
Hall, John W., 2074
Hall directors, 341–342
Halliday, M. A. K., 1388–1389
Halpern, Diane, 1426
Halpin, Andrew, 2122
Hambleton, Ronald, 140
Hambrecht, William, 167
Hamburg, David, 1633
Hamilton, David, 307
Hamlin, Herbert, 76
Hammer, Carol Schneffer, 1511
Hampshire College, 1214
Hampton Institute, 2664
Hancock, John, 87
Handbook II. See Financial Accounting for Local and State Schools Systems (Fowler)
The Handbook of Alternative Education (Mintz), 85
The Handbook of Research of Multicultural Education (Banks and Banks), 1706
Handicapped students. *See* Disabled students
Handwriting, **987–990**
Hanna, Paul R., **990–991,** 2266
Hannah, Larry, 2433
Hannam, Shaftsburg v. (England), 280–281
Hans Christian Andersen prize, 289
Hanson, Thomas, 1906
Hanushek, Eric, 316, 551
Harassment, 758, 2076
Hare, Nathan, 67
Hare, Victoria, 1468
Hargens, Lowell L., 12
Harlem Renaissance, 611
Harley, Carolyn, 730
Harmon, Hobart L., 2088
Harms, Thelma, 271
Harper, William Rainey, **991–993**
college athletics, 349

community colleges, 442
research universities, 2042
University of Chicago, 2597–2598
Harris, Joseph, 2462
Harris, William T., **993–994**
Blow, Susan, 190
early childhood education, 622
efforts to stop Herbartianism, 1022
Froebel, Friedrich, 905
Harrison, Elizabeth, 190, 622
Harrison, Norwood v., 2424
Hart, Laurie, 305–306
Hartman, William, 1952
Harty, H., 2164
Harvard Graduate School of Education, 1365
Harvard University, **994–996**
admissions requirement, 2163
African-American studies, 66
beginnings, 389
Conant, J. B., 471–474
Eliot's presidency, 723–725
football, 348–349, 350
Hatano, Giyoo, 763–765
Hatch Act, 73
Hattie, John, 762, 2502
Hauenstein, Dean, 2433
Havighurst, Robert J., **996–998**
Hawaii, 2466
Hawkins -Stafford Amendments of 1988, 455
Haworth, Jennifer Grant, 521
Hayes, John, 2695
Hazelwood School District v. Kuhlmeier, 2425
Hazing, 2251, 2252–2253
HBCUs. *See* Historically black colleges and universities (HBCUs)
HCFA (Health Care Financing Administration), 844
Head Start program, **3081–3084**
benefits, 619
Bloom, Benjamin S., 188
compensatory education, 456–458
federal involvement in education, 844
infant schools' influence, 1135
National Association for the Education of Young Children (NAEYC), 1737
overview, 616
professional development and in-service training, 624
teachers, 618, 624
See also Early childhood education; Preschool education; Readiness, school
Health and nutrition, **998–999, 1821–1822**
academic performance, 1836–1837
child care, 273
dental health, **554–557**
HIV/AIDS, 2058–2059
immunization, **1106–1108**
poverty, 808, 1910–1911
school food programs, **2131–2136**
sexuality health, 2213–2217
sexually transmitted diseases (STIs), 2058, **2064–2066**
sleep, **2231–2234**
smoking, **2066–2068**
sports participation, 2314
television viewing, 1582
young children, 626–627
See also Health care; Health education; Health services
Health care, **1000–1003**
health maintenance organizations (HMOs), 1530–1532
insurance, 1837
Jeanes teachers, 1339
low-income children, 808
managed care for children, **1529–1534**
Medicaid, 1530–1531, 2674
State Children's Health Insurance Plan (SCHIP), 2674
See also Health and nutrition; Health education; Health services
Health Care Financing Administration (HCFA), 844
Health care paraprofessionals, 110–111
Health Care Quality First (initiative), 111
Health education, **1003–1012**
American Alliance for Health, Physical Education, Recreation, and Dance (AAHPERD), 88
American Association for Health Education (AAHE), 89
dental health, 555–556
World Health Organization (WHO), 1263
See also Health and nutrition; Health care; Health services; Physical education
Health Maintenance Organization Act, 1530
Health maintenance organizations (HMOs), 1530–1532
Health Research Extension Act of 1985, 2037
Health services, **1012–1017**
colleges and universities, **1016–1017**
school, 1005, **1012–1016**
See also Health and nutrition; Health care; Health education; School-linked services
Healthy Meals for Children Act, 2134
Healthy People 2000 (report), 1888
Healthy Start Initiative (California), 832
Healy, William, 2710
Hearing impairment, **1017–1021**
Gallaudet University, 469, 867
school programs, **1017–1019**
teaching methods, **1019–1021**
See also Disabled students
Heath, Shirley, 318, 319–320
Heckman, James, 620
Hegarty, Mary, 1442, 1499
Heinecke, Walter, 2455
Helplessness theory of ability, 1693
Help-seeking, 1866
Hemmings, Annette, 538
Henri, Victor, 185
Henry, Franklin, 1892
Henry Luce Foundation/ACLS Dissertation Fellowship in American Art, 106
Henscheid, Jean, 239
Hepatitis, 1107
Herbart, Johann, 695, **1021–1023**
Herbartianism
Herbart, Johann, 1022
McMurry, Charles, 1574–1575
Rice, Joseph Mayer, 2054
Heredity. *See* Genetics
Heritage model of language arts instruction, 1393–1394
Herman, Joan, 138
Herman the Bug, 1169, 1170

Hernandez v. Texas, 2094
Herpes simplex virus (HSV-2), 2065–2066
Herrnstein, Richard J., 1962
Hershey, Alan M., 731
Heslep, Robert D., 260
Heuristic knowledge, 1148
Heuristic strategy, 1546
HI-AYH (Hostelling International-American Youth Hostels), **2732–2733**
Hidden curriculum, **537–539**
Hidi, Suzanne, 1991
Hierarchical model of ability differences, 1114–1115
High Commissioner on National Minorities, 2248
Higher cognitive functions, 2659
Higher education
  AACSB International, 1–2
  academic advising, **2–5**
  academic calendars, **5–8**
  academic disciplines, **9–14,** 21–22
  academic standards, 1037
  accounting systems, **25–26**
  accreditation, **27–28,** 31–37
  accreditation corruption, 1660–1661
  affirmative action, **61–65**
  African Americans, 1036, 2666–2667
  agricultural programs, 78
  American Association for Higher Education (AAHE), **90–91,** 255, 415
  American Council on Education (ACE), 57, 102, **107–110**
  assessment, 2497–2498
  business education, 1–2
  Canada, 235–236
  capstone course, **239–241**
  career counseling, **241–243**
  commerce, **1314–1318**
  conferences, 90–91
  consortia, **475–478**
  corporate colleges, **492–494**
  costs, 1303
  credit transfer, 2683
  curriculum, **509–524**
  disability laws, 408–409
  distance learning, **589–593,** 2498
  East Asia and the Pacific, *636,* 637
  economic benefits, 339–340
  economics of, 198–199
  educational technology, **2521–2526**
  enrollment management, **748–751**
  entrance examinations, 2530–2531
  equality in, 673
  ethics, **756–760**
  European Union, 1252
  evaluation of programs and majors, 22
  federal funding, **861–865,** 871–872
  finance, **869–885,** 2360–2361
  general education, **923–925,** 1095
  grading systems, **960–962**
  Great Books program, 212, 1213–1214, 2366–2367
  Higher Education and Research Committee (Council of Europe), 1254
  Higher Education and the American Resurgence (report), 517–518
  Higher Education Center for Alcohol and Other Drug Prevention, 608
  Higher Education for American Democracy (report), 96
  Higher Education in the American Republics (Benjamin), 170
  high-performing Asian economies, 638–639
  historical development, **1034–1045**
  honors programs, **1086–1088**
  individual differences, 2496–2497
  institutional advancement, **1139–1144**
  institutional research, **1144–1146**
  interdisciplinary courses and majors, 1210–1214
  international issues, **1027–1034,** 1218–1219, 1302–1303, **2499–2501**
  internships, **1324–1327**
  Latin America, 1411
  local unit reorganization, 2343
  master's degrees
  medical education, **1585–1587**
  minorities, **1968–1971**
  moral development, 2496
  motivation, 2496–2497
  multicultural education, **1709–1716,** 2496
  National Association of Schools of Art and Design (NASAD), **1743–1745**
  National Center for Higher Education, 108
  National Conference on Higher Education, 90
  Netherlands, 1247
  nontraditional students, **1814–1816**
  nursing education, **1818–1821**
  Office of Postsecondary Education, Department of Education, 2618
  online education, 2524–2525
  organizational structure, 10
  postsecondary reform, 2434
  private sector's role, 1218–1221
  Professional and Organizational Development Network for Higher Education (POD), 255, 256
  psychosocial aspects, 2495
  race/ethnicity, **1968–1971**
  realization of goals, 334
  reforms, international, 1302–1303
  resource allocation, **2047–2052**
  rhythmic developmentalism, 2685–2686
  Rice, John A., 2052–2053
  risk management, **2074–2076**
  segregation, 2202
  service learning, **2205–2210,** 2656–2657
  Smithsonian Institution programs, 2240
  social fraternities and sororities, **2250–2253**
  societal influences, **1023–1027**
  South Asia, 2274, *2276*
  state education agencies and, 2345–2346
  state governments and, **2359–2364**
  state oversight, 2333, 2343
  strategic and long-range planning, **2367–2369**
  structural reorganization, 2343–2345
  student services, **2387–2394**
  study abroad, 1136–1138
  Sub-Saharan Africa, 2400–2401
  teaching and learning, **2493–2499**
  technology costs, 2523
  tuition, 2361

tutoring, **2583–2585**
United States system, **1041–1045**
universal, 421
Upward Bound (UB) program, **2603–2605**
Veteran's Upward Bound (VUB) program, 2604
western Europe, 2682–2684
Whitehead, Alfred North, 2685–2686
women's studies, **2688–2691**
See also Administration, educational; Admissions; Admissions tests; Application process; College athletics; Colleges and universities; College students; Community colleges; Faculty; Financial aid; Historically black colleges and universities (HBCUs); Nontraditional students; Public colleges and universities; Research universities; Tribal colleges and universities; Specific colleges and universities
Higher education, Sub-Saharan Africa, 2398
Higher Education Act
accreditation, 33–34
Accrediting Commission of Career Schools and Colleges of Technology (ACCSCT), 36
community colleges, 96
policy, 673
Title IV, 862
Title V, 1045
Title VI, 2619–2620
See also Title IX, Higher Education Act
Higher Education and Research Committee (Council of Europe), 1254
Higher Education and the American Resurgence (report), 517–518
Higher Education Center for Alcohol and Other Drug Prevention, 608
Higher Education for American Democracy (report), 96
Higher Education in the American Republics (Benjamin), 170
Higher mental functions, 575
Highlander Folk School. *See* Highlander Research and Education Center
Highlander Research and Education Center, 1090
High-performing Asian economies (HPAEs), 638–639
High-performing schools, 2540
High-risk neighborhoods, **1851–1856**
High School: A Report on Secondary Education in America, 200, 697
High School Achievement: Public, Catholic and Private Schools Compared (report), 1926
High School and Beyond (HSB) data set, 325, 326
High school equivalency test. *See* General Educational Development Test (GED)
High schools. *See* Secondary education
High school students
club participation, 317
college search and selection, **394–399**
dropouts, **599–602**
drug and alcohol use, 603
employment, **728–732, 735–737**
sexual orientation, 2220–2221
See also Secondary education; Youth
High Stakes: Testing for Tracking, Promotion, and Graduation (National Research Council), 1730
High-stakes assessment, 1301, 1730, **2533–2537**
Hilgard, Ernest, 1118–1119, 1120
Hill, Patty Smith, 190
Hill, Paul T., 692
Hillock, George, 2695
Himstead, Ralph E., 102
Hine, Darlene Clark, 67
Hioll, Patty Smith, 622
Hirsch, Eric D., 717, 2151, 2266
Hirschman, Albert, 2105
Hispanic Americans
culture, **1967–1968**
dropout rates, 599
early childhood education access, 618
educational attainment, 1966
faculty diversity, 776–778
faculty earnings, 18
gang members, 51, 52
Hispanic Association of Colleges and Universities (HACU), 1046, 1047
Hispanic-serving institutions, 776, 1044, **1045–1048**
immigrants, 1100
language, 1966–1967
Mexican-American education, 2094
migrant students, 1639
number sense and culture, 1564
population growth, 1966
Pura Belpré Award for children's literature, 289
race, 1967
Sanchez, George I., 2094
student employment, 728
uninsured children, 1000
See also Bilingual education; Language minority students
Hispanic Association of Colleges and Universities (HACU), 1046, 1047
Hispanic-serving institutions (HSIs), 776, 1044, **1045–1048**
Historians and history reading, 1986
Historical documents, 1732–1734
Historically black colleges and universities (HBCUs), **1048–1051**
African-American studies, 66–67
Bethune-Cookman College, 174
Bond, Horace Mann, 196, 197
faculty diversity, 776
Howard University, 867, 868
Morehouse College, 1570–1571
Office for the Advancement of Public Black Colleges, American Association of State Colleges and Universities, 100
overview, 1043–1044
Tuskegee Normal and Industrial Institute, 2665
Historical significance, defining, 1052, 1057
Historical thinking, 1052–1053
Historic colleges and universities, profiles of
Berea College, **171–172**
Harvard University, **994–996**
Johns Hopkins University, **1343–1344**
University of Chicago, **2597–2598**
University of Virginia, **2598–2600**
Yale University, **2697–2698**

Historic schools, profiles of
Dalton School, **541–542**
Lincoln School, **1484–1485**

History, educational
ability testing, 1112–1113
academic advising, 3
academic freedom, 14–15
academic majors, 20
accreditation, 31–32
Accrediting Commission of Career Schools and Colleges of Technology (ACCSCT), 36
African-American studies, 66–67
agricultural education, 72–78
Association of American Colleges and Universities, 152
Association of American Universities (AAU), 153–154
athletics, college and university, **347–353**
bilingual education, 177–178
business education, 215–216, 223
Canada, 234–236
Catholic schools, 250–252
character development, 259
coeducational colleges, 2226–2227
college and university student services, 2387–2388
common schools, 427–431
community colleges, 96, 442–446, 875
compulsory attendance, 465–466
Curti, Merle, 539–540
Department of Education, 2614–2615
developmental theory, **561–567**
early childhood education, 615–616
educational technology, 2514–2515
elementary education, **709–715**
English education, 740–741
experiential education, 760–761
faculty research and scholarship, 782–783
family and consumer sciences education, 803–804
federal participation, **836–840**
gay and lesbian studies, 917
General Educational Development Test (GED), 921–922
grading systems, 954–956
guidance and counseling, 975–976
handwriting, 987–989
Harvard University, 994–995
higher education, **1034–1045**
high-stakes testing, 2535–2536
historically black colleges and universities (HBCUs), 1048–1049
History of Secondary Education (Kandel), 1363–1364
home schooling, 1060–1061
infant schools (England), 11341135
institutional advancement, 1139–1140
instructional strategies, 1178–1179
intelligence tests, 1201–1202
interdisciplinary courses, 1211
international education agreements, 1277–1284
Islamic, 1328–1329
Jeanes teachers, 1337
Johns Hopkins University, 1343
kindergartens, 189–190, 621–622
land-grant colleges, **1380–1384**
Latin, 1414–1415
liberal arts colleges, 1476
libraries, 2137–2138
magnet schools, 1526–1527
master's degrees, 1537–1538
mental retardation, 1616–1617
middle schools, 1630–1632
military training, 1656–1657
moral education, 1683–1685
multicultural education, 1703–1704
Naval Academy, U.S., 1652
normal schools, 720
number sense, 1559
outdoor and environmental education, 1833–1834
physical education, 1886–1887
physical education teacher preparation, 1890–1891
private schools, 1923–1926
Protestant schools, 1941–1944
psychology, educational, 677
Public Education in the United States (Cubberley), 508–509
reading comprehension strategy instruction, 1977–1978
reading instruction, 1998–1999
reform reports, 695–697
religiously affiliated colleges and universities, 389
research universities, 2042
school curriculum, 532–533
school funding, **884–886**
science education, 2160–2161
science history, 2163–2164
secondary education, **2183–2190,** 2195–2196
segregation, 2199–2200
severe and multiple disabilities, students with, 2211
single-sex colleges and universities, 2225–2226
social fraternities and sororities, 2250–2251
special education, 1885–1886, **2278–2284**
special education teacher education, 2290
spelling instruction, 2303
state departments of education, 2323–2324
summer school programs, 2410
superintendents, 2412, 2415–2416
supervision of instruction, 2418–2419
teacher education, **2438–2444**
teacher evaluation, 2453–2454
textbooks, 2551–2552, 2554–2555
transportation, 2574–2575
urban superintendents, 2412
U.S. Coast Guard Academy, 1645
U.S. Merchant Marine Academy, 1648–1649
U.S. Military Academy, 1651
vocational and technical education, **2636–2642**
vocational education teacher preparation, 2647–2648
western Europe, 2680
writing instruction, 2693–2694
Yale University, 2697–2698

History, juvenile court, **1349–1352**

History education
learning, **1051–1055**
reading history texts, 1986–1987
teaching, **1055–1058**

History of Secondary Education (Kandel), 1363–1364

HIV/AIDS, **2058–2060**
international aspects, 627
risk behaviors, 2066, 2072–2073
school health services, 1015
sub-Saharan Africa, 2398
See also Sexually transmitted diseases (STDs)

Hmelo, Cindy, 1174
HMOs, 1530–1532
Hobbs, Renee, 1580–1581
Hoffer, Thomas, 950, 1926
Hofferth, Sandra, 317
Hoffman, Saul, 2062
Hofstetter, Carolyn, 2382
Holdzkom, David, 2164
Hollingworth, Leta, 931
Holmes, C. Thomas, 2263
Holmes County Board of Education, Alexander v., 2201
Holmes Group, 1931
Holt, John, **1059–1060**
Holton, Douglas, 1174
Holyoak, Keith, 1450
Home economics. *See* Family and consumer sciences education
Homeless children, 808
Homemakers Clubs, 1338
Home/school communication
  importance of, 1845
  language minority students, 1402
  sample practices, 822
Home schooling, **1060–1063**
  alternative schooling, 83, 84
  Holt, John, 1059–1060
  Virginia, 466
Homework, **1063–1065**
  learning at home, 823
  parental involvement, 1858
Homosexuality. *See* Sexual orientation
Homosexual studies. *See* Gay and lesbian studies
Honduras. *See* Latin America and the Caribbean
Hong Kong, 978–979
  See also East Asia and the Pacific
Honor societies, **1065–1086**
  Alpha Chi, **1065–1067**
  Alpha Mu Gamma, **1067**
  Alpha Omega Alpha, **1067–1068**
  Association for Women in Communications, **1068–1069**
  Association of College Honor Societies (ACHS), **1070–1071**
  Beta Phi Mu, **1071–1072**
  Delta Kappa Gamma Society, **1072–1073**
  Delta Sigma Rho-Tau Kappa Alpha, **1073–1074**
  Kappa Delta Pi, **1074–1075,** 2436
  Kappa Omicron Nu, **1075–1076**
  Lambda Iota Tau, **1076–1077**
  National Academy of Sciences, 1727
  National Art Honor Society, 1735
  National Honor Society (NHS), 1747, **1777–1780**
  National Junior Honor Society (NJHS), 1747, 1778–1780
  Phi Beta Kappa, **1077–1079**
  Phi Delta Kappa International, **1079–1080**
  Pi Kappa Lambda, **1080–1081**
  Pi Sigma Alpha, **1081–1082**
  professional, 2436
  Quill and Scroll Society, **2736–2737**
  Rho Chi, **1082–1083**
  Sigma Xi, **1083–1085**
  student involvement in, 2374–2375
  Tau Beta Pi, **1085–1086**
Honors programs, higher education, **1086–1088**
Honor system, 759, 1651, 1653
Hoops for Hearts, 88
Hoover-Dempsey, Kathleen V., 1844
Hope and Lifetime Learning tax credits, 863
Hopkins, L. Thomas, **1088–1089**
Hopwood v. State of Texas, 63, 64, 397
Horace's Compromise: The Dilemma of the American High School (report), 321, 697
Horn, John L., 1202, 1205
Horner, Robert H., 158
Horowitz, Board of Curators of the University of Missouri v., 2425
Horton, Myles, **1089–1091**
Hoskyn, Maureen, 2008–2009
Hossler, Don, 748
Hostelling International-American Youth Hostels (HI-AYH), **2732–2733**
House of Refuge, 1350
House Un-American Activities Committee, 102
Housing
  Association of College and University Housing Officers-International (ACUHO-I), 342
  college and university, 2044
  community colleges, 2392–2393
  high-risk neighborhoods, 1852
  instability, 808
  living and learning centers, **1518–1520**
  National Association of College and University Residence Halls (NACURH), 342
  residence halls, **340–344,** 2044
Houston, Texas, 694
Howard University, 867, 868
How Children Fail (Holt), 1059
How Children Learn (Holt), 1059
How Children Think and Learn (Wood), 575
How College Affects Students (Pascarella and Terenzini), 335–340, 2494–2496
How Gertrude Teaches Her Children (Pestalozzi), 1875
Howley, Craig B., 2088
How People Learn: Bridging Research and Practice (National Research Council), 2165, 2646
How Schools Shortchange Girls (report), 1125
How the Brain Learns: A Classroom Teacher's Guide (Sousa), 202
How to Change Colleges: Notes on Radical Reform (Taylor), 2434
How to Experiment in Education (McCall), 1573
How to Get More of Them (report), 698
How to Make a Curriculum (Bobbitt), 193
How to Measure in Education (McCall), 1573
How to Solve It (Pólya), 1546
HSB (High School and Beyond) data set, 325, 326
HSIs (Hispanic-serving institutions), 776
HSV-2 (herpes simplex virus), 2065–2066
Hubbard, Mabel, 1018
Hubble, Edwin, 93
Hubert H. Humphrey Fellowship Program, 847
Hughes, Raymond, 378
Huitt, William G., 261
Hull, Clark, 1691
Hull-House
  Addams, Jane, 41

family support services, 829
Putnam, Alice, 1957
Hull-House Labor Museum, 41
Human capital theory, 549, 647
Human ecology, 1214
Humanism, 1525–1526
Humanities
American Council of Learned Societies, **105–107**
gender equity, 1127
National Endowment for the Humanities (NEH), **1774–1776**
To Reclaim a Legacy: A Report on the Humanities in Higher Education (report), 514–515
Human life cycle, 752
Human Problem Solving (Newell and Simon), 1546
Human Resource Development Index (HDI), 634–635
Human services. *See* Family support services
Human subject protection, **1091–1092**
Hume, David, 1425, 1426
Hung, Shwu-Yong, 304–305
Hungary. *See* Eastern Europe and Central Asia
Hunter, John and Ronda, 1113
Hunter, Madeline Cheek, **1093–1094,** 2418
Hunter, Robert, 906
Huntington Corporation, 2582
Hutchins, Robert, **1094–1096**
Progressive education, 1937
University of Chicago, 2598
Hutchinson, Janice, 313
Hybrid classes, 590
Hyman, Ronald T., 1132
Hymes, Dell, 2462
Hyperactivity. *See* Attention deficit hyperactivity disorder (ADHD)

I

IAAUS (Intercollegiate Athletic Association of the United States), 364–365
IAEA (International Academy of Educational Accreditors), 30
IAEA (International Association for Educational Assessment), **1225**
IASA. *See* Improving America's Schools Act (IASA)
IBE (International Bureau of Education), 1277, 1278–1279
IB (international baccalaureate) diploma, 898, **1238–1241**
IBO (International Baccalaureate Organization), 1239
Iceland. *See* Western Europe
ICETEX (Colombia), 2380
ICFAD (International Council of Fine Arts Deans), 121–122
ICSAC (International Council of School Accreditation Commissions, Inc.), 29–30
ICTM (International Commission on the Teaching of Mathematics), 2237
IDB (Inter-American Development Bank), 1255–1256
IDEA. *See* Individuals with Disabilities Education Act (IDEA)
Idealism
Bode, Boyd H., 194
Froebel's idealist philosophy, 904–905
Plato, 1898–1899
Identity
college students, 337
Erikson, Erik, 752
families, 812–813
formation, 278–279
learning communities, 1162
IEA. *See* International Association for the Evaluation of Educational Achievement (IEA)
IEA (Independent Education Associations), 2478
IEP. *See* Individualized Education Programs (IEP)
IFFTU (International Federation of Free Teachers' Unions), 1319–1321
IGR (Institute for Government Research), 209
I Have a Future (initiative), 2062–2063
Ijaz, M. Ahmed and I. Helene, 1707
Ill-defined problems, 1442
Illinois Juvenile Court Act, 1350
Illustrated text. *See* Multimedia
Illustrators, children's book, 286
ILO (International Labor Organization), 1263
ILS (individualized learning systems), 2516
Ilutsik, Ester, 1564
An Image of the Future (Trump), 2095
Imagery and creativity, 507
Imanishi-Kari, Thereza, 2039
Imitation task, 1592
Immersion, foreign language, 896, 899
IMMEX system, 147
Immigrant education, **1097–1106**
bilingual education, 177–178
bilingualism, 183
Canada, 235, 237
common school movement, 711–712
community colleges, 445
dropout rates, 599
elementary education, 718
Hull-House, 41
international issues, **1104–1106**
language arts instruction, 1396
student educational aspirations and attainment, 1859
United States, **1097–1104**
See also Language minority students; Migrant students
Immigrants
Chinese, 1100–1101
Cuban, 1102
gangs, 51
German, 1098–1099
Latino, 1966–1968
Immigration and Nationality Act of 1952, 1312
Immigration and Naturalization Act, 1098
Immigration and Naturalization Service (INS), 846, 1312
Immoral conduct of teachers, 753
Immunization, **1106–1108**
Impact aid, **1108–1109**
federal involvement in education, 837
government schools, 866
Implementation
school reform, 692
study of program implementation, 2031–2032
Implicit memory, **1596–1600,** 1606, 1609–1610
Importing Oxford (Duke), 2046
The Improvement of Practical Intelligence: The Central Task of Education (Raup et al.), 170

Improving America's Schools Act (IASA)
compensatory education, 455
national achievement tests, 2546
statewide testing, 2538
Improving Student Learning: A Strategic Plan for Education Research and Its Utilization (National Research Council), 1730
Impulses and the philosophy of education, 1881–1884
In a Different Voice: Psychological Theory and Women's Development (Gilligan), 1682
Inagaki, Kayoko, 763–765
Incentives
bureaucratic accountability, 652
faculty service, 796–797
school performance, 551
teaching improvement, 256
test-based, 2536
See also Motivation; Reinforcement
Inclusion model of special education, 2293
Income
assistance, 1867–1868
poverty measures, 1910
support services, **833–836**
See also Low income families; Socioeconomic status
Incremental budgeting, 2049
"In Defense of Measurement" (Green), 1194
Independent Education Associations (IEA), 2478
Independent study, **1110–1112**
See also Self-directed learning
India
educational development, 2274–2275
Kerala Project, 1246
public *vs.* private schools, 951–952
See also South Asia
Indiana, 314, 316
Indian Education Act, 1109
Indicators
education, *1628*
Indicators of Education Statistics program (OECD), 1287, 1294–1295
Indicators of National Education Systems (INES), 1250–1251
social, **1291–1296**
Indicators of Education Statistics program (OECD), 1287, 1294–1295
Indicators of National Education Systems (INES), 1250–1251
Indifference, parental, 1849–1850
Indirect costs and research grants, **2019–2020**
Individual differences, **1112–1129**
abilities and aptitudes, **1112–1118**
affective and conative processes, **1118–1121**
attention, 157
ethnicity, **1121–1125**
gender equity and schooling, **1125–1129**
higher education, 2496–2497
motivation, 1697–1698
problem solving, 1443–1444
Individual Education Compacts, 1674
Individual interest, 705
"Individualization: The Hidden Agenda" (Hyman), 1132
Individualized attention, 2193
Individualized education programs (IEP)
adapted physical education, 37
assistive technology, 149–150
autistic students, 161
extended-year programs, 2409–2410
special education history, 2281
See also Individuals with Disabilities Education Act (IDEA)
Individualized instruction, **1129–1133**
Individualized learning systems (ILS), 2516
Individuals with Disabilities Education Act (IDEA), **3080**
accommodation, 407–408
adapted physical education, 37–39
assistive technology, 149
autism, 160, 161, 162
emotionally disturbed students, 726
foster children, 284
funding, 838
learning disabilities, 2008
overview, 1868–1869
physically disabled persons, 1885
severe and multiple disabilities, students with, 2211–2212
speech and language impairment, 2295–2296
See also Americans with Disabilities Act (ADA); Disabled students; Special education
Indonesia, 639
See also East Asia and the Pacific
Induction programs
international teacher education, 2473
learning to teach, 2487–2488
teacher evaluation, 2460
unions, 2480, 2481
See also Mentoring; Teacher education
Inductive reasoning, 678
Indulgent parents, 1849
Industrial-age instructional design, 1149
Industrial arts. *See* Technology education
Industrial engineering, 739
Industrialization, 670–671
Industrialized nations, 1296–1299
Industrial training boards (ITBs, Great Britain), 487
Industry-University Cooperative Research Projects Program (I/UCRPP), 2593
Industry-University Research Centers Program (I/URCP), 2593
Industry-university research collaboration, **2592–2597**
ethics, 757
faculty entrepreneurship, 770
faculty roles, 791
Rosenzweig study of, 154
Inefficiency, educational, 644
Inequities, instructional, 305–306
Inert knowledge
analogical reasoning, 1422–1423
constructivism, 1464
instructional design, 1151
problem solving, 1443
transfer of learning, 1449
INES (Indicators of National Education Systems), 1250–1251
Infants
attention, 156
causal perception, 1425
emotions, 60
maternal smoking, 2067

See also Child development; Developmental theory
Infant schools (England), **1133–1136,** 1823
InFocus Program on Strengthening Social Dialogue, 1263
Informal mathematics, 1563–1564
Informal reasoning, 1446–1448
Information-age instructional design, 1148–1149, *1149*
Information and communications technology
academic advising, 3
business education, 224–225
courses, 224
digital divide, **1296–1299,** 2519–2520
global economics, 424–425
higher education, 2521–2526
international issues, 1220–1221, **1229–1233, 1296–1299**
knowledge management, 1374–1375
school facility design and, 2127, 2129–2131
school libraries, 2139
trade, 1323
writing and, 1508–1509
See also Computer technology; Educational technology; Software
Information Clearinghouse, ECS, 686
Information dissemination
Department of Education, U.S., 2620
international higher education, 1031
Internet, 2522
National Education Association, 1770–1771
state education agencies, 2348
substance abuse, 603
teacher unions, 2481
Information processing, **567–571**
developmental theory, 564
individual differences, 1114
learning theory, 1462
Information Systems and Technology Division, ETS, 685
Informed consent, 757–758, 1092
Infrastructure. *See* Facilities
Infringement, copyright, 1189
Infusion approach to character education, 1686
Ingersoll, Richard, 745
Inglehard, Ronald, 664
Ingraham v. Wright, 2425
In-home child care, 271
Injury
liability, 1474
school health services, 1014, 1015
sports, 2308, *2312*
Inner-City Private Elementary Schools (report), 1925–1926
Innumeracy: Mathematical Illiteracy and Its Consequences (Paulos), 1559
Inquiry
educational technology and, 2517
Inquiry and the National Science Education Standards: A Guide for Teaching and Learning (National Research Council), 1729
learning, 2166–2168
mathematics teaching, 1555–1556
technological tools, 2178–2179
Inquiry and the National Science Education Standards: A Guide for Teaching and Learning (National Research Council), 1729
In re Gault, 1351
In re Winship, 1351
In-service training
continuing professional education (CPE), 484
mathematics education, 1540
microteaching, 1621
physical education teachers, 1892
school boards, 2110–2111
science teacher education, 2164–2165
social studies education, 2270–2271
vocational education teachers, 2648–2649
See also Field experience
Insight and Responsibility (Erikson), 752
Instead of Education (Holt), 1059
Instinct and language, 1386–1387
Institute for Government Research (IGR), 209
Institute for Statistics, UNESCO, 1294
Institute of International Education (IIE), **1136–1139**
Institute of Mental Measurements, 214
Institutional advancement, 192, **1139–1144**
Institutional culture, 783
Institutional drift, 1042
Institutionalization
disabled individuals, 2278–2279, 2281
juvenile crime, 1356
youth, 2709
Institutional nature of curriculum, 534–535
Institutional research, higher education, **1144–1146**
Institutional Review Boards (IRBs), 1091–1092
Institutional service, faculty, 792, 793, 796–797
Instruction
art, 166
assessment integration, 135
audio-tutorial, 1130–1131
calendar use and conversion, effect of, 6–7
causal reasoning skills, 1426–1427
classroom management and, 299–300
classroom observation and instructional processes, 304–305
conceptual change, 1430
disabled students, 2280
educational technology, 2522
flow of, 301
foreign language, 899
improvement, 306–307
individualized, **1129–1133**
inequitable, 305–306
instructional organizers, 1179
language arts, 1393–1394, 1396
Latin, **1413–1417**
learner-centered, 2494
literacy, 1515–1516
motivation and, **1695–1698**
objectives, **1176–1178,** 2493
open classrooms, 1823
pace, 1129
programmed, 1309–1310, 2230
reading, 1513–1517, **1998–2003**
reading comprehension, 1977–1983, 1995, 1999
receptive, 1160
schema theory and, 1468–1469
special education, 2282, 2291
spelling, 2303

strategies, **1178–1186,** 2100–2101
supervision, **2418–2422**
technology and, 2512
transfer and, 1450–1451
triarchic theory of intelligence, 1208–1209
undergraduate methods of, 512
vocabulary, 1505
wait-time, 312–313
whole-class, 305, 1410
writing and composition, 1507, 2693–2695
See also Curriculum; Teaching
Instructional aids. *See* Learning aids
Instructional design, **1146–1178**
anchored instruction (AI), 681, **1151–1154**
case-based reasoning, **1154–1159**
design-based learning, **1163–1169**
direct instruction, **1159–1162,** 1180–1181
Integrated Thematic Instruction model, 203
learning communities, **1162–1163**
Madeline Hunter Method, 1093–1094
overview, **1147–1151**
pedagogical agents and tutors, **1169–1172**
Pestalozzi, Johann, 1875–1876
problem-based learning, **1172–1175,** 1185–1186
See also Curriculum
Instructional materials
Middle East and North Africa, 1626–1627, *1630*
multiculturalism, 1706–1707
packages, 2553–2554
rural education, 2091
University Council for Educational Administration (UCEA), 2592
Instructional research offices, 749
Instructional technology. *See* Educational technology
Instructional Theory Into Practice (ITIP) model, 1093–1094
Instrumental conditioning, 1460–1461
Instrumental performance, 1722
INTASC (Interstate New Teacher Assessment and Support Consortium), 121, 122
Integrated governance, 2106
Integrated literacy instruction, 1515–1516
Integrated Thematic Instruction model, 203
Integrating Computer Technology into the Classroom (Morrison and Lowther), 1578
Integration, international, 1105
Integration, Its Meaning and Application (Hopkins), 1088
Integration, racial. *See* Segregation
Integrity in the College Curriculum: A Report to the Academic Community (report), 152, 515–516
Intellectual history, 539–540
Intellectual property, **1186–1190**
educational technology, 2519
faculty entrepreneurship, 770
international trade, 1323–1324
Intelligence, **1190–1209**
abilities and aptitudes, 1112–1116
accommodation, 1896
animal studies, 2564–2565
artificial intelligence, 1546
assimilation, 1895–1896
attention, 156–157
creativity, 506
emotional intelligence, **1191–1194,** 1199
genetics, 941, 1115, 1196–1197, 1204, 2567
Goddard, Henry H., 940
identification of gifted students by, 931, 934
immigrants, 1099
"Intelligence: A Very Short Introduction" (Deary), 1195
"Intelligence: Knowns and Unknowns" (Neisser et al.), 1205
Intelligence Reframed (Gardner), 1198
lead poisoning, 1911
myths, mysteries, and realities, **1201–1206**
naturalist, 1199, 1834
nature of, 680–681
poverty, 1913
Terman, Lewis, 2528–2529
triarchic theory, 1115, **1206–1209**
See also Intelligence testing; Multiple intelligences
"Intelligence: A Very Short Introduction" (Deary), 1195
"Intelligence: Knowns and Unknowns" (Neisser et al.), 1205
Intelligence quotient (IQ)
as determinant of giftedness, 930–931, 933
dynamic assessment, 128–130
foster care children, 819
learning disabilities, 2008–2009
measurement, 1194
myths, 1202, 1204
reading disabilities, 2008–2011
Intelligence Reframed (Gardner), 1198
Intelligence testing, **1201–1205**
Binet, Alfred, 186–187
educational psychology, 677–678
individual differences, 1113, 1115–1116
measurement, **1194–1198,** 2566–2567
overview, 1194–1197
standardized, 186–187
Thorndike, Edward L., 1936–1937, 2566–2567
See also Intelligence; Standardized tests; Testing
Intelligent Transportation Systems program, 850
Intended curriculum, 524
Intensification, school regulations and requirements, 691
Interaction: The Democratic Process (Hopkins), 1088
Interaction coding systems, classroom, 304
Interactive Physics (software), 2178
Inter-American Development Bank (IDB), 631, 1255–1256
Intercollegiate Athletic Association of the United States (IAAUS), 364–365
Interdisciplinarity
African-American studies, **65–69,** *68, 69,* 2691–2693
capstone courses, 240
courses, **1210–1215**
Cultural Foundations of Education: An Interdisciplinary Exploration (Brameld), 207
diversity, 1713
English, 742–743
gay and lesbian studies, 918
history education, 1057

majors, 21, 916–918
outcome based education, 1830
undergraduate, 512
women's studies, 2689–2690
Interdistrict school choice programs, 552
Interest
effort and, **704–707**
reading, **1989–1993**
Interest groups, 526, **662–664**
Intergovernmental relations, **1215–1218**
Intergroup Education in Cooperating Schools Project, 2428
Interim Policy on Research Misconduct (Public Health Service), 2037, 2038
Intermittent reinforcement, 1461, 1462
Internal accountability, 655
Internalizing behavior problems, 1911–1912
International Academy of Educational Accreditors (IAEA), 30
International Adult Literacy Survey (OECD), 642, 1408
International aid, 2276
See also International development agencies
International Association for Educational Assessment (IAEA), **1225**
International Association for Management Education. *See* AACSB International
International Association for the Evaluation of Educational Achievement (IEA), **1225–1238**
civics education, 296
comparative assessment, 1222–1223
international statistics, 1288, 1293
Latin America and the Caribbean, 1409
International baccalaureate (IB) diploma, 898, **1238–1241**
International Baccalaureate Organization (IBO), 1239
International Bank for Reconstruction and Development. *See* World Bank
International Board on Books for Young People, 289
International Bureau of Education (IBE), 1262, 1277, 1278–1279
International Commission on Intellectual Co-operation, 1278
International Commission on the Teaching of Mathematics (ICTM), 2237
International Conference on Public Education, 1278
International Council of Fine Arts Deans (ICFAD), 121–122
International Council of School Accreditation Commissions, Inc. (ICSAC), 29–30
International Covenant on Economic, Social and Cultural Rights, 1280
International Cultural Property Protection Program, ECA, 848
International development agencies, **1241–1265**
bilateral agencies, **1241–1249**
regional institutions, **1249–1259**
United Nations and international agencies, **1259–1265**
International education, 991, **1265–1276,** 1364, 1730, 2268
International Education for All program, 1407
International Federation of Free Teachers' Unions (IFFTU), 1319–1321
International Federation of University Women, 105
International Fellowships Program, 1138
International governments
educational spending, 547, 548, 629, 631, 632
higher education regulation, 27
role in education, **949–954**
See also Decentralization; Developing nations; International issues
International Indicators of Education Systems (INES), 1293–1294
International Institute of Statistics, UNESCO's, 1224
International issues
accountability, 951–952
accreditation, **27–28,** 30
adoption, 814
adult literacy, 642
alternative schooling, 85, 2500–2501
American Association for the Advancement of Science (AAAS), 92
American overseas schools, **112–115**
area studies, 106
assessment, **1221–1238**
basic education, 2196
bilingual education, 177
Boyer's achievements, 201
business education, 219
certification examinations, 2530–2531
civics education, 296, **1236–1238**
classroom questions, 310–311
college admissions rates, 2707
commerce of education, **423–426, 1218–1221**
continuing professional education (CPE), **486–489**
corruption, education, **1659–1668**
curriculum, **524–529**
democratization of education, 715
Department of Education, U.S., **2619–2620**
design oriented curricula, 1164
distance education, 425
dropout rates, 599–600
early childhood education, 620, **626–634**
East Asia and the Pacific, **634–640,** *636*
Eastern Europe and Central Asia region, **640–647**
economic analysis of decision-making, **546–550**
education agreements, **1276–1285**
educational change, 658–659
education development projects, **686–689**
education research, **1265–1276**
education statistics, **1285–1296**
elementary education, 716
entrance examinations, college and university, 2530–2531
foreign language education, 898–899
gender, **919–921**
global competencies, 511
globalism, 425–426
government funding of education, 547, 548, 629, 631, 632
government's role in education, **949–954**

graduation rates, 2707
Hanna, Paul R., 991
health and education, **998–999**
higher education, **1027–1034,** 1218–1219
homework, 1064
immigrant education, **1104–1106**
infant schools, 1135–1136
information and communication technology in the classroom, **1229–1233**
Institute of International Education (IIE), **1136–1139**
intergovernmental relations, **1215–1218**
International Association for Educational Assessment (IAEA), **1225**
international baccalaureate (IB) diploma, **1238–1241**
International Federation of University Women, 105
knowledge management competencies, 1232, *1233*
magnet schools, 1528
microteaching, 1621–1622
national achievement tests, **2545–2550**
Nongovernmental organizations and foundations, **1803–1811**
nontraditional students in higher education, 1814
number sense and culture, 1563–1564
peace education, **1860–1864**
population trends, 2704
private schools, 1219–1220
public *vs.* private schools, 950–951k
race/ethnicity, 2247–2249
reading literacy, **1228–1229**
recruitment of teachers, 2444
rural education, **2090–2092**
school counseling, 978–979
science and mathematics education, **1233–1236**
science education, comparative studies of, 2161
secondary education, 2188–2189, **2195–2198**
small nations, **2234–2236**
social cohesion, 2246–2249
social mobility of underprivileged groups, **1300–1307**
social studies, 2266–2267
special education, **2293–2295**
standard model of education, 2499–2500
standards and testing, 2531–2532
standards-based education, 2319–2320
standards of test development, **2550–2551**
student loans, **2377–2381**
teacher education, **2444–2448, 2470–2475**
teacher supply, 548
teaching and learning in higher education, **2499–2501**
teaching history, 1055–1057j
technology gap, **1296–1299**
telecommunications, 424–425
textbooks, 2551–2554
trade in education goods and services, **1321–1324**
tutoring, **2585–2587**
U.S. government's education activity, 839
vocational and technical education, **2651–2654**
vocational school fallacy, **2654–2656**
work readiness, 2639–2640
See also Comparative assessment; Decentralization; Developing nations; Globalization; International Association for the Evaluation of Educational Achievement (IEA); International students; International treaties and agreements; Third International Mathematics and Science Study (TIMSS); Specific countries; Specific regions

Internationalization. *See* Globalization

International Kindergarten Union, 190

International Labor Organization (ILO), 1263

International Reading Association (IRA), 741, **1307–1309,** 1394–1395

International Registry of Accredited Schools, 30

International School of Geneva, 1238

International Schools Association (ISA), 1238

International Schools Services (ISS), 115

International Society for Business Education, 219

International Society for Performance Improvement (ISPI), **1309–1310**

International students, **1310–1318**
country of origin, *1272*
education policy, 1271–1272
fields of study, *1273*
global commerce of higher education, **1314–1318**
source of higher education funds, *1271*
tertiary students, *1275*
U.S. colleges and universities, *1270, 1271, 1272, 1273,* **1310–1314**
See also Exchange programs; International issues; Study abroad

International Teachers Associations, **1318–1321**

International Technology Education Association (ITEA), 2506–2507

International Trade Administration (ITA), 841

International trade secretariats (ITSs), 1318–1319

International treaties and agreements
accreditation, 27–28
APEC Education Dialogue and Knowledge Sharing Network, 27
Bologna Process, 27
Convention Against Discrimination in Education, 1282
Convention on Technical and Vocational Education, 1283
Convention on the Elimination of All Forms of Discrimination against Women, 1280–1281
Convention on the Rights of the Child, 1281
Covenant of Civil and Political Rights, 1280
education agreements, **1276–1285**
General Agreement on Trade and Services (GATS), 423–424, 1322–1323

International Covenant on Economic, Social and Cultural Rights, 1280
Lisbon Convention on the Recognition of Qualifications Pertaining to Higher Education in the European Region, 27
Trade Related Aspects of Intellectual Property Rights (TRIPS), 1323–1324
The Treaty Establishing the European Community, 1251
International Visitor Program, ECA, 848
Internet
AskERIC, 683
availability, 2509
career services, 242–243
College Entrance Examination Board, 373
college recruitment, 383
Digital Millennium Copyright Act (DMCA), 1189–1190
distance learning, 593, 2511–2511
education sites, 1220
Electronic Access Project, National Archives and Records Administration, 1733–1734
international access, 1296–1299
international education, 1220–1221
Jason Project, 2510
learning and, 1495–1496
public broadcasting and, 658
research, 2510–2511, 2516
school access, international comparative study of, 1230–1232
science education, 2179–2180
sexuality information, 2217
small nations, 2236
student services, 2393
teacher learning communities, 2467
teachers, 2436
threaded discourse, 1371–1372
Virtual High School (VHS), 2179
writing instruction, 2695
See also Information and communications technology; Online education
Internships, **1324–1327**
career counseling, 242
Smithsonian Institution, 2240
See also Experiential learning
Interpersonal relationships
college students, 337–338
intelligence, 1199
middle childhood, 278
See also Peer relations; Social development
Interpretative techniques in assessment reporting, 141–142
Interpretive function of school, 211
Interstate New Teacher Assessment and Support Consortium (INTASC), 121, 122
Interstate School Leaders Licensure Consortium (ISLLC), 1921
Intersubjective mental activity, 575, 576
Intertextuality, **1489–1493**
Interuniversity Committee on Superior Students (ICSS). *See* National Collegiate Honors Council (NCHC)
Intervention. *See* Prevention and intervention
Interviews, educational research, 2028
Intradistrict school choice programs, 552
Intramural athletics, 348, **361–364,** *363, 364*
See also College athletics; Sports
Intramural Athletics (Mitchell), 362
Intrapersonal intelligence, 1199
Intrasubjective mental activity, 575, 576
Intrinsic motivation, 1696–1697
Inuits, 419
Investing in Our Children (report), 697
Investing in Teaching (report), 698
Investment in Learning (Bowen), 334
Involvement in Learning: Realizing the Potential of American Higher Education (report), 515, 2046
Iowa, 2450–2451
Iowa Testing Programs, 496, 537, 1485–1486
IQ. *See* Intelligence quotient (IQ)
IRA (International Reading Association), 741, **1307–1309,** 1394–1395
Iran. *See* Middle East and North Africa
Iraq. *See* Middle East and North Africa
Ireland. *See* Western Europe
Iron deficiency, 1822
IRT (item response theory), 140
Irvine, Jacqueline Jordan, 1963
ISA (International Schools Association), 1238
ISBE (International Society for Business Education), 219
Ishler, Margaret, 313
Isidore of Seville, 160
Islam, **1327–1330,** 1627
ISLLC (Interstate School Leaders Licensure Consortium), 1921
Isolation in the Schools (Young), 2702–2703
Isolation of minority faculty, 777
ISPI (International Society for Performance Improvement), **1309–1310**
Israel, youth trips to, 1342
ISS (International Schools Services), 115
Issues of Secondary Education (report), 696
"Is the Fuss about Brain Research Justified?" (Sousa), 204
ITA (International Trade Administration), 841
Italic handwriting forms, 989
Italy. *See* Western Europe
Itard, Jean-Marc-Gaspard
education methods, 2211
Montessori, Maria, 1676
Wild boy of Averyon, 2278, 2279
ITBs (industrial training boards, Great Britain), 487
ITEA (International Technology Education Association), 2506–2507
Item response theory (IRT), 140
ITSs (International trade secretariats), 1318–1319
ITTE: Education Technology Programs and Technology Leadership Network, 1785
I/UCRPP (Industry-University Cooperative Research Projects Program), 2593
I/URCP (Industry-University Research Centers Program), 2593

Ivory Coast. *See* Sub-Saharan Africa
Ivy Group (League), 351

J

Jackson, Anthony, 1633
Jackson Board of Education, Wygant v., 63, 64
Jacobs, Jerry, 2070
Jacobsen, Doug, 201
Jacobson, Cathy, 1165
Jaffree, Wallace F., 2423
Jamaica. *See* Latin America and the Caribbean
James, Edmund J., 1416
James, William, **1331–1337**
  attention, 155
  Bode, Boyd H., 194
  Educational psychology, 677, 681
  Progressive education, 1934
Jankuniene, Zita, 317
Janssen, Rianne, 142
Japan
  AACSB International tour, 2
  continuing professional education (CPE), 488
  elementary education, 716
  higher education reform, 1029
  high school counseling, 978
  international student recruitment, 1316
  Japan International Cooperation Agency (JICA), 1245–1246
  school architecture, 909
  See also East Asia and the Pacific
Japan International Cooperation Agency (JICA), 1245–1246
Jason Project, 2510
Jasper Project, 1165
Javacap (software), 1157
JCCA (Jewish Community Centers Association of North America), 2739–2740
JEA (Journalism Education Association), **1346–1347**
Jeanes teachers, **1337–1339**
Jefferson, Thomas
  common schools, 428
  elementary education history, 710–711
  immigrants, 1098
  literate citizenry, 2245
  University of Virginia, 2598–2599
Jencks, Charles, 118–119
Jenkins, Esther J., 2628
Jenkins, John, 987
Jenkins v. Missouri
  segregation, 2202
  states and the U.S. Constitution, 480
  Supreme Court cases, 2424
Jensen, Arthur, 1196, 1202
Jewish Community Centers Association of North America (JCCA), 2739–2740
Jewish education, U.S., 390, **1340–1343**
Jewish youth organizations, **2720–2721, 2739–2741**
JICA (Japan International Cooperation Agency), 1245–1246
Job fairs, 242
Job Opportunities and Basic Skill (JOBS) Program, 2677
Job search skills, 242
JOBS (Job Opportunities and Basic Skill) Program, 2677
Job skills
  Eastern Europe and Central Asia, 642
  Job Training Partnership Act (JTPA), 488
  student employment, 730–731, 733–734
  See also Employment; Workforce training
Job Training Partnership Act (JTPA), 488
Johns Hopkins University, **1343–1344**
  academic majors, 20
  education partnerships, 826
Johns Hopkins University Press, 2600
Johnson, Lyndon B., 188, 2687
Johnson, Marietta Pierce, **1344–1346**
Johnson, Richard, 2220
Johnstone, R. F., 72
Joining Forces (Levy and Copple), 2141
Joint degree programs, 221
Joint Professional Military Education Program, 1655
"Joint Statement on the Education Summit with the Nation's Governors in Charlottesville, Virginia," **3017–3020**
"Joint Statement on the Impact of Entertainment Violence on Children," 1581
Joliet Junior College, 96, 875
Jomtien Declaration and Framework for Action, 626
Jonassen, David, 1148, 1160
Jones-Evans, Dylan, 770
Jones International University, 2524
Jordan. *See* Middle East and North Africa
Jordan, David Starr, 443
Jordan, I. King, 867
Journalism education, **1347–1349**
  Journalism Education Association (JEA), **1346–1347**
  Quill and Scroll Society, **2736–2737**
Journalism Education Association (JEA), **1346–1347**
Journal of Educational Psychology, 164
Journal of Environmental Education, 1831
Journal of Negro History, 66, 2692
Journal of Speculative Philosophy, 993
Joyce, Bruce, 1179, 2446
JTPA (Job Training Partnership Act), 488
Judd, Charles, 681
Judicial services, community college, 2390
Julius Rosenwald Fund, 196
Jump Rope for Hearts, 88
Jungeblut, Ann, 2543–2544
Junior colleges. *See* Community colleges; Higher education
Junior high schools. *See* Middle schools
Just communities, 1377–1378, 1681–1682
Justice/caring dispute, 755
Juvenile justice system, **1349–1361**
  contemporary system and alternatives, **1352–1358**
  history of juvenile courts, **1349–1352**
  juvenile courts, 282, **1349–1352**

juvenile crime and violence, **1358–1361**
mental health services, 1614
See also Crime; Gangs; Violence

K

Kaestle, Carl, 430
Kafai, Yasmin, 1165
Kagan, Jerome, 261
Kagan, Sharon Lynn, 2041
Kahler, A., 77
Kahn, Si, 435
Ka Lama Teacher Education Initiative, 2466
Kalamazoo case, 2184
The Kallikak Family: A Study in the Heredity of Feeble-Mindedness (Goddard), 941
Kandel, Isaac L., **1363–1365**
Kane, Mary Jo, 1451
Kanner, Leo, 161
Kansas State University, Nero v., 2075
Kaplan organization, 2582
Kaplin, William A., 2074
Kappa Delta Pi, **1074–1075,** 2436
Kappa Omicron Nu, **1075–1076**
Karenga, Maulana, 68
Karier, Clarence J., 173
Kawata, Jennifer, 2536
Kazakhstan. *See* Eastern Europe and Central Asia
Keele, Steven, 1702
KEEP Project, 1511
Keizai Koho Center, 2
Keliher Commission, 708
Keller, Helen, 1387–1388, 2278
Keller, John, 2497
Keller Plan, 1130–1131
Kellogg Foundation, 108
Kelly, Robert L., 152
Kendall, Amos, 867
Kennedy, John F., 1365
Kentucky, 694, 2326
Kent v. United States, 1350–1351
Kenya. *See* Sub-Saharan Africa
Keogh, Rosemary, 762
Keppel, Francis C., 131, **1365–1367**
Kerala Project, 1246
Kerr, Clark, 936, 1038, 1041, 2042, 2367
Kerschensteiner, Georg, **1367–1369**
Kettering Foundation, National Commission on the Reform of Secondary Education, 697
Keyboarding, 217–218
Keyes v. School District No. 1, 2201, 2424
Keyword mnemonic technique, 1670–1671
"Key Work of School Boards" (initiative), 1786
KIDLINK project, 2511–2512
Kidmap, *144*
Kihlstrom, John, 1191
Kilgore, Sally, 950
Kilpatrick, William H., **1368–1369**
Bagley, William C., 164
Benne, Kenneth D., 170
Childs, John L., 293
Montessori, Maria, 1679
project method, 1939
Kilpatrick discussion group, 170
Kindergarten
Blow, Susan, 189–190
curriculum, 905
early childhood education, 615–616
Froebel, Friedrich, 903–906
gifts and occupations, 905
The Kindergarten (report), 190
Putnam, Alice, 1957–1959
teacher education, 621–622
See also Early childhood education
The Kindergarten (report), 190
Kinetic City Super Crew (radio program), 92
King, Alison, 490
King, Mary A., 1326
Kingdon, Geeta, 951
King v. Board of Education, 1391
Kintsch, Walter, 1972, 1993
Kiribati. *See* East Asia and the Pacific
Kirst, Michael, 2141
Kirwan v. Podberesky, 63, 64
Kjolseth, Rolf, 178
Klebanov, Pamela, 1905
Klein, Pnina, 128
Klein, Stephen, 2536
Klingner, Janette K., 1982
Klofsten, Magnus, 770
Klopsteg Memorial Lecture, 98
Knight Foundation Commission on the Future of Intercollegiate Athletics, 352
Knitzer, Jane, 727
Knowledge
acquisition, representation, and organization, **1431–1435**
in Bloom's taxonomy, 311
building, 1370–1373
consequences of, 41
construction, 1705
creativity, 507
dissemination, 1031
learning communities, 1163
local *vs.* generalizable, 1149–1150
organization, **2169–2173**
student presentations of, 2517
tacit, 1207–1208
teaching, knowledge bases of, **2482–2485,** 2486
See also Inert knowledge; Prior knowledge
Knowledge-based approaches to transfer, 1449–1450
Knowledge Forum, 1372
Knowledge management, 1232, *1233,* **1373-1376**
Knowledge Services, AACSB International's, 1
Knowles, J. Gary, 2491
Knox v. O'Brien, 1062
Knudsvig, Glenn, 1415
Kobasigawa, Akira, 1471
Koch, Will, 2046
Kohlberg, Lawrence, **1376–1378**
justice, 755
moral development, 1681–1682
moral education, 1685
Kolb, David A., 762
Kolbe, Lloyd, 1013, 2495
Kolodner, Janet, 1155, 1157, 1174
Koran, 1327–1328
Korea. *See* East Asia and the Pacific
Kornhaber, Mindy, 1200
Kounin, Jacob, 301
Kovalik, Susan, 203
Kramer, Santosky v., 282
Krampe, Ralf, 766
Krashen, Stephen, 176–177
Krathwohl, David, 2430–2432
Kraus-Boelte, Maria, 622
Krefeld Model of ethnic integration, 1105
Kreisel, Philip, 2314
Kriege, Matilda, 621
Krueger, Scott, 2076
Kuh, George D., 2046
Kuhl, Julius, 1120

Kuhlmeier, Hazelwood School District v., 2425
Kuhn, Thomas S., 10–11
Kurtzman, Lemon v., 2337, 2423
Kuwait. *See* Middle East and North Africa
Kyrgystan. *See* Eastern Europe and Central Asia

L

Labeling
  disabled students, 2286
  gifted and talented, 934
Laboratory of Comparative Human Cognition (LCHC), 469
Laboratory of Experimental Pedagogy (Paris), 187
Laboratory School, University of Chicago, 1689, 1833
Laboratory schools, nursery, 623
Labor issues. *See* Collective bargaining; Unions
Labor market, academic, **17–19**
  See also Teacher supply and demand
Labrant, Lou L., **1379–1380**
Ladson-Billings, Gloria, 1564
Lake, Peter F., 2075
Lamda Iota Tau, **1076–1077**
Lampert, Magdalene, 1546
Lancaster, Joseph, 711
Lancaster Method of instruction, 1178
Land-grant act. *See* Morrill Act
Land-grant colleges and universities, **1380–1384**
  agricultural education, 72–74
  extension services, 804
  faculty research and federal funding, 854–855
  federal funding for higher education, 861
  federal involvement in education, 837
  higher education finance, 871
  history of higher education, 1036
  listed by state, *1382–1383*
  National Association of State Universities and Land-Grant Colleges (NASULGC), 100, 101, **1749–1750**
  vocational education and, 2636–2637
  See also Morrill Act; Public colleges and universities
Land Ordinance of 1785, **3039–3043**
Laney, Lucy Craft, 174
Langer, Judith A., 2001
Language
  African-American Language, 1391–1392
  Ebonics, 1391–1392
  education and, **1388–1392**
  Hispanic Americans, 1966–1967
  school readiness, 2148–2149
Language acquisition, **1384–1388**
  developmental theory, 562, 565
  early childhood, 277
  language minority students, 1401
  reading, 1974
  secondary, 175–177
  Vygotsky, Lev, 575
Language arts, 713–714, **1392–1396**
Language change, 1399–1400
Language development, 1385–1386
Language minority students, **1396–1403**
  impact on education, **1400–1403**
  scope, **1396–1400**
  See also Bilingual education; English as a second language (ESL); Language; Language acquisition
Lanham Act
  early childhood education, 623
  federal involvement in education, 837
  immunizations, 1108
Lanier, Judith, 2441
Lao People's Democratic Republic. *See* East Asia and the Pacific
Laos, 639
  See also East Asia and the Pacific
Larson, Katherine, 2382
Larson, Reed, 46
Lassiter v. Department of Social Services, 282
"Last Will and Testament" (Bethune), 174–175
Latchkey children, **1403–1407**
Latency stage, 277–278
Latent class (LC) model, 141
Latent learning, 1461
Latent semantic analysis (LSA), 148, 1973
Latin America and the Caribbean, **1407–1413**
  compensatory education, **458–464**
  decentralization, 544, 546
  early childhood education, 627, 628
  gender issues, 920
  health and nutrition of young children, 627
Latin for Reading (Knudsvig), 1415
Latin instruction, **1413–1417**
Lattuca, Lisa, 521, 923, 925
Latvia. *See* Eastern Europe and Central Asia
Laubach Literacy, 2581
Laura Ingalls Wilder Award, 288
Lau v. Nichols, **2948–2951**
  bilingual education, 177–178
  immigrant education, 1101, 1102
  policy, 672
Lauver, Kristy, 733
Lave, Jean, 2462
Law
  ethics, 753
  journalism, 1349
  legal accountability, 653–654
  legal liability, 2075–2076
  liability for negligence, **1472–1475**
Law education, **1417–1419**
Lawlor, Edward, 2712
Law of effect, 1460
Law of the development of higher mental functions, 575
Lawrence, William, 1140
Law School Admission Test (LSAT), 1417, **1419–1420**
Laws (Plato), 1900
LCHC (Laboratory of Comparative Human Cognition), 469
LC (latent class) model, 141
LCME (Liaison Committee on Medical Education), 1586
Le, Huy, 733
Leaders' Center, National Conference of State Legislatures, 1761
Leadership
  academic deans, 9
  department chairpersons, 560–561
  development, 2193

educational, 234
Kappa Omicron Nu, **1075–1076**
planning and higher education, 2369
religiously-affiliated colleges and universities, 391–392
rural education, 2087
school, **664–668,** 1921
school boards, 2115
school principals, 1921
state departments of education, 2327
teacher styles, 973–974

Lead poisoning exposure, 1911

League of Nations, 1277–1278

Learn and Serve America program, 762

Learned helplessness, 1693, 2372

Learner-centered instruction, 2494
See also Child-centered education

Learning, **1421–1452**
analogical reasoning, **1421–1424,** 1429, 1450
assessment, 761–762
Bloom's taxonomy, 188, 311
categories, 248
causal reasoning, **1425–1427**
classroom assessment, 124
class size, **314–317,** *315*
collaborative, 2494
conceptual change, **1427–1431**
cultural expectations, **1961–1966**
democratic authority, 170
development, 575
direct instruction, 1160–1161
emotions, 60–61
environment, 300–302, 1179
failure, 1154–1155, 1158
foster care, 819
goals and international curriculum, 527–528
higher education, **2493–2499**
high-stakes testing, 2536
instructional strategies, 1180
insufficient sleep, 2233
interest, 1990–1991
knowledge acquisition, representation, and organization, **1431–1435**
knowledge building as distinct from, 1370–1371
language, 1390–1391
learning-by-doing, 1935
learning to teach, **2485–2488**
mastery learning, 188–189, 765–766
meaningful, 1443
metamemory, 1604
motor skills, *1701,* **1701–1703**
multimedia sources, **1493–1497**
neurological foundation, **1436–1437**
organizations, 1148
peer relations, **1864–1867**
perceptual processes, **1437–1441**
prior knowledge, 1151
problem solving, **1441–1444**
reading, 1996–1998
reasoning, **1444–1448**
science learning, **2166–2181**
strategy instruction, 1470–1471
teacher' knowledge of, 2483
teaching, **2492–2501**
technology, 2515–2516
from text, **1993–1995,** 1996–1997
transfer of, **1449–1452**
undergraduate education, 510, 515
See also Brain-based education; Learning aids; Learning theory

Learning aids
animated, 1169–1170, 1494–1495, 1577
Comenius, Johann, 421
instructional media, 2514–2515
mathematics, 1544, **1550–1552**
science education, 2177–2181
software, 1577
tutorial, 2582–2583
visual and aural, 1577
See also Educational technology

Learning a Living: A Blueprint for High Performance (report), 216

Learning by Design, 1156–1158, 1165

Learning communities, **1162–1163**
community-based organizations, 437
constructivism, 1465
higher education curriculum, 512
knowledge management, 1374–1375
Learning Communities: Creating Connections among Students, Faculty, and Disciplines (Gabelnick et al.), 1453
residential, 2044
teacher learning communities, **2461–2469**
undergraduate curriculum and, **1452–1457,** *1454*
See also Cooperative and collaborative learning

Learning Communities: Creating Connections among Students, Faculty, and Disciplines (Gabelnick et al.), 1453

Learning disabilities
brain scans and educational intervention, 205
college students, **410–413**
discrepancy model, 2008–2009
dyslexia, 989–990, 2008
handwriting, 989–990
identifying, 2008–2009
Learning Disabilities Act, 2008
low-income children, 808
reading disabilities, **2007–2013**
students, **1457–1458,** 2286

Learning Disabilities Act, 2008

Learning for Life Curriculum, 1688

"Learning for Mastery" (Bloom), 188

Learning from Media (Clark), 1576

Learning materials. *See* Instructional materials

Learning objectives. *See* Instruction, objectives

Learning outcomes
efficiency in education, 701–702
instructional strategies, 1179–1180
international statistics, 1288–1289
language arts, 1394
pedagogical agents, 1170
poverty and, 1905–1907, *1906,* 1913–1914
school climate and, 2123
student athletes, 358–361
See also Outcome Based Education (OBE)

Learning Sciences Institute, Vanderbilt University, 147

Learning theory, **1458–1469**
adaptive expertise, 764–765
behavioral views, 678–679, 680
behaviorism, 563, 678–679, 680, 1458–1461, 2493
cognitive, 679, 680
constructivist, 679–680, **1463–1467**
dynamic assessment, 128
historical overview, **1458–1463**

How People Learn: Bridging Research and Practice (National Research Council), 2646
How the Brain Learns: A Classroom Teacher's Guide (Sousa), 202
mediated learning experience (MLE), 128
motivation, 680
primary and secondary abilities, 572–573
schema theory, **1467–1469**
Thorndike, Edward Lee, 677
zone of proximal development (ZPD), 128
Learning to Be (report), 1481
Learning to learn, **1470–1472**
Learning to Read: The Great Debate (Chall), 258
Least restrictive environment (LRE), 37, 39
Lebanon. *See* Middle East and North Africa
Lecture, 1182–1183
Lederman, Leon, 93
LeDoux, Joseph, 203
Lee, Barbara, 794, 2074
Lee, Carol, 1512, 1706
Lee, Valerie, 2382
Lee v. Weisman, 2423
Left-handedness, 989
Legal accountability, 653–654
Legal Advocacy Fund, American Association of University Women, 104
Legal liability, 2075–2076
Legislation
Adoption and Safe Families Act, 269, 282, 284
Adoption Assistance and Child Welfare Act of 1980, 282, 284
affirmative action related, 63–64
Airport and Airway Development Act, 849
Americans with Disabilities Act (ADA), 149, 409, 1868–1869
Arts and Humanities Act of 1965, 1771
Bayh-Dole Act, 856
Bennett Law (Wisconsin), 1924
Bilingual Education Act, 178, 182
Carl D. Perkins Vocational Education acts, 216–217, 838, 2329, 2638–2639
Child Abuse Prevention and Treatment Act (CAPTA), 267
Child Nutrition Act of 1966, 2134
Civil Rights Act of 1964, 64
Civil Rights acts, 62, 178, 1868, 2424
Civil Rights Restoration Act, 2571
Constitution Act (Canada), 234
Copyright Act of 1976, 1187–1189
Custody of Infants Act (England), 281
Day Law (Kentucky), 171
Department of Education Organization Act, 2616–2617
Digital Millennium Copyright Act (DMCA), 1189–1190
Economic Opportunity Act of 1964, 2677
Education Act of 1944 (England), 1134
Educational Television Facilities Act, 657
Education for All Handicapped Children Act, 40, 719, 726, 838, 1617
Education Reform Act (England), 1134–1135, 1135
Elementary and Secondary Education Act (ESEA), 177, 314, 715, 837–838, 886, 1108, 1365–1366, 1801–1802, 1948–1949, 2545
Employment and Training Act (Great Britain), 487
Equal Access Act, 2375–2376
Equal Educational Opportunities Act of 1974, 178
Equity in Athletics Disclosure Act of 1996, 2571
Family Education Rights and Privacy Act (FERPA), 2013–2015
Family Preservation and Support Initiative, 269
Family Support Act of 1988 (FSA), 2677
Family Violence Prevention and Services Act, 2633
Federal Highway Safety Act, 598
Foreign Assistance Act, 1242
Foreign Service Act, 113
Fulbright-Hays Act, 113, 2619–2620
George-Barden Act, 2647
George-Deen Act, 976, 2647
Goals 2000: Educate America Act, 118, 216, 217, 277, 294–295, 838, 2155, 2174, 2546
Government Employee Training Act, 840
Hatch Act, 73
Hawkins -Stafford Amendments of 1988, 455
Health Maintenance Organization Act, 1530
Health Research Extension Act of 1985, 2037
Healthy Meals for Children Act, 2134
Higher Education Act, 33–34, 96, 673, 862, 2619–2620
Illinois Juvenile Court Act, 1350
Immigration and Nationality Act of 1952, 1312
Immigration and Naturalization Act, 1098
Improving America's Schools Act (IASA), 455, 2538
Indian Education Act, 1109
Individuals with Disabilities Education Act (IDEA), 37–39, 149, 161, 162, 284, 407–408, 726, 838, 1868–1869, 1885, 2008, 2280, 2285–2289
Job Training Partnership Act (JTPA), 488
Lanham Act, 623, 837, 1108
Learning Disabilities Act, 2008
Maritime Education and Training Act, 851
Mondale Lifelong Learning Act, 1481
Montgomery G.I. Bill, 930
Morrill Act, 72–73, 215, 216, 837, 854, 861, 871, 1036, 1049, 1380, 1381, 2636–2637
National and Community Service Act, 2205–2206, 2207
National Childhood Vaccine Injury Act (NCVIA), 1107
National Defense Education Act (NDEA), 862, 2325, 2538, 2615
National Origins Act of 1924, 1097–1098
National Research Act, 1091
National School Lunch Act (NSLA), 2131–2132
National Sea Grant College and Program Act, 2182
National Traffic and Motor Safety Act of 1966, 2574

National Vocational Education Act, 73–74
No Child Left Behind Act, 228, 663, 714, 718, 838, 1783, **1801–1803,** 2033, 2435–2436, 2538, 2540, 2546
Northwest Ordinance, 710, 837
Old Deluder Satan Act (Massachusetts Bay Colony), 710, 2636
Parental Notification law, 607–608
Personal Responsibility and Work Opportunity Reconciliation Act (PRWORA), 833–834, 2673–2675, 2677–2678
Poor Law Act (England), 281
Proposition 209 (California), 64
Proposition 227 (California), 179, 182
Public Broadcasting Act, 657
Public Law 91-248, 2132
Public Law 94-142, 2635
Public Law 103-448, 2133–2134
Public Laws 81-815 and 81-874, **1108–1109**
Ready to Learn Act of 1994, 200
Rehabilitation Act, 149, 408–409, 1868–1869
School Education Law of 1947 (Japan), 716
School-to-Work Opportunities Act (STWOA), 217, 731, 736–737, 838, 844, 2329, 2639
"Secondary Schools Achievement Act" (proposed), 2193–2194
Second Morrill Act of 1890, 1049
Servicemen's Readjustment Act, 837, 838, 861–862, **928–930**
Sheppard-Towner Act of 1921, 2676
Smith-Hughes Act, 73–74, 216, 804, 837, 2637, 2647
Smith-Lever Act, 73, 804, 2088
Smith-Sears Veterans' Rehabilitation Act of 1918, 1867
Social Security Act, 834, 1106, 1867–1868, 2676–2677
special education, 2280–2281
Taxpayer Relief Act of 1997, 863
Technology Education and Copyright Harmonization Act (proposed), 1189
Technology-Related Assistance for Individuals with Disabilities Act of 1988, 149
Tenures Abolition Act (England), 281
Title I, Elementary and Secondary Education Act (ESEA), 454–456, 457–458, 837–838
Title IV, Education and Secondary Education Act (ESEA), 2017
Title IV, Higher Education Act, 862
Title V, Elementary and Secondary Education Act of 1965, 2325
Title V, Higher Education Act of 1965, 1045
Title VI, Civil Rights Act of 1964, 64, 65
Title VI, Higher Education Act, 2619–2620
Title VII, Civil Rights Act of 1964, 64
Title IX, Goals 2000: Educate America Act, 2017
Title IX, Higher Education Act, 64, 351–352, 673, 804, 837, **2569–2573**
Transportation Equity Act for the 21st Century, 850
Tribally Controlled Community College Assistance Act, 2579
Veterans Readjustment Act of 1952, 929
Veterans Readjustment Benefits Act of 1966, 929
Violence Against Women Act of 1994 (VAWA), 2633
Vocational Act of 1963, 216
Vocational Education Act, 2637–2638
Vocational Rehabilitation Act, 838
Vocational Training Act of 1963, 77
Workforce Investment Act (WIA), 488, 730, 2329
See also Specific legislation
Legislative appropriations, 2339–2341
Legislative Corps, 99
Legislative earmarking, 2342
Lehman, Andreas C., 765
Lehrer, Richard, 1165
Lehrfreiheit, 14, 20, 2042
Leisure and recreation, 89
Lemke, Jay, 2462
Lemon v. Kurtzman, 2337, 2423
Leong, Deborah, 576
Leont'ev, Alexei, 576
LEP (limited English proficient) students, 1397–1398, 1400–1403
See also Bilingual education; Bilingualism; English as a second language (ESL); Language minority students
Lernfreiheit, 14, 20
Lesbian students. *See* Sexual orientation
Lesbian studies. *See* Gay and lesbian studies
Leslie, Alan, 1425
Leslie, Larry, 770, 795, 797, 2527
Lesotho. *See* Sub-Saharan Africa
Lesser, Gerald, 1580
Lesson for Life: Responsibility, Respect, Results (initiative), 110
The Lessons of Experience: How Successful Executives Develop On the Job (McCall et al.), 733
Lester, James, 1169
Level of capacity and efficiency, 702
Leveraging Educational Assistance Partnerships program, 837
Leveson, Lynne, 733
Levin, Henry M., 551
Levin, Joel R., 1980
Levine, Arthur, 239
Levstik, Linda, 1057
Levy, Frank, 690
Levy, Janet, 2141
Lewin, Kurt, 170, 973, 1817
Lewis, Marva, 2628
Lexicography, 2671
Li, Xiaoming, 2628
Liability, **1472–1475,** 2074–2076
Liaison Committee on Medical Education (LCME), 1586
Liberal arts colleges, **1475–1477**
Liberal education
Association of American Colleges and Universities commitment, 151–152
Augustine, St., 160
Bestor, A. E., Jr., 173
Buchanan, Scott, 213

The Challenge of Connecting Learning (report), 517
curriculum, 522–523
curriculum considerations, 522–523
general education *vs.*, 923
St. John's College, 2366–2367
teacher learning and, 2486
Ties That Bind: Integrating Undergraduate Liberal and Professional Study (report), 517

Liberation theology, 1571–1572

Liberia. *See* Sub-Saharan Africa

Liberty, 670, 674–676, 723–724

Libraries
consortia, 476–477
income and library distribution, 2712
librarians, 2139–2140
National Library of Education, 683
National Transit Library, 850
school libraries, 287, **2137–2141**
teaching center, 256

Library and information science, 1071–1072

Libya. *See* Middle East and North Africa

Licensing, driver, 597–598

Lichten, William, 58

Lickona, Thomas, 261

Lieberman, Ann, 2461

Life-adjustment education, 1937–1938

Life experience for college credit, **1477–1480**

Lifelong learning, **1480–1483**
community education, 448, 449
Smithsonian Institution, 2240–2241
See also Adult education; Nontraditional students

Life stages, eight, 752

Light, Richard, 1711

Lighted schools. *See* Full-service schools

Lilly Endowment, 1808

Limited English proficient (LEP) students, 1397–1398, 1400–1403, 2638
See also Bilingual education; Bilingualism; English as a second language (ESL); Language minority students

Lincoln School, **1484–1485**

Linden, Wim van der, 140

Lindholm-Leary, Kathryn, 180

Lindquist, E. F., **1485–1487**

Line-item budgeting, 1953

Lingua program (European Union), 1252

Linguistic intelligence, 1198

Linkages terminology, 1793

Link mnemonic method, 1671

Linn, Robert, 2458

Lipka, Jerry, 1564

Lippitt, Ronald, 973

Lipsey, Michael, 2030

Lipsitz, Joan, 1633

Lisbon Convention on the Recognition of Qualifications Pertaining to Higher Education in the European Region, 27

Listening, active, 1979

Literacy, **1487–1509**
Clark, Septima Poinsette, 299
computer, 714, 743, 2518
culture and, **1509–1513**
early experience and, 566
education, 742
emergent literacy, **1487–1489**
English language learners (ELLs), 182–183
integrated literacy instruction, 1515–1516
International Reading Association, **1307–1309**
intertextuality, **1489–1493**
language minorities, 1398
Literacy Volunteers of America, 2581
media, 1580–1581, 2520
Middle East and North Africa, 1625
multimedia, **1493–1497, 1497–1500**
narrative comprehension and production, **1500–1504**
reading and, **1513–1518**
science, 2159–2160
South Asia, 2273, *2274*
tutoring, 2581
United States rates, 1289
vocabulary, **1504–1507**
writing and composition, **1507–1509**
See also Adult literacy; General Educational Development Test (GED); Reading; Reading comprehension

Literacy Volunteers of America, 2581

Literature
Lambda Iota Tau, **1076–1077**
narratives, 1500–1503
reading literature texts, 1988
See also English education

Literature as Exploration, 288

Lithuania. *See* Eastern Europe and Central Asia

Littell, Julia, 2712

Little, Judith, 2441

Little Albert Study, 2669

Littleton, Colorado, school shootings, 2310

Living and learning centers (LLCs), **1518–1520,** 2044

Lloyd-Jones, Esther, 2388

Loans, student. *See* Student loans

Lobbying
American Association of Colleges for Teacher Education, 93
American Association of School Administrators (AASA), 99–100
American Association of State Colleges and Universities (AASCU), 100
American Association of University Women, 104
American Council on Education (ACE), 107, 109
American Federation of Teachers (AFT), 111
Association of American Universities, 154
Council for Exceptional Children, 500
Council of Chief State School Officers (CCSSO), 502, 503
National Business Education Association, 1753
National Education Association, 1770
National Science Teachers Association, 1792
teacher unions, 2479–2480

Localism, 2259

Local Only Teacher Unions (LOTUs), 2478

Local *vs.* generalizable knowledge, 1149–1150

Locido, Marguerite, 1470

Locke, John, 562

Locke, Larry, 1891

Lodahl, Thomas, 10

Loeber, Rolf, 1360

Logic, 116
  See also Formal reasoning
Logical-mathematical intelligence, 1198
Logical model of intellectual development, 1896–1897
Long, Huey, 350
Longitudinal Study of Structured English Immersion Strategy, Early-Exit and Late-Exit Programs for Language-Minority Children, 179
Long-range planning in higher education, **2367–2369**
Lonigan, Christopher, 1489
Looping, **1520–1522**
The Looping Handbook (Grant et al.), 1521
Lopez, Goss v., 2425
Lopez, United States v., 478
Lord, Frederick, 140
Lorentz, Elizabeth, 2143
LOTUs (Local Only Teacher Unions), 2478
Louisiana State University, 350
Louisville Kindergarten and Training School, 622
Lounsbury, John H., 1521
Love, G. M., 77
Low, Juliette, 2731
Low, Seth, 229
Low achieving students
  dynamic assessment, 127–130
  social promotion, 2262–2264
  See also Academic achievement
Lowenfeld, Viktor, **1522–1524**
Low-income families
  academic performance, 1836
  at-risk youth, 2709–2710
  child care cost, 274–276
  Child Care Development Fund (CCDF), 616–617
  college attendance encouragement, 395–396
  community violence exposure, 2627–2630
  compensatory education, 453–463
  dental health, 555–556
  digital divide, 2519–2520
  early childhood education access, 618–619
  Eastern Europe and Central Asia region enrollment rates, 643
  elementary education, 718
  equality of opportunity, 1948–1949
  health care, 1000–1001
  income support services, **833–836**
  inequitable instruction, 306
  literacy and culture, 1510–1511
  Rightstart project, 1562
  student employment, 728, 729, 730, 736
  Success for All programs, **2405–2407,** *2406*
  teachers of students from, 2449
  teenage pregnancy, 2061–2063
  Upward Bound (UB), **2603–2605**
  welfare reform, **2673–2676**
  See also Family support services; Poverty; Socioeconomic status; Urban education
Low-performing schools
  lack of leadership, 667
  statewide testing, 2540
Lowther, Deborah, 1578
Loyalty oaths, 751
LSA (latent semantic analysis), 148, 1973
LSAT (Law School Admission Test), 1417, **1419–1420**
Lubart, Todd, 1207
Lubbock, John, 212
Lunch programs, 2131–2134
Lutheran schools, 1941–1942
Lutz, Pamela B., 2164
Luxembourg. *See* Western Europe
Lynton, Ernest A., 796, 797
Lyon, G. Reid, 2009
Lyotard, Jean Francois, 1210

M

M2RCML approach to psychometric modeling, 142
Macabbi USA, 2740
Macau. *See* East Asia and the Pacific
Macdonald, James, **1525–1526**
Maclure, William, 1876
MACOS ("Man: A Course of Study"), 2267
Macy, Anne Sullivan, 2278
Madagascar. *See* Sub-Saharan Africa
Madeline Hunter Method, 1093–1094
Madison, James, 674
Madison Metropolitan School District Classroom Action Research Professional Development Program, 2466
Maggs, Jennifer, 1405
Magnet School Assistance Program, 1528–1529
Magnet schools, **1526–1529**
  arts schools, 1719
  career-theme, 82, 83, 85
  Magnet School Assistance Program, 1528–1529
  Magnet Schools of America (MSA), 1528
  See also Alternative education; School choice
Magnet Schools of America (MSA), 1528
Magolda, Marcia Baxter, 521
Mainstreaming, 2281–2282, 2285–2286
Maintenance, facility, 2126, **2128–2131**
The Maintenance of High Ethical Standards in the Conduct of Research (report), 2037
Major gifts to colleges and universities, 1141–1142
Majors, academic, **19–23**
  African-American studies, **65–69,** *68, 69,* 2691–2693
  business education, 220–222
  classics, 1414
  curriculum, 523
  engineering, 737–740
  evaluation, 22
  exponential, 1087
  interdisciplinary, **1210–1215**
  U.S. Air Force Academy, 1644–1645
  See also Degree programs; Disciplines; Interdisciplinarity
Making Connections: Teaching and the Human Brain (Caine and Caine), 202
Making Students Matter (report), 110
Making the Grade (report), 697
Malawi. *See* Sub-Saharan Africa
Malaysia, 639, 2585–2586
  See also East Asia and the Pacific
Maldives, 2236, 2275
  See also South Asia
Mali. *See* Sub-Saharan Africa
Malnutrition, 1911
  See also Health and nutrition

Maloney, Michael, 360–361
Malpractice, 1475
Malta. *See* Western Europe
"Man: A Course of Study" (MACOS), 2267
Managed care, **1529–1534**
Management
  department, 560
  facility, 2126
  school-based decision-making, **2099–2102**
  See also Business education
Management Education Career Marketplace, 2
Mann, Horace, **1534–1537**
  common schools, 429–430, 2245–2246
  education reform reports, 695
  elementary education history, 712
  moral education, 1684
  reading instruction, 1999
Mannheim, Karl, 949
Manpower Services Commission (MSC, Great Britain), 487
Manualism, 1018, 1020
Manual training, 915–916
Manuscript writing, 988–989
Map reading, 927
MARAD (Maritime Administration), 851
Maran, Steven, 2628
Maratea, Italy workshop, 469
March, H. W., 762
March, Herbert W., 2502
March, James, 2042
Marijuana use, 606
Maritime Administration (MARAD), 851
Maritime Education and Training Act, 851
Market accountability, 653
Market-based allocation, 2049
Market-based reforms, 552–553
Market economies *vs.* command economies, 641–645
Marketing. *See* Recruitment
Markman, Ellen M., 1977, 1979
Marlowe, John, 1111
Marsh, Herbert W., 730
Martin, R. A., 78
Martinez, Pedro, 2628
Martinique. *See* Latin America and the Caribbean
Marwedel, Emma, 622
Marxism, 901–902
Maryland School Performance Assessment Program (MSPAP), 2539
Mary Sharp College, 2225
Marzano, Robert, 2433, 2644
Maslow, Abraham, 1865
Massachusetts
  compulsory school attendance, 465
  Mann, Horace, 1535–1536
  public high schools, 2184
  school organization, 2332
Massachusetts, Prince v., 465
Mass production of goods and services, 641–642
Masters, Geoffrey, 141
Master's degree programs, **1537–1539**
  "Adviser of Women," Teachers College, 2388
  business administration, 221, 222
  Carnegie Classification, 244, 245
  divinity, 594
  education, 968, 969
  engineering, 738–739
  National Board for Professional Teaching Standards, 1751
  nursing, 1819
  overview, 965–966
  See also Graduate education
Mastery learning
  Bloom, Benjamin S., 124, 188–189
  motivation, 1694, 1697
  Outcome Based Education, 1829
  See also Expertise
Math and Science Partnerships program (National Science Foundation), 1790
Mathematical Problem Solving (Schoenfeld), 1546
Mathematics education, **1539–1569**
  Adding It Up: Helping Children Learn Mathematics (National Research Council), 1729
  The Adventures of Jasper Woodbury (middle school mathematics series), 1151–1153
  algebra, **1542–1545,** *1544*
  brain imaging and mathematical ability, 205
  complex problem solving, **1545–1548**
  computer technology classroom use, 305
  culture and number sense, **1563–1566**
  Curriculum and Evaluation Standards for School Mathematics (National Council of Teachers of Mathematics), 1547, 1548, 1559, 2174, 2320
  elementary schools, 714
  Fawcett, Harold P., 835–836
  figure problem, *1561*
  gender equity, 1126–1127
  geometry, **1548–1550**
  history, 2237–2238
  inequitable instruction, 305–306
  learning theories, 1553
  learning tools, **1550–1552**
  Mathematics Education Trust (MET), 1768
  Middle-School Mathematics through Application Project (MMAP), 1164–1165
  myths, mysteries, and realities, **1552–1558**
  National Council of Teachers of Mathematics (NCTM), **1767–1768**
  National Research Council studies, 1729
  The Nature of Proof (Fawcett), 835, 836
  number sense, **1558–1566,** 1567
  poetry, relationship to, 212
  school readiness, 2149–2150
  Smith, David Eugene, 2236–2238
  standards, 717–718, 1767, 2174
  static *vs.* dynamic curricula, *528*
  story problems *vs.* anchors, 1152
  studies, 1729
  teacher preparation, **1539–1542**
  textbooks, 2556
  Trends in Mathematics and Science Study (TIMSS), 1226, 1227, **1233–1236**
  undergraduate curriculum reform, 512
  Upward Bound Math/Science program (UBMS), 2604
  word problems, **1566–1569**
  See also Third International Mathematics and Science Study (TIMSS)

Mathematics Education Trust (MET), 1768
Matthew effect, 1372
Mauritania. *See* Sub-Saharan Africa
Mauritius. *See* Sub-Saharan Africa
Mayer, John D., 1191–1192
Mayer, Richard, 1442, 1577, 1595
Mayer, Salovey, and Caruso Emotional Intelligence Test (MSCEIT), 1192
Mayer, Susan, 1905
Mays, Benjamin, **1569–1572**
Mazurek, Kas, 2294
MBDA (Minority Business Development Agency), 841–842
MCAT (Medical College Admission Test), 1585
McCall, William A., **1572–1574**
McCarthy, Joseph P., 102
McCarthyism
  academic freedom, 15
  American Association of University Professors (AAUP), 102
  Du Bois, W. E. B., 612
McClintock, Barbara, 104
McCloy, Charles, 1887
McCormick, Robert, 360–361
McCrary, Runyoon v., 2424
McCulloch, Warren, 1562
McCullough, David, 2439
McDill, Edward, 48
McDonald, Dale, 1928
McEneaney, Elizabeth, 534–535
McEwan, Patrick, 551
McFadden, Kathleen L., 733, 734
McFadyen-Ketchum, Steven, 70
McGregor, Josette, 1707
McGuffey Readers
  elementary education history, 713
  reading instruction, 1999
  textbooks, history of, 2555
McGuire, Frederick, 1113
McKeachie, Wilbert J., 254
McKiever v. Pennsylvania, 1351
McKnight, John, 2462
McLanahan, Sara, 1906
M-CLASS (Multicultural Collaborative for Literacy and Secondary Schools), 2466
McLaughlin, Daniel, 1511
McLaughlin, Milbrey
  academic clubs, 319–320
  education reform, 692
  program evaluation, 2030, 2031
McLaurin v. Oklahoma State Regents, 64
McLuhan, Marshall, 936
McMillan, Margaret and Rachel, 622–623
McMurry, Charles, 1022, **1574–1575**
McMurry, Foster, 173
McNamara, Danielle, 1426
McNeil, Linda, 2536
McNichol, Theresa, 819
Mead, Margaret, 93
Meaningful learning, 1443
Measles, 1107
Measurement
  chronometric information processing, 568–569
  classical test theory (CTT), 140
  competencies, 2523
  cost-effectiveness analysis, 495–496
  decentralization, 543–544
  economic benefits of education investment, **647–651**
  educational, 1573–1574
  Educational Measurement (Lindquist), 1486
  educational outcomes, 701
  efficiency, 703–704
  faculty research and scholarship performance, 784
  generalizability theory, 140
  How to Measure in Education (McCall), 1573
  Institute of Mental Measurements, 214
  intelligence, **1194–1198,** 2566–2567
  item response theory (IRT), 140
  Lindquist, E. F., 1486
  portfolio assessment, 138
  readability, 1972–1973
  research, 2022
  school board performance, 2106–2107
  school climate, 2122–2123
  school-linked services effectiveness, 2145–2147
  teaching and research quality, 2502–2503
  theory, 1486
  See also Psychometrics
Mechanical engineering, 739
Mechanical view of the mind, 1332–1333
Media
  impact on adolescent development, 279
  influence on children, **1579–1583**
  learning and, **1575–1579**
  literacy, 1580–1581, 2520
  school library program goals, 2138–2139
  specialists, 2139–2140
Mediated learning experience (MLE), 128, 130
Mediating structures, 434
Medicaid, 1001, 1530–1531, 2674
Medical care. *See* Health services
Medical College Admission Test (MCAT), 1585
Medical education, **1585–1587**
  accreditation, 33
  Alpha Omega Alpha, 1067–1068
  Flexner, Abraham, 891–893
Medical model of special education, 2293
Medicare Learning Network, 844
Medication
  aggressive behavior, 70
  attention deficit hyperactivity disorder, 158
  mental health, 1615–1616
Medley, Donald M., 308–309
Mednick, Sarnoff A., 506
Medsker, Leland, 96, 332
Meeting the Need for Quality Action in the South (report), 697
Meier, Kenneth, 663, 1964
Meiklejohn, Alexander, 212, **1587–1588**
MEIS (Multidimensional Emotional Intelligence Scale), 1192
Meister, Carla, 313, 1982
Mellon Foundation, 352
Memory, **1588–1613**
  autobiographical memory, **1588–1591**
  context dependency, 1449
  development, **1591–1593**
  graphics, diagrams, and videos, **1594–1596**
  implicit memory, **1596–1600,** 1606
  information processing, 568
  knowledge acquisition, 1433–1434
  memorization, 1993
  mental models, **1600–1602**

metamemory, **1602–1605**
mnemonic techniques, **1669–1672**
myths, mysteries, and realities, **1605–1609**
neurology, 1436–1437, *1437*
structures and functions, **1609–1613**
words, 1335
MENA region. *See* Middle East and North Africa
MENC: The National Association for Music Education, 1720
Mennonite schools, 1943–1944
Meno (Plato), 1899
Mental health
academic performance, 1836–1837
counseling services, college and university, **1869–1871,** 1873–1874, 1970
family members, 810–811
family support services, 832
foster care children, 284
poverty, 1911–1914
See also Emotionally disturbed students
Mental health services
children's, **1613–1616**
full-service schools, 907
school, 1006–1007
Mental imagery and reading comprehension, 1979–1980
Mental Measurements Yearbook (Buros), 214
Mental models, 1560–1561, **1600–1602**
Mental representation and comprehension, 1977
Mental retardation, **1616–1618**
Binet, Alfred, 186–187
severe and multiple disabilities, 2210, 2211
special education, 2287
See also Disabled students
Mental speed, 1114
Mentkowski, Marcia, 521
Mentoring, **1618–1620**
teacher education, 912
teacher evaluation, 2460
tutoring, 2581
youth organizations and clubs, 318, 319
See also Induction programs
Mentor Prize, 92
MEP (Migrant Education Program), 1640–1641
Merchant Marine Academy, U.S., 851, **1646–1649**
Mergens, Board of Education of Westside Community Schools v., 2423
Merit and teacher evaluation, 2454
Merrill, David, 1160, 2432
Messiah College, Boyer Center at, 201
Messick, Samuel, 2543–2544
Meta-analysis, 2025
Metacognition, **1470–1472**
complex problem solving, 1546
higher education learning, 2493–2494
knowledge acquisition, 1434–1435
Meta-ethics, 755
Metallurgical engineering, 740
Metamemory, **1602–1605**
Meta-professionals, college teachers as, 415
Methodology
classroom observation, 307–308
cost effectiveness measurement, 495–496
Eight-Year Study, 708
information processing research, 568–569
method of loci, 1434, 1671
Methods of Teaching (Charters), 263
projecture of educational expenditures, 659–661
for studying teaching, **2488–2492**
teacher evaluation, **2457–2461**
See also Research methods
Methods of Teaching (Charters), 263
MET (Mathematics Education Trust), 1768
Metzler, Michael, 1891
Mexican Americans. *See* Hispanic Americans
Mexico, 459–463
See also Latin America and the Caribbean
Meyer, John, 534–535, 2454
Meyer, Linda, 2005
Meyer, Robert, 2335
Meyer v. State of Nebraska
child protective services, 282
compulsory education, 464
home schooling, 1061
immigrant education, 1100
private schools, 1924–1925
state relations to private schools, 2335–2336
Supreme Court cases, 2422
MFY (Mobilization for Youth) Program, 436
MHSA (Mine Safety and Health Administration), 847
Michaelis, John, 2433
Michaels, Sarah, 1510, 2467
Michigan, 2540
Microteaching, **1620–1623,** 2447
Middle Ages, 1414
Middle Atlantic colonies, 710
Middle childhood development, 277–278
Middle East and North Africa, 628, **1623–1630**
Middle school
principals, 1634
Middle-School Mathematics through Application Project (MMAP), 1164–1165, 1166
Middle schools, **1630–1635**
art education, 119
Core Knowledge Sequence, 535–537
emergence of, 2186
foreign language education, 897–898
guidance and counseling, 977
health programs, 1003–1004
independent study, 1110–1111
Learning by Design, 1156–1158, 1165
looping, 1521–1522
mathematics teachers, 1539
Middle-School Mathematics through Application Project (MMAP), 1164–1165
music education, 1720–1721
scheduling, 2096, *2097,* 2098
science, 2160, 2161
urban, 2609
Middle States Association of Colleges and Schools (MSA), 28, 30
Middleton, James, 1165
Midwest Middle School Association, 1631
Miel, Alice, **1635–1638**
Migrant students, **1638–1642**
Migrant Education Program (MEP), 1640–1641
Migrant Head Start program, 844
See also Immigrant education

MILES (Multiple Integrated Laser Engagement System), 1657–1658
Military, U.S.
  Impact Aid Program, 1108–1109
  intelligence tests, 1113
  military academies, 843, **1642–1653**
  professional education, **1653–1655**
  research, 861
  segregation, 63
  training doctrine, **1655–1658**
  U.S. Air Force Academy, **1642–1645**
  U.S. Coast Guard Academy, **1645–1646**
  U.S. Merchant Marine Academy, **1646–1649**
  U.S. Military Academy, **1649–1652**
  U.S. Naval Academy, **1652–1653**
  U.S. War Colleges, **2620–2621**
  See also Department of Defense, U.S.; Specific branches
Milk program, 2134–2135
Miller, Lynn, 2461
Miller Analogies test, 968–969
Millet, John, 385
Millikan Medal, 98
Milliken v. Bradley, 2424
Mills, Caleb, 695
Mills v. Board of Education of the District of Columbia, 672, 1868, **2877–2892**
Milwaukee school system, 2155
Mine Safety and Health Administration (MHSA), 847
Minimum competency testing, 2535
Ministries of education
  Middle East and North Africa, 1624–1625, 1627
  standards-driven reform model, 2319–2320, 2322
Minnesota, 82
Minorities
  admissions, 397
  Boys and Girls Club participation, 319
  Catholic schools, 325
  college student retention rates, 403
  dental health, 555–556
  equity in public schools, 1948–1949
  faculty diversity, 776–778
  faculty roles and responsibilities, 793
  graduation rates, 2706, 2707
  higher education, 1024–1025, **1968–1971**
  intelligence testing, 1115–1116
  Labrant, Lou L., 1380
  language minorities, **1396–1403**
  parenting, 1850–1851
  population trends, 2705
  poverty rates, 2707
  principals, 1922
  private school enrollment, 1922–1923, 1927
  public high schools, 2186–2187
  rural education, 2086
  sexual orientation, 2219
  teachers, 2449
  See also Multiculturalism; Race/ethnicity; Specific groups
Minority Business Development Agency (MBDA), 841–842
Minors tried as adults, 1351, 1356, 1358
Minsky, Marvin, 1467
Mintz, Jerry, 85
MIRM (multidimensional item response model), 141
Misbehavior, classroom, 301–302
Misconceptions and categories, 248
Misconduct
  allegations of faculty, 758
  college athletics, 370
  research, **2037–2041**
  See also Corruption
The Mis-Education of the Negro (Woodson), 2692
Mislevy, Robert, 139
Missions
  chief academic affairs officers, 265
  community colleges, 446–447
  Department of Education, 2617
  faculty senates, 794–795
  liberal arts colleges, 1476
  schools and civics education, 294
  urban schools, 2610
Mississippi Freedom Schools, **1668–1669**
Missouri, 830
Missouri ex rel Gaines v. Canada, 2423
Missouri v. Jenkins, 480, 2202, 2424
Mitchell, Elmer, 362
Mitchell, Maria, 93
Mixed teaching style, 160
MLA (Modern Language Association of America), **1672–1674**
MLE (Mediated learning experience), 128, 130
MMAP (Middle-School Mathematics through Application Project), 1164–1165
Mnemonics, 1434, **1669–1672,** 1980
Mobility, student, **2381–2385**
Mobility training, 2635
Mobilization for Youth (MFY) Program, 436
Model-It (software), 2178–2179
Models
  alternative school, 84–85
  behavior, 1462–1463
  instructional design, 1165
  mathematics, 1568
  memory, 1610–1611
  neighborhood, 1793–1794
  student departure, 403–406
  technology, 2178–2179
Moden, Gary, 265
Modern era reform reports, 697–698
Modernization of school facilities, **2128–2131**
Modernization theory, 937
Modern Language Association of America (MLA), **1672–1674**
Modern Red Schoolhouse (MRSh), **1674–1675**
Modern reform period school funding, 886
Modern warfare, 1657
Moe, Terry, 1927, 2105
Moje, Elizabeth B., 2002
Moldova. *See* Eastern Europe and Central Asia
Moll, Luis, 1511, 1564
Molnar, Alex, 949
Mondale Lifelong Learning Act, 1481
Monitorialism, 711
Monitoring students, 301
Monitor model of second language acquisition, 176
Monk, Christopher, 1442
Monographs, 2601

Montessori, Maria, 84, 942, **1675–1680**
Montessori Accreditation Council for Teacher Education (MACTE), 1679–1680
Montessori Reexamined (Kilpatrick), 1679
Montessori schools, 84, 1678–1679
Montgomery G.I. Bill. *See* Servicemen's Readjustment Act
Mood
  adolescence, 279
  emotions, 58
  sleep, 2233
Moore, Mary Sue, 2628
Moral development, **1680–1683**
  accountability, 652
  higher education, 2496
  Kohlberg, Lawrence, 1376–1378
  Plato, 1900
  See also Character development; Civics and citizenship education; Moral education
Moral discussion, 1377
Moral education, **1683–1688**
  See also Character development; Civics and citizenship education; Moral development
Morality of care, 1682
The Moral Judgment of the Child (Piaget), 1680
Morehouse College, 1570–1571
Moreno, Roxana, 1170
Morgan, Thomas Hunt, 93
Morine-Dershimer, Greta, 2491
Morocco. *See* Middle East and North Africa
Morrill Act, **3060–3062**
  African American education, 63
  agricultural education, 72–73
  agricultural research, 854–855
  business education, 215, 216
  higher education aid, 837
  higher education history, 1036
  historically black colleges and universities, 1049
  state university support, 861, 871
  utilitarian support, 923
  See also Land-grant colleges and universities
Morrisett, Lloyd, 1580
Morrison, Coleman, 1999
Morrison, Gary R., 1578
Morrison, Henry C., 886, **1688–1690**
Morrison Plan, 1689–1690
Mort, Paul, 886
Mortimer, Jeylan T., 728, 730, 731
Moss, Beverly, 1510
Mossman, Lois Coffey, 0, 2506
Mosteller, Frederick, 315
Mother-child interactions, 130
Mother Play, 190
Motion pictures, 2514
Motion Pictures and Youth (Charters), 264
Motivation, **1690–1701**
  adaptive expertise, 764
  classroom climate, 301
  developmental theory, 572–573
  higher education, 2496–2497
  high-stakes testing, 2536, 2539–2540
  instruction, **1695–1698**
  learning, 680
  media, 1577–1578
  overview, **1690–1695**
  peer relations, 1865
  self-regulated learning, **1698–1701**
  See also Affective and conative processes; Incentives; Reinforcement
Motor learning, *1701,* **1701–1703**
Moulton, Mark, 2107
Mousavi, Samual, 1577
Movement-based physical education curriculum, 1888
Movies, influence of on children, 264
Mozambique. *See* Sub-Saharan Africa
MRSh (Modern Red Schoolhouse), **1674–1675**
MSA (Magnet Schools of America), 1528
MSA (Middle States Association of Colleges and Schools), 28
MSCEIT (Mayer, Salovey, and Caruso Emotional Intelligence Test), 1192
MSC (Manpower Services Commission, Great Britain), 487
MSPAP (Maryland School Performance Assessment Program), 2539
Mueller v. Allen, 2423
Mulhall, Peter, 1405
Mullins v. Pine Manor College 2075
Multiage student grouping, 1813, 1824
Multicultural Collaborative for Literacy and Secondary Schools (M-CLASS), 2465–2466
Multiculturalism, **1703–1716**
  academic achievement, 1962
  activities, 375
  Canada, 237
  children's literature, 286
  Dimensions of Multicultural Education (Banks), 1705
  English, 743
  family composition, 812
  higher education, 2496
  Intergroup Education in Cooperating Schools Project, 2428
  music education, 1725
  peace education and, 1863
  social organization of schools, 2255–2256
  social studies, 2268
  teachers, 2436
  testing, 685
  women's studies, 2688–2689
  See also Culture; Diversity; Race/ethnicity
Multidimensional Emotional Intelligence Scale (MEIS), 1192
Multidimensional item response models (MIRM), 141
Multidisciplinarity. *See* Interdisciplinarity
Multigenre English, 743
Multilingual English, 743
Multimedia
  English, 743
  learning, **1493–1497**
  literacy, **1497–1500**
Multiple cognitive abilities, 680–681
Multiple disabilities, students with, **2210–2213**
Multiple Integrated Laser Engagement System (MILES), 1657–1658
Multiple intelligences, **1198–1201**
  alternative education, 84
  individual differences, 1115
  outdoor and environmental education, 1834
  triarchic intelligence theory as different from, 1209

Multipurpose academic consortia, 475–476
Multiversity, 385
Mumford, Lewis, 207
Mumps, 1107
Murnane, Richard, 690
Murphy v. State of Arkansas, 1061
Murray, Charles, 1196, 1962
Murray, Harry G., 416
Murray, John P., 256
Muscular movement handwriting, 988
Musculoskeletal conditions, 1885
Museums, **1716–1718**
  Hull-House Labor Museum, 41
  school museums, 2514
  Smithsonian Institution, 854, **2238–2241**
Museums for a New Century (American Association of Museums), 1717–1718
Music education, **1718–1726**
  activities, 2375
  MENC: The National Association for Music Education, 1720
  music intelligence, 1198
  overview, **1719–1723**
  Pi Kappa Lambda, **1080–1081**
  teacher preparation, **1723–1726**
Muslims. *See* Islam
Muthen, Bengt, 141
Mutual instruction, 711
Myanmar, 639
  See also East Asia and the Pacific
Myers, Michele, 1477
My Pedagogic Creed (Dewey), 581, **3004–3010**
Myths
  intelligence and intelligence tests, **1201–1206**
  learning to teach, 2485–2486
  mathematics learning, **1552–1558**
  memory, **1605–1609**

N

NAACP (National Association for the Advancement of Colored People), 197, 610–612
NABTE (National Association for Business Teacher Education), 224
NABT (National Association of Biology Teachers), **1737–1739**
NACAC (National Association of College Admission Counseling), 383
Nachtigal, Paul, 2085
NACURH (National Association of College and University Residence Halls), 342
NAEA. *See* National Art Education Association (NAEA)
NAEP. *See* National Assessment of Educational Progress (NAEP)
NAESP (National Association of Elementary School Principals), **1739–1741**
NAEYC. *See* National Association for the Education of Young Children (NAEYC)
NAGB (National Assessment Governing Board), 133, 134
Nagel, Kris, 1157
Naglieri, Jack A., 570
NAICU (National Association of Independent Colleges and Universities), 152, **1741–1742**
Naismith, James, 348
NAIS (National Association of Independent Schools), **1742–1743**
Namibia. *See* Sub-Saharan Africa
NAM (National Association of Manufacturers), 2637
Nannies, 271
NARA (National Archives and Records Administration), **1731–1734**
Narration and sound effects, 1494–1495
Narratives
  comprehension and production, **1500–1504**
  as method of studying teaching, 2491
  in texts, 1996
NASAD (National Association of Schools of Art and Design), **1743–1745**
NASA (National Aeronautics and Space Administration), 858
NASC (National Association of Student Councils), 1747
NASC (Northwest Association of Schools and Colleges), 28
Nasir, Na'ilah, 1451
NAS (National Academy of Sciences), **1727–1731**
NAS (National Association of Scholars), 517
NAS (New American Schools), **1798–1800**
NASPE. *See* National Association for Sports and Physical Education (NASPE)
Nasr, Seyyed Hossein, 1329
NASULGC (National Association of State Universities and Land-Grant Colleges), 100, 101, **1749–1750**
National Academy of Early Childhood Programs, 1737
National Academy of Education, 133
National Academy of Sciences (NAS), **1727–1731**
  evaluation of National Assessment of Educational Progress (NAEP), 133
  federal funding for academic research, 854
  research misconduct definition, 2038
National Achievement Scholarship Program, 1781
National achievement tests, **2545–2550**
National Aeronautics and Space Administration (NASA), 858
National Alliance for Civic Education, 296
National and Community Service Act, 2205–2206, 2207
National Archives and Records Administration (NARA), **1731–1734**
National Art Education Association (NAEA), **1734–1736**
  art education expectations, 118
  art teacher preparation standards, 121, 122
National Art Honor Society, 1735
National Assessment Governing Board (NAGB), 133
National Assessment of Educational Progress (NAEP), **131–134**
  business involvement in education, 227
  Civics Assessment, 295, 296
  Council of Chief State School Officers (CCSSO), 502

elementary education, 719
geography assessment, 926
as high-stakes assessment, 2533–2537
history learning, 1057
Keppel's role in, 1366
main, 132–133
as "national" achievement test, 2547–2548
public school students, 1949
reauthorization of, 2546
score trends, 2547–2548
Trend Report, 296

National Association and Council of Business Schools, 36

National Association for Business Teacher Education (NABTE), 224

National Association for Nursery Education. *See* National Association for the Education of Young Children (NAEYC)

National Association for Sports and Physical Education (NASPE)
health education, 1006
overview, 89
physical education, 1889, 1890–1891

National Association for the Advancement of Colored People (NAACP), 197, 610–612

National Association for the Education of Young Children (NAEYC), 273, 623, 624, 625, **1736–1737**

National Association of Biology Teachers (NABT), **1737–1739**

National Association of College Admission Counseling (NACAC), 383

National Association of College and University Residence Halls (NACURH), 342

National Association of Colored Women, 174

National Association of Elementary School Principals (NAESP), **1739–1741**

National Association of Independent Colleges and Universities (NAICU), 152, **1741–1742**

National Association of Independent Schools (NAIS), **1742–1743**

National Association of Manufacturers' (NAM), 2637

National Association of Scholars (NAS), 517

National Association of Schools of Art and Design (NASAD), **1743–1745**

National Association of School Superintendents, 100

National Association of Secondary School Principals (NASSP), **1745–1747**
National Honor Society, 1778–1780
as representative body, 1920
secondary education history, 2193–2194

National Association of State Boards of Education (NASBE), **1747–1749**

National Association of State Universities and Land-Grant Colleges (NASULGC), 100, 101, **1749–1750**

National Association of Student Councils (NASC), 1747

National Association of Trade and Technical Schools, 36

National Association to Promote Library Service to the Spanish Speaking, 289

National Board Dental Examination, 559

National Board for Professional Teaching Standards (NBPTS), **1750–1753**
social studies teachers, 2271
teacher employment, 2450–2451
teacher evaluation, 2456, 2458–2460
vocational education, 2649

National Business Education Association (NBEA), **1753–1754**
business education, 215–216, 218
teacher education, 224

National Cancer Institute, 1092

National Catholic Educational Association (NCEA), **1754–1756**

National Catholic Forensic League, 2300–2301

National Catholic Welfare Conference, 251

National Center for Education Statistics (NCES), **1756–1757**
Carnegie Classification data, 243
dropout rates, 599
educational expenditures resources, 662
Educational Testing Service (ETS), 684–685
faculty diversity, 777–778
international comparative studies, 1223–1224
revenue for higher education institutions, 25–26
rural education, 2084
school choice, 82–83
service learning, 2203
student community service participation, 296
See also National Assessment of Educational Progress (NAEP); Statistics

National Center for Higher Education, 108

National Center for Policy Analysis, 467

National Child Abuse and Neglect Data System, 268

National Childhood Vaccine Injury Act (NCVIA), 1107

National Coalition for Education in the Arts, 118

National Collegiate Athletic Association (NCAA), **364–368**
athletic department revenues and expenses, 346
championships, 345, 366
CHAMPS/Life Skills program, 357
formation, 349–350
Graduation Rates Report, 359–360
regulatory power, 351, 352
rules and regulations, **368–371**
scholarship provisions, 356

National Collegiate Honors Council (NCHC), 1086–1087

National Commission for the Protection of Human Subjects of Biomedical and Behavioral Research, 1091

National Commission of Civic Renewal, 296

National Commission on Excellence in Education (NCEE)
art education, 118
education reform, 689–690

policy, 673
See also A Nation at Risk: The Imperative for Educational Reform (report)
National Commission on the Reform of Secondary Education, 697
National Commission on the Role and Future of State Colleges and Universities, 518
National Committee for Children and Youth (NCCY), **1757–1758**
National Committee on Nursery Schools, 623
National Communication Association (NCA), **1759–1760,** 2299
National Conference of State Legislatures, **1760–1762**
National Conference on Education, 99
National Conference on Higher Education, 90
National Consortium for Physical Education and Recreation for Individuals with Disabilities (NCPERID), 38
National Consortium on Preparing Graduate Students as College Teachers, 910
National Council for Accreditation of Teacher Education (NCATE), **1762–1763**
constituent member organizations, *1763*
health education standards, 1009
professional development schools, 1931
specialized associations' challenge of, 34
state licensure reciprocity, 33
teacher education, 2442
National Council for Private School Accreditation (NCPSA), 30
National Council for the Social Studies (NCSS), **1764–1765,** 2265–2266, 2269–2270
National Council of Negro Women, 174
National Council of Teachers of English (NCTE), **1765–1767**
academic standards, 1394–1395
English education history, 741
National Council of Teachers of Mathematics (NCTM), **1767–1768**
academic standards, 1545
elementary education, 717–718
number sense, 1565
teacher education, 1541
National Council on Education Standards and Testing (NCEST), 2154–2155
National Dance Association (NDA), 89, 90
National defense and secondary education, 2187–2188
National Defense Education Act (NDEA)
higher education funding, 862
state departments of education, 2325
statewide testing, 2538
vocational guidance, 976
National Defense Research Committee (NDRC), 473
National Defense University (NDU), 843, 2621
National Educational Longitudinal Study (NELS), 1405–1406, 1529
National Education Association (NEA), **1769–1771**
academic freedom and tenure, 15
American Alliance for Health, Physical Education, Recreation, and Dance, 89–90
American Association for Higher Education and, 91
Buetler presidency, 230
Cardinal Principles of Secondary Education, 193, 696, 2185–2186
Code of Ethics for the Education Profession, 753–754
Committee of Ten, 696, 725, 2184–2185, 2693
Department of Kindergarten Education, 622
Department of School Superintendence, 100
educational expenditures resources, 662
Educational Policies Commission (EPC), 696
overview, 2476–2478, 2479–2481
Rankings and Estimates, 662
reports, 696
rural education, 2084–2085
school infrastructure needs, 2128
social studies education, 2265
Superintendents Division, 2416
women's rights, 984
National Education Goals Panel
education statistics, 1286
federal involvement in education, 838
Goals 2000, **3084–3087**
standards-based education, 2320
National Education Policy Network, 1785
National Education Standards and Improvement Council (NESIC), 2155
National education summits. *See* Education summits
National Endowment for the Arts (NEA), 657, **1771–1773**
National Endowment for the Humanities (NEH), **1774–1776**
American Council of Learned Societies, 106
educational broadcasting, 657
undergraduate curriculum, 514–515
National Federation of High School Activities, 2300
National Federation of the Blind, 2635
National Foreign Affairs Training Center, 848
National Foreign Language Week, 1067
National Forensic League (NFL), 2300–2301, **2733–2734**
National Foundation for the Arts and Humanities. *See* National Endowment for the Arts (NEA); National Endowment for the Humanities (NEH)
National Future Farmers of America Organization, **2734–2736**
National Governors Association (NGA), **1776–1777**
school reform, 2153
standards-based education, 2319
undergraduate curriculum reports, 518
National Health Education Standards, 1005

National Highway Traffic Safety Administration (NHTSA)
driver education, 598
educational activities, 850
school bus transportation, 2575
National Historical Publications and Records Commission, National Archives and Records Administration, 1733
National history, teaching of, 1055–1056
National Home Education Research Institute, 1062
National Honor Society (NHS), 1078, 1747, **1777–1780**
National Immunization Program (NIP), 1106
National Institute for Literacy, 921
National Institute for Staff and Organizational Development (NISOD), 255
National Institute for Standards and Technology (NIST), 842
National Institute of Child Health and Human Development (NICHD), 183
National Institute of Education (NIE), 839, 2017
National Institute of Medicine, 831
National Institute on Drug Abuse, 92
National Institutes of Health (NIH)
educational activities, 845
federal funding for faculty research, 855, 857
National Cancer Institute, 1092
research misconduct policy, 2039–2040
National Intramural Association (NIA), 362
National Intramural-Recreational Sports Association (NIRSA), 362
National Junior Honor Society (NJHS), 1747, 1778–1780
National Library of Education, 683
National Longitudinal Study of Adolescent Health, 295, 1004
National Longitudinal Survey of Youth (NLSY), 729
National-Louis University, 622
National Mental Health and Special Education Coalition, 726
National Merit Scholarship program, **1780–1782**
National Middle School Association, 1631
National Network for Educational Renewal, IEI, 121, 122
National Network of Partnership Schools, Johns Hopkins University, 826
National Oceanic and Atmospheric Administration (NOAA), 842
National Ocean Service, 842
National Origins Act of 1924, 1097–1098
National Paideia Center, 1841
National period school funding, 885
National Policy Board for Educational Administration (NPBEA), 99–100, 1920–1921
National PTA, **1782–1784**
National Public Radio (NPR), 657
National Reading Panel (NRP)
reading and literacy, 1514–1515
reading comprehension strategies, 1977–1983
reading instruction, 2000, 2002
word recognition skills, 2005
National Research Act, 1091
National Research Council (NRC)
Committee for the Study of Research-Doctoral Programs, 379
early childhood education study, 617–618
families, 831
National Academy of Sciences, 1727–1728
National Science Education Standards, 1729, 2175, *2176*
vocational education, 2646
National Resource Center for the First-Year Experience and Students in Transition, 239
National School Boards Association (NSBA), **1784–1786**
National School Lunch Act (NSLA), 2131–2132
National School Lunch Program (NSLP), 2131–2136, *2135, 2136*
National School Public Relations Association (NSPRA), **1786–1788**
National Science Education Standards (National Research Council), 1729, 2175, *2176*
National Science Foundation (NSF), **1788–1790**
academic R&D support, 857–858
curriculum reform study, 512
federal funding for faculty research, 855
federal involvement in education, 839
industry-university research collaboration, 2593
research misconduct definition, 2038
research misconduct policy, 2037, 2038
science teacher education, 2163–2165
Zacharias, Jerrold, 2745–2746
National Science Teachers Association (NSTA), **1791–1792,** 2174–2175
National Sea Grant Program, 842, **2181–2183**
National Skills Standards Board, 217
National Society for Programmed Instruction. *See* International Society for Performance Improvement (ISPI)
National Society for the Promotion of Industrial Education, 73
National standards. *See* Academic standards; Standards-based education
National Standards for Civics and Government, 295
National Standards for Physical Education, 1006
National Standards for Professional School Counselors (ASCA), 977
National Study of Indian Education, 997
National Study of School Evaluation (NSSE), 29
National Summit on Agricultural Education, 77–78
National Survey of Postsecondary Faculty (NSOPF99), 774–775, 777
National Survey of Student Engagement, 381

National Teachers Association, 100, 1771
  See also National Education Association (NEA)
National Teaching and Learning Forum, AAHE, 91
National Technical Information Service (NTIS), 842
National Technological University, 592
National Telecommunications and Information Administration (NTIA), 657, 842
National Traffic and Motor Safety Act of 1966, 2574
National Training Center (NTC), U.S. Army, 1657–1658
National Transit Library, 850
National Undersea Research Program, 842
National Vocational Education Act, 73–74
National Vocational Guidance Association, 975
National Weather Service (NWS), 842
National Writing Project (NWP)
  English education, 744
  teacher education, 746
  teacher learning communities, 2465
  writing and composition, 2694
National Youth Administration, Division of Negro Affairs, 174
National Youth Sports Program (NYSP), 367
A Nation at Risk: The Imperative for Educational Reform (report), **3010–3017**
  art education, 118
  business involvement in education, 226
  Department of Education and, 2616
  education policy, 673–674
  elementary education, 718
  foreign language education, 895
  high-stakes testing, 2535
  historical significance, 697
  homework, 1063
  as impetus for reform, 689–690
  international education, 1266–1267
  international education statistics, 1286
  large-city superintendents, 2414
  national achievement testing, 2545–2546
  National Assessment of Educational Progress (NAEP), 132
  public school organization and, 2259–2260
  school boards and policy, 2113
  school reform, 2152–2153
  science education standards, 2173–2174
  secondary education reform, 2188
  standards movement, 838
  state departments of education and, 2325
  statewide testing programs, 2538
  summer school programs, 2410
  superintendents, 2417, 2644
  teacher unions and, 2222
  textbooks, 2557
  undergraduate curriculum, 514
  vocational education, 2638, 2644
A Nation Prepared: Teachers for the Twenty-first Century (report), 697, 2154
The Nation's Report Card (report), 132
Native Americans
  American Indian Head Start program, 844
  boarding schools, 712, 2187
  cross-cultural education, 418–419
  culture and literacy, 1510, 1511
  Diné College, 868
  elementary education, 712
  faculty diversity, 776–778
  federal schools, 866
  KEEP Project, 1511
  National Study of Indian Education, 997
  The People: A Study of the Navajo (report), 2094
  public high schools, 2187
  Public Laws 81-874 and 81-815, 1109
  school system improvement, 199
  vocational education, 2638
  See also Tribal colleges and universities
Native Hawaiians, 1564
Nativism, 1439
Natural approach to secondary language acquisition, 177
Natural education, 1875–1876
Naturalist intelligence, 1199, 1834
Natural Resources and Environment (NRE), 841
The Nature of Proof (Fawcett), 835–836
Nature study, 74
Nature *vs.* nurture, 562–563
Navajo Community College. *See* Diné College
Naval Academy, U.S., **1652–1653**
Naval War College (NWC), 2620
NBEA. *See* National Business Education Association (NBEA)
NBPTS. *See* National Board for Professional Teaching Standards (NBPTS)
NCAA. *See* National Collegiate Athletic Association (NCAA)
NCAA Manual, 368
NCA (National Communication Association), **1759–1760,** 2299
NCA (North Central Association of Colleges and Schools), 28
NCATE. *See* National Council for Accreditation of Teacher Education (NCATE)
NCCY (National Committee for Children and Youth), **1757–1758**
NCEA (National Catholic Educational Association), **1754–1756**
NCEE. *See* National Commission on Excellence in Education (NCEE)
NCHC (National Collegiate Honors Council), 1086–1087
NCOES (Noncommissioned Officers Education System), 1653–1655
NCPERID (National Consortium for Physical Education and Recreation for Individuals with Disabilities), 38
NCPSA (National Council for Private School Accreditation), 30
NCSS (National Council for the Social Studies), **1764–1765,** 2265–2266, 2269–2270
NCTE. *See* National Council of Teachers of English (NCTE)
NCTM. *See* National Council of Teachers of Mathematics (NCTM)

NCVIA (National Childhood Vaccine Injury Act), 1107–1108
NDA (National Dance Association), 89, 90
NDEA. *See* National Defense Education Act (NDEA)
NDU (National Defense University), 843, 2621
NEA. *See* National Education Association (NEA)
NEA (National Endowment for the Arts), 657, **1771–1773**
NEASC (New England Association of Schools and Colleges), 28, 32, 2185
Nebraska, Meyer v. See Meyer v. State of Nebraska
Nebraska University, 66
Need-based financial aid, 376–377
Needs based schools, 84–85
Neef, Joseph, 1876
Negative changers, 332
Negative reinforcement, 1460
Neglect. *See* Child abuse and neglect
Negligence, **1472–1475,** 2075–2076
Negro History Bulletin, 2692–2693
Negro History Week, 66
The Negro's Church (Mays and Nicholson), 1570
The Negro's God: As Reflected in His Literature (Mays), 1572
NEH. *See* National Endowment for the Humanities (NEH)
Neighborhoods, **1793–1796, 1851–1856,** 1907
  See also Communities
Neill, A. S., 84, 942, **1796–1798**
Neill, James T., 762
Neisser, Ulric, 1205
NELS (National Educational Longitudinal Study), 1405–1406
Nelson, Katherine, 1589
Nelson, Laurie, 1148
Neoliberal policies, 1302
Neo-Piagetian theory, 564
Nepal. *See* South Asia
Nero v. Kansas State University, 2075
NESIC (National Education Standards and Improvement Council), 2155
Netherlands
  Coordination Dutch-Russian Cooperation in Education (CROSS) program, 1267
  higher education restructuring, 1029
  Netherlands Organization for International Cooperation in Higher Education (Nuffic), 1247
  university restructuring, 1029
  See also Western Europe
Networking, 242
Network of Outcome Based Schools (NOBS), 1829
Neural Organization Technique, 1457
Neurology
  claims by brain-based education proponents, 202–204
  learning, **1436–1437**
  neuroimaging, 156
  neurological conditions, 1885
New American Schools (NAS), 1674, **1798–1800**
New basic skills, 690
Newbery, John, 286
Newbery Medal, 288
Newby, Timothy, 1149
New College, 2370
Newcomb, Simon, 93
Newcomb, Theodore, 332–333
Newcomb Cleveland Prize, 92
Newcomer centers, 1640
New Deal, 297–298
New Deans Seminar, AACSB, 1
Newell, Allen, 567, 1546
Newell, Karl, 1702
Newell, William H., 1210
New England
  common school movement, 712
  elementary education history, 710
  school organization, 2232
  town schools, 427
New England Association of Colleges and Preparatory Schools, 725
New England Association of Schools and Colleges (NEASC), 28, 32, 2185
New England Primer, 713, 740
"New History," 539–540
New Jersey v. T.L.O., 2425
Newlon, Jesse, **1800–1801**
Newman, Katherine S., 731, 736
Newmann, Fred, 2712
New School for Social Research, 554
Newsline (newsletter), 2
News media, 1353
New Standards Consortium, 2321
New Students and New Places (report), 243
A New Vitality for General Education (report), 516–517
New York Children's Aid Society, 282, 2709
New York City, 2222
New York Free School Society, 711
New York State Agricultural Society, 72
New York Teachers Guild, 2477
Next Steps for TIMSS: Directions for Secondary Analysis (National Research Council), 1730
Next Steps for TIMSS: Directions for Secondary Analysis (report), 1730
Neyhart, Amos, 597
NGA. *See* National Governors Association (NGA)
NGOs (Nongovernmental organizations). *See* Nongovernmental organizations (NGOs) and foundations
NHS. *See* National Honor Society (NHS)
NHTSA. *See* National Highway Traffic Safety Administration (NHTSA)
Niagara Movement, 610
NIA (National Intramural Association), 362
Nicaragua. *See* Latin America and the Caribbean
NICHD (National Institute of Child Health and Human Development), 183
Nichols, Lau v. See Lau v. Nichols
Nicomachean Ethics (Aristotle), 117
NIE (National Institute of Education), 839, 2017
Niger. *See* Sub-Saharan Africa
Nigeria. *See* Sub-Saharan Africa
NIH (National Institutes of Health), 845, 855, 857
1990 World Conference on Education for All, 626, 687

NIRSA (National Intramural-Recreational Sports Association), 362
NISOD (National Institute for Staff and Organizational Development), 255
NIST (National Institute for Standards and Technology), 842
NJHS (National Junior Honor Society), 1747, 1778–1780
NLSY (National Longitudinal Survey of Youth), 729
NOAA (National Oceanic and Atmospheric Administration), 842
NOBS (Network of Outcome Based Schools), 1829
No Child Left Behind Act, **1801–1803, 3087–3090**
  accountability, 2191
  assessment, 2190
  business involvement in education, 228
  current trends in elementary education, 718
  elementary education history, 714
  federal involvement in education, 838
  interest groups, 663
  national achievement tests, 2546
  National PTA, 1783
  program evaluation, 2033
  teacher education, 2538, 2540
  teachers, 2435–2436
Nolan, Aretas, 74
Noller, Patricia, 55
Nonbroadcast television, 657–658
Noncommissioned Officers Education System (NCOES), 1653–1655
Non-English speaking population, *1398, 1399,* 1639
  See also Bilingualism; Immigrant education; Language minority students
Nonequivalent comparison group designs, 2024–2025
Nongovernmental organizations (NGOs) and foundations, **1803–1811**
  Canadian International Development Agency (CIDA) partners, 1242–1243
  education development projects, 688, 1261
  equalization aid, 548
  gender and international education, 920–921
Nongradedness: Helping It to Happen (Anderson and Pavan), 1813
Nongraded schools, **1812–1813**
Nonprofit private schools, 1219
Nonroutine problems, 1442
Nontraditional students
  college and university, 1024, **1814–1816**
  college teaching, 416
  community colleges, 445–446
  distance education, 2498
  learning, 2493
  life experience for college credit, 1477
  master's programs, 1538
  NTL Institute for Applied Behavioral Science, 1817
  recruitment, 383
  student retention, 404–405
  See also Adult education; Lifelong learning
NORAD (Norwegian Agency for Development Cooperation), 1246–1247
Norberg, Katarina, 2472
Norland, Emmalou, 320
Normal schools
  early childhood education teacher education, 622
  elementary education teacher education, 720–721
  Hampton Institute, 2664, 2666–2667
  junior colleges and, 443–444
  Mann, Horace, 1536
  teacher education history, 2439
Normative philosophies of education. *See* Theory of education
Norm-referenced teacher evaluation, 2454
Norms, classroom, 974
North Africa. *See* Middle East and North Africa
North Central Association of Colleges and Schools (NCA), 28, 30
Northwest Association of Schools and Colleges (NASC), 28, 30
Northwest Ordinance, 710, 837, **3043–3046**
Norway, 1246–1247, 2681
  See also Western Europe
Norwegian Agency for Development Cooperation (NORAD), 1246–1247
Norwood v. Harrison, 2424
No Shame in My Game: The Working Poor in the Inner City (Newman), 736
Nosofsky, Robert M., 248
Notification of rights and student records, 2015
NPBEA (National Policy Board for Educational Administration), 99–100, 1920–1921
NPR (National Public Radio), 657
NRC. *See* National Research Council (NRC)
NRE (Natural Resources and Environment), 841
NRP. *See* National Reading Panel (NRP)
NSBA (National School Boards Association), **1784–1786**
NSF. *See* National Science Foundation (NSF)
NSLA (National School Lunch Act), 2131–2132
NSLP (National School Lunch Program), 2131–2136, *2135, 2136*
NSPRA (National School Public Relations Association), **1786–1788**
NSSE (National Study of School Evaluation), 29
NSTA Handbook, 1999-2000 (National Science Teachers Association), 2159–2160
NSTA (National Science Teachers Association), **1791–1792,** 2174–2175
NSTA Press, 1792
NSTA Reports! (periodical), 1792
NTIA (National Telecommunications and Information Administration), 657, 842
NTIS (National Technical Information Service), 842
NTL Institute for Applied Behavioral Science, **1817–1818**
Nuclear engineering, 740
Nuffic (Netherlands Organization for International Cooperation in Higher Education), 1247
Number sense, **1558–1566,** 1567

The Number Sense: How the Mind Creates Mathematics (Dehaene), 1559
Numeracy. *See* Number sense
Nuns. *See* Sister-teachers
Nursery schools. *See* Early childhood education; Head Start program; Preschool education
Nursing education, **1818–1821**
Nutrient standards, school lunch, 2133–2134
Nutrition. *See* Health and nutrition
Nutrition services, school, 1006, 1013–1014
NWC (Naval War College), 2620–2621
NWP. *See* National Writing Project (NWP)
NWS (National Weather Service), 842
Nyerere, Julius, 2091
Nyquist, Committee for Public Education v., 2423
NYSP (National Youth Sports Program), 367

O

Oakes, Jeannie, 1964
Oakes, Lisa, 1425
Oakland School Board, 1391–1392
OAPBC (Office for the Advancement of Public Black Colleges), 100
O'Banion, Terry, 2
OBEMLA (Office of Bilingual Education and Minority Languages Affairs), Department of Education, 2618
OBE (Outcome based education), **1827–1831,** 2429–2430
Obesity, 1822
Objectives, instructional, **1176–1178,** 2493
  See also Bloom, Benjamin S.; Taxonomies of educational objectives
Objectivism, 1463
Object lessons, 1875–1876
OBRA (Omnibus Budget Reconciliation Act), 1106
O'Brien, Eileen, 1537
O'Brien, Knox v., 1062
Observational research, 2023, 2027–2028, 2489
  See also Classroom observation
Occupational Safety and Health Administration (OSHA), 846–847
Occupational stress, 777
OCDQ (Organizational Climate Description Questionnaire), 2122
Oceanography, 2181–2183
O'Connor, Carla, 1964
O'Donnell, Angela, 490
OECD. *See* Organisation for Economic Co-Operation and Development (OECD)
OEO (Office of Economic Opportunity), 2603, 2677
OERI. *See* Office of Educational Research and Improvement (OERI)
Oersted Medal, 98
OFCCP (Office of Federal Contract Compliance Programs), 62
Offenders, juvenile, 1359–1360
Office for Civil Rights, Department of Education, 2619
Office for the Advancement of Public Black Colleges (OAPBC), 100
Office of Administrative Services, National Archives and Records Administration, 1732
Office of Bilingual Education and Minority Languages Affairs (OBEMLA), Department of Education, 2618
Office of Citizen Exchanges, ECA, 848
Office of Civil Rights, Department of Education, 2571
Office of Community Oriented Policing Services (COPS), 846
Office of Economic Opportunity (OEO), 2603, 2677
Office of Education, U.S., 838–839, 2614–2615
Office of Educational Research and Improvement (OERI)
  bilingual education, 183
  federal involvement in education, 838
  overview, 2618
  Regional Educational Laboratories, 2088
  regional research and development centers, 2017–2018
Office of Elementary and Secondary Education, Department of Education, 2618
Office of English Language Programs, ECA, 848
Office of Federal Contract Compliance Programs (OFCCP), 62, 64
Office of Global Education Programs, 847
Office of Indian Education Programs (OIEP), 866
Office of Justice Programs, 846
Office of Juvenile Justice and Delinquency Prevention, DOJ, 1354–1355
Office of Legislative and Congressional Affairs, Department of Education, 2618
Office of Naval Research (ONR), 855
Office of Overseas Schools (OOS), State Department, 112, 113
Office of Postsecondary Education, Department of Education, 2618
Office of Presidential Libraries, National Archives and Records Administration, 1733
Office of Records Services, National Archives and Records Administration, 1732
Office of Science and Technology Policy (OSTP), 2038
Office of Scientific Research and Development (OSRD), 855
Office of Special Education and Rehabilitative Services, Department of Education, 2619
Office of the Chief Financial Officer, Department of Education, 2618
Office of the Chief Information Officer, Department of Education, 2618
Office of the Federal Register, 1732
Office of the General Counsel, Department of Education, 2617
Office of the Inspector General, Department of Commerce, 842
Office of the Inspector General, Department of Education, 2617

Office of Vocational and Adult Education, Department of Education, 2619
Office of Vocational Rehabilitation and Employment, VA, 852
Officer Candidate Schools, 1654
Officer Professional Military Education (OPME), 1653–1655
Offices of institutional research, college and university, 1144–1146
Office space, teacher, 2127
Ogbu, John U., 1859, 1964
Ohio, 837
OHI (Organizational Health Inventory), 2122–2123
Ohio State University
- academic calendar, 6–7
- African-American studies, 66
- Alberty, H. B., 80–81
- Barkan, Manuel, 165
- Bode, Boyd H., 195
- Charters, W. W., 264
- Fawcett, Harold P., 835
- resource allocation, 2050
- Taba, Hilda, 2428
- Tyler, Ralph W., 2588
- Zirbes, Laura, 2747

Ohlin, Lloyd, 2710
OIEP (Office of Indian Education Programs), 866
Oil producing countries. *See* Middle East and North Africa
OISE (Ontario Institute for Studies in Education), 469
OJJDP (Office of Juvenile Justice and Delinquency Prevention), 1354–1355
Oklahoma State Regents, McLaurin v., 64
Old Deluder Satan Act (Massachusetts Bay Colony), 710, 715, 2636
Olson, David, 1488
Olweus, Dan, 1359
Oman, 1624
- *See also* Middle East and North Africa

Omnibus Budget Reconciliation Act (OBRA), 1106
Onafowora, Laura, 1752
O'Neil, Harold F., Jr., 733
One-room schools, 712
One Sky Many Voices, 2179
One Stop Centers, 488–489
Online education
- academic advising, 3
- community colleges, 2393
- distance learning, 591
- educational technology, 2517
- higher education, 2524–2525
- law school, 1418
- public school courses and programs, 84
- *See also* Distance education; Internet; Virtual universities

Online Exhibit Hall, National Archives and Records Administration, 1734
ONR (Office of Naval Research), 855
Ontario Institute for Studies in Education (OISE), 469
OOS (Office of Overseas Schools), State Department, 113
Open access at community colleges, 876–880
Open classrooms, **1823–1824,** 1824–1825
Open education, **1824–1827**
- alternative schooling, 84
- distance education, 591

Open enrollment of public schools, 84, 1951, 2260
Operant conditioning, 1460–1461, 2229
Operating budget, 2047–2048
OPI (Oral Proficiency Interview), 894
OPME (Officer Professional Military Education), 1653–1655
Oral communication education. *See* Speech and theater education
Oral health. *See* Dental health
Oralism, 1018, 1020
Oral language
- culture, 1510
- school readiness, 2148–2149

Oral mathematics skills, 2149–2150
Oral Proficiency Interview (OPI), 894
Ordered associations, 1671
Ordered information mnemonic method, 1671
Ordinary Least Squares (OLS) Regression Analysis, 660–661, *661*
Orelove, Fred, 2210
Orfield, Gary, 663
Organic education, 1344–1346
Organisation for Economic Co-operation and Development (OECD)
- Adult Literacy Survey (IALS), 642
- Centre for Educational Research and Innovation (CERI), 1250–1251, 1266–1267
- decentralization, 543
- *Education at a Glance: OECD Indicators,* 1287, 1291, 1293
- education development projects, 687
- education statistics, 1287, 1292, 1293, 1295
- international assessment, 1223, 1224
- lifelong learning, 1481
- reading assessment, 1229
- research, 1266–1267
- special education, 2293–2294

Organizational Climate Description Questionnaire (OCDQ), 2122–2123
The Organizational Climate of Schools (Halpin and Croft), 2122
Organizational Health Inventory (OHI), 2122–2123
Organizational structure of colleges and universities, **384–389**
- academic majors, 21
- disciplines, 10
- enrollment management, 749–750
- governance, 946–947

Organizational structure of schools, 2186, 2257
Organization for Security and Cooperation in Europe (OSCE), 1254–1255, 2248
Organizations
- climate, 2122
- development, 1817
- knowledge management, **1373–1376**
- organizational change, 170
- schools as, 2256
- social cohesion, 2244
- *See also* Associations, educational; Youth organizations and clubs

Organizers, instructional, 1179
Orientation
- professional advisers, 4

school board members, 2120
student, 44, 749, **2385–2387,** 2391
See also First-year seminars
Orphans, 281, 2709
Orthodox Jews, 1340–1341
Orthophrenic School (Italy), 1675–1676
Ory, John, 786
OSCE (Organization for Security and Cooperation in Europe), 1254–1255, 2248
OSHA (Occupational Safety and Health Administration), 846–847
Osofsky, Joy, 2628
OSRD (Office of Scientific Research and Development), 855
O'Sullivan, Julia T., 1470
Oswego Training School, 2224–2225
O'Toole, Margot, 2039
Our Enemy the Child (De Lima), 553
Outcome Based Education (OBE), **1827–1831,** 2429–2430
See also Learning outcomes
Outdoor adventure programs, 761, 762
Outdoor and environmental education, **1831–1835**
See also Outward Bound
Outline for an Institute for the Education of Teachers (Carter), 1535
Out-of-school influences, **1835–1839**
Outsourcing of student services, 2388–2389
Outward Bound, 85, 761, 762
See also Outdoor and environmental education
The Overcrowded Curriculum (International Center for Leadership in Education), 2644–2645
Overlapping waves of development, 564
Overstreet, Stacy, 2629
Owen, Robert, 430, 1134, 1876
Oxfam International, 1804–1805

P

Pace, C. Robert, 332
Pace, instructional, 1129
PACE (Policy Analysis for California Education), 82–83
Pacific Islands, 635, 639
Padrón, Yolanda, 304–305
Pagani, Linda, 1906
Page, Walter Hines, 2054
Paideia Program, 84, **1841–1842**
The Paideia Proposal (Adler), 697
Painter, Sweatt v., 64
Pakistan. *See* South Asia
Palinscar, Annemarie S., 1604, 1978
Palloff, Rena, 2498
Palmer, Alice Freeman, **1842–1844**
Palmer, George, 1843
Palmer Method of handwriting, 988
Pan-Africanism, 611–612
Panama. *See* Latin America and the Caribbean
Pangburn, Jesse May, 720
Pansophy, 419–421
Papua New Guinea. *See* East Asia and the Pacific
Paradigm development and academic disciplines, 10–11
Paraguay. *See* Latin America and the Caribbean
Parallel block schedule, 2098
Parallel Distributed Processing (PDP) model, 1610–1611
Parameters in standard psychometric models, 140–141
Paraprofessional staff, 110–112
Parens patriae doctrine, 281, 1350
Parental Notification law, 607–608
Parent News, 683
Parents and parenting, **1847–1860**
academic performance, influence on, 1835–1836
adolescent peer culture, **54–56**
aggression prevention and intervention, role in, 71
attitudes towards student employment, 730
behavior problems and, 2246
child care involvement, 273
children and media, 1581
college choice, 394, 395
education level, 628, 777–778, **1856–1858**
factors in children's success, 811–813
high-risk neighborhoods, **1851–1856**
involvement in education, **1844–1847,** 1854–1855
juvenile offenders, 1359–1360
mental health, 1907, 1912–1913
mental illness, 810–811
mother-child interaction, 130
National PTA, **1782–1784**
organizations, 823–824
overview, **1847–1851**
parental rights, 280–282, 284
school communication, 822
school involvement with, 821
sexuality education of children, 2215
single parents, 808, 833, 2705
student's educational aspirations and attainment, **1858–1860**
styles, 55
substance abuse, 268, 809, **815–817,** 815–818
teen sexual activity and, 2063–2064
urban schools, 2610
volunteers, 822
welfare reform and, 2674
See also Families
Park, Robert, 433
Parker, Francis W., 1935, 1999
Parkhurst, Helen, 541
Parnell, Dale, 96
Parochial schools. *See* Catholic schools
PAR (Peer Assistance and Review), 2481
Parsons, Frank, 975
Partnership for Civic Change (PCC) program, 2016
Partnerships, school/family/community, **821–828,** 1845, 2016
"Partners in Progress," 2466–2467
Part-time faculty, **779–782**
diversity, 777
gender, *778*
statistics, 19
Pasadena (California) Public Schools, 943–944
Pascarella, Ernest
extracurricular activities, 374
formal and informal learning, 2493
general education, 924

How College Affects Students (Pascarella and Terenzini), 335–340
psychosocial changes in college students, 2495
residence hall living, 2046
student adjustment to college, 43, 924
student-faculty interaction, 452
PASS (Portable Assisted Study Sequence), 1641
Patent and Trademark Office (PTO), 842
Patents and licensing, 856, 2527
PATHS (Promoting Alternative Thinking Strategies), 1192–1193
Pathways Out of Poverty program, 1808
Patrick Henry College, 1062
Patterns of Educational Philosophy: A Democratic Interpretation (Brameld), 207
Patton, Michael, 2032
Paulos, John Allen, 1559
Pavlov, Ivan, 1459, 2229
PBL (Phi Beta Lambda), 219, **2729–2730**
PBL (problem-based learning), **1172–1175,** 1185–1186, 1544
PBS (Public Broadcast Service), 657
PBTE (performance-based teacher education), 2441–2442, 2447
PCC (Partnership for Civic Change) program, 2016
PDP (Parallel Distributed Processing) model, 1610–1611
PDSs (professional development schools), **1930–1933,** 2441
PEA. *See* Progressive Education Association (PEA)
Peabody, Elizabeth, 621, 905
Peace education, **1860–1864**
Peace Information Center, 612
PEA (Progressive Education Association)
Pearson, P. David, 1978
Pedagogy
anchored instruction, 1152
Comenius, Johann, 419–422
comparative research studies, 2054–2055
content knowledge, 414, 1179
critical, 1124
culturally responsive, 1124, 1511–1512
English education, 746
equity, 1705–1706
first-year seminars, 400
Freire, Paulo, 900–903
geometry, 835–836
Herbart, Johann, 1021–1022
Herbartarian, 1574–1575
history, 1053–1054, 1056–1057
James, William, 1331–1336
mathematics, 1561–1562
multiculturalism, 1705
pedagogical agents, **1169–1172**
Progressive education, 1934–1935
teacher knowledge of, 2483
See also Curriculum; Instruction; Philosophy of education; Theory of education
Pediatricians, 1614
Peer-advisers, 4
Peer Assistance and Review (PAR), 2480
Peer culture, adolescent, **45–56**
gangs, **51–54**
overview, **45–51**
parents' role, **54–56**
peer pressure, 812
stages of growth, 279
Peer learning, 2179–2180, 2582
See also Cooperative and collaborative learning
Peer relations
clubs, 318
college students, 335
educational aspirations, 1859
health education involvement, 1009
juvenile crime, 1360
learning, **1864–1867**
See also Interpersonal relationships; Peer culture, adolescent; Social development
Peer review
accountability, 652
faculty research, 154
federal research funding, 860
Pegword mnemonic method, 1671
Pellegrino, James, 2517
Pell Grants, 377, 837, 862–863
Pena, Adarand Constructors, Inc. v., 2424
Penick, John, 1751
Penmanship. *See* Handwriting
Pennsylvania, McKiever v., 1351
Pennsylvania Association for Retarded Children (PARC) v. Commonwealth of Pennsylvania, 672, 1868, **2853–2864**
The People: A Study of the Navajo (report), 2094
People's Institute, 212
People's Republic of China. *See* China
Percentage grading, 955
"Perceptual Learning: Differentiation or Enrichment?" (Gibson and Gibson), 1439
Perceptual processes, **1437–1441,** 1597–1598
Performance assessment, **134–137**
accountability, 654–655
faculty research, 787–788
Performance audits, 1955
Performance-based teacher education (PBTE), 2441–2442, 2447
Performance-based teachers' pay, 2480
Performance goals, 1694
Performance guidelines, ACTFL, 894, 897
Performance improvement, 765–766
Performance standards, 2315–2316
Pergamit, Michael, 729
Perkins, David, 1148, 1174
Perkins Act. *See* Carl D. Perkins Vocational Education acts
Perkins Loans, 862
Permanent records, 2013–2014
Permission slips, 1474
Permissive parents, 55
Perot Commission, 226
Perry Preschool program, 619
Person, Natalie, 1170
Persona effect, 1170
Personal development, 2208
Personality disorder, 268
Personalized System of Instruction, 1130–1131
Personalized year education, 2700
Personal problems, college students', **1871–1874**
Personal Responsibility and Work Opportunity Reconciliation Act (PRWORA)
income support, 833–834
welfare reform, 2673–2675, 2677–2678

Person-based approaches to transfer, 1450–1451
Personnel
liability, **1472–1475**
school-based decision-making, 2100
state education agencies, 2346–2347
Pertussis, 1107
Peru. *See* Latin America and the Caribbean
Pestalozzi, Johann, 904, 1833, **1874–1876,** 1934, 2224
Peters, Ellen E., 1980
Peterson, Marvin, 2367
Peterson, Paul, 662–663
Peterson, Penelope, 305
Peter W. v. San Francisco Unified School District, 1475
Pew Charitable Trusts, 91, 1808–1809
PFF (Preparing Future Faculty) program, 255, 910–911
Pharmaceutical education, 94–95, 1082–1083
Pharmacy education, 95
Pharm.D. degree, 94–95
Ph.D. programs. *See* Doctoral degree programs; Graduate education
Phi Beta Kappa, **1077–1079**
Phi Beta Lambda (PBL), 219, **2729–2730**
Phi Delta Kappa International, **1079–1080**
Philadelphia Housing Authority, 845
The Philadelphia Negro, A Social Study (Du Bois), 66, 610
Philadelphia Society for Promoting Agriculture, 72
Philadelphia Teachers' Learning Center Cooperative, 2467
Philadelphia Writing Project (PhilWP), 2466
Philanthropy, educational. *See* Institutional advancement
Philip Hauge Abelson Prize, 92
Philippines. *See* East Asia and the Pacific
Phillips, Deborah, 1907
Phillips, Susan, 1510
Philosophers, 1878–1879
Philosophy of education, **1877–1885**
Addams, Jane, 41
Aderhold, Omer, 76
agricultural education, 74–79
alternative schooling, 84–85
Aristotle, 116–117
Augustine, St., 159–160
Bagley, William C., **163–165**
Bailey, Liberty Hyde, 74, 75
Barrick, R. Kirby, 78
Brameld, Theodore, 206–207
Broudy, Harry S., 210–211
Childs, John L., 292–294
Comenius, Johann, 419–422
constructivism, 118
Cook, Glen, 75
current trends, **1880–1885**
democracy in education, 195, 206–207
democratic, 210–211
Dewey, John, 75, 578–582
Eaton, Theodore, 74–75
essentialist, 164–165, 207
ethics, 754
Freire, Paulo, 902–903
Harris, William T., 993–994
historical overview, **1877–1880**
James, William, 1331–1337
Kahler, A., 77
Love, G. M., 77
Martin, R. A., 78
multiple intelligences theory, 119
Nolan, Aretas, 74
open education, 1825
postmodernism, 118–119, 120
reconstructionism, 207
Steiner, Rudolf, 2364–2366
Stewart, R. M., 75–76
Whitehead, Alfred North, 2684–2686
Williams, David, 78
See also Learning theory; Pedagogy; Theory of education
PhilWP (Philadelphia Writing Project), 2466
Phipps, Lloyd, 76–77
Phoenix Police Department, 54
Phonemic awareness, 2149, 15514
Phonics, 258, 681, 1514
Phonological awareness
emergent literacy, 1488–1489
language acquisition, 1385
reading, 569, 572, 1974–1975
Photography, 417–419
PHS (Public Health Service), 2037, 2038
Physical abuse. *See* Child abuse and neglect
Physical education, **1886–1894**
adapted physical education (APE), **37–40**
American Alliance for Health, Physical Education, Recreation, and Dance (AAHPERD), **88–90,** 1888
American Association for the Advancement of Physical Education, 89
American Physical Education Association, 89–90
health education, 1006
health services, 1013
motor learning, 1702
National Association for Sports and Physical Education (NASPE), 89
overview, **1886–1890**
teacher preparation, **1890–1894**
See also Health education
Physical growth
adolescence, 278
early childhood, 276–277
middle childhood, 278
Physical Sciences Study Committee (PSSC), 2745–2746
Physics, folk, 572
Physics education
American Association of Physics Teachers (AAPT), **97–98**
awards, 98
Constructing Physics Understanding, 2179
history of science education, 2160
Interactive Physics (software), 2178
Zacharias, Jerrold, 2745–2746
Piaget, Jean, **1894–1898**
child development, 1825
cognitive development theory, 678
early childhood education, international aspects of
educational psychology, 678
history of developmental theory, 563–564
intelligence, 1202–1203
moral development, 1680–1681
science process, 2171
scientific process, 2171
spatial concepts, 926
transformation, 1463
See also Child development; Cognitive development; Developmental theory

Pianfetti, Evangeline, 2472
Pickering, Susan J., 568
Pico, Board of Education Island Trees Union Free School District No. 26 v., 2425
Picture books, 286
Pierce, David, 96
Pierce, Mohn, 695
Pierce v. Society of Sisters, 466, 1061, 1925, 1942, 2336, 2422, **2785–2789**
Pi Kappa Lambda, **1080–1081**
Pine Manor College, Mullins v., 2075
Pintrich, Paul R., 1700
Piracy, software, 2518–2519
Pirolli, Peter, 142
PISA. *See* Program for International Student Assessment (PISA)
Pi Sigma Alpha, **1081–1082**
Pits, Freeman v., 2202
Pittman, Karen J., 2710
A Place Called School (report), 697
Placement
  physical education, 38–39
  special education, 2281–2282, 2285–2286
Placement services and career counseling, 242
Plagiarism, 757
Planned giving, college and university, 1142
Planning
  facilities, 2124–2126
  higher education, **2367–2369**
  school health programs, 1008
The Planning of Change (Bennis et al.), 170
Plants, Robert T., 1578
Plato, **1898–1901**
  Aristotle compared to, 116
  educational psychology, 676
Platoon schools. *See* Gary Plan
Play, importance of
  Froebel, Friedrich, 905
  Hall, G. Stanley, 986
  James, William, 1333–1334
Plessy v. Ferguson, **2772–2785**
  historically black colleges and universities (HBCUs), 1049
  legal aspects of segregation, 2200
  secondary education history, 2186
  separate but equal doctrine, 63
  Supreme Court cases, 2423
Plimpton, George A., 2237
Plomin, Robert, 1196–1197
Plowden Report (England), 1134, 1825–1826
Pluralism, 662–663, 754
  See also Diversity; Multiculturalism
Podberesky, Kirwan v., 63, 64
POD (Professional and Organizational Development Network for Higher Education), 255, 256
Poetry and Mathematics (Buchanan), 212
Point-of-service (POS) plans, 1530
Poland. *See* Eastern Europe and Central Asia
Policy, education
  Benjamin, Harold R. W., 168–169
  business community and federal education policy, 227–228
  Department of Education, U.S., 2620
  design oriented curricula, 1164
  Education Commission of the States (ECS), 685–686
  efficiency, 703–704
  ethics, 754–755
  gender equity, 920–921
  interest groups, 662–664
  international education, 1269–1272
  Latin America, 1411–1412
  learning through design, 1164
  National Governors Association (NGA), 1777
  policy and procedures manuals, 355
  poverty, 1913–1914
  program evaluation and, 2032–2033
  rate of return on investment in education and, 650
  reform, 692
  rural education, 2087
  school-based decision-making, 2102
  school boards, 2113, 2114–2116
  South Asia, 2275–2276
  state boards of education, 2357–2358
  states, 703–704
  structural adjustment, 937–938
  testing, **2530–2533**
  textbooks, 2552–2554
  United States, **668–676**
  See also Administration, educational; Decision-making; Governance
Policy Analysis for California Education (PACE), 82–83
Policy Studies and Programs Division, ECS, 686
Polio, 1107
Political model of standards-based reform, 2319, 2320, 2322
Political science, 1081–1082
Political socialization and history education, 1055–1056
Politics
  ethics, 116–117
  large-city superintendents, 2414
  participation and community organization, 435
  political accountability, 653
  superintendents and, 2417
  teacher unions, 2476–2477, 2479–2480
  urban education, 2606
Politics (Aristotle), 116–117
Pólya, George, 1545–1546
Ponce de León, Pedro, 1019
PONSI (Program on Noncollegiate Sponsored Instruction), 1478, 1479
Poor Law Act (England), 281
Popkewitz, Tom, 307
Popovic, Mikulas, 2039
Popular music, 1724–1725
Population trends, **1901–1903,** 2703–2707
Portable Assisted Study Sequence (PASS), 1641
Portes, Alejandro, 1100
Portfolio assessment, **137–139**
  Coleman, James S., 324, 326–327
  English education, 744
  experiential learning, 1478, 1479
  faculty, 788, 800
  teachers, 414–415
Portfolio Project, American Association for Higher Education, 91
Portugal. *See* Western Europe
Positive reinforcement, 1460
Posner, Jill, 1405

POS (point-of-service) plans, 1530
Post–Civil War period school funding, 885
Postconventional moral development level, 1681
Postdoctoral education, **1903–1904**
Postlethwait, Samuel N., 1130–1131
Postmaterialism and interest groups, 664
Postmodernism
art education, 118–119, 120
ethics, 755
Freire, Paulo, 903
Post-Vietnam Era Veterans' Educational Assistance program (VEAP), 929–930
Potter, David, 1073
Poverty, **1904–1915**
children and adolescents, **1910–1915**
compensatory education, 453–463
effect on children, 808
foster care, 818
health and nutrition, 808, 1910–1911
international data, 1303–1304
overview of poverty and education, **1904–1910**
rates, 2707
reduction, 549, 1303–1304
See also Low-income families; Socioeconomic status
Powell, John Wesley, 93
Powell, Marjorie, 2454
Powerful Learning approach, 23, 24
The Power of Video Technology in International Comparative Research in Education (National Research Council), 1730
PPBS (program-planning-budgeting systems), 1953
PPOs (preferred provider organizations), 1530
PPP Persona, 1169
Practical intelligence, 1207–1208
The Practical (Schwab), 2157–2158
Practice and performance improvement, 765–766
The Practice of Teaching in the Secondary Schools (Morrison), 1690
Practicum, teacher, 2445–2447
Pragmatic communication, 586–587
Pragmatics, 1385
Pratt, Conrad and Anne M., 521
Pratt, Keith, 2498
Praxis Series examinations, 2455
Prayer. *See* Church-state issues
Preconventional moral development level, 1681
Prediction, research for, 2022
Predominantly white institutions (PWIs), 776
Preferential race-based admissions treatment, 64
Preferred provider organizations (PPOs), 1530
Pregnancy, teen, 978, **2060–2064,** 2067, **2071–2074**
Prejudice, racial, 1707
Preliminary SAT/National Merit Scholarship Qualifying Test (PSAT/NMSQT), 1781–1783
Prenatal drug exposure, 815
Preparing Future Faculty (PFF) program, 255, 910–911
Preschool education
dental health, 556
elementary school readiness, 716
emerging literacy, 1488–1489
English literacy development for English language learners, 183
funding, 275–276
infant schools' influence, 1135
overview, 616–620
programs, 277
school readiness, 200
Tools of the Mind (Bodrova and Leong), 576
See also Early childhood education; Head Start program
Prescott, Suzanne, 46
Prescriptive advising, 3
Prescriptive impulse and the philosophy of education, 1881–1882, 1883
Presentation, 1182–1183
Pre-service teacher programs, 2472
Presidency, college and university, **1915–1917**
decision-making, 946
in organizational structure, 386
Presidential Appointee Initiative, 209
Presidential libraries, 1733
Presidential papers, 1732
Presidential Task Force on the Arts and Humanities, 1773, 1774, 1776
President's Commission on White House Fellowships, 2686–2687
Presses, university, **2600–2603**
Pressey, Sidney L., **1917–1919,** 2230
Pressley, Michael, 1470, 1978, 1982
Pressure groups, 435
Presswood, Colleen S., 2491
Preventing Reading Difficulties in Young Children (National Research Council), 183, 1729–1730
Prevention and intervention
aggressive behavior, 71, 72
child abuse, 268–270
corruption, education, 1665–1666, *1666*
dental disease, 555–557
disabled students, 2288
dropouts, 601, 2581
early childhood problems, 831–832
full-service schools, 907
gang activity, 53–54
guidance and counseling, school, 977–978
health problems, 1007–1008, 1014
hearing impairment, 1019
HIV/AIDS, 2058–2059, 2072–2073
juvenile crime, 1354–1355
reading disabilities, 2009–2010
school counselors, 977–978
stress and depression, 2373
substance abuse, 816–817, 2056–2057
suicide, 2070
teenage pregnancy, 2062–2064, 2072–2074
violence exposure, 2626
Price, Joseph, 47
Priest, Serrano v., 481, 889
Primary and secondary abilities, 572–573
Primary care physicians, 1614
Prime Time project, 314, 316
Priming, memory test, 1596–1598

Princeton Review college rankings, 1644
Prince v. Massachusetts, 465
The Principal, Keystone of a High-Achieving School: Attracting and Keeping the Leaders We Need (report), 1746
Principal Leadership (periodical), 1746
Principal (periodical), 1739, 1740
Principals, **1919–1922**
  control, 2257
  leadership, 665–668
  middle school, 1634
  National Association of Elementary School Principals (NAESP), **1739–1741**
  National Association of Secondary School Principals (NASSP), **1745–1747,** 1778–1780
  secondary schools, 2192
  urban schools, 2606
Principals Center, Harvard Graduate School of Education, 666
Principles and Standards for School Mathematics (National Council of Teachers of Mathematics), 1545, 1767–1768
Principles of good practice, 415
Principles of Perceptual Learning and Development (Gibson), 1437
The Principles of Psychology (James), 1331–1332
Print, children's concepts about, 1974
Prior knowledge
  constructivism, 1464
  knowledge acquisition, representation, and organization, 1434
  learning, 1151
  mental models, 1600
  reading and, **1996–1998**
  reading comprehension and, 1979
  in reasoning, 1445
  transfer, 1450
Prisoners of Time (report), 698
Pritchett, Henry S., 892
Privacy, technology and, 2519
Private colleges and universities
  Canada, 236
  finance, 1024
  junior colleges, 876
  National Association of Independent Colleges and Universities (NAICU), **1741–1742**
  revenue, 25–26
  state aid, 873
  structure, 1042–1043
  See also Religiously affiliated colleges and universities
Private schools, **1922–1930**
  accreditation, 30
  compulsory school attendance and, 466
  Dalton School, **541–542**
  elementary, 712
  National Association of Independent Schools (NAIS), **1742–1743**
  principals, 1922
  public *vs.,* 950–953
  South Asia, 2276
  state administrative agencies and, 2348
  state funded, 953
  state relations to, **2335–2338**
  Sub-Saharan Africa, 2401–2402
  See also Catholic schools; Protestant schools; Voucher programs
Private speech, 575
Private textbook publishers, 2552
Private tutoring, 2581–2582, 2585–2587
Private Wealth and Public Education (Sugarman), 671–672
Privatization, school
  accountability, 653
  criticism, 547
  gender issues, 920
  international commerce of education, 1220
  Middle East and North Africa, 1629
  policy, 674
  private schools, 1927–1928
  school choice, 552–553
  social organization of public schools, 2260
Probation, 1356
Probationary period in tenure process, 16
PROBE Team, 951–952
The Problem Child (Neill), 1797
Problems and Theorems in Analysis (Pólya and Szegö), 1545–1546
Problem solving, **1441–1444**
  adaptive expertise, 763–764
  assessment, 147
  case-based reasoning, 1154–1158
  complex problem solving, **1545–1548**
  experts *vs.* novices, 569
  Human Problem Solving (Newell and Simon), 1546
  problem-based learning (PBL), **1172–1175,** 1185–1186, 1544
  problem-posing method of education, 901
  See also Instructional design
Procedural component of metamemory, 1603
Procedural knowledge, 1432, 1434–1435
Process, scientific, 2170–2171
Process model of language arts instruction, 1393–1394
Process views of emotions, 59–60
Productive thinking, 1443
Productivity, 549
Professional advisers, 4
Professional and Organizational Development Network for Higher Education (POD), 255, 256
Professional development
  AACSB International, 1
  accelerated schools, 24
  business teachers, 1, 223–224
  early childhood education teachers, 624
  elementary school teachers, 721, 722
  English education, 746–747
  part-time faculty, 780–781
  Phi Delta Kappa International, 1080
  professional development schools (PDSs), **1930–1933,** 2441
  Smithsonian Institution programs, 2240
  social studies education, 2270–2271
  studies of, 1729
  teacher learning communities, 2461–2467
  teachers, 721, 2470–2473
  teacher training *vs.,* 2470
  teacher unions, 2480
  teaching improvement centers, 254–256
  urban teachers, 2611
  vocational education teachers, 2648–2649

See also Continuing professional education (CPE)
Professional development schools (PDSs), **1930–1933,** 2441
Professional education
accreditation, 33
continuing, **483–489**
graduate, 967
military, **1653–1655**
professional doctoral degrees, 596
See also Higher education
Professional honor societies, 2436
Professionalism, 754
Professional misconduct, 1664
Professional negotiations, 2476
Professional Preparation Network, 517
Professional status
part-time faculty, 781–782
women and minority faculty, 777
Proficiencies, curriculum, 511
Proficiency, foreign language, 893–894
Proficiency Guidelines (American Council on the Teaching of Foreign Languages), 893–894
Program compliance audits, 1955
Program elimination
art education, 117, 118
business education, 224
Program evaluation, **2030–2034**
Program for International Student Assessment (PISA)
national achievement tests, 2548
social indicators, 1295
statistics, 1287–1288
Program implementation, 2031–2032
Programmatic curriculum, 531
Programmed instruction, 1309–1310, 2230
Program on Noncollegiate Sponsored Instruction (PONSI), 1478, 1479
Program-planning-budgeting systems (PPBS), 1953
Program-specific grants, 891
Progressive education, **1933–1938**
character development, 259–260
criticism, 172–173, 994, 1364
Dalton School, **541–542**
De Lima, Agnes, 553–554
Eight-Year Study, 80, **707–709,** 2427–2428, 2588
Gary Plan, **915–916**
geography, 926
Goslin, Willard E., 943–944
instructional strategies, 1178–1179
international conferences, 1278–1279
kindergarten, 189–190
Labrant, Lou L., 1379–1380
Miel, Alice, 1636
Progressive Education Association (PEA), 80–81, 696–697, 707
Progressive Education at the Crossroads (Bode), 195
project method, 1938–1939
rural, 297–298
textbooks, 2555
vocational education, 1940
See also Child-centered education
Progressive Education Association (PEA)
Aiken Commission, 707–708, 2427–2428
Alberty, H. B., 80–81
Commission on Human Relations, 708
reports, 696–697
Progressive Education at the Crossroads (Bode), 195
Progressive educator's biographies
Alberty, H. B., **80–82**
Bagley, William Chandler, **163–165**
Bode, Boyd H., **194–196**
Childs, John L., **292–294**
Counts, George S., **503–505**
De Lima, Agnes, **553–554**
Hahn, Kurt, **981–982**
Hopkins, L. Thomas, **1088–1089**
Johnson, Marietta Pierce, **1344–1346**
Kerschensteiner, Georg, **1367–1369**
Kilpatrick, William H., **1368–1369**
Labrant, Lou L., **1379–1380**
Putnam, Alice, **1957–1959**
Rice, Joseph Mayer, **2053–2055**
Snedden, David, **2241–2242**
Taylor, Harold, **2433–2435**
Thayer, V. T., **2560–2562**
Progress maps, 141, *142*
Progress portfolios, 138
Project 2000 (Kahler et al.), 77
Project 2061, 91–92, 2174–2175
Project Chata, 1053
Project Follow Through, 2000
Project method, 1368, **1938–1939**
Project model for educational aid, 687
Project on the Status and Education of Women, 152
Project STAR (Student Teacher Achievement Ratio), 314–315, 316
Project Zero, Harvard University's, 1200
Promoting Alternative Thinking Strategies (PATHS), 1192–1193
Promotion, social, 2191, **2262–2265**
Promotion and Participation for Economic Cooperation (Proparco, France), 1244
Proparco (Promotion and Participation for Economic Cooperation, France), 1244
Property, educational, 1664–1665
Property crime, 1354, 1359
Proposition 209 (California), 64
Proposition 227 (California), 182
Proprietary schools, American overseas, 113–114
Prospect research, development office's, 1142–1143
Prospect School, Vermont, 2467
Prosser, Charles, **1940–1941**
Protection and education suppliers, 1662–1663
Protestant schools, 429, **1941–1945**
See also Private schools; Religiously affiliated schools; Voucher programs
Protocol analysis of information processing, 569
Provost. *See* Chief academic affairs officers
PRWORA. *See* Personal Responsibility and Work Opportunity Reconciliation Act (PRWORA)
Psacharopoulos, George, 549
PSAT/NMSQT (Preliminary Sat/National Merit Scholarship Qualifying Test), 372, 1781–1783
Pseudospeciation, 752
PSSC (Physical Sciences Study Committee), 2745–2746
Psychoanalysis, 751–752

Psychological problems and counseling, **1869–1871, 1871–1874**

Psychologists, school, **1945–1948**

Psychology
- animal studies, 2564–2565
- Binet, Alfred, 185–187
- community psychology, 433–435
- folk, 572
- Rogers, Carl, 2076–2079
- Vygotsky, Lev, 2658–2660
- *See also* Educational psychology

Psychometrics, 138, 139–143
- *See also* Intelligence testing; Measurement

Psychomotor objectives, 1177

Psychosexual development, 2061, 2063–2064

Psychosocial aspects
- development, 751–752
- eight-stage model of development, 752
- group processes, 972–973
- learning, 627, 630, 730–731
- student employment, 730–731
- substance abuse, 2055–2056
- undergraduate learning, 2495

Psychotherapy, 1869–1870, 2077–2079

Psychotropic drugs, 1615–1616

PTFP (Public Telecommunications Facilities Program), 657

PTO (Patent and Trademark Office), 842

Public and Private High Schools: The Impact of Communities (Coleman), 326, 1926

Publication of faculty research
- academic freedom, 17
- expectations at research universities, 17

Publications offices, college and university, 1140

Public broadcasting, **656–658**

Public Broadcasting Act, 657

Public Broadcast Service (PBS), 657

Public colleges and universities
- American Association of State Colleges and Universities (AASCU), **100–101,** 1750
- chartered colleges, 1035
- finance, 1023–1024
- international privatization, 1032
- National Association of State Universities and Land-Grant Colleges (NASULGC), 100, 101, **1749–1750**
- Office for the Advancement of Public Black Colleges (OAPBC), 100
- revenue, 25–26, 2340–2341
- state funding, 872–873
- structure, 1042–1043
- teacher education programs, 2439–2440
- *See also* Colleges and universities; Higher education; Land-grant colleges and universities

Public domain, 1187

Public Education in the United States (Cubberley), 508–509

Public good, 949–950

Public health. *See* Health education

Public Health Service (PHS), 2037, 2038

Public kindergarten, 189–190

Public Law 91-248, 2132

Public Law 94-142, 2635

Public Law 103-448, 2133–2134

Public Law 107-87. *See* No Child Left Behind Act

Public Laws 81-815 and 81-874, **1108–1109**

Public libraries, 287, 2137

Public museums, **1716–1718**

Public-private partnerships, 1220

Public relations
- AACSB International conference, 1
- higher education, 1140
- National Education Association, 1770–1771
- National School Public Relations Association (NSPRA), **1786–1788**

Public Report on Basic Education in India (PROBE Team), 951–952

Public School Administration (Cubberley), 508

Public schools
- accountability, 651–655
- administration, 508–509
- African Americans, 2199–2202
- alternative schooling, **82–86**
- Beacon Education Management, Inc., **167–168**
- Canada, 235–236, 236
- capacity, 1770
- Catholic schools and, 250, 252, 325–326
- character development, 259–261
- common school movement, 711–712
- community education, 448–451
- contracting out services, 952–953
- Council of Chief State School Officers (CCSSO), **501–503**
- criticism, 172–173, **1948–1952**
- curriculum and state education agencies, 2345
- decentralization, **542–546**
- demographics, 2706
- efficiency, 950–951
- emancipated slaves, 2665–2666
- finance, **1952–1957**
- funding, 236
- Gary Plan, **915–916**
- governance, 693
- health services, **1012–1016**
- hidden curriculum, 537–538
- homicides, 1355, 1358–1359
- immigrants, 1098–1103
- Jewish students, 1340
- kindergarten, 615–616, 622
- language diversity, 1400–1403
- large-city superintendents, **2411–2415**
- leadership, **664–668**
- lifelong learning, 1481
- looping, 1521
- magnet schools, **1526–1529**
- Mann, Horace, 1535–1536
- mental health services, 1613–1614
- minorities and public high schools, 2186–2187
- museums, 1717–1718
- National PTA support, 1783–1784
- physical education programs, 1887–1888
- police/school partnerships, 1355
- preschool, 617
- principals, 665–668
- Progressive education, 1935
- public support, 694
- records and reports, **2013–2015**
- recreation programs, **2015–2017**
- restructuring, 2638
- school boards, **2102–2121**
- secondary education, 2184–2185, 2186–2187
- segregation, 324–325, 430
- social organization, **2253–2261**
- special education, 2279–2289

standards, 950–951
standards movement, 674
state departments of education, **2323–2331**
state educational systems, **2331–2334**
statewide testing programs, 2538–2541
subject centered curriculum, 993–994
superintendents, 666–668, 2107–2111
See also Charter schools; Common schools; Education reform; Magnet schools; Privatization, school; School choice; School reform

The Public-School System of the United States (report), 2054
Public sector employees
cost/benefit analysis, 648–649
Middle East and North Africa, 1624, *1626*
Public service role, faculty, 792, 796–797
Public speaking. *See* Speech and theater education
Public Telecommunications Facilities Program (PTFP), 657
Publishing
faculty, 785–786, 788
textbook, 2552–2553
university presses, **2600–2603**
Puerto Ricans, 1098
Puerto Rico. *See* Latin America and the Caribbean
Punishment and operant conditioning, 1460
Pupil weighting, 891
Pura Belpré Award, 289
Puritans, 710
The Purposes of Education in American Democracy (report), 696
Purposes of schooling, 2254–2256
Putnam, Alice, 190, 622, **1957–1959**
Putnam, James Jackson, 190
PWIs (predominantly white institutions), 776

Q

Qatar. *See* Middle East and North Africa
Qualitative approach to research, **2026–2030**
Quality Counts (Survey), 270–271, 274, 275
Quality Initiatives, AAHE, 90
Quality of education
child care, 273
decentralization, 544
Education Quality Institute, 1798–1799
Latin America, 1408–1410
school-parent-community partnerships, 825–826
teacher quality, 1770
texts, 1997
Quantum Opportunities Program, 2713
Quarter calendar. *See* Academic calendars
Quasi-experimental research, 2024–2025, 2031
Quebec, 235
Queer theory, 918
Question answering and reading comprehension, 1980–1981
Questions, classroom, **310–314**
classroom discourse, 583
cognitive perspective, 588
language, 1390
Questions, research, 2027
Quill and Scroll Society, **2736–2737**
Quincy Grammar School, 1812
Quinn, Bill, 496

R

Race/ethnicity, **1121–1125**
academic labor market, 18
adjustment to college, 44
affirmative action, **61–65,** 397, 2424
court cases, 2423–2425
cultural expectations and learning, **1961–1966**
culture, **1961–1971**
decentralization, 544
discrimination, 609–610
faculty consulting, 774
faculty diversity, 776–778, *778*
gang membership, 53
graduate study in education, 967
Harvard, 724
higher education, **1968–1971**
inequality in school funding, 298
inequitable instruction, 305–306
intelligence quotient scores, 1204
literacy, 1509–1512
number sense and culture, 1564–1565
nursery school enrollment, 618
parenting, 1850–1851
population trends, 2705
poverty and behavior problems, 1912
poverty rates, 2707
private school students, 1922–1923
"Racial Problems and Academic Programs," 152
rural education, 2086
salaries, faculty, 18–19
school boards, 2106
school choice, 90
school sports participation, *2309*
social cohesions and, 2247–2248
teacher educators, 2441
transracial adoptions, 815
Young Women's Christian Association's fight against discrimination, 2742
See also Demographics; Minorities; Multiculturalism; Specific groups

"Racial Problems and Academic Programs," 152
Radcliffe College, 995
Radio, 656, 657, 2514
RAND Change Agent study, 2030–2031
Randolph, Virginia Estelle, 1337
Randomized Field Experiments for Planning and Evaluation: A Practical Guide (Boruch), 2024
Rankings, college and university, **378–381**
college rankings, 397
consumerism, 1024
research universities, 2042–2043
U.S. Air Force Academy, 1644
Rankings and Estimates (National Education Association), 662
Raphael, Taffy E., 1981
Rasch model, 141
RAs (resident assistants or advisers), 341
Rate of return on investment. *See* Cost/benefit analysis
Ratings, media, 1580

RAT (Remote Associations Test), 506
Raudenbusch, Steve, 999
Raven's Colored Progressive Matrices (RCPM), 128
Ravitch, Dinate, 1057
Rawls, John, 754
Ray, Edward, 2049
Razor, Jack, 1892
RCE (responsible conduct of research), 2039–2040
RCPM (Raven's Colored Progressive Matrices), 128
Readability indices, **1972–1973**
Readiness, employment, **732–735**
Readiness, reading, 1487, **2003–2007**
Readiness, school, **2148–2151**
  current trends in elementary education, 716
  family support services, 831–832
  stages of growth, 277
  See also Early childhood education; Head Start program; Preschool education
Reading, **1973–2007**
  ABC reading method, 1999
  acquisition, 1513–1515
  attention, 157
  beginning, **1974–1977**
  brain imaging and reading ability, 205
  Chall, Jeanne, 257–259
  children's literature, 288
  content areas, **1985–1989**
  disabilities, **2007–2013**
  educational psychology, 681
  elementary education history, 713–714
  elementary school, 713
  Gray, William Scott, 970–971
  guided reading, 2005
  instruction, **1998–2003**
  instruction studies, 1729–1730
  interest, **1989–1993**
  international assessment, 1223, **1228–1229**
  International Reading Association, **1307–1309**
  Labrant, Lou L., 1379
  learning from text, **1993–1995,** 1996–1997
  literacy and, **1513–1518**
  National Research Council studies, 1729–1730
  parents' role, 811–812
  politicization of the process, 901–902
  Preventing Reading Difficulties in Young Children (National Research Council), 183, 1729–1730
  prior knowledge and, **1996–1998**
  readability indices, **1972–1973**
  readiness, 1487, **2003–2007**
  reading aloud to children, 2004–2005
  Reading and Writing for Critical Thinking (RWCT) Project, 1308
  reading engagement, value of, **2003–2007**
  Reading One-to-One, 2581
  Reading Recovery (initiative), 2581
  reciprocal listening/reading, 576–577
  SQ3R reading technique, 1978
  Starting Out Right: A Guide to Promoting Children's Reading Success (National Research Council), 1729–1730
  student-generated strategies, 1988–1989
  teacher-directed strategies, 1988
  textbooks, 713
  tutoring, 2581
  whole language instruction, 258, 681, 741
  See also Language arts; Literacy; Reading comprehension
Reading and Writing for Critical Thinking (RWCT) Project, 1308
Reading comprehension, **1977–1985**
  beginning readers, 1975–1976
  causal reasoning, 1426
  instruction, 1999
  interest, 1990–1991
  learning from texts, 1993–1995
  literacy, 1515
  narratives, 1501–1502
  reciprocal listening/reading, 576–577
  strategies, 1977–1983, 1995, 1999
  text comprehensibility, 1994
Reading One-to-One, 2581
Reading Recovery (initiative), 2581
Ready to Learn: A Mandate for the Nation (report), 200
Ready to Learn Act of 1994, 200
Reagan, Ronald, 2152, 2153
Realizing the Educational Potential of Residence Halls (Smith), 2046
Reallocation of school resources, 551
Reasoning, **1444–1448**
  analogical, **1421–1424,** 1429, 1450
  case-based, **1154–1159**
  causal, **1425–1427**
  deductive, 678
  mathematics as, 1554
  moral, 1680–1683
  syllogisms, 1444–1445
Recall. *See* Memory
Reception classes, immigrant, 1104
Receptive instruction, 1160
Recession, economic, 883
Recidivism, juvenile crime, 1356
Reciprocal listening/reading, 576–577
Reciprocal peer tutoring (RPT), 490
Reciprocal teaching of comprehension, 1978
Reciprocity licensing, 2436
Reckase, Mark, 141
Recommendations, student, 329
Reconstructionism, 207–208
Reconstructive memory, 1589, 1608
Recording and playback technology, 592
Records, educational, 1641, **2013–2015**
Recreation activities
  academic performance, 1837
  school programs, **2015–2017**
Recruitment
  college practices, **382–384,** 396, 397–398
  community colleges, 2390–2391
  international students, 1314–1317
  records, 1144
  school bus drivers, 2576
  teachers, 2444, 2449–2450
Reder, Lynn, 1466
Redistricting, 2344–2345
REE (Research, Education, and Economics), 841
Rees, Mina, 93

Reference sources, digital, 2516
Reflection
  case-based learning, 1157–1158
  English instruction, 744
  internships, 1326
  learning, 762
  problem-based learning, 1174
  Reflective Learner (software), 1157
  reflective thinking, 579
Reflections (National Council of Teachers of Mathematics), 1768
Reflective Learner (software), 1157
Reform. *See* Education reform; School reform; Social reform; Welfare reform
REFORMA, 289
The Reform of Secondary Education (report), 697
Refugees, 1264–1265
Refuge movement, 281
Regents of the University of California v. Bakke, 62–63, 64, 2424, **2951–3004**
Regional Educational Laboratories, 2088
Regional international development institutions, **1249–1259**
Regional laboratories and research and development centers, **2017–2019**
Regional Records Services centers, National Archives and Records Administration, 1732–1733
Regional school accrediting commissions, 28–29, 32
Regional service centers, 2348–2349
Regression analysis, 660–661, *661*
Regular decision admissions, 328
Regular Education Initiative (REI), 2281–2282
Regulation and state government, 2326, 2336–2338
Rehabilitation Act
  assistive technology, 149
  disabled college students, 408–409
  federal assistance programs, 1868–1869
Reid, Bill, 349
Reid, Community for Creative Non-Violence (CCNV) v., 1188
Reiguluth, Charles, 1147, 1149, 1160
Reimbursement
  After-School Snack Program, 2135
  School Breakfast Program, 2134
  school lunch, 2132–2133
  Special Milk Program (SMP), 2134–2135
Reimer, Bennett, 1723
Rein, Wilhelm, 1022
Reinforcement
  classical conditioning, 1460
  educational psychology, 2565
  instruction, 1695–1697
  learning theory, 678–679, 680
  See also Incentives; Motivation
Reinventing government, 691
REI (Regular Education Initiative), 2281–2282
Reis, Sally, 931
Reisert, John, 314, 316
Relationships, interpersonal
  college students, 337–338
  intelligence, 1199
  middle childhood, 278
  See also Peer relations; Social development
Relationships, peer
  clubs, 318
  college students, 335
  educational aspirations, 1859
  health education involvement, 1009
  juvenile crime, 1360
  learning, **1864–1867**
  See also Interpersonal relationships; Peer culture, adolescent; Social development
Re:Learning project, 323
Relevance, school, 601
Religion
  common schools, 430
  freedom of religion and compulsory school attendance, 466
  higher education and, 1026, 1034
  Islam, **1327–1330**
  Jewish education, **1340–1343**
  moral education, 1684
  See also Church-state issues; Court cases
Religiously affiliated colleges and universities, **389–393**
  academic freedom, 15
  colonial America, 1034
  Harvard University, 724
  liberal arts, 1476
  See also Private colleges and universities
Religiously affiliated schools
  academic freedom, 15
  American overseas church schools, 114
  Christian day schools, 1944
  elementary schools, 712
  government aid to, 1925
  immigrants, 1099
  Jewish schools, **1340–1343**
  National Catholic Educational Association (NCEA), **1754–1756**
  state regulation, 2336–2337
  See also Catholic schools; Private schools; Protestant schools; Voucher programs
Remedial Cases in Reading: Their Diagnosis and Correction (Gray), 971
Remediation
  accelerated schools, 23
  college students, 44
  summer school, 2409
Reminiscence bump, 1589–1590
Remote Associations Test (RAT), 506
Removal of children from their homes, 809–810
Renaud, Robert D., 416
Renzulli, Joseph, 931
Reorganizing Secondary Education (report), 2561
Reorganizing the High School Curriculum (Alberty), 81
Replication, research for, 2022
Reporting
  faculty consulting, 773–774
  financial, 26
  research findings, 2029
Report of the Association of American Universities Committee on the Integrity of Research (report), 2037
Report of the Committee of Ten (Committee on Secondary School Studies, NEA), 696
Report of the Hadow Committee (England), 1134
Report of the National Commission on Aid to Vocational Education, 1940

Report of the National Reading Panel, 1514

Reports and publications
Academic Preparation for College, 697
Adventures in Learning, 708
American College Athletics, 350
American High School Today, 473, 697
An American Imperative: Higher Expectations for Higher Education, 518
America's Competitive Challenge, 697
Belmont Report, 1091
Bond, Horace Mann, 196–197
Boyer, Ernest, 200–201
Breaking Ranks: Changing an American Institution, 1746, 1778, 2191
The Challenges of Connecting Learning, 517
Children and Their Primary Schools (England), 1134, 1825–1826
Children in Need, 698
Classroom Assessment and the National Science Education Standards, 1729
Coleman Report, 324–325, 326, 673, 728
College: The Undergraduate Experience in America, 200
college sports, 352–353
A Comparative Study of Intramural Programs in Negro Colleges (Wasson), 362
Conant, J. B., 473–474
Condition of Education, 843
The Conditions of Children in California, 2141
curriculum guides, 525
Digest of Education Statistics, 843
The Dissolution of General Education, 517
Does School Quality Matter, Beyond Rhetoric: A New American Agenda for Children and Families, 698
Eager to Learn: Educating Our Preschoolers, 1730
early childhood education, 617–618
economic, 841
Educating Americans for the 21st Century, 697
Educating One and All: Students with Disabilities and Standards-Based Reform, 1730
Educational Policy, 474
Educational Resources Information Center (ERIC), 683
Education at a Glance: OECD Indicators (OECD), 1287, 1291, 1293
Education for All American Youth, 697
The Education of American Teachers, 474
education reform, **695–700**
Equality of Education Opportunity, 697, 1835
The Essential Profession, 698
Excellence and Equity, 1717–1718
expenditure projections, 662
Facing the Challenge: The Report of the Twentieth Century Task Force on School Governance (report), 2105, 2115
fact books, college and university, 1145
Faure Report, 1481
50 Hours: A Core Curriculum for College Students, 515
foreign language education, 895
Functions of Secondary Education, 696
Global Perspectives for Local Action: Using TIMSS to Improve U.S. Mathematics and Science Education, 1730
Hadow Report (England), 1825
Higher Education and the American Resurgence, 517–518
High School: A Report on Secondary Education in America, 200, 697
High School Achievement: Public, Catholic and Private Schools Compared, 1926
High Stakes: Testing for Tracking, Promotion, and Graduation, 1730
Horace's Compromise: The Dilemma of the American High School, 321, 697
How People Learn: Bridging Research and Practice, 2165, 2646
How Schools Shortchange Girls, 1125
How to Get More of Them, 698
Improving Student Learning: A Strategic Plan for Education Research and Its Utilization, 1730
institutional advancement, 1140
Integrity in the College Curriculum: A Report to the Academic Community, 152, 515–516
Investing in Our Children, 697
Investing in Teaching, 698
Involvement in Learning: Realizing the Potential of American Higher Education, 515, 2046
Issues of Secondary Education, 696
Joining Forces, 2141
juvenile crime, 1360
The Kindergarten, 190
Learning to Be, 1481
The Maintenance of High Ethical Standards in the Conduct of Research, 2037
Making the Grade, 697
Meeting the Need for Quality Action in the South, 697
mental health services, 1006–1007
Museums for a New Century, 1717–1718
National Academy of Sciences, 1728–1730
National Reading Panel (NRP), 2005
A Nation Prepared: Teachers for the Twenty-first Century, 697, 2154
A New Vitality for General Education, 516–517
Next Steps for TIMSS: Directions for Secondary Analysis, 1730
The Paideia Proposal, 697
patents and trademarks, 842
A Place Called School, 697
Plowden Report (England), 1134, 1825–1826
The Power of Video Technology in International Comparative Research in Education, 1730
Presidential papers, 1732
Preventing Reading Difficulties in Young Children, 183, 1729–1730
Prisoners of Time, 698
Public and Private High Schools: The Impact of Communities, 326, 1926

Public Report on Basic Education in India, 951–952
The Public-School System of the United States, 2054
The Purposes of Education in American Democracy, 696
The Reform of Secondary Education, 697
Report of the Association of American Universities Committee on the Integrity of Research (report), 2037
Report of the Committee of Ten, 696
Report of the Hadow Committee (England), 1134
Report of the National Commission on Aid to Vocational Education, 1940
Report of the National Reading Panel, 1514
research integrity reports, 2037
Science in General Education, 80
Science Teacher Preparation in an Era of Standards-Based Reform, 1729
Science—the Endless Frontier: A Report to the President on a Program for Postwar Scientific Research, 855
Scientific Inquiry in Education, 1730
service-needs, 2141
Single Source: Towards an Inventory of Federal Education Programs, 864–865
Slums and Suburbs, 473
The Social Ideas of American Educators, 539
Strengthening the Ties That Bind: Integrating Undergraduate Liberal and Professional Study, 517
Strength through Wisdom, 895
Strong Foundations: Twelve Principles for Effective General Education Programs, 517
"The Supply and Demand of Elementary and Secondary School Teachers in the United States," 2087
The Surgeon General's Report on Physical Activity and Health, 1888
The Teachers We Want, 698
Theory and Practice in Historical Study: A Report of the Committee on Historiography, 539
Time for Results, 518, 697
Tomorrow's Teachers, 697
To Reclaim a Legacy: A Report on the Humanities in Higher Education, 514–515
To Secure the Blessings of Liberty, 518
Transforming the State Role in Undergraduate Education: Time for A Different View, 518
Truman Report, 96
Turning Points, 1632–1633, 1746, 2096, 2191
undergraduate curriculum, **514–519**
The Undergraduate Experience in America, 516
The Unique Functions of Education in American Democracy, 696
The Uses of the University, 1038
What Matters Most: Teaching for America's Future, 2155
Wingspread Report, 790
World Development Report, 998
"The Yale Report of 1828," 1476
See also Eight-Year Study; *A Nation at Risk: The Imperative for Educational Reform* (report)

Representation, scientific, 2171
Representational systems, 1563
Reproductive thinking, 1443, 1589
Republic of China. *See* China
Republic of Congo. *See* Sub-Saharan Africa
Republic of Georgia. *See* Eastern Europe and Central Asia
Republic of Macedonia. *See* Eastern Europe and Central Asia
Republic (Plato), 1899
Reputational diversity in higher education, 1044
Required Education in the Protection of Human Research Participants (NIH), 2040
Requirements
- diversity requirements, 1711–1713
- general education, 925
- graduate education degrees, 969–970
- graduation, 2539–2540, 2657
- master's programs, 1538
- service learning, 2203–2204
- speech education, 2298–2299

Research. *See* Educational research; Faculty research; Research methods; Research universities; Studies, research
Research, Education, and Economics (REE), 841
Research About Teacher Education (RATE) Study, 721
Research and development. *See* Faculty research; Research universities
Research and development centers and regional laboratories, **2017–2019**
Research and Special Programs Administration, DOT, 851
Research grants, **2019–2020**
Research in Higher Education (Feldman), 416
Research methods, **2020–2036**
- data analysis, 2028–2029
- data collection, 2027, 2034–2036
- experimental research, 2023–2024, 2031, 2229
- human subject protection, **1091–1092**
- Internet, 2510–2511, 2516
- language acquisition study, 1385
- Lindquist, E. F., 1486
- misconduct, **2037–2041**
- overview, **2020–2026**
- qualitative and ethnographic approach, **2026–2030**
- school and program evaluation, **2030–2034**
- scientific *vs.* program evaluation, 2030
- study design, 2027
- verbal protocols, **2034–2036**
- *See also* Faculty research; Research universities

Research universities, **2041–2043**
- Carnegie Classification, 244, 245
- consortia, 477
- faculty research, 783, 785–786
- Johns Hopkins University, **1343–1344**
- junior colleges and, 443
- land-grant, 1383–1384
- misconduct, research, 2037–2040
- teaching centers, 255
- technology transfer, **2526–2528**

See also Faculty research; Research methods
Research within Reach: Science Education (Holdzkom and Lutz), 2164
Residence halls, **340–344, 1518–1520,** 2044
Residencies, medical, 1586
Resident assistants or advisers (RAs), 341
Resident directors. *See* Hall directors
Residential colleges, **2043–2047**
Residential learning communities, 2044
Residential programs, academic, 2044
Residential public high schools, 84
Resiliency and high-risk environments, 1853
Resistance approach to substance abuse education, 604
Resnick, David P., 2255
Resnick, Lauren, 1149, 1559, 2255
Resnick, Mitchell, 1165
Resnik, Judith, 104
Resolving Conflict Creatively, 1193
Resource allocation, 702, **2047–2052**
Resource cost model, 1954–1955
Resources in Education (Educational Resources Information Center), 683
Resource units, 81
Respecting Differences Resource Guide (National PTA), 1783
Responsibility Center Management, 2051
The Responsible Conduct of Research in the Health Sciences (Institute of Medicine), 2039
Responsible conduct of research (RCR), 2039–2040
Responsible Officers (ROs), 1313–1314
Responsiveness, parental, 55
The Restoration of Learning (Bestor), 172–173
Restrained teaching style, 160
Restraining orders, 2633–2634
Restructuring, school, 691, 2638
"Results-Oriented Professional Development: In Search of an Optimal Mix of Effective Practices" (Guskey), 2471
Retention
  college, **401–407**
  community colleges, 402, 2391
  commuter students, 452
  enrollment management, 749–750
  promotion *vs.*, 2191
  school bus drivers, 2576–2577
Retrieval, memory, 1606, 1607–1608, 1611
Rettig, Michael, 2097–2098
Revenue
  community colleges, 876
  distribution by institution type, *877, 879*
  federal revenue for degree-granting institutions, *873*
  higher education, 25–26, 870–871, *872,* 2047–2048
  public school organization and, 2258
  school modernization, 2130
  state administrative services, 2340–2342
  state revenue for degree-granting institutions, *874*
  tuition and fees by institution type, *880*
  See also Budgeting; Economics of education; Finance; Funding
Reverse engineering and copyright infringement, 1190
Review, records, 2015
Revised Standards and Policies for Accrediting Colleges for Teacher Education (American Association of Colleges for Teacher Education), 2442
Revolutionary War, 1656
Reward system, academic, 796–797
Reynolds, Cecil R., 2294
Rho Chi, **1082–1083**
Rhodes, Richard, 794
Rhythmic developmentalism, 2685–2686
Rice, Gong Lum v., 1100
Rice, John A., **2052–2053**
Rice, Joseph Mayer, 696, **2053–2055**
Richards, Ellen H., 803–804
Richards, Garry E., 762
Richardson, Adams v., 776
Richmond County School Board, Georgia, Cummings v., 2186, 2200
Rich Schools, Poor Schools (Wise), 671
Richter, John E., 2628
Rickel, Jeff, 1169
Riecken, Henry, 2031
Right brain/left brain learning, 204
Rightstart project, 1562
Rigsby, Leo, 48
Riley, Richard, 2616
Risk assumption, 1474
Risk behavior, **2055–2074**
  community violence exposure, 2629
  health education, 1004
  HIV/AIDS, **2058–2060,** 2066
  sexual activity, 2058, **2060–2064,** 2064–2066, 2071–2074
  sexually transmitted diseases (STDs), **2064–2066**
  smoking, 2066–2068, **2066–2068**
  substance abuse, *2055,* **2055–2058**
  suicide, **2068–2071**
  teen pregnancy, **2060–2064,** 2071–2074, **2071–2074**
Risk factors
  adolescents, 1837
  suicide, 2069
Risk management, higher education, **2074–2076**
Ritalin, 158
Ritual, fraternity and sorority, 2252
Robert F. Sibert Informational Book Award, 288
Robertson, Roland, 936
Roberts v. City of Boston, 2200
Rochester, New Hampshire, School District, Timothy W. v., 2212
Rockefeller Foundation, 996–997, 1809
Rodriquez, San Antonio Independent School District v., 481, 2113
Roehler, Laura R., 1978
Rogers, Carl, 976, **2076–2079**
Rogers, William B., 1939
Role models, teachers as, 753

Roles
  college faculty, 414–415, 417, **789–794, 796–798**
  role theory, 1859
  student, 43
Rolling admissions, 328
Rollins College, 2052
Roman education, 1414
Romania. *See* Eastern Europe and Central Asia
Romney, Kim, 1620
Ronan, Michael B., 167
Ronning, Royce, 1604
Ronsenshine, Barak, 1981, 1982
Roommate assignments, residence hall, 342–343
Roosevelt, Eleanor, 298, 1069
Roosevelt, Theodore
  agricultural education, 73
  Barnard, Frederick A. P., 230
  college athletics, 349, 364
Roosevelt v. Bishop, 888
Root, Elihu, 1138
Root, Lewis S., 801
Ropers-Huilman, Becky, 521
Roschelle, Jeremy, 469–470
Rose Bowl Game, 350
Rosenberger v. University of Virginia, 2423
Rosenblatt, Louise, 288
Rosenshine, Barak, 313
Rosenthal, Hilary, 1174
Rosenwald Schools, 1338–1339
Rosenzweig, Robert M., 154
Rose v. Council for Better Education, 672
Ross, Steven M., 1578
Rosseau, Jean-Jacques, 562
Rossi, Peter, 2030
Rote learning, 1443
Roth, Jodie, 2713
Rothstein, Richard, 2263
Rousing Minds to Life: Teaching, Learning and Schooling in Social Context (Tharp and Gallimore), 576
Rousseau, Jean-Jacques, 1833, **2079–2081**
Routine problems, 1442
Rowan, Brian, 2454
Rowe, Mary Budd, 312
Rowley, Board of Education of the Hendrick Hudson Central School District v., 2281
Royal Agricultural Society (England), 72
RPT (reciprocal peer tutoring), 490
Rubella, 1107
Rubin, David C., 1589
Ruchs, Ralph F., 102
Rugg, Harold, 1484, **2081–2083**
Rugg textbooks, 2556
Rugh, Andrea B., 2446
Rule assessment method, 569
Rules and procedures, classroom, 300–301
Rules and regulations, NCAA, **368–371**
Rumbaut, Ruben G., 1100
Rumberger, Russell, 2382
Rumelhart, David, 1467–1468
Runyon v. McCrary, 2424
Rural education, **2083–2092**
  arts programs, 1772–1773
  Clapp, Elsie Ripley, 297–298
  Four-H Programs, **2727–2728**
  international context, **2090–2092**
  Jeanes teachers, **1337–1339**
  one-room schools, 712
  overview, **2083–2090**
  public school demographics, 2706
  Rural Education: In Search of a Better Way (Nachtigal), 2085
  Rural Education: Issues and Practices (DeYoung), 2088
  Rural School and Community Trust, 2087
  rural/urban differences, *2085*
  state departments of education, 2324
Rural Education: In Search of a Better Way (Nachtigal), 2085
Rural Education: Issues and Practices (DeYoung), 2088
Rural improvement, 74
Rural School and Community Trust, 2087
Rush, Benjamin, 428, 1098
Rushes, class, 348
Russia
  cognitive development theory, 576
  Coordination Dutch-Russian Cooperation in Education (CROSS) program, 1267
  international education assistance for, 1267
  zemstvo schools, 712
  See also Eastern Europe and Central Asia
Rutter, Robert, 2712
Rwanda. *See* Sub-Saharan Africa
RWCT (Reading and Writing for Critical Thinking) Project, 1308
Ryan, Kevin, 261

S

Saarni, Carolyn, 1191
Sabbath schools, 2665
The Saber Tooth Curriculum (Benjamin), 168–169
Sacred music, 594
SACS (Southern Association of Colleges and Schools), 28, 32
Sadoski, Mark, 1991
Safe and Drug-Free Schools Program, 603
Safety
  child care, 273
  low-income children, 808
  school bus, 2574–2575
  school sports, 2308
  urban schools, 2611
Sagan, Carl, 2162
The Sage of Petaluma (Benjamin), 169
SAGE (Student Achievement Guarantee in Education), 315
Salaries. *See* Earnings
Salish I and II studies, 2164
Salomon, Gavriel, 1174, 1499, 1578
Salovey, Peter, 1191–1192
The Salterton Trilogy (Davies), 2439
Saltus Model, 142
Samoa. *See* East Asia and the Pacific
Sampson, Geoffrey, 1488
SAM (Search of Associate Memory) model, 1610
Samuel, Michael, 2472
Samuels, Spencer Jay, 1494
San Antonio Independent School District v. Rodriquez, 481, 2113, **2908–2948**
Sanchez, George I., **2093–2095**
Sanctions, NCAA, 370
Sanders, John R., 2088
Sanders, Mavis G., 1846
Sanders, William, 2458
Sanderson, Allen R., 966

Sandler, Howard M., 1844
Sanford, Dred Scott v., 2199
San Francisco State University, Black Student Union, 67
San Francisco Unified School District, Peter W. v., 1475
"Sanity Code," NCAA, 366
Santa, Carol Minnick, 1983
Santa Fe Independent School District v. Doe, 2423
Santosky v. Kramer, 282
São Tomé & Príncipe. *See* Sub-Saharan Africa
Sarah Lawrence College, 2434
Sarason, Seymour, 2143
SAT
  college admissions use, 329
  College Entrance Examination Board, 372, 373
  as high-stakes test, 2535
  as "national" examination, 2545, 2546
  overview, 330–331, 2531
  student individual difference, 1113
  test preparation programs, 2543–2544
  value as admissions criteria, 1203
  See also Admissions tests; Application process
SAT-9 (Stanford Achievement Test), 2539
Satcher, David, 2068
Satellite television and radio, 657–658
Satellite transmission, 592–593
Saudi Arabia. *See* Middle East and North Africa
Saunders, Robert L., 378
Savage, Howard, 350
Savannah-Chatham County Board of Education, Stell v., 480
Save the Children, 1805
SBB (site-based budgeting), 1953
Scaffolding, 312, 1390, 1448
SCANS (Secretary's Commission on Achieving Necessary Skills), 732
Scarborough, Hollis, 2004
Scavenger gangs, 51–52
Schallert, Diane, 1468
Schank, Roger, 1148, 1155, 1468
Schauble, Leona, 1165, 1426
Schedules, reinforcement, 2229
Scheduling, **2095–2099**
  block schedule, *2098*
  Carnegie units, 246
  secondary education history, 2189
  traditional seven period schedule, *2097*
Schemas, 1606–1607, 1611
Schema theory, **1467–1469**
Schempp, School District v., 2422
SCHIP. *See* State Children's Health Insurance Program (SCHIP)
Schizophrenia, 810
Schlesinger, Arthur, Jr., 1052
Schlossberg, Nancy, 43
Schmidt, Richard, 1702
Schneider, Barbara, 730, 731, 736
Schneider, Carol Geary, 1713
Schnotz, Wolfgang, 1494
Schoen, David, 764
Schoenhals, Mark, 730
Scholarly societies
  American Academy of Arts and Sciences, **86–87**
  American Council of Learned Societies, **105–107**
Scholarship Assessed: Evaluation of the Professoriate (Glassick et al.), 200
Scholarship of teaching, 255, 415
Scholarship Reconsidered: Priorities of the Professoriate (Boyer)
  college teaching, 415
  faculty preparation, 910 (*See also* Boyer, Ernest L.)
  faculty research, 784
  faculty roles, 797
Scholarships
  Alpha Chi, 1066
  Alpha Mu Gamma, 1067
  athletic, 351–352, **356–358,** 2309
  Beta Phi Mu, 1071
  Bill and Melinda Gates Foundation, 1808
  Delta Kappa Gamma Society, 1072
  department chairpersons, 560
  Distributive Education Clubs of America (DECA), 2727
  engineering, 1085
  faculty, **782–789,** 796–797
  Kappa Delta Pi, 1075
  library and information science, 1069
  National Achievement Scholarship Program, 1781
  National Art Education Association, 1735
  National Council of Teachers of Mathematics, 1768
  National Forensic League, 2733
  National Honor Society, 1780
  National Merit Scholarship program, **1780–1782**
  Phi Beta Kappa, 1078
  Phi Delta Kappa International, 1080
  sports, 2309
  statewide testing and, 2540
  Tau Beta Pi, 1085
  women in education, 1072
  See also Fellowships; Financial aid; Grants; Nongovernmental organizations (NGOs) and foundations
Scholastic Aptitude Test. *See* SAT
Scholastic Assessment Test. *See* SAT
School, Family, and Community Partnerships (Epstein), 1845
The School Administrator, 99
School and College Services Division, ETS, 684
School and life, 580–581
The School and Society (Dewey), 578, 580
School-based community centers, 2711
School-based enterprises, 2641
School-based services. *See* School-linked services
School Board News, 1785
School Board of New Kent County, Green v., 480, 2201
School boards, **2111–2121**
  accountability, 653
  authority of, **2111–2118**
  community/school board relations, **2104–2107**
  control of schools, **2103–2104**
  duties and responsibilities, 2113–2114
  member selection and education, **2118–2121**
  National School Boards Association (NSBA), **1784–1786**
  relations, **2102–2121**
  superintendents/school board relations, **2107–2111**

urban, 2413, 2606

School Breakfast Program, 1006, 2134, *2135, 2136*

School-business partnerships, 226–227

School busing, **2573–2577**

School changes, **2381–2385**

School choice
- accountability, 653
- alternative schooling, 82–83
- Catholic school advocates, 253
- Coleman, James, S., 325
- funding, 552–553
- interdistrict programs, 552
- international issues, 953
- policy, 674, 675–676
- private schools, 1927–1928
- public schools criticism, 1950–1951
- school organization and, 2260
- school reform, 2155–2156
- special education, 2285
- *See also* Charter schools; Magnet schools; Voucher programs

School climate, 1706, **2121–2124**

School culture. *See* School climate

School District Budgeting (Hartman), 1952

School District No. 1, Keyes v., 2201, 2424

School districts
- accelerated schools, 24
- consolidation, 673, 2332
- grants programs, 890–891
- liability for negligence, **1472–1475**
- reorganization, 2344–2345
- school boards, 712
- state education agencies and, 2347–2348
- states *vs.* school boards, 701
- *See also* Superintendents

School District v. Schempp, 2422

School Education Law of 1947 (Japan), 716

School effectiveness, 305

School evaluation, **2030–2034**

School facilities. *See* Facilities

School finance theory, 8886

School food programs, **2131–2136**

School funding. *See* Funding

School health coordinators and councils, 1008

School Health Index for Physical Activity and Health eating: A Self-Assessment and Planning Guide (Division of School and Adolescent Health), 1008

School/home communication
- importance of, 1845
- language minority students, 1402
- sample practices, 822

School improvement programs
- accreditation and, 30
- rural education, 2086–2087
- *See also* School reform

School libraries, 287, **2137–2141**

School-linked services
- full-service schools, 908, **2141–2147**
- high-risk neighborhoods, 1855
- intergovernmental relations, 1217
- outcomes, **2145–2147**
- types of, **2141–2145**
- *See also* Family support services

School Mental Health Project, UCLA, 2147

School museums, 2514

School personnel liability, **1472–1475**

School prayer, 2423
- *See also* Church-state issues

School psychologists, **1945–1948**

School readiness, **2148–2151**
- current trends in elementary education, 716
- family support services, 831–832
- stages of growth, 277
- *See also* Early childhood education; Head Start program; Preschool education

School records and reports. *See* Records, educational

School reform, **2151–2156**
- Accelerated Schools, **23–25**
- Coalition of Essential Schools, **321–324**
- Comprehensive School Reform Demonstration (CSRD) programs, 1798–1800, 2018
- computers, 2518
- curriculum, 531
- New American Schools (NAS), **1798–1800**
- schools as societies, 2661–2662
- special education, 2285
- state departments of education, 2325–2326
- state revenue services, 2341–2342
- teacher education, 2471
- teacher unions, 2480–2481
- urban schools, 2608
- vocational education, 2644–2645
- *See also* Academic standards; Accountability; Education reform; School improvement programs; Standards-based education

Schools Council history project (Great Britain), 056

School size
- alternative schooling, 83
- rural, 2086
- school structure and, 2257
- secondary education, 2189

Schools Without Walls, 85

School-to-Work Opportunities Act (STWOA)
- business education, 217
- Department of Education, U.S., 844
- federal involvement in education, 838
- state departments of education, 2329
- student employment, 731, 736–737
- vocational education, 2639

School-to-work transition of disabled students, 2288

School violence
- alternative public schools, 83
- juvenile justice system, 1358–1359
- prevention, 978
- *Zero Tolerance* (initiative), 110

Schorr, Lisbeth, 830, 2142

Schraw, Gregg, 1604, 1990

Schulman, Madelyn, 733

Schumm, Jeanne S., 1982

Schurz, Margarethe, 615, 621

Schuster, Jack, 777

Schutte, Niccola, 1191

Schwab, Joseph, **2156–2158**

Science education, **2158–2166**
- American Association for the Advancement of Science (AAAS), **91–93**, 854, 2174–2175
- developing countries, 2197–2198

elementary schools, 714
explanation and argumentation, **2166–2169**
federal support for, 854–860
Future Scientists and Engineers of America (FSEA), **2730**
gender equity, 1126–1127
knowledge organization and understanding, **2169–2173**
Learning by Design, 1156–1158, 1165
learning science, **2166–2181**
National Academy of Sciences (NAS), **1727–1731**
National Association of Biology Teachers (NABT), **1737–1739**
National Science Foundation (NSF), **1788–1790,** 1790
National Science Teachers Association (NSTA), **1791–1792**
overview, **2158–2163**
reading science texts, 1987–1988
real world *vs.* school science, 1464
Science in General Education (report), 80
Science Teacher Preparation in an Era of Standards-Based Reform (National Research Council), 1729
scientific thinking, 2167–2169
Sigma Xi, **1083–1085**
standards, 1729, **2173–2177,** *2176*
studies, 1729
teacher preparation, **2163–2166**
textbooks, 2556–2558
tools, **2177–2181**
undergraduate curriculum reform, 512
Upward Bound Math/Science program (UBMS), 2604
Zacharias, Jerrold, **2745–2747**
See also Third International Mathematics and Science Study (TIMSS)

Science in General Education (report), 80

Science (periodical), 92, 93

Science Plus Literacy for Health Drug Education Project, 92

Science Teacher Preparation in an Era of Standards-Based Reform (National Research Council), 1729

Science/Technology/Society as Reform in Science Education (Zuga), 2159
Science—the Endless Frontier: A Report to the President on a Program for Postwar Scientific Research, 855
Science Update (radio program), 92
Scientific experimentation, 1426–1427
Scientific Freedom and Responsibility Award, 92
Scientific Inquiry in Education (National Research Council), 1730
Scientific thinking, 2167–2169
Scope, Sequence, and Coordination: The Content Core (NSTA), 2174
Scopes, State v., 2556
Scoring performance assessment, 135
Scotland, 1134
See also Europe; Western Europe
Scripted cooperation, 490
Scriven, Michael, 2031
Sea Grant program, **2181–2183**
Seal, Robert, 777
SEAMEO (Southeast Asian Ministers of Education Organization), 1255
Search and selection, college, **394–399**
Search of Associative Memory (SAM) model, 1610
Seat-time, 246
Seattle Central Community College, 1455
Seattle Social Development Project, 1192–1193
Sebesta, Judith, 1415
Secondary education, **2183–2198**
academic rigor, 2193
academic standards, 2188, 2190
accreditation, 28–31, 2185
advanced placement courses, 57
agricultural programs, 78
Alberty, H. B., 80–81
alternative schooling, **82–86**
art education, 119–120
business education, **215–220**
Cardinal Principles of Secondary Education (National Education Association), 193, 696, 2185–2186
career education courses, 805–806
Carnegie units, **246–247**
certification examinations, 2530–2531
China, 638
civics or government courses, 295
Coalition of Essential Schools (CES), **321–324**
commencement, **422–423**
Committee of Ten, 696, 725, 2184–2185, 2693
comprehensive high schools, 2185–2186, 2187–2188
current trends, **2190–2195**
curriculum, 80–81, 172–173, 532–535, 707–708, 2184–2186
dental health, 556
Distributive Education Clubs of America (DECA), **2726–2727**
driver education, 597–598
dropouts, **599–602**
East Asia and the Pacific, *636,* 637
Eight-Year Study, **707–709**
employment/school integration, 731
family and consumer sciences education, **802–807**
federal, 866
first-year seminars, **399–401**
foreign language education, 898
Future Business Leaders of America-Phi Beta Lambda (FBLA-PBL), **2729–2730**
Future Scientists and Engineers of America (FSEA), **2730**
General Educational Development Test (GED), **921–923**
geometry, 1549
graduation rates, 2706, 2707, *2708*
graduation requirements, 2539–2540, 2657
guidance and counseling, 977
health education, 1003–1009
high-performing Asian economies, 638–639
High School: A Report on Secondary Education in America, 200
High School Achievement: Public, Catholic, and Private Schools Compared (Coleman), 1926
High School and Beyond (HSB) data set, 325, 326

history, **2183–2190**
independent study, 1110–1111
international baccalaureate (IB) diploma, **1238–1241**
international issues, **2195–2198**
interscholastic sports and Title IX, **2569–2570**
journalism teachers, 1346–1347, **1347–1349**
junior colleges and, 443–444
mathematics teachers, 1539–1540
Middle East and North Africa, 1626
Morrison, Henry C., 1689–1690
music, 1719, 1722
National Association of Secondary School Principals (NASSP), **1745–1747,** 1778–1780
National Forensic League (NFL), **2733–2734**
National Future Farmers of America Organization, **2734–2736**
National Honor Society (NHS), 1747, **1777–1780**
Office of Elementary and Secondary Education, Department of Education, 2618
physical education, 1889
Portable Assisted Study Sequence (PASS), 1641
principals, 2192
Quill and Scroll Society, **2736–2737**
reports, 696–697
role in college choice, 395
school sports, **2305–2315,** *2310, 2311*
science, 2160, 2161
Secondary School Evaluative Criteria, 29
"Secondary Schools Achievement Act" (National Association of Secondary School Principals), 2193–2194
service learning, *2203,* 2203–2205
sexual orientation, 2220–2221
Smithsonian Institution programs, 2239–2240
social studies, 2266
South Asia, 2274, *2276*
speech and theater education, 2297–2301
student mobility, 2382
Sub-Saharan Africa, 2400
summer enrichment programs, **2407–2409**
super high schools, 1527
transcripts, 329
vocational education, 1940, 2328–2331
volunteerism, 2656–2657
western Europe, 2681
writing instruction, 2693
See also High school students
Secondary language acquisition, 175–177, 183–184
Secondary research analysis, 2025
Secondary School Evaluative Criteria, 29
"Secondary Schools Achievement Act" (National Association of Secondary School Principals), 2193–2194
Secondhand effects of college substance abuse, 607
Second-hand smoke, 2067, 2068
Second International Mathematics Study (SIMS), 524, *525*
Second International Technology in Education Study (SITES)
international statistics, 1288
Internet access by country, *1231*
knowledge management competencies, *1233*
overview, 1230–1232
three modules, *1230*
Second language acquisition, **181–185**
Second Morrill Act of 1890, 1049, **3062–3064**
Secretary of education, 2616, 2617
Secretary's Commission on Achieving Necessary Skills (SCANS), 732
Sector-wide approach to educational aid, 688
Security, campus, 2075–2076
SED (serious emotional disturbance), 1613–1614
See also, Vouchers
Sega Enterprises Ltd. v. Accolade, 1190
Segregation
Berea College, 171
Coleman Report, 324–325
desegregation, 478–480, 552, 671
Gary schools, 915–916
legal aspects, **2199–2202**
magnet schools, 1526–1527
public schools, 430
secondary education history, 2186–2187
Supreme Court cases, 2423–2425
urban education, 997
See also African Americans; Court cases; Equal protection clause
Séguin, Édouard, 1676, 2211
Selected Professions Fellowships, AAUW, 104
Selection, college, **394–399**
Selection corruption, 1659–1660
Selective attention, 155
Self-assessment, student, 125
Self care children, **1403–1407**
Self concept, 1861
Self-determination, 1694
Self-directed learning, **1698–1701**
alternative schooling, 84
complex problem-solving, 1546
continuing professional education, 485
individual differences, 1119–1120
metamemory, 1604
Vygotsky, Lev, 2659
See also Independent study
Self-efficacy theory of ability, 1692–1693
Self-esteem, 1582
Self-help community organizing, 435
Self-modification processes, 568
Self-paced learning, 2662–2663
Self-regulation, emotional, 60
Self-reporting and emotional intelligence, 1191–1192
Self-reports, teacher, 800
Seligman, Martin, 1693, 2373
Semantic memory, 1610
Semantic processing, 1431–1433, *1432, 1433*
Semantics, 1385
Semester calendar, 2097
Seminars, college, 399
Senates, faculty, 793, **794–796**
Senegal. *See* Sub-Saharan Africa
Senge, Peter, 1148
Senior Executive Service, 847
Senior seminars. *See* Capstone courses
Senior Service Colleges. *See* War Colleges, U.S.
Sense making. *See* Number sense

Sensori-motor period, 1897
Separate-but-equal theory, 2200–2201
September 11 attacks, 1317
Sequencing and science education, 2172
Serious emotional disturbance (SED), 1613–1614
Serrano v. Priest, 481, 889
SER (The Society for Educational Reconstruction), 208
Service academies, military, 843, **1642–1653**
Service clubs, 2375
Service learning, **2202–2210**
  Alternative Spring Break (ASB), 2207
  Campus Compact, 2207
  clients of, 2204–2205
  community, 437–438
  community service, 2656–2657
  diversity and, 1712–1713
  experiential learning, 762
  higher education, **2205–2210**
  learning communities, 1454–1455
  moral education, 1686–1687
  school, **2202–2205,** *2203*
  Service Learning Project, 90
  teen pregnancy reduction, 2073
  undergraduate education, 518
  See also Community service; Experiential learning
Service Learning Project, 90
Servicemen's Readjustment Act, **928–930**
  community colleges, 96
  Department of Veterans Affairs, 852
  federal funding, 861–862
  federal involvement in education, 837, 838
Service role, faculty, 792, 793, **796–798**
Sesame Street (television show), 200, 1580
Seton, Elizabeth, 250
Settlement houses
  Addams, Jane, 41
  family support services, 829
  Putnam, Alice, 1957
"Seven Principles for Good Practice in Undergraduate Education" (Chickering and Gamson), 2495
Seven Sisters, 2226, 2227
Seventh-day Adventist schools, 1943
Severely disabled students, **2210–2213,** 2287
Sex discrimination. *See* Discrimination
Sex education, **2213–2218**
  international issues, 919–920
  sexual activity, 2062–2063
  teen pregnancy, 2072–2074
Sexual abuse, 267, 284, 2061–2062
Sexual activity, youth, **2060–2064**
  HIV/AIDS, 2058
  sexually transmitted diseases, 2064–2066
  teen pregnancy, 2071–2074
Sexual content in the media, 1582
Sexual harassment, 758, 2076
Sexually transmitted diseases (STDs), 2058, **2064–2066,** 2072–2073
Sexual maturation, 278–279
Sexual orientation, 44, 919–920, **2218–2221**
  See also Gay and lesbian studies
Seychelles. *See* Sub-Saharan Africa
Shaftsbury v. Hannam (England), 280–281
Shaken baby syndrome, 268
Shallow comprehension, 586
Shallow constructivism, 1371
Shanahan, Timothy, 1513
Shanker, Albert, **2221–2223,** 2477
Shaping the College Curriculum: Academic Plans in Action (Stark and Lattuca), 521
Share, David, 2004
Shared governance, 945–948
Shared learning experiences, 521–522
Sharing time, 1390
Sharp, Lloyd B., 1833
Sheldon, Edward, 1876, **2223–2225**
Sheppard-Towner Act of 1921, 2676
Shipley, Christopher, 569
Shkurti, William, 2049
Shore, Bruce, 933
Shorthand, 215
Short-term memory, 1591
Show-and-tell, 1390
Showcase portfolios, 138
Showers, Beverly, 2446
Shulman, James, 352–353
Shulman, Lee, 1179
Siblings and intelligence, 1196
SIDA (Swedish International Development Cooperation Agency), 1243–1244
SIDS (Sudden Infant Death Syndrome), 2067
Siedentop, Daryl, 1891
Siegler, Robert S., 564, 569
Siek-Toon, Khoo, 141
Sierra Leone. *See* Sub-Saharan Africa
Sigma Xi, **1083–1085**
Silliman, Benjamin, 2697
Silver, Judith A., 818
Silverberg, Marsha K., 731
Simon, Herbert
  complex problem solving, 1546
  constructivism, 1466
  expertise, 765
  information processing, 567
  verbal protocols, 2035
Simon, Théodore, 185, 186–187, 1112–1113
Simulations
  combat, 1657–1658
  instructional strategies, 1181–1182
  as method of studying teaching, 2491
  multimedia, 1495
Singapore. *See* East Asia and the Pacific
Single parents, 808, 833, 2705
Single-sex colleges and universities, 1037, 1044, **2225–2228**
Single Source: Towards an Inventory of Federal Education Programs (FICE), 864–865
Sipuel v. Board of Regents, 64
Sirotnik, Ken, 304–305
Sister-teachers, 251
Site-based budgeting (SBB), 1953
SITES (Second International Technology in Education Study). *See* Second International Technology in Education Study (SITES)
Situational interest, 705, 1989
Situation model of discourse processing, 586
Sizer, Theodore R., 321, 322–323, 761, 2151
Skill development, early childhood, 277

SkillsUSA-VICA, **2737–2738**
Skinner, B. F., **2228–2231**
International Society for Performance Improvement (ISPI), 1309–1310
learning theory history, 1460–1461
See also Behaviorism
Skyline High School, 1527
Slaughter, Sheila, 770, 795, 797, 2527
Slaves
education, 710
emancipated, 2665–2666
Emancipation Proclamation, 63
segregation, 2199
U.S. Constitution, 63
Slavin, Robert, 489, 491, 1706
Sleep, **2231–2234**
Sloane, Kathryn, 141
Slovak Republic. *See* Eastern Europe and Central Asia
Slovenia. *See* Eastern Europe and Central Asia
SLSDC (St. Lawrence Seaway Development Corporation), 850–851
Slums and Suburbs (report), 473
Small nations, **2234–2236**
Smart buildings, 2127, 2129–2131
SMILE (Supportive Multi-User Interactive Learning Environment) Design, 1156
Smith, Christian, 1927
Smith, David Eugene, **2236–2238**
Smith, Judith, 1905
Smith, Julia, 2382
Smith, Julian, 1833
Smith, Mary Katherine, 1504
Smith, Mary Lee, 314
Smith, Terry B., 2046
Smith-Hughes Act
agricultural education, 73–74
business education, 216
family and consumer sciences education, 804
federal involvement in education, 837
vocational education, 2637
vocational education teacher preparation, 2647
Smith-Lever Act
agricultural education, 73
family and consumer sciences education, 804
rural education, 2088
Smith Richardson Foundation, 1809
Smith-Sears Veterans' Rehabilitation Act of 1918, 1867
Smithsonian Institution, 854, **2238–2241**
Smoking, 606, 2066–2068
See also Substance abuse
SMP (Special Milk Program), 2134–2135
SMPY (Study of Mathematically Precocious Youth), 2408
Snack Program, After-School, 2135
SNCC (Student Nonviolent Coordinating Committee), 1668
Snedden, David, **2241–2242**
Snelbecker, Glenn, 1149
Snow, Richard, 1120, 1196
Soar Training Expert for Virtual Environments (STEVE), 1169, 1170
Sobol, Bradstreet v., 1062
Sobsey, Dick, 2210
Social activism, 2690
Social adjustment, 1312–1313
Social capital
Coleman, James S., 325–326
community ecology, 434–435
parenting, 1853–1854
private schools, 1926, **2242–2243**
social mobility, 1301–1302
Social change and vocational school fallacy, 2654–2655
Social cohesion, **2243–2250**
Social competencies, 812
Social connectedness of faculty, 11
Social contract, 2244–2245
The Social Contract (Rousseau), 2079–2080, 2081
Social demands, students', 43–44
Social-democrats (western Europe), 2682
Social development
attention, 157
domestic violence exposure, 2632
educational aspirations and attainment, 1858
middle childhood, 278
school readiness, 2148
sexual orientation, 2219–2220
sports participation, **2312–2316**
stages, 571
violence exposure, 2626
See also Interpersonal relationships; Peer relations
Social Development Priorities: A Framework for Action (initiative, Canada), 1243
Social divisions, 41
Social efficiency, 193, 194, 2241–2242
Social engineering, 1113
Social Experimentation (Riecken and Boruch), 2031
Social Foundations of Education (Smith, B. et al.), 170
Social fraternities and sororities, **2250–2253**
The Social Frontier (periodical), 206, 293
Social historians, 1052
Social humanism, 1525
The Social Ideas of American Educators (report), 539
Social indicators and education statistics, **1291–1296**
Social Indicators Research (periodical), 1292, 1293
Social integration, 404
Social invention, 2229–2230
Socialism, 612, 629
Socialization of college students, 43
Social learning theory, 1461–1462, 1865
Social life and school, 2256
Social mobility of underpriveleged groups, **1300–1307**
Social organization of schools, **2253–2261**
Social philosophy and education, 195
Social promotion, 2191, **2262–2265**
Social reconstruction, 293
Social referencing, 60
Social reform
Addams, Jane, 41–42
Clark, Septima Poinsette, 299
Counts, George S., 504
disabled individuals, 2278–2279
education for, 504
juvenile justice, 1350, 1352
movement, 975
Social resistance approach to substance abuse education, 604
Social Responsibilities Round Table of the ALA, 289

Social responsibility and service learning, 2209
Social Science Research Council, 1291–1292
Social sciences, 1057
Social Security Act
disabled individuals, 1867–1868
immunization, 1106
income support, 834
welfare reform, 2676–2677
Social self-realization, 207
Social services
academic performance and, 1838
high-risk neighborhoods, 1855
intergovernmental relations, 1217
Social settlements, 41
Social studies education, **2265–2272**
elementary schools, 714
Miel, Alice, 1637
National Council for the Social Studies (NCSS), **1764–1765**
overview, **2265–2269**
textbook controversies, 2556
textbooks, 990–991, 2082
See also Civics and citizenship education; History
Social support for secondary school completion, 601
Social transformation, 901–903
Social values and educational policy, 670
Societal type and educational change, 668–669
The Society for Educational Reconstruction (SER), 208
Society for the Prevention of Cruelty to Children (SPCC), 281–282
Society for the Study of the Child, 186
Society of Sisters, Pierce v., 466, 1061, 1925, 1942, 2336, 2422
Sociocultural theory, 574–575, 2658–2660
Socioeconomic status
academic achievement, 1122, 1836
adult literacy, international aspects of, 642
digital divide, 2519–2520
high-risk neighborhoods, 1852
international early childhood education enrollment trends, 628–629
library distribution, 2712
mobility of underpriveleged groups, **1300–1307**
self care children, 1404, 1406
Slums and Suburbs (report), 473
test preparation programs, 2544
youth development programs, 2712–2713
See also Low income families; Poverty
Socioemotional skills, 277
Sociological Determination of Objectives in Education (Snedden), 2241–2242
Sociological development, 1895
Sociology of education
Coleman, James S., 324–327
Counts, George S., 504
public school reform, 692
Waller, Willard W., 2661–2662
The Sociology of Teaching (Waller), 2661–2662
Sociopolitical use of history teaching, 1055
Sociosystemic theory, 1124
Socrates, 312, 2438
Socrates program (European Union), 1252, 2682, 2683
Software
algebra, 1544
AutoTutor, 1169–1170
case-based reasoning, 1155–1158
copyright, 1190
Interactive Physics, 2178
mathematics, 1551
Model-It, 2178–2179
pedagogical agents, 1169–1170
piracy, 2518–2519
science education, 2177–2181, 2179–2180
tutorial, 2582–2583
visualization, 2179
WorldWatcher, 2179
See also Animated learning aids; Computer technology; Information and communications technology; Learning aids
Soldiers' Field, 349
Solomon Islands. *See* East Asia and the Pacific
Somalia. *See* Sub-Saharan Africa
Soman, Vijay, 20399
Sophists, 1899
Sororities. *See* Fraternities and sororities
Soros Foundation, 1809–1810
The Souls of Black Folk (Du Bois), 610
Sousa, David A., 202, 203, 204–205
South Africa. *See* Sub-Saharan Africa
South Asia, **2272–2277,** *2273*
South Baltimore Youth Center, 2714
Southeast Asian Ministers of Education Organization (SEAMEO), 1255
Southeastern Association of Colored Women, 174
Southern Association of Colleges and Schools (SACS), 28, 32
Southern Association of College Women, 105
Southern Baptist colleges and universities, 391
Southern United States
education of emancipated slaves, 2665–2666
elementary education, 710
school organization, 2332
Southern Workman (periodical), 2667
Soviet Union, 611, 612
Sowder, Judith, 1559, 1560
Spady, William, 404
Spain, 544
See also Western Europe
Spatial concepts, 926–927
Spatial intelligence, 1198–1199
SPCC (Society for the Prevention of Cruelty to Children), 281–282
The Speaking, Listening, and Media Literacy Standards and Competency Statements for K-12 Education (National Communication Association), 2299, *2300*
Spearman, Charles
individual differences, 1113, 1114
intelligence measurement, 1194, 1195, 1202
Spearman-Brown Prophecy formula, 1194
Special education, **2278–2295**
adapted physical education, **37–40**
attention deficit hyperactivity disorder, students with, 158

Council for Exceptional Children (CEC), 499–500
current trends, 2284–2289, **2284–2290**
equality in education, 672
general education *vs.*, 1458
hearing impaired students, 1020
history, **2278–2284**
international context, **2293–2295**
least restrictive environment (LRE), 37, 39
Office of Special Education and Rehabilitative Services, Department of Education, 2619
physically disabled persons, 1885–1886
placement, 2285–2286
policy, 672
radical restructuring, 2282
school choice, 2285
school psychology and, 1946
school reform, 2285
secondary education, 2189
severe and multiple disabilities, students with, **2210–2213**
speech and language impairment, **2295–2297**
standards-based education, 2285
teacher education, **2290–2293**
teachers, 314
transition issues, 2288
urban education, 2608–2609
See also Disabled students; Emotionally disturbed students; Gifted and talented students; Individualized education programs (IEP)

Specialization. *See* Majors, academic

Specialized accreditation, 32–33

Special learning needs, **410–413**

Special Milk Program (SMP), 2134–2135

Speech and language impairment, **2295–2297**

Speech and theater education, **2297–2302**
Association for Women in Communications, **1068–1069**
Delta Sigma Rho-Tau Kappa Alpha, 1073–1074
Middle East and North Africa, 1624, *1627*
National Communication Association (NCA), **1759–1760**

Spelling education, 1391, **2302–2305,** 2670–2672

Spence, Kenneth, 1691

Spencer Foundation, 1811

Sperling, Melanie, 2695

Spiegel, Daisy L., 1981

Spilhaus, Athelstan, 2182

Sponsorship, faculty consulting, 774

Sports
Macabbi USA Jewish youth athletic competitions, 2740
school sports, **2305–2315,** *2310, 2311*
social and emotional development and, **2312–2315**
Title IX, **2569–2573**
See also College athletics; Intramural athletics; Student athletes

Sports medicine, 358, 367

Spoth, Richard, 2056

Springfield College, 348

Spurs to Creative Teaching (Zirbes), 2748

Sputnik
ability grouping, 681
American High School Today (report), release of, 473
bilingual education, 177
community education, 449
curriculum reform, 118, 166, 173, 1826, 2030, 2196
educational research, 677
federal R&D involvement, 855
gifted education, 931
guidance and counseling, 976
homework, 1063
instructional strategies, 1179
international education, 1266
life adjustment education, 1938
National Defense Education Act (NDEA), 862, 2615
secondary education, 2187–2188
social studies, 1637
summer school programs, 2410
supervision of instruction, 2418

SQ3R reading technique, 1978

Sri Lanka, 2247, 2275
See also South Asia

S-R learning theory, 1459

SSI (Supplemental Security Income), 834, 1868, 2674

St. Edward's University (Texas), 1712

St. John, Edward, 405

St. John's College, 212–213, 1213–1214, **2366–2367**

St. Kitts and Nevis. *See* Latin America and the Caribbean

St. Lawrence Seaway Development Corporation (SLSDC), 850–851

St. Lucia. *See* Latin America and the Caribbean

St. Vincent and the Grenadines. *See* Latin America and the Caribbean

Stability and Change in Human Characteristics (Bloom), 188

Stages of Reading Development (Chall), 258

Stage theories of development, 562, 563–564

Stagg, Amos Alonzo, 349

Stahl, Robert, 2432

Stahl, Steve, 2005

Stakeholders and program evaluation, 2031–3032

Standard Issue Scoring Manual (Kohlberg), 1376

Standardization, high school curriculum, 2184–2185

Standardized tests, **2530–2551**
ability tests, 1112–1116
accountability movement, 2321–2322
admissions, **330–332,** 372, 1039, 2530–2531, 2543–2544
Army Alpha and Beta tests, 1201
college admissions, 329, **330–332**
Core Knowledge Sequence, 536–537
dynamic assessment *vs.*, 127, *129*
educational psychology and, 681
Educational Testing Services (ETS), **684–685**
elementary education, 719
emotional intelligence, 1192
England, 1135
English language arts, 742
General Educational Development Test (GED), **921–923**
Graduate Record Examination (GRE), **962–965,** 968

graduation test requirements, 2539–2450
guidance and counseling credentialing, 977
high-stakes assessment, **2533–2537**
introduction, 975
language minority students, 1402–1403
Law School Admission Test (LSAT), 1417, **1419–1420**
Lindquist, E. F., 1485–1486
Mayer, Salovey, and Caruso Emotional Intelligence Test MSCEIT), 1192
measurement, 1573–1574
Miller Analogies test, 968–969
Multidimensional Emotional Intelligence Scale (MEIS), 1192
Preliminary SAT/National Merit Scholarship Qualifying Test (PSAT/NMSQT), 1781–1783
Pressey, Sidney L., 1917–1919
purposes, 2539–2540
reading instruction and, 2002
scoring technology, 1485–1486
shortcomings, 127
standards of test development, international, **2550–2551**
statewide programs, **2538–2542**
Sternberg Triarchic Abilities Test (STAT), 1208
teaching to the test, 719
Terman, Lewis, 2528–2529
test development, 2429–2430
test preparation programs, **2542–2545**
Tyler, Ralph W., 2587–2589
urban schools, 2609
writing education, 2694–2695
See also Achievement tests; Assessment; Assessment tools; Educational Testing Service (ETS); Intelligence testing; National Assessment of Educational Progress (NAEP); Testing

Standards. *See* Academic standards; Standards-based education

Standards-based education, **2318–2323**
business involvement in education, 227
Council for Basic Education (CBE), 498
federal involvement, 838
high-stakes testing, 2535
initiatives, 700–701
international issues, 1301
movement, 674, 2154–2155
reform, 227, 691–692
state boards of education and, 2357–2358
studies of, 1729
teacher education, 498
teacher evaluation, 2455–2456
testing, 2530
textbooks, 2320
urban schools, 2609
See also Academic standards; Accountability; Education reform; School reform

Standards-Based Teacher Education (STEP), 498

Standards for Educational and Psychological Testing, 2536, 2550

Standards for Foreign Language Learning in the Twenty-First Century, 894, 897, 898

Standards for Technological Literacy (International Technology Education Association), 2176

The Standards for Technology Education (International Technology Education Association), 2507

Standards for the English Language Arts (National Council of Teachers of English and International Reading Association), 741–742, 1394–1395

Standards in Science for New Teachers: A Resource for State Dialogue (Interstate New Teacher Assessment and Support Consortium), 2176

Stanford Achievement Test (SAT-9), 2539

Stanford-Binet intelligence tests, 1201

Stanford University, 66, 2044

Stanley, Julian, 2031

Stanley v. Darlington School District, 479–480

Stanovich, Keith, 2005

Stapp, William B., 1831

Stark, Jerry A., 2046

Stark, Joan, 521, 923, 925

Starting Out Right: A Guide to Promoting Children's Reading Success (National Research Council), 1729–1730

Start-up companies, 2595–2596

Start-up programs, financing, 551–552

State Board of Education, Giardino v., 887–888

State boards of education, 1747–1749, **2350–2359,** *2352–2356*

State Children's Health Insurance Program (SCHIP), 1001–1002, 1530, 2674

State colleges and universities. *See* Land-grant colleges and universities; Public colleges and universities

State Constitutions and Public Education Governance, **3020–3039**

State departments of education. *See* Departments of education, state

State legislatures, 1760–1762

"A Statement of the Association's Council: Freedom and Responsibility" (American Association of University Professors), 758

Statement on College and University Government (American Association of University Professors), 102, 794

Statement on Distance Education (American Association of University Professors), 590

Statement on Principles of Academic Freedom and Tenure (American Association of University Professors), 14–15, 387, 756

"Statement on Professional Ethics" (American Association of University Professors), 756–757

State of Arkansas, Murphy v., 1061

State of Nebraska, Meyer v., 1100, 2335–2336

State of Texas, Hopwood v., 63, 64, 397

State of Wyoming v. Campbell County School District, 888

States, **2335–2364**
administrative services, **2338–2350**
boards of education, 2350–2359

budget cutbacks, 883
business involvement in education policy, 226–227
capital outlay funding, 887–888
chartered colleges, 1035
child care funding, 275–276
child protection systems, 282–283
Colleges and Classrooms: State Strategies for Redesigning Teacher Preparation Policies (initiative), 1777
common school movement, 711–712
compulsory school attendance, 464–467
constitutional responsibility for education, 478–482, 710, 712
Council of Chief State School Officers (CCSSO), 501–503
curriculum and instruction, influence on, 2345–2346
decision-making discretion, 675
departments of education, 2339
domestic violence laws, 2633–2634
driver education, 598
early childhood education licensure, 624
economic development programs, 2596
Education Commission of the States (ECS), **685–686**
education policy, 703–704
efficiency in education, 700–701
equity and adequacy lawsuits, 481–482
expenditures services, 2342
financial aid, 377
funding of preschool programs, 275–276
higher education, 1025, **2359–2364**
higher education funding, 25, 872–873, *874*
higher education oversight, 2333, 2343
home schooling laws, 1061
immunization laws, 1106
international comparisons, 1289
juvenile crime codes, 1351
kindergarten funding, 615–616
land-grant colleges by, *1382–1383*
leadership and educational standards, 667
local school boards *vs.*, 701
local unit reorganization, 2343–2345
National Assessment of Educational Progress (NAEP), 132, 2547
National Governors Association (NGA), **1776–1777**
preschool initiatives, 617
private schools and state relations, **2335–2338**
public school accountability, 1950
public school systems, **2331–2334**
reform results, 693
revenue services, 2340–2342
role in college choice, 395
rural education, 2087
school boards, 2113
school board takeovers, 2119–2120
school funding, 671–672, 885–886, **889–891**
secondary education standards, 2191
standards, 227, 654–655, 700–701, 1216, 2320–2321
State Children's Health Insurance Plan (SCHIP), 2674
state-level educational progress assessment, 132, 133
superintendents, 2324
testing programs, **2538–2542**
undergraduate education, 518
vocational education, 73, 2328–2331
See also United States
States Services, ECS, 686
State superintendents, 2416
State University of New York (SUNY), 199, 1712
State v. Bailey, 465
State v. Edgington, 1062
State v. Scopes, 2556
State v. Whisner, 2336–2337
Static allocation systems, 2049
Statistics
advanced placement courses/exams, 57
African-American studies, 67, 68
age demographics, 2703–2707
Air Force Academy faculty, 1643
alternative schools, 82–83
Bureau of Education, U.S., 2615
Canadian education, 235–236
capstone courses, 239
child dependency cases, 284–285
child mortality, 998–999
children's health insurance, 1000–1001, 1837
children's vocabulary, 1386
class size, 314, 316
Coast Guard Academy, 1646
college and university presidents, 1915
community college enrollment, 875
community college expenditures, 880–882, *881–882*
community college revenues, 876, *877, 878,* 880
community service, 2203, 2207
community violence, 2627–2628, 2629
commuter students, 451
comparability, 1286–1287
comparative assessment surveys, 1223
dentistry education, 557
Department of Defense educational activities, 843
Department of Health and Human Services educational activities, 844
developing nations higher education, 1218–1219
disabled children, 1885
doctoral degrees, 17–18
domestic violence, 2628, 2632
dropout rates, 599
early childhood education enrollment, 628
East Asia and the Pacific, *636*
educational attainment by region, *1305*
educational demographics, 2705–2706
education indicators, Middle East and North Africa, *1628*
engineering degrees, 18
enrollment and retention, Middle East and North Africa, 1625, *1629*
enrollment rates, Eastern Europe and Central Asia, *643*
expenditures, South Asia, 2275, *2277*
expenditures, Sub-Saharan Africa, *2403*
facilities, 2086
faculty consulting, 774–775
faculty demographics, 18, 776–778, *777, 778*

faculty research, 784–785
family and consumer science programs, 806
family composition, 2705
federal higher education funding, 861–863
financial aid, 377, 862–863
foster care, 817, 819
fraternities and sororities, 2251, 2252
gangs, 51, 52
gender and school access, 919
GNP/education expenditure relationship, 1662, *1662*
Graduate Record Examination (GRE) scores, 964
graduate study in education, 967
graduation rates, 2706–2707, *2708*
gross domestic product, Middle East and North Africa, *1625*
Head Start, 456–457
health, 1910–1911
health education, 1003–1004
health insurance, 1000–1001
hearing impaired students, 1018
higher education, Sub-Saharan Africa, 2397
higher education demographics, 1024–1025
higher education expenditures, 25, 870
higher education revenues, 871, *872, 873, 874, 877, 879*
Hispanic Americans, 1966–1967
Hispanic-serving institutions, 1045, 1046
historically black college and university graduates, 1050
HIV/AIDS, 2066
home-schooled children, 1060
homework, 1064
impact aid, 1108–1109
Indicators of National Education Systems (INES), 1250–1251
injury rates in school sports, *2312*
institutional research, 1144–1145
intercollegiate sports participation, 2571–2572
interdisciplinarity in higher education, 1211–1212
international, 1250–1251, 1272–1273, **1285–1296**
international baccalaureate diploma, 1239
international health and education, 998–999
international higher education enrollment, 1027
International Institute of Statistics, UNESCO's, 1224
international Internet access, *1231*
international students, *1270,* 1270–1272, *1271, 1272, 1273,* 1310–1311, *1315*
international students in England, France and Japan, 1316
international trade in education services, 1322
Internet access, international comparison, 1297
Internet content providers, 1296
Internet users by region, *1297*
Jeanes teachers, 1337
Jewish education, 1341, 1342
juvenile crime, 1353–1354, 1358–1359
kindergarten enrollment, 615
language minority population, 1397–1398, *1398, 1399*
latchkey children, 1403–1404
Latin enrollment, 1413–1414
liberal arts colleges, 1475–1476
literacy, Middle East and North Africa, 1624
literacy, South Asia, *2274*
majors, 21
malnutrition, 1911
managed care, 1530, 1532–1533
master's degrees, 1538
measurement theory, 1486
mental health services, 1006, 1613
Merchant Marine Academy, 1646–1647
middle schools, 1632
migrant children, 1638–1638
minorities, 2086, 2605
minorities in higher education, 1968
music course enrollment, 1719
National Center for Education Statistics (NCES), **1756–1757**
National Sea Grant Program, 2182
new teacher mentoring, 1619
nontraditional college students, 1482, 1814–1815
nursery school enrollment, 618
Organisation for Economic Co-operation and Development (OECD), 1250–1251
part-time faculty, 779
population demographics, U.S., 1707, 1709–1710
poverty, 1904, 1910–1911, 2605, 2707
primary education, South Asia, *2275*
primary education, Sub-Saharan Africa, 2398–2399, *2399*
private education, Sub-Saharan Africa, 2401
private schools, 1922–1923
Protestant schools, 1941–1944k
psychological disorders, 1873
public school enrollment, 887
public sector workers, Middle East and North Africa, *1626*
race/ethnicity, 1121, 1968, 2705
rate of return on investment in education, *649, 650*
reform results, 693–694
regional expenditure growth, *1663*
religiously-affiliated colleges and universities, 389–390
research and development funding, 853, *854, 856,* 856–859, *858, 859*
research universities, 2041
revenue for higher education institutions, 25–26
rural America, 2083–2087
rural education, 2084–2085
school food programs, 2133–2136, *2135, 2136*
school health services, 1005
school principals, 1921–1923
school sports participation, 2306–2307, *2307, 2308, 2309, 2310, 2311,* 2569
school transportation, 2573
secondary education, Sub-Saharan Africa, 2400
severe and multiple disabilities prevalence, 2211
sex education support, 2213
sexually transmitted diseases, 2064
sexual risk behavior, 2065, 2071–2072
single-sex institutions, 2225–2226
smoking, 2066–2067
social indicators, **1291–1296**

South Asia education, *2273*, 2273–2275, *2274*, *2275*, *2276*, *2277*
special education teachers, 2290
speech problems, 2298
statewide testing programs, 2538
Statistics and Research Division, Educational Testing Service, 684
student athlete graduation rates, 359–360
study abroad students, *1274*, *1275*
substance abuse, 603, 606, 817, *2055*
Success for All reading assessment, *2406*
suicide, 2068–2069
teachers, 2087, 2436–2437, 2448
teacher unions, 2477, 2478
teen pregnancy, 2071
telephone coverage, Middle East and North Africa, *1627*
tertiary education, Sub-Saharan Africa, 2400–2401
tuition, *880*
Upward Bound programs, 1971, 2604
urban education, 2605
U.S. Military Academy, 1649
U.S. population demographics, 1707, 1709–1710
U.S. research and development funding, *856*, 856–859, *857*, *858*, *859*, 863
violence exposure, 2623, 2627–2628, 2629, 2632
visually impaired students, 2634
vocabulary, 1386, 1504
vocational education, 2329, 2640, 2641
welfare, 2678
workforce, 883
Workforce Incentives Program, 2677
World Education Indicator (WEI) project, 1251
world population, 2704
youth employment, 729–730
See also Enrollment; National Center for Education Statistics (NCES)

Statistics and Research Division, Educational Testing Service, 684

STAT (Sternberg Triarchic Abilities Test), 1208

Steadman, Mimi, 2497

STDs (sexually transmitted diseases), 2058, **2064–2066,** 2072–2073

Steele, Claude, 1115

Steenwyk, Fern L., 1981

Steering committees, 2124–2125

Steinberg, Laurence, 49, 1848, 1849, 1859

Steinberg, Zine, 727

Steiner, Rudolf, 84, 953, **2364–2366**

Stell v. Savannah-Chatham County Board of Education, 480

Stepien, William, 1174

STEP (Standards-Based Teacher Education), 498

Sterilization, forced, 941

Stern, David, 729

Stern, William, 1194

Sternberg, Robert, 506, 1115, 1206–1208

Sternberg Triarchic Abilities Test (STAT), 1208

Steuben, Friedrich von, 1656

Stevens, Rommiett, 310

Stevens, Ron, 147

Stevenson, David, 731, 736

STEVE (Soar Training Expert for Virtual Environments), 1169, 1170

Stewardship offices, college and university, 1143

Stewart, Joseph, Jr., 1964

Still, George F., 158

Stipek, Deborah, 705

Stoehr, Taylor, 942

Stone, Margaret, 48

Stopouts, college, 402

Storage, memory, 1606, 1607

Storyboard (software), 1157

Story structure and reading comprehension, 1981

Stowe, Calvin, 695, 1098

Stoy, Karl Volkmar, 1021–1022

The Strategic Management of College Enrollments (Hossler and Bean), 406

Strategic planning in higher education, **2367–2369**

Strategies, instructional, **1178–1186**

Stratemeyer, Florence, **2369–2371**

Straus, Murray, 2627–2628

Strauss, Alfred, 158

Strauss syndrome, 158

Streaming, 2255, 2257

Strengthening the Ties That Bind: Integrating Undergraduate Liberal and Professional Study (report), 517

Strengths-based community organizations, 438

Strength through Wisdom (report), 895

Stress
depression, **2371–2374**
poverty and, 1912–1913

Strict scrutiny test, 64

Strong Foundations: Twelve Principles for Effective General Education Programs (report), 517

Stroop effect, 155

Structural adjustment policies, 937–938

Structural diversity in higher education, 1042–1043

Structural inequality and academic achievement, 1963–1964

Structure, college and university. *See* Organizational structure of colleges and universities

Structure, memory, **1609–1613**

Structure, school. *See* Organizational structure of schools

Stuart, Charles E., v. School District No. 1 of the Village of Kalamazoo, **2765–2771**

Stuart, Debra, 380

Stuart, Walter, 2039

Stuart Foundation, 1810

Student activities, **2374–2377**
academic, 2375
community colleges, 2393
financing, **2376–2377**
overview, **2374–2376**
See also Extracurricular activities; Youth organizations and clubs

Student affairs, 192, 341–342

Student athletes
academic outcomes, **358–361**
academic performance, 344–345
academic support, **353–356,** 356–357
drug and alcohol abuse, 607
eligibility requirements, 369–370
extracurricular activities, 375

high school, 2306–2315, *2307, 2308, 2309*
nutritional needs, 358
residential affairs, 357
scholarship provisions, 356–357
tutoring, 2584
as unpaid professionals, 352
See also College athletics; Intramural athletics; Sports

Student Bill of Rights, 2376

Student body funds, 2376–2377

Student-centered teaching, 761

Student exchange programs. *See* Exchange programs; Study abroad

Student government
college and university, 374–375
National Association of Student Councils (NASC), 1747
participation, 2374
residence hall, 342

Student housing. *See* Residence halls

Student loans, **2377–2381**
community colleges, 2392
higher education account systems, 26
subsidized, 377
See also Financial aid

Student mobility, **2381–2385**

Student Nonviolent Coordinating Committee (SNCC), 1668

Student orientation, **2385–2387,** 2391

Student Personnel Point of View (American Council on Education), 2388

Student personnel workers, 2388

Student Press Law Center, 1349

Student protests, 67, 1039

Student questions, 588

Student ratings of teaching, 414, 415–416

Student records and reports, 1144, **2013–2015**

Student responsibility, 1119–1120

Student retention. *See* Retention

Students
academic demands, 43
adjustment to college, **42–45**
adviser/student relationship, 2–3, 4
at-risk, 23–24
business education organizations, 218–219
classroom expectations, 300–301
class rushes, 348
community service, 295–296
commuter, **451–453**
discipline, 2436
early warning systems, 44–45
effort and interest, **704–707**
faculty evaluation, 254
freshmen interest groups, 44
gay, lesbian, and bisexual, 44
individual differences, **1112–1129**
individualized attention, 2193
inequitable instruction, 305–306
learning assessment as measurement of teacher effectiveness, 801
migrant, **1638–1642**
misbehavior, 301–302
monitoring, 301
performance standards for educational progress assessment, 133
portfolio assessment involvement, 138, 139
presentations, 2511
relationships, 43
rights, 2425
roles, 43
school governance participation, 295
self-assessment, 125
service learning, 2204
sexual orientation, **2218–2221**
social demands, 43–44
subpopulations, 44
support services, 44
teacher evaluation, 799
teacher responses to student answers, 312–313, 583
teacher/student role, 761
urban schools, 2610–2611
See also College students; High school students; International students; Nontraditional students; Teacher/student interaction

Student services, **2387–2394**
colleges and universities, **2387–2389**
community colleges, **2389–2394**

Students without Teachers (Taylor), 2434

Student/teacher interaction
classroom discourse, 583, 588
classroom observation, 304–305
gender equity, 1126
group processes, 973–974

Student-teacher ratio
class size, 314
Coalition of Essential Schools, 323
dropout rates, 600
East Asia and the Pacific, *636,* 638
South Asia, 2274
United States, 1288

Student teaching, 1724, 2446–2447, 2449

Student visas, 1138, 1312

Studies, research
academic calendars, 5–6
academic performance of student athletes, 360–361
adolescent peer culture, 47–48
anchored instruction, 1152–1153
attention, 155–156
attention deficit hyperactivity disorder (ADHD), 70–71, 158
bilingual education, 179–180
Catholic schools, 253
classroom observation, 304–307
cognitive and information processing research, 568–570
college athletics, 350, 352–353
college teaching, 415–416
community college growth, 96
community education, 450–451
commuter students, 451–452
compensatory education in Latin America, 461–463
cost-effectiveness, 496–497
creativity, 505–507
curriculum reform, 512
disruptive behavior, 70–71
domain expertise, 765–766
early childhood care, 1836
early childhood education, 1730
educational attainment of parents, 1857
educational interest groups, 663
education development programs, 687
education research, 1730
English education teacher preparation, 745–746
English infant school reform, 1135
faculty scholarly performance, 784–786
foster care children, 819
globalization, 938–939
hearing impairment programs, 1019
hidden curriculum, 538

high-stakes testing, effects of, 2536
homework effectiveness, 1064–1065
immigrants and language, 1100
industry-university research collaboration, 154
intelligence heritability, 941
international studies, 1730
juvenile crime and violence, 1360
language of instruction, 182–183
latchkey children, 140501406
learning from multimedia sources, 1494–1495
life-span development, 997
literacy and culture, 1510–1512
mathematics education, 1729
media and learning, 1577
media influence on children, 1581–1583
middle school education, 1633
National Academy of Sciences, 1729–1730
parenting and child's educational aspirations, 1859
pedagogical agents effectiveness, 1170
poverty's effect on children, 1905
private *vs.* public education, 950
problem-based learning, 1174
race/ethnicity and academic achievement, 1122–1124
RAND Change Agent study, 2030–2031
reading aloud to children, 2004–2005
reading disabilities, 2008–2009
reading instruction, 1729–1730
Research About Teacher Education (RATE) Study, 721
residential colleges, 2046
school/family/community partnerships, 826–827
school readiness, 831–832
school sports and emotional development, 2313–2314
science education, 1729
service learning, 2204, 2207–2209
sleep, 2232
special education, international studies of, 2294
standards-based reform, 1729
strategies to prepare work-bound youth, 2639–2640
student employment, 728–731
student extracurricular activities, 318–320
student mobility, 2382–2383
substance abuse prevention program effectiveness, 603–605
superintendents/school board communication, 2109
teacher education faculty, 2441
teacher professional development, 1729
teaching assessment, 1752
testing and assessment, 1730
test preparation programs, 2543–2544
triarchic intelligence theory, 1207–1209
violence exposure, 2627–2630
working students, 736–737
youth development programs, 2712–2714
youth gangs, 51–52
See also Comparative assessment; Educational research; Eight-Year Study; Reports and publications
Studies in Art Education (periodical), 1735
Study abroad, **2394–2396**
curriculum innovation, 511
Department of Education, U.S., 2620
Institute of International Education (IIE), 1136–1139
statistics, *1274*
See also Exchange programs; International students
Study hours, 355
A Study of Graduate Schools of America (Hughes), 378
Study of Mathematically Precocious Youth (SMPY), 2408
Study of the U.S. Branch, ECA, 848
Stuebing, K. K., 2009
Sturgis, George, 886
STWOA (School-to-Work Opportunities Act), 2329
"The Subjective Necessity for Social Settlements" (Addams), 41
Subjectivity and grading, 957–958
Subject-matter competence, college students', 336
Subjects, concept of, 115–116
Submemories, 1610
Sub-Saharan Africa, **2396–2405**
African Development Bank (AfDB), 1258
early childhood education enrollment trends, 628
Economic Commission for Africa (ECA), 1257–1258
gender and access to education, 919
higher education, 1027
rate of return on investment in education, 649
student exchange programs, 1138
vocational school fallacy, 2655
See also Specific countries
Subsidized student loans, 377
Substance abuse, **602–609, 815–817, 2055–2058**
child abuse and neglect, 268
college students, **606–609,** 1872–1873
HIV/AIDS, 2058
juvenile drug offenses, 1354
media, 1582
prevention, 978
risk management, 2075–2076
school education and prevention programs, **602–605**
Science Plus Literacy for Health Drug Education Project, 92
sexual activity and, 2062
social fraternities and sororities, 2253
trends, *2055*
See also Tobacco use
Substitution and resource allocation, 2051
Success, factors in, 811–813
Success for All programs, **2405–2407,** *2406,* 2580–2581
Sudan. *See* Sub-Saharan Africa
Sudden Infant Death Syndrome (SIDS), 2067
Suelzle, Marijean, 1326
Suffrage, women's, 2703
Sugarman, Stephen, 672, 1927
Sugrue, Brenda, 1576
Suicide, 404, **2068–2071**
Sullivan, Henry Stack, 1864
Sulzby, Elizabeth, 1487
Summarization and reading comprehension, 1981–1982
Summative assessment, 138

Summative teacher evaluation, 2454
Summer employment, 730, 736
Summer enrichment programs, **2407–2409**
Summerhill, 1797–1798
Summerlin, William, 2038
Summer school, **2409–2411**
Sunday schools, 711
Sunrise Semester (television show), 592
SUNY (State University of New York), 199
Super high schools, 1527
Superintendents, **2411–2418**
  Goslin, Willard E., 943–944
  large-city school systems, **2411–2415**
  leadership, 666–668
  Morrison, Henry C., 1688–1690
  Newlon, Jesse, 1800–1801
  school board relations, **2107–2111,** 2121
  state, 2324
  urban schools, 2606
  Washburne, Carleton, 2663
  Young, Ella Flagg, 2702
Supervision in the Secondary School (Alberty and Thayer), 80
Supervision of instruction, **2418–2422**
Supplemental Security Income (SSI), 834, 1868, 2674
Supplies, education, 1661–1663
Supply and demand, teacher. *See* Teacher supply and demand
"The Supply and Demand of Elementary and Secondary School Teachers in the United States" (report), 2087
Supply-side honors, 1087
Supportive Multi-User Interactive Learning Environment (SMILE) Design, 1156
Support services. *See* Family support services; School-linked services
Support services for nontraditional students, 1815–1816
Supreme Court, U.S., **2422–2425**
  See also Court cases
Surface code, 586
The Surgeon General's Report on Physical Activity and Health, 1888
Suriname. *See* Latin America and the Caribbean
Surveys
  Campus Computing Survey, 2521
  employment readiness, 733–734
  faculty consulting, 774–775
  High School and Beyond Survey, 2025
  India, education in, 951–952
  as method of studying teaching, 2490
  multiculturalism in higher education, 1711
  proposed Master's Degree Program for teachers, 1751
  reading instruction, 1999–2000
  research, 2022–2023
  Research About Teacher Education (RATE) Study, 721
  school, 508
  student employment, 729
  violence exposure, 2628
  Youth Risk Behavior Surveillance System (YRBS), 1004, 2058, 2307, 2308, 2629
  See also Studies
Survivors' and Dependents' Educational Assistance Program, 852, 930
Susan Harwood Training Grants, 846
Sustainable development, 1264
Svinicki, Marilla, 2493–2494
Swanborn, Machteld, 1504
Swann v. Charlotte-Mecklenburg Board of Education, 480, 2424, **2864–2877**
Swanson, H. Lee, 2008–2009
Swanson v. Guthrie Independent School District, 1062
Swarthmore College, 1086
Swaziland. *See* Sub-Saharan Africa
Sweatt v. Painter, 64
Sweden. *See* Western Europe
Swedish International Development Cooperation Agency (SIDA), 1243–1244
Switzer, H. Frederick, 1326
Switzerland. *See* Western Europe
Sylvan Learning, 2582
Symbolic Distance in Relation to Analogy and Fiction (Buchanan), 212
Symbols and learning, 2658–2659
Synagogue education, 1341–1342
Synchronous communication, 592
Synn, Joan, 2712
Synthesis in Bloom's taxonomy, 311
Syria. *See* Middle East and North Africa
System diversity in higher education, 1041–1042
Systemic educational change, 658–659

T

TAAS (Texas Assessment of Academic Skills), 2536
Taba, Hilda, 521, **2427–2429**
Tabachnick, Robert, 307
Taba Spiral of Curriculum Development, 2428
Tacit knowledge, 1207–1208
Tactics, instructional, 1179
Taiwan. *See* East Asia and the Pacific
Tajikistan. *See* Eastern Europe and Central Asia
Take Charge of Your TV (initiative), 1783
Talbani, Aziz, 1328
Talent development, 932
Talent Search programs. *See* Summer enrichment programs
Talks to Teachers (James), 1333
Tall, David, 1561
TANF (Temporary Assistance for Needy Families), 2673–2674, 2678
Tanzania, 2446
  See also Sub-Saharan Africa
Tarasoff v. Board of Regents of the University of California, 2075
Tash, Constance, 819
Task-sampling ability tests, 1113
TA (Technology Administration), 842
Tatsuoka, Kikumi, 141
Tau Beta Pi, **1085–1086**
Tax Commission, Walz v., 2423
Taxes
  corruption, 1664–1665
  school funding and, 885–886
  for secondary education, 2184
  tax credits, 377, 834–835, 863, 1951
  Taxpayer Relief Act of 1997, 863
  taxpayers as an interest group, 663

Taxonomies of educational objectives, **2429–2433**
classroom questions, 311
educational psychology, 678
higher education learning, 2493
instructional strategies, 1180–1186
See also Bloom, Benjamin S.
Taxonomies of instructional methods, 1180, *1181*
A Taxonomy for Learning, Teaching and Assessing: A Revision of Bloom's Taxonomy of Educational Objectives (Anderson and Krathwohl), 2430–2432
Taxonomy of academic disciplines, Biglan, 11
Taxpayer Relief Act of 1997, 863
Taxpayers as an interest group, 663
Taylor, Carl, 51–52
Taylor, Frederick Winslow, 193
Taylor, Harold, **2433–2435**
TBE (Transitional bilingual education), 1102
Teachable agents, 147
TEACH Act (proposed), 1189
The Teacher as World Citizen: A Scenario of the 21st Century (Brameld), 207
Teacher education, **2438–2448**
accreditation, 1762–1763, 2442
adaptive physical education, 40
American Association of Colleges for Teacher Education (AACTE), **93–94,** 2442
business education, **222–226**
Canada, 236–237
Catholic schools, 251
coaches, 2308–2309
Colleges and Classrooms: State Strategies for Redesigning Teacher Preparation Policies (initiative), 1777
competency-based teacher education (CBTE), 2441–2442, 2447
credentialism, 237
curriculum, 2370–2371
Delta Kappa Gamma Society, **1072–1073**
early childhood education, 618, **621–626,** 632
elementary school, **720–722**
English education, **745–748**
field experience, 2440–2441
future faculty preparation programs, **909–913**
Gallaudet University, 867
gender issues, 920
health education, 1008–1009
history, **2438–2444**
induction programs, 2473, 2487–2488
in-service and staff development programs for early childhood educators, 624
Instructional Theory Into Practice (ITIP) model, 1093–1094
international issues, **2444–2448, 2470–2475**
job placement, 76
journalism, 1348
Ka Lama Teacher Education Initiative, 2466
Kappa Delta Pi, **1074–1075**
kindergarten, 621–622
Latin America, 1410–1411
learning to teach, 2485–2488
mathematics, **1539–1542,** 1729, 2237–2238
microteaching, **1620–1623,** 2447
middle school, 1634
Montessori Accreditation Council for Teacher Education (MACTE), 1679–1680
moral education, 1687
music, **1723–1726**
National Council for Accreditation of Teacher Education (NCATE), **1762–1763,** *1763*
Nolan, Aretas, 74
nursery schools, 622–623
Oswego Training School, 2224–2225
parental involvement, 1846
performance-based teacher education (PBTE), 2441–2442, 2447
Phi Delta Kappa International, **1079–1080**
physical education, **1890–1894**
as preparation for teaching, 2486
problems in, 722
professional development and continuing education, 721, 722, 2470–2473
professional development schools, **1930–1933**
reform and, 2471
science, 1729
science education, **2163–2166**
sexuality education, 2215–2216
social studies education, **2269–2272**
special education, 2288, **2290–2293**
speech education, 2301
standards, 498, 1763, 1770
Stewart, R. M., 75–76
student teaching, 2446–2447, 2449
supervised training, 76
Teacher Education (Gage and Winne), 2442
The Teacher Educator's Handbook (Feiman-Nemser and Remillard), 2438
teacher learning communities, 2461–2462
text comprehension instruction, 1982
training *vs.* professional development, 2470
vocational education, 74, 75–76, **2647–2651**
See also Certification and licensure; Continuing professional education (CPE); Professional development
Teacher Education (Gage and Winne), 2442
The Teacher Educator's Handbook (Feiman-Nemser and Remillard), 2438
Teacher evaluation, **2453–2461**
college teaching, 254, 414–416, 788, **798–802**
employment, 2450–2451
methods, **2457–2461**
new teachers, 2460
overview, **2453–2457**
performance assessment, 787, 788
social organization of public schools, 2260
supervision of instruction, 2418–2421
See also Classroom observation
Teacher Exchange Program, 847
Teacher learning communities, **2461–2469**
Teacher networks. *See* Teacher learning communities
Teacher of the Year program, 502

Teachers, **2435–2437**
accountability, 652–655, 2319, 2321–2322
alternative public schools, 83
American Association of Educators (AAE), 2478
American overseas schools, 114–115
art education, **121–123**
Board certified teachers, 2450–2451, 2458–2460
Canada, 236–237
certification, 1751–1752
control, 2257–2258
decentralization, 544
early childhood, 618
Eleanor Roosevelt Teacher Fellowships, 104
employment, **2448–2453**
English language arts, 742
equalization of pay, 298–299
ethics, **753–756**
evaluation, 2450–2451
foreign language, 895, 1672–1673
Global Educators Program, 2718
health promotion programs, 1007, 1014
immoral conduct, 753
induction period, 2460
inequitable instruction, 305–306
in-service training, 1892
international associations, **1318–1321**
international comparisons, 1288
learning, teacher, 2485–2488
learning community role, 1162
mathematics, 1565
mentoring, **1618–1620**
middle school, 1633–1634
minorities, 2449
National Writing Project (NWP), 2465, 2694
new teachers, 2460
observational feedback, 306–307
office space, 2127
parental involvement and, 1845–1846
peer supervision, 2420
professional development, 223–224
professionalism, 236–237, 2456
quality, 1770
recruitment, 2449–2450
responses to student answers, 312–313, 583
as role models, 753
rural schools, 2087
salaries, 544, 2448, 2450–2451
school reform, 2154
secondary school, 2192
Smithsonian Institution programs, 2240
social studies, 2269–2271
special education, 2288
state education agencies and, 2346–2347
student/teacher role, 761
subroles, 415
supervision of instruction, **2418–2422**
teacher learning communities, **2461–2469**
teacher questions, 310–311
unions, 2222–2223
urban schools, 2610
See also Classroom management; Classroom observation; Faculty; Teacher evaluation

Teachers College of Columbia University
Bagley, William C., 164–165
Benne, Kenneth D., 170
Brameld, Theodore, 206
Butler, Nicholas M., 230
Childs, John L., 293
Council for Exceptional Children, 500
Curti, Merle, 540
Dewey, John, 578–579
Kilpatrick, William H., 1369
Lincoln School, **1484–1485**
Master's degree for "Adviser of Women," 2388
McCall, William A., 1572–1574
Miel, Alice, 1636
Newlon, Jesse, 1801
Rugg, Harold, 2082
Smith, David Eugene, 2237
Snedden, David, 2241–2242
Stratemeyer, Florence, 2370
Thorndike, Edward L., 2563–2564

Teachers Guild, 2221–2222

Teacher shortages. *See* Teacher supply and demand

Teachers International Union of America, 111

Teachers Learning Collaborative Network, 2466

Teacher/student interaction
classroom discourse, 583, 588
classroom observation, 304–305
gender equity, 1126
group processes, 973–974

Teacher-student ratio
class size, 314
Coalition of Essential Schools, 323
dropout rates, 600
East Asia and the Pacific, *636*, 638
South Asia, 2274
United States, 1288

Teacher supply and demand
American overseas schools, 114–115
business education, 219, 224
Canada, 237
developing nations, 548
early childhood education, 624–625
employment issues, 2448–2449, 2451
faculty, college, 17–18
Latin teachers, 1415
professional development schools, 1932
rural education, 2087
secondary education, 2192
special education, 2291–2291
teacher education and, 2440
urban schools, 2607
vocational education, 2648
See also Academic labor market

The Teachers We Want (report), 698

Teacher Union Reform Network (TURN), 2478, 2481

Teacher unions. *See* Unions

Teaching, **2482–2492**
adaptive, 1120
college, **413–417,** 790–791
constructivist classrooms, 1465–1466
consulting, impact of, 775
deaf education, **1019–1021**
dialectical method, 1899
didactic *vs.* evocative, 2438–2439
geography, **926–928**
higher education, **2493–2499**
history, **1055–1058**
improvement programs, college and university, **254–257**
in-service training, 1621
international comparisons, 1288
journalism, **1347–1349**
knowledge bases of, **2482–2485,** 2486
language arts, **1392–1396**
Latin America, 1410
leadership styles, 973–974

learning and, **2492–2501**
learning to teach, **2485–2488**
mathematics, 1553–1557
methods for studying, **2488–2492**
microteaching, **1620–1623**
Middle East and North Africa, 1626
National Board for Professional Teaching Standards, **1750–1753**
national commission on, 691
open classrooms, 1823
problem solving, 1443
as profession, 2456
reading, 1998–2003
research, **2501–2504**
styles, 159–160
thinking, teacher, 2484
word problems, 1568
See also Instruction; Teacher evaluation; Team teaching

Teaching and Learning Division, ETS, 685

Teaching assistants
future faculty preparation programs, 910–912
graduate study in education, 969
teaching improvement programs, 255

Teaching Initiatives, AAHE, 90

Teaching machines, 1918, 2230

The Teaching of Agriculture (Nolan), 74

Teaching to the test
academic standards, 2321
accountability, 655
elementary education, 719
high-stakes testing, 2536
secondary education, 2191
statewide testing programs, 2541

Teaching units, 2555

Teaching with Technology (Brown), 2525

Teach Me to Sing of Winter (Benne), 169–170

Teale, William, 1487

Team teaching, **2504–2506**
interdisciplinarity, 1212–1213
nongraded schools, 1813
scheduling, 2096, 2098–2099

Tech Act, 149

Technical colleges, 441

Technical cooperation programs
German Organization for Technical Cooperation, 1248
Japan International Cooperation Agency, 1245–1246

Technical education. *See* Vocational and technical education

Technology
assistive, **149–151, 2518**
licensing, 2527
programmed instruction, 2230
special education, 2288
See also Computer technology; Information and communications technology

Technology Administration (TA), 842

Technology education, **2506–2509**
academic standards, 2176
science and technology education, 2159–2160, 2161, 2165
Technology Education and Copyright Harmonization Act (proposed), 1189
undergraduate curriculum reform, 512
vocational education, 2640

Technology Education and Copyright Harmonization Act (proposed), 1189

Technology-planning consortia, 476

Technology-Related Assistance for Individuals with Disabilities Act of 1988, 149

Technology transfer, **2526–2528**

Teen pregnancy, 978, **2060–2064,** 2067, **2071–2074**

Teich, Albert H., 853

Telecommunications, 424–425
See also Information and communications technology

Telecourses, 592

Telephone contact in recruitment process, 383

Television
educational, 592, 656–658, 2515
influence, 1580, 1581–1582
latchkey children, 1406

Temperament, 156

Temporary Assistance for Needy Families (TANF)
income support, 833–834
welfare reform, 2673–2674, 2678

Temporary student records, 2014

Tempus program (European Union), 1252

Tennessee, 314–315, 316

Tennyson, Robert, 1160

Tenure, **14–16**
See also Academic freedom

Tenures Abolition Act (England), 281

Teplin, Linda, 1360

Terenzini, Patrick T.
extracurricular activities, 374
formal and informal learning, 2493
general education, 924
How College Affects Students (Pascarella and Terenzini), 335–340
psychosocial changes in college students, 2495
residence hall living, 2046
student adjustment to college, 43, 924
student-faculty interaction, 452

Terman, Lewis, 931, 1195, 1201, **2528–2529**

Terra Nova test, 2539

Territorial gangs, 52

Terrorism, 978

Tesch-Römer, Clemens, 766

Testa, Mark, 2712

Testing, **2530–2551**
ACT tests, 329, 330, 331, 2543–2546
assessment of, 654
certification examinations, 2530–2531
competence, 2532
corruption, 1660
creativity, 506
educational policy, **2530–2533**
High Stakes: Testing for Tracking, Promotion, and Graduation (National Research Council), 1730
high-stakes assessment, 1301, 1730, **2533–2537**
international test development standards, 2550–2551
McCall, William A., 1572–1574
memory, 1596–1599, 1606, 1607–1608
Middle East and North Africa, 1628–1629
minimum competency, 2535

professional testing standards, 2536–2537
purposes, 2539–2540
standards and, 2531–2532
statewide programs, **2538–2542**
studies of, 1730
teacher, 2260
test preparation programs, **2542–2546**
test reviews, 214
test theory, 140
Thorndike, Edward L., 2566–2567
Tyler, Ralph W., 2587–2589
vocational education, 2645
writing education, 2694–2695
See also Assessment; Assessment tools; Educational Testing Service (ETS); Grading systems; Intelligence testing; National Assessment of Educational Progress (NAEP); Standardized tests
Test of Creative Thinking (TTCT), 506
Tests in Print (Buros), 214
Tetanus, 1107
Tetlow, John, 725
Texas, 314
Texas, Hernandez v., 2094
Texas Assessment of Academic Skills (TAAS), 2536
Texas Western, 350
Textbase, 586
Textbooks, **2551–2560**
African-American history, 1704
Basic Learning Materials Initiative (UNESCO), 1262
children's literature, 288
Cubberley, Elwood, 508
gender bias, 1126
genres, 1996
Hanna, Paul R., 990–991
history, 1986–1987
interest and learning, 1990–1991
Latin, 1415
learning from, **1993–1995**
mathematics, 2237–2238
mathematics teaching, 1540
multiculturalism, 1706–1707
New England Primer, 713, 740
overview, **2551–2554**
previewing, 1978
readability, 1972–1973
reading instruction, 2000–2001
resource units *vs.*, 81
Rugg, Harold, 2082
science, 1987–1988
standards-based education and, 2320
United States, **2554–2560**
Webster, Noah, 2670–2672
T-Groups, 170, 1817
Thailand
private *vs.* public schools, 950–951
school counseling, 978
secondary education, 639
Tharp, Roland G., 576
Thayer, V.T., 80, **2560–2562**
Thayer Commission. *See* Commission on Secondary School Curriculum, PEA
Theater education. *See* Speech and theater education
Thelen, Herbert A., 972
Theme residence halls, 342
"Theology as Public Performance: Reflections on the Christian Convictions of Ernest L. Boyer" (Jacobsen), 201
Theory, instructional design, 1147–1150
Theory, women's studies, 2690–2691
Theory and Practice in Historical Study: A Report of the Committee on Historiography (report), 539
Theory-based program evaluation, 2032
Theory of education
Freire, Paulo, 902–903
Kandel, Isaac L., 1364
motivation, 1691–1695
philosophy of education, 1877–1878
student departure theory, 403–406
See also Developmental theory; Learning theory; Pedagogy; Philosophy of education
Theosophical Society, 2364
Theta Sigma Phi. *See* Association for Women in Communications
Thinking, teacher, 2484
Third International Mathematics and Science Study (TIMSS), **1233–1236**
educational research, 1272–1273
International Association for Educational Assessment, 1226, 1227
international curriculum, 524–529
national achievement tests, 2548
public schools, 1950
secondary students, 2192
standards-based education, 2320
statistics, 1288, 1293
study of, 1730
Thirty-School Study. *See* Eight-Year Study
Thomas, Wayne, 179
Thomas Aquinas, 160
Thompson, David, 1954
Thomson, Elizabeth, 1906
Thoreau, Henry David, 93
Thorndike, Edward L., **2562–2569**
Bagley, William C., 164
educational psychology, 677
instrumental conditioning, 1460
McCall, William A., 1572–1573
Progressive education, 1936–1937
Thorne, Barrie, 1211
Thrasher, Frederic, 51
Threaded discourse, 1371–1372
Thresholds theory, 175
Through Art to Creativity (Barkan), 166
Thurstone, Lloyd L., 1202
Thurstone, Louis Leon, 680
Tibawi, Abdul, 1328
Tiebout, Charles, 2105
Tienda, Marta, 730
Tierney, Robert, 1513, 1978
Tierney, William G., 521, 793, 794
Tillery, Dale, 96
Time, homework, 1064
Time constraints and learning outcomes, 1828
Time for Results (report), 518, 697
Timeline of affirmative action, 63–65
Time management skills, 355
Time-series designs, 2024
TIMMS. *See* Third International Mathematics and Science Study (TIMSS)
Timothy W. v. Rochester, New Hampshire, School District, 2212
Tinker et al. v. Des Moines Independent Community School District et al., **2844–2853**
Tinto, Vincent, 374, 404
Titchener, Edward Bradford, 163

Title I, Elementary and Secondary Education Act (ESEA)
compensatory education, 454–456, 457–458
federal involvement in education, 837–838
tutoring, 2581
Title IV, Education Amendments, 862
Title IV, Elementary and Secondary Education Act, 2017
Title V, Elementary and Secondary Education Act of 1965, 2325
Title V, Higher Education Act of 1965, 1045
Title VI, Civil Rights Act of 1964, 64, 65
Title VI, Elementary and Secondary Education Act, 1868
Title VI, Higher Education Act, 2619–2620
Title VII, Civil Rights Act of 1964, 64
Title IX, Goals 2000: Education America Act, 2017
Title IX, Higher Education Act, **2569–2573, 3072–3075**
in affirmative action timeline, 64
collegiate sports, 351–352, **2570–2573**
education funding, 837
education policy, 673
family and consumer sciences, 804
school sports, **2569–2570**
Tjeerdsma, Bonnie, 1891
TLCs. *See* Teacher learning communities
T.L.O., New Jersey v., 2425
TMMS (Trait Meta-Mood Scale), 1191
Tobacco use, 606, 2066–2068
See also Substance abuse
Toennies, Ferdinand, 937
Togo. *See* Sub-Saharan Africa
Tokenism, 777
Tokushige, Farrington v., 1925, 2336
Tolan, Patrick, 2629
Tolman, Edward, 1461
Tomlinson, Carol A., 933
Tomorrow's Teachers (report), 697
To Move Forward, 121
Tonga. *See* East Asia and the Pacific
Tooley, James, 949
Tools of the Mind (Bodrova and Leong), 576
Tooth decay, 555
To Reclaim a Legacy: A Report on the Humanities in Higher Education (report), 514–515
Torgesen, Joseph, 2009
Torrey, H. A. P., 578
Torts, 1472
To Secure the Blessings of Liberty (report), 518
Total communication approach to deaf education, 1020
Tracking, 2255, 2257
Track plans, year-round education, 2699–2700
Trade agreements, 423–424
Trade of education goods and services, **1321–1324**
Trade Related Aspects of Intellectual Property Rights (TRIPS), 1323–1324
Trade schools. *See* Vocational and technical education
TRADOC (Training and Doctrine Command), U.S. Army, 1657
Trager, Helen, 1707
Training
groups, 170
school board members, 2120–2121
school psychologists, 1946
See also In-service training
Training and Doctrine Command (TRADOC), U.S. Army, 1657
The Training of Farmers (Bailey), 74
Trait Meta-Mood Scale (TMMS), 1191
Transcendentalism, 1526
Transcripts, 329, 1311–1312
Transfer, student records, 2015
Transfer of learning, **1449–1452**
analogical reasoning, 1422–1423
educational technology, 2515–2516
The Transformation of the School (Cremin), 554
Transforming the State Role in Undergraduate Education: Time for A Different View (report), 518
Transit City, U.S.A., 850
Transitional bilingual education (TBE), 1102
Transition and special education, 2288
Transition capstone courses, 240
Transition programs, higher education, 1969
Translation, Latin, 1414–1415
Transmission, HIV, 2058
Transparency in analogy, 1422
Transportation
commuter students, 451–452
public funding for private school students, 2337
school busing, **2573–2577**
Transportation Equity Act for the 21st Century, 850
Transportation Safety Institute, 851
Transportation Equity Act for the 21st Century, 850
Transportation Safety Institute, 851
Transracial adoptions, 815
Travel programs, foreign language, 898
Treadwell, Donald F. and Jill B., 734
Treatises of Aristotle, 115–116
The Treaty Establishing the European Community, 1251
TREE (Trust to Reach Education Excellence), 1747
Tremblay, Gilles, 819
Trend NAEP, 132
Trends. *See* Current Trends
Trent, James, 332
Triarchic theory of intelligence, 1115, **1206–1209**
Tribal colleges and universities, **2578–2580**
Carnegie classification system, 245
faculty diversity, 776
government schools, 868
See also Native Americans
Tribally Controlled Community College Assistance Act, 2579
Trimester calendars, 2097
See also Academic calendars
Trinidad & Tobago. *See* Latin America and the Caribbean
TRIO Programs, 1971, 2603
TRIPS (Trade Related Aspects of Intellectual Property Rights), 1323–1324

Truancy and attendance problems
child abuse and neglect, 269
compulsory attendance laws, 464
foster care children, 819
juvenile justice system, 1355
Truman, Harry S., 63
Truman Report, 96
Trump, J. Lloyd, 2095
Trustees, board of, **191–192**
in college organization, 385–386
decision-making, 946
state government, 2360–2362
Trust to Reach Education Excellence (TREE), 1747
TTCT (Test of Creative Thinking), 506
Tucker, Pamela, 2455
Tuition
community colleges, 876–880
higher education finance, 871, 873–874
by institution type, *880*
as revenue source, 25–26
state governments, 2361
See also Budgeting; Economics of education; Finance; Revenue
Tu Kappa Alpha. *See* Delta Sigma Rho-Tau Kappa Alpha
Tulving, Endel, 1589, 1606
Tunisia. *See* Middle East and North Africa
Turkey
early childhood education, 629
school counseling, 979
See also Western Europe
Turkmenistan. *See* Eastern Europe and Central Asia
Turn, Jennifer, 1157
Turner, Frederick Jackson, 350
Turner Elementary School, 167
Turning Points (Carnegie Council on Adolescent Development), 1632–1633, 1746, 2096, 2191
TURN (Teacher Union Reform Network), 2478, 2481
Tuskegee Normal and Industrial Institute, 2665
Tutoring, **2580–2587**
college athletes, 354, 355
discourse, 588–589
higher education, **2583–2585**
international trends, **2585–2587**
problem-based learning, 1173, *1173*
school, **2580–2583**
services, 1220
Success for All programs, 2405
tutors, **1169–1172**
Tuvalu. *See* East Asia and the Pacific
Two sigma problem, 189
Two-track school system, 710
Two-year colleges. *See* Community colleges
Tyack, David
Carnegie units, 246
education reform, 691
family support services, 829
school remediation, 906
Tyler, Ralph W., **2587–2590**
academic standards, 2316
Bloom, Benjamin S., 188
curriculum, 520–521
National Assessment of Educational Progress (NAEP), 131
types of understandings, 1994
Tyner, Kathleen T., 1497
Tyranny, 2244
Tzuriel, David, 128, 129

U

UAE (United Arab Emirates). *See* Middle East and North Africa
UBMS (Upward Bound Math/Science program), 2604
UCEA (University Council for Educational Administration), **2591–2592**
UCLA School Mental Health Project, 2147
UFT (United Federation of Teachers), 2222, 2477
Uganda. *See* Sub-Saharan Africa
U.K. Education brand, 1316
Ukraine. *See* Eastern Europe and Central Asia
Undergraduate education
curriculum innovation, **509–514**
curriculum reports, 515–516
engineering, 738
GEAR UP (Gaining Early Awareness and Readiness for Undergraduate Programs), 837
learning communities, **1452–1457**, *1454*
music teacher, 1723–1724
national reports on curriculum, **514–519**
physical education teacher education, 1891
"Seven Principles for Good Practice in Undergraduate Education" (Chickering and Gamson), 2495
teaching and learning, 2493–2498
The Undergraduate Experience in America (report), 516
Undergraduate Pre-Service Science Teacher Education Program (UPSTEP), 2164
See also Colleges and universities; Higher education
The Undergraduate Experience in America (report), 516
Undergraduate Pre-Service Science Teacher Education Program (UPSTEP), 2164
Undernutrition, 1821–1822
See also Health and nutrition
Understanding, scientific, **2169–2173**
UNESCO. *See* United Nations Educational, Scientific and Cultural Organization (UNESCO)
Unger, Chris, 1148
UNHCR (United Nations High Commissioner for Refugees), 1264–1265
UNICEF (United Nations Children's Fund), 1261–1262
Unified Model, 142
Uniformity of performance, 701–702
Uninsured children, 1000–1001
Union Leadership Institute, 111
Unions, **2475–2482**
American Council on Education, 110
decentralization, 544
faculty, 103
Haley, Margaret, 983–985
influence on education, **2479–2482**
interest groups, 663
overview, **2475–2479**
teacher, 544, 983–985, **1318–1321**
Teachers International Union of America, 111
United Federation of Teachers (UFT), 2222

See also American Federation of Teachers (AFT); Collective bargaining
The Unique Functions of Education in American Democracy (report), 696
Uniserv program (National Education Association), 2476
United Arab Emirates. *See* Middle East and North Africa
United Church of Christ, 389
United Federation of Teachers (UFT), 2222, 2477
United Kingdom. *See* England
United Methodist University Senate, 390
United Nations, **1259–1265,** 1280–1282
United Nations Children's Fund (UNICEF), 1261–1262
United Nations Educational, Scientific and Cultural Organization (UNESCO)
accreditation, 27
early childhood education, 627, 631
international agreements, 1277, 1279–1280
international comparative studies, 1222, 1224
international treaties, 1282–1284
Learning to Be (report), 1481
overview, 1262
peace education, 1860–1861
social indicators, 1294
United Nations Food and Agriculture Organization (FAO), 1264
United Nations High Commissioner for Refugees (UNHCR), 1264–1265
United Nations World Summit for Children, 1243
United States
accountability, 653–654
accreditation, **28–37**
agricultural education, 72–79
alternative schooling, 82–86
bilingual education, 175, 177–178
business schools, 220–222
Catholic schools, 250–253
child abuse and neglect, 267–268
child care, 274
child protective services, 283–285
civics education, 294–296
college athletics, 344–353, 361–364
college rankings, 378–381
common schools, 427–431
community colleges, 441–442
compensatory education, **453–458**
continuing professional education (CPE), **483–486**
demographics, 1707, 1709–1710
disabled college students, 407–409
dropout rates, 599
early childhood education, 615–617
educational demographics, 275–2706
educational psychology, 677
Education Commission of the States (ECS), **685–686**
education expenditures, 1288
education participation, 1288
education reform, **689–700,** 715–716
elementary education, 709–714, 715–720
ethnicity and achievement gap, 1121–1124
gang activity, 51
global competencies, 511
guidance and counseling, 975–976
hearing impaired students, 1018–1019, 1020
higher education, **1034–1041, 1041–1045**
higher education governance, 385
immigrant education, **1097–1104**
infant schools, 1135
interdisciplinarity in higher education, 1211–1212
international students, *1270,* 1270–1272, *1271, 1272, 1273,* 1314
language learning, 1389, 1401–1403
latchkey children, 1403–1404
Latino growth, 1966–1968
learning outcomes, 1288–1289
liberal arts colleges, 1477
literacy, 1289
magnet schools, 1526–1527
moral education, 259–260, 1663–1685
national education reports, **514–519, 695–700**
open education, 1826
outdoor and environmental education, 1833–1834
policy, education, **668–676,** 691–692
population demographics, 2704–2705
private schools, 712, 1923–1928
public education criticism, 1948–1951
public school authority, 664
school finance, 1216–1217
secondary education, 2195–2196
social cohesion and education, 2245–2249
southern, 710, 2332, 2665–2666
substance abuse, college, 606–607
teachers and teaching, 1288
textbooks, 2554–2559, **2554–2560**
trade agreements, 423–424
Vygotskian theory applications, 576–577
workforce development, 488–489
See also Colonial America; Government, U.S.; History, educational; States
United States, Barenblatt v., 102
United States, Kent v., 1350–1351
United States Advisory Board on Child Abuse and Neglect, 285
United States Agency for International Development (USAID), 113, 1241–1242
United States Commission on Immigration Reform, 296
United States Medical Licensing Examination (USMLE), 1586
United States v. Fordice, 2202
United States v. Lopez, 478
United States v. Virginia, 2202
Units of work, 2555
Universal Declaration of Human Rights, **3099–3104**
Universal education, 421
Universities: American, English, German (Flexner), 893
University 101, 44
University Council for Educational Administration (UCEA), **2591–2592**
University of California at Davis
academic calendars, 7

Medical School, 62
University of California system, 373
University of Chicago, **2597–2598**
African-American studies, 66
Bobbitt, Franklin, 192–193
Campbell, Roald F., 233
college athletics, 349
Counts, George S., 504
creation of the Association of American Universities, 153–154
Dewey, John, 578
Gray, William Scott, 970
Great Books program, 212
Harper, William Rainey, 992
Hutchins, Robert, 1094–1095
international education, 1265–1266
Palmer, Alice Freeman, 1843
Schwab, Joseph, 2156–2157
University of Chicago Laboratory School, 1689, 1833
University of Delaware, Furek v., 2075
University of Houston, 656
University of Illinois
affirmative action, 64
Benne, Kenneth D., 170
Bode, Boyd H., 194–195
University of Iowa, 198
University of Kentucky, 350
University of Maryland, 1712, 2044
University of Massachusetts, *363*
University of Memphis, 1712
University of Michigan, 63, 1711
University of Missouri, 66, 2044
University of Missouri-Columbia High School, 1111
University of Notre Dame, 350
University of Oklahoma, 66
University of South Carolina, 2584
University of Southern California, 350
University of Utah, Beach v., 2075
University of Virginia, 20, **2598–2600**
University of Virginia, Rosenberger v., 2423
University of Wisconsin Experimental College, 1587–1588
University of Wisconsin–Green Bay, 1214
University presses, **2600–2603**
University Scholar-in-Residence Award, 104
University Senate, 390
University Transportation Center Program, 850
Updegraff, Harlen, 886
Up from Slavery (Washington), 2668
UPSTEP (Undergraduate Pre-Service Science Teacher Education Program), 2164
Upton, Emory, 1656–1657
Upward Bound program, 1970–1971, **2603–2605**
Urban education, **2605–2612**
community violence exposure, 2627–2630
Havighurst, Robert J., 997
international early childhood education enrollment trends, 628
public school demographics, 2706
school boards and public confidence, 2105
school effectiveness, 305
school facilities, 2128
superintendents, **2411–2415**
youth development programs, 2712–2713
Urban Institute, **2612–2614**
Urbanization of China, 638
Urban Universities Portfolio Project: Assuring Quality for Multiple Publics, 91
Uruguay. *See* Latin America and the Caribbean
U.S. Agency for International Development (USAID), 1241–1242
U.S. Air Force Academy, **1642–1645**
U.S. Coast Guard Academy, 849, **1645–1646**
U.S. Military Academy, 836, **1649–1652**
U.S. Naval Academy, **1652–1653**
U.S. News and World Report college rankings, 379–381, *380*, 1644
U.S. War Colleges, **2620–2621**
USAID (United States Agency for International Development), 113, 1241–1242
USDA Graduate School, 868
The Use of Resources in Education (Clapp), 297
The Uses of Schooling (Broudy), 210, 211
The Uses of the University (Kerr), 1038
USMLE (United States Medical Licensing Examination), 1586
USMMA (U.S. Merchant Marine Academy), 851
Uzbekistan. *See* Eastern Europe and Central Asia

V

Vaccines. *See* Immunization
Vaccines for Children Program (VFC), 1106
Vadeboncoeur, Jennifer, 762
Valenzuela, Angela, 2536
Validity, logical, 1445
Value-added measurements of educational outcomes, 701
Value communities, 1854
Values
clarification, 1377, 1685
college students, 338
families, 812
reading textbooks' depiction of, 713
Values education. *See* Character development; Moral development; Moral education
Vandell, Deborah, 1405, 1855
Vanderbilt University, 2044
Vanderbilt University, Cognition and Technology Group, 681
Vanderbilt University Learning Sciences Institute, 147
Van Dijk, Teun A., 1977
Van Merriënboer, J. J. G., 1160
Van Mondfrns, Adrian, 496
Vanuatu. *See* East Asia and the Pacific
Variable career emphasis programs, 792
Varicella, 1107
Vaughn, Sharon, 1457, 1982
VAWA (Violence Against Women Act of 1994), 2633
Vending machines in schools, 1004
Venezuela. *See* Latin America and the Caribbean
Venger, Leonid, 576
Venture capital, 551–552

Verbal protocols, **2034–2036**
Vernon, Philip E., 1202
Vertical writing, 988
Vessels, Gordon G., 261
Veterans
  Department of Veterans Affairs, U.S., 852
  Veterans Readjustment Act of 1952, 929
  Veterans Readjustment Benefits Act of 1966, 929
  Veterans' Testing Service (VTS), 921
  Veteran's Upward Bound (VUB) program, 2604
  vocational rehabilitation programs, 1867
  See also Servicemen's Readjustment Act
Veterans Readjustment Act of 1952, 929
Veterans Readjustment Benefits Act of 1966, 929
Veterans' Testing Service (VTS), 921
Veteran's Upward Bound (VUB) program, 2604
VHS (Virtual High School), 2179
Vice chancellor. *See* Chief academic affairs officers
Vice president of academic affairs. *See* Chief academic affairs officers
Video technology
  goal-based scenario, 1155–1156
  mathematics learning tools, 1550–1551
  microteaching, 1622
  The Power of Video Technology in International Comparative Research in Education (National Research Council), 1730
  school buses, 2576
  videotapes, 592
  See also Educational technology; Visual media
Vietnam, 639
  See also East Asia and the Pacific
Vincent, Widmar v., 2423
Vincent (animated learning tool), 1169
Violence
  academic performance and, 1837
  college athletics, 349
  community violence, **2627–2631**
  domestic, 809, 818, 1837, **2631–2634**
  exposure, **2623–2634**
  gangs, 52–53
  general effects, **2623–2627**
  juvenile crime, 1353–1354
  media violence, 1360, 1581–1582
  school, 83, 110, 718, 978, 1358–1359
  school sports, 2309–2310
  See also Behavior problems; School violence
Violence Against Women Act of 1994 (VAWA), 2633
Viral sexually transmitted diseases, 2065–2066
Virginia, 466
Virginia, United States v., 2202
Virginia Military Institute (VMI), 2202
Virgin Islands. *See* Latin America and the Caribbean
Virtual agents, 147
Virtual High School (VHS), 2179
Virtual reality, 1495
Virtual tours and art education, 120
Virtual universities, 2368, 2524–2525
  See also Online education
Virtual violence, 1581
Visas, student, 1312
Vision problems of school children, 187
Visual anthropology, 417–419
Visual Anthropology: Photography as a Research Method (Collier), 417–418
Visualization software, 2179
Visual learning aids, 1577
Visually impaired students, **2634–2635**
Visual media and memory, **1594–1596**
Visual search tasks, 155–156
Vitale, Engel v., 2422
Vives, Juan Luis, 677
VMI (Virginia Military Institute), 2202
Vocabulary, **1504–1507**
  development, 1386
  early childhood, 277
  instruction and reading comprehension, 1980
  school readiness, 2149

Vocational Act of 1917. *See* Smith-Hughes Act

Vocational Act of 1963, 216

Vocational and technical education, **2636–2654**
  academic/vocational curriculum, 2640–2641
  African Americans, 2636
  agricultural, 73–74
  business education as, 216
  career clusters, 2643–2644, 2649–2650
  community colleges and, 444–445
  Convention on Technical and Vocational Education, 1283
  current trends, **2642–2647**
  in curriculum development, 193–194
  developing countries, 2198
  European Union, 1252
  German Organization for Technical Cooperation, 1248
  Hampton Institute, 2666–2667
  history, **2636–2642**
  home economics, 804
  international issues, 1029–1030, **2651–2654**
  Kerschensteiner, Georg, 1367–1368
  National Board for Professional Teaching Standards, 2649
  Office of Vocational and Adult Education, Department of Education, 2619
  Progressives, 1936
  Prosser, Charles, 1940
  rehabilitation programs, 1867
  rural education, 2091
  secondary schools, 2185–2186
  South Asia, 2274
  standards, 2329, 2644, 2645, 2649
  state education agencies, **2328–2331,** 2345
  streaming, 2255
  Sub-Saharan Africa, 2400
  teacher preparation, **2647–2651**
  technical preparation programs, 217
  technology education, 2640
  vocational aptitude tests, 113
  Vocational Educational Assistance Program, VA, 852

Vocational Education in Farming Occupations: The Part of the Public High School (Eaton), 74–75
vocationalism, 2640–2641
Vocational Rehabilitation Act, 838
vocational rehabilitation programs, 1867
Vocational school fallacy, **2654–2656**
Vocational Training Act (Germany), 488
Vocational Training Act of 1963, 77
western Europe, 2681
work-based learning, 2641–2642
See also Carl D. Perkins Vocational Education acts; Smith-Hughes Act
Vocational Educational Assistance Program, VA, 852
Vocational Education in Farming Occupations: The Part of the Public High School (Eaton), 74–75
Vocationalism, 2640–2641
Vocational Rehabilitation Act, 838
Vocational school fallacy, **2654–2656**
Vocational Training Act (Germany), 488
Vocational Training Act of 1963, 77
Volition. *See* Affective and conative processes
Volpe National Transportation Systems Center, 851
Voluntary accreditation, 27, 36
Volunteers
club leaders, 319
parents as, 822
school, 822–823
tutors, 2581
See also Community service; Service learning
Voter education, 1254
Voting rights, 63
Voucher programs
accountability, 552, 653
alternative education, 84
constitutional issues, 481
constitutionality, 479
international issues, 953
policy, 675–676
private schools, 1927–1928
public schools criticism, 1950–1951
social organization of schools, 2260
state administrative services, 2348
See also Catholic schools; Private schools; Protestant schools; Religiously affiliated schools; School choice
VTS (Veterans' Testing Service), 921
VUB (Veteran's Upward Bound) program, 2604
Vygotskian theory, **574–577,** 585
Vygotsky, Lev, **2658–2660**
classroom discourse, 585
communicative interactions, 1463–1464
constructivist theory, 679
developmental theory, 574–577
dynamic assessment, 128
early childhood education, international aspects of, 630
inner speech, 1978
mediated learning, 1865

W

Wade, Nicholas, 2039
Wade, Suzanne E., 2002
Wait list, enrollment, 328
Wait-time, 312–313
Walden Two (Skinner), 2230
Waldorf Schools
alternative education, 84
looping, 1521
Steiner, Rudolf, 2365–2366
Walker, David, 762
Walker, Lou Ann, 1019
Wallace v. Jaffree, 2423
Waller, Willard W., 2246, **2661–2662**
Walz v. Tax Commission, 2423
Wambold, Clark, 1470
Wankel, Leonard, 2314
War Colleges, U.S., 1655, **2620–2621**
Warmbrod, Robert, 76–77
Warning signs, suicide, 2070
WASC (Western Association of Schools and Colleges), 28
Washburne, Carleton, **2662–2664**
Washington, Booker T., **2664–2668**
Du Bois, W. E. B., 610
vocational education, 2636
Washington Department of Services for the Blind, Witters v., 2423
Washington State University, 2044
Wasson, William, 362
Water fluoridation, 555
Watkins, Kevin, 919
Watkins, Thomas, 1857
Watson, John B., **2668–2670**
Waxman, Hersh, 304–305
Way of Light (Comenius), 421
WCCI (World Council on Curriculum and Instruction), 1637
WCOTP (World Confederation of Organizations in the Teaching Profession), 1319–1321
WCT (World Confederation of Teachers), 1319–1321
Weaver, Marilyn, 1347
Webb, Noreen, 491
Web-based Integrated Science Environment (WISE), 2180
Weber, Lillian, 1135
Webster, David S., 378, 379, 380–381
Webster, Noah, **2670–2673**
common schools, 429
elementary education history, 711
reading instruction, 1998
spelling education, 2303
textbooks, 2554–2555
Weeks, Jeffery, 916
Wehlage, Gary, 2141
Weick, Karl E., 2258
Weiner, Bernard, 1692
Weiner, Michael, 1707
Weinstein-Shr, Gail, 1511
Weisman, Lee v., 2423
Weiss, Carol, 2032
WEI (World Education Indicators) project, 1251, 1267, 1294
Welfare reform, **2673–2679**
child care, 275
effects on families and children, **2673–2676**
income support, 833–834
preschool availability, 617
welfare-to-work mothers, 275, **2676–2679**
Welfare system, Middle East and North Africa, 1627–1628
Well-defined problems, 1442

Well-developed individual interest, 705–706
Wellesley College, 348, 1843
Wellness programs. *See* Physical education
Wells, William G., Jr., 854
Wenger, Etienne, 2462
Wenglinsky, Harold, 315
Werner, Heinz, 158
Wertheimer, Max, 1443
Wertsch, James, 1464
West, Edwin G., 949
West Bank-Gaza. *See* Middle East and North Africa
Western Association of Schools and Colleges (WASC), 28, 30
Western Europe, 1104–1105, **2679–2684**
  See also Europe; Specific countries
Western Governors University, 425
Westheimer, Joel, 2462
West Philadelphia Improvement Corps, 2712
West Point. *See* U.S. Military Academy
West Virginia Board of Education v. Barnette, 2425
What Americans Believe Students Should Know: A Survey of U.S. Adults (Marzano et al.), 2644
What is English? (Elbow), 745
What Matters in College (Astin), 334–335
What Matters Most: Teaching for America's Future (report), 2155
What's the Word? (radio series), 1673
Wheaton College (Massachusetts), 2050
When Teenagers Work (Greenberger and Steinberg), 728
Whiley, Calvin, 695
Whisner, State v., 2336–2337
White, Andrew D., 725
White, Julie, 2141
White, Ralph, 973
White, Walter, 174
White Americans. *See* Demographics; Race/ethnicity
White flight, 2201–2202
Whitehead, Alfred North, **2684–2686**
  inert knowledge, 1443, 1464
  instructional design, 1151
  potential of schooling, 1994
White House Conference on Children and Youth, 1757–17758
White House Conference on the Care of Dependent Children, 282, 283, 284, 2676
White House Fellows program, **2686–2688**
Whitehurst, Grover, 1489
White Paper on International Development (Great Britain), 1244
Whitney, Albert W., 596
Whole-class instruction, 305, 1410
Whole language reading instruction
  Chall, Jeanne, 258
  educational psychology, 681
  English teaching, 741
WHO (World Health Organization), 1263–1264
Why Is It? (radio program), 92
Why Johnny Can't Read —and What You Can Do About It (Flesch), 258
WIA (Workforce Investment Act), 488, 2329
WIBs (Workforce Investment Boards), 488–489
WICI (Women in Communications, Inc.), 1069
Wideen, Marvin, 2447
Widmar v. Vincent, 2423
Wigfield, Allan, 1513, 1694
Wiggin, Kate Douglas, 622
Wild boy of Averyon, 2278, 2279
Wilen, William, 312, 313
Wiley, David, 142
Wilkinson, Ian, 1513
William, Dylan, 124
Williams, David, 78
Williams, Emmett, 1631
Williams, Ralph M., 2304
Williams College (Massachusetts), 239
Williamson, Stephanie, 2536
Willis, Arlette Ingram, 2002
Willms, J. Douglas, 326
Wilson, Edmund B., 93
Wilson, Mark, 139, 141, 142
Wilson, Woodrow, 1727–1728
Wineburg, Samuel, 1986
Wingspread Report, 790
Wing units, 1631
Winne, Philip, 2442
Winnetka plan, 2663
Winnetka schools, 1935
Winship, In re, 1351
Winzer, Margaret A., 2294
Wirt, William A., 915
Wisconsin, class size reduction in, 315
Wisconsin v. Yoder, 466, 1061, 2336, **2892–2908**
Wise, Arthur E., 671
WISE (Web-based Integrated Science Environment), 2180
Within-group ethnic studies, 1122–1123
Witters v. Washington Department of Services for the Blind, 2423
Witty, Paul, 931
Wlodkowski, Raymond, 2497
Wolf, Theta, 185, 186
Wolfe, Pat, 204
Wolff, Phillip, 1421
Women
  academic freedom and tenure, 15
  Addams, Jane, **40–42,** 829
  American Association of University Women (AAUW), **103–105**
  Association for Intercollegiate Athletics for Women (AIAW), 351
  Association for Women in Communications, **1068–1069**
  athletic program equity, 351–352
  Bethune, Mary McLeod, **173–175**
  Blow, Susan, **189–191,** 622
  Chall, Jeanne, **257–259**
  Clark, Septima Poinsette, **298–299**
  Convention on the Elimination of All Forms of Discrimination Against Women, 1280–1281
  Coretta Scott King Fund, 104
  De Lima, Agnes, **553–554**
  Delta Kappa Gamma Society, **1072–1073**
  doctoral degrees, 596
  domestic violence, 2632–2633
  eating disorders, 1872
  economic benefits of education investment, 648

education for poverty reduction, 549
education of, 41–42
Eleanor Roosevelt Teacher Fellowships, 104
faculty roles and responsibilities, 793
family and consumer sciences education, 803–804
fertility and education, 1901–1903
Haley, Margaret, **982–985**
Harvard University, 724, 995
health and education, 998–999
higher education, 1024, 1036, 1040
Hunter, Madeline Cheek, **1093–1094,** 2418
international college enrollment, 1032
International Federation of University Women, 105
Jeanes teachers, 1337–1338
Johnson, Marietta Pierce, **1344–1346**
Miel, Alice, **1635–1638**
Montessori, Maria, 84, **1675–1680**
National Education Association (NEA), 984
nontraditional students, 1815
Palmer, Alice Freeman, **1842–1844**
Plato and role of, 1900
principals, 1922
Project on the Status and Education of Women, 152
Putnam, Alice, **1957–1959**
rate of return on investment in education, 648
scholars' awards, 104
sex-based segregation, 2202
sexually transmitted diseases (STDs), 2064–2066
sister-teachers, 251
social sororities, 2251
sports, 2313
Stratemeyer, Florence, **2369–2371**
suffrage, 2703
Taba, Hilda, **2427–2429**
Women in Communications, Inc. (WICI), 1069
Women's Army Auxiliary Corps, 174
Women's Bureau, Department of Labor, 847
women's colleges, 1037, 1044, 2225–2228
women's studies, **2686–2688**
Yale's admission of, 2697, 2698
Young, Ella Flagg, 984, **2701–2703**
Zirbes, Laura, **2747–2748**
See also Gender; Title IX, Higher Education Act
Women in Communications, Inc. (WICI), 1069
Women's Army Auxiliary Corps, 174
Women's Bureau, Department of Labor, 847
Women's colleges, 1037, 1044, 2225–2228
Women's studies, **2688–2691**
Wong, Kenneth, 2107
Wonnacott, Clydie A., 1981
Wood, Craig, 1954
Wood, David, 575
Wood, Thomas, 1887
Woodhouse, Howard R., 938
Woodring, Paul, 2442
Woodson, Carter Godwin, **2691–2693**
African-American studies, 66
multiculturalism, 1704
Woodward, Calvin M., 1939
Woodworth, Robert, 1701–1702
Word problems, 1543, **1566–1569**
Words and memory, 1335
Work-based learning, 731, 736–737, 2641–2642
Work conference model, 1817
Workforce Incentives Program, 2677
Workforce Investment Act (WIA), 488, 730, 2329
Workforce Investment Boards (WIBs), 488–489
Workforce training, 883
See also Employment; Job skills
Work-for-hire and copyright, 1187–1188
Working memory
individual differences, 1114
information processing, 568
memory development, 1591–1593
neurology of memory, 1436
Working mothers
parental involvement in education, 1845
preschool availability, 617
Work readiness, 2639–2640, 2645–2646
Works Progress Administration (WPA) nursery schools, 623
Work-Study-Play schools. *See* Gary Plan
Work-Study Program, VA, 852
World affairs, 295
The World as Teacher (Taylor), 2434
World Bank
early childhood education, 631
overview, 1259–1261
vocational school fallacy, 2656
World Development Report, 998
World Confederation of Organizations in the Teaching Profession (WCOTP), 1319–1321
World Confederation of Teachers (WCT), 1319–1321
World Council on Curriculum and Instruction (WCCI), 1637
World Declaration on Education for All, **3162–3167**
World Education Indicators (WEI) project, 1251, 1267, 1294
World Federation of Teachers' Unions (FISE), 1319–1321
World Health Organization (WHO), 1263–1264
The World in Pictures (Comenius), 420–421
World system theory, 937
World Vision, 1805–1806
World War I
Addams, Jane, 42
Army intelligence tests, 1113, 1195, 1201, 2566–2567
Conant's gas warfare work, 471–472
private schools, 1924–1925
standardized tests, 975
World War II
federal involvement in science, 855
General Educational Development Test (GED), 921
instructional media, 2514
National Defense Research Committee (NDRC), 473
state departments of education, 2324
See also Servicemen's Readjustment Act
WorldWatcher (software), 2179
World Wide Web. *See* Internet

Wort, William, 906
Worth, Blaine R., 496
WPA (Works Progress Administration) nursery schools, 623
Wrenn, C. Gilbert, 976
Wright, Benjamin, 141
Wright, Frances, 1707
Wright, Ingraham v., 2425
Wright State University, 845
Writing-Across-the-Curriculum, 2694
Writing and composition, **1507–1509, 2693–2696**
  assessment, 147–148, 2694–2695
  Graduate Record Examination (GRE), 963
  international assessment, 1223
  narratives, 1502
  Reading and Writing for Critical Thinking (RWCT) Project, 1308
  as weakness in employment readiness, 734
  See also English education; Journalism education; Language arts
Writing-to-Learn, 2694
Wundt, Wilhelm, 1458, 1459
Wygant v. Jackson Board of Education, 63, 64

Y

"The Yale Report of 1828," 1476
Yale University, 348, 349, **2697–2698**
Yamoor, Catherine, 731
Yarborough, Senator, 177
Yarrow, Marion, 1707
Yasin, Said, 2087
Yawkey, Thomas, 1707
Year-round education, **2698–2701**
  See also Calendars, academic
Yemen. *See* Middle East and North Africa
Yerkes, Robert, 1195
Yeshiva University, 390
Yield rate, 328
YMCA (Young Men's Christian Association), 1890, **2738–2739**
YM-YWHA (Young Men's Hebrew Association and Young Women's Hebrew Association), **2739–2741**
Yoder, Wisconsin v., 466, 1061, 2336
York, Darlene Eleanor, 1963
Young, Ella Flagg, 984, **2701–2703**
Young adult literature, 285
Young children. *See* Early childhood
Young Men's Christian Association (YMCA), 1890, **2738–2739**
Young Men's Hebrew Association and Young Women's Hebrew Association (YM-YWHA), **2739–2741**
Young Women's Christian Association (YWCA), **2741–2743**
Youth
  adoption, 814
  boys, 985–986
  community organizations, 436–438
  demographic trends, **2703–2708,** *2708*
  health education, 1004–1009
  HIV/AIDS, **2058–2060,** 2066, 2072–2073
  juvenile crime and violence, **1358–1361**
  poverty, 1906–1907, **1910–1915**
  risk behaviors, **2055–2074**
  risk factors, 1837
  self care, 1405–1406
  sexual activity, 2058, **2060–2064,** 2064–2066
  sexuality, 2214–2215
  sexually transmitted diseases (STIs), 2058, **2064–2066**
  sexual orientation, 2218–2221
  sleep, 2231–2233
  smoking, **2066–2068**
  stages of growth, 278–279
  substance abuse, *2055*, **2055–2058**
  suicide, **2068–2071**
  teen pregnancy, 978, **2060–2064,** 2067, **2071–2074**
  See also Gangs; High school students; Peer culture, adolescent
Youthbuild (initiative), 845
Youth development programs, 437–438, **2708–2717,** *2711, 2712*
Youth hostels, 2732–2733
Youth organizations and clubs, **317–321, 2717–2743**
  American Field Service, **2717–2718**
  Big Brothers Big Sisters of America, **2718–2719**
  B'nai B'rith Youth Organization, **2720–2721**
  Boys and Girls Clubs of America, **2721–2722**
  Boy Scouts of America, **2724–2725**
  Boys State and Girls State programs, **2722–2723**
  Camp Fire USA, **2725–2726**
  Distributive Education Clubs of America (DECA), **2726–2727**
  Four-H Programs, 320, 806, **2727–2728**
  Future Business Leaders of America-Phi Beta Lambda (FBLA-PBL), **2729–2730**
  Future Scientists and Engineers of America (FSEA), **2730**
  Girl Scouts of the USA, **2731**
  Hostelling International-American Youth Hostels (HI-AYH), **2732–2733**
  Jewish, 1342
  National Forensic League (NFL), **2733–2734**
  National Future Farmers of America Organization, **2734–2736**
  Quill and Scroll Society, **2736–2737**
  SkillsUSA-VICA, **2737–2738**
  student activities, 2374–2375
  student services, 2393
  Young Men's Christian Association (YMCA), 1890, **2738–2739**
  Young Men's Hebrew Association and Young Women's Hebrew Association (YM-YWHA), **2739–2741**
  Young Women's Christian Association (YWCA), **2741–2743**
  See also Extracurricular activities; Student activities
Youth Risk Behavior Survey (YRBS), 1004, 2058, 2307, 2308, 2629
Yup'ik Alaskans, 1564

YWCA (Young Women's Christian Association), **2741–2743**

Z

Zacharias, Jerrold, **2745–2747**
Zambia. *See* Sub-Saharan Africa
Zaporozhets, Alexander, 576
ZBB (zero-based budgeting), 1953
Zeichner, Kenneth, 307
Zeldin, Shepherd, 2710
Zemstvo schools, 712
Zero-based budgeting (ZBB), 1953
Zero Tolerance (initiative), 110
Zero to Three, 273
Ziller, Tuiskon, 1021–1022
Zimbabwe. *See* Sub-Saharan Africa
Zirbes, Laura, **2747–2748**
Zobrest v. Catalina Foothills School District, 2423
Zone of proximal development (ZPD)
  constructivism, 1464
  dynamic assessment, 128
  peer relations, 1865
  Vygotskian theory, 575
  See also Vygotsky, Lev
Zones of wishful thinking, 692
Zook, George, 96
ZPD. *See* Zone of proximal development (ZPD)
Zuga, Karen F., 2159
Zureich, Michael, 2129